AUSTRALIA
HANDBOOK

AUSTRALIA
HANDBOOK

SECOND EDITION

MARAEL JOHNSON
& ANDREW HEMPSTEAD

MOON
TRAVEL
HANDBOOKS

AUSTRALIA HANDBOOK
SECOND EDITION

Published by
Avalon Travel Publishing
5855 Beaudry St.
Emeryville, CA 94608, USA

Printed by
Colorcraft

ISBN: 1-56691-158-3
ISSN: 1088-6427

Editors: Gregor Johnson Krause, Marion Harmon
Production & Design: Carey Wilson
Cartography: Brian Bardwell, Chris Folks, Bob Race, Jason Sadler, Rob Warner
Index: Sondra Nation

Front cover photo courtesy of SuperStock, Inc., © 2000

All photos by Andrew Hempstead unless otherwise noted.
All illustrations by Bob Race unless otherwise noted.

Distributed in the United States and Canada by Publishers Group West

Printed in China

Although the author and publisher have made every effort to ensure that the information was correct at the time of going to press, the author and publisher do not assume and hereby disclaim any
liability to any party for any loss or damage caused by errors, omissions, or any potential travel dis-
ruption due to labor or financial difficulty, whether such errors or omissions result from negligence,
accident, or any other cause.

Please send all comments, corrections,
additions, amendments, and critiques to:

**AUSTRALIA HANDBOOK
MOON TRAVEL HANDBOOKS
5855 BEAUDRY ST.
EMERYVILLE, CA 94608 USA
e-mail: travel@moon.com
www.moon.com**

Printing History
1st edition—1997
2nd edition—March 2000
5 4 3 2 1 0

CONTENTS

MAPS

(continued on next page)

MAPS
(continued)

MAP SYMBOLS

─────	HIGHWAY
─────	MAIN ROAD
─────	OTHER ROAD
‐ ‐ ‐ ‐	TRACK
═════	BRIDGE
·—··—··—	STATE BORDER
+‐+‐+‐+	RAILROAD
·—·‐·—·‐	PATH

NOTE: NOT ALL ROADS INDICATED BY A
SOLID LINE ARE PAVED. CONDITION OF
UNPAVED ROADS OR TRACKS MAY VARY.

○	CITY
○	TOWN
■	POINT OF INTEREST
●	ACCOMMODATIONS/CARAVAN PARKS
C. P. =	CONSERVATION PARK
N. P. =	NATIONAL PARK
♪	GOLF COURSE

	NATIONAL HIGHWAY
	STATE HIGHWAY
	DRY LAKE
	WATER
▲	MOUNTAIN
△	CAMPING
	SHIPWRECK
✕✕	AIRPORT
♈	ABORIGINAL ROCK ART

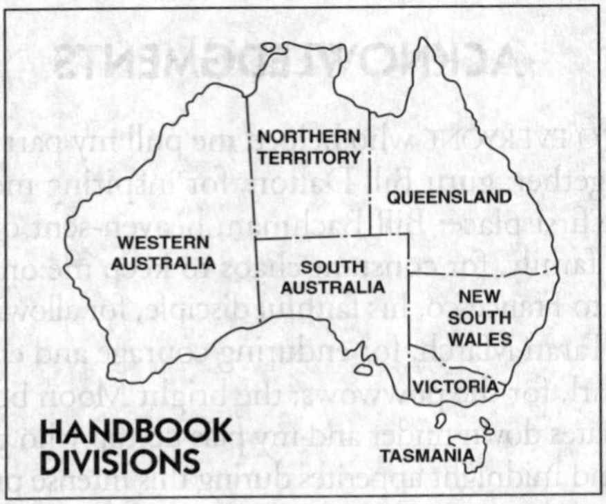

ABBREVIATIONS

ACT—Australian Capital Territory

B&B—bed and breakfast

BHP—Broken Hill Proprietary

C—Celsius

CWA—Country Women's Association

d—double

DC&NR—Department of Conservation and Natural Resources

F—Fahrenheit

4WD—four-wheel drive

NPWS—National Parks and Wildlife Service

NSW—New South Wales

NT—Northern Territory

P.O.—post office

pp—per person

RAA or **RAC**—Royal Automobile Association *or* Royal Automobile Club

QLD—Queensland

s—single

SA—South Australia

STA—State Transit Authority (South Australia) *or* Student Travel Association

TAS—Tasmania

tel.—telephone

VIC—Victoria

WA—Western Australia

YHA—Youth Hostel Association

YMCA/YWCA—Young Men's/Women's Christian Association

HELP MAKE THIS A BETTER BOOK

Though we strive to be as accurate as possible, things always change. If you discover an error—or, better yet, if you run across something new and exciting (a walking trail, dinosaur footprint, cache of diamonds, reflection of the man in the moon)—please let us know.

Australia Handbook
c/o Avalon Travel Publishing
5855 Beaudry Street
Emeryville, CA 94608
e-mail: travel@moon.com (please put Australia Handbook" in the subject line of your message)

ACKNOWLEDGMENTS

THANKS TO EVERYONE who helped me pull my part of this master-piece together: guru Bill Dalton, for inspiring me to be a travel writer in the first place; Bill Bachman, heaven-sent outback photographer; my family, for constant chaos to keep me on my toes; God (cat) and Santo Francesco, his faithful disciple, for allowing me to share their home; Taran March, for enduring courage and encouragement; Chris and Carl, for the powwows; the bright Moon beams in Chico; and all my mates down under and my pals up top who put up with my bad moods and midnight appetites during this intense project, *especially* the Argyle Street gang (happy now?).

—MARAEL JOHNSON

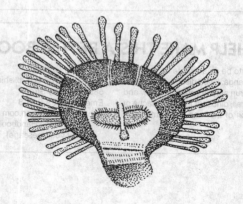

INTRODUCTION

Waltzing Matilda through Australia will take you to more places than the Great Barrier Reef and the Outback. The Great Southern Land is massive and, if you have a true swagman's spirit, limitless. Australia comprises six states and two territories, with Canberra, ACT, being the national capital and Sydney, NSW, the largest city (pop. four million). Well over half of Australia's total population of 18 million lives within 100 km of the Pacific shore, a 4,000-km stretch of beaches, bays, and rocky headlands. The Great Barrier Reef, 2,000 km of reef dotted with islands, and one of the world's greatest wonders, protects the northern half of Australia's east coast. Rural Australia and the Outback lie west of the Great Dividing Range, a spine of mountains that runs the entire length of the east coast. The Outback sprawls across five states, with the Northern Territory, Western Australia, and South Australia almost entirely desert. Along the coasts of these states cling their three capitals—Darwin, Perth, and Adelaide, respectively—each with a distinctive charm not found in the main eastern population centers. The Northern

Territory's Uluru (Ayers Rock), the world's largest monolith, rises from the heart of Australia. Australia is by no means just beaches and desert; at

AUSTRALIA
COMPARED TO
NORTH AMERICA

0   1,000 km

© AVALON TRAVEL PUBLISHING

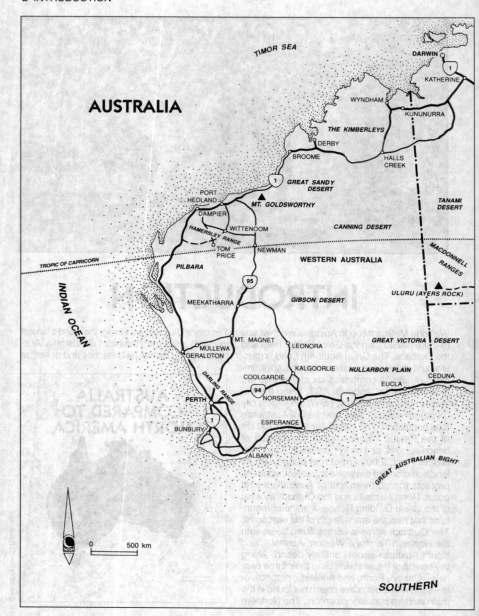

ARAFURA SEA

TORRES STRAIT

CORAL SEA

ARNHEM LAND

GULF OF CARPENTARIA

SOUTH PACIFIC OCEAN

LARRIMAH

DALY WATERS

CAPE YORK PENINSULA

CAIRNS

NORMANTON

BARKLY TABLELAND

TENNANT CREEK

87

66

TOWNSVILLE

CHARTERS TOWERS

PROSERPINE

MACKAY

GREAT BARRIER REEF

MT. ISA

78

NORTHERN TERRITORY

WINTON

GREAT DIVIDING RANGE

66

EMERALD

TROPIC OF CAPRICORN

ALICE SPRINGS

LONGREACH

QUEENSLAND

ROCKHAMPTON

GLADSTONE

71

SIMPSON DESERT

THE CHANNEL COUNTRY

CHARLEVILLE

MARYBOROUGH

17

MAROOCHYDORE

SOUTH AUSTRALIA

LAKE EYRE

CUNNAMULLA

TOOWOOMBA

58

BRISBANE

GOLD COAST

COOBER PEDY

FLINDERS RANGES

NEW SOUTH WALES

BOURKE

BYRON BAY

GRAFTON

87

LAKE TORRENS

71

TAMWORTH

39

15

COFFS HARBOUR

PORT AUGUSTA

32

BROKEN HILL

DUBBO

GREAT DIVIDING RANGE

PORT MACQUARIE

EYRE PENINSULA

MURRAY

MILDURA

39

32

SYDNEY

NEWCASTLE

PORT LINCOLN

YORKE PENINSULA

ADELAIDE

20

RIVER

31

CANBERRA

AUSTRALIAN CAPITAL TERRITORY

1

79

ALBURY

GREAT

8

VICTORIA

31

20

MT. KOSCIUSZKO

MT. GAMBIER

MELBOURNE

COOMA

TASMAN SEA

OCEAN

KING ISLAND

BASS STRAIT

FLINDERS ISLAND

BURNIE

DEVONPORT

LAUNCESTON

TASMANIA

HOBART

the southern end of the Great Dividing Range vast areas of high country are blanketed in snow each winter, offering Aussie-style alpine experiences. Different from anywhere else in the country, Tasmania, a 68,000-square-km island off the southeast coast of the mainland, is often missed by travelers down under, and even by many Aussies themselves. As well as having some of Australia's best-preserved convict-era villages, Tasmania, with its hiking, climbing, and sea-kayaking opportunities, is a mecca for zealots of the outdoors.

THE LAND

Australia is made of contradictions and conundrums. Is it the smallest continent or the biggest island on earth? Is it the oldest place in the world? Indeed it is, and you can stroll over rocks that were formed four billion years ago. But geologists will remind you that Australia didn't separate from the Asian landmass to become its own continent until recent, almost modern times—a mere 50 million years ago.

Its isolation in the remote southern ocean meant that Australia, aside from Antarctica, was the last continent to succumb to human occupancy (Aborigines arrived about 40,000 years ago); but long before Europeans arrived, philosophers from Athens to Alexandria postulated the existence of the "antipodes" on the theory that symmetry demanded a southern continent to balance the known world in the north.

Australia is a fragment of the ancient supercontinent Pangaea. Six hundred million years ago, South America, Africa, Antarctica, Australasia, and the Indian subcontinent were all hooked together. Over the millennia since, they have been drifting apart, as the massive tectonic plates float across the earth's mantle. Australia is riding in the middle of a plate whose leading edge in northern India is relentlessly smashing into central Asia, piling up the Himalayas. The eastern edge of the same plate runs alongside New Zealand, which experiences the volcanic consequences of two unimaginably vast slabs of rock grinding away at each other.

Being in the middle of this enormous plate has meant that the Australian continent has been comparatively free of volcanic and other cataclysmic upheavals. Consequently, Australia is the flattest of the continents; time and weather have eroded mountain ranges that once would have dwarfed Mt. Everest. Mount Kosciuszko in New South Wales, Australia's highest mountain (2,228 meters above sea level), would barely pass muster as a respectable foothill elsewhere in the world. Australia has an average height of only 200 meters, and one of the most powerful impressions the traveler experiences in Australia is of awesome, mind-numbing flatness.

Another impression is dryness. Australia is the driest of the continents; some areas are subject to more evaporation than precipitation. While 40% of its landmass lies in the tropics, almost 70% is arid, with an annual rainfall below 25 centimeters. These parched conditions are accompanied by a *big* load of sand; some of the longest sand dunes in the world run parallel for up to 200 km in the Simpson Desert. Where the sandy deserts give out, they are replaced by stony "gibber" deserts, relics of an ancient inland sea.

PROTECTING THE LAND

Protection Programs

The Register of the National Estate, compiled by the Australian Heritage Commission, provides annual grants for more than 200 projects within all states and territories. The 1990s have been dedicated the "Decade of Landcare" by the federal government, which has established environmental and conservation protection programs throughout the country—with all levels of government participating. This is a feather in the Green caps of the estimated 800,000 members of Australia's conservation societies (numbering nearly 1,000—up from 50 in the 1950s).

In 1974, Australia became one of the first signatories to the UNESCO World Heritage convention—signers and members are committed to identify, protect, and promote World Heritage properties. Australia's list consists of: the Great Barrier Reef, Kakadu National Park, the Willandra Lakes Region, the Tasmanian Wilderness,

PROTECTING THE NATIONAL PARKS

The Australian Nature Conservation Agency (formerly the National Parks and Wildlife Service) asks you to follow a number of simple rules to protect both you and the parks.

- Guard against fire. Use fireplaces where provided. Native timber is the home of small animals, so please preserve it by using a portable stove. No fires, including gas barbecues and stoves, may be lit when a fire ban is in force.
- Do not disturb, collect, or damage animals, wildflowers, vegetation, or earth or rock formations.
- Do not disturb or collect artifacts from Aboriginal sites. Sites and items may have sacred, ceremonial, mythological, and historical significance to Aboriginal people, as well as scientific value.
- Firearms are not permitted.
- Do not litter. Carry your rubbish out of the park when you leave, or use a litter bin.
- Leave your pets at home. Dogs and cats are not allowed in parks, as they disturb both native animals and park visitors.
- Drive carefully and observe all notices.
- Use of registered off-road vehicles is restricted to existing designated roads and tracks.
- Contact local rangers for camping permits and for information on local conditions for bushwalking.

Lord Howe Island Group, the Australian East Coast Temperate and Sub-tropical Rainforest Parks, Uluru-Kata Tjuta National Park, Wet Tropics of Queensland, Shark Bay in Western Australia, and Fraser Island in Queensland. State and territorial governments join with the federal entity to protect these ecologically diverse and magnificent regions.

Pollution-wise, the feds control dumping of waste in the sea, as well as imports and exports of hazardous waste, while state and territory governments hold main responsibility for pollution controls (though guidelines for permitted levels of pollution are a collaborative effort with the federal government). As for industrial pollution, the federal government offers "encouragement" for cleaner methods.

State and territory governments are accountable for native wildlife within their respective boundaries, with the federal government taking over for the critters inhabiting federal territories. The federal level also has the say-so regarding international import and export of wildlife, and holds the pen when it comes to international treaties and conventions dealing with nature conservation.

Conservation Organizations

Greenies and other concerned travelers have several ways to join or support Australia's environmental consciousness.

The **Australian Conservation Foundation** (ACF) is the country's largest private conservation organization. Often working in coalition with the Wilderness Society and other action groups, the ACF is concerned with ozone depletion and the greenhouse effect, rainforest preservation, logging, and land abuse. It even casts its (save-the) eagle eye on the fragile Antarctic region. Memberships, subscriptions, and individual donations constitute most of their funding (the government contributes only about 10%). For more information, contact ACF, 340 Gore St., Fitzroy, VIC 3065, tel. (03) 9416-1166.

The **Wilderness Society,** which began as the Tasmanian Wilderness Society in response to the forthcoming *damning* of the Franklin River, has expanded its causes to encompass the entire country. You can support their positions by purchasing goods such as T-shirts, posters, books, and postcards from shops in all states except the Northern Territory. For more information, contact the main office at 130 Davey St., Hobart, TAS 7000, tel. (03) 6234-9366.

The **Ecotourism Association of Australia,** P.O. Box 26, Paddington, QLD 4064, tel. (07) 3369-6099, promotes eco-sensitive tourism throughout the country.

National Parks

For information on Australia's more than 2,200 national parks, wildlife sanctuaries, and nature reserves, contact the following organizations.

Australian Capital Territory, Department of

Planning and Land Management, 16 Challis St., Dickson, ACT, tel. (02) 6207-1923, website: www.act.gov.au.

New South Wales, National Parks and Wildlife Service, 43 Bridge St., Hurstville, NSW 2220; G.P.O. Box 1967, Hurstville, NSW 2220, tel. (02) 9585-6333 or (1300) 36-1967; website: www.npws.nsw.gov.au.

Northern Territory, Parks and Wildlife Commission of the Northern Territory, P.O. Box 496, Palmerston, Darwin, NT 0831, tel. (08) 8999-5511, website: www.nt.gov.au/paw.

Queensland, Queensland National Parks and Wildlife Service, 160 Ann St., Brisbane, QLD 4000, tel. (07) 3227-7111.

South Australia, Department of Environment and Heritage, 91 Grenfell St., Adelaide, SA 5001; G.P.O. Box 667, Adelaide, SA 5001, tel. (08) 8204-1910.

Victoria, Department of Natural Resources and Environment, 8 Nicholson St., East Melbourne; P.O. Box 41, East Melbourne, VIC 3002, tel. (03) 9412-4745.

Tasmania, Tasmanian Parks and Wildlife Service, 134 Macquarie St., Hobart; P.O. Box 44a, Hobart, TAS 7001, tel. (03) 6233-3382; website: www.parks.tas.gov.au.

Western Australia, Department of Conservation and Land Management, 50 Hayman Rd., Como, WA 6152, tel. (08) 9334-0303.

For countrywide information, contact the **Biodiversity Group of Environment Australia,** G.P.O. Box 636, Canberra, ACT 2601, tel. (02) 6250-0200.

CLIMATE

The Seasons

Visitors from the Northern Hemisphere will immediately be struck by Australia's topsy-turvy seasons: summer officially begins on 1 December and winter on 1 June. This means that the academic and calendar years coincide, and both end with the summer holidays, in December. It also means you may experience the novelty of sitting down to a piping-hot Christmas dinner, perhaps of roast turkey or baked ham with all the trimmings, in the sweltering heat of high summer. And don't forget—here the sun rides across the northern sky and new rules

apply. If you get lost and look for the mossy side of trees, just remember you're pointed south instead of north.

Most of the country doesn't experience the climatic extremes of, say, North America, but, still, choosing the correct time of year to travel is important. For those planning an extended trip around the country, try to spend spring, summer, or autumn in the south and leave the Outback and the tropical areas of Queensland and the Northern Territory for the cooler months.

Australia straddles the tropic of Capricorn, and climatic conditions range from temperate in the south to tropical in the north. Sydney enjoys a climate similar to Southern California, with mild winters and summer heat tempered by cooling sea breezes. Heading north, the year-round temperature increases, and while summers in Brisbane are pleasant, after crossing the tropic of Capricorn (at Rockhampton) the summer heat can become unbearable for those unaccustomed to it. Being the tropics, summer in northern Queensland is the Wet (Aussie for the wet season), when torrential downpours are part of life, and travel up Cape York and in the Gulf Country is almost impossible. This far north, winters are comfortable, particularly near the coast, with dazzling days and dreamy nights. However, summer brings tropical rains and cyclones, some of which have been devilishly savage. In 1974, Cyclone Tracy—like a lover on a rampage—destroyed Darwin overnight, and most other coastal cities have suffered extensive damage from cyclones in the past. While traveling in these regions during the summer cyclone season, keep your ears open for radio weather reports, which give frequent updates

---

SEASONS

Seasons in the Southern Hemisphere are the reverse of those in the Northern Hemisphere. Also, they go by the exact months rather than by the solstices.

Spring: September-November
Summer: December-February
Fall: March-May
Winter: June-August

on the movements of cyclones as they develop. Perth's weather is some of the best: sunny, mild, and not too humid (conditions are mild by run-for-the-thermal-undies standards). Adelaide enjoys a mild, almost Mediterranean climate, with moderate winters and dry summers. Summer is the best season to travel through Victoria and Tasmania, although spring and autumn can be pleasant (and less crowded).

Weather conditions around the country and in surrounding waters are monitored by the government-sponsored **Bureau of Meteorology**, which regularly updates the website www.bom.gov.au with local weather reports, flood and cyclone warnings, satellite images, and interesting stories on Australia's climate.

The Aboriginal Seasons

The Aborigines who live around Kakadu National Park recognize six annual seasons rather than the "usual" four. The terms come from the Gundjeidmi (Maiili) language. *Gunumeleng,* the early storm season, is marked by hot, increasingly humid weather, along with building thunderstorms and scattered showers; *gudjewg,* the early monsoon season (known as the Wet), is usually a time of thunder and lightning, heat and humidity, and blossoming plant and animal life; *bangereng* is late monsoon season (also referred to as "knock 'em down" season) with violent storms, intense humidity, and a riot of flora and fauna; *yegge,* late storm season, brings early morning mists and water lilies, as well as strong winds

and the first fires; *wurrgeng,* the cool, dry season, sees continuing burning, drying billabongs, dewy nights, and the relatively low humidity and temperatures that bring prolific bird- and wildlife as well as flocks of tourists; *gurrung,* the hot dry season, is *very* hot with some wind, rapidly traveling fires, and building thunderheads, which signal the return of *gunumeleng.*

Droughts, Fires, and Floods

The vast interior is arid; this makes for clear skies, warm to hot days, and chilly (and amazingly starry) nights. Rain west of the Great Dividing Range is a hit-and-miss affair, and rarely falls in the Outback, but when it does the landscape responds spectacularly as dormant vegetation bursts into life. Australia's aridity is such that many areas are subject to drought, and it is common for some regions to struggle for as much as seven years without a drop of rain. Even the wetter coastal areas are not immune to occasional droughts, and water restrictions are something that most Australians are familiar with. In 1994, the weather reversed its geographical pattern, bringing bizarre summer rains to the Red Centre and South Australia and devasting drought (the worst in Australian history) to the east coast. The farming community was hard hit as cattle, crops, and wildlife bit the dust and farmers were forced both to slaughter livestock early and refrain from planting summer crops.

In the normally dry summer months in the south, bushfires are an annual danger, and the consequences of uncontrollable outbreaks have been devastating for some time. In 1982, incalculable damage was caused by the terrible fires that broke out, ironically enough, on Ash Wednesday of that year, in Victoria and South Australia. And, certainly, few Australians will forget 1994's out-of-control wildfires (the worst since European colonization 200 years ago), which snuffed out more than 400,000 hectares of bush and grasslands, destroyed 100-or-so homes, and roared within a few km of central Sydney. Ash and haze left the city's famous opera house a shade of dismal orange rather than its customary blinding white—but at least it was spared.

The flip side of the drought-and-fire coin is flood. Many agonizingly long droughts have been broken by catastrophic floods that can isolate outlying communities for weeks.

Australia's highest recorded temperature was a brain-frying 53.1° C (127.6° F) in Cloncurry, Queensland, in 1889, while Marble Bar, in Western Australia, had 160 sweltering days over 37° C (99° F) in 1923-24, still a world record. The highest rainfall in a 24-hour period was 108 cm in 1979 at Bellenden, Queensland, which also holds the Australian record for the highest annual rainfall—over 10 meters.

Sunshine and Ozone

Australia is exposed to more hours of sunshine than most countries. This has two important consequences. First, the anxiously observed hole in the protective ozone layer over the South Pole has extended at times to expose southern parts of the continent, and it is expected that the hole will only enlarge further. Scientific opinion about the negative effects of this startling development are divided. There is no doubt, however, about the consequences of exposure to high levels of sunshine on humans. Even before the rent in the ozone layer became a concern, Australia's rate of skin-cancer cases was abnormally high. The combination of a fashion for bronze suntans, an addiction to sunbathing, a beach culture, and a love of outdoor activities has led to a national health problem of major proportions. It is worth remembering the simple creed propounded in a recent public health campaign: Slip, Slop, Slap (slip on a shirt, slop on some sunscreen, and slap on a hat).

Harsh climatic conditions have helped to shape the national character, and, far from resenting the forces of nature that so often blight the lives of Australians, especially in the bush, many people have a strangely sentimental attachment to this rigorous and inhospitable land. The words of Dorothy Mackellar in this poem, which most Australians learn at school, sum up their ambivalent affection:

> *I love a sunburnt country,*
> *A land of sweeping plains,*
> *Of rugged mountain ranges,*
> *Of droughts, and flooding rains.*
> *I love her far horizons.*
> *I love her jewelled sea.*
> *Her beauty and her terror;*
> *A wide brown land for me.*

FLORA AND FAUNA

In wilderness is the preservation of the world. We need the tonic of wilderness, to wade sometimes in the marshes . . . we can never have enough of nature.
—HENRY THOREAU

Australia's 50 million years of geographic isolation has led to the evolution of a bewildering array of indigenous plant and animal life that has little in common with life-forms in relatively nearby parts of the world. It is one of the fascinations of travel in the Outback to be continually confronted with animals and plants that might easily spring from the fevered brains of science fiction writers.

FLORA

"The great quantity of plants Mr. Banks and Dr. Solander found in this place occasioned my giving it the name of Botany Bay." This brief entry in Captain Cook's 1770 journal does little justice to the excitement the two botanical gentlemen in his company must have experienced. The flora they collected was certainly novel and was the subject of lively academic interest in Europe. The following overview highlights some of the botanic marvels that Banks and Solander probably observed.

The Bush
The term "bush," which Australians bandy about so loosely, covers a variety of terrains and broad vegetation types, including rainforests, both temperate and tropical, mangrove swamps, savannahs, rolling scrub-covered hills, forests of eucalypt or conifer, grasslands, and deserts. Australian plants and trees are generally nondeciduous, and many species bear fragrant blossoms. After a desert rainstorm, the air is cloyingly sweet, and sailors say they can smell the sharp medicinal scent of gums (eucalypts) far out to sea.

Myrtles and Gums
The largest and most famous of Australian plant groups is the myrtle family. It contains more than

AUSTRALIA'S OFFICIAL PLANTS AND ANIMALS

Australia's national flower is the Golden Wattle (*Acacia pycnantha*). Individual state emblems are:

NEW SOUTH WALES

animal(s): Platypus (*Ornithorhynchus anatinus*) and Laughing Kookaburra (*Dacelo novaeguineae*)

plant: Waratah (*Telopea speciosissima*)

NORTHERN TERRITORY

animal(s): Red Kangaroo (*Macropus rufus*); Wedge-tailed Eagle (*Aquila audax*)

plant: Sturt's Desert Rose (*Gossypium sturtianum*)

QUEENSLAND

animal: Koala (*Phascolarctos cinereus*)

plant: Cooktown Orchid (*Dendrobium bigibbum*)

SOUTH AUSTRALIA

animal: Hairy-Nosed Wombat (*Lasiorhinus latifrons*)

plant: Sturt's Desert Pea (*Clianthus formosus*)

TASMANIA

plant: Tasmanian Blue Gum (*Eucalyptus globulus*)

VICTORIA

animal: Helmeted Honeyeater (*Meliphaga cassidix*)

plant: Common Heath (*Epacris impressa*)

WESTERN AUSTRALIA

animal(s): Numbat (*Myrmecobius fasciatus*); Black Swan (*Cygnus atratus*)

plant: Kangaroo Paw (*Anigozanthos manglesii*)

1,000 native species, from the ground-hugging heathlike kunzeas to the 500-odd species of eucalypt. It includes the tea-tree (so named by Captain Cook's crew, who made a tea-colored drink from its leaves), the picturesque paperbark with its white papery trunk, and the brilliantly colored bottlebrush. The hundreds of species of eucalypt, or gum tree, many with colorful scarlet, coral, and white blossoms, are now the most transplanted trees in the world. More than 100 years ago these fast growers, well-suited to arid climates, were planted in California and Arizona as windbreaks, and you can find Australian eucalypts in well over 70 countries, a tribute to their hardy adaptability.

Fewer than 100 species of eucalypt are found in the country's arid climes, many of them shorter and squatter than their relatives living in the bush, highlands, or coastal regions. These varieties have developed an ability to resist heat and preserve moisture. Many gum trees have leaves that turn their edges to the sun's rays to reduce evaporation, which, incidentally, makes them poor shade trees on scorching afternoons. Gum leaves are generally thick-skinned and equipped with oil glands to provide an oily film to resist the heat.

Commonly sighted eucalypts include: the snow gum, with a distinctive gnarled look, found in alpine regions; the ghost gum with sheeny, bleached-out bark and vibrant green leaves, a haunting vision around central Australia and the tropical north; the river (or "red") gum, a large-limbed giant of a tree with slick bark tattooed in tans and grays, found rooted in waterways; coolabahs, another water- and swamp-dweller, recognizable by its gnarly shape, lackluster leaves, and tough bark; the Darwin woollybutt, a tall lumbering tree with a two-toned, dual-textured trunk and seasonal orange blossoms, scattered coast-to-coast across the Top End; and mallee, a stunted eucalypt that thrives in the desertlike conditions of, appropriately enough, the Mallee in northwestern Victoria.

Other Plants and Shrubs

The wattle, Australia's floral emblem, belongs to the acacia family, which is represented by some 600 species across Australia. Mulgas, the most common arid-zone wattle, can grow in sparse clumps or thick groupings and look somewhat like scrawny eucalypts. In early days, colonists made wattle-and-daub huts, an ancient building technique involving interwoven saplings covered with mud, and the name "wattle" was attached to this profusely blooming species with its either spikey or rounded yellow flowers. Like a good Aussie football player, the wattle is extremely hardy and fast growing, and can thrive in the arid, bare interior where even eucalypts cannot compete, but its career is not long-lived. Some species have adapted to sand dunes drenched with salt spray, some to soggy ill-drained swamps, and others to stony exposed ridges. And like many Australian plants, they have adapted to fire.

The bushfire did not come to Australia with the Europeans. Since ancient times, lightning has started many a blazing inferno, and Aborigines used fire to flush animals out of dense foliage. Many species of Australian plants have developed a remarkable resistance to fire. Eucalypts have dormant buds beneath their bark that open immediately after a bushfire to restore foliage to a burnt tree. The seeds of other plant species do not readily germinate until the first rains after a fire, when great quantities of acacia seedlings spring up from the charred earth. The woody fruits of hakeas and banksias actually require the heat of fire before they will burst open and release the seeds.

The ubiquitous banksia trees and shrubs are named after Sir Joseph Banks, and they have a special place in the nightmares of Australian children after the artist May Gibbs created the wicked Banksia men for her popular bush fairy tales. Banksias belong to the Protaceae family, which has developed most abundantly in Australia. It is named after Proteus, the shape-changing Old Man of the Sea in Greek mythology, and it points to the enormous diversity of the family.

snow gum

Some banksias, for instance, grow half submerged in the sand, while others grow into trees 15 meters tall. Leaves and flowers of this family vary tremendously from the so-called spider flowers of the *Grevillea* genus to the dense heads of the waratahs. The most commercially valuable members of the family are the macadamia, which are grown in Queensland for their rich, yummy nut, and the silky oak, which produces a fine cabinet wood.

And yet there are still more wildly beautiful, utterly strange trees and shrubs to stumble across: spinifex, a hardy, prickly, spiky plant—and favorite reptilian hiding place—that blankets much of central Australia; some 30 varieties of saltbrush, a staple in the diets of Outback livestock that has a special fondness for the Birdsville and Oodnadatta Tracks; the boab tree, a squatty, gnarly-branched oddity with a bloated, water-retaining trunk, and a relative of the African baobab, expat-ing it in the northeastern Northern Territory and the southwestern Kimberley; the

desert oak, a tall, shady drama queen of a breed prevalent around arid spots like Ayers Rock and King Canyon; and a species of red cabbage palms, known as *Livistona mariae,* which has not been identified any place else on the planet! Groves of the palms as well as cycads—all left over from prehistoric times—are alive and well in the Northern Territory.

Late and Early Bloomers

Australia's native plants include profuse bloomers. Sturt's desert pea stretches like a red carpet across vast tracts of inland desert. More than 600 varieties of orchids, including the only two underground species in the world, lend their sensuous beauty to the steamy rainforests of the north, while water lilies float gently and dreamily atop Top End lagoons.

Western Australia alone grows more than 6,000 species of wildflowers and flowering shrubs and trees. For many eons, the southwest corner of Australia was virtually a floral island, isolated from the world by the Indian Ocean and the deserts to its north and east. Among the most colorful of Western Australia's flowers are the kangaroo paw, the Geraldton wax flower, the scarlet coccinea, the exquisitely scented boronias, and the pine grevillea with its enormous deep orange spikes that grow to six meters. Australia's Christmas tree is not a conifer, but a relative of the mistletoe, a parasite that

grass tree

blooms at Christmas in masses of orange balloon-like blossoms.

One reason for the very different configurations of Australian flowers, in which petals are often tiny or nonexistent while stamens and pistils are prominent, is that many have evolved in isolation where they are pollinated by birds, not bees, and have had to adapt to the demands of a host of honey-eaters' beaks.

The sight of Western Australian wildflowers, covering the earth as far as the eye can see, like the prolific blue leschenaultia (which Aborigines called "the floor of the sky"), is worth the cost of a dozen trips there. But there are fantastic botanical eye-poppers to be found elsewhere: the stately kauri and jarrah forests; the majestic mountain ash and beech myrtle of the temperate rainforests; ghost gums silhouetted against the setting sun; grass trees spiked with flowers; primitive tree ferns slowly inching their way up from the mossy, mist-shrouded forest floor; the sparse but fascinating vegetation of the Nullarbor Plain—so inhospitable but so alive; and for the ghoulish, two carnivorous species, the pitcher plant and the rainbow plant. The isolation and stress of a harsh climate have created plantlife in Australia that is unique, extraordinary, and well worth investigating.

FAUNA

The Extinct

Carnivorous lizards standing nine meters tall, eight-meter ichthyosaurs (or fish lizards), and three-meter labyrinthodonts (or frog lizards) in-

---

FOSSILS, FOOTPRINTS, AND OLD BONES

The land of Oz was home to some of the earth's earliest life-forms, and traces of many of them have been uncovered in the Outback (more are probably waiting to be discovered). Following is a sampling of discoveries and their sites.

NEW SOUTH WALES

Cretaceous period: carnivorous theropod—Lightning Ridge
monotreme (country's oldest mammal fossil)—Lightning Ridge

NORTHERN TERRITORY

extinct marsupials—Bullock Creek
Miocene epoch: fossils including enormous flightless birds, meat-eating thylacinids, a huge diprotodontid, and a marsupial lion—Alcoota Station, near Alice Springs
Ordovician period: vertebrate fish—Amadeus Basin

QUEENSLAND

extinct marsupials, kangaroos, and other mammals—Riversleigh
Cretaceous period: ichthyosaurs—Richmond; marine reptile (possibly the largest known specimen)—near Hughenden
Jurassic-period pliosaurs—Mount Morgan area
Permian-period fish—Blackwater
many dinosaur footprints—Lark Quarry, south of Winton

ornithopod ("Mutta," unalive and well in Queensland Museum)—Thomson River near Muttaburra
plesiosaurs—north of Wandoan
pterosaurs—near Boulia and Richmond
sauropod (Australia's first Jurassic-period discovery)—near Roma
theraspid (Australia's first)—Carnarvon Gorge

SOUTH AUSTRALIA

extinct marsupials—Lake Eyre basin
Pleistocene epoch: wombats—Cooper Creek, Lake Eyre, Lake Callabonna
Miocene epoch: river dolphins—Lake Frome region
Cretaceous period: carnivorous theropod—Andamooka; opalized pliosaur ("Eric," usually on tour)—Coober Pedy

WESTERN AUSTRALIA

dinosaur footprints—Gantheaume Point, near Broome
Triassic-period fish predators—Erskine Range, between Derby and Fitzroy Crossing
Devonian period: fish—The Kimberley; placoderms—Gogo Station, near Fitzroy Crossing
Archaean-era stromatolites (the planet's oldest life-form)—Shark Bay

habited prehistoric Australia. These creatures died out in the cataclysmic worldwide extinction of the dinosaurs, long before humans arrived. Their most dangerous descendants are the saltwater crocodile, the great white shark, and a gallery of the world's deadliest snakes. A class of creature known as megafauna, however, still roamed the land when the first Aborigines came ashore. The bones of gigantic wombats bigger than buffalos, huge saber-toothed marsupial lions, and outsized kangaroos that would dwarf their puny descendants have been found, and some of these creatures may well have entered the racial memory of the Aborigines, in the form of Dreamtime myths.

The Extraordinary

Some of Australia's native fauna are candidates for *Ripley's Believe It or Not!*. The silver barramundi, found in the Northern Territory's Kakadu National Park, spends the first six years of its life as a male and the rest as a female. Australia has the world's largest and most ferociously destructive termites, some of which build nests as high as six meters. The grand champion of termite mounds is near Hayes Creek in the Northern Territory, and others are scattered about the central deserts. The world's most venomous snake is the taipan, and its kissing cousin, which inhabits northeastern South Australia and southwestern Queensland, carries enough venom to kill more than 200,000 mice.

The rather unsavory platypus frog deserves a mention; the female carries her young in her stomach and gives birth by regurgitating them. Personally, this seems like a much more humane method than the labor-and-delivery hell that most women go through! Hmpf, Mother Nature must never have been pregnant.

Marsupials

The most famous of Australian animals are the marsupials—mammals that lack a placenta, give birth to offspring still in the gestative stage, and carry them in a pouch. Almost all the 150-odd marsupial species—most notably kangaroos, wallabies, possums, koalas, and wombats—are found in Australia.

Kangaroos, or 'roos, the largest of the marsupials, are the country's national symbol. They are also the most widespread; since the arrival

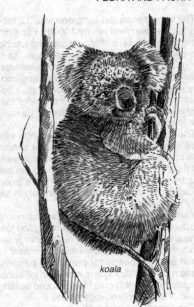

koala

of Europeans, their numbers have increased as pastoralists cleared land and drilled water bores for sheep and cattle. Australians now resort to "culling," a euphemism for massacring large numbers of native animals that interfere with graziers' interests and thereby earn the title of pest.

Despite the increasing numbers of some kangaroo species, it is a misconception that kangaroos can be seen loping down the main street of any town in Australia. In fact, they are timid creatures—usually hiding in forests—often most active at night, and they are seen about as often as a deer is in North America.

Kangaroos are hunted for their skins and meat by Aborigines, for whom they form an important food source. It used to be that most culled kangaroos would end up as dog food, but recent initiatives have allowed kangaroo steaks and burgers onto the menus of sophisticated (and some not-so-sophisticated) city restaurants. Reputedly, kangaroo meat is highly nutritious, containing no cholesterol and very little fat. So, dear travelers, you and your canine mates can now feast on the same chow.

The largest recorded kangaroo was 3.2 meters tall and weighed nearly 100 kg. Far from being the harmless, inoffensive creature gazing doe-eyed from a glossy tourist brochure, kangaroos are ready and able to defend themselves. When attacked, by dingoes or a rival kangaroo, they use their forepaws to immobilize their opponent and, rearing up on their powerful tail, they attempt to rip open their adversary's belly with knifelike hind claws.

The kangaroo has evolved a remarkably efficient means of locomotion: jumping. It cannot walk or run, though it can swim surprisingly well, but it can achieve speeds of up to 50 km per hour by just hopping along. The sight of a group of kangaroos loping across an open field in full flight is exquisite.

Kangaroos' powerful hind legs are cunningly structured with a system of counterweighted tendons and muscles that conserve the energy expended in motion, thus enabling the animal to travel at high speeds for prolonged periods. Some rural racetracks have stories to tell about kangaroos bounding onto the track and beating a field of thoroughbred race horses.

The female kangaroo, like some other marsupials, is able to control her reproductive cycle depending on the availability of food and water. A female can carry a "joey," or immature kangaroo, in her pouch and one in her uterus. Should conditions become unfavorable, she will terminate her unborn joey in utero. The joey at birth is about one inch long and must drag itself from the birth canal to the mammary gland in the pouch, a perilous journey during which the mother offers no assistance. Hairs on the mother's belly grow in a pattern that gives the joey directional aid, but should the joey fall off the mother, she will abandon it. Once the joey puts its mouth to the mammary gland, the nipple swells up and effectively locks the joey onto the teat until it has grown sufficiently to suck for itself. The joey will stay in the pouch for six to eight months until it is weaned, but it will continue to use its mother's pouch for safety and transportation until it is almost ridiculously big—a big, old pouch potato.

Kangaroo species range in size from the five-centimeter dusky hopping mouse to the giant two-meter red kangaroo. "Wallaby" usually denotes smaller kangaroos, while "wallaroo" usually denotes kangaroos that prefer a rocky or densely wooded habitat.

The sleepy, cuddlesome **koala**, beloved star of so many Australian tourist promotions, is not a bear but another marsupial. Despite its endearing good looks, koalas prefer not to be handled by kootchy-kooing humans, and they frequently outrage distinguished visitors, who pose for photo opportunities, by piddling on them. They are also equipped with formidable claws and are really much better left dozing in the trees where they belong, well-hidden atop a gum tree.

Koalas rarely drink water; they obtain their moisture from the 37 species of eucalypt leaves that form their sole diet. Their sleepy attitude is due in part to the sedative and hypnotic effect of a naturally occurring barbiturate in the eucalypt leaves. Koala numbers have rapidly declined since European settlement, and now they are a protected species. No longer hunted for their pelts, they are still under threat from loss of habitat and a venereal disease similar to chlamydia. Needless to say, that stuffed bear you take home will—hopefully—be a fake.

Wombats are stocky, thickset marsupials slightly bigger than the koala. They make their home in burrows on the forest floor. They are nocturnal animals, and consequently the headlights of cars upset their night vision.

Other marsupials include the tree kangaroo, the monkeylike cuscus, batlike flying foxes, a host of tree-dwelling possums (which are really the only marsupial to have adapted to city life), marsupial rats and mice.

One disturbing sight for drivers on rural roads is passing countless carcasses of wombats and other native animals. Road signs warn motorists of frequent crossing points, and not just for the animals' protection. Many drivers have cracked a radiator—or worse—in a collision with a kangaroo.

Monotremes

Monotremes are egg-laying mammals. There are only two in the world and they are both in Australia: the platypus and the echidna. The **duck-billed platypus** is perhaps the most intriguing of all Australia's odd creatures. The first specimens sent to the British Museum were dismissed as a hoax. Scientists thought that the web-footed, duck-billed creature with fur and claws had been intricately stitched together from the various parts of

The echidna, or spiny anteater, is a common sight in the bush, deserts, and mountains.

The other monotreme, the **echidna,** or spiny anteater, is much more accessible and a reasonably common sight in the bush, deserts, and mountains. It is named after Echidna, a monster of Greek mythology—part beautiful woman, part voracious serpent—whose offspring were even more monstrous than her own sweet self. The echidna resembles a North American porcupine, with a spine-covered body, a protruding snout, and a distinctive waddling gait, as it rolls along on its knuckles. It also has sharp claws, but its usual response to disturbance is to roll into a ball with its quills flexed.

several animals, like so-called mermaids made of monkey heads attached to fish bodies that travelers brought back from time to time from the East. However, the platypus is genuinely odd. It represents a possible link in the evolutionary chain between reptiles and mammals, since it both lays eggs and suckles its young. Its choice of home is also peculiar. The platypus, living within the confines of eastern Australia and Tasmania, seems equally happy whether basking in a tropical river or freezing its bill off in a nippy mountain stream. It lives in burrows in the banks of streams and feeds off the streambed. The platypus must close its eyes and ears under water and uses a mysterious electric sense to locate food. For protection against natural predators, the adult male has venomous spurs on its hind legs. The platypus is extremely shy and sensitive to pollution or any disturbance to its habitat. Naturally, since European settlement, its numbers are well down; so, now it is a protected species. It's not too likely that you'll see a platypus in the wild (Eungella National Park, Queensland, offers the best opportunity), but if you do, remember that these creatures are enormously sensitive and their existence is utterly dependent on being left alone.

Dingoes, Bats, and Bandicoots

Australia's native dog is the dingo, which was actually introduced from Southeast Asia about 6,000 years ago, well after the Aborigines arrived. Traditionally, Aborigines used dingoes for several activities, including sleeping beside them for warmth on cold nights—hence the expression "a three-dog night" for a particularly cold night. Nowadays the dingo roams the Outback in packs, and it is a difficult, though not impossible, animal to domesticate. The dingo earned worldwide notoriety through the Azaria Chamberlain case (wherein a dingo allegedly snatched—and, later, gnawed to death—baby Azaria from her family's Ayers Rock campsite), which only reinforced the need to take precautions when traveling in the more remote regions of the Outback. (Those dark-of-night dingo howls hardly inspire dreamy-bye lullabies.) Actually, sheep have more to worry about than newborn babes. Dingoes are known to wreak havoc (i.e. feast upon) whole flocks of sheep, inspiring a "shoot-to-kill" stance among many graziers. The famous Dingo Fence—the world's longest fence—stretches from the bottom of South Australia up to northwest Queensland. Inspectors regularly patrol about one-half of the fenceline, mending holes and setting traps, keeping the dingoes to the north and west of the barrier and out of southeastern Australia. The best chance of seeing dingoes is along the beaches of Fraser Island, off the Queensland coast.

Australia is home to about 50 species of bats, including the colossal fruit bat. These large bats congregate in huge colonies, often in the tops of trees, and feed at night.

platypus

dingo

Watching a colony wake up at sunset is a spectacle not to be missed: there is an all-pervading batty smell, and the sound of their bat cries as they fly in bat formation round the treetops is quite eerie. Gradually they disperse in search of fruit. Many species can be found grouped inside caves, and the rare golden horseshoe bat can be viewed at the Cutta Cutta Caves south of Katherine in the Northern Territory.

Both feral and domestic cats, unfortunately, have taken a vampire-ish liking to the rare—and getting rarer—rat-ish little bandicoot. The mostly nocturnal bandicoots, however, prefer a diet of insects with perhaps a bit of plant fiber to aid digestion. The short-nosed bandicoot, found around both eastern and western Australia, is the most common breed, while the rabbit-eared is a scarce sight in the Northern Territory.

Introduced Species

These are "the animals that ate Australia." Feral dogs, cats, pigs, goats, rabbits, and a host of other nonnative species, introduced by a series of intentional and accidental blunders, have brought with them economic and environmental devastation and a wave of extinctions unparalleled in the 50 million years since Australian life was cut off from outside influence by plate tectonics. Scores of native animals have been driven to near or complete extinction by competition with or attack from introduced species. Unique and irreplaceable creatures like the eastern hare-wallaby, the golden bandicoot, and the short-tailed hopping mouse have disappeared forever.

With today's population into the hundred millions, Australia's rabbits were first introduced by English colonists soon after settlement for the purpose of sport. The spry hippity-hops adapted marvelously to the semiarid areas that were cleared for pasture, and they soon out-ate the resident animals. Now, rabbit infestations regularly break out, producing tens of millions of rabbits at a time. Huge amounts of money and effort have been poured into the control and eradication of the rabbit, most notably for the construction of the "rabbit-proof fence," which extended for thousands of miles across the continent, and for the hideous virus myxomatosis, which wiped out millions of rabbits in the 1930s. These days rabbits are largely immune to myxomatosis and vast research programs seek new and more virulent solutions to the rabbit problem. In late 1995 a virus being tested on a small rabbit population on an island off the South Australian coast "escaped" to the mainland. In the ensuing months, the virus slowly spread in ever increasing arcs across the country.

An estimated 10 million feral pigs cause in excess of $100 million worth of damage annually and pose a nightmarish threat to Australia's lucrative livestock industry should they contract and spread diseases like foot-and-mouth disease or rinderpest.

Feral cats and dogs create havoc in national parks. In the trees, gorgeously colored native parrots, parakeets, and lorikeets are fighting a losing battle against introduced sparrows and starlings (the sparrows and starlings, however, have not yet made it into Western Australia, thanks to the sharpshooters on watch at the state's borders). Wild horses and feral goats roam at will, ravaging remote areas of wilderness. More than 70,000 feral donkeys are shot each year. Foxes—also introduced deliberately for sport—are a pest for farmers, but they are steadily wiping out native species as well.

In the arid zones, wild camels—one-hump dromedaries, descendants of animals brought here for cartage purposes—are actually captured for export to the Middle East; Australia now has the dubious distinction of being home to the last wild camels (approximately 100,000 of them) on earth.

Until the arrival of Europeans, Australia had never known a cloven-hoofed beast; the hard impact of hoofs breaks up the dry crusted earth in the arid regions so that annually millions of tons of topsoil simply blow away. In the Northern Territory, herds of wild buffalo and semiwild cattle roam across a fragile landscape that struggles to recover from the devastation.

Where feral animals encroach on the interests of agriculture, enormous efforts are made to control the situation. But where human population is thin, and livestock (and, consequently, livelihoods) are not affected, feral animal populations are quite literally out of control. Paradoxically, in areas that are declared national parks—and there are more than 500 of them—feral animals often thrive because they are no longer subject to the control mechanisms of agriculture, and park authorities rarely have sufficient resources to take over.

Birds

Australia's birds are a wonderful and unexpected surprise for many visitors— about 700 species, of which approximately 500 are endemic and 200 migrate to all parts of the world.

One of Australia's most distinctive birds is the flightless emu, which roams the open plains, often inside the Dingo Fence. It's slightly smaller than the ostrich. The male emu has sole responsibility in child-rearing from the time the eggs are laid. Most recently, the emu—part of the country's coat-of-arms, along with the kangaroo—is becoming trendy in the skin/feather/nouvelle cuisine arena.

Birdwatchers throughout the country will spot a large and exotic assortment of multicolored parrots (including the raucous cockatoo), budgerigars, and galahs. If you're hanging around the termite mounds you might glimpse the rare hooded parrot. Of the kingfishers, the largest is the kookaburra, found near permanent water sources. Its infectious laughing cry has earned it the nickname "the laughing jackass."

Most of Australia's 18 types of finch inhabit the tropic regions, but two renegades, the painted fireball and the zebra finch, have managed to adapt in the arid zone, usually close to permanent water sources. (Hint to Outback travelers:

kookaburra

zebra finches = nearby water.) The exquisitely colorful Gouldian finch, once a common sight across the Top End, is now almost extinct.

Common thoughout Australia are swans, ducks, geese, and pelicans, but they are most spectacular when rain falls in the interior and long-dry watercourses and lakes fill for a few months; millions of birds appear, feeding on the long-dormant creatures that have lain for years under the scorched clay.

Curvy-billed honeyeaters—67 species that range from small and colorful to big and drab—not only frequent the watercourses but are regulars around scrub, plains, and woodlands.

Around the coast, seabirds congregate in large numbers. Gulls and terns, the fairy penguins of Adelaide, Kangaroo Island, Phillip Island, and Tasmania, the muttonbird, and even the lonely albatross all may be seen in the southern oceans.

The bowerbird constructs an elaborate "bower" or display for mating purposes. It collects all manner of shiny and colorful objects for inclusion in its display, from flowers and berries to jewelry stolen from campsites. Some bowerbirds mix various substances into a form of paint to enhance their overall concept of interior decorating. The females select their mates from the most resourceful and tasteful males.

The lyrebird, so named after the fabulous lyreshaped display feathers of the male, is a great mimic and will deliver prolonged concerts imitating the sounds of the forest, other birdcalls, and even a tractor or a chainsaw. A single concert may contain up to 40 different calls.

The stately brolga (a large crane) is famous for its courtship dance, a spectacle of immense beauty.

Of the birds of prey, the keen-sighted, wedgetailed eagle is the largest, and hawks and kites are a common sight, hovering motionlessly above their intended victims or wheeling in pairs high over their territory. White-bellied sea eagles and ospreys do their preying along the remote coasts.

A fashion for native gardens that swept Australia in the '60s has meant that many species of native birds have returned to the suburbs of cities to feed on the flowering shrubs that replaced the hedges and annuals imported from Europe. Many previously unsighted species of native birds are now common in suburbs that once knew only sparrows and pigeons.

Unfortunately, many of Australia's exotic birds are highly prized by collectors overseas and, since the birds are protected, a cruel and illicit smuggling industry has developed. Snaring threatens to wipe out some species, especially of parrots, and the smuggling process itself kills more of these sensitive creatures than can satisfy this objectionable market.

Reptiles and Amphibians

Love lizards and snakes? Then you've come to the right place. Select from about 230 species of lizard, from the extraordinary frill-necked lizard to the lethargic two-meter-long goanna, plus 140 species of snake and two species of crocodile. Relatively few people are killed annually by snake bites, and occasionally an incautious swimmer is taken by a crocodile—sometimes beside a sign warning against swimming (or, worse, beside a sign that *used* to be there but was pinched by a thoughtless tourist!).

Fewer than 20 species of Australian **snakes** have the potential to kill humans. The taipan is the deadliest, although its bite is not necessarily fatal if an antivenin is administered soon enough. Other snakes to be wary of include the tiger snake, the copperhead, the death adder, the brown, and the red-bellied black snakes. Additionally, more than 30 species of poisonous sea snakes frequent coastal waters, though they are rarely encountered by humans. Remember that snakes are no more delighted to meet you than you are to meet them. Most snake bites are the result of humans trying to kill the snake, or stumbling across one suddenly and startling it into attack. When hiking it's sensible to wear boots, thick socks, and long pants. Never stick your fingers into holes and be especially careful when poking around wood or rocks (obviously). Tromp and stomp and any nearby snakes should sense your approach well in advance; most will simply move—hopefully in the opposite direction.

The two types of **crocodiles** found in Australia, freshwater and saltwater (or "salties"), are now protected since hunting severely depleted their numbers. The salties, inhabitants of tidal estuaries along Australia's northern coastline, occasionally creep into freshwater territory and are *extremely dangerous*. Big and bulky, and growing up to seven meters long, salties viciously attack and kill humans. And make no mistake—they move fast! More finely built, shorter in length (three to four meters), and with smaller teeth, the freshwater croc usually sticks to a diet of fish and frogs. It has, however, been known to attack humans, especially to defend its nests.

Good advice: No matter how inviting the river or pool, and no matter how tantalizing the prospect of diving into its limpid depths, if there are crocodile warning signs, *always* resist the temptation to swim there. Most victims of crocodile attacks have ignored the warnings. It is worth going out of your way to see these magnificent creatures, but always treat them with the greatest respect and give them a wide berth!

Lizards are harmless to humans, but you might not believe that when you look at them. The very size of the giant perentie goanna, almost 2.5 meters long, is enough to keep most of its foes at bay. The goanna inhabiting central Australia is a sleek-appearing critter with distinctive yellow spots on its back; its large gray cousin hangs out around northern riverbanks.

Lazing about the western arid zone, the fierce-looking thorny, or mountain devil, dragon can change color to a limited extent and is covered with spines so sharp that no predator would contemplate eating it. *It*, on the other hand, has a fetish for eating nothing except heaps of black ants. The Top End's frill-necked lizard is another whose hiss is worse than its bite; when threatened, it unfurls a vividly colored ruff of membrane, which makes it appear much larger, and sways menacingly from side to side, spitting and hissing with gusto. The bearded dragon has the ability to flatten its body while sunbathing in its favorite arid-zone turf.

Giant leatherback turtles (one of Australia's dozen or so species of freshwater tortoise and five types of marine turtle) breed on some northern beaches, but they are under threat from driftnet fishing and suffocation from floating plastic bags that impersonate their favorite kind of jellyfish. One of Australia's premier turtle-viewing spots is Mon Repos Environmental Park, east of Bundaberg (Queensland), where four species of turtles nest through the months of summer.

You can pick out 130 species of **frogs.** In the arid claypans where rains come only once every few years, some croakers survive by filling their bladders with water and burrowing into the mud just before it dries. There they coat their bodies with a mucilaginous secretion that seals in their juices for the next few years until rain falls again. In this way they might live for 40 years—unless they are dug up by Aborigines who use them as a source of fresh water.

Insects and Arachnids

Just as there are numerous bird species across Australia, there are some 50,000 insect species for them to feed on. These include 350 species of butterflies, 7,600 varieties of moths, and 18,000 types of beetles. New insect species are discovered with almost monotonous regularity.

Australia's 9,000 kinds of ants make it the mecca for ant scientists around the world. In some arid areas of Western Australia, there are more ant species in half a hectare than there are in the rest of the world.

Termites, also called "white ants" though they are not ants at all, are hard to miss; their humongous mounds, some in the shapes of pillars or tombstones (actually the topsides of nests), are eye-popping sights in the tropical north.

The various types of flies will soon become all too familiar to visitors with no interest in natural history, as will the staggering array of mosquitoes, midges, and other biting mites. Native bees and wasps are present as are the generally larger and more vicious European varieties. And, if the human race were to die out, cockroaches are already established in Australia, poised to take our place.

Mosquitoes cause the usual grief and are most bothersome in tropical areas. Ward them off with your choice of poisons, keep skin well covered, and sleep beneath netting; mosquito coils may or may not work. The rare but potentially fatal Ross River fever is a mosquito-induced malady with mononucleosis-like symptoms.

Thousands of spider species reside here, many of them large and hairy enough to feature in the most horrific Hollywood fantasy, but the only two posing a threat to life and limb are the infamous red-back (kin to the black widow) and funnel-web spiders. Popular mythology places the red-back squarely under the seats of outdoor lavatories so that uneasy thoughts of tiny red spiders haunt many Australians' more intimate moments. Scientists tell us that only the female red-back is venomous, but it is hard to tell the difference in a creature so small. The funnel-web spider is the most toxic in the world and is confined to Sydney and its environs. Still, very few people in Australia have died from spider bites in the last two decades. Other species to watch out for are the three varieties of scorpion, which like to hide inside shoes and clothing (clean or not), and the trap-door spider, which lives in underground holes.

The most ubiquitous, infuriating, and unsavory creature in the Australian biosphere is without a doubt the fly. In hotter months or after rains, flies descend like a nightmarish scene out of a Hitchcock film. They are relentless: they want your sweat, they want your tears, they want your moistest orifice, and they live for the moment you drop your drawers. They will irritate you into resorting to the most ridiculous contrivance of a hat fitted with dangling corks, or covering your head with a fly net, drawstring tied snugly around your neck (it's amazing how the sadistic creatures know exactly when you're going to sneak a bite of food or sip a drink!). Repellents, such as Aerogard, are moderately effective. Or simply resort instead to waving your hand constantly in front of your face, like everybody else. This is known as the Great Australian Salute. Blessedly, the little devils dissipate at nightfall.

Marinelife

Australia's seas are filled with such diversity and abundance that this topic deserves its own book. The first sea creature that most travelers heading to Australia think of is the **shark.** Australians love the beach and the danger of shark attack is instilled into all swimmers from a tender age. Consequently, the shark has been hunted mercilessly and undeservedly, without regard to the vital part it plays in the overall marine ecology. As a result, the existence of some shark species is threatened. In reality, Australia has had only 180 recorded deaths from shark attacks since 1791. (Drowning is much more of a danger in

Australia—almost twice the number of people drown *each year* as have been killed by sharks in the last *200 years*.) The largest sharks inhabit southern waters, the home of the white pointer that starred in *Jaws*. The best place to ogle these monsters is Dangerous Reef (hence the name) on South Australia's Eyre Peninsula. By the way, smaller sharks are the staple fish in fish and chips shops, where they are called "flake."

Swimmers should also beware of the deadly **box jellyfish** (a.k.a. sea wasp or stinger), prevalent along tropical coastal waters and estuaries between late October and May. Unfortunately these are the exact spots and months when the beach looks oh-so-inviting. Steer clear! The translucent box jellyfish is very difficult to see and its potentially fatal bite elicits horrific pain, red

welts, possible collapse, and the need for emergency medical help. Why do you think the locals stay away?

Most coastal areas of Australia are visited by **dolphins,** and surfers often tell of schools of dolphins frolicking with them while they surf. An isolated beach in Western Australia called Monkey Mia has become quite famous for the intimacy of its regularly visiting dolphins. Humans flock to this remote spot in such droves that there is a danger of the dolphins being frightened away or getting sick from too much human contact.

From June through October **southern right whales** can be seen during their annual breeding migration along the coastline between Yalata and the border.

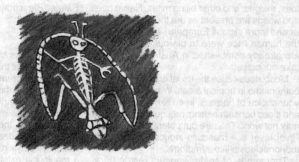

HISTORY

Australian history . . . does not read like
history, but like the most beautiful lies. And
all of a fresh sort, no mouldy old stale ones.
It is full of surprises and adventures and
incongruities, and contradictions and in-
credibilities; but they are all true, and they
happened.

—MARK TWAIN

FIRST SETTLERS

Contrary to the assertion of most Australian school textbooks published before 1980, Australia was not discovered by Europeans, and certainly not by the intrepid Captain Cook. Australia's first settlers were the Aborigines, who arrived from Asia at least 40,000 years ago, and possibly as early as 100,000 years ago.

At that time the sea levels were very much lower than they are today, and the Australian landmass was connected to Papua New Guinea in the north and Tasmania in the south. Nevertheless, the water distance separating what was then Asia from this extended Australian continent was 100 km at its very shortest. The sea journey necessary to reach and colonize Australia was a remarkable achievement, especially when you consider that early Europeans had not yet reached some Mediterranean islands where the distances involved were a lot shorter. Aborigines had arrived and populated the entire continent millennia before the great expansionary movements of either the Europeans or the Polynesians.

At least 1,800 generations of Aborigines have lived in Australia with a simple but appropriate technology—a stark contrast to the eight or nine generations of Europeans with their highly inappropriate mechanical and agricultural technologies.

Early Aboriginal Society

Much of the archaeological evidence revealing Aboriginal history comes from places like Lake Mungo, an ongoing living excavation in southwest New South Wales. Sites like this are natural treasures because their remoteness and aridity has left the fossil record undisturbed. Lake Mungo used to lie on the edge of a vast inland sea, even at the time of the earliest Aboriginal relics, and huge piles of discarded bones and seashells (known as "middens") found there provide a fairly detailed peek into the daily life of the Aborigines.

Aborigines dwelt in hunter-gatherer societies, following the kangaroos, wallabies, goannas, and fish and collecting "bush food" like witchetty grubs, roots, seeds, honey, nuts, and berries. Conditions in Australia seem to have been so favorable and the bounties of nature so prolific that Aborigines never developed permanent agricultural settlements as their cousins in Papua New Guinea did. Their main tools were spears, three types of boomerang, sharpened stones for digging and shaping wood, and a spear-thrower called a woomera. They fished with nets, traps, and hooks. Controlled fires were started to flush game and, it has been suggested, as a land-management practice, since some forests have adapted to periodic bushfires. The remnants of elaborate stone weirs designed to trap fish can be seen in parts of Victoria and New South Wales. In northern Australia's wetlands bamboo-and-cord nets trapped end-of-wet-season fish, while woven nets were employed to snag wallabies and 'roos galavanting the Queensland tablelands.

Aborigines were split up into clans—a practice that still occurs today. Clan members were considered to be descendants of a common ancestor, bound by ritual, tradition, law, and—most importantly—to designated spiritual sites. Their religious belief decrees that, after death, clan members' spirits will return to these sites. Consequently, clan rituals to honor their Dreamtime creators and ancestral spirits are supremely important events, as are their spiritual links to the land. Designated members of the clan are responsible for keeping the ancestral spirits happy by protecting the sacred sites (hardly an easy task with white settlers and, later, tourists trampling upon them) or else risk traditional punishments and/or the wrath of the ancestral ones—disasters, sicknesses, and droughts are often signs that the spirits are mighty annoyed.

DREAMTIME

Aborigines were telling stories about the land and animals around them long before the ancient Egyptians built the pyramids. Cave paintings of animals and spirits in Australia are at least as old as the earliest example in Europe. The paintings and stories tell how the great spirits made the land, animals, and plants, and how they taught the people to find food, perform ceremonies, dance, sing, paint, and keep the laws.

The spiritual interconnectedness of all living things is very powerful for Aborigines. For example, among some central Australian tribes, the Kadaitja—an elder sorcerer who wears boots of emu feathers that leave no tracks—enforces the decisions of the community. He has only to take a certain bone and point it at a miscreant to punish him. "Pointing the bone" will cause an offender to withdraw from the tribe, pine away, and eventually die. In other examples, certain painted images are vested with such power that their misuse can result in the deaths of those to whom the paintings are sacred. Disputes have arisen as recently as 1989, when some sacrosanct tribal designs were incorporated in the decor of the new Parliament in Canberra.

Dreamtime—not merely the ancient period of creation but an ongoing relationship between the land, Aborigines, and all living creatures—is essential to Aboriginal spirituality.

In the Dreamtime, animal spirits exist in human form, and eventually turn into the various animals that we know as kangaroo, snake, and so forth, while the spirits of their human kin remain related to them totemically. To the Aborigine, the Dreamtime is to be acknowledged, honored, and fortified with ritual.

Family groups or individual Aborigines have their own Dreaming, which can be a particular plant, animal, place, or natural force. Significant places where Dreamtime spirits lived or played out their destiny are marked by physical formations such as rocks, waterholes, trees, or the shape of the land. These are sacred sites, and recently some of these places have been protected from mining or other development by legislation.

An Aboriginal leader, Pat Dodson, describes the Dreaming this way:

Our dreaming in this country travels thousands of kilometres. It comes from the sea in the north to Uluru in the centre, and it spreads out in all directions, east, north, south and west. We relate to other people through the Dreaming tracks which form paths among the sacred places, and there is not just one Dreaming line, there are many.

Parts of Australia contain the harshest and most inhospitable environments on the planet, yet the Aborigines developed an affinity with the land that is a testament to their knowledge and skill. As recently as the mid-1980s, an Aboriginal family arrived at a remote Outback station, never before having had contact with whites. Their only possessions were two stone knives, two rubbing sticks to make fire, a container of dried worms, a boomerang, a spear, a woomera, and a dingo. In contrast, automobile clubs today advise travelers in the same terrain to carry the following equipment in their 4WD vehicles: long-range fuel tanks, water tanks, food for twice the expected stay, two spare wheels and tires, spare battery, tools, medicine, cooking gear, mosquito nets, blankets, maps, compass, and a radio!

Long before Captain Cook sailed into Botany Bay and formally "took possession" of their land

on behalf of the British Crown, there were 700 Aboriginal tribal groups using some 300 different languages. Their population then is estimated at anywhere up to a million people, distributed in subgroups of up to 40. By that time theirs was an ancient, complex culture, rich and finely tuned to the environment. Like their American Indian counterparts, the Aborigines lived in a spiritual communion with the land. Concepts of land ownership (like that icon of European social order—the fence) implicit in Captain Cook's first act of possession, are alien to Aborigines: "We don't own the land," says Aboriginal poet Oodgeroo. "The land owns us."

European Contact

Like white Americans, European Australians have historically accorded the native culture and heritage little or no value. This attitude was en-

The complexity of the Dreamtime for most non-Aborigines is not simply that it is obscure. Many aspects of the culture are accessible only by initiation, and taboos forbid some ceremonial and spiritual practices to even be discussed. Men and women often hold separate and exclusive ceremonies. Non-Aborigines often can only guess at the real significance and experience that underlies the Dreamtime stories. Here is a world where giant marsupials carve out the hills, the hills themselves are age-old marsupials frozen in moments of significance, the rivers are the tracks of the rainbow serpent, and the Milky Way is the river of the sky where, after the rainbow serpent has swallowed the sun, people fish for stingrays and turtles, and the stars are their campfires.

The Southern Cross is an especially significant constellation for all Australians. One Dreamtime myth gives this account of its creation: A father had four daughters. When he was old, he told his daughters that they had no one else to protect them and that when he died they might have to marry men they did not like. They agreed to meet him in the sky after he was dead. With the aid of a sorcerer, he spun a silver rope from the strands of his hair, and when he died, his four daughters climbed the rope to take up their positions as the four bright points of the Southern Cross. Their father is the brightest of the nearby pointers, Alpha Centauri, still watching over them.

capsulated in the earliest recorded commentary on the Aborigines by a European, the gentleman pirate William Dampier, when he wrote in 1688: "The Inhabitants of this country are the Miserablest People in the World. They are long visaged and of very unpleasing Aspect, having no one graceful Feature in their Faces."

The balance and harmony that Aborigines had developed and refined in their world was doomed to destruction with the first contact with land-owning Europeans who quickly "pioneered" beyond their first few coastal settlements. They brought in sheep and cattle, subsequently annihilating the waterholes that for millennia had supported many plants and animals—staples of the Aboriginal diet. Those sheep and cattle started looking mighty tempting to Aborigines, empty bellies growling with hunger. Thus the spears went a-flying, the cow pies hit the fan, and savage

retaliation by the settlers left many Aborigines dead. The dispossession of the Aborigines came with brutal suddenness and more from epidemics of introduced diseases to which they had no immunity than from gunfire and violence. Aborigines died by the thousands from smallpox, sexually transmitted diseases, tuberculosis, measles, and influenza, all of which spread rapidly through the nonresistant native community. In addition there was a policy of "dispersal," in which Aborigines were cynically cleared like any other pest from areas valuable to the pastoralists—a sickening practice tantamount to massacre. Aborigines were even hunted "for sport"—an unofficial sport, of course—as recently as the 1950s in isolated parts of Australia.

The Tasmanian example illustrates the deliberate policy of genocide instigated by the invading Europeans. Aborigines were either killed or simply rounded up and shipped to small island colonies "for their protection," where they died of disease, malnutrition, and mistreatment. Tasmania's Aboriginal population declined from an estimated 4,000 to fewer than 500 between 1800 and 1830. By 1847 only 40 remained.

Truganini, the last Tasmanian, died in 1876. Her body was preserved and displayed in a museum. Hers was not the only body to receive such ignominious treatment. Scientists in the learned universities of Europe were excited by the search for a "missing link" to demonstrate Darwin's novel theories of evolution, and thought that the Tasmanian Aborigines might prove to be that link. Bodies were purloined from burial sites to enhance the anthropological collections of faculties from Dublin to Leipzig. In 1803, the governor of New South Wales presented the preserved head of the Aboriginal warrior Pemulwoy to botanist Sir Joseph Banks, who wrote that the head "caused some comical consequences when opened at the Customs House but when brought home was very acceptable to our anthropological collections." Today, the remains of some 3,000 Aborigines, together with objects of immense cultural value, lie moldering in British museums; Aboriginal groups have been negotiating for some time, with little success, to retrieve the bodies for proper burial.

Not everybody contributed to this genocide. There were well-meaning, sometimes enlightened, but usually ineffectual efforts to help. Reservations were created, rations issued, and religious missions established, many of which are still the focus of Aboriginal settlements today. However, by the beginning of the 20th century, most Aborigines were beggars in their own country, dependent on handouts of food and clothing (without the latter they were not allowed in the white settlers' towns), or they worked for white bosses without pay. (Not too long ago, a newspaper photo of several Aboriginal entertainers on tour in America showed them posing in costume, i.e., nearly naked, while being presented with brand-new suitcases.)

White society, if it thought at all about Aborigines, took a paternalistic approach, which resulted in legislation aimed at the "benevolent" protection of an inferior race for its own good. Aborigines were under the control of official guardians in the bureaucracy until very recent

times. Children were sometimes taken from their families to be raised within the "civilizing" influence of urban, Christian folk. A form of segregation, with limits to movement, property restrictions, separate employment conditions, and regulated marriage, has existed in different forms from state to state until the last few decades. In fact, the infamous South African apartheid laws grew in part from the observations of a delegation, early this century, to Queensland, where the treatment of Aborigines was at its worst.

Up until 1939, official policy was still predicated upon the inhuman thesis that the Aborigines were a self-solving problem, meaning they would eventually die out. It was not until 1967 that Aborigines were granted the vote and the Department of Aboriginal Affairs was created by the government to legislate their needs. Australians are traditionally suspicious of attempts to alter the Constitution by referendum, and most referenda fail. So it is to Australia's credit that one of the very few to succeed was this landmark 1967 vote to grant Aborigines the same status as the rest of the community. Too bad it had to take so long. The full horror of the dispossession of the Aborigines is difficult for many Australians to grasp, and there is still an enormous gulf that separates the lives of white Australians from the ugly realities that Aborigines are laboring under even today.

ABORIGINES TODAY

Why change our sacred myths for your sacred myths?

—OODGEROO

Of the 18 million people who live in Australia today, fewer than two percent are Aborigines. The largest population of Aborigines (about 40,000) is in the Northern Territory where the first land-rights legislation returned some lands to their original owners. Altogether there are some 300 Aboriginal reserves totaling about 286,000 square km.

Most Australians seldom ever see an Aborigine, but political pressure from Aboriginal groups means that they are no longer psychologically invisible. Issues like land rights, unlawful discrimination, and Aboriginal deaths in custody are much more likely to gain media attention today than just 10 years ago. Hand in hand with increased political struggle is a renaissance of Aboriginal identity through art, dance, and music. The 1988 Bicentennial celebrations, which marked two hundred years since the establishment of the first penal colony, saw protests and demonstrations from highly visible and vocal Aboriginal groups who tried to point out that the country was a bit older than that. Still, there's a long struggle ahead.

In most states Aborigines make up 25-40% of prison populations; infant mortality among Aborigines is twice the national average; Aboriginal children are affected by serious diseases like trachoma and hepatitis B at rates well above the national average; Aborigines are still more vulnerable to sexually transmitted disease; Aborigines have a life expectancy 20 years below the national average; unemployment among Aborigines is four times the national average; access to education and health services in remote areas, where most Aborigines live, is minimal; racial discrimination, while outlawed theoretically, is a constant reality for many Aborigines. Under these demoralizing conditions many (especially young and middle-aged men) are vulnerable to alcohol abuse or, worse, petrol-sniffing. Not surprisingly, domestic violence follows in the heavy footsteps of substance abuse.

But thanks largely to Aboriginal women who have been victimized, many communities now ban booze, and rehab programs have been implemented. Inroads have also been made by the Royal Commission into Aboriginal Deaths in Custody which, in its report to the federal Parliament, acknowledged the need for big changes in police practice and the justice system as they pertain to Aborigines. The Aboriginal and Torres Strait Islanders Commission (ATSIC), created in 1990, authorizes elected Aboriginal representatives to give input and exercise some control over a number of federally funded employment and social-works programs.

Land Rights

Advances on the land-rights issue are slow but have gained momentum since the '60s when the Yolngu people of Yirrkala in northeastern Arnhem Land had the audacity to present a petition (on a sheet of bark, no less) to the federal government, demanding recognition of their original ownership. As you might imagine, that action was dismissed quickly. But the Yolngu people—

ABORIGINAL ARCHAEOLOGICAL SITES

The undisputed granddaddy of Aboriginal archaeological discoveries is Lake Mungo, a World Heritage site in the Willandra Lakes region of southwestern New South Wales. Though the lake has been dried up for about 20,000 years, the site itself is a very active excavation. Muddy, sandy embankments have eroded with time and weather, unearthing a veritable treasure trove of human and animal remains dating back about 38,000 years. Other ancient relics, such as fireplaces, tools, and leftover food (!) provide a good glimpse into the Aborigines' daily life. One extraordinary find was the 25,000-year-old cremated remains of a young woman—the world's first recorded cremation.

Northern Victoria's Kow Swamp has yielded a bounty of 10,000-12,000-year-old remains, while Keilor (near Melbourne and the international airport) has uncovered evidence of human occupation 40,000 years back. A relative baby (maybe 7,000 years old) was dredged up around Lake Nitchie in western New South Wales.

Tools and other artifacts, 20,000-40,000 years old, have been plucked from rock shelters at Miriwun on the Kimberley's Ord River, Mt. Newman in the Pilbara, and Malangangerr in Arnhem Land. Significant sites in southwestern Australia are the Swan Valley, where the oldest implements have been found, and Devil's Lair, near Cape Leeuwin in the very southwesternmost corner (near good surfing and vineyards).

Some of the oldest petroglyphs (ice age rock engravings) are located on the Nullarbor in South Australia's Koonside Cave. Other petroglyph-viewing spots include the Lightning Brothers locale (Delamere, Northern Territory), Early Man shelter (Laura, Queensland), Mutawintji National Park (far western New South Wales), and Burrup Peninsula (Damper, Western Australia).

Terra nullius, anyone?

a tough-nut bunch—fought the matter all the way to court where (surprise) it was quashed in the Yirrkala Land Case of 1971, wherein the courts upheld the Australian government's credo of *terra nullius*, i.e., no one had lived in the island-continent before 1788. This outrageously racist stance eventually pressured the government into passing the Northern Territory Aboriginal Land Rights Act of 1976.

Three Aboriginal Land Councils were established to reclaim Aboriginal lands; however, the act applied only to the dregs of the Territory, deserts or semideserts, nothing within town boundaries or owned or leased by anyone else, i.e., *anyone* else. Even Kakadu and Uluru-Kata Tjuta (Ayers Rock and the Olgas) were declared exceptions, albeit *big* exceptions, because the land fell within boundaries already designated as conservation reserves. Thus the lands were handed over with the provision that they were to be leased back to the Australian Nature Conservation Agency. The Aborigines do, however, constitute a majority of the management board and hold 99-year leases that are renegotiated in five-year increments. The co-managers, intrinsically knowledgeable about the delicate ecology and precious conservation of their formerly sacred sites, are snappy in their ranger uniforms as they give directions to ogling tourists.

The complex rules and regulations of the claiming process have meant years of haggles and hassles butting against the Territorial government, mining companies, and the federal conservation agency. Still, about one-half of the Northern Territory has been or is being "processed." Some enterprising Aborigines have started small businesses and, as for those mining rights, the Aboriginal owners have accepted the majority of the mining companies' proposals. This is progress, no?

In South Australia, the semi-obscure Aboriginal Land Trust Act of 1966 established small reserves with but few rights. More far-reaching was the Pitjantjatjara Land Rights Act of 1981, which bestowed the Anangu Pitjantjatjara and Yankunytjatjara people with title to the Anangu Pitjantjatjara Lands in the far north, about 10% of the state's area. This was followed by the Maralinga Tjarutja Land Rights Act of 1984, which returned another eight percent of the state known

as the Maralinga Lands to the Anangu people. This parcel, though conveniently located just south of the designated Anangu Pitjantjatjara Lands, is hardly choice property; it was widely contaminated in the 1950s and '60s by British nuclear testing. The Anangu retain the right to regulate liquor availability as well as access to their land. Mining is another story: an arbitrator makes the ultimate decision in any dispute between the Anangu people and the mining companies.

Land rights in the rest of Australia are still very limited. In Western Australia, where Aboriginal land constitutes about 13% of the state, the Aboriginal Affairs Department exercises dominion over only two-thirds of the Aboriginal reserves; they are granted 99-year leases for the remainder. Queensland allots less than two percent of that state to Aborigines, many of whom, because of the Queensland Aboriginal Land Act of 1991, are unable to claim their land. The Queensland Nature Conservation Act of 1992 commands that, should a claim to one of that state's parks prove successful, the Aboriginal owners must immediately lease it right back to the government—no future lease negotiations, no majority representation on the park management team, pretty much no nothing. New South Wales is not much better. That state's Aboriginal Land Rights Act of 1983 merely turned over the titles to already established Aboriginal reserves, with the possibility to claim a few other clumps of land as well as receiving some piddling privileges to the national parks. Provisions for land rights in Tasmania and Victoria are minuscule. (There *are* no Aborigines in Tasmania, you say? Guess what? They're back—well at least about 6,000 descendants are—and they're pushing to reclaim their land and heritage.)

On the national level, however, measures have been taken, if not to actually bond the Aborigines and the white folk, to at least reconcile them to one another's presence on the same land. A legal battle initiated in 1982 by Eddie Mabo and four other Torres Islanders over Queensland's Murray Islands culminated 10 years later with the groundbreaking Mabo Decision in which the High Court of Australia actually rejected *terra nullius*. This effectively acknowledged that Aborigines were the original owners of the land—yes, *before* the British! Nothing of the kind was ever done in the past. Despite adverse hoopla from pastoralists, mining companies, and other "special interest" groups, the Native Title Act was passed by federal Parliament in 1993 and implemented in 1994, paving the way for Aborigines to claim land that no one else owned or leased, or land to which they had long-term links. The many limitations and complexities surrounding the law were bound to create confusion. And they did. The first to make a significant claim under the Native Title Act were the Wik people of Cape York. Their claim included two pastoral leases that had never been permanently occupied for their purpose. Despite the Wik people having occupied the land for generations, under Queensland law, in 1996 it was decided that the granting of pastoral leases extinguished the rights of the native people. The following year the High Court overturned the decision, determining that while the Wik people had a right to the land, the pastoralists' leases would remain legitimate. And so after being dragged through the highest courts in Australia, and coming to national attention through what became known as the Wik Decision, the Native Title Act has come to be seen as ambiguous and as doing nothing to help the reconciliation of Australia.

EUROPEAN SETTLEMENT

The ancient Greeks, who were quite comfortable with the notion that the earth was round, proposed without any concrete evidence that a large southern continent was necessary to preserve the earth's equilibrium. In the 2nd century A.D., the mathematician Ptolemy, conjecturing, mapped the "Terra Incognita," the Unknown Land. It was not until the great age of European exploration, more than a thousand years later, that these intuitions were confirmed. Following the sea routes opened up by Magellan, who entered the Pacific while exploring South America, Portuguese navigator Cristoval de Mendonca made an unauthorized trip to map much of the north and east coasts of Australia. This expedition violated the treaty between Spain and Portugal, which gave Spain all the lands west of Brazil, and so the discovery was kept hush-hush. As a result no European saw the east coast of Australia until Cook's expedition 240 years later.

As early as 1606, the Spanish navigator Torres, approaching from the west around southern Africa, sailed through the straits that separate Australia from Papua New Guinea and now bear his name. Willem Janzoon followed in the same year and entered the Gulf of Carpentaria. Seventeen years later, Jan Carstensz followed Janzoon's route and mapped the western coast of Cape York. In 1642, the Dutch almost completed the coastal surveillance of Australia when Abel Tasman circumnavigated Tasmania, calling it "Van Diemen's Land," but he could see little potential for the mercantile interests that he largely represented.

By the end of the 17th century, the Dutch had poked about every part of Australia but the east coast. This was partly because they caught the prevailing westerlies as they rounded Cape Horn in Africa, sweeping them on to the lucrative markets of the East Indies. Interestingly enough, many of the Europeans who found their way to Australia had simply overshot their mark on the way to the Spice Islands to the north.

The first Englishman to visit Australia, William Dampier, landed near King Sound on the northwest coast in 1688 with a rather disreputable company that had lost its way and needed to stop for repairs. He was so unimpressed with the desolate country that he could see no reason to return or to encourage his countrymen to do so.

It was not until 82 years later that the celebrated navigator Capt. James Cook visited Australia and dragged it into the modern world. Cook had been sent to the South Pacific primarily to make astronomical observations of Venus and, while he was about it, to explore a region that was receiving more and more attention from the great powers of the day. After accomplishing his scientific mission, he returned, circumnavigating New Zealand. On 20 April 1770, he sighted the southeast coast of Australia. He turned north and charted the length of the east coast. His first landfall was "a fine bay," which Cook later called "Botany Bay" because of the numerous botanical specimens they were able to collect there.

Cook continued north for 3,000 km until his ship *Endeavor* ran aground on a coral reef near what is now Cooktown in north Queensland. It took his crew two months to repair the damage before they sailed north through Torres Strait. On

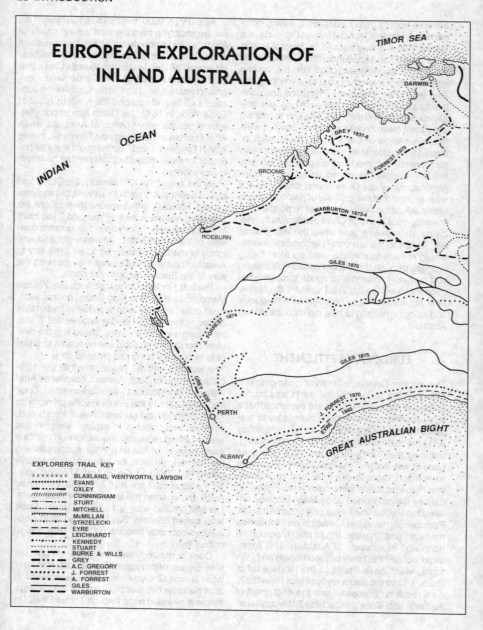

EUROPEAN EXPLORATION OF INLAND AUSTRALIA

TIMOR SEA

DARWIN

GREY 1837-8

A. FORREST 1879

INDIAN OCEAN

BROOME

WARBURTON 1873-4

ROEBURN

GILES 1876

J. FORREST 1874

GILES 1875

GREY 1839

A. FORREST 1870

PERTH

EYRE 1840

ALBANY

GREAT AUSTRALIAN BIGHT

EXPLORERS TRAIL KEY

×××××××	BLAXLAND, WENTWORTH, LAWSON
••••••••	EVANS
——————	OXLEY
////////	CUNNINGHAM
——————	STURT
‒‒‒‒‒‒	MITCHELL
▪▪▪▪▪▪	McMILLAN
——————	STRZELECKI
——————	EYRE
——————	LEICHHARDT
••••••••	KENNEDY
——————	STUART
——————	BURKE & WILLS
——————	GREY
——————	A.C. GREGORY
••••••••	J. FORREST
——————	A. FORREST
——————	GILES
‒‒‒‒‒‒	WARBURTON

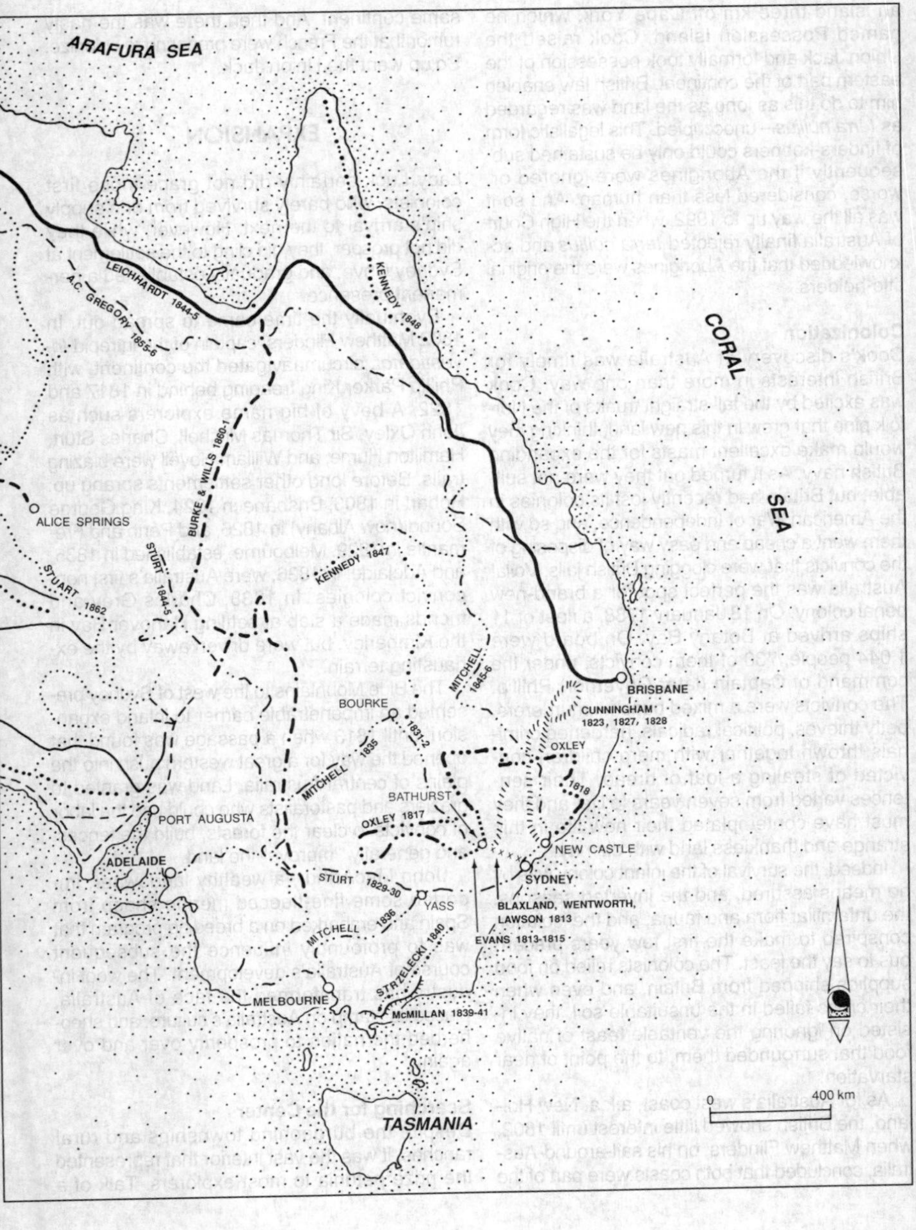
ARAFURA SEA
CORAL SEA
TASMANIA
LEICHHARDT 1844-5
A.C. GREGORY 1855-6
KENNEDY 1848
BURKE & WILLS 1860-1
ALICE SPRINGS
STURT 1844-5
KENNEDY 1847
STUART 1862
MITCHELL 1845-6
BRISBANE
CUNNINGHAM 1823, 1827, 1828
OXLEY
1818
BOURKE
1831-2
MITCHELL 1835
BATHURST
OXLEY 1817
PORT AUGUSTA
ADELAIDE
NEW CASTLE
SYDNEY
STURT 1829-30
YASS
BLAXLAND, WENTWORTH, LAWSON 1813
MITCHELL 1836
STRZELECKI 1840
EVANS 1813-1815
MELBOURNE
McMILLAN 1839-41
0
400 km

an island three km off Cape York, which he named Possession Island, Cook raised the Union Jack and formally took possession of the eastern part of the continent. British law enabled him to do this as long as the land was regarded as *terra nullius*—unoccupied. This legalistic form of finders-keepers could only be sustained subsequently if the Aborigines were ignored or, worse, considered less than human. And so it was all the way up to 1992, when the High Court of Australia finally rejected *terra nullius* and acknowledged that the Aborigines were the original title-holders.

Colonization

Cook's discovery of Australia was timely for British interests in more than one way. Cook was excited by the tall straight trunks of the Norfolk pine that grew in this new land, thinking they would make excellent masts for the expanding British navy. As it turned out they were not suitable, but Britain had recently lost its colonies in the American War of Independence, and so with them went a cheap and easy way of disposing of the convicts that were clogging British jails. Voila! Australia was the perfect spot for a brand-new penal colony. On 18 January 1788, a fleet of 11 ships arrived at Botany Bay. On board were 1,044 people, 730 of them convicts, under the command of Captain (later Governor) Phillip. The convicts were a mixed bunch—murderers, petty thieves, political radicals, hardened criminals thrown together with mere children convicted of stealing a loaf of bread. Their sentences varied from seven years to life, and they must have contemplated their new life in this strange and thankless land with dismay.

Indeed, the survival of the infant colony was by no means assured, and the inverted seasons, the unfamiliar flora and fauna, and the isolation conspired to make the first few years precarious to say the least. The colonists relied on food supplies shipped from Britain, and even when their crops failed in the unsuitable soil, they insisted on ignoring the veritable feast of native food that surrounded them, to the point of near starvation.

As for Australia's west coast, a.k.a. New Holland, the British showed little interest until 1802, when Matthew Flinders, on his sail-around-Australia, concluded that both coasts were part of the

same continent. And then there was the nasty rumor that the French were preparing to colonize. So up went the Union Jack.

EXPANSION

Lady Luck certainly did not grace those first colonists, who barely survived from one supply ship's arrival to the next. However, while they did not prosper, they did cling to the settlement at Sydney Cove, and gradually established a permanent presence.

Eventually the time came to spread out. In 1802 Matthew Flinders, captain of the intrepid *Investigator*, circumnavigated the continent, with Phillip Parker King treading behind in 1817 and 1822. A bevy of big name explorers such as John Oxley, Sir Thomas Mitchell, Charles Sturt, Hamilton Hume, and William Hovell were blazing trails. Before long other settlements sprang up: Hobart in 1803, Brisbane in 1824, King George Sound (now Albany) in 1826, and Perth and Fremantle in 1829. Melbourne, established in 1835, and Adelaide, in 1836, were Australia's first non-convict colonies. In 1838, Charles Grey and friends made a stab at settling Hanover Bay in the Kimberley, but were driven away by the exhausting terrain.

The Blue Mountains to the west of Sydney presented an impenetrable barrier to inland expansion, until 1813 when a passage was found that opened the way for a great western push into the plains of central Australia. Land was granted to graziers and pastoralists who could use the labor of convicts to clear the forests, build the fences, and generally "improve" the land.

John MacArthur, a wealthy landowner, imported some fine-fleeced merino sheep from Spain and embarked on a breeding program that was to profoundly influence the subsequent course of Australia's development. The wool industry has transformed the face of Australia, placed its stamp on Australia's culture, and shepherded the nation to prosperity over and over again.

Searching for the Center

Despite the burgeoning townships and rural ranches, it was the vast interior that represented the prize petunia to most explorers. Talk of a huge inland sea prompted a sort of magnetic pull to find the something; nothing; everything— somewhere in there!

Rummaging around the Flinders Ranges in South Australia in 1840, Edward John Eyre found not a big sea but an enormous salt lake. The lake, which he named "Torrens," prevented him from getting to his goal: Australia's center. So he had to trek south to Port Lincoln, then cross the continent to Albany in Western Australia. (Lake Torrens is actually only one in a group of lakes that includes Lakes Eyre and Frome.)

Taking up the challenge in 1844, Charles Sturt embarked on an 18-month odyssey that took him from lovely Adelaide, along the Murray and Darling Rivers, then northwest to Sturt Stony Desert where inferno-like heat, scurvy, and a variety of other horrific conditions drove him back to the city. Poor Charles never was the same, but he did end up with a forboding desert named after him.

Enter Prussian doctor Ludwig Leichhardt. Departing from Brisbane in 1844, Leichhardt and his men made a historic 14-month crossing between Darling Downs and Port Essington, near Darwin, and were credited with finding potential farmlands for pastoralist expansion. Unfortunately, the heroic Leichhardt vanished two years later while attempting another crossing. In the same year that Leichardt went poof, the Edmund Kennedy Expedition also met a dismal demise. Trekking from Rockingham Bay, south of Cairns, to Cape York in northern Queensland, a combination of bad strategy, illness, and Aboriginal attack wiped out Kennedy and most of his men.

In 1860 the Burke and Wills Expedition was running neck-in-neck with that of John McDouall Stuart, as they raced to conquer Australia's mysterious center and to forge the best route for the overland telegraph line soon to begin in Darwin.

Explorers Robert O'Hara Burke and William John Wills had money, men, and equipment aplenty, but still they did not fare very well. Departing Melbourne, Burke and Wills left most of their men at Menindee, southeast of Broken Hill. After establishing a depot at Coopers Creek, only four members of the expedition headed any farther: Burke, Wills, John King, and Charles Grey.

Summer. Ah, a marvelous time for a 1,100-km stroll through central Australia up to the Gulf of Carpentaria. They eventually achieved their goal—it was the return journey that was the killer. Grey bit the dust first, followed by Burke and Wills, who actually made it back to the Coopers Creek depot only to find their loyal mates had split back to Menindee that same morning. You can still visit the Dig Tree with its carved message on the Cooper Creek banks. John King, however, survived, thanks to nursing by local Aborigines.

Meanwhile, John McDouall Stuart turned out (in some ways) the big winner. A much better planner, Stuart had traveled round-trip from Adelaide to Chambers Bay on the north coast, east of Darwin—a route eventually mimicked by the original road, railway, and overland telegraph lines. He went down in history as the first explorer to reach Australia's geographical center, but then he just went down, period, losing his vision, memory, and his life soon after his journey.

As for that big inland sea, it turned out to be the vast, dry Outback interior. No oasis, just a *big* mirage.

Western Exploration

Except for settlements at Perth and Fremantle, the western half of Australia remained virtually unexplored by Europeans until the latter part of the nineteenth century, when a handful of intrepid explorers ventured into the region: William Gosse, aiming west from the Alice Springs telegraph station, stumbled upon Uluru (Ayers Rock); Ernest Giles bumped into Kata Tjuta (the Olgas) on his crossing attempt, then made a later expedition from between the Gascoyne River to Kata Tjuta and the telegraph line; Major John Warburton, also trying to locate a westward route from Alice Springs, eventually forged his way to the Oakover River; from the west coast, John Forrest made expeditions from Geraldton to the Overland Telegraph Line, and from Perth to Fowlers Bay in South Australia.

The 1890s brought a series of scientific expeditions into the region to check out flora and fauna, rocks and minerals, and lifestyles of the local Aborigines. Explorations were conducted northeast of Coolgardie by David Lindsay (in charge of the Elder Scientific Exploring Expedition), while the territory west and south of Alice Springs was covered by the Horn Expedition. Prospector David Carnegie staked a route from

Coolgardie to Halls Creek while, around the same time, the Calvert Expedition did not survive its foray around Western Australia's Great Sandy Desert.

It was Alfred Canning, in 1906, who mapped out his famous Canning Stock Route southwest from Halls Creek to Wiluna in Western Australia—a barren, treacherous track through the Great Sandy and Gibson Deserts and a thumbs-up favorite with diehard four-wheel-drivers.

THE GOLD RUSH ERA

The discovery of gold in the 1850s sparked a gold rush that brought huge numbers of hopeful prospectors from around the world.

Edward Hargraves began the fury in 1851. The news of even his relatively small find at Ophir, near Bathurst in New South Wales, was all it took to start the fever. Diggers came flocking, first to Ophir, and then to Turon. The Victorian government, none too happy with the migration to its neighboring state, offered a reward for gold discovery closer to, say, their own Melbourne. Within a month gold was discovered at Clunes, followed by the extraordinary finds at Ballarat, Castlemaine, and Bendigo, thereby establishing Victoria as a center of wealth and influence.

Spawned by an 1887 find in Southern Cross, Western Australia, the rush rushed westward. Five years later, Arthur Bayley staked an astoundingly huge claim near Coolgardie; then came an even larger find by three Irish prospectors at neighboring Kalgoorlie. This so-called "Golden Mile" is supposedly the world's richest area of gold-bearing earth. Once the country's poorest and most undeveloped state, Western Australia's population soared; the place was on the map—even European opera stars traveled to the wild mining settlements to have gold nuggets thrown at their feet. Even today, Western Australia is the country's richest state.

The opulence and grandeur of Melbourne and the cities that grew up around the gold mines were the exuberant expressions of an unprecedented boom. Vast fortunes were made and Australian society was transformed almost overnight. Gold fever brought Prussians, Americans, Italians, Chinese, and—of course—more English, Irish, Scottish, and Welsh. Today, Dar-

win's mix of more than 50 ethnic groups reflects the demographic wealth brought about by the gold rush. A tiny provincial society was inundated with intellectuals, merchants, entrepreneurs, professionals, artists, and adventurers ready to take advantage of new opportunities that seemed to be opening up everywhere.

Economic and social consequences aside, the gold rush gave birth to a peculiarly Australian ethos, that of "mateship." In many other parts of the English-speaking world, "mate" means a marriage partner; in Australia it also means a friend, and as a form of address, it carries an unspoken appeal to deep levels of devotion, loyalty, and affection that come from a tradition of interdependence that was born in the crucible of the goldfields. This fraternal tradition remains deeply entrenched in the Australian psyche.

It was on the goldfields near Ballarat that the Eureka Stockade incident took place. With easily extractable ore already mined, the "diggers" were forced to sink deeper and more elaborate shafts, causing mining costs to increase. As a result the gold miners' license fee became the subject of outraged protest. The dispute between the miners and the government agents became so heated that a group of diggers who refused to pay the fee built a stockade at a place called Eureka, and fought government troops on 3 December 1854. Thirty diggers died and the incipient rebellion was quashed, but the event remains significant as an expression of what author Thomas Keneally calls "that most Australian of birthrights, the Fair Go." This is a central concept for Australians, involving a sense of natural justice based on common sense, equality, and a healthy disregard for authority and ideology.

The Bushrangers

A passion for the "fair go" flows on as a sympathy for the underdog, the "battler." This accounts for the affection—almost reverence—rogues and outlaws command in the popular imagination, particularly the 19th-century bushrangers. The most famous of them was Ned Kelly, whose distinctive homemade helmet and suit of armor have become icons of Australian culture. Kelly came from an Irish family of small selectors (cockatoo farmers, or "cockies") whose frequent conflict with wealthy pastoralists, or "squatters," and the authorities led them into a miniature revolt. After seeing their mother imprisoned and serving time themselves for uncommitted crimes, the Kelly brothers took to the bush and began a brief but spectacular career as bank robbers. Ned Kelly often brazenly and singlehandedly captured entire townships for days at a time. His reputation grew until he was captured after a siege at Glenrowan in which he received 28 gunshot wounds. He was taken to Beechworth where a sensational trial took place, then transported to Melbourne to be hanged. "Tell them I died game," he said, awaiting execution. On the gallows his last words summed up the battler's philosophy: "Such is life."

There were many other bushrangers—Bold Ben Hall, Mad Dog Morgan, Frank Gardiner, Martin Cash (who was one of only a few to escape the infamous Port Arthur penal colony in Tasmania), Bogong Jack, Captain Midnight— and it is interesting to note that much of the mythology about them centers around the unfair and treacherous circumstances of their captures and deaths. Traditionally, Australians have tolerated almost every kind of social aberration, but they draw the line at the arbitrary exercise of power and privilege by the strong over the weak.

SOCIAL REFORM AND FEDERATION

By the end of the 19th century the scene was set for further social upheaval. Labor was organizing itself and leading the world in a militant struggle for workers' rights. The Australian Labor Party was founded in 1891, and that same year a wave of strikes for better wages and conditions culminated in the famous Shearers' Strike, which was ruthlessly put down by the wealthy landowners who employed scabs, or "blacklegs," to bring in the all-important wool clip (crop). Labor leaders were imprisoned, which led to the cry: "If they jail a man for striking, it's a rich man's country yet." If the cardinal virtue in Australia is mateship, the two deadly sins are scabbing and dobbing—informing against one's mates.

On 1 January 1901, after a decade of debate and negotiation, the six Australian colonies were joined in a federation of states with the passage of the Constitution by the British Parliament. The new federal government met in Melbourne until

moving to the new capital, Canberra (designed by the fashionable architect Walter Burley Griffin), in 1927. Australia continued to pioneer policies of social reform that did not go unnoticed elsewhere in the world. For example, Australia was the first country to elect Labor representatives and the first country to elect a Labor government. It was one of the first countries to grant women the vote.

These notable developments came to the attention of Lenin, who wrote a tract on the Australian Labor Party. He concluded that it was a tool of the bourgeoisie. Nevertheless, a number of progressive developments were enshrined in Australian legislation long before they were achieved elsewhere. The old-age pension, the eight-hour workday, the right to strike—all these became realities in Australia when other nations would not even tolerate their advocacy.

While Australia achieved its independence from Britain without bloodshed, it still remained emotionally and psychically bound to the mother country. Britain remained Australia's chief trading partner and military ally through two world wars. The decline of the British Empire and the emergence of the United States as a world power meant merely that dependence was transferred from one to the other.

MODERN TIMES

World Wars

The first world war terribly scarred the generation that took part in it. Australia's first action was at Gallipoli in the Dardanelles, where, hopelessly outnumbered and outpositioned by a firmly entrenched Turkish army, thousands of young Australians were slaughtered. The incident was so profoundly shocking to a young nation that the sacrifice and suffering of those Anzacs (Australia and New Zealand Army Corps) has never been forgotten.

Perhaps the most moving story of that conflict concerns a young soldier, Simpson, who with his donkey rescued the injured and dying without regard for his own safety. Eventually he fell to a sniper's bullet, but Simpson and his donkey have an honored place in the national consciousness.

Australians went on to fight on the battlefields of Europe, and, if nothing else, their experiences helped to open the eyes of an insular and isolated community to the wider world. This process was terribly gradual, and despite its proximity to Asia Australia for years regarded itself as an outpost of the British Empire.

The 1920s brought increased prosperity, largely through the export of primary produce. Refrigeration had made possible the shipment of frozen meat over the enormous distances necessary to reach markets in Europe; Australia was said to ride once again on the sheep's back. Unable to avoid the worldwide depression of the 1930s, Australians suffered all the hardships that were familiar to people in America and Europe, and—with the outbreak of WW II— once again took up arms for king and country. This time, however, there was a direct threat from Japan and, while Australians fought in Europe and Africa, they also had to defend their own land. An air raid on Darwin by Japanese bombers created an unprecedented response and helped cement a military alliance with the United States that continues today. General Douglas MacArthur's proud boast that he would return to the Philippines was made possible in part by retreating and regrouping on the Australian mainland.

Changing Times

After the war, social change picked up tempo. A positive immigration drive replaced the infamous White Australia Policy, which had restricted entry to Australia largely to white Anglo-Saxons. Displaced refugees from Europe were recruited to come for a new start in the land of opportunity. For many, the realities did not measure up to the promise, but, nevertheless, ever-increasing numbers of Italians, Greeks, Hungarians, Yugoslavs, and peoples from a host of other countries began to make their presence felt.

It is often hard now for Australians to appreciate just how staid, unimaginative, and limited their society was only a few decades ago. The isolated Outback, as might be expected, has almost always possessed a typically anarchic "we make our own rules" nature, while the Western Australians are plain and simply "laid-back," like their Southern California geographic counterparts. Other parts of the country, particularly the east coast, were slightly on the uptight side. In Melbourne, for example, no alcohol could be sold after six o'clock, which led to the degrading "six o'clock swill," as patrons rushed into hotels after work and downed as many beers as quickly as they could. "Wowserism," or puritanism, ensured that virtually no activity of any kind, except church-going, could take place on Sunday. A combination of the influx of more sophisticated migrants and the liberating influence of the youth culture of the '60s has irreversibly transformed the face of Australian society over the past two or three decades.

During the same period, Australia's traditional allegiance to Britain became more and more irrelevant. Meanwhile, Britain has gradually divested itself of its colonial heritage and turned more and more toward a future in Europe. With Britain's entry into the Common Market, Australia lost automatic access to its traditional markets and was forced to face the reality of its location on the edge of Asia. The increasing numbers of European and, later, Asian migrants felt no sentimental attachment to the British institutions that had figured so largely in the minds of Anglo-Saxon Australians.

Finally, Australia's strategic position in the South Pacific brought it into the sphere of American influence. Since the 1950s, Australian troops have answered the call from Washington, not London, first in the Korean War and more disastrously in the Vietnam War. Australia's longest-serving prime minister, Sir Robert Menzies, once said of Queen Elizabeth, "I did but see her passing by, and yet I love her till I die," much to the dismay of independence-minded Australians. Nothing could better illustrate the dramatic shift in cultural focus that has taken place in Australia than the words of his successor, Harold Holt, at the height of the Vietnam War: "All the way with L.B.J."

AUSTRALIA TODAY

Australia describes itself as a multicultural society, and it is perhaps the most cosmopolitan society in the world, with almost one-quarter of its present population having been born elsewhere. The benefits of such a wide mix of ethnic, cultural, and religious backgrounds are immense and, although the potential for social discord undoubtedly exists, somehow the friction that characterizes similarly heterogeneous communities has rarely occurred in Australia. Whether this is due to a tradition of easygoing tolerance, or to an ambience of apathy that infects all new arrivals, Australia's numerous ethnic communities have achieved a harmony that would be unthinkable in many parts of the world. That is not to say that discrimination and prejudice do not exist, but most Australians have grown to appreciate the differences that succeeding waves of migrants bring to their society—from the novelty of new foods (Australia boasts some fabulous ethnic restaurants) to the challenge of learning new languages, customs, and ways of thinking.

Economically, Australia is in the same circle of recession, unemployment, foreign debt blowout, and inflation as many other western countries. Having a small population, and a tax base that is minuscule compared to that of larger industrialized countries, Australia is helpless in the face of international economic developments. For decades, the country has relied on the export of primary produce and now finds that its markets are increasingly unreliable, while prices are out of control. A new drive to turn the "Lucky Country" into the "Clever Country" has been launched to stop the flight of its scientists and technicians to the universities and research companies of America and Europe, and at the same time develop the "sunrise" industries necessary for a high-technology future.

Australia, the Republic

For many Australians, looking toward the future means breaking ties with the past. The drive to make the final break with Britain and declare Australia a republic has been an issue for more than a decade, but has recently intensified. Former Labor Prime Minister Paul Keating began the push, but current Prime Minister John Howard is a monarchist. At the 1998 Constitutional Convention, it was voted overwhelmingly to sever ties with the British Monarchy. The next step is a public referendum to decide how an Australian president would be elected (the two most likely outcomes are that the president would be voted in by a general election or would be elected by the federal parliament).

She'll Be Right, Mate!

Australians have developed a unique laissez-faire attitude, embodied in the expressions "she'll be right" and "no worries," and it seems difficult to rouse them to action. The advantage of this approach is that life in Australia is remarkably relaxed and stress-free, even in the cities. Violence and the social blight of drug abuse have not quite reached the heights that most Americans would consider normal. Access to a comfortable standard of living is easier in Australia than almost anywhere else on earth. The price for such a self-satisfied lifestyle is indolence, apathy, and procrastination, and Australians are only just beginning to realize how precarious their delightful existence is.

Australia is changing, and never more so than now. The past has forced Australians to be innovative and adaptable because of their extreme isolation. Air travel, which so many Australians helped to pioneer, and the information superhighway have meant that Australia no longer must labor under the "tyranny of distance."

Despite its problems, Australia still has a refreshing, overriding sense of optimism—hey, South Australia still has its festivals; Northern Territory and Outback, their mystique; Queensland, the reef; New South Wales, its harbor; Victoria, her restaurants; Tasmania, its wild beauty; and Western Australia, the surfers and prospects of gold. So, what's the problem, mate?

GOVERNMENT

For a country of only 18 million people, Australia has an awful lot of government. It is a measure of Australians' political apathy that they have allowed themselves to become, according to some commentators, one of the most over-governed peoples in the free world. Australians labor under three tiers of government—federal, state, and shire or municipal. There are six state governments, two assemblies for the territories, and 900 local government bodies. All are accompanied by the appropriate bureaucracies, red tape, and seals of approval (or disapproval).

STRUCTURE

Australia follows the American example in the separation of powers, whereby the executive, legislative, and judiciary are independent. The federal government is an odd mix of the British Westminster system and the American congressional system. Australia's Constitution is an Act of the British Parliament, passed in 1901, which provides for a House of Representatives, whose members (divided on the basis of population) are elected every four years, and an upper house, the Senate, whose function is to act as a house of review and provide equal representation for each state, thereby preserving state rights. The political party with most members in the House of Representatives becomes the governing party and the prime minister is elected from within that majority. On 3 October 1998, the Liberal Party, under the leadership of John Howard, scraped into power for a second term. For general information on the Australian government and its structure, visit the website www.fed.gov.au. The **Commonwealth Government Directory,** listing all departments, including contact names and addresses, is also displayed on the web at www.gold.directory.gov.au.

Canberra (Australian Capital Territory, or ACT) is home to the federal Parliament and other government agencies, as well as foreign embassies. Surrounded on all sides by New South Wales and on its own piece of land, Canberra resembles Washington, D.C., but it's not nearly as exciting.

The formal head of state is still the Queen of England, although her powers are vested in the governor-general, who is nominated by the Australian government of the day. With all the current buzz about ditching the monarchy, however, the title Governor-General may soon transmute into President of the Republic of Australia. Under the Australian Constitution, the governor-general, being the chief executive, has the power to dissolve Parliament, ratify legislation, appoint ministers of the government, command the armed forces, and appoint judges to the high court. Under an unwritten convention, the governor-general acts, in a mainly titular capacity, under the instructions and advice of the prime minister, as does the queen.

Many Australians remember with outrage the events of 11 November 1975, when Governor-General Sir John Kerr dismissed the Labor government of Prime Minister Gough Whitlam, thus bucking the customary hierarchy. Right before a general election Whitlam couldn't pass supply bills through the hostile Senate, agitated by the governor-general. The intricacies and implications of that decision still reverberate in the corridors of Parliament House and the case is still a hotly debated point for many Australians.

The Senate is made up of 12 senators from each state and two from each territory. State senators are elected for six years, but only half the Senate faces the electorate every three years. Territory senators serve a maximum of three years, their terms coinciding with those of House members. Because the popular mandate only affects those senators who stand for re-election, this has often led to the situation in which the House of Representatives faces a hostile Senate. The Senate, while theoretically a house of review, is able to block legislation—as it did in the crisis of 1975.

State governments are microcosms of the federal structure and are bicameral, with the exception of Queensland, which disbanded its upper house as soon as it could. Numerous attempts in other states to follow that example have all been met with the in-built suspicion with which Australians treat politicians who start tinkering around with the system: it is axiomatic that politicians are not to be trusted, so if they want to do something it is much safer not to let them do it. Consequently, most states are lumbered with unwieldy edifices of government. With the exception of the Northern Territory, which is governed by a chief minister, the states are run by individual premiers. Aside from renegade Queensland and the Northern Territory, upper houses in the states are known as the Legislative Council; lower houses in New South Wales, Victoria, and Western Australia are the Legislative Assembly; lower houses in South Australia and Tasmania are the House of Assembly. The state governments are based in each capital city.

The struggle between the state and federal governments is ongoing. The Constitution gave the states considerable powers, many of which have been whittled away by the federal government over the years. States have responsibilities for health, housing, education, justice, and transport, but they have lost much of their power to raise revenue and must receive grants from Canberra, which controls the power of taxation. The control of natural resources is under the jurisdiction of the states, but the federal government has used its powers to make foreign policy (particularly by entering the World Heritage Treaty) to block development in environmentally sensitive areas of Tasmania and Queensland. Other federal controls consist of the usual matters concerning defense, foreign policy, immigration, the economy, and the postal service.

Australia has a plethora of local governments, responsible for collecting rubbish, mending holes in the road, giving out parking tickets, and holding up homeowners' plans to renovate their kitchens.

POLITICS

Parties
Historically, Australian politics has been effectively dominated by a two-party system. The Australian Labor Party (ALP) has traditionally drawn its support from the union movement but in recent times has extended its base to white-collar workers and liberals. The Liberal Party (LP), drawing its support from private enterprise,

small business, and the professions, is the principal partner in a conservative coalition with the rural-based National Party (formerly the Country Party). Recently, the Australian Democrats (AD), a centrist party with a strong environmental platform, various Green Independent parties, and One Nation have made inroads into the two-party system.

Voting
Because of the huge variations in population density across Australia, it has never been possible to achieve "one vote, one value." Rural electorates can be quite enormous in area but still have fewer electors than inner-city seats, so there is an inevitable gerrymander that favors rural communities, traditionally the most conservative voting block.

Voting is mandatory for all citizens over 18; electors who fail to vote are liable for a fine. Voluntary voting was tried until 1925, but the turnout was so abysmally low that it was abandoned. Voting is preferential and candidates on the ballot must be numbered in order of the elector's preference. This has made it necessary for political parties to produce "how to vote" cards and hand them out at polling booths, to instruct their supporters in the best manner of distributing their preferences. Some Senate ballot papers have had more than 60 candidates, and voters have had to number each one for their vote to be valid. This system has given rise to the "donkey vote" in which a lazy, bored, or hurried voter will simply number the candidates in order down the page. So widespread did this practice become that it has decided the outcomes of several close ballots, and candidates with names at the beginning of the alphabet enjoyed such an advantage that they have been known to change their names to secure the donkey vote. To counter this practice, candidates' positions on the ballot are now determined by random selection.

International Relations
The Australian government is signatory to a number of international treaties including ANZUS, a joint-defense pact between Australia, New Zealand, and the United States. Recently, New Zealand was suspended from this arrangement because of its refusal to allow nuclear-armed ships into its ports; still the Aussies

haven't abandoned the Kiwis—they have other agreements. Strategic commitments are also active in Papua New Guinea and nearby southwest Pacific islands.

The United States maintains three top-secret military bases in Australia—at Pine Gap, the North West Cape, and Narrungar. No rental is charged for these facilities (unlike U.S. bases in the Philippines); while they are described as joint facilities, access for Australians is limited. Many Australians believe these bases are first-strike targets and have lobbied for their removal. The North West Cape facility has currently been turned over to the Australians.

Australia is one of the senior members of the Commonwealth of Nations and has a long history of concerned involvement in international affairs through the United Nations and, more recently, the South Pacific Forum. The country lays claim to the largest area of the Antarctic and has been instrumental in ensuring that Antarctic Treaty nations agree to prevent mining and damaging development of the continent. Australia has also campaigned vigorously against French nuclear testing in the Pacific.

Acknowledging its identity as Asia-Pacific (and not part of the United States or Europe), Australia is taking steps to build relations with its northern neighbors. One example is dispassionate work for a solution to the terrible problems that beset

Cambodia; e.g., the Khmer Rouge. Australia's "good guy" reputation for being the first country to recognize the early 1970s Beijing government has been used to persuade the Chinese government to improve civil rights for its people. Similarly, relations with close neighbor Indonesia have been helped through two 1992 events: the creation of the Australia-Indonesia Ministerial Forum and the signing of the Timor Gap Treaty, which recognizes Timor's sovereignty and legitimacy as an Indonesian country. The government is also increasing dialogue regarding security and defense with important nations such as Malaysia, Singapore, and Indonesia, and continues to pursue mutual arrangements and agreements with Japan, China, the Republic of Korea, and Vietnam.

Relations with independent African nations are relatively friendly, as they are in parts of Latin America and the Carribean, and of course Europe. Australia is a supporter both of peace negotiations in the Middle East and the Israeli-Palestine Liberation Organization peace accord.

But don't think for a minute that Australia has softened its allegiance with the United States, despite occasional tensions over wheat subsidies and airline routes. Australia sent a battalion to join the U.S.-guided task force in Somalia and was also the first country to back the Gulf War.

ECONOMY

Official embassy statistics peg Australia fourteenth from the top of the world's economies, with a GDP (Gross Domestic Product) around 70% that of the United States. Agriculture and mining still account for much of Australia's wealth, but, increasingly, other sectors such as tourism, manufacturing, and service industries have shown big promise as "econo-boosters."

Life wasn't looking so rosy during the world recession of the early 1990s, which dragged Australia down with it. The usual greed, corruption, and rah-rah investments of the booming 1980s—most of them instigated by a few mega-rich Western Australian tycoons—lost big bucks for many—trusting senior citizens and hyped-up spendthrift yuppies alike. Few went unscathed. The result of those high-profile entrepreneurs

shuffling worthless pieces of paper back and forth was the same: huge stock market losses, wiped-out savings accounts, building societies and banking institutions gone belly-up.

Times were tough on the farm those days—not just because of the recession but because of an international trade war with potentially disastrous consequences for the land of Oz. Even rural Australia, while it might seem removed from the rest of the planet's concerns, gets heavily spun up in the buy-and-sell trade-war web. Cattle, wool, and mining (and now tourism) are major rural commodities, and rural Australia comprises a big chunk of the country, which relies heavily on global trade.

Australia has been working diligently to establish an internationally competitive economy, enabling it to compete with the United States and Europe, but most particularly with the rapidly exploding Asia-Pacific markets (Japan, which purchases more than one-fourth of the country's merchandise exports, remains the largest single export market). To enable primary export commodities to compete, Australia has greatly reduced tariffs on once heavily protected industries.

Overall, the increased-trade plan seems to be working and, happily, the country is pitting its growth against that of the top industrialized nations. In 1998 the economy grew by three percent. The knocking-down of the high tariff walls in the mid-1990s meant that Australian manufacturers, production having increased about 25%, now compete with traditional commodities to bring export revenue into the country. Latest statistics show that manufacturing and services exports have increased threefold, while overall exports have doubled.

An annual average inflation rate that hovered at about eight percent in the 1980s slid to below two percent in the late 1990s, below that of most of the country's largest trading partners. Interest rates have dropped considerably in the last decade. Official short-term rates plunged from about 18% in 1989 to about seven percent in 1999; long-term rates of about eight percent are at their lowest since the early 1970s. This is certainly good news in a country that boasts one of the highest levels of home ownership in the world.

Unemployment, however, has not fared too well in the numbers game. And, while a substantial number of jobs were created in the manufacturing and services sectors (1.4 million 1983-1990), the traditional arena saw massive layoffs and cutbacks. Optimists point to signs of a strengthening job market with the change of government, but the reality is that unemployment, which ranked a whopping 11% in late 1992, still occasionally drifts within the double-digit range. At the last election, in late 1998, just over six million people worked full-time, with women making up 41% of the labor force. Most employment fell within manufacturing, construction, community services, and wholesale and retail trade.

The pressure of international competition has inevitably eroded the hard-won conditions that a century of union activity had established. At one time more than 50% of the labor force belonged to one of 227 unions, affiliates under the umbrella of the national Australian Council of Trade Unions (ACTU). And even though membership has dropped some 25%, industrial relations—and the ubiquitous strikes—continue to be a thorny issue in Australian politics.

Employment discrimination because of race, color, sex, marital status, pregnancy, descent, or national or ethnic origin is illegal throughout Australia, and age discrimination is now squeaking its way onto the list as well. The average work week is 38 hours and almost every employee is entitled to four weeks per year of paid holiday time.

AGRICULTURE

Just two percent of Australia's workforce is involved in agriculture, and yet agricultural products account for nearly four percent of Australia's export revenue—as well as feeding the other 98% of Australians. Not too bad, considering that only about two-thirds of the country is suitable for any kind of agricultural or ranching enterprise, and half of *that* area can only handle pastoral activities. Nevertheless, advanced know-how in crop yields, pastoral output, and soil fertility, along with the related equipment and machinery, have inaugurated and/or boosted cultivation at many desert and semidesert stations (rural ranches). And, of course, Australia's so-called "cattle kings" of the late 1800s were instrumental to the inland's pastoral development; Sir Sidney Kidman, Nat Buchanan, the Durack family—all of them were successful cattle-station pioneers.

Stations are enormous. Numbering about 125,000, they encompass 60% of the country's total land area and are the breeding grounds for most of the cattle and sheep. South Australia's Anna Creek Station, for example, totals 31,000 square km and is the size of some European countries. Typically each station has a homestead, or headquarters, where the owners, managers, and other staff tend to their livestock.

Australia is the world leader in wool production and, with the majority of its sheep being that fine merino breed, most of that wool eventually threads its way into (warm) apparel, while skins off the sheeps' rears often end up cozying those of humans riding in cars or sprawled in front of a fireplace. Australia's major wool markets are Germany, Italy, France, Japan, and China.

In case any of you thought we were entering some sort of "cut your cholesterol, curtail your meat intake" era—forget it. As of the 1990s, Australia knocked out the entire European Community as the largest international exporter of veal and beef, with mutton and lamb following behind. And although exports are sent to more than 100 countries, guess who's stuffing down the most? Yes, the new "fat-free" United States. Skinny Japan, however, is the biggest spender. (Some consolation: Japan and the United States are also the main export markets for fish and seafood.) The Aussies, coming in third as the world's biggest meat-eaters, support their own country by consuming approximately 100 kg per person annually of beef, veal, chicken, lamb, mutton, and pork.

Dairy concerns, situated mainly around the high-rainfall southwestern and southeastern mainland coasts and northern Tasmania, pump out billions of liters of whole milk; two-thirds are made into cheese, butter, milk powders, and other related products.

Australia's massive wheatbelt, stretching across all five mainland states, produces more than 15 million tons of the grain, with nearly two-thirds exported to big buyers like India, Egypt, Japan, Korea, and China. Wheat production accounts for almost half of farmers' total income from field crops, but also important are rice, cotton, barley, sugarcane, oats, oilseeds, and field peas.

Fruit and vegetables are practically devotional commodities in Australia, and the country enshrines approximately 125,000 hectares of vegetables and 25 million fruit trees. Vineyards, planted on 65,000 hectares, produce millions of liters of wine annually and are receiving recognition—and occasional raves—from rapidly growing export markets in the United States, United Kingdom, New Zealand, Canada, Japan, and Sweden. Major winegrowing regions are in South Australia and New South Wales, but Tasmania, Victoria, and Western Australia each have noteworthy cellars. Australian beer has also been hopping.

Forestry, as in many other parts of the world, is a touchy subject. Three-quarters of Australia's native forests (mainly eucalypt forests, but significant areas of rainforest as well) have disappeared since the arrival of Europeans. Some have been destroyed by fire, but the majority have—as elsewhere—simply been logged. Parts of Tasmania look positively ravaged. Plantation forests are usually pine, which offer no food or habitat to native bird and animal life. Logging in native forests and reserves, the "national estate," has been increasingly opposed by environmental groups on the grounds that such activities are unsustainable, and bitter disputes rage between the Greens and proponents of the timber industry, who see their jobs and livelihoods threatened.

MINING

You name it, Australia probably mines it—the country has been mined for well over a century.

Once the only mineral of any interest to the prospector was gold, gold, and more gold; this is still one of the principal targets of the mining industry (after all, Australia is still the world's third-largest producer), and gold miners have tax-exempt status. There's still gold lurking (and luring) in the hills; every now and again some lucky fossicker trips over a nugget and sells it to a Las Vegas casino for a million dollars.

Now miners have turned their attention to the host of other valuable minerals still underground. Prices fluctuate and mining has its slumps and booms, but the only check on mining activities for the past decade has been the combination of environmental and Aboriginal land-rights issues.

Australia is the world's largest producer of

a man and his big monster—symbol of the rich Pilbara district

bauxite, which is mined mostly at Weipa, on Queensland's Cape York. The principal source of aluminum, bauxite is also a major player in the iron ore business, of which Australia, along with Brazil, is the world's largest exporter. Much of Australia's iron ore is mined from the remote Pilbara region of Western Australia and is a big reason for the state's wealth. Iron ore launched BHP (Broken Hill Proprietary) on the path that has made it Australia's largest company and a multinational corporation.

Australia has some of the world's largest reserves of black coal, most of it mined in Queensland and New South Wales where it was discovered in 1791. It's an energy source that becomes more significant as global supplies of oil are depleted. Like so many of Australia's raw materials, minerals are generally shipped offshore to the industrial powerhouses of Europe, Japan, and other Asian countries to be turned into consumer products like cars, television sets, and computers, and sold back to Australia, aggravating the problems of foreign debt and balance of trade. The government's "Buy Australian" admonishment is taken quite seriously by citizens.

Australia is a major producer of copper, which is mined in all states except Victoria. The largest deposits are at Queensland's Mount Isa and South Australia's Olympic Dam, with refineries in South Australia, Queensland, and New South Wales.

Nickel, another huge output, is mined largely in Western Australia, followed by Queensland. Groote Eylandt, in the Northern Territory, is home to one of the world's largest manganese mines, while Kunwarara in Queensland is a major cryptocrystalline magnesite reserve.

More megaproducers are the wealth of mineral sands that contain titanium minerals and byproducts such as zircon and monazite, minerals important in the development of new technology ceramics. These sands have traditionally been found and mined on the nation's beaches, and pristine areas of environmental importance have been ravaged in the past. Public pressure has resulted in the preservation of Fraser Island, Moreton Island, and other sensitive areas, while places like the Shelbourne Bay wilderness in Cape York, where mineral sands have been identified, are the subject of ongoing disputes.

Australia contains an estimated one-third of the world's known uranium ore, with the major deposits situated in South Australia, Queensland, Western Australia, and the Northern Territory. The government allows the mining and export of uranium from Northern Territory's Ranger Mine and South Australia's Olympic Dam—export conditions being that the raw "yellowcake" is to be used for peaceful purposes only. Further exploration for uranium threatens parts of Kakadu National Park in the Northern Territory, where environmentalists and Aboriginal activists have joined to oppose development.

Other mining activities bring much happier thoughts of future use: Australia is a leading producer of diamonds, sapphires, and opals. Sparkly, happy things!

ENERGY

Australia is ideally situated to take advantage of the development of solar energy, although progress in this field is slow; fewer than five percent of Australian homes are equipped with solar hot-water units. In the Northern Territory and Western Australia, where cloudless days are as numerous as anywhere on earth, the figure is much higher. Locally developed silicon solar cells power remote railway crossings. Telstra, the national telephone authority, has installed solar-powered telephones in isolated communities in the Outback. Interest in solar power is getting stronger in Australia, which is running low on traditional energy sources. In 1993, Perth (Western Australia) was designated the first United Nations Centre for Applications of Solar Energy, giving it a leading edge in international research.

Wind provides another environment-friendly energy option, particularly in the high-wind coastal areas of South Australia, Western Australia, Tasmania, and the Bass Strait. Its main uses are to power windmills and small turbine generators, and it is now the preferred choice over diesel at Outback homesteads.

Most of Australia's energy requirements are still supplied by coal, which is also exported in the millions of tons along with large quantities of liquefied natural gas and light crude oil. Australia is roughly two-thirds self-sufficient in oil and produces plenty of natural gas. Most petroleum comes from the Bass Strait and Timor Sea regions, while Western Australia's North West Shelf—Australia's largest development project—is pumping out millions of tons of liquefied natural gas (LNG). (More areas, showing potential for large gas and oil discoveries, have yet to be fully explored.) Light crude oil as well as LNG represent increasingly significant exports, most of it slicking toward the South Pacific and Japan. Heavy crude, however, is still on the import list, supplied by the Middle East but refined domestically.

Huge, easy-access coal reserves give Australia the benefit of substantial, low-cost electricity, most of it produced by coal-fired power plants bolstered by hydroelectric systems and natural gas-fired units. State public utilities have been the suppliers for most of the country's electricity; however, the federal government is geared up for a soon-to-come national electricity grid to provide a competitive market for business consumers.

Gas is becoming increasingly more important as a power source in Australia. The federal government's National Gas Strategy is encouraging free and fair trade between states, the dismissal of a lot of red-tape approvals, and a "casual" approach to pipeline regulations. Natural gas is supplied to all mainland capital cities via pipelines from producing fields.

Environmental Concerns
The looming greenhouse effect from carbon gas emission is becoming more critical, even to the normally apathetic Australian public. Several neighboring nations in the South Pacific face the prospect of literally sinking beneath the waves should global warming cause sea levels to rise even a meter or two.

Substantial hydroelectric systems operate in Tasmania and the Australian Alps in the southeastern corner of the mainland, but it is unlikely that further development of this energy source will be acceptable to a public that, thankfully, is growing more environmentally aware. It was the planned flooding of the Gordon River for hydroelectricity that placed environmental issues firmly on the agenda of every political party in Australia early in the 1980s.

And, remember that little problem with the ozone layer?

The good news is the politicians have been listening and maybe even *care* (at least about reelection). Concerned Greenies, innocent islanders, gasping asthmatics—help may be on the way!

In 1994 the Commonwealth Environment Protection Agency in Australia signed an agreement with the United States Environmental Protection Agency to help each other with mutual environmental concerns. This global stance will encourage joint research-and-development projects and an information-and-personnel network that will benefit both countries and thereby extend to the rest of the world, hopefully. Both countries are part of the Montreal Protocol on Substances that Deplete the Ozone Layer, which regulates trade in, and production of, ozone-depleting substances. Also, Australia is a signatory to the Climate Change Convention. Too, the federal government has developed a National Greenhouse Response Strategy and is preparing a National Strategy for the Conservation of Biological Diversity (for preservation of ecosystems, plants, and animals).

Ocean Rescue 2000, a 10-year program (guess when it's due to end), promotes conservation and sustainable use of Australia's marine environment; the Antarctica Treaty protects that region's fragile environment; and—hang on, you sinking South Pacific islands—Australia is a spirited member of the South Pacific Regional Environment Program, which hopes to promote conservation, protection, and sustainable development in the South Pacific countries.

TOURISM

Beloved travelers, *you* are the brightest stars in Australia's economic Southern Cross. Over the past decade, tourism has boomed, driven by the success of *Crocodile Dundee* and an aggressive marketing campaign in which juicy shrimp were tossed on the barbies of Europe, Japan, and the United States. Also helpful were the 1987 America's Cup Challenge at Fremantle (near Perth) and Expo 88 in Brisbane, both of which brought large numbers of tourists—and their large wallets—streaming into the country. And, though Paul Hogan's overused shrimp have been replaced by the Olympics 2000 in Sydney, Australia is still cookin'.

Tourism has consistently been the highest growth sector of the economy, and tourist dollars promise to be the country's largest source of foreign income. The setbacks of a crippling pilots' strike, which adversely affected many resorts in the late 1980s and nearly devastated Tasmania tourism, thankfully are over.

The Australian Tourist Commission (ATC), tourism-marketing arm of the government, has offices throughout the world from which it promotes Australia's glories as a tourist destination. Marketing endeavors have been particularly successful in Asia and Europe, with North Asia accounting for nearly one-third of short-term visitors.

The ATC hardly has a tough job—the land of Oz is an easy sell. It's safe, healthy, friendly, and full of spectacular scenery, fabulous beaches, and natural wonders.

The federal government, in fact, is aiming to promote the country's unique natural sites, and yet wants to ensure manageable ecotourism. Substantial funds have already been committed to spur regional tourism and expand opportunities for the rural and backpacker markets, prompting the Bureau of Tourism Research to project accommodation shortages by the late 1990s in the Outback areas of the Northern Territory, Perth, Brisbane, Far North Queensland, and the Gold Coast.

Australians are an amiable people and easygoing, but they've had to learn the rudiments of a service industry like tourism from the ground up—trying to master the "art" of commercial hospitality in a culture that does not readily distinguish between service and servility. So don't always expect them to do a kangaroo hop whenever a demanding tourist snaps his fingers. For the most part, tourists are treated with great openness and friendliness, and the delight that visitors generally take in Australia has stimulated the Aussies to take new interest in the natural wonders of their own country—wonders that had previously been taken for granted in a country that's a mix of Stone Age, New Age, and the 21st century.

MANUFACTURING

Australia's manufacturing industry has boomed during the past decade, since trade barriers and economic regulations have been dropped to make the country a more productive and competitive exporter. Manufacturing, which has seen a rapid rise of about 16% per year, now composes about 18% of the country's GDP (Gross Domestic Product), with about one-fifth of the goods being exported, mainly to Asian countries.

The broad range of manufactured items includes iron and steel products (BHP, the predominant producer, is Australia's largest company); engineering equipment and tools; telecommunications and electronic equipment; small- to medium-sized ships and vessels; chemicals and plastics; aerospace equipment; information technology; motor vehicles; processed foods; paper and woodchips; and aluminum.

Australia would like you to know that it is behind the scenes where least expected. The Swiss Stock Exchange and Frankfurt-based Lufthansa's ticketing system use Australian software; Aussie software also manages Heathrow, Schipol, and Manchester airports. Many BMW gearboxes are Australian-made, as are most of Europe's high-speed ferries and *all* of the public transport "smart cards" in Scandinavia and the United Kingdom.

Smaller entrepreneurs are cashing in also. One fast-growing company ships large cryogenic gas storage tanks to Thailand and other Asian markets, another supplies "Ronald on a Park Bench" figures to McDonald's outlets around the globe, and one outfit sends hundreds of thousands of singly wrapped cheesecake slices to Japan every year.

Increasing numbers of international companies already active in, or about to pounce upon, the booming Asian markets have already set up regional headquarters in Australia. Two such companies are Mars and Kellogg Australia. (Lifesaving Tip: Down under, your Mars and Snickers bars remain the same, but your Rice Krispies and Raisin Bran masquerade as Rice Bubbles and Sultana Bran.)

PEOPLE, RELIGION, AND LANGUAGE

Australia's population is about the same as Texas, and would fit between Los Angeles and San Diego, except it is spread over a continent roughly the size of the United States. Mostly the people are concentrated along the east coast between Cairns and Adelaide.

Almost the entire population lives in six or seven cities, most of them congested enough you'd scarcely sense that vast emptiness outside the urban limits. The current population breakdown is as follows: 6,008,000 in New South Wales; 4,315,000 in Victoria; 3,123,000 in Queensland; 1,677,000 in South Australia; 1,676,000 in Western Australia; 451,000 in Tasmania; 296,000 in Australian Capital Territory; and 164,000 in the Northern Territory. Aborigines and Torres Strait Islanders make up about 1.8% of the total population, with the majority residing in the Northern Territory.

Before World War II, the majority of Australians were of British and Irish origin. That mix, however, has changed drastically. After the war, migrants came in droves and the island continent soon included significant numbers of Italians, Greeks, Yugoslavs, Dutch, Germans, Lebanese, Turks, and Maltese. Melbourne is said to be the second-largest Greek city in the world, after Athens, and has the largest population of Italians outside Italy, with Sydney having the second-largest; Germans made stakes in the Barossa Valley; Chinese pearled around Broome; and Darwin is just one big cosmopolitan city, with people from just about everywhere.

Waves of migration occurred in the 1850s, 1880s, early 1900s, and 1920s. The Great Depression and World War II restricted immigration, and a low birthrate made necessary a renewed migration drive in the 1950s. This campaign brought three million people to Australia (mostly to the major cities) between 1947 and 1974.

The scrapping of the White Australia Policy along with Australia's humanitarian refugee program after the Vietnam War has brought a steady increase in Asian immigration, particularly Vietnamese refugees. Also, Hong Kong's reversion to China in 1997 saw many Hong Kong nationals immigrating to Australia.

Presently, as home to almost five million immigrants from approximately 160 countries, Australia is rich in cultural and ethnic diversity. Nearly 16% of Australians have parents who were both born in another country; four out of 10 Australians are first-generation children of migrants—or migrants themselves—and many come from non-English speaking households. Southeast and Northeast Asia contributed 44% of new immigrant arrivals in the 1990s and thousands more resettlement places have been allotted to refugees and displaced persons throughout the decade.

Outback Dwellers

Outback residents *are* rugged individualists taming a savage wilderness, *and* they are a unique breed. Hey, life in the middle of nowhere isn't especially easy—most residents live 500 km or more from the nearest corner store, and even farther from a school or physician.

In general, Outback men are very brusque and very strong. They work in the mines, operate big rigs and heavy equipment, and spend a lot of their free time in remote pubs where they spin dubious tales. The Outback women are saints.

Aborigines and Torres Strait Islanders

Though white Australians often refer to themselves as the "world's newest people," the Aborigines who began living there at least 50,000-60,000 years ago (and maybe as far back as 100,000 years ago) are surely the world's oldest people. The most current census shows that Aborigines and Torres Strait Islanders number 345,000, or about 1.8% of Australia's total population. The majority are concentrated in the remote Outback, many still living (or trying to live) according to their traditional ways; even Aborigines living in or near towns hang out primarily with their own people.

There is dispute among anthropologists over the exact number of Aboriginal cultural groups: it could have been 11, it could have been twice that. Basically, groups were linked by common language, tools, art forms, social structure, and their environment—most of them lived in the desert or its fringes, along the coast or down in Tasmania. Political activism over the last two decades has inspired a cultural revival among surviving groups with a renewed commitment to those traditional common links. Consequently, these days many Aborigines prefer to be called by their self-designated names: Kooris (Victoria and New South Wales); Murris (Queensland); Anangu (western desert); Yappa (Warlpiris); Nunga (coastal South Australia); Nyoongah (southwest Australia); and Yolngu (northeast Arnhem Land). If you have any doubts about correct affiliation, it's probably best to simply refer to the traditional people as "Aborigines"—and that goes for those of mixed descent, as well. The terms "abo" and "coon" are hideously derogatory and unacceptable.

Though often lumped together with the Aboriginal people, the estimated 24,000 Torres Strait Islanders are mainly Melanesian and represent a separate cultural group with two distinct languages. Residing on the islands separating New Guinea and Cape York, the eastern islanders work the rich soil while the western islanders remain seminomadic. Thursday Island, a regularly scheduled ferry ride from Queensland's Cape York, is administrative center of Torres Strait. The gone but never-to-be-forgotten Eddie Mabo neoned the speck-size islands on the map when he had the gumption to suggest the Australian government acknowledge the Merriam people as rightful, traditional owners of Murray Island, sparking the landmark Mabo Decision and Native Title Act.

RELIGION

The First Fleet brought to Australia the alien concept of the separation of church and state in the form of an Anglican minister to service the religious needs of the convicts and their keepers. It was well over a week after their arrival before the immigrants got around to performing their first religious ceremony, however, and religion seems to have been consigned to the backseat of Australian life ever since. In this regard, Australia offers a curious contrast to America's pilgrim fathers, who knelt in prayer as soon as they stepped ashore.

This is not to say that religion doesn't play any part at all in Australian life—it's just not a starring role. Adherents of every major world religion practice their faith in an environment of freedom and tolerance. Not surprisingly, Christianity in all its variants and deviants is the principal religion. The largest group belongs to the Roman Catholic Church, followed by the Anglican. Anglicans have declined in number, possibly because the days when the establishment and Anglican Church went hand-in-hand are over. The Uniting Church now encompasses most of the Protestant sects. Roman Catholic numbers have been boosted since the war, with the arrival of Catholic migrants from Europe. However, the overall membership of any formal religious group is in decline in Australia, due in part to a secular, almost hedonistic, culture. Nevertheless, visitors who want to practice their religion and contact the Big Boss up top from the land down under will find plenty of opportunity.

Australia's major non-Christian faiths are Judaism, Buddhism, and Islam, but there are growing leagues of just about every California-meets-The East, New Age religion—replete with channelers, UFO-watchers, and surfing nudists.

Aboriginal Religion

To cast off the Aborigines' religion in a paragraph or two (or a century or two) is a real sacrilege. The early Christian missionaries couldn't fathom their beliefs at all; they simply assumed that the Aborigines—without any seeming belief in a white God and his crucified son, were Judgment Day goners.

Australia's first inhabitants, in isolation, had a spirituality that was inseparable from their way of life. In a sense their religion was and is an all-encompassing experience in which their life, their tribe, the land, the plants and animals around them, the past, and the great Dreamtime legends are inextricably interwoven.

LANGUAGE

English, with its distinct Australian accent and vocabulary, is the predominant language spoken throughout Australia. Of course, that's aside from hundreds of Aboriginal languages and dozens of other languages—Italian, Greek, Vietnamese, Turkish, you name it—spoken within various immigrant communities.

One advantage to visitors is that regional variants are very subtle, so if you can understand someone in Perth, you can understand someone in Cairns or Melbourne. Class-linked distinctions are more noticeable than regional ones; the upper middle classes affect a plummier accent closer to their English cousins, while the working classes are prone to exaggerate the idiosyncratic earthy tones that distinguish the Australian accent. But even these distinctions are much less dramatic than those that Americans are used to amongst themselves.

However, be warned. The Australian accent can be tricky for American or British visitors, at least at first. Australians love to tell stories about their compatriots traveling overseas and failing to make themselves understood; tales of Australians trying to explain to bewildered American barkeepers that they want to drink some "piss," or British hotel receptionists calling for the house translator to cope with Australian tourists.

One common misconception is that all Australians use a profusion of colorful idiomatic words and phrases, such as those that are regularly listed in travel books. Such words are well known to all Australians, but have a currency that may exist solely in the minds of the compilers of Australian slang dictionaries. Many words are used facetiously or ironically. "Bastard," for example, can mean several different things, depending on context: a bad bastard is someone who's bigger than you; good bastard, someone who's lent you money; lucky bastard, someone who has a better job than you; and a greedy bastard is someone with a better house. "Mate" may be the cheery greeting of long-lost chums *or* the signal for a barroom brawl. With the proviso that the words are often the fossilized relics of an Australia that may never have existed, and that they can sound quite peculiar in an American accent, refer to this book's glossary (but don't write us if you're laughed at).

You *won't* go wrong, however, if you shorten just about any word to one or two syllables and then add a "y," "ie," or "o" to the end. Examples: "television" becomes "telly"; "journalist," "journo"; and "surfers," "surfies."

Transatlantic variations that exist between English and American usage often occur in Australia, where generally the English version is preferred. However, from being regularly bombarded by American film, music, and television, Australians are familiar with all things American, and most people will understand that when you say "cookie" you really mean biscuit, and so on.

If it seems from these examples and this book's glossary that Australians use only the most insulting and derogatory terms for almost everything except alcohol and for everyone except themselves, be assured that for most Australians the use of many of these expressions would be unthinkable. The visitor to Australia will find a language with its own unique flavor that is riddled with delightful idioms while remaining basically English.

Aboriginal Languages

If you thought the shortening and rhyming and unique idioms discussed above were confusing, just wait! Aboriginal languages number at least 100 and have many dialects. This isn't quite so overwhelming when you realize that before the Europeans barged in the number was in the ballpark of 250 languages and 700 dialects—all thought to stem from just one language that changed and expanded as the traditional people broke off into groups and spread around the continent. Most languages were exclusively oral, not written, and subsequently died out along with their speakers. Others, such as Pitjantjatjara—the most common dialect of the western desert language group—were painstakingly transcribed. Pitjantjatjara (also known as Pitjantjara) is spoken in Uluru National Park (where visitors find it written phonetically on park signs), in Aboriginal communities from the Northern Territory/Western Australia border to the Simpson Desert's eastern border, and within the Anangu Pitjantjatjara traditional lands in South Australia. Pitjantjatjara contains three vowels (each having an additional long form) and 17 consonants, some of which require some tricky curling-tongue action.

Most Aboriginal languages contain about 10,000 words and some of these have also merged with Australian English: dingo, boomerang, kangaroo, kookaburra, barramundi, galah, mulga, mallee, and wallaby should be recognizable to most readers. Conversely, some English has found its way into Aboriginal speech, particularly in the relatively new Aboriginal Kriol, the "adopted" language of a growing contingency of younger people.

Many Outback Aborigines speak little or no English. They don't learn it in their communities—neither do they need to. Even on shopping trips to town, the Aborigines seem to get by, communicating adequately via fistfuls of money. Nonetheless, when speaking to Aborigines, use your normal English words and voice tones. The Aborigines will probably do the same for you—in their own language. Hopefully, *someone* will understand.

By the way, most Aboriginal languages do not contain words that mean "hello," "please," or "thank you," but if you need any kind of plant or animal, are looking for water, or want to say "sorry," you're in business.

ON THE ROAD
SPORTS AND RECREATION

Australians love sport. They love it so much that it's tempting to include this section under the "Religion" heading. They have a tradition of competitive sport that goes back to the earliest days of colonization, and they'll travel anywhere on earth if there's someone willing to play against them. Australia is one of only two countries (Greece is the other) to have been represented at every modern Olympiad, and in 2000, Australia will host the Olympics for the second time, in Sydney. The Olympic Games were held in Melbourne in 1956, where Australians won the third-most medals, an extraordinary feat for a nation with such a tiny population. Yet that is a measure of how seriously Australians treat athletic achievement. Australian champions regularly crop up in sports as diverse as golf, tennis, weightlifting, squash, yachting, cycling, and swimming.

A significant number of champion athletes enter public office after their sporting career is over, and political leaders of all persuasions find it necessary to publicize their allegiance to particular sporting clubs. Personal appearances at matches are a prerequisite to a successful career in politics. Australians can name past or present world champions in almost every sport, a phenomenon that causes their chests to swell with pride, even though sporting involvement for many Australians is confined to watching their idols on the telly.

HIKING

The unique sights, sounds, and smells of the "bush" make hiking in Australia a special experience, but there are plenty of "nasties" to be aware of. Tasmania is a mecca for hikers, with many routes easily completed in a day, while others such as the trail between Cradle Mountain and Lake St. Clair require back country skills. Tasmania's Freycinet Peninsula is considered one of Australia's finest day-hike destinations. Some of mainland Australia's better-known hiking is in the Blue Mountains (NSW), in the Australian Alps (NSW and Victoria), across Hinchinbrook Island (Queensland), through the Flinders Ranges (South Australia), and in Grampians National Park (Victoria).

HORSEBACK RIDING

In rural Australia, horses remain an important part of life; many rural folk spend half their life on a horse's back. This lifestyle was immortalized in the movie *The Man from Snowy River,* which was set in the high country of the Australian Alps. **Bogong Horseback Adventures,** tel. (03) 5754-4849, rides through the type of country depicted in the movie, including a visit to Craig's Hut. A full-day ride costs $120 pp, but to really get a feel for the lifestyle, you'll need to take a multiday trek, resting for the night in the remote huts that dot the mountains. These trips cost $150 pp per day. In the Blue Mountains, west of Sydney, **Packsaddlers,** tel. (02) 4787-9150, offers overnight horseback trips along the Megalong Valley for $100 pp per day.

Trail riding is possible throughout the country but is usually pretty tame, with the guide setting the pace to that of the less experienced riders. One exception is **Glenworth Valley Horse Riding,** north of Sydney on the Central Coast, tel. (02) 4375-1222, where riders can spend the day wherever they please on a large property of open fields, forested trails, and many rivers and streams with enticing water holes.

CAMEL TREKKING

Traveling on the back of a camel is more comfortable than it looks and is an experience not easily forgotten. Camels have a reputation for being aggressive, but this is not the case with those used in commercial operations. Camels were originally brought to Australia for Outback transportation, and today, most camel farms still are in this part of the country. **Alice Springs Camel Outback Safaris,** tel. (08) 8956-0925, charges around $35 per hour for a trek, with longer and overnight trips also offered. In South Australia, Rex Ellis of the **Flinders Range Outback Camel Company,** tel. (08) 8543-2280, is one of Australia's most respected "camel men." You can take half-day trip for $75, stay out

---

TRY A LITTLE FOSSICKING?

Fossicking is a favorite Australian adventure. Seek your pot of gold or cache of gems in river deposits, rock bars, along the bases of rock outcrops, or around old mine dumps. Stay out of old or abandoned mines!

Basic tools will suffice: pick and shovel, prospecting dish, small crowbar, sledgehammer, a gravel-washing container, and varied aluminum sieves.

All fossickers must have a fossicking permit or miner's right from either the state or territorial government, or, on private land, permission must be obtained from the landowner or leaseholder.

The following agencies will provide you with specific info on mining laws and can point you to fossicking guides and geological maps:

New South Wales, Dept. of Mineral Resources, P.O. Box 536, St. Leonards, NSW 2065, tel. (02) 9901-8888

Northern Territory, Dept. of Mines and Energy, P.O. Box 2901, Darwin, NT 0800, tel. (08) 8999-5511

Queensland, Dept. of Mines and Energy, 61 Mary St., Brisbane, QLD 4000, tel. (07) 3237-1435

South Australia, Dept. of Primary Industries and Resources, P.O. Box 151, Eastwood, SA 5063, tel. (08) 8274-7500

Victoria, Dept. of Energy and Minerals, P.O. Box 98, East Melbourne, VIC 3002, tel. (03) 9651-7799

Western Australia, Dept. of Minerals and Energy, 100 Plain St., East Perth, WA 6004, tel. (08) 9222-3333

---

overnight, or join Rex on a three-week expedition deep into the Simpson Desert for $2,500.

GOLFING

The game of golf is extremely popular in Australia. This is due to a number of factors, including inexpensive greens fees, a year-round season, and the high profile of Australian golfers overseas. Australia holds more than 1,400 golf courses, most of which are open to the public. A Letter of Membership and a handicap card from your home club goes a long way toward playing on semiprivate and even private courses. Some of these courses set aside a day for public play. Most courses hold club competitions for members three to five days a week, so call ahead to reserve a tee time.

Australia's best-known golf courses, along a strip in Melbourne known as the "sand belt," include **Royal Melbourne,** generally regarded as one of the world's top 10 courses. In Victoria, the course at seaside **Anglesea** is home to a large population of kangaroos that graze contentedly among the golfers. Sydney has a large number of courses, including the renowned **Australian,** as well as a string of semiprivate courses along the ocean that challenge all golfers. **New South Wales Golf Club** and **St. Michaels** are the best of these. Queensland's best golf courses are located in the major resort areas and have been developed especially for the tourist market. The best of these are on **Hope Island** on the Gold Coast, at the **Hyatt Regency Coolum** on the Sunshine Coast, at the **Capricorn International Resort** near Rockhampton, and the **Mirage Country Club** in tropical Port Douglas. In the west, Perth's best golf courses are private, but visitors can play them on a **Golf Escort** tour, tel. (08) 9357-5758. These day tours include everything from hotel pickups to greens fees.

Greens fees in Australia are remarkably inexpensive. Rarely does it cost more than $20 for a round on a public course, and most "resort" courses, such as those found on the Gold Coast, charge less than $100. Most courses offer club rentals, pull carts (known as "buggies" in Australia), and motorized carts. Each course has a resident professional who can link you up with local members.

North American-based companies **Classic Australian Golf Tours,** tel. (800) 426-3610, and **ITC Golf Tours,** tel. 310-595-6905 or (800) 257-4981, offer fully escorted golfing tours to Australia.

WATER SPORTS

Swimming is particularly important in a land where so much social activity takes place on the beach, and most Australian children are taught to swim very early. Let's face it—the country is filled with spectacular beaches. And, while the beaches are deserted and beautiful, the water may be dangerous. In surf areas, strong "rips" can sweep an unwary swimmer out to sea. Most popular beaches are patrolled by Surf Life Saving Clubs, which post flags to indicate safe swimming areas. (Swim between the flags.) Large swells often curtail swimming at the ocean beaches, but there are many other options, ranging from the clear blue water of Sydney Harbour to thermal hot springs bubbling out of the ground in the Outback town of Lightning Ridge.

Sailing and Boating
Taking to the water on the weekend is a national pastime for Australians. Some natives really get into the competitive water sports, but most simply find it a way to enjoy the great outdoors. Almost every coastal town has an operator renting some type of watercraft. Jet skis, windsurfers, rowboats, and motorboats can all be rented at reasonable rates and with few restrictions on their use. Queensland's **Whitsunday Islands** are the center of a huge cruising industry. Many old racing yachts have "retired" to these protected waters, and for $70-80 you can spend a leisurely day under sail on a yacht such as *Gretel,* which represented Australia at the America's Cup. You can also charter your own yacht for an extended trip through the islands. Known as "bareboat" cruising, these trips start at $280 per day. Call **Queensland Yacht Charters,** tel. (07) 4946-7400 or, from the U.S., contact **The Moorings,** tel. (813) 530-5424 or (800) 535-7289.

Scuba Diving
No question about it, Australia is one of the world's finest diving destinations. While the best-known spot is the Great Barrier Reef, there is great diving around the entire coastline. Airlie Beach and Cairns hold the largest concentration of dive operators, and in both cases, competition for business is strong. From Airlie Beach, a day trip to the outer reef costs $150-170, including lunch, equipment, and two dives. Basic Professional Association of Diving Instructors (PADI) open-water diving courses cost from $300 for three days. All resort islands on the Great Barrier Reef have a dive shop, with the chance to do day dives or complete a PADI dive

course. **Lady Elliot Island,** tel. (07) 4125-5344 or (1800) 07-2200, and **Heron Island,** tel. (07) 4978-1488 or 13-2469, or (800) 225-9849 from North America, feature some of the best diving on the entire Great Barrier Reef, with resorts set up expressly for the diving market. Across the country in Western Australia, the **Exmouth Diving Company,** tel. (08) 9949-1201, offers the unique opportunity to dive with whale sharks, which grow to 18 meters in length and can weigh up to 40 tons. A day trip costs $250 pp, which includes everything, including a spotter plane to help find the whales.

North American operators who specialize in diving down under include **Rothschild Dive Safaris,** tel. (800) 359-0747, and **Tropical Adventures,** tel. (206) 441-3483 or (800) 247-3483.

Surfing
In 1915, Hawaiian Duke Kahanamoku introduced the surfboard to Australia, and thus began one of the country's most popular sports. After Australian "Midget" Farrelly won the first world championship in 1964, Australian surfers started making their own innovations to the traditional longboard, creating more maneuverable short boards suited to Australian conditions. Superb surfing beaches surround the country. Queensland's Gold Coast is famed for long barreling waves such as **Burleigh** and **Kirra,** while to the north, the fun beach breaks of the **Sunshine Coast** are a great place to learn the sport. The entire New South Wales coast is lined with surfing beaches. The Sydney beaches of **Manly, Narrabeen,** and **Bondi** are renowned but also very crowded. Up the coast, **Byron Bay** has many different types of breaking waves and offers a number of learn-to-surf schools. The stretch of coastline southwest of Melbourne is known as the **Surf Coast,** which holds one of the world's best-known breaks at **Bell's Beach.** The nearby town of **Torquay** is home to Surfworld Australia, the country's only surfing museum. The coast around **Margaret River,** south of Perth, is a mecca for big-wave surfers, who ride on waves of up to four meters crashing into the shore.

World Surfaris, tel. (07) 3861-1163 or (1800) 61-1163, website: www.worldsurfaris.com.au, offers well-priced packages that include accommodations and rental cars at major surfing areas around the country. **North Coast Sur-**

faris, tel. (1800) 63-4951, has a five-day surfing trip between Sydney and Byron Bay. The cost of $435 pp includes accommodations, meals, and the use of surfboards.

FISHING
Fishing addicts, don't worry that Australia's aridity will prevent you from finding a catch of the day (or year). Whether your taste runs to game fishing à la Hemingway or dropping a line off the end of a pier, a fish waits for you! Fishing enjoys the highest participation rate of any recreational activity in Australia, and for many Australians, their earliest holiday memories involve dangling a line over the side of a sun-drenched wharf. And that is one of the advantages of fishing in Australia—the simplicity of the sport. No licenses are required for saltwater fishing, no special skills are needed, and fishing tackle and bait are readily available and inexpensive. Bream, whiting, taylor, flathead, and blackfish are common catches from wharves and breakwalls. Rock and beach fishing require more equipment, but the rewards are ample.

Summer is the prime game-fishing season. Black marlin is the most prized of all game fish, but tuna, sharks, sailfish, and barracuda can be caught by those in the know (or with the money to pay for a charter boat). Between August and December, gamefishers from around the globe descend on luxurious **Lizard Island Lodge,** off Cairns, tel. (07) 4060-3999 or (1800) 227-4411, from where many world records have been set and marlin weighing 600 kg are not uncommon.

Trout
Since 1864, Tasmania's fast-flowing streams and cold lakes have been stocked with trout, and in the years since, those of the southeastern mainland states have also been stocked. Spinning gear with artificial lures is the most popular trout fishing method, mainly because it is easiest to master.

Tasmania gets most of the attention from dedicated fly-fishers. In the northern part of the state, **London Lakes Fly-Fishing Lodge,** tel. (03) 6289-1159, is Australia's premier fly-fishing accommodation. **Arthurs Lake** and **Little Pine Lagoon** are two of Tasmania's better-known and more easily accessible trout lakes. Jindabyne, in southeastern New South Wales, is quickly gaining a reputation as a prime trout fishing destination, especially since hosting the World Fly-Fishing Championships in 1999.

All freshwater fishing requires a license. Each state has its own license system; these cost from $10 for a month to $45 for an annual permit. For licenses, as well as general freshwater fishing information, contact: NSW Fisheries, tel. (1300) 36-9365, the Inland Fisheries Commission, Tasmania, tel. (03) 6233-4140, or the Department of Natural Resources and Environment, Victoria, tel. (03) 9412-4011.

Barramundi

Fishing for the highly prized barramundi (or "barra") seems to reel in all types—from local pros and holiday-making Aussies to big-shot Hollywood celebrities and international politicians; catching it is a challenge and eating it is a treat. The barra teases fishers in coastal and river waters of the Top End, Kimberley region (Northern Territory), Cape York, and Gulf Country (Queensland). Enthusiasts seem to have very individual ideas regarding method, timing, and season—which is just as well or they'd be trampling over each other. Both novices and pros will find a myriad of organized fishing trips. For information regarding bag and size limits, permits, seasonal and other restrictions, contact: Amateur Fishermen's Association of the Northern Territory, tel. (08) 8981-5991; Northern Fisheries Centre, Cairns, QLD, tel. (07) 4052-9888; or Fisheries Western Australia, tel. (08) 9220-5333.

SPECTATOR SPORTS

Australians love and excel at many competitive sports and flock in droves to watch their favorites. So important is sport in Australia that federal and state governments appoint quite senior ministers to Departments of Sport. The federal government sponsors a kind of athletic university in Canberra, called the Australian Institute of Sport, where promising athletes are coached. Cricket and the three codes of football (see below) are followed with the keenest interest, but many other sports are watched, and the feats of champions heralded on the television and analyzed in the press.

On an international level, Australia competes with the best in the world at most sports. Tennis has a particularly high profile, with Australian players dominating the world scene in the 1950s and '60s, and a number of male players coming to prominence late in the 1990s. The Australian Open, held in Melbourne in January, brings these players back home and gives Australian fans the chance to see the best players in the world compete in a Grand Slam event. Summer is also the golf season. U.S. and European tour players head down under during their off season for tournaments across the country. Australia also has national baseball and basketball leagues.

Australia is often described as a nation of gamblers, and this is most evidenced by horseracing. Every city and most mid-sized towns have a horseracing track, where at least once a month "race day" attracts huge crowds. Bets are taken at the course and at TABs, which are betting shops found in pubs and in most towns. Horseracing takes place daily in the capital cities, including Sydney, Melbourne, and Brisbane. The most famous of all races is the Melbourne Cup, on the first Tuesday of November, when the whole country stops work and crowds into pubs and around radios for the duration of the race.

Football

Australians are very patriotic to their favorite code of football, and while the three main codes— **Australian Rules** (best known as Aussie Rules or footy), **Rugby League** (also known as footy), and **Rugby Union** (best known as, simply, rugby)—are played throughout the country, each code has a stronghold on particular parts of the country. In Victoria the most popular game—and one which visitors must not miss—is Australian Rules. Developed on the goldfields of central Victoria well over a century ago, it is a fast and exciting sport that everyone can enjoy. Visitors can look forward to witnessing the game being played at the very highest levels at grounds throughout Melbourne each Saturday through winter. Of the other two codes, Rugby League is most widespread, with most teams in the national competition based in New South Wales and southern Queensland.

Cricket

Unfortunately, footy is only played in the winter months, and Australians turn their attention in summer to their other great passion—cricket. Cricket is a relic of a colonial past and, although many Americans might be surprised to learn that the U.S. even has a national team, it is today strongest in Commonwealth countries. The Australian cricket team is generally regarded as the best in the world, but England, the West Indies, South Africa, New Zealand, India, Sri Lanka, and Pakistan all compete on an international level.

A leisurely and cerebral sport, matches can last up to five days. Teams of 11 players compete against each other, in an attempt to score the highest number of runs. On an international level, the most important games are **test matches.** These last up to five days, after which time, if there is still no result, the match is declared a draw. To the uninitiated it may seem like whole days may pass with very little actually happening. This provides the spectator with ample time to chat (and drink) with a neighbor and discuss the Byzantine intricacies of past controversies. International matches take place throughout the summer in all capital cities except Darwin and combine five-day test matches with "one day" matches. The shorter version of the game was developed in the 1970s especially for television audiences. They are lively and are guaranteed to end in a result; this provides a more suitable introduction to the game. **The Ashes,** which pits arch enemies Australia and England against each other every second year, is the most sought-after cricketing trophy. On a national level, the states compete for the **Sheffield Shield,** while at the local level, most towns have a team that competes on weekends against its neighbors on the local cricket ground.

ARTS AND ENTERTAINMENT

Australians have long been noted for a "cultural cringe," meaning they look to London and New York in matters of taste and style, slavishly following their lead. Americans will find that much of their culture has preceded them and taken root, to the point that Australia is beginning to export its own version of America's late-20th-century global techno-culture back to the United States. It has taken a long time, but Australians are making real advances in the creation of a national culture. Bolstered by the success of expatriates in all artistic endeavors (Dame Joan Sutherland, Nobel Laureate Patrick White, artist Sir Sydney Nolan, actress Nicole Kidman, and the band silverchair), artsy Aussies are growing more confident and ready to take their work to the outside world.

Australia offers one superb entertainment that you won't see in the Northern Hemisphere—the brilliant glow of a million stars lighting up the unfamiliar constellations of a strange southern sky, an impossibly classy act to follow.

Performing Arts

Each state capital has its own symphony orchestra, opera company, ballet company, theater, and art gallery, which are recipients of generous arts funding. Lovers of traditional Western art forms will be happily surprised at the high standards and support from a quite sophisticated public at the end of the earth.

Australia also is home to a lively "fringe" arts scene, mainly centered in the bohemian suburbs of Sydney, Melbourne, and Adelaide. Adelaide's Fringe Festival, which runs concurrently with the city's renowned and highbrow Festival of the Arts, honors the more avant-garde contributions to theater, music, art, and literature. And while it isn't Times Square or Haight-Ashbury, the low-key local color can be a lot of fun. The cultural melting pot of Australia's cities has meant that artists no longer need to travel to Europe or America to eke out a penurious living in a squalid garret; they can do it here!

Film

The world's first feature-length film, *The Story of the Kelly Gang,* was a 1901 Australian production, but the country's arrival on the international scene is a much more recent phenomenon. Filmmakers Peter Weir, Gillian Armstrong, Paul Cox, Jocelyn Moorehouse, Bruce Beresford, Baz Luhrmann, and P.J. Hogan, along with film stars Errol Flynn, Mel Gibson, Paul Mercurio,

Judy Davis, Bryan Brown, Nicole Kidman, Toni Collette, Oscar winner Geoffrey Rush, and Kate Blanchett lead a coterie of Australian artists who have dazzled star-bright Hollywood. They learned their craft in the domestic Australian industry, offering entertainment with not merely an Australian accent but with some fabulously quirky characters and fresh, innovative themes. Thankfully, in this respect, Australia does not lean heavily on the traditional box-office, crass-market models (*Crocodile Dundee* excepted) normally provided by the U.S. film industry. Some of the many well-known films include not only *Crocodile Dundee*, but *Mad Max I, II,* and *III, My Brilliant Career, Evil Angels (A Cry in the Dark), Breaker Morant, Walkabout, Chant of Jimmie Blacksmith, Strictly Ballroom, Romper Stomper, Muriel's Wedding,* the delightfully fashionable *Priscilla, Queen of the Desert,* and the 1996 smash hit *Babe,* about a talking pig.

Contemporary Music

Australia also has a vital and dynamic music industry, very much in evidence in the major cities and towns throughout the country. Hundreds of hopeful young musicians play nightly in every style you can name—and some you can't. In the 1950s, Johnny O'Keefe became Australia's first rock 'n' roll star, but it wasn't until the late 1960s, when The Seekers and the Bee Gees reached the height of their popularity, that Australian musicians made a name for themselves outside of their own country. Not long ago it was possible to see bands like Midnight Oil, AC/DC, Men at Work, Crowded House, and INXS playing in small suburban pubs, and you can bet the bands that play there now have big ambitions. Many of Australia's most popular bands through the 1970s and 1980s didn't attempt to break into the overseas market but gathered huge fan bases within Australia. These include the Skyhooks, Cold Chisel, and Australian Crawl. Today, Australian contemporary music embraces a dynamic diversity from jazz to hip-hop, rock to heavy metal. Current international headliners include silverchair, You am I, Soundgarden, and Nick Cave.

Although country music doesn't enjoy the mainstream popularity it does in the United States, it is popular throughout rural areas, and America's most popular country acts regularly tour Australia. With more than 50 albums to his credit, Slim Dusty is the father of Australian country music. Following in his footsteps is Lee Kernaghan, Gina Jeffreys, John Williamson, and Troy Cassar-Daley. Only one Australian, Olivia Newton-John, has had a song reach the top of the U.S. country charts. Sheree Austin is a more recent Australian success story in American country music, but she is almost unknown in her home country.

Aboriginal Music and Dance

Aboriginal music—an inspiring mix of political and racial statements, contemporary electronics, and traditional didgeridoo (a large wooden trumpet)—has been garnering international acclaim in recent years. Two of the best-known Aboriginal entertainment troupes are Tjapukai (performing daily outside of Cairns) and the rock band Yothu Yindi (lead singer Mandawuy Yunupingu was named 1993 Australian of the Year). Christine Anu, from the Torres Strait islands, is a contemporary Aboriginal singer currently enjoying commercial success.

Aboriginal dance is another resurgent art form, and new performances of established companies are eagerly awaited—particularly those of the Tjapukai company. Corroborees are ceremonial dances accompanied by the unearthly music of the didgeridoo. Non-Aborigines are rarely invited to authentic corroborees, but you can catch tourist versions at Darwin and a few other spots.

Artists and Art Galleries

The "Heidelberg School" of young artists who resided near Melbourne in the 1930s, along with a group of artists living up around Sydney Harbour, established the first uniquely Australian painting style. Working in oils and watercolors, using natural light to its full advantage, the painters captured the magic, starkness, and intensity of Australian life and landscape. Notable artists of that period were Julian Ashton, Louis Abrahams, Charles Conder, Frederick McCubbin, Tom Roberts, and Arthur Streeton. A later revolution in the 1940s brought fame and acclaim to Sir Sidney Nolan and Arthur Boyd—probably Australia's most well-known painters—and a bevy of other talents, including Pro Hart, who still strokes Outback images from his Broken Hill studio. The colorful art of Ken Done can be found on all manner of Australian souvenirs.

Aboriginal Art

Aboriginal art has its own aesthetics, which reflect the profound experience of life in Australia. Recently "discovered" by the West, Aboriginal paintings can command substantial prices on the world market.

Most Aboriginal art forms are spiritually based and concerned with the myths and totemic beliefs of the Dreamtime. Painting on bark and, more recently, canvas, Aboriginal artists employ a decorative dot technique that to Western eyes appears quite abstract, and representational images of animals and spirits are painted in the style of an X-ray, revealing internal organs. These techniques are incredibly ancient. Extremely old examples are found on the walls of caves in Arnhem Land. Often the actual rendering of these works is accompanied by songs that instruct the artist in the progress of the work and invest him with spiritual power. The full significance of such works is sacred and available only to the initiated. Aborigines also craft exquisite implements, from the aerodynamically perfect boomerang to ceremonial belts and headdresses.

Australia's most famous Aboriginal artist, Albert Namatjira (1902-59), hailed from Hermannsburg Lutheran Mission, west of Alice Springs. Learning European-style watercolor techniques from a non-Aboriginal painter, Namatjira became comparatively successful for what were considered to be European-style, central Australian landscapes; eventually he became the first Aborigine to "achieve" Australian citizenship. This achievement, however, did not accord him blanket privileges. Just one year later, in 1958, Namatjira was arrested for buying alcohol for other Aborigines; one year after that, he died. Still, he inspired other would-be artists with his technique, use of color, imagery—and his image.

The 1970s weren't exclusively prime time for American and European artists—the creative renaissance of that period also surfaced at Papunya, a tiny impoverished Aboriginal community northwest of Alice Springs. There, the painting of a mural—a children's school project—turned into a cross-generational creation when elders (with mixed feelings about their traditional symbols being splattered across a public wall) joined in and helped complete the piece. The result, *Honey Ant Dreaming*, became the first art piece in which traditional images were displayed on something other than a rock or human body. Pretty soon the community was passionately painting away and, though more murals were produced, acrylic paints on canvas eventually became the preferred medium. Central Australian painting has since evolved as an important source of religious and traditional instruction for Aboriginal children.

Other distinctive contemporary Aboriginal arts and crafts include: batiks, pottery, wooden sculptures and carvings in central Australia; bark paintings, painted log coffins, fiber art, Ngukurr acrylics on canvas in Arnhem Land; paintings and engraved pearl-shell pendants in the Kimberley; spears, bark baskets, carved and painted burial poles, sculptures, and bark paintings on the Tiwi Islands.

Aboriginal rock art can be found in all corners of rural Australia.

As some of us might expect, the works of city-dwelling Aboriginal artists tend to reflect either European influences or deep, raging, racially themed anger. In fact, the beginnings of Aboriginal urban art can be traced to the land-rights issues of the 1970s.

If you'd rather view Aboriginal art from earlier times, drawn or engraved on rocks rather than hanging on gallery walls, significant sites open to visitors are: Mutawintji National Park (New South Wales); Ewaninga (Northern Territory); Chambers Gorge and Cooper Creek (South Australia); The Grampians (Victoria); and Mersey Bluff near Devonport (Tasmania). Both the Australian Museum, in Sydney, and the South Australian Museum, in Adelaide, have outstanding collections of Aboriginal artifacts.

Gambling

Australians love to gamble—you can bet on it. Each of the major cities has its glitter-and-flash gambling mecca: Star City in Sydney, Casino Canberra, Brisbane's Conrad Treasury Casino, Townsville's Sheraton Breakwater Casino, the Reef Hotel Casino in Cairns, the MGM Grand Hotel Casino in Darwin, Perth's Burswood International Resort Casino, the Adelaide Casino, Melbourne's Crown Casino, and Wrest Point Hotel Casino in Hobart.

A huge industry has also grown up around horse racing, harness racing (pacing or trotting), and greyhound racing. Billions of dollars are invested annually either with trackside bookmakers or off-course government-run totalizators. Champion thoroughbred horses occupy as exalted a position in the galaxy of Australian sporting heroes as champion human athletes, and a racing subculture has long been established in which the uninitiated quickly find themselves lost in a strange land. The passion for horses culminates in the fabulous Melbourne Spring Carnival; the prized petunia of that meet is the Melbourne Cup, a race that few Australians fail to bet on—and a declared local holiday.

SHOPPING

Aside from Aboriginal arts and crafts, Australia is *not* shop-till-you-drop territory. In all the cities and most smaller towns, you will find everything you need, from flyspray to condoms. You'll find necessary and desired gear and clothing in most cities around Australia. Prices for most items are higher than in the U.S., and books and compact discs are *much* more expensive. Either bring books with you or buy them secondhand.

Distinctly Australian items include Blundstone boots (elastic sides; Aussie Doc Marten's), Akubra hats, and Driza-bone overcoats. You will just have to purchase at least one sheepskin item, a bottle of Australian wine, and an opal (or 10). One of the largest concentrations of down under souvenir shops is in the historic Rocks area of Sydney, where you'll find the colorful artwork of Ken Done and the distinctive landscape photography of Ken Duncan.

Normal shopping hours are Mon.-Fri. 9 a.m.-5 p.m., Saturday 9 a.m.-noon, but most of the major shopping centers stay open all day Saturday as well as Sunday. One night a week—either Thursday or Friday—is designated "late shopping night" with doors staying open until 9 p.m. In the Outback and in rural towns, shops basically open and close whenever.

Aboriginal Arts and Crafts

It is possible to buy Aboriginal art from cooperatives run by local communities; these are often the best sources. Much of what is passed off as Aboriginal art in the cities is worthless imitation and souvenir schlock. Some excellent Aboriginal-owned or -managed shops and galleries are the Papunya Tula Artists in Alice Springs, Maruku Arts and Crafts Centre in Uluru-Kata Tjuta National Park, and Mt. Ebenezer Roadhouse on the Lasseter Highway, en route to Uluru. In major cities, recommended outlets for authentic Aboriginal artworks are: Sydney's Aboriginal Art Centre, Queensland Aboriginal Creations in Brisbane, and Aboriginal Handcrafts in Melbourne. Most buyers will be able to take home a print, small carving, or T-shirt, but be prepared to pay dearly for gallery originals.

Opals

Be cautious when buying opals; try to get recommendations from tourist bureaus, and definitely comparison-shop. The three types of solid opal are: black opal, the most valuable, found at Lightning Ridge, New South Wales, and Mintabie, South Australia; white opal, also called "light" or "fire" opal, found at Coober Pedy and Andamooka, South Australia; and boulder opal, found at Quilpie in southwestern Queensland. All major cities have shops specializing in opals (and selling them to tourists with too much money), but you're better off buying them at their source. A "triplet" is a thin slice of opal layered between a clear dome capping of dark opal potch and crystal quartz.

Markets

A not-to-be-missed shopping experience is at the mostly outdoor, sometimes indoor markets held almost everywhere in the country. In Melbourne, Queen Victoria Market north of downtown is a prime example, as is Paddy's Market in Sydney, Adelaide's Central Market near Victoria Square, and Darwin's Big Flea Market, the city's oldest. These usually take place on weekends, though some city markets are open during the week. Depending on where you are and the type of market it is, you'll be able to pick up bargains on fruits and veggies, furniture, secondhand clothing, used tools, camping gear, and various bric-a-brac, like the ubiquitous plastic fish and fake handcuffs from Asia.

HOLIDAYS AND FESTIVALS

Australia is partyland, folks, and *any* excuse for a long weekend or a raucous rage is welcomed. Most public holidays fall on Monday, allowing for what is called a "long weekend." You can pretty much count on everything being closed for all three (or, in some instances, four) days.

Major National Holidays
New Year's Day: 1 January
Australia Day: 26 January
Good Friday, Easter Saturday, Easter Sunday, and Easter Monday: varies
Anzac Day: 25 April
Queen's Birthday: second Monday in June (Western Australia celebrates in late September/early October)
Melbourne Cup Day: first Tuesday in November (the whole country stops in its hooves for this all-important race—Melbourne stops for the entire day!)
Christmas Day: 25 December
Boxing Day: 26 December

Regional Holidays
Labour Day: second Monday in March (Victoria)
Labour Day: first Monday in March (Western Australia and Tasmania)
Labour Day: first Monday in May (Queensland)
Labour Day: first Monday in October (South Australia, New South Wales, and Australia Capital Territory)
May Day: 1 May (Northern Territory)
Adelaide Cup Day: third Monday in May (South Australia)

Foundation Day: first Monday in June (Western Australia)
Bank Holiday: first Monday in August (New South Wales)
Picnic Day: first Monday in August (Northern Territory)
Show Day: every municipality allots one day a year as Show Day for its residents. It is mostly now only given to schoolchildren, but the long-time tradition continues.

School Holidays

These are scheduled four times a year and fall on different dates throughout all the states and territories. Basically they run late December to early February, mid-April to mid-May, late June to late July, and mid-September to mid-October. It is especially important to book transport and accommodations ahead during school holiday periods, as that's when most Aussies hit the road or take to the skies.

Festivals and Seasonal Events

January: The New Year kicks off in Australia's largest city with the three-week **Sydney Festival,** celebrating all forms of performing arts. During this same period, Melbourne hosts the **International Jazz Festival.** The 10-day **Australian Country Music Festival** takes place in Tamworth in late January. The **Sardine Festival,** in Fremantle, features a wide variety of entertainment, but the main attraction is eating sardines. At Lake Jabiru, in the Northern Territory, the **Jabiru Regatta** features offbeat games and races.

February: The two-day **Kangaroo Island Racing Carnival** comes to Kangaroo Island's Kingscote (South Australia). In the Northern Territory, **race meetings and rodeos** take place at Alice Springs, Tennant Creek, and Darwin. The **Festival of Perth** is a cultural extravaganza in Western Australia, beginning in mid-February and lasting a month. The last weekend of February sees Sydney's downtown streets come alive with outrageous floats in the **Gay and Lesbian Mardi Gras,** one of the world's largest street parades.

March: Melbourne's **Moomba Festival** is a week-long cultural festival that culminates in dragon boat races down the Yarra River. The **Australian Formula One Grand Prix** burns rubber through Melbourne streets for four days (the race is on the last day). South Australia's famed **Adelaide Festival** (even-numbered years) offers three weeks of premier theater, music, comedy, dance, arts exhibitions, and fringe events. The **Port Fairy Folk Festival** in Victoria is Australia's largest such gathering.

April: **Anzac Day** is one of Australia's few public holidays that is celebrated with its true meaning in mind. The main street of most towns and cities is closed for a parade of Australians who have fought for the country, and, along with local marching bands and community groups, the true Aussie spirit is celebrated. After the parade, celebrations usually move to RSL Clubs or local pubs, where **two-up** is played (Anzac Day is the only day of the year when two-up is legal). In odd-numbered years, South Australia's **Barossa Vintage Festival** is a major weeklong taste-till-you-waste celebration in honor of the local grapes and vintners. Also in April Coober Pedy hosts its **Opal and Outback Festival.**

May: In mid-May, the **Melbourne International Film Festival** attracts contemporary films from around the world. In the Northern Territory, the **Alice Springs Camel Races** feature a variety of sporting competitions, fireworks, and—of course—camel races. **May Day** in Darwin signals the end of those treacherous box jellyfish and the beginning of beach parties.

June: The June long weekend heralds the official start to the Australian **ski season.** Resorts in New South Wales and Victoria kick off the season with a variety of fun events. Darwin's **Bougainvillea Festival** offers two weeks of flow-

ery events. The **Katherine Gorge Canoe Marathon** (Northern Territory) is a 100-km race along the Katherine River, organized by the Red Cross. Grab the opportunity to celebrate (non-alcoholically) with the traditional people at **Barunga Festival,** which features traditional dancing, sports, and arts and crafts.

July: Darwin is at the forefront again with its **Beer Can Regatta,** featuring sailing "craft" constructed entirely from empty beer cans. Almond-lovers will want to attend the **Almond Blossom Festival,** in Willunga, South Australia, with assorted nutty activities.

August: The first weekend of August brings the **Avon Descent.** Requiring a 133-km kayak descent of Western Australia's Avon River, this is Australia's premier whitewater race. **Shinju Matsuri** ("Festival of the Pearl") is a weeklong Asian-theme event held in Broome, Western Australia's old pearling port. The **Darwin Rodeo** is a well-attended international competition. And Darwin's **Mud Crab Tying Competiton** is another must on the cultural calendar.

September: The tiny Outback community at Birdsville, Queensland, hosts the hot-to-trot **Birdsville Races.** The **AFL Grand Final,** Australian football's final game, is in Melbourne but religiously followed by fans across the country. Watch it on the telly from your favorite pub. For the more active, consider entering Sydney's **City to Surf** marathon, which attracts more than 25,000 competitors. Also, Canberra and Perth blossom over their **Floriade** and **Western Australia Wildflower Festivals,** respectively.

October: Melbourne hosts three cultural festivals in September, bringing together fringe performers, artists, and writers. The **Henley-on-Todd Regatta** in Alice Springs (late August or early September) features bizarre and creative mock-ups of boats propelled by the racers' feet as they run along the dry Todd River bed. South Australia's **McLaren Vale Bushing Festival** commemorates the release of a new vintage with a variety of events including the crowning of a Bushing King and Queen. The **Kalgoorlie Cup** horse race is held in Western Australia's eponymous mining town.

December: December marks the start of summer holidays and, of course **Christmas,** which is usually celebrated in typical Aussie style with a barbecue, beer, and a lazy day on the beach.

Young travelers from around the world descend on Sydney's Bondi Beach for an unofficial Christmas celebration. The following day, Boxing Day, is the start of the **Sydney to Hobart** yacht race.

Bush Bashes

Rodeos are favorite rural and Outback entertainments. You'll see stockmen who are dead ringers for cowboys, Americano-style—10-gallon hats, chaps, spurs, struts, the whole shebang. Flies, dust, *lots* of beer, and monstrous steak sandwiches lend that unique Aussie flavor. The range of events includes calf roping, steer wrestling, bareback riding, saddle bronc riding, and bull rid-ing. Rodeo has become more commercialized in recent years, with many nonrural towns hosting watered-down rodeos once a year.

The other live-to-die-for event is the **B&S Ball.** The B&S have nothing to do with what's left after the rodeo—it actually stands for "bachelor and spinster," though the event is no longer confined to just single folk. The balls are grand social occasions where rural dwellers can socialize, renew old acquaintances, and kick up their dusty heels. In true Aussie style, the balls are one big, long party, with lots of drinking, eating, and carousing. Despite the fact they're held in big barns or open fields, ball-goers dress to the hilt.

ACCOMMODATIONS

Australian lodging is well represented by the cliché, "myriad of possibilities." Choices range from backpacker dorms to penthouse suites in luxury hotels—with motels, pubs, guesthouses, bed and breakfasts, holiday flats, caravan parks, and Outback stations tossed in between. You can get accommodation guides with up-to-date prices at branches of the automobile clubs or, often, at state tourist bureaus. It is advisable to book ahead during public and school holidays.

Hotels

These come in a few varieties—from older-style pubs to the big Hyatt-type places. The one common factor is that they are licensed to serve alcohol. Pubs are called "hotels" because originally they were required to provide lodging for travelers. Thus they are usually rather old, with simple rooms (no television or telephone), and share bathrooms, although most rooms have a sink. The most basic of these rooms cost $20-30 s, $25-40 d, rooms with private bathrooms are a few dollars extra, and the rate often includes breakfast. The Australian Hotels Association has initiated **Pubstay,** which promotes the accommodations offered in traditional pubs. For details, call (02) 9281-6922 or (1800) 80-7772; website: www.aha-nsw.asn.au. You'll also come across "private" and "boutique" hotels. These are traditional pubs that have been restored, offering old-style luxury but no longer serving alcohol.

Worldwide, national, and regional hotel chains and resorts are of international standard and feature all the requisite luxuries and amenities—pools, saunas, spas, room service, complimentary toiletries, restaurants, and bars. They can be found in central locations in all cities and major tourist areas. Rates at four- or five-star hotels start at $140-200 s or d, but they are generally lower on weekends. Major hotel chains represented throughout Australia include: **Best Western,** tel. (13) 1779 within Australia, tel. (800) 528-1234 from elsewhere in the world; **Country Comfort,** tel. (1800) 06-5064 within Australia; **Hilton International,** tel. (800) 445-8667 worldwide; **Holiday Inn,** tel. (800) 465-4329 worldwide; **Hyatt,** tel. (800) 233-1234 from North America; **Quality,** tel. (800) 228-5151 from North America; **Radisson,** tel. (800) 333-3333 from North America; **Regent International,** tel. (800) 545-4000 worldwide; **Sheraton,** tel. (800) 325-3535 from North America; and **Southern Pacific,** tel. (1300) 36-3300 within Australia, (800) 835-7742 from North America.

Motels

As in the U.S., motels are prevalent throughout Australia, owned either by independent operators or chain establishments (many motels belong to major chains but are privately run). Rooms—usually doubles—are serviced daily and have private bathrooms, radios, televisions, refrigerators, and the ubiquitous electric jug accompanied by packets of instant coffee and tea bags. Motels often have a swimming pool and attached restaurant, and some have family suites with cooking facilities.

AUSTRALIAN ACCOMMODATION PRICES AND TYPES

To make choosing a room that comes within your budget easy, all accommodations have been afforded a one-word "rating" in this book. The rating is based on double occupancy rates. In the off-season, prices will often drop to a less expensive category, as will many city hotels on weekends. The rating only indicates price and does not evaluate the facilities offered at each establishment.

> **Budget:** up to $30
> **Inexpensive:** $30-60
> **Moderate:** $60-90
> **Expensive:** $90-120
> **Premium:** $120-150
> **Luxury:** $150 and up

And to clarify just what is meant by different terms for different types of accommodations, here is a breakdown of the various options available.

- **Hotels:** Chain and independent establishments with all the creature comforts range from $70 up to $350, and higher for international resorts.

- **Motels:** Chain or locally owned, and ubiquitous throughout Australia; can be had for $35-55, single or double.

- **Serviced Apartments:** Good options for families, groups, and long-termers. Fully equipped at a variety of prices but usually located in cities or resort areas.

- **Pub "Hotels":** Older rooms with simple furnishings and shared baths, often in renovated or once-glorious buildings—in cities or country towns. Priced around $25-45.

- **Guesthouses and Bed and Breakfasts (B&Bs):** Intimate sharing experiences (sometimes *too* intimate). Can be cheap ($25) or way up there ($100).

- **Home and Farm Stays:** Again, a wide variety, from basic down-home to yuppie-ish pseudo-farms—around $50-150 per day.

- **Camping and Caravanning:** Figure campsites at around $8-15 per day, on-site caravans or cabins at $16-65 (prices are for two).

- **YHAs and Backpacker Lodges:** Average $10-18 per night.

Expect to pay from $35 s, $45 d for a basic room on the outskirts of town. Australia's major motel chains include: **Budget,** tel. (1800) 81-1223 within Australia; **Country Comfort,** tel. (1800) 06-5064 within Australia; **Flag International,** tel. (13) 2400 within Australia, (800) 624-3524 from North America; and **Golden Chain,** tel. (1800) 02-3966.

Serviced Apartments and Holiday Flats

Serviced apartments are usually found in the cities, while holiday flats (or units) are in resort or vacation areas. They range from basic motel-style rooms with kitchenettes to full-on posh apartments with several rooms. Cutlery, dishes, and cooking utensils are provided but, unless you're staying in one of the upmarket pads with daily or weekly maid service, plan on doing the cleaning yourself. Rented by the week or month, they cater mainly to those who plan an extended stay in one place, and can be an exceptionally good value for a group traveling together. In resort towns, bookings for holiday flats can be made through local real estate agents.

Bed and Breakfasts

Bed and breakfasts can be private residences, purpose-built lodgings, or restored guesthouses or hotels. They have one thing in common—they include breakfast in the rate. They are generally small, privately run operations, and bathrooms are often shared. Dinner can often be arranged. The bed-and-breakfast industry is flourishing in Australia, as travelers discover the joys of staying in a friendly environment with hosts more than eager to share their local knowledge. Rates at bed and breakfasts fluctuate wildly; expect to pay $30 s, $40 d for a basic room and from $50 s, $65 d for a more comfortable room with a private bathroom. This style isn't for everyone, especially if you're reclusive. Be prepared to hear the other guests' life stories or have your own dragged out of you over the morning's bacon and eggs.

Book bed and breakfasts directly, through local information centers, or with **Bed and Breakfast Australia,** tel. (02) 9499-5499; website: www.bnba.com.au.

Hostelling International

Increased competition in the budget travel market has seen the **YHA** change direction in recent years (and its name), ridding itself of the "youth" image, along with curfews and the need for guests to do chores. You can rely on YHAs to be well organized, efficiently run, and, best of all, inexpensive ($10-24 pp per night). They can be found throughout the country, including all major cities, ski resorts, national parks, and the Outback, and operate from an incredible variety of locations, including tiny shelters, railway cars, suburban mansions, and country churches. Even membership of the YHA ($44 per year) isn't compulsory anymore, although it only takes a few nights of discounted lodging to make up the difference. Other membership benefits include discounted air, rail, and bus travel; discounts on car rental; and discounts on some attractions and commercial activities. Join and pick up the handy booklet *YHA Accommodation Guide* at any YHA Travel Centre. These are located at the following addresses: 422 Kent St., Sydney, NSW, tel. (02) 9261-1111; 154 Roma St., Brisbane, QLD, tel. (07) 3236-4999; 69 Mitchell St., Darwin, NT, tel. (08) 8981-6344; 236 William St., Perth, WA, tel. (08) 9227-5122; 38 Sturt St., Adelaide, SA, tel. (08) 8231-5583; 205 King St., Melbourne, VIC, tel. (03) 9670-7991; and 28 Criterion St., Hobart, TAS, tel. (03) 6234-9617. The YHA website is www.yha.org.au.

Joining Hostelling International in your home country will entitle you to reciprocal rights in Australia, as well as at about 5,000 hostels in 65 countries around the world. In the United States, contact **Hostelling International-American Youth Hostels,** Suite 840, 733 15th St. NW, Washington, DC 20005, tel. (202) 783-6161, website: www.hiayh.org. In Canada, contact **Hostelling International-Canada,** 400-205 Catherine St., Ottawa, ON K2P 1C3, tel. (613) 237-7884, website: www.hostellingintl.ca. In the U.K., contact **Youth Hostels Association,** Trevelyan House, St. Stephen's Hill, St. Albans, Herts. AL1 2DY, tel. (0172) 785-5215, website: www.yha.org.uk. In New Zealand, contact **Youth Hostels Association of New Zealand,** P.O. Box 436, Christchurch 1, tel. (03) 379-9970, website: www.yha.org.nz.

Other Backpacker Accommodations

Until recently, the only accommodations in Australia designed specifically for budget travelers were Youth Hostels, run by the YHA. The last decade has seen private backpacker accommodations spring up around the country. Standards vary considerably; some are old downtown hotels with noisy bars downstairs, some are tacked onto the back of motels, and others are filled with seasonal workers, but for the most part they are excellent, with locations as diverse as the country. They are the ultimate for budget travelers ($10-28 pp per night), to say nothing of a superb clearinghouse for local information, job possibilities, and ride-sharing. Accommodations are in dormitories, double rooms, or twin rooms (two single beds). Each also offers communal cooking, lounging, and laundry facilities. "Extras" might include

---

HOME AND FARM STAYS

It's easy—you stay with Aussies in their homes or on their farms. In homes, you're treated like one of the family. You'll have a private bedroom, though you'll probably share bathroom facilities with your Aussie parents and siblings. Breakfast is almost always included, and other meals can often be arranged.

Farm stays can include just about anything, though. You might be lodged in the bunkhouse or shearers' quarters and expected to work alongside the jack- and jilleroos. Particularly on Outback stations, life is simple and often tough. Then again, you might arrange a motel-style farm stay, where you sit back on the veranda with a cold beer (or, more likely, *several* cold beers) and breathe in the scent of fresh cow and sheep dung. Ah, nature! If you're fussy, you should thoroughly check out specifics of places you're considering well in advance.

Book home and farm stays through state tourist centers or the following North American representatives: **Bed and Breakfast Australia** (Adventure Center, tel. 800-227-8747 U.S.); **Farmstays** (Sprint Australia, tel. 800-423-2880 U.S.); **Inta-Aussie Accommodation Service** (Inta-Aussie Tours, tel. 800-531-9222 U.S.); **Austravel** (tel. 800-633-3404 U.S.); **Goway Travel** (tel. 800-387-8850 Canada); and **SoPac** (tel. 800-551-2012 or 213-871-0747 U.S. and Canada).

bicycle, surfboard, and equipment rentals, as well as a pool, café, bar, and organized excursions and tour bookings. The two main private backpacker organizations in Australia are **VIP Backpackers Resorts**, website: www.backpackers.com.au, and **Nomads Backpackers International**, tel. (1800) 81-9883, website: www.nomadsbackpackers.com.

YMCAs and YWCAs
The YMCA and YWCA offer good-value city accommodations in central locations. Rooms are generally plain but adequately furnished. Some Ys have dorm rooms for travelers, but most are private with a private bathroom and linen. Rates start at $30 s, $40 d.

Camping and Caravanning
Australia's many commercial campgrounds (called "caravan parks" or "holiday parks") provide exceptional value. Many differ greatly from the North American variety, as they provide a wide range of lodgings and, in general, excellent facilities. They are located in most towns, along highways, near beaches and rivers, and on the city fringes. In coastal areas, holiday parks include basic communal facilities as well as swimming pools, playgrounds, recreation rooms, and a barbecue area. Some even feature bathrooms for each site. Along with tent and powered sites ($10-24 per site), the parks offer on-site vans ($25-40) and cabins ($30-100). Some cabins

may be nothing more than a couple of beds in a freestanding building, while others include a full kitchen, bathroom, and television. In coastal towns during summer and other school holidays, advance bookings are necessary.

Most of Australia's many national parks have campgrounds; facilities range enormously—from having to bring your own drinking water to those with hot showers and a laundry. In all cases a fee applies, either payable upon arrival or collected by the ranger in the evening. Camping is permitted on some islands of the Great Barrier Reef. This entails being totally self-sufficient, and often requires an expensive drop-off charge, but the thrill of being alone on a tropical isle is priceless.

In Queensland, camping is permitted at designated rest areas along all major highways. There are no fees involved, bathroom facilities are offered, and at busy times of the year volunteers are on hand to serve up tea and coffee each morning.

Other Accommodations
During academic holidays you might try scoring a room at one of the universities or colleges. It isn't that easy—you must book in advance and most of the places are inconveniently located. Students are given first preference and cheaper rates (about $25-40 for B&B, double for nonstudents).

For longer stays, inquire at real estate agencies, scan local newspaper's classified ads, or check bulletin boards at hostels.

FOOD AND DRINK

TUCKER

With the exception of major cities, tucker (food) is basic meat and potatoes fare. Just keep in mind that the "meat" may be crocodile, kangaroo, emu, camel, or buffalo! Seafood, especially the prized barramundi, John Dory, prawns, and Moreton Bay bugs (a type of crayfish), is popular around the coastal areas.

Although some progress has been made in recent years, this is *not* an easy country for cholesterol watchers—many foods are fried, breaded, cheesed, and buttered. Food labeling is not very detailed. For example, a label may pro-

claim "100% vegetable oil" but does not elaborate on what kind of vegetable.

Breakfast is an all-important meal down under, and Vegemite (a darkly colored concoction of yeast, salt, and malt) is the national spread. Whatever you do, don't malign Vegemite in Australia—it's worse than desecrating the flag. When out on the road, you'll find no better place for lunch than a **"takeaway"** (takeout), which typically offers roast chicken, fish and chips, chips with gravy, meat pies, pasties, sausage rolls, and hamburgers with "the lot" (meaning with egg, bacon, pineapple, cheese, lettuce, tomato, and a slice of red beet). Bakeries also provide an inexpensive and easy meal. And, thanks to the ethnic population, you'll find a large number of luscious Italian, Greek, Lebanese, Turkish, and Asian establishments for takeaway meals.

The bigger cities have supermarkets that rival even those in the United States, and smaller communities have a passable assortment of grocery stores. One of the joys of buying fresh food in Australia is its specialty stores. Most towns have a local butcher, baker, and green grocer (for fruit and vegetables). It's a very good idea to stock up before you go bush or Outback; otherwise you'll be at the mercy of roadhouses—far apart and high-priced. Quarantine regulations prohibit fruits, veggies, plants, and some other agricultural products from crossing state lines—eat them, plant them, or prepare to relinquish them at each border.

Restaurants

One of the best things about Australian dining is this: when you book a table in a restaurant, it's yours for the whole night. No one hovers vulture-like, intimidating you to gulp your meal so the table can be turned over to other diners. That's where the no-tipping stance really shines—no tips involved, no need to hurry the patrons. Consequently, dining out is popular entertainment for most Aussies. One of the most popular places for a meal is at a pub, where "counter meals" (commonly veal, chicken, steak, or sausages, with salad and chips) are normally available noon-2 p.m. and 6-8 p.m. Such meals can be eaten either at the counter or a table in the adjoining lounge (if there is one), or in an outdoor courtyard.

Other things to know: A licensed restaurant serves alcohol (though sometimes only beer and wine), while a BYO restaurant, though unlicensed, allows you to bring your own beer and wine; dinner is often called "tea"; entree means appetizer; and if you want ketchup, ask for tomato sauce.

DRINK

Australians love to drink. Walk into someone's house and the kettle is instantly put on the stove; make a deal and you'll invariably seal it at the local pub. Favorite nonalcoholic drinks include mineral waters, Coca-Cola, fresh juices, flavored milk, tea, and lots of coffee. "White" tea or coffee has milk in it; "flat white" or "flat black" coffee has milk in it, but no froth, as opposed to a cappuccino. Despite the ubiquitousness of the almighty espresso machine, out in the bush tea-and coffee-drinkers may have to resort to the trusty tea bag and instant coffee powder.

Ice Cold and Plenty of It!

No question about it—Aussies love their beer. As Slim Dusty, Australia's best-known country crooner, so memorably sang, "Be it ever so lonesome, morbid, or dear, there's no place on Earth like a pub with no beer." The country's reputation as a nation of beer guzzlers may be clichéd, but Aussies certainly do enjoy a drop of the "amber nectar," usually down at the "local" pub with their mates, who take it in turn to "shout" a round of drinks. Beer is Australia's most popular beverage (coffee comes in a distant second), with 115 liters consumed annually for every man, woman, and child. Australia's most famous beer drinker is Bob Hawke, who won the World Drinking Championship (and made the Guinness Book of World Records) in 1955 by consuming 2.5 pints of beer in 12 seconds. His name would probably have been lost to history, except for the fact that he later went on to become the Prime Minister of Australia.

Australians prefer draught (draft) beer straight from the tap. It comes in a dizzying variety of glasses—middies, pots, schooners, ponies, and goblets—so it's best to ask advice on what size to get from the publican or a friendly local. Liquor stores are known as "bottle shops." Most pubs have an attached "drive-through" liquor store, where beer comes in tinnies, stubbies, and twisties.

Though **Fosters** is the best-known Australian beer worldwide (mainly through extensive advertising), it is for the most part scorned in its country of origin, and loyalty for local brands prevails. Some states have their own special brew, though most are available throughout Australia, including: **Tooheys** (New South Wales), **XXXX** (called "FOUR X") and **Powers** (Queensland), **Victoria Bitter** (Victoria), and **Swan** (Western Australia). The smaller breweries also have loyal followings for their beers, which include: **Cairn's Draught** (Queensland), **Coopers** (South Australia), **Cascade** and **Brogues** (Tasmania), and **Redback** (Western Australia). In addition, boutique breweries have popped up in the major cities, but you'll only be able to taste their efforts at the hotel where they're made. Try 'em all.

Keep in mind that Australian beer is higher in alcohol content than American varieties (even the Foster's you buy in the U.S. has been watered down), so gauge your consumption accordingly. "Drink-driving" laws are tough in Australia; on-the-spot sobriety checks and booze buses (Breathalyzer vans) are common in urban areas (see below).

Australian Wines

Australia's premier wine-producing areas are the Hunter Valley in New South Wales and the Barossa Valley in South Australia. The Hunter has produced wines that have won awards around the world, but it is shiraz, Australia's favorite red, for which the valley is most renowned. While the Hunter Valley is known for quality, the Barossa is Australia's largest wine-growing region. More than 400 grape growers harvest 40,000 tons annually, with wine produced by 50 wineries. Most of these grapes finish up in inexpensive rieslings and classic wine styles such as semillons and chardonnays. Wines are are produced in many other parts of Australia, including South Australia's McLaren Vale and Clare Valley, Western Australia's Swan and Margaret River Valleys and throughout Victoria, which has well over 100 vineyards. Australian champagne (oops—*méthode champenoise* wine) is widely imbibed and a good value. Tour the vineyards for free tastings, then buy a bottle or two of your favorite wine or bubbly. Less expensive wines can be purchased in two- or four-liter casks.

Spirits

If you're on a budget, you'd best stick to beer and wine—spirits down here are expensive, at least compared to prices in the Unites States. If money is no object, you'll find most of your favorite brands readily available at bottle shops and bars. Australia also produces port, brandy, and sherry, as well as two types of Queensland rum (but beware of the alcohol content, which could be considerably more than the normal 33%). Australia's biggest selling spirit is **Bundaberg Rum.**

Drinking Laws

You must be 18 or older to buy or consume alcohol. Liquor licenses vary from state to state (and territory). Pubs normally stay open for 12 hours (10 a.m.-10 p.m., or variations thereof) seven days a week. Other bars, clubs, and restaurants can offer alcohol until 2 or 3 a.m. Some establishments can serve you only if you're eating food, or else they are designated BYO (Bring Your Own). It is illegal to bring alcohol into an Aboriginal community or reserve.

GETTING THERE

Fly. It's the only way to get down under, unless you opt for an expensive cruise with a couple of one- or two-day port stops. Most international airlines operate wide-body aircraft to Australia. The main gateway cities are on the east coast, with Sydney (from North and South America, throughout the Pacific, Asia, and Europe) handling the majority of passengers. Other major gateways are Brisbane and Cairns (from throughout the Pacific and Asia), Darwin (from Asia), Perth (from Asia and Africa), and Melbourne (from North America, the Pacific, Asia, and Europe).

Other cities with international airports are Port Headland (from Indonesia), Adelaide (from Asia), and Hobart (from New Zealand). If you can avoid flying in over Christmas, Easter, or the middle of Australia's summer or school holiday periods, do so. Otherwise book well ahead as these are Australia's heaviest travel periods. Also, try to avoid weekend arrivals.

LOWERING FLIGHT COSTS

Before contemplating which travel agent to use, call individual airlines and do the comparisons yourself. Always ask for their best price for the time of year you wish to travel. The Internet is another good place to start searching out the cheapest fares. **Travelocity** (www.travelocity.com) displays airline schedules and their published fares. Also, check the Sunday travel section of most newspapers for an idea of current discount prices. Then shop around the travel agencies—you should be able to save 30-50% of the price you were quoted by the airline. Important questions to ask include applicable standby fares, accommodation packages, special promotions, allowed stopovers, and restrictions and penalties.

Many cheaper tickets have strict restrictions regarding changes of flight dates, lengths of stay, and cancellations. A general rule is: the cheaper the ticket, the more restrictions in place. Apart from airline promotional fares, consolidators—bucket shops as they are commonly called—consistently offer the lowest airfares. Once prevalent only in Asian cities such as Singapore and Bangkok and in the popular European travel hubs, this form of travel agent is now common throughout the world. They buy blocks of seats on scheduled flights that airlines decide they wouldn't normally be able to sell, then either sell them directly to the public or to other travel agents.

If you're not fussy about travel dates, say so. You can save plenty of bucks by traveling in the low or shoulder season instead of sky-high peak time. **Fare seasons** from the Northern Hemisphere are: 1 May-31 August, low; 1 December-28 February, high; everything else, shoulder. Some airlines vary these periods by a few weeks.

When you have found the best fare, open a **frequent flyer** membership with the airline—Australia is far enough from the rest of the world to make the rewards very obtainable.

APEX, Round-the-World, and Circle-Pacific Fares

Most travelers flying down under do so on an APEX (advance-purchase excursion) fare. These are usually the best value, though some (and, occasionally, many) restrictions apply. These might include minimum and maximum stays, and nonchangeable itineraries (or hefty penalties for changes); tickets may also be nonrefundable, once purchased.

Other travel options to consider are Round-the-World or Circle-Pacific fares. Round-the-World tickets—usually combining two airlines—allow travel in the same direction (with no backtracking) around the world anywhere on their combined route systems. Tickets ordinarily require that the first sector be booked in advance and that travel be completed within one year. The number of stops permitted may vary, and cancellation penalties may apply. Circle-Pacific tickets work pretty much the same as round-the-worlders except that they circle only the Pacific rather than the whole world. A sample itinerary might encompass San Francisco, Honolulu, Auckland, Sydney, Singapore, Bangkok, Hong Kong, Tokyo, then back to San Francisco. Contact travel agents for participating airlines and current fares; both types of tickets can prove an exceptionally good value.

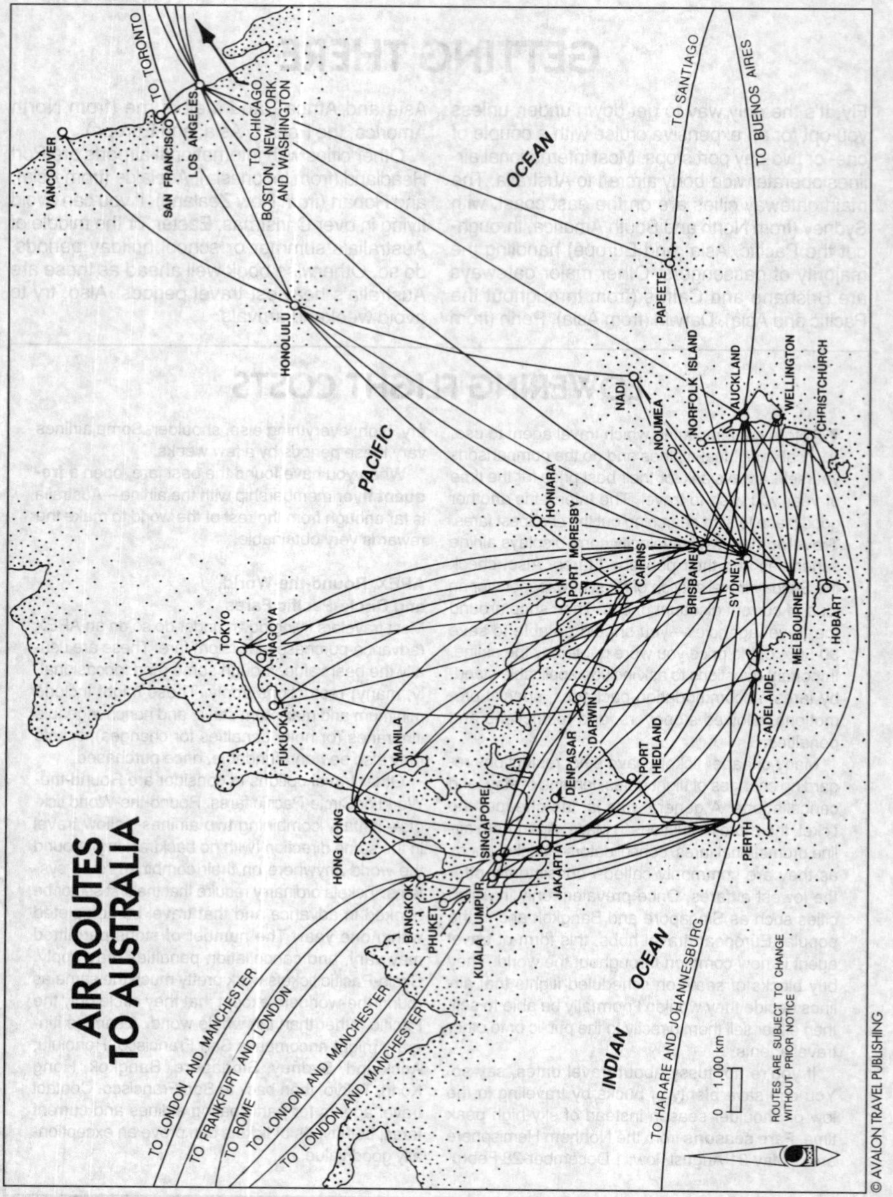

AIR ROUTES
TO AUSTRALIA

TO TORONTO

VANCOUVER

SAN FRANCISCO
LOS ANGELES
TO CHICAGO,
BOSTON, NEW YORK,
AND WASHINGTON

TO SANTIAGO

TO BUENOS AIRES

OCEAN

HONOLULU

PAPEETE

PACIFIC

AUCKLAND
WELLINGTON
CHRISTCHURCH
NORFOLK ISLAND
NADI
NOUMEA

TOKYO
NAGOYA

FUKUOKA

HONIARA

PORT MORESBY
CAIRNS
BRISBANE
SYDNEY
MELBOURNE
HOBART

MANILA

ADELAIDE

HONG KONG

DENPASAR
DARWIN
PORT
HEDLAND

BANGKOK
PHUKET
KUALA LUMPUR
SINGAPORE
JAKARTA

PERTH

TO LONDON AND MANCHESTER
TO FRANKFURT AND LONDON
TO ROME
TO LONDON AND MANCHESTER
TO LONDON AND MANCHESTER

INDIAN
OCEAN

TO HARARE AND JOHANNESBURG

ROUTES ARE SUBJECT TO CHANGE
WITHOUT PRIOR NOTICE

0   1,000 km

© AVALON TRAVEL PUBLISHING

FROM NORTH AMERICA

Direct nonstop flights (15-16 hours) between North America and Australia are offered by Air New Zealand, Qantas, and United Airlines, which each have daily services between Los Angeles or San Francisco and Sydney. Qantas and Air New Zealand also offer a staggering variety of stopover possibilities, such as Honolulu/Tahiti/Fiji with Qantas; and Honolulu/Western Samoa/Tahiti/Fiji Islands/Cook Islands/Tonga/Auckland with Air New Zealand. From the west coast, fares to Sydney start at US$1,100 roundtrip in the low season and US$1,300 in the high season.

From Canada, Canadian Airlines has a codesharing agreement Qantas, which entails a change of carrier in Honolulu. Many other airlines cross the Pacific Ocean between Canada and Australia but are routed via their home country. For example, Malaysian flies via Singapore, and Cathay Pacific flies via Hong Kong. The fare from Vancouver starts at $1,700 roundtrip in the high season and at $1,400 in the low season. Canadian Airlines charges from around $200 extra for the roundtrip. A less expensive option is charter operator Canada 3000, which often advertises fares as low as $999, but with many restrictions.

Travel Agents

Austravel, 51 East 42nd St., Suite 616, New York, NY 10017, tel. (212) 972-6880 or (800) 633-3404, www.austravel.net, specializes in travel to Australia. **STA Travel,** tel. (800) 777-0112, website: www.sta-travel.com, started life as a travel agency for university students but caters to all comers, with discounted fares for students and those under 26. They operate 150 agencies worldwide, include 16 within the United States. The Sydney STA Travel office is at 732 Harris St., Ultimo, Sydney, tel. (02) 9281-2604. **Council Travel,** tel. (800) 226-8624, also specializes in student and youth travel. They have agencies in most major U.S. cities.

Travel Cuts began life as a student travel agency, but it has long since slipped into the mainstream and now has 40 agencies across Canada. Head office is at 187 College St., Toronto, tel. (416) 979-2406.

FROM THE UNITED KINGDOM AND EUROPE

From the United Kingdom and Europe, the following airlines fly to Australia: Air France, Air India, Air New Zealand, Alitalia, British Airways, Cathay Pacific, Garuda Indonesia, JAL, KLM Royal Dutch Airlines, Lauda Air, Malaysian Air System, Qantas, Scandinavian Airlines, Singapore Airlines, and Thai International. The cheapest flights between London and Australia are offered by Britannia Airways, which operates charter flights between November and April from £399 roundtrip. Scheduled airlines charge from £600 in the low season and £700 in the high season.

Travel Agents

London holds many bucket shops (advertised in *Southern Cross, Time Out,* and *TNT*) offering discounted fares. A long-running and reliable favorite with travelers heading to Australia is **Trailfinders,** 194 Kensington High St., London, tel. (0171) 938-3366. Other reliable agencies include: **Campus Travel,** 52 Grosvenor Gardens, London, tel. (0171) 730-3402, website: www.campus-travel.co.uk, and **Council Travel,** 28A Poland St., Oxford Circus, London, tel. (0171) 287-3357.

FROM OTHER PARTS OF THE WORLD

New Zealand

Direct Qantas and Air New Zealand flights link Auckland, Wellington, Christchurch, and (in winter) Queenstown to most Australian capital cities. The high season fare between Auckland and Sydney is NZ$680 roundtrip, but with so many flights and competition from other transpacific airlines that make a stop at Auckland on the way to Australia, discounting is common. Shop around; flights can cost around NZ$500 roundtrip.

Asia

An exotic way to enter Australia is to hop over to Darwin from Bali with Garuda Indonesia. This airline also flies to Sydney, Brisbane, Cairns, Perth, Adelaide, and Melbourne from major Indonesian cities. Garuda also flies out of Los Angeles to

Australia, via Honolulu, and Bali or Jakarta, as well as from the following cities: London, Amsterdam, Tokyo, Beijing, Seoul, Hong Kong, Bangkok, Singapore, Kuala Lumpur, and Manila. For **Circle-Pacific** ticket holders, Garuda's partners are Delta and Cathay Pacific. (If traveling through the Indonesian archipelago, you will want to explore the country with Moon's *Indonesia Handbook,* Bill Dalton's bible to the country, or with *Bali Handbook,* Dalton's smaller volume.)

Other international carriers serving Australia from Asian cities are Air France, Air India, Air New Zealand, Air Niugini, All Nippon Airways, Ansett Australia, British Airways, Cathay Pacific Japan Airlines, KLM Royal Dutch Airlines, Malaysian, Philippine Airlines, Qantas, Singapore Airlines, and Thai International. The roundtrip airfare between the main Asian hub of Singapore and Sydney is S$1,050, with fares to Perth and Darwin slightly less expensive. The least expensive flight between Asia and Australia is operated by **Merpati** between Kupang in Timor and Darwin; $400 roundtrip.

Airline ticket consolidators can be found throughout Asia, especially in Singapore, Bangkok, and Hong Kong, but be aware that companies can fold overnight. The best source of

information regarding reliable agencies is other travelers.

South America

You have two options for flying between South America and Australia, and both will land you in Sydney. Lan Chile flies from Santiago via Easter Island and Tahiti (the last leg, between Tahiti and Sydney, is aboard Qantas). The other is with Aerolineas Argentinas, which flies nonstop between Buenos Aires and Auckland, before making the final hop across the Tasman Sea to Sydney. Neither way is particularly cheap; expect to pay from US$1,800 for the roundtrip fare.

Africa

The only direct flights between Africa and Australia originate in Johannesburg and Harare and terminate in Perth. Airlines that fly these routes are Qantas, South African Airways, and Air Zimbabwe. Air Mauritius flies between Johannesburg and Perth via Mauritius. Fares start at US$1,300 roundtrip in the low season. A less expensive option from southern Africa is to fly with Singapore Airlines or Malaysian via Singapore and Kuala Lumpur respectively, but the flight is much longer.

GETTING AROUND

Australia is enormous. Distances between places are vast and destinations often totally isolated—don't try to see the whole continent on a 10-day tour. Australia is also not a dollar-a-day country. Allow yourself plenty of time, plan at least a tentative itinerary, and budget your funds accordingly.

Travel Times Australia is a comprehensive transport timetable with rail, coach, and ferry schedules, as well as reservation numbers, addresses, and maps. Purchase it from newsagents, or get a copy in advance by sending A$8.95 (which includes airmail postage) to Traveltime Publishing, 3 Goodwin St., Glen Iris, VIC 3146, tel. (03) 9889-3344.

BY AIR

The main domestic carriers are **Ansett Australia,** tel. (13) 1300, website: www.ansett.com.au, and

Qantas, tel. (13) 1313, website: www.qantas.com.au. To book from North America, call (800) 366-1300 or (800) 227-4500, respectively. These two giants of Australian air travel have undergone massive upheavals since deregulation, taking many smaller regional airlines under their wing and blasting upstarts, such as ill-fated Compass Airlines, out of the sky. The bottom line for travelers is that the price of flying within Australia has dropped considerably in the last few years. The days of paying $1,200 to fly across the continent are long gone; today the roundtrip between Sydney and Perth is about $500 and the airlines will throw in a couple nights' accommodation as part of the deal. As well as regular APEX fares (the cheapest tickets available), both airlines offer some excellent package deals (most travel agents will have details), such as less than $350 pp for travel between Sydney and Tasmania inclusive of three nights' accommodations and a rental car.

DOMESTIC AIR ROUTES

INDIAN OCEAN

PACIFIC OCEAN

DARWIN · GOVE · WEIPA

KATHERINE

KUNUNURRA

CAIRNS

BROOME

TENNANT CREEK

QUEENSLAND

TOWNSVILLE

HAMILTON ISLAND

KARRATHA

PORT HEDLAND

NORTHERN TERRITORY

MT. ISA

PROSERPINE

MACKAY

WESTERN AUSTRALIA

ALICE SPRINGS

LONGREACH

ROCKHAMPTON

PARABURDOO

YULARA (AYERS ROCK)

BIRDSVILLE

BUNDABERG

BRISBANE
COOLANGATTA

SOUTH AUSTRALIA

NEW SOUTH WALES

COFFS HARBOUR
ARMIDALE

KALGOORLIE

BROKEN HILL

DUBBO

PORT MACQUARIE

PERTH

NEWCASTLE

ADELAIDE

WAGGA WAGGA

SYDNEY

VICTORIA

CANBERRA

COOMA

MELBOURNE

DEVONPORT

HOBART · LAUNCESTON

TASMANIA

0   500 km

© AVALON TRAVEL PUBLISHING

Regional Airlines

While Ansett and Qantas handle flights between major centers, about a dozen smaller airlines shuttle passengers to smaller centers from the main gateways. The easiest way to get schedule information and make reservations is through the central booking services of Ansett, tel. (13) 1300, and Qantas, tel. (13) 1313. The main subsidiaries of Ansett are: **Airnorth,** serving the Northern Territory; **Flight West,** serving Queensland's Outback and far north; **Hazelton,** serving central and Outback New South Wales; and **Kendell,** serving Victoria, southern New South Wales, and northern Tasmania. Those tied in with Qantas are **Eastern Australia, Southern Australia,** serving South Australia, and **Sunstate,** serving coastal Queensland. **Impulse,** tel. (13) 1381, is a small airline based in Newcastle with flights to all major centers between Melbourne and Brisbane.

Air Passes

Domestic passes don't offer the exceptional value they once did, what with the advent of deregulation. Once you're in Australia, you'll most likely see a number of advertised special fares and promotions. Also, international ticket holders are eligible for up to 30% discounts off regular economy fares on domestic routes with Ansett's **See Australia** fares and Qantas' **Discover Australia** fares.

The **Visit Australia Pass** (Ansett) and the **Boomerang Pass** (Qantas) are similar. In both cases, two to 10 sectors must be bought, and the passes must be purchased outside Australia. Each has slight variations in the definition of a "sector," but in both cases a one-zone sector costs $200 and a two-zone sector $250. Basically, all flights within the east are considered one-zone sectors, while flights to the west are two-zone sectors, as are flights between east coast cities and New Zealand and, in the case of Qantas, Fiji.

If you're already in the country, head to any travel agency and request either the Ansett or Qantas holiday brochures. Packages offered are often no more than the standard airfare.

From the Airport

Major cities offer inexpensive public bus service to, from, and between international and domestic airports. A variety of shuttle companies operate convenient door-to-door minivan service, usually operating till the last flight arrives. These are cheaper than taxis if you're traveling alone, but if you're with one or more companions, a taxi is probably better value. Larger hotels, as well as many motels, provide free pickup service for their guests. In smaller towns, you'll have to rely on whatever you can—a taxi, passing local, or your good looks.

BY TRAIN

Australia's main rail "events" are the transcontinental Indian-Pacific (Sydney-Perth, 65 hours), the Ghan (Adelaide-Alice Springs, 20 hours), and the Queenslander (Brisbane-Cairns, 32 hours).

The **Indian-Pacific** spans 4,350 km between the Pacific and Indian Oceans, crossing the vast Nullarbor Plain and the world's longest length of straight railway track (478 km). It's one of the few remaining great rail journeys.

The **Ghan** is, alas, the "new Ghan" of the 1980s. The original Ghan, begun in the late 1800s, was built along creek beds that were assumed to be bone-dry—that is, until the rains came and the route became regularly flooded. It was supposed to run from Adelaide to Darwin, but it still hasn't made it beyond Alice Springs.

The original broad-gauge line went only to Marree, becoming a narrow-gauge all the way to Oodnadatta, where passengers were escorted to Alice Springs via Afghani-guided camel trains, thus the name "Ghan." By the late 1920s the railway was extended to the Alice—but the rains still flooded the original lines. Often the train was left stranded, and supplies had to be parachuted down to waiting travelers. The old Ghan was rarely used after its film scene in *Mad Max III*. The new Ghan is still a good trip, but without the risk and romance.

The **Queenslander** is a luxurious, yuppy-ish scoot up the coast from Brisbane to Cairns (1,680 km). You can get off at Proserpine (gateway to the Whitsundays) or go to the end of the line. You'll be pampered with great views, gourmet cuisine, and sophisticated entertainment.

Other rail services include the **Sunlander** (Brisbane-Cairns, 32 hours), the **Spirit of the Tropics** (Brisbane-Cairns, 32 hours), the **Spirit of the Outback** (Brisbane-Longreach, 24 hours), the **Westlander** (Brisbane-Cunnamulla-Quilpie, 22 hours), the **Inlander** (Townsville-Mount Isa, 19 hours), the **XPT** (Sydney-Brisbane, 14 and one-half hours), the **Overland** (Adelaide-Melbourne, 12 hours), the **XPT** (Sydney-Melbourne, 10 and one-half hours), the **Xplorer** (Sydney-Canberra, four and one-half hours), the **Prospector** (Perth-Kalgoorlie, eight hours), and the **Silver City Link** (Melbourne-Mildura, Broken Hill, 13 hours).

First- and economy-class seats and berths are available on all long-distance services and must be booked in advance. First-class twinette cabins have seats that turn into two sleeping berths; most have private shower, toilet, wash basin with hot and cold water, and electric shaver outlet. First-class single cabins only have toilets and basins—showers are down the hall. Economy-class sleepers in Queensland accommodate three people, with toilets and showers available in each car. Available on the Ghan and Indian-Pacific only, "holiday class" offers two-berth cabins with economy sleepers. Coach-class cars feature reclining seats and, on many hauls, also provide showers. Meals are included with first-class accommodation fares. All long-distance trains have dining cars, bars, buffet cars, and lounges with a variety of entertainment.

For scheduling and ticketing information as well as reservations, call **Countrylink** in New South Wales and the ACT, tel. (13) 2232; **Queensland Rail** in Queensland, tel. (13) 2232; **V/Line** in Victoria, tel. (13) 2232; and **Westrail** in Western Australia, tel. (13) 1053. **Great Southern Railways,** tel. (13) 2147, website: www.gsr.com.au, is a private company that operates the Ghan, Overland, and Indian-Pacific services. For all overseas inquiries, scheduling information, fares, and pass purchases, contact **Rail Australia** in the United States, tel. (800) 423-2880; Canada, tel. (800) 387-8850; or the United Kingdom, tel. (0171) 828-4111.

Rail Passes

The **Austrailpass** allows unlimited rail travel within 14, 21, or 30 days in Economy class, including metropolitan trains, and are good deals if you plan to do a lot of rail travel. They must be purchased outside Australia and cost between $545 and $850. As the name suggests, the **Austrail Flexipass** is more flexible. It allows limited travel within a six-month period, but only on a certain number of days. Costs are: eight days, $450; 15 days, $550; 22 days, $780; and 29 days, $1,020. The eight-day pass does not allow travel on the Ghan or Indian-Pacific from Adelaide to Perth. Passes do not cover charges for

sleeping berths or meals. The **NSW Discovery Pass** is a good value for travel within that state. Unlimited travel for one month costs $249.

If you want to catch a train but don't have a rail pass, inquire about advance-purchase fares, which, if booked more than seven days in advance, can save you up to 40% off regular rail fares.

BY COACH

Modern air-conditioned coaches (buses) are an easy and comfortable way to see the country. Most of them have bathroom facilities, overhead video monitors, piped-in music, on-board hostesses, and drivers who double as tour guides. Buses are usually the cheapest way to travel *and* they go to a far wider range of places than trains and planes—to all capital cities, country towns, provincial centers, and most Outback regions. If there's a place they don't travel, they can usually hook up with a local bus system (which might be a mail truck) that will get you where you're going. Coach travel is a good way to kick back and relax, see the countryside, and meet other Aussie and international travelers.

Greyhound Pioneer, tel. (13) 2030, website: www.greyhound.com.au, has Australia's most extensive network of routes, serving all mainland capitals and just about everywhere in between. The other large company is **McCafferty's,** tel. (13) 1499, website: www.mccaffertys.com.au, based in Toowoomba, west of Brisbane. Its routes cover the entire east coast, Adelaide, Alice Springs, and Darwin. Anywhere not served by these two giants can be reached by local companies, often with connecting timetables and through-fares. Greyhound Pioneer and McCafferty's offer services in all states except Tasmania. For travel around the island state, **Tasmanian Redline Coaches,** tel. (03) 6331-3233, offers daily runs to all major towns and cities, and Tasmanian Wilderness Travel (see below) serves the out-of-the-way places.

Sample daily express traveling times and fares include: Sydney-Brisbane (16 hours, $84); Brisbane-Cairns (25 hours, $162); Sydney-Melbourne (15 hours, $64); Sydney-Adelaide (23 hours, $110); Melbourne-Adelaide (10 hours, $56); Adelaide-Alice Springs (20 hours, $155);

Alice Springs-Ayers Rock (six hours, $68); Alice Springs-Darwin (19 hours, $151); Darwin-Cairns (42 hours, $275); Darwin-Perth (34 hours, $354); and Adelaide-Perth (35 hours, $244).

Bus Passes
Again, you have an almost infinite assortment of bus passes—local, regional, national, and bus and train combination passes—explorer passes, backpacker discounts, bargain fares, etc. Some you have to buy outside Australia; others you can only buy once you're there.

The **Aussie Kilometre Pass** offers travel over a certain number of km on the Greyhound Pioneer national network. Simply work out your route and how many kilometers it covers, then purchase the relevant pass. Costs are: 2,000 km, $185; 10,000 km, $735; and 15,000 km, $1,065. These passes are valid for 3-6 months. The other option with Greyhound Pioneer is the **Aussie Explorer Pass,** which can be purchased for fixed itineraries. They range from a Sydney-Brisbane two-month pass for $105 to a 12-month, all-system pass for $1,555. The McCafferty's **Aussie Roamer Pass** is a similar setup, saving about 50% on regular fares. The pass is available for 2,000 km, $165; 10,000 km, $660; and 15,000 km, $957. McCafferty's also offers passes for certain routes where you are free to get on and off as you please. A pass for travel between Sydney and Cairns via Adelaide, Alice Springs, and Darwin costs $515. All McCafferty's passes are valid for 12 months.

These passes are available in the United States through **ATS Tours,** tel. (800) 423-2880, and in Canada through **Goway Travel,** tel. (800) 387-8850.

Other Bus Companies
A new breed of "adventure" buses has spawned within Australia. They are as much of a tour as a way to get between places. They head off the beaten path, carry small groups, and ease—rather than rush—you along. Based in Adelaide, the **Wayward Bus,** tel. (08) 8232-6646 or (1800) 88-2823, leads the way in comfort, cost, reliability, commentary, and widespread appeal. The main routes link Sydney, Melbourne, Adelaide, and Alice Springs. They stop at all major attractions, national parks, and towns, and passengers can get on and off as they please. A number

of different trips are offered, ranging from a five-day Sydney-Melbourne run ($170) to an eight-day, all-inclusive adventure between Adelaide and Alice Springs ($640). **Oz Experience,** tel. (9368) 1766 or (1300) 30-0028, website: www.ozex.com.au, follows in the footsteps of its New Zealand counterpart, Kiwi Experience. It attracts a young backpacker crowd, often emphasizing partying rather than seeing the sights, but the price is right. They offer services along the entire east coast, across to Adelaide, and north as far as Darwin. Passes come in more than 20 configurations; a Sydney-Cairns pass, valid for nine days' travel within a six-month period, is $300. Or have unlimited travel on the entire network for 12 months for $1,100.

For travel between Adelaide and Perth, consider the **Nullarbor Traveller,** tel. (08) 8364-0407 or (1800) 81-6858. With a maximum of 20 passengers in each bus, stops at all the best natural attractions and national parks, camping and hostel accommodations, and plenty of bush tucker, Nullarbor offers a great way to travel safely across one of the world's largest deserts. The cost is $750 pp, which includes transportation, accommodations, and meals. In the other Outback state, the **Blue Banana,** tel. (08) 8945-6800; website: www.taunet.au/banana, travels to the national parks in the north of the Northern Territory. A three-month pass is just $170 pp—a great value. **Tasmanian Wilderness Travel,** tel. (03) 6334-4442, website: www.tassie.net.au/wildtour, offers transport around Tasmania, including to national parks and major trailheads. Their Wilderness Passes range from five days' travel in seven days ($100) to 30 days' travel in 40 days ($220).

BY BOAT

The *Spirit of Tasmania* links Port Melbourne, Victoria, and Devonport, Tasmania, three times weekly. The 14-hour overnight trip offers everything from hostel-style dormitories to private cabins. The *Devil Cat* is a high-speed catamaran that crosses from Port Melbourne to George Town in just six hours. Travel costs the same on both services. Fares range $103-308 pp each way depending on the season and level of accommodations. Vehicles are also transported.

Since the implementation of the Bass Strait Passenger Vehicle Equalization Scheme, the cost has been reduced to $30-50 per standard-sized vehicle. For fare details, see the chart in the Introduction of the Tasmania chapter. For information and reservations, contact **TT-Line,** tel. (13) 2010, website: www.tt-line.com.au.

Kangaroo Island Sealink, tel. (13) 1301, operates two roll-on roll-off ferries daily between Cape Jervis, South Australia, and Kangaroo Island; $30 pp one way, $62 per vehicle one way.

Western Australia's Rottnest Island is serviced daily by three companies, including **Oceanic Cruises,** tel. (08) 9325-1191, from Perth's Barrack St. jetty for $40 roundtrip.

BY CAR

Car Rental
Outside the major cities, cars are about the only practical way to go. Rentals are not cheap, but if you're with a group the cost can work out more favorably. Avis, Budget, Hertz, and Thrifty are well represented and can be booked ahead from North America, but you'll often get a better deal from smaller, independent concerns after you've arrived. One advantage of the big conglomerates is that you can pick up and return your car at the airport and, in many cases, drop your car off at a destination other than your pickup place (one-way rentals are not usually available in Western Australia, the Northern Territory, or other remote locations).

Before renting a car, find out if it includes unlimited km and insurance. If you're paying by credit card, check with your company to see if you qualify for CDW (Collision Damage Waiver), which can save you considerable money. For U.S. residents, your regular auto insurance policy also might cover this charge.

All major car-rental companies are represented in Australia. Daily rates range from about $75 for a small car (Toyota Corolla, Ford Laser), $90 for a medium size (Toyota Camry, Holden Camira), and $105-plus for a larger vehicle like the Holden Commodore. Long-term rentals are less expensive. Companies include: **Avis,** tel. (1800) 22-5533, website: www.avis.com; **Budget,** tel. (13) 2727, website: www.budgetrentacar.com; **Dollar,** tel. (02) 9223-1444; **Hertz,** tel. (13) 3039, website: www.hertz.com; **National,** tel. (13) 1045; and **Thrifty,** tel. (1800) 65-2008, website: www. thrifty.com. In most cases, vehicles can be rented before arriving in Australia. Contact numbers are: Avis, tel. (800) 831-2847 U.S.; Budget, tel. (800) 527-0700 U.S., tel. (0800) 18-1181 U.K.; Hertz, tel. (800) 654-3001 U.S., tel. (0345) 55-5888 U.K.; and National, tel. (800) 227-3876 U.S., tel. (0345) 022-2525 U.K. Rates with local companies are much lower than with the international conglomerates. In Sydney, **Ascot,** tel. (02) 9317-2111, has vehicles from $30 a day and $36 for medium-sized cars for long-term rentals. In the middle of the pack are Australian-based companies with outlets in major centers, including **Discount,** tel. (02) 9212-3111, and **Lets,** tel. (02) 9331-5033.

Four-wheel-drive vehicles are available for more adventurous travel, but they are costlier than conventional cars ($100-150 daily, many with limited km). Also, insurance can add considerably to the cost. When tallying up the cost and equipment of a 4WD journey, travelers may find that organized tours are more economical and less stressful. Reputable rental agencies include Brits: Australia, tel. (1800) 33-1454; Oz Rentals, tel. (03) 9877-2986, Victoria; Cairns Rent-a-Car, tel. (07) 4051-6077; and South Perth 4WD Rentals, tel. (08) 9362-5444, Western Australia.

Campervan Rental
Campervans (two to four berths) range in price from $900 to $1,400 per week, with unlimited mileage. Most come equipped with refrigerator, sink, gas stove, and water tank, and some have showers and toilets. **Maui Campervans,** tel. (02) 9597-6155 or (1800) 22-7279, has depots in all major cities and often offers special deals to get vans back from certain centers. For example, most people travel up the east coast from Syd-

ney or Melbourne to Cairns, leaving a surplus of vans in Cairns. At last report, the rental rate for all size of campervan from Cairns to just about anywhere in Australia was $90 per day inclusive of unlimited mileage and insurance. **Brits: Australia,** tel. (1800) 33-1454, also operates a large fleet of vehicles, including many 4WD campervans. A highly recommended local operator is **Backpacker Campervans,** which rents small campervans from $70 per day including unlimited mileage. Head office is in Melbourne, tel. (03) 9417-1341, or in Sydney, call (02) 9693-2079, and in Darwin, call (08) 8941-1811.

Purchasing a Car
Buying a car, especially for the short-term visitor, can be a pain—an *expensive* pain. New ones, whether locally manufactured or imported, are not cheap; used ones can turn out to be unreliable lemons. This is not like going to Sweden or Germany to pick up a shiny new Saab or Porsche and drive off into the sunset. Buying a car, particularly a used one, can be the same kind of arduous, time-consuming hell in Sydney or Perth as it is in Los Angeles or Detroit. And, as you ride off into that central Australian sunset, and the car blows its head gasket or cracks the block, your salty tears will do nothing more than blur your written guarantee.

The **buy-back** plan is another option: you buy a car (or motorcycle) at a fixed rate, put down a deposit equal to the vehicle's value, return it after a specified period, and get your money back, less the agreed-upon fee. Most prices include a set number of km, limited warranties, and short-term insurance. One Sydney company that is set up especially for this type of transaction is **Travellers Auto Barn,** 177 William St., Kings Cross, tel. (02) 9360-1500, website: www.travellers-autobarn.com.au, which offers a 5,000 km warranty on all vehicles. Companies that specialize in both car and motorcycle buy-backs are **Car Connection,** RSD Lot 8, Vaughan Springs Rd., Glenluce, VIC 3451, tel. (03) 5473-4469, and **Boomerang Cars,** 579 Grand Junction, Adelaide, SA, tel. (08) 8262-3700.

Highways and Byways
City expressways and thoroughfares are just about as hectic and expletive-in-

ROAD WARNING SIGNS

CROSSING HERE

NEXT 15 km

SPEED LIMIT ENDS

spiring as those in any other first world metropolis and come complete with rush-hour (peak) traffic, which, increasingly, seems to last early morning until late at night. The major highways are sealed (called "bitumen") with asphalt or tar and well-maintained—though they are often only two-lane affairs (in the Outback, bitumen roads can barely accommodate even one vehicle). Only since the 1980s have Highway 1 (the around-Australia road) and the Stuart Highway (up the center) been completely surfaced.

Filling stations (also known as petrol stations and service stations) are plentiful in cities, suburbs, and townships, but can be few and far between in the Outback. Petrol, sold by the liter, comes in leaded and unleaded grades and costs 70-80 cents per liter (A$3-3.50 per gallon) in populated areas, though in desolate areas prices can go much higher (what are you going to do, shop around?). Diesel and leaded premium are usually available. Distances between Outback petrol pumps can be considerable; check with each roadhouse and service station before assuming a fill-up will be available at your next stop when traveling in remote regions.

Laws and Licenses
First rule to remember: Drive on the left side of the road! (And for you four-on-the-floorers, this means you shift with your *left* hand.) Second rule: The vehicle on your right has right-of-way, as does any vehicle on a roundabout. Play it safe and watch carefully.

The maximum **speed limit** in cities and towns is 50-80 kph, increasing to 100-110 km/h on country roads and highways, unless signs say otherwise. **Seat belts** are mandatory and must be worn by the driver and all passengers; small children must be harnessed into a safety seat. **Motorcyclists** need a special license, as well as a helmet (check with state automobile clubs). **"Drink-driving" laws** are strict and spot checks, including Breathalyzer tests, are commonplace. Drivers having blood-alcohol levels 0.05 percent or higher (0.08 percent in the Northern Territory) will incur large fines, a court appearance, and loss of driving privileges.

Tourists can get away with using their valid overseas driver's license (along with a passport) if driving the same class of vehicle. International Driver's Licenses are only recognized if used in conjunction with a valid driver's permit (so, why bother?).

If you're a member of an official Automobile Club in your home country, bring your membership card to receive reciprocal rights from Australian automobile clubs.

CYCLING

Both long-distance and round-the-city cycling are popular in Australia. Most cities have designated bike routes, and flat country roads can be sheer heaven. Remote areas and Outback tracks require careful planning, extra equipment, and excellent health—always check with locals and notify police or park rangers before venturing into desolate regions. Make certain to drink heaps of water, wear plenty of sunscreen, and use a bicycle helmet (mandatory). You can bring your own bike from overseas (check with your airline

ROAD SIGNS

| NATIONAL HIGHWAY | NATIONAL ROUTE | STATE ROUTE | TOURIST DRIVE |

regarding packing and costs) or buy a touring or mountain bike once you get to Australia.

For route maps, trail suggestions, and information on bicycle touring, contact the **Bicycle Federation of Australia,** GPO 792, Adelaide, SA 5001, tel. (08) 6355-1724, website: www.oze-mail.com.au/~bicycle. State bicycling organizations can provide similar information. These are: **Pedal Power ACT,** tel. (02) 6248-7995; **Bicycle New South Wales,** tel. (02) 9283-5200; **Bicycle Institute of Queensland,** tel. (07) 3899-2988; **Bicycle Institute of South Australia,** tel. (08) 8411-0233; **Bicycle Tasmania,** tel. (03) 6233-6619; **Bicycle Victoria,** tel. (03) 9328-3000; and **Western Australia Cycle Touring Association,** tel. (08) 9384-7409.

OTHER OPTIONS

Motorcycles

Read the info above regarding car purchases; the same applies to motorcycles. You can ship your own over (special permit necessary, and expensive) or buy one out of the classifieds—April or May, the beginning of the Australian winter, is a good time to shop. Rentals are usually available only in the cities, but the same buy-

back scheme for cars (see above) can be had for motorcycles. A favorite is the Yamaha Ténéré, a long-distance cruiser and off-road beauty.

It is *not* recommended that bikers solo into the Outback. Tag-along tours, similar to those for 4WD vehicles are available for motorcylists. Rates for motorcycles range $60-95 per day and $300-500 per week, depending on engine size; a refundable deposit—around $500—is required.

Hitchhiking

Don't. Hitchhiking is illegal in most states and strongly discouraged throughout Australia. Check the bulletin boards at YHA hostels and other backpacker lodges for rides, though this, too, has its risks.

Mail Trucks and Planes

Outback mail runs, whether by truck or plane, are one of Australia's most enduring traditions. The weekly runs—covering hundreds or thousands of kilometers—often provide the only outside human contact for Outback dwellers. Besides being a reliable source for important information and juicy gossip—and, of course, the mail—the service also delivers everything from Vegemite to spark plugs.

TOURS

The range of tours available in Australia is as vast as the country, as wild as your imagination, as extravagant or economical as you wish, and as environmentally conscious or politically correct as you choose. The place to begin is at each state or territory's government tourist office. These offices are glorious resources for all kinds of information, and will not only recommend and seek out a suitable tour for you, but will book it as well. Major cities offer the usual tourist-friendly range of commercial "city sights," "by day," and "by night" tours, either in a big bus, minivan, or hop-on-and-off shuttle.

Since its humble beginnings in Melbourne in 1927, **Australian Pacific Tours,** tel. (03) 9277-8444, (1800) 65-5220, or, in North America, (800) 290-8687, has grown to become Australia's largest tour operator. The buses are luxurious and accommodations of a superior standard. **AAT Kings,** tel. (03) 9274-7422, (1800) 33-4009, or (800) 353-4525, is a similar operation. **Globus,** dating from 1928, is a North American company specializing in escorted and independent first-class tours to Australia, tel. 303-797-2800 or (800) 221-0090. **Contiki,** tel. (02) 9511-2200 or (1300) 30-1835 or, from North America, (800) 266-8454, website: www.contiki.com, specializes in bus tours for the 18-35 age group. In Australia, the tours operate in Queensland, Northern Territory, Tasmania, and Western Australia.

ABORIGINAL TOURS

Certainly one of the most rewarding opportunities of travel through Australia is to visit one or more of the Aboriginal lands. Tourism plays an important economical role for the Aborigines. The tour companies listed below are owned, managed, and/or led by the traditional people. Focus might be on religion, the rudiments of "Dreaming," art and culture, the use of plants and animals, or bush tucker. Be prepared to abide by special customs and rules of behavior (i.e., do not spit out the food—unless you're *supposed* to).

NORTHERN TERRITORY

Ipolera Community, tel. (08) 8956-7466: short culture-oriented walks and talks

Ntaria Aboriginal Community, tel. (08) 8956-7402: self-guided tours of historical Hermannsburg

Oak Valley Tours, tel. (08) 8956-7411: day tours to areas south of Alice Springs

Wallace Rockhole Aboriginal Community, tel. (08) 8956-7415: short walks and talks about culture and rock art

NORTHERN TERRITORY—TOP END

Aussie Safaris, tel. (08) 8981-1633: day tours of Peppimenarti Aboriginal Community

Manyallaluk Aboriginal Corporation, tel. (08) 8975-4727: tours and meetings with Jawoyn traditional owners, leaving from Katherine

Tiwi Tours, tel. (08) 8981-5115: trips to Vathurst and Melville Islands, off of Darwin

Umorrduk Aboriginal Safaris, tel. (08) 8948-1306: flying and driving art-and-culture tours of northwest Arnhem Land and Kakadu National Park

QUEENSLAND

Ang-gnarra Aboriginal Corporation, tel. (07) 4060-3214: guided tours of Split Rock Gallery and other rock sites, departing from Laura

SOUTH AUSTRALIA

Desert Tracks, tel. (08) 8956-2144: excellent—but costly—cultural tours of Anangu-Pitjantjatjara Lands, departing from Yulara (NT)

WESTERN AUSTRALIA

Derby Tourist Bureau, tel. (08) 9191-1426: arrangements can be made to cruise Geikie Gorge with Bunuba traditional people

Karijini Adventure Tours, tel. (08) 9188-1670: adventure trips in the Pilbara's Karijini National Park

Flak Track Tours, tel. (08) 9192-1487: Aboriginal community visits departing from Broome

Accommodations are in lodges, motels, or cabins (often four-share), the coaches are modern and comfortable, and the crowd is fun-loving.

Many smaller companies offer tours through specific regions. The following is a small cross-section of these. **Coolabah Tours,** tel. (1800) 50-5265, operates a three-day trip between Sydney and Byron Bay, which combines coastal attractions with two nights' accommodation at Bakers Creek Station, where horseback riding and hiking through the rainforest are highlights. The price of this tour is typical of those aimed at backpackers—$250 includes transportation, two nights' accommodation, and all meals. **Sahara Outback Tours,** tel. (08) 8953-0881 or (1800) 80-6240, runs five-day camping tours from Alice Springs to destinations such as Ayers Rock, the Olgas, and Ormiston Gorge. Also in the Territory, **Gondwana Adventure Tours,** tel. (1800) 24-2177, takes small-group tours into Kakadu National Park. **Craclair Tours,** tel. (03) 6424-7833, offers lodge-based hiking tours through Tasmania's most spectacular national parks. A good resource such tours is the **Outdoor Tour Operators Association** website at www.otoa.com.au.

Aerial Tours

From the comfort of a six- or 10-seater Piper, fly high above the parched land, peering down at the ant-like climbers at Uluru or the Bungle Bungles. Tours from a few days to a few weeks can be arranged through the state tourist offices; **Air Adventure Australia,** tel. (1800) 03-3160; **Aircruising Australia,** tel. (02) 9693-2233; **Aviatour,** tel. (03) 9589-4097; or **Outback NT Touring Co.,** tel. (08) 8979-2411 or (1800) 08-9113.

Fishing Tours

North American companies that specialize in fishing tours, including to Australia, are **Anglers Travel,** tel. 702-324-0580 or (800) 624-8429, and **Rod and Reel Adventures,** tel. 209-785-0444. For more specialized fishing tours, contact **Lizard Island Lodge,** tel. (07) 4060-3999 or (1800) 227-4411, for game fishing off Cairns; **Arafura Safaris,** tel. (08) 8948-2663, for barramundi fishing in the Northern Territory; or Tasmania's **London Lakes Fly-Fishing Lodge,** tel. (03) 6289-1159, Australia's premier fly-fishing accommodation.

Volunteer Programs and Eco Tours

WWOOF (Willing Workers On Organic Farms) will trade you bed and board in exchange for several hours' daily work. The farms, numbering more than 700, are not always organic, nor are they always farms; an occasional pottery or other enterprise might sneak in there. Some farms are in Outback areas, though most are in more built-up regions. Membership ($30 outside Australia, $25 within the country) is required. Send the fee and you'll receive a membership number and WWOOF directory in return. For more information, contact WWOOF, Mt. Murrindal Co-op, Buchan, VIC 3885, tel. (03) 5155-0218, e-mail: wwoof@ozemail.com.au.

Volunteer conservation projects are available through **ATCV** (Australian Trust for Conservation Volunteers). This is a wonderful opportunity for travelers to do something constructive for the environment, meet other like-minded souls, and visit some roads less traveled. Projects are often situated in the Outback and can include track construction, tree planting, and cataloging natural habitation. Volunteers make a contribution to help cover costs and, in return, are supplied with transportation, accommodations, and food. You can join for a week, weekend, or several weeks. For more information, contact ATCV, 534 City Rd., North Melbourne, VIC, tel. (03) 9686-5554.

Operators specializing in organized ecotours include **Ecotour Travel,** tel. (02) 9261-8984, and **Tailored Tours,** tel. (08) 8363-0367. In North America, contact **Earthwatch,** tel. 617-926-8200 or (800) 776-0188, or **Naturequest,** tel. 714-499-9561 or (800) 369-3033.

VISAS AND OFFICIALDOM

Keep up to date on current red tape by contacting the nearest embassy or consulate, as well as your country's customs service. See "Australian Embassies and Consulates," below, for addresses.

PASSPORTS AND VISAS

Every visitor must have a valid passport for entry into Australia. In addition, visas are required for everyone except holders of Australian and New Zealand passports.

Tourist visas are issued free of charge for stays of three months or less, at Australian consulates and embassies throughout the world. If you plan to stay for more than three months, you must pay a fee (US$25-30, depending on the exchange rate). Modern technology has caught up with the visa-issuing process, and residents of most western countries need not apply in person or by post. The Electronic Travel Authority issues visas through the airlines and travel agencies, or you can download an application from the Internet (www.anzac.com/aust/visa.htm). If applying in person, a visa will probably be issued on the spot; if applying by mail, be sure to enclose the completed application, any necessary fees, and a stamped, self-addressed envelope large enough to accommodate your passport. Also, allow at least 21 days for processing. If you want special services, such as your documents returned via first-class, certified, registered, or express mail, enclose the appropriate forms and postage. Mail that is marked "insufficient postage" will be returned, unprocessed.

Whether applying in person or by mail, you must present your passport and a signed application form (they don't seem to want your photograph anymore).

Within Australia, visas can be extended (often on the whim of the official you approach) in major cities. Do this well ahead of your visa expiration date, as the process can be lengthy. The application fee for the further extension of a three-month visa is $100-200, depending which country's passport you hold. These fees are *not* re-turned should your extension be denied. You may be required to have a personal interview and produce bank statements and other proof of financial solvency, including medical insurance and an onward ticket. The maximum stay, including extensions, is one year.

The tourist visa, no matter how long it's good for, does not allow you to be employed or take formal study in Australia. If you want to reapply as a resident, you'll probably have to go home and do it—the old pay-someone-to-marry-you-and-stay-forever technique is pretty much a thing of the past.

Visitors from Britain, Ireland, Canada, Japan, or the Netherlands, aged 18 to 26 (sometimes a bit older), may be eligible for a **working holiday visa.** This visa, which should be applied for in the applicant's home country, allows casual employment for a period of three months, though the visa is good for up to 12 months. **Student visas** entitle the holders to study full-time and work part-time, up to 20 hours per week. Application must be made in person—and in advance—at an Australian consulate. Individuals who have approved sponsorship from an employer or organization in Australia can apply for a **temporary working visa** at their nearest Australian consulate—be forewarned, the requirements are stringent.

WORK

Regular tourist visas clearly state that *no* employment of *any* kind is allowed during your stay. A lot of travelers used to think, "sure, sure—I'll just work 'under the table.'" Unfortunately, with Australia's high unemployment rate, this is no longer a reliable option—there are too many "legit" citizens looking for jobs.

Holders of working holiday visas are officially allowed to work for three out of 12 months. You are also required to have a "Tax File Number" (i.e., a Social Security card); forms are available at the Taxation Department office or post office (be prepared to show your passport and visa). Without a tax file number, you'll pay the high-

PERMITS

You may need special permits to enter, pass through, or camp in certain areas of Australia.

Aboriginal Lands

The laws vary—on some lands you can pass through on "main roads" or stop in a community for fuel, on others you need a permit just to put your little toe on the land. If you're on an organized tour, the operator or guide will probably have taken care of all the red tape, otherwise apply well in advance (allow a couple of months) to the following land councils (you must apply to each state or territory that you wish to visit): Permits Officer, Department of Aboriginal Affairs, P.O. Box 7770, Perth, WA 6850, tel. (08) 9235-8000; Administration Officer, Maralinga-Tjarutja Inc., P.O. Box 435, Ceduna, SA 5435, tel. (08) 8625-2946; Permits Officer, Central Land Council, P.O. Box 3321, Alice Springs, NT 0871, tel. (08) 8951-6320, for central and southern areas; Permits Officer, Northern Land Council, P.O. Box 42921, Casuarina, NT 0811,

tel. (08) 8920-5178, for northern areas and Arnhem Land; Aboriginal Coordinating Council, P.O. Box 6512, Cairns, QLD 4870, tel. (07) 4031-2623; Permits Officer, Tiwi Land Council, Snake Bay, Bathurst Island via Darwin, NT 0822, tel. (08) 8978-3733, for Melville and Bathurst Islands.

National Parks and Desert Parks

Obtain camping and visitor permits in advance (see destination chapters for more info). If you're planning a visit to Simpson Desert Conservation Park, Simpson Desert Regional Reserve, Lake Eyre National Park, Innamincka Regional Reserve, and/or Witjira National Park in South Australia, you'll need a Desert Parks Pass. The pass, which costs around $50 per vehicle, includes camping and visiting permits, essential maps, and mini-travel guides. Purchase one at various shops in the northern part of the state, or through Flinders Ranges-based South Australian National Parks and Wildlife Service, Far Northern Region, tel. (08) 8648-4244.

est rate of tax—48.9%. Visitors with a working holiday visa can take advantage of **Employment National,** the government employment agency that has branches or representatives in virtually every city and town. Casual labor is what you'll probably be offered—possibilities are fruit-picking, bar and restaurant work, ski resorts jobs, nannying, as well as some skilled positions for carpenters, electricians, plumbers, mechanics, and such. Another option is to register with a recruitment agency. The best chance of securing work in capital cities is with: **Recruitment Solutions,** tel. (02) 9377-6666, offering secretarial and accounting positions; **Medistaff,** tel. (03) 9510-1444, specializing in the nursing field; and **Dunhill Personnel,** tel. (02) 9602-4680, advertising positions in all fields.

Harvesting is the best possibility for casual work. Opportunities are: South Australia—Barossa Valley grapes (Feb.-April), Riverlands citrus and soft fruits (all year); Western Australia—west coast seafoods (March-Nov.), Kununurra-area fruits and vegetables (May-Oct.), southwest-region grapes (Oct.-June); Queensland—central coast fruits and vegetables (May-Dec.), New South Wales border area grapes and orchard

fruits (Dec.-March), Bundaberg-area fruits and vegetables (all year), northern coast bananas, tobacco, and sugarcane; New South Wales—northern coast bananas (all year), central eastern-area asparagus, cottons, onions, orchard and other fruits (Nov.-April); Victoria—Shepparton-area orchard and soft fruits, grapes, tobacco, and tomatoes (Nov.-April); Tasmania—grapes, hops, orchard and soft fruits (Dec.-March).

AUSTRALIAN CONSULATES AND EMBASSIES

United States

The **Australian Embassy** is at 1601 Massachusetts Ave. NW, Washington, DC 20036-2273, tel. (202) 797-3000. You'll find Australian consulates in the following cities:

Honolulu, 1000 Bishop St., Penthouse, Honolulu, HI 96813, tel. (808) 524-5050

Los Angeles, Century Plaza Towers, 2049 Century Park East, 19th floor, Los Angeles, CA 90067, tel. (310) 229-4800

New York, 34th Floor, 150 E 42nd St., New York, NY 10017-5612, tel. (212) 351-6500

San Francisco, Suite 700, 1 Bush St., San Francisco, CA 94104, tel. (415) 362-6160

Canada
Ottawa, Suite 710, 50 O'Connor St., Ottawa, ON K1P 6L2, tel. (613) 236-0841
Toronto, Suite 316, 175 Bloor St. East, Toronto, ON M4W 3R8, tel. (416) 323-1155
Vancouver, Suite 1255, 888 Dunsmuir St., Vancouver, BC V6C 3K4, tel. (604) 684-1177

New Zealand
Auckland, 32-38 Quay St., Auckland 1, tel. (09) 303-2429
Wellington, 72-78 Hobson St., Thorndon, Wellington, tel. (04) 473-6411

Asia
Indonesia, Jalan H.R. Rasuna Said, Kav. c 15-16, Jakarta Selatan 12940, tel. (021) 522-7111
Hong Kong, 25 Harbour Rd., Wanchai, tel. (2827) 8881
Japan, Osaka, 2-1-61 Shiromi, Chuo-ku 540, tel. (06) 941-9271; Tokyo, 2-1-14 Mita, Minato-ku, tel. (03) 5232-4111
Malaysia, 6 Jalan Yap, Kwan Seng, Kuala Lumpur 50450, tel. (03) 242-3122
Philippines, 104 Paseo de Roxas, Makati, Metro Manila, tel. (02) 750-2850
Singapore, 25 Napier Rd., Singapore 258507, tel. 737-9311
Thailand, 37 S. Sathorn Rd., Bangkok 10120, tel. (02) 287-2680

Europe
Denmark, Kristianagade 21, 2100 Copenhagen, tel. (035) 26-2244
France, 4 rue Jean Rey, Paris 15, tel. (01) 4059-3300
Germany, Godesberger Allee 105-107, 53175 Bonn, tel. (0228) 81-030
Great Britain, Australia House, The Strand, London WC2B 4LA, tel. (0171) 379-4334
Ireland, Fitzwilton House, Wilton Terrace, Dublin 2, tel. (01) 676-1517
Netherlands, Carnegielaan 14, 2517 KH The Hague, tel. (070) 310-8200
Sweden, Sergels Torg 12, Stockholm, tel. (08) 613-2900
Switzerland, 29 Alpenstrasse, Berne, tel. (031) 351-0143

South Africa
Pretoria, 292 Orient St., Arcadia, Pretoria 0083, tel. (012) 342-3740

FOREIGN CONSULATES AND EMBASSIES

Canberra (Australian Capital Territory), Australia's equivalent to Washington, D.C., is where you'll find the foreign embassies. Wieldy connections such as New Zealand, Great Britain, the United States, and significant others, maintain consulates in other capital cities such as Sydney and Melbourne; an Indonesian consulate resides in Darwin. Canberra offices include:

Austria, 12 Talbot St., Forrest, tel. (02) 6295-1533
Canada, Commonwealth Ave., Canberra, tel. (02) 6273-3844
Germany, 119 Empire Circuit, Yarralumla, tel. (02) 6270-1951
India, 3 Moonah Pl., Yarralumla, tel. (02) 6273-3999
Indonesia, 8 Darwin Ave., Yarralumla, tel. (02) 6250-8600
Ireland, 20 Arkana St., Yarralumla, tel. (02) 6273-3022
Japan, 112 Empire Circuit, Yarralumla, tel. (02) 6273-3244
Malaysia, 7 Perth Ave., Yarralumla, tel. (02) 6273-1543
Netherlands, 120 Empire Circuit, Yarralumla, tel. (02) 6273-3111
New Zealand, Commonwealth Ave., Yarralumla, tel. (02) 6270-4211
Norway, 17 Hunter St., Yarralumla, tel. (02) 6273-3444
Papua New Guinea, Forster Crescent, Yarralumla, tel. (02) 6273-3322
Singapore, 17 Forster Crescent, Yarralumla, tel. (02) 6273-3944
South Africa, State Circle, Yarralumla, tel. (02) 6273-2424
Sweden, 5 Turrana St., Yarralumla, tel. (02) 6270-2700
Switzerland, 7 Melbourne Ave., Forrest, tel. (02) 6273-3977
Thailand, 111 Empire Circuit, Yarralumla, tel. (02) 6273-1149

United Kingdom, Commonwealth Ave., Yarra-lumla, tel. (02) 6270-6666

CUSTOMS

Australian Customs

Visitors may bring personal clothing and effects into Australia duty-free. If you're over 18 years old, you're also allowed 250 cigarettes or 250 grams of cigars or tobacco, in addition to one liter of wine, beer, or spirits (you must carry these items on you to qualify). Other taxable goods (up to $400 worth per adult and $200 per child under 18 years old) may be admitted duty-free if included inside personal baggage.

Drugs, weapons, and firearms are prohibited or restricted in Australia. Eager (and possibly kinky) German shepherds will be sniffing you as you wait to clear immigration. Drug laws are strictly enforced. Also, certain quarantined items such as meats (including dried meats), vegetables, honey, fruit, and flowers will be confiscated. Forget about bringing in items made from endangered species (an ivory mojo man in a polar bear fur pouch, for example), live animals (endangered or not), and certain types of nonapproved telecommunication devices. If you're not sure of something, *don't* try to smuggle it in—ask a customs agent. And if that doesn't suit you, drop the questionable article in the amnesty box before passing through customs.

Since you will probably not want to drop cash into the amnesty box, you should also know that persons carrying or sending cash and coins valuing A$10,000 or more (in *any* country's currency) into or out of Australia must declare the money and fill out a report with the Australian Customs Service, tel. (02) 9213-2000 or (1300) 36-3263, at the airport. Traveler's checks in any amount of Australian or foreign currency are exempt from this rule.

Aside from international customs, quarantines on fresh fruit, vegetables, and plants are in effect between states and territories. Eat everything up before you reach the state line.

International Customs

Each family member is allowed to bring back into the U.S. up to US$400 in duty-free goods; that is, if you're out of the U.S. for a minimum of 48 hours and haven't taken any other international journey in 30 days. Family members may combine their exemptions. Goods between $400 and $1,400 are assessed at a flat 10% rate. If you're at least 21 years old, your allowance may include 100 cigars (no Cuban brands), 200 cigarettes, and one liter of wine, beer, or spirits. You may mail gifts, valued under $50, duty-free to friends or relatives—but don't send more than one package per day to any one person. For further information, consult the U.S. Customs Service, tel. (202) 927-6724, website: www.customs.ustreas.gov.

Canadians who have been abroad for less than eight days may bring back up to C$100 of goods duty-free. Those who have been away for eight days or more are allowed up to C$500 in merchandise. The duty-free allowance for Canadians includes up to 1.1 liter of spirits, one carton of cigarettes, and 50 cigars. Canada Customs can be reached at (613) 993-0534 or (800) 461-9999, or visit the Revenue Canada web site: www.revcan.ca.

Travelers from the United Kingdom may bring home up to £145 of goods duty-free. In addition, goods such as wine, tobacco, and perfume are duty-free, and so is anything you've owned for longer than six months. The same regulations apply to items that are mailed home. For information, call Customs and Excise, tel. (0181) 910-3602, website: www.open.gov.uk.

Departure Tax

Unless you're a transit passenger who's been in the country less than 24 hours (in which case you probably wouldn't be reading this book), every person 12 years and older must pay a $27 departure tax when leaving Australia. To offset the cost of insulating houses under a new flight path, all passengers departing from Sydney must also pay an Airport Noise Levy of $3.40. In most cases, departure tax for all countries that you visit is added, or hidden, in the cost of your ticket.

SPECIAL INTERESTS

WOMEN

Aussie men have a reputation for being pretty brusque and gruff, and for putting their cars and sport atop the pecking order, with the women coming in last—though they're not always that way deep under down under. As with anywhere else in the world, exercise common sense: don't walk alone late at night in the city (also city trains at night are not particularly safe), try to blend in as much as possible, don't tell anyone you're traveling alone, and most definitely don't hitchhike alone. There are women's resource centers, health clinics, and hotlines in every major city for help and assistance.

GAY AND LESBIAN

Well, *Priscilla, Queen of the Desert*, managed quite well, thank you, in her Outback travels. But will *you* if you're gay or lesbian?

Oddly enough, despite all of Australia's machismo, Sydney has one of the world's largest and most active gay and lesbian scenes. Other cities and many country areas have gay-and-lesbian havens. Parades, gatherings, networks, and club-life are all part of the open lifestyle.

The Outback, however, is not quite so accepting—those miners, ranchers, and truckers have been known to be a wee bit intolerant. Consequently, it might be best to keep your sexual preference under wraps in those circumstances.

Monthly gay and lesbian mags such as *Outrage* and *Campaign* provide current information as well as lists of services and resources. The **Australian Gay and Lesbian Tourism Association,** P.O. Box 2174, Fitzroy, VIC (www.aglta.asn.au/index.htm) publishes a homosexual-friendly accommodation guide. In North America, the International Gay and Lesbian Travel Association, tel. (954) 776-2626 or (800) 448-8550, website: www.iglta.org, represents gay-friendly travel agents and accommodations in Australia and across the world.

TRAVELERS WITH DISABILITIES

Many of Australia's accommodations, restaurants, cinemas, and tourist attractions provide facilities and access for travelers with disabilities. Most newer buildings are equipped with wheelchair access. Guides and booklets for travelers with disabilities, which include state and local organizations and travel specialists, can be obtained from **National Information Communication Awareness Network** (NICAN), P.O. Box 407, Curtin, ACT 2605, tel. (02) 6285-3713, e-mail: nican@spirit.com.au.

HEALTH AND SAFETY

Yes, you can drink the water and eat your fruit unpeeled—Australian hygiene standards are high. Most city hospitals are well equipped, though you might run into problems in country towns, particularly on weekends, when some hospital emergency rooms are closed. It is imperative to buy **travel insurance,** which is usually cheapest in your home country. **Medicare** is Australia's government-run health organization. Citizens of New Zealand, the United Kingdom, Ireland, Sweden, and the Netherlands enjoy the same benefits as Australians, but should still invest in general travel insurance.

Pharmacies (chemists) are readily available and stock most drugs, though often by their generic name. If you're taking medication, bring a supply and duplicate prescriptions with generic equivalents with you—and that goes for eyeglasses, too.

Take it easy until you get acclimated, especially if the weather is hot or humid, if you're traveling into the Outback, or if you're planning any strenuous physical activities. Go slow, and work up to a pace you're comfortable with. Always carry a good first-aid kit and handbook (auto clubs and St. John Ambulance service sell a selection of kits; and consider taking Moon Publications' *Staying Healthy in Asia, Africa, and Latin America,* an informative, practical first-aid handbook). In Sydney the **Traveller's Medical & Vaccination Centre,** Level 7, 428 George St., tel. (02) 9221-7133, is a good source of local medical information and sells a range of medical kits to suit all purposes.

The **International Association for Medical Assistance to Travellers** (IAMAT) provides a list of doctors worldwide with U.S. standards of medical training. For more information, contact IAMAT, 417 Center St., Lewiston, NY 14092, tel. (716) 754-4883. If you find yourself in a real medical nightmare, contact your country's consulate or embassy for emergency help.

Vaccinations
Vaccinations are not necessary if you're traveling from the United States, Canada, or the United Kingdom. If you've visited a yellow fever-infected country within six days of your arrival in Australia, you'll need appropriate inoculations.

FIRST AID

Prevention
Be sensible! The ultraviolet rays are intense, the ozone hole wide, and the skin cancer rate very high. Even cloudy skies can cause a bad burn. As for the super-bright Outback, wear a hat and sunblock, drink plenty of water to avoid dehydration, and go easy on booze and cigarettes. Follow these simple rules and you should be right, mates.

Exhaustion and Heat Exposure
It's *hot* in the Outback. Keep a slow pace until you become acclimated. Get lots of rest, fill up on water, include enough salt in your diet, and avoid overexposure to the harsh sun. Wear loose cotton clothing and a hat, of course. Beware of heatstroke. Symptoms include increased body temperature, a reduction in sweat, and occasional vomiting or nausea. Heatstroke is an emergency situation: the victim should be taken to a cool place, then doused, fanned, and sponged with cold water until body temperature drops to at least 39° C (102° F).

Traveler's Diarrhea
It doesn't matter how clean the place is, unfamiliar foods, overeating, too much drinking, and various other factors can cause the runs. Again, be sensible until you get used to your new environment. If you do come down with Bali Belly or Montezuma's Revenge, ward off dehydration by drinking lots of fluids such as clear broth or soup, weak tea, or juice (*no* alcohol or coffee). Gradually add bland and boiled grub to your diet—rice, biscuits, bread, bananas.

Stings and Bites, Snakes and Beasties
Oz is renowned for its numerous evil snakes. Most won't attack unless provoked, but exceptions are the "fierce" tiger and taipan snakes (the most dangerous). For bites, apply a pressure bandage and splint, keep the victim calm and immobilized, and get medical help fast. Don't move the victim if at all possible; make sure someone stays behind in case artificial respiration is required.

Spiders to watch out for are the red-back (usually found in dunnies and toilets), the trap-doors (usually lurking in holes, with or without trap-door lids), and the funnel-web (only found in Sydney). Place ice on the affected area and seek prompt medical attention.

Know your nasty sea critters before wiggling your toes in the water. The box jellyfish can inflict a fatal sting. Douse the area with vinegar, pull out tentacles, and procure immediate medical attention. Some other poisonous marine dwellers are the sea snake, the blue-ringed octopus, the scorpion fish, and the stonefish (which masquerades as a harmless piece of rock). Treat stings as for snake bites.

Finally, if you're attacked by a saltwater croc, well . . . adios.

Sexually Transmitted Diseases
There is AIDS in Oz. Use condoms. Period.

Help!
To summon emergency help, dial 000 from any telephone (the call is free). The Royal Flying Doctors can be contacted any time, any day, via HF (high-frequency) radios. These units can and should be rented by anyone venturing into very remote areas.

For expert first-aid information, see Moon Publications' Staying Healthy in Asia, Africa, and Latin America, by Dirk G. Schroeder, ScD, MPH.

Health Hazards

This is a country with one of the highest rates of skin cancer in the world. The sun is intense and the hole in the ozone layer is *wide*—wear sunblock and a hat whenever you're outdoors. Also, drink plenty of fluids to ward off possible dehydration. When traveling in Outback areas, check in first with the automobile club, local police, or park rangers.

Other potential dangers include drowning (more than 300 people drown annually in Australia), Australia's infamous poisonous snakes, those faster-than-you'd-care-to-imagine saltwater crocs, a few poisonous spiders, and the box jellyfish. Obey all warning signs and, when in doubt, ask the locals.

Animals on the road, particularly at night, can also be deadly. When walking on coral reef, protect your feet with sturdy shoes. Seek prompt medical treatment for any coral cuts.

Health Insurance

Though a visit to the doctor's office might only cost $40 or so, other medical expenses can be quite hefty (for example, if you need an ambulance or search-and-rescue team). Make sure you have health insurance to adequately cover possible accidents and illness before you leave home; if you plan to take part in any dangerous sport or activity, make sure the policy covers it. Health insurance is usually part of a **travel insurance** policy that typically includes emergency transportation, lost luggage, and trip cancellation. Travel insurance is usually purchased in conjunction with airfare or a tour, but companies such as American Express offer policies for cardholders. North American travel insurers include: **Access America,** tel. (804) 285-3300 or (800) 284-8300; **Carefree Travel Insurance,** tel. (516) 294-0220 or (800) 323-3149; and **TravelGuard International,** tel. (715) 345-0505 or (800) 826-1300.

MONEY

Note: All prices quoted in this guide are in Australian dollars (A$) unless otherwise noted.

Currency

Australian currency is based on the dollars-and-cents decimal system (100 cents equal one dollar). Notes, of different colors, come in denominations of $5, $10, $20, $50, and $100. Originally made of paper, all denominations except the $100 bill have been replaced by unique plasticky and indestructible versions. Coins are in denominations of 5 cents, 10 cents, 20 cents, 50 cents, $1, and $2.

You may bring in or take out any amount of personal funds; however, if you're carrying or sending $10,000 or more in Australian or foreign currency, you must file a form with the Australian Customs Service. You may also be required to furnish a report with customs agents in other countries.

Changing Money

Currency exchange facilities are available at all international airports, though many open only for incoming and outgoing flights. Larger hotels and most banks will also exchange foreign cash and traveler's checks (traveler's checks fetch a slightly higher exchange rate). Traveler's checks are easily cashed in the city (have identification with you) but can be a pain in rural communities. You'll always get a better rate by exchanging foreign currency to Australian dollars *within* Australia.

Banking hours are generally Mon.-Thurs. 9:30 a.m.-4 p.m., Friday 9 a.m.-5 p.m. A few of the larger city banks are open on Saturday morning—but don't count on it.

Credit Cards

The most commonly accepted credit cards are American Express, Bankcard, MasterCard, and Visa, and it shouldn't be a problem using them anywhere in Australia (but always carry some cash to be safe). Also, many rental agencies will only rent vehicles to customers with recognized credit cards.

Another advantage to the credit card is the ability to pull cash advances from ATMs (automatic teller machines), which are prevalent throughout Australian cities and towns.

Bank and Passbook Accounts

Another way to handle your funds (and to ensure easy access) is to open a local bank ac-

AUSTRALIAN EXCHANGE RATES

As of June 1999, the Aussie dollar was being traded at about US66 cents per A$1 (exchanging at about A$1.49 per US$1). Travelers with currency other than the almighty greenback should be able to exchange funds at most banks and airport money-changing facilities without problem. On the Internet, check current exchange rates at www.rubicon.com/passport/currency/currency.html. Current exchange rates (into A$) for other major currencies are:

C$1 = $1.03
DM1 = 80 cents
EURO = $1.57
HK$10 = $1.90
NZ$1 = 87 cents
UK£ = $2.42
¥100 = $1.25

count, especially if you'll be in the country for several months. Commonwealth, National, ANZ, and Westpac are located nationwide. If you're a foreigner, you can open an account within six weeks of arrival in Australia, using just your passport for identification. After that the ante is upped—you'll need your passport, birth certificate, driver's license, credit cards, etc. Make sure to apply for an ATM (or cash) card. It takes a couple of weeks (you'll need an Australian address for delivery). Many of the banks accept each other's cards, so you'll have access to plenty of ATM machines across the country. Also, as in the U.S., many establishments such as petrol stations and supermarkets accept cash cards for payment.

Your home ATM card should work in Australia if it is designated for one of the following systems: Star, Cirrus, Plus, or Interact. Check with your issuing bank regarding use and service charges.

Costs
You've probably guessed, transport is the most expensive. The country is huge and transportation costs are comparatively high. Buying a rail, air, or coach pass, or going in on a car with others can be a real money saver. Fuel is more expensive than in the U.S. and Canada, but cheaper than in Europe; however, you'll probably use large quantities of it. Clothing is also fairly expensive. On the other hand, food and accommodations are both relatively cheap.

Tipping and Bargaining
Tipping is not mandatory in Australia. Your waitperson will not follow you into the street, meat cleaver in hand, for the extra 15-20%. Normally, tipping is done only in an expensive restaurant, or when service has been extra good—and then 10% will suffice. Leave taxi drivers the extra change to make the tab an even amount and they'll be happy.

Bargaining is confined to flea markets and some of the larger secondhand shops. It is downright offensive to do so with Aborigines for their arts and crafts.

Student and Senior Discounts
Students and seniors with proper photo identification (such as an International Student Identity Card) are eligible for "Concession" rates on many transportation services and at attractions, cinemas, and entertainment venues.

Check with the ticket office before you purchase your ticket.

COMMUNICATIONS AND MEDIA

POSTAL SERVICES

The mail averages a whopping seven to 10 days or longer between Australia and North America or Europe—going either direction. Domestic service, however, is relatively efficient (barring postal strikes).

General post offices and branches will hang onto your mail, free of charge, for up to a month. Check all Australian post codes (zip codes) on the Internet at www.auspost.com.au. Alternatively, American Express cardholders can have mail sent to city American Express offices, to be held for later pickup.

Post office hours are Mon.-Fri. 9 a.m.-5 p.m. There is no Saturday mail delivery. Stamps can also be purchased at some hotels, motels, and from newsagents. A domestic stamp costs 45 cents; to the U.S. and Canada, stamps are 95 cents for postcards and $1.05 for letters.

Main post offices have philatelic desks, which sell sets of souvenir stamps ranging from poignant and historical to political and colorful.

TELEPHONE

Telstra (formerly Telecom Australia) has followed the deregulation path of AT&T. A second company, Optus, now offers alternative service—on long-distance and international calls—in the big-user cities. The result is the same kind of confusion, special access codes, varying rates, and endless advertising perks and bribes that occurred after U.S. telephone deregulation.

Local calls from pay phones (i.e., coin boxes) cost 40 cents. Telstra phone cards can also be purchased in $5, $10, $20, and $50 amounts from chemists (pharmacies), newsagents, and other shops. Some phones accept only credit or bank cash cards and, though convenient, are more expensive.

Almost all public phones are equipped for STD (subscriber trunk dialing) and IDD (international direct dialing). Just keep feeding coins into the slots (you can use one-dollar pieces, if you like). There is no three-minute minimum and unused change will be returned when you hang up.

When placing international calls, dial 0011 (the international access code), the country code, the city code, and then the desired phone number. From private phones it's about $1.50 per minute to the U.S. or U.K. (discounted midnight-8 a.m. and on Sunday); on pay phones it's much more.

Operator-assisted calls can be placed from any phone, though fees for reverse-charge (collect) and person-to-person calls run $6-8. Credit card phones are now installed in many airports, hotels, and post offices. Refer to the front pages of the local telephone book for dialing information and charges. Try not to make any long-distance calls from big hotels—the surcharges are usually astronomical and can double or triple the actual cost of the call.

Toll-free numbers have the prefix 1800; companies such as airlines and other transport services often have six-digit numbers beginning with 13, or nine-digit numbers beginning with 1300, meaning it is charged as a local call even if it's cross-country; the prefix 018 is an example designation for nine-digit mobile phone numbers; and nine-digit numbers, beginning with 0055, are usually psychic, sex, lonely-hearts, or do-it-yourself lines.

In this land of few and far between, **fax** machines are used everywhere, including the Outback. Almost every post office provides a fax calling and receiving service.

In remote Outback locations, both CB and HF (high-frequency) radios play an important part in communications. CBs are used mainly for vehicles to keep in contact with each other, while HF radios are used to summon medical help, provide education, spread community information—and gossip. Licenses are necessary for both types of radio. Telstra (OTC), with government-controlled frequencies, will most likely take over future communications for the Royal Flying Doctor Service.

Mobile Phones

Australia is the land of the mobile phone. Everyone seems to have one—from suited city businesspeople, to school-age children, to construction workers. For travelers, the y make a handy tool for booking tours or accommodations while on the road. The **Travellers Contact Point,** with offices in major cities including at 428 George St., Sydney, tel. (02) 9221-8744, website: www.travellers.com.au, has prepaid mobile phones for sale. No contracts need to be signed; you simply select the plan best suited to your needs.

Country Direct

Country Direct allows travelers to access operators in their home countries (more than 40 countries are hooked up to the service) for easier, and maybe cheaper, credit card, calling card, or collect calls. To the U.S. operator, call (1800) 88-1011 (AT&T), (1800) 88-1877 (Sprint), or (1800) 88-1100 (MCI). To Canada, call (1800) 88-1490. To the U.K., call (1800) 88-1640. For other countries, refer to the local telephone book or call the international operator.

E-MAIL

The easiest and least expensive way to keep in touch with the folks back home is via e-mail. Most libraries now offer public Internet access for a minimal charge, and "cybercafés," found throughout the country, allow you to access the Internet while sipping a cup of coffee. Cafés usually charge $2-3 per 10 minutes or $10-12 per hour. This is the only charge you incur—the actual connection is free. The website www.cyberiacafe.net/cyberia/guide/café.htm lists cybercafés worldwide. All you need is an e-mail address. **Hotmail** offers web-based addresses for free. Go to the website www.hotmail.com, where easy-to-follow instructions will take you through the registration process step by step. With your own address, it is possible to access your e-mail from any computer in the world that is linked to the Internet.

MEDIA

Newspapers and Magazines

The most respected daily newspapers are *Sydney Morning Herald* and Melbourne's *Age.* Catch up with the latest Australian news at their respective websites, www.smh.com.au and www.theage.com.au. Ordinarily available in the major cities and many small towns (even if a day or so old), they might not hit the Outback stands at all. Other city newspapers are Brisbane's *Courier Mail,* Adelaide's *Advertiser,* Darwin's *Northern Territory News,* and Perth's *West Australian.* Australia has two national dailies: the *Australian* and the *Australian Financial Review.*

Australian editions of *Time, Vogue, Cosmopolitan,* and other international magazines, plus worldwide newspapers (like *USA Today*) and foreign-language press are sold at many news agencies. Most newsagents, in fact, stock an astonishing array of specialty magazines. Two "women's mags," *New Idea* and *Woman's Weekly,* will assure that you never are out-of-touch with the U.K.'s latest royal scandals.

Each city has free street-happening music and entertainment newspapers. They are found in hotel lobbies, bars, clubs, and music shops.

TNT (www.tntmag.com.au) comprises six regional magazines aimed at the backpacker market. They are produced quarterly and include current issues, traveling tips, and classifieds. They are distributed free through information centers and backpacker lodges.

Radio and Television

The independent, government-funded ABC (Australian Broadcasting Corporation) is the national television and radio network. Often its programs are all you will hear or see in rural areas, though the major cities and towns will feature two or three regionally based commercial stations. Stations frequently televise nearly-first-run movies, as well as some excellent foreign films. The government-sponsored SBS beams excellent multicultural news and entertainment, along with uncensored films, to all state capitals.

American look-alike programming includes the *Today Show, 60 Minutes,* and several genre dating game, newlywed, quiz, and love connection shows—plus MTV. You can also catch the U.S. *Oprah, Entertainment Tonight,* and *Late Show with David Letterman* in many locales, and—never fear—those U.S. dramas are part of the regular programming (although it's about a year or so behind).

Alice Springs-based Imparja is an Aboriginal-run station that broadcasts many types of programs, including some produced by and for Aborigines, over about one-third of Australia.

The ABC, which operates radio stations in many of the cities, can be picked up in all parts of Australia. Other listening options (AM and FM) include everything from rock and Muzak to talk shows and community services.

INFORMATION

There's no lack of Tourist Information Centres in Australia. All of the states and territories have branch offices in major city centers—veritable treasure troves of details on tours, attractions, sports, accommodations, package deals, car and campervan rentals, and local and interstate transportation. Most of these centers will make bookings for you, and all will load you with brochures. Additionally, almost every country town has an information center—albeit an office, petrol station, or museum—marked by the international "I" sign. Hours are usually Mon.-Fri. 9 a.m.-5 p.m., Saturday 9 a.m.-1 p.m. Centers in heavily touristed areas are often open on Sunday as well.

State Tourist Offices
Every state and territory has a government department or government-sponsored agency promoting tourism. Some states have walk-in information and booking centers, while others only take phone inquiries and reservations.

Contact names, numbers, and addresses are:
Tourism NSW, tel. (13) 2077, website: www.tourism.nsw.gov.au
Canberra Tourism, Northbourne Ave., Canberra, tel. (02) 6205-0044 or (1800) 06-1666, website: canberratourism.com.au
Northern Territory Tourism Commission, tel. (08) 8981-4300 or (1800) 62-1336, website: www.nttc.com.au
Queensland Tourism and Travel Corporation, tel. (13) 1801, website: www.qttc.com.au
South Australian Tourism Commission, 1 King William St., Adelaide, tel. (08) 8303-2222 or (1300) 36-6770, website: www.tourism.sa.gov.au
Tasmanian Travel and Information Centre, 20 Davey St., Hobart, tel. (03) 6230-8233, website: www.tourism.tas.gov.au
Tourism Victoria, Town Hall, corner of Little Collins and Swanston Streets, Melbourne, tel. (03) 9658-9036 or (13) 2842

Western Australia Tourism Commission, corner Forrest Place and Wellington St., Perth, tel. (08) 9483-1111 or (1300) 36-1351, website: www.tourism.wa.gov.au

Australian Tourist Commission
The Australian Tourist Commission is a government-operated department that promotes travel to Australia throughout the world. In recent years, it has been closing overseas offices in all but the biggest marketplaces. The head office is at Level 4, 80 William St., Woolloomooloo, Sydney, NSW 2011, tel. (02) 9360-1111. Their website, www.aussie.net.au, features links to thousands of tourist operators within Australia.

Overseas offices are:
United States, 27911 West Franklin Parkway, Valencia, CA 91355, tel. (805) 775-2000
United Kingdom, Gemini House, 10-18 Putney Hill, London, England SW15 6AA, tel. (0891) 07-0707
New Zealand, 22 Centre St., Auckland 1, tel. (09) 527-1629

Aussie Helplines
Aussie Helplines work in conjunction with the Australian Tourist Commission to answer questions, offer travel tips, assist with itinerary planning, and mail out brochures. Free travel information sheets are available on many aspects of Australia, including sports, beaches, diving, Aboriginal Australia, nightlife, backpacking, surfing, etc. In North America, call (847) 296-4900 or (800)-333-4305; in the United Kingdom, call (0990) 02-2000; in New Zealand, call (0800) 65-0303.

Automobile Associations
Australian automobile clubs offer reciprocal rights to members of the American Automobile Club and the United Kingdom's RAC and AA (bring your membership card with you). The **Australian Automobile Association**'s services include free roadside emergency breakdown service (within

certain city limits), route maps, touring information, discounted travel guides, and accommodations and camping directories. Many offices will make tour and accommodations reservations for you.

The **main state offices** are: **Australian Automobile Association** (AAA Head Office), G.P.O. Box 1555, Canberra, ACT 2601, tel. (02) 6247-7311; **National Roads and Motorists Association** (NRMA), 151 Clarence St., Sydney, NSW, tel. (02) 9892-0355 or (13) 1122, or 92 Northbourne Ave., Canberra, tel. (02) 6240-4620; **Automobile Association of the Northern Territory** (AANT), 79-81 Smith St., Darwin, tel. (08) 8981-3837; **Royal Automobile Club of Queensland** (RACQ), 300 St. Pauls Terrace, Fortitude Valley, tel. (07) 3361-2444 or (13) 1905; **Royal Automobile Association of South Australia** (RAA), 41 Hindmarsh Square, Adelaide, tel. (08) 8202-4600; **Royal Automobile Club of Tasmania** (RACT), corner Patrick and Murray Streets, Hobart, tel. (03) 6232-6300; **Royal Automobile Club of Victoria** (RACV), 360 Bourke St., Melbourne, tel. (03) 9642-5566 or (13) 1955; and **Royal Automobile Club** (RAC), 228 Adelaide Terrace, Perth, WA, tel. (08) 9421-4444.

WHAT TO TAKE

Clothing

Australians are casual dressers. Follow the old, basic rule: Dress for comfort and climate. If you're going to the tropical north, take lightweight cottons, which are suitable year-round. (Shorts are okay most places.) The southern temperate regions also call for cottons and other natural fibers during summer months; winters can be very cold there, so pack a heavy sweater and jacket. The Outback will be searing during the summer, giving way to chilly nights in winter. And rain can drop any time, unexpectedly, and in great torrents; you might want to include a light raincoat and an umbrella in your suitcase. It's always well advised to dress in layers, particularly due to rapidly changing weather conditions in many regions.

Dressing for the Outback

For the authentic Outback Aussie look in warmer months, outfit yourself in a singlet (sleeveless T-shirt), a pair of shorts, heavy socks, and Blundstone boots (they have elastic sides and last forever but are somewhat costly). You'll definitely need a hat, so, if you still have some clothing budget left, pick up an Akubra (the Aussie working-bloke's Stetson).

Et Cetera

Other articles to bring along are a sunhat, sunglasses, sunscreen, sturdy walking shoes (again, broken-in *before* arrival), and waterproof sneakers for coral reef-walking. You might also want to pack a voltage converter, adapter plugs, insect repellent, prescription medications, and an extra pair of eyeglasses or contact lenses. Most brands of cosmetics, toiletries, and over-the-counter medications are readily available at chemist shops (pharmacies).

Other Points

Pack light. Leave room in your backpack or luggage for necessities (and souvenirs) that you'll collect along the way. Bring a sheet sack if you'll be doing the hostel routine, as well as your usual camping gear. Don't forget any required permits (which you should have obtained beforehand), maps, and a good, ahem, *guidebook*. Special equipment, swags or other camp bedding, cooking equipment, first-aid kits and such, can all be purchased in Australia—and may be better suited to the unique environment than the closer-to-civilization gear you may be used to. Often you can pick up good deals on used equipment from departing travelers at hostels. If you sign up for an organized tour, many operators provide many needed items. You can pick up the fly net to wear over your face after you arrive in Australia.

FILM AND PHOTOGRAPHY

Film and Processing

Film, processing labs, and photo equipment are easy finds in Australian cities. Bring your own 35mm camera and lenses. Unless you're coming in via Singapore or Hong Kong, it's unnecessary to stock up on film beforehand; Australian film costs about the same as in North America or Europe. You'll also find many "one-hour" photo shops with speedy processing for those on the move.

Photo Tips

Special conditions to be aware of are: intensity of light, particularly in the Outback; temperature extremes (try to keep film cool and dry); Outback dust; and, in the country's far north, tropical humidity.

Best times for taking photos are early morning and late afternoon. A polarizing filter will help minimize washout.

As for those airport X-ray machines—if you're worried about your film (especially any over 400 ASA), carry it in a lead-lined bag and/or request hand inspection.

Photo Etiquette

Do not photograph Aboriginals without their permission—which you probably won't get. They do not like having their photos taken—and that includes crowd and distance shots.

© AVALON TRAVEL PUBLISHING

WEIGHTS AND MEASURES

Measurements

Australia uses the metric system, like almost every other country in the world. Temperatures are in Celsius (C). (See the conversion tables at the back of this book.)

Electrical Voltage

Australia's electrical current is 240/250 volts, 50Hz AC. You'll need a **three-pin adapter plug** (different from the British three-pronger) for any 110-volt appliances you intend to bring, as well as the appropriate **voltage converter.** It's best to purchase adapter plugs and converters before arrival, though both are available in the larger cities. If you're bringing a computer or other specialized equipment, be sure to check with the manufacturer for exact requirements.

Time Zones

Australia has three time zones. New South Wales, Australian Capital Territory, Victoria, Tasmania, and Queensland operate on **eastern standard time** (EST); South Australia and the Northern Territory use **central standard time** (CST); and Western Australia has its very own **western standard time** (WST).

Here is the confusing part: central standard time is half an hour behind eastern standard time, while western standard time is two hours behind eastern standard time. And all of the states except Western Australia, Queensland, and the Northern Territory go on **summer time** (daylight saving time) from October to March, when clocks are set ahead one hour. And Tasmania keeps to daylight saving time one month longer than the others. It's no wonder the Aborigines keep to Dreamtime!

NEW SOUTH WALES
INTRODUCTION

Although New South Wales is the most populous of Australia's six states and two territories, in many places it's remarkably remote, especially west of the Great Dividing Range, a ridge of ancient mountains that parallels Australia's entire east coast. Because of New South Wales's relatively small size (10% of the continent's total area), most destinations are within one day's drive of the state capital, Sydney. The beaches are one of New South Wales's best-known features, but the state boasts more than sun, sand, and surf. Whether it be schussing down snow-covered slopes, fishing and boating on magnificent river systems, exploring ghost towns, sampling world-class wines, or hiking through lush rainforests, New South Wales has something for everyone.

LAND

New South Wales, on the east coast of Australia, is bordered by Queensland to the north, Victoria to the south, and South Australia to the west, with the eastern border a 1,400-km stretch of magnificent coastline. Most of the state's residents live along the coast, with more than half of the population living in Sydney, the birthplace of modern Australia and Australia's largest city. Sydney lies on a convoluted harbor, with downtown concentrated around Sydney Cove, and it's surrounded on three sides by land set aside as national park. South of Sydney are long stretches of unspoilt and uncrowded beaches and small seaside communities. The Australian Capital Territory, home to the national capital Canberra, 250 km southwest of Sydney, boasts many fine civic buildings. Beyond Canberra are the Snowy Mountains, including Mt. Kosciuzko, Australia's highest point, and a winter playground of ski resorts. West of Sydney are the Blue Mountains, a vast expanse of spectacular wilderness right on Sydney's back doorstep. Beyond the mountains is the Golden West, an area of stately old towns dating from successive gold rushes. Much of western New South Wales is Outback and the entire western portion of the state comprises a flat, dry, and barren land dominated by sheep farms and the odd town or settlement. Immediately north of Sydney is the industrial city of Newcastle, gateway to a string of beautiful beaches and the wine-producing Hunter Valley. From Newcastle there are two routes north to Queensland. The inland route, the New England Highway, passes through north-central New South Wales and the country music capital of Australia, Tamworth. The Pacific Highway, the coastal route, extends the entire length of the north coast, along a seemingly endless stretch of seaside towns, national parks, and long strips of sand. Few travelers on the route between Sydney and Brisbane fail to stop at Byron Bay, a melting pot of Australian cultures backed by a beautiful hinterland of rainforested national parks.

Climate

Temperatures in Sydney are pleasant year-round, but the city is far enough south to get relatively cold in winter. During the months of summer, the climate can be very humid, especially along the coast north of Sydney. West of the Great Dividing Range summer temperatures can be unbearably hot, making travel unpleasant and, in the extreme west, dangerous. Spring and fall are pleasant throughout the state, and these are probably the best times of year to travel (and you'll miss the maddening summer crowds). Winter on the far north coast, with day-time temperatures averaging 15° C (59° F), is pleasant, while in the mountainous region in the state's south, a blanket of snow extends thousands of square kilometers. Snow occasionally falls as far north as Armidale.

HISTORY

Archaeological finds in Mungo National Park, in the southwest of the state, point to human habitation up to 30,000 years ago. Aboriginals probably lived throughout the state during this time, their nomadic lifestyle changing with long-term weather patterns, such as successive ice ages. The Aboriginals' first contact with Europeans came in 1770, when Capt. James Cook landed at Botany Bay, claiming possession of the east coast for England. A few years later, with British jails overcrowded, the British government decided to send prisoners to the unknown continent down under. The First Fleet, of which more than half of the people were convicts, found life at Sydney Cove difficult. Crops failed, more and more convicts arrived, and a succession of governors was unable to control the rebellious officers. Expansion was at first slow, and by the early 1800s, the only other settlements were a few penal colonies along the coast north of Sydney Town; inland exploration had been nonexistent. That all changed in 1813, when three landowners crossed the Blue Mountains in search of greener pastures. Settlers streamed

New South Wales is dotted with historic sandstone buildings from the convict era, including this one, the Surveyor General Inn, Berrima.

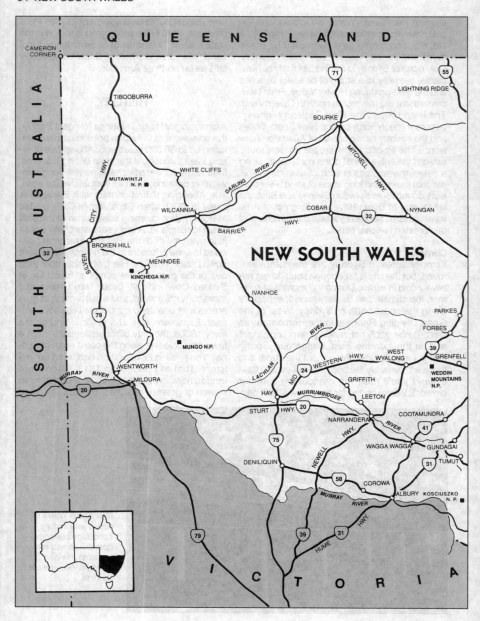

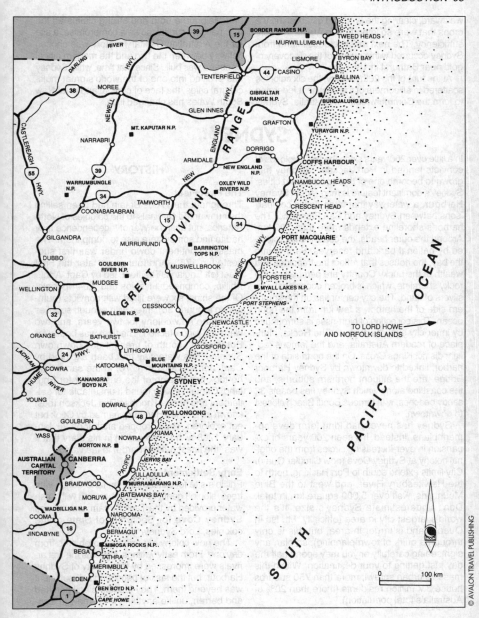

westward, clearing the land and establishing the crops that were so important to Australia's self-sufficiency. The next mass exodus inland from Sydney occurred within weeks of the discovery of gold near Bathurst in 1851.

At the turn of the 20th century, the six colonies scattered in all corners of the continent federated to form the Commonwealth of Australia. Sydney and Melbourne both had strong claims as the new national capital, so as a compromise, a site for the Australian Capital Territory was chosen halfway between the two and the modern city of Canberra was built. Since that time, while Sydney has evolved into one of the world's great multicultural cities, the face of coastal and rural New South Wales has changed little.

SYDNEY

In a little over 200 years since the first shiploads of convicts landed in Port Jackson, Sydney has grown to become one of the world's great cities. Sydney's dominant feature is magnificent **Sydney Harbour,** a waterway that often draws comparisons between Sydney and San Francisco. The harbor's shoreline extends more than 300 km. Around the outer heads, the coastline is protected by national park and reserves. Farther into the bay, the houses that reflect the trappings and wealth of the Lucky Country are perched on the rocky shoreline, which is broken occasionally by slivers of sand. The city center lies on the southern side of the harbor, a few km from the open ocean. This collection of high-rises is surrounded by inner-city suburbs such as The Rocks, birthplace of modern Australia, and the famous red-light district Kings Cross. On the north side of the harbor, linked to downtown by Sydney Harbour Bridge, are the affluent northern suburbs, and the coastline along which Sydney lies boasts 32 sandy beaches, with famous Bondi Beach closest to downtown.

Sydney has never had long-term development plans. Instead, it's seen 200 years of expansion in ever-increasing circles from the original colony at Sydney Cove (now Circular Quay). City limits extend south to Port Hacking, north to the Hawkesbury River, and west to the Blue Mountains, well over 5,000 square km in total. Don't underestimate Sydney's size. It's the world's largest city in area (officially, Mt. Isa in Queensland is larger in area, but this is only through a quirk of town planning), so plan any sightseeing carefully or you may spend half the day just getting to your destination. Within this massive urban sprawl, more than 750 suburbs house 3.7 million residents (more than 20% of Australia's total population).

HISTORY

The First Fleet

Throughout the 1700s Britain had been selling their unwanted criminals to the colonies of North America, but after the War of Independence they had to find somewhere else to dump them. The massive continent down under was first suggested in 1783. And four years later the First Fleet left England. The fleet, led by Capt. Arthur Phillip, comprised 11 ships and 1,044 people. Of the ships, six were filled with convicts (numbering around 730), three with enough supplies to last the new colony for two years, and two warships for protection. The fleet was bound for Botany Bay, south of present-day downtown Sydney. This waterway had been explored by Capt. James Cook in 1770, at the same time he took possession of the east coast for England. Captain Phillip found it unsuitable for settlement and headed north to Port Jackson (best known as Sydney Harbour), named by Cook but not explored. They dropped anchor on 26 January 1788 with Phillip noting in his diary that it was "the finest natural harbor in the world."

Early Settlement

Phillip's site for settlement, on land dense with trees, sloping gently to the harbor, and with fresh water provided by the Tank Stream, was named **Sydney Cove** for Secretary of State of the colonies, Lord Sydney.

The new colony experienced problems from day one. From early writings, it seems the first arrivals were impressed by the beauty of Sydney Harbour, but the task of becoming self-sufficient was beyond them. They found the soil parched and barren, unlike anything they knew in Eng-

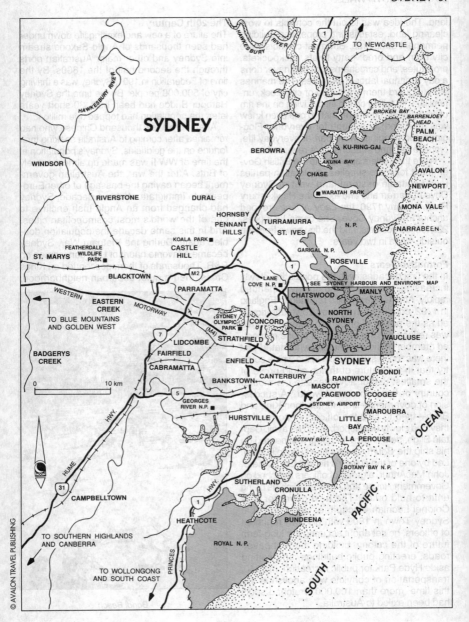

SYDNEY

TO NEWCASTLE

HAWKESBURY RIVER

WINDSOR

BROKEN BAY

BARRENJOEY HEAD

PALM BEACH

BEROWRA

KU-RING-GAI

AVALON

NEWPORT

CHASE

AKUNA BAY

RIVERSTONE

DURAL

WARATAH PARK

N.P.

MONA VALE

HORNSBY

NARRABEEN

PENNANT HILLS

TURRAMURRA

ST. IVES

GARIGAL N.P.

KOALA PARK

CASTLE HILL

FEATHERDALE WILDLIFE PARK

ROSEVILLE

LANE COVE N.P.

SEE "SYDNEY HARBOUR AND ENVIRONS" MAP

ST. MARYS

BLACKTOWN

M2

CHATSWOOD

MANLY

PARRAMATTA

NORTH SYDNEY

WESTERN

EASTERN CREEK

MOTORWAY

3

CONCORD

VAUCLUSE

TO BLUE MOUNTAINS AND GOLDEN WEST

SYDNEY OLYMPIC PARK

(M4)

STRATHFIELD

SYDNEY

7

LIDCOMBE

BADGERYS CREEK

FAIRFIELD

ENFIELD

BONDI

CABRAMATTA

0   10 km

CANTERBURY

RANDWICK

BANKSTOWN

MASCOT

COOGEE

5

GEORGES RIVER N.P.

PAGEWOOD

SYDNEY AIRPORT

MAROUBRA

HURSTVILLE

LITTLE BAY

HUME HWY.

31

CAMPBELLTOWN

BOTANY BAY

LA PEROUSE

BOTANY BAY N.P.

OCEAN

SUTHERLAND

CRONULLA

PACIFIC

TO SOUTHERN HIGHLANDS AND CANBERRA

HEATHCOTE

BUNDEENA

© AVALON TRAVEL PUBLISHING

PRINCES HWY.

ROYAL N.P.

TO WOLLONGONG AND SOUTH COAST

SOUTH

land. The idea was to put the convicts to work clearing land, establishing crops, and building permanent structures. But most convicts were city born and bred: petty thiefs, pickpockets, prostitutes, and cardsharps that had never done a day's manual labor in their lives. The marines sent to guard them were also of city stock, unfamiliar with toiling on the land. Living on the rim of an unknown continent (that no one even knew was an island) was tough for everyone. Floggings and hangings were part of everyday life, crops failed, and seasons were reversed.

While the settlers appealed to the British Government for more supplies, exploration parties found suitable pastoral land west of Sydney Cove at Parramatta and along the Hawkesbury River. In early 1790, the *Lady Juliana* dropped anchor in Sydney Cove. She carried supplies, 225 female convicts, and the first news from the outside world in two years.

Formative Years

In the first decades, with the population slowly increasing, the area of the colony expanded rapidly. After Captain Phillip returned to England in 1792, conditions in Sydney Town deteriorated as the power of officers increased. Morale was reflected in the comments of one respected member of the community, who stated that there was "not a single article in the whole country that in the nature of things could prove of the smallest use or advantage to the mother country or the commercial world." A succession of governors—first Hunter, then King and Bligh—tried to strip the officers of power that they had slowly developed, but to no avail. Captain Bligh, best known for being mutineered on his ship the *Bounty,* was a strict disciplinarian. Led by one of the colony's richest landowners, John MacArthur, a group of officers marched on Government House and arrested Bligh as being unfit to hold office. The next governor was Colonel Lachlan Macquarie. Upon arrival in Sydney Town in 1809 with his own regiment of officers, he set about securing the long-term future of the colony, building the first paved roads, erecting public buildings, and setting aside Hyde Park for public recreation. In 1840, transportation of convicts was abolished. By this time, more than 100,000 wretched souls had been exiled to Australia.

The 20th Century

The allure of a new and exciting life down under had seen thousands of Anglo-Saxons stream into Sydney and other major Australian ports through the second half of the 1800s. By the time of Federation in 1901, Sydney was a thriving city of 500,000 people. By the time the Sydney Harbour Bridge had been built, 30 short years later, the population had topped one million.

Apart from a few thousand Chinese who had remained after coming to Australia seeking their fortune on the goldfields, Sydney's population at the time of WW II was made up almost entirely of Brits. After the war, the Australian government began paying the passage of other Europeans to immigrate. Within a decade, Sydney had changed from an Anglo-Irish enclave to one of the world's most cosmopolitan cities. And in this same decade the population doubled again. During the Vietnam War, Sydney became a favorite haunt of U.S. servicemen on R&R. Thousands of them descended on Kings Cross, then a quiet suburban neighborhood,

Bondi Beach

St. Mary's Cathedral

turning it into a 24-hour party zone of strip joints, bars, and brothels. In this same period, a building boom saw the construction of many downtown high-rise buildings, and the urban sprawl continued marching westward. By the time the 1980s had rolled around, Sydney had grown to become one of the world's great cities. The city, and Australia, celebrated its bicentenary in 1988 with much fanfare, an event that was greeted with as much enthusiasm as the announcement that Sydney was to host the 2000 Summer Olympic Games.

CITY CENTER SIGHTS

Downtown extends from Central Station in the south to Circular Quay in the north and is bounded by Hyde Park and Macquarie St. to the east and Chinatown and Darling Harbour to the west. The city has no real "center," but Martin Place, a five-block-long pedestrian mall, is pretty central and a popular meeting place. The business district, where the head offices of many major banks and insurance offices lie, is between King St. and Circular Quay. The original Government House, now long gone, was at the junction of Bridge and Phillip Streets, with the original layout of streets leading like spokes to the center of a wheel. Some of the "spokes" remain, now leading nowhere. **George St.,** the city center's main thoroughfare, was originally a track used by convicts hauling bricks along the west bank of the Tank Stream. This street runs the entire length of downtown. Halfway along is the French Renaissance-style **Town Hall** (1889), which houses one of the world's largest pipe organs. Adjacent, the magnificent **Queen Victoria Building,** originally the city markets, was restored to its former glory in the mid-1980s. From Town Hall, Park St. leads east through Hyde Park to William St., which is lined with car showrooms and car rental outlets, to Kings Cross. Apart from the bustle of Chinatown, the area south of Park St. is uninspiring, an area where future urban planners have their work cut out.

AMP Tower

On top of the Centrepoint complex, in the heart of the city, is AMP Tower, the Southern Hemisphere's highest public building. This distinctive 300-meter-high landmark is topped by a massive viewing gallery and two revolving restaurants. At street level, high-speed elevators whisk visitors from the Centrepoint complex (easiest entrance is from Market St.) to the Podium Level, then it's all aboard double-decker lifts to the Observation Level. Needless to say, views from the top are magnificent, extending west to the Blue Mountains, east over the Pacific Ocean, and south to Wollongong. The Observation Level, tel. (02) 9231-1000, is open Sun.-Fri. 9:30 a.m.-9:30 p.m., Saturday 9:30 a.m.-11:30 p.m.; access costs adult $10, child $4.50. On the other levels of AMP Tower are Australia's highest coffee lounge and two other restaurants.

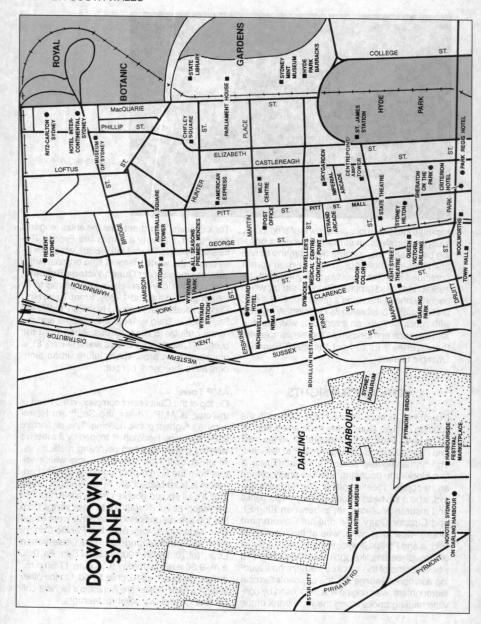

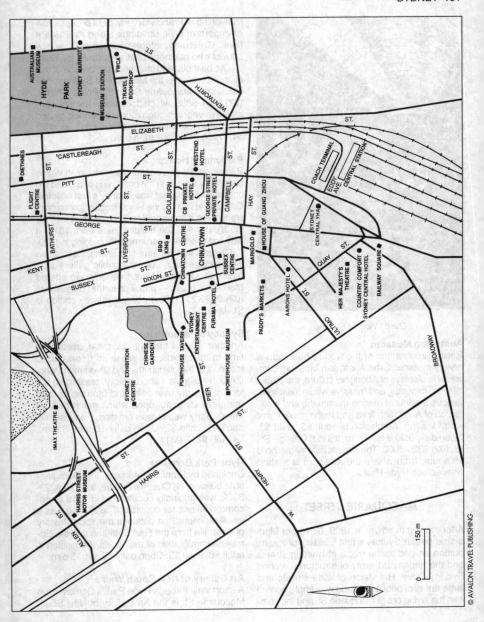

Queen Victoria Building

Australian Museum

Recognized as one of the world's best natural history museums, the Australian Museum's impressive displays of Aboriginal culture, the Pacific Islands, minerals, and massive whale skeletons, various models of marine mammals, and a collection of Australian flora and fauna make it well worth visiting. Admission is adult $5, child $3. Open daily 9:30 a.m.-5 p.m. It's at 6 College St., tel. (02) 9320-6000. The closest railway station is Museum, from where the museum is a short walk across Hyde Park.

MACQUARIE STREET

After coming to power in 1809, Governor Macquarie began Sydney's first building program, putting an end to the maze of twisting streets and the haphazard array of structures around Sydney Cove. His vision of wide streets and large areas of public parkland was implemented with the laying out of Macquarie St. and the commissioning of Francis Greenway to design a row of important civic buildings along its eastern flank. Greenway, interestingly enough, was a convict who had been sent to Australia for fraud.

The best place to start your exploration of this historic precinct is the **Museum of Sydney,** one block from Macquarie St. at 37 Phillip St., tel. (02) 9251-5988, which documents the city's formulative years through modern technology and interactive exhibits. Admission is adult $6, child $4. Open daily 10 a.m.-5 p.m.

Parliament House

Parliament House, seat of the New South Wales state legislature, is in the north wing of a grand old colonial building that was Sydney's first hospital. Originally known as the Rum Hospital (contractors were given a monopoly on the rum trade for their labor), parts of the building date from 1811. It was first used as a parliamentary building in 1829.

On days that parliament is sitting, visitors can view proceedings from the public gallery after 9:30 a.m. On other days, free tours are offered Mon.-Fri. 10 a.m.-4 p.m. For further details, call (02) 9230-2111. The nearest railway station is St. James.

Sydney Mint Museum

Another wing of the Rum Hospital, used for a time to mint coins, is a museum dedicated to the work of the goldsmiths and silversmiths who, through Australia's short history, created an astonishing array of jewelry and ornaments from the precious gems upon which much of Australia's early wealth was created. Admission is adult $5, child $2. Open daily 10 a.m.-5 p.m., tel. (02) 9217-0311.

Hyde Park Barracks

Designed by Francis Greenway, this Georgian-style building, on Queen's Square, tel. (02) 9223-8922, was originally constructed in 1819 as accommodations for convicts. Today it houses a small museum that catalogs the social history of Australia from the First Settlement to the European immigration to the 1950s. Admission is adult $6, child $3. Open daily 10 a.m.-5 p.m.

Art Gallery of New South Wales

A short walk through Hyde Park's Domain from Macquarie St. is the Art Gallery of New South

Wales on Art Gallery Rd., tel. (02) 9225-1744. The complex consists of two wings. The earlier one, built at the turn of the century, houses European and Australian art from the early 1900s and Aboriginal art and artifacts. The new wing contains contemporary art, including works by Sidney Nolan, Russell Drysdale, and William Dobell. A small theater screens art films, and a café overlooks Sydney Harbour; you can pick up gifts at the souvenir shop. Admission to the gallery is free. Open daily 10 a.m.-5 p.m.

Royal Botanic Gardens

When the First Fleet arrived at Sydney Cove in 1788 the convicts were put to work planting vegetable gardens, but the important project met with little success. The gardens were moved west, to Parramatta, and in 1816 the original site was set aside as a botanic garden. Popular with workers at lunchtime, the gardens are home to 400 species of plants from around the world. Within the park is **Government House,** completed in 1844 and home to successive state governors until 1996. Since that time it has been used for public functions. Tours are conducted Fri.-Sun. 10 a.m.-3 p.m. For bookings, call (02) 9931-5222. In the same vicinity is the Conservatorium of Music, originally built as horse stables. The main road through the park is Mrs Macquarie's Rd., which ends at **Mrs Macquarie's Chair,** cut into a rocky outcrop nearly two centuries ago for the governor's wife to watch for

incoming ships. The park is open between 7 a.m. and dusk.

CIRCULAR QUAY

Circular Quay, transportation hub of Sydney Harbour, sits at the head of Sydney Cove and at the north end of the City Circle rail line. The Quay is always busy, with tourists and workers boarding and alighting from a seemingly never-ending parade of ferries, trains, and buses. There, you are also in sight of Sydney's two most famous landmarks, the Opera House and the Bridge.

Sydney Opera House

Described by many as "the most beautiful building of the 20th century," this architectural masterpiece is one of the few buildings worldwide that immediately identifies a city. It lies east of Circular Quay on Bennelong Point, named by Governor Phillip for an Aboriginal he had befriended and taken back to England. Danish architect John Utzon won an international competition to design a building for the site, which had been used as a tram depot until 1956. His design was imaginative and unique: "I had white in mind when I designed the Opera House. And the roof, like sails, white in the strong day, the whole thing slowly coming to life as the sun shone from the east and lifted overhead. In the

Sydney Opera House

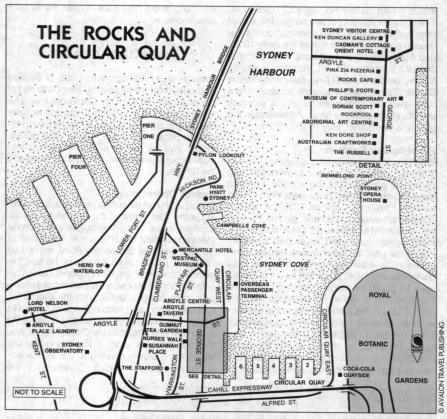

THE ROCKS AND CIRCULAR QUAY

SYDNEY HARBOUR

SYDNEY VISITOR CENTRE
KEN DUNCAN GALLERY
CADMAN'S COTTAGE
ORIENT HOTEL

ARGYLE ST.
PINA ZIA PIZZERIA
ROCKS CAFE
PHILLIP'S FOOTE
MUSEUM OF CONTEMPORARY ART
DORIAN SCOTT
ROCKPOOL
ABORIGINAL ART CENTRE
KEN DORE SHOP
AUSTRALIAN CRAFTWORKS
THE RUSSELL

GEORGE ST.

DETAIL

BENNELONG POINT

SYDNEY OPERA HOUSE

© AVALON TRAVEL PUBLISHING

NOT TO SCALE

hot sun of the day it will be a beautiful, white shimmering thing—as alive to the eyes as architecture can make anything, set in the blue-green waters of the harbour. And at night the floodlit shells will be equally vibrant—but in a softer, more majestic way." But troubles started early when the old two-hectare tram site was deemed unstable. Costs blew out considerably, and to fund the massive project a lottery was set up (the winner of the first lottery had his son kidnapped then murdered before a ransom could be paid).

The Opera House's shell had been completed by 1966, when because of contention with the actors and artists over the interior's furnishings

and the cladding, John Utzon went home, leaving the project only half-finished. Even the name, "Opera House," was settled upon to appease factions—the main hall had always been planned as a venue for orchestras. The Opera House was finally completed in 1973, but with a budget that had blown to more than 1,000% of the original.

The Opera House is most spectacular from the outside, viewed from the promenade that surrounds it or, better still, from a harbor ferry. Inside is the main auditorium, which is capable of seating 2,800, and three performance halls. Guided tours are offered daily 9:15 a.m.-4 p.m.; adult $10, child $7. The booking office is on the Lower Forecourt Level, tel. (02) 9250-7111. On

Sunday jazz is performed free outside, and craft markets are at the front entrance. The closest railway station is Circular Quay.

Coca-Cola Quayside

Between the Opera House and Circular Quay Ferry Terminal is this small museum cataloging the history of the world's best-known soft drink. As well as displays of advertising paraphernalia dating from the 1920s, there's a booth to make your own Coca-Cola advertisement and a Coca-Cola retail shop. Admission is adult $6, child $3. Open daily 10 a.m.-5 p.m. For further information, call (02) 9259-6700.

THE ROCKS AND VICINITY

The Rocks are both picturesque and of historical importance. In 1788 Captain Phillip came ashore with a few hundred marines and 736 convicts and set up a shanty town on the slopes of a rocky sandstone outcrop overlooking the bay Phillip had named Sydney Cove. As development spread slowly inland, The Rocks evolved into an area of disrepute, known to seamen around the world for the brothels, rowdy taverns, and cheap liquor. The area later became a port facility, with many large warehouses. When bubonic plague broke out in 1900 many original buildings were demolished, and in later years the construction of the Sydney Harbour Bridge saw entire streets disappear under tons of con-

crete. In the early 1970s, preservation began, with the oldest buildings restored and innumerable cafes and tourist shops opened.

The best way to get a feel for the Rocks is on a 90-minute **Unseen Sydney** walking tour, tel. (02) 9555-2700, which run Tues.-Sat. at 5 p.m. and 7 p.m. For $13 pp you get an entertaining insight into the Rocks, its history, its convict-era buildings, and the colorful characters who once called the area home. The tour ends with a free drink at the historical Hero of Waterloo Hotel.

Historic Buildings

Beside the Sydney Visitor Centre on George St. is **Cadman's Cottage.** Built in 1816 for former convict John Cadman, who was superintendent of the governor's boats, it is Sydney's oldest standing house. At the time of construction, the cottage stood on a small sandy beach, but the land in front has since been reclaimed. The house now serves as an information center for the National Parks and Wildlife Service, tel. (02) 9247-8861. Open daily 9 a.m.-5 p.m. The center of The Rocks is the junction of Argyle and George Streets. On this corner is the **Orient Hotel,** built in 1844 and operating as a hotel since 1851. Uphill from the Orient are many more historic buildings. Along Nurses Walk is a narrow lane known as **Suez Canal,** one-time haunt of the "Rocks Push," a gang of notorious thugs who terrorized passersby late last century. The **Argyle Centre,** farther up Argyle St., is a se-

Cadman's Cottage

THE SYDNEY HARBOUR BRIDGE

The Sydney Harbour Bridge, linking the city center to the northern suburbs, is, along with the Opera House, a symbol of Sydney. Known locally as the "Coathanger," it looks a little old-fashioned today, with the four massive stone pylons built purely for decoration not the least bit decorative. A harbor bridge was talked about for much of the second half of the 19th century, but not until 1932 was one completed. The bridge spans 550 meters (one of the world's longest single-span bridges), rises 120 meters above the harbor, weighs more than 50,000 tons, and is supported entirely by the distinctive span girders. Since its inception, traffic across the bridge has increased dramatically. For many decades, various proposals were put forward to ease bridge congestion, including building a brand-new bridge and adding an additional level to the existing bridge. The least popular suggestion—increasing the bridge toll from 20 cents to $2 in one stroke—was implemented, but it had little long-term effect on the problem. Money collected from the toll helped pay for a tunnel beneath the harbor, which opened in 1992.

Bridge Views

Good views of the bridge are available from many vantage points around the harbor foreshore, including the north end of the Rocks (at the south end of the bridge) and Kirribilli (at the north end). In both cases, paths lead under the bridge and beyond to where it can be appreciated in all its glory. From sea level, catch a ferry between Circular Quay and Darling Harbour ($3.20 one way), and you'll pass right under it. Catch a ferry back from Manly to Circular Quay, and the bridge becomes part of a magnificent harbor panorama.

Walking across the bridge takes about 20 minutes (the east side of the bridge has a pedestrian walkway, the west side a cycleway). Pedestrian access is from Cumberland St. in The Rocks. The pylon closest to The Rocks is open to the public daily 10 a.m.-5 p.m. Inside is a small museum telling the bridge's story and a 200-step stairway that ends at a lookout. Admission is $2.

Bridge Climb

In 1998, the company Bridge Climb began taking visitors to the very top of the bridge for a 360-degree panorama that is nothing less than awe-inspiring. The climb is not for the faint of heart—much of the trek to the top is made on the outside of the span, high above the traffic and the harbor. The cost is $98 pp, which includes a commemorative photo. The popularity of the climb exceeded all expectations (up to 500 people a day were reaching the peak in 1999), so make bookings well in advance by calling (02) 9252-0077.

ries of warehouses dating from as early as 1840. Today they house shops selling arts, crafts, and souvenirs. At the top of the street is **Argyle Cut,** an excavation through a massive slab of sandstone that convicts cut by hand to connect Sydney Cove with what is now known as Darling Harbour. Immediately south of the Cut, at 58 Gloucester St., tel. (02) 9241-1893, is **Susannah Place,** a small terrace built for a working-class family back in 1844. It's open for inspection Sat.-Sun. 10 a.m.-5 p.m.; admission is adult $6, child $2. At the end of Playfair Street, a cobbled pedestrian mall, is the **Westpac Museum,** tel. (02) 9251-1419. The museum, in an old bank building, features the story of Australian currency. It's open daily noon-4 p.m.

Museum of Contemporary Art

This museum at 140 George St., tel. (02) 9252-4033, is contained in a large art deco building overlooking Circular Quay (walk around to the back entrance to appreciate its size). Displays include anything from today's world of art, from modern Aboriginal works to the art of Andy Warhol to computer-created art. Admission is adult $9, child $6. It's open daily 10 a.m.-6 p.m.

Sydney Observatory

On Observatory Hill, reached by passing through the Argyle Cut and climbing a steep flight of stairs, this observatory is an old graystone structure dating from 1857. Part of the observatory's original function was as a timekeeper for the new colony. Daily at 1 p.m. the ball at the top of the weather vane was dropped simultaneously with the firing of a gun on Fort Denison, allowing settlers on land and sailors on ships out on the harbor to check their timepieces. As Sydney expanded, the bright lights of the city pushed the observatory past its use-by date, and it is now open daily for tours 10 a.m.-5 p.m. (free) and nightly except Wednesday for telescope viewing at 8:30 p.m. (adult $8, child $3). For further information, call (02) 9217-0485.

DARLING HARBOUR

Originally a shipping and storage area for the city, Darling Harbour, a narrow inlet immediately west of downtown, was an eyesore for

decades until a massive redevelopment program in the 1980s saw the birth of a stylish waterfront shopping and entertainment complex. The centerpiece is **Harbourside Festival Marketplace,** a massive complex of 200 shops, restaurants, and bars, alive with color of clowns, musicians, dancers, and mime artists. On the harborfront are long promenades, gardens, and parkland as well as a variety of other attractions. Access from downtown is at the end of Market St. over the Pyrmont Bridge (pedestrians only). Another option is the **monorail,** which circles Darling Harbour and links it to the city center. The one-way fare is $3, or ride it all day for $7. Beside Harbourside is the Exhibition Centre, a massive expanse of space protected by a suspended roof canopy seven stories high, and beyond this an IMAX theater.

Sydney Aquarium

Located on the city side of Darling Harbour, this aquarium complex is the largest in the Southern Hemisphere. It contains 5,000 Australian specimens, including one of the world's largest collections of sharks, as well as Barrier Reef fish and crocodiles. Other features are the mock river system and a touch pool where visitors are encouraged to get their hands wet. Two massive tanks moored in the harbor contain larger species, such as sharks and rays, while other tanks contain marinelife found in Sydney Harbour. Admission adult $16, child $8. Open daily 9:30 a.m.-10 p.m. For more information call (02) 9262-2300.

Australian National Maritime Museum

This museum catalogs Australia's shipping history and the influence the ocean has had on the country. Displays include the relationship between Australian and North American marine history, Aboriginal canoes, the victorious 1983 America's Cup wing-keeled yacht *Australia II,* the role of lifesavers, beach culture through the years, the world's fastest boat *Spirit of Australia,* and the anchor from the *Sirius,* wrecked on Norfolk Island in 1790.

Tied up at the museum's docks are a number of vessels, including a Russian navy submarine, the destroyer HMAS *Vampire,* a Vietnamese refugee boat, a tug boat, and a couple of old racing yachts. Admission is adult $9, child

One of the highlights of the National Maritime Museum is the display of boats tied up at the wharf.

$4.50, which includes a free museum tour, and it's open daily 9:30 a.m.-5 p.m. For more information, call (02) 9552-7777. Tours of the historic waterfront suburb of Pyrmont depart the museum at 10:30 a.m. on the first Tuesday of every month; $15 pp.

Powerhouse Museum
Housed in an enormous building that once generated power for Sydney's trams, this, Sydney's most spectacular museum, definitely shouldn't be missed. Displays encompass Australia's entire social history, and it's easy to spend an entire day wandering through the building, large enough to house entire airplanes, trains, and houses. Exhibitions are expertly displayed, with many interactive displays encouraging visitors to push buttons and pull levers. As well as the science and technology upon which the country has been built, displays show an old settler's hut, an old arena, and a suburban grocery store.

Admission is a worthwhile adult $8, child $3. Open daily 10 a.m.-5 p.m. It's at 500 Harris St., Ultimo, immediately south of Darling Harbour, tel. (02) 9217-0111.

Harris Street Motor Museum
Behind Darling Harbour, at 320 Harris St., tel. (02) 9552-3375, this museum is devoted entirely to the automobile, with around 160 machines on display. Classic cars are exhibited, along with motorcycles, vans, and vehicles with famous former owners. Also in the museum is a two-km-long slot-car track for enthusiasts to test their skills. Admission is adult $10, child $5. Open Wed.-Sun. 10 a.m.-5 p.m. Easiest access is from the Convention Centre monorail station.

SIGHTS AND SUBURBS EAST OF DOWNTOWN

Kings Cross
Sleaze. Porn. Drugs. The Underworld. You name it, "The Cross," has it. Australia's best-known suburb is in fact not an official suburb, but has come to be known as one. Located immediately east of the Domain, this famous red-light district is Australia's answer to London's Soho. The main drag is Darlinghurst Rd., a continuous stretch of strip joints, porn shops, nightclubs, and late-night restaurants. Although things are seedy and sleazy after dark, it's a lively place 24 hours a day. Darlinghurst Rd. is reasonably safe, but you definitely wouldn't want to wander down too many dark alleys. The Cross attracts a great array of people, from overseas tourists to drugged-out teenage hookers. It is a popular travelers' center and has Australia's largest concentration of backpacker accommodations. **El Alamein Fountain,** a local landmark and popular meeting place, is on the corner of Darlinghurst Rd. and MacLeay Street.

Darlinghurst
Southeast of downtown along Oxford St., this old suburb features restaurants, lively nightlife, and many restored Victorian-era terraces. The main attraction is **Sydney Jewish Museum** at 148 Darlinghurst Rd., tel. (02) 9360-7999. Jews were among the first fleet of convicts to land on Australian soil. While telling the history of these

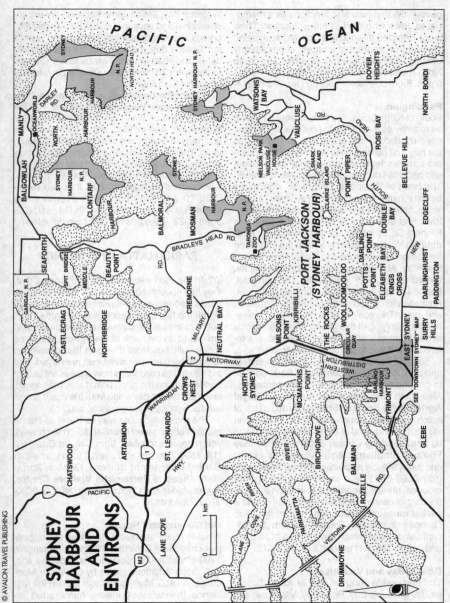

PACIFIC OCEAN

SYDNEY HARBOUR AND ENVIRONS

© AVALON TRAVEL PUBLISHING

PORT JACKSON (SYDNEY HARBOUR)

MANLY

OCEANWORLD

DARLEY RD.

NORTH HARBOUR

BALGOWLAH

SEAFORTH

SYDNEY HARBOUR N.P.

NORTH HEAD

SYDNEY HARBOUR N.P.

CLONTARF

SPIT BRIDGE

GARGAL N.P.

MIDDLE HARBOUR

CASTLECRAG

NORTHBRIDGE

BEAUTY POINT

BALMORAL

MOSMAN

SYDNEY HARBOUR N.P.

BRADLEYS HEAD RD.

TARONGA ZOO

CREMORNE

MILITARY RD.

NEUTRAL BAY

SYDNEY HARBOUR N.P.

WATSONS BAY

NELSON PARK

VAUCLUSE HOUSE

VAUCLUSE

NEW SOUTH HEAD RD.

SHARK ISLAND

CLARKE ISLAND

DOVER HEIGHTS

NORTH BONDI

ROSE BAY

BELLEVUE HILL

DOUBLE BAY

EDGECLIFF

POINT PIPER

DARLING POINT

ELIZABETH BAY

POTTS POINT

KINGS CROSS

DARLINGHURST

PADDINGTON

WOOLLOOMOOLOO

THE ROCKS

KIRRIBILLI

MILSONS POINT

MCMAHONS POINT

NORTH SYDNEY

CROWS NEST

WARRINGAH

CHATSWOOD

ARTARMON

ST. LEONARDS

PACIFIC HWY.

LANE COVE N.P.

LANE COVE RIVER

PARRAMATTA RIVER

DRUMMOYNE

M2

BIRCHGROVE

BALMAIN

ROZELLE

VICTORIA RD.

CIRCULAR QUAY

WESTERN DISTRIBUTOR

EAST SYDNEY

SURRY HILLS

SEE "DOWNTOWN SYDNEY" MAP

DARLING HARBOUR

PYRMONT

GLEBE

SEE "DOWNTOWN SYDNEY" MAP

MOTORWAY

2

1

1

0   1 km

people, the museum also functions as a memorial to Jews who died in the Holocaust. Their story, depicted through interactive displays and stunning photographic images, is particularly moving. Admission adult $6, child $3. Open Mon.-Thurs. 10 a.m.-4 p.m. and Sunday 11 a.m.-5 p.m. From downtown take bus no. 373 or 374.

Paddington

South of Kings Cross, this suburb, very run-down as recently as the 1970s, is now one of the inner city's most desirable areas to live. The streets are hilly and twisted, lined with narrow Victorian-era terraces featuring ornamental plasterwork and balconies decorated with cast-iron lace work. The heart of "Paddo" is Oxford St., dominated by fashionable boutiques, antique shops, art galleries, cafes, and bric-a-brac stores. The downtown end of Oxford St., around the corner of Flinders St., is the gay center of Sydney. **Paddington Village Bazaar** is held in the church on the corner of Newcombe and Oxford Streets every Saturday. Also of interest is **Victoria Barracks,** Oxford St., tel. (02) 9339-3445. The barracks, finished in 1848, were built using convict labor. Australian forces currently occupy the barracks, and every Thursday at 10 a.m. there is a ceremonial changing of the guard. After this weekly event, tours of a small military museum are offered. Admission to the barracks is free.

South of Paddo is Sydney's largest stretch of parkland, 220-hectare **Centennial Park,** opened to commemorate Australia's 1888 centenary. Also south of Paddington is the original **Royal Agricultural Society Showground,** parts of which have been transformed into a Foxtel movie studio. The north end of the showground is taken up by the **Sydney Cricket Ground** and **Sydney Football Stadium,** premier venues for cricket and rugby league respectively. **Sportspace,** tel. (02) 9360-6601, is a tour that takes in both grounds, dressing rooms, players' tunnel, security control center, 1886 Member's Stand, and a cricket museum. Tours depart from the Club Lounge in the Sydney Football Stadium daily except Sunday and match days at 10 a.m., 1 p.m., and 3 p.m. The cost is adult $18, child $12.

Double Bay and Vaucluse

The harborside suburbs east of Kings Cross, including Double Bay, Rose Bay, Vaucluse, and Watsons Bay, are all upmarket and very expensive to live and shop in. Double Bay, especially, boasts shops representing some of the world's top fashion designers as well as many trendy cafes and restaurants. Ferries leave Circular Quay every 20 minutes for Double Bay; for details call (13) 1500.

Toward the headlands is the swank suburb Vaucluse, where **Vaucluse House** lies. This imposing mansion was built for William Charles Wentworth, who in 1813 was a member of the first party of Europeans to cross the Blue Mountains. The house, set on 11 magnificent harborside hectares, is furnished from that period, with original outbuildings and stables still in place. Admission is adult $6, child $3. It's open Tues.-Sun. 10 a.m.-4:30 p.m., with afternoon tea served daily. It's on Wentworth Rd., tel. (02) 9388-7922. Take bus no. 325 from downtown.

PARRAMATTA AND VICINITY

When the First Fleet arrived at Sydney Cove, they had enough supplies to last two years. This made becoming self-sufficient a top priority. When the first crops failed, search parties sent out from the colony discovered a fertile area 30 km inland on the bank of the Parramatta River. Many buildings from the town that developed around the gardens have been preserved, and the site of the gardens is now a pleasant strip of parkland along the river. (What was then a wild, unknown area a day's ride from the coast is now *east* of Sydney's geographical center.)

The most enjoyable way to travel to Parramatta is aboard the ***RiverCat*** ($5.80 each way), which departs regularly from Circular Quay, tel. (13) 1500. You can also catch a train from either Central or Wynyard Stations. Once in Parramatta, head to **Parramatta Visitors Centre,** corner Market and Church Streets, tel. (02) 9630-3703. Open daily.

Old Government House

What is now Parramatta Park was the original plot chosen by Governor Phillip for farming. In 1790 Phillip had a residence built on the site, with major additions made by Governor Macquarie in 1815. Many governors lived in the residence, the intricate paneling, handcrafted furniture, and expensive furnishings attesting to their grand tastes. On the western side of the house are fruit trees and grapevines dating from the era of Phillip's reign as governor. Admission to the house is adult $5, child $3. It's open Tues.-Fri. 10 a.m.-4 p.m., Sat.-Sun. 11 a.m.-4 p.m., tel. (02) 9635-8149.

Elizabeth Farm
Built in 1793 as a home for John MacArthur, founder of the merino wool industry, this is the oldest existing house in Australia. Featuring wide verandas, it's typical of Australian homestead construction. Restored, and decorated with many pieces of original furniture, the house is open for inspection daily 10 a.m.-4:30 p.m. Admission adult $6, child $3. It's at 70 Alice St., Rosehill, tel. (02) 9635-9488.

Australia's Wonderland
This, Australia's largest theme park, is west of Parramatta on Wallgrove Rd., Eastern Creek, tel. (02) 9830-9100. Set on more than 200 hectares (that's larger than Disneyland), it has six themed areas, including one containing cartoon characters, an International Village, fun park, water slides, and the Australian Wildlife Park. Admission is adult $26.95, child $19.95. Admission to the wildlife park only is $10, worthwhile for the viewing of goannas from underground walkways and an excellent nocturnal house. Wonderland is open daily during school holidays (the rest of the year weekends only) 10 a.m.-5 p.m. The nearest railway station is Rooty Hill, from where buses run to Wonderland every half hour.

SIGHTS NORTH OF THE HARBOR

Taronga Zoo
Overlooking the harbor and a short ferry ride across the harbor from Circular Quay, this is Australia's premier zoological garden, having what is often described as the best setting of any zoo in the world. Across 30 hectares are 4,000 animals from around the world. Highlights include the seal pool, underwater platypus house, noctarium, Friendship Farm, and, yes, they have all the usual lions, tigers, bears, elephants, giraffes, and monkeys. Admission is adult $16, senior $10, child $8.50. A Zoo Pass,

available at Circular Quay, includes ferry transfers, the Aerial Safari, and zoo admission for adult $21, senior $13, child $10.50. Road access is from Bradleys Head Rd. off Military Rd., Mosman, tel. (02) 9969-2777. The zoo is open daily 9 a.m.-5 p.m.

Oceanworld
In the bustling seaside suburb of Manly, this four-million-liter aquarium features a unique moving walkway that runs underneath the main tank. This allows visitors the unusual angle of looking *up* at large sharks and stingrays. Other tanks contain reef fish, octopuses, eels, lobsters, crabs, and poisonous dwellers of the deep. A highlight of Oceanworld is the daily shark feeding at 12:15 and 2:30 p.m. Admission is adult $14.50, child $7.50. Open daily 10 a.m.-5:30 p.m. It's on West Esplanade, Manly Cove, tel. (02) 9949-2644. The most enjoyable way to get there is aboard a ferry from Circular Quay.

Other Manly Sights
Manly is almost a self-contained resort rather than a suburb, and boasts one of Sydney's most popular beaches. Access from Circular Quay is easy aboard ferries, which dock at Manly Wharf, Manly Cove. From there a 500-meter-walk extends along the **Corso**, a pedestrian mall, to the oceanfront. On West Esplanade is **Manly Art Gallery and Museum,** tel. (02) 9949-2435, with local memorabilia and photographs of the beaches' earliest swimmers and surfers. Admission is adult $2 (free with an Oceanworld ticket). It's open Tues.-Fri. 10 a.m.-4 p.m., Sat.-Sun. noon-5 p.m. Darley Road through Manly leads to **North Head,** at the entrance to Sydney Harbour and within Sydney Harbour National Park. On the headland, the **Quarantine Station** housed new immigrants suspected of carrying diseases as recently as 1984. The only way to visit is on a guided tour. These depart Mon.-Fri. at 10.40 a.m., Sat.-Sun. at 11.40 a.m., and cost $10 pp. After dark, the "Ghost Walk" tour Wednesday and Fri.-Sun. at 7:30 p.m. costs $17 pp, which includes a light snack. For bookings, call (02) 9977-6522. Also on the headland is the **Royal Australian Artillery Museum,** tel. (02) 9976-1138, displaying guns and cannons used by Australian forces in colonial times. Admission adult $4, child $2. It's open on weekends only 10 a.m.-4 p.m.

NATIONAL PARKS

Not only is Sydney blessed with one of the world's great harbors, but within the city limits are no less than seven national parks. Combined with the six national parks along the city limits, well over 800,000 hectares of native bushland are protected in the Sydney area. The best source of information about all parks is the National Parks and Wildlife Service office in **Cadman's Cottage,** 110 George St., The Rocks, tel. (02) 9247-8861; open Mon.-Fri. 9 a.m.-5 p.m.

Sydney Harbour National Park

This, the closest national park to downtown, protects various sections of undeveloped coastline around Sydney Heads, including **Gap Bluff** at Watsons Bay; **Shark** and **Clarke Islands; Bradleys** and **Middle Heads** near Mosman; **Dobroyd Head** at Balgowlah Heights; and **North Head,** south of Manly.

Ku-ring-gai Chase National Park

When residents of Sydney's northern suburbs feel like escaping the crush of city living, they needn't travel far, for this 14,880-hectare national park is right on the back door (in some cases, literally). The park extends from the leafy outlying suburbs of the North Shore to the Hawkesbury River and east from the Pacific Highway to Pittwater. It's part of an area known geographically as the Sydney Basin, once part of the ocean floor until uplift created the high plateau through which watercourses have carved deep valleys. Many of these valleys have flooded to become part of Broken Bay. Most larger species of mammals are long gone (although gray kangaroos are often seen at dawn and' dusk along Bobbin Head Rd.), but possums, gliders, echidnas, and bandicoots are present. Three main access roads lead into the park. Bobbin Head Rd. begins at Mt. Colah, descending to the far reaches of Cowan Creek, where the Halverson Boat Sheds are located. Beyond the boat sheds, toward Terrey Hills, is the **Visitors Centre,** tel. (02) 9457-9322, with displays of park fauna and an audiovisual. The other park access is north off Mona Vale Rd. to West Head, from where views extend across Broken Bay to Lion Island and across Pittwater to the narrow spit of sand joining

Barrenjoey Head to Palm Beach. From West Head, the 3.5-km Garigal Aboriginal Heritage Walk passes various sites sacred to Australia's first inhabitants. Camping is possible at the Basin on Pittwater, accessible on foot from West Head Rd. or water taxi from Palm Beach.

Royal National Park

Disastrous fires in January 1994 left this 15,080-hectare park a charred wasteland. Human intervention in the natural cycle of fires—as was the case in the U.S.'s Yellowstone Park a few years earlier—encouraged the park to become overly dense, making it susceptible to quick-spreading fires. First gazetted (proclaimed) in 1879, Royal National Park is the world's second-oldest national park. The early preservation of this coastal landscape allows visitors the unique chance to explore the same environment that early European visitors did. The park extends between the Princes Highway and the Pacific Ocean and south from Port Hacking to Wollongong's northern suburbs. For 8,000 years before the arrival of Europeans, the Dharawa tribe lived around the bays of Port Hacking, fishing and collecting shellfish. Piles of empty shells (known as middens), a burial site, and rock art are reminders of their presence.

One of the most enjoyable ways to reach the park is on the regular ferry service between Cronulla and **Bundeena,** a small town at the southern entrance to Port Hacking and surrounded by the park. From Bundeena, the Coast Track leads 28 km south to Otford, on the main southern rail line. The trail passes many delightful bays and beaches and is easily completed in two days. For day trippers, Marley Headland and Big Marley Beach (three km one-way) are popular destinations from Bundeena, as is Jibbon Point (one km one-way), where Koori rock art is carved into a rock platform. The main road into the park passes Audley Weir (boat rentals and picnic areas), then divides: one fork ends at Bundeena, the other winds through the park's southern reaches. Side roads access the coastline at Wattamolla Beach and Garie, both popular picnic and bushwalking spots.

Other National Parks

Garigal National Park extends from the lower reaches of Middle Harbour north to the suburb of St. Ives. The park has boat rentals near Roseville Bridge and more than 100 km of hiking trails, including one along Middle Harbour Creek.

Smallest of the city national parks, at just 372 hectares, is **Lane Cove National Park,** which protects an area of bushland west of Chatswood. Trails lead along Lane Cove River, and more than 30 picnic areas dot the park.

South of Bankstown, 330-hectare **Georges River National Park** features riverside hiking trails and picnic areas. Yerambi Lagoon is home to a prolific number of birds.

Botany Bay National Park protects the tip of Kurnell Peninsula as well as a small section of coastline at the north entrance to Botany Bay. The park is best known as the landing place of Captain Cook. At the **Discovery Centre,** tel. (02) 9668-9111, the story of Cook, his landing, and the effect it had on the local natives is told; open Mon.-Fri. 11 a.m.-3 p.m., Sat.-Sun. 10 a.m.-4:30 p.m.

WILDLIFE PARKS

One of the world's great zoos is Taronga Zoo (see above), with many displays of animals from around the world, but Sydney has three other wildlife parks. These specialize in the unique fauna of the Australian continent.

Waratah Park
More of a nature reserve than a park, this place is good for viewing kangaroos, wallabies, emus, and wombats as they wander around freely in their natural environment. Other native species, such as Tasmanian devils and dingos, are caged. The 10-hectare site is adjacent to Kuring-gai Chase National Park. Cuddle the koalas in the Koala House, and take the Bush Railway, which winds through eucalypts and bushland typical of the area. The park also has a cook-your-own steak bistro, a restaurant, and souvenir shop. Admission is adult $12.50, child $6.60, and it's open daily 10 a.m.-5 p.m. Waratah Park is on Namba Rd., Duffys Forest, tel. (02) 9450-2377. Many city day tours include the park on their itinerary. Otherwise take a train to Chatswood in time to meet the 11:45 a.m. Forest Coach Lines bus.

Koala Park
For more than 65 years, Koala Park has helped preserve Australia's favorite native animal. It was the state's first such sanctuary and has been instrumental in the species' survival. As well, the park houses kangaroos, wallabies, wombats, dingoes, and colorful birds. Attend one of their knowledgable talks about the koalas. Admission to the sanctuary is a reasonable adult $9.50, child $5. Open daily 9 a.m.-5 p.m. Located at 84 Castle Hill Rd., West Pennant Hills, tel. (02) 9484-3141. By public transportation take the train to Pennant Hills (via Strathfield), then bus no. 651 or 655 to the park entrance.

Featherdale Wildlife Park
Although farther from the city, this park has Australia's largest collection of native fauna. Large enclosures containing all the usual species are spread through extensive native bushland. Highlights are the native-bird aviaries, koala-cuddling, crocodile-feeding (daily at 3:30 p.m.), fairy penguins, and a large collection of raptors. Admission to the park is adult $10.50, child $5.25. It's open daily 9 a.m.-5 p.m. The park is on Kildare Rd., Doonside, tel. (02) 9622-1644. By public transportation, take the train from Central Station to Blacktown and jump aboard bus no. 725.

OUTDOOR ACTIVITIES AND SPECTATOR SPORTS

Boating and Fishing
"Heading out on the harbor" is a favorite Sydneysider pastime and on any given weekend, Sydney Harbour is alive with sea craft of all shapes and sizes, from colorful windsurfers to speeding 18-footers to luxurious motor cruisers.

Northside Sailing School, at the southern end of the Spit Bridge, Mosman, tel. (02) 9969-3972, rents small boats and sailboards from $18 an hour. They offer sailing lessons in all manner of craft, including racing yachts. From the Middle Harbour Yacht Club, also at the Spit Bridge, **Ausail Yacht Charters,** tel. (02) 9960-5511, rents yachts from eight to 20 meters. Continuing north, various places rent boats, including **Skipper a Clipper,** based at the Gibson Marina, 1710 Pittwater Rd., Bayview, tel. (02) 9979-6188. This operation rents large cruisers, complete with kitchen, electric anchor, radios, linen, fuel, and a dinghy, for $50-160 pp per day. These boats are perfect for exploring the many estuaries and coves of the Hawkesbury River and busy Pittwater. On the Hawkesbury River, **Brooklyn Central Boat Hire,** tel. (02) 9985-7155, rents small aluminum boats with fishing gear for around $50 a day.

2000 SUMMER OLYMPIC GAMES

Word came in September 1993 that Sydney had been chosen to host the Summer Olympic Games in the year 2000, and Sydneysiders have been celebrating—and preparing—ever since. (Talk about optimism—some 65% of competition sites were underway or had already been constructed when the announcement was made!)

Upon arriving in Sydney today and seeing all the bumper stickers, flags, and T-shirts, you'll find it all but impossible to miss the fact that Sydney is hosting the Olympics, to be held from Friday 15 September to Sunday 1 October. The games will bring together more than 10,000 athletes competing in 28 sports and be televised to an estimated 3.5 billion viewers. (Following soon thereafter are the **Paralympic Games,** which run 18-29 October.) Australia last hosted the games in 1956, in Melbourne. This is the only country besides Greece to have been represented at every summer Olympics since the advent of the modern games in 1896.

Sydney Olympic Park

Homebush Bay, a disused industrial site beside the Parramatta River 15 km west of the city center, has been transformed into Sydney Olympic Park, a sporting and residential complex for the games. Incorporating more than 500 hectares of parkland, the facility is designed to be user-friendly and constitute a legacy for the city of Sydney long after the athletes of 2000 have left.

Start a visit to Sydney Olympic Park at the **Homebush Bay Visitors Centre,** in the heart of the village at 1 Herb Elliot Ave., tel. (02) 9735-4800; open daily 9 a.m.-5 p.m. Across Olympic Blvd. from the visitors center is **Sydney International Aquatic Centre,** tel. (02) 9752-3666. As well as competition pools, this complex features leisure pools, spas, saunas, a fitness facility, and a café. Immediately to the north is **Stadium Australia,** the park's showpiece. This 110,000-seat stadium will host the opening and closing ceremonies as well as track and field events, the end of the marathons, and the soccer final. The 18,000-seat **Super Dome,** Australia's largest indoor sports center, will host basketball and gymnastics competitions. Other components of Sydney Olympic Park include **Sydney Showground,** which will host the equestrian events and become the permanent home of the Royal Easter Show; the **State Sports Centre** for field hockey; as well as a tennis center, an archery park, golf driving range, and two large hotels.

Other Olympic Sites

While most Olympic events will be hosted within Sydney Olympic Park, a few will occur farther afield: west at Penrith, the newly constructed **Sydney International Regatta Centre** will host rowing and whitewater kayaking. Boxing, weight lifting, wrestling, and judo will take place in the **Darling Harbour** exhibition halls. **Sydney Harbour** will set the scene for sailing events. And beach volleyball will be held at **Bondi Beach.**

Practicalities

From Homebush Bay Visitors Centre, walking tours of the park are conducted between 10 a.m. and 2:30 p.m. The tours give a good overview of the facilities before setting off on foot yourself. The tour costs $10 pp.

Even though the park is a ways from downtown, getting there is easy by road, rail, or water. By car, simply follow the M4 out of the city and take the Homebush Bay Dr. exit. A brand new railway station has been built for the games, making the train a good way to travel to the park. From Central Station, **CityRail,** tel. (13) 1500, runs a train service to **Olympic Park Station.** This service is somewhat infrequent, so consider alighting at Strathfield, from where buses make the final leg of the journey. The state-run *RiverCat* stops at Sydney Olympic Park on its run between Circular Quay and Parramatta. The **Olympic Explorer** bus makes 10 stops along a loop route through the park, and for adult $10, child $5, you can get on and off all day.

The **Sydney Organizing Committee for the Olympic Games (SOCOG)** is responsible for the planning and staging of the games and handles all ticketing and marketing. Contact SOCOG at (02) 9297-2000 or visit the official website at www. sydney.olympic.org.

Swimming

No city in the world has a string of ocean beaches as beautiful as Sydney does, extending from Cronulla in the south to Palm Beach in the north. All major beaches have shark nets (the last recorded shark attack on a Sydney beach was 30 years ago), and volunteer lifesavers patrol beaches all summer and weekends year-round. Within the harbor are good beaches, including **Nielson Park** and **Watsons Bay,** and on the north side of the harbor, **Balmoral** and **Reef Beaches.**

BEACHES IN AND AROUND SYDNEY

Visitors to Australia usually need little prompting to "head down the beach," and with 32 beaches at Sydney's doorstep, there is no better place to experience distinctive Aussie culture. Sydney's beaches can get very crowded, especially on weekends, but this disadvantage is far outweighed by the advantages—golden sand, clear and warm water, and accessibility to the city itself. You can swim in the ocean year-round, but it's most pleasant Dec.-April, when water temperatures rise as high as 21° C (70° F). Sydney has three distinct groups of beaches—within the harbor, south of the harbor, and north of the harbor—extending 60 km from Cronulla in the south to Palm Beach in the north. And while at the beach, you may notice you feel overdressed. At many of the area's beaches, topless sunbathing is both legal and accepted (do, however, make sure that this is the case where you are before tossing your top).

Harbor Beaches

A number of remarkably beautiful beaches lie within the harbor, with some, such as **Nielson Park** at Vaucluse, just minutes from downtown yet surrounded by native forest. Nielson Park is protected by netting and has change sheds, lockers, and a kiosk. East, toward the heads, is **Watsons Bay,** where a small area of beach is netted. Immediately north, around a rocky headland, is **Camp Cove,** a trendy little spot popular with families. Busy **Balmoral Beach,** east of Mosman, on the north shore of the harbor, has two netted sections and plenty of parking.

Beaches South of the Harbor

The coastline between Sydney Harbour and Botany Bay is dotted with beautiful stretches of beach, but high cliffs and rugged headlands prevent extensive coastal views. Development is extensive and haphazard, with no decent road linking the beaches.

Australia's best-known beach, and closest to downtown, is **Bondi.** Like other beaches south of the harbor, it's surrounded by ugly high-rise development in various states of disrepair, though it's popular with travelers, and many New Zealanders and Brits live in the area. South of Bondi are two small beaches, **Tamarama** and **Bronte;** the former is often plagued by strong currents that make swimming inadvisable. Farther south, **Coogee** is another popular beach, with a large pub on the foreshore. All the above southern beaches can be reached by bus from Circular Quay.

Within Botany Bay lies a long stretch of beach at **Brighton Le Sands,** with netted swimming areas making it perfect for families. Southernmost of Sydney's beaches is **Cronulla,** a magnificent stretch of sand backed by pristine sand dunes that stretch from a developed area in the south along a narrow peninsula to Kurnell, landing site of Captain Cook in 1770. Cronulla is Sydney's only beach accessible by train; these depart Central Station every half-hour.

Beaches North of the Harbor

The 30 km of coastline north of the harbor is less developed but no more beautiful than that south of the harbor. **Manly,** reached by ferry from Circular Quay, has a real seaside resort atmosphere, with its tree-lined foreshore and many outdoor cafés and restaurants. From Manly, a crescent of sand extends two km to **Queenscliff Beach.** Beyond Queenscliff is **Curl Curl,** a popular family spot, then **Dee Why,** backed by a large lagoon and wildlife reserve. The crescent ends in the north at **Long Reef Point,** which has a spectacular oceanfront golf course. Beyond is **Narrabeen,** a legendary surf spot (and the only Australian beach mentioned in a Beach Boys' song). Farther north is another excellent surfing beach, **Newport,** with some of Sydney's most consistent surf—you may even find yourself sharing a wave with former world surfing champion Tom Carroll, a longtime resident. Newport lies at the southern end of a narrow peninsula that ends at Barrenjoey Heads. Along the peninsula are **Bilgola, Avalon, Whale,** and **Palm Beaches,** all backed by the calm waters of Pittwater, an arm of the Hawkesbury River.

The closest swimming pools to the city are: **Andrew Boy Charlton Pool,** in the Domain, Woolloomooloo, tel. (02) 9358-6686; **Prince Alfred Park Swimming Pool,** Chalmers St., Surry Hills, tel. (02) 9319-7045; and **North Sydney Olympic Pool,** Alfred St., Milsons Point, tel. (02) 9955-2309.

Scuba Diving

Water in Sydney Harbour is remarkably clear, and many hundreds of established dive sites exist. The best way to arrange a dive trip and equipment rental is through one of the following operators: **Dive 2000,** 2 Military Rd., Neutral Bay, tel. (02) 9953-0520; **Pro Dive,** 227 Victoria Rd., Drummoyne, tel. (02) 9819-7711; or **Pro Dive,** 39 Old Pittwater Rd., Manly, tel. (02) 9976-3499.

Golfing

Sydney is blessed with 80 golf courses, including a string of famous courses immediately south of downtown. Some of the better courses that allow visitors are: **Moore Park Golf Club,** corner Cleveland St. and Anzac Parade, tel. (02) 9663-4966, greens fees $20-25; **The Lakes,** King St., Mascot, tel. (02) 9667-3558, $65-100; **Concord Golf Club,** Majors Bay Rd., Concord, tel. (02) 9743-0265, $65; **Bonnie Doon Golf Club,** Banks Ave., Pagewood, tel. (02) 9344-5835, $55; **St. Michael's,** Little Bay, tel. (02) 9661-7549, $68; and **Bondi Golf Club,** 5 Military Rd., North Bondi, tel. (02) 9130-3170, $12. Northwest of the city, **Riverside Oaks,** Cattai, tel. (02) 4560-3299, is a resort-style course charging $80 for 18 holes.

Rugby League

Sydney is a stronghold of rugby league, hosting many competitions with teams across Australia and New Zealand. Crowds are never as large as those at Aussie Rules matches in Melbourne, but are no less fanatic. Closest of the grounds to downtown is the Sydney Football Stadium, which hosts the Grand Final every September. The main season runs March-Sept., with most games on Sunday afternoon. Contact the individual clubs for tickets.

Cricket

With Australia heading toward becoming a republic, the leisurely paced game of cricket may soon be the country's strongest link to England. During summer, cricket is played across the country, from kids playing on quiet backstreets to Internationals at the Sydney Cricket Ground. For match information at this and other major venues, contact the New South Wales Cricket Association at (02) 9339-0999.

Horse Racing

Sydney has four racecourses. They are: **Royal Randwick Racecourse,** Alison Rd., Randwick, tel. (02) 9663-8400; **Canterbury Park Racecourse,** King St., Canterbury, tel. (02) 9930-

---

HAZARDS OF THE BEACH

Australia's infamous wild animals should be the least of your worries when heading down to the beach. Sharks are occasionally present, but attacks off Sydney beaches are rare because offshore meshing and regular aerial patrols protect the masses from the marauding monsters of the deep. In fact, sunburn presents a much greater threat (Australians have the world's highest incidence of skin cancer), especially for visitors who have fled a Northern Hemisphere winter. Most of the popular beaches have nearby kiosks and general stores selling sunscreen (ask for one with a 15+ rating), but even with this protection, a wide-brimmed hat or beach umbrella is also recommended.

In the water, **bluebottles** are the biggest danger. Known locally as "stingers," they are often confused with box jellyfish. These annoying critters float in with summer's northeasterly breezes, en masse, and are easily recognizable as bright blue sacks with tentacles trailing up to two meters. Stings are not fatal but can cause intense local pain lasting 10-15 minutes and do leave long red welts where the tentacles touched you. Rubbing the affected area with wet sand removes many of the unbroken stinging sacks, but the poison that's already been discharged will run its course. Dousing the wound with Methylated Spirits or vinegar may ease the pain (surf clubs always have a supply).

Most Sydney beaches are patrolled between October and Easter by volunteer **surf lifesavers.** Distinctive red and yellow flags are set up on the beach to indicate safe swimming areas.

the clear water of
Sydney Harbour at
Nielson Park

4000; **Rosehill Gardens Racecourse,** Grand Ave., Rosehill, near Parramatta, tel. (02) 9930-4066; and **Warwick Farm Racecourse,** Hume Hwy., Warwick Farm, tel. (02) 9602-6199. Races are held at one of these venues every Wednesday and Saturday year-round. Racing starts at 12:30 p.m. (in summer at 2:30 p.m.), with the last race run around 5 p.m. Each course offers a Tote, or a bookmaker, through whom you can bet, as well as restaurants, bars, and plenty of parking. Another good place to bet on the horses (via a television screen), as well as see a cross-section of Sydneysiders, is at one to the many licensed clubs throughout the city.

ARTS AND ENTERTAINMENT

Art Galleries

Along with large public galleries, such as the Art Gallery of New South Wales and the Museum of Contemporary Art, Sydney has dozens of commercial galleries, many concentrated in Paddington and The Rocks. The **Aboriginal Art Centre,** 117 George St., The Rocks, tel. (02) 9247-9625, sells native artifacts, ranging from traditional art to contemporary paintings. Open daily 10 a.m.-5 p.m. Also in The Rocks is **Australian Craftworks,** 127 George St., tel. (02) 9147-7156, housed in an old police station from the Colonial era. It features arts and crafts for sale in all mediums. More good Australian art is for sale at **Watters Gallery,** 109 Riley St., East Sydney, tel. (02) 9331-2556,

which is open Tues.-Sat. 10 a.m.-5 p.m. Australia's most infamous contemporary artist was Brett Whiteley. After his sudden death in 1992, his studio opened as the **Brett Whiteley Studio Museum,** 2 Raper St., Surry Hills, tel. (02) 9225-1881. Admission is $6; open weekends 10 a.m.-4 p.m. For a bizarre range of glass sculptures, head to **Glass Artist's Gallery,** 70 Glebe Point Rd., Glebe, tel. (02) 9552-1552.

Theater

In Sydney, live theater has never reached the heights of popularity it enjoys in Melbourne, and it didn't really catch on at all until the 1960s. Also, Sydney has no "theater district," and many of the old playhouses have been bulldozed. That said, Sydney now has 25 theater companies, which perform more than 200 plays and musicals annually. Downtown theaters include: **Her Majesty's,** 107 Quay St., tel. (02) 9212-3411, a large theater, seating 1,500, that features musicals, Christmas pantomimes, and historical productions; **Kent Street Theatre,** 420 Kent St., tel. (02) 9529-5333, an old church featuring Australian and British productions; **Theatre Royal,** MLC Centre, King St., tel. (02) 9224-8444, a large and lavish venue featuring international musicals; **Lyric Theatre,** in Star City, Pyrmont, tel. (02) 9777-9150, features much of the same; and **Wharf Theatre,** Pier 4, Hickson Rd., Millers Point, tel. (02) 9250-1700, home to the Sydney Theatre Company, which puts on a broad spectrum of productions.

For regular drama, comedy, and modern dance, head to the **Seymour Theatre Centre,** corner City Rd. and Cleveland St., Chippendale, tel. (02) 9364-9400. Tickets range $15-25. The **Footbridge Theatre,** tel. (02) 9320-9000, is named for a footbridge that spans Parramatta Rd., Glebe. It's on the University of Sydney campus, catering mostly to the student crowd through comedy and a cynical look at the establishment. The **Belvoir Street Theatre,** 25 Belvoir St., Surry Hills, tel. (02) 9699-3444, features a wide range of Australian productions, from Aboriginal themes to children's shows; tickets are $15-20.

Music and Dance

Sydney's premier music venue is also its most recognizable, the **Sydney Opera House,** on Bennelong Point near Circular Quay. It hosts a broad range of productions, including those performed by the Australian Opera, Australian Ballet, Sydney Dance Company, and Sydney Symphony Orchestra. For bookings, call (02) 9250-7777. The **State Theatre,** 49 Market St., tel. (02) 9373-6655, built as a grand picture palace in the 1930s, has been restored to its former glory and now hosts visiting dance groups, musicals, and movies.

Cinemas

The main concentration of movie houses is at the southern end of George St., between Bathurst and Liverpool Streets. Here you'll find **Village,** tel. (02) 9264-6701; **Greater Union,** tel. (12) 3456; and **Hoyts,** tel. (13) 2700. Ticket prices at these mainstream cinemas ranges $9-12, with Tuesday night generally half price. A center of alternative movies, the **Valhalla,** 166 Glebe Point Rd., Glebe, tel. (02) 9660-8050, is a social center for fans of all movie genres including comedy, science fiction, and animation. The **Panasonic IMAX** theater, at Darling Harbour, tel. (13) 3462, features an eight-story-high screen (one of the world's largest) showing three one-hour feature films daily 10 a.m.-10 p.m. Tickets are $14 per film.

Casino

In late 1997, **Star City,** Sydney's first casino complex, opened on Pyrmont St., Pyrmont, tel. (02) 9777-9000 or (1800) 70-0700. Although not as large as its Melbourne counterpart, this Aus-

tralian-themed, Las Vegas-style complex lacks nothing in the ritz and glitz department. Gamblers have the option of blackjack, roulette, pai gow, and sic bo as well as two-up. Star City also holds a dozen restaurants and just as many bars, boutique shops, the biggest names in entertainment performing in a 2,000-seat theater, and a five-star hotel. It's open daily 24 hours.

Hotels and Bars

Sydney has literally hundreds of hotels and bars, many with high-quality live music performed nightly. The best source of entertainment information is the Metro pull-out in Friday's *Sydney Morning Herald*.

For a quiet drink downtown, there are a few options, including the longtime favorite **King George Tavern,** corner King and George Streets, tel. (02) 9232-3144, an upmarket drinking hole that attracts local white-collar workers. It's open from noon daily. Another stylish place is **Marble Bar** in the Sydney Hilton at 259 Pitt St., tel. (02) 9266-0610. This bar has an interesting history. Slated for demolition in the 1970s, after almost 100 years of use, it was moved—marble arches, intricate woodwork, and all—to a ground-floor location in the Hilton Hotel. **Arizona,** 247 Pitt St., tel. (02) 9261-1077, has a more casual atmosphere. This—and the daily drink specials and free pool—makes it popular with travelers.

Sydney's oldest pub, the **Lord Nelson Hotel,** corner Argyle and Kent Streets, The Rocks, tel. (02) 9251-4044, brews its own beer, while the **Mercantile Hotel,** George St., tel. (02) 9247-3570, is the best place to head for a pint of Guinness.

At Darling Harbour *the* place for a drink is the **Pumphouse Tavern,** 17 Little Pier St., tel. (02) 9281-3967, with beer brewed on site and served in old-style pint glasses. The tavern is built around an old water-pumping station that dates from 1891. The old cast-iron water tank remains, with a beer garden built around it. Also at Darling Harbour, the **Craig Brewery,** tel. (02) 9281-3922, is a popular hangout.

Friend in Hand Hotel, 58 Cowper St., Glebe, tel. (02) 9660-2326, has cheap beer nights and a packed entertainment program, including crab racing on Wednesday nights. Also in Glebe is the **Nag's Head,** 162 St. Johns Rd., tel. (02) 9660-

1591, with lots of British beers and live entertainment Wed.-Sunday.

It's after dark when Kings Cross really comes alive, with streets bustling through the night. Crowds make the main streets relatively safe, but still be careful. Before disappearing into a crowded and smoky bar, check out El Alamein Fountain, which is beautifully floodlit after dark. The most famous of the Cross's many drinking holes is the **Bourbon and Beefsteak,** 24 Darlinghurst Rd., tel. (02) 9358-1144, which attracts everyone from visiting celebrities to off-duty strippers. Happy hour is 4-7 p.m. For a cheap beer head to the **Darlo Bar,** on the corner of Darlinghurst and Liverpool Streets. At the 24-hour **Hampton Court Hotel,** 9 Bayswater Rd., tel. (02) 9357-2711, beer is $2 after 7 p.m. Backpackers flock to the **Kings Cross Hotel,** 248 William St., tel. (02) 9358-3377, for cheap drinks, Internet access, and big-screen televisions that seem to always be showing UK soccer matches. For something with a bit more style, the **Civic Club,** 44 Macleay St., Potts Point, tel. (02) 9358-4347, sells drinks at bar prices and has live entertainment; open daily 10 a.m.-5 a.m.

Nightclubs

Most downtown nightclubs cater to the upmarket or over-30 crowd, providing an enjoyable but often expensive night out. Trendy **Riva,** Sheraton on the Park, Castlereagh St., tel. (02) 9286-6666, is a dressy nightclub with ultramodern decor and the latest dance and jazz music. It opens Wed.-Sat. 10 p.m.-5 a.m. Cover charge $12. **Rokoko** is a popular place with tourists. The great variety of entertainment includes jazz, comedy, raffles, and plenty of dancing. Admission is free before 9 p.m. and varies after. It's at 16 Argyle St., The Rocks, tel. (02) 9251-1579.

Kinsela's, 383 Bourke St., Darlinghurst, tel. (02) 9331-3100, a renovated funeral parlor, has entertainment on three floors. Dancing is on the third-floor disco; the second floor has a cocktail bar and the ground floor features pool tables. Disco admission is $10. The **Metropolis,** 99 Walker St., North Sydney, tel. (02) 9929-8222, is the spot for those on the North Shore. Serious nightclubers head to Kings Cross, and places such as **Soho X Site,** 171 Victoria St., tel. (02) 9358-6511, a trendy dance club with a scene similar to an English rave party. The **Rhino Bar,**

24 Bayswater Rd., tel. (02) 9357-7700, has DJs spinning dance music, with an African-theme decor. It's open all night. The **Kings Cross Hotel,** 248 William St., tel. (02) 9358-6677, popular with budget travelers, features a nightly DJ, with UK pop on Friday and retro on Sunday.

Rock

Sydney has some legendary rock venues, mostly large pubs with an auditorium out back. Admission varies with the act but is rarely more than $10-15, even for international performers. The biggest big-name acts perform at the **Sydney Entertainment Centre** or **State Theatre.** **Selina's,** in the Coogee Bay Hotel, 253 Coogee Bay Rd., Coogee, tel. (02) 9665-0000, is a classic Aussie rock venue, with big-name acts every Friday and Saturday, with the action usually ending around 3 a.m. This venue also has six bars and a disco capable of holding 3,000 people. The **Bridge Hotel,** 135 Victoria Rd., Rozelle, tel. (02) 9810-1260, is a little more upmarket, but no less rowdy, and often attracts international rock acts. Bands play nightly with cover charges ranging $5-15. The **Hard Rock Café** is at 121 Crown St., Darlinghurst, tel. (02) 9331-1116. This shrine to music memorabilia has happy hour 5-7 p.m., with rock bands kicking off around 8 p.m.

Jazz, Blues, and Folk

The **Real Ale Cafe,** 66 King St., tel. (02) 9262-3277, is one of Sydney's premier jazz venues, with local and international acts performing Tues.-Saturday. Happy hour (5-7 p.m.) features half-price drinks; jazz starts at 8 p.m. and the action continues to as late as 4 a.m. on weekends. **Strawberry Hills Hotel,** 453 Elizabeth St., Surry Hills, tel. (02) 9698-2997, features contemporary jazz in fine surroundings with performances nightly as well as weekend afternoons. The **Basement,** 29 Reiby Place, Circular Quay, tel. (02) 9251-2797, hosts many international jazz and blues acts, usually kicking off at 8:30 p.m. Admission is from $5. Folk fans flock to the **Rose, Shamrock, and Thistle Hotel** (known locally as "The Three Weeds"), an old pub with a pleasant atmosphere and live folk, reggae, or blues most nights. Admission ranges $5-16, and the action runs 8-11 p.m. It's at 193 Evans St., Rozelle, tel. (02) 9810-2244.

Comedy

The **Harold Park Hotel**, 115 Wigram Rd., Glebe, tel. (02) 9692-0564, is a great entertainment venue with stand-up comedians performing Mon.-Fri.; admission $10. The **Comedy Store**, corner Crystal St. and Parramatta Rd., Petersham, tel. (02) 9564-3900, presents a smorgasbord of comedy talent ranging from local amateurs, overseas acts, and all-female shows (Thursday night). Admission averages $10. The **Double Bay Comedy Club**, 16 Cross St., Double Bay, tel. (02) 9327-6560, is an upmarket venue featuring dinner and stand-up comedians most nights.

SHOPPING

The three main strips of retail shops in downtown Sydney are along George, Pitt, and Castlereagh Streets (but for touristy souvenirs you're better off heading to Darling Harbour or The Rocks). For overseas visitors, the only real bargain shopping will be at duty-free stores along these streets, including **Downtown Duty Free** at 84 Pitt St., tel. (02) 9221-4444. Sydney's largest and most fashionable department store is **David Jones**, on the corner of Elizabeth and Market Streets. It features a wide range of retail items, with this store containing a travel agency, food court, restaurant, and beauty parlor. Down-market from David Jones is **Grace Bros.**, at 436 George Street. Sydney has many fine shopping arcades but, by far, the most magnificent is the **Queen Victoria Building** (QVB) on George Street. Built in 1898, it has been restored and now contains a stylish food court, fashion boutiques, and specialty shops. The **Strand Arcade**, built in 1892, connects Pitt and George Streets. It features 82 distinctive shops and is a pleasant escape from the busy footpaths. Worth visiting for the stylish decor is **Skygarden**, connecting Pitt St. Mall to Castlereagh Street, where a massive glass dome covers upmarket specialty shops and a trendy mix of cafes and restaurants. **Harbourside Festival Marketplace** is a bright, colorful complex at Darling Harbour with around 200 shops selling all sorts of items from tacky souvenirs to designer-label fashion accessories. It's open daily until 9 p.m.

Markets

After a few years' absence, **Paddy's Markets** have returned to their former home of 150 years adjacent to Chinatown. These markets attract both locals and tourists with more than 1,000 stalls selling just about everything you could imagine. The markets operate Sat.-Sun. 9 a.m.-4:30 p.m. **Paddington Markets,** held in the church grounds on the corner of Oxford and Newcombe Streets every Saturday, has a great atmosphere with locally crafted works, books, handmade toys, and clothing by young designers for sale. The buskers are the other attraction of these markets. A similar atmosphere prevails at **Glebe Market,** held on the corner of Glebe Point Rd. and Derby Place every Saturday. There's also a market at the top end of George St. in The Rocks every Saturday and Sunday.

Australiana

Sydney has several Aboriginal galleries. The biggest and best is the **Aboriginal Art Centre,** 117 George St., The Rocks, tel. (02) 9247-9625. It features a wide range of authentic Aboriginal and Melanesian artifacts including weaponry, jewelry, clothing, carvings, and paintings.

R.M. Williams, 389 George St., tel. (02) 9262-2228, is a legendary Aussie bush wear shop selling oilskins, hats, boots, and belts. Closed Sunday. This company has another outlet down at the airport on the Departure Level of the International Terminal. The **Ken Done Shop,** 123 George St., tel. (02) 9251-6099, sells the work of Ken Done, whose colorful designs appear on just about everything. A few doors away, at 105 George St., tel. (02) 9221-8145, is **Dorian Scott,** whose colorful clothing is a great Australian souvenir. A similar distance north is the **Ken Duncan Gallery,** 73 George St., tel. (02) 9241-3460, selling the works of Australia's premier landscape photographer.

If you're after opals, there are plenty of duty-free jewelers around The Rocks and Circular Quay. A better option if you're downtown is **Costello's** at 280 George St., tel. (02) 9221-1770.

FESTIVALS AND EVENTS

The entire month of January is taken up by the **Sydney Festival,** featuring open-air concerts in the Domain, contemporary music at Hyde Park, a variety of performances at the Opera House, and outdoor movies in Hyde Park. The monthlong **Gay and Lesbian Mardi Gras** culminates in a colorful parade along Oxford St. with all manner of floats on the first Saturday night in March. It is claimed to be the world's largest nighttime parade, with 800,000 spectators lining the streets.

The most eagerly awaited of Sydney's festivals is the **Royal Easter Show,** a 12-day agricultural extravaganza. The show provides an opportunity for the bush to come to the big smoke, and for city folk to experience life on the farm. The agricultural society was formed in 1822. Its chief goal was to ensure that levels of stock and produce resources were sufficient to support the fledgling colony. The first show put on by the society was held out at Parramatta in 1823. It was then moved closer to the city, to the Royal Agricultural Society Showground, south of Paddington, where it stayed for more than 100 years. The logistics of holding the show within walking distance of downtown Sydney finally took their toll on the event, and in 1998 it was moved to the new **Sydney Showground,** at Sydney Olympic Park, Homebush Bay. Originally showcasing livestock and agricultural machinery, the show now also features a fun park, polo, rodeo, cooking competitions, wood chopping, and a pavilion full of showbags. Show attendance averages around 900,000, so try to plan your visit on a weekday. The show runs for 12 days, ending the day after Easter Monday. Entry is adult $15, child $12. For details call (02) 9704-1111.

The **Biennale of Sydney,** held every two years (even-numbered years), brings together the world's leading artists with lectures, workshops, and lectures.

Held in theaters throughout the city, the **Sydney Film Festival** brings together filmmakers for two weeks through June.

Christmas Day on Bondi Beach is an unofficial event, drawing thousands of young overseas visitors to Australia's most famous beach. A combination of too much sun and too much booze has given the gathering a bad name, but things seem to have quieted down the last couple of years. Each Boxing Day dozens of yachts flanked by hundreds of spectator craft assemble in the harbor for the **Sydney-Hobart Yacht Race,** a spectacular event that sees the harbor foreshore lined with Sydneysiders.

HOTELS AND MOTELS

Downtown—Inexpensive
Sydney has no downtown budget accommodations, and few in the inexpensive range, but south of the city center, around Central Station, are several old pubs offering accommodations. **George Street Private Hotel,** 700 George St., tel. (02) 9211-1800, a rambling old place with basic but clean rooms, a laundry, and a kitchen. Rates are $40 s, $54 d, with shared facilities. In the same area is **CB Private Hotel,** 417 Pitt St., tel. (02) 9211-5115, with more than 200 rooms; $40 s, $55 d.

Downtown—Moderate
Of a higher standard than the pubs listed above, but in the same vicinity, is the **Westend Hotel,** across from the CB Private Hotel at 412 Pitt St., tel. (02) 9211-4822. Rooms with private facilities start at $65 s, $75 d. At the north end of downtown, and one block from Wynyard Station, **Wynyard Hotel,** corner Clarence and Erskine Streets, tel. (02) 9299-1330, has a reasonable standard of rooms with shared facilities for $55 s, $65 d.

Downtown—Expensive
The best value in this price range is **Aarons Hotel** (formerly the Sydney Travellers Rest), 37 Ultimo St., tel. (02) 9281-5555 or (1800) 02-3071, close to Darling Harbour and Chinatown. Rooms are small but were renovated in 1997, and all have bathrooms; rates start at $98 s or d, which includes breakfast.

East of Hyde Park, but still well within walking distance of downtown, are a number of well-priced accommodations. Best-value of these is **Oxford Koala Hotel,** corner Oxford and Pelican Streets, tel. (02) 9269-0645, comprising motel-style rooms and self-contained apartments for $110-155 s or d. All rooms are well-furnished, air-conditioned, and have hair dryers. On the 13th floor is a pool. A little farther out is **Cambridge Hotel,** 212 Riley St., tel. (02) 9212-1111, three blocks east of Hyde Park. It has a pool, spa, sauna, and secure parking as well as a few rooms with kitchenettes. Rates start at $120 s or d, including breakfast.

Downtown—Premium

Opposite Central Station and a short walk to Darling Harbour is **Country Comfort Sydney Central Hotel,** corner George and Quay Streets, tel. (02) 9212-2544. Facilities are good and parking is free; $141 s, $156 d. Directly opposite the Sydney Entertainment Centre and close to a monorail station is **Furama Hotel,** 68 Harbour St., tel. (02) 9281-0400 or (1800) 80-0555, with all the facilities you'd expect of a four-star hostelry; $148 s or d. **Park Regis Hotel,** 27 Park St., tel. (02) 9267-6511 or (1800) 22-1138, has a central location and has recently been refurbished; $150 s or d. It also features a pool and free parking.

Downtown—Luxury

Most guests of the hotels in this category survive on business expense accounts and pre-booked accommodation packages, but often reduced rates and weekend packages are offered, reducing costs considerably. **All Seasons Premier Menzies,** 14 Carrington S, tel. (02) 9299-1000, is in the heart of the city center, one block from Wynyard Station, Facilities include an indoor pool, gym, laundry, restaurant, and bar; $185 s or d. Least expensive of Sydney's 10 five-star accommodations is the **Sydney Marriott,** 36 College St., tel. (02) 9361-8400 or (1800) 02-5419, which overlooks the southeast corner of Hyde Park. Rooms are

spacious and well-furnished, and each has a large bathtub. On the top floor is a pool and a sundeck with city views. Rates start at $225 s or d. Farther north, overlooking the Royal Botanic Gardens and 200 meters from Circular Quay, is the **Hotel Inter-Continental Sydney,** 117 Macquarie St., tel. (02) 9230-0200 or (1800) 22-1828, a 31-story hotel that incorporates the old 1849 Treasury building. Rooms are large and well-furnished, and many have views. Rates in standard rooms range $245-285 s or d. Open since 1990, the elegant **Ritz-Carlton Sydney,** 93 Macquarie St., tel. (02) 9252-4600, overlooks the same gardens. Rates start at $399 s or d, but good weekend packages are offered. The **Regent Sydney,** 199 George St., tel. (02) 9238-0000, is a luxurious hostelry featuring king beds, marble bathrooms, and oak furnishings in every room. It is also home to Kable's, one of Sydney's best restaurants. Rates start at $270 s or d. **Novotel Sydney on Darling Harbour,** 100 Murray St., tel. (02) 9934-0000, 100 meters from the attractions of Darling Harbour and with a monorail station on the doorstep, has comfortable rooms (request city views), a large pool area, gym, restaurant serving a high-quality buffet breakfast and a la carte dinner, and free guest parking. Rooms start at $245 s or d.

The Rocks

A continuation of downtown, the historic Rocks area is close to many sights and the public transportation hub of Circular Quay, making it an ideal alternative to staying in the city center. The **Lord**

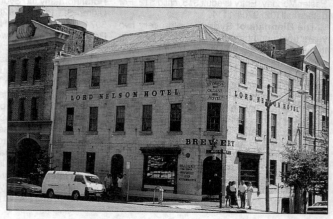

Lord Nelson Hotel is a moderately priced accommodation just a five-minute walk from the heart of The Rocks.

Nelson Hotel, 19 Kent St., tel. (02) 9251-4044, Sydney's oldest licensed hotel, has six rooms above a popular bar. Each has a private bathroom and is decorated with antiques. Guests have use of communal tea- and coffee-making facilities. Rates range $60-100 s or d, depending on room size, and include a continental breakfast. Moderate. In the heart of The Rocks is **The Russell,** 143A George St., tel. (02) 9241-3543, not luxurious but oozing Victorian charm with bright furnishings, antique iron beds, and a rooftop garden with views over Circular Quay. Rates are $100-230 d, depending on room size and facilities. All rates include a daily newspaper and light breakfast in the downstairs café. Expensive. **The Stafford,** 75 Harrington St., tel. (02) 9251-6711, comprises 54 apartments spread through six floors and seven renovated 100-year-old terraces. All units are well furnished and self-contained with kitchens. Some rooms have balconies. The complex also boasts a laundry, outdoor pool, spa, and gym. Rates are $200 for a studio, rising to $235 for a one-bedroom apartment or a Terrace Room. Luxury. **Park Hyatt Sydney,** 7 Hickson Rd., tel. (02) 9241-1234 or (1800) 22-2188, on Campbells Cove, is absolute waterfront. It's a low-rise development in the heart of The Rocks, with most rooms having water views. Rooms are luxurious and start at $490 s or d, rising to $3,500 per night for the Governor Suite, which boasts no less than six private balconies. Luxury.

Kings Cross and Vicinity

As well as being home to many backpacker lodges, Kings Cross has a range of accommodations for those who like to be in the center of a lively nightlife. Immediately north, and just a short walk from the action, is the suburb of Potts Point. **Kingsview Motel,** 30 Darlinghurst Rd., tel. (02) 9358-5599, is a good-value choice in the heart of the action. Rooms are of a high standard and range $75-108 s or d. Moderate. Top of the range in Kings Cross is the **Millennium Hotel Sydney,** William St., tel. (02) 9356-1234, with rooms from $230. Luxury.

In Potts Point, **Challis Lodge,** 21 Challis Ave., tel. (02) 9358-5422, is two adjacent terraces offering basic but clean rooms. Rates are $34 s, $42 d with shared facilities; $44 s, $58 d with private facilities. Weekly rates start at $180 for a double. Inexpensive. Similarly priced is **Bernly**

Private Hotel, 15 Springfield Ave., tel. (02) 9358-3122. Inexpensive. The friendly **De Vere Hotel,** 46 Macleay St., tel. (02) 9358-1211, is a good choice for overseas visitors as staff are more than happy to make tour arrangements. Rates are $94-130 s or d. Expensive. **Victoria Court Hotel,** 122 Victoria St., tel. (02) 9357-3200, is a boutique hotel of two adjoining terraces dating from 1881. Each room has its own character, and all rooms are decorated in Victorian style. Guests have use of a cozy sitting room where daily papers are supplied and a conservatory where tea- and coffee-making facilities are provided. Rates start at $75 s, $99 d, rising to $230 in a suite with a four-poster bed and private balcony. All rates include a continental buffet breakfast. Expensive.

Elizabeth Bay

Northeast of Kings Cross, this upmarket suburb is a good choice for those who don't mind a short cab ride into the city. **Roslyn Gardens Motor Inn,** 4 Roslyn Gardens, tel. (02) 9358-1944, comprises 29 rooms, each air-conditioned and with a fully equipped kitchen; from $64 s, $78 d. Moderate. On a residential backstreet is the art-deco **Manhattan Park Inn,** 8 Greenknowe Ave., tel. (02) 9358-1288, a large accommodation dating from the 1940s but renovated and having a modern feel. Rooms are comfortable, and some have harbor views. Rates are $104 s or d. Expensive. Overlooking busy Rushcutters Bay Marina is **Sebel of Sydney,** 23 Elizabeth Bay Rd., tel. (02) 9358-3244 or (1800) 22-2266, well priced for the standard of facilities, but long the choice of theater and showbiz personalities. Standard rooms are spacious and well furnished; $225-295 depending on the view. Suites have spectacular water views, kitchens, and are luxuriously outfitted; these rooms start at $350 (these rates on weekends include breakfast and dinner). Luxury.

Bondi

The old **Hotel Bondi,** 178 Campbell Parade, tel. (02) 9130-3271, has been extensively renovated on the outside and in the downstairs bar and restaurant areas, and although the rooms have seen better days, they are comfortable and clean. Standard pub-style rooms are $50 s, $75 d. Rooms with beach views start at $95, while the best rooms are $130. Moderate. Also overlooking the beach is **Bondi Beachside Inn,** 152 Campbell Parade, tel. (02) 9130-5311, where basic rooms are $75 s, $95 d. Expensive. Bondi's most luxurious accommodation is **Swiss Grand,** corner Campbell Parade and Beach Rd., tel. (02) 9365-5666, where self-contained apartments start at $230 s or d. **City Beach Motor Inn,** 99 Curlewis St., tel. (02) 9365-3100, with a tropical-looking facade a five-minute walk from famous Bondi Beach, has rooms of a good standard from $130 s or d.

Glebe
Glebe is a leafy suburb immediately west of downtown and with regular bus links to all the sights of downtown. Among the rows of cafes and restaurants are a couple of good-value accommodations. **Alishan International,** 100 Glebe Point Rd., tel. (02) 9566-4048, set back slightly from busy Glebe Point Rd., features 19 rooms, some with bathrooms, a recreation room, barbecue area, communal kitchen, and laundry; $70-80 s, $80-90 d. Moderate. **Rooftop Motel,** 146 Glebe Point Rd., tel. (02) 9660-7777 or (1800) 22-7436, has a pool, barbecue, and large rooms for $85 s, $95 d. Expensive.

Airport and Vicinity
Airport Sydney International Motor Inn, 35 Levey St., tel. (02) 9556-1555, within easy walking distance of the International Terminal, has comfortable rooms for a reasonable $129 s or d, and offers a day rate (6 a.m.-6 p.m.) for $60 s or d. Rates include airport transfers. Premium. One km north of the airport is **Parkroyal Sydney Airport,** tel. (02) 9330-0600 or (1800) 62-1859, with all the facilities expected of this international chain. Rates start at $165 s or d. Luxury. A few km east of the airport is **Trade Winds Hotel,** 200 Maroubra Rd., Maroubra, tel. (02) 9344-5555 or (1800) 80-6760, an elegantly furnished accommodation, with a pool, security parking, and airport transfers; $120-150 s or d. Premium.

North Shore
Centra North Sydney, Blue St., tel. (02) 9955-0499 or (1800) 80-1989, has spectacular harbor and city views and is in the perfect location for a walk over the Bridge to begin a day's sightseeing. Rates start at $155 s or d, but good

weekend packages are offered. Luxury. Immediately west of North Sydney is **Harbourside Apartments,** which comprise 82 fully self-contained luxurious units right on Sydney Harbour. The main feature is a harborside pool with sundeck. The complex also features a private jetty served by regular ferry services. Rates begin at $141 s or d, rising to $220 for two-bedroom units. It's at 2 Henry Lawson Ave., McMahons Point, tel. (02) 9963-4300. Premium.

Heading north on the Pacific Highway through the North Shore, most suburbs have motels. Pick of the bunch is **Killara Inn,** corner Pacific Hwy. and Commonwealth Rd., Killara, tel. (02) 9416-1344 or (1800) 22-6980, which has a wide range of facilities and comfortable rooms from $140 s or d. Premium.

Manly and the Northern Beaches
Manly Paradise Motel, 54 North Steyne, tel. (02) 9977-5799, is a stone's throw from the beach and is the best choice for mid-priced accommodation north of the harbor. Motel-style units are well equipped, and guests have use of a rooftop pool and sundeck. Rates are $95 for a standard room. Facing the beach are huge two-bedroom fully self-contained apartments for $210 s or d. Expensive/Luxury. Similarly priced and 50 meters from the beach is **Manly Beach Resort,** 6 Carlton St., tel. (02) 9977-4188. Expensive. Overlooking the beach is **Manly Pacific Parkroyal,** 55 North Steyne, tel. (02) 9977-7666, an upmarket establishment with a resort feel about it. Rates start at $190 s or d. Luxury. **Periwinkle-Manly Cove Guest House,** 18 East Esplanade, tel. (02) 9977-4668, is a small privately owned accommodation on the harbor side of Manly. Rooms are clean, comfortable, and large, and some have harbor views. Guests have use of a communal kitchen, lounge room, and barbecue area in a central courtyard. Rates are $75 s, $90 d, which includes a continental breakfast. Moderate. All of the above accommodations are within walking distance of both the beach and Manly Wharf.

Newport Mirage, corner Queens Parade and Kalinya Streets, Newport, tel. (02) 9997-7011, is on the quiet waters of Pittwater yet just minutes from famous Newport Beach. A large pool, barbecue area, and sundeck right on the harbor are the main features, while rooms are bright and airy. Rates start at $155, with waterfront rooms for $185. Luxury.

BACKPACKER ACCOMMODATIONS

The largest concentration of backpacker lodges is in Kings Cross, a couple of kilometers east of downtown. Staying in one of the world's most infamous red-light districts isn't to everyone's liking; other choices are the YHA in the heart of downtown, inner city Glebe, west of the city center, and the suburbs scattered along the beachside where the pace is slower.

Downtown

Directly opposite Central Station and an easy walk to all downtown attractions, **Sydney Central YHA,** corner Pitt St. and Rawson Pl., tel. (02) 9281-9111, is the world's largest hostel, with 532 beds and every service imaginable. Spread over nine floors are numerous lounges and communal kitchens, a rooftop swimming pool and barbecue area, a games room, Internet terminals ($10 per hour), a bistro, a bar, a general store, and a travel agency. Accommodations include eight-bed dorms ($17 pp), six-bed dorms ($18 pp), four-bed dorms ($21 pp), twins ($28 pp), and doubles ($29-33 pp). Nonmembers pay an additional $3 pp per night. Parking is $7 per night. Check-in is at noon, check-out at 10 a.m., and the maximum stay is 14 days. Inexpensive.

Y on the Park, in the YWCA building at 5 Wentworth Ave., tel. (02) 9264-2451 or (1800) 99-4994, offers safe, clean, and convenient accommodations for both men and women. Rooms are spartan, but have recently been redecorated in pleasing pastel colors, and the location and price are right. Guests have use of a communal TV lounge and laundry. Rates with shared bathrooms are $52 s, $60 d; with private facilities $60 s, $85 d. Inexpensive.

Kings Cross

With no less than 20 backpacker lodges, you'll always be able to find a bed in this lively part of the city. Most lodges are along Victoria St., but on the main drag are another couple of choices. **Highfield Private Hotel,** 166 Victoria St., tel. (02) 9358-1552, is a popular choice with overseas visitors. Dorms are $15-18 pp, and private rooms

(shared facilities) $25 s, $40 d. Budget. Heading north, next door but one, is **Original Backpackers,** 162 Victoria St., tel. (02) 9356-3232, with a friendly atmosphere and reasonable facilities; dorms $17 pp, private rooms $44 s or d. Inexpensive. Farther down the street is **Travellers Rest,** 156 Victoria St., tel. (02) 9358-4606, one of Kings Cross's best hostels. Facilities are excellent and some rooms have balconies opening to leafy Victoria Street. Dorms are $17 and private rooms are $35 s, $38 d. Inexpensive. **Jolly Swagman** is another good choice. Facilities are modern, beds comfortable, and on the roof is a sundeck and barbecue area with city views. Dorm beds are $18, and there are a few private rooms for $44. It's at 144 Victoria St., tel. (02) 9357-4733. Inexpensive.

Backpackers Connection, 2 Roslyn St., tel. (02) 9358-4844, an old motel off Darlinghurst Rd., has a modern kitchen, rooftop sundeck, and large rooms each with a bathroom and television; some are even air-conditioned. Rates start at $15 pp, with singles and doubles for $48. Inexpensive. Of an equal standard is the **Pink House,** 6 Barncleuth Square, tel. (02) 9358-1689, in a quiet location adjacent to the Travellers Car Market. Dorms are $15, private rooms $35 s or d. Budget.

Newtown

Newtown, an old suburb south of the city center, is home to **Billabong Gardens,** 11 Egan St., tel. (02) 9550-3236, one of Sydney's best budget accommodations. It's just off busy King St., home to lively pubs, cafes, and many alternative-fashion boutiques. Facilities include indoor and outdoor dining areas, laundry, modern kitchen, comfortable TV lounge, pool, spa, and barbecue area. Each room has a private bathroom. Dorms are $17, doubles $38. Inexpensive.

Glebe

This historic suburb west of downtown features many cafes and restaurants, plenty of nightlife, and two of Sydney's four YHA hostels. **Glebe Point YHA,** 262 Glebe Point Rd., tel. (02) 9692-8418, has a rooftop sundeck, lounge and TV rooms, laundry, and lots of organized activities. Rates in four- and six-bed dorms are $18 and $20 pp, respectively, and a bed in a twin or double room is $25 pp. Inexpensive. **Hereford**

Lodge, the other YHA hostel, has rooms with private bathrooms and a small rooftop pool. Rates are $18-25 pp depending on the number of beds in each room. This hostel is at 51 Hereford St., tel. (02) 9660-5577. From downtown, along George St., buses no. 431 and no. 433 pass both hostels. From the airport, catch the Kingsford Smith Transport bus and the hostels will deduct the fare from your room cost. Inexpensive. Across the road from Hereford Lodge is **Wattle House,** 44 Hereford St., tel. (02) 9552-4997, with dorm beds from $19 pp and doubles for $50. Inexpensive.

Bondi and the Southern Beaches
Bondi Beach Guesthouse, 11 Consett Ave., tel. (02) 9389-8309, just two blocks from the beach, is very central to Bondi attractions. Each room has a TV and fridge, and the communal kitchen is spotlessly clean. Dorm beds are $18 and doubles $42. Inexpensive. **Nomads on Bondi,** 2-8 Campbell Parade, tel. (02) 9130-1366 or (1800) 81-4885, is in a great central position and features large and comfortable common areas, including a rooftop patio. Dorm beds cost $15 pp, single rooms $35, and doubles $45. Budget.

The best backpacker accommodation along the southern beaches is **Surfside Backpackers,** 186 Arden St., Coogee, tel. (02) 9315-7888, right by the beach. Rates are $16 in dorms and $36 for a double. Inexpensive. Up the hill from the beach is the **Original Coogee Beach Backpackers,** 94 Beach St., tel. (02) 9665-7735, also of a high standard and similarly priced. Inexpensive.

Cremorne Point
Harbourside Hostel, 41 Cremorne Rd., tel. (02) 9953-7977, is in leafy Cremorne Point, north of the harbor and east of North Sydney. It's right on the harbor, and popular with those who don't need a raging nightlife. Rates start at $18 pp, mostly in twins, and include a light breakfast. The easiest access by public transport is to get a ferry from Circular Quay to Cremorne Wharf and walk up the hill. Inexpensive.

Manly and the Northern Beaches
Manly Bunkhouse, 46 Malvern Ave., tel. (02) 9976-0472 or (1800) 65-7122, is the pick of the backpacker accommodations north of the harbor.

It's a small facility, with a maximum of four beds in a dorm, each of which has its own bathroom, kitchen, and television. Common areas include a rooftop patio and an outdoor courtyard. Dorms are $18 pp, twin rooms $25 pp. Inexpensive. Of a similar standard, in an anonymous red brick building, is **Manly Backpackers Beachside,** 28 Raglan St., tel. (02) 9977-3411. Inexpensive.

Avalon Beach Backpackers Hostel, 59 Avalon Parade, Avalon, tel. (02) 9918-9709, has a relaxed atmosphere and is a short walk to Avalon Beach. The hostel has all the usual facilities as well as surfboard and mountain bike rentals. Dorm beds are $16-18, doubles $42. Inexpensive.

Sydney's most unique hostel is **Pittwater YHA,** tel. (02) 9999-2196. It's at Morning Bay, in the heart of Ku-ring-gai Chase National Park, and accessible only by boat from Church Point, at the southern end of Pittwater. The lodge is rustic but comfortable. Rates are $16-20 pp. Call ahead for transportation details. Inexpensive.

CAMPGROUNDS

North
The closest campground to the city center is **Lane Cove River Caravan Park,** Plassey Rd., North Ryde, tel. (02) 9888-9133, set among eucalypts adjacent to Lane Cove National Park. Facilities are excellent and include a pool, laundry, kiosk, and barbecue area. Unpowered sites are $20, powered sites $24, on-site vans $52, and air-conditioned, fully self-contained cabins go for $80. To get there take Delhi Rd. off Epping Rd. immediately west of the Lane Cove River, then take the second left. Budget-Inexpensive. Continuing north, on the old Pacific Hwy. near Berowra, is **La Mancha Cara-Park,** tel. (9456) 1766, with an excellent standard of facilities, including a large pool area, squash court, games room, lounge area, communal kitchen, and lots of barbecues; sites are $16-22, self-contained sites $27, and cabins range $64-69. Budget/Moderate.

West of Pacific Highway, in the rural area of Dural, is **Dural Village Caravan Park,** 269 New Line Rd., tel. (02) 9651-2555, with similar rates and facilities (as well as a tennis court), but is unsuitable for tent camping. Budget-Inexpensive.

Just 400 meters from North Narrabeen Beach

is **Lakeside Caravan Park,** Lake Park Rd., tel. (02) 9913-7845. Facilities are modern. Sites are $17-22, while comfortable cabins range $70-135. Budget/Moderate.

South

At Lady Robinsons Beach (safe swimming) on Botany Bay is **Grand Pines Caravan Park.** Facilities are good and there's a city bus stop just around the corner. Sites are $19 (no tents), on-site vans $30, and cabins $40-65. It's at 289 Grand Parade, which runs along Botany Bay, but access is one block west on Alfred St., tel. (02) 9529-7329. From the Princes Highway in Blakehurst, Ramsgate Rd. passes the park. Budget.

Farther south, in the picturesque township of Bundeena, is **Bundeena Caravan Park,** tel. (02) 9523-9520, in a quiet location a few blocks from the beach. Sites are $14-18, and cabins are $40-55. Budget-Inexpensive. The road to Bundeena passes through Royal National Park, where camping is at Bonnie Vale, two km from Bundeena. Facilities here include toilets, showers, and a laundry. For bookings, call (02) 9521-2230. Budget.

DOWNTOWN DINING

Cafés

The old officer's mess of **Hyde Park Barracks,** Queens Square, Macquarie St., has been converted to a pleasant café with tables tucked into a sunny corner of a large courtyard. Lunch averages around $10-12. As the name suggests, **Uptown Brasserie, Bar, & Cafe,** Level 3, Skygarden, Pitt St. Mall, has a section for all occasions. The café features strikingly innovative furniture that's worth a look even if you don't plan on eating. The café is good for those in a hurry, with fast efficient service and all the usual café fare (try for one of the tables overlooking busy Castlereagh Street). Also on Pitt St. Mall is the Strand Arcade, filled with stylish boutiques and a couple of cafes, including the **Old Sydney Coffee Shop,** where coffee is ground on the premises. The style and elegance of the Queen Victoria Building, on George St., is continued within its many small cafés. The pick of these is **Bar Cupola,** at street level. Highlights are the specially blended coffees, healthy breakfasts, and gourmet meat pies.

Food Courts and Other Cheap Eats

These popular eating spots are the best places in the city for quick and inexpensive meals, and there are generally enough choices to suit all tastes. One of the best food courts is on the ground floor of the Queen Victoria Building on George Street. While most food courts are buried in the lower floors of large complexes, **Skygarden,** on Pitt St. Mall, is in a stylish setting on the top floor. Outlets serve food from four continents, and there's even a bar serving champagne. In Chinatown, at the corner of Dixon and Goulburn Streets, is the **Chinatown Centre,** with a wide range of eateries; most dishes are less than $6. It's open daily 10 a.m.-10 p.m. Another Chinatown food court is in the **Sussex Centre,** between Dixon and Sussex Streets.

The **YWCA,** 5-11 Wentworth Ave., has a small inexpensive café. The setting is plain, but no dish costs more than $9. Open daily 7:30 a.m.-7 p.m. With similar prices and atmosphere is the cafeteria in **Woolworths,** on the corner of George and Park Streets. Down Park St. one block is the **Criterion Hotel,** with lunchtime counter meals from $5 and steak and salad for $8.50. **Bar Ace,** 624 George St., has a friendly atmosphere, pastas from $6.50, and steaks from $12. Opposite the Strand Arcade is **Soup Plus,** 383 George St., where four different soups are offered daily along with a blackboard menu with lunch dishes, including soup and lasagna for $5. Most dinner dishes are $7-12. The decor is plain, but the atmosphere is good. Open Mon.-Sat. noon-late. Live jazz is performed nightly. **Brasserie Cassis,** at street level in Chifley Square, corner Hunter and Elizabeth Streets, is a popular breakfast stop for local office workers, with cooked breakfasts from $9.

For vegetarian meals, head to **Bodhi,** 187 Hay St., tel. (02) 9212-2828, where dishes such as eggplant fritters start at $3 and main dishes range $5-12. It's open daily 11 a.m.-3 p.m. and 5-10 p.m. Slightly more expensive is **Minar Sona Restaurant,** 16 Wentworth Ave., tel. (02) 9283-4634, toward Darlinghurst, which offers a wide variety of vegetarian and Indian cuisine. It's best known for tandoori dishes ($11-15), but there are plenty of other choices.

Steak

For reasonably priced steaks cooked to perfection head to **Daniel's Steakhouse,** 1 Bent St., tel. (02) 9251-6977. The beef is all grain-fed, raised on the rich pastures of Queensland's Darling Downs. It's open weekdays only for lunch and dinner. Built as a candle factory in the 1830s, **Kingsley's,** 29 King St., tel. (02) 9262-4155, features exposed sandstone blocks decorated with prints of Australian folk heroes, such as Captain Cook and Ned Kelly, and polished wooden floors. Steaks are thick and juicy and cooked to perfection. Expect to pay from $22 for a main meal. Steaks come no better than those cooked at **Kable's** in the Regent of Sydney, 199 George St., tel. (02) 9238-0000. The setting is a long art deco room with tables set as if for royalty, including crystalware and silverware. As well as steak, the menu includes such delicacies as lobster from Tasmania and lamb from the Victorian Gippsland; main dishes range $24-40. Desserts are delicious and begin at $8. Open Tues.-Fri. noon-2:30 p.m. and Tues.-Sat. 6-10:30 p.m.

Australian

Few countries in the world encourage the consumption of their national emblem, but in Australia kangaroo and emu appear on many restaurant menus. **Edna's Table II,** Lobby Level, MLC Centre, Martin Place, tel. (02) 9231-1400, features decor that reflects the stunning ochre colors of the Outback and cool colors of the ocean, with grass trees decorating the room. The menu reflects typical bush tucker, cooked using native herbs. Open Mon.-Fri. for lunch and Tues.-Sat. for dinner.

Harbor Views

Harbour Take-out is on the west side of the Opera House (past the entrance to the Drama Theatre) with seating both under cover and out on the promenade. It's a good place for inexpensive seafood. Fish and chips starts at $6.50 and the filling Seafood Box is $10.50. Otherwise, cake and coffee is $4. It's open daily 10 a.m.-5:30 p.m. Also on the promenade is **Bennelong,** tel. (02) 9250-7300. This restaurant attracts a wide variety of diners but is most popular with tourists, mostly because of its location at Sydney's top tourist attraction. The atmosphere is casual yet smart, with seating inside or out,

dining in the shadow of the Opera House

and some of the best harbor views. The menu is eclectic, suiting the tastes of as many cultures as possible. Main dishes range $18-37, and wine can be bought by the glass. It's open Mon.-Sat. 10 a.m.-11 p.m., Sunday 10 a.m.-5 p.m. Above the main dining area is a cocktail lounge, where you can take in the stunning harbor panorama for the price of a beer.

Sydney has three revolving restaurants. Two of these are on the top of AMP Tower. The **International Restaurant,** on Level One 85 stories above the city streets, has (for a revolving restaurant) excellent food. The same menu is offered at lunch and dinner, with the former less expensive. On Level Two is a less-expensive restaurant with the same spectacular views. This eatery is self-service, with a large buffet that includes more than a dozen main courses, including a carvery, grills, seafood, and Asian dishes. Lunch is a reasonable $27.50 ($32.50 on Sunday) and dinner is $36.50 ($38.50 Saturday and Sunday). For bookings at either restaurant, call (02) 9233-

3722. The world's largest revolving restaurant is the **Summit,** on the 47th floor of Australia Square Tower, George St., tel. (02) 9247-9777. Needless to say, the views are stunning. Food is a little more expensive than the other two revolving restaurants, but there's also a buffet. Open daily for lunch and dinner.

Chinatown

Chinatown lies at the south end of downtown, in an area known as Haymarket, and is centered on Dixon Street. The street vendors, food halls, and bakeries provide inexpensive meals, but there is no lack of choice in any price category. For inexpensive no-frills Chinese food, try **Hingara Restaurant,** 82 Dixon St., tel. (02) 9212-2169, where the menu is pretty standard—dozens of soups and sweet and sour everything—but portions are good and the service is efficient. For similarly priced Cantonese-style Chinese head to **New Tai Yuen,** 31 Dixon St., tel. (02) 9212-5244. A longtime Chinatown favorite is **BBQ King,** 18 Goulburn St., tel. (02) 9267-2433, which, as the name suggests, specializes in barbecued meats. The atmosphere and decor are nothing special, but this restaurant is a good spot for a quick meal. The **Lantern Restaurant,** 515 Kent St., tel. (02) 9267-1153, has a lunchtime buffet for $7.90. **Marigold,** 683 George St., tel. (02) 9281-3388, an upmarket restaurant that wouldn't be out of place in Hong Kong, occupies two floors and seats around 800 diners at one sitting. It's the place to come for *yum cha,* a traditional form of eating small courses wheeled around from table to table on a trolley. Open daily 10 a.m.-3 p.m. and from 6 p.m. for dinner. Popular with locals is the bright and breezy **Emperor Garden,** 213 Thomas St., tel. (02) 9281-9899. Around the corner is **House of Guang Zhou,** 76 Ultimo St., tel. (02) 9281-2205, a well-established restaurant famed for its local seafood cooked Chinese-style.

Other Asian Restaurants

The streets around Chinatown are dotted with many Asian restaurants. **Minh-Hai,** 615 George St., tel. (02) 9281-1875, is a Vietnamese restaurant in the heart of Chinatown. Aside from garish lighting and plain decor, the food is delicious and very inexpensive. Most meals are around $7 (adventurous diners may want to try the fish por-

ridge). It's open Mon.-Sat. 10 a.m.-9:30 p.m. **Malaya,** 761 George St., tel. (02) 9211-0946, has been around for decades and was recently redecorated. The food, though, has stayed the same—the choice of cuisine from China, Malaysia, and Indonesia.

Matsukaze, Level 1, Chifley Plaza, Chifley Square, tel. (02) 9229-0191, specializes in tempura, a traditional method of deep-frying all manner of meats and vegetables in special oils. The lunch menu is simple and inexpensive ($20 for the set lunch), but it's the dinner that most people come for. Open weekdays only.

Greek

Diethnes, 336 Pitt St., tel. (02) 9267-8956, is an old favorite that has been serving up delicious Greek salads, calamari, moussaka, and lamb dishes for more than 40 years. Service is fast and friendly and the food reasonably priced. Closed Sunday. The **Hellenic Club,** 251 Elizabeth St., tel. (02) 9261-4910, is a staid, old restaurant, good for souvlaki. The dining room has unimpeded views across Hyde Park.

Italian

A Sydney institution is **Machiavelli,** 123 Clarence St., tel. (02) 9299-3748. This well-patronized restaurant is cavernous, with hanging sausages and hams adding a delicate touch. Lunch's main dishes average $18-20 (the antipasto is delicious), but there are a couple of offerings for around $15. Open for lunch Mon.-Fri. and for dinner Wed.-Friday. Another good choice for a casual Italian meal is **Primo's,** Queen Victoria Building, tel. (02) 9283-5093, decorated in mellow green and white with a few tables looking down on the bustle of shoppers. Light lunches are priced from $6.50 with more filling Italian specialties from $12.

If you've spent the morning exploring the Australian Museum, a great place for lunch is **Beppi's,** corner Stanley and Yurong Streets, tel. (02) 9360-4558, which celebrated 40 years of service in 1996.

Spanish

Around the intersection of Liverpool and Kent Streets is a small enclave of Spanish cafes, restaurants, and tapas bars. **Casa Asturiana,** 77 Liverpool St., tel. (02) 9264-1010, is a dimly lit, always-crowded restaurant with rows of solid wooden tables that draw diners to indulge in tapas, a Spanish specialty of small servings (two to three tapas with a salad will fill most stomachs). The 30-odd different tapas are priced $4.50, $5.50, and $6.50, making keeping to a budget easy. Open for lunch Tues.-Fri. and dinner Tues.-Sunday. A couple of doors away is **Capitan Torres,** 73 Liverpool St., tel. (02) 9264-5574, formerly one of Sydney's great cheap eats. Prices have risen over the last few years, but it's still good value. Seafood is the specialty, with portions generous. The mixed grill of seafood is especially good. Open daily for lunch and dinner.

The Rocks

This historic area west of Circular Quay has Sydney's largest concentration of cafes and restaurants but, unlike those in inner-city suburbs, they are geared mostly to tourists, and there are no real dining bargains. The **Rocks Cafe,** 99 George St., is a cozy little place with breakfasts that are surprisingly cheap for this popular tourist area. Next door is **Phillip's Foote,** 101 George St., tel. (02) 9241-1485, an English-style restaurant featuring a barbecue with grill-your-own steak, and a salad, for $18. Smaller meals are available in the café section from $6. It's open between noon and midnight. In an 1830s convict-built sandstone cottage with sloping wooden floors and crooked walls, the **Gumnut Tea Garden,** 28 Harrington St., has an authentic atmosphere. Seating is in one of many small rooms or outside along a wide shaded veranda. This is a great place for breakfast ($5-12), and it gets crowded at lunchtime, especially on weekends. For a no-frills pub-style meal head to **Orient Hotel,** at 89 George St., tel. (02) 9251-1255. Typical Aussie fare, such as meat pies, is on the menu, and no meal is more than $14. The most-pleasant eating area is a courtyard out the back of the pub.

In the Argyle Centre is the **Argyle Restaurant,** tel. (02) 9247-7782. The original structure, dating from 1828, remains, a good surrounding for the nightly "Jolly Swagman Show," which includes a three-course meal, sing-along, and sheep-shearing demonstration for adult $54, child $27. **Pina Zia Pizzeria,** 93 George St., tel. (02) 9247-2255, is a small restaurant that seems continuously full. The menu consists of two sizes of pizza, but a staggering variety of toppings are offered, with the most expensive $18. It's open for lunch and dinner daily.

Originally built as a jail, **Hero of Waterloo,** 81 Lower Fort St., tel. (02) 9252-4553, has been a licensed hotel since 1815. In its earlier days it was a rough-and-tough hangout, and while the look remains, today it's a lot tamer. Off the main bar is the Duke's Room, an old-world restaurant with lots of polished brass, old wooden tables, and gas lamps hanging from the rafters. The menu is varied and the food good. Expect to pay around $12-15 for a main meal. Friday-Sun. nights, folk musicians entertain diners.

Probably the best-placed of Sydney's restaurants is **Quay** in the Overseas Passenger Terminal at Circular Quay West, tel. (02) 9251-5600. Harbor views are stunning from all tables, with large wraparound glass windows. Apart from the views, friendly staff, and efficient service, it's recommended for the consistently good food upon which the restaurant has built its reputation. Specializing in modern Australian cuisine with a French influence, the steak is the major drawcard, but the menu changes regularly and features cuisine from any of a dozen countries. Expect to pay from $60 pp for a three-course dinner; lunch is markedly less expensive. In the same top-end price range is **Rockpool,** 107 George St., tel. (02) 9252-1888, featuring modern Australian cuisine with an Asian and Mediterranean influence. While "in" restaurants come and go almost overnight, Rockpool has remained a favorite place for a splurge with Sydneysiders for over a decade. The restaurant lacks for nothing—the service, atmosphere, and most important, the food are rarely faulted. It's open weekdays for lunch and Mon.-Sat. for dinner.

Darling Harbour Dining

Along the promenade of Harbourside Festival Marketplace is a string of restaurants with seating inside and out, but the prime location means prices are high. Best of the bunch is **Jordon's,** tel. (02) 9281-3711, offering fish and chips from $17.50. On the southern promenade is **Wockpool,** tel. (02) 9211-9888, a very stylish Chinese restaurant where the service is impeccable and the food renowned. It's also very expensive; the noodle bar costs $15 pp, otherwise mains range $28-40. Near the Chinese Garden is the **Pump-**

house Tavern, tel. (02) 9281-3967, best-known for its in-house brewery, but it also serves up good counter meals ranging $8.50-16.

RESTAURANTS IN OTHER PARTS OF THE CITY

East Sydney

Within this old suburb east of Hyde Park is an enclave of bistro-style restaurants that come alive each lunchtime with the business crowd. **The eDGE,** 60 Riley St., tel. (02) 9360-1372, is a large, noisy eatery best-known for delicious pizza (from $14), but also for offering crisp salads, a great variety of pastas, and a legendary seafood antipasto. The desserts are especially delicious. No reservations are taken, but there's a bar where you can wait for a table. Around the corner, on Stanley St., is a string of small restaurants. **Two Chefs on Stanley,** 115 Riley St., tel. (02) 9331-1559, is a stylish eatery with large windows overlooking the leafy streets. The emphasis is on good food, and best value is the fixed-price lunch for $19.50. It's also open for dinner. **No Name,** 2 Chapel St., tel. (02) 9360-4711, which can be entered from Stanley St. through the Arch Cafe, is the ultimate no-frills restaurant. No reservations are taken, and there's basically no decor, but the food is surprisingly good, and most meals are less than $8. Open daily for lunch and dinner.

Darlinghurst

Immediately south of East Sydney, **Onde,** a small French bistro, lies at 346 Liverpool St., tel. (02) 9331-8749. You'll find all sorts of diners here, but it's most popular with the locals. The atmosphere is casual—no bookings are taken, and most people choose from the blackboard menu. It's open for dinner only. In Darlinghurst proper, **Silver Spoon,** 203 Oxford St., tel. (02) 9360-4669, is a great little restaurant serving up the gently spiced food of Thailand, much of it prepared using local seafood. Expect to pay around $12-15 for a main meal. It's open daily for lunch and dinner. **Kim's,** 235 Oxford St., tel. (02) 9357-5429, is a very small two-story Vietnamese restaurant where the food and atmosphere are surprisingly good for the price you pay—$8-10 for a main meal. It's open for dinner only and closed Tuesday.

Oh Calcutta, 251 Victoria St., tel. (02) 9360-3650, which features dishes from across the subcontinent, has some very hot tandoori choices. Main dishes are from $8. Open for dinner daily. In the same part of Darlinghurst is **Dov,** corner Forbes and Burton Streets, tel. (02) 9360-9594, a small, stylishly decorated place serving a wide range of dishes, but all well-prepared and inexpensive. Most dishes are about $12. Open Mon.-Sat. 6:30 a.m.-10 p.m. One block south is Victoria Park and the **Bandstand Café,** 301 Victoria St., tel. (02) 9360-9266. This converted bandstand is surrounded by outdoor tables, or dine inside and upstairs. Lunch is a casual affair, with salad platters ($8-15) a favorite, but it's also open for dinner.

Kings Cross

The **Lazy Owl Café,** 220 William St., is an inexpensive, no frills breakfast hangout. A cooked breakfast is $5, while the rest of the day pastas, salads, and sandwiches start at $6. The **Astoria Restaurant,** 7 Darlinghurst Rd., tel. (02) 9358-6327, is a no-frills place with roast dinners for around $5, and desserts, such as canned fruit with a dollop of ice cream, from $1. It's open Mon.-Sat. 10:30 a.m.-2:30 p.m. and for dinner 4-8:30 p.m. Developed to suit the demands of U.S. servicemen on R&R in the 1960s, the **Bourbon and Beefsteak Bar,** 24 Darlinghurst Rd., tel. (02) 9358-1144, still rages 24 hours a day. The breakfast menu could be right out of a U.S. roadside diner—hash browns, pancakes, and omelettes—while the rest of the day dishes such as Son-of-a-bitch Cowpoke Stew are offered.

The casual **Bayswater Brasserie,** 32 Bayswater Rd., tel. (02) 9357-2177, is a popular spot, considered by many to be the best bar/bistro in the city. Food is reasonably priced, service friendly, and it's one place that retains its popularity through the years. It's possible to just drop by for a cappuccino. The Sunday brunch (10 a.m.-5 p.m.) is very popular, while the rest of the week it's open for lunch and dinner. Tiny **Cafe Pralinka,** 4 Roslyn St., tel. (02) 9358-1553, is an inexpensive spot with just five tables. The fare is pretty standard but portions are good, and no dish costs more than $8. Open Tues.-Sat. 11 a.m.-9 p.m.

At the south end of Kings Cross is **Sirocco,** 23 Craigend St., tel. (02) 9332-4495, a wide-open restaurant with an open kitchen and a hint of

Mediterranean style. The setting is stylish and the food modern Australian, which usually means local ingredients cooked in a style from overseas. Open daily except Monday for lunch and dinner.

Along Kellett St. are nightspots and late-night restaurants. Pick of the bunch is **Lime and Lemongrass**, 42 Kellett St., tel. (02) 9358-5577, a Thai restaurant and cocktail bar open daily 6 p.m.-4 a.m. Tables are inside and out and the food is very good. Main meals are a reasonable $10-16.

Woolloomooloo

One of Sydney's legendary eating spots, **Harry's Cafe de Wheels**, on Cowper Wharf Rd., has no tables and doesn't even open until 9 p.m. But for decades this pie wagon has been serving pies and hot drinks to regular clientele that vary from shift workers to visiting celebrities. Once the haunt of only thirsty wharfies, the **Woolloomooloo Bay Hotel**, 2 Bourke St., tel. (02) 9357-1177, now has a stylish bistro with an interesting blackboard menu and a pianist tickling the keys every evening. Open daily 11 a.m.-9 p.m.

Surry Hills

This revitalized suburb extends from the back streets around Central Station through leafy streets lined with terraces to a large Lebanese community centered on the junction of Cleveland and Elizabeth Streets. The Lebanese restaurants in this area differ greatly in quality. **Gazal Restaurant**, 286 Cleveland St., tel. (02) 9318-1982, is one of the best, with a great variety of dips for about $5 and main meals about $9. For takeaway, try **Abdul's**, across the road.

One block up Crown St. from the Lebanese restaurants, at Devonshire St., is **Rustic Cafe**, a popular spot (with a distinctive bright yellow exterior) where the coffee is ground on the premises daily and they serve tasty pastries. One block to the east, at 633 Bourke St., is **La Passion Du Fruit**, a great little café with a few tables on the sidewalk and plenty of reading material inside. As well as serving great coffee, they serve light snacks, with the emphasis on healthy eating. Soups are $5, and other dishes average $10. Desserts range $3-5. Open Mon.-Sat. 8 a.m.-5 p.m., Sunday 11 a.m.-4 p.m. **Dolphin Hotel**, 412 Crown St., tel. (02) 9331-4800, has fantastic pub food and a good beer

garden. The T-bone steaks are particularly good, and for an extra $7 you can have unlimited servings of salad. Open daily for lunch noon-2 p.m., dinner 6-9 p.m. With a very different atmosphere, **MG Garage**, 490 Crown St., tel. (02) 9383-9383, has quickly gained a following, for its setup as much as the food. The restaurant doubles as a showroom for MGs, with tables set around the showroom floor. **Strelitzia**, 26 Buckingham St., tel. (02) 9698-3349, is a terrace dating from early this century that has been transformed into a cozy restaurant with an open fire and balcony. Some of the best dishes are char-grilled, including chicken breast and kangaroo. All main dishes are $18 and desserts are $8. Open weekdays for lunch and Tues.-Sat. for dinner.

Glebe

In recent times, the main street of this old inner-city suburb has been transformed to a trendy café and restaurant precinct. Many places cater to the university folks who hang out at cafes like **Well Connected**, 35 Glebe Point Rd., which allows coffee-guzzlers to surf the Internet. **Rose Blue Cafe**, 23 Glebe Point Rd., is seemingly out of place in Glebe, with a relaxed atmosphere and plenty of room between tables. Out back is a large courtyard terrace, the perfect place to relax with a slab of one of many delicious cakes and a strong coffee ($6.50). Other meals are available, including breakfasts from $3, with many American-style choices such as eggs Benedict and omelets from $8.50. The rest of the day a wide variety of dishes are offered, with the Caesar salad ($10.50) especially good. **Yak and Yeti**, 41 Glebe Point Rd., tel. (02) 9552-1220, is a small eatery serving up the traditional Nepalese cuisine in a simple yet stylish setting. Open daily 6-10:30 p.m.

Eastern Suburbs

In Double Bay is **The Cleveland**, 63 Bay St., tel. (02) 9327-6877, one of Sydney's most stylish Chinese restaurants. The restaurant is divided in two sections—downstairs is Bhuddist-style vegetarian and upstairs is Sichuan. Open daily for lunch and dinner.

In Nielson Park, Vaucluse, opposite a beautiful little beach and surrounded by Moreton Bay figs, an old kiosk has been converted to a stylish

Italian restaurant with a casual atmosphere. Open for a hot or cold buffet breakfast on Sunday, lunch Tues.-Sun., and dinner Fri.-Sunday. Located on Graycliffe Ave., tel. (02) 9337-1574.

Doyle's on the Beach

Eating at this famous restaurant is a Sydney dining experience you shouldn't miss. The restaurant, overlooking Watsons Bay, is a hive of activity in summer and a peaceful retreat the rest of the year. The best way to arrive is by water taxi from Circular Quay (last one departs at 3 p.m.). Seafood is what draws the crowds, and they rarely leave disappointed. The selection is varied, ranging from grilled fish to a mixed seafood platter. Desserts are also good. It's open daily noon-3 p.m. and 6-9:30 p.m. Located at 11 Marine Parade, tel. (02) 9337-2007.

Bondi Beach

The year-round summer atmosphere of Bondi makes this seaside suburb a good place for outdoor dining. If you're staying at the Alice Motel (or even if you're not) don't miss breakfast in the small restaurant overlooking Tamarama Bay. Located at 30 Fletcher St., tel. (02) 9130-5231. Another popular spot with locals for breakfast is **Bondi Diggers Café,** 232 Campbell Parade, open daily from 7 a.m.

Right on busy Campbell Parade is a string of cafés and restaurants of very different standards. Lunch in Bondi is typically fish and chips. For this, head to **Bondi Surf Seafoods** at 128 Campbell Parade, where it'll cost from $4.50. One of Bondi's original cafes is **Bates Milk Bar,** at 126 Campbell Parade, with surf murals on the walls, chrome chairs, and speckled laminex tables. Service is friendly and efficient, and the burgers are as good as they get for less than $5. At the opposite end of the to-be-seen-at scale are the cafes clustered around the corner of Campbell Parade and Lamrock Avenue. Right on the corner of these streets is trendy **Le Crepe Cafe,** while next door is a similar set-up, **Hugo's.** Despite walls covered in sporting memorabilia, the **Sports Bard,** 32 Campbell Parade, tel. (02) 9130-4582, manages to retain a sense of style and has a definite casual "Bondi" vibe. The menu isn't extensive, but is varied and moderately priced. It's open Sat.-Sun. 10 a.m.-3 p.m. and daily for dinner from 5 p.m.

Toward North Bondi and overlooking the beach is **Bondi Aquabar,** 266 Campbell Parade, tel. (02) 9130-6070. This place is bright, casual, and has a varied menu. A couple of doors farther north, **Sean's Panorama,** 270 Campbell Parade, tel. (02) 9365-4924, looks fairly nondescript from the street, but inside the decor is funky and the food prepared by one of Sydney's most highly respected up-and-coming chefs. The breakfasts here are legendary.

Away from the beach is **Love in a Cup,** 106 Glenayr Ave., a popular local hangout for sipping coffee in the sun; open daily from 7 a.m. Also away from Campbell Parade are a couple of good restaurants. Opposite City Beach Motor Inn is **Intra Thai,** 90 Curlewis St., tel. (02) 9130-3342, a budget restaurant with surprising style, right down to its white tablecloths and attentive waiters. Expect to pay less than $40 for a filling meal for two. In the same area is **Little Snail,** 96 Curlewis St., tel. (02) 9365-4847, an inexpensive French restaurant open Mon.-Fri. for lunch and nightly for dinner. The best deal is the fixed-price three-course dinner for $28.

Southern Beaches

Coogee isn't exactly the culinary center of Sydney, but **Barzura,** 62 Carr St., tel. (02) 9665-5546, has plenty of choices, is licensed, and, best of all, has great ocean views. **Boatshed Cafe** is exactly that—an old boatshed overlooking Botany Bay. It's right on the beach at La Perouse, tel. (02) 9661-9315.

North Shore

Since being bypassed by the freeway a few years back, Crows Nest, immediately north of North Sydney, has become a lot quieter. But that hasn't changed the brisk trade at **Eric's Seafood Cafe,** 316 Pacific Hwy., tel. (02) 9436-4906, which has been serving fish and chips since the 1920s. Surprisingly, one of Sydney's best-loved Chinese restaurants is in the commercial area of Crows Nest, well away from Chinatown. It's **Peacock Gardens,** 100 Alexander St., tel. (02) 9439-8786, where the local specialty is *sang choy bow* with seafood substituted for the usual generic meat.

For an intriguing mix of cuisine from Morocco and Sri Lanka, head to **Mosquito Bar,** 142 Spit Rd., tel. (02) 9968-1801. Main meals are a reasonable $8-14. Open for dinner Mon.-Sat. 6-10 p.m.

Manly and the Northern Beaches

For inexpensive fish and chips, deep-fried to perfection in olive oil, head to **Manly Fish Market and Cafe,** at 25 South Steyne; fish, chips, and a salad is around $8. Along the Corso are other casual seafood joints, including **Cristals,** 90 the Corso, tel. (02) 9977-3758, with tables spread around the Corso. Seafood dishes start at $11 and it's also open for breakfast (croissants here are delicious). Along the Steyne, either side of the Corso, are trendy cafes and restaurants. South of the Corso is the large **Rimini Fish Cafe,** 35 South Steyne, tel. (02) 9977-3880, with tiered levels of tables opening to ocean views. Diners have a choice of Land or Ocean menus, with the Grilled Barramundi especially good for $17.50. It's open daily for all meals. Farther along, at 25 Wentworth St., is **Cafe Nice,** tel. (02) 9976-3658, serving up good coffee and with daily newspapers to read.

On North Steyne are still more eateries, including **Wi Marn,** 47 North Steyne, tel. (02) 9976-2995, specializing in seafood cooked in Thai style. **Manly Pier Restaurant,** Commonwealth Ave., tel. (02) 9949-1994, is a stylish and simply furnished restaurant where the main feature is the view across Manly Cove through massive glass windows. Seafood is the specialty, with most main meals about $20 and all desserts $8.50.

Traditionally, meat pies have been a staple at breakfast for many Australians. But, the pies at **Sylvia and Fran's Upper Crust,** at 1003 Pittwater Rd., Collaroy, deserve better. They are very popular and many varieties are offered. **Surfside Pie Shop,** 383 Barrenjoey Rd., Newport, is equally good, and the cooks use real cream in their cream buns. Farther north, at 231 Whale Beach Rd., Whale Beach, is **Whaley's,** tel. (02) 9974-4121, a good place for a healthy burger.

A great luncheon spot on Sydney's northernmost beach, Palm Beach, is **La Palma,** 1108 Barrenjoey Rd., tel. (02) 9974-4001, which has a lovely outdoor eating area. The food is well-prepared and the freshest of ingredients are used. Dinner main dishes average $18-20, with lunchtime prices considerably lower. Open daily for lunch and dinner.

GETTING THERE

Air

Sydney Airport (officially known as **Kingsford Smith,** but also called Mascot, for the suburb it's in) is on Botany Bay, surrounded by urban sprawl 15 km south of the city center. More passengers pass through this gateway than any other Australian airport, and for more than a decade there has been talk of developing a brand-new airport. A site, 40 km west of downtown at Badgerys Creek, had been decided upon, but, at last report, the airport will be remain at Mascot for at least another decade. A third runway has been developed at Sydney to handle ever-increasing passenger numbers. Road links were also upgraded, including to downtown, with a tunnel diverting northbound traffic away from the congested downtown streets.

In the International Terminal you'll find car rental companies, **Tourism NSW** information and booking desks (both are open daily 6 a.m. until the arrival of the last flight; ask for hotel discounts), a post office, currency exchange, lockers, duty-free shops, showers, restaurants, and bars.

The best way to arrive in Sydney is aboard the flying kangaroo, **Qantas,** tel. (13) 1313 or, from North America, tel. (800) 227-4500. Qantas flights originate from major centers around the world, providing a little Aussie culture before arriving down under. Other international carriers arriving in Sydney are: **Air Italia, Air New Zealand, Ansett Australia, British Airways, Canadian Airlines, Japan Air Lines, Lauda Air, Malaysian Air System, Singapore Airlines,** and **United Airlines,** as well as many Pacific Island airlines. Around a dozen domestic carriers serve Sydney Airport, but, with the exception of **Impulse,** tel. (13) 1381, flying to rural and coastal New South Wales, flights to all centers can be booked through **Ansett Australia,** tel. (13) 1300, or **Qantas,** tel. (13) 1313. To call these airlines from North America, call (800) 366-1300 and (800) 227-4500, respectively.

The distinctive green and yellow **Airport Express,** tel. (13) 1500, operates a regular service between both airport terminals and downtown (Route 300) and Kings Cross (Route 350), stopping at points throughout the city. Departures are every 10-20 minutes between 6 a.m. and 1 p.m. The fare is $6 one-way, $10 roundtrip. A transfer between the two terminals is $2.50. **Kingsford Smith Transport,** tel. (02) 9667-3221, operates from both terminals, dropping passengers right at the door of all city and inner suburban accommodations. The fare is $6 each way. A cab between the airport and downtown runs about $25-30.

Rail
Countrylink, tel. (13) 2232, operates an extensive rail service throughout the state, with bus connections to smaller centers. **Central Station,** at the south end of downtown, is the main interstate and intrastate terminal. Fares are comparable to traveling by bus, with transport and accommodation packages often making rail travel even cheaper. Within New South Wales, rail services run along the north coast, west to Bathurst and Dubbo, and south through Canberra to Albury.

Bus
Also at Central Station is the **Sydney Coach Terminal,** on the corner of Eddy Ave. and Pitt Street. **Greyhound Pioneer,** tel. (13) 2030, operates the most extensive network of bus services, with daily service from Sydney to all state capitals as well as most major towns throughout the country. The other major carrier is **McCafferty's,** tel. (13) 4499, which also runs throughout Australia.

    Oz Experience, tel. (02) 9907-0522, operates an alternative bus service along the east coast, with stops made at points of interest en route and nights spent at backpacker lodges. The trip between Sydney and Cairns takes nine days. Within North America bookings can be made through any STA agent.

GETTING AROUND

Transport around Sydney is provided by the **State Transit Authority,** with information desks at Central Station, Circular Quay, and at the Queen Victoria Building on George St., tel. (13) 1500. The best deal for extensive sightseeing is a **SydneyPass,** which allows unlimited travel on buses, ferries, the *RiverCat* to Parramatta, Airport

Express services, some harbor cruises, and the Sydney Explorer bus. The cost is three days $70, five days $95, and seven days $110. Call (13) 1500 for details. The passes can be purchased from both airport terminals, Circular Quay booking agents, and all Tourist Information Centres.

Rail
The suburban rail service covers most parts of the city (except the northern beaches), and, because of heavy road traffic, it's often quicker than bus travel. The City Circle line runs underground, linking Central Station to Town Hall, Wynyard, Circular Quay, and Hyde Park; $1.30 per sector. Other main routes from Central are to Bondi, Cronulla, Parramatta, and across the Harbour Bridge to North Sydney and the North Shore. A City Hopper ticket ($2.20) allows one day's unlimited train travel Mon.-Fri. after 9 a.m. and all weekend. For all local rail travel, call (13) 1500.

Bus
State Transit buses run throughout the city but travel is slow compared to trains, especially during peak hours. The main downtown bus stops are at Circular Quay, Railway Square (Central Station), and Wynyard Park. The best source of bus information is the kiosk on Alfred St., Circular Quay. Fares start at $1.30 per sector (about four km), with the maximum you'll pay $4.40 for the 44-km trip between downtown and Palm Beach. Buses run daily 4:30 a.m.-11:30 p.m., with less-frequent weekend services.

    The easy-to-recognize red **Sydney Explorer,** operated by State Transit, runs every 20 minutes on a 90-minute loop between 24 of the city's top attractions. The ticket price of $25 (included in the SydneyPass; see above) includes discounts at many attractions. They can be bought onboard the bus or at any State Transit office. The service runs daily 9 a.m.-7 p.m. The blue **Bondi & Bay Explorer** has a similar format, running from Circular Quay through Kings Cross, Double Bay, and Watsons Bay to famous Bondi Beach every 30 minutes. Tickets are $25.

Monorail
The state-of-the-art monorail connects Darling Harbour with Chinatown, George St., and Pitt St. (travel is counterclockwise), whisking passengers along high above the congested streets

below. It operates Mon.-Wed. 7 a.m.-10 p.m., Thurs.-Fri. 7 a.m.-midnight, Saturday 8 a.m.-midnight, Sunday 9 a.m.-8 p.m. Travel costs $3, with no limit to how far you can travel. A day pass is $7.

Ferry

The ferries of Sydney Harbour are the most scenic way to travel around the city. From Circular Quay Ferry Terminal ferries run to Balmain, Sydney Aquarium, Darling Harbour, McMahons Point, Kirribilli, Cremorne Point, Mosman, Taronga Zoo, Manly, Rose Bay, and Watsons Bay. Fares range $3.20 for the trip to Darling Harbour to $4 for the 35-minute trip across to Manly. Another way to get to Manly is aboard the high-speed *JetCat;* $5.20 each way. The high-speed *RiverCat* runs up the Parramatta River to Parramatta ($5.80), passing Sydney Olympic Park. All the above services are covered on the SydneyPass. Ferries run daily 5:30 a.m.-midnight. For further ferry information, head to the small information center behind Wharf 4 at Circular Quay or call (13) 1500.

Taxi

Cabs run throughout the city 24 hours a day. Flag charge is $3, then $1.75 per km. Taxi ranks are throughout the city, but the best places to look for a cab are outside railway stations and major downtown hotels. Otherwise, call: **Legion Cabs,** tel. (13) 1451; **RSL Taxis,** tel. (13) 1581; or **Taxis Combined,** tel. (02) 9332-8888.

Water taxis run around the harbor but are expensive. Sample fares from Circular Quay are Kirribilli $8 pp, Darling Harbour $10, Watsons Bay $40. For bookings, call **Taxis Afloat** at (02) 9955-3222.

Car

The major car rental companies have desks at both the International and Domestic Terminals of Sydney Airport. Otherwise call: **Avis,** tel. (02) 9353-9000; **Budget,** tel. (13) 2727; **Dollar,** tel. (02) 9223-1444; **Hertz,** tel. (13) 3039; or **Thrifty,** tel. (02) 9380-5399. Rates from these companies range $75-105 per day depending on car size, km allowances, and insurance inclusions, but rates are often lower. With branches throughout the city, **Ascot,** tel. (02) 9317-2111, is a lot cheaper, with new cars from $30 a day and $36 for medium-sized cars for long-term rentals. A number of companies rent second-hand cars, including **Down Under Rent-a-car,** tel. (02) 9971-8447. **Maui,** tel. (02) 9597-6155 or (1800) 22-7279, operates a massive fleet of campervans that can be rented from $85 per day.

If you plan a long stay in Australia, buying a car is the best option. A car market popular with travelers is on the corner of Ward Ave. and Elizabeth Bay Rd., Kings Cross. Sellers are charged $35 per week to display their vehicles there; open daily. On a Sunday, Flemington Car Market, right by Flemington Railway Station, is a good bet for a wide range of vehicles.

Circular Quay is the terminus of all manner of boats, from cruise ships to commuter ferries.

Pyrmont Bridge

Bicycle

Sydney certainly isn't the best city in the world for cycling, but there are a few interesting routes around the inner city. Centennial Park makes for good downtown cycling; **Centennial Park Cycles,** tel. (02) 9398-8138, rents both bikes and in-line skates for $10 per hour. **Inner City Cycles,** 31 Glebe Point Rd., Glebe, tel. (02) 9660-6605, has good bikes for $35 a day, $55 for a weekend, and $125 a week. Similarly priced is **Bicycles in the City,** Orwell St., Kings Cross, tel. (02) 9380-2939. On the north side of harbor, **Manly Cycle Centre,** 36 Pittwater Rd., Manly, tel. (02) 9977-1189, is well priced with bikes for $6 an hour and $75 a week.

Tours

Apart from the Sydney Explorer (see above), many private operators offer tours of the city and its surrounds. The main companies are **Clipper Gray Line Tours,** tel. (9252) 4499; **Murray's,** tel. (02) 9252-3590; and **Australian Pa-**

cific Tours, tel. (13) 1304. Typically, a tour of the city and Northern Beaches is $44-55, of the city and Bondi is $38-45, and a full-day tour including lunch and a harbor cruise is around $90-100. These companies also offer night tours that take in various lookouts with the option of dinner or a visit to Star City. Look for their brochures at all information centers and pick an itinerary that best suits your needs. **Australian Pacific Tours,** tel. (13) 1304, has a popular Night Lights and Sights tour in a double-decker bus for $40 and the famous After Dark Tour, which includes dining in AMP Tower Restaurant, viewing Les Girls Revue, and visiting Kings Cross; $115 pp.

Harbor Cruises

Captain Cook Cruises, based at Wharf 6, Circular Quay, tel. (02) 9206-1111, offers a great variety of cruises to destinations around the harbor. The Coffee Cruise passes all the major points of interest, departing daily at 10 a.m. and 2:15 p.m.; adult $32, child $20. The Harbour Highlights Cruise is shorter, passing sights around the Harbour Bridge. Departures are five times daily; adult $18, child $12.50. Other tours include Fort Denison (departs 10 a.m., noon, and 2 p.m.; adult $10, child $7.50), a Luncheon Cruise (departs 12:30 p.m.; adult $50, child $37), which features fresh seafood, and the Showtime Dinner Cruise (departs 7:30 p.m.; adult $89, child $52). This company also operates the hourly **Sydney Harbour Explorer,** which stops at six major harbor attractions between 9 a.m. and 5 p.m.; adult $20, child $12.

SERVICES

Sydney's **general post office** is in Martin Place, between Pitt and George Streets. It's open Mon.-Fri. 8:15 a.m.-5:30 p.m., Saturday 8:30 a.m.-noon. Computer terminals have been set up for visitors to check General Delivery (address to General Delivery, GPO, Sydney, NSW 2001). **Travelex Australia** has foreign money exchange outlets throughout the city, including at both airport terminals, in Martin Place at 37 Pitt St., 167 Macquarie St., and 182 George St., and in Kings Cross at 48 Darlinghurst Road. **American Express** is at 92 Pitt St., tel. (02) 9239-0666. All major banks will also cash traveler's checks; those in a foreign currency often entail a fee.

Without a doubt, **Global Gossip,** 770 George St., tel. (02) 9212-1466, is the best place to go for your Internet needs. Public access is $10 an hour. They also offer an inexpensive phone and fax service, scanning, and photocopying. **Travellers Contact Point,** Suite 11-15, 7th Floor, 428 George St., tel. (02) 9221-8744, is also centrally located and offers the same services. In Darlinghurst, head to the **Internet Café,** Top of the Town Hotel, 227 Victoria St., tel. (02) 9360-1911.

One-hour photo developing shops are scattered throughout the city, but one that I've found to be very professional is **Jadon Digital** on Level 6, 89 York St., tel. (02) 9262-1114. For purchasing photographic equipment, **Paxton's,** 285 George St., tel. (02) 9299-2999, is well priced, with some good duty-free buys.

Along Kent St., behind Town Hall, are shops specializing in adventure travel. This is also the location of **YHA Travel,** 422 Kent St., tel. (02) 9261-1111.

The **Flight Centre** is the best place to search out inexpensive tickets for onward travel. The branch at 580 George St., tel. (02) 9267-2999, is central, or call (13) 1600 for quotes over the phone. The folks at **Surf Travel Co.,** 2/25 Cronulla Plaza, tel. (02) 9527-4722, specializing in travel for surfers and snowboarders, are experts in onward travel through Indonesia and the Pacific Ocean, as well as adventure tours through New Zealand. The airfares they offer are also competitive.

Most better accommodations and backpacker lodges have a laundry for guest use. Otherwise, try: **Tina Coin Laundry,** 148 Glenayr Ave., Bondi; **Soap Sud City,** 56 Bayswater Rd., Kings Cross; **St. Johns Laundromat,** 176 St. Johns Rd., Glebe; **Pacific Laundry,** 10 Campbell Parade, Bondi Beach; **Manly Beach Laundrette,** 28 Darley Rd., Manly; **Argyle Place Laundry,** 9 Argyle Place, The Rocks.

Travellers Contact Point

Located at Suite 11-15, 7th Floor, 428 George St., tel. (02) 9221-8744, website: www.travellers.com.au, Travellers Contact Point deals with all travel questions, including accommodations, employment, Sydney tourist information, travel insurance, visa and immigration informa-

tion, and tips on buying and registering a car. Also available is public Internet access and a mail holding service. They're also an agent for adventure tour operators, major bus companies, and New Zealand tour operators. They are open Mon.-Fri. 9 a.m.-6 p.m., Saturday 10 a.m.-4 p.m.

Emergency Services

Sydney's main hospitals are: **Sydney Hospital,** Macquarie St., Sydney, tel. (02) 9382-7111; **St. Vincents Hospital,** corner Victoria and Burton Streets, Darlinghurst, tel. (02) 9339-1111; **Royal Prince Alfred Hospital,** Missenden Rd., Camperdown, tel. (02) 9515-6111; and **Children's Hospital,** Hawkesbury Rd., Westmead, tel. (02) 9845-0000. The **Traveller's Medical & Vaccination Centre** is on Level 7, 428 George St., tel. (02) 9221-7133. It's open Mon.-Wed. 9 a.m.-6 p.m., Thursday 9 a.m.-8 p.m., Friday 9 a.m.-6 p.m., Saturday 9 a.m.-1 p.m.

INFORMATION

State Library of New South Wales

This magnificent library faces Macquarie St., tel. (02) 9230-1414, and is sandwiched between a line of colonial-era buildings. The original library, now known as the **Mitchell Wing,** is a cavernous room housing rare and antiquarian books on shelves around a three-story-high atrium that's lit by a massive skylight. On this wing's lobby floor is a mosaic reproduction of Abel Tasman's map of Australia. Through a walkway and past the library café is the modern wing, with the main collection of general reference books, audiovisuals, and newspapers and magazines from around the world. The library is open Mon.-Fri. 9 a.m.-9 p.m., Sat.-Sun. 11 a.m.-5 p.m.

Bookstores

The **Travel Bookshop,** 175 Liverpool St., tel. (02) 9261-8200, has an extensive range of books to all Australian destinations, including cycling, hiking, climbing, and cruising guides. It's open daily. **Angus and Robertson** has a bookshop in the Imperial Arcade, 174-186 Pitt St., tel. (02) 9235-1188, and **Dymocks** is at 428 George St., tel. (02) 9235-0155. Specializing in rare and antiquarian books is **Berkelouw Book Sellers,** 19 Oxford St., Paddington, tel. (02) 9360-3200. If

Mitchell Wing,
State Library

you're heading south on the Hume Highway, it's worth stopping at their main shop, **Berkelouw** in Berrima, tel. (02) 4877-1370. Another antiquarian bookseller is the **Old Church Bookshop,** at 346 Marsden Rd., in the western suburb of Carlingford, tel. (02) 9872-3802.

Information Centers
Coming off an international flight, the first place you should stop is the **Travellers Information Centre,** in the International Terminal. It's open every day of the year from 6 a.m. until the arrival of the day's last flight. The **Sydney Visitor Centre,** 106 George St., The Rocks, tel. (02) 9255-1788 or (1800) 06-7676, website: www.scvb.com.au, in a

building dating from the 1860s, has lots of brochures as well as books and maps for sale; open daily 9 a.m.-6 p.m. In the adjacent Cadman's Cottage is a **National Parks and Wildlife Service information center,** tel. (02) 9247-5033, website: www.npws.gov.au. Out in beachside Manly is **Manly Visitors Information Bureau,** South Steyne St., tel. (02) 9977-1088, open daily 10 a.m.-4 p.m. The New South Wales automobile club is the **National Roads and Motorists Association** (NRMA), with an office at 151 Clarence St., tel. (02) 9260-9222. For members of affiliated clubs, maps and accommodation guides are free. This office is open Mon.-Fri. 8:30 a.m.-5 p.m., Saturday 8:30 a.m.-11:30 a.m.

SOUTH COAST

Two main roads connect Melbourne and Sydney: the Hume Highway, which is the most direct, and the Princes Highway, which follows the coast. Along the Hume Highway, the trip between the two cities can be done in one day, while the Princes Highway takes longer, passing small seaside towns, glorious stretches of beach, and many coastal national parks. A good compromise is to take the Hume Highway through the southern highlands, before crossing to the coast at Kiama. As you get farther from Sydney, crowds become nonexistent (except in summer) and the beaches more appealing. Some of the better spots are the holiday towns of Kiama, Merimbula, Tathra, and Eden, while the national parks of Jervis Bay, Murramarang, and Ben Boyd protect long stretches of spectacular coastline.

Sydney to Wollongong

Southbound travelers are presented with two very different options for the short drive to Wollongong. The Princes Highway follows the ridge of the Illawarra Escarpment, with panoramic views of the coast at places like Stanwell Tops (a favorite spot for hang-gliding enthusiasts). The other option is a winding road that passes through a string of coastal communities sandwiched between the ocean and escarpment. Northernmost of these communities is **Stanwell Park,** which lies behind a sandy beach where offshore sandbars create waves popular with surfers.

WOLLONGONG

Located 80 km south of Sydney, Wollongong (pop. 221,000) is Australia's seventh-largest city. It has been a major industrial center since the 1940s, with **Port Kembla** the industrial heart.

Wollongong's main thoroughfare is **Crown St.,** part of which is a pedestrian mall. In the mall is an information center, which has walking tour maps outlining the many historic buildings around downtown. On Market St., one block from Crown St., is a small **museum.** Before Port Kembla was developed, coal was shipped from a small harbor at the end of Marine Drive. Out on the point stands a lighthouse built in 1872; open for inspection Sat.-Sun. 1-4 p.m.

Accommodations and Food

Beach Park Motor Inn, 10 Pleasant Ave., tel. (02) 4226-1577, overlooks the beach at North Wollongong; $55 s, $65 d. Moderate. If you must stay close to the city center, try **Downtown Motel,** 76 Crown St., tel. (02) 4229-8344, where rooms are small but clean; $65 s, $68 d. Moderate. North from Wollongong, Corrimal and Bulli have council-run campgrounds, with sites for $15 and cabins from $50. Budget-Inexpensive. Another option is **Wollongong Surf Leisure Resort,** Pioneer Rd., tel. (02) 4283-6999, right on the beach at Fairy Meadow. Facilities include an indoor heated pool, tennis court, spa, sauna, and laundry. Sites are $15-25, cabins $65-115. Budget/Moderate.

Down Crown St. from the information center are a number of cafés and restaurants. Closest is **Café on the Mall,** with inexpensive light meals while across the road is the **Glasshouse Tavern,** 90 Crown St., for something more substantial. One block further east is **Café Suraz,** 121 Corrimal St., featuring a menu of modern Australian cuisine. Next door is **Il Mondo De Caffe,** 119 Corrimal St., tel. (02) 4227-2006, where pastas range $8-15 and Italian specialties start at $14.50. Dining is inside or out. Continuing east is **City Beach Brasserie,** in the Wollongong Entertainment Centre, a large restaurant offering great ocean views.

Transportation, Services, and Information

City Rail, tel. (13) 1500, runs trains regularly between Sydney and Wollongong.

Greyhound Pioneer, tel. (13) 2030, runs a coastal route between Sydney and Melbourne, stopping at Wollongong; the terminal is on the corner of Keira and Campbell Streets.

Just east of the pedestrian mall, at the corner of Crown and Kembla Streets, is the **Tourist Information Centre,** tel. (02) 4227-5545 or (1800) 24-0737; open daily 9 a.m.-5 p.m.

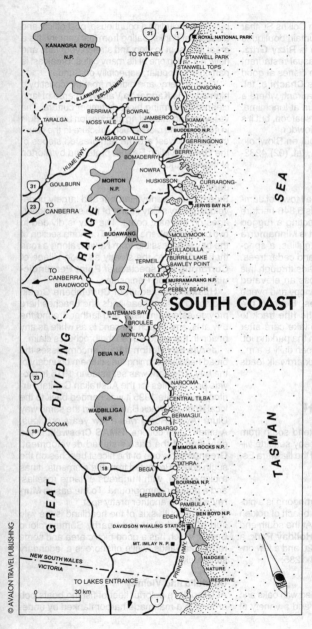

KIAMA AND VICINITY

Kiama's biggest attraction is a **blowhole** (Kiama is an Aboriginal word meaning "where the sea makes a noise"), but it has not been performing that well in recent years. When a heavy southerly is running and the tide is right, water is sucked under a ledge, exploding through a narrow crevice high into the air (up to 50 meters when conditions are right). Much of the blowhole's force has been lost in the last 20 years as water action has enlarged the crevice. Also on the point is a lighthouse dating from 1887. The original lightkeeper's cottage is now a small museum open Fri.-Mon. 11 a.m.-3 p.m. The town's commercial center is within walking distance of the blowhole, while immediately south are small beaches protected from wave action by deeply indented bays.

Practicalities

Kiama appeals mainly to holidaying families and is especially busy in January and during Easter week. At other times of the year, the town reverts to its sleepy self, and getting a room or campsite is no problem. Rooms at **Briggdale Seaside Motel,** 18 Hothersall St., tel. (02) 4232-1767, on Bombo Beach one km north of town, all have beach views; $50 s, $65 d. Moderate. **Easts Beach Caravan Park,** south of Kiama, tel. (02) 4232-2124, has excellent facilities and is right on the beach. Sites are $15-21 and cabins start at $50 s or d. Budget-Inexpensive.

Built in 1885 to house mining families, The Terraces are a

© AVALON TRAVEL PUBLISHING

row of weatherboard houses on Collins St. that have been restored and now contain boutiques and restaurants. One of these is **Ritzy Gritz,** tel. (02) 4232-1853, a small, casual restaurant specializing in modern Mexican dishes at good prices. Also at The Terraces is **Chachi's,** tel. (02) 4233-1144, an Italian restaurant, where a few outside tables catch the sun at lunchtime. The menu features lots of local seafood, but it's hard to go past the Seafood Chowder.

Kiama Visitors Centre is out on Blowhole Point; open daily 9 a.m.-5 p.m., tel. (02) 4232-3322 or (1800) 80-3897.

Budderoo National Park

West of Kiama, beyond the small town of Jamberoo in the Jamberoo Valley, is 5,846-hectare Budderoo National Park, protecting a rugged sandstone plateau. The highlight is **Minnamurra Rainforest,** with its fern-filled gullies, a spectacular waterfall, and giant fig and cedar trees. The 1.6-km Rainforest Walk leads through this subtropical environment, across an elevated boardwalk that leads into the canopy and over a couple of suspension bridges. Beyond the boardwalk is **Minnamurra Falls** (the track to the falls is steep in places, so take care after rain), a three-km roundtrip from the parking lot. At the the **Rainforest Centre,** open daily 9 a.m.-4 p.m., tel. (02) 4236-0469, a boardwalk leads out above the canopy.

SHOALHAVEN

These 150 km of coastline extend south from Gerringong. It's a stretch of sleepy seaside villages backed by dairy farms and the Illawarra Escarpment.

Gerringong

With a population of 2,900, Gerringong is a picturesque village spread along a beach of golden sand surrounded by pastures. At the south end of the beach is **Werri Beach Holiday Park,** a campground with sites for $15-20 and a few onsite vans for $45, tel. (02) 4234-1285.

Berry and Vicinity

The town of Berry has streets lined with oaks and elms planted by early settlers, and a variety of

buildings, including a courthouse, post office, and a couple of banks, dating from last century. It's a great little spot to stop and stretch your legs and have a meal in one of its many cafés. Breakfast is particularly popular, especially on Sunday.

West of Berry, and hidden from the coast by a high ridge, is **Kangaroo Valley,** an area of land cleared for farming by early timber cutters. The valley has an interesting suspension bridge. Built in 1898, it's the oldest such structure in the country. Farther west are the rainforested slopes of the Great Dividing Range, protected by Morton National Park.

Jervis Bay

Bigger than Sydney Harbour and largely undeveloped, Jervis Bay is one of the safest anchorages on the east coast. The bay is divided in two by **Currumbene Creek.** The north section of the bay is accessible from Nowra, along a road that leads out to the sleepy seaside village of **Currarong** and spectacular **Point Perpendicular,** on Beecroft Peninsula.

Huskisson is south of Currumbene Creek. Protected by long headlands, the beaches here provide safe swimming, and farther around the bay at Hyams Beach the sand is as white as any beach in the world—or so the brochures claim.

Jervis Bay National Park encompasses the broad headland forming the southern boundary of the bay. The park was set aside in 1915 to provide port facilities for the Australian Capital Territory, but in late 1995 it was handed back to the local Koori of Wreck Bay, in much the same way Uluru (Ayers Rock) was a few years previous. A small naval college, **HMAS Creswell,** is the only sign of the base's stalled development. **Greenpatch** is one of the nicest beaches on the south coast. Protected from the elements, it has a picnic area, with hundreds of tame rosellas, and a popular campground. To the east is **Murray's Beach,** another pretty spot.

On the south side of the headland is the wild surf of Wreck Bay and nearby Summercloud Beach, which has a good picnic area and some rocky headlands, while offshore is a legendary surf break.

Ulladulla and Vicinity

At Ulladulla a colorful fleet of fishing boats bob around in a manmade harbor flanked by undeveloped headlands. One of the nicest accommodations along the entire South Coast is **Uladulla Guest House,** off South St. at 30 Burrill St., tel. (02) 4455-1796 or (1800) 70-0905. The rooms are large and luxuriously appointed, each adorned with original artwork. Guests also can use a heated saltwater pool, sauna, small fitness room, and lounge decorated with African art. Rates are a reasonable $70-120 s or d, which includes a cooked breakfast. Moderate. On the Princes Highway south of town is **Beach Haven Holiday Resort,** tel. (02) 4455-2110, right on the beach and with a heated pool, spa, tennis court, and barbecue area. Rates are $12.60-23, on-site vans $25-45, and cabins from $47. Budget-Inexpensive.

Farther south is **Burrill Lake,** a small community sandwiched between the lake's outlet and the ocean. The lake is particularly picturesque; easiest access is Kings Point (turn off 500 meters north of Burrill Lake township), where watercraft can be rented.

Murramarang National Park

Extending along the coast between Bawley Point and Batemans Bay, this 1,757-hectare park is of exceptional beauty, featuring beaches, rugged headlands, tidal platforms, and extensive warm-temperate rainforest. Six access points lie between Termeil and Cullendulla on the Princes Highway. From Kioloa a road leads to **Pebbly Beach,** where kangaroos feed on the beach. This beach has a campground with sites costing $12 per night; call (02) 4423-9800 for bookings. Budget. **Depot Beach,** to the south, is another good camping spot.

EUROBODALLA COAST

The Eurobodalla Coast, extending from Batemans Bay to Narooma, has more of those great south coast beaches, and, chances are, outside of the summer school holidays you'll have them to yourself. The Princes Highway runs through the area about four km from the coast, but access to the many beaches is easy. West of the highway is 82,926-hectare **Deua National Park,** which protects remote forested valleys, high ridges, limestone outcrops, and limestone caves. Access is from Moruya.

Batemans Bay

Batemans Bay is a fishing town of 10,000 at the mouth of the Clyde River, which starts high in Budawang National Park to the north. The town is popular with people from Canberra, who regularly make the two-hour run over the Great Dividing Range from the landlocked national capital. Batemans Bay itself has little of interest, but swimming, surfing, fishing, boating, and golfing are all popular. From below the bridge over the Clyde River, the *Clyde Princess,* tel. (02) 4478-1005, departs daily at 11 a.m. for a three-hour cruise upstream to Nelligen. The cruise only costs $15 pp, with lunch an optional $5 extra. Southeast of town, **Observation Head** has a lookout where panoramic views extend across the bay to offshore rock stacks.

Mariners Lodge, Orient St., tel. (02) 4472-6222, is right in town and overlooks Clyde River. It also has a pool. Many rooms have ocean views; from $55 s, $65 d. Moderate. **Lincoln Downs,** Princes Hwy., tel. (02) 4472-6388, one km north of downtown, is a stylish retreat boasting the best of everything in a magnificent country-style setting—landscaped gardens run down to a lagoon alive with waterbirds, and pathways link rooms to the main lodge with a restaurant, lounge, cocktail bar, and billiards room. Rates are $150 s or d. Luxury. Campers have many choices along the coast south from Batemans Bay; best of the bunch is **Coachhouse Resort,** on a beach and across from the golf course at the south end of town, tel. (02) 4472-5187. All facilities are excellent and a grassed area is set aside for tents; sites are $14-18, on-site vans $32-40, and cabins $45-80. Budget-Inexpensive.

On the main highway through town is **Batemans Bay Visitor Centre,** tel. (02) 4472-6900 or (1800) 80-2528; open daily 8:30 a.m.-4:30 p.m.

Braidwood

Braidwood, 63 km northwest of Batemans Bay on the highway linking Canberra to the coast, was founded in the mid-1830s. Many buildings from this era remain, including **Doncaster Inn,** which dates from 1837. After functioning as a nunnery for many years, it was recently restored and now operates as a guesthouse. Rooms have been furnished with iron four-posters, and each opens to a veranda. Rates are $65 s, $110 d, which includes a hearty cooked breakfast.

For bookings, call (02) 4842-2356. Expensive. The inn restaurant is open for dinner Fri.-Sat. nights only, providing the town's best dining experience.

Broulee

Broulee is southernmost of a string of small townships along George Bass Dr., which branches off the Princes Hwy. at Batemans Bay. Broulee itself is bordered to the north by Tomaga River and to the south by a stumpy headland, which at low tide is linked to **Broulee Island.** Before a port at Batemans Bay was established, shipping docked at a jetty on the north side of the island; all that remains are foundations of a hotel and a lone grave.

Narooma

Narooma is a small seaside town of 3,400 at the mouth of Wagonga River, 350 km south of Sydney. Like so many other towns on the south coast it comes alive in summer, while the rest of the year it's a sleepy seaside village. North of the river are several short beaches, and snorkeling at the headland is excellent in calm weather. Above the high cliffs east of downtown is Narooma's golf course, which has many difficult holes, including one which requires a very accurate shot over a deep chasm.

Amooran Court, 30 Montague St., tel. (02) 4476-2198, is a small motel opposite the golf course and has views of the ocean; $55-100 s or d. Inexpensive. Facilities at **Surf Beach Caravan Park,** Ballangalla St., tel. (02) 4476-2275, aren't anything special, but the location is excellent; sites are $14-20, cabins start at $35. Budget-Inexpensive.

Montague Island

Located nine km east of Narooma, this 82-hectare island is a nesting site for crested terns, shearwaters (muttonbirds), silver gulls, and around 20,000 little penguins. Before Europeans, Koori often visited the island to collect bird eggs. In 1881 a lighthouse was built there to allow shipping a safer passage up the treacherous coast. Visiting the island is possible on a tour ($50 pp) operated by the National Parks and Wildlife Service; the office is on the corner of Princes Hwy. and Field St., Narooma, tel. (02) 4476-2888.

SAPPHIRE COAST

At Narooma the Princes Highway heads inland to **Bega,** rejoining the coast at Merimbula. A pleasant alternative to the inland route is along the Sapphire Coast, passing three national parks and a number of picturesque towns.

Wallaga Lake

The coastal road south from Narooma crosses an outlet channel of Wallaga Lake. The lake, which formed when a wide valley flooded at the end of the last ice age, is deeply indented, its shoreline stretching more than 100 km. Access to the lake is possible from the east and north.

Part of the shoreline through here is protected by 1,237-hectare **Wallaga Lake National Park,** which has a high concentration of wildlife, including koalas, swamp wallabies, and lyrebirds, and is dotted with Koori middens. Access to the park is on foot from Regatta Point or by boat.

Bermagui

The picturesque fishing village of Bermagui (pop. 1,000) is fronted by an area of parkland that separates the main street from the quiet waters of **Horseshoe Bay.** The Continental Shelf, off which the ocean floor drops dramatically, is closest to mainland Australia east of Bermagui.

Bermagui's manmade harbor is home to a large commercial fishing fleet and a number of game-fishing boats, including many for charter (if you're interested, contact the Tourist Information Centre for charter details). Marine Dr., running east from the main street to a high headland and out of town to the south, passes **Blue Pool,** an ocean-fed swimming pool, **Beares Beach,** and several rocky headlands. Other activities in town include fishing, golf (call 02-6493-4340 for tee times), and scuba diving. Held over Easter weekend, **Four Winds Easter Concert** is a unique combination of classical and Aboriginal music. For details call (02) 6493-4105.

Beachview Motel, 12 Lamont St., tel. (02) 6493-4155, is close to everything and has modern facilities; rates are $60 s, $70 d, except in holiday periods when they rise to more than $100 for a double. Moderate. **Zane Grey Caravan Park,** Lamont St., tel. (02) 6493-4382, overlooks the bay and is within easy walking distance of town. Sites are $17.50-22 in summer holidays, and $5 less the rest of the year. Cabins here are excellent, and each has a TV and microwave; from $60 s or d. Other facilities include free gas barbecues and a laundry. Budget-Inexpensive.

The fish shop on the harbor should have great fish and chips. But it doesn't. And unfortunately, in a town so famous for its seafood, there's really nowhere else to recommend for inexpensive seafood. For somewhere more formal, head to **Roly's Wharf Restaurant,** Cutajo St., tel. (02) 6493-4328, for seafood; open daily for lunch and dinner. For Chinese, head to the Country Club on Tuross St., tel. (02) 6493-4177.

Mimosa Rocks National Park
A 17-km stretch of coastline between Bermagui and Tathra is protected by this 5,230-hectare park, which also extends eight km inland from Nelson Lagoon. The Tathra-Bermagui Road passes through only a small section of the park, but the coast can be accessed in many places. Northernmost of these, Aragunnu Rd., 20 km south of Bermagui, leads to a sandy beach surrounded by dark volcanic rock and the deep blue of the Pacific Ocean. From the campground at the end of this road, it's easy to scramble around a rocky bay to the stack of volcanic rock for which the park is named. At the end of Wapengo Lake Rd., the next access road, is a campground, picnic area, and trail leading to a headland. The next two roads off the Tathra-Bermagui Road lead to Middle Beach and Gillards Beach, both of which have camping. At the park's southern end is **Nelson Lagoon,** and at the end of Nelson Lakes Rd. trails lead to pleasant sandy beaches at the lagoon's outlet. None of the park's camping areas have drinking water. For further park details, call (02) 4476-2888.

Tathra
Flanked by two national parks and nestled in the protected northeast corner of a long headland, Tathra is one of the south coast's most picturesque villages. Out on the headland is **Tathra Wharf;** dating from 1862, it's the oldest sea wharf on the east coast. It has been extensively restored, with the two-story storehouse given a coat of red paint to spruce it up. The storehouse is open and contains a small museum, a

Tathra Wharf

general store selling everything from fishing gear to fresh prawns, and an information center, tel. (02) 6494-4062. Views from the wharf extend across the bay to Tathra and around a beautiful sandy beach to the mouth of the Bega River.

Tathra Hotel Motel, Bega St., tel. (02) 6494-1101, is on Tathra Head, and every room has panoramic ocean views; $55 s, $65 d. Moderate. **Tathra Beach Tourist Park,** between the beach and Andy Poole Dr., is spread along the foreshore near the surf club. Rates are $14-18 for camping and $34 for on-site vans; call (02) 6494-1302 for bookings. Budget-Inexpensive.

Opposite the caravan park is **Mimosa Rocks Restaurant,** 61 Andy Poole Dr., tel. (02) 6494-1483, which serves light lunches and dinner (seafood dishes are especially good) daily. Up on the headland in a residence dating from 1906 is **Tathra Harbour Master Restaurant.** The elegant setting and fine food combine to make it an excellent choice for dinner. It's at 15 Bega St., tel. (02) 6494-1344.

Bournda National Park

This 2,378-hectare park extends from south of Tathra to Tura Beach, north of Merimbula, and encompasses wetland areas around **Wallagoot Lake.** In the north of the park, forests of eucalypt extend to the deeply indented coastline, accessible along a gravel track leading south of Tathra.

Hobart Beach, near the south end of Wallagoot Lake, has a picnic area and campground (bring drinking water). This part of the park is crisscrossed with hiking trails, including one around Bondi Lake.

SAPPHIRE COAST HINTERLAND

Early settlers found the narrow strip of land wedged below the foothills of the Great Dividing Range ideal for running cattle, and for more than 150 years the land has provided its farmers with a healthy living.

Tilba Tilba

In the shadow of **Mt. Dromedary** (860 meters), this historic town boomed during an 1852 gold rush and is today a picturesque village, home to many artisans who sell their wares in period-style buildings along the main street. The village boasts a cobbler, wood-turner, leadlight artist, leatherman, and small cheese factory. Behind the cheese factory is **Wirrina,** tel. (02) 4473-7279, a small B&B where rates are $60 s, $78 d. Moderate.

Cobargo

Cobargo developed as a dairy town in the 1860s, and with the abundance of wattle a prosperous tanning industry thrived. Today this charming town's main street is lined with buildings from all eras of Cobargo's history, including a bakery, pharmacy, saddlery, grain store, and newsagency.

Wadbilliga National Park

Primarily protecting Wadbilliga Plateau, this large 79,000-hectare park is in a remote part of the Great Dividing Range west of Cobargo. From the plateau's highest reaches flow the Wadbilliga, Tuross, and Brogo Rivers. Each of these has carved a deep gorge, with that of the Tuross

being the most accessible. Elevation changes in the park provide habitat for a variety of vegetation—from temperate rainforests on the valley floor to subalpine forests of snow gum at higher elevations. The only two-wheel drive access is west from Cobargo, along a road that ends at Wadbilliga Crossing, where there's a picnic area and basic campground.

Bega

Bega is synonymous with cheese, an industry upon which the town has grown into the largest commercial center between Wollongong and the Victorian border. The highlight of a visit to the town is **Bega Heritage Centre,** in a historic cheese factory on Lagoon St., tel. (02) 6492-1444. Cheese tastings are offered daily 9 a.m.-5 p.m. On the outskirts of town is **Grevillea Estate Wines,** also open for tasting and home to a fair-sized herd of dairy cows milked daily at 3 p.m. Located on Buckajo Rd., tel. (02) 6492-3006.

MERIMBULA AND VICINITY

Merimbula (pop. 4,400) is a popular holiday town set around the sparkling waters of a narrow channel that drains Merimbula Lake into the ocean. Jutting out from the township are Short and Merimbula Points, ochre-colored headlands that drop vertically into the ocean. Merimbula grew as a private port for the Twofold Bay Pastoral Association, and boomed when gold was discovered in the Snowy Mountains.

On the headland at the lake's entrance is a wharf, which is a good fishing spot and home to **Merimbula Aquarium** (a bit much at adult $8, child $6); open daily 10 a.m.-5 p.m., tel. (02) 6495-3227. To get out to the headland, follow Main St. out of town to Lake Street. The surrounding national parks offer many hiking opportunities, but the town itself is the starting point for many walks. One leads along the western shore of Merimbula Lake to a beach where Boggy Creek drains into the lake. Birdlife abounds in this area, and around dusk kangaroos and wallabies feed in the open. Merimbula is known for its beaches; the best of these are either side of Short Point and **Bar Beach,** a protected spot along Lake St. facing the channel and backed by a grassed picnic area.

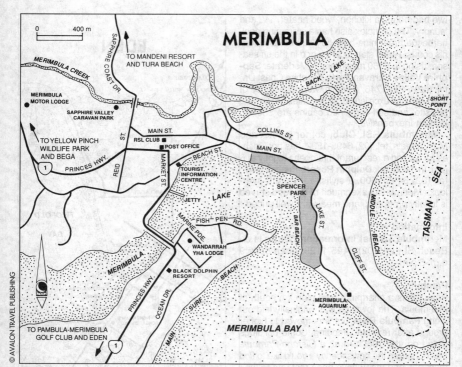

Recreation

The least expensive way to get out on the lake is a cruise on the glass-bottomed *Merimbula Princess,* tel. (02) 6493-2057, departing from the jetty daily 2 p.m.; adult $15, child $10. A tour desk at Merimbula Marina, tel. (02) 6495-1686, makes bookings for dolphin watching ($22 pp), whale watching ($45 pp), and a variety of fishing excursions.

Yellow Pinch Wildlife Park is set in native bushland nine km west of Merimbula. Apart from the usual array of Australian animals, there are rides for the kids and a café with picnic area. Admission is adult $9, child $6. Open daily 10 a.m.-5 p.m., tel. (02) 6494-9225.

Pambula-Merimbula Golf Club has one of the best courses on the south coast and is open to the public most days, tel. (02) 6495-6280. North of town is **Mandeni Resort,** tel. (02) 6495-9644, featuring a nine-hole golf course and a unique deepwater driving range, where balls are hit into a lake.

Accommodations and Food

Merimbula Motor Lodge is one of the town's better motels; rates start at a reasonable $45 s, $50 d; located at 131 Princes Hwy., tel. (02) 6495-1748 or (1800) 02-5612. Inexpensive. **Fairway Motor Inn,** 386 Princes Hwy., tel. (02) 6495-6000, is, as the name suggests, right opposite the golf course. Rooms are large with modern facilities, and rates are $64 s, $72 d. Moderate. **Wandarrah YHA Lodge** is a purpose-built backpacker accommodation one block from the beach and a 10-minute walk from downtown. Rates are $16 pp for a dorm, and $28 s, $40 d; located at 18 Marine Parade, tel. (02) 6495-3503. Inexpensive. A good accommodation deal is **Mandeni Resort,** eight km north of town on Sapphire Coast Dr., tel. (02) 6495-9644. Rooms are self-contained; each has two bedrooms, a kitchen, wood heater, TV, and laundry. The complex also has a swimming pool, barbecue area, nine-hole golf course, and tennis courts. Rates start at $65 s or d in the off season, rising to $160 midsummer. Moderate. **Sapphire Valley Caravan Park,** Sapphire Coast Dr., tel. (02) 6495-1746, is within walking distance of town and has excellent facilities. Rates are $15-22 per site, and self-contained cabins are $35-85. Budget-Inexpensive.

Merimbula RSL Club, corner Market and Main Streets, tel. (02) 6495-1502, has hot lunches for $5 and a restaurant that opens nightly at 6 p.m. In the **Black Dolphin Resort,** Princes Hwy., tel. (02) 6495-1500, a stylish restaurant overlooks Merimbula Lake; much of the food served is locally produced, and meals are well priced.

Information

Merimbula Tourist Information Centre is on Beach St., tel. (02) 6495-1129; open daily 9 a.m.-5 p.m.

Pambula

Pambula is a charming town nine km south of Merimbula. The townsite was originally laid out along **Pambula River** but was moved to higher ground after repeated flooding. Some buildings date from the 1860s (grab a *Historic Pambula* brochure from the newsagency if you'd like to find them all), and many have been restored to their former grandeur. **Pambula Beach,** at the mouth of Pambula River two km east of Pambula, is at the end of a beach stretching north to Merimbula.

Merimbula has a better range of accommodations than Pambula, although Pambula Beach has a caravan park. As for food, though, Pambula excels, with excellent restaurants. The elegant restaurant in **Covington's Retreat,** 26 Quondola St., tel. (02) 6495-6543, a historic inn dating from 1850, is open for breakfast, lunch, and dinner daily (except Tuesday). **The Grange** on the road out to Wyndham, tel. (02) 6495-6169, was built in 1844 and is open for lunch and dinner. Closed Monday.

EDEN AND VICINITY

The sparkling blue waters of Twofold Bay and the dense forests that flank the town are Eden's

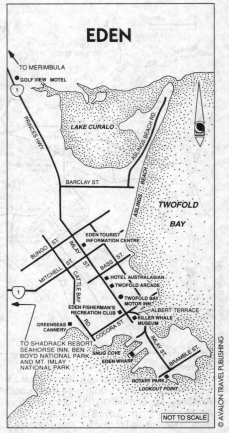

© AVALON TRAVEL PUBLISHING

major tourist drawcard and also the lifeblood of the area's sometimes-grisly past as well as present economy. The town itself, 490 km south of Sydney and 50 km north of the Victorian border, is spread over a narrow spit of land extending into Twofold Bay, a deep body of water lined by beaches and rocky headlands.

The first in a long line of entrepreneurs who tried to make their fortunes from Eden's bountiful natural resources was Englishman Ben Boyd, whose ambitious plan to build a city rivaling Sydney in importance began in 1843 with the construction of an inn, a church, and houses at the southern corner of Twofold Bay, eight km south of present-day Eden. But by 1849 Boyd was broke, and all that remains of his dream is an inn and the ruins of a church. Farther around the bay, **Davidson Whaling Station** was faring much better, landing around a dozen whales each season. They operated until 1929, by which time whale numbers had been decimated and the station had become uneconomical to run. The station has been partially restored, with interpretive panels describing the "processing" of the whales. On the road out to the old station, it's impossible to miss **Harris Daishowa Mill,** where trees are wood-chipped for export. If scrambling around piles of woodchips sounds enticing, tours are offered on Thursday; book through the Tourist Information Centre. The other mainstay of Eden's economy is fishing, and there can be few sights as peaceful as watching the fleet of boats bobbing around the wharf. Commercial fishing is a dangerous, year-round operation, as the **Seamen's Memorial Wall** in Rotary Park will attest. Most of the fish are transported to Sydney or processed at the **Greenseas Cannery,** down on the harbor.

Killer Whale Museum

Whaling has long since ended in Australia, and this museum catalogs its history. The main feature is a skeleton of Old Tom, a killer whale that hunted in Twofold Bay. Also on display is a whaleboat, and in the Viewing Gallery descriptions of today's fishing industry adorn a room overlooking the bay. You'll find displays of seashells and the Koori, and an audiovisual in other galleries. The museum is open Mon.-Sat. 9:15 a.m.-3:45 p.m., Sunday 11:15 a.m.-3:45 p.m. Admission is $4. It's at 94 Imlay St., tel. (02) 6496-2094.

Whalewatching has really caught on in the last few years, but the season runs only two months—October and November. The humpback whales can be seen from *Cat Balou* but often come right into the bay where they can be watched from vantage points around town. During the season, the boat departs daily at 7 a.m. for a five-hour cruise. The boat is not allowed within 100 meters of whales, but the whales, disregarding the rules, often surface alongside the boat. Cruise cost is adult $45, child $30; book through the Tourist Information Centre, tel. (02) 6496-1953, or call direct at (02) 6496-2027.

Accommodations

The **Seahorse Inn,** built by Ben Boyd in 1840, is a Tudor-style mansion overlooking Twofold Bay. Although rooms are fairly basic, its historic charm and beachfront location make it the best place in the Eden area to stay. Rooms are $70-75 s, $85-120 d, including breakfast. It's at Boydtown Park, eight km south of Eden, tel. (02) 6496-1361. Moderate.

Golf View Motel, Princes Hwy., tel. (02) 6496-1601, is one km north of downtown Eden and has the least expensive rooms in town; $40 s, $45 d. Inexpensive. Of a higher standard, and overlooking the bay, is **Twofold Bay Motor Inn,**

Seahorse Inn,
Boydtown Park

166 Imlay St., tel. (02) 6496-3111, which has an indoor pool and spa; rates are from $65 s, $75 d. Moderate.

Eden Tourist Park, Aslings Beach Rd., tel. (02) 6496-1139, fronts both the beach and lake. Sites are $11-17, basic on-site vans are $28-40, and cabins are $52 and up. Budget. **Shadrack Resort,** south of Eden, is one of three campgrounds on the shore of Twofold Bay. This large park has all the facilities you'll need. Sites are $18, and those with bathrooms are $24. The cabins are excellent and start at $44 d, tel. (02) 6496-1651. Budget-Inexpensive.

Food

Although Eden is one of the state's largest fishing towns, most of the catch is transported to markets in Sydney. Still, if it's seafood you want, Eden excels. Down on Eden Wharf, **The Wharf Fish Shop** has a selection of battered and grilled fish from $4 and prawns for $18-24 per kg; open daily 8 a.m.-5 p.m. **Wheelhouse Restaurant,** also on the Wharf, tel. (02) 6496-3392, is a more formal joint, with views of all the activity and generous portions of the freshest seafood from $14 for dinner. The **Hotel Australasian,** 60 Imlay St., tel. (02) 6496-1600, has good bar meals for $5-10 and is least rowdy of the town's many pubs. The hotel is also home to **Bianca's Bistro,** in the old dining room, where the seafood dishes are of an exceptional standard. **Eden Fishermen's Recreation Club,** Imlay St., tel. (02) 6496-1577, has a popular bistro and restaurant with higher-than-usual club prices.

Transportation, Services, and Information

Edward's Bus Service, tel. (02) 6496-1422, runs between Merimbula and Eden Mon.-Sat., with some services via Bega and others along the coast; buses stop outside Twofold Arcade on Imlay Street.

Eden Tourist Information Centre is on the corner of Imlay and Mitchell Streets, tel. (02) 6496-1953; open daily 9 a.m.-5 p.m. At the back of Twofold Arcade on Imlay St. is an **NPWS** office, tel. (02) 6496-3248, and an **Eden Forestry Office,** tel. (02) 6496-1500, a good information source on the many interesting forest drives between the south coast and Snowy Mountains.

Ben Boyd National Park

This 9,750-hectare park extends along 40 km of coastline from Pambula in the north to Disaster Bay in the south and is divided in two by Twofold Bay. This stretch of coastline is nothing less than spectacular, with folding and faulting of the bedrock creating a rugged shoreline. The main feature of the park's north section is **The Pinnacles. Haycock Point,** at the park's northern tip, has a picnic area protected from prevailing nor'easters. The park's most recognizable feature is **Boyd Tower,** in the southern section. The tower was built in the 1840s for spotting whales, and was later used mostly as a lighthouse. The main access to the tower, and other features of this part of the park, is Edrom Rd., spurring east from the Princes Hwy. 18 km south of Eden. Campgrounds at **Saltwater Creek** and **Bittangabee** are reached off this road. For more information on the park, head to the NPWS office in Twofold Arcade on Imlay St., tel. (02) 6496-3248.

Mount Imlay National Park

The 886-meter peak for which this park is named rises high above the surrounding forests and provides an excellent vantage point. Changes in elevation create habitat for a wide variety of vegetation within the park, including the newly discovered *Eucalypt imlayensis*. For most people, the main purpose of a visit to the park is climbing Mt. Imlay. The climb is only three km each way, with an elevation gain of 600 meters, but it's a hard slog, with the final ascent along an exposed ridge. The summit track trailhead is at the park's only facilities—a picnic area—located at the end of Burrawang Rd., which spurs off the Princes Hwy. 19 km south of Eden.

SOUTHERN HIGHLANDS AND GOULBURN

The original Hume Highway, the main route between Sydney and Melbourne, has been re-routed in many places, bypassing towns established to serve early travelers. Immediately south of Sydney's southwestern suburbs, a turnoff to Mittagong signals the old highway, which passes through a string of charming towns, offering the chance to browse antique shops, eat in historic cafés, and stay overnight in luxurious guesthouses. **Morton National Park,** south of these towns, is a rugged and remote wilderness with some spectacular waterfalls and a good range of hiking for all levels of fitness.

For information on this region, contact **Southern Highlands Tourism,** tel. (02) 4871-2888 or (1300) 65-7559, website: www.wsc.nsw.gov.au/tourism.

Wombeyan Caves

Jenolan Caves may be Australia's best-known cave system, but there are others of equal beauty, the difference being that access is more difficult. Wombeyan Caves, 65 km northwest of Mittagong, is one such system. The final 40-km stretch is along a rough gravel road that passes through a convict-built sandstone tunnel. Almost 230 caves make up the system, of which five are open to the public. **Fig Tree Cave** has a self-guided trail through it, with buttons to press for commentary and, more importantly, light. Of the other four, **Wollondilly Cave,** featuring a 25-meter-high cathedral, is regarded as the most spectacular. Admission to self-guided caves is $10, guided caves $12. They are open daily 8:30 a.m.-4:30 p.m.

At the caves' entrance is a wide open area (*wombeyan* is Aboriginal for "grassy flat between two mountains") with a campground that features a camp kitchen, hot showers, kiosk, and laundry. Unpowered sites are $10, powered sites $15, on-site vans $40 s or d. For campground bookings and cave tour information, call (02) 4843-5976.

BERRIMA

Berrima lies beside a sweeping bend of the Wingecarribee River, 120 km southwest of Sydney. Established in 1828 to serve travelers, the township developed with the construction of a stone courthouse, post office, and a number of inns. In 1850, when the rail line between Sydney and Bowral bypassed Berrima, the town's prosperity came to an abrupt end. Since that time, Berrima has become a popular getaway for Sydneysiders, but has changed little. A certain amount of peace came to the streets in the late 1980s when the Hume Highway was diverted north of town, leaving the sleepy village almost traffic free.

Sights

Berrima is one of Australia's best remaining examples of a 19th-century town, remarkably unchanged since the 1840s. The town's most impressive building is the **courthouse,** which dates from 1838. Within the grand sandstone structure are displays explaining court proceedings in colonial Australia. It's open for tours and an audiovisual presentation daily 10 a.m.-4 p.m., tel. (02) 4877-1505. Behind the courthouse is Australia's oldest remaining jail. For most of the 1800s it was among the most dreaded of all jails, mainly for the fact that for the first nine months of his sentence a prisoner wasn't allowed to talk to anyone, lest he be flogged. On the south side of the jail is **Bull's Head Fountain,** designed to catch runoff from the roof. Down the hill is the **Surveyor General Inn.** Open since 1835, it is Australia's oldest continually licensed hotel. **Harper's Mansion,** on Wilkinson St., is a fine example of a large Australian home from early last century; open Sat.-Mon. 11 a.m.-4 p.m. At least 20 other buildings of historic significance are detailed in the *Two Foot Walking Tour* brochure, available from the courthouse.

Berkelouw Book Dealer, three km north of Berrima, tel. (02) 4877-1370, has more than 200,000 books, including many rare early Australian works; open daily 8:30 a.m.-3 p.m.

Accommodations and Food

Walden Wood, Old Mandemar Rd., tel. (02) 4877-1164, is an 1860 sandstone cottage set on three hectares. Two rooms, each with private bathroom, are offered, and the lounge area has an open fire. Rates are $75 s, $95 d, which includes a cooked breakfast. Expensive. A little less expensive is **Berrima Bakehouse Motel,** right in the heart of town, tel. (02) 4877-1381; $56 s, $69 d. Moderate.

Cottage Kitchen is open daily 9 a.m.-5 p.m. for light lunches and Devonshire teas in a country atmosphere. For something a bit more formal, head to **Colonial Inn,** tel. (02) 4877-1389, a sandstone structure dating from 1842 and built by convict labor. Tables are set in five rooms, four with fireplaces. Main dishes start at $15 (less at lunch). Open daily noon-3 p.m. and 6-9:30 p.m. **Surveyor General Inn,** tel. (02) 4877-1226, is worth visiting, if only to have a beer in Australia's oldest pub. Meals are served at lunch and dinner, with a wide choice of cook-your-own steaks for $12-16.

BOWRAL

While Berrima is noted for its historic charm, Bowral (pop. 5,500), 10 km east, is renowned for magnificent gardens, tree-lined avenues, and as the childhood home of the world's best-known cricketer, Sir Donald Bradman. The population of Bowral is markedly different from almost all other country towns in that almost all residents are wealthy or retired, giving the town an air of pomp. Bowral grew from a subdivision of land owned by Australia's first Surveyor General, John Oxley. By the 1920s the town had become a popular getaway for Sydneysiders, and to cater to them guesthouses and inns were established.

Sights
Bowral is a fitting site for the **Bradman Museum,** St. Jude St., tel. (02) 4862-1247, dedicated to, arguably, the finest cricketer the world had ever seen. Overlooking the town's main cricket ground and across the road from Bradman's childhood home, the museum catalogs not just his career but development of cricket through Australia, and is filled with memorabilia from all eras—from a 1750s cricket bat to the modern equipment used by today's test cricketers. Admission is adult $7, child $3. The museum is open daily 10 a.m.-4 p.m. Bradman lived opposite the oval, at 20 Glebe Rd., as well as two blocks east, at 52 Shepard Street. Back near the center of town, on

Sir Donald Bradman grew up in Bowral, playing cricket on this ground, which now has a museum in his honor.

the corner of Boolwey and Bendooley Streets, is **Bowral Schoolhouse Museum,** set up as a mid-1800s school room. On Bendooley St. are many other historic buildings, including a courthouse, police station, and rectory. Bowral has many fine shops, most around the town center and in **Grand Arcade.** For views over town and surrounding rolling farmland, head to 980-meter **Mt. Gibraltar,** a rocky outcrop accessible along Oxley Dr., off Mittagong Road.

Tulip Time Festival, the first weekend of October, attracts thousands of visitors to Bowral. The highlight is 60,000 blooming tulips in Corbett Gardens, but many private gardens are also open for inspection, and musicians play in various venues through town; call (02) 4861-3133 for details.

Accommodations
Port O'Call Motor Inn, corner Bong Bong and Bundaroo Streets, tel. (02) 4861-1779, is the

least expensive motel in town; rooms start at $50 s or d midweek. Inexpensive. Built in 1925, **Berida Manor,** 6 David St., tel. (02) 4861-1177, is a large boutique hotel surrounded by well-tended gardens on the edge of the golf course and is just a five-minute walk from downtown Bowral. Rooms are well-furnished, and guest facilities include a pool, spa, sauna, gym, tennis courts, snooker rooms, and mountain bikes. Rates are $100 s, $160 d. Luxury. **Links House,** 17 Links Rd., tel. (02) 4861-1977, is a small, colorful hotel in a lovely setting of landscaped gardens. Each room has a private bathroom and costs $145 s, $200 d, including dinner and breakfast. Luxury.

Food
Bowral Cafe, 336 Bong Bong St., has an old-world atmosphere but, more importantly, a delicious array of cakes, pastries, and ice cream; closed Tuesday. At 326 Bong Bong St. is **Bowral Country Kitchen,** tel. (02) 4861-4560, a casual restaurant with coffee and cake around $6. On Friday and Saturday nights a three-course dinner is offered for $15 pp. **Truffles,** Highlands Arcade, Bong Bong St., tel. (02) 4861-1257, is a small, casual restaurant, with breakfast $7-11, lunch $6-14, and dinner $12-18.

MOSS VALE AND VICINITY

Moss Vale
Moss Vale, a thriving country town, lacks the pretensions of Bowral and Berrima, but with tree-lined streets and many historic buildings, it's still a pleasant place to stop. **Cecil Hoskins Nature Reserve,** along the Wingecarribee River, two km northeast of Moss Vale, is home to waterbirds and platypuses. Walking tracks make access to all corners of this 80-hectare reserve possible, with a number of hides for birdwatching located at strategic locations.

Bundanoon
Bundanoon (pop. 1,500), 26 km south of Moss Vale, is a sleepy southern highlands village where two lookouts provide spectacular views across Morton National Park. To the east is a **glowworm cave,** well signposted from town. Early this century, Bundanoon was a popular

mountain getaway, and many sandstone buildings remain from that era.

Brigadoon Highland Gathering, in mid-April, celebrates the coming of autumn with pipe bands, a street parade, haggis hurling, and other traditional highland games.

The best value accommodation is **Bundanoon YHA,** one km northeast of downtown along Railway Ave., tel. (02) 4883-6010. Located in an Edwardian-era home, this hostel is set on extensive grounds and features comfortable beds, a well-equipped kitchen, and cozy lounge area with an open fire. Dorm beds are $16 pp while doubles are $36. Inexpensive. **Mildenhall Guesthouse,** 10 Anzac Parade, tel. (02) 4883-6643, dates from the 1920s and is just 500 meters from the center of town. Rates are $50-75 pp for bed and breakfast; dinner is an additional $25-35 pp. Expensive.

Morton National Park
This large but little-known park occupies 162,000 hectares of a rugged and almost inaccessible section of the southern highlands. Access is from the Illawarra Highway, which links the southern highlands to the south coast, or from **Bundanoon,** south of Moss Vale. Dominant geological features are the deep gorges around the headwaters of the Shoalhaven River and its tributaries and a large plateau in the center of the park. **Fitzroy Falls,** a 250-meter walk from Nowra Rd., is a park highlight, plunging 81 meters. From the same parking lot, trails lead along the East and West Rims to lookouts above the falls; the 3.5-km East Rim trail is the easier of the two routes. **Fitzroy Falls Visitors Centre,** tel. (02) 4887-7270, is open daily 8:30 a.m.-5 p.m. Also at the center is a café and campground.

The park's remote southern section protects the ancient **Budawang Range,** providing the opportunity for experienced hikers to explore an area of extraordinary sandstone formations and long, forested valleys. In the far south is 719-meter **Pigeon House Mountain,** a volcanic plug towering high above surrounding forest.

GOULBURN

Located 190 km south of Sydney, this large inland city of 24,000 is the center of a rich wool-

Big Merino

growing area—but you won't need anyone to tell you that after seeing the massive fiberglass sheep that towers over the main drag though town.

Goulburn was gazetted in 1833, and for years it was base for large numbers of police officers hunting for bushrangers. By the early 1860s free settlers from Sydney were moving to the area, and as early as 1885 Goulburn had been proclaimed a city. Many buildings from that era remain, including the courthouse (1887), surrounded by the landscaped gardens of Belmore Park.

Goulburn's major attraction is, undoubtedly, the 15-meter-high **Big Merino,** tel. (02) 4821-8800, a grotesque monument to the lifeblood of the city. Inside its fiberglass hulk are displays describing the wool-growing process, and you climb into the head for city views. Part of the same complex is an agridome, where several times daily sheep shows are conducted, which include a shearing exhibition.

Practicalities

Along freeway access roads north and south of Goulburn is a variety of accommodations. **Lilac City Motor Inn,** Hume Hwy., tel. (02) 4821-5000, has rooms of a good standard, with all the expected services for $55 s, $68 d; it's two km north of downtown. Moderate. **Centretown Motel** is on the opposite side of the Hume Hwy. and closer to downtown, tel. (02) 4821-2422. Facilities include an indoor pool, restaurant, and bar; $76 s, $84 d. Moderate.

South of Goulburn, in the historic village of Bungendore, is **The Carrington,** tel. (02) 6238-1044 or (1800) 04-6079. Built in 1885 as a stopping point for coaches traveling between Sydney and Melbourne, the inn has been totally restored with luxurious rooms for $105 s, $120 d. Meal packages in their renowned restaurant are also available. Premium.

Goulburn Visitors Centre is downtown at 6 Montague St., tel. (02) 4823-0492 or (1800) 35-3646.

CANBERRA AND THE AUSTRALIAN CAPITAL TERRITORY

Midway between Sydney and Melbourne is the Australian Capital Territory, home to the country's capital, Canberra. The site was a compromise between the powers of Sydney and Melbourne, who, after Australia's federation in 1901, both claimed their city as the rightful capital. Today, Canberra, which lies away from the ocean (Canberra is Australia's largest inland city), away from a major river, and away from mineral deposits, exists for no other reason than to serve the politicians and bureaucrats running Australia, but don't let that put you off visiting—it's a unique and oddly beautiful city with many fine museums and attractions.

Canberra is a planned city. From the original plans submitted by architect Walter Burley Griffin to the newest row of trees, nothing is out of place. Arterial roads bypass all political, commercial, and residential areas, which, in turn, are separate from each other. It's possible to drive through the city's heart without spotting a petrol station, shopping mall, fast food outlet, or neon sign. Political buildings such as the High Court, National Gallery, and National Library are within the **Parliamentary Triangle,** bordered by Parkes Way, Kings Way, and Commonwealth Ave., the latter two forming and an apex at Capital Hill, site of Parliament House. The city proper surrounds the triangle. To the north, across manmade **Lake Burley Griffin,** lies **Civic,** Canberra's commercial heart. The city's 300,000 or so residents live in decentralized suburbs, each with its own commercial center and completely bypassed by arterial roads. All suburbs have blocks of land varying in size, and therefore, in theory, there are no "rich" or "poor" suburbs.

Through all this, politicians are only small in number, and are only in town when parliament is sitting. Most of the population consists of public servants, who serve the large infrastructure of government and related services.

History
At federation in 1901, and until a permanent site had been decided upon, Melbourne was deemed temporary capital of Australia. Various existing towns through the southeast were considered, but eventually it was decided to build the capital from scratch. The site chosen, a wide floodplain on the Molonglo River, was halfway between Sydney and Melbourne, the two cities most vocal about becoming the nation's capital. The land, granted to a free settler as a reward for helping with the capture of a bushranger, was bought by the Commonwealth and named Canberra, Aboriginal for "Meeting Place." The creation of the new capital began in 1911 with an international design competition. American architect Walter Burley Griffin was declared the winner, but it would be half a century before his original plan was fully implemented.

To coincide with the 9 May 1927 opening of a temporary parliament, 1,000 families were moved to Canberra. But Canberra was no boomtown; it wasn't until after WW II that the city took the form it does today, and in 1960 the population was only 50,000. And the temporary Parliament House? It wasn't until 1988 that the permanent structure was completed.

PARLIAMENTARY TRIANGLE SIGHTS

Within the Parliamentary Triangle, bounded by Commonwealth Ave., Parkes Way, and Kings Ave., lie the federal buildings. Parliament House, on Capital Hill, forms the triangle's apex. Across Lake Burley Griffin, and beyond the base of the triangle, is Anzac Parade, which ends at the Australian War Memorial. Scattered around the leafy streets west of Capital Hill are the embassies of many countries. **The Lodge,** on Adelaide Ave., is the official residence of Australia's prime minister.

Parliament House
After eight years of construction and $1 billion of taxpayers' money, Australia's Parliament House, the culmination of Walter Burley Griffin's city plan, opened in 1988. The building is very dis-

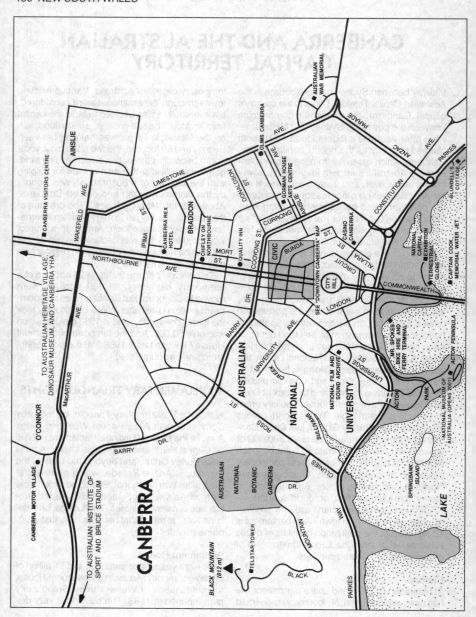

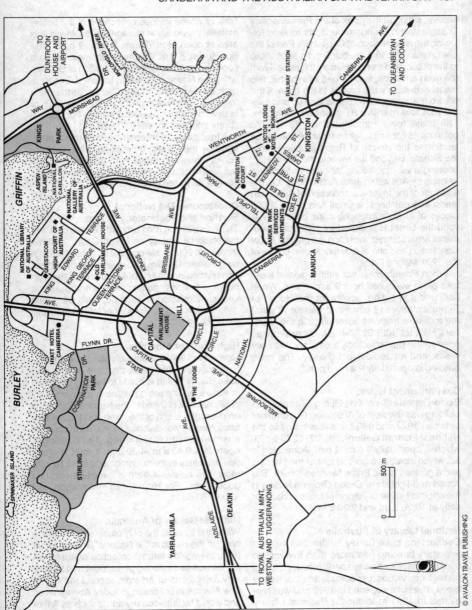

© AVALON TRAVEL PUBLISHING

tinctive, sitting at the apex of the Parliamentary Triangle and half-underground, its roofline following the natural slope of Capital Hill. Part of the design plan was that the building be accessible to the public, and this is definitely the case. From the main entrance, submerged into the hill, two massive granite walls radiate to the base of the hill, from where grassed banks lead up and over the roof to a massive 81-meter-high flagpole. The main foyer, dominated by 48 marble columns, is flanked by grand marble staircases leading to the House of Representatives and the Senate. Beyond the foyer is the Great Hall, housing a 20-meter-long tapestry based on a painting by Australian artist Arthur Boyd. On the first floor of the foyer is a collection of Australian landscape paintings, a small part of the 3,000 pieces of artwork throughout the building. Beyond the Great Hall important historical documents are displayed, including the original Act of Constitution and one of only four known copies of the 1297 Magna Carta.

When Parliament is not sitting, guided tours take place every half hour 9 a.m.-5 p.m. When parliament is sitting, tickets for the House of Representatives (3 p.m.) and Senate (2 p.m.) are available from the ticket office in the Members Hall, tel. (02) 6277-4889. Other facilities open to the public include a cafeteria with city views, and an audiovisual display. The main building is open daily 9 a.m.-5 p.m.

Old Parliament House
Below Capital Hill, on King George Terrace, this building was the seat of Australian Government between 1927 and 1988. It's now home to the **National Portrait Gallery,** tel. (02) 6273-5130, which is open daily 9 a.m.-4 p.m. Admission is $2, which includes a guided tour of the building and a glimpse of the Prime Ministerial suite. The sound-and-light show *Order! Order!* is shown in the original House of Representatives chamber daily at 10:30 a.m. and 2:30 p.m.

National Library of Australia
Overlooking Lake Burley Griffin, this elegant five-story building has more than five million books, as well as newspapers, maps, pictures, prints, films, videos, periodicals, and oral history tapes. The library opened in 1968 and was renovated in 1991 to include a National Library

Gallery where various collections of the library material previously in storage are displayed; this area is open Mon.-Thurs. 9 a.m.-9 p.m., Fri.-Sun. 9 a.m.-5 p.m. The main reading rooms are open similar hours, with the exception of Sunday, when the Newspaper Room is closed. The Kenneth Baillieu Myer Visitor Centre, at the main foyer, has information on the many collections, or take a library tour (weekdays only). For general library information, call (02) 6262-1111.

Kinetica is an Internet-based project managed by the library. It catalogues the library's books along with those from libraries throughout Australasia. Surf the Web to website: www.nla.gov.au to see project details.

Questacon—The National Science and Technology Centre
This museum, on King Edward Terrace between the National Library and High Court, features more than 200 hands-on exhibits spread through six galleries. The aim is to give everyone a basic understanding of scientific concepts through pushing buttons, pulling levers, and pressing knobs. Admission is adult $8, child $4. Open daily 10 a.m.-5 p.m. For further information, call (02) 6270-2800.

High Court of Australia
Opened in 1980, this uniquely shaped 40-meter-high concrete-and-glass structure overlooking Lake Burley Griffin is home to the highest court in Australia. The main feature is a seven-story public hall that is linked to the National Gallery by an overpass. Each of the three courtrooms features elegant woodwork, and in Courtroom One a large tapestry is displayed. The building is open daily 9:45 a.m.-4:30 p.m. If court is sitting you must stay in the courtrooms at least 10 minutes. The cafeteria here is excellent and has good views. For High Court information, call (02) 6270-6811.

National Gallery of Australia
Within the triangle, the only other federal building open to the public is the National Gallery. It displays the world's largest collection of Australian art, as well as featuring permanent and temporary exhibitions of art from around the world. The Australian collection includes Aboriginal art and works by 20th-century artists such as Arthur

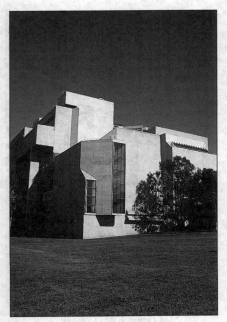

High Court of Australia

Boyd and Sidney Nolan (look for his distinctive Ned Kelly works). Photographs, sculptures, prints, drawings, and fashions are also displayed. For details on the program of regular lectures and film screenings, call (02) 6271-2502. The gallery is open daily 10 a.m.-5 p.m., with guided tours at 11 a.m. and 2 p.m. Admission is $3 pp.

National Capital Exhibition and Vicinity
This small center at Regatta Point on the north side of the lake (signposted from Commonwealth Ave.) tells the story of Canberra's development through photographs, models, and an audiovisual display. It's open daily 9 a.m.-5 p.m., and admission is free. For information call (02) 6257-1068.

Along the lakefront west of the center is **Terrestrial Globe,** where Captain Cook's three world journeys are traced. In front of the globe is the **Captain Cook Memorial Water Jet,** which throws water a spectacular 140 meters in the air. It operates daily 10 a.m.-noon, 2-4 p.m., and

during summer 7-9 p.m. **Blundell's Cottage,** 800 meters east of the National Capital Exhibition, is a six-room sandstone cottage that was built for a family that worked a local landowner's property before Canberra existed. Dating from 1860, it was moved to the site and restored in 1964. Admission is $2. Open Tues.-Sun. 10 a.m.-4 p.m. Farther around the lake, on Aspen Island, is the **National Carillon,** a three-column bell tower. Comprising 53 bells, including one weighing six tons, they are rung weekdays 12:45-1:30 p.m. and Sat.-Sun. 2:45-3:30 p.m.

OTHER SIGHTS

Canberra Museum
The main attraction of downtown Canberra is the newly opened **Canberra Museum,** London Circuit, tel. (02) 6207-3968. Through six small galleries the capital's entire history is told in a dynamic way. One gallery is reserved for changing exhibits. Admission is free. Open Tues.-Sun. 10 a.m.-5 p.m. (Friday until 9 p.m.).

Royal Australian Mint
This is where Australia's coinage is minted, and, naturally, you're not free to wander round the place or collect free samples. The closest you'll get to the coins is looking through a plate-glass window to the area where the minting process takes place. In the foyer are displays cataloging the development of Australian currency, including the story of Governor Macquarie who, in 1813, punched out the center of coins to create double the currency. Admission is free. Open Mon.-Fri. 9 a.m.-4 p.m., Sat.-Sun. 10 a.m.-3 p.m. The mint has an interesting gift shop and a café. It's southwest of Capital Hill on Denison St., tel. (02) 6202-6819.

Australian Federal Police Museum
Through displays of badges, uniforms, vehicles, and memorabilia from well-known police operations, this small museum catalogs the history of the Federal Police Force through a dozen-odd name changes. It's open Mon.-Fri. 9 a.m.-3 p.m., and admission is free. Located in the Police Services and Training Centre off Unwin Pl. in Weston, southwest of downtown, tel. (02) 6287-0618.

Australian National University

The grounds of this 10,000-student university sprawl over 145 hectares between City Hill and Black Mountain. The information center at Balmain Crescent, tel. (02) 6249-0794, has maps and entertainment programs. The grounds themselves are pleasant to wander through, and there are a couple of art galleries, restaurants, and cafés. On McCoy Circuit is the **National Film and Sound Archive,** tel. (02) 6209-3111, a collection of Australia's cinematographic and audio history. Old movie house equipment is on display, and old news bulletins run in a small theater. Open daily 9:30 a.m.-4 p.m. Admission is $3 pp.

Australian National Botanic Gardens

These gardens, on the lower slopes of Black Mountain west of the university, cover 50 hectares and are devoted entirely to the unique flora of Australia. Features include 600 species of eucalypts and a garden planted with species used by the Aborigines. Guided tours depart from the gardens' Visitor Information Centre, tel. (02) 6250-9540, weekdays at 11 a.m. and Sat.-Sun. at 11 a.m. and 2 p.m. The center is open daily 9:30 a.m.-4:30 p.m. To get there, take bus no. 904 to Clunes Ross Street.

Black Mountain

The best place for city views is 812-meter Black Mountain, immediately west of Civic. A sealed road leads to the summit and to **Telstra Tower,** which features displays of Australia's telecommunications history and has a revolving restaurant. Admission is $3, and it's open daily 9 a.m.-10 p.m., tel. (02) 6248-1911. Access is off Clunes Ross St., or take bus no. 904.

Australian War Memorial

This in one of Canberra's top attractions, housing an impressive collection of wartime memorabilia, photographs, and exhibitions as a tribute to the wars in which Australians have been involved, including Gallipoli, where thousands of Anzacs were killed, and the wars in which Australians have fought alongside Americans, such as WW II in the Pacific Ocean. The memorial reopened in 1999 after a $20 million refit, which saw the addition of a research center and the Bomber Command Experience, a mock-up of the cockpit of a Lancaster bomber. The memorial is on the

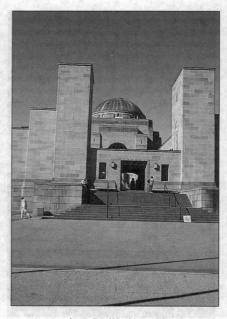

Australian War Memorial

north side of Lake Burley Griffin, at the foot of Mt. Ainslie at the top end of Anzac Parade, looking down to Parliament House. Along Anzac Parade are 11 memorials, commemorating different wars and the Australians who fought in them, including one dedicated to wartime nurses.

Another part of the memorial is the Hall of Memory, where the body of the unknown Australian soldier, symbolizing all those Australians lost in action, lies. Admission is free, and the museum is open daily 10 a.m.-4:45 p.m. Tours are held regularly. To get there take bus no. 901 or 302 from the city. Call (02) 6243-4211 to contact the memorial.

Duntroon House

This was the home of the first settler along the Molonglo River, and it is now part of the **Royal Military College,** established in 1911. Parts of the stone house date from the 1830s. For tour details, call (06) 275-9545. To get there from Civic, take Parkes Way southeast to Morshead Drive and turn onto Jubilee Avenue.

Australian Institute of Sport

This facility provides the training facilities for the cream of Australia's athletes. The indoor and outdoor training facilities and stadiums are of the highest standard and include swimming pools and tennis courts. Athletes in training lead tours daily at 1:30 p.m. and 2:30 p.m. For bookings, call (02) 6214-1010. Located five km northeast of City Hill on Leverrier Crescent. Get there on bus no. 431 from downtown.

Australian Heritage Village

North of Canberra, on the corner of the Federal Hwy. and Antill St., this place is a re-creation of a rural Australian village of late last century. With cobbled roads linking stone and timber buildings around a small lagoon, the village also boasts a large collection of buggies, carts, and carriages. On the grounds are various Australiana shops, galleries, a tavern, café, restaurant, and antique shops. Admission is free. Open daily 9 a.m.-5 p.m.

National Dinosaur Museum

Australia's only museum dedicated only to the prehistoric animals that once roamed the earth, this private collection includes 300 exhibits including 10 full-size dinosaur replicas. Mike Durrant, the founder, has collected specimens from around the world for display, with many bones and other fossils and minerals displayed to illustrate this period of the earth's history. Admission is $8. Open daily 10 a.m.-5 p.m. Located 11 km north of downtown on Gold Creek Rd., off Barton Hwy., tel. (02) 6230-2655 or (1800) 35-6000.

Canberra Space Centre and Vicinity

This interesting exhibit lies on the grounds of the Canberra Deep Space Communication Complex, southwest of downtown near Tinbinbilla. The main complex is operated by the CSIRO (Commonwealth Scientific and Industrial Research Organization) on behalf of NASA. It is one of three worldwide communication complexes (the others are in California and Spain) that together monitor space missions. The Space Centre, tel. (02) 6201-7880, is a public facility, holding a collection of space-exploration memorabilia, a few chunks of the Moon, details of all

the latest missions, and general space-related displays. It's open daily 9 a.m.-5 p.m.

To the north, an observatory opened in 1924 on Mt. Stromlo, high in the Brindabella Range, and for many years it was a world leader in space exploration. Today, the site has been transformed to **Stromlo Exploratory,** Cotter Rd., tel. (02) 6249-0232, with guided tours (four times daily), hands-on exhibits, and slide shows. It's open daily 9:30 a.m.-4:30 p.m.

OUTDOOR ACTIVITIES AND SPECTATOR SPORTS

Biking

Canberra is probably Australia's best city for biking, with more than 120 km of cycleways winding through the city and around Lake Burley Griffin. The best map for biking is *Canberra Cycleways* ($2.50), available from the main Tourist Information Centre and many bookshops.

Mr Spokes Bike Hire, in Acton Park, tel. (02) 6257-1188, rents mountain bikes for $8 an hour and $24 a day.

Canoeing and Boating

At the Acton Park Ferry Terminal, on the north shore of Lake Burley Griffin and immediately west of Commonwealth Ave., is **Lake Burley Griffin Boat Hire,** tel. (02) 6249-6861, which rents canoes and surf-skis for $10 an hour and catamarans for $20 an hour. **SS** *Maid Marion,* tel. 017-82-8355, cruises around the main body of the lake four times daily. The cost is $12 pp, and the departure point is the wharf by the National Library.

Swimming

The **Australian Institute of Sport** (see above) has a 50-meter heated pool open to the public; call for times; $3.50 per session; located eight km northwest of Civic on Leverrier Crescent, tel. (02) 6252-1444.

Rugby League

The **Canberra Raiders** were Australia's most successful rugby league team of the 1990s. They play home games every second week March-Sept. at Bruce Stadium, Battye St., Bruce. Call (02) 6253-2111 for ticketing information.

ARTS AND ENTERTAINMENT

Theater

The **Canberra Theatre,** London Circuit, Civic, tel. (02) 6257-1077, is the city's main venue for performing arts. The large theater seats around 1,200, and performances range from Shakespeare to international rock acts. Tickets range $30-70. **Gorman House Arts Centre,** Ainslie Ave., Braddon, occasionally has theater and dance performances. For ticketing details, call (02) 6249-7377.

Cinemas

A few cinemas are scattered around Civic Square, and the **National Library of Australia** screens films Tuesday and Thursday at lunchtime.

Casino Canberra

This European-style casino is on Constitution Ave., tel. (02) 6257-7074 or (1800) 80-6833. Games played are baccarat, blackjack, keno, pai gow, roulette, and sic bo. Dress regulations include no denim jeans or sports shoes, and blokes must wear a jacket and tie after 7 p.m. It's open weekends 24 hours, weekdays noon-6 a.m.

Bars and Nightclubs

The **Canberra Tradesmen's Union Club,** 2 Badham St., Dickson, tel. (02) 6248-0999, is a workingman's club four km north of downtown. It has rows and rows of pokies (slot machines), regular bingo sessions, a snooker room, and, best of all, beer for just $2 a schooner. The club also boasts a large collection of historic bicycles. **Mooseheads,** 105 London Circuit, tel. (02) 6257-6496, features a downstairs bar and an upstairs nightclub where the Top 40 is the drawcard. **Pandora's,** on the corner of Alinga and Mort Streets, tel. (02) 6248-7405, is a large dance club. Another nightclub, **Private Bin,** 50 Northbourne Ave., tel. (02) 6247-3030, is popular with the younger set. Inside this tri-level entertainment complex is a pool room, disco, and piano bar.

Festivals and Events

The **Canberra National Multicultural Festival,** the first three weeks of March, celebrates the city's birth and its cultural diversity. The festival opens with a colorful street party, while other features include an outdoor film festival, a nighttime street parade, fireworks display, hot-air balloon competition, entertainment in Glebe Park, and an evocative nighttime reading of Canberra's history. Every Easter the **National Folk Festival** takes place throughout the city, including on the streets and in the pubs, as well as at larger venues. In September, **Floriade** is a spectacular collection of springtime flowers.

SHOPPING

The **Canberra Centre** encompasses four blocks between City Walk, Ballumbir St., Petrie St., and Akuna Street in Civic. It has more than 150 shops, all surrounding a three-story glass-roofed atrium. In the **City Market** section, you'll find fresh produce and a food court. On the first floor is **Craftsman's Collection,** tel. (02) 6257-4733, crammed with Australiana, including pottery, glasswork, woodcarving, and jewelry. On the weekend, the **Old Bus Depot Markets,** Wentworth Ave., Kingston, is the place to head for local arts and crafts as well as fresh produce.

ACCOMMODATIONS

Getting a motel room close to the city center can be difficult midweek, so you should try to make advance reservations. On weekends the city is deserted and most motels offer reduced rates.

Hotels and Motels

You'll find several hotels and motels in and around Civic. Least expensive of the downtown motels **City Walk Hotel,** corner City Walk and Mort St., tel. (02) 6257-0124, right in the heart of the action. Rooms are small and basic, and while each has a private bathroom, kitchen and lounge facilities are shared. That aside, the price is right, with rooms from just $55 s, $59 d. Inexpensive. **Acacia Motor Lodge,** 65 Ainslie Ave., tel. (02) 6249-6955, a five-minute walk from the city center, is also well priced. Rates are $72 s, $78 d, which includes a continental breakfast. Moderate.

Other Moderately priced motels are on Northbourne Ave., immediately north of downtown, including **Quality Inn,** 82 Northbourne Ave., tel.

(02) 6249-1388, which has undergone a name change and been renovated. Rates are $80-105 s or d. **Olims Canberra,** corner Ainslie and Limestone Avenues, tel. (02) 6248-5511, first opened its doors in 1927 and is as close as you'll get to a historical accommodation in the capital. It's been totally renovated, and many rooms overlook a landscaped courtyard. Rates are $105-140 s or d, but on weekends rates drop to $75. Expensive. Other more expensive options north of Civic are: **Canberra Rex Hotel,** 150 Northbourne Ave., tel. (02) 6248-5311 or (1800) 02-6103, where rooms are $105-135 s or d (Expensive), and **Chifley on Northbourne,** 102 Northbourne Ave., tel. (02) 6249-1411, with large rooms and a range of facilities, $138 s or d (Premium).

Moving away from the city, **Hyatt Hotel Canberra,** Commonwealth Ave., Yarralumla, tel. (02) 6270-1234, adjacent to the Parliamentary Triangle and Lake Burley Griffin, is in a 1924 art deco heritage-listed building. This is the city's most luxurious hotel; rooms are $300 s or d. Luxury.

Victor Lodge, 29 Dawes St., Kingston, tel. (02) 6295-7777, is a small place two km from Parliament House. Meals are available, and guests can rent bikes. Rooms, with shared bathrooms, are $36 s $46 d. Inexpensive. Next door is **Motel Monaro,** 27 Dawes St., tel. (02) 6295-2111 or (1800) 24-1721, with large rooms and modern facilities for $79 s, $89 d. **Kingston Court,** 4 Tench St., tel. (02) 6295-2244, has 36 self-contained apartments each measuring close

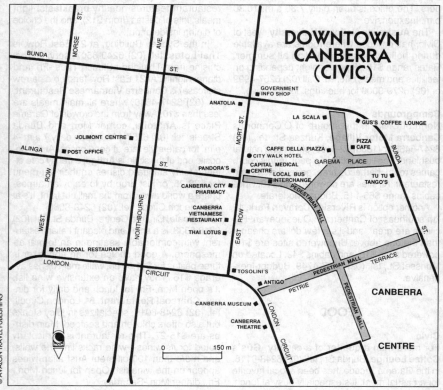

DOWNTOWN CANBERRA (CIVIC)

BUNDA ST.
MORSE ST.
AVE.
ST.
GOVERNMENT INFO SHOP
ANATOLIA
LA SCALA
GUS'S COFFEE LOUNGE
MORT ST.
PIZZA CAFE
JOLIMONT CENTRE
CAFFE DELLA PIAZZA
ALINGA
POST OFFICE
CITY WALK HOTEL
GAREMA PLACE
BUNDA ST.
ROW
ST.
PANDORA'S
CAPITAL MEDICAL CENTRE
LOCAL BUS INTERCHANGE
TU TU TANGO'S
CANBERRA CITY PHARMACY
WEST
NORTHBOURNE
EAST ROW
PEDESTRIAN MALL
CANBERRA VIETNAMESE RESTAURANT
THAI LOTUS
CHARCOAL RESTAURANT
LONDON
CIRCUIT
PEDESTRIAN MALL
TERRACE
TOSOLINI'S
ANTIGO
PETRIE
PEDESTRIAN MALL
CANBERRA
CANBERRA MUSEUM
LONDON CIRCUIT
CANBERRA THEATRE
CENTRE
MOON
0   150 m

© AVALON TRAVEL PUBLISHING

to 100 square meters and with a modern kitchen, balcony or courtyard, and laundry facility. The pool, half tennis court, and barbecue are for communal use. Rates are $110 s, $130 d. Premium.

The modern and stylish **Manuka Park Serviced Apartments** is set around a large pool. Each unit has a well-equipped kitchen, laundry, and separate bedroom area. Rates are $115 s or d. It's at 1 Oxley St., Manuka, tel. (02) 6285-1175 or (1800) 68-8227. Expensive.

Backpacker Accommodations
Canberra YHA, Dryandra St., O'Connor, tel. (02) 6248-9155, is a beautiful hostel six km northwest of Civic. All facilities are modern and well kept. Bikes can be rented, and there's a travel desk. Dorm beds are $16 pp, $18-23 pp in a twin room, and it's $5 pp extra for nonmembers. The office is open daily 7:30 a.m.-10:30 p.m. Inexpensive.

The **Australian National University,** west of Civic, has colleges where rooms are available during holiday breaks, including all summer. Rates range $18-48 pp per night depending on facilities and meals offered. Call (02) 6267-4999 or (02) 6279-9000 for bookings. Inexpensive.

Campgrounds
North of Civic, in the suburb of O'Connor, is **Canberra Motor Village,** Kunzea St., tel. (02) 6247-5466 or (1800) 02-6199, set among natural bushland. Facilities include a pool, tennis court, games room, barbecue area, general store, and restaurant. All sites are powered and $18, while cabins range $65-115. Budget/Moderate.

Another option is **Riverside Caravan Park,** 12 km southeast of Canberra in Queanbeyan. Facilities are great, and it's a few dollars cheaper than the one above. Unpowered sites are $10, powered sites $15, and cabins $42. Located on Morisset St., tel. (02) 6297-4749. Budget-Inexpensive.

FOOD

Civic
For more than a quarter of a century, **Gus's Coffee Lounge,** Bunda St., tel. (02) 6248-8118, in the Garema Arcade, has been a local favorite for a casual meal. It's especially busy at lunch,

when those in the know come to feast on focaccia and other European delights as well as a wide variety of desserts. Prices are excellent, with soup for $4.50 and most main dishes less than $10. Open daily 7:30 a.m.-midnight. Another popular breakfast hangout is **Tu Tu Tango's,** 124 Bunda St., tel. (02) 6257-7100, a modern café with tables inside and out and a wide variety of breakfast dishes.

One of Canberra's busiest cafés is **Caffe Della Piazza,** on Garema Place, tel. (02) 6248-9711. Tables are spread around the cobbled square and are perpetually filled with coffee-drinking locals. Across the mall is **Pizza Cafe,** tel. (02) 6248-9131, where a slice of pizza is $3 and a full pizza ranges $10-20. A favorite for Italian is **Tosolini's,** on the corner of East Row and London Circuit, tel. (02) 6247-4317. This bistro-style restaurant features healthy breakfasts, light meals, lots of pastas (from $12), and the choice of dining inside or out.

In the Sydney Building, at 27 East Row, is **Thai Lotus,** tel. (02) 6249-6507, serving Thai cuisine from Thailand at lunch Tues.-Fri. and dinner nightly. At 21 East Row (and up a narrow staircase) is **Canberra Vietnamese Restaurant,** tel. (02) 6247-4840, where all main meals are less than $10. Away from the crowds of Garema Place is **Anatolia,** corner Mort and Bunda Streets, tel. (02) 6257-1100, open daily 7 a.m.-4 p.m. for café-style fare at good prices. At the opposite end of the scale is **Antigo,** a trendy café offering fairly standard dishes on their set menu for $22-26; or just drop by to enjoy an atmosphere a world away from the mall out front. It's at 143 London Circuit, tel. (02) 6249-8080.

La Scala, Cinema Centre, Bunda St., tel. (02) 6248-8338, is a small and elegant Italian restaurant with comfortable seating in an formal atmosphere. A good choice for an appetizer is three pastas for $11.50 pp, while main dishes average $16. They have an extensive wine list. It's open Mon.-Fri. for lunch and daily for dinner. **Charcoal Restaurant,** 61 London Circuit, tel. (02) 6248-8015, specializes in juicy steaks but also offers chicken and seafood. Main dishes are $15-27. This restaurant is particularly noted for its wines—wine racks line the walls, and more than 100 different Australian wines appear on the wine list. Open for lunch Mon.-Fri., dinner Mon.-Saturday.

Parliamentary Triangle

The **Public Dining Room** in Parliament House has surprisingly good food, including all the usual Aussie fare, at reasonable prices. It's open daily 9 a.m.-5 p.m. (between 11 a.m. and 2 p.m. a $7.50 carvery is offered. **Sufficient Grounds,** in the High Court of Australia, has similar choices, as well as inexpensive afternoon teas. A popular politician hangout is **The Lobby Restaurant,** opposite Old Parliament House on Queen Victoria Terrace, tel. (02) 6273-1563. It's only open for lunch weekdays and dinner Tues.-Saturday.

Manuka

Manuka is a suburb south of Lake Burley Griffin, with services for politicians, bureaucrats, and embassy staff from around the world. In Manuka Arcade on Franklin St. is **My Café,** a quiet place with healthy snacks around $7. **La Grange,** tel. (02) 6295-8866, also on Franklin St., is a stylish bistro with main dishes $10-17. In Style Arcade is **Chez Daniel,** tel. (02) 6295-7122, with main dishes from $18. **Atlantic,** 20 Palmerston Lane, tel. (02) 6232-7888, offers a variety of meat dishes, but is best known for its seafood platters.

Black Mountain

Apart from an inexpensive café with excellent views, Telstra Tower boasts **The Tower Restaurant,** tel. (02) 6248-6162, a revolving restaurant with spectacular views, especially at sunset. At lunch an extensive buffet is offered for $27.50, while in the evening dinner plates average $20.

GETTING THERE

Air

Canberra Airport is on Pialligo Ave., 12 km east of downtown. **Ansett Australia,** tel. (13) 1300, and **Qantas,** tel. (13) 1313, have regular flights between Canberra and all major Australian cities. A taxi to downtown runs $15, or catch an **Airport Shuttle,** tel. (02) 6291-4592; $5-8.

Rail

The **Countrylink Xplorer** operates daily between Sydney and Canberra; four hours one-way; call (13) 2232 for bookings. **Canberra Link** is a combined rail/bus service from Melbourne. For details you should call V/Line at (03) 9619-

5000 or 13-2232. The railway station is on Wentworth Ave., Kingston, three km southeast of Capital Hill.

Bus

Long-distance buses arrive and depart from the **Jolimont Centre,** on the corner of Northbourne Ave. and Alinga St., Civic. **Greyhound Pioneer,** tel. (13) 2030, has regular services between Sydney and Canberra for $35 one-way (some services depart from Sydney Airport). **Murray's,** tel. (13) 2251, offers a quicker service (four hours) for a few bucks less and also runs east to the south coast town of Batemans Bay ($21).

GETTING AROUND

Bus

Canberra's local bus service, **ACTION** (ACT Internal Omnibus Network), runs throughout the city and suburbs Mon.-Sat. 7 a.m.-11 p.m. and Sunday 8:30 a.m.-6 p.m. A free brochure available from the information center details all attractions, including current hours and how to reach them by bus. The main terminal is at the west end of Garema Place on the corner of Alinga St. and East Row. The basic sector fare is $2, or pay $17 for a 10-trip ticket. For further information, call (13) 1710.

Taxi

The city has just one taxi company, **Aerial.** Call (06) 285-9222 for pickups.

Car Rental

Canberra has a good public transportation system, and tours (see below) cover most popular sights, but if you need to rent a car, call: **Avis,** tel. (02) 6249-6088; **Budget,** tel. (13) 2727; **Hertz,** tel. (02) 6257-4877; **National,** tel. (02) 6247-8888; or **Thrifty,** tel. (02) 6247-7422. For something cheaper, try **Value Rent-a-car,** tel. (02) 6295-6155, where cars are $45 per day and $200 per week.

Tours

The **Canberra Explorer,** tel. (13) 2251, makes 18 stops around a 25-km circuit, and there's a commentary along the way. The fare is adult $15, child $8. From the main terminal, bus no.

901 runs to sights around the Parliamentary Triangle.

SERVICES

The main **post office** is on Alinga St., Civic; it's open Mon.-Fri. 9 a.m.-5 p.m. **60 Minute Cleaners** is on Bailey's Corner, Civic, tel. (02) 6248-0521. **Thomas Cook Currency Exchange** is in the Canberra Centre, Bunda St., tel. (02) 6247-9984; open Mon.-Fri. 9 a.m.-5 p.m., Saturday 9:30 a.m.-12:30 p.m. Internet access is free at the National Library, but a 30-minute time limit is imposed. The main coach terminal, the **Jolimont Centre,** on Northbourne Ave., has a couple of computer terminals where public Internet access is $2 for 10 minutes.

Emergencies

Canberra Hospital is on Yamba Dr., Garran, tel. (02) 6244-2222. For medical emergencies, call (06) 244-2611. **Capital Medical Centre** looks after nonurgent cases; it's at 2 Mort St., Civic, tel. (02) 6257-3766; open Mon.-Fri. 8:30 a.m.-5 p.m. **Canberra City Pharmacy** is on the corner of Alinga St. and East Row, tel. (02) 6248-5469.

INFORMATION

Books

The **National Library of Australia** has more than five million books. It's open Mon.-Thurs. 9 a.m.-9 p.m., Fri.-Sat. 9 a.m.-4:30 p.m., and Sunday 1:30-4:30 p.m. Call (02) 6262-1111 for more information.

The **Government Info Shop,** 10 Mort St., tel. (02) 6247-7211, website: www.ausinfo.gov.au, is filled with government surveys and reports, but also has a wide range of natural and human history titles, coffee table books, and videos. **Dalton's,** in the Capital Centre, tel. (02) 6249-1844, is a good choice for general reading.

Information Centers

Canberra Visitors Centre is on Northbourne Ave., the main road into the city from the north. As well as tons of brochures on the city and its attractions, colorful interpretive boards display the best of everything the capital has to offer. Staff are helpful and friendly and are more than happy to make accommodation bookings. It's open daily 9 a.m.-5 p.m., tel. (02) 6205-0044 or (1800) 02-6166, website: www.canberratourism.com.au.

SNOWY MOUNTAINS

While Australia is best known for its red center, endless beaches, and the Great Barrier Reef, there is another side to this land of extremes, an area of alpine country that extends across the far south of New South Wales into Victoria. Many visitors from the Northern Hemisphere are surprised to find that many thousands of square kilometers of Australia are blanketed in snow for part of the year. But unlike the European Alps or North America's Rocky Mountains, there are no dominant peaks. Instead, Australia's Snowy Mountains are a high plateau, with only 10 peaks higher than 2,000 meters, and the highest, **Mt. Kosciuszko** (koz-ee-OS-ko), rising to just 2,228 meters. The entire area is protected by 690,000-hectare **Kosciuszko National Park.**

The mountains may not have the height of ranges on other continents, but in their own distinct way they are spectacular, an ancient landscape of alpine meadows, alive each spring with a carpet of wildflowers, providing almost unlimited opportunities for hiking in summer, while in winter lifts crank up on four ski resorts, including **Perisher-Blue,** whose network of lifts serves an area larger than any North American ski resort.

The Land

Volcanic activity deep below the earth's surface began pushing the Great Dividing Range upward around 350 million years ago. Around 20 million years ago, further uplift occurred, and the high plateau of today took shape. This final uplift pushed the plateau to elevations double those of today. Erosion from wind, rain, and snow saw the range slowly breaking down to its present height, while also forming its rugged topography.

During two successive ice ages, beginning 50,000 years ago, the area was covered in a deep sheet of ice. The last ice age was less severe, with glaciers confined to a combined total of less than 40 square km at the heads of the highest valleys. A number of lakes around Mt. Kosciuszko were gouged out by glaciers, with moraines of rock blocking the flow of water. These lakes provide the only clearly visible signs of glaciation on the Australian mainland.

Flora and Fauna

The most identifiable feature of the Snowy Mountains is the gnarled **snow gum,** but this is only one of 700 flora species in the park. While much of the Monaro region has been cleared for pastoral use, within the boundaries of Kosciuszko National Park many east-facing valleys are naturally devoid of trees. On the opposite side of the range, where rainfall is high, forests of towering mountain ash, stands of stringybark, and even a small area of rainforest are able to be supported. At higher elevations, between 1,500 and 1,800 meters, dense forest gives way to open forests of alpine ash and snow gum. Above 1,800 meters, treeless alpine meadows are dominated by heathlands, and grasslands of snow grasses, daisies, grand orchids, and violets are found, broken only by ferns and sphagnum bogs.

The great diversity of vegetation provides ideal habitat for many species of fauna. Gray kangaroos, red-neck wallabies, wombats, koalas, and the rare tiger quoll live at lower elevations. Only small rodents and marsupials such as the rare mountain pygmy possum, which lives in scree-covered slopes, live above the treeline.

HISTORY

The First Visitors

Around 15,000 years ago, as Australia's climate warmed, the mountains became habitable for humans year-round. For thousands of years, Aboriginal people living in the valleys would head for the high country to feast on **bogong moths,** a great delicacy rich in protein.

Exploration, Gold, and Settlement

Explorers Hume and Hovell were the first Europeans to visit the mountains. Paul Edmond Strzelecki later surveyed much of the high country, naming Mt. Kosciuszko for the patriot of his Polish homeland. The talk of all Australian colonies in the 1850s was gold, and many a high-country stockman kept his eyes peeled for the precious metal. The first gold strike in the mountains was made by the Pollock brothers in

November 1859. The area experienced no sudden rush, but as finds in neighboring Victoria declined, thousands of diggers crossed the mountains to try their luck at the field that became known as **Kiandra.** A year later, at the height of the rush, 10,000 diggers lived in the shantytown. As finds were made elsewhere and the harsh winter climate came upon them, the diggers moved on.

With the diggers gone, the pastoral service towns of Cooma, Jindabyne, and Adaminaby continued to grow. The rail line reached Cooma in 1889, opening up the mountains to tourists who came to hike in summer and ski in winter. A small area of the mountains was set aside for public recreation in 1906, but it was not until 1944 that the foundation of the national park as it is today was proclaimed.

The Snowy Mountains Scheme

Best known through the poetry of Banjo Patterson, the Snowy River is much altered from its original state, especially its upper reaches, which have been diverted to form an important part of the Snowy Mountains Scheme, which harnesses the river's hydroelectric power as well as providing water for inland irrigation in one of Australia's greatest engineering feats.

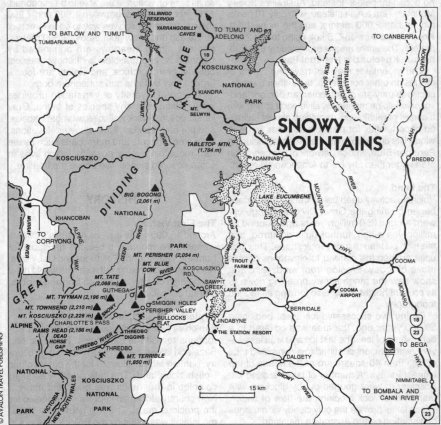

AUSTRALIA—BIRTHPLACE OF COMPETITIVE SKIING?

For early residents of the gold-rush town of Kiandra, skiing was a great way to break up the long, cold winter. Skis were made from alpine ash, and although ski poles weren't used, a single sapling was pushed into the snow to propel the skier forward, then straddled to control braking. In 1878, Kiandra hosted a skiing carnival, an event that is claimed to make Australia the point of origin for competitive downhill skiing.

As early as the 1880s, plans were being made to change the river's direction to divert its waters to what was then an agricultural wasteland in southwestern New South Wales. These plans became financially viable in the 1920s, when the river's hydroelectric power was harnessed to supply electricity to Canberra, the nation's new capital. The scheme was launched on 17 October 1949 with the first stage, a five-km tunnel completed to Guthega Dam. A 60,000-kilowatt power station was constructed at the dam. Eucumbene Dam was completed in 1958, along with another power station, and on 1 April 1966 the Snowy River finally flowed westward, changing the face of Australian agriculture forever.

COOMA

Descending into Cooma (pop. 7,500), in the heart of the Monaro, your first impression will be the profusion of ski shops and billboards advertising the ski resorts a farther 80 km away. Cooma itself rarely gets snow, but for four months each year, tens of thousands of snowbound Sydneysiders pass through town.

The Monaro's first permanent settlers were squatters who had secured massive cattle runs in the region. Cooma was the name of one of these original runs and has grown from a small village. After the Snowy Mountains Authority established its headquarters there, the population boomed, rising for a time to above 15,000.

Sights

Construction of the Snowy Mountains Scheme may have finished 20 years ago, but day-to-day operations employ more than 600 people. Many of these are based at the scheme's headquarters on Cooma's northern outskirts. A modern complex replaced the old in 1987, and within its walls is the **Snowy Information Centre**, tel. (02) 6453-2004 or (1800) 62-3776, with models of the scheme's various aspects, a video presentation, and display boards detailing its workings. This is the place to book tours of the scheme's various operations or pick up the self-guided driving tour brochures. The facility is open Mon.-Fri. 8 a.m.-5 p.m., Sat.-Sun. 8 a.m.-1 p.m.

The streets of Cooma are dotted with historic buildings, many of which are along the main drag. On the corner of Sharp and Lambie Streets is the **Royal Hotel**, a sandstone structure dating from 1858. Lambie Street boasts a number of Victorian-era terraces, while Barrack St., parallel to Lambie, has several civic buildings, including a post office (1877), courthouse (1879), and jail (1867).

Accommodations and Food

Except for winter weekends, accommodation in Cooma is easy to come by. **Dodd's Hotel**, Commissioner St., tel. (02) 6452-2011, has rooms above a noisy bar for $24 s, $40 d, including breakfast. Inexpensive. A step up in quality is the **Family Motel**, 32 Massie St., tel. (02) 6452-1414, where rooms with private bathrooms are $32 s, $42 d in summer, and $45 s, $55 d in winter. Rates include breakfast. Inexpensive. Another inexpensive place is **Bunkhouse Motel**, 28-30 Soho St., tel. (02) 6452-2983, featuring self-contained units and a laundry for $35 s, $45 d. The **Swiss Motel**, 34 Massie St., tel. (02) 6452-1950, has rooms of a reasonable standard for $37 s, $47 d. Inexpensive. **Nebula Motel**, 42 Bombala St., tel. (02) 6452-4133, is a well-kept accommodation with modern rooms and a range of handy facilities; rates are $54 s, $62 d and slightly higher in winter. Moderate. The best accommodation in town is the **Cooma Motor Lodge**, on the northeast approach to town at 6 Sharp St., tel. (02) 6452-1888; $75-100 s or d. Moderate.

The Monaro Highway through town is lined with roadhouses and cafés and, although park-

Cooma Courthouse

ing is often difficult in the center of town, that is where the best eateries are. **Cafe Upstairs,** at 121 Sharp St., tel. (02) 6452-4488, serves lunches for $6-8 and dinners under $14. This place gets crowded at lunch. Across the road are two bakeries; try **Rolf's** for the best meat pies. **Cooma Ex-serviceman's Club,** 106 Vale St., tel. (02) 6452-1144, serves bistro meals from $4-8 and has a more formal restaurant open Fri.-Sun. 6-9 p.m. Cooma has a couple of good Asian restaurants, including **Grand Court Chinese Restaurant,** Snowstop Village, Sharp St., tel. (02) 6452-4525.

Transportation, Services, and Information
Getting to the mountains by air is not very practical. Cooma has the closest airport taking scheduled flights, but there is no scheduled bus service into the mountains from this airport. **Eastern Australia,** tel. (13) 1313, flies daily between Sydney and Cooma, and **Kendell,** tel. (13) 1300, flies into Cooma from Melbourne. **Greyhound Pioneer,** tel. (13) 2030, operates services between Cooma and: Sydney, Canberra, and Jindabyne.

Cooma Visitors Centre is in the center of town on Sharp St., tel. (02) 6450-1742 or (1800) 63-6525; open daily 9 a.m.-5 p.m.

JINDABYNE

The service town of Jindabyne is 65 km west of Cooma and a 30-minute drive from the major ski areas. It's not a pretty town, nor is the surrounding scarred landscape anything to write home about, but it provides an excellent off-mountain base during the ski season. The town's official name is New Jindabyne. The original Jindabyne was in a valley that flooded when a dam for the Snowy Mountains Scheme was built in the 1960s. Residents were moved to a planned town at a higher elevation, overlooking the lake that was their nemesis.

Fishing
In summer, fishing is by far the most popular activity. In the earliest days of the Snowy Mountains Scheme, rainbow and brown trout were stocked in many waterways. Today, within a close proximity to Jindabyne, trout can be found in all manmade lakes and many of the rivers that flow into them, including Lakes Jindabyne and Eucumbene. In the warmer months of summer, the fish tend to stay in deeper waters, making trolling and downrigging the preferred fishing method. In the evenings, though, fish tend to rise to the surface and feed. Thus the edge of the lakes and, for experienced fly-fishers, the rivers provide a challenge year-round. **High Country Fly Fishing,** Nugget's Crossing, tel. (02) 6456-2989, offers guided fishing on local lakes and sells tackle. Steve Williamson of **Trout Fishing Adventures,** tel. 018-02-4436, comes highly recommended for guided river trips.

Eucumbene Trout Farm, on the road out to Lake Eucumbene, tel. (02) 6456-8866, is a com-

NEW SOUTH WALES SKIING

Skiing in Australia is unlike skiing anywhere else in the world. Australian skiers are unbelievably keen; most travel great distances to reach the mountains, prices are high, and the slopes crowded in even the most atrocious conditions. That said, after a fresh fall of snow, skiing through massive granite boulders and stands of gnarled snowy gums on a cloudless day is an unforgettable experience. Heading to the mountains is known as "going to the snow," and when fresh snow has fallen and the weekend forecast is good, Friday night sees cars bumper to bumper from Sydney's southwestern suburbs to Jindabyne. On-snow accommodations are at a premium all winter and must be booked well in advance. The opening of the ski season, the first weekend of June, is infamous for a lack of snow, but no one seems to mind too much, especially the publicans, who do a roaring trade. Generally, good snow conditions can be relied on July to mid-September, while snowmaking allows skiing a month either side of these dates.

The four ski areas are **Thredbo**, a stylish European-style village with mostly intermediate terrain and some of Australia's longest runs; **Perisher-Blue**, a conglomeration of four ski areas that combined in 1995 to form Australia's largest resort; **Charlottes Pass,** accessible only by snowcat; and **Mt. Selwyn,** popular with families and beginners. New South Wales is not the only state with skiing; Victoria has five resorts with a great variety of skiing, and Tasmania has two small ski areas.

Thredbo

Thredbo is considered the most upmarket of Australia's ski resorts, mainly due to the self-contained European-style village overlooking the lower slopes. Twelve lifts access 175 hectares of skiing for all levels of expertise. Karel's T-bar rises to 2,037 meters, making it the highest lift point in Australia. From the summit, trails up to five km long descend to the valley floor. Thredbo is also the only Australian resort to host a World Cup Event (1989 World Cup Giant Slalom and Slalom). Although Thredbo's season runs early June to early Oct., generally only from July to mid-Sept. are all lifts operational. Lift tickets are adult $62, child $33, with five-day passes adult $270, child $158. Thredbo is also a good resort for seniors; those over 65 pay only $10 for a day pass. Other costs to budget for are park entry ($18 per car) and rental equipment ($20-50 per day).

For further resort information, call (02) 6459-4100 or visit www.thredbo.com.au.

Perisher-Blue

The combining of four existing ski resorts in 1995 to create Perisher-Blue was the ski news of the decade, creating a megaresort of more than 50 lifts spanning seven mountains and 1,605 hectares. The original resorts (Perisher Valley, Smiggin Holes, Blue Cow, and Guthega) are linked by lifts and trails, but it's most practical to ski in just one area. One of the great advantages of Perisher-Blue is **Skitube,** an underground rail service linking Bullocks Flat, along Alpine Way, to Perisher Valley and Blue Cow. This allows skiers to avoid paying the national park entrance fee ($18 per car), while parking below the snowline. Perisher Valley is heart of the ski area, with Front Valley suited to beginners and Mt. Perisher to intermediates. Smiggin Holes and Guthega are also well suited to beginners, while Blue Cow has runs for all abilities, including Kamikaze, claimed to be Australia's steepest run. Lift tickets are priced the same as Thredbo, with the Skitube an extra $10 pp. For resort information, call (02) 6456-2010 or visit www.perisherblue.com.au.

Charlottes Pass

Australia's oldest ski area, Charlottes Pass sits well above the treeline at the end of Kosciusko Road. While not extensive nor particularly steep, the slopes are uncrowded and the scenery is beautiful. The resort road is snowed over for most of the winter; access is by snowcat and limited to those staying at the resort's two lodges. **Stillwell Lodge,** tel. (02) 6457-5073, charges $140 pp per night, including meals, and **Kosciusko Chalet,** tel. (02) 6457-5245, runs $159 pp. For general resort information, call (02) 6457-5247.

Mount Selwyn

Skiing in Australia began just around the corner from this small day-use resort along the Snowy Mountains Hwy. west of Kiandra. Cooma is 100 km to the southeast, and the closest accommodation is 50 km away at Adaminaby. Twelve lifts access 45 hectares of beginner and easy-intermediate skiing. The day lodge has ski rentals, a ski school, and a restaurant. But probably the best aspect of skiing at Mt. Selwyn is the cost—day tickets are only adult $32, child $18. For resort information, call (02) 6454-9488.

mercial operation open to the public for trout fishing. Two trout ponds are open for fishing. One is large and requires some fishing expertise, while in the small one you can't miss. Either way, you'll end up with a juicy trout to be cooked on the spot or prepared to take away. Also at the trout farm is a horseback riding center, good for beginners. Both are open daily 9 a.m.-7 p.m.

Accommodations

Winter is high season in all parts of the Snowy Mountains. Rather than offer greatly reduced rates in non-skiing months, most accommodations offer packages, which are a good deal if you want to spend three or four days in the mountains. That said, summer rates at the ski areas themselves are an even better deal and are closer to the action. Bookings in the ski season are essential, especially during school holidays and on weekends. The easiest way to secure a room during this period is through a booking agent, such as **Alpine Resort and Travel Centre,** tel. (02) 6456-2999 or (1800) 80-2315, while the rest of the year you should contact the accommodations directly.

Since being refurbished in 1994, **Lazy Harry's Lodge,** 18 Clyde St., tel. (02) 6456-1957, is the best of the budget accommodations in town. Each room has private facilities, and many have lake views. The communal kitchen is large and modern. Other facilities include a drying room and lounge area with a log fire. Rates in summer are $50 s or d, while in winter they start at $70 s or d. Four-share dorms are $15 pp in summer, $30 pp in winter. Inexpensive. Another inexpensive accommodation is **Aspen Chalet,** Kosciuszko Rd., tel. (02) 6456-2372 or (1800) 04-6275, where summer rates are $55 s, $65 d, and double in winter. Moderate.

Lake Jindabyne Hotel, Kosciuszko Rd., tel. (02) 6456-2203, best known as Jindabyne's favorite drinking hole, has basic motel units on the lake side of the complex. Summer rates are $50 s, $70 d, including breakfast, but they double and even triple in winter. Moderate. **Nettin Chalet,** 24 Nettin Circuit, tel. (02) 6456-2692, has excellent summer rates; $42 pp, with most rooms having balconies and lake or mountain views, and guest facilities including a spa, sauna, game room, bar, and bistro. Moderate. **Enzian Lodge,** 42 Gippsland St., tel. (02) 6456-2038, is

a pleasant guesthouse within walking distance of all services. With just eight rooms, the atmosphere is personal and relaxed. Summer rates are $40 s, $65 d, rising to $85 s, $130 d in winter. All rates include breakfast. Moderate.

On the road out to Dalgety, six km south of Jindabyne, is **The Station Resort,** tel. (02) 6456-2895 or (1800) 02-0808, a sprawling complex of 1,500 beds under the same ownership as Perisher-Blue ski area. Accommodation is sparse; most rooms are six- to 10-bed dorms, but there are also a few doubles available. The resort is best suited for those looking for a cheap place to sleep and a raging nightlife. Other features include a bistro and restaurant, bar, nightclub, and laundry. Summer rates are $70 s or d, while in winter packages for two days' accommodation, breakfasts, and skiing start at around $140 pp. Moderate.

Also out of town, but on the road to Thredbo, is the upmarket **Lake Crackenback Resort,** Alpine Way, tel. (02) 6456-2960 or (1800) 02-0524. Built over a lake, this Novotel property features facilities such as a par-three golf course, indoor pool, fitness room, and tennis courts. The rooms are spacious and luxurious, with each holding a kitchen and laundry. Summer rates start at $180 s or d. Luxury.

Snowline Caravan Park is on Kosciuszko Rd. two km southwest of Jindabyne, tel. (02) 6456-2099 or (1800) 24-8148. Grassed tent sites are spread among trees and overlook the lake ($14-22), and while basic cabins are $38, there are some new ones up by the road for $85. Budget-Inexpensive.

Food

Restaurants are in some motels, but most are in **Jindabyne Shopping Centre,** overlooking the lake, and **Nugget's Crossing,** toward the mountains. A great place for breakfast is **Sundance Bakehouse,** in Nugget's Crossing. **Mario's Mineshaft Restaurant,** Lakeview Plaza Motel, 2 Snowy River Hwy., tel. (02) 6456-2727, is the place to head for pizza. Other Italian dishes are offered and tables are set around a log fire. The **Brumby Bar,** Jindabyne Shopping Centre, tel. (02) 6456-2526, is a popular steakhouse, where you choose a steak and cook it on a central chargrill. A restaurant in the Station Resort has a similar setup.

Information

Snowy Region Information Centre is beyond Jindabyne Shopping Centre toward the mountains, tel. (02) 6450-5600.

JINDABYNE TO CHARLOTTES PASS

Beyond Jindabyne, Kosciuszko Rd. passes the Kosciuszko National Park gate, where an entrance fee of $18 per vehicle will be collected (or pay $90 for an annual pass), and climbs steadily to a lookout over Lake Jindabyne, then continues into the park's interior.

Sawpit Creek

Sawpit Creek, 15 km from Jindabyne along Kosciuszko Rd., is home to **Park Headquarters,** tel. (02) 6450-5600. The center has displays on the park's natural wonders and an audiovisual. It's open daily 8 a.m.-6 p.m. Beyond the center is a pleasant picnic area with barbecues and the trailhead for a 1.6-km hike through a subalpine environment.

Adjoining park headquarters is **Kosciuszko Mountain Retreat,** tel. (02) 6456-2224, a large national park campground set among eucalypts. Unpowered sites are $18, powered sites $26, and cabins range $65-150 depending on the season.

Blue Cow

Blue Cow, part of the massive Perisher-Blue ski area, is accessible only by **Skitube,** tel. (02) 6456-2010, a rail system built to transport skiers from below the snowline to Blue Cow. The Skitube begins from Bullocks Flat, on the Alpine Way, and reaches a depth of up to 550 meters under the ground as it makes its six-km trek to Blue Cow. At Blue Cow you'll find many hiking opportunities, and mountain bikes can be rented for $12 per hour. The half-day ($38) and full-day ($52) bike rental rates include travel on the Skitube. A bistro at Blue Cow is open daily 10 a.m.-4 p.m. Outside of the ski season, Skitube operates between Christmas and May four to seven times daily except Monday. The roundtrip fare from Bullock's Flat to Blue Cow is adult $22, child $12. From Perisher, the fare is adult $16, child $9.

Charlottes Pass and Nearby Hiking

Kosciuszko Road ends on a high ridge overlooking the alpine village of Charlottes Pass. In winter, the road is snowed over and village access is by snowcat from Perisher Valley. In summer, Charlottes Pass becomes a popular staging area for hikes, including to the summit of Mt. Kosciuszko. This part of the national park has a complex trail system, and because of the high elevation of the road, most of the hard work has been done. The main trails are the **Main Range Track** and **Summit Walk.** Both end at the summit of Australia's highest peak, **Mt. Kosciuszko.** The Main Range Track descends to the headwaters of the famous Snowy River before climbing to a lookout over Blue Lake, one of five glacial features around the peak. This lookout is five km from Charlottes Pass, with Kosciuszko's summit a farther seven km. The Summit Walk is a more direct route, following an old four-wheel drive track to the summit; eight km one-way.

In Charlottes Pass village is **Kosciuszko Chalet,** tel. (02) 6457-5245 or (1800) 02-6369, a relaxed accommodation where summer rates are $95 pp, including meals.

THREDBO

Thredbo is the only New South Wales ski area actively promoting summer activities, but with Australia's beach-loving population, it's a hard task, and outside of winter, the village is quiet. Thredbo lies on the Alpine Way 36 km southwest of Jindabyne, spread along a steep north-facing hill, overlooking the valley floor and ski area.

Summer Sights and Recreation

A great variety of activities are possible in the village; most can be booked through the **Thredbo Centre,** tel. (02) 6459-4100, website: www.thredbo.com.au. The **Crackenback Express** chairlift rises from the village to an elevation of 1,930 meters, providing an excellent starting point for hiking through the high country. The most popular trail is to the summit of Mt. Kosciuszko (seven km one-way). The summit trek is steep, but can be done by anyone with a reasonable level of fitness. Another good hike is the 10-km **Dead Horse Gap/Thredbo River Track,** which follows a ridge from the top of the chairlift to the summit of the Alpine Way, returning to the village along the Thredbo River. A full-day ticket for the chairlift costs $18, but the wide variety of multi-activity passes provide the best value. For example, the chairlift, three bobsled rides, and a game of golf is $35. The **Alpine Slide,** a twisting 700-meter bobsled run on which speeds of 50 kph can be reached, is located at the base of the village. A single ride is $4, three rides $9, and 10 rides $20. Other resort facilities include a challenging nine-hole golf course (greens fees $12), tennis, guided walks, horseback riding, whitewater rafting, mountain biking, and fishing.

Raw NRG, tel. (02) 6457-6282, rents mountain bikes for $16 per hour or $48 per day. This company offers a good deal for beginning riders—a day's instruction, guided rides, rentals, and a chairlift pass for $100 pp.

Events

A packed schedule of events takes place each summer, commencing with the Thredbo Summer Cup, the weekend after Christmas—if there's any snow left. **Thredbo Blues Festival,** in mid-January, is a weekend of music and entertainment. In late January the **Alpine Wildflower Festival** features guided walks, a photographic display, and painting workshop. **Thredbo Adventure Week,** the last week of February, is an opportunity to try a variety of adventure activities, including mountain biking, climbing, abseiling, and fly-fishing. Events thin out after this, with the **Australian Mountain Bike Championships** held mid-March, the **Adventure Film Festival** in late March, a golf tournament early April, and the **Legends of Jazz Festival** the first weekend of May.

Accommodations

During the ski season accommodations in Thredbo are at a premium. In summer, things are very different and some excellent packages are offered. For bookings and current rates, either contact the accommodations direct or call Alpine Accommodation Reservations at (02) 6457-2066 or (1800) 81-1351.

Thredbo YHA Lodge, Jack Adams Path, tel. (02) 6457-6376, is the cheapest lodging option in the village. The hostel was purpose-built, with a modern kitchen, lounge area, laundry, and drying

room. Summer rates are $16 pp in a dorm or $20 pp twin. In the ski season rates rise to $38 pp per night. During this time a ballot (lottery) system is in place, with reservations needed months in advance. Inexpensive.

Thredbo Alpine Hotel, tel. (02) 6459-4200 or (1800) 02-6333, is a three-story complex in the heart of the village. Rooms are spacious and comfortable. Summer rates are $115 s or d including breakfast. Expensive.

Many of Thredbo's most-popular accommodations are European-style ski lodges. **Bernti's,** tel. (02) 6457-6332 or (1800) 50-0105, is a central lodge with a relaxed atmosphere and a real mountain charm. Facilities include a café, bar, restaurant, sauna, spa, and large lounge area. Summer rates are $80 s, $100 d, including breakfast, but their various packages, from $90 pp, are a better deal. Expensive.

All rates quoted below are for high season (August); rates in July and September will be markedly lower (around 25%)—and in June up to 50% lower.

powder day at Thredbo

One of the best deals is **Riverside Cabins,** tel. (02) 6457-6700, set alongside Thredbo River away from the village. Each unit is fully self-contained. Rates are $599-899 pp for five nights' accommodation and a corresponding five-day lift pass.

Thredbo's many self-contained apartments come into their own during the ski season when rates in the village are phenomenally high, ranging $350-1,200 per night. In the heart of the village and also self-contained is **Thredbo Alpine Apartments,** Friday Dr., tel. (02) 6457-6414; $549-849 pp for five nights with ski passes.

Between Thredbo and Bullocks Flat is Thredbo Diggings, site of a short-lived gold rush and now a small riverside campground.

Transportation
In winter, **Greyhound Pioneer,** tel. (13) 2030, operates daily services between Sydney and Thredbo.

WEST FROM THREDBO ON THE ALPINE WAY

From Thredbo, the Alpine Way climbs steadily through the Thredbo Valley to Dead Horse Gap, atop the Great Dividing Range, before descending into a remote part of the national park that was only opened up with the construction of the Snowy Mountains Scheme. The road then changes direction sharply to the north and descends into the rugged hill country around Khancoban.

A long stretch of road beyond the pass is unsealed and can be rough going in a two-wheel drive. This section of road is closed in winter, reopening when the snow melts (usually October).

Khancoban
Khancoban, 113 km northwest of Jindabyne along the Alpine Way, is a small high country town that exists to serve workers on the Snowy Mountains Scheme. Water from the upper reaches of the Snowy River is pumped westward to two massive power stations near Khancoban, before being discharged into the Murray River. Part of this system, **Murray One Power Station,** is open for tours daily 9 a.m.-4 p.m. Book through the Snowy Information Centre in Cooma, tel. (02) 6453-2004. Khancoban's proximity to

some of the country's best trout fishing makes it an excellent base for anglers. The town also has a nine-hole golf course, tennis courts, and **Khancoban Trail Rides,** tel. (02) 6076-9455.

Khancoban Alpine Inn, tel. (02) 6076-9471, is the town's only motel and has a bar and restaurant; rooms are $55 s, $68 d. Moderate. Camping is through town to the west at **Khancoban Lakeside Caravan Resort,** tel. (02) 6076-9488, where sites are $11-13 and cabins $40-60. Budget-Inexpensive.

SOUTHWEST SLOPES

The southwest slopes, as they are called, encompass the northern end of Kosciuszko National Park as well as the **Tumut Valley,** an important link in the Snowy Mountains Scheme. From Cooma, access to the region is along the **Snowy Mountains Highway.** From Jindabyne, you can take the Alpine Way (see above), a longer yet more scenic alternative.

Kiandra
The ghost town of Kiandra, in the north end of Kosciuszko National Park, is 90 km northwest of Cooma and at the junction of a road through the mountains to Khancoban. Kiandra provides a graphic reminder of gold-rush days, when thousands of diggers would converge on a newly discovered field and just as quickly move to the next. In Kiandra's case, the year was 1859, and it was around 16,000 diggers who came to try their luck. Through pastoral use and the Snowy Mountains Scheme, the landscape surrounding Kiandra has changed considerably in the last 100 years, but buildings in varying degrees of disrepair remain. **Kiandra Heritage Trail** leads through the once-thriving town, with boards describing the original purpose of each building.

Yarrangobilly Caves
This extensive system of limestone caves is at the floor of the Yarrangobilly River Valley, 20 km north of Kiandra. The cave system extends over an area of 12 square km and includes more than 200 caves. The limestone that the caves are in is estimated to be up to 450 million years old, and during all that time, spectacular formations have developed. The **Glory Hole Cave** is open for self-

guiding tours daily 9 a.m.-5 p.m. ($4 pp), while tours of the other caves are offered weekdays at 1 p.m. and weekends at 11 a.m., 1 p.m., and 3 p.m. ($8-12 pp). For details, call (02) 6454-9597.

Tumut

Tumut (meaning "Quiet Resting Place by the River") boomed with construction of the Snowy Mountains Scheme, although it was the hard work of settlers from as early as the 1820s that cleared the vast tracts of land along the valley floor. Two of the scheme's largest dams are close to town, and **Tumut Three Power Station,** boasting the largest generating capacity of all the power stations, is open for tours 10 a.m.-2:30 p.m.

Fishing in lakes and streams around Tumut is legendary. The most accessible spots are along the Tumut River, where experienced fly fishers rate this river as among the best in the country. **Blowering Dam,** 10 km north of Tumut, is stocked with trout, cod, and perch.

Around town are interesting cottage industries worth visiting. Locally grown millet is prepared and processed at **Tumut Broom Co.,** 30 Adelong Rd., tel. (02) 6947-2804; open Mon.-Fri. 9 a.m.-4 p.m. for factory tours. Stock whips are made at **Tumut Valley Whipworks and Saddlery,** 139 Wynyard St., tel. (02) 6947-3889, and you can try cracking a whip yourself; open Mon.-Fri. 9 a.m.-5 p.m., Saturday 9 a.m.-3 p.m. Locally excavated marble, which is renowned for its amazing colors, is cut and polished at a factory on Adelong Road; it's open to the public Mon.-Fri. 3-4 p.m.

The **Commercial Hotel,** 103 Wynyard St., tel. (02) 6947-1040, has high-standard rooms, each with private facilities, for $50 s, $65 d, including breakfast. Moderate. None of the town's half dozen motels are particularly good value, although standards are generally good. Try **Ashton Townhouse Motel,** 124 Wynyard St., tel. (02) 6947-1999, where facilities include a pool;

$70 s, $82 d. Moderate. **Riverglade Caravan Park** is spread along the Tumut River. Unpowered sites are $12, powered sites $16. It's right in town on the main highway through town, tel. (02) 6947-2528. Budget.

Tumut has a surprisingly large number of cafés and quality restaurants. One of the best is **Brooklyn on Fitzroy,** 10-12 Fitzroy St., tel. (02) 6947-4022, housed in an old homestead restored to an upmarket restaurant, elegantly decorated in turn-of-the-century style. Main meals start at $13.50, or for $18 you get the three-course Squatters Meal. Open Tues.-Sat. for lunch and dinner.

Tumut Region Visitors Centre is in an old butter factory on Adelong Rd., tel. (02) 6947-1849; open daily 8 a.m.-6 p.m.

Adelong

With a population that hovers around 1,000, Adelong is a far cry from the 1860s when 20,000 diggers lived on surrounding goldfields. Like most other fields, miners left as quickly as they arrived, but, in Adelong's case, the town had already gained an air of permanency. These prosperous beginnings can be seen along the main drag, where many National Trust-classified buildings have been restored. During the original rush, claims were made on every stream and gully in the region; at Adelong Falls traces of the diggers' frantic activities can be seen.

Batlow

If you like apples and apple cider, you'll love Batlow, a small town of 1,500 in the Tumut Valley surrounded by Australia's largest concentration of apple orchards. Thousands of tons of apples are processed into apple juice and canned for apple pie each year under the famous Mountain Maid brand. To sample the apples and see the packing complex, head to **Batlow Fruit Co-op,** Forest Rd., tel. (02) 6949-1408, weekdays 9 a.m.-4 p.m.

SOUTH-CENTRAL NEW SOUTH WALES

In 1817, while exploring west of the Snowy Mountains, John Oxley planted a couple of oak and apricot trees to commemorate the king's birthday and noted in his diary that the trees would "serve to commemorate the day and situation, should these desolate plains ever again be visited by civilized man of which, however, I think there is little probability." But how wrong he was. As traffic on the Sydney-Melbourne route increased, towns such as **Yass, Gundagai,** and **Albury** thrived. In later years, the untapped potential of the vast, empty tracts of land along the **Murray** and **Murrumbidgee Rivers** was realized as modern technology developed a complex irrigation system that transformed the countryside. The **Murrumbidgee Irrigation Area** became among the most intensely farmed regions of the country, with crops including more than 90% of Australia's rice, 80% of the state's wine grapes, and every single gherkin you'll ever eat at an Australian McDonald's.

GOULBURN TO WAGGA WAGGA

Yass

The area around Yass was opened up to settlers after the explorers Hume and Hovell returned to Sydney with reports of land suitable for grazing. Hume ended up settling in Yass. His home, **Cooma Cottage,** one of the oldest houses still standing in this part of the state, has been restored to its 1870s colonial glory and is open daily except Tuesday 10 a.m.-4 p.m. Admission is $4, and about that amount again will get you tea and scones in the tearooms. The house is five km east of Yass along the Hume Hwy., tel. (02) 6226-1470. **Hamilton Hume Museum,** Comur St., tel. (02) 6226-2557, which has displays on the explorer and his expeditions through New South Wales, is open daily except Tuesday and Thursday 10 a.m.-4 p.m.

Thunderbird Motel, on the north side of town, tel. (02) 6226-1158, has modern rooms, a swimming pool, and restaurant; $67 s, $74 d. Moderate. In Coronation Park, along the main drag, is the **Tourist Information Centre,** tel. (02) 6226-2557.

Vicinity of Yass

Much of the water used on farms in the Murrumbidgee Irrigation Area is stored at **Burrinjuck Dam,** southwest of Yass. At the time of construction, in 1927, it was one of the world's largest dams, capable of storing more than one million megaliters and with a shoreline of around 500 km. **Burrinjuck State Recreation Area,** on a southeastern arm of the lake, is one of the few areas of natural bushland around the lake. It has a number of bushwalks and is the departure point for lake cruises, tel. (02) 6227-7270. **Lake Burrinjuck Leisure Resort,** along the same access road, features a swimming pool, boat rentals, and excellent facilities for campers. Tent sites are $14-18, on-site vans $30, and cabins $40-55; call (02) 6227-7271 for bookings.

Wee Jasper is a town of 150 in a wooded valley 54 km southwest of Yass along the road to Tumut. Apart from the tranquil surroundings, **Carey's Caves** make the detour worthwhile. These deep limestone caves are open to the public Sat.-Sun. noon-3 p.m. Admission is $8 pp, tel. (02) 6227-9622. Wee Jasper is also the gateway to remote **Brindabella National Park,** which protects 12,280 hectares of the Great Dividing Range immediately north of Kosciuszko National Park. Formerly the police station, **The Stables,** tel. (02) 6227-9619, a classic limestone building on Wee Jasper's main street, serves meals and beer, and offers accommodation in three cabins out back; $65-75 s or d. Moderate.

Back on the Hume Highway, 12 km west of Yass, is **Bowning,** a small hamlet where the original Cobb and Co. Coaching Station still stands. In **Binalong,** a charming town of 250 northwest of Bowning, is **The Black Swan,** which has an excellent reputation for food. Open Wed.-Sun. 7 p.m.-midnight and for lunch on Sunday; call (02) 6227-4236 for bookings.

Gundagai

Originating as a crossing point of the Murrumbidgee River, Gundagai has seen few changes in the last 100 years. Drovers, and in later years diggers, rested on the riverbank before crossing and heading into the frontier farther

MEMORIALIZING GUNDAGAI

The little town of Gundagai has received an outsize measure of attention in song and verse. The chorus of the most famous song, written by local poet Jack O'Hagan and now part of Australian legend, immortalized it in this way:

There's a track winding back to an old-fashioned shack,
Along the road to Gundagai;
Where the blue gums are growing and the Murrumbidgee's
Flowing beneath that sunny sky,
Where my daddy and mummy are waiting for me
And the pals of my childhood once more will I see;
Then no more will I roam when I'm heading right for home,
Along the road to Gundagai

Also at Gundagai is one of Australia's best-known monuments, the **Dog on the Tucker-box,** which—as every Australian knows—sits "five miles from Gundagai." Its origins were also in a poem, penned from an old yarn about a bullock driver who got bogged by Five Mile Creek. Then, to top his troubles off, his "dog sat on the tuckerbox, five miles from Gundagai," although, in the original version, the bullocky's dog did more than just *sit* on his tuckerbox.

south. The river was also the settlement's downfall—on 23 June 1852 the river flooded the town, destroying most buildings and killing 89 people, almost a third of the population. Below the town is **Prince Alfred Bridge,** one of Australia's longest timber bridges. Built in 1866 over the Murrumbidgee River, it has long since been bypassed by the highway but is still open to foot traffic. A gravel road leads to the summit of **Mount Pernassus,** from where the layout of the town and area of the disastrous flood can be clearly seen.

Gundagai's best-known attraction, the **Dog on the Tuckerbox** is, as every Australian knows, five miles from Gundagai. At the same site is a statue of **Dad and Dave,** fictional bush characters immortalized in a series of Australian pre-WW II films, which later turned into a radio serial that still runs in some parts of the country today.

WAGGA WAGGA

Straddling the Murrumbidgee River 478 km southwest of Sydney and 48 km west of the Hume Highway, Wagga Wagga (WAU-ga WAU-ga) is the hub of southern New South Wales, and with a population of 58,000, it's one of Australia's largest inland cities. The area was first inhabited by the Wiradjuri, the state's largest tribe. After exploration by Capt. Charles Sturt, settlers streamed into the region looking for prime pastoral land, and by the 1850s hundreds of farms had been established, with Wagga Wagga, originally a river crossing point, growing into the region's transportation and service hub.

Sights

You won't need to spend long in Wagga to see why it's called the "Garden City." The largest formal garden is **Wagga Wagga Botanic Gardens,** set on nine hectares at the base of Williams Hill, south of town. Trails lead through the gardens to an open-air chapel, traditional Japanese chapel, café, petting zoo for kids (free admission), an aviary, and an area of rainforest. At the top of the gardens is the **Historical Museum,** tel. (02) 6925-2934, with indoor and outdoor displays; open Tuesday, Wednesday, Saturday, and Sunday 2-5 p.m. Admission is adult $3, child $1.

Wagga Wagga City Art Gallery, Gurwood St., tel. (02) 6923-5419, is worth visiting to view a large collection of contemporary glass sculpture and the Carnegie Print Collection. Open Tues.-Fri. 11 a.m.-5 p.m., Saturday 10 a.m.-5 p.m., and Sunday noon-4 p.m.; admission is free. For history buffs, three walking trail brochures, available from the Tourist Information Centre, detail buildings of historical importance.

Murray Cod Hatcheries and Fauna Park, tel. (02) 6922-7360, is a 10-minute drive east of Wagga along the Sturt Highway. Murray cod grow to legendary sizes, and a couple of fine specimens are displayed, along with a variety of other Australian freshwater fish. The fauna park boasts koalas, kangaroos, wombats, and dingos. A small fossil museum displays the fossilized remains of a four-meter fish. Admission adult $6, child $3. Open daily 9 a.m.-5 p.m.

Accommodations

Most of the hotels along Baylis and Fitzmaurice Streets have rooms, but most are a bit rough around the edges. Try **Romano's Hotel,** corner Fitzmaurice and Sturt Streets, tel. (02) 6921-2013, which has been restored; $55 s, $65 d. Moderate. Motels are located on all the main routes into town. One of the least expensive is **Club Motel,** 73 Morgan St., tel. (02) 6921-6966, just north of downtown; $48 s, $58 d. Inexpensive. **Centralpoint Motel,** across from the information center at 164 Tarcutta St., tel. (02) 6921-7272, is another good option. It has a handy location, across from the Tourist Information Centre and one block from the main commercial strip. Each room has cooking facilities; $62 s, $74 d. Moderate. One of the nicest places to stay is **Country House Motor Lodge,** five km east of town on the Sturt Hwy., tel. (02) 6922-7256. Set among two hectares of gardens, it features a pool and spa, laundry, and restaurant, and rooms are furnished with handcrafted heritage-style furniture; $81 s, $84 d. Moderate.

Crepe Myrtle Bed and Breakfast, 102 Kincaid St., tel. (02) 6921-4757, retains much of its original 1870s charm. The four rooms have period furniture and shared facilities; $75 s, $95 d. Expensive.

Riverview Caravan Park, two km east of town on the Sturt Hwy., tel. (02) 6921-4287, is adjacent to the Murrumbidgee River and has excellent facilities. Shaded sites range $8-14, basic on-site vans are $34, and great little cabins start at $48 d. Budget-Inexpensive.

Food

Of the many downtown cafés, **Street Cafe,** 32 Fitzmaurice St., has the most character. It's open weekdays from 7:30 a.m., weekends from 9 a.m.

For a more substantial meal, head to the **Victoria Hotel** on Baylis St., tel. (02) 6921-5233, or **Golden Grill Family Restaurant,** in the Wagga RSL Club on Kincaid Street. **Pavilion Garden Restaurant,** in the Pavilion Motor Inn on Kincaid St., tel. (02) 6921-6411, is an upmarket dining room in a garden atrium. Breakfast is served daily from 7 a.m., lunch daily except Sunday, and each evening the good cutlery comes out with an a la carte menu. For something more exotic, try **Bahn Thai Restaurant,** 73 Morgan St., tel. (02) 6921-4177.

North of town, over the Murrumbidgee River toward Junee, is **Wagga Wagga Winery,** 427 Oura Rd., tel. (02) 6922-1221. As well as daily winetasting, a restaurant serves lunch and dinner daily with an excellent steak and salad deal for only $12.50 pp.

Information

The **Tourist Information Centre** is in a pleasant area of parkland on Tarcutta St., tel. (02) 6926-9621.

SOUTH FROM WAGGA WAGGA

The quickest route south from Wagga is back out on the Hume Highway, from where it's 140 km to the Victorian border. Just over halfway is **Holbrook.** In town is **Woolpack Inn Museum,** tel. (02) 6036-2131, a two-story hotel on the main drag with displays depicting life in the late 1800s; open daily 9:30 a.m.-4:30 p.m.

Ettamogah Pub, 50 km south of Holbrook and 15 km north of Albury, tel. (02) 6026-2366, is arguably Australia's most famous hotel. To appreciate just why, pick up a copy of *Post* magazine (from any newsagency), where the Ken Maynard's Ettamogah Pub cartoon has been featured since 1959. Originally the figment of a cartoonist's imagination, the cartoon has been converted to reality, leaning walls and all. Typical bar meals such

---

WHY THE DOUBLE-BARRELED NAMES?

You will notice that many Australian towns and landmarks bear what might be termed double-barreled names. The Aboriginal language had no plurals, so when the natives gave names to their sites and settlements, in order to convey quantity or size, they simply repeated the words requiring emphasis. Hence Wagga Wagga (lots of crows) and others.

Ettamogah Pub

as pie and chips are served, and, as the famous sign says, "The beer is free. Tommorow."

Morgan Country

The alternative route south from Wagga is Highway 41 (Olympic Way), which passes through the heart of a territory once roamed by the notorious bushranger Dan "Mad Dog" Morgan.

For three days each September, the small town of Henty comes alive for **Henty Machinery Field Days.** The event began with a few equipment salesmen displaying machinery to local farmers, and has now grown into one of Australia's largest agricultural events. Everyone's welcome, and non-farmers will find plenty of interest on the 150-hectare site, with machinery trials, animal judging, and displays of historic equipment. For details, call (02) 6929-3305.

Culcairn, 18 km south of Henty, is the region's largest town. The sprawling redbrick **Culcairn Hotel,** opposite the railway station, was the largest hotel between Sydney and Melbourne for many years after its construction in 1891. Nearby **Morgan's Lookout** was used by the infamous bushranger. Access to the lookout is from Walbundrie, west of Culcairn.

ALBURY

On the northern bank of the Murray River, 559 km southwest of Sydney and 310 km northeast of Melbourne, Albury (pop. 41,000) is the largest center on the Hume Highway. Explorers Hume and Hovell, the first Europeans to travel overland from Sydney to Port Phillip Bay, crossed the Murray River in 1824, where Albury now lies. Within a few years a settlement first known as the Crossing Place had become established.

Sights

Much of the floodplain between the commercial center of Albury and the Murray River is open parkland, with river red gums lining the riverbank and a few picturesque barbecue areas spread around. The **PS *Cumberoona,*** a replica of a wood-fired paddlesteamer, once the main form of river transport, cruises the river a couple of times daily; for departure times, call (02) 6041-5558. Where the highway parallels the river through town, you'll find **Albury Regional Museum,** tel. (02) 6021-4550, occupying the 1884 Turks Head Hotel on Wodonga Place. It features an interesting collection of locally collected memorabilia; open daily 10:30 a.m.-4:30 p.m.

Monument Hill, off Memorial Drive west of downtown, provides views of the city and sweeping bends of the Murray River.

Accommodations

Motels line either side of the Hume Hwy. north of town, including **Sodens Australia Hotel/Motel,** corner David and Wilson Streets, tel. (02) 6021-2400. It has pub rooms with shared facilities for $28 s, $42 d, which includes breakfast, and motel units (no breakfast) for $38 s, $45 d. Inexpensive. Off the main drag to the north of downtown is **Albury Golf Club Motor Inn,** 530 North St., tel. (02) 6041-1211. The motel is set in a quiet area, with rooms overlooking the pool and an 18-hole golf course. Rooms are large and of a high standard, each with coffee-making facilities and a fridge; $72 s, $79 d. Moderate. **Country Comfort Albury,** corner Dean and Elizabeth Streets, tel. (02) 6021-5366, lies one block from the botanic garden and within walking distance of the river. Facilities include a pool, sauna, spa, restaurant, and bar; $95-135 s or d. Expensive.

Albury Central Tourist Park has a pool, tennis court, and shop, but sites are small; sites $12-14, cabins $30-45 d. It's on North St., tel. (02) 6021-8420. Budget. As an overnight stop for campers, this place is fine, but for a nicer environment, it's worth the 32-km drive out to **The Great Aussie Resort,** on Jingellic Rd. east of Bowna, on the Hume Hwy. north of Albury, tel. (02) 6020-3236. This large park is spread around the shore of Lake Hume and has enough facilities to keep you busy for days—from golf to grass skiing and boat hire to bingo games. Sites are $14-20, depending on the season; basic cabins start at $40, and on-site tents, complete with cooking facilities, are $50. Budget-Inexpensive.

Food
There are a few **Matilda's Family Steakhouses** spread around this part of the country, and wherever you see one, you'll get a decent meal at a good price. A lunch buffet is $8.95, and a steak dinner, with all-you-can-eat soup, salad, and dessert, is $13-18.50. In Albury, Matilda's is at the corner of the Hume Hwy. and David St., tel. (02) 6041-4400. **Cultura Cafe & Restaurant,** 515 Kiewa St., tel. (02) 6041-3884, has a trendy interior with a variety of dishes from around the world. Each dish is offered in varying sizes, with large portions running $14.50-18.50 and desserts around $6 (including an excellent Mississippi Mudcake).

Transportation, Services, and Information
Mylon Motorways, tel. (02) 6056-3100, operates a different tour every day of the week. For example, the Friday tour visits historical areas north of Albury ($45 pp), and the Sunday tour takes in town sights ($28 pp). Book through the information center.

The **Gateway Visitor Information Centre** is located on the Hume Hwy. toward Wodonga, tel. (02) 6041-3875 or (1800) 80-0743. Open daily 9 a.m.-5 p.m.

WEST OF ALBURY
ALONG THE MURRAY RIVER

Corowa
Corowa (pop. 5,500) is a quiet town 52 km west of Albury. Popular as an inland holiday destination, it boasts a challenging 27-hole golf course, and just across the river is the Rutherglen, one of Australia's premier wine producing areas. Fans of lawn bowling may want to visit **Corowa Bowling Club** in Ball Park. It has 54 rinks on seven greens, the world's largest such complex.

Tocumwal
Tocumwal is a sleepy little town where the Newell Highway crosses the Murray River, with a picturesque park between the river and the main street. Many shops date from the late 1800s, including one that has been restored to an antique emporium and tearoom. Next door to this store is the sprawling **Tocumwal Hotel,** 17 Deniliquin St., tel. (03) 5874-2025, where rooms are $34 s, $44 d, including a light breakfast. Inexpensive.

Jerilderie
A small article published in an 1868 edition of the *Jerilderie and Urana Gazette* about a shortage of police did little to prompt government action, but news of the police shortage filtered through to Ned Kelly. On 8 February 1869 the infamous Victorian bushranger and his gang rode into town. They locked the town's two policemen in their own cells and spent the day walking around town in police uniforms, even helping a policeman's wife to set the church for Sunday service. On that Monday morning they bailed up staff of the Royal Mail Hotel, shooting drinks at the bar while two gang members emptied the coffers of the bank next door. Thumbing their noses at authority, the gang rode out of town, raising their hats to the cheers of those they'd held hostage in the hotel. Before the gang left town, they visited the Telegraph Office to cut telegraph wires; that building, on Powell St., still stands, and is open daily 9:30 a.m.-4:30 p.m. Next door is **The Willows,** a historic home serving lunch and Devonshire teas.

Deniliquin
Straddling the Edward River, at the junction of the Cobb and Riverina Highways and 204 km

west of Albury, this town of 8,000 is in the heart of a rich rice- and wool-growing area. **Deniliquin Rice Mill** is the largest such mill in the Southern Hemisphere, with 750,000 tons of rice milled annually. A visitor center at the mill features an audiovisual and cooking demonstrations; open daily 9 a.m.-5 p.m. It's south of town, off the road to Barmah, tel. (03) 5881-2477. The **merino** breed of sheep, resilient to the harsh and dry conditions of Australia and now the backbone of the country's rural economy, was pioneered by the Deniliquin-based Peppin family. **Peppin Heritage Centre** catalogs the family and their successful breeding program, which literally changed the face of Australia. Displays are housed in an old school building, while, outside, the grounds are stocked with those famous merinos. The center is open daily 9 a.m.-4 p.m.; located on George St., tel. (03) 5881-4150.

Globe Hotel, 280 Cressy St., tel. (03) 5881-2030, has basic but clean rooms for $25 s, $30 d. Budget. The nicest place in town is **Deniliquin Country Club Motor Inn,** 68 Crispe St., tel. (03) 5881-5299, which is close to the golf course and clubs and has large rooms with king-size beds; $57 s, $70 d. Moderate. Camping is at **Pioneer Tourist Park,** north of town, tel. (03) 5881-5066, or at **McLean Beach Caravan Park,** Butler St., tel. (03) 5881-2448.

MURRUMBIDGEE IRRIGATION AREA

Known as the **Riverina,** the region west of Wagga Wagga is able to sustain high yields of a great variety of crops through the workings of the massive Murrumbidgee Irrigation Area (M.I.A.), named for the river that is central to its success. The first stage of the project was the construction of Burrinjuck Dam, on the higher reaches of the Murrumbidgee River. Once this dam was completed, a complex system of more than 3,500 km of canals was dug. This opened up a huge tract of land west of Narrandera and north of the Murrumbidgee River for farming. Today, more than 500,000 hectares are irrigated, transforming the once-dry land to one of Australia's richest food-producing regions. The main crops are rice, a variety of fruits, and cereals.

Narrandera

Narrandera is a midsized town of 4,800 on the north bank of the Murrumbidgee River, 95 km west of Wagga Wagga. Within the grounds of **Narrandera Park,** in the heart of town, is an information center housing the world's largest playable guitar. **Parkside Cottage Museum,** Twynam St., tel. (02) 6959-1372, is a two-story building with a variety of local relics; open Mon.-Tues. 2-5 p.m., Wed.-Sun. 11 a.m.-5 p.m. Admission is $2. Along Lake Dr., off the main drag through town, is **Lake Talbot Complex,** tel. (02) 6959-1211, comprising swimming pools, water slides, a picnic area, and a small colony of koalas. Near the complex entrance is **Bundidgerry Walking Track,** which winds around a lake and down to the Murrumbidgee River. **John Lake Centre,** five km east of town toward Wagga, tel. (02) 6959-9021, carries out research on various species of freshwater fish found in local rivers; open Mon.-Fri. 9 a.m.-4 p.m. with tours ($5 pp) at 10:30 a.m.

Historic Star Lodge, corner Newell Hwy. and Arthur St., tel. (02) 6959-1768, is a classic Aussie hotel with well-furnished pub rooms for $38 s, $58 d. This place is also an associate YHA, with dorms for $15 pp. Budget-Inexpensive. **Country Roads Motor Inn,** Newell Hwy. and East St., tel. (02) 6959-3244, features modern rooms and is within walking distance of town; $50 s, $60 d. Inexpensive. **Lake Talbot Caravan Park,** Broad St., tel. (02) 6959-1302, has unpowered sites for $15, powered sites for $16, on-site vans for $27, and cabins for $45-55. Budget-Inexpensive.

For an inexpensive feed, head to **Narrandera Hotel** at 183 East St., tel. (02) 6959-2057, or the **Murrumbidgee Club** at 43 Douglas St., tel. (02) 6959-3832, where a juicy T-bone steak with vegetables or salad is $10.

Narrandera Tourist Centre is in Narrandera Park on the Newell Hwy., tel. (02) 6959-1766 or (1800) 67-2392; open Mon.-Fri. 9 a.m.-5 p.m., Sat.-Sun. 10 a.m.-4 p.m.

Leeton

Laid out in the early 1900s as part of the Murrumbidgee Irrigation Area project, this town of 6,500, 24 km northwest of Narrandera, is home to a number of large food-processing companies. **Sunrice Country Visitors Centre** is at a

Historic Star Lodge,
Narrandera

working rice mill on Calrose St., tel. (02) 6953-0596. Along with an audiovisual describing the growing, harvesting, and distribution processes, the Centre has displays, talks, and tastings. It's open Mon.-Fri. 9 a.m.-5 p.m., with tours at 9:30 a.m. and 2:45 p.m. **Sunburst Foods Juice Factory** offers tours weekdays at 10:45 a.m. Tours through **Historic Hydro Motor Inn,** Chelmsford Place, are offered daily at 2 p.m. Book all tours through **Leeton Visitor Centre,** Yanco Place, tel. (02) 6953-6481. One of many wineries in the M.I.A. is **Lillypilly Estate,** out on Lillypilly Rd., tel. (02) 6953-4069. Guided tours of the vineyard are conducted Mon.-Fri. at 4 p.m., with the winery open for tastings Mon.-Sat. 10 a.m.-5:30 p.m.

Leeton Visitor Centre, 10 Yanco Place, tel. (02) 6953-6481, is open Mon.-Fri. 9 a.m.-5 p.m., Sat.-Sun. 9:30 a.m.-12:30 p.m.

Griffith

This, the largest town of the M.I.A. (pop. 25,000), should be best known for colorful gardens and surrounding rich agricultural land; but that is not the case. Most Australians know Griffith as "Drug Capital of Australia" and "Chicago of the Outback," long after the 1970s when the waters of the Murrumbidgee River were irrigating crops a lot different than those the founders intended.

Pioneer Park, a large area of native bushland north of town, is dotted with 40 historic buildings dating from the late 1800s. Although the buildings have been relocated to the site, together they create an authentic reproduction of what an early Riverina town would have looked like. The complex is open daily 8:30 a.m.-5 p.m. and admission is a worthwhile $6; it's two km north of town on Airport Rd., tel. (02) 6962-4196.

The area's many wineries are also a major attraction. **McWilliams Wines** offers tours Friday at 2 p.m. This winery also has a barrel-shaped tasting room open Mon.-Sat. 9 a.m.-5 p.m. Located eight km south of Griffith, tel. (02) 6963-1001. (The unusual smell often hovering around the winery will horrify vegetarian winetasters—it comes from nearby Bartter Enterprises, Australia's largest egg producers and supplier of 60,000 chickens a week). **Cranswick Estate,** Walla Ave., tel. (02) 6962-4133, produces wine purely for export, with the colorful labels and "Barramundi" name synonymous with Australian wine overseas; tastings are daily 10 a.m.-4 p.m.

Held over Easter, the **Griffith Wine & Food Festival** celebrates the popularity of the area's wineries with activities throughout town and at the wineries, including "grape-treading" at McWilliam's Wines. Another big event is the **Festival of Gardens,** held in mid-October, when many local families open their gardens to the public.

Motel accommodation in Griffith isn't particularly cheap, with **A-line Motel,** 187 Wakaden St., tel. (02) 6962-1922, having rooms for $50 s, $60 d. Inexpensive. If you want to spend a little extra, the **Kidman Wayside Inn,** 58 Jondaryan Ave., tel. (02) 6964-5666, is of a higher standard. Each of the 60 units is well furnished and air-conditioned, while guest facilities include a pool, restaurant, and bar. Rates are $75 s, $90 d, which includes a buffet breakfast. Moderate. **Griffith Caravan Village,** on the road out to Leeton, tel. (02) 6962-3785, has tent sites for $10, on-site vans for $25, and a swimming pool, barbecue area, and laundry.

Pasticceria Bassano, 449 Banna Ave., is open daily 8 a.m.-5:30 p.m., serving a variety of coffees, great bowls of pasta, and healthy sandwiches. Also try the bread—it's baked daily in the wood-fired oven. **La Scala,** 455 Banna Ave., tel. (02) 6962-4322, is a pizzeria, with most pizzas costing $12-20.

Griffith Visitors Centre is at the eastern entrance to town on the corner of Banna and Jondaryan Avenues, tel. (02) 6962-4145. Available here are wine-tour maps and information on the far southwest of the state. Open Mon.-Fri. 9 a.m.-5 p.m., Saturday 9 a.m.-3 p.m., Sunday 10 a.m.-2 p.m.

Cocoparra National Park

This 8,358-hectare park northeast of Griffith protects a section of the ancient Cocoparra Range. The range comprises sediments laid down on the ocean floor 400 million years ago and uplifted by movements beneath the earth's surface in the ensuing years, with erosion sculpting the present landscape. Cliffs and gullies along the park's western border are great for exploring, with the trail through **Ladysmith Glen** among the most accessible.

The first European to penetrate the range, John Oxley, had scant appreciation for the area's flora and fauna, commenting in his diary that the mountains had been "abandoned by every living creature capable of getting out of them." The main access is from Yenda north to a stock route along the park's western boundary. This road leads to Mt. Bingar, Woolshed Flat Camping Area, and a number of shaded picnic areas. In the park's southeast corner an access road leads to **Spring Hill Picnic Area,** from where a 1.2-km trail leads into a canyon and Falcon Falls.

WEST FROM GRIFFITH

The Sturt Highway passes 32 km south of Griffith before passing through Hay and Balranald; then it crosses the Murray River at Mildura and continues to Adelaide. The highway was named for Capt. Charles Sturt, who followed much the same route on his 1829-30 expedition tracking the Murrumbidgee River to the Murray River and following it to the Great Australian Bight.

Hay

Hay (pop. 3,000) is at the junction of three main highways midway between Sydney and Adelaide. Unlike other river towns, Hay is set back a few blocks from the waterway, and wandering around town there's little indication that the Murrumbidgee River flows so close. The town has a colorful history—from its early days as a river crossing, then as a major Cobb and Co. coach stop, and during WW II as home to 20,000 prisoners of war. One of many historic buildings on the main street is **Hay Gaol,** an imposing structure dating from 1878 that through the years has served as a holding area for WWII prisoners, a mental asylum, and a minimum security women's prison. It now serves as a museum, tel. (02) 6993-1003; open daily 9 a.m.-5 p.m.

BLUE MOUNTAINS AND VICINITY

The Blue Mountains might not have the height of the North American Rockies or the tradition of the European Alps, but in their own rugged way they're awe-inspiring and one of Australia's great natural wonders. Named for a blue haze caused by sunlight reflecting from evaporating eucalyptus oil, they are part of the Great Dividing Range that runs along Australia's east coast. Although most areas of the mountains can be reached in less than two hours' driving time, much of the area is rugged and remote. More than 240,000 hectares are protected by **Blue Mountains National Park,** and the only development is along the Great Western Highway, constructed along a high ridge linking Sydney to the western plains. Along this 70-km stretch of road are 26 towns and villages, the largest being Katoomba, just two km from Echo Point, vantage point for viewing the Three Sisters and trailhead for a number of hikes leading into the vast valley below. Wentworth Falls, Leura, and Mt. Victoria are other picturesque Blue Mountains villages, and each has a wide range of historic guesthouses, charming restaurants, and plenty of nearby hiking.

For a country addicted to the coastline, it's surprising how busy the Blue Mountains can get, especially on weekends; try to plan your visit midweek, and apart from more room to move, you'll benefit from good deals on accommodation packages.

SYDNEY TO WENTWORTH FALLS

The most direct route from Sydney to the Blue Mountains is the Great Western Highway, which bypasses the sprawl of Sydney's western suburbs before crossing the Nepean River and climbing steadily to Glenbrook, easternmost of the Blue Mountains' communities.

Glenbrook

Glenbrook provides a gateway to the middle section of Blue Mountains National Park. Immediately south of town an access road leads into the park, passing a **park information center** (open Sat.-Sun. and school holidays 8:30 a.m.-5 p.m.). Along this road are a variety of picnic areas, bush camping at **Euroka Clearing,** Koori hand stencils at **Red Hands Cave,** and a couple of lookouts.

Norman Lindsay Gallery and Museum

Norman Lindsay was an imaginative artist and author who spent much of his life in the Blue Mountains. He died in 1969 at the age of 90, his infamous lifestyle portrayed in the 1994 movie *Sirens.* Lindsay's former home is classified by the National Trust and is open for inspection Wed.-Mon. 10 a.m.-4 p.m.; admission is adult $6, child $2. On display are many of his works as well as a display of his best-known writing, *The Magic Pudding,* and many of his sculptures are scattered around the landscaped gardens. It's located on Norman Lindsay Cres., north of Faulconbridge, tel. (02) 4751-1067.

PENETRATING THE WESTERN MOUNTAINS

Hemmed in by the ocean to the east and mountains to the west, Sydney Town struggled to expand for the first 25 years of its existence. Many attempts were made at crossing the Great Dividing Range, but it wasn't until 1813 that the crossing of what Governor King described as "a formidable barrier impassable for man" was successful.

Gregory Blaxland, William Lawson, and William Charles Wentworth, all holders of land at the base of the mountains, set out westward on 11 May 1813 in search of better pastures. Their innovative idea was to follow ridges rather than valleys, which had been the downfall of earlier expeditions. Each man brought a different talent to the expedition, and together they crossed the Great Dividing Range in less than two months.

Just six months after the official route had been mapped, a gang of 30 convicts was put to work constructing a track over the mountains. Within six months, a trail was completed, the convicts had been pardoned for their good, hard work, and settlers began streaming west.

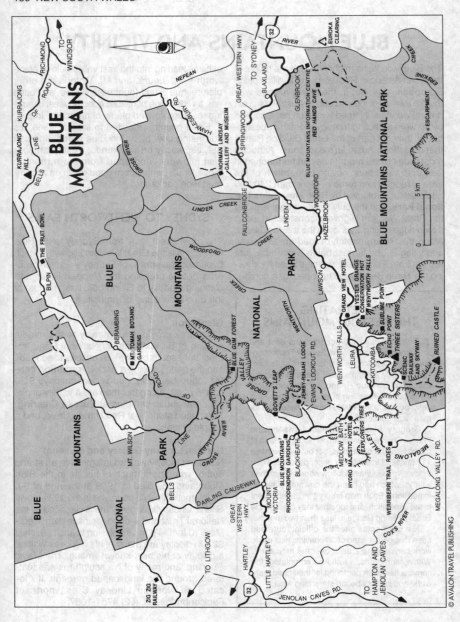

BLUE MOUNTAINS

TO WINDSOR

TO RICHMOND

KURRAJONG HILL

KURRAJONG

BELLS LINE OF ROAD

NEPEAN RIVER

HAWKESBURY RD.

GREAT WESTERN HWY.

32

RIVER

TO SYDNEY

BLAXLAND

GLENBROOK

EUROKA CLEARING

ERSKINE CREEK

NORMAN LINDSAY GALLERY AND MUSEUM

SPRINGWOOD

BLUE MOUNTAINS INFORMATION CENTRE

RED HANDS CAVE

= ESCARPMENT

THE FRUIT BOWL

GROSE RIVER

FAULCONBRIDGE

LINDEN CREEK

WOODFORD

HAZELBROOK

BLUE MOUNTAINS NATIONAL PARK

5 km

BILPIN

BLUE

BERAMBING

MT. TOMAH BOTANIC GARDENS

MOUNTAINS

WOODFORD CREEK

LINDEN

BLUE GUM FOREST

NATIONAL

LAWSON

WENTWORTH CREEK

GRAND VIEW HOTEL

YESTER GRANGE
CONSERVATION HUT
WENTWORTH FALLS

MT. WILSON

PARK

VALLEY

GROSE

GOVETT'S LEAP

JEMBY-RINJAH LODGE

EVANS LOOKOUT RD.

WENTWORTH FALLS

LEURA

KATOOMBA

SUBLIME POINT

ECHO POINT

THREE SISTERS

SCENIC RAILWAY AND SKYWAY

RUINED CASTLE

BLUE
MOUNTAINS

NATIONAL PARK

MT. WILSON

BELLS LINE OF ROAD

GROSE RIVER

DARLING CAUSEWAY

MOUNT VICTORIA

GREAT WESTERN HWY.

BLUE MOUNTAINS RHODODENDRON GARDENS

BLACKHEATH

MEDLOW BATH

HYDRO MAJESTIC HOTEL

EXPLORERS TREE

VALLEY

WERRIBERRI TRAIL RIDES

MEGALONG

MEGALONG VALLEY RD.

COX'S RIVER

TO LITHGOW

ZIG ZIG RAILWAY

HARTLEY

LITTLE HARTLEY

32

TO HAMPTON AND JENOLAN CAVES

JENOLAN CAVES RD.

© AVALON TRAVEL PUBLISHING

WENTWORTH FALLS

Named for the youngest member of the successful expedition across the Great Dividing Range, the falls tumble 300 meters from a high escarpment into a remote valley. The town Wentworth Falls (pop. 5,000) is less commercialized than those farther west and is the starting point for some excellent hikes.

Yester Grange

Nestled in beautiful landscaped gardens above Wentworth Falls, Yester Grange is one of the finest Victorian-era houses in the Blue Mountains. Dating from the 1870s, it has been restored to its former glory. It now combines an art gallery, museum, and tearooms in a setting with glorious views over the Jamison Valley. Morning and afternoon teas are served in a former ballroom, and in summer tables are set around the veranda. Admission to the gardens and house is $5 pp; open Mon.-Fri. 10 a.m.-4 p.m., Sat.-Sun. 10 a.m.-5 p.m. Located on Yester Rd., off Tableland Rd., tel. (02) 4757-1110.

Hiking

Conservation Hut, on Fletcher St., is the main trailhead, with trails leading east along the escarpment to the end of Falls Rd., west to Inspiration Point, and south into the valley below. From Falls Rd. a short trail leads to various lookouts, with a one-km trail crossing Jamison Creek and ending at Rocket Point Lookout. From Conservation Hut the shortest route into the valley is two km one-way, but it's a *very* strenuous return climb, so allow three hours' roundtrip. Another option is to descend from the hut to **National Pass,** below the main ridge, and follow it beyond Wentworth Falls, returning along the top of the escarpment (six-km roundtrip, allow four hours).

Accommodations and Food

Grand View Hotel, on the Great Western Hwy., tel. (02) 4757-1001, is in the heart of Wentworth Falls, right opposite the railway station and shopping area. It dates from last century; its solid mass and distinctive pink color make it a Blue Mountains landmark. Rooms are $60 s, $96 d, which includes breakfast. Expensive.

Grand View Hotel has a bistro open daily and a restaurant open Saturday night. **Conserva-

tion Hut Cafe,** Fletcher St., tel. (02) 4757-3827, is an informal mud-brick place, perfect for relaxing after a hike into the valley below. Back in town, at 30 Station St., is **Conditorei Patisserie,** baker of fine cakes and pastries.

LEURA

Leura, five km west of Wentworth Falls, is arguably the mountains' most charming town. Spread between the Great Western Highway and the escarpment, its tree-lined streets are dotted with fine examples of early Australian architecture, and spectacular **Cliff Drive** provides access to picnic areas and hiking trails. The highlight of Leura is **Leura Mall,** directly south of the railway station, lined with tearooms, boutiques, cafés, and gift shops—the largest concentration of such shops in the Blue Mountains.

Lookouts and Hiking Trails

One of the best viewpoints is **Sublime Point,** south of the golf course and signposted from town. The panorama extends 270 degrees, from Wentworth Falls in the east, to remote stretches of Warragamba Dam in the south, and Echo Point and the Three Sisters in the west. West of Sublime Point, at the end of Olympian Parade, is **Gordon Falls Lookout** and a shaded picnic area. **Prince Henry Cliff Walk** leads from here to Echo Point; it's about four km one-way and passes numerous lookouts. For the keen, it's possible to return on the valley floor along **Dardanelles Pass** (nine km roundtrip; allow four hours). East from Gordon Falls Lookout a trail leads up Gordon Creek to **Lyrebird Dell;** two km roundtrip.

Accommodations

Historic guesthouses dot the streets of Leura, and although weekend rates are high, midweek packages are a good deal. **Leura House,** 7 Britain St., tel. (02) 4784-2035, is a three-story Victorian-era guesthouse faithfully restored and set among rambling landscaped gardens. Its 12 rooms are furnished with antiques, and many have views. On the first floor is an enormous lounge area and dining room. Rates Sun.-Thurs. are $125 pp for two nights, including breakfast, and from $226 pp weekends, which includes breakfast and dinner. Luxury.

Little Company Retreat, 2 Eastview Ave., tel. (02) 4782-4023, is a series of small cottages set on a two-hectare property and centered around The Nunnery, a rambling old house with 12 large rooms of the highest standard. Rates of $155 pp per night include breakfast and dinner. Luxury.

Fairmont Resort, overlooking the valley on the road out to Sublime Point, tel. (02) 4782-5222, is the largest resort-style development in the mountains. It boasts all modern conveniences, including a health club and 18-hole golf course; rates start at $175 s or d. Luxury.

Food

The Ferns, 130 Megalong St., tel. (02) 4784-3256, is a federation-style restaurant specializing in international cuisine in an elegant atmosphere. Open daily except Wednesday for lunch and dinner. More casual is **Silk's Brasserie,** in Leura Mall, tel. (02) 4784-2534, a country-style restaurant open daily for lunch and dinner.

KATOOMBA

Katoomba is the largest tourist and commercial center in the Blue Mountains, and although it lacks the charm of Leura, it has many of the best-known sights, including the **Three Sisters,** an impressive rock formation floodlit daily until 10 p.m. Echo Point is the best place to start a visit to the area, not only for the information center, but for the variety of hiking in the immediate vicinity.

Scenic Railway and Skyway

Although not designed as such, these two commercial attractions give an adrenalin rush as well as any fun park can. Originally built in the 1880s to haul coal and shale from the valley floor, the Scenic Railway is claimed to be the steepest railway in the world, operating on an incline of 45 degrees. Mine management began giving early tourists the ride of their lives in sooty coal skips; mining has long since ceased, and the coal skips have been replaced by more comfortable cars. The fare is $4.50 roundtrip, but the one-way fare ($3) allows you to descend to the valley floor on foot and catch the train back up to Katoomba. Starting from the same complex is the Skyway, an aerial cable car that glides horizontally over a 280-meter-deep valley; $4.50 roundtrip. Both operate daily 9 a.m.-4:50 p.m. Also at the complex, tel. (02) 4782-2699, is a large, tacky souvenir shop and a revolving restaurant.

Hiking

Views of the Three Sisters are best from the parking lot at Echo Point; to get a closer look, take the 500-meter trail around the back of the information center to another lookout. This trail is also the beginning of **Prince Henry Cliff Walk,** which follows the escarpment to Leura Falls and Gordon Falls Lookout in Leura (four km one-way). From Echo Point, the **Giant Stairway** accesses the valley floor from where Federal Pass Walk leads to the base of the Scenic Railway and the Dardanelles Pass Walk heads northeast toward Leura. Also from Echo Point, a trail leads westward to **Katoomba Falls** (two km one-way) and around to the Skyway and Scenic Railway. For experienced hikers, the six-km (one-way) trail from the base of the Scenic Railway to a rocky outcrop known as **Ruined Castle** is a good way to escape the crowds.

the Three Sisters

Skyway

One of the most interesting overnight hikes is the 45-km **Six Foot Track** linking Katoomba and Jenolan Caves. Four campgrounds are located along the trail, but it can easily be completed in three days. **Country Walks,** tel. (02) 4784-3266, operates a guided walk along its entire length; $195-275 pp, including meals and transportation.

Other Activities

A number of mountain climbing and abseiling (rappelling) companies based in Katoomba offer full-day adventure-packed activities as well as a variety of training courses. The **Australian School of Mountaineering,** in the Paddy Pallin shop at 166 Katoomba St., tel. (02) 4782-2014, offers a beginners abseiling course, which includes an 80-meter jump, lunch, and transport; $79 pp. A two-day rock climbing course is $180. Thursday and Saturday Oct.-March, the company offers a canyoning experience, abseiling into a water-filled canyon and swimming/scrambling out; $75 pp.

A great way to explore the more remote portions of the Mountains is on a 4WD safari with **Cox's River Escapes,** tel. (02) 4784-1621. They offer full-day trips (eight to 10 hours) four-wheel driving in Megalong Valley, combined with easy bushwalking, lunch and a light snack, and swimming in the clear water of Cox's River; $95-120 pp. Other options are a half-day tour ($65) and a Twilight Tour, which includes dinner and spotlighting animals ($95).

Edge Maxvision, Great Western Hwy., tel. (02) 4782-8900, is an IMAX-style movie theater featuring a six-story-high screen. *The Edge,* a 40-minute-long film on the Blue Mountains, includes some incredible footage from a helicopter and of an abseiler. Two other features are shown daily. All showings are $12 pp.

Yulefest

For those from the Northern Hemisphere, celebrating Christmas in the middle of summer probably doesn't seem right, so each winter (June-Aug.) up in the Blue Mountains, Yulefest celebrations make up for Australia's climatic reversal. No official celebrations are held, but many accommodations offer special packages that include Christmas dinners, a visit by Santa, and, you never know, it may even snow.

Historic Guesthouses

Along the Great Western Highway are a few motels, but these are generally expensive, and for the same price you can stay at a historic guesthouse or B&B. The least expensive of these is **Katoomba Mountain Lodge,** 31 Lurline St., tel. (02) 4782-3933, close to the town and with basic but adequate facilities, including a large lounge area, free tea and coffee, and game room. Rates are $42-50 s, $67-83 d for bed and breakfast, and a three-course dinner is an extra $18 pp. Moderate. Dating from 1876, **Balmoral House,** 196 Bathurst Rd., tel. (02) 4782-2264, has 10 basic rooms, a dining area, and small lounge furnished with antiques. Rates are $65 pp Mon.-Fri., $85 weekends, which includes breakfast and dinner. Expensive. **Megalong Lodge,** 40 Acacia St., tel. (02) 4782-2036, has a real homey feel and is set in a large property, right by Katoomba Golf Course. Rates are $55 s, $100 d for bed and breakfast. Expensive. The **Clarendon,** 68 Lurline St., tel. (02) 4782-1322, is a

but elegant rooms for $50 pp midweek. Weekend rates of $195 pp include two nights' accommodation, breakfast, and dinner with theater performance. Expensive. **Avonleigh Country House,** 174 Lurline St., tel. (02) 4782-1534, dates from the turn of the century and has been restored to its former glory, yet retains a homey ambience. Rates are $110 pp midweek, which includes a delicious three-course dinner and cooked breakfast. Luxury. **Mountain Heritage Country House Retreat,** corner Apex and Lovel Streets, tel. (02) 4782-2155, is 100 meters from Katoomba's main street; rooms are large and furnished to the highest standard. Rates for bed and breakfast are $138-248 s or d. Premium.

Other Accommodations
What **Blue Mountains YHA** lacks in historic grandeur it makes up for in location, halfway between town and Echo Point and within walking distance of both. Facilities include a communal kitchen, game room, lounge area with log fire, and bike rental. Rates are $14 in dorms and $18

pp twin or d. It's at 66 Lurline St., tel. (02) 4782-1416. Budget. Another option for budget travelers is **Gearins Hotel,** right opposite the railway station, tel. (02) 4782-6028, where dorms are $14 and doubles are $38. Budget.

Katoomba Falls Caravan Park, Katoomba Falls Rd., tel. (02) 4782-1835, has a laundry and barbecues. Sites are $12 and cabins $60 s or d. Budget-Inexpensive.

Food
Along Katoomba St., the main drag through town, are some great cafés scattered among an otherwise ordinary strip of shops. One of the most interesting is **The Paragon,** 65 Katoomba St., which has been in operation since 1916. This art-deco masterpiece with wood-paneled booths for privacy has a distinct air of historical importance. It's best-known for English-style afternoon tea; open daily 10 a.m.-5 p.m. **Bodd's** is a more modern eatery. The décor is bright and breezy and the food inexpensive. It's in Katoomba Plaza at 43 Waratah Street.

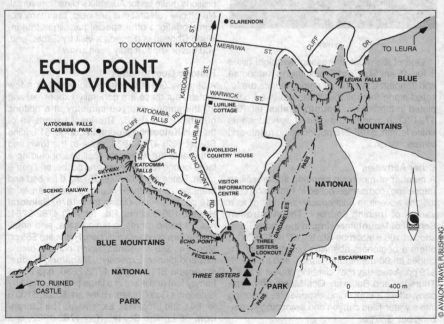

Lurline Cottage, 132 Lurline St., tel. (02) 4782-2281, features that great Swiss invention, the fondue, as well as a variety of other Swiss-influenced dishes. It's only open for dinner Fri.-Sat., but Wed.-Sun. light lunches and afternoon tea are served. For a splurge, consider **Darley's,** on Lilianfels Ave., tel. (02) 4780-1200. The restaurant is within an upmarket guesthouse, but nonguests are made welcome (reservations required).

Transportation and Tours
A regular rail service links Sydney's Central Station and Katoomba, but a better deal are the combined rail/bus tours, including Blue Mountains Explorer Link; call (13) 2232 for details. All major tour companies offer day trips from Sydney to the Blue Mountains from $60 pp.
    Katoomba's **Fantastic Aussie Tours,** tel. (02) 4782-1866, offers a three-hour tour of all major sights for adult $30, child $15, as well as a full-day tour for adult $60, child $48. They also operate the **Blue Mountains Explorer Bus,** which runs daily 9:30 a.m.-5 p.m. between 17 major sights around Katoomba and Leura for $18 pp. If you just want to get from one point to another **Katoomba Leura Bus Service,** tel. (02) 4782-3333, runs regular weekday services. **Blue Mountains Adventure Company,** tel. (02) 4782-1271, rents mountain bikes for $30 a day. If you're staying there, Katoomba Hostel also has a few bikes. **Katoomba Radio Cabs** can be reached at (047) 82-1311.

Services and Information
The **post office** is at 95 Katoomba Street. **Blue Mountains District Hospital** is up the Great Western Hwy., tel. (02) 4782-2111. **Katoomba Washing Well,** Pioneer Place (near Kmart), has laundry services; open daily 7 a.m.-7 p.m.
    If you visit just one bookstore in Australia, make it **Brian's Books,** 44 Katoomba St., tel. (02) 4782-5115. Apart from two floors of secondhand books on every subject imaginable, you'll often have background ambience of Brian tapping away at his piano or giving lessons in one of many ancient languages; after hours scrabble games are often held. **Blue Mountains Visitor Information Centre** is at Echo Point, tel. (02) 4782-0756, website: www.lisp.com.au/~bmta, open daily 9 a.m.-5 p.m.

KATOOMBA TO HARTLEY

Immediately west of Katoomba is **Explorers Tree,** engraved by Blaxland, Wentworth, and Lawson. It is, in fact, less interesting than you may think. A wall built around the tree killed it, so the dead trunk was removed, leaving a stump, from which the explorers' initials have long since rotted away. Near the tree are sandstone headstones on graves of convicts who died during construction of the road.

Hydro Majestic Hotel
The community of **Medlow Bath,** six km northwest of Katoomba, consists of a cluster of houses that would be inconspicuous if it wasn't for the Hydro Majestic Hotel, an ochre-colored Edwardian monolith set in 80 hectares of landscaped garden right on the escarpment. Built late last century as a luxurious health resort, it features a cavernous lounge, dining room, two bars, swimming pool, and tennis courts. Rates are $130 pp midweek, $150 pp weekends, which includes breakfast and dinner. For bookings, call (047) 88-1002. Luxury.

Blackheath
The natural beauty of the Blue Mountains certainly doesn't end at Katoomba, for Blackheath (pop. 4,000), 14 km farther northwest, is gateway to the glorious Grose Valley to the north and Megalong Valley to the south. The town itself is a good base for exploring these areas, has a great number of historic buildings, and is noted for rhododendron gardens, many planted in private residences. **Blue Mountains Rhododendron Garden,** north of the highway off Sturt St., features 18 hectares of landscaped gardens; open daily 9 a.m.-5 p.m.
    Norwood Guesthouse, 209 Great Western Hwy., tel. (02) 4787-8568, is a small B&B dating from 1888. Rates are $75-105 s or d midweek, $95-135 weekends. Moderate. **Rowan Brae Guesthouse,** 284 Great Western Hwy., tel. (02) 4787-8296, is a romantic getaway surrounded in English-style gardens just a short walk from town; $110 pp Mon.-Fri., $130 pp weekends, which includes breakfast and a delicious three-course dinner. Luxury. **Jemby-Rinjah Lodge,**

336 Evans Lookout Rd., tel. (02) 4787-7622, is a series of log cabins set in native bushland, each with a kitchen and bathroom, and the complex has a laundry, lounge area with log fire, and plenty of native animals. It's only a short walk from Govett's Leap (see below). Cabins are $95 Mon.-Thurs., $130 Fri.-Sunday. Expensive. **Blackheath Caravan Park,** Prince Edward Rd., tel. (02) 4787-8101, has sites for $10 and cabins from $45. Budget-Inexpensive.

Vulcan's, 33 Govett's Leap Rd., tel. (02) 4787-6899, has all the modern style of a big-city restaurant but the feel of a small-town café. The menu features everything from seafood to vegetarian, all prepared and presented with flair. Although not cheap, Vulcan's is one of the Blue Mountains' finest restaurants.

Grose Valley
The northern section of Blue Mountains National Park encompasses spectacular Grose Valley, a deep box canyon carved through millions of years of erosion by the Grose River and its tributaries. The valley has no railway accessing the valley floor, and no famous landmark such as the Three Sisters, but views from various lookouts at the top of the escarpment are nothing short of breathtaking. The main lookout is **Govett's Leap,** at the end of Govett's Leap Road. The story behind the leap is that a bushranger pursued by troopers chose death rather than capture and spurred his horse over the 450-meter cliffs. From the lookout, trails lead north to Horseshoe Falls (800 meters one-way) and Pulpit Rock (2.5 km one-way), and south past Bridal Veil Falls, which can be seen from Govett's Leap, to Evans Lookout (three km one-way). The trail down into the valley is extremely steep and in places narrow (one km each way, but allow two hours roundtrip). If you are confident enough to negotiate this track, it would be a pity not to continue to Junction Rock, from where one trail branches south, climbing the escarpment at Evans Lookout (nine km roundtrip, allow five hours), and one branches north along Govett's Creek to the Blue Gum Forest (eight km one-way). Although not the valley proper, **Grand Canyon** is an interesting and moderately difficult five-km roundtrip from Evan's Lookout, perfect if you're staying at Jemby-Rinjah Lodge.

Along Govett's Leap Rd. is the **NPWS Heritage Centre,** displaying different aspects of the mountain's human and natural history; open daily 9 a.m.-4:30 p.m., tel. (02) 4787-8877.

Megalong Valley
The Megalong Valley, south of Blackheath, is not part of Blue Mountains National Park and is mostly cleared farmland, but driving into the valley allows a different perspective on the escarpment.

In the valley, **Werriberri Trail Rides** offers horseback riding for all levels of expertise, and charges $15 pp per half hour or $80 for a full day. An overnight ride is $170 pp. Open only on weekends and school holidays, tel. (02) 4787-9171.

Mount Victoria
Westernmost village of the Blue Mountains, Mt. Victoria is a charming place with a small museum behind the railway station (open 2-5 p.m. Sat.-Sun.) and a few grand buildings along the main street. On the eastern outskirts of the town is the **Toll Keepers Cottage,** built in 1849 to collect one shilling six pence from every coach—heavy vehicles (those without springs) were not required to pay the toll as they helped crush the stones and form the road. Built in 1878, the **Imperial Hotel,** tel. (02) 4787-1233, has rooms with shared facilities for $41 s, $62 d, private facilities for $48 s, $74 d, including breakfast, with weekend packages only slightly higher. Moderate.

From Mt. Victoria, the Great Western Highway continues to Lithgow and Bushranger Country, or you can return to Sydney along the Bells Line of Road (see below) or head to Jenolan Caves, south of Hartley.

Hartley
On the western slopes of the Blue Mountains, and beyond Little Hartley, Hartley, totally devoid of 20th century development, is one of Australia's best examples of an early 1800s town. Established in 1815 as a stopping point for travelers heading to the newly opened western plains, Hartley thrived within 20 years, with a courthouse, police station, hotels, and churches constructed. The town's fate was reversed in 1869 when it was bypassed in favor of a northern route for the rail line. Today, 17 buildings remain as a symbol

of the town's short but prosperous past. The most impressive is the **courthouse,** completed in 1837. Many notorious bushrangers were sentenced here, and the graffiti-lined walls of the cells allow an insight of early guests. Across the road is a well-preserved church, sandstone hotels, a post office, and other residences. The post office operates as an information center (open daily 10 a.m.-4:30 p.m.), and the courthouse is open for inspection, with tours daily 10 a.m., 11 a.m., noon, 2:15 p.m., and 3:30 p.m.

JENOLAN CAVES AND VICINITY

These caverns, nestled in a valley on the western slopes of the Blue Mountains 160 km west of Sydney, are among the most spectacular cave systems in Australia. They're especially popular because a couple are floodlit and have stairs leading through them. A bushranger was the first to discover the caves, and by 1866 the government had opened them to visitors, who made an arduous three-day trek on horseback from Katoomba.

From the Great Western Highway, the final descent to the main caves complex is through **Grand Arch,** an impressive open-ended cave more than 100 meters long and 20 meters high. Parts of the cave system are still unexplored, and of the 22 main caves, 12 are open for inspection—nine on a guided tour, three on a self-guided basis. The caves themselves are magical, with all the formations associated with limestone caverns. Tours run every 15-30 minutes (9:15 a.m.-5 p.m.) and last up to 90 minutes; $16-20 pp. Entry to self-guided caves is $10-12 pp. For more information, call (02) 6359-3311.

Accommodations

Open for visitors since 1906, **Caves House** is a three-story guesthouse built of locally quarried sandstone. Although extensive renovations have been done, rooms are still fairly basic; $80-150 s or d, including breakfast. Moderate. A cheaper option, 24 km north of the caves at the small village of Hampton, is **Hampton Halfway Hotel Motel,** tel. (02) 6359-3302. Motel-style rooms are basic, and there's a restaurant and bar on the premises; $38 s, $65 d. Moderate.

Kanangra Boyd National Park

An extension of Blue Mountains National Park, this 68,644-hectare park is a vast wilderness of sandstone cliffs, gorges, limestone caves, and the impressive **Kanangra Walls,** equal in beauty to areas around Katoomba but totally undeveloped. The walls are 33 km south of Jenolan Caves along a rough gravel road. A lookout here allows spectacular views across **Grand Gorge** and is the starting point of three short walks.

BELLS LINE OF ROAD

Originally built to provide a link between Windsor and the western plains, Bells Line of Road, north of the Great Western Highway, is an alternative route across the Blue Mountains.

Zig Zag Railway

The major problem engineers had with construction of a rail line across the Blue Mountains was the final descent into Lithgow. Eventually, a Z-shaped line, with two reverse stations, two tunnels, three sandstone viaducts, and a grade of 1:42, was completed. The line operated 1869-1910, falling into disrepair after a 10-tunnel deviation of the main line was constructed. The original route has been restored; steam trains run weekends and school holidays, and a diesel-powered train runs on other days. All trips start at Clarence Station; $12 pp. For bookings and timetable information, call (02) 6351-4826; for information on packages from Sydney and Katoomba, call City Rail at 13-1500.

Mount Wilson

In 1868 an area of crown land at the base of Mt. Wilson was subdivided and sold off to Sydneysiders who subsequently built cottages and planted extensive gardens reminiscent of England. Today the community remains a beautiful hideaway, different from anywhere else in the Blue Mountains. Exotic trees line most avenues, with rows of elm, beech, liquid amber, and lime dominating Church and Queens Avenues. In spring and autumn many private gardens are open to the public. Many hiking trails begin from Mt. Wilson, including one-km Waterfall Creek

Trail and, through town, the 400-meter Cathedral of Ferns Trail.

Mount Tomah Botanic Gardens

Maintained by the Sydney Royal Botanic Society, these gardens were developed on the site of a nursery once operational as a flower farm. Sections of the original garden remain, including a corner devoted to species of the Southern Hemisphere, but the highlight is the view from the Visitor Centre, which extends right across Sydney. The gardens are open daily 10 a.m.-5 p.m., tel. (02) 4567-2154. The restaurant here comes highly recommended.

Bilpin to Windsor

Bilpin is famous for its apples, or more precisely, its apple juice; both can be bought from the **Fruit Bowl,** a large fruit stall east of town. Farther east, on Kurrajong Hill, is a fabulous view across the city; on a clear day the skyscrapers of downtown Sydney can be seen. **Kurrajong,** the last community before crossing the Nepean River eastbound for Windsor, has a main street lined with tearooms, antique emporiums, and a few craft shops.

HAWKESBURY RIVER

The Hawkesbury is the largest river system draining into the Pacific Ocean from the Great Dividing Range. The eastern slopes of the Blue Mountains are its watershed, from where it flows northward along the base of the Great Dividing Range, looping around Sydney's outlying suburbs, flanked by a number of national parks, then draining into the ocean at **Broken Bay,** a wide body of water separating Sydney from the central coast.

Windsor

Windsor, located 56 km northwest of Sydney at the eastern end of Bells Line of Road, has seen much development in recent years, but the main street is lined with historic buildings. Windsor is one of five **Macquarie Towns** established along the Hawkesbury Valley by Governor Lachlan Macquarie in the late 1700s as a source of farmland for the new colony on Sydney Cove. Head first to the **Hawkesbury Museum,** in the old inn on Thompson Square, tel. (02) 4577-2310, which catalogs the history of the Macquarie Towns and has maps for exploring the whole area; open daily 9 a.m.-5 p.m. On nearby George St. is **Macquarie Arms Hotel,** which first opened in 1812. Farther along George St. is **St. Matthew's Anglican Church,** designed and built by convicts in 1822. On Palmer St. is **Tebbutt Observatory,** named for a keen astronomer who built an observatory on the site in 1879 (look for his face on the Australian $100 note).

North from Windsor

Hawkesbury Heritage Farm, six km north of Windsor in the Macquarie Town of Wilberforce, is a re-creation of an early Hawkesbury Valley township. Many buildings are original, including an 1811 timber cottage, the oldest such structure in the country. The park is open Thurs.-Sun. 10 a.m.-5 p.m. and admission is $10. Located on Buttsworth Lane, tel. (02) 4575-1457.

Wilberforce is on the west side of the Hawkesbury River, and if you continue north along Putty Rd., you'll finish at Singleton, in the Hunter Valley west of Newcastle. The alternative is to travel along the east bank of the Hawkesbury on Cattai Rd. to Wisemans Ferry through the delightful towns of **Pitt Town** and **Cattai.**

GOLDEN WEST

West of the Great Dividing Range are the western slopes, a rich agricultural land sandwiched between the mountains and the Outback. European settlement west of the Great Divide was at first slow; townships developed up and down the coast from Sydney Town before any movement west was made. Three landowners from the base of the range, Wentworth, Blaxland, and Lawson, were the first to make the crossing. Within months convicts were put to work constructing a road, and upon completion settlers began streaming west. The new settlers cleared vast tracts of land, opening it up for cereal crops, cattle, and sheep. In 1851, when Edward Hargraves discovered gold on Lewis Ponds Creek, north of Bathurst, thousands more flowed west, seeking fame and fortune. As at other goldfields of the same era, only a few struck it rich, and within a few years, life in the Golden West returned to normal.

Bathurst, Australia's first inland city, is a fine example of an Australian country town, with impressive buildings lining wide streets. To the north is the best-preserved of the gold-mining towns, Hill End, while to the south is Carcoar, scene of many daring bushranging exploits. South of Carcoar is Cowra and the grand town of Forbes. The northernmost town of the Golden West is Dubbo, home to Australia's largest open range zoo.

Lithgow and Vicinity

The first town west of the Blue Mountains is Lithgow (pop. 11,000), once an important coal-mining town and now a large manufacturing and industrial center. First settled in 1824, coal mining commenced in 1869, peaking in 1980 when 240,000 tons per day were extracted. Relying on the coal supply, industries such as steel, copper, brickworks, and pottery were also established.

Built in 1864, **Eskbank House,** corner Bennett and Inch Streets, tel. (02) 6351-3557, the home of one of Lithgow's earliest settlers, still stands. As well as original furniture, the house contains a coal-mining exhibit, while other relics are scattered around the grounds. Open Thurs.-Mon. 10 a.m.-4 p.m. A good source of information on the entire Golden West is the **Greater Lithgow Visitors Centre,** located in an old railway station on Cooerwull Rd., tel. (02) 6353-1859.

North of Lithgow, in Wollemi National Park, is a **glowworm tunnel.** The tunnel itself is man-made, having been constructed for a rail line, but the glowing worms are completely natural. To get there take Inch Street out of Lithgow, turning onto Atkinson St. and following this road onto Newnes Plateau. From the parking area, it's five km to the tunnel, but it's possible to continue a farther four km by road. A trail through the tunnel continues 11 km to the former shale-mining town of Newnes.

BATHURST

Bathurst lies 200 km west of Sydney. It is Australia's oldest inland city, and while other population centers of the same era have slid into oblivion, Bathurst continues to thrive and is now an important rural center of 26,000.

History

Construction of a road west from Sydney began within months of the explorers Wentworth, Blaxland, and Lawson's crossing the Blue Mountains. By 1815, less than two years after the first crossing, a rough track had been completed over the mountains and as far west as the Macquarie River, where the township of Bathurst developed. As a pastoral center, Bathurst grew steadily in its formulative years, but it wasn't until the 1850s, with nearby gold discoveries, that the town boomed. Gold strikes to the north of Bathurst brought thousands of prospectors through the town, as well as a number of bushrangers. The rush for gold has long since ended, but Bathurst remains a thriving city, serving the large agricultural industry and becoming the focus of national attention for the running of Australia's most popular motor race.

Mt. Panorama Sights

A racing circuit was first developed on Mt. Panorama, southwest of town, in the 1930s. It's Australia's only public road-racing circuit, meaning you're free to drive around the 6.2-km circuit year-round. All normal road rules apply, so chances are you won't break the lap record of two minutes and 12 seconds.

Near the starting line is the **National Motor Racing Museum**, tel. (02) 6332-1872, featuring bikes and cars dating from 1930, photographic displays of the track's winners and losers, and other racing memorabilia. It's open daily 9 a.m.-4:30 p.m. Admission is adult $5, child $1.50.

At the top of Mt. Panorama is **Sir Joseph Banks Nature Park,** a 41-hectare enclosure of native bushland that's home to kangaroos, koalas, wombats, dingos, emus, quolls, and a variety of birds. Admission is $3 pp, and it's open daily 9 a.m.-4:15 p.m.

Off the Conrod Straight section of the motor racing circuit is **Bathurst Gold Fields,** a replica of an 1850s goldfield. All aspects of mining techniques have been reconstructed as well as a blacksmith's shop, ore stamper, and traditional miner's hut. Admission is adult $8, child $4, which includes gold panning. The goldfields are only open in conjunction with guided tours operated by the local information center. Book these at (02) 6332-1444.

A split in the motor racing world in 1997 saw the demise of Australia's most famous race, the Tooheys 1,000. Today, two offshoots of this long-

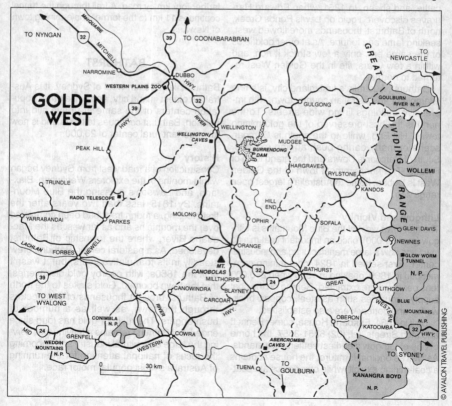

© AVALON TRAVEL PUBLISHING

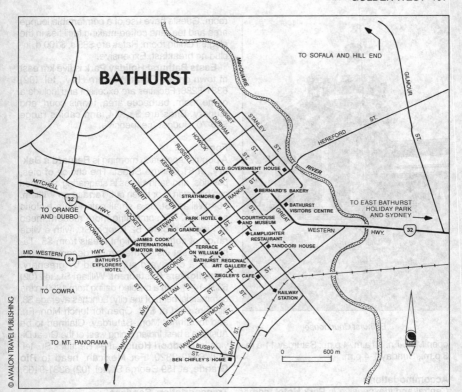

BATHURST

TO SOFALA AND HILL END

GILMOUR ST.

MACQUARIE ST.

MORRISSET ST.

DURHAM ST.

STANLEY ST.

HOWICK ST.

RUSSELL ST.

KEPPEL ST.

LAMBERT ST.

HEREFORD ST.

RIVER

OLD GOVERNMENT HOUSE

BERNARD'S BAKERY

BATHURST VISITORS CENTRE

TO EAST BATHURST HOLIDAY PARK AND SYDNEY

MITCHELL

32

TO ORANGE AND DUBBO

HWY.

ROCKET ST.

BROWNING ST.

PIPER ST.

RANKIN ST.

GREAT WESTERN HWY.

32

STRATHMORE

PARK HOTEL

COURTHOUSE AND MUSEUM

RIO GRANDE

LAMPLIGHTER RESTAURANT

STEWART ST.

JAMES COOK INTERNATIONAL MOTOR INN

TERRACE ON WILLIAM

TANDOORI HOUSE

MID WESTERN HWY.

24

BATHURST EXPLORERS MOTEL

BRILLIANT ST.

GEORGE ST.

BATHURST REGIONAL ART GALLERY

ZIEGLER'S CAFE

TO COWRA

WILLIAM ST.

BENTINCK ST.

SEYMOUR ST.

RAILWAY STATION

PANORAMA AVE.

HAVANNAH ST.

BUSBY ST.

BANT ST.

TO MT. PANORAMA

BEN CHIFLEY'S HOME

0   600 m

N

© AVALON TRAVEL PUBLISHING

running race attract the crowds—up to 30,000 for each event. The **AMP Bathurst 1,000** is held the first weekend of October and the **Australian 1,000 Classic** in mid-November. Both are 161-lap races. A general admission ticket to the final day's racing is $30, $120 if you want to sit on Pit Straight. For ticketing information, call the information center at (02) 6332-1444.

Town Sights

Ben Chifley, one of Australia's great prime ministers, was born and raised in Bathurst. He ran the country between 1945 and 1949. His small, unpretentious Bathurst home is open to the public Mon.-Sat. 2-4 p.m. and Sunday 10 a.m.-noon. Admission is adult $2, child $1. It's on the corner of Busby and Bant Streets.

Bathurst's oldest building is **Old Government House,** at the northeast end of George St., which dates from 1820. Many of the city center's other buildings, including commercial, civic, and residential, date from the Victorian era (1840-1900). **Bathurst Courthouse,** Russell St., is the most impressive of these and is open Mon.-Fri. 9:30 a.m.-4 p.m. In the courthouse's east wing is **Bathurst and District Historical Museum,** tel. (02) 6332-4755. Open Saturday 9:30 a.m.-4:30 p.m. and Sunday 9:30 a.m.-4:30 p.m.; admission $1.

Many of Australia's greatest artists have drawn inspiration from Bathurst's natural surroundings and nearby ghost towns. Works displayed at **Bathurst Regional Art Gallery,** 70 Keppel St., tel. (02) 6331-6066, depict this environment. It's

Bathurst Courthouse

open Mon.-Fri. 10 a.m.-4 p.m., Saturday 11 a.m.-3 p.m., Sunday 1-4 p.m.

Accommodations
Central and inexpensive is **Park Hotel,** corner George and Keppel Streets, tel. (02) 6331-3399, where rooms with private facilities are $39 s, $60 d, including breakfast. Inexpensive. Most motels are at least one km from downtown, including a few on the road out to Cowra. Of these, **Bathurst Explorers Motel,** Mid Western Hwy., tel. (02) 6331-2966, is least expensive, with basic rooms for $52 s, $68 d. Moderate. One block east is **James Cook International Motor Inn,** tel. (02) 6332-1800, Bathurst's best motel. Rooms are of the highest standard, with an indoor pool, laundry, health club, and fine-dining restaurant. Rates are $118 s or d for a standard room, $145 with a private spa. Expensive.

Built as a private residence in 1882, **Strathmore,** 202 Russell St., tel. (02) 6332-3252, is one of Bathurst's many historic B&Bs. Each of the five refurbished rooms has a private bath-

room. Guests have use of a comfortable lounge area and tea- and coffee-making facilities in the elegant dining room. Rates are $85 s, $100 d, including breakfast. Expensive.

Easts Bathurst Holiday Park is five km east of town on the Great Western Hwy., tel. (02) 6331-8286. Facilities are excellent and include a game room, barbecue area, tennis court, and laundry. Sites are $12-14, and cabins range $40-70. Budget-Inexpensive.

Food
A popular spot each morning is **Bernard's Bakery,** at 81 George Street. The choice of pies, pastries, and sandwiches is staggering, and food can be eaten in or taken out. **Terrace on William,** 164 William St., is a small café with a historic ambience. For something more modern, head to **Ziegler's Cafe,** 52 Keppel St., with a wide range of coffees and light meals from $5. Tables are set inside the simply decorated café and in a courtyard surrounded by greenery. **Lamplighters Restaurant,** William St., tel. (02) 6331-1448, is in a building dating from 1890 in the commercial heart of the city. Lunches average $8, dinners start at $12. Open for lunch Mon.-Fri. and for dinner Mon.-Saturday. Claimed to be Australia's best Indian dining west of the Great Divide is **Tandoori House** at 94 Bentinck St., tel. (02) 6332-3320. For Mexican, head to **Rio Grande,** at 159 George St., tel. (02) 6331-9136.

Transportation, Services, and Information
Hazelton, tel. (13) 1300, the main airline carrier west of the Great Divide, has daily flights between Sydney and major centers in the region. The flight between Sydney and Bathurst takes 40 minutes and costs $140 one-way. **Countrylink,** tel. (13) 2232, runs the **XPT** between Sydney's Central Station and Bathurst Railway Station at the end of Keppel Street. All long-distance buses stop in town.

Bathurst Visitors Centre is at 28 William St., tel. (02) 6332-1444. Open daily 9 a.m.-5 p.m.

NORTH FROM BATHURST

The area north of Bathurst was the scene of frenzied gold rushes in the 1850s but is today a quiet destination, well off the beaten track. The first village north of Bathurst is **Sofala**, a picturesque settlement on the Turon River. At the height of the gold rush, in the late 1850s, 40,000 people lived in Sofala. The town has aged naturally, with very little changing since late last century. The main street, lined with buildings in varying states of disrepair, features a general store, post office, small museum, and a couple of cafés.

Hill End

Walking through the deserted streets of Hill End, about 36 km west of Sofala, it's difficult to imagine the atmosphere that must have prevailed between 1871 and 1874 when thousands of hopeful diggers descended on the remote valley in hope of making their fortune. When gold was found at **Hawkins Hill** in 1871, word of the enormous amount of gold spread quickly around the world. The reef of gold uncovered was 400 meters long, 100 meters wide, and 80 meters deep. It brought fortune to those lucky enough to arrive early, and as merchants, tradesmen, and miners established themselves, the town gained an air of permanence. Within two years, though, the supply of gold had dwindled, and the newly established town saw a mass exodus of diggers. Those who remained searched the mullock heaps for gold missed in the initial rush and panned for alluvial gold in the creek beds.

Where Hill End differs from other historic goldmining towns is that there has been virtually no development since the boom years. The streets are lined with buildings from the 1870s. Each is marked with a plaque describing its history, while the sites of those demolished buildings are marked with photos of the original structures. A two-km trail leads around Hawkins Hill and to an old mine on Bald Hill. In the old hospital on Bathurst Rd., the NPWS, caretaker of the town, operates an excellent **museum**, tel. (02) 6337-8206. It's open daily 9:30 a.m.-4:30 p.m.

Dating from 1872, the **Royal Hotel**, tel. (02) 6337-8261, sits atop a small rise overlooking town. Rooms, with shared facilities, are of an excellent standard and open to a wide balcony. Rates are $35 s, $50 d; $43 s, $66 d, with breakfast. Inexpensive. The NPWS operates three campgrounds in town, including one within walking distance of the pub and general store. Out back of the hotel is a bistro counter—either eat at tables set around the beer garden or in the small room off the main bar.

Mudgee

Farther north, the medium-sized country town of Mudgee (pop. 8,200) lies in a shallow valley through which the Codgegong River flows. While it was gold that saw other towns thrive, Mudgee's wealth is centered on agriculture, in particular wine and honey. The wide main street, typical of country towns, features a number of impressive civic buildings, including a town hall dating from 1880. **Colonial Inn Museum**, 126 Market St., is in the old West End Hotel. Parts of the old hotel have been restored—including the bar, parlor, and a kitchen—using relics from a nearby inn. It's open Saturday 2-5 p.m., Sunday 10 a.m.-5 p.m. **Mudgee Honey Co.**, 28 Robertson St., tel. (02) 6372-2359, is a good place to view the honey production process. Open daily 9 a.m.-5 p.m.

The **Paragon Hotel**, corner of Gladstone and Perry Streets, tel. (02) 6372-1313, has a few basic rooms with shared facilities for $28-30 pp, including breakfast. Inexpensive. The nicest place in town is **Country Comfort–Mudgee**, Cassilis Rd., tel. (02) 6372-4500 or (1800) 06-5064, with a bar, bistro, and restaurant; $99-136 s or d. Expensive.

Mudgee boasts a surprising number of good cafés and restaurants. **Mudgee Country Bakehouse**, 79 Market St., has all the usual pies and pastries as well as healthy sandwiches. For a pub meal, head to **Lawson Park Hotel**, 1 Church St., tel. (02) 6372-2183, where a good roast is offered Monday and Tuesday. **Elton's Café**, in a historic chemist shop at 81 Market St., has a friendly small-town atmosphere and good food at the right price. For something a bit more formal, try **Craigmoor Winery Restaurant**, Craigmoor Rd., tel. (02) 6372-2208. The restaurant, built of native timbers and overlooking the winetasting area, is open daily for lunch and on weekends for dinner. The winery itself is renowned as the home of Australia's oldest Chardonnay plantings. Another winery option is **Augustine Vineyard Restaurant**, George Campbell Dr., tel. (02) 6372-6816. Morning and afternoon teas ($7.50) are the highlight, with cheese plates ($8) also available. Lunch dishes are prepared using mostly local produce and range $12-15.

Mudgee Visitors Centre is at 84 Market St., tel. (02) 6372-5875 or (1800) 81-6304. It's open Mon.-Fri. 9 a.m.-5 p.m., Saturday 9 a.m.-3:30 p.m., Sunday 9:30 a.m.-2 p.m.

Gulgong

While most Australians took the introduction of plastic banknotes in stride, it was a sad time for Gulgong, the town on the old $10 note. Gold was discovered at nearby Red Hill in 1870, and a prosperous town soon developed. The streets of Gulgong, about 29 km north of Mudgee, are narrow and winding, lined with a variety of one-story buildings. **Gulgong Pioneer Museum,** 73 Herbert St., tel. (02) 6374-1513, is one of the best small-town museums in the state. On display is a blacksmith's shop, settler's cottage, Cobb & Co. coach, and a collection of Aboriginal artifacts. It's open daily 9 a.m.-5 p.m.

Stables Guest Rooms, 149 Mayne St., tel. (02) 6374-1668, is a late-Victorian accommodation, and while a couple of rooms are in the original stables others are in the main house. Rates are $80 s, $105 d. Expensive.

Wellington

This medium-sized town of 5,000 is on the Macquarie River between Bathurst and Dubbo. The town's main drawcard is **Wellington Caves,** eight km south of town. The caves were discovered by Europeans in 1828 and for most of this century have been a popular tourist destination. Cathedral and Gaden Caves are lit for public inspection, while River Cave is only open to cave divers. Tours are conducted seven times daily, tel. (02) 6845-1733. Around the caves' entrance are tourist attractions, including a house made entirely from bottles, and a golf course. Also here is a campground with good grassy and shaded sites; $10-12 per night, and cabins are $45-55. For bookings, call (02) 6845-2970. Budget-Inexpensive.

DUBBO

Dubbo is a city of 30,000 on the Macquarie River, 400 km northwest of Sydney. It's the hub of western New South Wales and gateway to the Outback. Dubbo, meaning "Red Earth" to the

Aborigines, is an important wheat and wool center but is a transportation point for a great variety of other agricultural industries. Prior to European settlement, the region was inhabited by the Wiradhuri Aborigines. The first Europeans arrived in 1824, settling land along the Macquarie River. By 1840 a general store had opened, followed by a hotel and courthouse. A decade later the town had been surveyed and blocks of land were for sale.

Western Plains Zoo

Australia's largest open-range zoo, this facility features animals from six continents roaming more than 300 hectares six km south of Dubbo. As well as more than 1,000 Australian animals, there are lions, tigers, cheetahs, rhinos, a herd of elephants, bison, oryx, monkeys, and giraffes. None of the animals are caged; instead they are contained subtly—by moats, for example. Kids can pet animals at the Friendship Farm. Because of the zoo's large area, you may want to rent a bike ($8 four hours) or mini-moke ($30 for three hours) to get around. Admission is adult $15, child $7.50. Open daily 9 a.m.-5 p.m. For park information, call (02) 6882-5888.

Other Sights

Old Dubbo Gaol, right downtown between the Commonwealth and State Banks, tel. (02) 6882-8122, has held some of Australia's most notorious bushrangers. Established in 1847, the jail was in use until 1966. Many of the cells have been restored, and along with gallows, padded cells for condemned prisoners, and a hangman's kit, the place makes for a grisly yet interesting attraction. Animated models of prisoners tell of their crimes and tragic endings. Admission is adult $5, child $1. Open daily 9 a.m.-4:30 p.m.

In a sandstone building dating from 1876 is **Dubbo Museum** at 232 Macquarie St., tel. (02) 6882-5359. It features a coach-building display, Aboriginal relics, and memorabilia from early settlers. Admission is adult $5, child $1. Open daily 9 a.m.-4:30 p.m.

Accommodations and Food

Of the cheap hotels, **Castlereagh Hotel** is the best, with basic rooms for $27 s, $45 d, including breakfast. Inexpensive. It's at the corner of Talbragar and Brisbane Streets, tel. (02) 6882-4877. Also basic is **Park Vue Motel**, 131 Bourke St., tel. (02) 6882-4253, where rooms are $40 s, $48 d. Inexpensive. Most other motels are strung along Cobra St., south of downtown. Of these, one of the best values is **Golden West Motor Inn**, 87 Cobra St., tel. (02) 6882-2822, which has all the usual facilities, a pool, spa, and barbecue area. Rates are $58 s, $66 d. Moderate. Similar in standard, and with an excellent pool area, is **Palms Motor Inn**, 35 Cobra St., tel. (02) 6881-8155; $64 s, $74 d. Moderate. **Dubbo YHA**, 87 Brisbane St., tel. (02) 6882-0922, is on the north side of the rail line a short walk from downtown. Facilities are fine, and dorm beds are $14 pp. Budget. Bikes can also be rented. **Dubbo City Caravan Park** is across the river from town on Whylandra St., tel. (02) 6882-4820. Sites are $12-19, on-site vans $30, and cabins $36-48. Budget-Inexpensive.

Along Macquarie St. are good cafés, including **Grape Vine Cafe**, opposite the courthouse at 144 Brisbane Street. **Village Hot Bake Bakery Café**, 113 Darling St., offers three distinct dining areas, including an outdoor courtyard. The breakfast menu is extensive, with full-cooked breakfasts from $8.50. **Jule's Crepes**, 213 Macquarie St., tel. (02) 6882-9300, is a heritage-style restaurant with an informal atmosphere. Savory crepes are a reasonable $10-13.50 pp, with the all-important dessert crepes averaging $6. Further along Macquarie, at No. 177, is **Echidna**, tel. (02) 6884-9393, a modern city-style bistro open daily except Monday. It's the newest kid on the block when it comes to Dubbo dining, so it has a real buzz about it. Throughout the day it offers specialty sandwiches and salads, while the dinner menu is more extensive and uses mostly local produce. For an inexpensive meal, head to **Dubbo RSL Club Resort** on Brisbane St., tel. (02) 6882-4411.

Transportation, Services, and Information
Countrylink, tel. (13) 2232, operates **XPT** rail services between Sydney and Dubbo. Countrylink also offers packages, including travel from Sydney, one-night accommodations, meals, and entry to Western Plains Zoo, for $275 pp. Dubbo Railway Station is on Talbragar Street. The main bus depot is on Erskine Street. It is served by **Greyhound Pioneer**, tel. (13) 2030, and **McCafferty's**, tel. (13) 1499. The fare from Sydney is around $45 each way.

Dubbo Visitors Centre is on the corner of Macquarie and Erskine Streets, tel. (02) 6884-1422 or (1800) 67-4443, website: www.dubbo.com.au. It's open daily 9 a.m.-5 p.m. There's plenty of parking at the center, making it a good place to base yourself for exploring downtown, a 400-meter walk away.

ORANGE AND VICINITY

Once considered as the site of the national capital, Orange, 260 km west of Sydney, is a thriving fruit-growing center of 35,000. Orange's dominant natural feature is 1,395-meter **Mt. Canobolas**, one of the continent's highest peaks away from the Great Dividing Range. Oranges are not grown at Orange (the city is named for William of Orange, former King of Holland); instead apples, pears, and cherries are the major crops, thriving in the rich volcanic soil. Australian poet Banjo Patterson was born in town.

The **Tourist Information Centre** is in the Civic Centre on Byng St., tel. (02) 6361-5226.

Ophir
When news of gold discoveries west of the Great Divide first filtered through to Sydney in the late 1840s, the government tried to keep the news quiet, afraid that settlers would desert their farms for the diggings. The situation changed dramatically when gold was discovered in California. Fearing a mass exodus across the Pacific, the government reversed its decision and offered a reward for the discovery of a payable goldfield. On 12 February 1851 Edward Hargraves found traces of gold on Lewis Ponds Creek, 20 km northwest of Orange. While he rushed off to Sydney to claim the reward, his partners, William Tom and John Lister, found the mother lode. This first rush was short and sweet. A few thousand diggers worked the creek and tributary, but within months they were lured away by finds elsewhere.

A few foundations and depressions at the junction of Lewis Ponds and Summer Hill Creeks are all that remain of the Ophir township. Walking tracks lead through the old workings, and a primitive campground has been developed above Fitzroy Bar, site of the original find.

Millthorpe

The historic village of Millthorpe, 25 km southeast of Orange, features numerous Victorian-era buildings and a small commercial center with cobbled sidewalks and winding streets. Buildings such as the school, a couple of hotels, and banks have changed little in more than 100 years. At the top end of Victoria St. is **Rosebank Guesthouse,** tel. (02) 6366-3191. Built in 1902, it's one of Millthorpe's more-modern buildings, but it lacks nothing in grandeur, with spacious rooms, a cozy lounge area, and extensive gardens. Rates are $75-100 pp, including breakfast, and dinner is available for an extra $25 pp. Luxury. The **Old Mill Cafe,** just down the hill from Rosebank at 32 Victoria St., tel. (02) 6366-3188, is one of many restored buildings. It serves delicious morning and afternoon teas ($4-8) and is also open for lunch (closed Monday).

BATHURST TO COWRA

Abercrombie Caves

South from the Mid Western Highway, on a rough road linking Bathurst and Goulburn, is Abercrombie Caves. Koori were the first to explore the remote cave system, but it wasn't until bushrangers began using them as a hideout that they came to the attention of officialdom. A massive limestone arch is the dominant aboveground feature of the cave system, and two caves are lit for public inspection. They are open daily 9 a.m.-4 p.m., with guided tours departing at 2 p.m. At the caves' entrance are campsites for $12 and cabins $40-45. Facilities include hot showers, a laundry, kiosk, and barbecue area. For tour information and campsite bookings, call (02) 6368-8603. Budget-Inexpensive.

Tuena

This small gold-mining village lies on the Tuena River 20 km south of Abercrombie Caves. Gold was discovered on the river in the mid-1850s, and although many permanent buildings were established, the field never amounted to much. **Parson's General Store,** dating from 1860, is Tuena's oldest building. It still operates as a general store and is good for supplies and hints on fossicking areas. Dating from 1866, the **Goldfields Inn,** tel. (02) 4834-5214, is an original wattle-and-daub building offering meals and inexpensive lodging.

Carcoar

Straddling the Belubula River, 50 km southwest of Bathurst, this charming old village of 400 was at one time the second-largest town west of the Blue Mountains. Established in 1838 to curb the activity of bushrangers, it grew steadily in importance, but when gold was found to the north its population steadied. As transport links became better, the need for the local banks and the courthouse lessened.

The biggest concentration of historic buildings is along Belubula St., which slopes down to the river. The Commercial Bank (1862) was often the target of bushrangers. Other historic buildings are the courthouse (1882) and Royal Hotel (1891). On the opposite side of the river is **Stoke Stable,** dating from 1849. It's now a small but interesting museum open daily 10 a.m.-4 p.m.

Farther down Naylor St. is **Dalebrook Bed and Breakfast,** tel. (02) 6367-3149. Facilities are shared; $85 s, $95 d. Expensive. On the north side of the river is **Bridges Tea Rooms,** serving good hamburgers and some light meals in an antique-filled room.

COWRA

Best known as site of the greatest prisoner escape in British military history, Cowra is a quiet country town on the Lachlan River, 300 km southwest of Sydney and 200 km north of Canberra. During WW II Cowra was the site of four prisoner-of-war camps. In the early hours of 4 August 1944 a mass breakout took place from one of two camps holding Japanese prisoners. In the darkness, confusion reigned, and guards manning machine guns were helpless against hundreds of marauding Japanese. Of the 1,104 prisoners, 378 escaped. Many were killed on the spot, others escaped and committed suicide, and still others were recaptured. Four guards were killed. Although little remains of the camp, photographs of the original compounds and a few foundations make the site worth visiting. It's northeast of town

Carcoar

on Sakura Avenue. North of the camp, on Doncaster Dr., are the Cowra and Japanese War Cemeteries, where victims of the breakout lie. At the southern end of Sakura Ave. is the **Japanese Garden,** tel. (02) 6341-2233. The gardens have been developed through years of close ties between Japan and the people of Cowra, officially opening in 1979. The gardens include ponds, cascading waterfalls, pathways, a Japanese cottage, a cultural center, a restaurant serving light meals, and a gift shop. Admission is adult $7, child $5. Open daily 8:30 a.m.-5 p.m.

Cowra Museum, five km east of town, tel. (02) 6342-2666, combines the region's railway, war, and rural history into one large and interesting museum. It's open daily 9 a.m.-5 p.m.

While most of the land around Cowra has been cleared for agriculture, 7,590 hectares within **Conimbla National Park,** 27 km west, are protected. Within the park, Ironbark Walking Track leads to a lookout above the surrounding open forests.

Practicalities

Alabaster Motel, 20 Lynch St., tel. (02) 6342-3133, has large modern units, a pool, spa, and barbecue area; $57 s, $59 d. Inexpensive. **Cowra Holiday Park** is five km east of Cowra toward Bathurst, tel. (02) 6342-2666. It has all the usual facilities and is adjacent to the museum. Sites are $12-15, on-site vans $40, and cabins $50. Budget-Inexpensive. The other alternative for campers is Conimbla National Park, 27 km west of Cowra.

Ilfracombe Restaurant, 127 Kendal St., tel. (02) 6341-1511, in a private residence dating from 1879, retains the authentic charm from the Victorian era. A coffee house open from 11 a.m. provides light snacks while the restaurant proper offers steak, chicken, and seafood from $15.50. Closed Sunday.

The **Visitor Information Centre,** on the Mid Western Hwy., tel. (02) 6342-4333, website: www.cowra.gov.au, features breakout memorabilia. Open daily 9 a.m.-5 p.m.

VICINITY OF COWRA

Grenfell, west of Cowra, grew from a gold rush on nearby Emu Creek, and relics from this time can be viewed at **Grenfell Museum** on Camp Street. Australia's best-known poet, Henry Lawson, was born in his parents' canvas tent at the Emu Creek goldfields. A cairn on Lawson St. marks the site, and each June long weekend the event is celebrated during the Henry Lawson Festival, a gathering of poets and songwriters.

Weddin Mountains National Park

Protecting the rugged Weddin Range, this 8,360-hectare park was an ideal hideout for bushrangers who took refuge in its dense cover and many caves. The most famous of these was Ben Hall, who with his gang often hid out at a cave in the west of the park. A 500-meter trail leads up to the cave from Nowlands Road. On the range's eastern slopes, at the end of Holy Camp Rd., is a campground.

West Wyalong
At the junction of the Newell and Mid Western Highways, this small country town of 4,000 is in the heart of a rich wool- and wheat-growing region. The town was never officially surveyed, so early residents dug the main street around tree stumps, and as a result West Wyalong's main drag is strangely crooked. A small museum downtown displays relics from the town's gold-mining history. It's open daily 2:30-5 p.m., tel. (02) 6972-2117. Southeast of town, toward Temora, is a mineral pool, good for a relaxing dip. **Lake Cowal,** 47 km northeast of town, is a shallow body of water covering 200 square km. More than 150 species of birds have been reported there. Access is from Clear Ridge Road.

Best value of the dozen motels in town is **Colonial Motor Inn,** on the Mid Western Hwy. 500 meters west of downtown, tel. (02) 6972-2611; $56 s, $66 d. Moderate. The **Tourist Information Centre** is in a train carriage in McCann Park, at the junction of the Newell and Mid Western Highways, tel. (02) 6972-3645. It's open daily 10 a.m.-4 p.m.

Forbes
Forbes, 90 km northwest of Cowra, is a stately town of 8,000 on the Lachlan River. Having been founded in the 1840s, many historic buildings line the streets, including the town hall, post office, courthouse, and a number of churches and hotels. Bushranger Ben Hall and his gang were active in the Forbes area, with Hall being brought down in a hail of bullets 20 km west of Forbes. He's buried in the cemetery northwest of town on Bogan Gate Road. On Cross St. is **Forbes Museum,** holding many Ben Hall relics. It's open 3-5 p.m.

The **Vandenberg Hotel,** Court St., tel. (02) 6852-2015, has basic rooms with shared facilities for $25 s, $39 d, including breakfast. Inexpensive. **Country Mile Motor Inn,** 14 Cross St., tel. (02) 6852-4099 or (1800) 80-3748, is the best motel in town; $62 s, $72 d. Moderate. Campers should head to **Lachlan View Caravan Park,** two km southeast of town toward Cowra, tel. (02) 6852-1055. Facilities include a pool, laundry, shop, and camp kitchen. Sites are $12-14, on-site vans $33, and cabins $33-50. Budget-Inexpensive.

The **Tourist Information Centre** is in the railway station on Union St., tel. (02) 6852-4155; open daily 9 a.m.-5 p.m.

Parkes
The highlight of a visit to Parkes, 55 km north of Forbes, is the **radio telescope,** 20 km north of town. The telescope's massive 64-meter-wide dish collects radio waves from throughout the galaxy and beyond, analyzing the signals on a computer to produce images. This telescope has been involved in various international projects, including the 1969 Moon Landing and the Voyager II journey to Neptune. In conjunction with NASA, the most recently completed project involved receiving data from the Galileo spacecraft, sent to photograph Jupiter's moons. A visitor center at the telescope is open daily 8:30 a.m.-4:30 p.m., with the film *The Invisible Universe* shown hourly, tel. (02) 6861-1777.

OUTBACK NEW SOUTH WALES

To the government, the Outback of New South Wales is known by the rather uninspiring name **Western Division,** an area encompassing more than 40% of the state and with a population that hovers around 50,000 (half of which live in Broken Hill). Although it is generally accepted that the "real" Outback lies west of the Darling River, which flows in a southwesterly direction from up near Lightning Ridge to the Murray River west of Mildura, the only official boundaries of Outback New South Wales are the borders of Queensland to the north and South Australia to the west.

Outback Tours

If you only have a few days to spare, the best way to cover the great distances of Outback New South Wales would be to fly into Broken Hill and take a tour. Many companies offer tours taking in all the best features of this part of the country. **Silver City Tours,** tel. (08) 8087-3310, operates day tours from Broken Hill out to Mutawintji and Kinchega National Parks and White Cliffs. The six-day tour includes all the above, plus it takes in sights closer to Broken Hill and provides basic motel accommodations for $520 pp. **Broken Hill's Outback Tours,** tel. (08) 8087-7800, is another option. A four-day Outback National Parks tour departs twice weekly and costs $635 pp. The most comprehensive tour is offered by **Centrek Safaris,** tel. (03) 9775-2211, and includes the Dingo Fence and Cameron Corner in a seven-day 4WD safari; $1,095 pp, including airfare from Melbourne.

BARRIER HIGHWAY

The Barrier Highway heads west from Nyngan through to Broken Hill and on to Adelaide and is sealed the entire way. The scenery is fairly mundane, featuring low undulating scrub-covered hills until the highway crosses the Darling River at Wilcannia, where red soils, typical of the Outback, dominate.

Nyngan

Nyngan, at the junction of the Mitchell and Barrier Highways 167 km northwest of Dubbo, is best-

known to Australians for the disastrous floods in April 1990, when water from the usually dry **Bogan River** rose to such a height that the town all but disappeared, and the 2,000 residents had to be airlifted by helicopter to Dubbo. During these same floods, an area larger than Great Britain was underwater north of Nyngan. The only reminders of the flooding are a sandbag levee constructed between the Bogan River and town, a couple of memorial cairns, and a helicopter in Vanges Park. A part of the railway station is a small museum, and the old stationmaster's cottage has been restored.

Country Manor Motor Inn, 145 Pangee St., tel. (02) 6832-1447 or (1800) 81-9913, is the best place to stay in town. Facilities include a saltwater pool, and across the road is the RSL Club, a good place for a meal; $48 s, $58 d. Inexpensive.

Information about the town and other Outback destinations is available from **Burn's Video and Gift Shop** at 105 Pangee St., tel. (02) 6832-1155; open seven days.

Cobar and Vicinity

Cobar (pop. 6,000) thrives on its tremendous mineral wealth, and unlike other towns of Outback NSW (except for Broken Hill) it's far away from any natural river source. The mineral outcrop around which the town was founded in 1871, with 920,000 tons of copper, lead, and zinc extracted annually. **Great Cobar Outback Heritage Centre** has some excellent displays pertaining to the history of the area and the people who settled in this harsh part of the country. An Aboriginal display shows the various bush tucker to be found in the Outback, while upstairs is devoted to mining and the mineralogy of the land upon which Cobar was built. It's located on a rise overlooking the town, on the Barrier Hwy., tel. (02) 6836-1452, and is open Mon.-Fri. 8 a.m.-5 p.m., Sat.-Sun. 10 a.m.-5 p.m.

The **Great Western Hotel,** built in 1898, has always been the grandest establishment in town. Rooms have shared facilities and are $28 s, $40 d, with breakfast $6 pp extra. Located on the corner of Linsley and Marshall Streets, tel. (02) 6836-2503. Inexpensive. The best lodging in

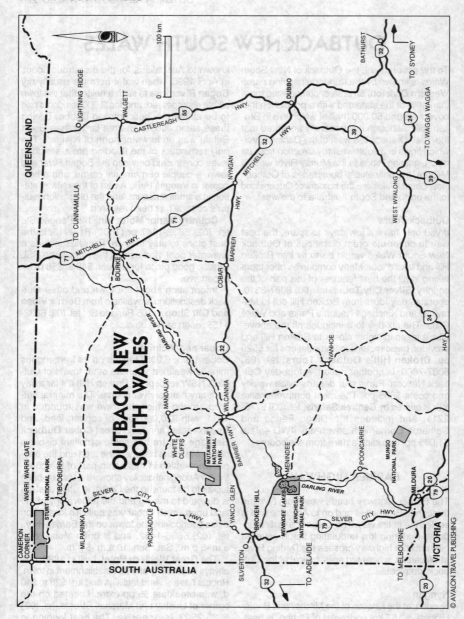

OUTBACK NEW SOUTH WALES

town is the **Sundowner Barrier Motel,** west of downtown, tel. (02) 6836-2203, with a pool and restaurant; $75 s, $85 d Moderate. **Longworth Restaurant and Bar,** 55 Linsley St., tel. (02) 6836-2611, is a formal eatery in a house built in 1899 for Thomas Longworth, one of the original directors of the Great Cobar Copper Mine. The setting is historically authentic, with pressed-metal ceilings and period furnishings. The menu features a wide variety of dishes ranging $13-21; open daily 7 p.m.

If you are passing through Cobar in early August, the detour to **Louth,** 132 km northwest of Cobar, is worthwhile. The first or second Saturday in August (call Louth Hotel at 02-6874-7422 to check dates) is the annual Louth race meeting, which has grown in stature to boast more than $30,000 in prize money and live television coverage across Australia. West of Cobar, 40 km along the Barrier Highway, a 35-km road spurs north to **Mt. Grenfell Historic Site,** where more than 1,300 pieces of Koori rock art are scattered over rock walls and overhangs. Toilets and water are supplied for campers.

Wilcannia

Wilcannia, 265 km west of Cobar and 200 km east of Broken Hill, spreads out along the west bank of the Darling River. The town grew as a staging point for wheat and wool transported from Outback stations and sent downriver on massive barges. Today's 800 inhabitants still rely heavily on the sheep and cattle industry, along with the tourist trade, to make up the local economy. The timber wharf used by paddlesteamers still stands, as does a historic jail, courthouse, and post office. The town has two inexpensive motels and a couple of hotels that offer meals.

White Cliffs

White Cliffs is as famous for its housing as for its black opals. Most of the population lives underground, escaping the climatic extremes of unbearably hot summers and near-freezing nights during winter. The town is very remote, 100 km north of Wilcannia along a gravel road that leads up to the northwestern corner of New South Wales. The sign at the edge of town records the population at 300, but, besides during the searing heat of summer, it's many times this number

as hopeful miners descend on the town to find their fortune. The surrounding landscape is dotted with hundreds of mullock heaps—the remains of small-scale opal mining operations that characterize the elusive nature of opal mining.

White Cliffs Dug-Out Motel is just that—underground, where temperatures remain constant at 22° C (72° F), day and night, winter and summer. Rooms are small but adequate and have shared facilities; $45 s, $70 d. Located one km south of town, tel. (08) 8091-6677 or (1800) 02-1154. Moderate. Camping is permitted in Opal Pioneer Reserve, to the north of the post office.

SOUTH OF THE BARRIER HIGHWAY

Menindee

Menindee is accessed by gravel road from Wilcannia (160 km) or by sealed road from Broken Hill (110 km). The town has lost much of its original charm, but one of its oldest features, **Maidens Menindee Hotel** stands proudly on the main street. In 1860, explorers Burke and Wills arrived, resting in Maiden's Menindee Hotel for a few nights before heading north on their ill-fated expedition across the continent. Apart from the hotel and coal-stained riverbanks, signs of the settlement's earlier days have all but disappeared—so there's nothing really to do in town except have a beer in the pub or a meal in the historic dining room.

Menindee lies in an area surrounded by shallow lakes that act as an overflow when the Darling River floods. The flow of water is now controlled, creating a water supply for Broken Hill and an ideal spot for water sports. To explore the river and its wetlands, contact **Burke & Wills Boat Expeditions,** tel. (02) 8091-4383.

Accommodations are provided at **Burke & Wills Menindee Motel,** Yartla St., tel. (02) 8091-4313, which charges $43 s, $53 d for a basic room. Inexpensive. Campsites are spread out along the lakeshore north of town, or head south into Kinchega National Park.

Kinchega National Park

This 44,260-hectare park surrounds Menindee and Cawndilla Lakes, whose waters are regulated by a complex system of weirs. At one time, 140,000 sheep were run on the property that is now the park. The former woolshed and out-buildings are now a living museum. Apart from the lakes, the park's landscape consists of mostly sandy plains and black river soils, and although the park's eastern boundary, the Darling River, is lined with impressive river red gums, the vegetation is generally prickly wattle, bluebush, and canegrass. Waterfowl congregate around the lakes and, of course, 'roos are prevalent.

When you visit, take **River Drive,** a 16-km loop that follows the Darling River from west of Menindee; **Lake Drive** traverses sections of the two major lakes' shorelines. Campsites are spread along both roads, and the historic woolshed houses a park information center, or call (08) 8088-5933.

Mungo National Park

Little known outside the world of anthropology, the ancient landscape of this remote 27,840-hectare park seems, at first, uninspiring. But the geology and human history will fascinate even the most casual observer. Although the park is on the "wrong" side of the Darling River to be classed as the real Outback, a sense of isolation prevails. From all directions it is a long, dry, and dusty drive to the park—the closest town of more than a handful of people is Mildura, 110 km to the south-west, while Balranald, on the Sturt Highway, is 150 km south and Menindee 210 km north.

Around 35,000 years ago the Lachlan River

THE REVELATIONS OF MUNGO WOMAN

In 1968, a geologist stumbled upon ancient human bones in the sand dunes of Willandra Lakes. The discovery led to some of the most important anthropological finds ever made, including the burnt bones of a young woman, dated at 26,000 years. Proof of early habitation was a sensation in itself, but the fact that the bones had been burnt and "buried" was of special significance, since it was the world's earliest known evidence of cremation. That conclusion established the fact that Mungo Woman lived in a society that had and followed cultural and spiritual practices. Since that find, more than 100 others have been made, including a whole skeleton dated at 30,000 years.

---

brought so much water off the Great Dividing Range that it spilled into the **Willandra Lakes,** a vast area of water and wetlands that remained for 15,000 years. The lakes, filled with fish and mollusks, attracted thousands of waterbirds and provided a food source for giant marsupials, such as seven-meter-tall kangaroos. With dramatic climatic changes at the end of the last ice age, rainfall lessened, rivers changed course, and over thousands of years the lakes dried up. **Lake Mungo,** once 200 square km in area, has been dry for 15,000 years. During that time, prevailing southerly winds have blown sediments from the dry lakebed into crescent-shaped sand dunes, known as the **Walls of China,** extending for more than 30 km along the eastern edge of dried-up Lake Mungo.

At the park entrance is an unmanned park information center (open daily 9 a.m.-5 p.m.) with panels showing the park's natural and human history, including life-size replicas of the gigantic mammals that once inhabited the Willandra Lakes. Beside the center is a woolshed dating from 1869. From the main facility area, a road leads through the dry lakebed to the Walls of China. It's easy to spend a few hours in and around the dunes' bizarre landscape. A 60-km loop road leads over Lake Mungo, and along and over the Walls of China.

The main camping area, near the park information center, is spread through a cleared area with drinking water and basic facilities. Another camping area is along the loop road. The modern **Mungo Lodge,** a privately owned operation three km from the visitor center, has rooms for $78 s, $88 d including breakfast, and self-contained cottages for $98. Moderate. Also at the lodge is a restaurant; for reservations, call (03) 5029-7297. For general park information, call (03) 5023-1278.

BROKEN HILL

Once described as the city of "Silver, Sin, and Six-Penny Ale," Broken Hill may have changed over the years, but this legendary Outback city in the middle of nowhere typifies the hardships of life in Australia and, through a colorful past, boasts a distinctive Australian character. The extravagant civic buildings and tree-lined boulevards of Bro-

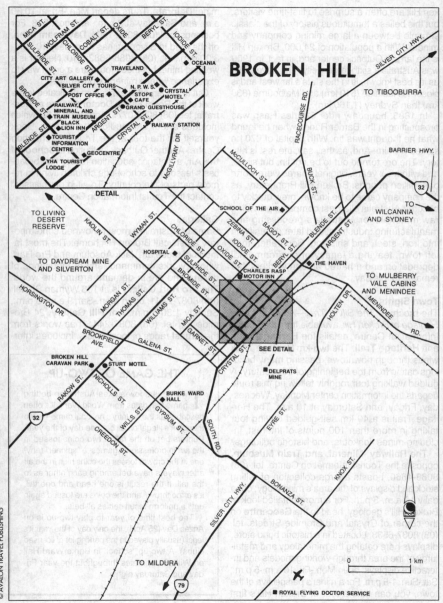

BROKEN HILL

DETAIL

MICA ST.
WOLFRAM ST.
SULPHIDE ST.
CHLORIDE ST.
COBALT ST.
OXIDE ST.
BERYL ST.
IODIDE ST.

OCEANIA

TRAVELAND

CITY ART GALLERY
SILVER CITY TOURS
POST OFFICE
BROMIDE ST.

N.P.W.S.
STOPE
CAFE

CRYSTAL
MOTEL

RAILWAY,
MINERAL, AND
TRAIN MUSEUM
BLACK
LION INN

ARGENT ST.
GRAND GUESTHOUSE

BLENDE ST.
CRYSTAL ST.
RAILWAY STATION

TOURIST
INFORMATION
CENTRE
GEOCENTRE

YHA TOURIST
LODGE

McGILLIVRAY DR.

SILVER CITY HWY.

TO TIBOOBURRA

RACECOURSE RD.

BARRIER HWY.

BUCK ST.

McCULLOCH ST.

SCHOOL OF THE AIR

BLENDE ST.
ARGENT ST.

32

TO
WILCANNIA
AND SYDNEY

TO LIVING
DESERT
RESERVE

KAOLIN ST.
WYMAN ST.

ZEBINA ST.
BAGOT ST.
BERYL ST.

THE HAVEN

TO DAYDREAM MINE
AND SILVERTON

HOSPITAL

CHLORIDE ST.
OXIDE ST.
SULPHIDE ST.
IODIDE ST.

CHARLES RASP
MOTOR INN

TO MULBERRY
VALE CABINS
AND MENINDEE

HORSINGTON DR.
MORGAN ST.
THOMAS ST.
WILLIAMS ST.
BROMIDE ST.
MICA ST.
GARNET ST.

HOLTEN DR.
MENINDEE RD.

BROOKFIELD
AVE.
GALENA ST.
CRYSTAL ST.

SEE DETAIL

BROKEN HILL
CARAVAN PARK
STURT MOTEL

DELPRATS
MINE

EYRE ST.

RAKOW ST.
NICHOLLS ST.
WILLS ST.
GYPSUM ST.

BURKE WARD
HALL

32

CREEDON ST.

SOUTH RD.

KNOX ST.

BONANZA ST.

SILVER CITY HWY.

TO MILDURA

79

0   1 km

ROYAL FLYING DOCTOR SERVICE

© AVALON TRAVEL PUBLISHING

ken Hill are often a surprise to first-time visitors, but this belies a tumultuous history of the classic struggle between a large mining company and miners. With a population of 24,000, Broken Hill is the largest Outback center and, in fact, in 1900 was Australia's sixth-largest city. The Silver City, as it's best known, is in the state's far west and is closer to Adelaide (510 km) and Melbourne (830 km) than Sydney (1,160 km).

In 1883, boundary rider Charles Rasp was prospecting in the Barrier Range when he found what he thought was tin. With capital of £70 he staked a claim. And, as they say, the rest is history. The ore turned out to be not tin, but silver, and within six years, original shares were worth one million pounds. Broken Hill Proprietary, as the company came to be known, grew quickly to become Australia's largest company, providing raw materials for Australia's processing and manufacturing industries, and later diversifying into iron, steel, and shipping. Soon after, they left town, leaving a legacy of environmental depredation and a hatred among workers that remains to this day.

Town Sights

The brochure *The Silver Trail—A Guide to the Heritage of Broken Hill,* available from the Tourist Information Centre, details the **Heritage Walk** and **Heritage Trail.** The two-km Heritage Walk winds through downtown, passing many buildings dating from the beginning of this century. A guided walking tour roughly following this route departs the information center Monday, Wednesday, Friday, and Saturday at 10 a.m. The Heritage Trail is a 40-km self-guided driving tour taking in more than 100 points of interest, including mines, lookouts, and historic buildings.

The **Railway, Mineral, and Train Museum,** opposite the Tourist Information Centre, tel. (08) 8088-4660, boasts a large collection of rolling stock and displays of the area's mineralogy; open daily 10 a.m.-3 p.m. For a more detailed look at Broken Hill's geology, head to the **Geocentre** on the corner of Crystal and Bromide Streets, tel. (08) 8087-6538. Located in a historic bond store, displays here catalog the mineralogy and metallurgy of the area through working models and interactive displays; open Mon.-Fri. 10 a.m.-5 p.m., Sat.-Sun. 1-5 p.m. For a miner's perspective of the town, you can take a tour of Broken Hill's first

mine, **Delprats.** Tours depart Mon.-Fri. at 10:30 a.m. and Saturday at 2 p.m., and cost $18. For bookings, call (08) 8088-1604. **Daydream Mine,** off the road to Silverton, has tours daily 10 a.m.-3:30 p.m., tel. (08) 8088-5682; $10. Neither is a working mine, but these tours are a great way to experience what a miner's work entails.

Out at the airport is a museum dedicated to the work of the **Royal Flying Doctor Service of Australia,** tel. (08) 8088-0777. Admission is $2, which includes a tour and audiovisual display. Book yourself for the tour at the Tourist Information Centre. Another Outback institution is **School of the Air,** a distance-education facility that broadcasts lessons to school-age children living in remote parts of the country. To sit in on "classes" contact the Tourist Information Centre.

Galleries

Some of Australia's most renowned contemporary artists call Broken Hill home. The most famous of these are Jack Absolum and Pro Hart, whose works command tens of thousands of dollars and are in demand around the world. The **Pro Hart Gallery** is at 108 Wyman St., tel. (08) 8087-2441; open Mon.-Sat. 9 a.m.-5 p.m., Sunday 1:30-5 p.m. **Ant Hill Gallery,** 24 Bromide St., tel. (08) 8087-2441, has works from the largest range of local artists. Includes inter-

THE GAME OF TWO-UP

Two-up is a low-stakes Australian betting game that dates from World War I. It's often described as the country's national game—even though it's illegal on all but one day of the year. Punters bet on the fall of two coins tossed in the air; in professional games, a "spinner" (anyone in the crowd) tosses the coins high in the air after players have bet among each other as to the fall. If the result is one head and one tail, it's a "no throw," and the coins are tossed again until a uniform result settles all bets.

The best time of year to play two-up is on Anzac Day (25 April), the only day of the year it's legal (usually played in the parking lot of licensed clubs). A two-up "school" in Burke Ward Hall on Wills St. operates throughout the year Friday and Saturday nights.

Broken Hill's Railway, Mineral, and Train Museum

esting pottery; open Mon.-Sat. 9 a.m.-5 p.m., Sunday 1:30-5 p.m. The stunning Outback landscapes of Eric and Roxanne Minchin are displayed at **Team Minchin,** 105 Morgan St., tel. (08) 8087-5853, open daily 9 a.m.-5 p.m. The only gallery with an admission charge is **Broken Hill City Art Gallery,** corner Blende and Chloride Streets, tel. (08) 8088-5491, but it's only $2. The gallery has a huge collection of works, all by local artists, spread through three galleries. Open Mon.-Fri. 10 a.m.-5 p.m., Saturday 9 a.m.-1 p.m.

Living Desert Reserve, five km north of town, comprises 12 large sculptures scattered on a rocky outcrop. They were created by sculptors during a 1993 symposium.

Silverton

Through the Barrier Range, 26 km northwest of Broken Hill, is Silverton. Promoted in tourist literature as a ghost town, there is in fact not an empty building in town. At its peak, in 1880, the town boasted a population in excess of 3,000, and hotels with names like Silver King and Nevada reflected the early dreams of entrepreneurs who came to make a fortune in this harsh country. The gold rush lasted less than a decade, with most miners moving back to Broken Hill. The only prospecting done around town today is for tourists. You can still get a beer in the sandstone and brick **Silverton Hotel,** and many of the other original buildings remain—making this pho-

togenic town the perfect setting for movies, including *Mad Max II, A Town Like Alice, Razorback, Hostage,* and more recently *Race the Sun* starring James Belushi. Two museums (one in the jail), a historic school building, and four good art galleries are scattered along the main street.

Camel rides are offered at the **Silverton Camel Farm,** tel. (08) 8088-5316. A 15-minute ride is $8, a one-hour ride is $30.

Accommodations

Grand Guesthouse, 317 Argent St., tel. (08) 8087-5305, has an excellent standard of pub-style rooms with shared facilities. Rates start at $45 s, $54 d, and rooms with private facilities are $80, including a continental breakfast. Inexpensive. The least expensive motel in town is the **Sturt Motel,** 153 Rakow St., tel. (08) 8087-3558, which has a pool, but it's three km west of town; $44 s, $50 d. Inexpensive. **Crystal Motel,** 328 Crystal St., tel. (08) 8088-2344, has the most comfortable rooms in town and a ton of facilities; rates of $72 s, $79 d include a cooked breakfast. Moderate. **Mulberry Vale Cabins,** Menindee Rd., tel. (08) 8088-1597, are located five km east of town. Set among native bushland, each cabin is self-contained with rates at $50-60, including a cooked breakfast. Inexpensive. The **YHA Tourist Lodge,** 100 Argent St., tel. (08) 8088-2086, 100 meters from the bus depot and Tourist Information Centre, features a communal kitchen, lounge and recreation rooms, laundry, and shaded courtyard; rates are $14-18 for members, $17-21 nonmembers. Budget. **Broken Hill Caravan Park** is three km west of downtown on Rakow St., tel. (08) 8087-3841; sites are $12-16, and cabins go for $32-42. Budget-Inexpensive.

Food
The clubs are the best place for an inexpensive meal. The **Musicians Club,** 276 Crystal St., tel. (08) 8088-1777, is open daily for lunch and dinner and most meals are less than $10. The **Barrier Social and Democratic Club,** 218 Argent St., tel. (08) 8088-4477, is another good option. Of the hotels, **Black Lion Inn,** across from the information center on Bromide St., has counter meal lunches from $5 and dinners for $10-14.50. The **Stope Café,** 243 Argent St., is the best bakery in town, with a wide range of cakes, pastries, meat pies, and sandwiches. The coffee here is also good. **Oceania,** 423 Argent St., tel. (08) 8087-3695, is a Chinese joint open for lunch and dinner with specials starting at $6. **The Haven,** 577 Argent St., tel. (08) 8088-2888, is a casual seafood and steak restaurant open seven nights a week.

Transportation and Tours
Hazelton, tel. (13) 1713, has daily flights between Sydney and Broken Hill ($337 one-way), and Kendell, tel. (13) 1300, connects Broken Hill to Adelaide. **Traveland,** 350 Argent St., tel. (08) 8087-1969, is the Broken Hill agent for both these airlines. The **Indian-Pacific,** Australia's transcontinental train service, stops in town twice weekly, departing Sydney Monday and Thursday. The railway station is on Crystal St., tel. (13) 2829. All major bus companies stop at Broken Hill on the Sydney-Adelaide run.

Silver City Tours, 328 Argent St., tel. (08) 8087-3310, operates a dozen different tours around town (from $20), to Silverton, and out to nearby national parks.

The various car rental agencies are: **Avis,** tel. (08) 8087-7532; **Hertz,** tel. (08) 8087-2719; and **Thrifty,** tel. (08) 8088-1928. For a taxi, call **Yellow Radio Cabs** at (08) 8088-1144.

Services and Information
Broken Hill Base Hospital is at 174 Thomas St., tel. (08) 8088-0333. A **laundromat,** at 241 Oxide St., is open daily 7 a.m.-10 p.m. For camp-

ing gear, head to **Disposals of Broken Hill** at 55-57 Oxide St., tel. (08) 8088-5977. **Outback Books,** 309 Argent St., tel. (08) 8088-1177, stocks a lot of local and general Outback literature. **Charles Rasp Memorial Library** is on Blende St., tel. (08) 8088-9291.

The **Tourist Information Centre** is located right downtown at the corner of Blende and Bromide Streets, tel. (08) 8087-6077. As well as all the usual literature, there's a historic display and a café, and all long-distance buses use the center as a depot; open daily 8:30 a.m.-5 p.m. The **NPWS** has an office at 5 Oxide St., tel. (08) 8088-5933; open Mon.-Fri. 8:30 a.m.-4:30 p.m.

NORTHWEST CORNER

The northwest corner of New South Wales is the state's least visited and most remote region; an area larger than many European countries, yet with only a few towns where the population exceeds five. Only gravel roads lead into the area, and although the main ones are passable in two-wheel drives, travel after rain is impossible. From Broken Hill, **Silver City Highway** is the main access with other two-wheel drive roads leading north from Wilcannia and west from Bourke. Like all Outback areas, travel requires forward planning—spare tires, extra fuel, and water are the basic prerequisites for safe travel.

Mutawintji National Park
Dominated by the knobbed and broken **Bynguano Range** rising from the surrounding stark landscape, this large 68,912-hectare park is dotted with Aboriginal rock art and intriguing geological formations. The Bynguano Range is a sloped layer of sedimentary rock, laid down in a seabed 400 million years ago. Over time, erosion has gouged out gullies and cliffs and formed contorted geological features. The Wilyakali people took shelter in the range, protecting themselves from the elements while feasting on the flora and fauna living around the rock pools that remained after other water sources had dried up.

More than 300 Koori sites are scattered through the range—but vandalism has taken its toll and two of the most concentrated areas are accessible only on a ranger-led tour. The tour takes in **Snake Cave,** featuring an eight-meter serpent. Hiking through the magical Bynguano Range is a highlight of Mutawintji. One of the most interesting, yet easiest, hikes is through **Homestead Gorge,** on a loop track following a dry creek bed up through crumbling cliffs. Watch overhangs anywhere along the route for rock art. Up near the entrance to the gorge is rock art from a more recent time—the initials of William Wright, who guided Burke and Wills through the range. This trail begins north of the campground. On the opposite side of the access road is the **Western Ridge Trail,** which climbs to a low summit from where sunrise and sunset can be seen in all their glory. The return trip takes three hours. Another interesting area to explore is **Old Mootwingee Gorge,** south of the campground. This narrow gorge, one km from the carpark, marks the end of the marked trail, but if you want to take to the water, swimming up the gorge is a unique experience.

The campground is well equipped, with drinking water, showers (you'll need some Outback common sense to operate them), and a handful of gas barbecues. Fees are $12 per night, plus a park-use fee of $7.50.

Ask at the Tourist Information Centre in Broken Hill about tours out to the park—apart from these, you're by yourself. The park is 130 km northeast of Broken Hill; turn off Silver City Highway 55 km north of the city.

Near the park entrance is a covered area with information boards and camping registration slips. Also look for details on tours into the restricted Mutawintji Historic Site (usually Wednesday and Saturday) or call (08) 8088-5933.

Milparinka

It is 296 km from Broken Hill to Milparinka along the Silver City Highway. Gold was found in the Milparinka area in 1880; within a few years a minor gold rush had taken place and the township gained an air of permanence, with three hotels, a few stores, and a stone courthouse

petroglyph in Mutawintji National Park

serving 3,000 miners. By the mid-1930s, the Albert Hotel was the only business still operating—and it's been open ever since. Rooms are $23 pp, the beer is cold, and basic pub meals are inexpensive; call (08) 8091-3963 for bookings. If you'd like to have a look inside the courthouse, pick up the key at the hotel.

A worthwhile detour is northwest to **Depot Glen,** a waterhole where Capt. Charles Sturt and his party were forced to rest for six months in the summer of 1844-45. The area is a small oasis surrounded by dry plains—it is easy to see why Sturt chose it. A couple of kilometers east of Depot Glen is a grevillea tree with "J.P. 1845" carved into its trunk, marking the final resting place of James Poole, who died during the ordeal.

Tibooburra

Meaning "Place of Granite" in the language of local Koori, Tibooburra is New South Wales's most remote town, being 340 km north of Broken Hill and 1,500 km northwest of Sydney. It is also the state's hottest place, with summer temperatures occasionally topping 50° C (122° F). Tibooburra is in an area known as Corner Country, more than a million hectares of sandhills and mulga. Tibooburra resembles a town of the U.S. Wild West, with a smattering of buildings along a small section of paved road.

Tibooburra grew from a gold rush in the 1890s, but the gold proved elusive, and after a couple of decades the population had dipped perilously low. The pastoral industry kept Tibooburra alive. Then, in the 1950s, the town served as a service center for natural gas exploration across the northeast part of South Australia.

Tibooburra's most famous buildings, and those that locals and tourists alike spend the most time in, are the two hotels. The **Family Hotel,** tel. (08) 8091-3314, was the home of Outback artist Clifton Pugh for most of the 1960s. He spent his time decorating the walls with his distinctive style of art for free beer. Across the road is the no-less-grand **Tibooburra Hotel,** tel. (08) 8091-3310, known locally as the "two-story."

Both pubs have accommodations for about $25 s, $30 d (Budget), or you can stay in **Granites Motel,** tel. (08) 8091-3305, which lacks atmosphere but has a pool; $46 s, $56 d. Inexpensive. At the north end of town is **Dead Horse Gully Campground.** It is officially within the border of Sturt National Park (see below) and has toilets and a few broken tables in an area of unusual boulders.

Before leaving Tibooburra, visit Sturt National Park Visitor Centre, Briscoe St., tel. (08) 8091-3308, for road conditions, an excellent interpretive display, and park literature.

Sturt National Park
For many, the stark desert landscape of this 340,000-hectare park may be monotonous, but this is the Outback at its best, with desolate gibber plains extending seemingly forever. The park is a conglomeration of six sheep stations, stretching for 80 km along the Queensland border from Cameron Corner. Since the removal of stock, the park has regenerated quickly, with native grasses covering much of the park, attracting large numbers of red kangaroos, flocks of emus, a variety of lizards, and other birds such as wedge-tailed eagles and kestrels. The park is divided into two halves by its most dominant geological feature, the **Grey Range,** bluffs of sandstone rising 150 meters above the red plains. For these rises, this area is known as "jump-up country," as the bluffs seem to jump up from the surrounding landscape.

The biggest attraction west of the jump-ups is the long dusty drive out to Cameron Corner, but in the east, the land is more varied and there are two interesting circuits to drive around. **Gorge Loop Road** begins in Tibooburra and heads west to Mt. Wood Homestead, where you'll find camping and a small **Pastoral Museum** featuring a whim, which is turned by horses to draw water from bores deep below. The road continues north to a spectacular gorge before rejoining Silver City Highway. From this junction, it's south to Tibooburra. But most people would want to drive the **Jump-up Loop Road;** short interpretive trails start from a campground along the way.

Access to the western portion of the park is

from two km south of Tibooburra. It is 140 km from the Silver City Highway to Cameron Corner. **Fort Grey,** 30 km from the corner, is a camp set up by Charles Sturt in 1845 on his journey to find an inland sea. At this site is a seven-km trail and campground.

Before heading into the park, stop at the **Sturt National Park Visitor Centre** in Tibooburra, tel. (08) 8091-3308.

Cameron Corner
Cameron Corner, 140 km northwest of Tibooburra, is the spot where three states—New South Wales, Queensland, and South Australia—meet. It was surveyed by John Cameron in 1880. His unenviable task that year was to survey the entire border of NSW and Queensland (when resurveyed in 1969, his pegs were found to be accurate within the meter). Until 1990, the corner boasted only a marker peg, but in that year the **Corner Store,** transported from South Australia, opened for road-weary travelers to quench their thirst and gas up.

BOURKE AND VICINITY

You need only look at a map of New South Wales to understand how the saying "Back o' Bourke" has come to mean a long way from anywhere. This remote town of 2,800 is on the eastern bank of the **Darling River,** 780 km northwest of Sydney. In the 1890s, when famous bush poet Henry Lawson lived in one of the town's 22 pubs, Bourke was a bleak frontier town, where locally grown wool was loaded onto barges for the long trip down the Darling River to Echuca and then on to England.

Bourke has changed little since Lawson's days, and many buildings remain from that era, including an impressive stone courthouse, built in 1899. The main drag is Mitchell Street, but service and civic buildings are scattered for four blocks between here and the Mitchell Highway. Many of the area's attractions are a fair drive from Bourke. **Mount Gunderbooka,** on Mulgowan Station, has Aboriginal rock art spread along a spectacular gorge, with three paintings in shallow caves directly across Mullareena Creek from the camping and picnic area. Up the gorge a couple of kilometers are a number of other paintings and from these it is possible to continue to the long ridge that forms the summit of the mountain. The mountain is signposted along the Bourke-Cobar road, but you'll need a mud map tours brochure (available from the information center) for details.

Rooms at the **Port of Bourke Hotel,** 32 Mitchell St., tel. (02) 6872-2544, are $31 s, $46 d with shared facilities and $66 for the rooms with private facilities. Inexpensive. **Darling River Motel,** 74 Mitchell St., tel. (02) 6872-2288, has rooms of a reasonable standard and is only a short walk to the center of town; $42 s, $53 d. Inexpensive. The flashiest place in town is **Major Mitchell Motel,** back out on the highway, tel. (02) 6872-2311. Facilities include a pool, laundry, and barbecue area; rates here start at $62 s, $72 d. Moderate. **Mitchell Caravan Park** is one km east of town, along the road out to Brewarrina, tel. (02) 6872-2791. Sites are $10, and the on-site vans are $25 d. **Paddlewheel Caravan Park,** Mitchell St., tel. (02) 6872-2277, is right in town and similarly priced. Both are in the budget category.

All the hotels serve counter meals, with the at-mosphere at the **Carrier Arms Hotel,** 71 Mitchell St., tel. (02) 6872-2040, being the most authentic. The restaurant area looks much the same as the days when Henry Lawson lived upstairs. Service isn't that slick, but for $10-12 you won't go hungry.

Buses run four times daily between Bourke and Dubbo. From there trains make connections to Sydney ($70 one-way). The local agent is **Lachlan Travel** at 35 Oxley St., tel. (02) 6872-2092.

The **Tourist Information Centre** is on Anson St., tel. (02) 6872-1222, and is open daily.

North from Bourke

From Bourke to the Queensland border is 138 km, but the first full-service town is **Cunnamulla,** 119 km north of the border. The only community before the border is **Enngonia,** a small settlement with a pub and a petrol pump. The grave of bushranger Midnight, whose "gentlemanly" conduct and dashing attire were the inspiration for the character Captain Starlight, of the book and movie *Robbery Under Arms,* is 35 km west of Enngonia.

CENTRAL COAST, NEWCASTLE, AND VICINITY

CENTRAL COAST

The Hawkesbury River is the official northern boundary of Sydney. What begins there is the Central Coast, a 50-km stretch of beautiful but developed beaches and large areas of rugged coastline protected as national parks. A freeway skirts the entire coast, ending west of Newcastle at the junction of the Pacific and New England Highways.

Brooklyn

On the southern bank of the Hawkesbury River is the small village of Brooklyn, a world away from city living, which is just a 20-minute drive away. Brooklyn was named after the hometown of American workers who built the adjacent railroad bridge. **Hawkesbury River Ferries,** tel. (02) 9985-7566, delivers supplies and mail to families living at in-accessible locations along the river. They take passengers for $24 pp. Departures are Mon.-Fri. at 9:30 a.m., returning just after 1 p.m.

Old Sydney Town and Australian Reptile Park

Take the first exit north of the Mooney Mooney River Bridge (look for the big, bright dinosaur on the hill) to find two worthwhile stops. Old Sydney Town, tel. (02) 4340-1104, an excellent attraction that re-creates Australia's original European settlement. The streets are lined with re-creations of early 1800s buildings, and dozens of people in period costume stroll the town, living life as they would have in the early 1800s. They encourage visitors to inquire about life in the old days. The most popular reenactments are floggings and hangings (even visitors may get flogged if they don't behave themselves), and there are wagon rides, bullock-driving, and a large sailing ship to explore. Also on site is a gift shop, bar, and restaurant. Admission is adult $17, child $10. It's open Wed.-Sun. 10 a.m.-4 p.m., daily during school holidays.

Adjacent is the **Australian Reptile Park,** tel. (02) 4340-1146, one of the country's premier such parks, and home to much more than just reptiles. The park began its life as a research facility, and under the leadership of Eric Worrell became a world leader in the development of antivenin. It has grown to become a full-scale wildlife park, home to koalas, kangaroos, dingoes, cassowaries, and "Eric," the world's largest crocodile kept in captivity. Animal-handling demonstrations, feeding sessions, and picnic tables in a setting of native bush make the experience even better. Admission is adult $14, child $8.

Sydney tour operators include Old Sydney Town and the Australian Reptile Park in their itinerary, or catch the train to Gosford and hop aboard a connecting bus service.

Gosford and Vicinity

Descending from the freeway to protected **Brisbane Water,** you'll pass West Gosford and

NEWCASTLE AND VICINITY

© AVALON TRAVEL PUBLISHING

Henry Kendall Cottage, named for its one-time resident, one of Australia's most prolific poets. At the north end of Brisbane Water is the central coast's largest town, **Gosford.**

Off the Entrance Rd., beyond the turnoff to Terrigal, is the rural hamlet of Matcham, home to **Ken Duncan Australia Wide Gallery,** displaying works of Australia's premier landscape photographer. It's on Oak Rd., tel. (02) 4367-6777.

Beaches and National Parks
Immediately north of the Hawkesbury River is 11,370-hectare **Brisbane Water National Park,** extending east from the freeway to Broken Bay and north to Somersby. The best way to experience the park is along a hiking trail linking **Wondabyne** (accessible only by train) to the coastal village of **Patonga** (10 km one-way). On a narrow finger of land between Brisbane Water and the ocean is **Bouddi National Park,** a long stretch of undeveloped coastline with hiking trails leading from Killcare to **Tallow Beach** and from park headquarters at Killcare Heights to picturesque **Maitland Bay,** named for a ship that wrecked on an offshore reef (look for wreckage around the northern headland).

North of the national park, high rocky headlands are linked by long stretches of golden sand; popular surfing and swimming spots include **Mac-Masters, Avoca,** and **Terrigal Beaches.** The latter is a resort town with trendy cafés and boutiques on a beach lined with stately Norfolk pines. Adjacent to the beach is the Haven, a protected bay backed by a grassed headland with panoramic views.

Continuing north is a string of beaches, including secluded **Spoon Bay** and long **Shelley Beach,** which is backed by a coastal golf course. **The Entrance,** immediately north of protected **Toowoon Bay,** is on a spit of land flanked by shallow **Tuggerah Lake** to the west and the ocean to the east. It is a popular holiday spot, especially for families. The main street overlooks a grassed reserve where boats can be rented, lake cruises are offered, and hundreds of pelicans gather for a frenzied 3:30 p.m. fish-feeding session.

North of The Entrance, on a low sandy spit of land that extends to Norah Head, is 597-hectare **Wyrrabalong National Park,** which protects a stretch of undeveloped coastline and an impressive stand of red gums. Farther north

A pelican waits for the daily fish-feeding at The Entrance.

is **Munmorah State Recreation Area,** a coastal reserve encompassing Birdie Beach and Frazer Park, both beautiful little spots with rocky headlands to explore, picnic areas, and camping. The north end of the central coast is timeless **Catherine Hill Bay,** dominated by coal-loading facilities at the southern end of the main beach. The south end of town has changed little this century, with old wooden cottages dotting the hill and a great pub overlooking the bay.

Accommodations
The central coast has long been a popular weekend getaway for jaded Sydneysiders, and it boasts a number of upmarket resorts, as well as accommodations to suit all other budgets.

Terrigal has a few choices. **Clan Lakeside Lodge,** 1 Ocean View Dr., tel. (02) 4384-1566, overlooks Terrigal Lagoon and is just 100 meters from the beach; $80-105 s or d. Moderate. **Terrigal Pacific Motel,** 224 Terrigal Dr., tel. (02) 4385-1555, a little farther from the beach but still within easy walking distance, has modern facilities, a landscaped pool area, a restaurant, and friendly front-desk staff. Rooms are $100-130 s or d, but many packages are offered, including golf, fishing, or horseback riding. Expensive. Terrigal's premier accommodation is **Crowne Plaza Terrigal,** Esplanade, tel. (02) 4384-9111, an eight-story, five-star resort separated from the beach by a row of towering Norfolk pines. The resort is totally self-contained, with a pool, bar, nightclub, restaurants, gym, lounge, and staff to organize local activities. All but six of 196 rooms have ocean views, and all are large with private balconies. Rates start at $240 s or d, but look for off season and mid-week package deals. Luxury. For those wishing to stay on Terrigal Beach for markedly less money, head to **Terrigal Beach Lodge,** on Campbell Crescent, directly behind the main shopping precinct and 100 meters from the beach. Dorm beds are $17, doubles $45. For bookings, call (02) 4385-3330; with advance notice, pickups can be arranged from Gosford railway station.

The Entrance also has a concentration of accommodations. Most have seen better days, but locations are generally excellent. **Pinehurst Caravillas,** 11 The Entrance Rd., tel. (02) 4332-2002, offers self-contained units opposite the lake; rates are $60-75 most of the year, rising to $90 in summer. Moderate. **El Lago Waters Resort,** 41 The Entrance Rd., tel. (02) 4332-3955, is one of the better motels; rooms here start at $75 s or d. Moderate.

Kim's Beachside Retreat, at Toowoon Bay between The Entrance and Terrigal, is, without being pretentious, one of the state's most luxurious hideaways. It comprises 34 bungalows spread among lush vegetation on a beachfront property. Each room has a private balcony, most have spas, and some have fireplaces. Rates start at $180 pp (more on weekends), which includes all meals. For bookings, call (02) 4332-1566. Luxury.

Many coastal communities have caravan parks. From north to south, the best are: **Blue Lagoon Beach Resort,** Bateau Bay, tel. (02) 4332-1447 or (1800) 68-0036; **Toowoon Bay Tourist Park,** overlooking North Shelly Beach, tel. (02) 4332-2834; **Dunleith Caravan Park,** at The Entrance, tel. (02) 4332-2172; and **Budgewoi Tourist Park,** Budgewoi, tel. (02) 4390-9100. All of these parks are on or near the beach, offering campsites in the budget category and cabins in the inexpensive and moderate categories.

Food and Drink
Terrigal has two excellent takeaway fish and chip shops: the **Co-op** is above the boat ramp at Terrigal Haven and the **Snapper Spot** is on the Esplanade. Head to the **Boatshed,** on the Es-

planade, for a wide variety of breakfast choices, healthy sandwiches, or coffee and cake on the sidewalk. Crowne Plaza Terrigal, tel. (02) 4384-9111, has a wide range of eateries, including the **Conservatory,** serving buffet breakfast and lunch; and the formal, silver-service **La Mer,** specializing in fresh seafood prepared with a French flair. **The Galley,** in Terrigal Haven, tel. (02) 4385-3222, with a stunning beach panorama from the outdoor deck, is renowned for excellent seafood.

The street-level beer garden at **Crowne Plaza Terrigal** attracts folks from as far away as Sydney for its sunny outlook, casual atmosphere, Sunday afternoon entertainment, and well-priced beer. This hotel complex also has an upstairs cocktail bar and a downstairs disco. Otherwise, it's the **Terrigal Pub,** overlooking the lake on Terrigal Dr., where the beer's always cold and the food is good.

At The Entrance, **La Terazza,** tel. (02) 4332-9082, is a stylish Italian restaurant with main dishes from $14 and seafood dishes from $17.50. Open daily from 6 p.m.

Transportation, Services, and Information
City Rail, tel. (13) 1500, operates hourly services from Sydney's Central Station to Gosford, from where **Busways,** tel. (02) 4392-6666, operates regular bus services to Terrigal and **Entrance Red Bus Services,** tel. (02) 4332-8655, runs to The Entrance. This company also operates an **Airbus** between the domestic and international terminals of Sydney airport and the central coast.

The coast's main **Tourist Information Centre** is in front of Gosford railway station, at 200 Mann St., tel. (02) 4325-2835 or (1800) 24-5734, website: www.cctourism.com.au. Others are on Terrigal Dr., a short walk along the lagoon from Terrigal Beach, and along the foreshore at The Entrance.

NEWCASTLE

Newcastle is best known as an industrial city, but away from the smelters and loading docks of Australia's second-largest port are some worthwhile attractions. It's the state's second-largest city (pop. 280,000), a massive sprawl of industry and residential suburbs centered at the mouth of the Hunter River. Downtown is Newcastle's redeeming feature. Few cities in the world can boast a commercial and civic heart such as Newcastle's, right on the ocean, and with a main street and rail line ending a stone's throw from magnificent sandy beaches. A freeway bypasses the city completely, but the old Pacific Highway follows the coast north from the central coast through **Swansea** and **Redhead Beach** to Newcastle proper.

History

Massive seams of coal lie under the area, and although coal was first mined in 1801, Newcastle, then known as Coal Harbour, was officially established in 1804 when the worst members of Sydney's ever-growing convict population were transported to the site. The government soon realized the wealth of the region's natural resources, so the convicts were transported farther

north, and mining and settlement along the river began in earnest.

Newcastle's recent history has been almost as infamous. In late December 1989 residents were shaken by a massive earthquake. In a country where fire and flood are a part of life, the shock of this type of natural disaster was hard to comprehend, especially as the epicenter was immediately west of downtown. As well as killing 12 people, the quake destroyed dozens of commercial buildings, damaged thousands of homes, and changed the face of the city forever.

Sights

An extensive redevelopment program along the mouth of the Hunter River has brought a much-needed boost to Newcastle's pride. Officially known as the Foreshore, it extends between the easternmost dockyards and the golden sands of **Nobby's Beach.** Along the Foreshore is a replica of *William IV,* the first steamer built in

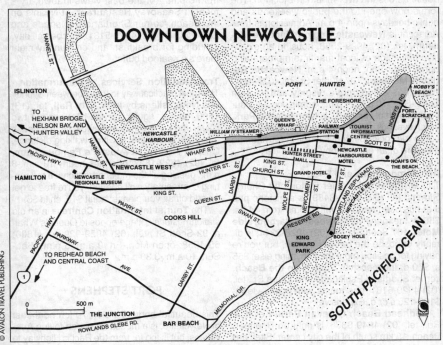

DOWNTOWN NEWCASTLE

Australia. Toward the ocean is **Queen's Wharf,** combining a small marina, bar, restaurant, and a tower from where views extend along the river. Take a pleasant walk from here to **Nobby's Head.** When Captain Cook first sailed up this way, Nobby's Head was an island; it was reduced to aid shipping and, in 1846, connected to the mainland by a breakwall as the Hunter River was developed as a port. At the southern end of Nobby's Beach is **Fort Scratchley,** tel. (02) 4929-3066. Completed in 1886 as part of a defense system around Australia's coastline, it consists of various sandstone and brick structures and a system of underground tunnels originally built to repel a perceived Russian invasion (that never came). The guns were fired, though, in 1942, when a Japanese submarine attacked Newcastle in an attempt to destroy the steelworks. The Japanese missed their intended target, and when the Australians replied with gunfire, they made just one direct hit—on a house across the river mouth in Stockton. The fort is now open to the public weekends and public holidays noon-4 p.m. Admission is free. Adjacent is **Newcastle Region Maritime Museum,** tel. (02) 4929-2588, housing an extensive collection of local maritime memorabilia; open Tues.-Sun. noon-4 p.m. **Newcastle Regional Museum,** 787 Hunter St., tel. (02) 4962-2001, has a supernova display and is open Tues.-Sun. 10 a.m.-5 p.m.; admission $4. Four blocks south of Hunter St. is **King Edward Park,** which overlooks the ocean, and the **Bogey Hole,** cut in the rocks by convicts for the swimming pleasure of an early colony commander.

Accommodations and Food

The **Grand Hotel,** corner Bolton and Church Streets, tel. (02) 4929-3489, is a historic pub that has been restored with rooms from $44 s, $50 d. Inexpensive. **Newcastle Harbourside Motel,** 107 Scott St., tel. (02) 4926-3244, is directly opposite the railway station, but you're paying for position more than anything else; $55 s, $60 d. Inexpensive. **Noah's on the Beach,** corner Shortland Esplanade and Zaara St., tel. (02) 4929-5181, has rooms with ocean views; $105-125 s or d. Expensive.

Redhead Beach Caravan Park, Kallaroo Rd., tel. (02) 4949-8306, is right on Redhead Beach, 15 km south of the city center. Sites are

$14-17, basic on-site vans $30, and cabins $45-75. Budget-Inexpensive. If you don't need to be right downtown, a couple of good choices present themselves on the north side of the river. On Fern Bay Rd., and right next to excellent Stockton Golf Course, is **Newcastle Links Motel,** tel. (02) 4928-2366. Rooms here are of a good standard and there's a pool; $66 s, $72 d. Moderate. In the same vicinity is **Stockton Beach Caravan Park,** Pitt St., tel. (02) 4928-1393, close to the beach. Budget-Inexpensive.

Many cafés are centered around the corner of Queen and Darby Streets, but closer to downtown are those along Hunter Street Mall. At Queen's Wharf is **Scratchley's on the Wharf,** tel. (02) 4929-1111, a stylish restaurant featuring seafood; open daily for lunch and dinner. Also at the wharf is a brewery pub with chairs and tables overlooking the water. For pizza and pasta, head to **The Etna,** 115 King St., tel. (02) 4926-1159, open for lunch Wed.-Fri. and for dinner daily from 6 p.m. For the best views in town, try a meal at **Seaspray Restaurant,** at Noah's on the Beach, corner Shortland Esplanade and Zaara St., tel. (02) 4929-5181. It's open all day, including for breakfast, and on Sunday night there's a seafood buffet.

Transportation, Services, and Information

The most practical way to travel between Sydney and Newcastle is by train. **City Rail,** tel. (13) 1500, runs a regular service between the two cities, and once you're in Newcastle, the beach and other sights are all within walking distance. Once in the city, **Newcastle's Famous Tram,** tel. (02) 4929-1822, operates hourly 10 a.m.-3 p.m., passing all the major attractions. If the running commentary isn't enough, you're free to get on and off as you please; adult $10, child $5.

The **Tourist Information Centre** is in an old stationmaster's cottage opposite Queen's Wharf at 92 Scott St., tel. (02) 4929-9299 or (1800) 65-4558; open Mon.-Fri. 9 a.m.-5 p.m., Sat.-Sun. 10 a.m.-3:30 p.m.

PORT STEPHENS

This beautiful body of water, 70 km northeast of Newcastle, is a mecca for ocean-loving Australians, but is too far from the Pacific Highway to

Jewfish are highly sought after by anglers along the New South Wales coast.

where calm waters are dotted with catamarans and sailboards. At the eastern end of the beach is **Tomaree Head** and the mouth of Port Stephens. On the ocean side of this headland is a string of short beaches with often-rough waters. These beaches are separated by high headlands rising to 150 meters. The only official summit track is up Tomaree Head. **Fingal Bay,** farther south, is a long crescent-shaped beach ending at Point Stephens, where a lighthouse has been guiding ships since 1862. Access to the headland is only possible at low tide, when a finger of sand is exposed. Fingal Bay is part of **Tomaree National Park,** 900 hectares of coastal heathland extending south to **Anna Bay.**

The best way to get out on the water is aboard the *Tamboi Queen,* tel. (02) 4982-0707, which departs Nelson Bay daily at 10:30 a.m. for a two-hour dolphin-watching cruise, with swimming and snorkeling included in the cost; adult $9, child $7.

Golfers are drawn to Port Stephens for two challenging courses. The narrow fairways of **Nelson Bay Golf Course** wind their way through native bushland above the main street of Nelson Bay, tel. (02) 4981-1132, while **Horizons,** tel. (02) 4982-0188, is a well-manicured resort course at Salamander Bay. Greens fees are $28 and $54 respectively.

attract great crowds. The main access is from the south, along a spit of land, with the ocean side linked to Newcastle by a magnificent stretch of sand. As well as being picturesque, the bay's calm and clear waters are excellent for scuba diving, swimming, fishing, and boating. Just a few kilometers' drive from the main body of Port Stephens are long stretches of beach, surfing breaks, and rocky headlands. Development on the bay side is mostly around Nelson Bay and Shoal Bay. On the north side of Port Stephens things are a lot quieter, with the twin towns of **Tea Gardens** and **Hawks Nest,** at the mouth of the Myall River, being the only development.

Sights and Recreation
The largest settlement on the shores of Port Stephens is **Nelson Bay** (pop. 8,000), with a steep main street that ends at a large marina chock-full of fishing boats and pleasure cruisers. To the west is a string of protected sandy beaches, while to the east is **Halifax Point,** a popular scuba-diving spot. East of this point is **Shoal Bay,** a two-km stretch of golden sand

Accommodations
One of the best-value accommodations in Port Stephens is **Beaches Serviced Apartments,** 12 Gowrie Ave., Nelson Bay, tel. (02) 4984-3255. Each apartment has a large living area, separate bedroom, modern kitchen, laundry, and a private balcony overlooking a pool and landscaped gardens. Rates start at $100 per unit but rise dramatically on weekends and holidays. Expensive. **Marina Resort,** 33 Magnus St., Nelson Bay, tel. (02) 4981-4400 or (1800) 65-9949, with panoramic water views, features rooms of high standard, but without kitchens; $78-169 s or d, depending on the season. Moderate. **Santa Catalina Motel,** 9 Shoal Bay Rd., Shoal Bay, tel. (02) 4981-1519, is an inexpensive place opposite the beach; from $55 s or d.

Fingal Bay Holiday Park, tel. (02) 4981-1473, is a sprawling campground opposite delightful Fingal Bay, offering long beach walks and protected swimming areas. Sites range $16-21 and cabins $40-105. Budget-Inexpensive. Another good spot, and similarly priced, is **One Mile Beach Holiday Park,** tel. (02) 4982-1112, with a large tenting area and absolute beachfront.

Information
Port Stephens Visitors Centre is on Victoria Parade, Nelson Bay, tel. (02) 4981-1579 or (1800) 80-8900. It's open daily 9 a.m.-5 p.m., or check out their web site: www.portstephens.org.au.

BARRINGTON TOPS NATIONAL PARK

Protecting the highest peaks of the Mount Royal Range, this 62,449-hectare park northwest of Newcastle encompasses a large chunk of rainforest between the coast and the Hunter Valley. Standing apart from the Great Dividing Range, the range was formed through a combination of uplift and lava flows. But it is erosion, aided by an annual rainfall of more than 2,000 mm, that has formed the deep gorges that are the park's most impressive features. The park's highest peak is **Polblue Mountain** (1,577 meters), at the north end of a high plateau.

The park's higher elevations are dominated by ancient Antarctic beech up to 2,000 years old. Other flora present in the subtropical rainforests include ferns, rosewood, corkwood, strangler figs, and palms.

A variety of access roads lead into the park, but none climb to the park's higher elevations. From Gloucester, a road leads to a facility area in the east of the park, while another loops around from the north to the main hiking area. From Dungog, a road leads north to Barrington Guest House.

Hiking
From the end of Gloucester Tops Rd., beyond the campground at Gloucester River, a short trail leads to Gloucester Falls and a spectacular lookout, while back at the campground, a five-km (one-way) trail leads upstream to a couple of swimming holes. The gravel track off Barrington Tops Forest Rd., linking Gloucester and Scone, winds past Mt. Barrington (1,556 meters) to an area with many hikes, including to Careys Peak and the 22-km Link Trail across Gloucester Tops.

Practicalities
Camping is at Gloucester River, 40 km west of Gloucester. Facilities are limited to toilets and fireplaces. At the south end of the park, 40 km northwest of Dungog, is **Barrington Guest House,** tel. (02) 4995-3212. This historic guesthouse has basic rooms and a few activities such as tennis. Rates are a reasonable $79 pp, including activities. Meal packages at the restaurant are extra.

For further park information, call (02) 4987-3108 or stop by the **Gloucester Visitor Information Centre** in Gloucester, tel. (02) 6558-1408.

HUNTER VALLEY

For thousands of years the Hunter River has washed rich soils down from the peaks of the Great Dividing Range, depositing them along its banks and creating the largest lowland plain on the NSW coast. The soil and a temperate climate provide the ideal conditions for growing grapes, which, in turn, has turned the valley into one of Australia's premier winemaking regions.

The valley's first grapevines were planted by the Tyrrell family more than 150 years ago, but it's only since the 1950s, when wine became popular among Australians, that the industry has boomed. Although the valley produces less than five percent of Australia's wine, its reputation for high quality rather than high quantity extends across the world. The valley itself is delightful to explore, with country lanes linking 70 wineries, stylish accommodations, and a great variety of restaurants. In stark contrast to the rolling hills of the valley are three rugged and remote national parks that border it to the south.

Cessnock, a rural service center, is the valley's largest town. The other major town of the Lower Hunter is **Maitland,** established in 1818 and once destined to rival Sydney in importance. The largest concentration of wineries is west of Cessnock in the **Pokolbin** area. North of Pokolbin is the New England Highway, which passes through the Hunter Valley and Upper Hunter towns of **Singleton, Muswellbrook,** and **Scone.**

Visiting the Vineyards
Probably the best part of visiting the wineries of the Hunter Valley is that you don't need to be a

wine snob to appreciate their products, and although winegrowers are in the business of selling wine, most appreciate that not everyone is an expert and are happy to help tasters make decisions. To encourage patronage, many wineries have picnic areas, and a couple offer tours or displays of winemaking equipment. Until recently, the wineries were mostly the destination for day trippers, but in the last decade many accommodations have been developed, some within the vineyards themselves, and a whole range of other activities developed. Without a teetotaling driver, getting around the wineries can be a problem, because, although they are relatively close together, walking isn't practical. **Vineyard Shuttle,** tel. (02) 4991-3655, makes a loop between major accommodations and vineyards. The cost is $28 pp for a full day—a good value considering they run on-demand. Alternatively, **Cessnock Radio Cabs,** tel. (02) 4990-1111, rents cabs for $30 an hour. For the more energetic, **Grapemobile,** tel. (02) 4991-2339, offers bike tours of the wineries for $98 pp, including lunch.

Visitor centers in all surrounding towns are good sources of information for visiting the Hunter Valley, or visit the website www.winecountry.com.au.

Maitland

Pardoned convicts and free settlers first arrived in the Lower Hunter Valley around 1818. The town of Maitland was established soon after, with its importance growing as traffic up the valley increased. Coal mining commenced late last century and created much wealth. These early riches are reflected in many impressive civic buildings, including the post office (1889), which boasts an ornate clock tower, and the courthouse (1895). **Brough House,** on Church St., was built in 1870 by a local merchant and is today an art gallery. Other historic buildings are along **Maitland Heritage Mall.**

Windsor Castle Hotel, George St., tel. (02) 4933-7276, is in East Maitland; rooms are very basic but are just $35 s, $48 d. Inexpensive. The best place to stay is **Country Comfort Monte Pio,** just off the New England Hwy. two km north of downtown, tel. (02) 4932-5288 or (1800) 06-5064, located in a building dating from the middle of the 19th century. Rooms have been renovated and are well-equipped, while facilities include a tennis court, pool, billiard room, lounge, bar, and restaurant. Rates are $90-120 s or d. Expensive. For more of a personal touch, **Old George and Dragon,** 48 Melbourne St., East Maitland, tel. (02) 4933-7272, a historic hotel restored magnificently, offers accommodations in five rooms. The rooms are elegantly decorated, complete with oak furnishings and original paintings. The rate of $120 s, $200 d includes breakfast and dinner. Luxury. Room-only packages are available, but because the hotel holds one of the Hunter Valley's premier restaurants, you'll want to eat there anyway. The restaurant is open to nonguests for dinner Tues.-Saturday.

Maitland Tourist Information Centre is in King Edward Park, East Maitland, tel. (02) 4933-2611; open daily 9 a.m.-5 p.m.

Morpeth

Although the streetscape of Morpeth, eight km northeast of Maitland, hasn't changed for more than 100 years, its vendors have; blacksmiths, bakeries, and leather merchants have been replaced by more than 20 specialty craft shops, making it one of the state's premier towns for shopping.

Cessnock

South of the New England Highway, and gateway to the winegrowing Pokolbin region, Cessnock (pop. 17,500) was first settled in 1826 by Scottish settler John Campbell, who named the town after a castle in his homeland. The town grew as the coal-mining industry developed. It has little of interest to travelers, although the excellent **Wine Country Information Centre,** southeast of town on Aberdare Rd., tel. (02) 4990-4477, is worth visiting. Cessnock is also an alternative to staying in the Pokolbin vineyards area; try **Hunter Valley Motel,** 30 Allandale Rd., tel. (02) 4990-1722; $49 s, $59 d. Inexpensive.

Pokolbin

As you approach Pokolbin from the south, the most noticeable sight is a distinct lack of vineyards. Even through the mining town of Cessnock, the cleared land is only partly planted, but once you have turned off the New England Highway onto Broke Rd. there's a sudden profusion of wineries, restaurants, and guesthouses; enough to warrant large maps and up to 40 confusing signs at each intersection. Pokolbin as such is not a town, but rather an area of vineyards. The center of the action is the junction of Broke and McDonalds Roads.

At the south end of Pokolbin, on Marrowbone Rd., is **McWilliams Mt. Pleasant Estate,** tel. (02) 4998-7505, part of Australia's largest family-run wine company. Tours of the winery are offered daily at 11 a.m., and, as well, there's winetasting and a café. In the same area, **Lindemans,** tel. (02) 4998-7684, part of a winemaking empire known throughout the world, was started by Dr. Henry John Lindeman, who planted vines in the valley in 1843. A museum at the winery displays a large collection of winemaking equipment; it's open Mon.-Fri. 9 a.m.-4:30 p.m., Sat.-Sun. 10 a.m.-4:30 p.m. Over the hill to the north is **Tulloch's Winery,** tel. (02) 4998-7580, also more than 100 years old and open daily for tasting. **Tyrrell's,** tel. (02) 4993-7000, owned by the same family since 1858, has a great range of wines for all budgets and has tours of the winery daily at 1:30 p.m. Also on the grounds is the slab-hut family home of the founder, which dates from 1864, as well as a barbecue and picnic area with great views across vineyards to the distinctive Brokenback Range. The above wineries are only a sampling of the larger operations; others worth visiting are **Pepper Tree Wines,** Halls Rd., tel. (02) 4998-7539, with a tasting area in a delightful barn surrounded by colorful gardens, and **Oakvale Winery,** Broke Rd., tel. (02) 4998-7520, which has a bookshop featuring a great variety of wine-related literature.

If possible, arrange your trip to the Hunter Valley midweek. On weekends, prices of all accommodations rise dramatically—up to 100%—and a minimum stay of two nights is required. Prices quoted below are midweek unless otherwise stated.

The best value accommodation in the Pokolbin area is **Grapeview Villas,** Thompsons Rd., tel. (02) 4998-7630, set on 10 hectares of natural bushland, with views across the valley and west to the Brokenback Range. It is also central to all the wineries and the closest accommodation to Cypress Lakes Golf & Country Club. (The owners are keen golfers, so they'll give you the inside running on the course as well as organize a discount for greens fees.) Each of the eight split-level villas is self-contained with a

modern kitchen, private balcony with outdoor furniture, separate bedroom, and a small bathroom; other facilities include a pool and barbecue area. Midweek rates are $70 s, $75 d, rising to $135 weekends. Moderate. A little cheaper, but more basic and farther from the action, is **Hunter Hideaway,** Tuckers Lane, tel. (02) 4938-2091; $35-45 pp. Moderate. If you prefer the facilities of a small resort, including a restaurant, bar, and tennis court, **Tallawanta,** Broke Rd., tel. (02) 4998-7854, is a good choice; $85-125 s or d. Moderate. **Hunter Resort,** Hermitage Rd., tel. (02) 4998-7777, is part of Hunter Estate, the Valley's largest winery. Rooms aren't huge, but are well-furnished and have a large sliding door opening to a balcony overlooking a small part of the vineyard. Rates are $120 s or d, rising to $160 weekends. Premium. **Casurina Country Inn,** Hermitage Rd., tel. (02) 4998-7888, is one of Australia's few five-star accommodations outside of a city. Set among vineyards, it features well-furnished rooms, each with a king-size bed and private verandah, a beautifully landscaped pool area, and a tennis court. Rates start at $160 s, $190 d. Luxury.

The Hunter Valley's wineries are complemented by a variety of restaurants, many within the larger winery complexes. **Blaxland's Restaurant,** Broke Rd., tel. (02) 4998-7550, built from sandstone blocks hand-hewn by convicts, has a colonial atmosphere. The menu changes daily, but the choice is always varied with main dishes generally less than $20; open daily for lunch and dinner. For a splurge, consider **Chez Pok,** in Peppers Guest House, Ekerts Rd., tel. (02) 4998-7596, a country-style restaurant where mostly local produce is presented with a French flair. Dining is inside or out; open daily for lunch and dinner. **Arnold's,** Pokolbin Village, Broke Rd., tel. (02) 4998-7619, is a little less pretentious and serves a great rack of lamb ($17.50). **Hunter Coffee Lounge,** in Pokolbin Estate Vineyard on McDonalds Rd., has a small bistro serving healthy sandwiches and burgers; it's also open for breakfast.

National Parks
On the southern edge of the Hunter Valley, around the foothills of the Great Dividing Range, are three remote and almost inaccessible national parks that protect a landscape dominated

WOLLEMI PINE

For scientists, discovering new species is always exciting, but not particularly unusual. In 1995, when rangers exploring a remote gully within Wollemi National Park stumbled upon a stand of Wollemi pine, the find was of dramatic importance. For, like the coelacanth fish discovered off Madagascar earlier this century, the species was already known to scientists—but only through fossils, and in this case fossils 150 million years old. Study of these ancient trees is only in its infancy, but at the very least, the Wollemi pine allows us a glimpse of living vegetation that was present when dinosaurs roamed the earth.

by outcrops of sandstone. Extending between Blue Mountains National Park and the Hunter Valley is 492,000-hectare **Wollemi National Park,** the state's largest national park. To the east of Wollemi is 139,861-hectare **Yengo National Park,** featuring deep gorges among the sandstone. Smallest of the three parks, at 70,161 hectares, is **Goulburn River,** dissected by the river for which it's named. Wildlife such as gray kangaroos, wombats, and emus are prolific, while platypuses live in slow-flowing sections of the river. Access is south from Merriwa.

The Upper Hunter

West of the historic New England Highway town of **Singleton,** the Hunter River flows through picturesque rolling hills backed by the wilderness of three remote national parks. The area features wineries that attract fewer crowds and are more casual than those downstream. The center of the area is the small town of **Denman.** Best known of the wineries is **Rosemount Estate,** dating from 1864. Tastings are Mon.-Sat. 10 a.m.-4 p.m., Sunday 10:30 a.m.-4 p.m. It's on Rosemount Rd., west of Denman, tel. (02) 6547-2467. The only accommodation in town is **Denman Motor Inn,** at 8 Crinoline St., tel. (02) 6547-2462; good value at $44 s, $52 d. Inexpensive. **Denman Visitors Centre** is in a railway carriage in the center of town, tel. (02) 6547-2731.

The northern reaches of the Hunter River, around the towns of **Scone** and **Muswellbrook,** are the heartland of Australia's thoroughbred industry, with the scenery of green fields and white fences seemingly never-ending. Scone is known as "Horse Capital of Australia" and has a popular Horse Week each May. **Russley,** a charming B&B, was originally built as the manager's residence for Segenhoe Stud. Although the historic house has lost none of its original charm, rooms are decorated in a modern style; rates are $85-115 s or d. It's east of Scone, just off the road out to Glenbawn Dam, tel. (02) 6543-7230.

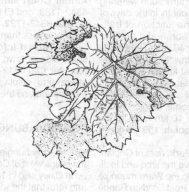

NORTH-CENTRAL NEW SOUTH WALES

In the north of the state, between the western slopes of the Great Dividing Range and endless plains to the west, is an area rich in mineral deposits and cleared for a thriving agricultural industry. The most interesting feature of this part of the state is the Warrumbungle Range, ancient mountains rising from surrounding plains in astounding formations. Farther west, along the Castlereagh Highway, is Lightning Ridge, a small town serving miners working the world's largest known concentration of black opal. From Sydney, the quickest way to access north-central New South Wales is through the Hunter Valley on the New England Highway or, from the south, the Newell Highway, the most direct route between Melbourne and Brisbane.

To the east is the New England region, a high plateau along the Great Dividing Range north of the Hunter Valley. On its eastern slopes are spectacular escarpments, waterfalls, and gorges, most of which are protected by national parks. The main route through the region is the New England Highway, which starts in Newcastle and runs north through the Hunter Valley to Queensland. Tamworth, largest of the New England towns, is the Australian capital of country music.

Beyond the Black Stump

The Black Stump Wine Saloon, named for a nearby creek, was one of many such watering holes scattered across the country in the days of horse travel. Located at the junction of trails leading west to Coonabarabran and north to Gunnedah, it traded for only 40 years, and today no sign of it remains, but, unwittingly, it has become one of Australia's best-known pubs. "Beyond the Black Stump," meaning beyond civilization, has become part of the Australian language. The site of the saloon is marked with a black stump at a rest area 10 km north of the small agricultural town of **Coolah,** 159 km northwest of Muswellbrook.

Coolah Tops National Park, east of Coolah, is worth exploring if you have the time and inclination. Linked geologically to the Warrumbungle Range to the west and the Great Dividing Range

to the east, the area is a high ridge rising to an elevation of 1,240 meters. The main access is **Warung Forest Rd.;** it follows a north-facing escarpment and passes waterfalls, lookouts, two camping areas, and a forest of snow gums.

Coonabarabran

They say the night sky around Coonabarabran is bigger and blacker and the stars brighter than anywhere else in the country. And after camping out in the Warrumbungles, you'll probably agree. A low horizon and high percentage of cloudless nights combine to make Coonabarabran an ideal location for stargazing. The 17-story **Siding Spring Observatory,** housing Australia's largest optical telescope, is located on 610-meter Siding Spring Mountain from where it is claimed you can see one-sixth of the state. Tours of the complex are offered daily 9:30 a.m.-4 p.m.; $5 pp. It's located 15 km west of town on National Park Rd., tel. (02) 6842-6211. **Skywatch Exploratory** is a commercial operation taking advantage of the dark skies. Night viewing is at 7 p.m. and 8 p.m., but the complex is open from 2-5 p.m. for you to wander around various displays. Admission is adult $10, child $6. Located two km west of town, tel. (02) 6842-3303.

Imperial Hotel, 70 John St., tel. (02) 6842-1023, has the least-expensive rooms in town; $28 s, $44 d includes breakfast. Inexpensive. **Amber Court Motel,** north of town, tel. (02) 6842-1188, and **El Paso Motel,** south of town, tel. (02) 6842-1722, both have inexpensive double rooms less than $60.

The **Tourist Information Centre** is on the south side of town and is open daily 9 a.m.-5 p.m., tel. (02) 6842-1441. Within the center are interesting displays of the region's extinct megafauna and the disastrous 1997 bushfire.

WARRUMBUNGLE NATIONAL PARK

The Warrumbungle Range rises abruptly from the plains west of Coonabarabran in, as explorer John Oxley said in 1818, "[E]very variety of shape and form that the wildest imagination could ever

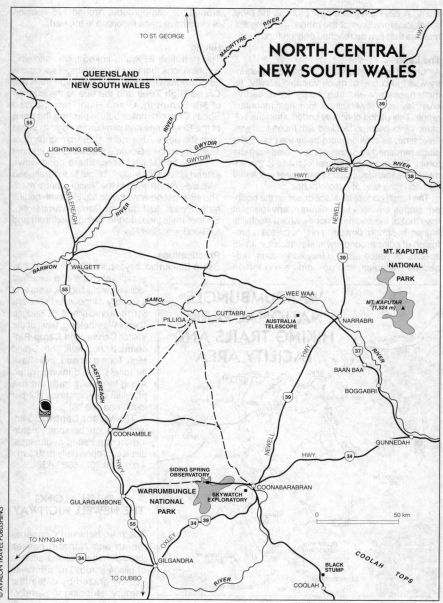

NORTH-CENTRAL NEW SOUTH WALES

TO ST. GEORGE

QUEENSLAND
NEW SOUTH WALES

MACINTYRE RIVER

GWYDIR RIVER

GWYDIR

55

LIGHTNING RIDGE

MOREE

HWY.

RIVER

39

38

NEWELL

RIVER

CASTLEREAGH

BARWON

WALGETT

55

NAMOI

MT. KAPUTAR
NATIONAL
PARK

MT. KAPUTAR
(1,524 m)

PILLIGA

CUTTABRI

WEE WAA

AUSTRALIA
TELESCOPE

NARRABRI

37

RIVER

CASTLEREAGH

BAAN BAA

BOGGABRI

39

HWY.

COONAMBLE

NEWELL

GUNNEDAH

HWY.

34

SIDING SPRING
OBSERVATORY

WARRUMBUNGLE
NATIONAL
PARK

SKYWATCH
EXPLORATORY

COONABARABRAN

GULARGAMBONE

34

39

0   50 km

55

TO NYNGAN

OXLEY

34

GILGANDRA

RIVER

TO DUBBO

BLACK
STUMP

COOLAH

COOLAH TOPS

© AVALON TRAVEL PUBLISHING

paint." A 22,945-hectare park protects the most spectacular features of the range, including formations that can be reached only on foot.

The Land

Around 13 million years ago this part of the country was the center of much volcanic activity. As molten rock spewed from faults in the earth's crust, layers of lava built up, forming a mountain range. This period of activity ended when the volcanic vents became blocked with tough trachyte. Over time, as erosion wore away the crater, the plugs remained as spires of rock rising from the forest. The most spectacular of these is the 90-meter **Breadknife,** a cast of a massive crack that formed in the side of a main crater.

The harsh climate and lack of soil on the northern slopes create a very different environment than that of the southern slopes where rainfall is higher. In spring, flowering plants create a profusion of color around lower elevations, with 25 species of wattle alone. Gray kangaroos, red-necked wallabies, and possums are common around the campground. Around 175 species of birds have been recorded in the park.

Hiking

The park has 35 km of linked trails, allowing combinations that take in all the most spectacular geological features. The two main trails are **Grand High Tops** and the one to the summit of **Mt. Exmouth.** Grand High Tops crosses Spirey Creek 12 times before passing the base of the Breadknife and climbing a ridge to some fantastic views. This trail is 12.5 km roundtrip, or 15 km if you take **Gould's Circuit** to the summit of Febar and Macha Tors, where good views extend across the valley. To get to the trailhead take the first left west of the Visitor Centre road. The six-km (one-way) trail to Mt. Exmouth begins farther west, just beyond Camp Wambelong. Shorter trails lead around Camp Blackman and to Belougery Split Rock.

Practicalities

Camp Blackman, beyond the Visitor Centre, has semiprivate sites and excellent facilities, including showers and a laundry. Unpowered sites are $10, powered sites $15. Budget. **Camp Wambelong,** west of the Visitor Centre, and **Camp Pincham,** a short walk from Grand High Tops trailhead, both have pit toilets and drinking water. Along the hiking trails are five primitive campgrounds ($2 per night) and one hut.

The **Visitor Centre,** 33 km west of Coonabarabran, featuring an interesting audiovisual display, is open daily 8:30 a.m.-4 p.m., tel. (02) 6825-4364.

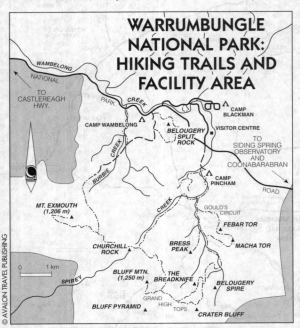

WARRUMBUNGLE NATIONAL PARK: HIKING TRAILS AND FACILITY AREA

NORTH ALONG THE NEWELL HIGHWAY

The road between Coonabarabran and Narrabri passes through half a million hectares of pilliga scrub. The area was heavily grazed by cattle last century, stripping the land of the soil, encouraging the growth of a hardy cypress pine-like tree, and rendering the land virtually useless.

Narrabri and Vicinity

This town of 7,500, 118 km north of Coonabarabran, is in an area famed for cotton-growing. The cotton industry in the Narrabri region didn't begin until the 1960s but now dominates the landscape, and is especially picturesque in late fall when the cotton balls have opened.

The **Australia Telescope,** 20 km west of Narrabri on Yarrie Lake Rd., tel. (02) 6790-4070, is the most powerful telescope in the country. It is a radio telescope, using images from radio signals received in six massive dishes that move along an eight-km rail line. The radio signals are processed by computers that translate them into visual pictures. An information center at the facility is open daily 8 a.m.-4 p.m.

At **Cuttabri,** beyond the telescope and along the road to Walgett, is Australia's only remaining wine shanty. Predating the era of beer in Australia, wine shanties were scattered along all major bush roads. This particular one served travelers on the road between Narrabri and Walgett and, unlike all others, is still operational. Drinkers have a choice of two drinks, Red Dog (port and Coke) or Brown Dog (muscat and Coke). It's open whenever the licensee has a customer to serve, which, more often than not, is most of the time.

Mount Kaputar National Park

Mt. Kaputar (1,524 meters), protected by a 36,817-hectare national park, is Australia's highest peak away from the Great Dividing Range—and you can drive right to the summit. The Nandewar Range, part of which the park encompasses, is an ancient volcano that has long since eroded, leaving only the layer of lava that spewed from its vents 18 million years ago. The main access road leads east from Narrabri, ending at the summit (53 km one-way) and **Dawsons Spring Campground,** which has hot showers; $15 per site. Budget. For bookings, call (02) 6799-1740. At the north end of the park (access from the Newell Hwy. north of Narrabri) is **Sawn Rocks,** a 40-meter-high basalt wall comprising octagonal rock columns that soar skyward.

Moree

Moree is a large agricultural service center straddling the Gwydir River 100 km north of Narrabri. Artesian bores in town are tapped into baths for therapeutic spa bathing; $2.50. Open during daylight hours.

CASTLEREAGH HIGHWAY

Beginning at Dubbo, 410 km northwest of Sydney, the Castlereagh Highway heads in a northerly direction before turning into a dusty track somewhere near the Queensland border north of Lightning Ridge.

Gilgandra is a good starting point for traveling the Castlereagh Highway, as it's an easy day's drive from Sydney. The town's main attraction is **Gilgandra Observatory,** operated by Steve Schier, a local resident whose zest for astronomy never seems to wane. The observatory is open for viewing Mon.-Sat. 7-10 p.m. It's on Willie St., tel. (02) 6847-2646.

Walgett

Walgett is on the Barwon River, one of a dozen rivers that flow westward from the Darling Downs to the Darling River. Walgett was the birthplace of the **Wolseley Shearing Machine,** which radically changed the face of the shearing industry. Today, the town has 2,500 residents and is popular as a base for fishing the Barwon, Narran, Castlereagh, and Macquarie Rivers.

The pubs in town can't really be recommended for a quiet night's sleep; instead, stay at the **Walgett Motel,** 14 Fox St., tel. (02) 6828-1355; $50 s or d. Inexpensive. For town information, head to **Walgett Shire Council Chambers,** also on Fox St., tel. (02) 6828-1399; open Mon.-Fri. 8:30-4:30 p.m.

LIGHTNING RIDGE

Lightning Ridge, a dry, dusty frontier town of 2,000, near the end of the Castlereagh Highway, 780 km northwest of Sydney, is synonymous with opal. Hundreds of small-scale mining operations around the area produce most of the world's black opal, Australia's national gemstone. Opal is found in varying qualities in the United

States, Mexico, and Brazil, but the black opal of Lightning Ridge, reflecting all colors of the spectrum off the dark body of rock, has few equals in the world. Its name, Lightning Ridge, originated in the 1870s when a drover was killed by lightning while sheltering from a storm on a ridge.

Sights

Surrounding the town are an estimated 1,000 claims, each mined by small-time operators, hoping against hope for the same success that prospectors had at Nebea Hill in the 1970s when $3 million worth of opal was extracted from one mine in two years. You don't need a license to fossick on abandoned mullock heaps—they are strewn with chips of boulder opal, and there's always a chance of finding a good one. Stephen and Lesley Henley offer tours of their mine and a demonstration of opal cutting daily at 10 a.m.; the mine is on Three Mile Rd., tel. (02) 6829-0247. Walk-in Mine, on Bald Hill, tel. (02) 6829-0473, is a similar setup, with tours departing at 9 a.m. and an audiovisual shown regularly. Spectrum Opal Mine, Bald Hill Rd., tel. (02) 6829-0581, has an underground showroom chock-full of spectacular opals, including one worth more than $80,000. They show a film here hourly, and aboveground is an area for fossicking and a picnic area with barbecues.

If you want to buy opal, Lightning Ridge is the place to do it, as prices often double by the time the opals reach the east coast. Opal shops line Opal and Manilla Streets. Often, cheaper opals are from other parts of Australia, so, if having an opal from Lightning Ridge is important to you, ask before you buy. You can buy good chunks of "solids" for less than $100. Top-quality black opal sells for about $3000 per carat.

The Ridge is also known for artesian bores, bubbling out of the ground at around 40° C (104° F). The therapeutic powers of the water have soothed the muscles of work-weary miners for a hundred years, but also attract visitors whose arthritic conditions are claimed to improve in the water. On Pandora St., the pools are open 24 hours; admission is free.

Accommodations and Food

Lightning Ridge Motor Village is a four-hectare complex with accommodation styles to suit all budgets. Motel rooms with private facilities are $50-59 s, $65-69 d; unpowered sites $10, powered sites $12. On-site is a bistro, bar, and restaurant, and a small area is set aside for fossicking. It's west of town on Onyx St., tel. (02) 6829-0304. Budget/Moderate. **Black Opal Motel,** Opal St., tel. (02) 6829-0518, has basic rooms for $51 s, $59 d, each with a safe for those precious opals. Inexpensive. Another good option is **Lightning Ridge Caravan Park,** Harlequin St., tel. (02) 6829-0532, where basic on-site vans are $28, cabins are $45, and sites for tents and vans are $10-12. Budget-Inexpensive.

If you're after steak and mashed potatoes go to the **Digger's Rest Hotel,** Opal St., or the **bowling club** on Morilla Street. The Ridge's finest dining (remember, things are relative out here) is at the **Wild Dingo,** 4 Opal St., tel. (02) 6829-0215. There's the choice of a café, bar, restaurant, and outdoor patio, all of which share similar menus offering pasta, steak, and even seafood.

Transportation, Services, and Information

Log Cabin Opal Shoppe, 47 Morilla St., tel. (02) 6829-0277, is the agent for long-distance bus companies serving the town, including Transcity, McCafferty's, and Sid Foggs, and rail bookings.

Apart from its remote location, Lightning Ridge is like any similar-sized town, with all expected services including a doctor, tel. (02) 6829-0416, post office, supermarket, bakery, banks, butchers, and gas stations (80-90 cents a liter for fuel). The **Tourist Information Centre** is on Fred Reece Way, tel. (02) 6829-1462 or (1800) 63-9545, website www.lightningridge.net.au; open Mon.-Fri. 8:30 a.m.-4:30 p.m.

TAMWORTH

This sprawling city of 38,000, 400 km northwest of Sydney, is Australia's country music capital. Country music in Australia doesn't have the following it does in the United States, but each January, when thousands of fans descend on Tamworth for the Australian Country Music Festival, the spirit is certainly there. For the other 51 weeks of the year, Tamworth uses its reputation as the home of country music to lure visitors off the highway.

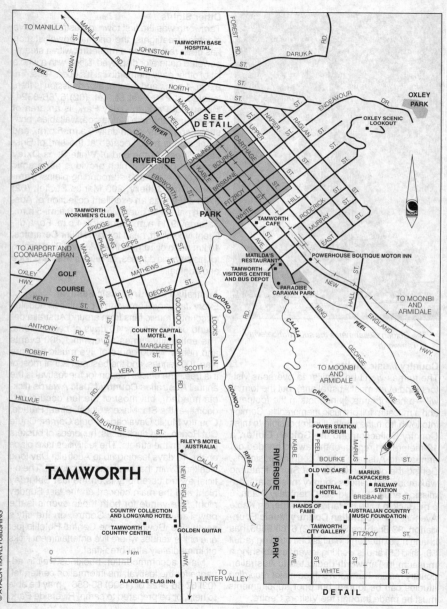

TO MANILLA

TAMWORTH BASE HOSPITAL

OXLEY PARK

OXLEY SCENIC LOOKOUT

SEE DETAIL

RIVERSIDE

PARK

TAMWORTH WORKMEN'S CLUB

TAMWORTH CAFE

TO AIRPORT AND COONABARABRAN

GOLF COURSE

MATILDA'S RESTAURANT

POWERHOUSE BOUTIQUE MOTOR INN

TAMWORTH VISITORS CENTRE AND BUS DEPOT

PARADISE CARAVAN PARK

TO MOONBI AND ARMIDALE

COUNTRY CAPITAL MOTEL

TO MOONBI AND ARMIDALE

RILEY'S MOTEL AUSTRALIA

TAMWORTH

COUNTRY COLLECTION AND LONGYARD HOTEL

TAMWORTH COUNTRY CENTRE

GOLDEN GUITAR

0   1 km

ALANDALE FLAG INN

TO HUNTER VALLEY

DETAIL

POWER STATION MUSEUM

RIVERSIDE

OLD VIC CAFE

MARIUS BACKPACKERS

CENTRAL HOTEL

RAILWAY STATION

HANDS OF FAME

AUSTRALIAN COUNTRY MUSIC FOUNDATION

TAMWORTH CITY GALLERY

PARK

The Golden Guitar marks the southern gateway to Tamworth.

Country Music Sights

The names won't be familiar to overseas visitors (and even most Australians), but the format will—a hall of fame, handprints in the footpath, and a museum full of music memorabilia. Coming into town from the south, it is impossible to miss Country Collection and the **Golden Guitar,** a 12-meter-high replica of the award handed out annually to Australia's best country musicians. Behind the guitar is **Gallery of Stars,** featuring wax models of various country music stars; admission adult $5, child $2. Open daily 9 a.m.-5 p.m. Back in town is **Hands of Fame,** on Kable Avenue. The **Australian Country Music Foundation,** 93 Brisbane St., tel. (02) 6766-9696, has changing exhibitions in a historic building (adult $8, child $5) and is working toward establishing a museum in Tamworth dedicated to Australian country music. Tamworth's three major recording studios can be toured, but prior appointments must be made through the Visitors Centre.

Other Sights

Tamworth was the first town in Australia to have electric streetlights; the original power station has been restored as a **museum,** with a steam-powered generator displayed, along with a whole lot of other early memorabilia. It's open Tues.-Fri. 9 a.m.-1 p.m., and, best of all, admission is free; located at 216 Peel St., tel. (02) 6766-8324. **Marsupial Park,** in Oxley Park, is an area of native bushland with kangaroos, wallabies, possums, and birds; open daily 8 a.m.-5 p.m., and admission is free. Located at the end of Brisbane Street. At the end of White St. is **Oxley Scenic Lookout,** which provides panoramic views of the city and surrounding plains. **Tamworth City Gallery,** 203 Marius St., tel. (02) 6768-4459, has an excellent collection of Australian paintings; open Mon.-Fri. 10 a.m.-5 p.m., Saturday 9-11 a.m., Sunday 1-4 p.m. For a different type of art, head to **Fred Hillier Ceramics,** 18 km north of Tamworth at Moonbi. Best known for his ceramic dunnies, all Hillier's work is unique and original.

Australian Country Music Festival

Every January, Tamworth's population doubles as country music fans from around Australia descend on the city for 10 days of celebrations. The entire city comes alive with 1,800 events and nearly 7,000 hours of live music at more than 100 venues, and the best part is that most of it is free. The official reason for the festival is the annual **Australian Country Music Awards** (tickets needed), but most of the fun occurs outdoors—at the Star Makers Quest, Street Parade, Country Music Cavalcade, Poets Corner, Chute Out Rodeo, and duck races; hundreds of buskers perform on the streets. The festivities take place on the 10 days leading up to Australia Day long weekend, with that weekend the busiest. The official award ceremony is on the last Saturday night and the main concert on the last Sunday night. The venue for both these events is the new Tamworth Country Centre, on the city's south side. Downtown, the Central Hotel is just one of the venues where live entertainment kicks off immediately after breakfast.

Make accommodation bookings well in advance for the festival; the information center, tel. (02) 67-66-9422 or (1800) 80-3561, may be able to help, or be prepared to camp. Riverside Park, within stumbling distance of downtown, opens up for camping, as do sporting and school grounds. The event hotline is tel. (02) 6766-6481.

Accommodations
Central Hotel, corner of Peel and Brisbane Streets, tel. (02) 6766-2160, has rooms with shared bathrooms for $25 s, $35 d and with private bathrooms for $35 s, $45 d. Inexpensive. Tamworth has dozens of motels, and although none are cheap, the standard is generally high. **Country Capital Motel,** 193 Goonoo Goonoo Rd., tel. (02) 6765-5966, has excellent facilities and is only $50 s, $55 d. Inexpensive. **Riley's Motel Australia,** 354 New England Hwy., tel. (02) 6765-9258, is a couple of km south of town but has reasonable rates at $48 s, $54 d. Inexpensive. Farther south, beyond the Longyard Hotel, is **Alandale Flag Inn,** tel. (02) 6765-7922, famous for its guitar-shaped swimming pool; $77 s, $85 d. Moderate. **Powerhouse Boutique Motor Inn,** on the New England Hwy. within walking distance of downtown, tel. (02) 6766-7000, is Tamworth's most luxurious accommodation. Rooms are large and elegantly furnished, many having a private spa; $100-105 s or d. Expensive.

Country Backpackers, 169 Marius St., tel. (02) 6761-2600, offers basic but clean accommodations in a very central position. It features an in-house art gallery. Dorm beds are $15 pp, doubles $35. All rates include breakfast. Inexpensive.

Paradise Caravan Park, Peel St., tel. (02) 6766-3120, fronts the Peel River and has a pleasant area set aside for tents. All sites are $16, basic on-site vans are $31, and cabins start at $50. Budget-Inexpensive.

Food
Many of Tamworth's eateries are on Peel St., while better restaurants are located in the motels. **Tamworth Cafe,** 282 Peel St., has fast efficient service and good food; open daily 9 a.m.-9 p.m. Farther along, at 261 Peel St., tel. (02) 6766-3435, is **Old Vic Cafe,** serving healthy breakfasts ($5-9) and lunches ($6-11). **Matilda's Restaurant,** corner Peel and Murray Streets, tel. (02) 6766-5133, is a great buffet restaurant with lunches starting at $8 and dinners at $10. Tamworth's many clubs offer some great dining bargains; try **Tamworth Work-**

men's Club, Reserve Place, West Tamworth, tel. (02) 6765-9291.

South of town, behind the Golden Guitar, **Longyard Hotel,** tel. (02) 6765-3411, has a large beer garden and bistro that serves meals daily from 11 a.m. Of the motel restaurants, **Monty's,** in the Powerhouse Boutique Motor Inn, New England Hwy., tel. (02) 6766-7000, is the pick of the bunch. The menu features mainly seafood, but steak and chicken dishes are also excellent and prices of main dishes run mostly $14-19; their breakfast is also good.

Transportation, Services, and Information
Eastern Australia, tel. (13) 1313, has regular daily flights between Sydney and Tamworth. The airport is west of town (a $12 cab ride). The **bus depot** is part of a modern guitar-shaped complex on the corner of Peel and Murray Streets, which also holds the information center. All major bus lines stop at Tamworth, each with at least one service daily. **Tamworth Railway Station** is on Bridge St., tel. (13) 2232, with daily Xplorer service south to Sydney and north as far as Moree.

From the main bus depot, **Tamworth Coaches,** tel. (02) 6762-3999, runs around the city and to outlying towns. For a rental car, call **Avis,** tel. (02) 6765-2000, or **Budget,** tel. (02) 6766-7255.

Tamworth Base Hospital is on Dean St., tel. (02) 6766-1722. The excellent **Tamworth Visitors Centre** is at the corner of Peel and Murray Streets, tel. (02) 6766-9422 or (1800) 80-3561; open daily 9 a.m.-5 p.m.

VICINITY OF TAMWORTH

Fossickers Way
The Fossickers Way, so named for a variety of gemstones that you can find en route, is a designated tourist route between Tamworth and Inverell, rejoining the New England Highway at Glen Innes. The information center at Barraba has details of all the best fossicking areas; 30 km west of this town is **Horton Falls.**

Bingara and the surrounding area are noted for diamonds. The town has some historic buildings along the main drag. At **Upper Bingara** to the south, once a thriving town of thousands of miners, gold can still be found.

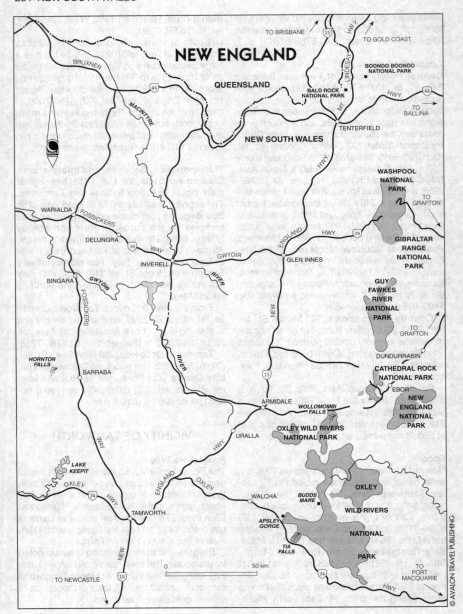

TO BRISBANE

NEW ENGLAND

TO GOLD COAST

BOONOO BOONOO
NATIONAL PARK

BRUXNER

QUEENSLAND

BALD ROCK
NATIONAL PARK

TO
BALLINA

MACINTYRE

NEW SOUTH WALES

TENTERFIELD

WASHPOOL
NATIONAL
PARK

TO
GRAFTON

WARIALDA   FOSSICKERS

DELUNGRA

GIBRALTAR
RANGE
NATIONAL
PARK

GLEN INNES

WAY

GWYDIR
RIVER

INVERELL

ENGLAND   HWY.

GUY
FAWKES
RIVER
NATIONAL
PARK

BINGARA

GWYDIR

FOSSICKERS

TO
GRAFTON

HORNTON
FALLS

RIVER

DUNDURRABIN

CATHEDRAL ROCK
NATIONAL PARK

EBOR

BARRABA

NEW
ENGLAND
NATIONAL
PARK

ARMIDALE

WOLLOMOMBI
FALLS

URALLA

OXLEY WILD RIVERS
NATIONAL PARK

LAKE
KEEPIT

OXLEY

OXLEY

WALCHA

BUDDS
MARE

OXLEY

ENGLAND   HWY.

TAMWORTH

NEW

WILD RIVERS

APSLEY
GORGE

NATIONAL

TIA
FALLS

PARK

TO
PORT
MACQUARIE

TO NEWCASTLE

0   50 km

© AVALON TRAVEL PUBLISHING

Farther north, on the Gwydir Highway, is **Warialda,** where agate, jasper, and petrified wood are also found. **Cranky Rock,** eight km east of Warialda, is a group of massive granite boulders through which Reedy Creek flows. The unusual name is said to come from a cranky Chinese man who jumped to his death from one of the rocks.

The last town along the Fossickers Way, and also the largest, is **Inverell,** located in an area known for sapphires.

Oxley Wild Rivers National Park

This 117,349-hectare park encompasses a number of spectacular gorges and escarpments along the Great Dividing Range east of Tamworth. The park, a high plateau through which more than 500 km of rivers flow, is divided into many sections, all accessible by regular vehicle. **Apsley Gorge,** 18 km east of Walcha, is one of the park's most spectacular features. Viewing platforms have been set up around a waterfall at the head of the gorge, and a teahouse is open daily 10 a.m.-5:30 p.m. Farther east is **Tia Falls. Budds Mare,** accessible on a gravel road from Walcha, provides more panoramic views and access to a remote part of the park. Some areas of the park extend north to Armidale, and include **Wollomombi Falls,** Australia's highest waterfall, located 40 km east of Armidale. Camping is permitted at all picnic areas. For park information, call (02) 6773-7211.

Uralla

The rolling hills around Uralla were the stomping grounds for **Thunderbolt,** one of the Australia's most infamous bushrangers. His reign of terror through the New England region spanned two decades in the mid-1800s. His favorite haunt was a jumbled pile of granite boulders south of Uralla, from where he had views of approaching travelers and mail coaches. Now buried in Uralla Cemetery, he met his demise east of the rocks when he was brought down by gunfire from a plucky constable. **McCrossin's Mill,** tel. (02) 6778-3022, a three-story building dating from 1870, houses memorabilia from Thunderbolt's era, including gold-mining and Aboriginal relics; open daily noon-5 p.m., and admission is $4.

Bushranger Motor Inn, tel. (02) 6778-3777 or (1800) 06-4795, features large rooms with modern facilities; $65 s, $70 d. Moderate. **Café La Quoi,** Bridge St., is a quirky little diner-style restaurant in a renovated turn-of-the-century general store. The food here is exceptionally good—lunch is the usual country-style fare such as a ploughman's platter, while the dinner menu is more varied (the lamb is delicious) and relatively inexpensive. Closed Monday and Tuesday. The other option is **Lindon House Antiques and Tea Rooms,** on the main drag, open daily for Devonshire teas. **Uralla Visitors Centre,** in the center of town, tel. (02) 6778-4496, is open Mon.-Fri. 9 a.m.-6 p.m.

ARMIDALE

Armidale is a large educational and agricultural service center of 21,500 on the New England Highway 110 km north of Tamworth. Located at an altitude of 1,000 meters, summers are relatively cool. The town's main employer is the **University of New England,** established in 1938 and now with an enrollment of 14,500 students.

Sights

Within a dozen blocks of downtown are many historic buildings, most of which are seen on the **Heritage Walking Tours;** a brochure available from the Tourist Information Centre details each one. **Saumarez Homestead,** southwest of town on Saumarez Rd., tel. (02) 6772-3616, is an impressive home built late last century for a wealthy grazier family; open for tours daily at 10:30 a.m. and 2 p.m. Back in town, on the corner of Faulkner and Rusden Streets, is **Armidale Folk Museum,** tel. (02) 6773-8536, open daily 1-4 p.m. **New England Regional Art Museum,** Kentucky St., tel. (02) 6772-5255, boasts an impressive collection of Australian artworks; open Mon.-Sat. 10 a.m.-5 p.m., Sunday 1-5 p.m.

Accommodations and Food

Wicklow Hotel, corner Marsh and Dumaresq Streets, tel. (02) 6772-2421, is right opposite the bus station and near downtown. Basic rooms start at $26 s, $36 d. Inexpensive. Armidale has no really cheap motels; most start at around $60 d. **Cedar Lodge,** 119 Barney St., tel. (02) 6772-9511 or (1800) 06-7829, is right downtown, and rooms start at $55 s, $65 d. Moderate. **Deer Park**

Motor Inn, 2.6 km north of town on the New England Hwy., tel. (02) 6772-9999, has large rooms of an excellent standard, a heated indoor pool, cocktail bar, and spa; $65 s, $75 d. Moderate. **Pembroke Tourist and Leisure Park**, corner Grafton and Cooks Roads, tel. (02) 6772-6470, two km east of town, has facilities of an excellent standard; unpowered sites $12.50, powered sites $15.50, on-site vans $27-35, cabins $38-85. Budget. Another option for campers is to head east to the national parks detailed below.

Being a university town, there's a wide variety of inexpensive cafés and restaurants to choose from, many spread along Beardy St. pedestrian mall. **Rumours**, 190 Beardy St., a popular student hangout, has good, inexpensive food. **Chocolates and Fine Things**, 119 Beardy St., tel. (02) 6771-2171, has a variety of coffees and mouthwatering homemade cakes and chocolates. For a casual lunch, head four km south of Armidale to **The Berry Best**, a café/restaurant on a berry farm. Everything is homemade, and if the tempting array of fruit pies isn't enough, sandwiches and hot dishes are also offered, tel. (02) 6772-5974. **Jitterbug Mood**, 231 Beardy St., tel. (02) 6772-3022, is one of Armidale's better restaurants; the setting is elegant, the food and service excellent, with choices ranging from Middle Eastern to vegetarian; open Tues-Sat. from 6:30 p.m.

Transportation, Services, and Information

All major bus lines stop at Armidale on the main Sydney-Brisbane route. The coach terminal is on the corner of Marsh and Dumaresq Streets, tel. (02) 6773-8527.

Armidale Visitor's Centre is in the coach terminal, tel. (02) 6772-4655 or (1800) 62-7736. They have a ton of local information and a large parking area (a good place to leave your car if heading into town); open Mon.-Fri. 9 a.m.-5 p.m., Saturday 9 a.m.-4 p.m., Sunday 10 a.m.-4 p.m.

ARMIDALE TO THE COAST

From Armidale, a road winds eastward across the Great Dividing Range to the coast south of Coffs Harbour (172 km) or, spurring north beyond Ebor, to Grafton (205 km). Three very different national parks are accessed from this road, but the first stop should be **Wollomombi**

Falls, 39 km east of Armidale. This waterfall, the highest in Australia, is in Oxley Wild Rivers National Park (see above).

New England National Park

Often shrouded in mist and totally undeveloped, this 55,989-hectare park encompasses a vast tract of rainforest along the eastern extremity of the New England Plateau, and includes many peaks more than 1,500 meters that become capped by a light layer of snow in winter. Wildlife is varied and abundant, with 110 species of birds alone recorded. One of the most panoramic viewpoints is **Point Lookout**, at the end of the park access road, where the panorama extends to the Pacific Ocean. From its Banksia Point, seven-km **Lyrebird Walk** follows the escarpment through a fern-filled gully (with the chance to see lyrebirds) and returns along the ridge.

Near the park entrance is **Thungutti Campground;** facilities include cold showers and drinking water. Three rustic cabins are also available; call (02) 6657-2309 for reservations.

Cathedral Rock National Park

The main features of this 6,529-hectare park are impressive granite tors for which the park is named. The easiest access to the tors is from Barokee Rest Area, at the end of a 10-km gravel road spurring north off the Armidale-Grafton Road. The 5.8-km summit-circuit trail crosses a wetland before climbing through a forest of eucalypts and banksias and emerging among the massive granite boulders. Camping is available at Barokee or on the other side of Cathedral Rock at Native Dog Creek Rest Area.

Guy Fawkes River National Park

With road access from northwest of Dundurrabin ending at the park border, this 63,395-hectare park is one of the least-visited of the New England national parks. Protecting the watershed of Guy Fawkes River, it is a favorite destination for wilderness whitewater canoe adventurers. From the headwaters, near Ebor, you can travel on the river for days, eventually flowing into the Nymboida then Clarence River. The only designated hiking trails begin from the end of the main access road, where a primitive campground is located. For canoeing information, contact the NPWS in Dorrigo, tel. (02) 6657-2309.

ARMIDALE TO QUEENSLAND

Glen Innes

As the name suggests, many of this town's earliest settlers were Scottish. They were attracted by the prospect of making their fortunes from the wealth of minerals in the area. Although agriculture keeps this town of 6,000 alive today, fossicking for gems is still productive, and a good reason to stop by. Sapphires are the region's best-known gemstone, but garnet, beryl, and topaz are all found in areas set aside for public use. If you don't have any luck, try the gem shops along Main Street.

Central Motel, named for its location right opposite the post office, tel. (02) 6732-1035, has rooms of a high standard for $55 s, $60 d. Inexpensive. **Poplar Caravan Park,** New England Hwy., tel. (02) 6732-1514, has a covered kitchen area; powered sites $12, on-site vans $28, cabins $38. Budget.

Gibraltar Range and Washpool National Parks

These two parks straddle the Gwydir Highway east of Glen Innes. In 1967, soon after construction of the road between Glen Innes and Grafton, a 17,273-hectare chunk of land was set aside to protect the virgin forests of the Gibraltar Range. Rainforests of the Washpool Creek watershed were at the mercy of loggers until 1982 when a further 28,000 hectares were protected. The park boundaries have continued to expand ever since, and today, combined, protect more than 73,000 hectares, the largest remaining area of rainforest in New South Wales. Plantlife in both parks is amazingly diverse, and includes sassafras, corkwood, lilly pilly, yello carabeens, strangler figs, and the largest stand of coachwood in the world. Many rare species of mammals live in the parks, including the long-nosed potoroo and the parma wallaby.

The five-km **Dandahra Falls Walk,** south of the highway, is the most interesting of the many hikes. It follows Surveyors Creek through a beautiful rainforest. On the north side of the highway is the 1.5-km **Coombadjha Nature Walk,** beginning from Coachwood Picnic Area and passing through rainforest to a swimming hole.

Campgrounds are located north and south of the highway, and the **Visitor Centre,** at the parks' entrance, is open daily 8:30 a.m.-4 p.m., tel. (02) 6732-1177.

Tenterfield

Tenterfield is a surprisingly pretty town, at the junction of the New England and Bruxner Highways. It was the birthplace of entertainer Peter Allen, and the saddlery, run by his grandfather for 50 years, was the source of inspiration for one of his best-known songs, "Tenterfield Saddler." The saddlery is open to the public Mon.-Fri. 9 a.m.-5 p.m.; it's on High St., tel. (02) 6736-1478.

From Tenterfield the most direct route to Queensland is the New England Highway, but a more interesting route is Mt. Lindesay Highway (gravel), the original inland route between Sydney and Brisbane.

Boonoo Boonoo National Park

Located 25 km north of Tenterfield along Mt. Lindesay Highway, this 2,695-hectare park is in the heart of "Granite Country," an area of the northern tablelands strewn with granite boulders. Morgan's Gully, along the park access road, was site of a short-lived gold rush late last century, but the most spectacular feature of the park is the Boonoo Boonoo River, which cascades across dozens of granite rock pools (near Cypress Rest Area) before plunging 210 meters to the valley floor. At the very end of the access road, a 300-meter trail leads to a viewing platform over the falls and the spectacular gorge beyond, or you can continue along a steep and often slippery track to the valley floor. Camping is allowed at both rest areas.

Bald Rock National Park

West of Mt. Lindesay Highway, this little-known 5,451-hectare park contains one of the most impressive geological features of New England—Bald Rock. From the park access road, the massif is hidden by towering eucalypts; the only way to appreciate its size is by scrambling to the summit. Rising 200 meters above the surrounding forest, it is Australia's second-largest rock (behind Uluru), measuring 500 meters wide and nearly one km long. Two trails lead to the summit: the most direct route is, naturally, the steepest, and can be slippery early in the morning (follow the white dots); a longer trail climbs steadily but at an easier gradient. Both trails begin from the picnic area. Beyond the picnic area is a campground (bring drinking water).

MID-NORTH COAST

The drive between Sydney or Newcastle and the far north coast of New South Wales can be easily completed in one day, but the 600-odd km of coastline in between offer a variety of national parks, beaches, and charming seaside towns, worthy of as much time as you can afford. The main route north, the **Pacific Highway,** takes a direct route, parallel to the Great Dividing Range and inland from the coast and most seaside towns.

Along the highway are dozens of roads spurring east to towns that come alive during January before reverting to their sleepy selves the other 11 months of the year. One of the least-developed towns is also the southernmost; Seal Rocks has changed little in 80 years. Others, such as Forster and Port Macquarie, are popular year-round. North from Port Macquarie the highway passes a string of picturesque coastal villages, including Crescent Head, Hat Head, and South West Rocks, before it descends to Coffs Harbour, halfway between Sydney and Brisbane and the largest town on the north coast. When the thrills of this activity-packed town wear off, continue north to the national parks of Yuraygir, Bundjalung, and Broadwater.

NEWCASTLE TO PORT MACQUARIE

Myall Lakes National Park
This 31,777-hectare park protects the state's largest coastal lagoon system, separated from the ocean by a sandy strip of beach extending between Port Stephens and the picturesque fishing village of **Seal Rocks.** Around 10,000 years ago the Pacific Ocean extended farther inland than today, and higher areas such as Seal Rocks, Bombah Point, and Violet Hill were islands. Wave action pushed sand around these islands, eventually creating the sand dunes that are such a dominant part of the park today. **Broughton Island,** two km offshore (one of the original islands that didn't become part of the mainland) is part of the park and a popular dive site. The lagoon system comprises three main lakes—Myall, Boolambayte, and Broadwater—

linked by narrow inlets and forming the headwaters of the Myall River, which flows southward behind the dune system for many kilometers before draining into Port Stephens at Tea Gardens. Much of the dune system is covered in grasses, while lower elevations support forests of eucalypts, wattles, banksias, and paperbarks. Gray kangaroos, red-necked wallabies, koalas, and dingos call the park home. Birdlife is prolific, too, with waterbirds such as black swans, herons, egrets, cranes, and pelicans common.

Access to the park is from Hawks Nest, Bulahdelah, or Seal Rocks. An unsealed road traverses the length of the park, but it is generally in bad shape and not recommended for two-wheel drives. From Hawks Nest, a road leads to **Mungo Brush,** a popular camping area. At Mungo Brush, a 500-meter hiking trail leads through a littoral rainforest, and access to both the lake and beach is possible. Accessed from Bulahdelah, **Myall Shores Eco-Tourist Resort,** at Bombah Pt., tel. (02) 4997-4495, is a basic campground ($10-14 per site) but also has canoe and boat rentals. From this point, a small ferry runs across to the Mungo Brush area of the park ($3 pp one way). From Seal Rocks, off the Forster Rd., an unsealed road leads south into the park to **Yagon,** where a great little campground is nestled behind the dunes. The small seaside community of Seal Rocks is worth visiting. The community has restricted development almost completely (even the access road remains unpaved), and comprises a general store, campground, and a few dozen old cottages, most right on Boat Beach.

Forster
Forster (pop. 12,500) and the smaller town of **Tuncurry** straddle the outlet of **Wallis Lake,** 66 km northeast of the highway town of Bulahdelah. Holidayers flock to Forster for great fishing, surfing, and long sandy beaches. Wallis Lake is also famous for oysters, producing two million annually. Some of the best fishing is just meters from the main street. Another way to explore the lake is on the cruiser *Amaroo II;* call (02) 6554-7743 to check departure times.

Accommodation will be very difficult to find in summer and during school holidays, so make bookings well in advance. **Lakes and Ocean Hotel,** 10 Little St., tel. (02) 6554-6005, has pub-style rooms of a good standard, most with a balcony, for $35 s, $52 d. Inexpensive. Just 150 meters from the beach, **Great Lakes Motor Inn,** 24 Head St., tel. (02) 6554-6955, has large comfortable rooms for $44 s, $58 d. Inexpensive. **Dolphin Lodge,** 43 Head St., tel. (02) 6555-8155, is affiliated with the YHA; dorm beds are $15, doubles $34. Inexpensive. Guests have free use of bikes and surfboards.

Local prawns and oysters are sold at various outlets around town; for something casual head to **Little Shell Restaurant,** 6 Head St., tel. (02) 6555-6890; open Tues.-Sun. from 6 p.m.

Taree and the Manning Valley

Even after being bypassed by the Pacific Hwy. in early 1999, Taree remains a busy service town of 16,000. There's nothing to see in town, but it makes an inexpensive overnight stop. Along the old Pacific Hwy. north of downtown, **Rainbow Gardens Motel,** tel. (02) 6552-1312, charges just $40 s, $44 d for rooms of a reasonable standard. Along the same strip of road is the **Manning Valley Tourist Information Centre,** tel. (02) 6552-1900 or (1800) 80-1522; open daily 9 a.m.-5 p.m.

West of Taree, **Wingham** and other small Manning Valley towns are interesting. Many historic buildings line Wingham's streets, and a museum, tel. (02) 6553-5823, is on Farquhar St.; open daily 10 a.m.-4 p.m. Behind the town

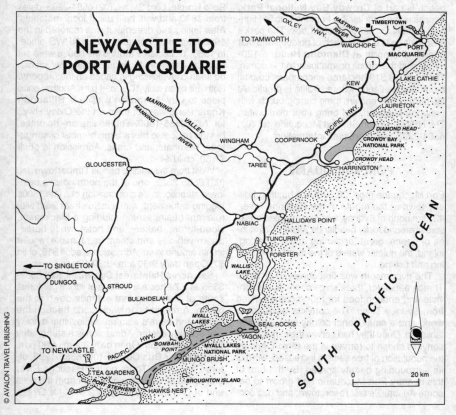

NEWCASTLE TO PORT MACQUARIE

and alongside the Manning River is Wingham Brush, an area of old-growth subtropical rainforest that has escaped logging. Many thousands of gray-headed flying foxes live in the reserve and their call can be deafening, especially Sept.-April.

Taree to Port Macquarie

It is only 85 km between these two towns, but interesting detours abound. The first is at Coopernook, 22 km north of Taree, where a road follows the north bank of the Manning River to the coastal community of **Harrington.** Beyond Harrington is **Crowdy Head,** named by Captain Cook for a crowd of Aboriginals he sighted on the headland. Views from this spot are spectacular, extending north along Crowdy Beach. This beach is part of **Crowdy Bay National Park.** Access to the park itself is from the Pacific Highway eight km north of Coopernook. The park's main feature is a long beach of golden sand that ends in the north at **Diamond Head,** a 120-meter bluff that drops dramatically to the ocean. The park's 9,519 hectares encompass coastal heath and wetlands where birdlife is prolific. At the park's north end are three campgrounds with firewood supplied, but bring your own water. The NPWS, Horton St., Port Macquarie, tel. (02) 6584-2203, has more park information.

PORT MACQUARIE

Port Macquarie (pop. 26,500) is a bustling holiday town at the mouth of the Hastings River, 420 km north of Sydney, where developed areas sprawl around rocky headlands linked by stretches of beach, great for surfing and sunbaking. Inland, the quieter waters of the river foster boating and fishing.

The river mouth was first surveyed in 1818. Three years later, three ships chock-full of convicts and enough food for four months arrived from Sydney Town. The convicts were put to work, and a small penal colony was soon established. Once they had served their time, many convicts chose to remain in the region, and as the population of free settlers increased, word of its surrounding beauty spread. By the turn of this century Port Macquarie had grown to become Australia's first resort town, and has continued to attract tourists for almost a century, mostly families looking for a quiet getaway.

Sights and Recreation

Port Macquarie's commercial area is sandwiched between Kooloonbung Creek and the ocean. The main drag, Clarence St., loops around the mouth of the river, passing a grassy headland with views northward and Town Beach below. Overlooking Town Beach is an old pilot's cottage that has been converted to a small **maritime museum.** It's open daily 10 a.m.-4 p.m., and admission is $2. **Port Macquarie District Museum,** 22 Clarence St., tel. (02) 6583-1108, has interesting relics, some dating from convict days.

One of Port Macquarie's oldest buildings, **Roto House,** Lord St., tel. (02) 6584-2203, dates from 1890 and was built using local materials. After falling into disrepair it was restored in the 1980s and now operates as an NPWS office. In 1966, 12 hectares around the house were set aside as a reserve for injured koalas, which can be seen convalescing in cages on the property. Both are open daily 10 a.m.-4 p.m. Another good place to view Australian wildlife is **Billabong Koala Park,** west of town on the Oxley Hwy., tel. (02) 6585-1060. The koalas are favorites, but the park also has a large number of kangaroos, wombats, and emus. Admission is adult $7.50, child $4.

West from this wildlife park is **Timbertown,** tel. (02) 6585-2322, one of the north coast's best-loved attractions. It's a re-creation of a late 1800s logging settlement, with a main street lined with relevant businesses, including a blacksmith, wood-turner, bakery, and hotel, while horse-drawn vehicles and steam trains make regular jaunts around town. Admission is adult $16, child $7. Open daily 9:30 a.m.-3:30 p.m.

Sea Acres Rainforest Centre, tel. (02) 6582-3355, is a 72-hectare reserve of littoral rainforest south of downtown that extends down to the beach. A raised boardwalk leads through the forest, and there's also an audiovisual display and ecology center. Admission is a steep adult $8.50, child $4.50. Open daily 9 a.m.-4:30 p.m.

The **Water Bus Co.,** tel. (02) 6583-1293, offers Everglades Tours on the Hastings River and its tributaries. Cruises depart from the west end of Clarence St. daily at 2 p.m. for Oyster

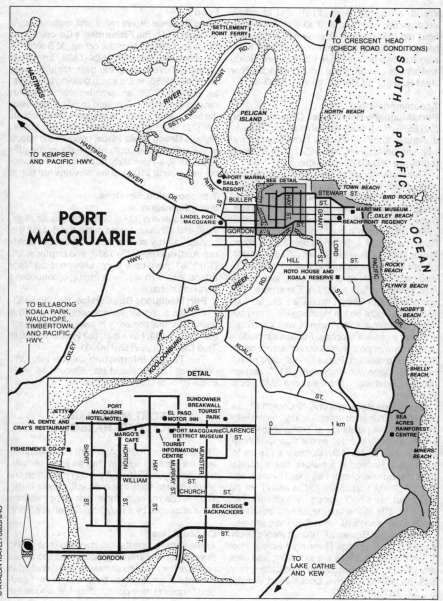

TO CRESCENT HEAD
(CHECK ROAD CONDITIONS)

SOUTH PACIFIC OCEAN

SETTLEMENT
POINT FERRY

SETTLEMENT POINT RD.

HASTINGS RIVER

PELICAN
ISLAND

NORTH BEACH

TO KEMPSEY
AND PACIFIC HWY.

HASTINGS RIVER

PARK DR.

PORT MARINA
SAILS RESORT.

SEE DETAIL

TOWN BEACH
BIRD ROCK

BULLER ST.

HAY ST.

STEWART ST.

GRANT ST.

MARITIME MUSEUM
OXLEY BEACH
BEACHFRONT REGENCY

**PORT
MACQUARIE**

LINDEL PORT
MACQUARIE

GORDON

HWY.

CREEK RD.

LAKE

HILL ST.

LORD ST.

ROTO HOUSE AND
KOALA RESERVE

PACIFIC DR.

ROCKY BEACH

FLYNN'S BEACH

TO BILLABONG
KOALA PARK,
WAUCHOPE,
TIMBERTOWN,
AND PACIFIC
HWY.

OXLEY HWY.

KOOLOONBUNG CREEK

KOALA ST.

NOBBY'S BEACH

SHELLY BEACH

DETAIL

SEA ACRES
RAINFOREST
CENTRE

MINERS BEACH

JETTY
AL DENTE AND
CRAY'S RESTAURANT

FISHERMEN'S CO-OP

PORT MACQUARIE
HOTEL/MOTEL

MARGO'S
CAFE

SHORT ST.

HORTON ST.

WILLIAM

HAY ST.

SUNDOWNER
BREAKWALL
TOURIST
PARK

EL PASO
MOTOR INN

TOURIST
INFORMATION
CENTRE

MURRAY ST.

MUNSTER ST.

PORT MACQUARIE
CLARENCE
DISTRICT MUSEUM ST.

CHURCH ST.

BEACHSIDE
BACKPACKERS

0   1 km

GORDON

TO
LAKE CATHIE
AND KEW

MOON

World, an oyster farm ($18), and Monday, Wednesday, Fri.-Sun. at 9:30 a.m. for a four-hour trip ($34) farther upstream. Children are half price. **Port Venture,** tel. (02) 6583-3058, also has two-hour cruises up the river. Boats and canoes can be rented from **Hastings River Boat Hire** at Port Marina, tel. (02) 6583-8811.

Accommodations

Port Macquarie Hotel/Motel, Clarence St., tel. (02) 6583-1011, is right downtown and close to the cruise docks. Pub-style rooms, basic and with shared facilities, are $25 s, $35 d. Motel rooms are $50 s, $60 d. Inexpensive.

The motels close to the beach are reasonably priced, but rooms must be booked in advance for all holiday periods. One of the best values and a short walk to the beach is **Beachfront Regency,** 40 William St., tel. (02) 6583-2244, set around a pool and barbecue area. Rooms are $55 s, $67 d. Moderate. **El Paso Motor Inn,** 29 Clarence St., tel. (02) 6583-1944, is right on the waterfront in town. Facilities include a pool, spa, recreation room, and restaurant; rates are $85 s, $95 d. Expensive. The upmarket **Sails Resort** is on Park St., tel. (02) 6583-3999, right on the Hastings River and beside the marina. Each room is well appointed and has a private balcony. Facilities include a large riverfront pool, tennis courts, steam room, spa, and restaurant. Rates for standard rooms are $125, those with kitchenettes $150, and executive rooms with water views are $245 s or d. Premium.

Beachside Backpackers, 40 Church St., tel. (02) 6583-5512, is an associate YHA hostel within easy walking distance of both the town and beach. A variety of activities are organized there, and it's clean and friendly. Dorms are $16 pp. Inexpensive. Housed in a historic home, **Lindel Port Macquarie,** corner Hastings River Dr. and Gordon St., tel. (02) 6583-1791, is away from the beach but has a pool, guests have use of bikes, and drop-offs to the bus depot and beach are made. Dorms are $16, twins $38. Inexpensive.

Sundowner Breakwall Tourist Park stretches along the Hastings River right across from Town Beach. Facilities are excellent, and sites are $17-29, on-site vans $40, and cabins from $45. Budget-Inexpensive. Located at 1 Munster St., tel. (02) 6583-2755.

Food

Along Clarence St. are cafés and restaurants. At the west end is the **Fishermen's Co-op,** where fish is sold straight from the ocean. **Al Dente,** 74 Clarence St., tel. (02) 6584-1422, an Italian restaurant overlooking the river, features pastas from $12.50. In the same building is **Cray's,** tel. (02) 6583-7885, an upmarket seafood restaurant. In the historic Garrison Building, opposite the information center, is **Margo's Restaurant,** tel. (02) 6583-5145. It's open daylight hours. **Flynn's Beach Pasta Place,** opposite the beach of the same name south of downtown, tel. (02) 6581-2679, is open daily from 5 p.m. Most pastas are around $10, and the servings are huge.

Transportation, Services, and Information

Port Macquarie is 20 km east of the Pacific Highway, and although buses make the detour, the closest railway station is at Wauchope. **Eastern Australia,** tel. (13) 1313, and **Impulse,** tel. (13) 1381, have daily flights between Port Macquarie and Sydney, with Impulse continuing north to Brisbane.

Port Macquarie Bus Service, tel. (02) 6583-2161, has a regular service around town. The main car-rental company in town is **Budget,** tel. (02) 6583-5144. For a cab, call **Port Macquarie Taxi Cabs,** tel. (02) 6581-0081.

The **Tourist Information Centre** is on the corner of Clarence and Hay Streets, tel. (02) 6583-1077 or (1800) 02-5935.

PORT MACQUARIE TO COFFS HARBOUR

The most direct route north from Port Macquarie is the Pacific Highway, but an interesting alternative, if you don't mind a rough road, is an unsealed coastal track that ends at Crescent Head. The road begins on the north side of the Hastings River, accessed by a ferry from Settlement Point.

Crescent Head

As the name suggests, this township is on a long sweeping beach. The magnificent beach continues unbroken for many kilometers to the north. When the swell is large, waves bend around the headland becoming near-perfect, often breaking all the way to the beach. The waves are ideal for long-boards, and in the 1950s and '60s surfers on the long haul north would make a customary stop at Crescent Head to check out the waves. The town of 1,200 remains much as it was then, a sleepy holiday hideaway with a well-positioned nine-hole golf course, and a bowling club that comes alive whenever an out-of-town band plays.

Crescent Head Holiday Park, tel. (02) 6566-0261, is definitely *the* place to stay. Cabins with cooking facilities are $50-85 per night, and sites are $13-21 (advance bookings necessary in January). Budget-Inexpensive. **Wombat Beach Resort,** Pacific St., tel. (02) 6566-0121, has well-appointed rooms for $60 s, $65 d, rising to $85 s, $110 d on holidays. Moderate.

Kempsey

Kempsey is a large town of 9,500 on the Pacific Highway, 50 km north of Port Macquarie. The town serves the farming communities of the rich Macleay Valley, but, for tourists, it has little of interest. **Macleay River Museum and Cultural Centre** is at the south end of town. Next door is **Kempsey Tourist Information Centre,** tel. (02) 6563-1555 or (1800) 64-2480.

Hat Head National Park

This 7,220-hectare park stretches along a strip of undeveloped coast northeast of Kempsey. The park is rich with birdlife, which thrives in low coastal scrub, while inland are freshwater lagoons and thick tea tree forests. In the middle of

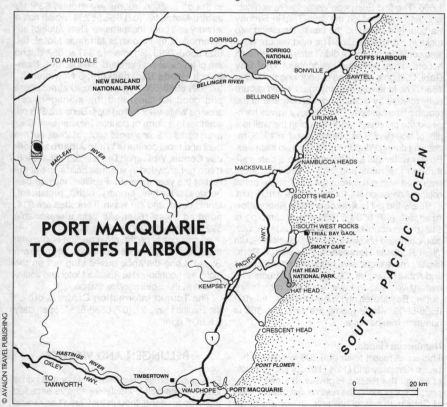

PORT MACQUARIE TO COFFS HARBOUR

© AVALON TRAVEL PUBLISHING

the park is the small community of **Hat Head,** spread along a sandy peninsula, bordered on one side by the sparkling waters of the Pacific Ocean and on the other by the tea tree-stained waters of Korogoro Creek. A hiking trail out to the headland takes in a unique coastal rainforest and sea caves. The town has no motels, but **Hat Head Holiday Park,** tel. (02) 6567-7501, has campsites for $13-21 and cabins for $45-65. Budget-Inexpensive. Within the park, camping is at **Smoky Cape,** in the north end of the national park.

South West Rocks
At the mouth of the Macleay River, overlooking Horseshoe Bay, is this small holiday town of 1,500. The first European visitors were convicts who had mutinied on the ship *Trial* in Sydney Harbour and sailed up the coast, smashing into rocks in Horseshoe Bay. The next visitors were also convicts, but these didn't arrive of their own accord. They were the residents of **Trial Bay Gaol,** built on a headland overlooking the bay in 1880. The idea was that prisoners would secure early release by working on a breakwater at the mouth of the Macleay River. Heavy waves hampered the prisoners' work, reducing the wall to a pile of boulders. The prison closed in 1903, reopening during WW I to house German internees. Prison walls still stand, and visitors can walk through the ruins and visit a small museum crammed with relics from the days of the penal colony. Admission is $4. Open daily 9 a.m.-5 p.m.

Below the jail is **Arakoon State Recreation Area,** tel. (02) 6566-6168, where camping is $12 (prices double during school holidays), with coin-operated showers. Budget. Back in South West Rocks is **Horseshoe Bay Beach Park,** slightly more expensive but with better facilities and right in town, tel. (02) 6566-6370. Budget-Inexpensive. Also in town are three motels, including **Bay Motel,** on Livingstone Ave., tel. (02) 6566-6909, where rooms are $50, and $85 in summer. Inexpensive.

Nambucca Heads
This small resort town of 6,200 is halfway between Kempsey and Coffs Harbour and a couple of km off the Pacific Highway. It's one of the prettier spots along the north coast, and outside of Christmas school holidays, things are pretty quiet. The town is spread along the braided mouth of the **Nambucca River,** which drains into the ocean between the long sweep of Forster Beach and the high bluffs of North Head. Shifting sands made the river mouth difficult to cross for loggers in the 1840s, so a breakwater was constructed along the northern river bank. Today logs are transported by road, and the only vessels using the river are pleasure craft. Fishing for flathead, bream, and whiting is great anywhere along the breakwall, while the main surf beach is at the end of Liston Street. Golfers visiting town can enjoy the unique opportunity of playing a course on an island in the river.

If all you're after is an inexpensive room for the night, the motels out on the highway will suffice. In the off season, rooms are around $35; try **Jabiru Motel,** tel. (02) 6568-6204, which has a laundry and pool. Inexpensive. Best value of accommodations in town is **Miramar Motel,** tel. (02) 6568-7899. Rooms are $47 s, $57 d, and are of an excellent standard. Inexpensive. **Nambucca Heads Backpackers,** 3 Newman St., tel. (02) 6568-6360, has a relaxed atmosphere and good facilities, and the managers can arrange whitewater rafting trips. Beds are $16 pp, whether in a dorm or double. Inexpensive. Caravan parks are strung out south of town, but the best and most central is **White Albatross Holiday Centre,** Wellington Dr., tel. (02) 6568-6468. It can get crowded in summer holidays, but the rest of the year it's quiet. Facilities include barbecues, a kitchen, laundry, bistro, restaurant, tennis court, and car wash. Tent sites are $14, powered sites $16, on-site vans a reasonable $22, and cabins $42-54. Budget.

Nambucca is on the main rail line north, with the station three km west of town, out on Bowra Street. Long-distance buses stop out on the highway; northbound at Aukaka Motel and southbound at the Shell service station.

The **Tourist Information Centre** is out on the Pacific Hwy., tel. (02) 6568-6954; open daily 9 a.m.-5 p.m.

BELLINGEN AND VICINITY

Bellingen, a small town west of Urunga, is home to many alternative-lifestylers who've escaped mainstream living, though they aren't as radical as those farther north. Their arts and crafts, mostly displayed at the **Old Butter Factory,** definitely make a detour worthwhile. Also here is the **Oasis Café,** with a pleasant outdoor dining area—the perfect place to enjoy a Devonshire tea ($5). The town also has a museum open weekdays 2-4 p.m. On the third Saturday of each month the town hosts a large market.

Dorrigo National Park

Well away from the coast, and west of Bellingen, this park of 7,885 hectares encompasses part of the Dorrigo Plateau and an escarpment that drops 900 meters into the Bellinger Valley. The steep-sided valleys off the plateau are covered in a lush subtropical rainforest, thriving in an area receiving 2,500 mm of rainfall annually. Dominant trees are strangler figs with chunky aboveground root systems, towering red cedars, and black booyangs, easily recognizable for their buttresses. Fauna is less diverse, and most species in the park are nocturnal; look for pademelons and gray kangaroos feeding in cleared areas at dusk.

Dorrigo Rainforest Centre, tel. (02) 6657-2309, has impressive displays explaining the various rainforest types. As well, an elevated boardwalk extends from the center above the rainforest canopy. The center is at the park entrance on the Dorrigo-Bellingen Road; open daily 9 a.m.-5 p.m.

The 5.8-km **Wonga Walk,** beginning from the rainforest center, passes waterfalls and a look-out before returning through a forest of towering eucalypts. At the end of the park access road is **Never Never Picnic Area** and more hiking opportunities, including the 6.4-km **Cedar Falls Trail.**

Camping is not allowed in the southern section of the park, although near the end of Slingsbys Rd., northeast of Dorrigo township, bush camping is possible. Between the park entrance and Dorrigo is **Dorrigo Mountain Resort,** tel. (02) 6657-2564, where powered sites are $12.50, and great little log cabins are $44-52. Budget-Inexpensive.

COFFS HARBOUR

Coffs Harbour, 550 km north of Sydney, is a large resort town of 59,000. It sprawls along 10 km of coastline, sandwiched between the Pacific Highway and the Pacific Ocean. The many beaches along this stretch of coast coupled with an ideal year-round climate have led to extensive tourism development, including world-class golf courses and big resorts.

The city was named for John Korff, an early settler, and through time the present spelling has become dominant. Loggers were the area's first permanent settlers, their job made easier in 1892 when a jetty was constructed in front of town. Banana plantations, first developed at the turn of the century, dominate the landscape around Coffs Harbour, and, with the development of the industry, have made Coffs Harbour Australia's major banana-growing area.

the most recognizable feature in Coffs Harbour

Sights

With all the surrounding natural beauty, it's ironic that Coffs Harbour's most recognizable feature is manmade. It's the **Big Banana,** once voted one of the world's 10 grossest tourist attractions, a monument to the area's biggest industry. What was once a convenient photo-session and banana-smoothie stop has grown into a small theme park, with three different tours offered. The basic tour includes a short bus ride to a lookout and a wander through the plantation ($5). The other tours take in a hydroponic glass house ($6.50) or, on the Grand Tour ($10), all of the above as well as a train ride. The complex is three km north of town on the Pacific Hwy., tel. (02) 6652-4355.

Small islands immediately offshore from the city are the breeding grounds of shearwaters (called muttonbirds by hungry settlers). Spring is the main breeding season. The most accessible of the islands is **Muttonbird,** a nature reserve linked to the mainland by a breakwall. Birds remain on the island through April when parents and newly hatched chicks head north for the winter. Also on the island is a platform for watching migrating whales (June and September). North of Muttonbird Island is a string of beautiful beaches; head to **Park Beach** for proximity to the city and north to **Sapphire Beach, Emerald Beach,** and **Korora Bay** to escape the crowds.

On the same side of the city as the Big Banana is **Coffs Harbour Zoo,** tel. (02) 6656-1330,

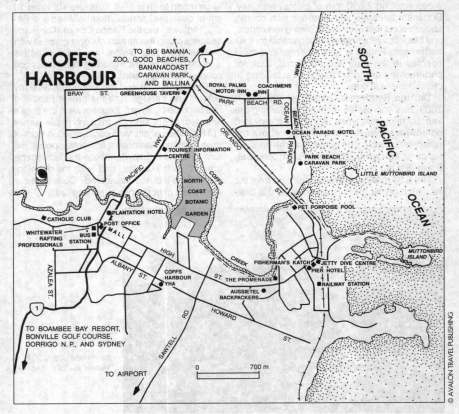

COFFS HARBOUR

TO BIG BANANA, ZOO, GOOD BEACHES, BANANACOAST CARAVAN PARK, AND BALLINA

BRAY ST. GREENHOUSE TAVERN

ROYAL PALMS MOTOR INN COACHMENS INN

PARK BEACH RD. OCEAN

OCEAN PARADE MOTEL

TOURIST INFORMATION CENTRE

PARK BEACH CARAVAN PARK

LITTLE MUTTONBIRD ISLAND

NORTH COAST BOTANIC GARDEN

PACIFIC

PET PORPOISE POOL

CATHOLIC CLUB

PLANTATION HOTEL

POST OFFICE

WHITEWATER RAFTING PROFESSIONALS

BUS STATION

MALL

HIGH

ALBANY ST.

COFFS HARBOUR YHA

CREEK ST. FISHERMAN'S KATCH

JETTY DIVE CENTRE

PIER HOTEL

THE PROMENADE

RAILWAY STATION

AUSSIETEL BACKPACKERS

AZALEA ST.

HOWARD ST.

SAWTELL RD.

TO BOAMBEE BAY RESORT, BONVILLE GOLF COURSE, DORRIGO N.P., AND SYDNEY

MUTTONBIRD ISLAND

SOUTH PACIFIC OCEAN

TO AIRPORT

0   700 m

© AVALON TRAVEL PUBLISHING

a large facility in a native bushland setting. Suited for kids, it features pony rides and animal petting. Admission is adult $12, child $6. Right downtown, at the end of Hardacre St., is **North Coast Botanic Garden.** Bordered on three sides by water, the park is a pleasant place for a quiet walk or picnic lunch. **Pet Porpoise Pool,** Orlando St., tel. (02) 6652-2164, has shows daily at 10:30 a.m. and 2:15 p.m. ($11), with dolphins, seals, and penguins on display.

Solitary Islands

Named by Captain Cook in 1770, the Solitary Islands, northeast of Coffs Harbour, are protected as a marine park. This 75-km-long stretch of uninhabited islands is the largest archipelago off the New South Wales Coast. The islands lie at the confluence of warm tropical currents and cooler southern ones, creating a haven for nearly 300 species of fish as well as turtles, dolphins, and whales—and a paradise for divers. **Jetty Dive Centre,** 398 High St., tel. (02) 6651-1611, organizes dive trips out to the islands, as does **Dive Quest,** tel. (02) 6654-1930, which operates out of Mulloway, farther up the coast. For nondivers, *Spirit of Coffs Harbour,* tel. (02) 6650-0155, makes a three-hour cruise to and among the Solitary Islands Monday, Thursday, and Friday; $30 pp.

Recreation

A profusion of water-based activities are offered down on the harbor; inquire at the **Marina Booking Centre,** tel. (02) 6651-4612, for all the details. Also at the harbor is **Coffs Harbour Parasailing,** tel. (02) 6651-5200, charging $55 for a half hour of parasailing; they also rent jet skis.

Inland is the remote **Nymboida River,** New South Wales's premier whitewater rafting destination. Its rapids challenge all levels of expertise, but all guides are professionals and anyone with a sense of adventure will have the time of their lives. **Whitewater Rafting Professionals,** 20 Moonee St., tel. (02) 6654-4066, operates full-day (12-hour) trips on the river for $135 pp, including transport from Coffs Harbour. This trip passes through the newly created **Nymboi-Binderay National Park,** protecting large areas of old-growth rainforest.

Golfers have the choice of a half dozen courses, with **Bonville International Golf and Country Club,** tel. (02) 6653-4544, the pick of the bunch.

Accommodations

A few years ago, the only choice was one of a dozen caravan parks or about 40 strip motels lining the Pacific Hwy., but today many world-class resorts have been constructed and two excellent backpacker lodges cater to budget travelers.

Pier Hotel, High St., tel. (02) 6652-2110, has large rooms with shared facilities for $18 pp and is close to the harbor and shopping areas. Of the motels out on the highway, many offer advertised rates of $40 d most of the year, doubling in price during school holidays. Other motels are near Park Beach, including **Coachmens Inn,** 93 Park Beach Rd., tel. (02) 6652-6044 or (1800) 35-8133, with a high standard of rooms and a swimming pool and spa; $44 s, $48 d. Inexpensive. In the same area is **Ocean Parade Motel,** 41 Ocean Parade, tel. (02) 6652-6733, right on the beach and only a couple of dollars more. Inexpensive. **Royal Palms Motor Inn,** 87 Park Beach Rd., tel. (02) 6652-4422, has large rooms for $50 s or d. Inexpensive.

The large resorts are north and south of the city. They cater mostly to prebooked holidayers, although good standby rates are offered. **Boambee Bay Resort,** tel. (02) 6653-2700 or (1800) 02-8907, is a 10-minute drive south of Coffs Harbour, but everything you need is here, so the distance from town doesn't really matter. Rooms are huge, and each has a balcony, TV and video, microwave, washing machine, and kitchen. Resort facilities include tennis and squash courts, gym, canoes, snooker rooms, coffee shop, bistro, and restaurant, and the beach is just a short walk away. Rates are $145 s or d. Premium.

Coffs Harbour YHA, 110 Albany St., tel. (02) 6652-6462, is one km from the center of town and has a laundry, game room, and lots of sporting equipment for guest use; staff often arrange day trips to Dorrigo National Park. Dorm beds are $15 pp per night. Budget. **Aussietel Backpackers,** 312 High St., tel. (02) 6651-1871, has similar facilities, as well as a pool, and, although farther from town, is closer to the harbor and beaches. Dorms there are $15 pp, and there are a few doubles for $17 pp. Budget.

Caravan parks line the Pacific Hwy. south and north of town, but the most central is **Park Beach Caravan Park,** Ocean Parade, tel. (02) 6652-3204, right opposite a great swimming and surfing beach. All sites are $12, on-site vans $26, and basic cabins $45. Budget. **Banana-coast Caravan Park,** four km north on the Pacific Hwy., tel. (02) 6652-2868, has a pool and tennis court; sites are $12-16, cabins start at $32. Budget-Inexpensive.

Food and Entertainment
Banana smoothies at the Big Banana are delicious, but mankind can not live on milk shakes alone, so for something more substantial, you'll need to head into town. Along the mall at the top end of High St. are casual eateries, including the **Short Black Coffee Shop** (Monterey Arcade), which serves healthy lunches daily and often has live music Thursday and Friday. Toward the harbor and linked by hiking trails to the botanic garden and Muttonbird Island is the **Promenade,** a creekfront development of shops and cafés.

Most of the seafood garnered from the ocean around Coffs Harbour finishes up in Sydney, but there are still a number of good seafood joints. The **Fisherman's Katch,** 394 High St., tel. (02) 6652-4372, is both a takeaway and restaurant. An order of fish and chips is $5 takeaway, while the restaurant boasts a wide variety of seafood with main dishes ranging $13.50-24. At this end of town are restaurants serving cuisine from France, China, and Thailand.

Each of the resorts has bars open to nonguests, but you should check dress regulations before charging in with thongs and boardshorts on. **Greenhouse Tavern,** corner Pacific Hwy. and Bray St., tel. (02) 6651-5488, is a casual place with three eateries and three bars, including one with a maritime theme, complete with a 12-meter yacht above the bar. Bands often play there weekends. Other places for live music are **Park Beach Hotel,** Ocean Parade, tel. (02) 6652-3833, and **Plantation Hotel,** Grafton St., tel. (02) 6652-3855.

Transportation, Services, and Information
The airport is south of town on Hogbin Dr., a $7 cab ride from the town center. It is served by **Ansett Australia,** tel. (13) 1300, and **Impulse,** tel. (13) 1381, with regular services between major north coast centers and Sydney. Often no more expensive than the airfare, packages offered by Ansett start at $285 pp, including airfare from Sydney and three nights' accommodation.

Countrylink, tel. (13) 2232, runs the **XPT** between Sydney and Coffs Harbour daily. As with the airlines, packages are the way to go: roundtrip fare and two nights' accommodation start at $159 pp. In Coffs Harbour, the railway station is at the end of High St. (six blocks from Aussietel Backpackers).

All long-distance buses stop at Coffs Harbour. The main bus stop is on Moonee Street.

The **Tourist Information Centre** is north of downtown and just off the Pacific Hwy. on Marcia St., tel. (02) 6652-1522 or (1800) 02-5650; open daily 9 a.m.-5 p.m.

COFFS HARBOUR TO BALLINA

The first town north of Coffs Harbour is **Woolgoolga,** nestled around the southern corner of a sweeping beach, with the Solitary Islands clearly visible a few kilometers offshore. This holiday town of 2,000 has a high population of East Indians, and the unmistakable onion-shaped dome of Guru Nanak Sikh Temple dominates the turnoff to town.

Immediately north are the quiet coastal villages of **Mulloway** and **Arrawarra,** perfect places to laze on the beach for a few days. **Arrawarra Beach Holiday Park,** tel. (02) 6649-2753, has unpowered sites for $10-17, powered sites for $13-21, and basic cabins for $39-75; it's within walking distance of the beach and a small general store serving delicious fish and chips. Farther north, before the Pacific Highway heads inland to Grafton, is **Red Rock,** named for an abundance of jasper around a headland at the mouth of Corindi River.

Yuraygir National Park
From Red Rock, the Pacific Highway heads inland to Grafton, with the next main coastal access at Yamba, more than 100 km to the north. The long stretch of undeveloped coastline in between is protected by Yuraygir National Park, broken by a few small holiday towns that provide basic services for holidaymakers and park visitors. The

COFFS HARBOUR TO BALLINA

© AVALON TRAVEL PUBLISHING

park currently encompasses 23,119 hectares of beaches, headlands, coastal heath, impenetrable forests of tea tree, and many areas of wetland, with plans to link the three existing sections. Birds such as emus, brolgas, storks, and lorikeets are present, as are gray kangaroos.

Access to the park's central section is along Wooli Rd., which branches off the Pacific Highway 32 km north of Red Rock and 14 km south of Grafton. Picnic and camping areas are available at Minnie Water. For details of the park's northern section, see "Yamba and Vicinity," below.

Grafton

Nestled in the Clarence Valley 85 km north of Coffs Harbour, this proud country town of 22,000 is dominated by streets lined with jacaranda trees. The mighty Clarence River makes a wide loop around town before emptying into the Pacific Ocean at Yamba, to the northeast. Many stately buildings stand around town in testimony to the wealth created by farming through the city's 140-year history. The jail and cathedral are both National Trust-classified and **Schaeffer House,** at 192 Fitzroy St., tel. (02) 6642-5212, is open for inspection Tues.-Sun. 10 a.m.-4 p.m. **Grafton Regional Art Gallery,** 158 Fitzroy St., tel. (02) 6642-3177, is in 1880 Prentice House. Each Spring, the jacarandas come alive with color, an annual event celebrated during the October **Jacaranda Festival.**

One of the least expensive places to stay is **Crown Hotel/Motel,** Prince St., tel. (02) 6642-4000, where rooms are $24 s, $32 d; $30 s, $38 d with private bathrooms. Inexpensive. Back out on the highway are a couple of inexpensive motels.

Also on the Pacific Highway side of the river is **Clarence River Tourist Centre,** tel. (02) 6642-4677; open daily 9 a.m.-5 p.m.

Yamba and Vicinity

Located 14 km east of the Pacific Highway, this resort and fishing town may lack the hype of Coffs Harbour, but its picturesque setting makes it a worthwhile detour. The town is at the mouth of the Clarence River, one of New South Wales's largest waterways. While commercial fishers use the river only as shelter for their boats, it's a prime fishing spot for amateurs, who pull out flathead, flounder, and bream. Just $10 spent at a fishing store, along with some local advice, ensures a good day's fishing. For an extra $20-35 per hour, boats can be rented from **BP Bait Place** on Yamba Road. Town beaches are partly protected by Yamba Point, especially Yamba Beach, which has a grassy picnic area overlooking it and a rock pool for safe swimming. In the river mouth is **Hickey Island,** which has a stretch of sandy beach.

A few kilometers south of Yamba is **Angourie** and the northern section of Yuraygir National Park. At the very end of the road into Angourie Township is a parking lot overlooking **Angourie Point,** a legendary surf spot that has been drawing surfers with its steep long waves for more than 30 years. As the road first enters town, a road forks left to **Blue** and **Green Pools.** Originally quarries for a breakwall at the mouth of the Clarence River, they have long since filled with water, creating safe swimming areas. Blue Pool is the larger of the two and has a natural platform for diving. South of Angourie is Yuraygir National Park (turn off one km before Angourie, then take the first left). The stretch of beach there is beautiful and generally uncrowded. A

10-km one-way trail traverses a spectacular section of coastline, taking in coastal heathland, deserted beaches, and rocky headlands, with backcountry camping allowed at three spots en route.

Pacific Hotel, on the best chunk of real estate in town, is on a high bluff overlooking Yamba Beach. Rooms are $24 s, $32 d. It's at 18 Pilot St., tel. (02) 6646-2466. Inexpensive. **Surf Motel,** 2 Queen St., tel. (02) 6646-2200, is also good value at $40 s, $45 d, although prices double during school holidays. Inexpensive. **Moby Dick Waterfront Resort,** 27 Yamba Rd., tel. (02) 6646-2196, is a two-story motel with an absolute riverfront location. Each room has a balcony, while guest facilities include a private jetty, pool, and tennis court; $80-120 s or d. Moderate. **Easts Calypso Holiday Park,** Harbour St., tel. (02) 6646-2468, is right in town and on the river. Sites are $12-15 and cabins $35-75. Budget-Inexpensive.

Iluka

Iluka, over the Clarence River from Yamba, is a small fishing town. An interesting way to travel between the two is on a ferry departing River St., Yamba, four times daily; $3 pp; call (02) 6646-6423 for times. Of special interest in Iluka (apart from a great pub overlooking the river) is the largest chunk of littoral rainforest in New South Wales. It's protected by Iluka Nature Reserve, which extends between town and Iluka Beach. **World Heritage Rainforest Walk** traverses a large section of it before ending at a rocky headland.

Bundjalung National Park

This 17,896-hectare park, extending between Iluka and Evans Head, features 38 km of unspoilt beach backed by coastal heathland and a dune system containing ancient Aboriginal campsites. The road into Iluka skirts the park's southern boundary and passes **Woody Head camping area,** where sites are spread out around a headland flanked by beaches. Facilities at the campground include a kiosk and hot showers; $13 per site. For reservations, call (02) 6646-6143.

The main park access is farther north and is signposted from the Pacific Highway south of Woodburn. This road ends at **Black Rocks,** where outcrops of black rock rise from the beach.

Evans Head

Like so many small townships along this coast, fishing and tourism provide a thriving economy for Evans Head. Surfing on the tame beach breaks is popular with tourists, as is fishing in the Evans River. Of special significance to the local Koori is **Goanna Headland,** on the south side of the river. Legend has it that this is where their race first settled in Australia. Farther in-

land, at the end of Bundjalung Rd., a footbridge leads over the waters of Oyster Creek to an ancient Koori campsite with shell middens. Also at Oyster Creek is a kurrajong tree, of special significance to historians because this species is otherwise only found at high elevations of the Great Dividing Range, so it is thought local Koori accidently brought back the seed during a trip inland.

FAR NORTH COAST

Mother Nature has managed to cram some of the country's most spectacular and diverse scenery into a 100-km stretch of coastline in the far north of New South Wales. The southern gateway to the far north coast is Ballina, a popular seaside holiday destination. Immediately north is Byron Bay, where the cultural clash of mainstream dropouts, sunburnt tourists, and the wealthy creates a colorful atmosphere found nowhere else in the country. From Byron Bay to the border, the coast is dotted with small holiday villages, starkly different from the development of the Gold Coast immediately north of the border. Extending 80 km inland from the coast is the hinterland, a region of lush subtropical and temperate rainforests dominated by Mt. Warning, the magma vent of an enormous volcano that erupted more than 20 million years ago.

BALLINA

This coastal city of 17,500 is concentrated on a low island at the mouth of the Richmond River. The island is almost entirely developed, but immediately north is a stretch of beautiful beaches rivaling any in the country.

A long breakwall was constructed at the mouth of the river in the 1880s, stabilizing its mouth, and allowing clear transit for shipping. Unintentionally, the wall created a protected swimming beach at **Shaws Bay** and a consistent surf break at **Lighthouse Beach.** The former outlet, under Ballina Head, is now a low-lying area where a deep tidal lagoon provides shark-free swimming and a pleasant shaded area with picnic tables.

Sights
Behind the Tourist Information Centre is **Ballina Naval and Maritime Museum,** tel. (02) 6681-1002, featuring *La Balsa,* a small raft that made an epic journey from Ecuador to Ballina; open daily 9 a.m.-4 p.m. Admission by donation.

North of Ballina is a commercial attraction worth visiting. **Thursday Plantation,** four km north, was the world's first tea-tree farm. Tea-tree oil was used by the Koori for its medicinal

properties and is now a popular remedy for head colds, blocked sinus, ulcers, cuts, and even arthritis. An audiovisual explains the farming process, and tours of the farm and nursery are offered. Open daily 9 a.m.-5 p.m., tel. (02) 6686-7273.

Recreation
Ballina Quays Marina, west of Ballina near the Big Prawn, is the departure point for *River Princess* and *Richmond Princess,* which regularly cruise the Richmond River; call (02) 6686-3484 for details. Also at the marina are rental boats. Rates start at $65 per day for a small runabout and $170 for a large riverboat; for bookings, call (02) 6686-4289.

Bream and flathead are easily caught in the Richmond River (a favorite fishing spot is along North Creek between Worm's Old Place and Cherry St.), and North Wall is a good spot for deepwater fishing.

Ballina Golf Course, Jameson Ave., tel. (02) 6686-2766, is open to the public during the week but is generally busy; $18 for 18 holes. **Royal Teven Golf Course** isn't really "royal," but that's the way it's known; greens fees $14. Located at Teven, west of Ballina, tel. (02) 6687-8386.

Accommodations
Central to downtown is **Ballina Heritage Inn,** 229 River St., tel. (02) 6686-0505. This place opened in 1993, so there isn't anything historic about it. Rooms are large and elegantly furnished, some with spas. Other facilities include a laundry and pool; from $63 s, $68 d. Moderate. Off the main road and just 200 meters from Lighthouse Beach is **Ballina Beach Resort,** Compton Dr., tel. (02) 6686-8888, which has a swimming pool, tennis court, restaurant, and bar. Rates are at $99 s or d, rising to $149 during school holidays. Expensive. Less expensive is the **Australian Hotel,** 103 River St., tel. (02) 6686-2015, with pub-style rooms of a decent standard for $35 s, $40 d. Inexpensive. Cheap motels are along the Pacific Hwy. west of downtown. **Ballina Motel,** tel. (02) 6686-2208, is the least expensive of these, with basic rooms for $40 s or d. Inexpensive. **Ballina Centrepoint Motel,** 285

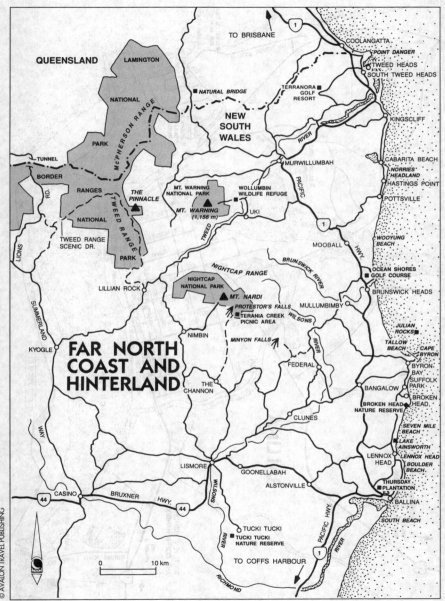

QUEENSLAND

LAMINGTON

NATIONAL

PARK

McPHERSON RANGE

TUNNEL
BORDER
RANGES
NATIONAL
PARK

RD.

TWEED RANGE

THE PINNACLE

TWEED RANGE SCENIC DR.

LIONS RD.

SUMMERLAND WAY

KYOGLE

WAY

CASINO

44

■ NATURAL BRIDGE

MT. WARNING NATIONAL PARK

MT. WARNING (1,156 m)

WOLLUMBIN WILDLIFE REFUGE

UKI

NEW SOUTH WALES

TERRANORA GOLF RESORT

RIVER

MURWILLUMBAH

TWEED RIVER

PACIFIC HWY

NIGHTCAP RANGE

NIGHTCAP NATIONAL PARK

MT. NARDI
PROTESTOR'S FALLS
■ TERANIA CREEK PICNIC AREA

MINYON FALLS

LILLIAN ROCK

NIMBIN

THE CHANNON

BRUNSWICK RIVER

WILSONS

WILSONS RIVER

MOOBALL

MULLUMBIMBY

FEDERAL

CLUNES

BANGALOW

FAR NORTH COAST AND HINTERLAND

LISMORE

GOONELLABAH

ALSTONVILLE

BRUXNER HWY

44

WILSONS RIVER

TUCKI TUCKI
■ TUCKI TUCKI NATURE RESERVE

TO COFFS HARBOUR

RICHMOND

TO BRISBANE

1

COOLANGATTA
POINT DANGER
TWEED HEADS
SOUTH TWEED HEADS

KINGSCLIFF

CABARITA BEACH
NORRIES HEADLAND
HASTINGS POINT
POTTSVILLE

1

WOOYUNG BEACH

OCEAN SHORES GOLF COURSE
BRUNSWICK HEADS

JULIAN ROCKS ■
TALLOW BEACH
CAPE BYRON
BYRON BAY
SUFFOLK PARK
BROKEN HEAD
BROKEN HEAD NATURE RESERVE

SEVEN MILE BEACH
LAKE AINSWORTH
LENNOX HEAD
BOULDER BEACH
LENNOX HEAD

THURSDAY PLANTATION
BALLINA
SOUTH BEACH

PACIFIC HWY

RIVER

1

0   10 km

MOON

© AVALON TRAVEL PUBLISHING

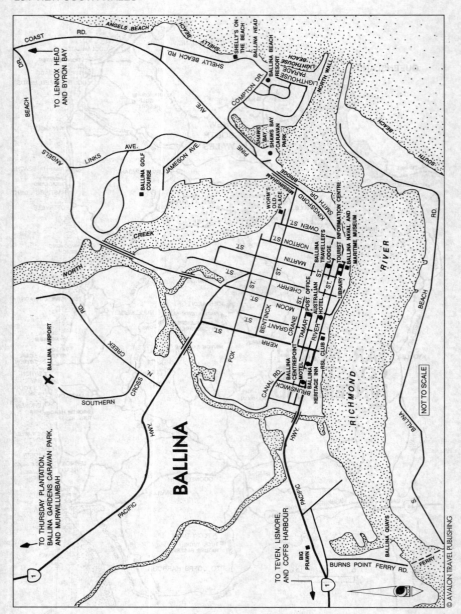

BALLINA

© AVALON TRAVEL PUBLISHING

River St., tel. (02) 6686-6877, is right downtown and has rooms from $40 s, $45 d. Inexpensive.

Ballina Traveller's Lodge, 36 Tamar St., tel. (02) 6686-6737, is a modern YHA hostel two blocks from downtown. All facilities are of a high standard, and guests have the free use of bikes. Dorm beds are $16 pp. Inexpensive.

Shaws Bay Caravan Park, by Missingham Bridge, has tent sites for $12 and basic cabins for $28-45, tel. (02) 6686-2326. Budget. Farther out, on the Pacific Hwy. north of town, is **Ballina Gardens Caravan Park,** tel. (02) 6686-2475. Although not suited to tents, facilities are excellent. Sites are $13.50 and cabins start at $28. Budget.

Food
Without a doubt, the best place for a casual meal is **Shelly's on the Beach.** Tables are indoors and out, and overlook Ballina Head and Shelly Beach; open daily 7:30 a.m.-3:30 p.m. **Ballina RSL Club,** River St., tel. (02) 6686-2544, has both an inexpensive bistro and the more formal **Spinnakers,** a seafood restaurant open daily 6-10 p.m. Lunch in the bistro is inexpensive, and Friday noon-2 p.m. fish and chips and dessert is just $3.

Transportation, Services, and Information
Ballina has no official bus depot, but all major bus lines stop at the Big Prawn, west of downtown. **Blanch's,** tel. (02) 6686-2144, serves Lennox Head and Byron Bay. **Ballina Motel,** tel. (02) 6686-2208, has rental cars from $48 per day.

The **post office** is at 85 Tamar Street. **Ballina Public Library,** beside the Tourist Information Centre, is open Mon.-Fri. 10 a.m.-5 p.m., Saturday 9 a.m.-noon. **Ballina Tourist Information Centre** is a modern facility located at the east end of River St. on the corner of Norton St., tel. (02) 6686-3484; open daily 9 a.m.-5 p.m.

North to Lennox Head
The most interesting route north from Ballina is along a coastal road through the picturesque village of Lennox Head, which overlooks a long grassy headland of the same name. The ceaseless motion of the ocean has pulled sand from the town's main beach, exposing long reefs of black rock. **Seven Mile Beach** extends north from Lennox Head and is backed by **Lake Ainsworth,** a freshwater lagoon.

The town has a couple of motels, but **Lennox Head Beach House,** 3 Ross St., tel. (02) 6687-7636, a purpose-built hostel, is the least expensive place to stay. Bikes, boats, and surfboards are available free for guest use, and Lake Ainsworth is a short walk away. Dorm beds are $16, and the double room is $36. Inexpensive.

The bakery on Ballina St. has great meat pies and pastries, and **Lennox Head Hotel** has live music on weekends.

North of Lennox Head is **Broken Head Nature Reserve,** an area of subtropical rainforest extending right to the ocean. At the north end of the reserve is a hiking trail leading along a cliff and descending to King's Beach.

BYRON BAY

A north coast sojourn wouldn't be complete without a stop at Byron Bay, 800 km north of Sydney and 100 km south of the Queensland border. "Byron," as it's best known, sprawls along a spectacular stretch of coastline dominated by **Cape Byron,** the easternmost point of mainland Australia. It's difficult to pinpoint exactly what makes the place so popular; originally it was the surf and setting, which is picture-postcard perfect—long sandy beaches flanked by a hinterland of rainforest. Today the town is a unique blend of lifestyles, with drifters and dreamers mixing with celebrities and overseas tourists, and one of Australia's most expensive suburbs a stone's throw from fibro houses full of surf bums.

Byron wasn't seen as anything more than a working-class seaside village until the 1960s, when rapid development hit the Gold Coast to the north and jaded Queenslanders escaped by migrating south. This coupled with an influx of hippies during Nimbin's 1973 Aquarius Festival began a counterculture that continues to this day. Things remained relatively low-key until the mid-1980s, when developers began investing in the town, a trend that has continued into the 1990s. Today the population stands at 5,400.

Cape Byron
The **lighthouse** on Cape Byron has been a landmark since its construction in 1901. A road leads right to the cape but **Cape Byron Walking Track** is a more interesting option. This trail begins at

Captain Cook Lookout and follows the shoreline to The Pass and Wategos Beach before it climbs steeply to the lighthouse. Although the lighthouse compound is locked at dawn (open daily 8 a.m.-5:30 p.m.), the headland commands fantastic views of the sun rising over the Pacific Ocean. The cape is also a good vantage point for whalewatching.

Beaches

Main Beach extends along the front of downtown and is a safe swimming area. To the northwest is **Belongil Beach** and a favorite surfbreak known as **The Wreck,** named for the *Wollongbar,* which is partly visible beyond the breaking

waves. East of Main Beach is **Clarks Beach,** where the sandy headland **The Pass** is a popular surf spot. Behind The Pass is **Wategos Beach,** one of the few beaches on Australia's east coast that faces north. South of the cape is **Tallow Beach,** accessible along a gravel track off Lighthouse Road. This stretch of beach is open to the fury of the ocean, and seas can be rough. Farther south is a long stretch of beaches, including **Suffolk Park.**

Recreation

Julian Rocks, three km off Cape Byron, is a popular diving spot. The area around the rocks has been declared a marine reserve, protecting a

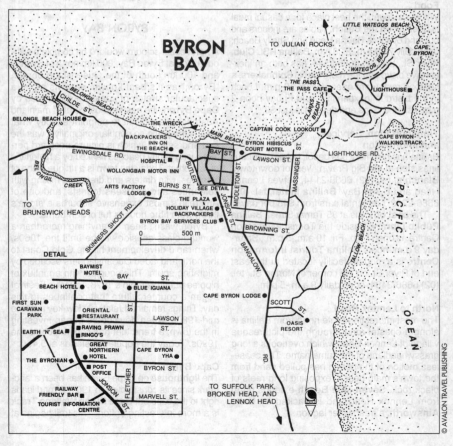

Cape Byron

Not all recreation need cost a fortune; spend your time swimming, surfing, snorkeling, sunbaking, and fishing, or, for the price of a beer at the Beach Hotel or a coffee at Ringo's, watch the world of Byron Bay go round.

Entertainment

Beach Hotel, corner Bay and Jonson Streets, tel. (02) 6685-6402, is definitely *the* place for a drink. In summer patrons spill out of the hotel onto the lawn overlooking Main Beach. **Railway Friendly Bar,** at the railway station, tel. (02) 6685-7662, has live music most evenings, but things generally wrap up early. The **Carpark,** in the parking lot of The Plaza, Jonson St., tel. (02) 6685-6170, is Byron's most popular nightclub, with the atmosphere of a big-city dance venue.

Hotels and Motels

The **Great Northern Hotel,** Jonson St., tel. (02) 6685-6454, has rooms for $55 s or d. Inexpensive. **Byron Hibiscus Motel,** 33 Lawson St., tel. (02) 6685-6195, is the least expensive of the motels close to downtown. Rooms are $69 d, rising to more than $100 during school holidays. Moderate. **Baymist Motel,** 12 Bay St., tel. (02) 6685-6121, is also central; $89 s, $99 d. Expensive. Farther out, **Wollongbar Motor Inn,** 19 Shirley St., tel. (02) 6685-8200, has a pool, barbecue, and rooms with basic cooking facilities; from $65 s, $70 d. Moderate. Since the last edition of this handbook, the **Beach Hotel,** Bay St., tel. (02) 6685-6402, has added Byron's most luxurious accommodations to the town's most popular drinking spot. Very separate from the pub, the rooms share the same fantastic location across from the beach. They are set around a beautifully landscaped pool, and each features a private balcony. Rates range $165-240 s or d. Luxury.

The Oasis Resort

South of town is The Oasis, 24 Scott St., tel. (02) 6685-7390. It offers accommodations in fully self-contained two-bedroom apartments, with a massive pool, tennis courts, three-story game room, gym, spa and masseuse, and outdoor barbecue area. Rates for apartments range $525-609 per week, rising to $1295 during summer school holidays; the nightly rate is $105-115. Expensive.

vast number of marine species. **Byron Bay Dive Centre,** 111 Lawson St., tel. (02) 6685-7149, has been established the longest of the five dive operators in town; two boat dives, including equipment rental, runs about $95 pp. **Cape Byron Marine Charter,** tel. (02) 6685-6858, and **Byron Boat Charter,** tel. (02) 6685-5474, offer daylong fishing trips starting at $100 pp.

Byron Bay is the perfect place to learn to surf, and **Swell Surf Co.,** tel. (02) 6685-5352, will help you do just that. They offer a variety of lessons, including a 90-minute group lesson for $12 pp and private lessons for $30 per hour. **Byron Surf School,** tel. (02) 6685-7536, also offers lessons and rents boards from $20 per day.

Hang gliders can often be seen soaring around the cape, and the recent introduction of **tandem hang gliding** has made this adventure sport more accessible; for details, call **Flight Zone,** tel. (02) 6685-8768. Instruction is included and rates start at $70 per half hour. For the less adventurous, kites can be hired at **Byron Kites,** on Byron St., tel. (02) 6685-5299.

Magnificent cedar **Treetop Houses** are part of the same resort. Each gives you ocean views and three stories of casual luxury, including two bedrooms, two bathrooms, a private pool on the deck, large lounge area with television and VCR, and full kitchen. The minimum stay is seven nights; $980-1099 per unit, rising to $2,415 during summer school holidays. Premium.

Backpacker Lodges

Byron Bay has an excellent selection of backpacker accommodations, many as good or better than motels twice their price. All hostels are busy year-round and bookings are essential in summer. **Cape Byron YHA** is a new place just 150 meters from Jonson St.; excellent facilities include a large modern kitchen area, lounge, outdoor deck, barbecue, laundry, shops, heated pool, Internet access, and bikes and surfboards for rent. Dorms are $18 pp and double rooms $48-60. Inexpensive. Located at the corner of Middleton and Byron Streets, tel. (02) 6685-8788. Also associated with the YHA is **Cape Byron Lodge**, 78 Bangalow Rd., tel. (02) 6685-6445, two km south of town toward Suffolk Park and a short walk to Tallow Beach; dorm beds $15-18, doubles $40. Budget.

Holiday Village Backpackers, 116 Jonson St., tel. (02) 6685-8888, is, in our opinion, the pick of the bunch. Facilities are of the highest standard, rooms are large and brightly decorated, and bikes, surfboards, and boogie boards are available for guest use. Rates are $17 pp, $38-45 d. Inexpensive. **Backpackers Inn on the Beach** is close to both the beach and downtown and has all the facilities of the above hostels. Rates are $18 in dorms and $45 d. Located at 29 Shirley St., tel. (02) 6685-8231. Inexpensive.

Belongil Beach House, Childe St., tel. (02) 6685-7868, is a relaxed place a couple of km west of town and just across the road from Belongil Beach. All facilities are of a high standard, and the café (open daily 8 a.m.-10 p.m.) serves healthy food at excellent prices. Rates are $17 in dorms, $38 s, $45 d, and rise a few dollars during school holidays. Inexpensive.

Arts Factory Lodge is farthest from the beach, but the atmosphere is laid-back and guests have free use of bicycles to get into town. Dorms are $16; you can camp for $10 pp, or stay in a tepee or covered wagon for $30-50 s or d. Budget-Inexpensive. The newest hostel-style accommodation is offered by **Blue Iguana**, right opposite Main Beach at 14 Bay St., tel. (02) 6685-5298. This is the smallest hostel, but facilities are adequate and views from the deck are nothing short of spectacular. Rates start at $18 pp in a four-share dorm, $60 d. Inexpensive.

Campgrounds

First Sun Caravan Park, Lawson St., tel. (02) 6685-6544, is in a prime location on Main Beach right downtown, with some unpowered sites on the absolute beachfront. Sites are $10-25 and small cabins are $44-86. Budget-Inexpensive. Facilities at **Cape Byron Van Village** are of a higher standard, but this place is farther out—located 2.4 km northwest of town on Ewingsdale Rd., tel. (02) 6685-7378—and more suited to vans. Sites range $12-30, cabins $40-70. Budget-Inexpensive. **Suffolk Park Caravan Park**, six km south of Byron, tel. (02) 6685-3353, is in a great spot surrounded by Broken Head Nature Reserve and fronting a long sandy beach; sites are $12-18, cabins $38-75. Budget-Inexpensive.

Food

Byron has a huge choice of cafés and restaurants; some have been around for years and have become landmarks while others seem to come and go with the seasons. **Ringo's**, 29 Jonson St., is a cavernous place with poster-covered walls and an eclectic crowd. Open daily 8:30 a.m.-9 p.m. **The Byronian**, 58 Jonson St., tel. (02) 6685-6754, is another casual place, with tables indoor and out. One of Byron's most relaxing and enjoyable places for a meal is **The Pass Cafe**, Brooke Dr., tel. (02) 6685-6074, off Lighthouse Rd. and an easy half-hour walk from town along Main and Clarks Beaches. Breakfast is served in summer only and ranges $5-10, while lunch and dinner feature European cuisine and seafood. Back in town, the Great Northern and Beach Hotels serve counter meals, while the bistro in **Byron Bay Services Club**, Jonson St., tel. (02) 6685-6878, has a daily $3.50 lunch special (probably the best dining deal in town); open noon-2 p.m. for lunch and 6:30-9 p.m. for dinner, with other specials Tues.-Thursday.

The **Raving Prawn** is a casual seafood restaurant in Feros Arcade on Jonson St., tel. (02) 6685-6737. Most main dishes are about $15, with appetizers and desserts $5-8; open Tues.-Sat. from 6 p.m. For the best pizza in town head to **Earth 'N' Sea,** Jonson St., tel. (02) 6685-5011, with indoor/outdoor dining and large pizzas from $15. **The Orient,** 3 Lawson St., tel. (02) 6685-7771, is a second-floor restaurant, with tables inside and out on the balcony of what was originally a hotel. The food is renowned (especially the oysters), with a menu featuring Asian and Australian dishes priced from $18 for a dinner main. Open daily for lunch and dinner.

Transportation, Services, and Information

Byron Bay is on the Sydney-Murwillumbah rail line. An XPT service departs Sydney daily at 7:05 a.m., arriving in Byron at 7:30 p.m. Byron is also a stopping point for all the major bus companies. The departure point is the Tourist Information Centre on Jonson Street. Additionally, **Kirklands,** tel. (02) 6622-1499, runs from Byron Bay to Lismore and north to Brisbane via Surfers Paradise.

Cheap rental cars are available from **Earth Car Rental,** where rates start at $35 per day with 200 free km; book through any hostel or call (066) 85-7472. All hostels have bikes for guest use, or hire them from **Byron Bay Bicycles,** The Plaza, Jonson St., tel. (02) 6685-6315, for $10-15 per day.

The **post office** is at 61 Jonson Street. **Global Gossip,** 84 Jonson St., tel. (02) 6680-9140, has public Internet access and inexpensive long-distance phone calls. **Byron District Hospital** is on Shirley St., tel. (02) 6685-6200.

The **Tourist Information Centre** is at 80 Jonson St., beside the railway station, tel. (02) 6685-8050; open daily 10 a.m.-4 p.m.

BYRON TO THE BORDER

Brunswick Heads and the Tweed Coast

Colorful fishing boats at the mouth of the Brunswick River mark this small seaside town, a popular tourist stop 40 km north of Byron Bay. Immediately north is the sprawling residential estate of **Ocean Shores,** which has a challenging 18-hole resort-style golf course. Greens fees are $20; call (066) 80-1247 for tee times.

A few kilometers north of Brunswick Heads, the Pacific Highway heads inland. The coastal route (turn off north of Brunswick Heads on Wooyung Road) is more picturesque, passing numerous holiday towns and long sandy beaches. **Pottsville** and **Hastings Point** are low-key towns with good beaches, fishing, and a choice of accommodations. Heading north, the next township is **Cabarita Beach,** overlooking a rocky headland and a popular surf break. It was known as "Bogangar" until a developer decided he could sell more land by changing the town's name.

North of Cabarita Beach the road traverses a narrow strip of scrub-covered dunes, crossing Cudgen Creek at the resort town of **Kingscliff,** with an atmosphere so relaxed it is hard to believe the Gold Coast is a half hour's drive north. **Kingscliff Motel,** 80 Marine Parade, tel. (02) 6674-1780, opposite the beach, has rooms for $40 s, $45 d, rising to $90 s, $95 d in January. Inexpensive. Along a narrow strip between the main road through town and the beach is **Kingscliff Beach Caravan Park,** tel. (02) 6674-1311, where sites are $11-21 and cabins are $55-110. Budget-Inexpensive. The best place in town for inexpensive food and beer is **Kingscliff Bowls Club,** right on the beach, tel. (02) 6674-1404.

Tweed Heads

Although the towns of Tweed Heads and Coolangatta merge to become one long residential strip, they are markedly different, courtesy of development restrictions on the New South Wales side of the border. Tweed Heads extends along the west bank of the Tweed River, much of it on reclaimed mangrove swamps. The state border hits the coast at **Point Danger,** a high bluff overlooking **Duranbah,** Tweed Heads's only beach, and where views extend north to Surfers Paradise. The point's dominant feature is an 18-meter-high monument to Captain Cook. At the monument's base is a replica of the capstan from the *Endeavour,* Cook's ship.

At South Tweed Heads is **Minjungbal Aboriginal Cultural Centre,** tel. (02) 5524-2109, located in an area of historic importance to the Koori. The area provided ample food for generations of their people, and a sacred ceremonial site within the grounds remains. From the center, a two-km trail leads through native bushland and to a boardwalk out on a mangrove swamp; open daily 10 a.m.-4 p.m. Admission is adult $8, child $4. Located at the end of Kirkwood Rd., off the Pacific Hwy. beside Tweed City Shopping Mall.

Tweed Heads has a few motels, but those in Coolangatta are much cheaper. On the other hand, campers are well catered to at **Border Caravan Park,** Boundary St., tel. (07) 5536-3134, which overlooks the Tweed River and is just two blocks from Coolangatta Beach. Sites are $15-19 and on-site vans $28-40.

The licensed clubs are a haven for budget-conscious diners, with each offering a variety of good deals. For example: **South Tweed Bowls Club,** Pacific Hwy., tel. (07) 5524-3655, has $2.50 lunches daily, and roast dinners are offered Sun.-Tues. for just $6.90; **Terranora Golf Resort,** Marana St., tel. (07) 5590-9242, offers $3 lunches and two-course dinners for $7.50 in the bistro. The club has a restaurant and Thurs.-Fri. $12.50 three-course meals are offered, and at Sunday lunch and dinner a $10 buffet is laid out. Both the above clubs have a courtesy bus from Gold Coast hotels.

The **Tourist Information Centre,** tel. (07) 5536-4244, is on the east side of the Pacific Hwy. in the middle of Tweed Heads and is open Mon.-Fri. 9 a.m.-5 p.m., Sat.-Sun. 9 a.m.-3:30 p.m.

HINTERLAND

The far north coast hinterland, extending from Lismore to the Queensland border and about 70 km west from the coast, is an area of unrivaled beauty, of lush subtropical forests and picturesque towns with high populations of those who have attempted to escape the boundaries of modern life. It all began with the 1973 Aquarius Festival at Nimbin, and while many of the original hippies still live in the area's many communes, they have been joined by many others, including people who like to be known as ferals—wanderers who make the remaining hippies look conservative, completely rejecting the outside world, moving around the hinterland worshipping the earth (and one plant in particular) in an almost primitive existence.

Colorful festivals such as the Growers Cup, Mardi Grass, and Pope of Dope, which take place throughout the year, are a highlight of life in the hinterland.

The Land
The dominant feature of the hinterland is **Mt. Warning,** the central magma vent of volcanic action 20 million years ago. The area was a shield volcano, twice as high as Mt. Warning and covering an area of 5,000 square km. Since the volcanic action ceased, wind and rain erosion have carved out an enormous caldera, with Mt. Warning rising to 1,156 meters in the center. This enormous basin is bordered by the **Nightcap Range** to the south and the **Tweed** and **McPherson Ranges** to the west, forming escarpments bordering high country beyond.

Lismore
Self-proclaimed capital of the far north, Lismore (pop. 32,000) is 35 km west of Ballina on the southern slopes of the caldera. Much of the town is subject to the flooding of the Wilsons River, and many houses are raised to counteract this annual cycle. Down on the river the excellent **Lismore Information and Heritage Centre,** corner Bruxner Hwy. and Molesworth St., tel. (02) 6622-0122, has an interesting rainforest display; admission $1. Just up the road, on Molesworth St., is **Richmond River Historical Society Museum,** and next door is a **regional art gallery.** The *Bennelong* cruises the Wilsons and Richmond Rivers on a variety of itineraries, including a lunch cruise (departs 11 a.m., $27 pp) and a full-day cruise from Lismore to Ballina, with morning and afternoon teas, lunch, and return bus transport (departs 10 a.m., $50 pp). For details call (066) 21-7729, or book through the Tourist Information Centre. A worthwhile side trip from Lismore is to **Tucki Tucki Nature Reserve,** 16 km south of town, which protects a small colony of koalas.

Currendina Lodge, 14 Ewing St., tel. (02) 6621-6118, is a good choice for budget travelers; dorm beds are $15 pp, $22 s, and $35 d. Budget. The atmosphere is friendly and communal cooking and laundry facilities are offered. Best value of the area's many motels is **Arcadia Motel,** six km east of Lismore in the village of Goonellabah, tel. (02) 6624-1999; $47 s, $57 d. Inexpensive.

Lismore Lake Caravan Park, two km east of town on the road out to Ballina, tel. (02) 6621-2585, has excellent facilities; sites are $15, and small cabins start at $32 d. Budget-Inexpensive.

Mecca Cafe, 80 Magellan St., tel. (02) 6621-3901, is a 1950s-style diner; it was open before the '50s became a novelty. **Northern Rivers Hotel,** corner Bridge and Terania Streets, offers typical pub grub at incredibly low prices. Lunches start at $2, dinners start at $3, and you can cook your own steak for $8; all of this can be enjoyed in a plant-filled courtyard. Across the road, **20,000 Cows,** 58 Bridge St., is one of a number of vegetarian places in town; funky decor and an interesting and inexpensive menu make it a local favorite.

Nimbin

Nimbin was a dairy town in decline when, in 1973, a group of students descended on the town and convinced the council to let them hold a festival. Little did locals realize that the **Aquarius Festival** would change the town forever and mark the beginning of a hinterland counterculture movement that continues to this day. The festival attracted about 5,000 people, young and old, who came to dance, listen to music, and discover themselves. Many festival-goers were so impressed with the beauty and peacefulness around Nimbin that they bought up cheap dairy farms and settled in communes where everything was shared and life made as simple as possible. Communes still exist, as such, scattered around the district in remote areas that casual visitors would be lucky to find.

Colorful murals along the main street are the dominant characteristic of Nimbin. **Nimbin Museum,** near the Rainbow Cafe, tel. (02) 6689-1123, is an eclectic collection of memorabilia from the Aquarius Festival, and with admission only $2 pp, it shouldn't be missed. Also on the main street, shops sell the weird and wonderful work of local artisans.

Nimbin Motel, four km north of town on Crofton Rd., tel. (02) 6689-1420, has basic rooms for $28 s, $44 d. Inexpensive. **Granny's Farm** is a YHA hostel in a relaxed atmosphere, a 10-minute walk north of town, tel. (02) 6689-1333. Dorm beds are $13-15 pp, private rooms $30 d, or you can camp for $8 pp. Budget. Behind the hotel is a council-operated caravan park

with sites for $12 and on-site vans for $28, tel. (02) 6689-1402. Budget.

The legendary **Rainbow Cafe** on Cullen St. has been around for years and is the most popular of a half dozen cafés in town. Healthy meals start at around $6; open daily at 9 a.m. Farther down the street is **Nimbin Rocks Cafe,** which is a little more mainstream.

Nightcap National Park

A long fight between environmentalists and the government was finally resolved in 1983, when this 4,950-hectare park, 15 km northeast of Nimbin, was proclaimed. The park encompasses the Nightcap Range, part of the southern rim of the Mt. Warning caldera. The main access road from Nimbin leads to the summit of **Mt. Nardi,** from where panoramic views extend over the park and valleys to the south. The other access is north from **The Channon,** along a gravel road that ends at Terania Creek Picnic Area, where a 500-meter trail leads through a lush rainforest to **Protestor's Falls.** Camping is allowed at the picnic area.

Mullumbimby

Although not as extreme as Nimbin, the alternative lifestyle of many of "Mullum's" 2,000 residents can be appreciated by spending time on the main street or lounging in the cafés. The forests around town are subtropical, with the most spectacular feature, **Minyon Falls,** dropping nearly 100 meters into a heavily forested gorge. A gravel track off the main Mullumbimby-Lismore Road (signposted) leads to within a few minutes' walk of the falls.

Mount Warning National Park

The summit climb of 1,156-meter Mt. Warning is a highlight of a trip to the far north coast, but, be warned, the final ascent is *very* steep. The summit trail is just five km one-way, but you should allow five hours for the return trip. If you leave early enough to watch the sun rise over the Pacific Ocean, you'll be the first to do so on mainland Australia. All flanks of Mt. Warning are covered in rainforests—subtropical at lower elevations and temperate closer to the summit. Even if you aren't attempting a summit climb, the park is worth visiting for these rainforests, best appreciated along a short trail beginning

NIMBIN'S AQUARIUS FESTIVAL

—17-28 April 1973

Rumors had been circulating around the country for weeks about an arts festival in a small town called Nimbin in the hills of New South Wales. Communes, hippies, and travelers were converging on the site from all over Australia. Stuck in Cairns after seven years' traveling to more than 70 countries, I hitched a ride south in a car that had "Nimbin or Bust" spelled out in the dust on its rear window. Driving deep into the countryside, we at last arrived at Nimbin. A fountain of red paint spurted above a store-front, psychedelic motifs ran from building to building all along the main street, and outlandishly dressed people emerged barefoot from all manner of wheeled contraptions. As I surveyed the scene, I realized that I had happened upon an Australian Woodstock, a landmark event of the 1970s, a wondrous once-in-a-lifetime experience.

Nimbin perched on top of a small hill. Below lay a broad valley cut in two by a winding river. Scattered across the valley floor were hundreds of tepees, tents, multicolored domes, makeshift plastic shelters, vans, and RVs, all under tall, bushy eucalyptus trees. I was invited to stay in a huge communal plastic orange igloo with a gang of bikers. Late into the first night, chillums sparked in the darkness as a New Zealand organist pierced the night air with Christian rock music. The next morning I woke to the sound of flutes and chanting Hare Krishnas. A heavy mist encircled the trees and drifted over a sea of bodies crashed everywhere on the damp grass. Smoke puffed above a small Aborigine tribe from central Australia camped on a nearby hill where they performed dances and told stories. The Aborigines considered Nimbin a holy place inhabited by departed spirits and refused to pay the admission fee to enter land they felt had been stolen from them.

That day hundreds of celebrants—each one a character—arrived. Fred Robinson, an amazing white-haired 83-year-old Moses figure from Perth, gave talks on the Grand Order of the Universe, flying saucers, and Right Diet in order to save the world by 1978—which promised to be a very heavy year. In a nearby field, peddling furiously, a man attempted to get an absurd spiral-shaped flying machine off the ground. As the crowds swelled, a mushroom-eating greeter called out "Hello Bruce!" to everyone. Webster, a sexual activist, revolutionary, and spiritualist, enthused on his soapbox in his faultless British accent: "What we need is not a new Christ but a new Robin Hood! Not pie in the sky! Pie *now!*" A bedraggled band of crazy long-haired flautists and bongo drummers from Melbourne, who called themselves "The White Company," poured out of a long white bus. All shared food and whatever

at the end of the access road. Camping is not allowed within the park, but **Wollumbin Wildlife Refuge,** tel. (02) 6679-5120, along the park access road, has sites set among towering forests of eucalypts; park facilities are modern; tent sites $12, on-site vans $28, and cabins $34-46. Budget. Other accommodation is available at Uki, a historic and picturesque village spread along the Tweed River east of the park and nine km southwest of Murwillumbah.

Murwillumbah

Largest of the Tweed Valley towns, Murwillumbah (pop. 8,000), out on the Pacific Hwy., is in an area of lush subtropical rainforests and many banana and sugar plantations. At the turnoff to town is the **World Heritage Rainforest Centre,** tel. (02) 6672-1340, featuring interesting displays and a good relief map of the entire caldera. It's open Mon.-Sat. 9 a.m.-4:30 p.m., Sunday 9:30 a.m.-4 p.m. On Queensland Rd. is a small museum (open Wed.-Fri. 10 a.m.-3 p.m.), and at the east end of Murwillumbah St. on Tumbulgum Rd. is **Tweed River Regional Art Gallery** (hours same as museum).

A good place to stay is **Mt. Warning YHA,** 1 Tumbulgum Rd., tel. (02) 6672-3763, where the managers organize hinterland tours. Basic dorm beds are $14, twins $16 pp. Budget.

Border Ranges National Park

The largest of the caldera national parks, this 31,683-hectare park encompasses a portion of the New South Wales side of the McPherson Range, the western rim of the caldera. Like other hinterland parks, subtropical and temperate rainforests dominate, with other features including spectacular escarpments, waterfalls,

else they had; at the communal privies, guys and girls—complete strangers—shared the toilets and took showers together. Everyone was repeating "It's working, it's working!" Nimbin was to become a metaphor for a whole generation of Australians.

The hilltop swarmed with people and hummed with activity. Rock concerts, be-ins, peak experiences, spontaneous dances swirled around us. Shops sold oatmeal cookies and stir-fry veggies on paper plates (the locals called whole-wheat flour "hippie flour" and brown rice "hippie rice"). The Learning Exchange held workshops on silversmithing, transcendental meditation, instrument- and batik-making, mime by the White Company, and others such as "Sex—The Virile Sport." A massage tent had opened up, and in the afternoon at the Butter Factory, vehement diatribes were underway on racism, gay and feminist liberation, radical sociology, and anti-psychiatry. At the Nimbin Pub, packed with freaks and farmers from 10 in the morning until 10 at night, the till was white hot. And the din! A few doors down, a poetry group read Yevtushenko by candlelight in the middle of the street. Dollar Brand, an African pianist, played a wild improvisation in Nimbin Hall, taking the audience to a crescendo, then down to the nadir. In the Central Cafe, the New Zealand jug band Blertha sent a hundred people rockin' with their shivering electric guitars. It was a scene of mind-boggling freshness and innocence.

By the 10th day, the media got hold of the event and turned it into a real circus. Straight tourists walked down the main street warily as if they were in a lion park. Keeping their kids close to their sides, they stood gaping at the goings-on, laughing nervously. Plainclothesmen drove the dirt roads, and notices divulging their license plate numbers circulated. Cameramen worked the throngs. An official-looking man asked me, "Where's the main attraction?" Later that morning, news spread of an orgiastic be-in on the soccer field. It started as a snake-like procession winding in and out of all the tents—a freak parade with everyone singing and playing musical toys. In the center, the crowd danced and gyrated, a naked, free-spirited frenzy, while a shaggy, bare-ass photographer with an oversized 16 mm movie camera recorded the climax for posterity. That was Australia's Summer of Love.

—Bill Dalton

*W*hile many festival-goers remained in the area after the Aquarius Festival ended, Bill Dalton headed to Sydney to self-publish in booklet form A Traveler's Notes: Indonesia, *which he had been flogging on the streets of Nimbin. Little did he realize that in the ensuing years what had begun as six pages of mimeographed notes would grow into Moon Publications, a publishing organization with a series of more than 80 guidebooks covering Asia, the South Pacific, and the Americas.*

and deep gorges. The most easily accessible section of the park is the Tweed Range, in the south of the park. **Tweed Range Scenic Drive,** which begins at Lillian Rock midway between Murwillumbah and Kyogle, follows the rim of the caldera on a 100-km loop. Along this route, lookouts provide panoramic views of the entire region and the many short walks are worthwhile. The park's dominant geological feature is **The Pinnacle,** a sheer-sided sliver of volcanic rock that towers above the rainforest. A lookout provides views of the rock, but those with a sense of adventure (and balance) will want to continue hiking out to the pinnacle itself. Along the scenic drive are numerous picnic areas as well as camping at Forest Tops and Sheepstation Creek.

The rest of the park is remote; the only road access is Lions Road north from Kyogle. For further park information, call (02) 6628-1177.

OFFSHORE ISLANDS

New South Wales may have nothing like the number of offshore islands that neighboring Queensland boasts, and apart from numerous uninhabited rocky outcrops close to the mainland, you have to travel a long way from the coast to find anything resembling an island paradise, but two such islands exist, very different from each other and little known outside of Australia. **Lord Howe Island,** 600 km from the mainland, a subtropical paradise surrounded by fringing reef, has a relaxed atmosphere unlike anything you'll find on the Great Barrier Reef. The other is **Norfolk Island,** a remote outpost where the worst of Sydney Town's convicts were once sent and where descendants of *Bounty* mutineers now live.

LORD HOWE ISLAND

Few people who have visited this unique subtropical island would argue that it lacks anything intrepid island-hoppers could ask for. It's a gem of composition, with towering peaks rising abruptly from the ocean, lush rainforests, a colorful coral lagoon, and a menagerie of birds, caged only by the island's location—all this condensed on an island of just 1,455 hectares and enjoyed by a permanent population of 300, plus a maximum of 400 visitors at any one time. The island is also popular for what it *doesn't* have: snakes, spiders, biting insects, crime, litter, poverty, or traffic jams. The island is linked to the mainland by daily flights from Australia's east coast and has a wide range of tourist facilities including accommodations (no camping), restaurants, and recreation as diverse as golfing and game fishing.

The Land and Climate
Lord Howe Island lies a little less than 600 km east of Port Macquarie, New South Wales, and 700 km northeast of Sydney. It's 1,455 hectares in area, 11 km long, and three km across at its widest point. The island formed around six million years ago when volcanic activity left a scattering of barren peaks in the middle of the ocean. Lord Howe's two highest points, **Mt. Lidgbird** (777

meters) and **Mt. Gower** (875 meters), were two such peaks. Since volcanic activity ceased, the actions of wind and water have laid alluvial sediments around these peaks, linking them to lower outcrops to the north. Over time, these materials compressed to form sedimentary rock and the low topography that dominates the center of the island today.

Lord Howe Island has the world's southernmost coral reef. It survives at the southern latitude due to warm currents of water moving down the Queensland coast. A lagoon of fringing reef encloses a wide part of the island's west shore, which boasts a great variety of beaches; within the lagoon, coral debris has washed ashore to form beautiful sandy beaches. On the island's east

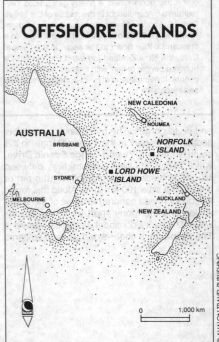

OFFSHORE ISLANDS

AUSTRALIA

NEW CALEDONIA
NOUMEA

BRISBANE

NORFOLK ISLAND

SYDNEY

LORD HOWE ISLAND

MELBOURNE

AUCKLAND

NEW ZEALAND

0   1,000 km

© AVALON TRAVEL PUBLISHING

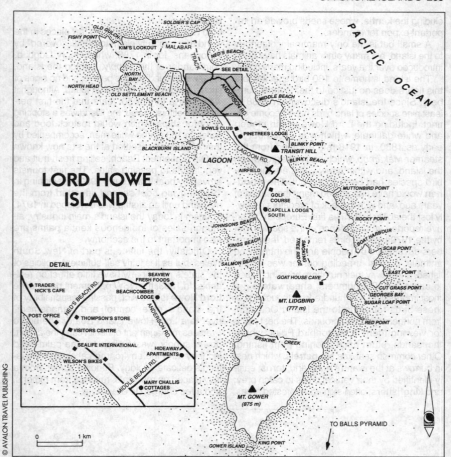

LORD HOWE ISLAND

© AVALON TRAVEL PUBLISHING

coast, beaches are made up of small volcanic rocks and, in the case of Boat Harbour, large basalt boulders smoothed over by wave action.

The 551-meter **Balls Pyramid,** 23 km south of Lord Howe itself, is the most spectacular of the isolated outcrops of rock north and south of the island.

The island's climate is oceanic. Summer temperatures rarely exceed 30° C (86° F), while even in the dead of winter 15° C (59° F) is considered a cold day. The best time to visit the island is spring and fall—most rain falls in winter,

and in summer moderate easterly winds blow almost unabated.

Flora and Fauna

Seeds transported by birds and ocean currents have transformed what was once nothing more than a rocky outcrop into a forested paradise. Seeds came from Australia, New Zealand, and other islands of the South Pacific, adapting over time and creating an environment found nowhere else on the earth. Valleys cloaked in subtropical rainforest are dominated by a variety of palms, including the **kentia,** whose seeds provide an important export for islanders.

A small bat is the only mammal indigenous to the island, but many other animals have been introduced over the years, including many cows.

The island is home to 130 bird species, but this figure does no justice to their overall numbers. Since the island's discovery in 1788 at least nine species of land birds have become extinct, including the Lord Howe Island pigeon and white gallinule, which was wiped out as early as 1830. In 1918 rats escaped from the steamer *Makambo,* which had run aground on the island, and within a few years another five bird species had been wiped out. The **woodhen** would have first arrived many thousands of years ago, and with the lack of predators it slowly lost the ability to fly. The first Europeans to arrive reported an abundance of the species, but by the 1970s just 30 birds remained, their numbers devastated by people and the introduced animals. A small breeding center was established, and slowly their numbers have increased to about 250. For numbers, **shearwaters** are most impressive, with hundreds of thousands of these birds returning to the island Oct.-April from northern wintering grounds. The best place for viewing them is Muttonbird Point, where thousands return each evening from fishing. Other common seabirds are **petrels,** which nest in burrows at the island's north end; **terns,** easily identified by their vertical dives to catch prey; and **kingfishers,** often sighted in forested areas.

History

Lord Howe Island is one of the few places in the world that can truly claim to be "discovered" by Europeans, for in 1788, when Henry Lidgbird, commander of the *Supply,* sighted the island, there were no indigenous people, and no signs of such a culture have ever been found. Although it wasn't for a further 50 years that the first permanent settlers arrived, the island was a stopping point for ships, which would restock food and water. In 1834 three white men, accompanied by their Maori wives, settled at the site now known as Old Settlement Beach, selling fresh fruit and vegetables to passing ships. The first tourists arrived by boat in the early 1930s. Beginning in 1947 a flying boat service operated from the mainland until an airstrip was developed in 1974. Tourism is today the island's main industry, although sales of indigenous kentia palms are also important to the economy.

Officially, the island is part of New South Wales, but as it is fairly self-sufficient, policies of the state's ruling party have little effect on residents. In 1953, the NSW parliament passed the **Lord Howe Island Act,** passing responsibility of the island's "care, control, and management" over to a Lord Howe Island Board. The board oversees management of health care, the airport, power supply, waste disposal, the palm-seed industry, and the environmental care of the island's delicate ecology. Funding comes from a levy placed on residents, revenue from exports, and a fee charged to all visitors.

Lord Howe Island

NADINA PURDON

Hiking

Hiking is by far the most popular activity on the island, with trails to the southern peaks testing the fittest hikers. An easy yet interesting trail is the four-km (roundtrip) **Malabar Track**. Beginning near the end of Ned's Beach Rd., the trail climbs steadily through open pastures to a lookout on Malabar Ridge, before continuing along the headland to Kim's Lookout and descending back to Lagoon Road. The finish of the trail is the beginning of another, this one ending at North Bay, where you'll find a pleasant beach with picnic tables and good snorkeling offshore. From North Bay, it's 300 meters across a low ridge to **Old Gulch,** a narrow inlet backed by a boulder-strewn beach.

The longer and more difficult hiking is at the island's rugged southern end. Beginning from Kings Beach, the strenuous climb to **Goat House Cave,** perched high in the sheer eastern face of Mt. Lidgbird, is less than three km one-way, but is very steep. For the first one km the trail climbs steadily, branching south from a trail to Boat Harbour before climbing Smoking Tree Ridge. The final ascent is up a scree slope to a cave from where the spectacular view extends across the island and lagoon. If you found that the climb to Goat House Cave tested your stamina and stretched your fear of heights to the limits, read no further—the ascent of **Mt. Gower** is steeper, longer, and scarier, so much so that it *must* be made with a guide (ask at your accommodation, the Island Administrative Office, or call Jack Shick, tel. (02) 6563-2218; $25 pp). The trail starts at Salmon Beach, skirting the ocean for 1.4 km before the first test of nerves, a narrow ledge with a 100-meter drop on one side and a rope for guidance on the other. The trail then ascends steadily through a thickly vegetated valley and climbs, climbs, and climbs an excruciatingly steep slope, almost vertical in places (there's a rope for guidance), to the summit.

Other Outdoor Activities

With crystal-clear water, 100 species of coral, and 500 species of fish, the lagoon is fantastic for snorkeling. Rent gear from **Thompson's Store.** If you'd like to view life in the lagoon without getting wet, a glass-bottomed boat tour costs adult $15, child $9. **Prodive,** tel. (02) 6563-2154, operates scuba diving on the island, with an eight-meter dive boat to access all the best spots. They also offer PADI dive courses. Fish feeding takes place each afternoon at Ned's Beach. Fishing around the island can be very productive (it's prohibited in the lagoon); buy equipment at Thompson's Store. **Wilson's Bikes** rents bikes and paddle skis from $5 per day.

South of the airfield is a nine-hole **golf course.** Club rental and payment of greens fees ($20) is on an honor system. A competition is conducted each Sunday from 1 p.m.; call (02) 6563-2054 to book. The **bowls club** is open to the public and racquets for the **tennis court** can be rented from Thompson's Store.

Accommodations and Food

All island accommodations are operated by local families. They range from motel-style rooms to fully self-contained units. Central to all island services is **Hideaway Apartments,** tel. (02) 6563-2054, one of the least expensive options and with a kitchen in each unit. **Mary Challis Cottages,** tel. (02) 6563-2076, just 50 meters from the lagoon, features two large cottages surrounded in lush greenery. Each has a kitchen with microwave. Rates are similar to Hideaway Apartments. **Pinetrees Lodge,** tel. (02) 6563-2177, the island's largest accommodation, has been operating since 1900. Rooms lack cooking facilities, but rates include meals. The all-inclusive rate at **Beachcomber Lodge,** tel. (02) 6563-2032, is slightly lower.

The island has a couple of grocery stores and a bakery; groceries are more expensive here than on the mainland, but less expensive than eating at island restaurants. **Thompson's Store** sells pies, pastries, and cakes. Generally, accommodations without self-contained units have a restaurant. Of these, head to **Capella Lodge South,** tel. (02) 6563-2008, for a huge breakfast layout ($18 pp) between 8 and 9 a.m. Lunches here average $8-10, and a three-course set menu is offered 6:30-8 p.m. for $40 pp. The Beachcomber Lodge, tel. (02) 6563-2032, has a restaurant open daily 7 a.m.-10 p.m. **Trader Nick's Cafe,** tel. (02) 6563-2002, is open Tues.-Sun. 10 a.m.-4:30 p.m. and has cappuccinos and all the typical big-city fare.

Booking a Trip to Lord Howe Island
Eastern Australia, tel. (13) 1313, flies daily between Sydney and the island. The regular airfare is $700 roundtrip in summer and $620 the rest of the year, but the smart way to visit the island is on a package. Rather than contacting the resorts directly, book through one of the following agents: **Fastbook Pacific Holidays,** tel. (02) 9958-2799 or (1300) 36-1153; **Pacific & International Travel,** tel. (02) 9244-1811 or (13) 2747; or **Pacific Unlimited Holidays,** tel. (02) 9233-3311 or (1800) 22-1260. In the high season (Dec.-Jan.), airfare from Sydney and five nights' accommodation start at $1,200 pp. With full board, rates start at $1,600 pp. Outside of summer holidays, rates are markedly lower, with five-night packages from $750 (check the Travel Section in Thursday's *Sydney Morning Herald* for even cheaper deals). Departure tax is $20 pp.

Services and Information
The **post office** is on the corner of Ned's Beach and Lagoon Roads; open weekdays. The island has three banks; open varying hours Mon.-Friday. For a doctor, call (02) 6563-2000. A bus service operates along the island's road system weekdays only; $8 for an all day ticket; call (02) 6563-2120 for times.

The **Visitors Centre,** on the corner of Lagoon Rd. and Ned's Beach Rd., tel. (02) 6563-2114, features displays of the island's geology and unique flora and fauna, as well as showing audiovisuals on request. It's open Mon.-Fri. 9 a.m.-12:30 p.m. A bulletin board outside the center has bus timetables, weather forecasts, and other island information. The island has no official website, but Fastbook Pacific Holidays offers a good overview of the island on its site: www.fastbook.com.au.

NORFOLK ISLAND

An elevated plateau of lush green rolling hills encircled by steep cliffs that drop straight into the raging ocean and steeped in a tragic yet romantic history, Norfolk Island is like no other place in the world. Its tragic history and remote location alone make it an interesting destination, but the small things that visitors are left to

discover for themselves make it all the more so: the annual horse race around the golf course, a phone book that lists nicknames, and unique cuisine developed over 100 years of isolation, just to name a few. Although the island attracts surprisingly few younger travelers (only newlyweds and nearly deads, the locals say), there is something to suit nearly everyone, including hiking, snorkeling, scuba diving, surfing, tours of the island's many convict-era buildings, and cheap booze. Most visitors arrive as part of a package and stay in self-contained units. While package cost is slightly higher than on Lord Howe Island, cost of living is generally less expensive. (The island is tax free, meaning inexpensive shopping.)

The Land
Norfolk Island is 1,600 km northeast of Sydney and on the same latitude as Byron Bay. About eight km long and up to five km wide with 30 km of coastline, the island is 3,455 hectares in area. Volcanic in origin, it is a high point along the Norfolk Ridge, a range of submerged mountains extending between New Zealand and New Caledonia. Norfolk is not your typical South Pacific paradise; its shoreline is dominated by high cliffs rising to a plateau of rolling hills and the peaks of **Mt. Bates** (321 meters) and **Mt. Pitt** (320 meters). The only section of the coastline without cliffs is at the island's southern end.

Nepean Island is a chunk of rock that rises to a massive plateau. It lies 800 meters from Norfolk's southern tip, and through the years there's been talk of constructing a breakwall linking it to the mainland to create a safe anchorage for visiting ships. Farther south is **Phillip Island.** Rugged and surrounded in precipitous cliffs, it's inhabited only by seabirds.

Flora and Fauna
After volcanic activity ended around 2.3 million years ago, forces of erosion began breaking down the island and creating a rich volcanic soil. Over time, seeds arrived on ocean currents and germinated. At the time of European settlement, in 1788, 178 species of plants had colonized the island, many of which had evolved to be better suited to the environment. Most dominant of endemic species is the **Norfolk Island pine,** a majestic tree that grows to a height of 50 meters.

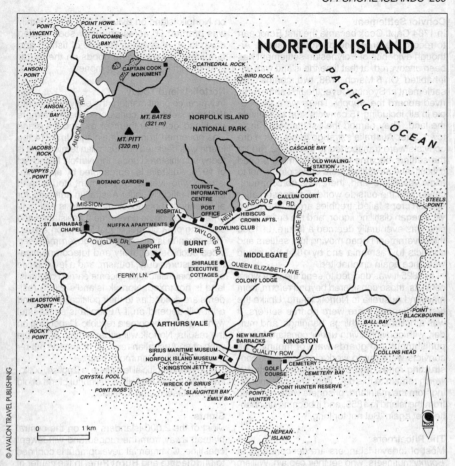

NORFOLK ISLAND

Dense stands of tree ferns and palms once covered most of the island but are now restricted to Norfolk Island National Park, where a canopy of greenery and an understory of creepers, vines, and ferns thrive. Another endemic species of interest is the **sharkwood tree,** which gives off a rotten onion smell.

Only two animals are native to the island, geckos and skinks, and both are very rare. Birdlife is prolific, with 45 species nesting on Norfolk Island, including both sea- and land birds. Rarest of the land birds is the **green parrot,** which is endemic. At one time their population dipped to 20, but a breeding program is slowly increasing numbers. At one time even more endangered was the **Norfolk Island mopoke,** whose population numbered just one in 1987. A breeding program with a closely related species from New Zealand has been successful. Of the seabirds present, some live year-round along the coastline while others are migratory. **Gannets** are common on offshore rock stacks, and **terns,** a variety of **petrels, shearwaters,** and **noddies** are present.

Convict Settlement

In 1784 Capt. Cook became the first European to record the presence of Norfolk Island. Although evidence of Polynesian settlement has been uncovered, at that time the island was uninhabited. On 6 March 1788, two months after settlement at Sydney Cove, the first settlers arrived aboard the *Supply*. There were 24 people in all, including 15 convicts sent to cultivate the land. They named their settlement King's town, after Australia's first governor. As more convicts were transported to the island, life for the settlers became tougher. Farming proved difficult, and as settlers were under orders not to allow vessels to land, there was no communication with the outside world. For season after season crops failed, troubles arose when convicts began distilling liquor, and the entire exercise was eventually deemed a failure. In 1806 the government began moving free settlers and convicts to Tasmania and by 1814 the island was once again uninhabited.

In 1825 it was decided to send the very worst convicts, those considered beyond reform, from mainland Australia to Norfolk Island. Unlike the first settlement, there were no free settlers. It was a hellhole of lashings, hangings, and murder, with convicts living under constant fear of punishment and guards wary of mutiny. The convicts were put to work clearing land, constructing roads, and building stone structures, which remain to this day. With pressure mounting from the mainland, prisoners were removed from the island in 1855, and it became uninhabited yet again. But not for long.

The Pitcairners

Most of today's islanders are descendants of *Bounty* mutineers, who set their captain, William Bligh, adrift on 28 April 1789, and under the leadership of 24-year-old Fletcher Christian sailed for the uninhabited island of Pitcairn, halfway between South America and New Zealand. Their life on Pitcairn Island was a violent one and within a decade only one of the original mutineers was alive. But they had brought a swag of Polynesian women with them and by 1854 the island's population had grown to nearly 200, putting pressure on food and water supplies. The British government decided to move them all to Norfolk Island. They came ashore on Norfolk Island on 8 June 1856. Each family was granted 50 acres and they soon settled down to an easy-going lifestyle of fishing and farming and exchanging goods on the barter system with no real use for money.

Norfolk Island Today

In typical colonial fashion, the early New South Wales government considered the Pitcairners unable to look after themselves, and the island was governed from the mainland. In 1914 the island was declared an Australian territory and is today administered under the Norfolk Island Act of 1979. Australia is represented by an administrator who lives at Government House. And although officially under Australian authority, for all intents and purposes the island is self-governed, receiving no government assistance and surviving on a budget of just $8 million a year. This revenue is raised through government services such as electricity and telecommunications, customs duty, tourism, and a levy placed on financial institutions. Income earned on the island is not taxed. Norfolk Island's 2,000 residents are divided as to their political future, and a lot will depend on if Australia is successful with its push to become a republic. Depending on the results, Norfolk will either remain under the wing of an Australian republic or secede but remain under the Commonwealth.

The island's official language is English, but locals also speak Norfolk, a delightful blend of old English, Gaelic, and Tahitian.

Sights

Most of the 2,000 islanders live on the central plateau away from the rugged and windswept coastline. Commercial development is confined to **Middlegate** and **Burnt Pine,** in the center of the island. South of this area is **Kingston,** site of settlement of the second wave of convicts. A variety of stone structures from this era remain, many along **Quality Row.** Some stone buildings have been restored and are open museums, including the original storehouse, which houses **Norfolk Island Museum,** tel. (1800) 23-088. It's open Mon.-Fri. 9 a.m.-4 p.m., Sat.-Sun. 10 a.m.-1 p.m. Open similar hours is **Sirius Maritime Museum,** housed in an old chapel. At the east end of Quality Row is a cemetery, with graves nearest to the ocean predating the arrival of the Pitcairners. **Emily Bay,** in front of Kingston, is backed by a crescent of golden sand. At low tide it's possible to walk from the beach onto the reef to view rock pools. The *Sirius* was wrecked on this reef in 1790; its anchor was salvaged and is now mounted in the New Military Barracks.

Beyond the airport, on Douglas Drive, is **St. Barnabas Chapel,** part of an 1866 Melanesian Mission established to train Melanesians in the ways of Christianity. This impressive church features intricate stonework, marble floors, kauri pews, and stained glass windows.

Norfolk Island National Park encompasses 460 hectares, the greater part of the island's north section. Hiking trails lead through the most interesting areas, including to Mt. Bates (500 meters each way) and a monument to Captain Cook's landing in 1774 (three km each way). At the park's southern end is a **botanic garden,** developed to ensure the future of the island's unique flora.

Recreation and Events

Fishing is a popular island pastime, with snapper and kingfish most sought after. Although the island is not renowned for waves, surfers occasionally arrive with their boards looking for surf; the most consistent breaks are in the south. The island has a large population of windsurfing enthusiasts, and although you can't rent boards, ask around and you should be able to borrow one. Waters away from Emily Bay are often rough, but good dive sites do exist; call **Bounty Divers** at 6723-22-751 for details. Bounty Divers also rents snorkeling gear for $10 per day. The nine-hole **Norfolk Island Golf Club** is down in Kingston, right on the oceanfront, tel. (6723) 22-354. Greens fees are $12, as are club rentals. In August, a $30,000 Pro-Am golf tournament attracts professional golfers from throughout Australasia. The clubhouse is the old magistrate's house. **Cheryl Tennis Club** is on Queen Elizabeth Ave., Middlegate, tel. (6723) 22-966. A good way to see the island's north end is on horseback with **Silky Oaks Stables,** tel. (6723) 22-291, where a two-and-a-half-hour ride with billy tea and damper is $25 pp.

Anniversary Day commemorates the Pitcairners' arrival on Norfolk Island. The 8 June celebrations include a re-creation of the landing at Kingston Jetty and a procession of islanders dressed in period costume to the cemetery where hymns and a prayer written by John Adams, one of the original mutineers, are read. Then everyone heads to the ruins of Quality Row for a picnic and game of cricket. The day ends with the Bounty Ball. Norfolk Island is the only place outside of the United States to officially celebrate **Thanksgiving Day,** a throwback to the days when a U.S. whaling station operated on the island.

Accommodations and Food

The island has dozens of accommodations. Most are motel-style units or self-contained apartments, and although none are overly luxurious, all are adequate and comfortable. Bookings are best made in conjunction with airfare (see below). Room rates alone for the following properties range $70-150 s or d. Moderate-Premium.

One of the least expensive places to stay is **Colony Lodge,** tel. (6723) 22-256, featuring basic self-contained apartments. Similarly priced are the self-contained **Hibiscus Crown Apartments,** tel. (6723) 22-325, with a tennis court. **Nuffka Apartments,** tel. (6723) 23-513, is also a good value. **Callum Court,** New Cascade Rd., tel. (6723) 22-850, comprises comfortable self-contained units with a wide range of facilities. For more than two people, the luxurious three-bedroom Callum House, on the same property, is an excellent deal at just $150 per night. For large self-contained units of a high standard and just a short walk from town stay at **Shiralee Executive Cottages,** on Taylors Rd., tel. (6723) 22-118.

While most motels offer food service for guests, enjoying the more than 20 restaurants is the best way to experience everyday island life. Both the bowling and golf clubs are open daily for lunch and are inexpensive (the bowling club has an $8 fish fry Sunday night). Another cheap choice is the bistro in the **South Pacific Resort Hotel,** Taylors Rd., tel. (6723) 23-154, which offers a $10 roast Monday, Tuesday, Thursday, and Saturday nights. Milk produced at the island's dairy is smooth, creamy, and delicious, but grocery stores generally sell out by lunchtime. Also look for locally made Cascade lemonade. As well as locally grown fruit, the island specialty is fish, and many restaurants have traditional fish fries once a week. **Christian's,** at the Castaway Hotel, tel. (6723) 22-625, has a fish fry Saturday night, a Pitcairn/Norfolk dinner Tuesday, and a roast dinner Sunday. **Bishop's Court,** tel. (6723) 22-211, features a traditional dinner and live entertainment Monday night for $32 pp. **Branka House Restaurant,** tel. (6723) 22-346, is in an old jail building, with foundations of cells below the main dining room. Main meals are well-priced at $15-18.

Transportation and Tours

Australia's newest airline, **Norfolk Jet Express,** tel. (02) 9251-3972 or (1800) 81-6947, flies to the island six times weekly from Sydney and three times from Brisbane. **FlightWest,** from Brisbane, and **Air New Zealand,** from Auckland, also have scheduled flights to Norfolk. The roundtrip fare from Sydney is $750, but as with Lord Howe Island, almost everyone buys airfare in conjunction with an accommodation package. These start at $800 pp for airfare from Sydney, four nights' accommodation, and transfers in the off season, rising to $1,400 in January. Book packages through **Fastbook Pacific Holidays,** tel. (02) 9958-2799 or (1300) 36-1153. Airport departure tax is $25 pp.

Getting Around

Car rentals on Norfolk Island are among the most inexpensive in the world—a small car starts at just $17 per day, plus $3 for insurance. Try **Aloha Rent-a-car,** tel. (6723) 22-510. Many accommodation packages include a rental car. **Bill's Hire,** tel. (6723) 22-139, rents bikes for $6 per day. For a cab, call **Pacific Taxi,** at (6723) 22-182.

Pinetree Tours, tel. (6723) 22-424, and **Bounty Excursions,** tel. (6723) 23-693, offer a variety of island tours from $20 pp, a sound and light show depicting the convict past for $25, and din-

ner theater shows for $40. Flightseeing starts at $50 pp for a short flight around the island.

Services and Information

The island provides all services of a midsized Australian country town. The **post office** is opposite the police station in Burnt Pine. (Colorful stamps issued by Norfolk Island are prized by philatelists the world over.) The Commonwealth and Westpac Banks operate branches in Burnt Pine; hours are Mon.-Thurs. 9:50 a.m.-4:30 p.m., Friday 9:30 a.m.-5 p.m.

As Norfolk Island has no import restrictions, all booze, electronic equipment, and other exotic goods can be purchased duty-free. Duty-free shops as such don't exist, but these items can be purchased at discounted prices from shops in Burnt Pine. The maximum liquor allowance is three bottles per person, but you must purchase them at one time.

Shops are generally closed Wednesday and Saturday afternoons and all day Sunday. **Australian currency** is used, but most major credit cards also accepted. Norfolk Island is on a time zone 90 minutes ahead of Australian Eastern Standard Time and 18 hours ahead of Pacific Standard Time. While on the island you do not need to dial the 6723 phone prefix.

A small **hospital** is off Grassy Rd., tel. (6723) 22-091; it's open Mon.-Fri. 9 a.m.-5 p.m., but emergencies are seen to any time.

The **Tourist Information Centre** is beside the post office on Taylors Rd., Burnt Pine, tel. (6723) 22-147; it's open Mon.-Fri. 9 a.m.-5 p.m., Sat.-Sun. 9 a.m.-noon. For information before arriving, write **Norfolk Island Government Tourist Bureau,** Box 211, Norfolk Island 2899 (tel. 6723-22-147). The website for Norfolk Island (www.nf) has no links to local businesses but gives a fantastic overview of the island, including its natural and human history, and everything there is to do and see.

THE NORTHERN TERRITORY
INTRODUCTION

Ah, beware Australia's last frontier. Take just one look and it's likely to itch clear through your bones and sting your spirit, and not even the venerable Royal Flying Doctors will be able to cure you. Long after the red dust has settled and you've put Aboriginal myths to rest, your Dreamtime will be influenced forevermore by this superlative land with its big rocks, big crocs, and big thirst.

This barren-but-bewitching region, encompassing 1,346,200 square km, is a veritable dynamo of contrasts—the tropical Top End and the arid Red Centre, sacred grounds and tourist meccas, Stone Age culture and Kmarts—inhabited by fewer than one percent of Australia's population (about 150,000), a quarter of them Aboriginal, and the remainder residing mainly in Darwin or Alice Springs.

Touring
Remote though the Territory is, you'll have no problem getting there on a number of scheduled flights into Darwin (which is closer to Indonesia and the Philippines than it is to Melbourne or Sydney), The Alice (Alice Springs), and, yes, even The Rock with its nearby airstrip. The Ghan will rail you from Adelaide to Alice Springs, while coaches, cars, caravans, and trucks can take the straight-as-an-arrow, bitumen Stuart Highway, a.k.a. the Track, all the way to Darwin. From Darwin, it's easy to rent a car or sign up for an organized tour to Top End sites (almost mandatory for Aboriginal lands), and from The Alice you have the option of humping 'round the Red Heart on a friendly camel or riding through the desert on a horse with no name.

Don't come here expecting to find an Aboriginal guru to take you under his wing and impart Stone-Age-old knowledge while you're on holiday. But don't despair. Aboriginal-led tours and "experiences" are available at a variety of sites throughout the Territory.

And you can easily be your own guide—just find your way here, lose yourself immediately, and let your imagination run wild. You may find

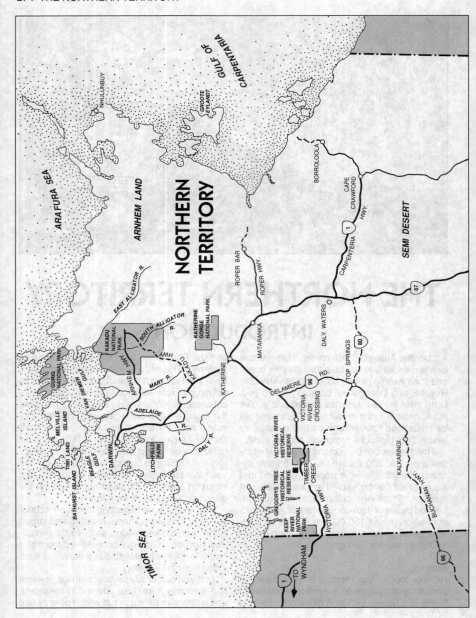

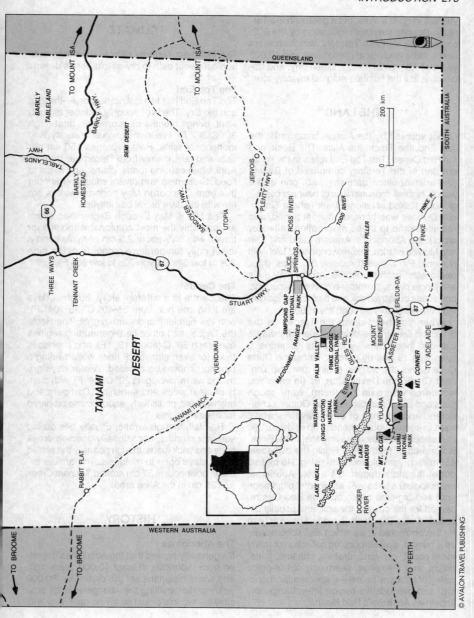

© AVALON TRAVEL PUBLISHING

yourself in quite a state, but it goes with the Territory. Despite inevitable infiltration by the 20th century, the Northern Territory, with its ancient lands, eerie geological formations, and 40,000 years of Aboriginal history, ceremony, and tradition, is still the ultimate magical mystery tour.

THE LAND

Orient yourself by the Aussie buzzwords: the Top End, the Track, the Alice, The Rock, and the Red Centre. The Top End refers to the northern part of the Territory comprised of Darwin (the cosmopolitan gateway, with one of the world's highest consumptions of beer per capita), glorious Kakadu National Park (where *Crocodile Dundee* was born, or at least filmed, and real-life home to those man-eating saltwater crocs), the Aboriginals' Arnhem Land and Tiwi and Melville Islands, nature wonderland Litchfield National Park, plus turquoise beaches, thick rainforests, profuse birdlife, raging waterfalls and jungle rivers, six-meter-high termite mounds, and scads of native rock and bark paintings dating from prehistory through the 1960s.

When you head down the Track—as the 3,188-km Darwin-to-Adelaide Stuart Highway is called in these parts—you'll pass Katherine, a town with 13 nearby gorges, limestone Cutta Cutta Caves, the old gold-mining township Tennant Creek, the Devils Marbles (in case you wondered where he lost them), some rough pubs and petrol pumps, assorted Outback characters, and a bunch of other travelers who'll want to know if you're "headin' up or down."

It should go without saying that "The Rock" is none other than Ayers Rock, the awesome 650-million-year-old monolith rising 348 meters out of the stark desert. It's a holy Aboriginal mythological site as well as visitors' pilgrimage spot and big-time photo op. The Red Centre, named for the color of the soil, and usually associated with The Rock, is really a blanket term for the whole vast area, which also encompasses a surreal, eyeball-popping collection of many more rocks, canyons, craters, chasms, gaps, pillars, and a strange, seemingly out-of-place valley of cabbage palms—a spectacular, inspiring, and provocative region interchangeably known as Australia's Red Heart.

CLIMATE

The Northern Territory climate runs from subtropical sweat bath to dry-as-old-bones desert.

The Top End
The Top End has two distinct seasons—the Wet and the Dry. The Wet, roughly October through April, brings months of oppressive heat (high 30° C, 90° F), live-in-the-shower humidity, and monsoonal rains. Rain averages 150 cm per year and falls mainly from December through April, often causing roads, plains, and rivers to flood. Swimmers and divers should remember that from October to May northern waters are rife with the dangerous box jellyfish.

The Dry is May through September, which are probably the most comfortable months for travel, with only about 2.5 cm of rainfall and a lower daily temperature range, from the high 20s to low 30s C (high 70s to low 90s F).

The Centre
The Centre is a different story. Summer days are long and hot, from 35-40° C (95-104° F), with low humidity and warm nights. The Rock, the Olgas, and other heat-generating regions can reach 50° C (about 120° F), and strenuous treks (or even piggyback rides while twirling a parasol) should be avoided. Winter days are mild to warm, averaging 20° C (54° F), with plenty of clear skies and sunshine. Campers and bushwalkers, particularly, should come prepared for freezing nights.

Rainfall, though erratic, usually hits during summer months, occasionally flooding creek beds and back roads, though normally the sealed Track stays open to motorists. The annual average downpour is 37 cm around Tennant Creek and 29 cm in the Alice area.

HISTORY

The Aborigines
It's generally agreed that the Aborigines migrated from Indonesia at least 40,000 years ago, and some historians set the date even 80,000 years earlier, making the Aborigines quite possibly the world's oldest surviving race. Any way

you look at it, they've been in Australia a long time, with Arnhem Land in the Territory's northeast corner marking the spot of tropical Australia's first human settlement.

For several centuries the Aborigines enjoyed a sort of love-hate relationship with Macassarese fishers from Indonesia who visited regularly in search of trepang (sea slugs) until the early 1900s, when the Australian government told them to scoot.

Exploration and Colonization

In 1623, the Dutch ship *Arnhem* became the first recorded European contact, followed by Abel Tasman's exploration of the northern coast in 1644. Aside from naming some of the features, the Dutch didn't seem terribly interested in the region. Additional charting of the coast was undertaken by Matthew Flinders in 1803, and then navigator Phillip King 14 years later.

The British began the old colonial ball rolling when, in 1824, Captain Gordon Bremer—in the name of King George IV—claimed the land as part of New South Wales. After settlement attempts failed at Melville Island, Raffles Bay, and Port Essington (lousy climate, no trade), the northern coast was left alone for about 15 years. In 1863, on the heels of John McDouall Stuart's groundbreaking south-north continental crossing, the Northern Territory became a vested interest of South Australia (called Northern Territory of South Australia). Another settlement was created by the territory's first government resident, Colonel Boyle Finniss, at Escape Cliffs near the Adelaide River mouth. Another failure.

Finally, in 1869, Surveyor-General George Goyder decided to try out Darwin as a prospective site. Bingo! Good choice, especially when shortly thereafter gold was discovered at nearby Pine Creek—bringing with it a railway line, followed by the Overland Telegraph Line and, subsequently, the predictable array of cattle ranchers, Chinese laborers, pastoralists, and significant others. Additional mineral finds in the 1880s through the early 1900s cinched the area as "a go." The Track, lifeline between Alice Springs

and Darwin, was not constructed until the 1930s and not sealed for about another 20 years.

And as for the Aborigines, some tried to resist the colonization of their land—in vain. The hunters and gatherers who'd lived for so long in perfect harmony with the land were, by the early 1900s, herded onto government reserves, introduced to Christian charities, forced into hard labor for low pay, left to rot on the fringes of towns, and given a taste of alcohol. Only those few who lived in the most remote areas were left alone to practice their age-old traditions.

It took some time, but in the 1960s Northern Territory Aborigines began pressing for their rights—with various protests against mining, ranching, and other intrusions on their reserves—culminating in the passage of the 1976 Aboriginal Land (NT) Act, giving them control of their lands (i.e., designated reserves) and returning their sacred sites, including Kakadu and Uluru-Kata Tjuta (Ayers Rock and the Olgas). Currently, Aborigines make up a majority of the management board of these heavily touristed areas, and word has it that someday visitors will be banned from climbing the spiritual sites and will instead be able just to walk around them, gazing in wonder.

The Act also allowed for the appointment of Aboriginal Land Commissioners and the creation of administrative Aboriginal Land Councils. Presently the Aborigines own about one-third of the Territory. Many have returned to their traditional ways and stay on the reserves, out of white reach; others live in squalid conditions around townships, ravaged by the effects of racism and alcohol; still others have turned militant or, worse, have become *capitalists.*

The 20th Century

The Australian Commonwealth government took over control of the Northern Territory in 1911. Though the region became self-governing in 1978, it still remains economically dependent upon the commonwealth. Agriculture, cattle-raising, mining (gold, bauxite, uranium), and booming tourism are the region's major moneymakers.

DARWIN

The Northern Territory's capital city was named for Charles Darwin, a shipmate of harbor discoverer John Lort Stokes, and the place has been in a state of evolution ever since.

Australians commonly joke about this Top End tropical city—with its difficult climate, transient population, and fabled thirst. Though true, those elements have also inspired a thriving frontier town, lively cosmopolitan center and, yes, lots of laughs as well as fisticuffs over that amazing intake of beer known worldwide as the Darwin Thirst. (Don't laugh—the Darwin stubby contains two liters of beer instead of the normal 375 milliliters; the average per capita intake is 230 liters per year, and that's a *low* estimate.)

People don't stick around here long, that's a fact. The weather and the isolation take their toll. Heck, not even the city stays put! During WW II, more than 60 bomb attacks by the Japanese pretty much turned Darwin into a pile of rubble. Then, in 1974, Cyclone Tracy paid a surprise Christmas Day visit, leveling practically the entire city. With indomitable Territorian pull-together spirit (and no doubt *many* thirst-quenchers under their tool belts), Darwin was rebuilt into a durable, modern center, punctuated here and there by the few surviving historical structures, accented by flowering bougainvillea, frangipani blossoms, and swaying palms.

Today's Darwin, with a population of approximately 80,000, is a conglomeration of 50 or so ethnic groups, including descendants of the Chinese miners, Japanese pearlers, Europeans who sought escape from postwar oppression, an onslaught of refugees from Southeast Asia, barramundi fishers, and a steady stream of travelers and backpackers headed to or from Asia, Top End attractions, or the rest of Australia. Most of the people who "do time" here work within some element of this Territorial administrative center's government, mining, or tourism sectors. Recent years, however, have seen an onslaught of younger Aussies move into town, just to give the place a shot. Consequently, it's become pretty cool to offhandedly tell mates you're shifting up to Darwin for a bit, will send them a postcard when you get there. Piggybacking on this phenomenon is the fact that the city is aburst with everyone

from the aforementioned transient travelers and workers to a new breed of yuppie-ish adventurers, artistes, and a burgeoning gay and lesbian contingency. It all sounds pretty cozy, but Darwin has its fair share of standard city problems.

The city center, compactly situated on a peninsula looking toward Darwin Harbour, is easily explored on foot. The Stuart Highway becomes Daly Street as it enters the city, bisecting Smith Street. Head one km toward the harbor to Smith Street Mall, the main shopping district and location of the Darwin Regional Tourism Association Information Centre. The majority of central Darwin sites and services—including Darwin Transit Centre, the general post office, and the Automobile Association of the Northern Territory—fall within a few blocks' radius of the mall. Noteworthy suburban attractions are mostly located at Larrakeyah, Palmerston, Fannie Bay, and East Point, all within 10 km to the north and east of city center. Head back away from the harbor and take a right turn off Smith St. onto Gilruth Ave. (which becomes East Point Rd.) to access most of these areas.

And, though you won't find the flair and sophistication of a highfalutin metropolis like Melbourne or Sydney, easygoing and eclectic Darwin can hold its own. And it can *certainly* hold its beer.

THE HISTORICAL TOUR

Yes, acts of war and God aside, a few dear structures—or pieces thereof—still stand. *A Walk Through Historical Darwin,* a booklet published by the National Trust, is a good source of information. This particular stroll may move your spirit as well as your feet. It starts off at the Tree of Knowledge, on the east side of downtown, continues in a loop around the Esplanade, heads down Smith Street Mall, and winds up at the Chinese Temple.

Tree of Knowledge

The ancient banyan behind the Civic Centre on Harry Chan Ave. is a longtime city landmark. Heralded as the Tree of Knowledge by Buddhists (Gautama received enlightenment while

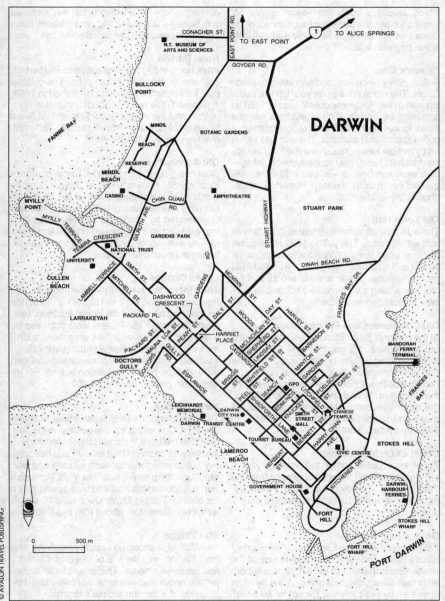

DARWIN

N.T. MUSEUM OF
ARTS AND SCIENCES

CONACHER ST.

EAST POINT RD.

TO EAST POINT

TO ALICE SPRINGS

GOYDER RD.

BULLOCKY
POINT

FANNIE BAY

BOTANIC GARDENS

MINDIL

BEACH

RESERVE

MINDIL
BEACH

CASINO

CHIN QUAN RD.

AMPHITHEATRE

STUART PARK

MYILLY
POINT

MYILLY TERRACE

TEMIRA CRESCENT

GILRUTH AVE.

GARDENS PARK

STUART HIGHWAY

DINAH BEACH RD.

NATIONAL TRUST

UNIVERSITY

SMITH ST.

MITCHELL ST.

LAMBELL TERRACE

CULLEN
BEACH

DASHWOOD
CRESCENT

GARDENS RD.

McMINN ST.

DAY ST.

HARVEY ST.

FRANCES BAY DR.

LARRAKEYAH

PACKARD PL.

PACKARD ST.

MAUNA LOA ST.

PEARY ST.

DALY ST.

WOODS ST.

McLACHLAN ST.

BARNESON ST.

HARRIET
PLACE

GULLY RD.

CAVENAGH ST.

SHEPHERD ST.

LINDSAY ST.

MANTON ST.

GARDNER ST.

MANDORAH
FERRY
TERMINAL.

DOCTORS
GULLY

DOCTORS GULLY RD.

ESPLANADE

BRIGGS ST.

WHITFIELD ST.

PEEL ST.

SEARCY ST.

GPO

LITCHFIELD ST.

FOELSCHE ST.

CAREY ST.

FRANCES
BAY

LEICHHARDT
MEMORIAL

DARWIN
CITY YHA

DARWIN TRANSIT CENTRE

TOURIST BUREAU

SHADFORTH LANE

EDMUNDS ST.

KNUCKEY ST.

SMITH
STREET
MALL

BENNETT ST.

CHINESE
TEMPLE

HARRY CHAN AVE.

STOKES HILL

LAMEROO
BEACH

HERBERT ST.

CIVIC CENTRE

KITCHENER DR.

DARWIN
HARBOUR
FERRIES.

GOVERNMENT HOUSE

FORT
HILL

STOKES HILL
WHARF

FORT HILL
WHARF

PORT DARWIN

0   500 m

© AVALON TRAVEL PUBLISHING

sitting beneath a bodhi tree—same genus, different species), this particular tree, survivor of cyclone and bombings, is serenely and defiantly spreading with age.

Brown's Mart
Follow Henry Chan Ave. and turn left onto Smith Street. The stone cottage on your left is a building with a past. Originally constructed in 1885 as a mining exchange, it changed hats several times to become a fruit and veggie market, a police station, and a brothel. The roof was blown off by two cyclones (though maybe from the action inside!). Today the reconstructed building—with exposed beams—is home to a well-regarded community theater. For information, phone (08) 8981-5522.

Old Town Hall
The old town hall, across the street, didn't fare as well with Cyclone Tracy. The 1883 rectangular building, used during WW II for naval administration and later as an art gallery, was flattened by the cyclone. Its stone walls are all that remain, providing a memorable backdrop for outdoor theater performances.

Old Courthouse and Police Station
At the corner of Smith St. and the Esplanade, the old courthouse is a classic 1884 South Australian building, originally constructed to house that government's offices, with the police station and cellblock connected behind. Used by the navy from WW II through Cyclone Tracy, the reconstructed rubble retains its external charm and now serves as offices for the Northern Territory's Administrator.

Christ Church Cathedral
Set on the opposite corner, this post-Tracy modern Anglican church incorporates ruins from the 1902 original. The porch was part of a 1944 addition to the earlier building. Hours are daily 7 a.m.-6 p.m.

Government House
Farther south along the Esplanade, Government House (a.k.a. the Residency and House of the Seven Gables), first built in 1870, was a superb bit of colonial architecture ravaged first by white ants, then by two cyclones. Except for the white-

ant demolition—after which timber was replaced with stone—the building and gardens have been continually restored to original splendor.

Hotel Darwin
Walk north along the Esplanade to Herbert St. and one of the city's oldest pubs. The original pub, known as the Palmerston, opened in 1883. The post-Tracy rebuild included lots of wicker, palms, and the tropically ubiquitous "just like a Somerset Maugham novel" slogan. For information, phone (08) 8981-9211.

Old Admiralty House
Continuing up the Esplanade, at the corner of Knuckey St., Admiralty House, former home to North Australia's naval commander, is one of Darwin's last remaining 1920s tropical houses. Undamaged by Tracy, the cypress pine building, elevated on stilts, houses an arts-and-crafts gallery with works by Top Enders, with an alfresco tearoom down below.

Lyons Cottage
The Georgian-revival-style bungalow across Knuckey St. was built in 1925 as a residence for the head honcho of the British Australia Telegraph Company (BAT), and later occupied by former Darwin mayor John Lyons. Now a BAT museum, the stone cottage features exhibits on Australia's history of telecommunications. Open daily 10 a.m.-5 p.m. Admission is free. For information, phone (08) 8981-1750.

Victoria Hotel
Take Knuckey St. to the Smith Street Mall and turn right. Occupying a prime position in the center of the mall, the Victoria Hotel (called the Vic, locally) was originally built in 1894 and painstakingly reconstructed after each cyclone and war. Still Darwin's premier pub, the Vic's Verandah Bar, overlooking the mall and busker action, is a top spot for that big Thirst. Open daily 10 a.m.-4 a.m. For information, phone (08) 8981-4011.

Star Village
Star Village, a shopping arcade across the mall from the Vic, was the site of The Star, Darwin's first open-air cinema. The original 1930s projection booth and entranceway have been incorporated within the arcade's facade.

Commercial Bank

At the mall's Bennett St. corner, only the 1884 stone colonnade was saved and restored when the bank's 1981 counterpart was built.

Chinese Temple

Continue along Bennett St. to Woods St., site of the post-Tracy temple that serves Darwin's large Chinese community. The original 1887 structure couldn't weather the storm, and only the floor, altar masonry blocks, and stone lions were spared. The current temple, built in 1978, has taken care to blend the old ruins within its steel and concrete replacement. Open Mon.-Fri. 8 a.m.-4 p.m., Sat.-Sun. 8 a.m.-3 p.m. Admission is free. **Note:** Please do not take photos while people are praying. For information, phone (08) 8981-3440.

OTHER CITY SIGHTS

Aquascene

Located on the Esplanade, at Doctors Gully, this is one of Darwin's best attractions. Almost every day at high tide, throngs of catfish, mullet, bream, milkfish, and others come along to nibble bread from the hands of knee-deep, wading tourists. This bizarre ritual began decades ago when a local denizen tossed some scraps to passing mullet (who told their friends, who told *their* friends). Anyway, talk about *wonder bread!* Open daily at high tide. Phone (08) 8981-7837 for each day's feeding time. Admission is $4.

Indo-Pacific Marine

This small aquarium, at Stokes Hill Wharf, is one of the few such facilities in the world with displays of isolated coral reef ecosystems. Other features include informative talks, a gift shop, and a small garden café. Open Tues.-Sun. 10 a.m.-5 p.m. (Nov.-March), 9 a.m.-5 p.m. (Apr.-Oct.). Admission is $10. For information, phone (08) 8981-1294.

Australian Pearling Exhibition

Housed in the same former garage as the Indo-Pacific Marine aquarium, the exhibition gives insight into the lives of pearl hunters and fortune seekers in this region, along with educational displays and presentations on this seductive

and dangerous industry. Of special interest are the jewelry settings. Open Mon.-Fri. 10 a.m.-4 p.m., Sat.-Sun. 10 a.m.-5:30 p.m. Admission is $10. For information, phone (08) 8999-6573.

National Trust

Consisting of four pre-WW II houses in the Myilly Point Heritage Precinct, just outside downtown, the National Trust buildings feature side-hung windows, louvres, feathered eaves, and other trappings of tropical architecture. Pick up booklets, brochures, good tips, and souvenirs at the information center and gift shop within. Open Mon.-Fri. 8:30 a.m.-4:30 p.m. Admission is free. For information, phone (08) 8981-2848.

Botanic Gardens

Just outside the city center on Gardens Rd. (off Gilruth Ave.), Darwin's botanic gardens, wiped out by three cyclones and a fire since their creation in 1879, have returned to glory with collections of figs, palms (nearly 400 species), and other tropical flora. Other noteworthy attractions include a rainforest and wetlands area, plus a greenhouse with ferns and orchids. The restored cottage of Dr. Maurice Holtze, the gardens' founder, houses a restaurant, and occasional live concerts are performed at the amphitheater. Open daily 8 a.m.-sunset. Admission is free. For information, phone (08) 8981-1958.

Northern Territory Museum of Arts and Sciences

The Territory's major museum, on Conacher St., Fannie Bay, features exceptional Aboriginal, Southeast Asian, and Oceanian galleries with arts and crafts, maps, photos, and artifacts (including a pearling lugger and Vietnamese refugee boat out front on the lawn). As a research and scientific institution responsible for cataloging plant and animal species, the museum also houses a comprehensive natural sciences section. One big attraction is Sweetheart, the five-meter, 780-kg saltwater crocodile that had terrorized trolling fishers until its capture in the late 1970s.

The art gallery features works by important Australian artists such as Russell Drysdale, Sir Sidney Nolan, and Donald Friend, as well as touring exhibitions. The museum bookshop has a good selection of local lore as well as gift items.

The Cornucopia Museum Café, set in tropical gardens, looking out at the Timor Sea, is a great spot for sunset-watching, contemporary cuisine, and good wines.

Open Mon.-Fri. 9 a.m.-5 p.m., Sat.-Sun. 10 a.m.-5 p.m. Closed Good Friday and Christmas Day. Admission is free. For information, phone (08) 8999-8201.

Fannie Bay Gaol
Farther along East Point Rd., Darwin's main prison from 1883 to 1979 is now a museum where visitors can reminisce about life in the cells and view the gallows where the last hanging took place in 1952. Comprehensive exhibitions devoted to Cyclone Tracy's devastation include newspaper clippings and videotaped news footage from that time. Open daily 10 a.m.-5 p.m. Admission is free. For information, phone (08) 8999-8290.

East Point
The north shore of Fannie Bay affords dramatic harbor, city, and sunset views. This peninsular reserve, with good bushwalking and cycling trails, is a popular spot at sunrise or twilight when wallabies frolic in the nearby field.

Check out heavy artillery, small arms, and other military memorabilia and relics of WW II at the **East Point Military Museum,** a former coastal defense complex adjacent to the reserve. Open daily 9:30 a.m.-5 p.m., closed Christmas Day and Good Friday. Admission is $6. For information, phone (08) 8981-9702.

Wharf Precinct
Stokes Hill Wharf, transformed first by war, then by tourism, offers historic walking paths, a war-era tunnel and lookout, and tourist creations such as cheap restaurants, trendy bars, live entertainment, and sports, which include bungee jumping and parasailing. It's also the site of the Indo-Pacific Marine aquarium and Australian Pearling Exhibition.

BEACHES

Watch your tootsies October to May—deadly box jellyfish season! Though you'll be tempted by Darwin's sparkling beaches (and the ever-present humidity)—*don't chance it.* Nightcliff Beach, off Casuarina Dr. in north Darwin, has a protective stinger net.

Nude bathing is allowed on a strip of beach at **Casuarina Coastal Reserve,** a 1,180-hectare area that also contains rainforests and WW II gun emplacements.

The first Sunday in May is the official opening of Darwin's beaches, and **Mindil Beach,** on Fannie Bay, is the place to be. Celebrations include rock bands, dancers, acrobats, foodstalls, fashion shows, and sandcastle-building contests. Mindil and nearby **Vesvey's** beaches stay crowded until the stingers return.

ACCOMMODATIONS

This gateway city with a frontier heart has accommodations to suit just about any lifestyle or pocketbook. The central city and surrounding suburbs feature a good selection of hostels, hotels, motels, and holiday flats, while most of the campgrounds and caravan parks are situated on the outskirts of town. If you're seeking a roommate, check out the downtown cafés or around the mall, where you're bound to meet other travelers.

Getting a room is usually not a problem, but advance bookings are a good idea if you plan to arrive during the more crowded Dry season and at festival times. Rates during the Wet are usually cheaper or at least up for bargaining.

City and Suburbs
Park Lodge, 42 Coronation Dr., Stuart Park, two km north of city center, tel. (08) 8981-5692, is a friendly 20-room guesthouse with four shared bathrooms, communal kitchen, dining room, TV room, laundry, pool, and spa. Inexpensive.

Very close to the transit center, **Value Inn,** 50 Mitchell St., tel. (08) 8981-4733, offers reasonably priced motel rooms for lone travelers and those who desire privacy without exorbitant rates. Rooms are simply furnished but have TVs, air-conditioning, private bathrooms, and small refrigerators. Inexpensive.

Coolibah Resort, 91 Aralia St., Nightcliff, about 12 km from city center, tel. (08) 8985-4166, is in the moderate price range, but the one-bedroom apartments with kitchen facilities can be a real steal if you share with one or two friends. Moderate. **Air Raid City Lodge,** (comforting name, eh?), 35 Cavenagh St., close to the GPO, tel. (08) 8981-9214, has plain but clean rooms, private facilities, air-conditioning, TVs, communal kitchen, and laundry room. Moderate. Small and cozy **Palms Motel,** 100 McMinn St., tel. (08) 8981-4188, is about one km north of the post office. Moderate.

Hotel Darwin, 10 Herbert St., tel. (08) 8981-9211, on the Esplanade, near the post office, is the city's former grande dame. The colonial building is somewhat worn but still has some charm, as well as the requisite wicker and cane decor. Facilities include TVs, phones, pool, restaurant, pub, and laundry. Expensive. **Asti Motel,** 7 Packard Pl., tel. (08) 8981-8200, with restaurant, pool, and spa, is large and comfortable. Expensive.

Ponciana Inn, on the corner of Mitchell and McLachlan in the center of town, tel. (08) 8981-8111, is a four-story motel with a pool. Expensive. **Comfort Inn Paravista,** 5 MacKillop St., Parap, tel. (08) 8981-9200, near Fannie Bay attractions, also has a pool and barbecue area. Expensive.

All of Darwin's top-notch hotels provide the usual luxury range of restaurants, bars, recreational facilities, and business services. **The Carlton Hotel Darwin,** (formerly the Beaufort) the Esplanade, tel. (08) 8980-0800 or (1800) 89-1119, has colorful desert architecture. Luxury. The **Novotel Atrium,** Peel St. and the Esplanade, tel. (08) 8941-0755, features—natch—a beautiful seven-story, glass-roofed atrium. Luxury. **MGM Grand Hotel Casino,** Gilruth Ave., Mindil Beach, tel. (08) 8943-8888, features interesting geometric shapes, beachfront accommodations and an action-packed casino. Luxury. The newer **Rydges Plaza Darwin,** 32 Mitchell St., tel. (08) 8982-0000 or (1800) 89-1107, the city's highest rise, is near the business district. Luxury.

Hostels

Darwin's hostels are perfect places to meet travelers from everywhere and pick up tips—and maybe a companion. Dorm beds average $15 per night.

Darwin City YHA, 69 Mitchell St., inside the coach transit center, tel. (08) 8981-3995, is one of the best deals in town. It's not gorgeous but it's

certainly convenient—the bus is practically at your bedside. This former workers' residence has been revived with refurbished rooms, cooking facilities, a pool, sauna, gym, laundry, and game room. Bathroom facilities are shared. The convenient on-site travel office offers discounted tour and bus tickets. Make sure you have your YHA membership card in hand.

Melaleuca Lodge, 50 Mitchell St., tel. (08) 8941-1395, is a long-established place with air-conditioned rooms, shared facilities, a pool, laundry room, complimentary airport shuttle, and free pancakes in the morning. Travelers seeking more privacy can book a double room for less than $45.

Well-known **Frogshollow Lodge,** 27 Lindsay St., tel. (08) 8941-2600, is largish, in a woodsy setting, with spa and continental breakfast included. **Gecko Lodge,** 146 Mitchell St., tel. (08) 8981-5569, is about a 20-minute walk from the transit center, but they'll pick you up from there or the airport. Air-conditioned rooms come with linens, and a pool, TV room, and kitchen are on the premises.

The popular **YWCA,** 119 Mitchell St., tel. (08) 8981-8644, accepts both women and men at its 42-room facility with clean rooms, communal bathrooms and kitchens, and TV lounges. Dorm beds and single or double rooms are available. Other hostels that draw crowds are: **Elke's Inner City Backpackers,** 112 Mitchell St., tel. (08) 8981-8399, with pool, spa, kitchen facilities, and airport pickup; and **Globetrotters,** 97 Mitchell St., tel. (08) 8981-5385—a bit dreary, but the bar, pool hall, and nightly meals make up for it.

Camping

Expect to pay $10-18 for tent sites for two; $40 and up for on-site vans.

Unfortunately, all of Darwin's campsites are about 10-15 km outside the city. The following parks allow tents as well as caravans: **The Overlander Caravan Park,** McMillans Rd., Berrimah, 13 km east, tel. (08) 8984-3025; **The Palms Caravan Park,** Stuart Hwy., Berrimah, 17 km east, tel. (08) 8932-2891; **Shady Glen Caravan Park,** Stuart Hwy. and Farrell Crescent, Winnellie, 10 km east, tel. (08) 8984-3330.

For additional camping opportunities in the Howard Springs area, 26 km from the city, see below.

Camping gear can be purchased from NT General Store, 42 Cavenagh St., tel. (08) 8981-8242.

FOOD

What's your favorite nosh—buffalo, crocodile, camel, or kangaroo? You'll find such territorial specialties listed alongside fish 'n' chips in some restaurants. Tasty barramundi, fresh from local waters, is plentiful also. And, as might be expected in this multinational city, ethnic foods are widely offered, with Asian cuisine ranking supreme. Supermarkets, small groceries, and takeaways are easy to spot throughout city and suburbs, and the Smith Street Mall area is full of coffee shops and lunch counters. Darwin's best dining value—and the most fun—is at the Asian-style markets held several times weekly.

City Dining

Head to Smith Street Mall, though keep in mind that most of the coffee shops shut down when the shops do, meaning 5 p.m. on weekdays (except for Thursday), Saturday afternoon, and Sunday. **Central City Café** is a popular breakfast and gathering spot. **Cosmopolitan Café,** in Anthony Plaza, serves up good breakfasts and lunches ($4-8). Next door, the **French Bakehouse** is open daily for coffee and light meals ($4-9). The historic **Victoria Hotel,** opposite Anthony Plaza, features a relatively cheap lunchtime carvery upstairs ($6-9 for a slab of roast), and good-value counter meals downstairs ($5-8).

Toward the Knuckey St. end of the mall, **Darwin Plaza** houses a glut of Lebanese, Thai, Chinese, and health food counters. The **Taco House,** within that same plaza, is where you can sample croc, buffalo, and 'roo burgers (about $4-6), along with tacos, of course (watch that filling!). The **Sate House,** in Victoria Arcade, across from Anthony Plaza, has cheap Indonesian dishes ($5-8).

Crepe lovers can feast on these thin pancakes ($6-8) for all meals at **Crepe Expectations,** on Mitchell St., across from the transit center. Open daily for breakfast, lunch, and dinner. **Oasis Café,** 50 Mitchell St., in the Melaleuca Lodge, also across from the transit center,

offers munchies 24 hours a day ($6 for sandwich and side salad).

Confetti's, 85 Mitchell St., is open late and serves homemade ice cream, cappuccino, pancakes, and a variety of smoothies, sundaes, and snacks. Open daily 11 a.m.-late. **The Pancake Palace,** Cavenagh St., is also open late every day to please pancake-heads ($3-5 for a short stack).

Hana Sushi Bar, 31 Knuckey St., will feed you traditional Japanese tidbits ($3 and way up).

Café Capri, 37 Knuckey St., between Smith and Cavenagh Streets, features pastas, vegetarian meals, and Mediterranean cuisine ($10-12 pastas, $8-14 veg specials). Open daily for lunch and dinner. **Rendezvous Café,** on Smith Street Mall, offers hot and spicy Malaysian meals. Open Mon.-Sat. for lunch, daily for dinner ($5-9 entrees).

Coyotes Cantina, inside the transit center, is very popular with travelers craving burritos, fajitas, and other Mexican fare ($9-16). Open daily for lunch and dinner.

Lindsay Street Café, 2 Lindsay St., serves contemporary cuisine either inside its historical building or outside in the lush tropical gardens. Open Tues.-Fri. lunch, Tues.-Sat. dinner, and Sunday brunch ($10-15 entrees).

Satisfy your pasta urge at **Guiseppe's,** Cavenagh St., with both regional and traditional Italian specialties ($6-12 for pastas). Open Mon.-Fri. lunch, Mon.-Sat. dinner. **Roma Bar Café,** 30 Cavenagh St., is a local favorite with an eclectic crowd, superb focaccias, pastas, and coffees (focaccias average $6). Open daily for breakfast and lunch.

Hanuman Thai Restaurant, 28 Mitchell St., tel. (08) 8941-3500, only opened in 1992 but has already been declared one of the country's finest dining establishments. Heavenly prepared Thai and Nonya delicacies are placed before you with grace and style ($12-16 for delectable entrees). Open Mon.-Fri. lunch, nightly dinner.

Siggi's, at the Carlton Hotel Darwin, tel. (08) 8999-1179, is the city's classical-French star (entrees range $20). Intimate settings and a changing menu keep the fat wallets coming back for more, more, and still *beaucoup plus.* Open Tues.-Sat. for dinner.

The Boardroom, atop the MGM Grand Hotel, tel. (08) 8943-8888, is a super-expensive (though not super-plus) spot for cozy dining on contemporary regional cuisine and superb desserts, accompanied by an impressive Australian wine list. Expect to pay about $40 pp, more with wine. Open nightly for dinner, Mon.-Sat. for lunch.

The Wharf Precinct
Christo's on the Wharf, in the Wharf Precinct, tel. (08) 8981-8658, has fabulous seafood (try the garlic prawns for $14) and is a splendid place to view the sunset. Open Tues-Fri. lunch, Tues.-Sun. dinner.

Kafe Neon, in the Wharf Precinct, is a casual eatery with superb Greek salads ($6-10). Open daily for lunch and dinner.

The Barra Bar, 15 Knuckey St., is a good, cheap, fish 'n' chippery. **Fisherman's Eatery,** on Fisherman's Wharf, specializes in takeaway barramundi 'n' chips, and you'll find many other inexpensive choices in the Wharf Precinct. Depending on the type and quantity of fish, you're looking at $4-12 for takeaways.

Markets
Darwin's thriving, colorful markets can be categorized equally under Food, Shopping, and Entertainment listings.

The foodaholics come early to set up folding tables and chairs beachside, watch the sunset, socialize, then tease their taste buds at the **Mindil Beach Market.** Foodstalls serve up Thai, Indian, Malaysian, Chinese, Indonesian, South American, and other ethnic cuisine, as well as cakes, breads, fruits, and veggies at very reasonable prices. The market is held Thursday 6-10 p.m. during the Dry.

Other sniff-and-gobble markets are: **The Big Flea Market,** Darwin's oldest, held Sunday 8 a.m.-2 p.m. at Rapid Creek Shopping Centre; **The Parap Market,** held Saturday 8 a.m.-2 p.m. at Parap; and **Palmerston Markets,** held Friday 5:30-9:30 p.m. at Frances Mall, Palmerston. Except for Mindil Beach, the markets are open year-round.

ENTERTAINMENT AND EVENTS

Don't expect big city culture, but there is a range of theaters, cinemas, pubs, clubs, and the casino for amusement. On the other hand, special events in this isolated region can be a whole lot of fun. The *Northern Territory News* provides listings of all the current doings. Again, if you're looking for companionship for a night on the town, scout around the Smith Street Mall, surrounding coffee shops, or the hostels. This is an easy town in which to meet people.

Cinemas
You can catch the usual commercial showings (several months or so old) at **Darwin Cinema Centre,** 76 Mitchell St., tel. (08) 8981-3111. **Deck Chair Cinema,** an open-air cinema with artsy films—which are sometimes upstaged by a showy night sky—are screened in a sunken amphitheater, not far from Darwin Harbor. For information and directions, phone (08) 8981-0700.

Pubs and Clubs
The oldies are goodies. The **Vic,** on the mall, features live bands in the upstairs veranda bar, Wed.-Saturday. The **Darwin Hotel,** on Mitchell St., hosts live bands on Friday night, piano in the lounge Wed.-Sat. and a jazz barbecue on Sunday. On Sunday afternoons and Fri.-Sat. nights you can alternate between indoor and outdoor bands at the **Beachfront Hotel,** Rapid Creek. Or get down and grungy at the infamous **Nightcliff Hotel,** corner of Bagot and Trower, about 10 km north of the city center. Depending on which night you visit, entertainment consists of live bands, wrestling females covered in a variety of cooking sauces, very thirsty men, and wild women. The Nightcliff is what's referred to as a Darwin "experience."

Favorite discos, most open nightly, are: backpacker-infiltrated **Rattle 'n' Hum,** 65 The Esplanade, between Knuckey and Herbert Streets; **Time,** Edmunds St., between Smith and Cavenagh Streets; and **Beachcombers,** corner of Daly and Mitchell Streets. Trendies should check out the array of nightclubs, piano lounges, and discos in the chichi hotels. Neat, casual dress is required.

Gay clubs include **Railcar Bar,** on Gardiner St, at the end of the block, and **Pandora's,** in the Don Hotel, Cavenagh and Bennett Streets (with drag performances held on Saturday nights).

Expect to pay a cover charge of about $5-7 in the pubs (when bands are on), $8-10 in the discos, and $12 or more at the five-star spots.

The Casino

Depending on your inclination, wardrobe, luck, and budget (or *lack* of a budget), the **MGM Grand Hotel Casino** might be the only entertainment you need. All the games are represented, including two-up. The 350-seat Cabaret Room hosts a variety of theatrical entertainment, along with bar service and elaborate buffets; a coffee shop is open round-the-clock. During the Dry, the casino puts on a Sunday afternoon poolside barbecue with live jazz.

Dress regulations are strict: neat, clean, tidy clothing at all times; no shorts, thongs, running shoes, or denim wear of any kind (not even your best hole-in-the-knee Levi's); and, it should go without saying—keep your shirt on your back, even if you lose it in the casino.

MGM Grand Hotel Casino is on Gilruth Ave., Mindil Beach. Casino hours are daily noon-4 a.m. For information, phone (08) 8943-8888.

Corroborees

You're in your own Dreamtime if you're waiting for an invite to an authentic Aboriginal corroboree. These sacred spiritual ceremonies are off-limits to the general public. You *will* be able to join tours that feature a kind of pseudo event, with traditional dancing, singing, and didgeridoo-ing.

Theater, Dance, and Concerts

The **Darwin Performing Arts Centre,** 93 Mitchell St., next to the Beaufort Hotel, tel. (08) 8981-1222, regularly stages theater, musical, and dance performances. The playhouse (capacity 1,070) also houses a rehearsal room, exhibition gallery, and dance studio. Phone the center, or check the daily newspaper. The center can also provide details of upcoming events at the botanic gardens outdoor amphitheater.

Events

This isolated laid-back city takes every opportunity to come together for just about any occasion. **The Northern Territory Barra Classic,** a premier "tag-and-release" tournament held by the Darwin Game Fishing Club, is held about the first of May. The **Mindil Beach Carnival** in May (see above) celebrates the departure of the box jellyfish and the opening of the beaches. More than a decade old, the **Bougainvillea Fes-**

tival is held for 18 days in late May or early June, the flower's peak blossoming time. Numerous festivities include a Mardi Gras, grand parade, concerts, photography contest, art exhibitions, music and film festivals, a food and wine fair, picnics, ethnic events, and daily doings on the mall. A weekend Festival Fringe Club produces alternative music, dance, theater, and literature events.

Darwin's famous **Beer Can Regatta** hits town in early August, and is certainly an event to inspire the Darwin Thirst. Empty beer cans are used to construct rafts and boats, which then "race" in the local sea. Using full cans of beer to build the craft is strictly *verboten!*

Other big-turnout annual events—all falling in August—are the barefoot **Mud Crab Tying Competition,** the **Darwin Cup** horse racing meet, and the internationally known **Darwin Rodeo.**

SPORTS AND RECREATION

You'll find a wide range of sports and recreation opportunities in the city and suburbs, but bear the heat and humidity in mind if you're not fit or not used to the climate. Joggers and cyclists will find plenty of good, scenic tracks. Best bets are the waterfront area that follows the Esplanade, and the shoreline reserve from Fannie Bay to East Point.

Water sports and fishing are favorites here, but heed those box jellyfish and crocodile warnings! For information on any Darwin sport, phone the **Sports Hotline,** tel. (08) 8981-4300.

Scuba Diving

Divers can explore the litter of WW II wrecks, as well as the large coral reef off Darwin's

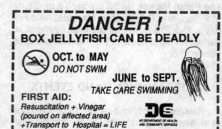

DANGER !
BOX JELLYFISH CAN BE DEADLY
OCT. to MAY
DO NOT SWIM
JUNE to SEPT.
TAKE CARE SWIMMING
FIRST AID:
*Resuscitation + Vinegar
(poured on affected area)
+Transport to Hospital = LIFE*
NT DEPARTMENT OF HEALTH AND COMMUNITY SERVICES

shores. Good dive shops are **Cullen Bay Dive,** 66 Marine Blvd., Cullen Bay, tel. (08) 8981-3049, and **Sand Pebbles Dive Shop,** De Latour St., Coconut Grove, tel. (08) 8948-0444.

Fishing

Top End waters are jumping with sport fish, particularly Australia's famous **barramundi.** The best time to score a catch is from Easter through May. The prime spots near Darwin are around the harbor arms, Leader's Creek, Bynoes Harbour, and in the creeks and estuaries of Shoal Bay. Other common species are queenfish, Spanish mackerel, longtail tuna, giant trevally, threadfin salmon, and barracuda. **Mud crabbing** in the estuaries is another favorite local activity.

For information on **licenses, regulations,** and **fishing tours,** contact the Department of Primary Industry and Fisheries, Bennett St., tel. (08) 8999-5511.

Swimming Pools

Practically every hostel, motel, and hotel has its own pool. In addition, you'll find public pools at Darwin, Casuarina, Nightcliff, and Winnellie. One of the better locations is on Ross Smith Ave., Fannie Bay, tel. (08) 8981-2662.

Sporting Facilities

Tennis: Four courts are available for public use at the **Darwin Tennis Centre,** Gilruth Ave., Botanic Gardens, tel. (08) 8985-2844. Courts are also available outside the casino, near Mindil Beach. For information, phone (08) 8981-2181.

Golf: Darwin Golf Club, Links Rd., Marrara, tel. (08) 8927-1322, has the only 18-hole course in town. Nine-hole courses are available at **Gardens Park Golf Links,** Botanic Gardens, tel. (08) 8981-6365, and **Palmerston Golf and Country Club,** Dwyer Crescent, Palmerston, tel. (08) 8932-1324. Equipment can be rented on-site.

For information on other sporting facilities, phone the Sports Hotline, above.

Other Sports

Sailboards are available for rent in front of the Diamond Beach Hotel Casino at Mindil Beach. For **sailboat** hire, contact the Darwin Sailing Club, tel. (08) 8981-1700. For information about weekend **hiking** expeditions, contact Darwin Bushwalking Club, tel. (08) 8985-1484. **Time Out Fitness Centre,** 5-2798 Dashwood Pl., tel. (08) 8941-8711, features workout and fitness equipment.

The most prominent spectator sport in Darwin is **horse racing,** with greyhounds placing, and an occasional touch football game making quite a show.

SHOPPING

Darwin's major shopping areas are **Smith Street Mall, Darwin Plaza, The Galleria,** and **Casuarina Shopping Square,** in the northern suburbs. Just about any creature comfort or service can be purchased at any of these places (and Casuarina has a Kmart, too). City shopping hours are Mon.-Fri. 9:30 a.m.-5:30 p.m., Saturday 8:30 a.m.-1 p.m., late-night trading Thursday until 9 p.m. Casuarina shopping hours are daily 9 a.m.-5:30 p.m., late-night trading Thursday and Friday until 9 p.m.

Markets

Darwin's markets hold a lot more than just foodstalls. You can pick up crafts, books, plants, dolls, knickknacks, Indian and Balinese clothing, and other goodies.

Crafts

Aboriginal art collectors will find a large variety of arts and crafts in Darwin. **Framed: the Darwin Gallery,** 55 Stuart Hwy., is the place to pick up fine Top End and central Australian bark paintings, sand paintings, weavings, didgeridoos, baskets, and hand-blown glass. Open Mon.-Sat. 8:30 a.m.-5:30 p.m., Sunday 11 a.m.-5 p.m. The **Raintree Gallery,** 29 Knuckey St., sells similar wares, specializing in items made by the Tiwi people from Bathurst and Melville Islands.

Purchase T-shirts printed with Aboriginal designs, as well as Tiwi printed fabrics, at **Indigenous Creations,** 35 Mitchell Street.

Weavers Workshop, Parap Place, Parap, sells locally made handknits, pottery, natural soaps, and toiletries. **Shades of Ochre** (in the Old Admiralty House), 70 the Esplanade, displays and sells fine local arts and crafts.

Darwin Shipstores, Frances Bay Dr., sells flags from all over the world, including the Boxing Kangaroo and Northern Territory state flags.

Other Shops

Photo Supplies: You'll find camera houses at just about every turn in this photo-op territory. **Camera World,** in Darwin Plaza, Smith Street Mall, offers fast passport service, a good range of photo supplies, and one-hour film processing. **Palm Photographics Drive-in Transit Shop,** on Mitchell St., right next to the Transit Centre, provides film processing and sales daily 8:30 a.m.-10 p.m.

New Age: Center yourself at **Inner Dreams Book and Gift Shop,** Parap Shopping Village, with quartz crystals, incense, flower essences, oils, books, tapes, and videos.

Gear: Everything you need for going bush is stocked at the **Northern Territory General Store,** 42 Cavenagh St., tel. (08) 8981-6737. Inventory includes tents, boots, maps, compasses, knives, tarps, sleeping bags, mosquito nets, etc.

Surf Wear: Purchase top Australian brands at **Fannie Bay Beach Bums,** 2/5 Fannie Bay Pl., Fannie Bay. Open daily 10 a.m.-6 p.m.

Bookshops: Conveniently located in the transit center, **Planet Oz** stocks travel guides and traveler's fiction. **Bookworld,** on Smith Street Mall, has a good selection of all-around titles, while **Angus and Robertson,** in the Galleria on Smith St., is the mega-bookstore.

SERVICES

Branches of national and territorial banks are located on and around the Smith Street Mall. Many have suburban offices and automatic teller machines. Banking hours are Mon.-Thurs. 9:30 a.m.-4 p.m., Friday until 5 p.m. Be sure to take your passport or other identification.

Darwin's glossy **general post office,** 48 Cavenagh St., tel. (08) 8980-8226, has instigated computerized postal services, including self-selection service, electronic counters, and digital readouts. Postal officers stand by to assist with any problems. Operating hours are Mon.-Fri. 8:30 a.m.-5 p.m.

Casual labor opportunities fluctuate. Check with the hostels or other travelers for up-to-date info. Working with an ordinary tourist visa is illegal in Australia.

INFORMATION

The **Darwin Regional Tourism Association,** Beagle House Bldg., corner of Mitchell and Knuckey Streets, tel. (08) 8981-4300, will quite likely be your one-stop shop for any information about the Territory. The bureau also provides free maps and informative booklets, and arranges accommodations, car rentals, and a variety of tours to fit all budgets. Hours are Mon.-Fri. 8:30 a.m.-6 p.m., Saturday 9 a.m.-3 p.m., Sunday 10 a.m.-2 p.m. In addition, there's a visitor office at Darwin's airport.

The **Environment Australia Biodiversity Group (EABG),** formerly the Australian Nature Conservancy, 81 Smith St., tel. (08) 8946-4300, provides information about the Territory's parks, regulations, and required permits. Alternately, the **Parks and Wildlife Commission,** Gaymark Building, Mansfield Lane, tel. (08) 8999-5511, is out in suburban Palmerston, about 20 km from the city center.

For permits to visit Aboriginal lands, contact **The Northern Land Council,** 9 Rowling St., Casaurina, tel. (08) 8920-5100.

Disabled travelers might want to get in touch with ACROD (Australian Council for Rehabilitation of the Disabled). ACROD offers an information and referral service for disabled visitors. For assistance in Darwin and the Northern Territory, phone (08) 8945-9054.

Darwin Gay and Lesbian Society, tel. (08) 8981-6812, offers info on social activities, counseling and health facilities, and other pertinent topics.

Maps, up-to-date road information, and camping and accommodation guides can be obtained from the **Automobile Association of the Northern Territory,** 79-81 Smith St., tel. (08) 8981-3837. The NTAA has reciprocal arrangements with both Australian and overseas automobile associations. Bring your membership card for free and discounted services.

Emergencies: Dial 000, or contact the **police,** tel. (08) 8927-8888, or **ambulance,** tel. (08) 8927-9000. **Royal Darwin Hospital,** Rocklands Dr., Casaurina, tel. (08) 8922-8888, has a 24-hour accident and emergency center. **Night and Day Medical and Dental Surgery,** in the Casaurina

Shopping Center, tel. (08) 8927-1899, handles everything from tooth to toe. For **Travel and Immunization Services,** contact the Australian Government Health Service, tel. (08) 8981-7492.

The **Northern Territory Library,** inside the Parliament Building, at the corner of Mitchell and Bennett Streets, tel. (08) 8999-7177, has shelves full of books, photos, magazines and other documents relating to the Territory. Interstate and international newspapers are available for browsing. Open Mon.-Sat. 10 a.m.-6 p.m.

Darwin's local daily newspaper is the *Northern Territory News.*

TRANSPORTATION

Air
Airlines serving Darwin from North America are **Qantas,** tel. (13) 1313, with a change of plane in Cairns, and **Garuda Indonesia,** tel. (08) 8981-6149, with a change of plane in Bali or Jakarta. Other international carriers include **Singapore Airlines, Qantas,** and **Royal Brunei** from Asia.

From other Australian states, Darwin is easily reached on **Ansett Australia,** Shop 19, Smith St. Mall, tel. (08) 8941-3666 or (13) 1300, and **Qantas,** 16 Bennett St., tel. (08) 8982-3316 or (13) 1313. Sample fares to major domestic cities are: Adelaide ($425); Alice Springs ($275); Broome ($260); Cairns ($340); Melbourne ($475); Perth ($490); and Sydney ($495).

All international and domestic flights arrive and depart from **Darwin International Airport,** just eight km north of the city center. Services include rental car desks, money exchange, and a visitor center. Airport **shuttles,** tel. (08) 8981-5056 or (08) 8945-1000, will shuttle you to or from the city for $6-8. Taxis are ready and waiting; fare to the city is about $13-15.

Due to airline deregulation, flying within the country has become much more affordable. Check with both the YHA and the visitor center, as well as with **Ansett Australia** and **Qantas**— both airlines are booking agents for the small commuter carriers, which seem to change with the seasons.

Bus
Greyhound Pioneer, tel. (13) 2030, offers the most frequent service to Darwin from Australia's capital cities and Outback communities. The **three**

routes into the city are: up the Track from Alice Springs, with stops at Tennant Creek and Katherine; the Barkly Highway from Townsville, Queensland, via Mt. Isa, joining the Track at Three Ways; and the Victoria Highway from Western Australia through Broome, Derby, and Kununurra. One or more of the coach companies make daily runs along all routes. On Queensland routes it's sometimes necessary to change coaches at Tennant Creek or Three Ways.

McCafferty's Coaches, tel. (08) 8941-0911 in Darwin or (13) 1499, provides service along and from the east coast, and closes a Townsville/Darwin/Alice Springs/Adelaide loop.

Fares vary little among the coach lines and they all offer stopovers and money-saving passes (some need to be purchased outside the country). Sample fares include: Alice Springs ($245); Cairns ($265); Melbourne ($325); Perth ($415); and Sydney ($430).

All intercity coaches arrive and depart at **Darwin Transit Centre,** 69 Mitchell Street.

Darwin Bus Service operates weekdays and Saturday morning, connecting the city with the suburbs. Fares are $1-2; and the city terminal is between Harry Chan Ave. and Bennett Street. For information, phone (08) 8924-7666.

Car
See the "Bus" section above for routes into the city. The main highways are sealed with asphalt and have roadhouse facilities. But remember—it's a long way to the Territory Tipperary: 350 km from Katherine, 978 km from Tennant Creek, 1,482 km from Alice Springs, 3,215 km from Adelaide, 2,489 km from Townsville, and 4,430 km from Perth. Don't venture off the main roads without a good 4WD vehicle, emergency supplies, and a phone call to the nearest police facility.

Taxis are available at the airport, or phone **Darwin Radio Taxis** at (08) 8981-8777.

Major **car rental** firms such as Budget, Hertz, and Thrifty have airport and city locations. Better deals might be had at **Territory Rent-a-Car,** tel. (08) 8924-2442; **Rent a Rocket,** tel. (08) 8941-3733; or **Nifty Rent-a-Car,** tel. (08) 8981-2999. Rates start at about $35 per day with 150 free km—20 cents to 30 cents per km after that. Rates are higher if you take the car more than about 70 km outside Darwin—which is probably just about everywhere you want to go. Be sure to inquire about weekend specials or extended-rental deals. Check with Territory Rent-A-Car for 4WDs (starting at $75 per day, plus kilometer and insurance charges).

Bicycle

Check first with the backpackers hostels—either they'll have cheap deals or, if you're a guest, they might lend you one for free. Otherwise, try **Freedom Cycles,** 89 Mitchell St., tel. (08) 8981-9995, or **Darwin Bike Rentals,** 57 Mitchell St., tel. (08) 8941-0070. Rates are about $4 per hour, or $15 per day.

Boat

Take a ride across the harbor to Mandorah on **Darwin Harbour Ferries.** Service operates Mon.-Fri. year-round, from Stokes Hill Wharf. Fare is $22 roundtrip, and the journey takes 30-40 minutes each way. Two-hour sunset and harbor cruises are also available. For information and schedules, phone (08) 8978-5094.

Tours

The organized tour offerings in and around Darwin are numerous—Litchfield National Park, Kakadu National Park, Cobourg Peninsula, Arnhem Land, Bathurst and Melville Islands, crocodile farms, and other destinations and activities

can be explored by plane, boat, jeep, chopper, canoe, or foot, for one day or longer. The visitor center has reams of info describing tours and operators, including prices and departure days. The **YHA** travel office also makes recommendations and bookings. Some tours operate infrequently, or not at all, during the Wet.

Getting Away

Due to its close proximity, Darwin is a popular gateway to Indonesia. **Garuda Indonesia** flies twice weekly between Darwin, Denpasar, and Jakarta (about $600 roundtrip to one or the other city). Garuda's city ticket office is at 9 Cavenagh St., tel. (08) 8981-6422.

Scour the newspaper listings and check with travel agents about the many APEX and excursion fares and package deals available to Indonesia.

Also check out special deals with **Singapore Airlines,** 48 Smith Street Mall, tel. (08) 8941-1799.

Unless you're in the big bucks, cruises are not a practical option.

Hitching

It's not so easy (and it's illegal). Track traffic is sparse outside cities and towns. Many hitchhikers report long waits at Three Ways, junction of the Track and the road to Mt. Isa.

THE TOP END

Keep your hat on and knock your socks off. Ever since ad rep Paul Hogan was reincarnated as Crocodile Dundee, the Northern Territory's tip-top has become one of Australia's most popular tourist destinations. Most of the moviedom believers head straight for Kakadu National Park and its realer-than-film-reel glories, with the spillover forging onward, upward, and backward to Arnhem Land, the Cobourg Peninsula, Litchfield National Park, and Bathurst and Melville Islands. Most of these spots can be visited on day trips from Darwin, but at some you'll no doubt want to stay longer. Make the most of your visit to this ancient and extraordinary region—there will be no sequel.

VICINITY OF DARWIN

Mandorah

Situated 10 km across the harbor from Darwin, this small resort on the northeast tip of Cox Peninsula is noted for its sandy beaches, superior fishing, and the tourist-oriented Aboriginal corroborees performed by the local Kenbi community and hosted by Mandorah Beach Hotel, tel. (08) 8978-5044. Otherwise, hop on a Darwin Harbour ferry for an easy day trip from the city. If you're driving up the Cox Peninsula road, you'll encounter magnetic anthills on the way into town. (By the way, they're called "magnetic" because they point north.)

Howard Springs

This nature reserve, 27 km southeast of Darwin along the Stuart Hwy., features a refreshing spring-fed pool set amid lush rainforest and is often crowded with city escapers. Additional features include a fish-viewing area, short bushwalking tracks, birds and wildlife, a kiosk, and barbecue facilities. The facilities are open daily 7 a.m.-5 p.m. For information, phone (08) 8983-3155.

Campsites are available at **Coolalinga Caravan Park,** Stuart Hwy., tel. (08) 8983-1026, and **Howard Springs Caravan Park,** 290 Whitewood Rd., tel. (08) 8983-2907. Budget. **Nook Caravan Park,** Morgan Rd., tel. (08) 8983-1048, has campsites and on-site vans. Budget-Inexpensive.

Darwin Crocodile Farm

I hate to tell you—many of the thousands of saltwater and freshwater crocs you see here are annually killed. But don't despair! You'll soon be able to admire them on someone's designer feet, slung over a fashion-setting arm, or inside tomorrow's burger. Come at feeding time when these beasts display their feelings about the future! Located 40 km from Darwin, on the Stuart Hwy., the farm is open daily 9 a.m.-5 p.m., with tours at 11 a.m. and 2 p.m. Feeding time is daily at 2 p.m., with an extra on Saturday and Sunday at noon. Admission is $10. For information, phone (08) 8988-1450.

Berry Springs

Two top attractions make this spot worth the 56-km journey (take the turnoff from Stuart Hwy.). **Berry Springs Nature Park** offers spring-fed, croc-free swimming sites with fewer people than Howard Springs, plus rainforest, picnic areas, and barbecue facilities. The springs are open daily 8 a.m.-7 p.m. year-round, except after extremely heavy rains. Admission is free. For information, phone (08) 8988-6030.

Territory Wildlife Park, next door, is a 400-hectare open-range sanctuary housing kangaroos, wallabies, water buffalo, dingoes, and other Northern Territory species, as well as a 20-meter-high walk-through aviary, an aquarium, natural lagoon with waterbirds and a viewing blind, and a nocturnal house. A motor train transports visitors along a four-km link road. Open daily 8:30 a.m.-6 p.m. (no admittance after 4 p.m.), except Christmas Day and Good Friday. Admission is $12. For information, phone (08) 8988-7200.

Litchfield National Park

Long overshadowed by Kakadu, this becoming-more-and-more-developed 65,700-hectare reserve, just a two-hour drive from Darwin, is now basking in the tourist limelight.

Dominated by the vast sandstone Tabletop Range and escarpment, some of the notable features of this awesome region include four major waterfalls cascading over the plateau (each with its own swimming pools and rainforest), creeks, caves, abundant flora, birds, and other wildlife, gigantic magnetic termite mounds, and numerous excellent bushwalking trails.

The **Lost City,** about six km east of Tolmer Falls, is a mysterious area of gigantic sandstone outcrops that resemble buildings, pillars, and humans. Adding to the mystique is the fact that no Aboriginal settlement has been traced here. The "city" is accessible by foot or 4WD.

Swimming is safe in the park's falls area (i.e., no crocs), but saltwater crocs *do* inhabit Sur-

prise Falls as well as the Finniss and Reynolds Rivers, so watch your tail there. **Camping** is permitted at Wangi Falls (very popular June through August), Florence Falls, Buley Rockhole, and Tjaynera Falls; bush campsites are available at Walker and Bamboo Creeks.

Privately owned **Petherick's Rainforest Reserve,** 10 km north of Wangi, features thick monsoon rainforest, waterfalls, rock pools, and wildlife. A series of marked walking trails includes a special botanist trail where trees are identified. Entrance and camping fees total $5 pp.

To reach Litchfield National Park, take either the Cox Peninsula/Wangi Road (beyond Berry

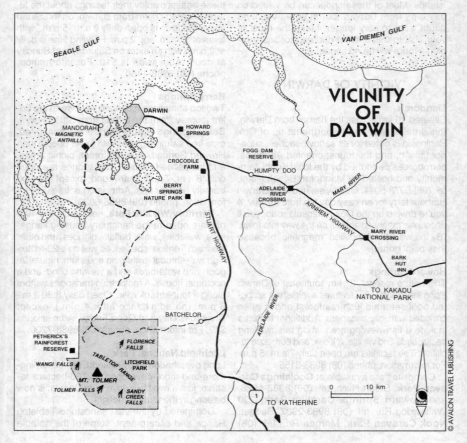

VICINITY OF DARWIN

Springs) or the Stuart Hwy. to Batchelor and into the park. It's possible to make somewhat of a loop, entering at the northern boundary (which has a ranger station), continuing about 18 km to Wangi Falls, 10 km to Tolmer Falls, 20 km to Florence Falls on the eastern edge, and out through Batchelor to the Track. Conventional vehicles should have no problem on the ring road, but a 4WD is necessary for access to other areas.

Ranger-conducted activities during winter months (June through August) include slide shows, guided walks, and informative lectures.

For information, phone the **Parks and Wildlife Commission,** tel. (08) 8999-4411, or the ranger station at Batchelor, tel. (08) 8976-0282.

A plethora of tours operate out of Darwin to Litchfield National Park.

THE TIWI ISLANDS: BATHURST AND MELVILLE ISLANDS

These two flat islands (pop. 2,500), about 80 km north of Darwin and divided by narrow Apsley Strait, comprise an area of 8,000 square km. As with much of the Top End, the seasons produce dramatic changes in this region. In the Dry, grass withers, turns to straw, and burns; the Wet brings monsoon rains and lush greenery.

History

Strange as it seems, these islands and their Tiwi owners not only had little contact with Europeans but, until the late 1800s, had limited dealings with mainland Aborigines. The British attempted to establish their first settlement on Melville Island in 1824, but disease, isolation, and the animosity of the Tiwis sent the new residents quickly packing. Other visits were made by Macassarese fishers, possibly the Portuguese, and a Japanese pilot who crashed onto Melville during WW II. Nguiu, a Catholic mission begun in 1911 in Bathurst's southeast, is the main settlement, followed by Milikapiti and Pularumpi, both on Melville.

Crafts

Tiwi culture is particularly rich and relatively unscathed. Locally produced arts and crafts include unique carved totems and burial poles, screen printing, bark painting, pottery, and interesting ethnic clothing.

Tours

Permits are not given to independent tourists, so the only way to visit these islands is through an all-inclusive organized tour that will fly you over from Darwin. Other than watching the Tiwis create their art (with, of course, an opportunity to make purchases), many tours allow visitors to experience traditional Aboriginal living, including the preparation and ingestion of typical bush tucker (*not* for the dietarily squeamish). A swim and lunch stop at **Turacumbie Falls** is another recreational feature.

Tiwi Tours, tel. (08) 8981-5115 or (1800) 811-633, the largest local operator, has a wide range of half- or full-day "Tiwi experience" excursions, costing $175-240; two- to three-day tours, $450-600, include accommodations at **Putjamirra Safari Camp** on the northwest tip of Melville Island, where guests are given the opportunity to really share in the Aboriginal lifestyle. For more information and a listing of other tour operators, contact **Darwin Regional Tourism Association,** tel. (08) 8981-4300.

It's best to bring necessities with you from Darwin. Stores stocking incidentals are located at Nguiu and at Barra Lodge at Port Hurd. Except for the bar at Barra Lodge, no alcohol is permitted on the islands.

ALONG ARNHEM HIGHWAY

The Arnhem Highway joins the Stuart Highway 34 km southeast of Darwin, traveling 217 km to Jabiru in the heart of Kakadu National Park. City buses go out as far as Humpty Doo, but you'll have to rely on the Kakadu-bound coaches or a car for other sites.

Humpty Doo

You can't miss this little service town (pop. 3,000) 10 km into this stretch—a massive replica of a croc decked out with red bulb-eyes and boxing gloves signals your arrival.

Turn west four km to **Graeme Gows Reptile World,** where you can see one of Australia's largest collections of snakes and lizards. Of special interest are Goddess Marael and Psycho, two of the world's deadliest snakes, and *Crocodile Dundee* python-stars Hoges and Strop. Informative talks are given each day. Open daily 9 a.m.-5 p.m. Admission is $5. For information, phone (08) 8988-1661.

Stop in at **Humpty Doo Hotel,** home of the annual Darwin Stubby Drinking Competition (31 July). Any time of year this pub is full of local color, serves counter meals, has an occasional live band, and is adorned with Territorial memorabilia.

Fogg Dam

Once an experimental rice farm, this 1,569-hectare conservation reserve, 11 km east of Humpty Doo, is an important refuge for waterbirds such as magpie geese, herons, ducks, egrets, brolgas, and rainbow pitta. Other wildlife includes jabirus, wallabies, frilled-neck lizards, file snakes, and pythons. Dawn and dusk during the Dry are the best viewing times. Camping is not allowed.

Adelaide River Crossing

Another eight km along the Arnhem Highway, the *Adelaide River Queen*, tel. (08) 8988-8144, departs from the western bank for 90-minute upstream cruises to view crocs (who leap for morsels being dangled from poles), buffalo, pigs, and birds. The two-story vessel has an air-conditioned lower deck and snack bar. Cruises operate May-Aug. daily at 9 a.m., 11 a.m., 1 p.m., and 3 p.m.; Sept.-Oct. daily at 11 a.m. and 2:30 p.m. Cost is $26 at the jetty. **Darwin Day Tours,** tel. (08) 8981-8696, offers excursions from Darwin (about $50).

Leaning Tree Lagoon

Off the highway, some 13 km from the river crossing, Leaning Tree Lagoon Nature Park (101 hectares) is another waterbird refuge during the Dry. The locals come here to picnic, canoe, and camp (no facilities).

Mary River Crossing

Continue another 25 km to this 2,590-hectare reserve, shelter to barramundi, saltwater crocs, waterbirds during the Dry, and wallabies who peek from the granite outcrops. Boating, fishing, and camping are permitted.

Bark Hut Inn

Built in the 1970s, this favorite roadside pub (two km beyond Mary River Crossing) is the replica of a 1918 Annaburroo Station homestead and is decorated with all the Territorial trappings. An on-site wildlife enclosure houses dingoes, donkeys, kangaroos, wallabies, emus, buffalo, and pigs. Accommodations are in the moderate range, but campsites are also available. For information, phone (08) 8976-0185 or (08) 8978-8988. Budget-Moderate.

The **YHA Annaburroo Lodge and Backpackers Hostel,** off the Arnhem Hwy., lies in the wetlands on Annaburroo Billabong. Tours are available to Kakadu and Mary River, as are bushwalks to Aboriginal sites and wildlife areas. With prior arrangement, Greyhound Pioneer will drop you off at the hostel. For information, phone (08) 8978-8971, or inquire at the Darwin YHA hostel. Budget.

KAKADU NATIONAL PARK

Hallelujah—you've arrived at one of Australia's most majestic, mystical natural wonderlands, a tropical wilderness encompassing 1,307,300 hectares and six major topographical regions stretching some 100 km to the western border of Aboriginal-controlled Arnhem Land. Listed as a World Heritage site for its important wetlands and cultural significance, Kakadu's spectacles include a fortress-like sandstone escarpment, thick-as-thieves woodlands and forests, magnificent rock formations, lowland savannah, wide floodplains, amazing birds and wildlife, gorges, waterfalls, caves, lagoons, mangrove-covered tidal flats, plentiful fish, flowers, and crocs, and an exquisite collection of Aboriginal rock art—some dating back 30,000 years or more.

It is recommended that, if possible, visitors experience the park during both the Wet and Dry seasons as features undergo drastic metamorphoses. During the oppressively humid Wet, rain falls in thunderous sheets over the weathered Arnhem Land escarpment, causing floodplains to swell, landscapes to green, posies to blossom, birds to breed, fish to jump, and all the beasties of the jungle to send out invites to fertility rites. In the height of the Dry, however, the searing sun cracks the earth, plants wither away, the fish die off, the abundant birds fight over the last bit of feed. (Secret: Shaded gorges and billabongs off the main roads are still green and filled with wildlife.)

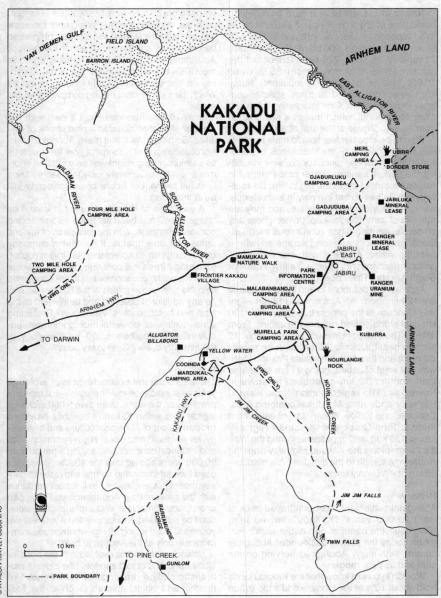

KAKADU NATIONAL PARK

VAN DIEMEN GULF

FIELD ISLAND

BARRON ISLAND

ARNHEM LAND

EAST ALLIGATOR RIVER

WILDMAN RIVER

SOUTH ALLIGATOR RIVER

MERL CAMPING AREA

UBIRR

BORDER STORE

DJABURLUKU CAMPING AREA

JABILUKA MINERAL LEASE

FOUR MILE HOLE CAMPING AREA

GADJUDUBA CAMPING AREA

RANGER MINERAL LEASE

TWO MILE HOLE CAMPING AREA

(4WD ONLY)

MAMUKALA NATURE WALK

JABIRU EAST

JABIRU

RANGER URANIUM MINE

ARNHEM HWY

FRONTIER KAKADU VILLAGE

PARK INFORMATION CENTRE

MALABANBANDJU CAMPING AREA

TO DARWIN

BURDULBA CAMPING AREA

KUBURRA

ALLIGATOR BILLABONG

MUIRELLA PARK CAMPING AREA

ARNHEM LAND

YELLOW WATER

(4WD ONLY)

NOURLANGIE ROCK

COOINDA

MARDUKAL CAMPING AREA

KAKADU HWY

JIM JIM CREEK

NOURLANGIE CREEK

JIM JIM FALLS

BARRAMUNDIE GORGE

TWIN FALLS

0   10 km

N

TO PINE CREEK

GUNLOM

----- = PARK BOUNDARY

Nature lovers will have a hard time getting bored here at any time of year. Kakadu is home to a staggering variety of flora and fauna, with species numbering 1,000 plants, 50 mammals, 75 reptiles, 25 frogs, 275 birds (check out the massive flocks of magpie geese), 55 fish, and 10,000 insects (bring lots of repellent). Many are rare or endangered, and new species continue to be identified. One interesting fish is the silver barramundi, which makes a sex change from male to female at the age of about six.

Wanna-be croc hunters should have no problem spotting some of the thousands of freshwater and saltwater dinosaur cousins inhabiting the park. It's the saltwater croc ("saltie," in Aussie parlance) that's the big threat. **Be forewarned:** Salties do not live only in saltwater but wherever they damn well please, and they are masters of camouflage. Also, do not ignore any crocodile-warning signs (don't steal them, either!), and don't leave food scraps anywhere near the water. A safe way to see these prehistoric descendants is on a Yellow Water or South Alligator River boat cruise.

Approximate distances to and through Kakadu are 120 km from the Arnhem and Stuart Highways junction to the park entrance, another 100 km east along sealed roadway to Jabiru. From Jabiru: The Ranger Uranium Mine is about 10 km southeast; Ubirr is 38 km north on mostly dirt road; and turn onto the sealed Kakadu Highway just west of Jabiru, going 21 km south and then another 12 km southeast, to arrive in Nourlangie. The sealed portion of the Kakadu Highway ends near Mardukal camping area, Cooinda, and Yellow Water; it's unsealed from there to Pine Creek and the Stuart Highway (about 160 km), and impassable during the Wet. It's 20 km along the Kakadu Highway from the Nourlangie turnoff to the Jim Jim Falls detour—60 km of 4WD-only track.

History

Aboriginal settlement has been traced back at least 25,000 years. "Kakadu" derived from "Gagadju," the name of one of the area's first tribes; today the park is back under Aboriginal control, with many Aborigines serving on the staff and as park rangers.

Wouldn't you just know that the Kakadu lands hold about 10% of the whole world's top-grade uranium ore? Three major mine sites—Ranger, Jabiluka, and Koongarra—sitting near the eastern edge, were leased to outside companies before the establishment of either the park or Aboriginal land rights. Land rights granted in the 1970s did not include the yea or nay of mining on sacred territory, only leasing terms by which the independent mining companies would abide.

In 1978, the Aborigines cut a deal with the Ranger Mine that included a nice chunk of royalties. So nice, in fact, that many Aboriginal owners of Jabiluka and Koongarra now feel that a little uranium mining might well be worth the enormous royalties. Currently, only the Ranger Mine is in full swing, but future operations may still be in the offing.

A vast area of Kakadu, in what is known as "stage three," has been set aside as a protected conservation zone, with the exception of mineral rights—for now, that is. If no mining company comes forth with an acceptable plan in due course, then stage three will continue life as a national park. Naturally, environmentalists are concerned over the destructive forces of the Ranger, as well as any additional pollution and defilement of the land and heritage sites. Who'll win? Protesting conservationists, powerful mining interests, unduly influenced politicians, sell-out Aborigines, or the almighty dollar? Care to lay odds?

Rock Art

The park's natural environment is of profound spiritual significance to Aborigines—just read the paintings on the walls. More than 5,000 archaeological sites within Kakadu's confines provide a rock-art record of Aboriginal culture and mythology, as well as a picture of changing environmental and historical conditions, spanning a period from 20,000 years ago up until the 1960s. Aborigines used their art forms and natural canvases to convey messages and myths, to link past centuries with the present day. And though you'll happen upon tours, pamphlets, and explanations galore, don't be surprised or disappointed if you feel like you're still missing something—many works communicate only to the Aboriginal heart.

Distinctive styles that evolved with the ages include hand and object imprints (the oldest), naturalistic outline drawings of stick-figure-like hunters and extinct animals (such as the Tasmanian tiger), dynamic "in motion"-type drawings with naked women and mythological beings, strange yam-shaped figures, and "X-ray" images showing skeletal structures and internal organs of mostly barramundi and crocs (the most recent at 1,000-9,000 years old).

More elaborate "X-ray" studies, produced within the last 1,000 years, convey the Aboriginal contact with Macassarese fishers and European "discoverers." Yellow, red, and white powdered minerals, blended with water, are the predominant colors in all the works. Other artifacts include little odds and ends like 20,000-year-old edge-ground stone axes.

Though contemporary Aboriginal artists have pretty much abandoned rocks as a medium, opting to work on sand or bark commercial creations, the ancient sites are revered and carefully guarded. Visitors are allowed at three major locations: both Nangoloar and Anbangbang galleries at Nourlangie, and Ubirr. A number of sacred sites are kept private and off-limits to the public. Visitors are asked to stay on marked paths, follow signs, and to refrain from touching or interfering with any site.

All Seasons Frontier Holiday Village
Set amid rainforest and bushland, this tourist complex features a range of motel accommodations, shady campsites, dining facilities, rainforest walking tracks, tennis courts and swimming pool (for paying guests only), souvenir shops, and petrol stations. For information and booking, phone (08) 8979-0166. Budget-Moderate.

South Alligator River cruises depart daily from the nearby crossing. Popular two-hour tours depart daily during the Dry. Cost is $25. For information and bookings, check with Frontier Holiday Village.

Jabiru
Jabiru (pop. 1,300) was established in 1982 to provide housing and services for the miners working at nearby Ranger. With the onslaught of tourism, however, the township now offers visitor facilities as well, including shops, a lake with sandy beach, picnic areas, golf, tennis, and car-rental agencies.

One-hour tours of the **Ranger Uranium Mine** depart twice daily, May-Oct., from the Jabiru Airport, six km east. Cost is $10. For schedules and bookings, phone **Kakadu Air Services,** tel. (08) 8979-2731 or (1800) 089-113.

Jabiru is also the location of **Gagudju Crocodile Hotel Kakadu,** Flinders St., tel. (08) 8979-2800. This is the crocodile-shaped hotel where guests enter through the "jaws," then pay through the nose to sleep and eat inside the belly and brains. The croc "head" houses shops, restaurants, and bars. It's definitely worth a look just for the reptilian kitsch angle. Luxury.

Frontier Kakadu Lodge and Caravan Park, tel. (08) 8979-2422, offers various hotel rooms and cabins, dorm beds ($25), and reasonable camping facilities ($8 pp). Budget-Expensive.

For emergencies, contact: **police,** tel. (08) 8979-2122, or **medical aid,** tel. (08) 8979-2018 or (08) 8979-2102.

Ubirr
Also known as Obiri Rock, this major rock-art site is home of some of the country's most important works, which are contained within six different sheltered areas. A one-km path leads visitors to all of the sites, but most impressive is the main gallery with its exquisitely preserved "X-ray" paintings that depict jungle and sea wildlife, as well as several haughty white boys in a 15-meter frieze. Another path leads to the top of The rock and magnificent views of Kakadu and Arnhem Land (some *Crocodile Dundee* scenes were shot up there).

Facilities include picnic grounds and a park headquarters with interpretive display and informative brochures. Park rangers lead tours during the Dry. Near Ubirr sit a border store and 20-bed **Kakadu Hostel,** closed during the Wet. Beds are $15, and on Thursday evenings park rangers host a slide show. For information and opening dates, phone (08) 8979-2232. Keep in mind that the gravel road to Ubirr is impassable for conventional vehicles—and often 4WDs—during the Wet.

Nourlangie Rock
The other major art site, reached via a short jog off the Kakadu Highway, is open year-round. The Aborigines call this rock Burrung-gui, and the surrounding area Nawulandja, both of which somehow were bastardized into Nourlangie.

Rising from the Arnhem Land escarpment, this massive weathered sandstone, sheer-cliffed outcrop features several formidable areas: **Anbang-**

bang, an Aboriginal shelter for at least 20,000 years, where mythological figures such as Namarrgon, "Lightning Man," are friezed in time; **Anbangbang Gallery,** behind the shelter, with works created by Najombolmi (a.k.a. Barramundi Charlie) as recently as the 1960s; and **Nangaloar Gallery,** reached by a three- to four-km walk, with styles including "X-ray" paintings, hand stencils, and stick figures with subjects ranging from mythical beings and fish to European ships.

On the way back to the highway, a turnoff to the left leads a short walk's way to **Nawulandja lookout,** where park rangers will guide you to the only known blue paintings.

Facilities include interpretive displays, guided walks, and a picnic area.

Jim Jim Falls

You'll take a 4WD-only road, then walk one km across boulders to reach these dramatic falls, which plunge 200 meters over the Arnhem Land escarpment, thundering during the Wet and, in comparison, trickling during the Dry.

Visitors come trekking here for the grand scenery, deep-plunge pool, freshwater crocs, sandy beach with shallow swimming area, breathtaking bushwalks, and for excellent camping.

Twin Falls

It's not quite so easy to reach Twin Falls, 10 km south of Jim Jim Falls, where access is gained by fording Jim Jim Creek. Take your choice of the two double-dare routes: make a few short swims and rock climbs up the gorge and hope you don't run into any freshwater crocs (no one said they were *safe,* just *safer*); or scramble, climb, and walk your way across Jim Jim Creek. On arrival you'll be rewarded by the glorious vision of the crystal falls (yes, two of them), lush ferns and greenery, and a sandy palm-lined beach.

Twin Falls Gorge, Kakadu National Park

Yellow Water

No worries—despite its name, this billabong derives its color from an algae that, when concentrated, produces a distinctive yellow tinge. These wetlands are a sanctuary for a large number and variety of waterbirds (whistling ducks, jabiru, egrets, pelicans, magpie geese, spoonbills, etc.), as well as crocs, and boat trips on the mangrove-lined billabong are one of the park's highlights.

Access to Yellow Water is through Cooinda, about four km off the Kakadu Hwy., 48 km from its junction with the Arnhem Highway. Accommodations at Cooinda are either at the **Gagudju Lodge Cooinda,** tel. (08) 8979-0145, or at the adjacent caravan park, which also has campsites and a bunkhouse section. Other facilities in the tourist complex include a restaurant, bistro, bar, takeaway, small supermarket, souvenir shop, petrol station, Tourist Information Centre, car rental agency, and airstrip. Budget-Expensive.

Gagudju Lodge Cooinda Tours operates two-hour Yellow River cruises departing four times daily. Cost is $27. Twice-daily 90-minute tours are a few bucks less. If you can keep your eyes open early in the morning, shoot for the first trip (around 6:30 a.m.) when birdlife is most active (you know who catches the worm). Advance bookings are essential for this popular outing. Phone the hotel for information, and don't forget to wear plenty of insect repellent.

To Pine Creek

Just past the Cooinda turnoff, the Kakadu Highway becomes mostly dirt for the 208-km, southwesterly "back way" to Pine Creek on the Stuart Highway. The road is often closed during the Wet; check with park rangers or police at either end for current status. **Barramundie Gorge,** about 35 km along the highway from Cooinda, then a 10-km turnoff on 4WD track, is lush with rainforest patches, gorge pools and beaches, freshwater crocs, and abundant birdlife. Camping is allowed.

Farther south and west, and often inaccessible during the Wet, **Waterfall Creek** (also known as Gunlom, and once known as Uranium Development Project Falls) was another site locale for *Crocodile Dundee*. Features include a 100-meter waterfall, interesting flat rocks, a large pool bordered by paperbark and pandanus, freshwater crocs, aerobic bushwalks, camping, and picnic areas.

WATCH OUT FOR CROCODILES

Know your crocs, and take the warning signs seriously! There are two kinds: saltwater ("salties") and freshwater. The smaller, freshwater croc is usually harmless unless provoked, while the larger saltie poses a definite danger. Worse, the saltie also inhabits freshwater! My opinion—don't trust either of them. They're smart and *fast*.

Aside from the obvious swimming hazards, avoid hanging out around water's edge, and don't clean fish or leave food waste near the water. Also, crocs seem to get upset around dogs and teasing boaters.

Camping

Aside from the privately run campgrounds mentioned above, Kakadu has a variety of campsites under jurisdiction of the national parks system. Major sites with showers, flush toilets, hot water, and drinking water are at **Merl** (near the border store), **Muirella Park** (near Nourlangie Rock), and **Mardugal** (just south of the Cooinda turnoff). Other camping areas are Djaburluku, Gadjuduba, Melabanbandju, Burdulba, Jim Jim Falls, Barramundie Gorge, Gunlom (Waterfall Creek), Alligator Billabong, Black Jungle Spring, Two Mile Hole, and Four Mile Hole.

All of the campgrounds except Mardukal are subject to wet-season closures. Permits (get them at park headquarters) are required for bush camping outside of designated areas. Camping fees are $7 per person, per night, and are payable at the park information center. Bush camping is free.

Information

The newer **Bowali Information Centre** is on the Kakadu Highway, a few km south of the Arnhem Highway. The center provides extensive literature, guide maps, and tour info (particularly the ranger-led art and nature tours), as well as audiovisual displays and video screenings. The center is open daily 8 a.m.-5 p.m. For information, phone (08) 8938-1121.

Tourist information is also available at Jabiru Airport and at the hotels. In Darwin, contact **Darwin Regional Tourism Association,** Beagle House, Mitchell and Knuckey Streets, Darwin 5744, tel. (08) 8981-4300.

The $15 entry fee to the park is good for two weeks' stay. Impromptu checkpoints are set up throughout the park, so do the right thing.

Transportation

Kakadu Air Services, tel. (08) 8979-2411 or (1800) 089-113, provides regular service between Darwin and Jabiru, as well as scenic flights over the park.

Greyhound Pioneer, tel. (13) 2030, runs daily between Darwin and Kakadu, stopping variously at Humpty Doo ($18), Bark Hut ($27), Jabiru ($52), and Nourlangie Rock and Cooinda ($56). Service may be delayed or suspended during the Wet.

Rental cars and 4WD vehicles can be procured in Darwin or within the park from Territory

Rent-A-Car, Gagudju Crocodile Hotel Kakadu, tel. (08) 8979-2800.

Bushwalkers can choose from marked trails or isolated terrain. Or join one of the walks organized by **Darwin Bushwalking Club,** tel. (08) 8985-1484—visitors are welcome. **Willis's Walkabouts,** tel. (08) 8985-2134, organizes two-day to two-week bushwalks led by experienced guides.

Tours

For visitors arriving by bus or conventional vehicle, there are a number of tour companies longing to take you around. Aboriginal-owned **Magela Tours,** tel. (1800) 089-113, conducts day tours around the park's lesser-traveled areas, but the price is a pretty hefty $250-plus (includes Jabiru pickup). **Kakadu Gorge and Waterfall Tours,** tel. (08) 8979-2025, offers 4WD jaunts from Jabiru or Cooinda to Jim Jim and Twin Falls for around $120 during the Dry.

Most tours depart Darwin, are of two-day duration (in the $200-plus range), and embrace the typical Nourlangie Rock, Jim Jim Falls, and Yellow River-cruise itinerary. Respected tour companies include: **Hunter Safaris,** tel. (08) 8981-2720; and **Kakadu Adventure Safaris,** tel. (1800) 672-677. **Backpacking Australia Tours,** tel. (1800) 652-628, specializes in organizing treks for the budget-conscious, while **Wilderness 4WD Adventures,** tel. (1800) 808-288, offers four- and five-day tours that emphasize biology.

The **Darwin Regional Tourism Association Information Centre** in Darwin has an exhaustive listing of Kakadu tour operators. The park information center, Kakadu Holiday Village, Gagudju Lodge Cooinda, and Gagudju Crocodile Hotel Kakadu all book a number of excursions within the park.

For **boat trips,** see above.

ARNHEM LAND AND BEYOND

Within this huge region (pop. 20,000), comprising the entire eastern half of the Top End, scattered groups of Aborigines keep their traditional fires burning in a homeland filled with escarpments and plateaus, gorges and rivers, an abundance of rock-art sites and birdlife.

The district was named by Matthew Flinders in 1803 for one of the Dutch ships that "discovered" the coast in 1623—though earlier "discoverers" were most likely Malaccans, Indonesians, and Portuguese on a visit.

Don't even try to go onto these designated Aboriginal lands without the necessary permit— and don't count on getting one very easily either. Permits are seldom given to curious tourists, but several tour operators can take you up to the Cobourg Peninsula and to Bathurst and Melville Islands, and a couple of companies offer trips deep into Arnhem Land. (Stop in at the Darwin Regional Tourism Association Information Centre for more tour info.)

If flying in, you won't need a permit to visit Gove Peninsula, at the northeast tip.

Gurig National Park

Isolated on the Cobourg Peninsula, 200 km northeast of Darwin, Gurig National Park (220,700 hectares) embraces exquisite virgin wilderness, important wetlands, protected coral reefs and marinelife, vast numbers of migratory birds, relics of the Macassarese trading days, and, of course, rich Aboriginal culture. The park is operated by the Parks and Wildlife Commission in conjunction with traditional owners (the Gurig people, made up of about 40 clans), many of whom live near Black Point and work within the tourist sector.

The Cobourg Peninsula was the location for several of those pre-Darwin, failed European settlements. Ruins of **Victoria Settlement,** the 1838 British garrison community at Port Essington, include building foundations, walls, stone chimneys, and a half-buried powder magazine. An interpretive walking track incorporates many sights; pick up informative pamphlets at the **Visitors Centre and Museum** at Black Point, tel. (08) 8979-0244.

The British left more than just their ruins— imported livestock still roaming the peninsula include Indian sambar deer, Timorese ponies, Balinese banteng cattle, and Javanese buffalo and pigs. Saltwater crocs, turtles, sea cows, and numerous tropical fish inhabit the coastal waters (though the Brits shouldn't be credited for those.) Along the sandy shores, beachcombers are apt to walk away with some primo shells for their collections. Fishing is idyllic year-round, but swimming is not recommended, unless you don't mind playing Russian roulette with the sharks, saltwater crocs, and box jellyfish.

A small **campground** near the shore at Smith Point has showers, toilets, a picnic and barbecue area, jetty, and nearby store with sporadic hours. Budget. At Smith Point, overlooking Port Essington, **Cobourg Cottages,** tel. (08) 8979-0214, sleeps four, but the $100 per night fee doesn't include supplies. Expensive.

The peninsula is about a nine-hour drive from Darwin along the Arnhem Highway, turning northwest from Jabiru. It's 4WD only from East Alligator River to Gurig, and the road is closed during the Wet. Advance permits (about $220 per vehicle for seven days) to enter Arnhem Land are mandatory. For information, contact the **Black Point Ranger Station,** Gurig National Park, Parks and Wildlife Commission, P.O. Box 496, Palmerston, NT 0831, tel. (08) 8979-0244, or the **Northern Land Council,** P.O. Box 42921, Casuarina, NT 0811, tel. (08) 8920-5100. Be forewarned: Only 15 vehicles per week are allowed access, and bookings are now running one to two years behind (most of the permits are snatched up way in advance by fishers on their way to Smith Point).

If you have a fat wallet (or a gold card), indulge yourself at **Seven Spirit Bay,** a super-remote, super-luxurious eco-resort that's accessible by light aircraft or boat. Gourmet cuisine is part of the $350 pp double-deal, as are various eco-activities. This is a favorite hideaway for celebs and type-A's (who probably go nuts after half a day). For information and bookings, phone (08) 8979-0277. Luxury.

An **organized tour,** all-inclusive of air or land transport, accommodations, and necessary permits, is really the easiest way to go. Again, check with the tourist center and YHA Travel Centre.

"Mini-tours" into Arnhem Land from Kakadu are offered by **Kakadu Parklink,** tel. (08) 8979-2411, for about $150, including a local Aboriginal guide.

Gove Peninsula

This remote region on Arnhem Land's very far away northeastern tip was first charted in 1803 by Matthew Flinders, but only settled at Nhulunbuy as late as 1969—when the bauxite mining began. The local Yirrkala Aborigines protested the intended rape of their traditional land and, though mining proceeded anyhow (surprise, surprise), a government inquiry and subsequent compensation award attracted national attention, planting a seed for the ongoing land-rights movement.

Visitors come to this balmy, tropical region expressly because it is so isolated and untouristy. White-sand beaches, wildlife, reef and big-game fishing, varied sports facilities, and saltwater croc and buffalo safaris are the big attractions. In addition, **Yirrkala,** a former mission, displays and sells art and artifacts produced by local Aborigines. Free half-day tours of the **Nabalco Mine** are given on Thursday mornings.

The only practical way to get up to Gove is by air. Flights depart Darwin and Cairns daily for Nhulunbuy, and no permit is necessary. The cheapest fares are in conjunction with land packages, which include accommodations and sightseeing. Driving up here is not practical because of the long distances (800 km of pretty lousy road from Katherine) and the number of complicated permits involved. Coastline explorers who fly in can rent cars in Nhulunbuy.

For information on tour operators to the peninsula, contact the **Darwin Regional Tourism Association Information Centre,** tel. (08) 8981-4300. Most tours depart from Darwin or Jabiru.

DOWN THE TRACK

It's about 1,500 km from Darwin to Alice Springs on the Stuart Highway (National Route 87). Closely paralleling explorer John McDouall Stuart's path (its namesake) and the 1872 Overland Telegraph Line, the Track has grown from a pre-WW II dirt stretch to a two-lane, sealed, all-weather highway. Sights on or near the road add interest to the long drive.

DARWIN TO KATHERINE

See above for towns and attractions on the Track within about 50 km south of Darwin.

Manton Dam
This huge reservoir, 42 km down the Track from Darwin and another few km along the turnoff, was originally built for WW II military personnel stationed in the Territory. The 440-hectare recreation area features sailing, swimming, waterskiing, and barbecue facilities. Open Mon.-Fri. 9 a.m.-5 p.m., Sat.-Sun. 8 a.m.-7 p.m. For information, phone (08) 8999-5511.

Lake Bennett
Situated 80 km down the Track and then seven km east, this 404-hectare human-made lake provides a large range of water activities, including windsurfing, swimming, sailing, canoeing, and fishing. Other features include prolific birdlife, tropical wilderness areas, bushwalks, and barbecue facilities. Accommodations at **Lake Bennett Holiday Park,** tel. (08) 8976-0960, consist of campsites or camp-o-tels (a combination tent and motel). Budget-Inexpensive.

Batchelor
This Litchfield National Park gateway (pop. 600) and former service town to the defunct Rum Jungle uranium and copper mine lies 84 km from Darwin and another 13 km to the west, in a lush forest setting with colorful birdlife. Nearby is an old airstrip, used from time to time by General Douglas MacArthur during WW II, as well as other wartime memorabilia. **Karlstein Castle,** a miniature replica of a Bohemian castle, sits

oddly out of place across from the police station. **Rum Jungle Lake,** six km from town, is a popular center for sailing, swimming, and canoeing. This town is also the site of an **Aboriginal Teacher Training College** and base for the **Top End Aerial Sports Association's** parachuting and gliding activities.

Accommodations are available at **Rum Jungle Motor Inn,** Rum Jungle Rd., tel. (08) 8976-0123. Moderate. **Batchelor Caravillage,** Rum

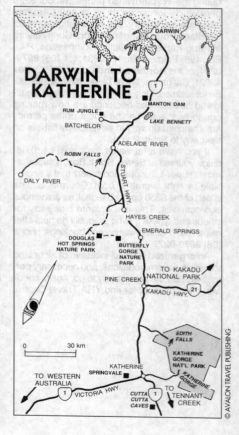

THE RECIPE FOR BILLY TEA

Want to brew your own "cuppa," just like the original Outback pioneers? It's an easy picker-upper from the land down under. Here's how:

Equipment
one Billy can (a small metal bucket)
a campfire
cups
one hand with a limber wrist

Ingredients
water
loose black tea
milk
sugar

Fill the Billy can with cold water. Allow it to boil on the campfire. Add a big old handful of tea (three to four heaping tablespoons). Grab the Billy by its handle and swing that baby around and around to blend the tea. Place the Billy back on the campfire and allow the tea leaves to settle and steep. Pour tea into cups, adding lots of milk and sugar.

Jungle Rd., tel. (08) 8976-0166, offers on-site vans and campsites, and also arranges tours of the Rum Jungle Mine. Budget-Inexpensive.

Adelaide River

Located on the Adelaide River (but not the crossing on Arnhem Hwy.), 110 km south of Darwin, this tiny township (pop. 200) was a hub of WW II military activity, undoubtedly due to its railway depot and prime position. Relics and armaments still in evidence include the **Snake Creek Arsenal**, a major armaments depot and wartime military camp; **Adelaide River War Cemetery,** Australia's largest such graveyard where most of the Darwin dead have been laid to rest; and a host of old airstrips scattered around the Track. The restored **Railway Station** (built 1888-89) is a designated National Trust property, housing a **Tourist Information Centre,** tel. (08) 8976-7010, open Wed.-Sun. 8:30 a.m.-5 p.m. The **Railway Bridge,** built the same year as the station, occasionally doubled as a road bridge during the Wet.

Adelaide River Inn, Stuart Hwy., tel. (08) 8976-7047, offers clean rooms, while **Shady River View Caravan Park,** War Memorial Dr. (same phone), has campsites. Budget-Inexpensive.

For emergencies, dial 000; the **police,** tel. (08) 8976-7042; or an **ambulance,** tel. (08) 8927-9000.

The Scenic Route

From Adelaide River you can continue on the Track or take the scenic Old Stuart Highway, an extra 14-km jog slightly to the west, for a variety of interesting attractions—though during the Wet, access is sometimes impossible.

First stop is **Robin Falls,** 17 km southwest of Adelaide River and a short walk from the road. Aside from the 12-meter-high falls (which are but a few drips and trickles during the Dry), this spot features a monsoon-forested gorge, good swimming, and, for those up to the climb, excellent views from the top.

The **Daly River** area is a bit of a detour (109 km southwest of the highway at Adelaide River), but it's worth the drive for several attractions. The town of Daly River (pop. 250), an 1880s copper mine, was the scene of a bloody race riot between Aborigines, who opposed the mine, and white miners. Though the mine did not stick around for long, the Jesuit mission, established around the time of the conflict, did—today it is run by the local Aboriginal council. The town has a variety of services, including a supermarket, Aboriginal art center, roadside inn, takeaway food, and petrol and camping gas.

Nearby attractions are: **Daly River Nature Park,** tel. (08) 8978-2347, a 60-hectare reserve with barramundi fishing, boating, picnic and camping facilities; **Bamboo Creek Rainforest Park,** tel. (08) 8978-2410, 13 km from Daly River on Woolianna Track, featuring fishing, canoeing, guided motorbike and boat tours, camping, and moderately priced cottage accommodations; and **Daly River Mango Farm,** tel. (08) 8978-2464, five km south of Daly River and another seven km from the turnoff, offering a variety of scenic, wildlife, croc-spotting, fishing, and hunting tours, plus safari tents, campsites, and moderately priced cabins. Be sure to inquire at the Aboriginal council office in Daly River to travel on local tribal lands.

Travel back to the old highway and turn another 35 km southwest (just before the junction with the Track) to reach **Douglas Hot Springs Nature Park,** tel. (08) 8973-8770. The top attraction of this 3,107-hectare park is the thermal pools, particularly **Hot Springs Lagoon,** with 40° C (104° F) bathtub water. Swimming, bushwalks, and camping are also popular here. **Butterfly Gorge Nature Park,** tel. (08) 8989-5511, 17 km farther along a 4WD track, is a 104-hectare tranquil woodland reserve with swarming butterflies, deep rock pools, and a high-cliffed gorge ideal for bushwalking, fishing, and swimming. As crocs may be present, check first with the **ranger station,** located about five km from the park's turnoff. Next to the ranger station, **Corn Patch Riverside Holiday Park,** tel. (08) 8975-3479, offers a variety of facilities including general store, petrol, bar, restaurant, takeaway, camping gas, and campsites.

Back on the Track, keep your eyes peeled for one of Australia's largest **termite mounds** (6.7 meters tall and 7.35 meters around the base) set in the bush near **Hayes Creek.**

Pine Creek

This historic township (pop. 500) 230 km south of Darwin was the site of a massive gold rush during the 1870s. Discovery of the precious metal during the building of the Overland Telegraph Line brought not merely an influx of gold diggers but the accoutrements that follow—Chinese coolies to do the hard labor, and lots of Chinese-run stores and butcheries. At one point the Chinese so outnumbered the Europeans that a law was passed in 1888 forbidding Chinese admittance to the Northern Territory. Originally named Playford in 1888, the town was renamed Pine Creek for—obviously—the pines that used to grow by the creek. Though Pine Creek was hardly even noticed during the world wars, the 1960s and '70s' uranium and iron ore mining brought renewed activity, followed by present gold-mining ventures and increased tourism.

Your first stop should be **Pine Creek Museum** in the old repeater station on Railway Terrace, the oldest surviving prefab building in the Territory. The National Trust, located within the museum, has identified approximately 140 historic sites in and around the town and provides visitor guides and heritage trail maps. Hours are daily April-Sept. 11 a.m.-1 p.m., closed Oct.-March. Admission is $2. For information, phone (08) 8976-1221.

Opened in 1889, **Playford Club Hotel** is the Territory's oldest surviving pub, now a private residence. Also located on Main Terrace is the 1888-89 **Railway Precinct,** including the station, weigh bridge, crane, water tank, sheds, and employee housing. **Miners Park,** next door, features assorted mining relics.

Pine Creek Hotel/Motel, Moule St., tel. (08) 8976-1288, has adequate rooms. Inexpensive. **Pine Creek Caravan Park,** Moule St., tel. (08) 8976-1217, features campsites as well as a fully equipped bunkhouse. Budget.

In case you forgot—or haven't read that part yet—Pine Creek is also the "back road" gateway to Kakadu Highway and Kakadu National Park. Pine Creekers fish for barramundi, black bream, and catfish at Mary River, at the park's edge.

KATHERINE

This third-largest Northern Territory center, 350 km south of Darwin, has practically doubled in population, from 6,200 to about 10,000, with the 1988 opening of RAAF Tindal, Australia's largest air base. Other than military activities, Katherine is a booming tourist town renowned for nearby Katherine Gorge and Cutta Cutta Caves as well as being a service town and turnoff point for the Kimberley region in Western Australia.

Set amidst tropical woodland and along the Katherine River banks, the town grew up in conjunction with the installation of the Overland Telegraph Line and railway. World War II brought a number of airstrips to the area and, more recently, regional administration, agriculture, cattle stations, and service facilities have added prosperity to this middle-of-nowhere tourist center.

Katherine Museum and Historical Park, off Giles Rd., opposite the hospital, features a variety of local history displays and architectural relics, in a former airport terminal building. Hours are Mon.-Fri. 10 a.m.-4 p.m., Sunday 2-5 p.m. (March-Oct.); Mon.-Fri. 10 a.m.-4 p.m. (Nov.-Feb.). Admission is $3. For information, phone (08) 8972-3945.

Katherine Railway Station, on Railway Terrace, houses railroad memorabilia and the local branch of the National Trust. Pick up a self-guided tour brochure to 10 heritage sites. Hours are Mon.-Fri. 1-3 p.m. late April-Sept., closed public holidays. For information, phone (08) 8972-3956.

Watch teachers in action with their Outback students at **School of the Air,** Giles Street. Guided tours are available Apr.-Oct., Mon.-Fri. 9 a.m.-5 p.m. Admission is $2. The **O'Keefe Residence,** on Riverbank Dr. across from Campbell Terrace, is an exceptional example of Territorial architecture, built of bush poles, corrugated iron, and asbestos(!). Hours are Mon.-Fri. 1-3 p.m. late April-Sept. Admission is $2. For information, phone (08) 8972-2204.

Orchid lovers might want to check the copious collection at **Katherine Orchid Nursery,** tel. (08) 8972-1905, across the highway from Victoria Backpackers Lodge.

Katherine Low Level Nature Park, a 104-hectare section of the Katherine River, is a local favorite for fishing, swimming (safe mainly during the Dry), and picnicking. Check locally about the possibility of freshwater crocs.

Knotts Crossing marks the site of Katherine's beginnings. Accessed via a turnoff past the hospital, the original settlement included a pub, store, telegraph, and police station. The old pub, located at the top of the riverbank, is now a private residence.

Springvale Homestead

Located eight km southwest of Katherine, on Shadforth Rd., Springvale, established in 1878, is reputedly the Territory's oldest original station homestead. Now a tourist facility, the homestead's features include period-costumed staff, walking tours, canoeing, croc-spotting, swimming (in the Dry), fishing, trail and pony rides, and Aboriginal corroborees (in the evening). Free tours of the homestead are given daily during the Dry at 9 a.m. and 3 p.m. (historical reenactments coincide with the afternoon tour). Croc cruises and corroboree nights cost $35. Canoe hire is $5 per hour or $20 for the day. For information, phone (08) 8972-1355.

Katherine Gorge National Park

This glorious park (292,008 hectares), 32 km northeast of Katherine township, ranks third—after Ayers Rock and Kakadu National Park—among the Territory's most visited attractions.

Now returned to the Jawoyn Aborigines, its traditional owners, the park is administered jointly by the Parks and Wildlife Commission and the Jawoyn people.

A total of 13 gorges, carved by the Katherine River through Arnhem Plateau sandstone merely 25 million years ago (though the base material is some 2.3 billion years old), are geological marvels with sheer rock faces rising 75 meters high, exquisitely patterned stone floors, and weathered canyon walls adorned with Aboriginal paintings and engravings. Aside from the magnificent gorges, the landscape encompasses rugged escarpments and plateaus, and a superb variety of flora and fauna, especially birds and aquatic life. This is an area of mosses and ferns, pandanus and paperbark, freshwater crocs and long-necked tortoises, red-winged parrots and blue-winged kookaburras—and bat caves. Ten **bushwalks,** taking from two hours to several days, cover approximately 100 km of always scenic, sometimes rugged, track. The longest walk is the 76-km trek to **Edith Falls,** a series of low falls and cool rock pools at the extreme western edge of the park. In case you're contemplating a swim, be forewarned: freshwater crocs inhabit these waters. Katherine Gorge is another place that changes markedly with the seasons, becoming thunderous during the Wet, drying into deep pools as the rains subside.

The **Nitmiluk Visitor Centre,** near the park entrance, provides area and bushwalking maps, informative displays, and literature, canoe rentals ($50 per day, $38 per half-day), and also issues the required permits for long-distance or wilderness hikes. For information, call (08) 8972-3604.

Cutta Cutta Caves

Situated west of the Track, 27 km south of Katherine, this series of limestone caverns dates back 500 million years, give or take a year or so. Classic stalactite and stalagmite formations and tower karsts are the primary characteristics of this protected nature park (1,499 hectares). Rare and strange cave dwellers include blind shrimp and the golden horseshoe bat. Though Katherine tour operators often include these caves in their excursions, if you come on your own you can sign up for an informative ranger-led tour (you can only enter the caves while on a guided tour). Ninety-minute ranger-led tours op-

THE EDIBLE, DRINKABLE DESERT

These notes (provided by the Northern Territory Conservation Commission) are a brief introduction to the traditional lifestyle and bush foods of central Australian Aborigines.

Do not eat any bush foods unless they have been positively identified as being edible. The desert areas contain many poisonous plants, some of which look just like their edible relatives.

Aboriginal Lifestyle

Aborigines have survived the harsh conditions of semiarid and desert lands for thousands of years. The secret to their survival lies in their detailed knowledge of the plants, animals, and water sources available in the country.

The women and children gathered fruits, roots, witchetty grubs, and small animals, while the men hunted larger game such as kangaroos and emus. Many of the traditional foods are still collected and eaten today.

cyclorana

Water

Knowledge of all available water sources is passed down from old to young. Water is not only found in local water holes and under the dry surface of creekbeds, but also in a variety of plants and certain animals. The succulent leaves of the parakeelya plant can be eaten in time of emergency. The graceful desert oak tree holds a secret store of water in its roots and in hidden hollows among its upper branches.

witchetty grub

The water-holding frog, **cyclorana,** burrows beneath the ground with an abdomen full of water and waits for the next heavy rains to fall. With their detailed knowledge of the land, the Aborigines can dig these frogs from their burrows and squeeze them for a thirst-quenching drink.

Protein

Witchetty grubs live in the roots of certain acacia bushes. These grubs, the juvenile stage of a large moth, contain large amounts of protein and fat, and can be eaten either raw or cooked. When roasted, the grub has a pleasant nutty flavor.

---

erate daily at 9 a.m., 10 a.m., 1 p.m., 2 p.m., and 3 p.m., except during the Wet, when caves are closed. Cost is $8. For information, phone (08) 8972-1940.

Accommodations

Knotts Crossing Resort, Cameron and Giles Streets, tel. (08) 8972-2511, offers the poshest accommodations in town, including a popular bistro and outside bar, and campsites are available ($8 pp). Expensive. For less costly accommodations, try **Kuringgai Motel,** Giles St., tel. (08) 8971-0266, or **Beagle Motor Inn,** corner Fourth and Lindsay Streets, tel. (08) 8972-3998. Moderate. The **Palm Court Backpackers Lodge,** corner of Giles and Third Streets, tel. (08) 8972-2722,

charges $12 pp for shared rooms with TVs and sagging mattresses. Budget. **Kookaburra Lodge,** corner Lindsay and Third Streets, tel. (08) 8971-0257, just a few blocks from the transit center, features $12-per-night dorm rooms. Budget. **Victoria Lodge,** 21 Victoria Hwy., tel. (08) 8972-3464, is a bit out of the way but offers good-value rooms with kitchenettes ($40), and dorms ($13). Budget-Inexpensive.

Campsites are available at **Katherine Gorge Caravan Park,** Katherine Gorge National Park, tel. (08) 8972-1253, **Frontier Katherine,** Cyprus St., south of town, tel. (08) 8972-1744, and **Knotts Crossing,** Cameron and Giles Streets, tel. (08) 8972-2511, and **Red Gum Caravan Park,** 42 Victoria Hwy., tel. (08) 8972-2385. Budget.

Both the **perentie** and its eggs are valuable sources of protein. The perentie is roasted whole in hot coals with the eggs, which are pierced to remove the whites before cooking.

Flour
The seeds of the **woollybutt** grass and **hakea** tree are just two of the many seeds that can be mixed with water to make damper or seed cake. The seeds are husked, ground, mixed with water, and then baked on hot coals. The result is a highly nutritious seed cake.

Fruits and Vegetables
The arid lands of central Australia provide an abundant supply of native fruits. The **ruby saltbush** bears a small red berry that can be eaten. The yellow **bush tomato** is very high in vitamin C and can be dried and stored for long periods. **Bush onions** can be

hakea

peeled and roasted on hot coals before being eaten, perhaps with seed cake or witchetty grubs.

Honey
There are many sources of honey in the bush. The tiny lac scale insects that live on the branches of the **mulga tree** appear as red bumps that exude sweet sticky honeydew. The dew is usually sucked directly from the mulga branch.

The flowers of the **honey grevillea** produce quantities of sweet nectar, which can be sucked straight from the flower or mixed with water in a *mimpu* (wooden bowl) to make a sweet drink.

A different source of honey comes from **honey ants.** These ants live in nests several meters underground and have honey-filled abdomens the size of small grapes. The honey can be eaten by biting off the honey pot or mixing the whole ant with flour to make a sweet damper.

Events
Though Aboriginal lands are normally off-limits to the public, everyone is invited to the big **Barunga Festival** at Beswick Aboriginal Land Trust, 130 km south of Katherine and an additional 29 km off the highway. Held over the Queen's Birthday weekend in June, it draws Aborigines from throughout the Territory for a four-day celebration of dancing, sports, arts and crafts, plus bushtucker stalls. Sunday is the best day, with firelighting as well as boomerang- and spear-throwing competitions.

Information
Pick up heaps of local info and maps at the **Katherine Region Tourist Association,** Stuart Hwy., tel. (08) 8972-2650. Hours are Mon.-Fri. 9 a.m.-5 p.m., Sat. 10 a.m.-4 p.m., Sun. 10 a.m.-3 p.m.

For emergencies, dial 000; the **police,** tel. (08) 8972-0111; or **hospital,** tel. (08) 8972-9294.

Transportation
Regularly scheduled flights are operated between Katherine, Alice Springs, and Darwin. Check with **Airnorth,** tel. (08) 8971-7277.

Greyhound Pioneer, tel. (13) 2030, and **McCafferty's,** tel. (08) 8972-2006 in Katharine or (13) 1499, stop in Katherine on their Port Au-

gusta-Darwin runs. Fare from Darwin is about $48 one-way; from Alice Springs, $125 one-way. You can also book through **Harvey World Travel,** in the transit center, tel. (08) 8972-1044.

Rental cars are available from **Avis,** tel. (08) 8971-0520; **Budget,** tel. (08) 8971-1333; **Hertz,** tel. (08) 8971-1111; and **Territory** (in the transit center), tel. (08) 8972-3183.

Inquire at the tourist bureau for best local tours. Most of the canoe rentals are made through **Nitmiluk Canoes,** tel. (08) 8972-3604 or (08) 8972-3150. **Nitmiluk Tours,** tel. (08) 8972-1044, operates a variety of two-, four-, and eighthour excursions up the Katherine River aboard a flat-bottom boat ($30-75). For more adventure, try the Aboriginal-guided **Manyallaluk Four-Day Trekking Adventure,** tel. (08) 8975-4727 or (1800) 644-727.

Bill Harney's Jankangyina Tours, tel. (08) 8972-2650, are excellent two-day, one-night Aboriginal outings including rock-art sites, bush foods, and campfire stories. Prices range $225-270.

TO WESTERN AUSTRALIA

It's 513 km southwest from Katherine to the Western Australia border along the **Victoria**

Highway. Though the road is bitumen all the way, it's extremely narrow and impassable during the Wet, when torrential rain causes rivers to flood bridges and roadways.

Note: Exercise caution when driving this route—if another vehicle approaches, so does an impending barrage of stones; slow down and pull as far off the road as possible.

It's 125 km along the Victoria Highway to the **Delamere Road** turnoff. **Top Springs** (pop. 15), 164 km south at the Buchanan Highway junction, features a popular beer-guzzler (an average of nine tons per week!) roadhouse, pools for swimming, moderately priced accommodations, campsites, and the usual range of services. For information, phone (08) 8975-0767. The Buchanan continues 170 km southwest to **Kalkaringi** (pop. 250), a service town for the Daguragu Aboriginal Land Trust, and another 222 km to the Western Australia border. Four-wheel-drives are recommended for this highway, which often floods during the Wet.

Back on Victoria Highway, **Victoria River Roadhouse,** tel. (08) 8975-0744, 196 km southwest of Katherine, sits at Victoria River Crossing, backed by smooth ranges and rugged cliffs. Known as the "friendliest pub in the scrub," facilities include a general store, supermarket, restaurant, pub, takeaway, petrol station, Tourist Information Centre, mechanic and towing service, campsites, and moderately priced motel rooms. **Red Valley boat tours** depart from here or Timber Creek three times daily (April-Oct.) on cruises of the scenic river and gorges. Cost is $10-20. Barramundi and bream fishing are good in these parts, but both freshwater crocs and salties live in the water as well, so stave off your temptation to swim.

Surrounding the Wayside Inn and Victoria River and stretching all the way to Timber Creek is more recently established **Gregory National Park** (10,000 square km), which encompasses much of the surrounding scenery, plus traces of Aboriginal and European presence, several historic homesteads, a few excellent camping spots (with no facilities), rare flora and fauna, abundant birdlife, and bushwalking trails. **Kuwang Lookout** offers spectacular views of Stokes Range. Access, at present, is mainly by 4WD. Park headquarters is in Timber Creek. For information, phone (08) 8975-0888.

Historic **Timber Creek** (pop. 100), 91 km from the Wayside Inn, was noteworthy for its Victoria River Depot and massive cattle stations. The old port, established in 1891, is now a historical reserve, located about eight km from town. The **Police Station Museum** presents displays, artifacts, and an occasional informal talk relating to police action and racial turmoil in the 1880s (tip: don't ask about those subjects *today!*). **Gregory's Tree Historical Reserve,** west of town, features a baobab tree carved with early explorers' initials.

Campsites and accommodations are available at **Timber Creek Hotel,** Victoria Hwy., tel. (08) 8975-0722. Budget-Moderate. A 16-bed **youth hostel** is located behind the police station. Budget.

Most basic services are available at Timber Creek. For emergencies, dial 000 or the **police,** tel. (08) 8975-0733.

Keep River National Park (59,700 hectares) is 190 km from Timber Creek, at the Western Australia border. The park, known for its extraordinary land formations and distinctive geology, also is characterized by tropical savannah, dramatic escarpments and plateaus, enormous baobab trees, Aboriginal art sites, volcanic rocks, and profuse plantlife, birds, and reptiles. Before embarking on bushwalks, make sure you are prepared for the searing heat and have plenty of water on hand. Check in with the park ranger located near the park entrance at Waters of Cockatoo Lagoon. **Camping areas,** with marked interpretive walking tracks, are located at **Gurrandalng** (15 km from Victoria Hwy.) and **Jarrnarm** (28 km within the park). Conventional vehicles can access the park, though roads may be closed during the Wet. For information, phone (08) 9167-8827.

TO TENNANT CREEK

Mataranka
Heading south on the Track, Mataranka (pop. 150) is 109 km from Katherine. Tropical bushland, crystal-clear thermal pools, a *very* colorful pub, and a chunk of literary history are the celebrated characteristics of this small cattle and service community.

Historic **Mataranka Homestead,** nine km east of town, is a wooded tourist resort bordering

Waterhouse River. Adjacent is **Mataranka Pool Nature Park,** a four-hectare reserve with relaxing thermal pools, plentiful birdlife, as well as palm, paperbark, pandanus, and passion fruit forest—and growing crowds of tourists.

Near the homestead stands a replica of **Elsey Station Homestead,** a set for the 1981 film *We of the Never Never,* based on the well-known Outback novel of the same name in which author Jeannie Gunn relates the life and times at the remote station she managed for a brief time. **Elsey**

Cemetery, 13 km south of Mataranka and eight km east of the Track, is the ashes-to-ashes, dust-to-dust home of *Never Never* characters including Jeannie and Aeneas Gunn, Fizzer the mailman, and Muluka.

Old Elsey Roadside Inn, the colorful pub on the Track, tel. (08) 8975-4512, features accommodations and counter meals. Inexpensive. **Mataranka Homestead,** tel. (08) 8975-4544, offers motel rooms, a **YHA Hostel,** and campsites. Budget-Moderate. Another choice is **Territory Manor,** Martin Rd., tel. (08) 8975-4516, with both motel rooms and campsites, and a pool. Budget-Moderate.

Canoes can be rented ($6 per hour) at Waterhouse River jetty. Historic **homestead walking tours** are available daily at 11 a.m. **Brolga Tours,** tel. (08) 8975-4538, offers a highly recommended four-hour tour of the Roper River, historic Elsey Station (the real one is at McMinns Bar on the Roper River), and Red Lily Lagoon ($60).

In emergencies, dial 000; the **police,** tel. (08) 8975-4511; or **ambulance,** tel. (08) 8972-1200.

Roper Highway

The Roper Highway intersects the Track seven km south of Mataranka. Another 185 km east—on mostly sealed road—is Roper Bar, a small tropical outpost (pop. six), popular for boating and barramundi fishing (not swimming, though—both salties and freshwater crocs call this place home). Facilities at "The Roper" include general store, takeaway, picnic and barbecue area, visitor information, boat ramp, airstrip, petrol station, Aboriginal art tours, moderately priced rooms, and campsites. For information, phone (08) 8975-4636.

Private Aboriginal lands begin just past Roper Bar.

Larrimah

Lots of WW II activity took place in this former railhead township (pop. 25), 68 km south of Mataranka. Apart from being a supply base, a top-secret airfield was located here, from where General Douglas MacArthur made some heavy-duty decisions. The original settlement was actually five km away at Birdum but, except for the 1920s Birdum Hotel which was moved to Larrimah, the rest of the town was abandoned after the war. The railway closed down in 1976, due to

KATHERINE
TO DARWIN
WATERHOUSE RIVER
MATARANKA
MATARANKA HOMESTEAD
ROPER BAR
ROPER HWY.
ELSEY STATION HOMESTEAD
WE OF THE NEVER NEVER GRAVES
LARRIMAH
DALY WATERS
DALY WATERS JUNCTION
CARPENTARIA HWY.
BUCHANAN HWY.
DUNMARRA
TO TENNANT CREEK
ELLIOTT
STUART HWY.
RENNER SPRINGS
BARKLY HWY.
JOHN FLYNN MEMORIAL
THREE WAYS
OLD TELEGRAPH STATION
DEVILS PEBBLES
TENNANT CREEK
TO ALICE SPRINGS
NOBLES NOB MINE

0   50 km

© AVALON TRAVEL PUBLISHING

lack of funding and Cyclone Tracy's devastation, but its remains, as well as those of the Overland Telegraph Station and old post office, are near the hotel. **Larrimah Hotel,** another old bush pub, is not to be missed for its dining specialties.

Campsites and cheap rooms are available at **Larrimah Wayside Inn,** Stuart Hwy., tel. (08) 8975-9931. Budget. **Green Park Tourist Complex,** Stuart Hwy., tel. (08) 8975-9937, offers campsites and is also a good clearinghouse for local information. Budget.

Daly Waters

First stop is **Daly Waters Pub,** 89 km from Larrimah and another three km off the highway. Known as one of the Territory's best and oldest Outback pubs, visitors are certain to soak up any color they desire amid a setting of Australian bush and traditional architecture, surrounded by tropical forest. The front bar "museum" displays pioneer and Aboriginal artifacts. A sign above the bar offers free credit to any 80-year-old woman who is with her mother. Inexpensive rooms and campsites are available. For information, phone (08) 8975-9927.

Daly Waters (pop. 20), two km beyond the pub, is a former campsite for Overland Telegraph Line workers and cattle drovers, as well as a refueling stop for Qantas Airways' first international route between Brisbane and Singapore in the 1930s.

Carpentaria Highway

Often mistaken for the real Daly Waters, **Daly Waters Junction** is another four km south, where the Stuart and Carpentaria Highways meet. The **Hi-Way Inn** roadhouse only dates back to 1974—thus many of us can well imagine both its history and the origins of its name. All the usual Outback roadside facilities are offered, including inexpensive accommodations, campsites, restaurant, shop, pub, beer garden, and petrol station. For information, phone (08) 8975-9925.

From the junction, the bitumen Carpentaria Highway travels 391 km east to Borroloola within the Narwinbi Aboriginal Land Trust, passing **Cape Crawford** (and the Heartbreak Hotel) 275 km along the way. The **Heartbreak,** tel. (08) 8975-9928, offers moderately priced rooms, campsites, restaurant, takeaway, shop, bar, picnic area, camping gas, and petrol station. From Cape Crawford, you can either turn south on the **Tablelands Highway** (also sealed) 378 km to Barkly Homestead on the Barkly Highway, or continue on the Carpentaria Highway, 116 km northeast to Borroloola.

Once a booming, colorful 1880s frontier town, today's **Borroloola,** set along the MacArthur River, is a famous barramundi fishing hole and site of the Easter **Barra Classic** barramundi fishing competition. Some of the old building ruins, including the former police station, can still be seen. Bunkhouse accommodations are available at **Borroloola Holiday Village,** tel. (08)

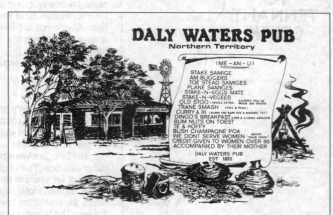

some daily fare at the Daly Waters Pub

DALY WATERS PUB
Northern Territory

(ME – AN – U)

STAKE SAMIGE
AM BUGGERS
TOE STEAD SAMIGES
PLANE SAMIGES
STAKE–N–EGGS MATE
STAKE–N–VEGEES
OLD STOO (FROGS EXTRA) ALLOWS YOU TO WALK ON WATER
TRANE SMASH (PIES & MASH)
CURRY & RI (BURN THE BUM OFF A BOEING 747)
DINGO'S BREAKFAST A PEE & A LOOK AROUND
BUM NUTS ON TOEST
TE & KOFFY
BUSH CHAMPAGNE POA
WE DON'T SERVE WOMEN (BRING YOUR OWN)
CREDIT GIVEN TO WOMEN OVER 80
ACCOMPANIED BY THEIR MOTHER

DALY WATERS PUB
EST 1893

8975-8742. Inexpensive. **McArthur River Caravan Park,** tel. (08) 8975-8734, offers on-site vans and campsites. Budget. Camping along the riverbanks is not advisable due to croc danger.

Dunmarra

It's 36 km along the Track from Daly Waters Junction to the Buchanan Highway turnoff (another route to Top Springs), and another eight km to Dunmarra, a WW II staging camp for southbound convoys from Larrimah. **Shell Wayside Inn,** tel. (08) 8975-9922, offers moderately priced accommodations, campsites, travelers' services, and facilities.

Elliott

The landscape gets drier as you near this Darwin-Alice Springs near-halfway point, 120 km south of Dunmarra and 23 km beyond **Newcastle Waters** historic cattle station. Also a former WW II staging camp, Elliott (pop. 600) is a low-key regional service center for the surrounding cattle-raising community. **Elliott Hotel,** tel. (08) 8969-2069, has well-kept, air-conditioned rooms. Moderate. **Halfway Caravan Park,** tel. (08) 8969-2025, offers campsites, and **Midland Caravan Park,** tel. (08) 8969-2037, has campsites and an inexpensive bunkhouse. Budget.

For emergencies, contact the **police,** tel. (08) 8969-2010; or **ambulance,** tel. (08) 8969-2060.

Renner Springs

The pub building is a typical example of postwar roadhouse architecture, and the pub interior is a prime example of wayside ambience—a few growls and a few giggles. Moderately priced rooms, campsites, dining, takeaway, petrol, and mechanical services are offered. For information, phone (08) 8964-4505.

According to Aboriginal mythology, Lubra Lookout, a flat-topped mesa four km south, was the place where local women kept watch for visitors. It is also considered the borderline between the wet Top End and the dry Centre.

Three Ways

Marked by a large stone memorial to Reverend John Flynn, founder of the Royal Flying Doctor Service, Three Ways, 134 km south of Renner Springs, sits at the junction of the Track and the Barkly Highway. A fabled "getting stuck" place,

this little hole in the Track is also known as hitch-hiker hell. **Three Ways Roadhouse,** right at the crossroads, tel. (08) 8962-2744, features bare-bones rooms and campsites, as well as a sign warning hitchhikers not to loiter. Budget-Inexpensive.

Barkly Highway

From Three Ways, the Barkly Highway travels 643 east to Mt. Isa, in Queensland. **Barkly Homestead,** 185 km along the way, is a modern roadhouse that provides basic facilities, including moderately priced accommodations, a caravan park, campsites, and petrol. For information, phone (08) 8964-4549.

TENNANT CREEK

Other than Katherine, Tennant Creek (pop. 3,600) is the biggest town between Alice Springs and Darwin. Situated 675 km south of Katherine and 507 km north of Alice Springs, Tennant Creek is a modern Outback cattle and tourist town as well as an important past and present gold-mining center.

According to legend, the town's location is attributed to the breakdown of a beer cart—instead of carting the beer and building materials back to the intended site, the camp was moved to where the beer had fallen! Another tribute to laziness is that the shops and pub were supposedly built closest to the creek because the miners didn't want to walk any farther than necessary.

After gold was discovered here in 1932, 100 mines sprang up before WW II (though most were small producers), followed by copper mining in the 1950s, which continues to the present day along with that of gold and silver. The Tennant Creek area, home to Warumungu Aborigines, who call the place Jurnkurakurr, features some interesting historic structures, working mines, and unique geological formations.

Sights

The **National Trust Museum,** Schmidt St., originally a WW II army hospital, features early memorabilia and historical displays. Open Mon.-Fri. 4-6 p.m. during the Dry. For information, phone (08) 8962-2340.

ROAD TRAINS
50 METRES LONG

Allow plenty of room to pass!

Church of Christ the King, Windley St., a classified historic corrugated-iron and wood structure, was originally built in Pine Creek in 1904 and eventually moved to its present location.

The 1872 stone **telegraph station,** 10 km north of town, has been renovated as a museum. For information, phone (08) 8962-3388.

Watch the ongoing action of gold-bearing ore being crushed and flushed at **Battery Hill,** about two km along Peko Road. Erected in 1939, it is one of Australia's few 10-head batteries still in operation. You can take a guided tour and nose around the museum, which features historical displays and other artifacts. Tours are daily at 9:30 a.m. and 5 p.m. Admission is $8. Tours into the newly constructed replica mine, complete with sound effects and authentic machinery, run daily at 11 a.m. For information, phone (08) 8962-3388.

The **Dot Mine,** Warrego Rd., is one of Tennant Creek's oldest mines. Originally leased in 1936 to German-born Otto Wohnert, the mine was signed away to friends after war broke out and Otto was interned. While Otto was tucked away, malicious rumors spread that he had poisoned the local waterholes. It's no surprise that after the war Otto returned to a burnt-out mine and home and a lot of missing machinery. It is still possible to glimpse gold extraction by the old gravitation method. Tours are daily Mon.-Fri., plus there's a special night descent. For information, phone (08) 8962-2168.

One of Tennant Creek's best views is at **One Tank Hill Lookout,** two km east along Peko Road. Eleven significant local sites are depicted on plaques embedded in a semicircular wall. **Purkiss Reserve,** corner of Ambrose and Peko Roads, has a shady barbecue and playground area, and a swimming pool. A better recreation spot is at **Mary Ann Dam,** six km north of town,

with a lake perfect for swimming and boating. Bicycle and bushwalking tracks plus boat and sailboard rentals are also offered.

Devils Pebbles, 11 km north on the Track and another six km left on a dirt road, are rounded boulders—weathered from a 1.7-billion-year-old granite mass—heaped across the landscape. Come at sunset when the combination of minerals and evening sun produces exquisite colors. Camping is permitted, but there are no facilities.

Accommodations and Food

Modern accommodations are available at **Eldorado Motor Lodge,** Paterson St., tel. (08) 8962-2402; **Goldfields Hotel Motel,** Paterson St., tel. (08) 8962-2030; **Bluestone Motor Inn,** Paterson St., tel. (08) 896-2617; and **Safari Lodge,** Davidson St., tel. (08) 8962-2207. Moderate-Expensive. Safari Lodge has cheap bunkhouse beds.

Campsites and on-site vans can be rented at **Outback Caravan Park,** Peko Rd., tel. (08) 8962-2459, and **Tennant Creek Caravan Park,** Paterson St., tel. (08) 8962-2325. Budget-Moderate. A 26-bed **YHA Hostel** is on Leichhardt St., tel. (08) 8962-2719. Budget.

Most restaurants and takeaways are on or around Paterson Street. **The Dolly Pot Inn,** Davidson St., a combination squash court/restaurant, is supposed to have the best food in town ($8-16), though **Margo Miles Steakhouse and Italian Restaurant** also has a good reputation for moderately priced fare (especially the kangaroo filet for $15, pastas around $7-10). The **Coffee Place** and **Gallery Restaurant,** 53 Paterson St. (in the Tavern), are the town's artsy/trendy attempts (nouvelle entrees range $12-18). For local ambience, try **Tennant Creek Memorial Club,** on Schmidt Street. It's supposedly "members only," but if you don't look grungy and act cool, you can fill up on moderately priced meals ($8-12) and the cheapest beer in town.

Tennant Creek's pubs beckon a heavy-duty drinking and fighting clientele. Unless you're game for that kind of action, stick to the tamer bars at the **Tavern, Swan,** and **Goldfields** hotels, all on Paterson Street.

Services and Information

The **Tennant Creek Battery Hill Regional Centre,** on Battery Hill, provides literature and information and also books tours and accommodations. Hours are Mon.-Fri. 9 a.m.-5 p.m., Sat. 9 a.m.-noon. For information, phone (08) 8962-3388.

In emergencies, dial 000; the **police,** tel. (08) 8962-4444; or **hospital,** tel. (08) 8962-4399 or (08) 8962-1900 (after hours).

Transportation

Ansett, tel. (13) 1300, operates regular flights into Tennant Creek.

Greyhound Pioneer, tel. (13) 2030, and **Mc-Cafferty's,** tel. (08) 8962-1070 in Tennant Creek or (13) 1499, stop in Tennant Creek on daily services between Darwin and Alice Springs.

Rent cars from **Outback Caravan Park,** Peko Rd., tel. (08) 8962-2459, or **Ten Ant Tours,** tel. (08) 8962-2168 or (08) 8962-2358. Cyclists can rent **bikes** ($10 per day) at **Bridgestone Tyre,** corner of Paterson and Davidson Streets, tel. (08) 8962-2361.

Ten Ant Tours offers various local excursions, including a popular two-hour fossicker and plant-lover expedition to Kraut Downs. Cost is $26. If gold is what lures you, check out the area's biggest goldmining sites with **Norm's Gold and Scenic Tours,** tel. (08) 8962-2388.

TO ALICE

Devils Marbles Conservation Reserve (1,828 hectares), 104 km south of Tennant Creek, is situated on both sides of the Track. These magnificent, precariously balanced granite boulders, spread across a wide shallow valley, were created from a single granite mass (similar to the Devils Pebbles). The Warumungu Aborigines believe the marbles are eggs that were laid by the Rainbow Serpent. Sunrise and sunset are the optimal visiting times to this Stonehenge-esque region. A short walking trail has signposts explaining the marbles' origins. Camping is allowed. For information, phone (08) 8951-8211.

Wauchope, 113 km south of Tennant Creek, is a 1938 characteristic bush pub, full of tall tales and imaginative stories. A one-time post office and store, Wauchope offers inexpensive rooms, campsites, and roadhouse facilities. For information, phone (08) 8964-1963.

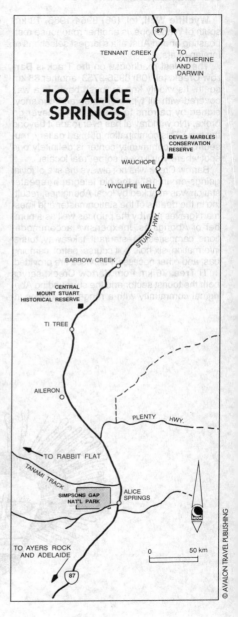

TENNANT CREEK

TO KATHERINE AND DARWIN

TO ALICE SPRINGS

DEVILS MARBLES CONSERVATION RESERVE

WAUCHOPE

WYCLIFFE WELL

STUART HWY.

BARROW CREEK

CENTRAL MOUNT STUART HISTORICAL RESERVE

TI TREE

AILERON

PLENTY HWY.

TO RABBIT FLAT

TANAMI TRACK

SIMPSONS GAP NAT'L PARK

ALICE SPRINGS

TO AYERS ROCK AND ADELAIDE

0   50 km

© AVALON TRAVEL PUBLISHING

Wycliffe Well, tel. (08) 8964-1966, 18 km south of Wauchope, is another roadhouse rest, boasting one of Australia's largest selections of foreign beers.

The oldest roadhouse on the Track is **Barrow Creek,** tel. (08) 8956-9753, another 88 km south. Its widely known "bush bank" is a wall covered with all types of notes and currency, signed by patrons to ensure they'll never go broke. (No withdrawal has ever made it beyond the bar.) This combination pub, art gallery, museum, and community center is definitely one spot where you'll meet some "real locals."

Barrow Creek was not always the site of jovial goings-on: in 1874 the old telegraph repeater station was attacked by local Aborigines, resulting in the deaths of the stationmaster and linesman (graves nearby the pub), as well as a number of Aborigines. Inexpensive accommodations, campsites, a restaurant, takeaway, tourist information, six-hole golf course, petrol, camping gas, and other necessary services are provided.

Ti Tree, 76 km from Barrow Creek, serves both the tourist sector and the surrounding Aboriginal community with a range of facilities including **Ti Tree Roadhouse,** tel. (08) 8956-9741, and the adjacent **Aaki Gallery,** which sells locally produced arts and crafts.

Last roadhouse stop before Alice Springs is **Aileron,** tel. (08) 8956-9703, which provides the necessary services.

Another 65 km farther, the Track meets the **Plenty Highway,** a part-sealed, part-gravel, and part-dirt track to the Queensland border and Mt. Isa. The first portion of the Plenty is a popular fossicking area. The **Sandover Highway** links up to the Plenty 27 km off the Track, heading farther north through Aboriginal land to a dirt track that eventually connects to the Barkly Highway.

The **Tanami Track** turnoff, 48 km past the Plenty Highway junction, travels 604 km northwest to Rabbit Flat in the Tanami Desert, near the Western Australia border. Fascinating plants and wildlife inhabit this region, but most of it sits on Aboriginal lands. Check with the Central Australian Tourism Industry Association in Alice Springs regarding necessary permits and other preparation, including good maps. The Tanami Track, with only about the first 100 km sealed, is suitable only for 4WD vehicles.

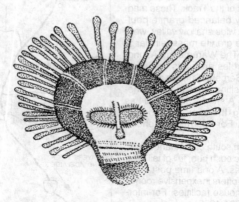

ALICE SPRINGS

Welcome to Alice (or "the Alice," as it's also known), the Red Centre of Australia. The thought can send chills up the straightest spine even in the most brain-meltdown heat. But, if you're thinking of the frontiersy Outback depicted in Neville Shute's slap-on-the-back novel *A Town Like Alice,* you'll be disappointed. However, the Alice isn't so bad, and, enclosed as it is within the Mac-Donnell Ranges, the surrounding area is downright astonishing. Just keep in mind that this is no longer an Outback town but a convenient tourist center for exploring the real Outback.

History

Originally a town called Stuart (after explorer John Stuart) and site of an important 1871 telegraph station built alongside normally dry Todd River (after telegraph superintendent Charles Todd) and its permanent spring (named Alice, after Todd's wife). When the repeater station was shifted into town in 1933, Stuart was renamed "Alice Springs." The town's growth was slow-going, particularly as supplies were delivered only once yearly by Afghan camel teams. Though the railway arrived in 1929, the European population was only about 250. Cattle and mining industries, as well as establishment of a government seat from 1926-31, still barely doubled Alice's population.

It was war and the WW II Darwin bombing that created a comparable population explosion. As a major military base, postwar rumors about the area's attributes were leaked, creating tourist interest and subsequent development. Presently the Alice Springs area is home to approximately 27,000 inhabitants. Besides being a service center to the neighboring Aboriginal and pastoral communities, and its obvious importance as a tourist base, nearby Pine Gap is home to a major (and controversial) hush-hush U.S. communications base.

A WALKING TOUR

Alice proper is easily explored on foot. The city center (including most accommodations and restaurants) is bordered by the Track (Stuart Highway) on one side, the Todd River (creek bed) on the other, Anzac Hill on the north, and Stuart Terrace on the south—about a five-square-block grid. Todd Street and its pedestrian mall between Wills and Gregory Terraces is the main shopping street and site of the general post office. The bus terminal and Central Australian Tourism Industry Association are nearby.

Old Telegraph Station

The original settlement site is now a 570-hectare historical reserve, featuring *the* Alice spring (you can swim in it), a small museum, several restored buildings, a walking trail to Trig Hill Lookout, picnic areas, and a wildlife enclosure. The reserve is an easy walk from town center along the path on the western edge of the Todd River bank. Hours are daily 8 a.m.-9 p.m. Oct.-April, 8 a.m.-7 p.m. May-September. Free ranger-guided tours are given Sunday 10 a.m., but book ahead. Admission is $4. For information, phone (08) 8952-1013.

School of the Air

Located on Head St., just before the Old Telegraph Station, School of the Air was founded in 1951 to educate children isolated in the Outback. You can tour the "school," but don't expect to find any kids there—all the teaching is done via CB radio. Still you can view the unique educational methods from this broadcasting station and peruse the artwork and other assignments submitted by the unseen students. Buy trinkets and souvenirs from the gift shop to help fund this unique school. Hours are Mon.-Sat. 8:30 a.m.-4:30 p.m., Sun. 1:30 p.m.-4:30 p.m., during the school term. Donations are accepted. For information, phone (08) 8951-6800.

Anzac Hill

Just north of the town center, Anzac Hill provides superb views of Alice and the surrounding ranges. Sunset and sunrise are the best viewing times. Walk up via "Lions" walk opposite the Catholic church on Wills Terrace.

ALICE SPRINGS

TO TENNANT CREEK

87

STUART HWY.

DIXON RD.

OLD TELEGRAPH STATION

WOODS TERRACE

CHARLES RIVER

ALICE SPRINGS TELEGRAPH STATION HISTORICAL RESERVE

SMITH ST.

SCHWARZ CRESCENT

ANZAC HILL

WILLS TERRACE

UNDOOLYA RD.

RAILWAY STATION

RAILWAY TERRACE

PARSONS ST.

BATH ST.

GREGORY TERRACE

POST OFFICE

PIONEER YHA

GEORGE CRESCENT

TOURIST OFFICE

STOTT TERRACE

TODD ST.

HARTLEY ST.

LARAPINTA DR.

ARALUEN ARTS CENTRE

STREHLOW RESEARCH CENTRE

BILLY GOAT HILL

AVIATION MUSEUM

MEMORIAL DR.

STUART TERRACE

ROYAL FLYING DOCTOR BASE

HOSPITAL

MELANKA LODGE BACKPACKERS

LEICHHARDT TERRACE

OLIVE PINK FLORA RESERVE

TUNKS RD.

BRADSHAW DR.

TELEGRAPH TERRACE

GAP RD.

SOUTH TERRACE

BARRETT DR.

LASSETER'S CASINO

TODD RIVER

TO AIRPORT, AYERS ROCK, AND ADELAIDE

87

HEAVITREE GAP

TO ALICE SPRINGS SOUTH

0   500 m

© AVALON TRAVEL PUBLISHING

Museum of Central Australia

On Todd Mall, at the corner of Parsons St., this museum of central Australia features natural history, Aboriginal culture, and early pioneering displays relating to the local region. Hours are Mon.-Fri. 9 a.m.-5 p.m., Sat.-Sun. 10 a.m.-5 p.m. Admission $2. For information, phone (08) 8951-5335.

Adelaide House

On the mall, across Parsons St., Adelaide House operated 1920-26 as the first Alice Springs Hospital, later became a convalescent home, and in 1980 was declared a museum. Established by Reverend John Flynn (founder of the Royal Flying Doctor Service) and his Australian Inland Mission, the stone radio hut behind the building marks the spot where Traeger and Flynn sent their first field transmission in 1926, prompting the invention of Traeger's Pedal Radio, which Flynn used for Outback communication in his Flying Doctor service. The **Flynn Memorial Church,** next door, was built to honor the good doctor. Hours are Mon.-Thurs. 10 a.m.-4 p.m., Fri.-Sat. 10 a.m.-noon. Admission $3. For information, phone (08) 8952-1856.

Old Government Homes

On Hartley St., between Stott and Stuart Terraces, these dwellings built for government officers in the 1930s were constructed of concrete blocks, timber, fly-wire verandas, and other architectural details indicative of that period. Hours are Mon.-Fri. 10 a.m.-4 p.m. For information, phone (08) 8952-6955.

Royal Flying Doctor Base

Straight ahead, across Stuart Terrace, this medical facility and lifeline to Outback residents offers educational tours including an informative film, displays, memorabilia, and a gift shop. Hours are Mon.-Sat. 9 a.m.-4 p.m., Sunday 1-4 p.m. Tours are given every half hour. Admission $3. For information, phone (08) 8952-1129.

Olive Pink Flora Reserve

Behind the Flying Doctor Base, near the hospital, follow Tunks Rd. across the Todd River causeway to see this excellent collection of central Australian native plants. Founded by Olive Pink, who lived with the local Aborigines, this arid-zone botanical reserve also features a visitor

DOCTORS WITH WINGS: THE ROYAL FLYING DOCTOR SERVICE

Medical care is provided by the Royal Flying Doctor Service (RFDS), which, since the 1920s, has been coming to the rescue of the Outback's sick and injured in an area equal to about two-thirds of the United States. Established in 1912 by John Flynn in Cloncurry, Queensland, the service is now a sophisticated network of 15 bases with twin-engine aircraft and a large staff of doctors, nurses, radio operators, pilots, aircraft engineers, and other personnel, with the capacity to arrive on the scene within a few hours. Funded by donations and government subsidies, the RFDS does not charge patients unless they have workers' compensation or accident insurance coverage. About 40% of RFDS patients are Aborigines.

High-frequency radio networks enable Outback residents to be in contact with doctors around the clock. Besides fly-in-fly-out emergency evacuations to base hospitals, the RFDS also supervises small nurse-run hospitals and community clinics and pro-

vides remote clinics, reserves, and homesteads with comprehensive first-aid and medicine chests. (Ah, how comforting to know a friend or relative could perform emergency surgery while getting radio instructions!)

Since 1951, when the first facility opened in Alice Springs, School of the Air has been educating school-age children living on Outback stations or in other remote parts of Australia. Lessons are a combination of high-frequency radio transmissions, correspondence courses (including audio and video materials), once-a-week "private" radio sessions, and at least one annual personal visit—when teachers swoop in via light planes or heavy vehicles.

The Royal Flying Doctor Service high-frequency radio network also provides an important social forum. Regular open broadcasts, called "galah sessions," allow far-apart residents to gab and gossip, share information, keep up on events, and send or receive telegrams.

center and several short walking trails. Hours are daily 10 a.m.-6 p.m. Donations requested. For information, phone (08) 8952-2154.

Billy Goat Hill
Back across Stuart Terrace (and the other side of the Royal Flying Doctor Base), Billy Goat Hill was an early goatherding location with goat yards built around its base and Aboriginal shepherds leading their flocks to wells near the present expanse of lawns.

Panorama Guth
Heading back toward town, on Hartley, Panorama Guth is a 360-degree realistic landscape painting of the Centre created by Dutch artist Henk Guth. Viewers can check out the scene from an elevated platform. But wouldn't you rather see the real thing? An art gallery exhibits a range of works by Hermannsburg School watercolorists. Hours are Mon.-Sat. 9 a.m.-5 p.m., Sunday (March-Nov.) noon-5 p.m., closed public holidays Dec.-February. Admission $3. For information, phone (08) 8952-2013.

Hartley Street School
Farther up the street, across Gregory Terrace, the first government school opened in 1929. Architectural contrasts between the original building and later octagonal addition depict typical Alice Springs '20s and '40s styles. The building houses the National Trust office. Hours are Mon.-Fri. 10:30 a.m.-2:30 p.m., closed public holidays. For information, phone (08) 8952-4516.

The Residency
On the other side of the post office, this 1927 stone structure, built for John Charles Cawood, Alice's first government resident, now serves as a museum with Territory history, Aboriginal art, and meteorite exhibits. Hours are Mon.-Fri. 9 a.m.-4 p.m., Sat.-Sun. 10 a.m.-4 p.m. For information, phone (08) 8951-5335.

Old Stuart Gaol
Across Hartley St., on Parsons St., the old gaol was built in 1907-08 and is the oldest building in Alice, having housed offenders from horse thieves to railway stowaways until its closure in 1938. Hours are Tuesday and Thursday 10 a.m.-12:30 p.m., Saturday 9:30 a.m.-noon. Admission is $2.

Old Court House
Across Parsons St. diagonally from the jail, this courthouse served as Administrator's Council Rooms 1926-31, and operated as Alice Spring's primary court until 1980, when a new facility was constructed. Viewing is from the outside only. For information, phone (08) 8952-9006.

Railway Terrace
Continue along Parsons St. to Railway Terrace. Toward your right, three 1920s concrete-brick **railway cottages** can be seen. Turn to the left to see the **Wild Dog** (Gnoilya Tmerga) sacred site, which depicts an Aboriginal legend about a great white Dog Man.

LARAPINTA DRIVE SIGHTS

Across the railway tracks from Billy Goat Hill, Stott Terrace becomes Larapinta Drive, a winding road with several additional attractions.

Pay your respects to some of the early pioneers at **Pioneer Cemetery,** the original Stuart Town graveyard on George Crescent, off Larapinta Drive.

The **Aviation Museum,** on Memorial Dr., just off Larapinta, is housed inside the former Connellan Hanger, site of Alice's first airport. Besides the predictable early aviation memorabilia, exhibits include a couple of (previously) missing aircraft and a road train. Open daily 10 a.m.-5 p.m. Free admission. For information, phone (08) 8951-5686.

Next to the Aviation Museum, also on Memorial Dr., **Memorial Cemetery** contains a few more interesting graves—most notably those of Aboriginal artist Albert Namatjira and Harold Bell Lasseter. (Lasseter was the fellow who claimed to have found a gold reef near Docker River on the Northern Territory/Western Australia border. The resulting hoopla was astounding and has continued from the 1930s to the present day, with the gold reef being lost, found, and lost again, many times over. Lasseter's reef may be folly, but his grave is well marked.)

Back on Larapinta Drive, you'll find the multimillion-dollar **Strehlow Research Centre,** opened in 1992 to commemorate the work of anthropologist Theodor Strehlow. Professor Strehlow devoted much of his life to studying the Aranda traditional people, ultimately being honored with the designation *ingkata,* or ceremonial chief. Much of the hands-on collection is hands-off due to its religious significance, but the public exhibits are still quite informative, giving a unique glimpse into the Aranda people's lifestyle and belief system. Hours are daily 10 a.m.-5 p.m. Admission is $4. For information, phone (08) 8952-8000.

Next door, **Araluen Arts Centre** houses two art galleries (one with paintings by noted Aboriginal artist Albert Namatjira), a craft center, restaurant, and bar, and presents a variety of performances. Hours are daily 10 a.m.-5 p.m. Admission is $2.50. For information, phone (08) 8952-5022.

Beyond the arts center, **Diorama Village** features gaudy displays of Aboriginal Dreamtime legends. Hours are daily 10 a.m.-5 p.m. Admission is $2. For information, phone (08) 8952-1884.

SOUTH ALICE SIGHTS

Yet another group of sights is clustered around the Stuart Highway, on Old South and Emily Gap Roads, south of the town center.

Pitchi Ritchi Aboriginal Experience
This open-air museum, south of the Heavitree Gap causeway, showcases a large collection of vintage machinery and other early relics, as well as Aboriginal sculptures by noted Victorian artist William Ricketts (most of Ricketts's work is in his sanctuary, outside Melbourne). A kiosk on the premises sells souvenirs. Hours are daily 9 a.m.- 2 p.m., and guided tours by local Aborigines are available. Admission $15 (!). For information, phone (08) 8952-1931.

Stuart Auto Museum
See restored vintage cars and motorcycles, as well as old phonographs, telephones, steam engines, and exhibits relating to Territorial motoring history (including the saga of the first car to cross the Territory back in 1907). A restaurant serves light meals and refreshments. Hours are daily 9 a.m.-5 p.m. Admission $3.

Mecca Date Gardens
Australia's only commercial date farm features more than 20 different varieties of this ancient tree crop, introduced to the area by the Afghan camel drivers. Dates are available for purchase, and tours are given regularly. Hours are Mon.-Sat. 9 a.m.-5 p.m., Sat. 9 a.m.-1 p.m. April-October. For information, phone (08) 8952-2425.

Frontier Camel Farm
This strange site includes a camel museum, camel rides and tours, and a big reptile house filled with goannas, lizards, and desert snakes. The staff offers informal talks. Hours are daily 9 a.m.-5 p.m., camel rides at 10:30 a.m. and 2 p.m., closed Christmas Day to New Year's Day. Admission is $10, $6 without the camel ride. For information, phone (08) 8953-0444.

Old Timer's Folk Museum
If you haven't had enough pioneering-day reminders, then stop in, pay a buck, and get another fix. Hours are daily 2-4 p.m., except summer months. For information, phone (08) 8952-2844.

Ghan Preservation/MacDonnell Siding
Come join other railway aficionados at this MacDonnell Siding site (built to original design specs), with restored and preserved classic 1929 Ghan locomotives and carriages along a 26-km stretch of the old train track. The Old Ghan, named for the Afghan camel drivers, operated between Alice and Adelaide for 51 years, until it was replaced by the New Ghan in 1980. Open daily 9 a.m.-5 p.m. April-Oct., 10 a.m.-4 p.m. Nov.-March. Admission is $3. Guided train journeys are $15; in July, night tours, including dinner, cost $50-90. Daily one-way journeys are also offered, with return by coach. For information, phone (08) 8955-5047.

Road Transport Hall of Fame
Adjacent to the Ghan, in the designated "Transport Heritage Area," this large warehouse features a collection of vintage vehicles and pays homage to the country's tough truckers. Among the displays are one of the Northern Territory's original road trains, as well as a 1911 Ford Model T and 1923 Rolls Royce. Hours are daily 9 a.m.-5 p.m. Admission $4. For information, phone (08) 8952-7161.

Chateau Hornsby Winery
Take the Colonel Rose Dr. turnoff from Stuart Highway, then hang a left at Petrick Rd., to visit

central Australia's only winery, where you can sip and taste shiraz, cabernet sauvignon, riesling, semillon, and chardonnay. A restaurant is open for lunch (with wine, of course). Hours are daily 9 a.m.-5 p.m., closed Christmas Day. For information, phone (08) 8955-5133.

ACCOMMODATIONS

Most Alice accommodations are conveniently located smack-dab in the center of town, while campsites and caravan parks are scattered around the fringes. If possible, book ahead—especially at the most and least expensive places. Rates are usually somewhat lower during the hotter-than-hell summer months.

The **Todd Tavern,** on Todd Mall, tel. (08) 8952-1255, features simple accommodations with shared facilities and continental breakfast, but beware the noise from live bands playing in the pub most weekends. Inexpensive. **Alice Lodge,** 4 Mueller St., tel. (08) 8953-1975, is a small seven-room establishment with weekly rates and a four-bed dorm. Facilities include a communal kitchen and laundry, plus pool and barbecue area. Inexpensive.

A pool and fully equipped, self-contained units with TVs are available at **The Swagmans Rest,** 67 Gap Rd., tel. (08) 8953-1333. Inexpensive. *Priscilla* fans can hang their wardrobe in one of the pleasant motel rooms at **Queen of the Desert Resort,** about two km south of the town center, tel. (08) 8952-6611. Those with less money in their pockets (or purses) can book a $16 dorm bed. Inexpensive.

Alice Sundown Motel, 39 Gap Rd., tel. (08) 8952-8422, features modern rooms with TVs, pool, barbecue area, and courtesy coach. Moderate. One of Alice's best values is **Desert Palms Resort,** Barrett Dr., tel. (08) 8952-5977, with large rooms, cooking facilities, pool, and half-court tennis. Moderate. **Desert Rose Inn,** 15 Railway Terrace, tel. (08) 8952-1411, has an inexpensive hotel section and a pricier motel with pool and spa. Moderate.

Rail buffs will appreciate **Larapinta Lodge,** 3 Larapinta Dr., tel. (08) 8952-7255, very close to the railway station, and equipped with single and double rooms. Moderate. **Territory Inn,** Leichardt Terrace, tel. (08) 8952-2066, in the heart of Todd

Mall "action," is a good choice for reasonable rooms with modern conveniences. Moderate.

For longer stays, **Alice Tourist Apartments,** corner Gap Rd. and Gnoilya St., tel. (08) 8952-2788, is also a good value, with a variety of rooms particularly well suited to groups of travelers who pool their resources. Pool, laundry, cooking, and barbecue facilities are available. Moderate.

Outback Motor Lodge, South Terrace, tel. (08) 8952-3888, offers clean, simple rooms with kitchen facilities as well as a pool and barbecue area. Moderate. A good choice near Alice South attractions is **Sienna Apartments,** corner Palm Circuit and Ross Hwy., tel. (08) 8952-7655. TVs, pool, and cooking facilities are included. Moderate.

Vista Alice Springs, Stephens Rd., tel. (08) 8952-6100, is about twice as far from town as the plushier Rydges Plaza Hotel, half the size, but not quite half the price. Amenities include a pool, tennis court, rental bicycles, gift shop, restaurant, and bar. Expensive.

The 90-room **Diplomat Hotel,** Gregory Terrace, tel. (08) 8952-8977, sits at the corner of Hartley St., putting it near but not *in* the town hub. All rooms are air-conditioned, with a pool and bar on the premises. Expensive.

Lasseter's Hotel Casino, 93 Barrett Dr., tel. (1800) 808-975, offers well-appointed rooms, tennis, pool, nightclub, and, of course, the casino. Premium.

The top choice for big budgets is **Rydges Plaza Hotel,** Barrett Dr., about 1.5 km from town, tel. (08) 8952-8000. This 243-room property with pastel decor and manicured grounds offers all the luxury comforts including TVs, videos, room service, pool, spa, sauna, tennis court, health club, restaurants, bars, live entertainment, and boutiques. Luxury.

Alice Springs Pacific Resort, 34 Stott Terrace, tel. (08) 8952-6699, located on the Todd River's east bank, sports 108 cheery rooms with cane furnishings, a wide expanse of lawn, a couple of bars, and a cool pool. Luxury.

Hostels
Backpackers will find plenty of options in Alice. Dorm beds average $10-14 per night and should be booked ahead during peak holiday periods. The **Pioneer YHA Hostel,** corner Parsons St. and Leichhardt Terrace, tel. (08) 8952-8855, is a busy, centrally located operation, housed inside

an old outdoor movie theater. Facilities include air-conditioned rooms, communal kitchen, recreation room, a laundry, and small food store. Travelers here will pick up all sorts of helpful information on the local scene.

Melanka Lodge, 94 Todd St., tel. (08) 8952-4744 or (1800) 819-110, is another popular choice, offering a variety of accommodations from backpackers' and dorm beds to guesthouse and motel rooms. **Toddy's Resort,** 41 Gap Rd., tel. (08) 8952-1322, also has a wide range of accommodations consisting of dorms, a bunkhouse, cabins, and double rooms with or without private baths.

Elke's Resort, 39 Gap Rd., tel. (08) 8952-8134, offers dorm rooms, each with a TV, bath, kitchenette, and balcony area. Breakfast is free, a pool is on the premises, and shuttle service is provided to and from the bus station or airport, making this a terrific deal.

Another backpacker's treasure is **Nomads Ossie's Homestead,** Lindsay Ave. and Warburton St., tel. (08) 8952-2308 or (1800) 628-111. Although situated in the "suburbs," this is a friendly alternative to the often crowded hostels in town. Breakfast and linens come with the deal.

Dorm and bunkhouse beds are also available at **Gapview Resort Hotel,** corner Gap Rd. and South Terrace, tel. (08) 8952-6611, with a pool, tennis courts, bar, and restaurant.

Camping

All of the following parks allow caravan and tent camping (about $15), and many rent on-site vans as well (approximately $35): **G'day Mate Tourist Park,** Palm Circuit, tel. (08) 8952-9589, near South Alice sights; **Greenleaves Tourist Park,** Burke St., tel. (08) 8952-8645, two km northwest of Todd River causeway; **Stuart Caravan Park,** Larapinta Dr., tel. (08) 8952-2547, near the arts center; **Wintersun Gardens Caravan Park,** Stuart Hwy., tel. (08) 8952-4080, two km north of the post office; **Carmichael Tourist Park,** Tmara Mara St., off Larapinta Dr., tel. (08) 8952-1200; **Heavitree Gap Caravan Park,** Emily Gap Rd., tel. (08) 8952-2370, adjacent to the Todd River; **MacDonnell Range Tourist Park,** Palm Pl., off Ross Hwy., tel. (08) 8952-6111, also near Alice South attractions; and **Ross River Homestead,** tel. (08) 8956-9711, at the end of Ross Highway.

FOOD

Foodies who'll die without nouvelle cuisine better steer clear of Alice—'cause steer is exactly what you'll find on most menus, and well-done, shoe leather steer at that. Along with the frozen barramundi and other occasional fish, it's good old meat and taters in mid-Oz—just like it is in middle America. (By the way, that Kentucky Fried Chicken place is at the corner of Todd St. and Stott Terrace.)

Inexpensive

Todd Street Mall is lined with coffee shops and takeaways and most are open seven days a week. **Jolly Swagman,** opposite Flynn Church, is open daily from 5:30 a.m. for breakfast, homemade cakes and dampers, and vegetarian and Asian-style meals ($6-9 entrees). **Thai Kitchen,** off the mall, offers decent Asian food.

The **Eastside Fish and Chips** shop, on Lindsay Ave., near the corner of Undoolya Rd., is highly recommended by locals ($4-8 for an average serving). **Eranova Cafeteria,** 70 Todd St., offers continental-style dining, a diverse selection, and good value ($9-15 entrees). Open Mon.-Sat. for breakfast, lunch, and dinner.

Alice Plaza lunch spots consist of **Fawlty's, Red Centre Chinese,** and **Doctor Lunch;** all cheap and casual (sandwiches around $4-6). For pub meals ($5-10), try **Stuart Arms Bistro,** upstairs in the Alice Plaza on Todd Street Mall.

Moderate

Lilli's, at Heavitree Gap Motel, Ross Hwy., tel. (08) 8952-2370, specializes in Australian delicacies (watch out for that witchetty grub sauce). Entrees run $10-15. **La Casalinga,** 105 Gregory Terrace, is an Alice favorite for pizza and Italian specialties ($8-13). Open daily for dinner. **Camel's Crossing,** in Fan Arcade, off Todd Mall, tel. (08) 8952-5522, features Mexican and vegetarian dishes ($9-14). **Swinger's Café,** 71 Gregory Terrace, is a show-off place, but with good pasta and curry ($11-15).

For Chinese meals, try **Chopsticks,** in Yeperenye Shopping Centre on Hartley St., tel. (08) 8952-3873; **Oriental Gourmet,** 80 Hartley St., tel. (08) 8953-0888; or **Golden Inn,** 9 Undoolya Road. Entrees average $9-16 and all are open daily.

If you care to get trendy in the Alice, try **Bar Doppios,** in the Fan Arcade, tel. (08) 8952-6252. Salads, curries, and marinated tofu dishes—not to mention the Mediterranean ambience—will make you feel as if you're in L.A. Entrees range $10-14.

Expensive
The **Overlanders Steakhouse,** 72 Hartley St., tel. (08) 8952-2159, serves up genuine Aussie tucker, including buffalo, camel, and kangaroo steaks (those slabs run a whopping $18-27), accompanied by live Australian folk entertainment.

Puccini's, corner Todd Mall and Parsons St., tel. (08) 8953-0935, offers fine Italian cuisine—surprisingly fine, in fact, for the Territory ($15-25 entrees).

Gourmet regional fare (entrees averaging $16-22) for both veg-heads and carnivores is served amid Aboriginal decor and music at the **Red Ochre Grill,** on Todd Mall, tel. (08) 8952-2066.

Rossini's, in the Diplomat Hotel, tel. (08) 8952-8977, is another unique find with its continental cuisine (entrees $16-26) and formal settings.

Balloons, in the Rydges Plaza Hotel, tel. (08) 8952-8000, and **Kings,** in Lasseter's Hotel Casino, tel. (08) 8952-5066, are other good choices. Expect to pay about $20 and up for entrees.

ENTERTAINMENT AND EVENTS

Cinemas
Films screen regularly at **Araluen Arts Centre,** Larapinta Road. The **Alice Springs Cinema,** at the end of Todd Mall, plays all the Hollywood favorites. For information, phone (08) 8952-4999.

Pubs and Clubs
The pub scene is somewhat limited; check *The Centralian Advocate* newspaper for current happenings. The **Todd Tavern,** corner Todd St. and Wills Terrace, features live piano-bar entertainment Thurs.-Sat., disco Thurs.-Sat., Monday night jam sessions, and Sunday night folk concerts. **Stuart Arms Bistro,** Todd Mall, occasionally presents cabarets and live weekend entertainment.

Legends, on the second floor of Alice Plaza, is one of the hottest local discos (especially on Fridays when the drinks are two bucks). It features live music nightly.

Simpsons Gap Bar, in the Rydges Plaza Hotel, a popular hangout for travelers, offers live entertainment every night and a DJ Thurs.-Saturday. Hipper-than-hip **Uncles,** corner of Hartley St. and Gregory Terrace, buzzes every night, but Friday is the big scene. **Alice Junction Tavern** (AJ's), at Heavitree Gap Tourist Resort, off Ross Highway, features disco Fri.-Sat., and **Bojangles Restaurant and Nightclub,** Todd St., also has occasional late-night disco.

Knight Moves, in the Queen of the Desert Resort, about two km south of town, offers cabaret-type entertainment.

Bush Entertainment
Chateau Hornsby Winery presents the long-running **Ted Egan Outback Show,** with tall tales, bush lore, and Outback songs. Performances are three times a week. Cost is $15, about twice that with dinner included. For bookings, phone (08) 8955-5133.

The **Overlanders Steakhouse,** 72 Hartley St., features local entertainers nightly, including sing-alongs and bush bands.

Often the big hotels will host a **Bush Tucker Night,** which typically includes campfire meals and storytelling.

Theater and Music
Araluen Arts Centre, Larapinta Dr., is Alice's venue for cinema, musical and theatrical performances, and visual arts. For schedules and ticket information, phone (08) 8953-3111.

Events
Alice hosts a variety of strange and colorful events, usually during the cooler winter months.

The end of June or early July brings the **Camel Cup,** a series of camel roundups and races on the Todd River bed, commemorating the old Afghan camel train days. A **Food and Wine Festival** takes place the day after Camel Cup on the lawns of Verdi Club, Undoolya Road. The **Alice Springs Cup** annual horse race runs the first Monday in May.

The **Bangtail Muster,** held the same day as the Alice Springs Cup, once glorified the cutting of horses' tails before they were shipped out, but today it's an excuse for a colorful and satirical parade.

In June, the **Finke Desert Race, Taps, Tubs and Tiles** is a 500-km, two-day endurance race for trail bikes and off-road vehicles.

Rodeo lovers will revel in August's weeklong **Alice Springs Rodeo,** with heaps of events, and cowboys and wanna-bes parading around town in full drag.

The **Henley-on-Todd Regatta,** in late September, is Alice's most famous event: competitors "race" along the dry riverbed in an amazing variety of bottomless boats, racers' legs poking out as they pick up their craft and speed along on foot. The series of peculiar events is followed the next day by the **Annual Beer Festival,** featuring live entertainment, children's activities, food, and many beer stalls.

SPORTS AND RECREATION

Swimming Pools
Almost every hotel and motel has its own pool. Alice Springs Swimming Centre, Speed St., tel. (08) 8952-3757, also has a water slide, trampoline, and aquarobics classes. Open daily mid-Sept.-April.

Sporting Facilities
Squash: Guests are welcome at Alice Springs Squash Centre, 13 Gap Rd., tel. (08) 8952-1277. Equipment is available for rent.

Tennis: Public courts and private coaching can be hired at Traeger Park, off Traeger Ave., tel. (08) 8953-2538.

Golf: Alice Springs Golf Club, Cromwell Dr., tel. (08) 8952-5440, welcomes visitors.

Gambling: Lasseter's Hotel Casino, tel. (1800) 808-975, is the venue for gaming tables and pokeys. A dress code is enforced (decent, not dressy).

Spectator Sports
Australian Rules **football** and **baseball** are played at Traeger Park, Gap Road. **Rugby League** meets at Anzac Oval, and Larapinta Oval, Memorial Dr., is the **softball** venue. The season for most sports is April-September.

For **flying and gliding,** contact the Alice Springs Aero Club, at the Aerodrome, tel. (08) 8955-5240.

SHOPPING

You've got a humongous Kmart, Woolworth, and a mall—those will take care of most immediate shopping needs. But Alice's big consumer draw, of course, is Aboriginal art. Alice is the place to pick up a didgeridoo or boomerang for that special someone. Distinctive works include Papunya sand paintings, batiks from the local Utopia settlement, as well as a good selection of weavings, carvings, and bark paintings.

Highly recommended outlets are **Jukurrpa Gallery and Artists,** 35 Gap Rd., both a gallery and working studio, and the **Original Dreamtime Gallery,** 63 Todd Mall, with an impressive range of Aboriginal arts and crafts. Other good shops are the **Papunya Tula Artists** shop, Todd St., south of the mall; **Gallery Gondwana,** on the mall; **Warumpi Arts,** on Gregory Terrace, near Todd St.; and the **Central Australian Aboriginal Media Association** shop, 101 Todd Street.

Opal buyers might enjoy the gems and jewelry at the **Gem Cave,** 85 Todd Street Mall.

Camping supplies can be purchased or rented from Alice Springs Disposals, off the mall, on Reg Harris Lane, tel. (08) 8952-5701. Centre Canvas, 9 Smith St., tel. (08) 8952-2453, manufactures quality swags (bed rolls).

SERVICES

Branches of national **banks** and automatic teller machines are located on Todd Mall, Todd Street, and Parsons Street. Almost all banks will change overseas traveler's checks, usually for $2-3 per transaction.

The **general post office,** Hartley St., is open Mon.-Fri. 9 a.m.-5 p.m. For information, phone (08) 8952-1020.

The **Wash-house Launderette,** corner Stuart Hwy., Parsons St., and Railway Terrace, provides coin-op machines for do-it-yourself washing and ironing, daily 8 a.m.-8 p.m. Almost every hotel, motel, or hostel has laundry facilities.

INFORMATION

The **Central Australian Tourism Industry Association,** corner Hartley St. and Gregory Terrace, tel. (08) 8952-5800, dispenses information, maps, and literature, and books tours and accommodations. Hours are Mon.-Fri. 9 a.m.-6 p.m., Sat.-Sun. and public holidays 9 a.m.-4 p.m.

Pick up maps, books, and information on ranger-led tours at the **Parks and Wildlife Commission,** either at the desk in the tourism office or at the main office, off the Stuart Hwy., several km south of town. For information, phone (08) 8951-8211.

In emergencies, dial 000; the **police,** tel. (08) 8951-8888; or **Alice Springs Hospital,** Gap Rd., tel. (08) 8951-7777. The hospital provides 24-hour emergency service, plus an outpatient walk-in clinic Mon.-Friday.

For details about local driving conditions (including those rough, unpaved "roads"), contact **Road Conditions Information,** tel. (08) 8952-3833.

The **public library,** near the corner of Leichardt and Gregory Terraces, tel. (08) 8950-0544, is open Mon.-Fri. 9 a.m.-6 p.m., Saturday 9 a.m.-1 p.m., Sunday 1 p.m.-5 p.m.

A branch of the **Angus and Robertson** bookshop chain is in the Yeperenye Centre. Other good shops are the **Arunta Gallery,** Todd St., south of the mall, and **Dymocks** in the Alice Plaza. For used books, seek out **Bookworm,** 76 Todd St., tel. (08) 8952-5843.

Stock up on even more maps at the **Automobile Association of the Northern Territory,** Gregory Terrace, tel. (08) 8953-1322, or at the **Department of Lands, Housing and Local Government,** also on Gregory Terrace, tel. (08) 8951-5743.

If you're looking for gay or lesbian services and have a call-back number, leave a message for **Gayline,** tel. (08) 8953-2844. Be forewarned: you must leave a number, and someone will call you back. For general crises, contact **Crisis Hotline,** tel. (1800) 019-116.

Almost every newsagent stocks *The Central Advocate,* Alice's local paper, which comes out on Tuesday and Friday, and many carry a large selection of air-freighted national dailies and mags.

GETTING THERE

By Air
Alice Springs Airport, 14 km southeast of town center, is served by **Ansett,** tel. (13) 1300, and **Qantas,** tel. (13) 1313, with daily scheduled flights from all capital cities. Offices are opposite each other at Todd and Parson Streets. In case you'd like to skip Alice and fly directly to The Rock, direct flights are available from both Sydney and Adelaide. **Airnorth,** tel. (08) 8952-6666, flies to destinations within the Northern Territory. Sample fares are: Ayers Rock ($370); Broome ($275); Cairns ($325); Melbourne ($485); Perth ($485); and Sydney ($485).

Alice Springs Airport Shuttle Service, tel. (08) 8953-0310, meets all flights and provides transport to the city center for $9. Book ahead for service to the airport. **Taxis** into the city cost about two bucks more. Taxi ranks are located at the airport, or phone **Alice Springs Taxis,** tel. (08) 8952-1877.

Left luggage storage lockers are available at the airport.

By Bus
Interstate coaches operated by **Greyhound Pioneer** arrive and depart from the Melanka Lodge, 94 Todd St.; **McCafferty's** terminal and office are located at 91 Gregory Terrace. Daily services between Alice, Darwin, and Adelaide are operated by Greyhound Pioneer, tel. (13) 2030, and McCafferty's, tel. (08) 8952-3952 in Alice Springs or (13) 1499. You can also pick up a daily connection to The Rock and the Olgas. Fares are approximately $145 from Darwin or Adelaide. Buses change at Three Ways Roadhouse for connections to Queensland, and at Katherine for the route to Western Australia.

By Train
The **Ghan** does not have quite the same flair and sense of adventure as its famous predecessor, but it's a terrific ride all the same. Half the fun of the original train was the dreadful track, frequent flooding, and the good chance of being stuck in the middle of nowhere and having emergency supplies parachuted in!

These days, darn it, the new track is fairly flood-proof, the train carries twice as many passengers in half the time (20 hours from Adelaide, instead of 50), and probably nothing exciting will happen along the trip. The scenery, however, and the ability to take a shower while choo-chooing through the central Australian desert, make this one of the country's great rail journeys.

Trains depart Adelaide on Monday and Thursday, returning to Adelaide on Tuesday and Friday; one additional service runs April-January. If you purchase a rail pass, the Ghan journey is included. Otherwise, one-way fares run about $150 economy sitting, $260 holiday-class berth, or $465 first-class berth, with meals included. For information and bookings, phone **Rail Australia,** tel. (13) 2232.

By Car, Thumb, Hook, or Crook

Basically it's the straight and narrow Track all the way from Adelaide or Darwin. Be careful hitching; traffic is light. Many hitchers report long waits at Three Ways. Women should not hitch around the Outback without a male companion. Check the Alice YHA notice board for possible rides.

GETTING AROUND

Other than taxis, Alice has no public transportation. **Alice Springs Taxis,** tel. (08) 8952-1877, offers local transport.

Rental cars will cost $30-80 per day, plus insurance and per-km charges; a 4WD will run about $125 and up per day, typically including 100 free km per day. Many vehicles cannot be taken outside a 50-km radius of town or on dirt roads without written permission—and extra fees. Read all fine print regarding insurance, as some coverages don't apply when vehicles leave paved roads (why else would you rent a 4WD in the Outback?).

Rental companies include **Avis,** tel. (08) 8953-5533; **Brits,** tel. (08) 8952-8814; **Budget,** tel. (08) 8952-8899; **Hertz,** tel. (08) 8952-2644; **Territory Rent-a-Car,** tel. (08) 8952-9999; and **Thrifty,** tel. (08) 8952-2400.

Most of the above offices are located on or near Todd Mall, and some have airport counters. Also inquire regarding moped, campervan, and motorhome rentals.

Rent **bicycles** (about $12 per day) from just about any of the backpacker hostels.

Tours

As with Darwin, you can choose from a seemingly endless array of organized tours to The Rock and other Red Centre sites, traveling by air-conditioned coach, 4WD, camel, balloon, or airplane. Call into the Central Australian Tourism Industry Association for advice and bookings, according to your specific interests. The Pioneer YHA also arranges tours.

Rod Steinert offers a variety of outings, including his ever-popular **Dreamtime Tour and Bushtucker Tour,** a half-day excursion that'll give you a taste of Aboriginal culture including bush food preparation, boomerang- and spear-throwing, and a "quickie" Dreamtime explanation. Cost is $65. For information, phone (1800) 679-418.

Tourists also flock to Alice for camel treks—everything from a quick ride to breakfast and dinner outings (yes, *on* the camel), to treks of several days. The tourist bureau will provide details and bookings, or contact **Frontier Camel Farm,** tel. (08) 8953-0444. Or saddle up on a horse with **Trail Rides,** tel. (08) 8952-2308.

Sign up for a day-time bushwalk or nighttime safari with **Trec Gondawana,** tel. (08) 8952-8248. Prices range $90-160, and the outings come fully equipped, whether you opt for a sunny picnic, campfire dinner, or view of the starry sky.

Sunrise **hot-air balloon** rides are particularly mesmerizing over the Red Centre. Costs run about $150 (including silver service breakfast) and are offered by **Outback Ballooning,** tel. (1800) 809-790, and **Ballooning Downunder,** tel. (08) 8952-8816.

The **Alice Wanderer,** tel. (08) 8952-2111, operates daily, on hourly rounds to most tourist sites in town. For $18, passengers can get on and off the bus at whim. A running commentary explains each point of interest.

VICINITY OF ALICE

Weathered gorges, rocky walls, and sheer cliffs of the ancient MacDonnell Ranges run east and west of Alice, with many of these scenic and mysterious spots an easy day trip or overnight away from the town center.

About the same age as Ayers Rock (650 million years old, give or take a few years), the mostly sandstone MacDonnells reach 400 km east to west and 160 km north to south. As babies, the ranges stood more than 3,000 meters above sea level, eroding over the millennia to an average height today of less than 500 meters. The rocky crags, crevices, and chasms are variegated with ferrous red, olive, and forest green—made even

more evident by sparse vegetation. In spring, wildflowers provide an even more spectacular sight, while shy wildlife, such as the black-flanked rock wallaby, is a bit more difficult to spot (try early morning or late afternoon). Whichever direction you travel in this majestic and meditative region, you'll end up gorged and centered.

TO THE EAST

Emily and Jessie Gaps

These two gaps, just east of Alice on the Ross Highway, form a 695-hectare nature park noted

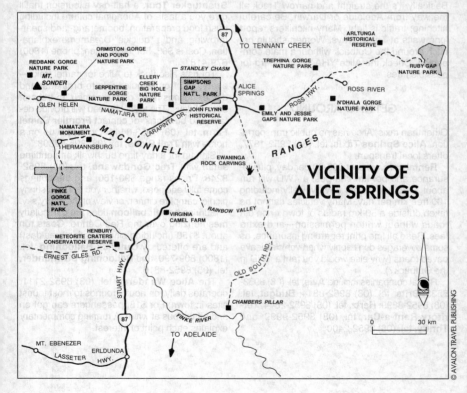

© AVALON TRAVEL PUBLISHING

for its scenic river red gums and waterholes. The area was also significant to Aborigines, who have left rock paintings along the eastern face of Emily Gap. The area is popular with picnickers, but also tends to beckon serious drinkers. For information, phone (08) 8952-1013.

Corroboree Rock

Local Aborigines used this limestone rock outcrop, located 46 km east of Alice on the Ross Highway, for both manhood rituals and as a storage area for sacred stones used in Dreamtime storytelling. The seven-hectare conservation reserve features a short walking trail and picnic and barbecue facilities. Camping is allowed. For information, phone (08) 8956-9765.

Trephina Gorge Nature Park

A few km north of the Ross Highway, and 80 km east of Alice, this 1,770-hectare nature park features two contrasting gorges: scenic Trephina Gorge with its tall river gums, gentle pool, and wide sandy creek bed, and, a few km west, shady and secluded John Hayes Rockhole, an area especially rich in birdlife.

The park offers grand campsites and walking tracks (one leads to John Hayes Rockhole); access for conventional vehicles may be limited in some areas. For information, phone (08) 8956-9765.

Ross River Homestead

Situated about 12 km east of Trephina Gorge, this 1898 whitewashed homestead (the original headquarters of Loves Creek Station) features a variety of tourist pleasures, including moderate to expensive accommodations, a budget bunkhouse, caravan park, country walking trails, horse and camel rides, a restaurant, and pub. Keep in mind that tour buses love it here also—even so, it's worth a stop. For information and bookings, phone (08) 8956-9711.

N'Dhala Gorge Nature Park

Continue about 10 km southeast of the homestead (4WD is necessary) to this 501-hectare park noted for its thousands of prehistoric rock carvings (at least 35,000 years old) decorating the gorge walls. Mystery fact: Present-day Aborigines have no inkling of what the designs mean or who the artists were! A short trail leads to the engravings. Picnic and barbecue facilities are available and camping is allowed, but you have to bring your own water. For information, phone (08) 8956-9765.

Arltunga Historical Reserve

Set along the eastern edge of the MacDonnells, 44 km northeast of Ross River Homestead, Arltunga preserves the remains of this particularly isolated gold-mining town, which was in operation 1887-1912 and held a population only of about 75 people during that period. Ruins within the 5,506-hectare reserve include mine offices, miners' graves, a police station, jail, assayer's residence, the old stamp batter and cyanide works, and many other sites. Walking tracks and picnic facilities are provided within the park. **Arltunga Tourist Park,** referred to as the "loneliest pub in the scrub," has a small campground and shop. The graded track to Arltunga is recommended for 4WD only, as is the 111-km northwest loop back to the Stuart Highway. For information, phone (08) 8956-9797.

Ruby Gap Nature Park

If you're in a 4WD, head 39 km southeast to Ruby Gap (also known as Ruby Gorge), an unusual geological site composed of ribbon-like quartz and limestone strata along glorious, rugged gorges that parallel the winding Hale River. Bush camping is allowed along the river, but take care of your own waste. For information, phone (08) 8956-9770.

TO THE WEST

Two different routes lead to sights in the western MacDonnell Ranges. You start off on Larapinta Drive and, about 54 km out of Alice (past Standley Chasm), either continue along Larapinta or turn onto Namatjira Drive. For information on any of the parks below, contact the **Parks and Wildlife Commission,** tel. (08) 8951-8211.

Alice Springs Desert Park

Opened in 1997, this 75-acre manmade park showcases 320 plant species and 120 animal species that thrive in the desert environment. A leading desert ecology research center, the park also contains the country's largest nocturnal house. Be sure to see the film depicting the evolution of the Outback landscape. Admission is $12. Open daily 7:30 a.m.-6 p.m. For information, phone (08) 8951-8788.

John Flynn Historical Reserve
What historical reserve? It's a half-hectare grave site on Larapinta Drive, where rest the ashes of Reverend John Flynn, founder of the Royal Flying Doctor Service. One of the Devils Marbles was imported to the site for effect.

Simpsons Gap National Park
Conveniently located only 18 km west of Alice, this is a great spot to get your gap-and-gorge fill if you're short on time, money, or energy. Comprised of purple-tinged mountains, steep ridges, huge white ghost gums, wooded creek beds, and colonies of rock wallabies, Simpsons Gap (30,950 hectares) is a favorite with tourists. A variety of good walking tracks begin at the excellent visitor center (pick up maps and other literature) and include 20-km unmarked climbing treks, 18-km roundabout bushwalks, and short, easy trails to lookout points. The park has picnic facilities but camping is not allowed.

Standley Chasm
Photographers love to shoot this steep, rusty-walled crevice, 50 km west of Alice, especially when the sun provides natural overhead lighting that turns the chasm fireball red. As you can probably imagine, it's not likely you'll be the only one clicking away. A kiosk sells snacks, refreshments, and souvenirs, and picnic facilities are available.

Namatjira Drive
Ellery Creek Big Hole Nature Park (1,766 hectares), 43 km beyond Standley Chasm, is another exquisite gorge with steep red cliffs and a large river-red-gum-shaded waterhole. This is an especially popular location for picnickers and energetic bushwalkers who climb to the ridge tops for majestic views.

Traveling another 11 km west will bring you to narrow, winding **Serpentine Gorge Nature Park** (518 hectares), which is actually two gorges with high rock walls, waterholes, and palmlike cycad vegetation. Picnicking and camping are allowed.

Next stop, 28 km down the road, is **Ormiston Gorge and Pound Nature Park** (4,655 hectares). The dominant two-km-long red cliff, rugged wilderness, permanent waterhole, and towering ghost gum and cypress pine forests have earned Ormiston its reputation as one of the most scenic and colorful gorges in the western MacDonnells. Features include wonderful walking tracks (the seven-km trail through the pound area is reputedly one of the country's finest wilderness treks), a visitor center, and small campground.

Glen Helen Gorge, just one km farther, is a 386-hectare nature park where the Finke River (supposedly the world's oldest, having run this same course for 350 million years) begins its journey through the MacDonnells to the Simpson Desert. An interesting walking track follows along the riverbed. **Glen Helen Lodge,** a restored 1930s homestead, provides a variety of accommodations in prices ranging from budget to expensive, including modern motel-style rooms, campsites, and a YHA-affiliated hostel. Other lodge facilities are a restaurant, bar, bistro, occasional live entertainment, takeaway, and petrol station. For bookings, phone (08) 8956-7489.

Redbank Gorge Nature Park (1,295 hectares) is situated 30 km west of Glen Helen; recommended for 4WD vehicles. Steep slopes with those mighty ghost gums hovering above this remote site provide the scenic beauty. If you intend to jump into one of the deep pools, be forewarned that the walls are slippery and the water is icy cold. Redbank also makes a good base for experienced climbers who wish to scale nearby **Mt. Sonder** (1,380 meters). Picnicking and camping are allowed.

Continuing along Larapinta Drive
The first sight you'll come to, about 100 km from Standley Chasm, is **Namatjira Monument,** which honors Albert Namatjira, one of Australia's most noted Aboriginal artists, famous for his central Australian landscape paintings.

Hermannsburg, another 30-40 km along, is the site of an 1880s mission brought to the Aranda people by Lutheran pastors. Though the Aranda own the mission now, this township still retains links with the Lutheran church. Historic buildings include the original church, Bethlehem church, schoolhouse, and smithy. A museum and tearooms are housed within two of the old residences, and a variety of local Aboriginal art and souvenirs can be purchased. The town also has a petrol station, garage, supermarket, and hardware store.

Finke Gorge National Park (36,000 hectares), 12 km south of Hermannsburg, can be reached only via 4WD vehicle. Within its protected wilderness, the park straddles the southward-bound Finke River and contains large waterholes, bird refuges, sculpted rock formations, more sandstone gorge, and a very comprehensive collection of central Australian plants. The park's most famous attraction, however, is **Palm Valley**, a strange and bizarre tropical area encompassing approximately 400 plant species, including the red cabbage palm *(Livistona mariae),* found nowhere else in the world. The valley is thought to be a remnant from the days (about 10,000 years ago) when the Centre supported a moister climate. An information and ranger station is near the entrance to Palm Creek. Picnicking and camping are allowed. For information, phone (08) 8951-8211.

TO THE ROCK

Back on the Track and aiming toward Ayers Rock, more fascinating sights await travelers willing to steer off the very well-beaten path. One route will take you along the Old South Road, which parallels the Old Ghan line shortly past the Ross Highway junction; the other is the Kings Canyon turnoff (Ernest Giles Road), a gravel road that cuts into the Track about 145 km south of Alice. (Be careful if driving this road during or after rains—it gets very slippery.) Or you can just keep on the Track all the way to Lasseter Highway (200 km south of Alice) and turn west 241 km to The Rock.

Along Old South Road
Ewaninga Rock Carvings are located within a six-hectare conservation reserve 39 km south of Alice. As with the N'Dhala Gorge site, these prehistoric engravings contain symbols so ancient that not even today's Aborigines can figure them out. Other features here include abundant plants, birds, and wildlife. Visitors are asked to not climb on the boulders.

With a 4WD you can access **Chambers Pillar Historical Reserve,** 104 km south of the carvings. This impressive sandstone pillar rises 58 meters out of the surrounding flat plain, casting a phenomenal glow at sunrise and sunset. Used as a landmark by early explorers, the pillar still bears the evidence of pioneers who scratched their names onto the surface. (Don't *you* do this!)

Still on Track
Virginia Camel Farm, 93 km south of Alice along the Stuart Hwy., is run by breeder Noel Fullerton, founder—and ofttimes winner—of the Camel Cup. Noel runs the outfit that can take you humping through the center on short rides or long safaris. He even arranges packages in which you can take your camel to breakfast, lunch, or dinner. Longer expeditions tour nearby **Rainbow Valley Nature Park** (2,483 hectares), a sublime region of richly colored, broken sandstone gorge. You can camp here on your own, but you'll need to bring a 4WD and your own water. For information about the camel farm and Rainbow Valley tours, check with the tourist bureau or phone (08) 8956-0925. Virginia Camel Farm is open daily 7 a.m.-5 p.m.

Along Ernest Giles Road
About 13 km from the Track (144 km southwest of Alice), follow the signpost to **Henbury Meteorite Craters,** a 16-hectare conservation reserve encompassing 12 separate craters, thought to have been created by a meteor shower 5,000 years ago. The craters range in size from two to 180 meters across, and one is a whopping 15 meters deep! An easy walking track offers explanatory signs. This is another "look but don't touch" site.

Next stop along this road—and probably a welcome one—is **Wallara Ranch,** about 85 km west of the meteor craters and about halfway to Kings Canyon. This rambling local pub is a winner with tourists who stop to soak up the local atmosphere and stock up on supplies. Facilities include moderately priced motel accommodations, a bunkhouse, campsites, a dining room, takeaway, a swimming pool, petrol station, and day tours of the canyon. For information, phone (08) 8956-2901. From Wallara Ranch, you can take an alternate route 70 km south to the Lasseter Highway or keep going to the canyon, at road's end.

Kings Canyon, often called Australia's Grand Canyon, is a dramatic gorge and escarpment situated 100 km past Wallara Ranch. Now called **Watarrka National Park,** some of the more unusual natural features of this 106,000-hectare area include the **Garden of Eden** palm shelter and the **Lost City,** a strange grouping of weathered outcrops that look like domed houses. A somewhat strenuous walking trail leads to most of the sights, or try the steep climb to the plateau for terrific canyon views. Park facilities include a ranger station and visitor center, plus picnic and camping areas. For information, phone (08) 8956-7460. **Kings Canyon Resort,** tel. (08) 8956-7442, near the canyon, offers very pricey hotel rooms ($250), four-bed dorms with shared facilities ($35 pp), and campsites ($10 pp). The "village" also contains a grocery store, gas station, restaurant, café, and medical center.

Lasseter Highway
You're almost there! **Erldunda Desert Oaks Resort,** at the junction of the Track and Lasseter Highway, offers roadhouse facilities including a range of motel accommodations, a caravan park, campsites, dining room, pub, takeaway, souvenirs, pool, tennis court, petrol station, and tourist information. For information, phone (08) 8956-0984.

Mt. Ebenezer is another roadhouse, 55 km west, owned by the neighboring Imanpa Aboriginal people. Aside from the normal roadhouse features, Mt. Ebenezer also houses a gift shop that displays and sells local artifacts and paintings. For information, phone (08) 8956-2904.

Another 100 km will bring you to the **Curtin Springs** roadhouse, which is also a working cattle station. Founded in 1943, this inn exudes local atmosphere while providing necessary services. For information, phone (08) 8956-2906.

Travel 82 more km west to Yulara, gateway to Ayers Rock and the Olgas.

AYERS ROCK AND THE OLGAS

Uluru National Park (132,566 hectares), by encompassing Ayers Rock and the Olgas, contains one of the world's great natural wonders and one of Australia's top tourist destinations. It is also the heart of Australia—the big red heart.

Uluru National Park encompasses more than 400 plant species, 150 types of birds, and about 25 mammal varieties in a sensitive geological landscape that contrasts drastically from sandy flat plains to those big old rocks. Though Uluru has been returned to its Aboriginal owners, the park is presently co-managed by the National Parks Service and the Anangu people.

Blissfully, all the "civilized" trappings are located in **Yulara,** a tourist village built in 1984 specifically to accommodate the hundreds-of-thousands of annual visitors from all over the world. Situated 20 km from The Rock, this complex—a joint government-private sector scheme—features all the comforts any modern-day traveler to a Stone Age site could desire.

Uluru (Ayers Rock)
I would like to be able to spew fluffy prose at you—to say that this incredible rock, of deep

spiritual and cultural significance to the Aborigines (who have lived here for at least 10,000 years), is a sacred shrine quite unlike any other. Though that is certainly no lie, it's not the complete truth either; this spectacular monolith is also the site of resorts, facilities, tourist buses, and tourists themselves, decked out in straw sun hats or beer-ad visors and printed T-shirts as they huff and puff their way up The Rock (supporting themselves on the specially installed safety chain). The traditional owners have been pushing, however, to get visitors off their rock and to, perhaps, admire it from a more reverent distance at or around its base.

Ayers Rock (Uluru, to the Aborigines), no matter who's crawling around it, is a pretty breathtaking sight—a 650-million-year-old sandstone behemoth, rising 348 meters above the pancakelike surrounding plain (and it's supposed to be about twice as big *beneath* the surface!). Its dimensions are indeed impressive—8.8 km around the base, 3.6 km long, and 2.4 km wide—but Uluru's most awe-inspiring feature is the ecstatic glow and haunting colors it exudes at different times of the day (sunrise and sunset are best).

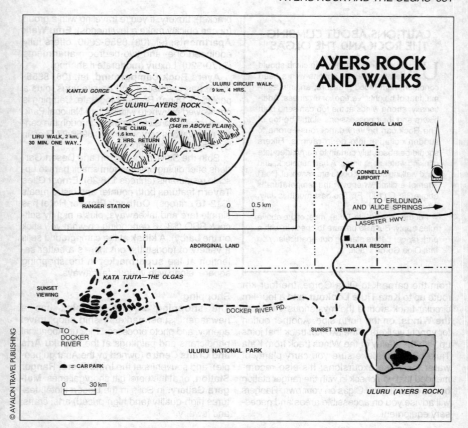

AYERS ROCK AND WALKS

KANTJU GORGE

ULURU—AYERS ROCK

ULURU CIRCUIT WALK,
9 km, 4 HRS.

THE CLIMB,
1.6 km,
2 HRS. RETURN

▲ 863 m
(348 m ABOVE PLAIN)

LIRU WALK, 2 km,
30 MIN. ONE WAY.

RANGER STATION

0   0.5 km

ABORIGINAL LAND

CONNELLAN
AIRPORT

TO ERLDUNDA
AND ALICE SPRINGS

LASSETER HWY.

YULARA RESORT

ABORIGINAL LAND

KATA TJUTA—THE OLGAS

SUNSET
VIEWING

DOCKER RIVER RD.

SUNSET VIEWING

TO
DOCKER
RIVER

ULURU NATIONAL PARK

= CAR PARK

0   30 km

ULURU (AYERS ROCK)

© AVALON TRAVEL PUBLISHING

The Rock also features weathered gullies, eerie caves, and Aboriginal carvings and paintings (some 10,000 years old). The public is not permitted access to some declared sacred sites.

If you want to climb The Rock, you are supposed to be in excellent physical condition (a real chuckle once you check out some of the climbers). Also be aware that the higher slopes are often hit by gale-force winds (climbers have died while trying to retrieve a Foster's visor). Check with the park rangers for necessary equipment. Another option is the three- to four-hour walk around the base, which is fringed with caves, waterholes, and a variety of desert vegetation. Admission is $15.

The Olgas

The Olgas (Kata Tjuta, or "Many Heads," to the Aborigines) lie about 27 km to the west and are also part of the protected Uluru National Park. These huge rocks, just as old and once much larger than Ayers Rock, are a jumble of more rounded monoliths, separated by gorges, valleys, and chasms. Many visitors enjoy exploring the Olgas more than The Rock because they have more hidden areas to discover and are a bit less intimidating and less touristed.

A favorite attraction is deep, narrow **Olga Gorge,** which runs between 546-meter-high Mt. Olga and slightly shorter Mt. Wulpa. The Olgas' three main **walking trails** are the two-km track

CAUTIONS ABOUT CLIMBING THE ROCK AND THE OLGAS

Uluru is extremely steep. The climb should not be attempted by anyone with a heart condition, high blood pressure, angina, asthma, fear of heights, vertigo, or dizziness. Additionally, strong winds at the top can send both hikers and their possessions aloft. The top of The Rock can be very dangerous—prone to sudden collapse into deep ravines. Hikers should be absolutely certain to carry adequate drinking water at all times. A hat, sunblock, and good walking shoes or boots are essential. Don't attempt a climb whenever the temperature is above 38° C (100° F). The best month is July, the worst January.

For the Olgas (Kata Tjuta), most of the above rules apply. But also be sure to check in with a park ranger before starting out—particularly on that Olga Gorge Track.

from the carpark to Olga Gorge, the four-km route up to **Kata Tjuta Lookout,** and a four-km circular track around the mysterious **Valley of the Winds,** on the north side. Another option for very fit walkers is the two-km track that joins up with the Valley of the Winds track from Kata Tjuta Lookout. Make sure you carry plenty of water for these excursions. It's also recommended that you check in with the ranger station before exploring the Olgas on your own. Rangers will advise you on accessible areas and necessary equipment.

PRACTICALITIES

Accommodations and Food
The cheapest place you'll find out here is the bunkhouse at **Outback Pioneer Lodge,** tel. (08) 8956-2170. Two dorms, each with 40 beds, run $18 pp. Budget. Within the same complex, the **Outback Pioneer Hotel** rents out air-conditioned hotel rooms for about $150 and up. Luxury. If you're not bothered by room rates almost as high as The Rock, your choices are **Sails in the Desert,** tel. (08) 8956-2200, or the **Desert Gardens Hotel,** tel. (08) 8956-2100. All the luxuries come with the price tag (in the $300-350

bracket). Luxury. If you're traveling with a group (or can quickly make a few friends), **Emu Walk Apartments,** tel. (08) 8956-2000, offers fully equipped one- and two-bedroom apartments ($170-320). Luxury (moderate if sharing).

Ayers Rock Campground, tel. (08) 8956-2055, has campsites and on-site vans, plus a pool ($10-16 pp). Budget-Moderate. Camping is not allowed anywhere within Uluru National Park.

All reservations can be made through the central reservations center, tel. (08) 8956-2737 or, in Sydney, tel. (02) 9360-9099.

Both the Sails in the Desert and Desert Gardens offer dining options from snack bars to upscale restaurants (entrees $16-26). **Ernest Giles Tavern** features both counter and bistro meals ($12-16 entrees). **Outback Pioneer Hotel** has simple fare and takeaways, plus a nightly self-cook BBQ ($8-16 depending on what you stick on the barby). A **kiosk** at the campground sells a variety of foodstuffs, but there's a better selection at the **supermarket** in the shopping square, along with various takeaways.

Shopping
The **shopping square complex** has a newsagent, supermarket, T-shirt shop, travel agency, and photo processor. Pick up Aboriginal handicrafts and paintings at the **Maruku Arts and Crafts Centre** (owned by the Anangu people), and souvenirs at the **Ininti Store, Ranger Station,** or at the hotel gift shop/galleries. **Mulgara Gallery,** in Sails in the Desert Hotel, features high-quality (and high-priced) arts, crafts, and jewelry.

Services and Information
A **bank, post office, police,** and **fire station** are located in Yulara Village.

The **Visitors Centre,** on Yulara Drive, features informative displays on the area's history, geography, flora, and fauna, and also presents regular slide shows. A variety of literature is available, including walking maps, visitor's guides, and *The Yulara Experience* newsletter. Open daily 8 a.m.-9 p.m. For information, phone (08) 8956-2240.

The **Uluru-Kata Tjuta Cultural Center,** one km before The Rock, on the road from Yulara, also dispenses maps, information, and helpful advice. For information, phone (08) 8956-3138.

A **medical clinic** at the Royal Flying Doctor base, near the police station, tel. (08) 8956-2286, is open Mon.-Fri. 9 a.m.-noon and 2-5 p.m., Sat.-Sun. 10-11 a.m.

In emergencies, dial 000; the **police,** tel. (08) 8956-2166; or **ambulance,** tel. (08) 8956-2286. An emergency alarm is located at the base of The Rock.

TRANSPORTATION

Getting There
Yulara's Connellan Airport, six km north of the village, is served by **Ansett Australia,** tel. (13) 1300; **Qantas,** tel. (13) 1313; and **Airnorth,** tel. (08) 8956-2093. Direct flights are available from Adelaide, Alice Springs, Cairns, Sydney, and Perth.

AAT Kings, tel. (08) 8952-1700, operates free shuttle coaches between the airport and the village. Taxi service between the resort and attractions is available from **Sunworth Shuttle Service,** tel. (08) 8956-2152.

Greyhound Pioneer, tel. (13) 2030, operates daily service between Alice Springs and Ayers Rock (450 km). Roundtrip day tours cost about $160, and a one-way bus ticket costs around half that. Many agencies offer all-inclusive packages, which include transportation, lodging, and sightseeing.

Holders of bus passes should book ahead as coaches fill up quickly.

Getting Around
It can cost big bucks to rent a car in Yulara—maybe $85-150 per day, including the "remote surcharge." Rental companies include **Avis,** tel. (08) 8956-2266; **Budget,** tel. (08) 8956-2121; and **Territory Rent-a-Car,** tel. (08) 8956-2030. **Sunworth Taxi Service, tel. (08) 8956-2152, also goes to The Rock.**

The Mobil station, in the village, rents bicycles (including safety helmet) for $20 per day and mopeds for $35 per half-day. Current identification and a $50-100 deposit are required.

If you're planning to head out to the Olgas, the road is *miserable!*

Organized Tours
Zillions are available but some of the best are the **ranger-conducted** tours, organized by the Na-

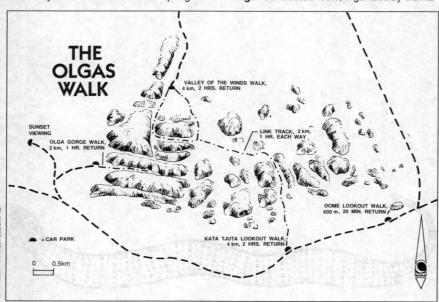

THE OLGAS WALK

VALLEY OF THE WINDS WALK, 4 km, 2 HRS. RETURN

SUNSET VIEWING

OLGA GORGE WALK, 2 km, 1 HR. RETURN

LINK TRACK, 2 km, 1 HR. EACH WAY

DOME LOOKOUT WALK, 600 m, 20 MIN. RETURN

= CAR PARK

KATA TJUTA LOOKOUT WALK, 4 km, 2 HRS. RETURN

0   0.5km

tional Park Service—and some of these are free. The two-hour **Liru Walk** led by Aboriginal rangers offers a traditional perspective of the land (daily 8:30 a.m., Oct.-April 7 a.m.). Take a 90-minute **Mala Walk,** starting from the climb's base, for an introduction to Arangu culture (daily 10 a.m., Oct.-April 8 a.m.). Book all of these tours well in advance. For information, contact the Visitors Centre, tel. (08) 8956-2240.

Anangu Tours, tel. (08) 8956-2123, the only Aboriginal-owned private tour company, offers a

variety of excursions including those focusing on bush foods and medicines, the environment, geology, cave paintings, as well as Aboriginal culture.

Flightseeing over The Rock and the Olgas is organized by **RockAyer,** tel. (08) 8956-2345, and **Airnorth**, tel. (08) 8956-2093. Cost is $75-175 pp for flights lasting 30-110 minutes. **Helicopter rides** cost $75 pp for 15 minutes over Ayers Rock, $100 for 20 minutes over the Olgas, or $145 for a pass over each. Contact RockAyer (above) or Jayrow, tel. (08) 8956-2077.

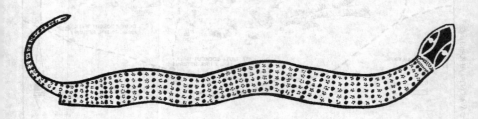

QUEENSLAND
INTRODUCTION

Second largest of the Australian states and twice the size of Texas, Queensland comprises the entire northeast corner of the continent. With 5,000 km of coastline and the magnificent Great Barrier Reef, it's not surprising that almost all of Queensland's attractions are water-oriented. Unless you're looking for snow, Queensland has something for everyone: you can scuba dive on the reef, soak up the rays on a Gold Coast beach, hike through a tropical rainforest, fish for barramundi, or go four-wheel driving through a remote desert national park. Known as the Sunshine State, the beaches, the reef, and the ideal climate attract tourists in droves; a string of cities and towns along the eastern seaboard serve the needs of travelers, some existing for no reason but tourism.

THE LAND

Queensland's most dominant feature is its coastline, the basis for the tourism industry and stepping stone for the Great Barrier Reef. The coast is paralleled by the Great Dividing Range, a low ridge of rugged peaks running along the eastern seaboard from the New South Wales border to the tip of Cape York. Along the range sprawl massive plateaus of fertile farming land while to the west lies the Outback, a vast and desolate landscape extending to neighboring Northern Territory.

Regions

Aside from the reef, Queensland's most appealing attributes are the beaches, especially those in the southeast of the state. Best-known of the beaches is the Gold Coast, a 30-km stretch of golden sand as beautiful as anywhere in the world and entirely backed by Waikiki-style high-rise resort developments. Northwest of the Gold Coast lies Brisbane, Queensland's capital and third-largest city in Australia. A young and vibrant city, Brisbane lacks the pretensions of its southern cousins. Heading north, beyond the beaches of the Sunshine Coast, is Hervey Bay, the center of a large whalewatching indus-

QUEENSLAND

TORRES STRAIT
THURSDAY ISLAND
CAPE YORK
BAMAGA
CAPE
WEIPA
YORK
CAPE WEYMOUTH
GULF
OF
CARPENTARIA
PENINSULA
GREAT DIVIDING RANGE
OSPREY REEF
CORAL SEA
WELLESLEY ISLANDS
COOKTOWN
BOUGAINVILLE REEF
MOSSMAN
PORT DOUGLAS
CAIRNS
HOLMES REEF
BURKETOWN
KARUMBA
NORMANTON
INNISFAIL
MISSION BEACH
TULLY
ROCKINGHAM BAY
CARDWELL
HINCHINBROOK ISLAND
INGHAM
PALM ISLANDS
MAGNETIC ISLAND
TOWNSVILLE
MARION REEF
CAMOOWEAL
ISA HIGHLANDS
CHARTERS TOWERS
AYR
BOWEN
FLINDERS HWY.
PROSERPINE
WHITSUNDAY ISLANDS
MOUNT ISA
CLONCURRY
HUGHENDEN
CUMBERLAND ISLANDS
REEF
LANDSBOROUGH
WINTON
LEICHHARDT RANGE
BRUCE HWY.
MACKAY
BO JLIA
SWAIN REEFS
CLERMONT
BARCALDINE
EMERALD
ROCKHAMPTON
YEPPOON
LONGREACH
CAPRICORN HWY.
MOUNT MORGAN
GLADSTONE
CAPRICORN GROUP
BLACKALL
MOURA
BUNKER GROUP
RANGE
BUNDABERG
MARYBOROUGH
FRASER ISLAND
CHARLEVILLE
MITCHELL
KINGAROY
GYMPIE
WARREGO HWY.
ROMA
NOOSA
CHINCHILLA
CALOUNDRA
DALBY
REDCLIFFE
CUNNAMULLA
TOOWOOMBA
IPSWICH
MORETON ISLAND
BRISBANE
GOONDIWINDI
WARWICK
SURFERS PARADISE
NORTHERN TERRITORY
SOUTH AUSTRALIA
BIRDSVILLE
DIAMANTINA RIVER
WARREGO RIVER
BALONNE RIVER
LISMORE
BYRON BAY
NEW SOUTH WALES
0   200 km

© AVALON TRAVEL PUBLISHING

try and gateway to the wilderness of **Fraser Island,** the world's largest sand island.

The Great Barrier Reef, extending from Bundaberg to the northern tip of Queensland, is made up of hundreds of islands. Many are protected as national parks, some are privately owned, and more than 20 have resorts. At the southern end of the reef, you'll find the Bunker and Capricorn Groups, some of the most beautiful island clusters on the entire reef. They are true coral islands; built entirely of reef debris, they sit on the reef itself, surrounded by magnificent coral reefs. More accessible than the cays, the continental islands lie between the mainland and outer reef. One of

the most accessible, and with great beaches and a variety of hiking trails, is Great Keppel Island, off Rockhampton. Best-known reef destination is the Whitsundays, 100-odd rugged continental islands rising magnificently from turquoise-colored waters off Proserpine. Townsville, north of the Whitsundays and Australia's largest tropical city, is home to the excellent Great Barrier Reef Wonderland. Cairns, 2,000 km north of Brisbane, is the capital of reef tourism. The city itself has nothing special to offer, but the reef is in close proximity and to the west are magnificent rainforests. The Great Barrier Reef extends beyond the tip of Cape York, but this section is only ac-

THE GREAT BARRIER REEF

The awe-inspiring Great Barrier Reef is one of Mother Nature's greatest masterpieces, a kaleidoscope of colorful marinelife that extends 2,000 km along Queensland's coast. And although the reef itself may seem inert, it is in fact a living organism—the world's *largest* living structure, in fact (about half the size of Texas). The reef's basic lifeform is **coral,** which comes in all shapes and sizes, and whose vivid colors range the full spectrum of the rainbow. The reef is also home to a colorful myriad of other creatures, including 1,500 species of fish and 4,000 species of mollusks.

The actual reef doesn't come in contact with the mainland; it comes very close, near the northern tip of Cape York, and is as far from the coast as 200 km off Mackay. While in the south the outer reef is almost continuous and narrow, in the north it is broken and up to 80 km wide.

Ironically, many visitors don't see the actual *barrier* reef (often called the outer reef), but instead limit their travels to the resort islands between the reef and the mainland. These islands are **continental** in origin, having been isolated from the mainland when the sea level rose at the end of the last ice age. Along the outer reef are more than 300 **coral cays,** low islands of coral debris that have built up on the barrier reef itself. Of the great variety of reef types found off Queensland's coast, three are very distinctive: **fringing** reefs develop around continental islands, **ribbon** reefs are narrow strips on the edge of the Continental Shelf, and **platform** reefs grow on the shelf as oval-shaped lagoons. As well as these common reefs, there's an array of other types, each a different shape due to

wave action, currents, and wind.

The reef's allure is undeniable. It's Australia's most popular holiday destination, with resorts on more than 20 islands, and towns such as Airlie Beach exist only to serve reef-bound travelers. But this popularity is also the reef's biggest enemy. The entire reef ecosystem is a delicate balance of nature that has evolved over thousands of years. Its importance is recognized by UNESCO, who has listed the entire reef as a World Heritage Area. Other large parts of the reef are protected by the Great Barrier Reef Marine Park.

Coral Cays

A coral cay is an island composed entirely of debris from the reef. While coral below the water surface is continually growing, dead coral is ground by wave and wind action onto the lee side of the reef, eventually building up above the high tide mark as a sand bank that constantly shifts with wind and water action. As the cay enlarges and becomes more stable, birds begin nesting on its apex. Seeds are brought to the island by nesting birds. Guano helps the seeds germinate, and on some cays, up to 30 species of plants thrive. Although cays become more stable as guano cements reef debris and vegetation takes hold, they are always changing shape. Of the Great Barrier Reef's 300 coral cays, 69 are vegetated.

Although the continental islands have fringing reefs, diving and snorkeling are better around the cays. Just three resort islands are cays—**Lady Elliot, Heron,** and **Green.** The rest are continental islands.

cessible by boat from Cairns. Although a large part of the state is Outback, Queensland also has vast areas of wild and inhospitable land around Cape York Peninsula accessible only by four-wheel drive, while to the west lies Gulf Country, a maze of rivers and streams draining into the Gulf of Carpentaria.

Climate

Of course, in a region spanning 20 degrees of latitude, climatic differences are immense, but all parts of the Sunshine State have a common thread—an abundance of sunny days. Even in Brisbane, in the state's south, daytime temperatures rarely drop below 20° C (68° F). The southern part of the state features ideal weather—summers are not unbearably hot, and winters are mild. The farther north from Brisbane you travel, the more tropical the climate, with rainfall restricted to the Wet (Jan.-March). North of the tropic of Capricorn, summer conditions can be unbearable for those used to cooler climates, with humid and hot days, punctuated by short and heavy rainfalls in the late afternoon. In the far north of the state, up to two meters of rain can fall in the Wet, with roads cut and land transportation impossible.

HISTORY

Like other Australian states, the European settlement of Queensland began with a penal colony.

Explorers sailed north from Sydney Town in the 1820s searching for a possible site. A spot was chosen on Moreton Bay, but the convicts and their guards moved inland to the present site of Brisbane shortly afterward. Free settlers followed in the mid-1930s, but the colony remained part of NSW until 1859 when the state of Queensland was formed. Settlement outside the state's southeast corner was slow. Travel to the north was by boat, and beyond the coastline the land was rugged and inhospitable. Aboriginals had crossed from Indonesia into what is now Queensland 40,000 years before the first Europeans arrived, and as new settlers encroached on their land many bloody battles ensued. Spears were no match for gun-toting Europeans, and the Aborigines were slowly forced to retreat to regions of the state unwanted by Europeans. By the turn of the century, the Aborigines had been completely driven from their land and were forced to live on reserves.

The settlers developed a thriving agricultural base, and while agriculture remains an important part of the economy (the state is a major producer of pineapples, peanuts, sugar, and wheat), Queensland built its modern-day wealth upon abundant mineral deposits. While NSW and Victoria boomed with 19th-century gold rushes, Queensland's mining industry has only developed this century, with lead, silver, copper, coal, and bauxite the main products.

Tourism is worth more than $10 billion annually to Queensland's economy. Climate and other natural attributes make tourism the sin-

typical
Queensland pub

gle biggest industry, and as many southerners discover the idyllic lifestyle Queenslanders enjoy, they move north. For more than two decades, until 1987, Queensland was ruled by the Na-

tional Party under the leadership of Sir Joh Bjelke-Peterson, a peanut farmer turned politician whose government was ultraconservative and always controversial.

GOLD COAST AND HINTERLAND

The Gold Coast is Australia's most popular and developed resort area. And although the sun almost always shines and the beaches are among the best in the country, rows of beachfront high-rise development, traffic jams, and crass commercialism mean the place has as many critics as fans. More than four million tourists flock to the Gold Coast annually, creating a year-round carnival atmosphere similar to that found at Miami Beach, Waikiki, or the south of France. The experience of visiting the Gold Coast definitely shouldn't be missed, but allow time to visit the Gold Coast hinterland and Lamington National Park.

The Gold Coast extends 30 km from the New South Wales border to a long sandy spit protecting the wide mouth of Nerang River. The southern end is a long strip of older resorts and residential areas, where suburbs such as Coolangatta, Currumbin, and Burleigh Heads have become one continuous sprawl along the Gold Coast Highway, which skirts the beach. From Miami, the highway heads inland a few blocks, entering a forest of high-rise apartments and massive hotels along a seemingly never-ending strip of neon signs known as Surfers Paradise. This is the center of the action, where scooters vie with towering tour coaches for room on the road, tanned surfers and hordes of sunburnt tourists pound the pavement, and elegant stores with outlets in Paris and New York stand beside fast-food restaurants. Love it or leave it, the Gold Coast is like no other place in the country.

History

In 1870 blocks of land were offered for sale at Southport, at the north end of the Gold Coast, for 10 pounds each, and, at first, developers couldn't find even one buyer. Over the years the lots began to sell, and a town grew on the west bank of the Nerang River. In 1923 a Brisbane developer paid 40 pounds for a block of land on the site that is now Cavill Mall. He built the **Surfers Paradise Hotel,** taking its name from a real es-

tate advertisement. In 1925, when a bridge was built over the Nerang River, carloads of Brisbane people, who up until that time spent their holidays on the beaches of Moreton Bay, flocked to the golden stretches of sand. After WW II, land prices on the coast soared, with developers building beachfront hotels and vast residential suburbs. Sarcastically, a journalist during this time called the strip the Gold Coast, and the name stuck. By the 1960s beachfront land all the way to the New South Wales border was built up, so developers headed inland, to the swamps and wetlands behind what was once sand dunes. Canals were dredged and millions of tons of fill were bulldozed into strips of land, turning nearly every residential block into waterfront property. Development today continues unabated, much of it at the northern end of the Gold Coast, where exclusive resorts and residential estates such as Hope Island and Sanctuary Cove sprawl over reclaimed wetland. The latest trend for developers is security-restricted housing estates; Sovereign Island (known as Griffin Island before developers arrived), right at the tip of Paradise Point, is the most outrageous of these.

SIGHTS AND BEACHES

South Gold Coast

Away from the glitz and gaudiness of Surfers Paradise are quieter stretches of beach and areas of natural bushland. North of where the Tweed River drains into the ocean, **Coolangatta** spreads over the headland of Point Danger, marking the point where the Queensland/New South Wales border hits the ocean. Views from the point extend south along the Tweed Coast and north to Surfers Paradise, giving a panoramic view of the Gold Coast. The town beach, **Greenmount,** is relatively protected, making this end of the coast great for families. North

TO SOUTH STRADBROKE ISLAND

TO SANCTUARY COVE, PARKWOOD GOLF COURSE, AND BRISBANE

NERANG HEAD

THE SPIT

NERANG SOUTHPORT RD

BROADWATER TOURIST PARK

SOUTHPORT

NERANG ST

SEA WORLD

SHERATON MIRAGE

HOSPITAL
TREKKERS
BACKPACKERS

MARINA MIRAGE

MAIN BEACH

MAIN BEACH TOURIST PARK

HEEB ST

SLATER AVE

MAIN BEACH

SURFERS PARADISE

TIKI VILLAGE

SOUTH PACIFIC OCEAN

NERANG RIVER

CAVILL MALL
SURFERS
TRANSIT
CENTRE

BROADBEACH WATERS

RIO VISTA BLVD

TO PALM MEADOWS GOLF COURSE

BROADBEACH

CONRAD JUPITERS CASINO

KURRAWA BEACH

MERMAID BEACH

MERMAID WATERS

MERMAID BEACH

GOLD COAST HWY

NOBBYS BEACH

MIAMI

MARINE PDE

MIAMI BEACH

BURLEIGH WATERS

WEST
BURLEIGH RD

REEDY CREEK RD

BURLEIGH HEADS

DAVID FLEAY WILDLIFE PARK

GOLD COAST

NPWS OFFICE

BURLEIGH HEAD NATIONAL PARK

WEST BURLEIGH

TALLEBUDGERA TOURIST PARK

MALLAWA DR

TO NERANG AND BRISBANE

TALLEBUDGERA BEACH

TALLEBUDGERA CREEK

0   2 km

PALM BEACH

PALM BEACH AVE.

CURRUMBIN WATERS

PACIFIC HWY

PALM BEACH

CURRUMBIN

CURRUMBIN CREEK

TUGUN BEACH

QUEENSLAND

CURRUMBIN SANCTUARY

TUGUN

GOLD COAST HWY

NEW SOUTH WALES

BILINGA BEACH

BILINGA

COOLANGATTA AIRPORT

GREENMOUNT BEACH

KIRRA

POINT DANGER

COOLANGATTA

TO BYRON BAY

TWEED HEADS

© AVALON TRAVEL PUBLISHING

from Coolangatta, Marine Parade hugs the ocean around **Kirra Point,** where sand has built up alongside two groins, forming what many surfers claim to be one of the world's top-10 waves. Thick swells break over the sandy bottom, spilling over to form tubing waves that break for more than 200 meters. Some of the world's best surfers call Kirra home, and if they're not in the water when the swell is up, there's sure to be 200-odd others.

Currumbin Sanctuary, tel. (07) 5534-1266, north of Kirra in an area of native bushland, is home to hundreds of Australian native birds as well as kangaroos, koalas, and emus. The sanctuary started by accident when a local horticulturalist began feeding rainbow lorikeets honey-soaked bread to keep them away from his nectar-bearing flowers. Now it's the tourists who feed the birds, a daily ritual that is one of the region's most-loved attractions. It's open daily 8 a.m.-5 p.m. Admission is $16 pp. The sanctuary is nestled in a strip of bushland that stretches to the beach, where Currumbin Creek drains into the ocean. This is another popular surf spot, known as the **Alley.** The strip between Currumbin and Burleigh Heads is **Palm Beach,** where sand has shifted northward in the last 20 years, leaving exposed rock.

Heading north, the next river crossing is **Tallebudgera Creek.** At its mouth is 28-hectare **Burleigh Head National Park,** an area of coastal bushland surrounded by Gold Coast sprawl. Short trails wind through the park and to the foreshore where you'll find columns of volcanic rock. Access is from beyond the National Parks and Wildlife Service office (turn right at the first set of traffic lights north of Tallebudgera Creek) or along Goodwin St. in downtown Burleigh Heads. Burleigh is another near-perfect barreling right-hand wave that breaks on swells up to three meters. North of Burleigh are **Miami, Mermaid Beach,** and **Broadbeach.**

Slightly inland is the **David Fleay Wildlife Park,** West Burleigh Rd., tel. (07) 5576-2411, operated by a local naturalist. More than four km of trails lead through rainforest and wetlands preserved in their natural state and home to a wide variety of Australian fauna, including koalas, platypuses, crocodiles, dingoes, and cassowaries. Admission is adult $9.50, senior $6.50. Open daily 9 a.m.-5 p.m.

BEWARE THE BOX JELLYFISH

Sharks and crocodiles may be Australia's best-known marine nasties, but the tropical waters of Queensland have a much less fearsome, yet just as deadly, danger—the **box jellyfish,** better known in the north as a "stinger." Found in tropical waters between Nov. and April, they live mainly around river mouths. However, it's not recommended to swim anywhere along the coast or even at many of the islands close to the mainland during this period (some beaches and resorts have stinger-free enclosures).

If stung, carefully remove tentacles with tweezers and douse the wounds liberally with vinegar. Get to a hospital as quickly as possible.

Surfers Paradise
Surfers Paradise Hotel, for which this area is named, has long since disappeared under waves of development that have turned a one-km stretch of beach into a jungle of skyscrapers. The beach at Surfers is particularly wide and crowded year-round. In winter months long shadows created by beachfront high-rise creep across the sand by early afternoon. **Cavill Mall,** the center of the strip, is sandwiched between the Gold Coast Highway and the foreshore. In Cavill Mall is **Ripley's Believe it or Not!,** tel. (07) 5592-0040, a museum of oddities from around the world, and a dinosaur gallery; open

daily 9 a.m.-10 p.m.; admission adult $9.95, child $5.25.

North of Surfers
Immediately north of Surfers Paradise is **Main Beach** and **The Spit,** a narrow strip of sand extending three km to Nerang Head, at the mouth of the Broadwater. Along Sea World Dr., which ends at Nerang Head, is **Marina Mirage,** the base of many water-oriented activities, and **Sea World** theme park (see below). North of Sea World, development has been restricted and the dunes retain a resemblance to what the area to the south would have looked like last century.

Across the Broadwater from the Spit is **Southport,** the Gold Coast's original settlement and still its commercial and administration center. From Southport, the Gold Coast Highway heads inland to the major theme parks (see below) and Brisbane while **Marine Parade** continues north through built-up residential estates with romantic names such as **Anglers Paradise, Runaway Bay,** and **Paradise Point.** West of Paradise Point is a maze of low-lying swamps around the Coomera River. Parts of **Hope Island** have been transformed in the last 10 years with the construction of **Sanctuary Cove,** an up-market residential and resort complex. **Village Square,** Hope Island, tel. (07) 5530-1885, is a lively arts and crafts market open daily 9 a.m.-5 p.m. Along with more than 250 shops

Burleigh Heads

and stalls, it features street performers, cafés, and restaurants. Admission is $2 pp.

South Stradbroke Island

Across the Broadwater from Paradise Point and immediately north of Nerang Head is long and narrow South Stradbroke Island. The *Maranoa,* a historic sailing vessel, departs Marina Mirage daily at 9:30 a.m. for a full-day cruise to South Stradbroke Island. The price, $45 pp, includes morning tea, buffet lunch, on-board entertainment, time to relax on the island, afternoon tea, and accommodation transfers. For bookings call (07) 5532-2439. On the island is the new **Couran Point Resort,** featuring a 1.5-square-km pool with a swim-up bar, hiking trails, tennis, and various water sports. It costs $60 pp for a day at the resort, including transfers from Marina Mirage. Call (07) 5591-1817 for details.

RECREATION

Cruises

Tiki Village, at the west end of Cavill Ave. in downtown Surfers Paradise, is the departure point for **Island Queen Showboat Cruises,** tel. (07) 5557-8800, with pickups also made at Marina Mirage. They depart regularly for a two-hour cruise around the canals and into the Broadwater ($28 pp) as well as at 9 a.m. and 10 a.m. for Sanctuary Cove and a buffet seafood lunch. **Shangri-la Cruises,** tel. (07) 5591-1800, departs from Marina Mirage on the Spit and offers similar options at the same prices.

Marina Mirage and Vicinity

This marina and shopping complex is the best place on the Gold Coast to indulge in water sports. **Aussie Bobs,** tel. (07) 5591-7577, based out on the marina, offers a variety of activities including a 10-minute speedboat ride ($35 pp), waterskiing ($30), jet skiing ($50), and parasailing ($50). **Popeye's Boat Hire,** tel. (07) 5532-5822, at adjacent Mariner's Cove, rents a variety of boats from $20 per hour.

Along Seaworld Dr. and anchored offshore is **Bungee Downunder,** tel. (07) 5531-1103, the world's only floating bungee jump. At just 50 meters, the tower is relatively low, but for $69 it's probably worth it for bungee enthusiasts.

Golf

Golfers migrate to the Gold Coast for its resort courses, some of which are the best in the country. **Parkwood,** four km northwest of Southport on Napper Rd., tel. (07) 5594-6835, is set among native bushland with water hazards on many holes; greens fees are $30 and club rental $25. Dotted with thousands of palm trees, **Palm Meadows** is a *very* long course; on Springbrook Rd., west of Surfers Paradise, tel. (07) 5594-2450 or (1800) 65-1117. Hope Island, north of Surfers Paradise, boasts three world-class courses, including two at Sanctuary Cove. The newest course on the Gold Coast is **The Links** on Hope Island, tel. (07) 5530-8988. Designed by Peter Thomson, it is styled on a Scottish links course with rolling fairways lined with tussocky grasses. Greens fees are $75 and clubs can be rented for $40.

Hooked on Golf, tel. (07) 5598-2788, will take you to a different course each day of the week, organize tee times and greens fees, and rent clubs.

Other Recreation

Mountain bike touring is popular in the hinterland, with a variety of tours offered from the Gold Coast. Typical of these is **Off the Edge,** tel. (07) 5592-6406, offering transportation to forested areas behind the Gold Coast, featuring a number of downhill rides and a van that takes you back up top each time. The cost is $45 pp.

A number of places offer horseback riding, including **Numinbah Valley Adventure Trails,** tel. (07) 5533-4137, 23 km southwest of Nerang. The scenic setting makes the three-hour, $45 trip out here well worthwhile.

Balloons Aloft, tel. (07) 5593-3291, offers hot-air balloon flights. Flights are weather dependent and generally last one hour (a fantastic way to watch the sun rise over the Gold Coast).

Queensland Climbing Centres, 38 Hutchinson St., Burleigh Waters, tel. (07) 5593-6919, is a large indoor climbing complex with more than 800 square meters of cracks and overhangs on walls rising 11 meters. Admission for climbers is $10, including basic tuition, but nonclimbers can come and watch for free; open daily 10 a.m.-10 p.m.

Theme Parks

Sea World may have the same name as its famous San Diego cousin, but the similarities stop there. Although there are animal shows, including penguins, sea lions, seals, and the massive Dolphin Cove, the emphasis here is on amusement rides, including a triple-loop roller coaster, monorail, and water slide park. Admission is adult $44, child $28, and it's open daily 9:30 a.m.-5 p.m. Located on the Spit, north of Surfers, tel. (07) 5588-2222.

Dreamworld, the most unique of the theme parks, has a Disney-Australian theme. Instead of being greeted by Mickey and Minnie, Kenny the Koala and his friends hang out hugging and kissing and posing for pictures. The 84-hectare park is divided into 11 theme areas, including Gum Tree Gully, Koala Country, Rivertown, and Gold Rush Country. The newest amusement ride here is claimed to be the fastest and tallest ride in the world: thrillseekers on the **Tower of Terror** drop 38 stories, reaching speeds of 160 km per hour in less than seven seconds. Admission is adult $44, child $28. This park is located on the Pacific Highway at Coomera, 30 km northwest of Surfers toward Brisbane, tel. (07) 5588-1111.

Just south of Dreamworld is the most popular of the theme parks, **Movie World,** which opened in 1991. Based on the famous Warner Bros. Hollywood studio, this park features re-creations of the movie sets for *Batman, Lethal Weapon,* and *Police Academy* as well as tours of a studio, a lively Main Street, and a few exhilarating rides. Admission is adult $40, child $24. Open daily 10 a.m.-5 p.m., tel. (07) 5573-3999.

Immediately south of Movie World is **Wet 'n' Wild,** tel. (07) 5573-2277, Australia's largest water-sports park. As well as long and twisting waterslides (including one reaching speeds of more than 50 km per hour), the park features a wave pool generating meter-high waves, a tropical island complete with sandy beaches and palm trees, a slow-moving river for tube riding, and Dive-in Movies, where you can watch a movie from the comfort of an inflated, waterborne tube. Admission to Wet 'n' Wild is adult $30, child $18. Open daily 10 a.m.-5 p.m. and Saturday until 9 p.m.

Entertainment

At last count, the Gold Coast held about 40 nightclubs, as well as numerous service clubs, a casino, and a handful of live theaters. The following clubs are all within a couple of blocks of Cavill Mall. **Cocktails and Dreams,** in the Mark shopping center on Orchid Ave., tel. (07) 5592-1955, is a longtime favorite of backpackers and a younger local crowd with a cross section of dance music played till 5 a.m. In the same complex is **The Party,** open the same hours. Both have theme nights and cheap drinks before 10 p.m. **The Penthouse,** Orchid Ave., tel. (07) 5538-1388, is a legendary place, with each of four stories offering a different style of nightlife, including a disco, pool room, and piano bar. **Benson's,** Orchid Ave., tel. (07) 5538-7600, is popular with the under-25s on Friday and Saturday nights, and attracts an older crowd the rest of the week.

Surfers Beergarden, upstairs on Cavill Mall, has a real beachside atmosphere, with surfboards hanging from the ceiling and old surfing photos adorning the walls. **Beach House Tavern,** in Iluka Beach Resort at the top end of Cavill Mall, is another casual place, open from 10 a.m. daily. **Hot Shots Saloon,** 51 Cavill Ave., tel. (07) 5592-2585, is open 11 a.m.-11 p.m., and you can bring your own booze.

Conrad Jupiters, tel. (07) 5592-1133, Queensland's first (legal) casino, is on Broadbeach Island, part of an artificial canal system three km south of Surfers Paradise. The casino holds just 114 gaming tables but boasts hundreds of video machines and "pokies" (slot machines). Although the casino is open 24 hours and is fairly casual, it's nothing like the glitz and glamour of those in Las Vegas. And as casinos are still a novelty in Australia, don't hold out for any dining or accommodation bargains (standard rooms start at $200). One of the most popular games is **two-up,** an Australian game where punters bet on the outcome of coins tossed in the air. The casino also has bars, restaurants, and an International Showroom where stage productions are performed nightly; for bookings call (07) 5592-1133. Jupiters also holds the stylish **Fortunes Nightclub,** open Tues.-Sat. from 9 p.m.

ACCOMMODATIONS

Motels, resorts, and caravan parks increase prices dramatically during Christmas school holidays (all of January) and other holiday periods. (Rates at backpacker accommodations remain steady year-round). Outside of Surfers, especially to the south toward Coolangatta, motels often advertise rooms for $35-40 d. The only way to *guarantee* a room is to book ahead, especially during school holidays, and year-round at backpacker lodges. **Accommodation Services,** tel. (07) 5592-0067, fax (07) 5592-1804, makes bookings for all standards of accommodations and charges only a small fee for the service.

Motels and Resorts in Surfers

The least expensive motel close to Surfers is **Delilah Motel,** 72 Ferny Ave., tel. (07) 5538-1722, where very basic rooms are $55 s, $75 d. Moderate. You'll find slightly more expensive but better quality rooms at **Paradise Inn,** 2826 Gold Coast Hwy., tel. (07) 5592-0585; many units have kitchenettes and there's a pool and laundry. Moderate. Located in the heart of Surfers is **Trickett Gardens Holiday Inn,** 24 Trickett St., tel. (07) 5539-0988 or (1800) 07-4290, where each apartment is fully self-contained, complete with laundry, and there's a pool; $92 s or d, rising to $120 at Christmas. Expensive. Moving up another notch is **Bahia Beachfront Apartments,** 154 Esplanade, tel. (07) 5538-3322, one km from Cavill Mall, where each unit is self-contained (request ocean views—from the third floor up); $95-110 s or d. Expensive. **Iluka Beach Resort Hotel** is centrally located, right opposite the beach and towering above Cavill Mall, tel. (07) 5539-9155 or (1800) 07-3333. Rooms are of a high standard and each has a private balcony; $140-260 s or d. Premium.

Gold Coast International Hotel, Staghorn Ave., tel. (07) 5592-1200 or (1800) 07-4020, is a five-star hostelry with a grand lobby and elegantly decorated rooms, many with balconies and ocean views. Rates are $195-215 s or d. Luxury. **Grand Mercure Broadbeach,** 81 Surf Parade, tel. (07) 5592-2250 or (1800) 07-4465, is two km south of Surfers and linked to Conrad Jupiters Casino by monorail; from $235 s or d. Luxury. **Sheraton Mirage Gold Coast,** Sea World Dr., tel. (07) 5591-1488, sprawls over 30 hectares and is right on the beach and across the road from Sea World. The resort has a tropical feel about it, with lagoons surrounding the units. Rates of $420-590 for a standard room include a buffet breakfast. Luxury.

Motels South of Surfers

Outside of summer holidays, motels along the "strip" south of Surfers Paradise are among the cheapest in Australia. Most advertise rates on boards out front, often less than $30 for a double. One of these is **El Rancho Holiday Apartments,** 2125 Gold Coast Hwy., Miami, tel. (07) 5572-3655, with a pool, laundry, gas barbecues, and rooms of a reasonable standard. During the research for this edition, rooms were just $28 d. Budget. More basic is the **Miami Motel,** 2117 Gold Coast Hwy., tel. (07) 5572-3083; from $30 s or d. Budget. For self-contained units right opposite the beach, consider **Miami Beach Apartments,** 12 Marine Parade, tel. (07) 5572-4444, which charges $75-120 s or d. Moderate.

Hyatt Regency

At Burleigh Heads, **Casino Motel,** 1761 Gold Coast Hwy., tel. (07) 5535-7133, offers all of the above facilities, and a couple of rooms have older-style kitchenettes. Rooms range $45-90. Inexpensive. **Fifth Avenue Motel,** also in Burleigh Heads, 1953 Gold Coast Hwy., tel. (07) 5535-3588, features rooms of an excellent standard and a pleasant pool area away from highway noise; $85-135 s or d. Moderate.

Tropic Sands on the Beach, 1295 Gold Coast Hwy., tel. (07) 5535-1044, is at the north end of Palm Beach. Many rooms yield ocean views. The rate of $85 s or d reflects the location rather than standard of the rooms. Moderate.

At the Beach Motel, Gold Coast Hwy., tel. (07) 5536-3599, is within walking distance of Kirra Beach and, at just $45 s, $55 d, is an excellent value. (Don't confuse this place with On the Beach Motel around the corner at Coolangatta.) Inexpensive.

Right on Coolangatta Beach is **Beach House Seaside Resort,** 52 Marine Parade, tel. (07) 5574-2800. Each unit is modern and fully self-contained, right down to dishwashers. Each room has a balcony with water views and can sleep up to six people; $135-185. Facilities include a squash court, half-size tennis court, pool, gym, barbecues, and an arcade with supermarket and choice of restaurants. Premium.

Sanctuary Cove
Hyatt Regency Sanctuary Cove, Manor Circle, tel. (07) 5577-1234 or (1800) 65-9994, is on Hope Island, away from the glitz of Surfers. It's part of a complex spread along the Coomera River and is well suited to golfers as guests have access to the 18-hole **Pines** golf course (otherwise open only to residents). Accommodations are in five three-story complexes surrounding a saltwater lagoon complete with sandy beaches. A standard room is $260, while Regency Club rooms at $390 include free booze and breakfast. Luxury.

Backpacker Accommodations
Without a doubt, the best backpacker lodge on the Gold Coast is **Surfers Paradise Backpackers** at 2835 Gold Coast Hwy., tel. (07) 5592-4677, just 100 meters from the beach and one km south of Cavill Mall. Communal facilities, all of the highest standard, include a large

pool area, modern kitchen, tennis court, game room with pool table, laundry, sauna, outdoor barbecue area, and small gym. All dorm beds are $15 pp, and in the off season a few doubles are offered. Budget. Most central of all hostels is **Nomads Islander Resort,** adjacent to the Surfers Transit Centre and across the road from the west end of Cavill Mall at 6 Beach Rd., tel. (1800) 07-4394. This converted multistory hotel features a large pool, spa, sauna, tennis, and squash. Dorm beds are $15-17, and doubles and twins are $18-22 pp. Budget. **Surf and Sun Backpackers,** Ocean Ave., tel. (07) 5592-2363, is on the north side of Surfers one block from the beach. This place has a pool and game room, and each four-bed dorm has a bathroom, TV, and fridge—courtesy of the days when it was a motel; $15 pp. Budget.

Continuing north is the YHA-affiliated **British Arms International Backpackers Resort,** right near the water at 70 Seaworld Dr., tel. (07) 5571-1776 or (1800) 68-0269. Plenty of activities and a free beer upon arrival make up for basic facilities. Dorm beds are $16-18 pp, doubles are $20-24 pp. Budget. Of a higher standard and also on the north side of Surfers is **Trekkers,** 22 White St., Southport, tel. (07) 5591-5616, where a bed for the night is just $14 pp, $30 d. The atmosphere here is more relaxed than at hostels in Surfers, and there's a great pool surrounded in greenery, as well as a game room. Staff organize activities most days, including trips to nightclubs. Budget.

Campgrounds
The Gold Coast City Council runs seven campgrounds, each in an excellent spot. Book as far ahead as possible, especially for summer; call (1800) 44-4474. The most central to Surfers Paradise is **Main Beach Tourist Park,** Main Beach Parade, tel. (07) 5581-7722. The beach is less than 100 meters away and Surfers is three km south. Sites start at $18, and for $26 the site comes with a private bathroom. Self-contained cabins start at $90 s or d. Budget-Moderate. Enjoy better facilities at **Broadwater Tourist Park,** on the Gold Coast Hwy. in Southport, tel. (07) 5581-7733. Unpowered sites are $12, powered sites $13-18. Budget.

South of Surfers, caravan parks are strung out at regular intervals all the way to Coolangatta, and like those above you'll need reservations in January. The best choices are beyond Burleigh Heads. **Tallebudgera Tourist Park,** 1544 Gold Coast Hwy., tel. (07) 5581-7700, is a five-minute walk from the beach and has a pool, laundry, and barbecues. Sites are $14-22. Budget.

FOOD

Surfers Paradise
The choice of restaurants in this area of the Gold Coast is staggering, but with millions of tourists to feed, it's not surprising. **Cavill Mall,** the pedestrian thoroughfare linking the Gold Coast Highway to the beach, offers the widest choice of casual eateries, many with outside tables, perfect for people-watching. **Paradise Centre** and **Raptis Plaza,** both off the mall, have food courts, the latter with **Seafood on the Beach,** a good fish and chips joint. In the Paradise Centre and facing the beach is **Pips,** a great little juice bar serving delicious smoothies.

Bavarian Haus Restaurant, corner Cavill Ave. and Gold Coast Hwy., tel. (07) 5531-7150, is authentically decorated and waitresses don traditional dress; all a bit corny, but it's popular and inexpensive, with lunches from $7.50 and dinners from $13.50. Another popular tourist restaurant is the **Rusty Pelican,** corner Elkhorn and Orchid Avenues, tel. (07) 5570-3073, with indoor and outdoor seating. The seafood-influenced menu is expensive, but before 7:30 p.m. everything is half price.

In the same vicinity, **Captain's Table,** 26 Orchid Ave., tel. (07) 5531-5766, offers a huge variety of seafood, including grilled barramundi for $17.50. Elkhorn Ave. also holds some ethnic restaurants, including the **Latin Quarter,** with Italian mains from $14. Another choice for Italian dining is **Grissini,** 3 Admiralty Dr., Paradise Waters, tel. (07) 5532-5788, a casual yet stylish restaurant with a reputation for excellent food.

Without a doubt, the best Mexican food in town is at **Margarita's on the Water,** 150 Bundall Rd., tel. (07) 5592-2100, on the west side of the Nerang River. The atmosphere is relaxing, with many tables offering river views, and the food delicious. Lunch is well priced (from $5) and the bar good for pre-dinner drinks, especially Mon.-Fri. 4:30-6:30 p.m. for happy hour. On

Sunday afternoons the restaurant hosts a Mexican barbecue.

Mango's, at the river end of Cavill Ave. in Tiki Village, tel. (07) 5531-6177, is an elegant Santa Fe-style restaurant on the Nerang River. Its size is cleverly disguised by the various dining areas, each with a distinct decor: the Santa Fe room for predinner drinks, the Terrace for river views, and the candlelit Courtyard for a romantic meal. The menu features mostly seafood, with dinner mains averaging $18-26.

La Porte Verte, 154 Scarborough St., Southport, tel. (07) 5591-4669, features provincial French cuisine in an intimate atmosphere; open Tues.-Sat. 6 p.m.-midnight and on Friday for lunch. Definitely worth the splurge.

Four Winds is a revolving restaurant atop Parkroyal Surfers Paradise at 2807 Gold Coast Hwy., tel. (07) 5592-9900. For such a fantastic setting, the plain decor is a bit disappointing and buffet-dining is the only option, but the food is good and the views don't come any better.

Even through a move from Marina Mirage to 2917 Gold Coast Hwy., **Omeros Brothers Seafood Restaurant,** tel. (07) 5538-5244, has remained one of the Gold Coast's most popular eateries. Main meals at lunch are $13-18 and at dinner $17-28.

The Spit
On the Nerang River side of The Spit are two adjacent marinas—**Marina Mirage** and **Mariners Cove**—linked by boardwalks running along the waterfront and offering a great variety of dining opportunities. **Grumpy's Grill,** Mariners Cove, is a casual joint with plastic chairs and tables scattered along the wharf (you fill out the check yourself and take it to the cashier), but what may lack in style is made up for in quality with great fish and chips for $6.50; Tuesday night features all-you-can-eat barbecue ribs and a drink for $12. Upstairs is **Grumpy's Wharf,** tel. (07) 5532-2900, a more formal steak and seafood restaurant. Both are open daily for lunch and dinner.

South of Surfers
Conrad Jupiters Casino, behind Broadbeach, tel. (07) 5592-1133, holds a number of eateries, including **Charters Towers,** one of the coast's finest fine dining restaurants. Nothing but the best china is used, each table is decorated with

colorful orchids, an entire wall is taken up by a glass wine rack, and service is impeccable. The menu features mostly steak and seafood. It's open daily from 6 p.m., and if you need to ask the price, you probably can't afford it. If that's the case, the casino has five other restaurants, including **Andiamo,** featuring dishes from the Tuscany region of Italy; the **Prince Albert,** an English-style pub; and **Food Fantasy,** a buffet restaurant open for breakfast, lunch, and dinner. Dinner and show tickets at the casino run $50-80 pp, depending on the restaurant of choice.

The **Great Khan,** 2488 Gold Coast Hwy., Mermaid Beach, tel. (07) 5572-9266, is a cavernous Mongolian restaurant; service is fast and efficient, although impersonal. Main meals start at $13, but for a few bucks more you can indulge in the buffet.

In Burleigh Heads, it's seafood and more seafood. **Paragon Seafood Restaurant,** 4 Goodwin Terrace, tel. (07) 5535-2300, has eat-in and takeaway sections, with fish and chips from $5. For lunch, the **Fish Monger,** on James St., is cheaper. Around the corner, on Connor St., are two excellent bakeries. **Burleigh Heads Hotel,** on the Esplanade, has inexpensive lunches and dinners, with a $9.95 buffet daily 6-9 p.m. **Oskar's on Burleigh** is an award-winning restaurant overlooking the beach. The eclectic menu features mainly seafood, but other meat and vegetarian dishes are also offered. Open daily for lunch and dinner; it's at 43 Goodwin Terrace, tel. (07) 5576-3722.

TRANSPORTATION

Getting There
The closest international airport to the Gold Coast is Brisbane, from where **Coachtrans,** tel. (07) 5588-8777, runs shuttles every 45 minutes to Surfers Paradise for $28 one-way. **Coolangatta Airport,** on the NSW/Queensland border, is a busy airport handling domestic flights from southern cities. It is served by **Ansett Australia,** tel. (13) 1300, and **Qantas,** tel. (13) 1313. Both airlines offer Gold Coast packages from Sydney starting at $289 pp for airfare and three nights' accommodation. Transfers between this airport and Surfers are $10 one-way.

The main coach terminal, **Surfers Transit Centre,** is on the corner of Gold Coast Hwy.

northbound and Beach Rd., one block from Cavill Mall and a $3-5 cab ride from all Surfers accommodations. The terminal has booking agents for onward travel, tour operators, lockers, a café, car rental agencies, and an accommodations booking service. All major bus companies stop at this terminal, including **Greyhound Pioneer,** tel. (13) 2030; **Kirklands,** tel. (07) 5531-7145; and **McCafferty's,** tel. (13) 1499. The fare between Sydney and Surfers is $78 one-way, but if you're continuing farther north, buy an onward ticket and ask for a free stopover. **Coachtrans,** tel. (07) 5588-8777, operates buses between Brisbane Transit Centre and Surfers at least once hourly ($15) and from Brisbane Airport ($28).

Queensland Rail has recently extended its services to the Gold Coast. Trains now run regularly between Brisbane's Roma St. Station and Nerang. The trip takes one hour, and although Nerang is inland from the coast, buses meet all trains, transporting passengers to Surfers Paradise for a few dollars. Queensland Rail has a booking office in Cavill Park Building on Beach Rd., tel. (13) 2232.

Getting Around
Surfside Buslines, tel. (07) 5536-7666, is the Gold Coast's public bus system, serving the length of the coast around the clock. The one-day Rover Pass is $8 and a weekly ticket is $26.

Airport Rent-a-Car has offices at Coolangatta, tel. (07) 5536-6300, and in the coach terminal, tel. (07) 5538-0700; pick up cars from Coolangatta Airport. Rates for a small car start at $55 per day. All other major rental companies operate on the Gold Coast, including **Avis,** tel. (07) 5539-9388; **Budget,** tel. (07) 5538-1344; **Hertz,** tel. (07) 5538-5366; **National,** tel. (07) 5592-0344; and **Thrifty,** tel. (07) 5538-6511.

Red Back Rentals, opposite the coach terminal, tel. (1800) 81-1268, rents mopeds for $18 per hour. For mountain bikes, head to **Green Bicycle Rentals,** Birt Ave., Surfers Paradise, tel. (0418) 76-6880.

For a cab call (07) 5591-5111.

SERVICES AND INFORMATION

The **post office,** at the beach end of the Paradise Centre on Cavill Mall, is open Mon.-Fri. 9

a.m.-5 p.m. **Thomas Cook Foreign Exchange,** tel. (07) 5531-7770, is also in the Paradise Centre. An **American Express** office is at 22 Albert Ave., Broadbeach, tel. (07) 5538-7588.

Gold Coast Hospital is on Nerang St., Southport, tel. (07) 5571-8211. You'll find the **24-hour Medical Clinic** in the Paradise Centre, tel. (07) 5538-8823, and a **24-hour pharmacy** at 94 Nerang St., Southport, tel. (07) 5591-2254.

The **Gold Coast Tourism Bureau** operates two information booths. One is on Cavill Mall, tel. (07) 5538-4419; open Mon.-Fri. 8 a.m.-5:30 p.m., Saturday 9 a.m.-5:30 p.m., and Sunday 9 a.m.-4 p.m. The other is on the ground floor of Beach House Seaside Resort on Marine Parade, Coolangatta, tel. (07) 5536-7765; open Mon.-Fri. 8 a.m.-4 p.m., Saturday 8 a.m.-1 p.m., and closed on Sunday. On the north side of Tallebudgera Creek, near Burleigh Heads, is an NPWS office with interesting displays on the ecology of the adjacent national park and information on hinterland parks; open daily 9 a.m.-4 p.m., tel. (07) 5535-3032.

GOLD COAST TO THE HINTERLAND

The heavily forested mountains rising behind the Gold Coast's urban sprawl are one of Queensland's hidden assets. The McPherson Range, which forms the northern and western rim of a massive volcano that erupted 20 million years ago, dominates the scene. To the north is **Tamborine Mountain,** an isolated plateau with spectacular views across the Gold Coast.

For those without transportation, a variety of companies offer tours to both destinations and will pick up at Brisbane and Gold Coast hotels. To save a few bucks, hire a car from the Gold Coast for $40-50 and spend the day exploring on your own.

Springbrook National Park
This 2,950-hectare park protects the Springbrook Plateau and, in a separate section, the geological wonder of the **Natural Bridge.** The rainforests, waterfalls, and lush fern-filled gorges around the park's southern boundary, the New South Wales/Queensland border, lend just a taste of what's to come farther west in Lamington

National Park. Access to the plateau is 29 km southwest of Mudgeeraba on the Pacific Highway. Along the park access road you'll find a campground ($5), park information center (open daily 8 a.m.-4 p.m.), and a number of picnic areas. Gwongorella picnic area is at Purling Brook Falls, a beautiful waterfall that cascades into a deep gully.

You can reach the Natural Bridge from the road that climbs up through the Numinbah Valley between Nerang and Murwillumbah. Years of water flowing over the top of an underwater cavern eventually wore a hole in it and formed the Natural Bridge out of the lip of the cavern's roof. Today a small creek plunges through the hole into a deep pool within the cavern. To contact the ranger, call (07) 5533-5147.

LAMINGTON NATIONAL PARK

Dense rainforests, hundreds of waterfalls, an extensive trail system, and excellent accommodations combine to make this 20,500-hectare park a great escape from the hustle and bustle of the Gold Coast 80 km to the east.

The Land
Around 20 million years ago, tremendous volcanic activity created massive changes in the landscape of the far northeastern corner of New South Wales. During the millions of preceding years, erosion broke down the volcanic basalt, leaving a circular rim of rock, with Mt. Warning in the middle. Lamington National Park is perched on the rim's northern edge (which also forms the Queensland/NSW border) from where escarpments drop hundreds of meters into heavily forested valleys of the caldera. Access to the park is only from the north. Two roads penetrate the park, both ending at points well north of the rim; at the end of each road is a camping and picnic area. Enter **Binna Burra** from Nerang (55 km) and to **Green Mountains** from Canungra (36 km), 22 km west of Nerang.

Flora and Fauna
The park encompasses one of the largest areas of subtropical rainforest in Australia. At higher altitudes you'll find stands of Antarctic beech trees, including some 2,500 years old, while in

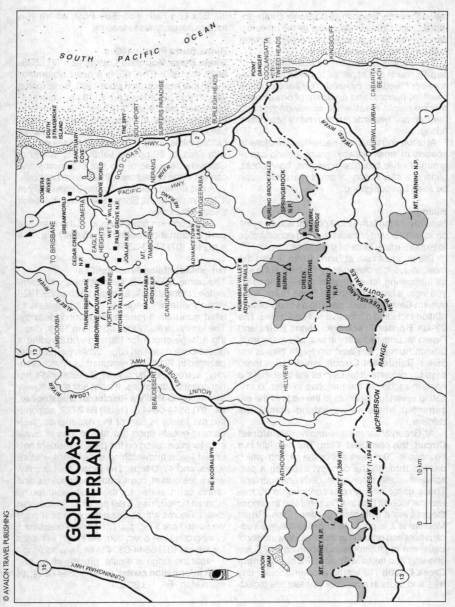

© AVALON TRAVEL PUBLISHING

GOLD COAST
HINTERLAND

SOUTH PACIFIC OCEAN

SOUTH STRADBROKE ISLAND

COOMERA RIVER

SANCTUARY COVE

THE SPIT

SOUTHPORT

SURFERS PARADISE

BURLEIGH HEADS

POINT DANGER
COOLANGATTA
TWEED HEADS

KINGSCLIFF

CABARITA BEACH

MURWILLUMBAH

TWEED RIVER

MT. WARNING N.P.

1

TO BRISBANE

COOMERA RIVER

DREAMWORLD

MOVIE WORLD

COOMERA

CEDAR CREEK N.P.

EAGLE HEIGHTS

WET 'N' WILD

PALM GROVE N.P.

JOALAH N.P.

MT. TAMBORINE

NERANG

GOLD COAST HWY

NERANG RIVER

PACIFIC HWY

MUDGEERABA

ADVANCETOWN LAKE

PURLING BROOK FALLS

SPRINGBROOK N.P.

NATURAL BRIDGE

1

2

THUNDERBIRD PARK

TAMBORINE MOUNTAIN

NORTH TAMBORINE

WITCHES FALLS N.P.

MACROZAMIA GROVE N.P.

CANUNGRA

NUMINBAH VALLEY ADVENTURE TRAILS

BINNA BURRA

GREEN MOUNTAINS

LAMINGTON N.P.

QUEENSLAND
NEW SOUTH WALES

ALBERT RIVER

JIMBOOMBA

13

BEAUDESERT

LINDESAY HWY

MOUNT LINDESAY

HILLVIEW

MCPHERSON RANGE

LOGAN RIVER

RATHDOWNEY

THE KOORALBYN

MT. LINDESAY (1,194 m)

MT. BARNEY (1,356 m)

MT. BARNEY N.P.

MAROON DAM

15

CUNNINGHAM HWY

13

10 km

0

© AVALON TRAVEL PUBLISHING

the valleys species such as booyong, carabeen, marara, and strangler figs make up the rainforest canopy, with ferns, mosses, and orchids thriving in the moist environment below.

The park is known for its colorful array of birdlife, much of it attracted to areas where visitors offer feedings by hand. You'll see crimson rosellas, parrots, and a variety of bower birds around picnic areas while currawongs, bush turkeys, and lyrebirds are commonly seen while hiking.

At dawn and dusk, red-necked pademelons (a species of small wallaby) graze around campgrounds while brushtail possums, bandicoots, gliders, and a variety of small marsupials can be seen by spotlighting.

Hiking

Naturally, hiking is the most popular activity in the park, with 160 km of trails providing opportunities to explore many of its best features.

The shortest hike at Binna Burra is also the most unique. It is designed for the blind but is just as interesting for sighted people—as long as you wear a blindfold. Also at Binna Burra is the five-km **Caves Circuit,** passing a variety of vegetation including a massive red cedar tree. The 22-km **Border Track** links Binna Burra and Green Mountains facility areas, and many trails branch from it. The best overnight hike is the 55-km **Rainforest Circuit,** which takes three days to complete. It takes in all the best that the eastern section of the park has to offer, culminating in various lookouts at the edge of the escarpment where views extend across the caldera.

At Green Mountains is another **Rainforest Circuit,** this one just 1.4 km. The highlight is a boardwalk, 30 meters above the ground, which passes through the canopy, allowing a perspective usually reserved for birds and possums. Those game enough can continue up 20 meters to a lookout high in a fig tree. Near the end of the trail lies a **botanical garden.** From Green Mountains it is possible to get to the main escarpment and return in one day along a variety of trails, the most interesting of which is 7.6 km one-way and takes in Toolona Falls. **Canungra Creek Circuit** (13 km) is another popular day hike and takes in a number of waterfalls includ-ing Box Log Falls and Blue Pool, where you might spot platypuses feeding.

Binna Burra Practicalities

Binna Burra Mountain Lodge, tel. (07) 5533-3622 or (1800) 07-4260, is a rustic accommodation that has operated since 1933. Basic rooms with shared bathrooms are $119 pp, while self-contained cabins are $165 pp. Rates include three hot meals, morning and afternoon teas, use of a game room, and daily activities such as guided hikes. Near this lodge is a campground with sites for $9 pp and safari tents at $36 d. Campers have use of modern bathrooms and can eat in the restaurant with advance bookings.

A bus departs Surfers Transit Centre daily at 1:15 p.m. for Binna Burra ($32 roundtrip); book through the lodge.

About one km from the end of the road is a **park information center,** open daily 8 a.m.-4 p.m., tel. (07) 5533-3584.

Green Mountains Practicalities

The name O'Reilly is synonymous with Lamington National Park, and has been since 1926 when the family began welcoming guests to what was then a remote mountain hideaway. The family originally took up land in 1911, clearing a large chunk for farming and building a guesthouse on a high ridge. When the park was gazetted in 1917, land remained as private property, surrounded by one of Queensland's top noncoastal attractions. It's not just the scenery that makes **O'Reilly's Rainforest Guesthouse,** tel. (07) 5544-0644 or (1800) 68-8722, so popular; the family is part of the experience, welcoming guests upon arrival and always available for information on the park. A resident naturalist leads birdwatching expeditions, nature walks, and 4WD trips. The lodge itself is cosy, with a restaurant, comfortable lounge area, and tennis court. Rates for the most basic rooms (shared facilities) are $129 pp, which includes all meals. Rooms with private bathrooms offer great views and are $169 pp. The NPWS operates a campground just down from the lodge, with sites for $9; call (07) 5544-0634 to make a booking.

Near the lodge is a café, grocery store, and **park information center,** tel. (07) 5544-0634; it's open Mon.-Fri. 1-3:30 p.m.

TAMBORINE MOUNTAIN

Tamborine isn't a mountain as such, but a plateau five km wide, eight km long, and rising 500 meters above the surrounding hinterland. It's a world apart from the Gold Coast, just 30 km to the east, with three picturesque mountain communities surrounded by nine small national parks. These parks are often referred to as Tamborine National Park but are in fact separate titles of land. The plateau is a spur of the McPherson Range and is the northernmost extent of lava flow from the Mount Warning Volcano. Much of the plateau has been cleared of original vegetation, but some small chunks of rainforest are protected by national parks.

National Parks

Most central of these is **Joalah National Park.** For parking, drive to the corner of Geissmann Dr. and Eagle Heights Rd., from where a short trail descends into a lush rainforest of tree ferns and orchids. The highlight is **Curtis Falls,** where Cedar Creek cascades over an outcrop of basalt into a deep blue pool. **Witches Falls National Park,** located on Tamborine Mountain Rd. just south of the township of North Tamborine, has a trail leading to the falls for which the park is named, passing lookouts where views extend west to the Main Range and south to Lamington National Park. For views north to Brisbane and the Glass House Mountains, head to **The Knoll National Park** at the end of Knoll Rd. (a continuation of Main St., which begins opposite the Visitors Centre). **Palm Grove National Park** features forests of towering palms interspersed with magnificent yellow carabeen trees. To get to this park continue east along Eagle Heights Rd., beyond the roundabout, and then take the first right.

The road up to the mountain from Nerang provides good views of the Gold Coast and Pacific Ocean. Also along this road, and flanking the village of Mount Tamborine, is **Macrozamia Grove National Park,** named for stands of macrozamia palms common in the area.

Thunderbird Park

Nestled below the northern flanks of the plateau in the valley carved by Cedar Creek is Thunderbird Park, tel. (07) 5545-1468, which holds the world's largest known deposit of **thunder eggs.** Volcanic in origin, thunder eggs have a hard outer shell protecting a cavity of semiprecious gems such as agate. This particular deposit, formed about 200 million years ago, is exposed as basalt from the Mt. Warning eruptions erodes. For $5 you get a bucket, a spade, and the chance to dig for the eggs. Most people find a few, and there's no real time limit. In a large shed set up in front of the deposit a lapidarist will cut and polish any eggs you find for $2-5 each. Also at Thunderbird Park is bird feeding daily at 3 p.m., an aviary, and mini-golf.

Practicalities

Tamborine Mountain has a wide range of accommodations, including a number of excellent B&Bs. For a basic, bland motel room, **Tall Trees Motel,** 9 Eagle Heights Rd., tel. (07) 5545-1242, should suffice; $60 s, $65 d. Moderate.

The sprawling **Tamborine Mountain Bed and Breakfast,** built of recycled timber including part of an old bridge, gives an air of rustic elegance. Guests may choose from four rooms spread out from the main house, each with a king-size bed, and take advantage of a large dining/lounge area and extensive verandas overlooking the lush rainforests of Palm Grove National Park; $95 s, $115 d. It's located at 19 Witherby Crescent, Eagle Heights, tel. (07) 5545-3595. Expensive. Another comfortable option is **Polish Place,** between Mount Tamborine and North Tamborine at 333 Main Western Rd., tel. (07) 5545-1603. Each of the five self-contained cottages is two stories, with a double bed in the loft, a kitchen, lounge area with TV, and a balcony with westward panoramic views catching the sunset in all its glory. Rates are $150-195 per unit. Luxury.

Around the main entrance of Joalah National Park, at the corner of Geissmann Dr. and Eagle Heights Rd., are places offering casual meals, including **Curtis Falls Cafe,** surrounded by lush palms, where Devonshire tea is $4.50 and most main dishes are less than $10. Across the road are more cafés and **Squires Inn,** tel. (07) 5545-1700, an English-style pub serving lunch and dinner. At Polish Place (see above), for the price of a coffee you can enjoy the same spectacular views as guests; open daily 10 a.m.-5 p.m. For dinner, don't pass up **Songbirds in the Forest** on Tamborine Mountain Rd., tel. (07) 5545-2563.

Tables circle an enclosed courtyard filled with greenery and within view of colorful rosellas feeding nearby. It's open for lunch Tues.-Sun. noon-3 p.m. and for dinner Fri.-Sat. from 6 p.m.

Tamborine Mountain Information Centre is in Doughty Park, across from the township of North Tamborine, tel. (07) 5545-3200; open daily 10 a.m.-3.30 p.m. For national park information, call the ranger at (07) 5545-1171.

MOUNT LINDESAY HIGHWAY

Beaudesert, 35 km west of Tamborine Mountain, is the main town along this highway, the original route between Brisbane and the New England region of New South Wales. On the main street you'll find a small museum and information center. South of town, check out **The Kooralbyn,** a resort that wouldn't look out of place in Cairns or on the Gold Coast. Accommodation is luxurious, but it's the 18-hole championship golf course, tennis courts, and the re-

laxed setting that attract most people. Rates are reasonable at $90-150 d for luxurious self-contained villas, rising to $200 s or d in the hotel proper. For reservations call (07) 5544-6222 or (1800) 07-3108. Expensive-Luxury.

Although not as accessible as Lamington, **Mt. Barney National Park** is just as rugged and provides experienced hikers a chance to explore the hinterland away from crowds. The main access to this 11,900-hectare park is west from Rathdowney, then south on Upper Logan Road. Along this road, a hiking trail branches along Barney Creek to Lower Portals, a water-filled gorge 3.7 km from the road. Experienced (and fit) hikers may want to climb 1,360-meter **Mt. Barney.** The trail, which begins from the end of the access road, is steep and often ill-defined. **Mt. Barney Lodge,** also near the end of the road, tel. (07) 5544-3233, is not a lodge but a campground, with sites for $12-15, bunk beds for $20 pp, and hot showers. The on-site owners offer a wealth of information on the adjacent park.

BRISBANE

In the last decade and a half Queensland's capital, Brisbane (BRIZ-bun), has grown into a dynamic and modern city of 1.3 million people, many of whom are expatriates from cooler southern states in search of a casual lifestyle in a modern metropolis. Brisbane is Australia's third-largest city and has come to prominence since hosting the 1982 Commonwealth Games and the 1988 World Expo. It sits on the Brisbane River, 33 km upstream from Moreton Bay. Sydney is 1,000 km south; Gladstone, gateway to the southernmost Great Barrier Reef Islands, is 550 km north; Cairns is 1,710 km north. The city center, restricted by a tight bend of the Brisbane River, mixes modern skyscrapers with some of Queensland's oldest buildings. Brisbane may lack the beauty of Sydney and the culture of Melbourne, but scattered across the city are enough sights to keep even the most desperate reef-bound traveler busy for a couple of days.

History

As Sydney's convict population increased, officials looked northward for somewhere to send the worst offenders. In 1824 a penal colony was established on Moreton Bay, near the mouth of the Brisbane River. The following year a lack of water and hostile natives forced a move upriver to the present site of Brisbane's city center. Though *not* the best place to build a city, the site was ideal for convict settlement—a remote location, surrounded on three sides by a river, and away from the ocean. But when the colony was closed in 1842 and the surrounding land opened to free settlers—who up to this time had not been allowed anywhere near the colony— Brisbane Town thrived. From a population of less than 1,000 in 1846, the town grew to well over 100,000 by the turn of the century. Gradually convict-built structures were replaced by permanent sandstone and granite buildings, many of which remain today.

Brisbane was headquarters of South Pacific operations during WW II, a time when thousands of U.S. troops were stationed in the city. Between WW II and the early 1980s, Brisbane's growth was due to newly discovered mineral wealth elsewhere in the state, but the 1982 Commonwealth Games, 1988 World Expo, and sun-seeking Sydneysiders and Melburnians moving north began a trend of development that continues to this day.

DOWNTOWN SIGHTS

Downtown Brisbane is bordered to the south, east, and west by the **Brisbane River,** with the extensive **Botanic Gardens** in the southern corner and ferry service across the river at various points. **South Bank,** over the Victoria Bridge and within walking distance of downtown, is a good place to park ($5 per day at South Bank Parklands) for a day's sightseeing around the city. City streets are laid out on a grid system, but driving downtown can be confusing as many streets are one-way and feed onto the **Riverside Expressway,** built along the river west of the city center to keep traffic out of downtown. **Queen Street Mall,** one block from Victoria Bridge, is the heart of downtown; it encompasses two blocks and includes a Hilton Hotel, an underground bus terminal, outdoor restaurants, entertainment stages, fountains, sculptures, and the massive $480-million **Myer Shopping Centre.**

Historic Buildings around Queen Street

Brisbane City Council publishes *Heritage Trail* brochures to 10 Brisbane suburbs and downtown, where you'll find the largest concentration of historic buildings. The best place to start a walking tour of downtown is **City Hall,** overlooking King George Square on Ann Street. Completed in 1930, it features a wide facade of Corinthian columns topped by an 85-meter-high clock tower. Tours of City Hall (adult $6, children free) depart from the foyer Mon.-Fri. at 10 a.m. and 2 p.m. Diagonally opposite City Hall stands the 1889 **Albert Street Uniting Church.** At 261-285 Queen St., beyond the end of the mall, is the 1871 **general post office,** formerly the site of a women's prison. On the first floor is the **GPO Museum,** cataloging the history of Brisbane's postal service; it's open Tues.-Fri. 9:30

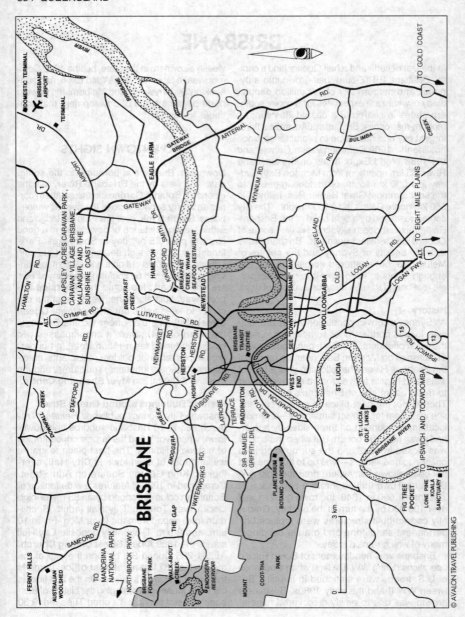

© AVALON TRAVEL PUBLISHING

a.m.-3:30 p.m., and admission is free. Through the post office arcade and across Elizabeth St. is **Old St. Stephen's Church;** built in 1850, it is Brisbane's oldest church. Next door is **St. Stephen's Cathedral,** built in English Gothic-style and featuring an elaborate facade flanked by two impressive spires.

Historic Sights along George Street

George St. runs parallel to the river and features some of the city's most impressive historic buildings. The **Treasury Building** was constructed in 1886 and was described at the time as "the most splendid public edifice in the Australian colonies." This Italian Renaissance-style building has been totally restored, and behind the colonnaded facade is a casino (see below). Behind the Treasury is the old **Land Administration Building.** Built in the same flamboyant style and fronted by **Queens Park,** it now serves as the hotel portion of the casino. Across from the park on William St. is the **Commissariat Stores,** one of only two Brisbane buildings dating from the convict era. **Parliament House,** at the end of George St., was built in 1868.

Sciencentre

This hands-on museum features many interactive displays endeavoring to make understanding science both easy and interesting. Admission is $7. Open daily 10 a.m.-5 p.m. It's located at 110 George St., tel. (07) 3220-0166.

SOUTH BANK

South Bank, across the Brisbane River from downtown, was the site of the 1988 World Expo and has since been developed into the city's premier recreation area. Head here to see the **Queensland Cultural Centre,** a sprawling low-rise development that includes the Queensland Museum, Queensland Art Gallery, State Library, and Performing Arts Complex. Adjoining is the **Brisbane Convention and Exhibition Centre** and Conservatorium of Music. Also at South Bank is an **IMAX Theatre,** Grey St., tel. (07) 3844-4222, complete with the latest 3-D technology. Spread out south from here is South Bank Parklands, featuring themed attractions, cafés, and restaurants.

Queensland Museum

Contained on three floors, this museum, tel. (07) 3840-7555, showcases the natural and human history of the state through modern and interesting displays. The highlight of the Lower Gallery is 3.6-meter *Acrohc Australis,* the smallest yacht to ever circumnavigate the world. Also on this floor is a realistic panorama of marine mammals, photography display, and a dinosaur skeleton. The next floor features the flora and fauna of Queensland, and a large area is set aside for temporary displays. The upper gallery looks at whales and whaling, with a display cataloging the climatic cycles of western Queensland and relics from Melanesian Culture. The museum is open daily 9:30 a.m.-5 p.m. and admission is free.

Queensland Art Gallery

In the same building as the museum is the state's largest art gallery, tel. (07) 3840-7303, boasting an extensive collection of works by all of Australia's best-known artists. It also hosts national and international touring exhibitions. The gallery is open daily 10 a.m.-5 p.m. and admission is free. Tours are offered Mon.-Fri. at 11 a.m., 1 p.m., and 2 p.m.

South Bank Parklands

Adjacent to the Queensland Cultural Centre and strung out along the river, this ever-expanding, 17-hectare park is Brisbane's most popular attraction. Admission is free (except to the themed attractions), making it the perfect place to escape city living. The park's unique feature is the swimming pool; its clear blue waters fringed with palms and a golden sandy beach could be straight out of a five-star resort—and there's even a lifeguard. On the far side of the park, small boats steam up and down a narrow canal, making access to all parts of South Bank easy (adult $5, child $2). South Bank Markets take place Friday night and Saturday and Sunday afternoons. **South Bank Wildlife Centre,** tel. (07) 3844-1112, contains an enormous collection of Australian butterflies, as well as many weird and wonderful insects. Admission is adult $7.50, child $4.50.

At the north entrance to the parklands is an information center, tel. (07) 3867-2051; open daily 8 a.m.-6 p.m.

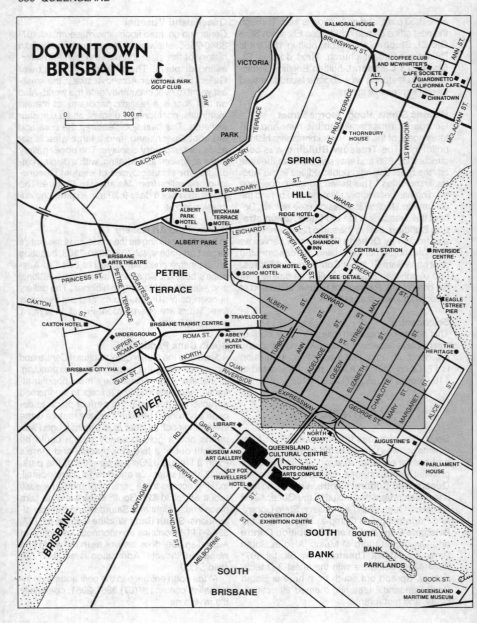

DOWNTOWN BRISBANE

FORTITUDE

VALLEY

NEW FARM

RIVER

BRISBANE

HARCOURT ST.
KENT ST.
ANNIE ST.
BROWNE ST.

PETE'S PALACE

RED HOT
CHILLI PACKERS

THE HOMESTEAD

BOWEN ST.

BOWEN

BRUNSWICK

ST.

MALT ST.

TERRACE

LANGSHAW

ST.

SOUTH PACIFIC
PALMS MOTEL

GOODWIN ST.

BRADFIELD

HWY.

ALT.
1

FERRY ST.

RYAN'S ON
THE RIVER

STORY BRIDGE
MOTOR INN

OLIMS HOTEL

DOCKSIDE
APARTMENT
HOTEL

KANGAROO

POINT

RIVER TERRACE

ALT.
1
15

BOTANIC GARDENS

CITY
GARDENS
CAFE

CAPTAIN COOK
BRIDGE

WALMSLEY ST.

QUALITY RIVER
PLAZA HOTEL

HILLCREST
APARTMENT HOTEL

VULTURE ST.

RIVERSIDE EXPRESSWAY

DETAIL

TURBOT ST.

BRISBANE
TRAVEL
CENTRE

ORIENT HOTEL

POST OFFICE
SQUARE

CREEK ST.

QUEENSLAND
GOVERNMENT
TRAVEL CENTRE

MALL

GENERAL
POST
OFFICE

OLD ST.
STEPHEN'S
CHURCH

DEPARTMENT OF
ENVIRONMENT

SHINGLES INN

ST.

KING GEORGE
SQUARE

EDWARD

ST.

CARLTON
CREST

TRAVELERS
CITY MEDICAL
HALL CENTRE

ALBERT ST.
UNITING CHURCH

ALBERT

ST.

METRO ARTS

ST.

ELIZABETH

CHARLOTTE

EXPLORERS INN

MAJESTIC
HOTEL

ANN ST.

CITY
PLAZA

ADELAIDE

QUEEN

ST.

MYER SHOPPING
CENTRE

BRISBANE
HILTON

ELIZABETH
ARCADE

MARY ST.

GEORGE

LENNONS
HOTEL

BRISBANE
BICYCLE HIRE

BRISBANE
ADMINISTRATION

MERCURE
HOTEL

MLC BUILDING

NORTH

QUAY

GOVINDA'S

BELLEVUE HOTEL

MARGARET ST.

TREASURY
BUILDING/CONRAD
TREASURY CASINO

QUEENSLAND ABORIGINAL
CREATIONS

LAND
ADMINISTRATION
BUILDING

SCIENCENTRE

COMMISSARIAT
STORES

© AVALON TRAVEL PUBLISHING

Queensland Maritime Museum
At the south end of the South Bank Parklands is this riverside museum, on Sidon St., tel. (07) 3844-5361, featuring the WW II frigate HMAS *Diamantina;* maritime memorabilia is also displayed. Admission is adult $5, child $2:50, and it's open daily 10 a.m.-5:30 p.m.

PARKS AND GARDENS

City Botanic Gardens
First established as a vegetable garden for the penal colony, 17 hectares of land at the south end of downtown, bordered by the Brisbane River, are now the city's botanic gardens. Part of the gardens' early aim was to grow seedlings for distribution to free settlers, and it wasn't until the early 1980s that the ordered look of today came about. Paved trails lead through the park to an area of rainforest, then to a boardwalk through mangroves, and end at a historic stone cottage that now houses a café. Guided tours leave the information desk, opposite the end of Albert St., Tues.-Sun. at 11 a.m. and 1 p.m.

Mt. Coot-tha Park
This 3,500-hectare park eight km west of downtown provides panoramic views of the city, Moreton and Stradbroke Islands, the Glass House Mountains, and the Gold Coast. Hiking trails crisscross the park and are accessible from Sir Samuel Griffith Dr., which circles the park. One of the most interesting is the Aboriginal Art Trail, a 1.6-km circuit along which all forms of native art— tree carvings, petroglyphs, and pictographs—are represented. At the foot of the mountain you'll find a **botanic garden** featuring a large dome-shaped greenhouse where a great variety of flora from the tropics thrives; open daily 8:30 a.m.-5 p.m., admission free. The garden is home to the **Sir Thomas Brisbane Planetarium,** tel. (07) 3403-2578, combining an observatory, astronomy displays, and the Cosmic Skydome, where special effects re-create the night sky across a 12-meter-wide dome. Show times are: Wed.-Sun. 3:30 p.m. and 7:30 p.m.; Saturday 1:30 p.m., 3:30 p.m., and 7:30 p.m.; and Sunday 1:30 p.m. and 3:30 p.m. Admission is adult $8, child $4.50.

To get to the gardens and lookout, take bus no. 471 from Adelaide St. at Albert Street.

Brisbane Forest Park
Few cities the size of Brisbane have an area of virgin bushland as large and as accessible as 28,500-hectare Brisbane Forest Park, which encompasses a large part of **D'Aguilar Range** and extends right to the outer suburb of The Gap. At the park entrance is **Walk-about Creek,** tel. (07) 3300-4855, a nature study center for viewing the flora and fauna of a typical subtropical creek, including turtles, snakes, barramundi, and the unique lungfish—which can breathe above the water. It's open Mon.-Fri. 9 a.m.-4:30 p.m., Sat.-Sun. 10 a.m.-4:30 p.m. Admission is a worthwhile $3.50 for adults, $2 for kids.

Northbrook Parkway extends from Walk-about Creek along the highest ridges of the D'Aguilar Range, passing lookouts, picnic areas, short hikes, and a small campground in Manorina National Park.

WILDLIFE PARKS

Lone Pine Koala Sanctuary
This 20-hectare wildlife park, 11 km southwest of downtown on Jesmond Rd., Fig Tree Pocket, tel. (07) 3378-1366, claims to have the world's largest collection of Australia's most popular native animal, the koala. They currently have 130 of the cuddly little critters, and for an extra $8 you *can* cuddle one. A variety of other indigenous Australian animals are kept here, including dingos, wombats, and a variety of birds including emus. Admission is adult $12.50, child $6.50; open daily 7:30 a.m.-5 p.m. By bus, take no. 445 from opposite City Hall on Adelaide Street. **Mirimar Cruises,** tel. (07) 3221-0300, departs daily at 11:30 a.m. in a historic 1930s ferry from North Quay for the sanctuary; $15 roundtrip.

Alma Park Zoo
This zoo features animals from around the world, as well as many native species, and has five feeding sessions daily, including time spent cuddling koalas. Within the zoo is a café and pleasant picnic area. Admission is a bit steep at $15.

It's 28 km north of downtown in the suburb of Kallangur; follow signs from Bruce Hwy., tel. (07) 3204-6566.

OUTDOOR ACTIVITIES

Biking
Brisbane Bicycle Hire, 87 Albert St., tel. (07) 3229-2433, rents mountain bikes for $10 per hour or $24 per day. A good place to head for riding is south along the river to the University of Queensland at St. Lucia.

Swimming
Spring Hill Baths, Torrington St., tel. (07) 3831-7881, is a throwback to an earlier era, where swimmers use poolside change rooms. It's open year-round Mon.-Fri. from 6:30 a.m., Sat.-Sun. from 8:30 a.m. Admission is $2. The pool at South Bank Parklands is complete with a sandy beach, palm trees, and a lifeguard.

Golfing
The closest golf course to the city is **Victoria Park Golf Club,** on Herston Rd. north of the city, tel. (07) 3252-9891. Greens fees are $22 for 18 holes and club rentals are $15. The city's other public course is **St. Lucia Golf Links** on Indooroopilly Rd., tel. (07) 3403-2557, along the Brisbane River. (This course was designed by Dr. Alistair Mackenzie, the same architect who designed Augusta National in Georgia).

ARTS AND ENTERTAINMENT

Australian Woolshed
Sheep, the backbone of Australia's economy since European settlement, are the stars of this attraction, which showcases the entire wool-growing industry. During the Ram Show, trained sheep of all breeds strut their stuff on the stage, a shearing exhibition is given, spinning is demonstrated, and sheepdogs show their skills. Shows take place daily at 10 a.m., 11 a.m., 1 p.m., 2 p.m., and 3 p.m.; adult $12, child $6. Other activities take place during the day, including feeding of Australian animals. Before the morning show, billy tea and damper ($3.50) are served, and lunch ($8-14) is also available. On Friday and Saturday nights there's a barn dance ($32, includes dinner). The woolshed is 13 km northwest of the city center at 148 Samford Rd., Ferny Hills, tel. (07) 3351-5366. The closest public transportation is Ferny Hills rail station, an 800-meter walk from the woodshed.

Theater, Music, and Dance
The **Performing Arts Complex** is the premier venue for all performing arts. Within the complex are three theaters—2,000-seat Concert Hall designed to hold a symphony orchestra, 2,000-seat Lyric Theatre for opera, dance, and musical comedy, and 300-seat Cremorne Theatre. Buy tickets in person at the center, or call (07) 3840-7444, or contact any Bass ticketing agency.

Princess Theatre, 8 Annerley Rd., Woolloongabba, tel. (07) 3891-6022, has presented both classical and Australian contemporary works for more than 100 years; tickets range $12-24. Other major theaters are **Metro Arts,** 109 Edward St., tel. (07) 3221-1527, for alternative theater and dance works, and **Brisbane Arts Theatre,** 210 Petrie Terrace, tel. (07) 3369-2344, home to the city's longest-running amateur theater company.

Cinemas
Alternative films are screened at the **Classic,** 963 Stanley St., East Brisbane, tel. (07) 3393-1066; the **Schonell,** University of Queensland, St. Lucia, tel. (07) 3371-1879; and **Metro Arts Cinema,** 109 Edward St., tel. (07) 3221-3505.

Casino
In April 1995 one of Brisbane's greatest historic structures, the Treasury Building, opened as **Conrad Treasury Casino.** Don't expect to see flashy neon signs and spectacular shows out front; one of the building's edicts prohibits outside signage. Once inside, though, things are different, with a six-story atrium welcoming gamblers. Games available are roulette, blackjack, baccarat, mini-baccarat, craps, sic-bo, big six, and two-up, as well as more than 1,000 slot machines. The casino also has a couple of restaurants, cafés, and bars. It's open daily 24 hours. Dress standards apply, including no shorts, tracksuit pants, sports shoes, or collarless shirts. It's on the corner of Queen and George Streets, tel. (07) 3306-8888.

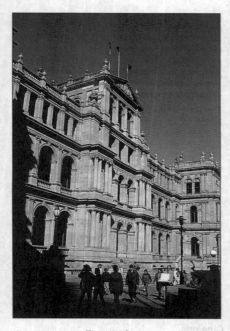

Treasury Casino

Hotels, Bars, and Nightclubs

Overlooking the confluence of Breakfast Creek and the Brisbane River is the **Breakfast Creek Hotel,** Kingsford Smith Dr., Breakfast Creek, tel. (07) 3262-5988, a classic Aussie pub that dates from the 1880s. Cold beer, hearty bar meals, a large outdoor beer garden, and ever-present crowds add to the already authentic atmosphere.

Most of the old downtown hotels have been replaced by high-rises, with the **Majestic Hotel,** 382 George St., tel. (07) 3229-0772, an exception. This casual place has live music some nights. Irish bar **P.J. O'Brien's,** 127 Charlotte St., tel. (07) 3210-6822, features Guinness on tap and weekend bands. Across the river at South Bank Parklands is the **Plough Inn Tavern,** tel. (07) 3844-7777, a pleasant place for a beer and meal during the day, with live entertainment Fri.-Sunday. Below Palace Backpackers, the **Down Under Bar & Grill,** 308 Edward St., tel. (07) 3211-9277, is the city's main budget-travelers'

hangout. The music is loud, the crowd rowdy, and the beer cheap.

The **Metro Nightclub,** housed in the old police barracks on Petrie Terrace, Paddington, tel. (07) 3236-1511, is the most popular of Brisbane's mainstream nightclubs and has been around since the late 1970s. It's open Wed.-Sun. until 3 a.m. and the cover charge is $5. Another, more stylish, choice is **Someplace Else** in the Sheraton Hotel at 249 Turbot Street. Adventurous nightclubbers should head to Fortitude Valley, the center of Brisbane's alternative scene, and to places such as **Tube** at 249 Brunswick St., tel. (07) 3852-1605, and **Arena** at 210 Brunswick St., tel. (07) 3252-5278.

Jazz, Blues, and Comedy

Call the **Brisbane Jazz Club,** tel. (07) 3391-2006, for a schedule of jazz performances throughout the city. The **Caxton Hotel,** 38 Caxton St., Petrie Terrace, tel. (07) 3369-5544, features all types of jazz and is most popular Saturday afternoons during jam sessions. The rest of the week it's '60s and '70s music and karaoke in the cocktail bar.

For blues, head to **Bakroom** in the Waterloo Hotel on the corner of Ann St. and Commercial Rd., tel. (07) 3852-1101, but call ahead as this place attracts a great variety of music styles.

Brisbane's main comedy venue is the intimate **Snug Harbour,** in the Dockside complex, Kangaroo Point, tel. (07) 3391-2045.

Festivals and Events

After the fireworks of New Year's Eve and nationwide celebrations of Australia Day, the next major event hosted by Brisbane is the **Caxton Street Seafood and Wine Festival,** in May. Also in May is the **Queensland Jazz Festival,** held at venues throughout the city, including a riverboat. Throughout winter (July-Aug.), the **Brisbane International Film Festival** showcases a wide variety of films, from short cartoons to documentaries. In early August, the **Royal Brisbane Show** brings the country to the city. The **Brisbane Festival,** one of Australia's premier arts and music festivals, features all types of music performed by national and international artists, the Brisbane Writers Festival, dramatic performances, as well as food and winetasting daily at South Bank Parklands. The festival takes place over 24 days from mid-August every second year (odd years).

SHOPPING

Brisbane's shopping mecca is definitely Queen Street Mall, including the Myer Shopping Centre, a five-story department store with 250 specialty shops, an eight-screen cinema, and massive food court.

Paddington, a historic suburb west of downtown, has a great variety of specialty boutiques, antique emporiums, art galleries, and cafés; most of these lie along Given Terrace. In the same area, at 167 Latrobe Terrace, more than 50 antique dealers display wares at **Paddington Antique Center.**

Markets
Each Friday evening and Saturday and Sunday afternoons **South Bank Markets** offer arts, crafts, and clothing at stalls spread along one or two narrow pedestrian streets (on Sunday a real carnival atmosphere prevails). **Riverside Crafts Market,** at the Riverside Centre on Eagle St., operates all day Sunday featuring arts, crafts, street performers, and foodstalls. **Paddy's Markets,** on the corner of Florence and MacQuarie Streets, New Farm, are undercover and feature all sorts of stalls—from handmade crafts to piles of secondhand junk; open daily 9 a.m.-4 p.m.

Australiana
Aboriginal-styled souvenirs are a dime a dozen throughout Australia, but the real thing, handcrafted by native Australians, is a lot harder to find—and also a lot more expensive. **Queensland Aboriginal Creations,** 135 George St., tel. (07) 3224-5730, sells original works by Aboriginal artists throughout the state, including pottery, paintings, and the more traditional bark paintings, weavings, and boomerangs and woomeras. The Supply Store, at the **Australian Woolshed** (see above) is the best place for Australian-made souvenirs, including woollen sweaters. **R.M. Williams,** in the Wintergarden Shopping Centre off Queen Street Mall, tel. (07) 3229-7724, stocks a wide range of true-blue Australian clothing. For souvenirs to send home, **Australia Post Shop,** in the main post office

on Queen St., specializes in gifts designed for posting. For opal, **Quilpie Opals,** Lennons Plaza, 68 Queen St., tel. (07) 3221-7369, is a good place to head—but you'll pay a lot more than out on the opal fields.

HOTEL AND MOTEL ACCOMMODATIONS

Accommodations downtown are limited to those in the higher price ranges, but immediately north, in Spring Hill, between Wickham and Gregory Terraces (a 10- to 15-minute walk to Queen Street Mall), is a wide variety of hotels and motels in all price ranges.

Downtown
The least expensive downtown hotel is the centrally located **Explorers Inn** at 63 Turbot St., tel. (07) 3211-3488 or (1800) 62-3288. Although it's housed in an older-style building, the rooms are an excellent value at $68 s or d. Moderate. The **Bellevue Hotel,** 103 George St., tel. (07) 3221-6044, two blocks from Queen Street Mall, is an equally good value. Views are limited by surrounding high-rises, but the rooms themselves are comfortable and have a tropical feel. Facilities include undercover parking, pool, spa, and restaurant. Standard rooms are $80 s or d, while larger rooms, some with kitchenettes, are $105. Moderate.

A couple of premium-priced options are near the Brisbane Transit Centre, northwest of Queen Street Mall. **Brisbane City Travelodge,** Roma St., tel. (07) 3238-2222, is on top of the Transit Centre, but seems a world away. Rooms aren't too big, but they are well-furnished and many have city views; from $125 s or d. Premium. Across the road is the modern **Abbey Plaza Hotel,** 160 Roma St., tel. (07) 3236-1444, with a small kitchen and microwave in each room. Also available is a pool, spa, gym, and security parking; all rooms are $130. Premium. **Lennons Hotel,** 66 Queen St., tel. (07) 3222-3222, is a 20-story hotel right on Queen Street Mall. Facilities include a pool, covered parking, and a restaurant and bar; $140-175 s or d. Premium. **Mercure Hotel Brisbane,** 85 North Quay, tel. (07) 3236-3300 or (1800) 77-7911, has a pool and restaurant. Some rooms offer river views, and three floors are reserved for nonsmokers; $147 s or d. Premium.

A step up in quality and price is **Carlton Crest,** corner Ann and Roma Streets, tel. (07) 3229-9111 or (1800) 77-7123, overlooking King George Square. Rooms are spacious and elegantly furnished in a heritage style; $160 s or d. Luxury. **The Heritage,** corner Margaret and Edward Streets, tel. (07) 3221-1999 or (1800) 77-3700, is Brisbane's most deluxe hostelry; its 230 rooms, decorated classical-style with king-size beds, exude a feeling of unpretentious luxury throughout. Also, each of the 21 floors has a butler. Rooms are $320 s or d and suites start at $570. Luxury. Another of the city's five-star hotels is the **Brisbane Hilton,** 190 Elizabeth St., tel. (07) 3231-3131, on Queen Street Mall, where a 20-story-high glass-domed atrium separates rooms with city views from those with river views; from $255 s or d. At the **Sheraton Brisbane Hotel & Towers,** 249 Turbot St., tel. (07) 3835-3535 or (1800) 07-3535, standard rooms are $250-350 s or d and those on the executive floor, with butler service, private lounge, and a buffet breakfast, are $450. Luxury.

Spring Hill

Immediately north of downtown, take an easy walk from Queen St. to find a good range of hotels and motels. The least expensive of these is the **Astor Motel,** 193 Wickham Terrace, tel. (07) 3831-9522, close to both Central Station and Brisbane Transit Centre. Rooms are basic, some with a microwave and toaster; $59 s, $69 d. Moderate. Similar in standard and price is **Soho Motel,** 333 Wickham Terrace, tel. (07) 3831-7722. Moderate.

A step up in quality is **Wickham Terrace Motel,** 491 Wickham Terrace, tel. (07) 3839-9611, with a pool and laundry; $88 s, $94 d. Expensive. Close by, the **Albert Park Hotel,** 551 Wickham Terrace, tel. (07) 3831-3111 or (1800) 77-7702, overlooking the park for which it is named, has recently been renovated; $95-129 s or d. Expensive. **Ridge Hotel,** 189 Leichhardt St., tel. (07) 3831-5000 or (1800) 06-1357, is a good-value accommodation within easy walking distance of downtown. Rooms are of a high standard, and many have views. Standard rooms are $100 s or d; those with kitchens are much larger and sleep four, $145. Expensive.

Fortitude Valley and New Farm

In Fortitude Valley, you'll find **Balmoral House,** 33 Amelia St., tel. (07) 3252-1397, off busy St. Pauls Terrace. Rooms are clean and comfortable and there's a communal kitchen; $30 s, $32 d, or $45 s or d with a private bathroom. Inexpensive.

South Pacific Palms Motel, corner Bowen Terrace and Langshaw St., New Farm, tel. (07) 3358-2366 or (1800) 67-9934, is in a quiet residential area, northwest of downtown. Each room has a kitchen and balcony and there's also a pool, barbecue, and laundry. Rates are $65 s, $72 d; great value if you don't mind being a few km from downtown. Moderate.

Kangaroo Point

The Point, a narrow finger of land formed by a bend of the Brisbane River, is home to the following three motels, all excellent alternatives to those in the city center as they are clustered above a ferry terminal linked to downtown by a regular ferry service. Least expensive of these is **Story Bridge Motor Inn,** 321 Main St., tel. (07) 3393-1433 or (1800) 77-3537, with a pool and laundry. Standard rooms are $72 s or d, but it's worth paying the extra $10-15 for those with better facilities. Moderate. Next door is **Olims Hotel,** 355 Main St., tel. (07) 3391-5566 or (1800) 80-0066, where rooms are $79. Moderate. **Ryan's on the River,** 269 Main St., tel. (07) 3391-1011, is the pick of the bunch, with 24 rooms on five floors; $99-139 s or d. Expensive.

On the east side of Kangaroo Point is **Dockside Apartment Hotel,** 44 Ferry St., tel. (07) 3891-6644 or (1800) 77-5005, comprising self-contained apartments of a very high standard with a tennis court, pool, spa, gym, and marina. Each room has a modern kitchen, dishwasher, and laundry. Rates are $150-210.

Farther south, along the Bradfield Highway, are a few inexpensive options, including the **Paramount Motel,** 649 Main St., tel. (07) 3393-1444, where each unit has a small kitchen; $68 s or d. Moderate.

South Brisbane

Sly Fox Travellers Hotel, 73 Melbourne St., tel. (07) 3844-0022, is really a backpacker place, with communal facilities, but basic rooms are also available for $32 s, $35 d. Inexpensive. Farther south, in the shadow of the Captain Cook Bridge, is **Quality River Plaza Hotel,** 21 Dock St., tel. (07) 3844-4455, a nonsmoking establishment in a good, quiet spot overlooking South Bank Parklands and with a pool and tennis court; rooms are $100 s or d, $145 with a kitchen. Expensive. A few blocks away is **Hillcrest Apartment Hotel,** 311 Vulture St., tel. (07) 3846-3000 or (1800) 67-8659, a small place of 16 large units, each with a well-equipped kitchen and laundry. There's also a tennis court and pool. One-bedroom units are $105, and two-bedroom units, each with a balcony, are $145. Expensive.

Hamilton

You'll find Brisbane's other main concentration of motels along Kingsford Smith Dr., paralleling the Brisbane River between downtown and Brisbane Airport. **Airport Motel,** 638 Kingsford Smith Dr., tel. (07) 3868-2399, is clean, comfortable, and offers airport transfers; $62 s, $68 d. Moderate. **Airport International Motel,** 528 Kingsford Smith Dr., tel. (07) 3268-6388, is of a higher standard and has a pool; $100 s or d. Expensive. The **Powerhouse Boutique Hotel,** on Kingsford Smith Dr. where it crosses the Brisbane River, tel. (07) 3862-1800, is a luxurious five-star hotel with all the trimmings. Rooms are $230 s or d. Luxury.

BED AND BREAKFASTS

Dating from 1854, **Annie's Shandon Inn,** 405 Upper Edward St., Spring Hill, tel. (07) 3831-8684, has managers who make an otherwise basic guesthouse feel like home. Rooms with shared bathrooms are $40 s, $50 d, with private bathrooms $50 s, $60 d (all rates include continental breakfast and use of a laundry). Inexpensive.

For Australian old-world charm at a reasonable price, consider **Thornbury House** at Thornbury St., Spring Hill, tel. (07) 3832-5985. This historic 1886 residence offers 10 rooms at $50 s, $90 d, which includes a cooked breakfast and use of an outdoor courtyard and comfortable lounge.

BACKPACKER ACCOMMODATIONS

Downtown

Brisbane City YHA, 392 Upper Roma St., tel. (07) 3236-1004, is 500 meters from Brisbane Transit Centre and a few blocks farther from the center of town. It has a large communal kitchen, laundry, reading room, cafeteria (dinner $5-9), and a small parking lot. Members pay $17 for a dorm, $20 pp in a double or twin room. Nonmembers pay $3-4 extra per night. The YHA is an easy 400-meter walk west along Roma St. from the transit center. Budget. Right downtown is **Palace Backpackers,** corner Ann and Edward Streets, tel. (1800) 67-6340. This rambling old place has been modernized and offers good accommodations, but can get noisy because Brisbane's only backpacker bar is in the same building. Dorm beds are $17, and private rooms are $25 s, $38 d. Budget.

Paddington

A few years ago Paddington had a handful of hostels; now there's just one to recommend, but it's a good one. In a quiet, off-the-main-road location is **Aussie Way,** a two-story, colonial-era house at 34 Cricket St., tel. (07) 3369-0711, with beds in four-bed dorms for $15 pp as well as a few single and double rooms for $27 and $34 respectively. Budget.

Spring Hill

Balmoral House, 33 Amelia St., tel. (07) 3252-5892, is a large guesthouse a short walk to the area's restaurants. Recently renovated, it now offers a few backpacker rooms with use of a large kitchen; dorms $10-12, singles $28, doubles $30.

New Farm

Beyond Spring Hill, past Fortitude Valley, in the riverside suburb of New Farm, is the city's greatest concentration of backpacker accommodations. The main route into New Farm is Brunswick St.—check out **Pete's Palace,** no. 515, tel. (07) 3254-1984, and **Red Hot Chilli Packers,** no. 569, tel. (07) 3392-0137, for adequate but not outstanding dorms for $13-15. Budget. **The Homestead,** 57 Annie St., tel. (07) 3358-3538, is the pick of the bunch, close to a couple of good cafés and restaurants on Brunswick St. and with excellent facilities including a small pool, laundry, kitchen, and game room. Transfers to the airport and into town can be arranged and tours are offered. Dorms are $14, doubles and twins $32. Budget.

West End

South of the Brisbane River and less than one km from South Bank Parklands, **Brisbane Backpackers Resort,** 110 Vulture St., tel. (07) 3844-9956 or (1800) 62-6452, is a three-story, purpose-built backpackers. As well as all the usual facilities, this place features a games room, pool, spa, small fitness room, sauna, tennis, nightly videos, bar, restaurant, travel agent, rental cars, laundry, and transit center pickups. Dorm beds are $15 pp, while private rooms are $30 s, $45 d. Budget. One block farther south is **Somewhere to Stay,** 45 Brighton Rd., tel. (07) 3846-2858 or (1800) 81-2398. It's a huge place, with a pool and landscaped barbecue area, Internet service, and a café. Some rooms have a TV and balcony. Rates are $13-16 for a dorm bed, $21-25 s, $28-35 d, and double rooms with bathrooms are $45. Budget.

CAMPGROUNDS

Most of Brisbane's caravan parks are full of permanent residents and offer only a few tourist sites. If you don't mind a lack of facilities, head 45 km west to **Manorina National Park,** beyond Mt. Nebo in Brisbane Forest Park. A small and primitive campground here has pit toilets and picnic tables.

North

The closest camping to downtown is at **Newmarket Gardens Caravan Park,** four km north at 199 Ashgrove Rd., Ashgrove, tel. (07) 3356-1458. Half the sites are taken by permanent residents, with the other half, all powered, going for $17 per night. On-site vans are $30 and cabins go for $50. Budget. In the suburb of Apsley, 13 km from downtown along the main route north, are a couple of choices, but tents aren't encouraged. **Caravan Village Brisbane,** 763 Zillmere Rd., tel. (07) 3263-4040 or (1800) 06-0797, offers powered sites for $17 ($25 with private bath) and excellent cabins for $58-70. Budget-Inexpensive. **Apsley Acres Caravan Park,** 1420 Gympie Rd., tel. (07) 3263-2668, is another good option, with powered sites for $18, on-site vans for $32, and cabins for $45-60. Budget-Inexpensive.

South

Dress Circle Mobile Village, 10 Holmead Rd., tel. (07) 3341-6133, in the suburb of Eight Mile Plains, 15 km south of the city on the Logan Freeway, is spread over 15 hectares and has an area set aside for tents; other features are three swimming pools, five laundries, a barbecue area, and nearby public transportation. Unpowered sites are $10, powered sites $17, and cabins $55-75. Budget-Inexpensive. Further south, in the suburb of Rochedale, is **Gateway Village,** 200 School Rd., tel. (07) 3341-6333, just south of the Brisbane bypass. Facilities here are also excellent and sites are $21, cabins $60-80. Budget-Inexpensive. Campgrounds are also located at Coomera, 54 km southeast of Brisbane, and on the north slope of Tamborine Mountain, 81 km south.

DOWNTOWN DINING

Cafés and Cheap Eats

Scattered along Queen Street Mall are many open-air cafés, including two **Jimmy's on the Mall** cafés. Service is fast and efficient and food fresh. Hot drinks and main meals are expensive, but light snacks such as nachos, sandwiches, and pastries are well-priced; each café is open daily 24 hours. **Cafe Mondial,** a trendy café on Elizabeth St. and just off Queen Street Mall, serves a vast array of coffees and cakes. The music can be loud, but the sound is muffled outside at tables spread along the sidewalk. The nicest place in the city to spend time over a coffee or lunch is **City Gardens Cafe,** an old caretaker's cottage in the botanic gardens south of Alice Street. Brunch is served daily 8-11 a.m. ($5-10) and lunch and afternoon tea are served till 5 p.m. ($4-9).

Between 11 a.m. and 2 p.m. lunch at the bistro on the ground floor of **Lennons Hotel,** Queen Street Mall, is only $7 (although dishes aren't that hot), which includes a beer or glass of wine.

A bunch of inexpensive restaurants lie along Elizabeth St., between George and Albert Streets. **Govinda's,** 99 Elizabeth St., tel. (07) 3210-0255, is a vegetarian restaurant run by the Hare Krishna; lunch is a good value at $5, and it's also open for dinner Friday. Elizabeth Arcade, 50 meters downhill from this restaurant, has a variety of inexpensive cafés and retro shops.

Restaurants

Near the north end of Queen Street Mall, **Shingles Inn,** 254 Edward St., tel. (07) 3221-9039, is a classic old restaurant that has been a favorite downtown haunt for more than 60 years, complete with waitstaff dressed in 1930s uniforms. The menu is fairly standard but well priced. Open daily except Sunday.

In the Novotel Brisbane, **Cilantro,** 200 Creek St., tel. (07) 3309-3364, is a casual Italian bistro with indoor and outdoor dining. On the ground floor of the Carlton Crest Hotel, corner Ann and Roma Streets, is **Picasso's,** a cavernous yet stylish bistro; open daily 9:30 a.m.-10 p.m. **Augustine's,** tel. (07) 3222-1128, is an elegant restaurant in the 1890s Mansions, a row of six terraces at the Parliament House end of George Street. Diners have a choice of eating in the parlor or surrounded by greenery in the courtyard. Main meals start at $20. Closed Sunday. For stylish contemporary dining, head to Brisbane's finest lodging, The Heritage, corner Margaret and Edward Streets, where you'll find **Siggi's,** tel. (07) 3221-4555. The high standard of food and service here attract the who's who of Brisbane society. Closed Sunday and Monday.

Riverside Centre and Vicinity

The Riverside Centre, on the east side of downtown and linked by ferry to Kangaroo Point accommodations, has a wide variety of restaurants to suit all budgets, including a number of top-end options. **Rivers Cafe & Bar,** tel. (07) 3831-4288, has lunches from $8 and, like all restaurants in the center, good views. Around the corner is **Marco's,** tel. (07) 3831-5555, a casual yet elegant Italian restaurant specializing in seafood dishes. Next door is one of Brisbane's most acclaimed restaurants, **Michael's,** tel. (07) 3832-5522, featuring cuisine from around the world but also specializing in seafood from Queensland waters prepared with an Asian flair (a cart filled with fresh ocean delicacies is presented to diners); main dishes range $22-34; open for lunch Mon.-Fri., dinner Mon.-Saturday. **Friday's,** tel. (07) 3832-2122, is a three-part restaurant including an outside grill ($9-22 for main dishes) and a lunchtime buffet ($26).

Along the promenade from the Riverside Centre is **Eagle Street Pier,** another large complex offering a great variety of restaurants. **City Rowers Fish Tavern,** on the second floor, tel. (07) 3221-2888, is an open air bistro-style restaurant with great views. Fish-of-the-day specials start at $13, with chicken and beef dishes similarly priced. Another seafood restaurant on the promenade, **Pier Nine,** tel. (07) 3229-2194, offers the very best of Australian seafood, including a variety of grilled fish dishes; for an appetizer, it's hard to go past their local oysters shucked on the spot. Also in this complex is **Il Centro,** tel. (07) 3221-6090, featuring stunning wooden floors and vibrant decor. This modern Italian restaurant has main dishes well priced at $15-23.

Kookaburra Queen

This wooden paddlewheeler, built using Australian timbers and traditional shipbuilding skills, departs daily from Eagle Street Pier for a variety of dine-aboard river cruises. Devonshire tea cruises depart daily 10 a.m. (also Sunday 3 p.m.) and include live entertainment; $17. The Luncheon Cruise departs daily at noon and returns at 2:15 p.m.; cost varies $26-49 depending on the lunch chosen. Dinner cruises depart Mon.-Sat. 7:30 p.m., Sunday 6:30 p.m. and range $26-60. For bookings call (07) 3221-1300.

RESTAURANTS IN OTHER PARTS OF THE CITY

South Bank

South Bank Parklands has about 20 eateries, including a string of fast-food places. **Capt'n Snapper,** tel. (07) 3846-4036, is a huge seafood restaurant at the south end of the Parklands. Basic fish and chips from the blackboard menu is $6.95, but many daily specials are also offered, with the Seafood Feast ($16.95) an especially good value. At the back of the restaurant is a takeaway section with a few tables; fish and chips here is $3.95, but tell the cashier to go easy on the spicy salt. Both are open daily for lunch and dinner. In the heart of South Bank Parklands, **Riverside Restaurants** is a complex of three stylish restaurants overlooking the river. **Cafe San Marco,** tel. (07) 3846-4334, has a large breakfast for $9.50, healthy sandwiches from $5, and Mexican dishes $8.50-13. **Wang Dynasty,** tel. (07) 3844-8318, specializes in kangaroo ($16) and crocodile ($23) cooked Asian-style. Upstairs is an elegant Italian restaurant, **Io Ti Amo,** tel. (07) 3846-4599.

In the Queensland Cultural Centre (below Victoria Bridge) is **Promenade Cafe,** with tables spread around a pleasant courtyard. All snacks are inexpensive and the coffee excellent; open daily 10 a.m.-5 p.m.

Paddington

One of Brisbane's oldest suburbs, Paddington has a variety of restaurants and cafés, most along Given Terrace, a continuation of Caxton St. from the city. **Sultan's Kitchen,** 163 Given Terrace, tel. (07) 3368-2194, is an Indian restaurant with curries ranging $14-18 and a lunchtime buffet for $13. Up the hill, and on the same side of the road, is **King Tut's,** 283 Given Terrace, tel. (07) 3369-9775, a trendy café with indoor and outdoor tables; open daily 8 a.m.-10:30 p.m. **Sweethearts,** 161 Latrobe Terrace, is a country-style café on the same stretch. At the junction of Given and Latrobe Terraces is **Kookaburra Cafe,** 280 Given Terrace, tel. (07) 3369-3300, in a building dating from 1888. Through the years it has seen a variety of uses, but is now an inexpensive café featuring pizza and pasta dishes from $6.50.

Fortitude Valley

Fortitude Valley, north of downtown, is a melting pot of cultures boasting some of the city's better ethnic restaurants, wildest nightclubs, and its most-famous breakfast hangout.

California Cafe, 376 Brunswick St., tel. (07) 3852-1026, is similar in appearance to many other 1950s-style diners, with one major difference—this one was actually around then, when Fortitude Valley was an outlying suburb and speckled laminex tabletops and chrome-colored chairs were de rigueur. It is now Brisbane's oldest café, open all day but most popular at breakfast when portions are legendary. Along Brunswick Street Mall are another couple of places open early including **Cafe Societe** and, farther down, **Coffee Club,** with large street-level windows perfect for people-watching. This café is part of **McWhirters,** a large emporium with a great food court, a number of small cafés, and trendy boutiques.

Brisbane's **Chinatown** is located between Wickham and Ann Streets, Fortitude Valley. **Universal Noodle Restaurant,** 145 Wickham St., tel. (07) 3854-1168, is one of Chinatown's least expensive eateries; most meals are less than $8. At the other end of the scale, in Duncan Street Mall, is **Chinahouse Seafood Restaurant,** tel. (07) 3216-0570, where main dishes range $13-20; open daily for lunch and dinner.

For a taste of Europe, head to **Giardinetto,** 366 Brunswick St., tel. (07) 3252-4750, a small Italian restaurant with pastas from $10 and seafood around $15.

Newstead

One of Brisbane's most popular places to head for seafood is **Breakfast Creek Wharf Seafood Restaurant,** northeast of town, tel. (07) 3252-2451. It's large, seating more than 300 diners, both indoors and out and overlooking Breakfast Creek. The main feature is a timber replica of the boat used by early Australian explorer John Oxley, which sits in the middle of the restaurant, and maritime memorabilia fills other parts. The seafood here is always fresh and prepared to perfection; coral trout and barramundi are especially good ($17). It's open daily noon-2:30 p.m., 6-10 p.m. You can also get takeout, or relax with a beer throughout the day and night.

For a splurge, **Roseville Restaurant,** 56 Chester St., tel. (07) 3358-1377, in a historic Victorian-era house, is worth every cent. Surrounded by immaculate gardens, the house has been totally restored, right down to period stained-glass windows and chandeliers. Service is impeccable and food excellent. It's open daily for lunch and dinner and although an a la carte menu is offered, a better deal is the fixed-price three-course lunch ($27) or dinner ($32).

GETTING THERE

Air

Brisbane Airport is 11 km northeast of downtown. The international and domestic terminals are two km apart and are both younger than 10 years old (a brand-new international terminal opened in September 1995), making the facilities among the most modern and efficient in the country. The international terminal has a currency exchange, bank, restaurant, cafés, and souvenir shop, but no lockers. Both terminals have all major car rental companies. International airlines flying into Brisbane include: **Qantas,** tel. (13) 1313; **Air New Zealand,** tel. (13) 2476; **British Airways,** tel. (07) 3232-3000; and **United Airlines,** tel. (07) 3221-7477. **Ansett Australia,** tel. (13) 1300, and **Qantas,** tel. (13) 1313, fly interstate. Within the state, **Flightwest,** tel. (13) 2392, serves Outback destinations, and **Sunstate,** tel. (13) 1313, runs up and down the coast.

Skytrans, tel. (07) 3236-1000, is a half-hourly bus service that operates daily 5:30 a.m.-8 p.m. between both terminals, and Brisbane Transit Centre and major downtown hotels ($6.50 one-way; $12 roundtrip). A cab between the airport and downtown will run $22-25, depending on traffic.

Brisbane Transit Centre
This excellent facility, located on Roma St. half a km from downtown and near many hotels, is the Brisbane terminus of all long-distance trains and buses. It has a restaurant, banks, lockers, car rental desks, an accommodation booking service (third floor), currency exchange, and information center.

Rail
The XPT departs Sydney for Brisbane twice daily with some services requiring a change to coach at Murwillumbah. Either way, the trip takes 14 hours.

Queensland's most popular rail trip is up the coast. The Sunlander, Spirit of the Tropics, and Queenslander all make the 32-hour journey to Cairns via Townsville. The Queenslander is more luxurious than other services; it departs each Sunday at 10 a.m. and arrives in Cairns 5:15 p.m. Monday. Other services from Brisbane are: Westlander to Charleville, Spirit of the Outback to Longreach, and Spirit of Capricorn to Rockhampton.

The best source of Queensland Rail information is **Brisbane Travel Centre,** 305 Edward St., tel. (07) 3235-1323 or (13) 2232.

Bus
All long-distance bus companies have booking offices in the Brisbane Transit Centre and are open daily till at least 6 p.m. **Greyhound Pioneer,** tel. (13) 2030, and **McCafferty's,** tel. (13)

1499, operate between Sydney and Brisbane with stops at major towns en route. The trip takes 16-19 hours on either the Pacific or New England Highway. Other major destinations served from Brisbane include: Bundaberg, Airlie Beach, Townsville, and Cairns. Discounts apply for YHA members and seniors, or, if you purchase tickets 15 days in advance, a 50% discount applies. To destinations north of Brisbane, a Greyhound Pioneer Sunseeker Pass, good for six months on the route to Cairns, is a good deal.

Coachtrans, tel. (07) 3236-1000, runs regular services from the airport and Brisbane Transit Centre to the Gold Coast; $15 one-way.

GETTING AROUND

Brisbane Transport
Brisbane Transport operates a network of rail, bus, and ferry services throughout the city. For ticketing, the city is divided into five zones, with all downtown falling in Zone 1. Travel on a single sector of this zone is $1.40. For unlimited travel on buses and ferries, a Day Rover is a good deal for $8, or $4 for travel 9-3:30 p.m. and after 7 p.m. A Roverlink ticket allows travel on bus, ferry, and rail; $8. For all local schedules, call the **Trans Info** hotline at (13) 1230.

Rail
Citytrains run along an extensive rail network to outer suburbs, daily 4:30 a.m.-1 a.m. They are mostly used by commuters and shoppers. All trains stop at Central Station, on Ann St., and Brisbane Transit Centre, on Roma Street.

Bus
Brisbane Transport operates bus services that radiate from the city center to the suburbs. The terminus of these routes is the bus station beneath the Myer Shopping Centre on Queen Street Mall. There are two main services: **City-xpress,** with limited stops, and **Citybus,** with multiple stops. The City Circle route runs along Adelaide, Eagle, Alice, and George Streets every five minutes (Mon.-Fri. only).

Ferry
Large blue catamarans known as CityCats run along the Brisbane River every 15-30 minutes.

Four routes run straight across the river, including from North Quay to South Bank, with the service extending as far upstream (west) as the university and as far downstream as Bretts Wharf. The cross-river fare is just $1.40.

Taxi

For a cab, call **Black and White Cabs,** tel. (13) 1008; **Brisbane Cabs,** tel. (07) 3360-0000; or **Yellow Cabs,** tel. (13) 1924.

Car

Driving in Brisbane isn't as frustrating as other Australian capital cities, although the Riverside Expressway can be confusing at times. Parking stations downtown charge from $4 an hour and $15 per day, with early-bird rates before 9 a.m. A good alternative is underground parking at the Queensland Cultural Centre ($8 per day) or at South Bank Parklands ($4 per day).

Rates for rental cars generally start at $39 per day with local companies, and rates for multiple days often include unlimited km and insurance. One of the cheapest is **A Aircond,** tel. (07) 3216-0303, with rates dropping to $30 per day over 21 days. Other cheapies include **Delta,** tel. (07) 3839-8180, and **Penny Wise,** tel. (07) 3252-3333. Major car rental companies with outlets in Brisbane include: **Avis,** tel. (07) 3221-2900; **Budget,** tel. (07) 3220-0699; **Hertz,** tel. (07) 3221-6166; **National,** tel. (07) 3854-1499; and **Thrifty,** tel. (07) 3252-5994. For small RVs, contact **Kangaroo Campervan Rentals,** tel. (07) 3899-3555 or (1800) 00-0133.

Tours

Brisbane Transport operates **City Sights** and **City Nights** tours, tel. (13) 1230, in a tram-on-wheels leaving from the Queen St. side of Post Office Square every half-hour 9 a.m.-4 p.m. Tickets are $15 and are valid all day, allowing you to get on and off at up to 19 stops of interest around the city including Wickham Terrace, Fortitude Valley, Kangaroo Point Ferry, the Maritime Museum, and the Queensland Cultural Centre. The City Nights tour departs City Hall at 6 p.m. and lasts two hours, taking in city lights as far away as Mt. Cootha. This tour is also $15.

Australian Pacific Tours, tel. (13) 1304, **Sunstate Day Tours,** tel. (07) 3236-3355, and **Boomerang Tours,** tel. (07) 3211-2484, operate tours of the city and its environs. Fares start at $42 for a half-day tour, which includes admission to a wildlife park.

SERVICES

The **general post office** is at 261 Queen St. and is open Mon.-Fri. 7 a.m.-7 p.m. Another post office operates out of the Brisbane Transit Centre. Cash traveler's checks at all major banks and hotels.

Emergency Services

For all emergencies call 000. **Royal Brisbane Hospital** is on Herston Rd., Herston, tel. (07) 3253-8111. **Travellers Medical Service** provides vaccinations for ongoing travel as well as first-aid kits and other travel accessories; it's at 245 Albert St., tel. (07) 3211-3611, and is open Mon.-Fri. 7:30 a.m.-7 p.m., Saturday 8 a.m.-3 p.m.

INFORMATION

Library

Located in the Queensland Cultural Centre on South Bank is the **State Library,** tel. (07) 3840-7666, with a large selection of current newspapers from around the world, magazines, audiovisual displays, a collection of historic maps, an Internet room (free; book a computer at 07-3840-7785), a research section, and café. It's open Mon.-Thurs. 10 a.m.-8 p.m., Fri.-Sun. 10 a.m.-5 p.m.

Bookstores

Dymocks has an outlet in Queen Street Mall, and **Angus and Robertson** is located in Post Office Square, Adelaide Street. **Hema Maps,** with a wide variety of travel guides and maps, is on the first floor of the MLC Building, 239 George St., tel. (07) 3221-4330. Another specialty bookstore is **World Wide Maps & Guides,** 187 George St., tel. (07) 3221-4330. **Archives Fine Books** is a large antiquarian bookstore spanning three shopfronts; it's at 38-42 Charlotte St., tel. (07) 3221-0491.

Information Centers

A small **information booth** operated by Brisbane City Council is on Queen Street Mall at Albert St., tel. (07) 3229-5918. It's open Mon.-Thurs. 8:30 a.m.-5 p.m., Friday 8:30 a.m.-8:30 p.m., and Sat.-Sun. 9 a.m.-5 p.m. **Brisbane Visitors & Convention Bureau,** tel. (07) 3221-8411, operates information centers at the arrivals level of the international terminal at Brisbane Airport, the foyer of City Hall, and Level 2 of Brisbane Transit Centre on Roma Street. The **Queensland Government Travel Centre,** corner Adelaide and Edward Streets, tel. (07) 3874-2800, books tours and attractions throughout the state; open Mon.-Fri. 8:30 a.m.-5 p.m., Saturday 9:30 a.m.-12:30 p.m.

The Department of Environment, caretaker of Queensland's national parks, operates the excellent **Naturally Queensland Information Centre** at 160 Ann St., tel. (07) 3227-8185; open Mon.-Fri. 8:30 a.m.-5 p.m.

The **RACQ** (Royal Automobile Club of Queensland), beside the post office at 261 Queen St., tel. (07) 3361-2565, is another good source of information, and members of associate motoring clubs—such as AAA—can fill their arms with maps and handy accommodation guides.

TOOWOOMBA AND VICINITY

Once known simply as The Swamp, Toowoomba (pop. 100,000) has grown into one of Queensland's largest regional centers. The city sprawls across the western slopes of the Great Dividing Range, 140 km west of Brisbane. It serves the farming communities of the Darling Downs as well as being home to the University of Southern Queensland. Best known for parks and gardens, tree-lined streets, art galleries, and historic buildings, Toowoomba exudes an air of elegance not usually associated with country towns.

Sights

The **Cobb & Co. Museum,** 27 Lindsay St., tel. (07) 4639-1971, boasts Australia's largest collection of horse-drawn vehicles, including many carts and buggies from early last century; admission $2.50. It's open daily 10 a.m.-4 p.m. Across the road is Queens Park, a large area of natural parkland. **Royal Bull's Head Inn** was built in 1847 as a resting stop for people traveling west from Brisbane to the Darling Downs. In its day, it would have gotten a five-star rating as one of the most comfortable stopping houses in Queensland. Although the building has undergone many changes since last century, it retains a historic charm; open Thurs.-Sun. 10 a.m.-4 p.m. Admission is $2. You'll find it in the suburb of Drayton, immediately west of the university campus, tel. (07) 4630-1869.

From **Picnic Point,** east of downtown at the end of Long St., views extend 360 degrees across the city and to the Great Dividing Range. There's a picnic area, and hiking trails lead down the escarpment. A park of a different type is **Ju Raku En,** a Japanese garden on the campus

of the University of Southern Queensland; open daily 7 a.m.-7 p.m. **Toowoomba Bicentennial Water Habitat,** on Mackenzie St., is an eight-hectare re-creation of the wetland environment before the arrival of white man in the area. Observation hides make viewing of the abundant birdlife possible at close range.

Accommodations and Food

Most of Toowoomba's 30-odd hotels and motels lie along Ruthven St. (New England Hwy.) north and south of downtown. **Settlers Inn Hotel,** 633 Ruthven St., tel. (07) 4632-3634, is the best in its class, with clean rooms for $24 s, $36 d. Inexpensive. **Motel Glenworth,** 1 Margaret St., tel. (07) 4638-1799, is also inexpensive and handy to downtown; $52 s, $59 d. **Allan Cunningham Motel,** 808 Ruthven St., tel. (07) 4635-5466, has large, comfortable rooms with modern conveniences, and a pool; $55 s, $65 d. Moderate.

Vacy Hall, 135 Russell St., tel. (07) 4639-2055, is an elegant home dating from 1883. Lovingly restored, each room has distinctive character and a comfortable brass bed. Standard rooms (shared bathrooms) are $88 s, $112 d, and much larger suites, with a fireplace and veranda, are $130 s, $165 d. Expensive.

Toowoomba Motor Village, 821 Ruthven St., tel. (07) 4635-8186 or (1800) 67-5105, has great facilities including a barbecue area and laundry; unpowered sites $12, powered sites $16, on-site vans $28, and cabins $32-60. Budget.

Dancing Bear Cafe, 1 Scholefield St., is the ubiquitous student hangout—sparsely furnished, notice boards crammed with Wanted to Rent notices, and a motley bunch of students sipping coffee while studying; open daily from 6:30 a.m. **Park House Café,** in Park House Gallery on Margaret St., is a more relaxed place with lunches served daily and morning and afternoon teas on weekends. **Banjo's** is a family-style steak and seafood restaurant at the corner of Ruthven St. and Hanna Court, tel. (07) 4636-1033. **Herries House,** 210 Herries St., tel. (07) 4632-7382, is an Italian restaurant with tables out on a covered veranda or inside around a log fire; open daily for lunch and dinner.

Transportation, Services, and Information
Australia's second largest bus company, **McCafferty's** was founded in Toowoomba in the 1940s and continues to use the inland city as its operational base. The company has at least two services daily from Brisbane and the Gold Coast to Toowoomba. The terminal is at 28 Neil St., tel. (07) 4690-9888 or (13) 1499.

Toowoomba Mapping Centre has a wide range of topographical maps and Australiana literature; it's at 185 Herries St., tel. 076-32-3848. The **Tourist Information Centre** is just over one km southeast of downtown at 86 James St., tel. (07) 4639-3797 or (1800) 33-1155; open Mon.-Fri. 8:30 a.m.-5 p.m., Sat.-Sun. 9 a.m.-5 p.m.

DARLING DOWNS

This area of far south Queensland, south of Toowoomba and immediately west of the Great Dividing Range, is a vast basin with all watersheds flowing in a southerly direction to form the **Darling River,** which drains into the Murray River and into the Southern Ocean, forming part of Australia's great river system. The especially fertile land provides an ideal environment for a variety of crops and stock. From Brisbane, the most direct access to the Darling Downs is through Ipswich, then southwest along the Cunningham Highway to the region's largest town, Warwick.

National Parks of the Main Range
Traveling west from Brisbane, the coastal plain in which the city lies soon gives way to the Great Dividing Range. This section of the range is protected by an almost continuous strip of national parks that continues southward into New South Wales. The largest is 11,500-hectare **Main Range National Park,** bisected by a road passing through **Cunningham's Gap,** a low pass flanked by peaks rising more than 1,100 meters. Apart from panoramic views, this section of the park seems uninspiring; but it is worth getting out at the **The Crest** for one of a number of short hikes. The **Rainforest Circuit** will take only 20 minutes, but this is only the beginning of an extensive trail system on the north side of the road. Off this track a 2.3-km trail leads to Mt. Cordeaux, not really a mountain at all, but a high ridge that comes alive with color in late spring when spear lilies bloom (allow two hours roundtrip). On the western flank of the gap is a campground and Park Headquarters, tel. (07) 4666-1133.

Ju Raku En gardens

East of the Main Range are four isolated peaks, each protected by a small national park and known wholly as **Moogerah Peaks National Parks.** The summit of each is accessible (784-meter Mt. Moon is the highest), and the cliff faces of **Mt. French** are popular with climbers.

Warwick

Warwick (pop. 10,000), largest community of the Darling Downs, is 162 km southwest of Brisbane, at the junction of the New England and Cunningham Highways. The city was first settled in 1840, making it Queensland's second-oldest settlement (only Brisbane has been established longer). Many sandstone buildings from this early era remain, including the courthouse, a number of impressive churches, and **Pringle Cottage,** on Dragon Street. The town's biggest drawcard is the **Warwick Rodeo Festival** in October. Events take place throughout the month, culminating in the rodeo on the last weekend. First run in 1851, it is Australia's oldest professional rodeo, and today cowboys compete for more than $10,000 in prize money.

Motels in town are of a surprisingly high standard, with **Country Rose Motel,** 2 Palmer Ave., on the road out to Brisbane, tel. (07) 4661-7700, being an especially good value at $58 s, $63 d. Moderate. **Kahlers Oasis Caravan Park,** on the New England Hwy. south of town, tel. (07) 4661-2874, has sites for $10 and on-site vans for $23. Budget.

Queen Mary Falls National Park

Located near Killarney, 44 km east of Warwick, this 333-hectare park encompasses two sections of natural bushland on the western slopes of the Great Dividing Range. The falls for which the park is named plunge 40 meters in a narrow ribbon of water that cascades photogenically over an escarpment. You'll find a privately operated campground at the park's entrance, yet within walking distance of the falls; unpowered sites $12, powered sites $14, and a few very basic on-site vans for $28.

Granite Belt

A landscape littered with granite boulders, a legacy of volcanic eruptions 200 million years ago, dominates this area, the southernmost part of the state, where the state border follows the peaks of the Roberts Range. The two national parks are the best places to experience this landscape, and if you come from the north, you'll pass through **Stanthorpe,** the center of Queensland's wine-producing area, highlighted during the **Granite Belt Spring Wine Festival** in October. Other fruits, such as pears, apples, and stone fruits were introduced by tin miners in the 1870s and now make up the other part of the local economy; in season, roadside stalls are the perfect places to indulge in this local produce. **Happy Valley Vineyard Retreat,** Glen Lyon Dr., tel. (07) 4681-3250 or (1800) 65-7009, four km west of Stanthorpe, features basic cabins and cozy cottages scattered around a natural bush setting, while other rooms, with shared facilities, are in the main building. Rates are $99-129 pp including breakfast and dinner.

The rugged 11,400-hectare **Girraween National Park,** 30 km south of Stanthorpe, typifies the granite belt. The access road climbs into an area of large granite boulders scattered through deep gullies and high ridges. More than 200 million years of erosion exposed the harder granite boulders, some balanced at impossible angles, looking as if they could roll at the slightest push. The park's highest point is the summit of 1,267-meter Mt. Norman, which in winter occasionally receives a light dusting of snow (yes, it does snow in Queensland). At the end of the sealed road are trailheads. The steep **Pyramid Trail** (three km one-way) passes through an area of exceptional beauty, ending at a particularly imposing boulder, deftly balanced on a high ridge. Girraween is Koori for "Place of Many Flowers," and for the flowers alone it is worth visiting the park in spring. The park has two campgrounds, both with hot showers, and there's a visitor center at Castle Rock, tel. (07) 4684-5157.

Also located on the NSW/Queensland border is 11,200-hectare **Sundown National Park,** known locally as "traprock country" for the ridges and gorges along Severn River. Access from the east is best suited to four-wheel drives (turn off at Ballandean) while from the west a good road leads to Broadwater Camping Area, south of Glenlyon.

Goondiwindi

Meaning "Resting Place for Birds" in the language of the Koori, Goondiwindi is a thriving country town on the MacIntyre River. The river is the lifeblood of the town, allowing agricultural industries such as cotton-growing to thrive. More than 30,000 hectares are irrigated for cotton-growing. MacIntyre Cotton Gin, one of the world's largest, is open for tours April-October. Also in town is an extensive botanic garden and small museum in the old customs house.

WEST FROM TOOWOOMBA

The Warrego Highway, the main route west from Toowoomba, passes through a number of large agricultural towns before ending at Charleville. This is also the most direct route between Brisbane and the Northern Territory.

Jondaryan Woolshed

Jondaryan (YON-dar-yan) was once part of one of Queensland's largest cattle stations but has long since been divided into smaller holdings. The original woodshed, along with other buildings, has been transformed into a heritage theme park featuring a massive collection of steam-powered farm equipment, carriages and buggies, antique tractors, and other pioneering memorabilia. The complex sprawls over 60 hectares, with demonstrations of sheep-shearing, blacksmithing, and agricultural techniques daily. Guided tours of the park depart daily at 1 p.m. and on weekends at 10:30 a.m., 1 p.m., and 3 p.m. Admission is adult $8, child $4, with billy tea and damper an extra $2.50 and full meals starting at $4.50. YHA members can bed down for the night at the old shearer's quarters for $9 pp, and campsites are $8-10. Budget.

On the last week of August the woolshed hosts the **Australian Heritage Festival,** when all the machinery is operating and literally thousands of people descend on the place. For more information call (07) 4692-2229.

Dalby and West to Charleville

Dalby is a major agricultural center of 7,000, 80 km northwest of Toowoomba on the Warrego Highway. You'll find a large display of antique and vintage farm machinery at **Pioneer Park**

The daily parade is a highlight of Jondaryan's Australian Heritage Festival.

Museum (open daily 10 a.m.-3 p.m.). Also of interest is **Jimbour House;** built in 1876, it is considered one of the finest examples of colonial architecture in the country. The house, although not open to the public, is north of Dalby in Jimbour, and the gardens are enjoyable to wander around. As well as celebrating the success of the region's largest industry, **Dalby Cotton Week,** the second week of March, offers horse racing, art displays, performances by some of Australia's leading country music stars, and a colorful street parade.

Chinchilla, the first major town west of Dalby, is renowned for extensive deposits of petrified wood.

The other large center along the Warrego Highway is **Roma** (pop. 5,700). First settled in the 1860s, Roma has long been associated with the grazing industry and is also located in an area rich in oil and natural gas. **Easter in the Country,** the town's biggest festival, features a goat race, rodeo, donkey derby, and rolling-pin throwing contest.

NORTH FROM TOOWOOMBA

Ravensbourne and
Crows Nest National Parks

Both of these parks are located off the New England Highway, north of Toowoomba. Ravensbourne is a 100-hectare park protecting an area of rainforest similar to that which once covered much of the surrounding area. A short trail leads through a stand of piccabeen palms and along the access road, east of Hampton, is a picnic area. The other park, Crows Nest Falls, is east of Crows Nest. The falls for which the park is named are one km from the picnic and camping area. Beyond the falls is a lookout over Valley of Diamonds. Further information on both parks can be obtained from the Department of Environment at 158 Hume St., Toowoomba, tel. (07) 4639-4599.

SOUTH BURNETT

Named for the Burnett River, which drains into the ocean at Bundaberg, this region of the Great Dividing Range, north of Toowoomba, is a bit out of the way, neither on the coastal route north nor the highway out west, so it's often bypassed.

Bunya Mountains National Park

Protecting a western spur of the Great Dividing Range, this 11,700-hectare park featuring lush rainforests and stands of distinctive bunya pines is well worth a detour. Bunya pines, once common through the mountains of southeast Queensland, are now confined to this park. Much of the park is more than 1,000 meters above

sea level, creating a climate very different from surrounding plains. This subtropical environment promotes rainforest growth including a canopy of dome-shaped bunya pines and a great variety of palms, ferns, orchids, and lichens. The park also boasts a variety of birds, and many of the more colorful species, such as king parrots and rosellas, can be seen around picnic areas. At dawn and dusk large numbers of red-necked wallabies feed in cleared areas along the road. The main park facility area is **Dandabah,** where a park information center, campground with hot showers ($7), and other accommodations are located. This is also the starting point for a variety of trails, including the four-km scenic circuit that takes in a variety of vegetation, a lookout, waterfall, and rock pools.

Other campgrounds lie to the north at Westcott Plain and Burton's Well, but facilities at these are more primitive. Not all the mountains are protected as a national park and a number of private homes rent by the night or week through the kiosk, tel. (07) 4668-3131. They range $55-95 per night, making them excellent values. The Hunch, one of these, is close to everything, sleeps nine, and is fully self-contained at $70 per night. Moderate. The park information center is at Dandabah, tel. (07) 4668-3127.

Kingaroy

Loved by some, hated by others, no one would argue that Joh Bjelke-Peterson, Australia's best-known peanut farmer and Queensland premier for more than 20 years, put his home town of Kingaroy on the map. More than 35,000 tons of peanuts are processed annually in town; the best place to taste this local delicacy is the peanut van on Kingaroy St., tel. (07) 4162-2737. The **Tourist Information Centre,** Haly St., tel. (07) 4162-3199, can arrange tours of local factories; open Mon.-Fri. 9 a.m.-5 p.m., Sat.-Sun. 10 a.m.-2 p.m.

MORETON BAY

For 500,000 years sand, washed down the river systems of northern New South Wales, has been pushed northward by ocean currents and prevailing southerly winds. Some of it is dumped on the Gold Coast, but most ends up farther north and has formed a chain of sand islands east of Brisbane. Moreton Bay, protected from the full force of the Pacific Ocean by this barrier, is dotted with islands, and along the mainland coast are historic coastal townships, but massive **North Stradbroke** and **Moreton Islands** are the most interesting. Although mostly undeveloped, access to both islands is inexpensive, with North Stradbroke having a short road system and three small towns while Moreton is mostly national park, with one small resort on the west coast.

BAYSIDE COMMUNITIES

The Bayside is a stretch of coast extending north and south from the mouth of the Brisbane River for about 40 km. The many seaside towns, once fishing villages and holiday destinations, are now really outer suburbs of Brisbane, with Queensland's capital less than an hour's drive west.

The towns of **Wynnum** and **Manly** are immediately south of the Brisbane River. To the north of Wynnum is **Fort Lytton**, built in 1877 to defend the mouth of the Brisbane River. Parts of the fort remain and are open to the public during daylight hours. In Manly, Cambridge Parade leads down a steep hill to a large harbor, chockfull of fishing trawlers, yachts, and motorboats.

Manly Hotel, Cambridge Parade, tel. (07) 3396-8188, is a 1950s-style place with basic rooms for $45 s, $55 d, and a good outdoor beer garden overlooking the bay. Inexpensive. Opposite, and overlooking the harbor, is **The Fish Cafe,** with dine-in and takeaway seafood.

South of Manly is **Cleveland,** departure point for ferries to North Stradbroke Island. For somewhere to stay, try the **Grand View Hotel,** built in 1851 and completely refurbished in 1992 to its original glory. It is Queensland's oldest pub; two rooms are available, each decorated in period furnishings. The hotel also has a few bars, including an outside deck overlooking the bay and a restaurant. Located on North St., tel. (07) 3286-1002. On the main road (Old Cleveland Rd.) out to the ferry terminal is **Redlands Tourism** office, tel. (07) 3821-0057; open Mon.-Fri. 8:30 a.m.-5 p.m., Sat.-Sun. 9 a.m.-4 p.m.

INNER ISLANDS

St. Helena Island

In the 1860s, when Brisbane's jails were overflowing, it was decided to send the worst prisoners to this 80-hectare island eight km from the mouth of the Brisbane River. Construction was extensive, with prisoners building two large cell blocks for themselves, as well as housing for the warders, and enough facilities to make the island self-sufficient. After 65 years the prison closed, and much of the construction material was shipped to the mainland. The stone and brick walls remain, as does Queensland's first tramway, and the island itself is pleasant (although much altered from its original tree-covered state).

Cat-o-nine-tails, tel. (07) 3396-3994, is a large catamaran that runs from the marina at Manly across to the island a few times a week; $30 pp includes a short island tour. If you're staying in Brisbane, the following may be a better option. From the BP Marina, on Kingsford Smith Dr., Breakfast Creek, **St. Helena Island Guided Tours,** tel. (07) 3262-7422, runs a day tour to the island for $35 pp.

Coochiemudlo Island

"Coochie," as it's best known, is a small residential island with sandy beaches and many water-based activities, making it a good day trip from the mainland. Within walking distance of the ferry terminal are boat and surf-ski rentals, cafés, and restaurants. Ferries run from Victoria Point (south of Cleveland) every half-hour 6 a.m.-6 p.m.; adult $1.50 one-way, child $1. For details call (07) 3820-7227.

NORTH STRADBROKE ISLAND

According to Captain Cook's 1770 charts, North Stradbroke (or "Straddie," as it's best known locally) was once part of a sand island that ran the length of Moreton Bay, with Moreton Island, to the north, breaking away first; then in 1896 North and South Stradbroke Islands separated during a storm.

This large island is a great place to escape from the mainland and is good for walking, diving, fishing, and surfing. Although sand is the dominant feature, much of the island is forested, with eucalypts, acacias, and banksias covering the dune system up to 100 meters high. Inland, swamps dominate, and on the island's inaccessible west coast mangroves reign.

Dunwich, the island's original settlement, initially served as a depot for processing goods bound for Brisbane in 1827, then an Italian mission, and later as a quarantine station. Just north of Dunwich, at One Mile, readable headstones in the cemetery tell a sad story of these early days, when a typhoid outbreak killed 27 people, including the Brisbane doctor sent to treat them. Today the island has three townships and a combined population of a little under 3,000. Settlement is restricted to the island's north end; the rest of the island is remote, inaccessible,

© AVALON TRAVEL PUBLISHING

and closed to the public due to ongoing mining of mineral sands.

Sights and Recreation

Upon landing, you'll come ashore at **Dunwich**, on the island's west coast. A visitor center is near the waterfront. Part of the original stone wharf built by convicts remains north of the main boat ramp. On Welsby St. is a small **museum.**

From Dunwich, the main road leads northeast to the island's other townships. Another leads east across the island, to **Blue Lake National Park.** A few km out of Dunwich on this road is **Brown Lake**, good for swimming and picnicking, with a nine-hole golf course. The 500-hectare park is best known for the intensely colored lake for which it is named. The lake is fairly shallow—10 meters at its deepest—and is encircled with paperbark trees. The lake is 2.7 km from the road, an easy walk for hikers seeking a refreshing swim.

At the end of the island's other sealed road is **Point Lookout,** Queensland's easternmost point. It's this rocky headland, part of an ancient volcano, upon which the island's sand has built up. From the point, views extend south to the end of the island and on clear days to Mt. Warning. Migrating humpback whales pass under the cape June-November. Surfers and, in calm weather, snorkelers and divers frequent this beach.

Accommodations and Food

Stradbroke Island Hotel, Point Lookout, tel. (07) 3409-8188, is a modern complex with basic rooms for $50 s, $70 d and motel-style rooms for a few bucks extra. Facilities include a pool, barbecue area, restaurant (see below), and bar. Moderate. An inexpensive option is **North Stradbroke Island Guesthouse** on East Coast Rd., just before it descends into Point Lookout, tel. (07) 3409-8888. Take advantage of the communal kitchen, free use of water sport equipment, and courtesy pickups from Brisbane Transit Centre Monday, Wednesday, and Friday at 2:30 p.m. (book ahead). Singles and doubles are $40 d and dorm beds are $16 pp. Budget. The local council operates five campgrounds on the island, including one in each of the three towns. Unpowered sites are $10 s, $13 d, with powered sites $5 extra; call (07) 3409-9025 for bookings. Budget.

At Point Lookout is **Stradbroke Tourist Park,** tel. (07) 3409-8127, away from the beach but with a kitchen, kiosk, and laundry; sites are $10-15, basic cabins are $50, and small self-contained cottages are $75. Budget-Inexpensive.

The best food in town is dished up at the place with the best views, the **Stradbroke Island Hotel,** tel. (07) 3409-8188, better known as "The Straddie." Daily lunch specials in the bistro are about $7, while the restaurant is a little dearer. **Point Lookout Bowls Club,** tel. (07) 3409-8182, has inexpensive lunches and dinners. Basic groceries are available from small stores in each town, but prices are high. Also look out for local seafood sold at roadside stands (including delicious crabs).

Transportation, Services, and Information

The mainland departure point for vehicular and passenger services to the island is Cleveland, 35 km east of Brisbane and connected to that city by regular bus and rail services. To get to Cleveland, catch a **Stradbroke Island Coach Service** bus, tel. (07) 3807-4299, from the Brisbane Transit Centre. They depart Mon.-Fri. at 9:15 a.m., 12:30 p.m., 4 p.m., and 5 p.m.; $4 one way.

Water taxis to the island are operated by two companies, **Stradbroke Ferries,** tel. (07) 3286-2666, and **Stradbroke Flyer,** tel. (07) 3286-1964; both depart from Cleveland with hourly services 7 a.m.-7 p.m. The fare is $10 pp roundtrip. **Stradbroke Ferries** also runs a vehicular ferry departing Cleveland nine to 11 times daily for Dunwich. The fare for a regular-sized car is $66 roundtrip including passengers. The last sailing Mon.-Thurs. and Saturday is 6 p.m., Friday at 8 p.m., and Sunday at 6:30 p.m. In summer you'll need advance bookings.

Stradbroke Island Coach Service, tel. (07) 3807-4299, operates regular links between the towns and meets all water taxi arrivals at Dunwich. For a cab call **Stradbroke Taxi Service,** tel. (07) 3409-9124; Dunwich to Point Lookout accommodations will be $30.

Stradbroke Visitors Information Centre is in Dunwich, tel. (07) 3409-9555, open Mon.-Fri. 8:30 a.m.-5 p.m., Sat.-Sun. 9 a.m.-4 p.m. On the mainland, on Old Cleveland Rd., is another information center with island information (open similar hours).

MORETON ISLAND

As sand-mining leases expire, this large sand island north of North Stradbroke Island is slowly reverting to the spectacular and remote wilderness it was before white settlers came. Compared to North Stradbroke, this island is a wilderness, much of it protected by national park, and with no designated roads; it's popular for four-wheel driving and camping. A great little resort sits on the west coast.

The island's east coast is one long beach, almost 40 km long. The island is 185 square km and rises to a height of 280 meters at **Mt. Tempest,** claimed to be the highest coastal sand dune in the world. Behind the ever-changing dune system is coastal heath of banksias, and at lower elevations swamps, while open woodlands dominate and along the west coast mangroves rise from tidal marshes. A lighthouse at the northeastern tip and scattered Koori middens are the most telling signs of human presence. **Tangalooma Wild Dolphin Resort** sits on the former site of Queensland's only whaling station, operational 1952-62. Without a four-wheel drive, the only way to get around is on foot; from the ferry dock, it's a one-day walk to the island's east coast (14 km one-way) and Mt. Tempest (16 km one-way).

Accommodations

Tangalooma Wild Dolphin Resort, tel. (07) 3268-6333, spread along a palm-fringed beach in the middle of the island's west coast, boasts many activities, including tennis, squash, sailing, diving, snorkeling, and bushwalking. Rooms are furnished with the mild climate and relaxed atmosphere in mind; cane furniture, slate floors, private balconies, and kitchenettes. Rates start at $160 d in the off season, rising to $220 on holidays; rooms with ocean views start at $180 d.

Camping at designated NPWS campgrounds is $7.50 per night; permits through the Department of Environment in Brisbane are essential, tel. (07) 3227-7111.

Transportation and Tours

Tangalooma Flyer, a high-speed catamaran, transports guests and day trippers to the resort. It departs from a wharf at the end of Holt St., Eagle Farm (northwest of downtown Brisbane), Tues.-Sun. at 9:30 a.m. returning from Tangalooma at 3 p.m. (except Saturday, 4:30 p.m.) for $30 roundtrip. June-Oct. this can be combined with whalewatching ($80, including lunch; Wednesday and Sunday only.). On Friday night there is an extra sailing at 5:30 p.m. for a Dolphin Cruise ($80 pp includes a four-course meal at the resort). Make bookings through the resort, tel. (07) 3268-6333. The other way of getting across to the island is aboard *Combie Trader,* a vehicular ferry that departs Scarborough, north of Brisbane, daily except Tuesday for Bulwer on the north end of the island. On Sunday, Monday, and Friday, the boat returns the same day; on other days you'll need to camp or stay in self-contained units, $60 per night; call (07) 3203-6399 for bookings. Passengers are $20 roundtrip, vehicles $90 including passengers. From Bulwer, **Moreton Island Taxi Service,** tel. (07) 3408-2661, offers drop-offs at campgrounds. The *Combie Trader* offers day tours Monday, Friday, and Sunday, including boat trip, lunch, and a 4WD tour for $55 adult, $35 child.

Sunrover Expeditions, tel. (07) 3203-4241, offers trips emphasizing the island's natural wonders, with a busy itinerary in a four-wheel drive including swimming in Blue Lagoon, visiting the lighthouse, climbing the sand dunes—and tobogganing back down—and snorkeling around a wreck. Rate of $105 pp includes pickup from Brisbane Transit Centre, boat trip, and lunch. And it really is a full-day trip, departing Monday and Saturday at 6:45 a.m. and Sunday at 7:45 a.m.

SUNSHINE COAST

The beautiful sandy beaches of the Sunshine Coast extend 70 km between Caloundra, 85 km north of Brisbane, and Rainbow Beach. Along the coastal route you'll find a string of laid-back residential and tourist developments and, most importantly, some of Australia's best beaches. The Sunshine Coast is often compared to the Gold Coast, but it's nowhere near as developed or hectic, with only a couple of pockets of high-rises and long strips of beachfront reserve. That's not to say things aren't going ahead on the Sunshine Coast; population growth runs about 10% annually and each summer hordes of holidaying Australians descend on the beaches. This stretch of coast is also the most northerly on the east coast open to the ocean, and, being so far north, it's T-shirt and shorts weather year-round.

The coastal resort towns of Caloundra, Mooloolaba, Maroochydore, and Coolum form a continuous string of development, while at the north end of the Sunshine Coast Noosa Heads forms the jewel in the crown; a small community with a beautiful national park on the doorstep and chic cafés, stylish boutiques, and luxurious accommodations.

BRISBANE TO CALOUNDRA

Caboolture

This town of 12,000, 40 km north of Brisbane, is a service town for a rich dairy industry. The town's most interesting feature is **Caboolture Historical Village,** a couple of km north of town on the old highway, tel. (07) 5495-4581. Around 70 historic buildings collected from around south-eastern Queensland have been relocated to the site, in a re-creation of a bush town. It's open daily 9:30 a.m.-3:30 p.m. and admission is $6 pp.

Bribie Island

Where the access road to Caboolture spurs west off Hwy. 1, another heads east to Bribie Island, linked to the mainland by a bridge spanning Pumicestone Passage. The island is flat and fairly uninspiring, with most of its northern end protected by a national park. The only develop-

ment is a smattering of fishing and holiday towns at its southern end, including the town of **Bongaree,** just south of the bridge. Across the island at **Woorim** is a long sandy beach and good camping at **Bribie Island Caravan Park,** tel. (07) 3408-1134, across from the beach. Sites are $16-18 per night and cabins $34-70. Budget-Inexpensive.

Glass House Mountains

This group of bizarrely shaped volcanic peaks dominates the western horizon north of Caboolture. Thirteen in total, the four largest are protected by small national parks. A 22-km forest drive, beginning at Beerburrum and ending at the township of Glass House Mountains, provides access to the base of each, as well as a lookout from where each peak can be recognized from a

The Glass House Mountains are best appreciated from the 22-km forest drive through their midst.

TO MARYBOROUGH

BRUCE HWY.

SUNSHINE COAST

GYMPIE

AMAMOOR

POMONA

COOROY

EUMUNDI

YANDINA

NAMBOUR

MAPLETON
KONDALILLA N.P.
FLAXTON
BLACKALL RANGE
MONTVILLE

MALENY

CONONDALE RANGE

TO KINGAROY

AUSTRALIA ZOO
BEERWAH

GLASS HOUSE MOUNTAINS
MT. COONOWRIN
MT. BEERWAH ▲
MT. TIBROGARGAN ▲
MT. BEERBURRUM ▲

MT. COOCHIN
MT. NGUNGUN
GLASS HOUSE MOUNTAINS

BEERBURRUM

TO BRISBANE

CABOOLTURE
HISTORICAL VILLAGE ■

CABOOLTURE

FRASER ISLAND

TIN CAN INLET

TIN CAN BAY

WIDE BAY

RAINBOW SHORES
• RAINBOW BEACH

DOUBLE ISLAND POINT

POONA LAKE

COOLOOLA NATIONAL PARK

NOOSA RIVER

FRESHWATER LAKE

COOLOOLA WAY

LAKE COOTHARABA

COOLOOLA BEACH

LAGUNA BAY

NOOSA HEADS
■ NOOSA N.P.

TEWANTIN
NOOSAVILLE

SUNRISE BEACH

COOLUM

MT. COOLUM (208 m) ▲
✕ SUNSHINE COAST AIRPORT

● NOVOTEL TWIN WATERS RESORT

SUNSHINE COAST MOTORWAY

BIG PINEAPPLE

MOOLOOLA RIVER

MAROOCHYDORE
MOOLOOLABA

DICKY BEACH

CALOUNDRA

LANDSBOROUGH

BULCOCK BEACH

GOLDEN BEACH

PUMICESTONE PASSAGE

BRIBIE ISLAND

BONGAREE

WOORIM

SOUTH PACIFIC OCEAN

N
Moon

0   10 km

© AVALON TRAVEL PUBLISHING

panoramic photo. The easiest peak to ascend is **Mt. Ngungun** (253 meters); allow one hour each way. **Mt. Beerburrum, Mt. Beerwah,** and **Mt. Coonowrin** are for rock climbers only. None of the four parks has camping, and only Mt. Tibrogargan National Park has picnic areas.

Lying in the northern shadow of the mountains is the **Australia Zoo,** just north of Beerwah, tel. (07) 5494-1134, a wildlife park best known for its creator, the **Crocodile Hunter,** Steve Irwin, who can be seen wrestling crocodiles and playing with deadly snakes on the Discovery Channel's Animal Planet. Steve and his wife, Terri, have amassed a large collection of unique Australian fauna, including crocodiles (fed daily at 1:30 p.m.), snakes, kangaroos, and koalas. The park is also home to Harriet, a massive Galapagos turtle. Admission is adult $12, child $6. Open daily 8:30 a.m.-4 p.m. Steve's has become so famous that he now has his own website: www.crocodilehunter.com.

CALOUNDRA

While other Sunshine Coast towns have developed on long stretches of sand, Caloundra (pop. 30,000) sprawls over a rocky headland and extends south along the Pumicestone Passage. Within the passage are two safe swimming beaches, Bulcock and Golden, protected from ocean swells by Bribie Island. These safe beaches make Caloundra an ideal destination for families and for those keen on water sports such as fishing, windsurfing, sailing, and swimming. Along Golden Beach, various operators rent water sport equipment during summer months. Right near downtown, at the mouth of the passage, a treed reserve overlooks a wide sandy bank with calm swimming on one side and the roar of the ocean on the other. Aside from the beaches, Caloundra's main attraction is **Queensland Air Museum,** at the airport on the main road into town. About 20 aircraft are on display, along with other aviation relics. It's open Wednesday, Saturday, and Sunday 10 a.m.-4 p.m., tel. (07) 5492-5930. Admission is $4.

Accommodation in Caloundra is geared mainly to holidaying families with six caravan parks and dozens of self-contained apartments available. **Rolling Surf Resort,** 10 Levuka Ave., tel.

(07) 5491-1300, overlooking all the best beaches, has rooms from $65 s or d, $75 with kitchens. Moderate. **Caloundra Holiday Resort,** Dicky Beach, tel. (07) 5491-3342, has sites for $16-26 and small motel-style units for $48. Budget-Inexpensive.

MOOLOOLABA

This resort town is one of the Sunshine Coast's most pleasant places, with a long stretch of parkland separating a strip of outdoor cafés, restaurants, and boutiques from a glorious beach of golden sand that curves southward from a rocky headland to the mouth of the Mooloola River. The river's course has been much changed through residential canal developments but near its mouth is a busy harbor, filled with a colorful collection of pleasure craft and fishing trawlers.

UnderWater World

This three-story complex, incorporating the world's largest oceanarium, is the Sunshine Coast's major commercial attraction. The main aquarium features species from the South Pacific. Other features are: aquariums re-creating river, reef, and swamp ecosystems; a marine mammal cove where seal shows take place five times daily; the chance to dive with sharks ($55 for certified divers); the Freshwater Billabong with crocodiles, barramundi, and the unique amphibious Queensland lungfish; a seashore display; and audiovisuals on life underwater. The center is open daily 9 a.m.-6 p.m. Admission is adult $18, child $10. It's on Parkyn Parade, tel. (07) 5444-8488. Shuttle buses depart daily from Noosa (9 a.m.) and other points along the way for UnderWater World; $12 roundtrip.

UnderWater World is part of **The Wharf,** a complex of cafés, restaurants, and souvenir shops spread along the harbor. Also on The Wharf are booking agents for a variety of river cruises, including a one-hour Canal Cruise for $9; call (07) 5444-7477 for bookings, diving trips, and jet skiing, as well as sea kayak rentals.

Practicalities

Central to UnderWater World, the beach, and shops is **River Esplanade Motel,** 73 Brisbane Rd., tel. (07) 5444-3855 or (1800) 80-7399, where rooms are $44 s, $52 d. Inexpensive. Closer to the beach, and with self-contained rooms, is **Sandcastles,** corner Parkyn Parade and River Esplanade, tel. (07) 5478-0666 or (1800) 80-1649. Each modern unit has a kitchen, laundry, separate living area, and balcony. Rates are $125-170 depending on the view. **Nautilus Mooloolaba,** River Esplanade, tel. (5444) 3877, is a similar setup. The rooms have only basic cooking facilities but are larger and more modern, and each has a spa bath and private balcony. This place also features a magnificent lagoon-style pool, complete with a waterfall and poolside café; rates range $125-180 s or d. Premium. Also central is **Maroochy Beach Park,** tel. (07) 5444-1201; unpowered sites are $13, powered sites $16.50. Budget.

For fresh fish and a good serving of chips, head out along Parkyn Parade beyond Under-Water World to **Fisheries on the Spit** for fresh seafood to eat in or take out. At UnderWater World itself and built over the marina is **Down the Hatch Café.** Shaped like a submarine, this brightly colored café provides a casual atmosphere and inexpensive dining. Under the Peninsula Apartments on Brisbane Rd. and opposite the beach, the **Coffee Club,** open early, is a good place for people-watching. On the corner of Brisbane Rd. and the Esplanade is **Montezuma's,** tel. (07) 5444-8444, a large Mexican restaurant where the food is always fresh and main dishes range $12-16; open daily for lunch and dinner.

A small **information booth** outside the Westpac Bank on the Esplanade operates daily 9 a.m.-5 p.m.

MAROOCHYDORE

The coastal strip between Mooloolaba and Maroochydore features some great beaches and surf breaks, but is also very developed. Maroochydore (pop. 28,000), spread around the braided mouth of the Maroochy River, is the commercial center of the Sunshine Coast. Downtown is an ugly urban sprawl, but the beach is gorgeous. **Cotton Tree Park,** on a sandy spit of land at the end of Alexandra Parade, is an undeveloped area of cotton trees and casuarinas—the perfect place for a picnic.

Accommodations and Food
Maroochydore has a good beachfront caravan park and a number of backpacker hostels, but for other types of accommodations you're better off heading north to Coolum or Noosa or south to Mooloolaba. If you want to stay in town, try **Blue Waters Motel,** 64 6th Ave., tel. (07) 5443-6700, close to the beach and with a pool. Outside holiday periods rooms are $60 s, $65 d. Moderate. On the north side of the river is **Novotel Twin Waters Resort,** a sprawling complex set around a 10-hectare lagoon lined with man-made beaches. The resort also boasts one of Australia's best golf courses (call 07-5448-8011 for tee times), free water sports, and an elevated restaurant in the middle of the lagoon. Rooms are large and of a high standard, many with kitchenettes and a spa; rates start at $170 s or d. For bookings call (07) 5448-8000 or (1800) 64-2244. Luxury.

Cotton Tree Beachouse, 15 Esplanade, tel. (07) 5443-1755, enjoys a great location across the road from the river and within 10 minutes walk of both the beach and downtown Maroochydore. Guests have free use of surfing equipment, and there's a large barbecue area, tropical courtyard, and Internet service. Dorm beds are $16, singles $32, and doubles $34. Budget.

Both the **Sea Breeze Caravan Park,** Melrose Parade, tel. (07) 5443-1167, right behind the Tourist Information Centre and backing onto the beach, and **Cotton Tree Caravan Park,** Esplanade, tel. (07) 5443-1253, on the riverfront, have unpowered sites for $13 and powered sites for $15 with all the usual facilities. Neither has on-site vans or cabins. Budget.

Most of the Sunshine Coast's fast-food outlets lie along Maroochydore's main drag; the **Maroochydore Hotel/Motel,** Duporth Ave., serves hearty lunches for $4-6 and dinners $8-11.

Transportation, Services, and Information
Travelers flying to the Sunshine Coast land at **Sunshine Coast Airport,** eight km north of Maroochydore. The airport is served by **Sunstate,** tel. (13) 1313, from Brisbane. From the airport, **Airport Bus Service,** tel. (07) 5443-3678, heads south ($5 to Maroochydore), but if you're staying at a resort transfers should be complimentary.

Suncoast Pacific, tel. (07) 3236-1901, operates about 10 buses daily between Brisbane Transit Centre and Maroochydore ($19 one-way), continuing to Noosa while **Sun-air,** tel. (07) 5478-2811, links Brisbane Airport to the Sunshine Coast.

Maroochy Information Centre is on the corner of Aerodrome Rd. and 6th Ave., right near the beach, tel. (07) 5479-1566. Hours are Mon.-Sat. 9 a.m.-4:30 p.m.

COOLUM

Coolum is usually bypassed for better-known Noosa to the north, but the long beach here is as good as any on the Sunshine Coast. The beach is screened from the main road through Coolum by coastal heath, but many unsealed roads provide access to the ocean.

At the northern end of Coolum an unsealed road spurs east to Stumers Creek, where a picnic and camping area sits alongside a shallow lagoon just a stone's throw from the beach. The western skyline is dominated by 208-meter **Mt. Coolum,** rising gently from the north to a vertical southern face.

Accommodations

Coolum Dreams, 28 Warran Rd., tel. (07) 5446-3868, is one of the Sunshine Coast's few bed and breakfasts. Within walking distance of the beach and Hyatt Regency (see below), it offers clean and comfortable rooms with a large outdoor area and a level of service not available at resort-style accommodations. Rates of $60 s, $90 d include a continental or cooked breakfast. Moderate.

Set on 140 hectares opposite Coolum Dreams, the **Hyatt Regency,** tel. (07) 5446-1234 or (1800) 22-2188, is a five-star hostelry modeled on North American health spa resorts. Along with one of Australia's top golf courses, sporting facilities include nine tennis courts, squash courts, a lap pool, aerobics classes, and a jogging track. And while physical activities are promoted, so is relaxation, as guests may take advantage of the pool, jacuzzis, sauna, and a myriad of beauty treatments. Rates start at $240 s or d, but the many package deals offer better prices. Luxury.

NOOSA

At the north end of the Sunshine Coast and 150 km from Brisbane is a conglomeration of communities known collectively as Noosa. Best known of these is **Noosa Heads,** which has grown from a 1960s surfing hangout to one of Australia's most stylish resort towns. Yet Noosa manages to offer something for everyone—hiking in an adjacent national park, fishing and boating in a maze of channels around the mouth of the Noosa River, surfing around the headland, swimming and sunbaking at a protected beach, shopping at fashionable boutiques, and dining at various restaurants.

Noosa Heads lies along a short north-facing beach, making it one of only two places along the east coast where resort guests and residents alike have views over a beautiful beach and the ocean while enjoying direct sunshine all day long (the other spot is Wategos Beach, Byron Bay). Sandwiched between this beach, the Noosa River, and a national park, future development is curtailed, forming an exclusive beachfront enclave along just one short street.

Noosa National Park

While tourist and residential development has destroyed most of southeast Queensland's original coastal habitat, an area of 442 hectares around Noosa Heads remains undisturbed, protected as a national park since 1879. It's a beautiful stretch of coast, punctuated by short beaches flanked by rocky headlands and accessed along short hiking trails leading through forests of eucalypt, open meadows, and areas of coastal heath. The popular **Coastal Track** (2.7 km one-way) begins at the end of Park Rd., closely following the coast past Tea Tree Bay, Dolphin Point, and Granite Bay, ending at Hells Gate. It's possible to return along **Tanglewood Track** through an area of rainforest 4.2 km back to the carpark. The park's main entrance is one km east of Noosa Heads along Park Road. A boardwalk also links town to the park. The **Park Information Centre,** at the end of Park Rd., tel. (07) 5447-3243, is open daily 9 a.m.-5 p.m.

From the south, a trail leads into the park from Parkedge Road. For an overview of the entire

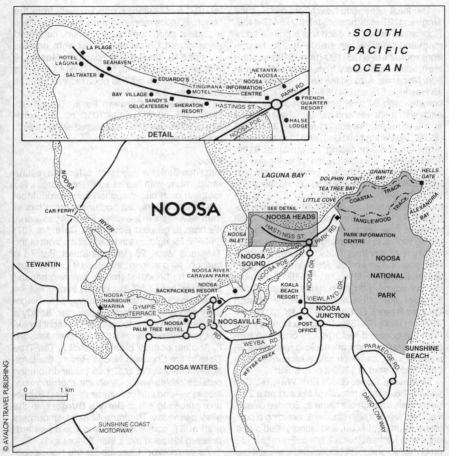

area, head to the lookout at the end of Viewland Dr. (off Noosa Drive).

Recreation

Swimming, surfing, fishing, and hiking—all the best things at Noosa—are free, but there are also a lot of activities you can pay for. The most worthwhile of these is a cruise on the Noosa River with **Everglades Waterbus Co.,** tel. (07) 5447-1838 or (1800) 68-8045. Cruises depart from various Noosa locations, including from the pontoon at the Sheraton. They last four hours and cost $45

pp. **Kingfisher Boat Hire,** tel. (07) 5449-9353, rents boats, kayaks, and jet skis from Noosa Harbour at Tewantin. **Noosa Sea Sports,** in Noosa Sound Shopping Centre, tel. (07) 5447-3426, rents surfboards and fishing gear.

Accommodations

Hastings Street is *the* place to stay in Noosa, but, naturally, it's not the cheapest and demand for rooms is particularly high throughout summer. During this period, prices also rise dramatically, up to 100% in some cases.

The least expensive beachfront motel is the **Tingirana,** 25 Hastings St., tel. (07) 5447-4455. Rooms are basic, but each has a private bathroom and small kitchen area. Rates for beachfront rooms are $135-160 (from $180 in summer), while those away from the beach start at $80. Moderate. Also on the beach is **Seahaven,** 13 Hastings St., tel. (07) 5447-3422, a modern complex with 66 one- and two-bedroom units, each with a kitchen and balcony. Rates for the smallest rooms (sleeping four) are $160-190 ($220-270 during holidays), and they also have a few small rooms facing the street for $100. The two-bedroom penthouses (sleeping six) are $350 per night and have a private rooftop garden. Luxury. **Netanya Noosa,** 75 Hastings St., tel. (07) 5447-4722 or (1800) 07-2072, is the most luxurious absolute-beachfront accommodation. As well as enjoying magnificent ocean views, its three levels are tiered, allowing each of the 48 rooms to have a large balcony bathed in sunshine all day long. It also features a beachfront pool, indoor and outdoor spas, and a great little restaurant. Rates start at $190 s or d, but rise considerably during summer. Luxury. Along the river side of Hastings St. lies the **French Quarter Resort,** 62 Hastings St., tel. (07) 5430-7100 or (1800) 67-4599. Still just a stone's throw from the ocean, it features 119 one- and two-bedroom suites, most overlooking a heated saltwater lagoon, and each with a kitchen and spa bath. Rates start at $220 s or d. Luxury.

Castaway Cove, David Low Way, tel. (07) 5447-3488, is six km south of Noosa and a 200-meter walk through bushland to Sunrise Beach. Facilities are of a high standard, including a pool, tennis court, barbecue, and laundry; $90 s or d; units with kitchenettes are $125. Premium. Out on Gympie Terrace, in Noosaville, are a string of cheaper motels; try the **Noosa Palm Tree Motel,** 233 Gympie Terrace, tel. (07) 5449-7311, for $55 s, $70 d. Moderate.

Backpackers have a few choices. Closest to Noosa Heads is the YHA-affiliated **Halse Lodge,** 2 Halse Lane, tel. (07) 5447-3377, a rambling old guesthouse that has been taking in travelers since the 1880s. Just 200 meters from the beach, the location is almost perfect. It features all the usual facilities, including a bar and restaurant; dorm beds are $15 pp, doubles $40. **Koala Beach Resort,** 44 Noosa Dr., Noosa Junction,

tel. (07) 5447-3355, a one-km walk from the beach, is much more of a party place. Facilities include a pool, communal kitchen, café, and bikes for rent. Dorms are $15 per night, doubles start at $42. **Noosa Backpackers Resort,** 9 William St. Munna Pt., tel. (07) 5449-8151, is farther from town but has good facilities. Dorms are $15 pp, doubles $32.

Noosa River Caravan Park, Russell St., Noosaville, tel. (07) 5449-7050, has an excellent riverfront location; unpowered sites are $16, powered sites $19.

Food

Hastings Street is lined with cafés and restaurants, many with tables scattered across the footpath or in sun-drenched courtyards. Most are casual affairs, but prices are often higher than elsewhere in the state. For position alone, it's hard to go past **Eduardo's Cafe,** tel. (07) 5447-5875, right on the beach at the front of the Tingirana Motel, 25 Hastings Street. Bathed in sunlight all day long, this casual café is most popular for breakfast (mouth-watering banana pancakes are $7.50), but is busy throughout the day, with dinner mains averaging $16. Diagonally opposite the information center, **Sandy's Delicatessen** is a good choice for a light breakfast; healthy muffins are $1.50 and breakfasts $4-8. Another popular breakfast spot is **Tea Tree Cafe** in the Sheraton Noosa Resort; the large hot and cold buffet is $21.95 pp, and from the outside tables you'll catch the morning sun. Noosa's—and one of Australia's—least expensive places to eat is **Betty's Burgers,** in the alley below the Tingirana Motel; hamburgers start at $1, coffee is free, and you'd be hard-pressed to spend more than $5 for lunch.

As you'd expect, seafood is the Noosa specialty. The least expensive way to savor the freshest of fresh is at **Noosa Junction Seafood Market,** corner of Cooyar St. and Lanyana Way, tel. (07) 5449-2655. On offer is a great selection of hot and cold seafood to go, such as a single serving of fish, chips, calamari, and salad for $8 or a platter of crab, prawns, oysters, and mussels for two for $40. For an extra $3 per order, they'll deliver it to your hotel room. For great takeout fish and chips right in downtown Noosa, head to **Saltwater,** at 8 Hastings St., tel. (07) 5447-2234. Upstairs is al fresco dining in a casual atmosphere and some of the most creative seafood dishes to be found in Queensland. Mains start at a reasonable $16. For a break from seafood, try the pasta or wood-fired oven pizza at **Cafe Vespa,** Bay Village, Hastings St., tel. (07) 5447-2473. **La Plage,** 5 Hastings St., tel. (07) 5447-3308, has a Mediterranean feel and features French cuisine using local seafood. Main meals are $17.50-25.

Over in Noosaville and right on the river is **Aquabar Café,** 271 Gympie Terrace, tel. (07) 5474-4888, decorated in typical "Noosa style"— simply furnished with bright pastel colors. The menu features mostly seafood and a few vegetarian dishes. Farther out, **The Jetty** is a long-time Noosa favorite. Overlooking the Noosa River, it features an intimate atmosphere and an innovative seafood menu. It is at Boreen Point, 28 km from Noosa, tel. (07) 5485-3167, but getting there is made easy with the companies that cruise regularly upriver, or call for complimentary transfers.

Transportation, Services, and Information
From Brisbane Airport, **Sun-air,** tel. (07) 5478-2811, and **Coachtrans,** tel. (07) 3236-1000, run regular bus services to Noosa. **Tewantin Bus Service,** tel. (07) 5449-7422, runs frequently between the communities of Noosa and Tewantin and Maroochydore. All major car-rental firms have outlets in Noosa. Contact **Sunshine 4WD Hire,** tel. (07) 5447-3702, for four-wheel drives ($100-150 per day) or

Sierra Mountain Bike Hire, tel. (07) 5474-8277, for bikes ($15 per day).

The small **Noosa Information Centre,** tel. (07) 5447-4988, is at the Hastings St. roundabout; open daily 9 a.m.-5 p.m.

SUNSHINE COAST HINTERLAND

Tropical fruit farms and endless fields of sugarcane dominate the part of the Sunshine Coast hinterland where the Bruce Highway runs through, but it is west of the highway in the Blackall Range where the scenery is most spectacular.

South of Nambour, along the Bruce Highway, are a number of commercial attractions including the **Big Pineapple,** part of a small theme park where you can visit a pineapple plantation and macadamia nut farm, ride a sugarcane train, and take a boat trip through the Harvest Boat Ride. Admission is free, but it's $15.50 for an all-day ride pass. It's six km south of Nambour, tel. (07) 5442-1333. North of Nambour, in Yandina, drop by the **Ginger Factory,** tel. (07) 5446-7096, the largest such factory in the world. Visitors watch a video, view work areas, and get another opportunity for a ride on a sugarcane train; $4.

Blackall Range and Montville
The Blackall Range rises dramatically west of the Bruce Highway; part of an ancient lava flow, its highest ridge is traversed by a scenic road that passes through the villages of **Maleny, Montville,**

Montville's relaxed atmosphere and many arts and crafts shops make the town a pleasant detour.

Flaxton, and **Mapleton.** The 50-km route through these villages begins at Landsborough, west of Caloundra, and ends in Nambour.

Styled on an English village, Montville is the most developed of the hinterland towns, with an 800-meter-long strip of tearooms, restaurants, and craft shops. Although a couple of artisans have lived in the town for years, it's only recently that tourism has taken off. Literally dozens of potters, sculptors, glassblowers, weavers, and other artists call Montville home. Also in the village are tearooms, cafés, restaurants, and numerous country-style accommodations.

Montville Mountain Inn, tel. (07) 5442-9499 or (1800) 67-1269, is a Tudor-style accommodation in the middle of all the action. Rooms are large, many have views, and there's also a pool and tennis court for guest use. Rates are $55 s, $70 d. Moderate. **Montville Country Cabins,** four km west of the village along Western Ave., tel. (07) 5442-9484, comprises seven private and luxuriously appointed self-contained cabins overlooking a small pond. Adding to the appeal is an adjoining national park. The nightly charge is $110-165 s or d. Expensive.

Just north of Montville is the turnoff to 353-hectare **Kondalilla National Park,** a remnant of rainforest that once covered the entire Blackall Range. The park's highlight is Kondalilla Falls. Reach a lookout above the falls along a 1.2-km trail from the picnic area. To get a different perspective of the falls, continue one km from the lookout to the valley floor.

Eumundi

Synonymous with a long-running market day, the picturesque village of Eumundi lies beside the Bruce Hwy. between Nambour and Gympie. Each Saturday between 6:30 a.m. and 2 p.m. the main street comes alive with local residents selling fresh fruit and vegetables, homemade jams, cooked snacks, and a wide variety of arts and crafts—more than 300 stalls in all. **Sun-air,** tel. (07) 5478-2811, provides transfers from Noosa.

NORTH FROM NOOSA

The Bruce Highway stays well inland, passing through the historic gold-mining town of Gympie. The coast is 60 km east of Gympie, but a detour to what is known as the Cooloola Coast, much of it protected by Cooloola National Park, is worthwhile for the colorful sand dunes and lack of crowds.

Gympie

In 1867 Queensland was on the verge of bankruptcy, so when James Nash found gold on the Mary River, the government took more than a passing interest. In the first few years, 15,000 diggers converged on the area. More than four million ounces were taken from the goldfields before operations closed in 1923. Today Gympie (pop. 10,900) is a popular stop on the long trek north, and it has all the services of a highway town.

The best place to get a feeling for the town's beginnings is at **Gympie Historical Museum,** through a park behind the information center, tel. (07) 5482-3995. A number of buildings have been moved to the disused mining site, as has rail rolling stock, horse-drawn buggies, and other pioneer relics. The museum is open daily 9 a.m.-4:30 p.m. and admission is $4. Adjacent to the museum is **Deep Creek Gold Fossicking Area,** but you need a fossicking license ($5.10), available from the Tourist Information Centre, to pan for gold. At the town's northern outskirts is **Woodworks,** tel. (07) 5483-7691, a forestry and timber museum that re-creates another local industry. The highlight is a working replica of a steam-driven sawmill. Admission is $3. Open weekdays 9 a.m.-4 p.m.

Tamworth may be Australia's country music capital, but Gympie's **Country Music Muster** is Australia's biggest single country concert, attracting about 30,000 fans to the state forest west of Amamoor for three days of music on the last weekend of August. (Get current information from the Tourist Information Centre.)

Great Eastern Motor Inn, 27 Geordie Rd., tel. (07) 5482-7288 or (1800) 07-2093, south of town opposite the Tourist Information Centre, has large modern rooms for $68 s, $75 d. Moderate. Campers should head to **Gympie Caravan Park,** west of the highway at 1 Jane St., tel. (07) 5483-6800, which has sites for $15-19, bunk beds for $12 pp, and cottages for $50 s or d. Budget-Inexpensive.

The **Tourist Information Centre** is adjacent to the fossicking area south of Gympie, tel. (07)

5482-5444. In the same building is a **Department of Environment** office, tel. (07) 5482-4189, good for Fraser Island information and permits. Both offices are open daily 8:30 a.m.-3:30 p.m.

Tin Can Bay

This small fishing town of 1,700, 45 km northwest of Gympie, is spread along a low-lying headland jutting into a maze of channels that make up the protected waters of Tin Can Inlet. Development has taken its toll on the surrounding landscape, with the road into town passing through cleared subdivisions and pine plantations, but once in the town, it won't take long to appreciate the slower pace of life. Commercial fishing is important to the local economy, but the sleepy village is also a popular holiday spot. Follow the main road through town to the end of the headland where a sprawling parking lot takes prime position on the point. Semi-tame dolphins swim into the shallows here on a regular basis; although they don't run to a schedule, staff at the little kiosk can advise as to what their recent patterns have been. **Luxury Afloat** operates yacht and houseboat rentals from the marina. Basic seafaring skills are required for rentals, but the area has nothing like those nasty reefs farther north, and you can explore hundreds of waterways and secluded sandy beaches. Rates start at $175 per day for a 10-meter yacht, rising considerably during holiday periods. For details call (07) 5486-4864.

Sandcastle Motel, Tin Can Bay Rd., tel. (07) 5486-4555, has rooms for $48 s, $58 d. Inexpensive. **Ace Caravan Park,** Esplanade, tel. (07) 5486-4152, is central and has sites for $14 and on-site vans for $28, but you'll need advance reservations in holiday periods. Budget. Overlooking the marina complex on Oyster Parade is **Marina Restaurant,** tel. (07) 5486-4400, a casual place with inside and outside tables and a menu featuring local seafood.

Rainbow Beach

As the crow flies, Rainbow Beach is just eight km east of Tin Can Bay, but by road it's closer to 40 km. The village overlooks the long sandy beach of Wide Bay, which extends to Inskip Point, southern gateway to Fraser Island (the town is jammed with four-wheel drive enthusiasts year-round). The beach in front of town is generally safe for swimming, but much of the best scenery is in Cooloola National Park (see below).

Rainbow Beach Hotel/Motel, tel. (07) 5486-3125, right on the beach, has rooms of a reasonable standard for $38 s, $49 d. Inexpensive. More upmarket, but worth every dollar, is delightful **Rainbow Shores,** tel. (07) 5486-3233, north of town in a forest of eucalypts and with a deserted sandy beach just meters away. Each two-story unit is fully self-contained, with views extending across the beach and to Point Danger as well as back to the landscaped pool area. Rates start at $80 per night for a one-bedroom beach house, rising to $150 for a three-bedroom unit. Moderate. **Rainbow Beach Holiday Village,** just across the road from the main beach, tel. (07) 5486-3222, has sites for $14-16, on-site vans for $25-32, and well-equipped units for $45-65; book in advance for the best sites. Budget-Inexpensive.

The town has a tavern, supermarket, petrol station, a couple of bakeries, and a good fish and chips shop. The **Tourist Information Centre** is on the south side of town, tel. (07) 5486-3227.

Cooloola National Park

As wind and rain erode the mountain ranges of northern New South Wales, sediment washes down rivers into the ocean. Prevailing winds and wave action have pushed masses of sand northward, creating a long stretch of sandy coastline and Fraser Island to the north. Over thousands of years, sand has blown off the beach and become entangled in the banksia and she-oak forests along the coast. This has built up, covering whole forests and forming sand dunes more than 200 meters high. One of the park's most famous features is its multi-colored sand, which lines many stretches of the coast. A different environment is found in the south of the park, along the Noosa River, where paperbarks, bloodwoods, and low-lying heaths and ferns thrive.

See the most colorful dunes along a two-km walk on the beach from Rainbow Beach. From the dunes, it's possible to continue to **Double Island Point** (10 km one-way), but check tides before setting out. Five km south of Rainbow

Beach, an unsealed track leads into the park, ending at a picnic area from where it's a short walk to **Poona Lake,** a body of trapped rainwater tinted brown by tea tree extractions. Cooloola Way is an unsealed route linking Rainbow Beach Rd. to Pomona, just off the Bruce Hwy. north of Cooroy. Off this road are more unsealed roads, leading to the Noosa River and Lake Cootharaba.

The **Park Information Centre** is in Rainbow Beach, tel. (07) 5486-3160; open daily 5:30 a.m.-4:30 p.m.

SUNSHINE COAST TO GLADSTONE

While tourist and residential development has blighted much of Queensland's beautiful coastline, development between the Sunshine Coast and Gladstone is contained in only a couple of areas, and the hinterland is scattered with many thousands of hectares of sugarcane.

The region's main tourist center is Hervey Bay, Australia's whalewatching capital and gateway to magnificent Fraser Island, the world's largest sand island and a paradise for nature lovers and four-wheel drive enthusiasts. The other main population center between the Sunshine Coast and Gladstone is Bundaberg, more famous for its rum distillery than for the thousands of turtles that nest on a nearby beach.

Maryborough

This historic city of 21,500 lies a few km inland and halfway between Gympie and Bundaberg. First settled in the 1840s as a port for wool and timber transportation, the Mary River has been the city's lifeblood for more than 150 years, but can also be its nemesis. In early 1999, heavy rainfall saw the river burst its banks and rise 15 meters above its normal level, flooding the city's low-lying areas. Many buildings from its early era remain, and along with tree-lined streets and Queenslanders, the city has a real sense of country charm. Many impressive historic buildings remain on Wharf St., including restored hotels, a customs house, post office, and court-

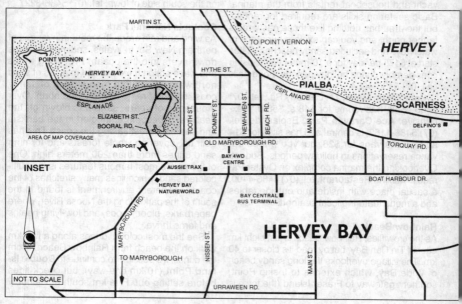

house. Also on Wharf St. is **Queens Park** (the perfect place for a picnic), sloping toward the river. **Brennan & Geraghty's Store,** on Lennox St., has operated as a general store for more than 100 years. Traffic down the main street is diverted every Thursday 8 a.m.-2 p.m. for the **Marlborough Heritage Market,** and in early April is **Heritage Week.**

Many historic downtown hotels, including the **Criterion,** tel. (07) 4121-3043, offer accommodation, or stay in one of the motels strung out along Ferry St., the main route into town from the south. Also on Ferry St. is **Wallace Caravan Park,** tel. (07) 4121-3970; sites are $9-14, cabins are from $28. Budget.

The **Tourist Information Centre** is at 30 Ferry St., tel. (07) 4121-4111; open daily 9 a.m.-5 p.m.

HERVEY BAY

Until a few years ago, the only reason to detour from the main highway to Hervey Bay (HA-vee Bay) was to hop aboard a ferry out to Fraser Island, but the development of a whalewatching in-

dustry has seen things change quickly. Until the mid-1980s, the shoreline of Hervey Bay was dotted with sleepy settlements off the main tourist route, seemingly a million miles from the hustle and bustle of other east coast resort towns. But in the last decade, shivering southerners discovered Hervey Bay's ideal climate, low land prices, and laid-back atmosphere. What were once five separate towns along the bay are now one long strip of development boasting a population of more than 30,000.

It's difficult to get lost in Hervey Bay. The main road into town from the Bruce Highway ends at **Pialba,** from where the Esplanade heads northwest to the town of **Point Vernon** and east to **Scarness, Torquay,** and **Urangan.** The marina at Urangan is the departure point for whale-watching day trips and foot passengers heading to Fraser Island.

Whalewatching
Between early August and mid-October migrating humpback whales rest in the calm and shallow waters of Platypus Bay, on the west coast of Fraser Island (a one- to two-hour boat trip from

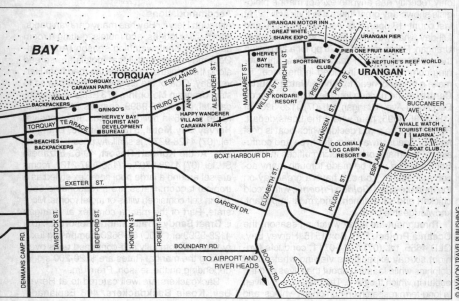

breeching humpback whale

Hervey Bay). During migration, whales can be seen at many places along the eastern seaboard, but the waters off Hervey Bay are the only place they stop for any length of time, allowing us humans the privilege of watching them frolic on their rest days. The whales have been following the same migration pattern for eons, but only recently has anyone except marine biologists shown any great interest in their activity. At last count, 18 operators were running half- and full-day whalewatching trips from the marina at Urangan. Prices range $60-70 pp for a full day on the water, with a lunch, tea and coffee, and running commentary all included in the price. To make a booking, head to **Whale Watch Tourist Centre,** at the parking lot side of the marina on Buccaneer Ave., Urangan, tel. (07) 4125-3287 or (1800) 35-8595, near where the boats depart. Here, they'll help you decide which boat is best for your needs, away from the hype and confusion of the many other booking offices in town. Bookings can also be made through many accommodations. You can have a great day on the medium-sized *Golden Phoenix,* with a cold chicken and salad lunch, and, most important, knowledgeable crew.

Throughout the whalewatching season, the **Oceania Project,** P.O. Box 1515, Hervey Bay, QLD 4655, tel. (07) 4124-0711, conducts five-night six-day expeditions viewing whales and dolphins while learning about their lives and the ocean in which they live. The project is involved in long-term research on humpback whales, and guests take an active role in collecting data. All meals and accommodation on board are included in the $1,050 pp price.

Other Sights
If whalewatching is called off for bad weather, the following commercial attractions may kill a few hours. **Hervey Bay Natureworld,** on the corner of Fairway Dr. and Maryborough Rd., Pialba, tel. (07) 4124-1733, features a variety of native fauna, including crocodiles fed daily at 11:30 a.m. The **Great White Shark Expo,** 533 Esplanade, tel. (07) 4128-9137, operated by Australian shark hunter Vic Hislop, features three frozen great white sharks, up to six meters long. Apart from justifying why they "need" to be killed, the display is interesting, in a gruesome kind of way. Admission is $10; open daily 8:30 a.m.-6 p.m. Farther along the Esplanade, toward the marina, is **Neptune's Reefworld,** tel. (07) 4128-9828, an aquarium with a living coral reef and variety of reef life, including a small shark; $8. Near the aquarium is **Urangan Pier,** extending more than one km into the bay. Originally built for loading sugar, it's now popular with anglers.

Accommodations
Although Hervey Bay has many caravan parks, backpacker lodges, and motels, getting a room during the whalewatching season (Aug.-mid-Oct.) may be difficult. Most motels are spread along the Esplanade, across the road from Hervey Bay. One of the least expensive places to stay, **Urangan Motor Inn,** 573 Esplanade, Urangan, tel. (07) 4128-9699, charges $40 s, $50 d, rising to $65 in holiday periods. Inexpensive. **Hervey Bay Motel,** 518 Esplanade, Urangan, tel. (07) 4128-9277, is similarly priced. Inexpensive. At the **Kondari Resort,** 49-63 Elizabeth St., tel. (07) 4128-9702 or (1800) 07-2131, rooms are set around a large pool complex styled as a tropical lagoon. Rates are a reasonable $60-100 in self-contained villas or motel rooms. Moderate. Part of the marina complex at Urangan is **Great Sandy Straits Marina Resort,** tel. (07) 4128-9999 or (1800) 65-3620, comprising luxury two-bedroom fully self-contained units overlooking the marina. Rates are $120-200 s or d, depending on the season. Premium.

Backpackers are well catered to at Hervey Bay. **Koala Backpackers,** 408 Esplanade,

Torquay, tel. (07) 4125-3601, is the largest hostel in town and has a real party atmosphere. Beds are clean and comfortable and there's also a pool. Dorm beds are $12-13 and double rooms $28. Budget. **Beaches Backpackers,** 195 Torquay Terrace, Scarness, tel. (07) 4124-1322, is away from the bay, but it has a pool, bar, and café, with good facilities; from $14 pp. Budget. YHA-affiliated **Colonial Log Cabin Resort,** Boat Harbour Dr., Urangan, tel. (07) 4125-1844, set among natural bushland, has all the usual facilities and is a short walk from the marina. Dorm beds are $13-16 and self-contained cabins are $50. Budget.

More than 20 caravan parks are scattered around the Hervey Bay area, but as always they cater to a wide range of budgets and not just to campers. The pick of the lot is **Happy Wanderer Village Caravan Park,** 105 Truro St., Torquay, tel. (07) 4125-1103, with the very best of facilities, including a good pool complex. Unpowered sites are $15, powered sites $18, and sites with private bathrooms $22. On-site vans are $32 and cabins and villas range $45-80. Budget-Inexpensive. **Torquay Caravan Park,** the Esplanade, tel. (07) 4125-1578, is right on the beach and central to the marina and shopping area of Pialba; unpowered sites $12, powered sites $15.

Food
Service clubs dish out the best bargain meals. **Hervey Bay Sportsmen's Club,** Pier St., Urangan, has lunch in the bistro from $4 and dinner from $5. They also offer a small buffet dinner for $10.45, Fri.-Sun. **Hervey Bay Boat Club,** Buccaneer Ave., has a similarly priced bistro and a restaurant with the best views in town. At the Great Sandy Straits Marina Resort in Urangan, **Mandy's** is a casual café built right over the water (for a unique dining experience, ask the staff to feed the resident fish below the verandah). On the marina proper, **The Deck,** tel. (07) 4125-1155, affords a similar panorama. Dinner is a seafood buffet, replacing a health-conscious lunch menu.

Back along The Esplanade in Torquay, at no. 449, **Gringo's,** tel. (07) 4125-1644, is a Mexican restaurant, with most main meals less than $10. The best of many seafood restaurants is **Delfino's,** 383 Esplanade, Scarness, tel. (07) 4124-

2466, open daily for dinner with live music on Friday and Saturday nights. For inexpensive Japanese, head to the **Black Dog Café,** 381 The Esplanade, tel. (07) 4124-3177.

Transportation, Services, and Information
Sunstate, tel. (13) 1313, flies daily between Brisbane and Hervey Bay. The airport is on Booral Rd., a $6 cab ride from most accommodations and the marina. The closest rail station to Hervey Bay is at Maryborough, from where a bus meets all arrivals. All major bus lines operate between Brisbane and Hervey Bay and also continue farther north. These buses terminate at **Bay Central Bus Terminal,** Central Ave., Pialba, tel. (07) 4124-4000. **Maryborough Hervey Bay Coaches,** tel. (07) 4121-3719, operates a regular service along the Esplanade (except Sunday). **Pier One Fruit Market,** 1 Pier St., Urangan, tel. (07) 4128-9471, rents bikes for $15 per day.

Hervey Bay Tourist & Development Bureau operates an information center at 10 Bideford St., Torquay, tel. (07) 4124-9609 or (1800) 81-1728. It's open Mon.-Fri. 9 a.m.-5 p.m. There are also many privately operated concerns, more interested in selling tours and tacky gifts than handing out information. One exception is **Whale Watch Tourist Centre,** behind the marina at Urangan, tel. (07) 4125-3287 or (1800) 35-8595. The office produces a handy reference sheet detailing all whalewatching trips and takes bookings for these trips, as well as for Fraser Island tours and permits. The office is open daily 6 a.m.-6 p.m.

FRASER ISLAND

Fraser Island, 120 km long, 22 km wide and totaling 165,000 hectares in area, is the largest sand island in the world. Apart from a few volcanic outcrops, the island is entirely composed of sand, with Seventy Five Mile Beach, on the island's east coast, one of the world's longest beaches. But the island is more than one great sand dune. Much of the 184,000 hectares is covered in vegetation, including many areas of rainforest and more than 25 species of mammals. More than one-third of the island is protected by **Great Sandy National Park,** and the entire island is listed with UNESCO as a World Heritage Area.

A network of sandy trails, accessible only by four-wheel drive, crisscross the island. If you don't have a four-wheel drive, you'll need to rent from the mainland or jump aboard one of the many tours offered. Access to the island is by barge (for vehicles) or fast catamaran, and once on the island a variety of accommodations are available or, for the self-sufficient, it's possible to camp.

History

When Europeans settled the Hervey Bay area in the 1850s, they herded the local Koori over to Fraser Island, using it as a kind of prison. For 30,000 years the island had been a seasonal hunting ground for the natives, who knew it as K'-gari, meaning paradise. But their paradise changed quickly and dramatically with the coming of white settlers in the 1800s. As loggers realized the island's potential, the Koori were herded

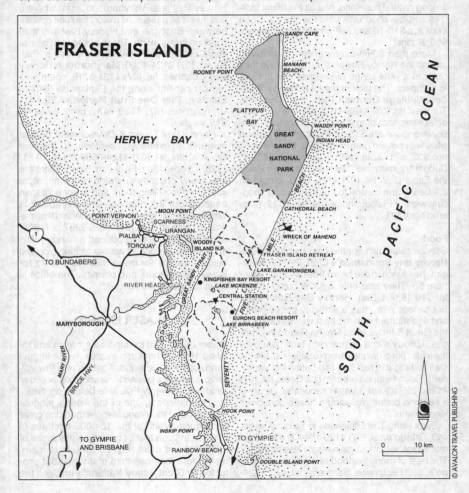

© AVALON TRAVEL PUBLISHING

THE NAMING OF FRASER ISLAND

Many ships were wrecked on Fraser Island after Captain Cook first sighted its east coast in 1770, but, ironically, the island is named for the survivor of a wreck that occurred off Mackay, 300 km north. The tragedy happened in 1836, when the brig *Stirling Castle* sank and the survivors drifted southward, coming ashore on the Great Sandy Island. Although cared for by Kooris, many died on the island before a rescue party managed to reach them two months later. One of the few survivors was the captain's wife, Eliza Fraser. On return to England, she told wild stories of torture and savagery by the island's natives, and, as a mark of her "bravery" in the situation, the name of the island was changed from Great Sandy to Fraser.

back to the mainland and by 1904 only a small mission of 200 remained.

Part of the island was put aside as a reserve in 1923, but the logging continued. In 1974 a license was granted for a large-scale rutile mining operation, provoking one of the most vicious battles between environmentalists and mining companies that Australia has ever seen. It ended in 1976 with a ban on mining.

In an ironic twist, the island's beauty, which environmentalists fought so hard to preserve, is now its own worst nightmare—attracting 350,000 visitors annually, up from around 10,000 in 1970.

Exploring the Island by Four-Wheel Drive

To get the most out of a trip to Fraser Island, you'll need to travel by four-wheel drive, whether in a vehicle rented from the mainland or on a tour. Four-wheel drives can be rented on the island and on the mainland. In Hervey Bay **Aussie Trax,** 56 Boat Harbour Dr., Pialba, tel. (07) 4124-4433, is among the cheapest, with ex-army Land Rovers for $80 per day (this is one of the few companies allowing one-day rentals). **Bay 4WD Centre,** 114 Boat Harbour Dr., tel. (07) 4128-2981, offers small four-wheel drives for $95 per day (seating two) and Land Cruisers (seating five) for $150. Rentals are also possible on the island, and although the cost of barging the vehicle

is saved, rates are higher. Small Suzukis at Kingfisher Bay Resort, tel. (07) 4120-3333, are $175 for a full day. For transportation details see below.

Driving on the island requires a permit ($30 per vehicle, or $40 if purchased on the island). These are available from the Department of Environment in Brisbane or Gympie, or the Whale Watch Tourist Centre, at the marina in Urangan, tel. (1800) 35-8595. The permit comes with an information packet, which is essential reading. Fraser Island beaches are registered as national highways, so all the normal road rules apply. Driving along the beach, while not particularly difficult, is fraught with hazards.

Exploring the Island on a Tour

For those without the necessary experience to drive off-road vehicles, a tour is the most convenient and enjoyable way to see the island. A great variety of day and overnight island tours operate from Hervey Bay. The tour offered by **Kingfisher Bay Resort,** tel. (07) 4125-5511, is typical and includes transport to the island, a four-wheel drive along part of Seventy Five Mile Beach, a visit to the wreck of *Maheno,* a peak at the colored sands of Cathedral Beach, and a swim in freshwater lakes. The $75 pp includes morning and afternoon tea and a buffet lunch. It departs Urangan daily at 8:30 a.m. and returns at 5 p.m. **Fraser Venture Day Tours,** tel. (07) 4125-4444, operates similar tours for a few dollars less. **Sun Safari Tours,** tel. (07) 5486-3154, operates from Rainbow Beach Caravan Park, departing daily at 8 a.m., and travels up Seventy Five Mile Beach as far north as Cathedral Beach. Lunch at Eurong Beach Resort is included in the price of adult $60, child $30.

Many overnight tours, operated by backpacker lodges in Hervey Bay, cost as little as $110 for three days (not including food and petrol). **Fraser Island Top Tours,** tel. (07) 4125-3933, offers an overnight tour inclusive of meals, transport, and accommodation at Fraser Island Retreat for $150 pp.

Accommodations

Kingfisher Bay Resort, the island's largest and most luxurious accommodation, has been designed to blend with the environment—using Australian timbers—and is spread over 65 hectares of natural bushland. Each of the spacious hotel rooms has a balcony, TV, and modern bathroom. Rates include resort activities, ranger-led hikes, and a hot buffet breakfast, while other options include whalewatching (in season), island tours ($65 pp), four-wheel drive rental ($175 per day), and scuba diving ($65, including equipment); $220-230 s or d. Package deals include many of the above options, such as accommodations, breakfast, dinner, and transfers for $130 pp. Luxury. The resort also features a general store, petrol supplies, bars, bakery, pizzeria, and three restaurants. Call (07) 4120-3333 or (1800) 07-2555 for bookings.

A couple of the old logging and sand-mining settlements have accommodations, including **Eurong Beach Resort,** tel. (07) 4125-4444, on the island's east coast. This absolute-beachfront property has two pools and a massive bistro-style restaurant. Old motel units are $70 s or d, while more modern self-contained units range $110-160. Moderate. Farther north at Happy Valley, **Fraser Island Retreat,** tel. (07) 4127-9144, is more luxurious. It features nine freestanding, self-contained lodges built of locally milled timber, as well as a pool, bar, and restaurant with indoor and outdoor dining, all just 100 meters from the beach; $140 s, $160 d. Luxury.

The island has six natural campgrounds (with drinking water, toilets, and showers), but camping is allowed just about anywhere on the island for $3.50 pp. **Cathedral Beach Resort,** tel. (07) 4127-9177, is a commercial operation with campsites for $20 and on-site vans for $50.

Getting to Fraser Island

For foot passengers, the easiest way to reach Fraser Island is aboard *Kingfisher 3,* a passenger catamaran, which jets between Urangan and Kingfisher Bay Resort for $30 pp roundtrip. This includes accommodation transfers to the departure point and guided walks at the resort. Kingfisher Bay also offers all-inclusive day trips, such as transfers and an extravagant seafood buffet Friday and Saturday night for a reasonable $38 pp. For bookings, call the resort at (07) 4125-5511.

From three points on the mainland, four vehicular ferries run to the island. Two depart three times daily from River Heads, south of Urangan. The *Fraser II,* tel. (07) 4125-5511, runs between this point and Kingfisher Bay Resort for $65 per vehicle roundtrip plus $5 pp, and the *Fraser Venture,* tel. (07) 4125-4444, crosses to Wanggoolba for $60 per vehicle roundtrip plus $5 pp. Another vehicular ferry is *Fraser Dawn,* tel. (07) 4125-3933, that departs Urangan twice daily for Moon Point, a remote area of the island's west coast. The fare on this barge is also $60 for a vehicle and $5 pp.

From Inskip Point, north of Rainbow Beach, *Rainbow Venture* makes regular crossings to the island's southern point. The fare is $25 one way for a vehicle, including passengers. Make bookings by calling (07) 5486-3227.

Information

Obtain island information and permits from Department of Environment offices on the mainland. Once on the island, there's a small information center at Eurong, tel. (07) 4127-9128, and the old forestry depot at Central Station has displays on the island's natural and human history. If you're looking for a book to while away the hours, try to get hold of Patrick White's *A Fringe of Leaves,* an intriguing account of Eliza Fraser's stay on the island. The *Fraser Island Sunmap* (available at most stores, $6) is essential for independent island exploration.

BUNDABERG

Bundaberg is a sugarcane-growing center of 48,000, 50 km east of the Bruce Highway and 370 km north of Brisbane. The Burnett River flows through town, draining into the ocean a few km east of the city center by a string of sleepy beachfront settlements. Unlike many other cane-growing regions, where raw cane is transported for processing, all parts of production take place in Bundaberg, including the distillation of Australia's most popular spirit, **Bundaberg Rum,** known throughout the land as "Bundy."

Mon Repos Environmental Park

East of Bundaberg is **Mon Repos Beach,** the largest and most accessible turtle rookery in mainland Australia. Four species of turtles nest on the beach; loggerhead are the most common, with green, flatback, and leatherback turtles also present. Between late November and early January, female turtles waddle up the beach

Bundaberg's main street

Avenue St., East Bundaberg, tel. (07) 4150-8684.

On the same side of town as the distillery is **Schmeider's Cooperage & Craft Centre,** Alexandra St., tel. (07) 4151-8233, which displays the art of making wooden barrels, wood-turning, pottery, and blacksmithing, as well as selling a wide range of interesting souvenirs. It's open Mon.-Fri. 9 a.m.-5 p.m., Sat.-Sun. 9 a.m.-3 p.m.

Bert Hinkler, an aviator best known for his 1928 solo flight between England and Australia, was born in Bundaberg. He lived part of his life in England, and a few years back his English house was transported to Bundaberg and turned into a museum featuring his life and feats, including media reports of his most famous flight. **Hinkler House** is open daily 10 a.m.-4 p.m. and admission is a worthwhile $4. It's on the road out to Gin Gin on Young St., tel. (07) 4152-0222. On the same side of the river are **mystery craters,** of an unknown origin and dated by geologists as being about 25 million years old. Admission is $3 and the site is open daily 8 a.m.-5 p.m.

The beaches east of Bundaberg won't win any beauty contests, but swimming at them is safe, and they are separated by rocky headlands of volcanic origin, home to interesting marinelife thriving in rock pools. The best beaches are at **Bargara** and farther south at **Elliott Heads.**

Accommodations

Grand Hotel, 89 Bourbong St., tel. (07) 4151-2441, has clean and comfortable rooms with shared facilities for $20 s, $28 d. Budget. **Matilda Motel,** 209 Bourbong St., tel. (07) 4151-4717, has rooms of a higher standard, as well as a pool and laundry; $56 s, $65 d. Moderate. The nicest place in town is **Sugar Country Motor Inn,** 220 Bourbong St., tel. (07) 4153-1166, with large, elegantly decorated rooms and all modern conveniences; $65 s, $72 d. Moderate. **Don Pancho Beach Resort** is an excellent alternative to Bundaberg's motels. Sandwiched between the ocean and a golf course, it is 13 km east of Bundaberg at 62 Miller St., Bargara Beach, tel. (07) 4159-2146, and features such facilities as a pool, fitness room, bar, and restaurant. Each of the 42 units is air-conditioned, and some have spa baths; $75-145 s or d. Moderate.

Bundaberg's backpacker lodges are geared mainly to seasonal workers, and if you've got

after dark to lay their eggs in the dunes beyond the beach. For two months from mid-January newly hatched turtles emerge from nests to make the long trek down the beach and into the water. Nearly all activity takes place after dark, with the most active times being an hour each side of high tide. When this tide falls between 7 and 9 p.m. the viewing areas can get very crowded. Access to the beach during nesting periods is restricted to ranger-led tours that leave from the park information center behind the beach. For further details call (07) 4159-2628.

Town Sights

The **Bundaberg Rum Distillery** is definitely the city's number-one attraction. Its connection to the cane-growing industry is molasses, a sticky (and smelly) syrup extracted from sugarcane at an adjacent factory. Tours of the distillery include a short video, a walk through all aspects of rum production, and, of course, a drink of rum. Tours depart four to five times daily between 10 a.m. and 3 p.m. and cost $5 pp. The distillery is on

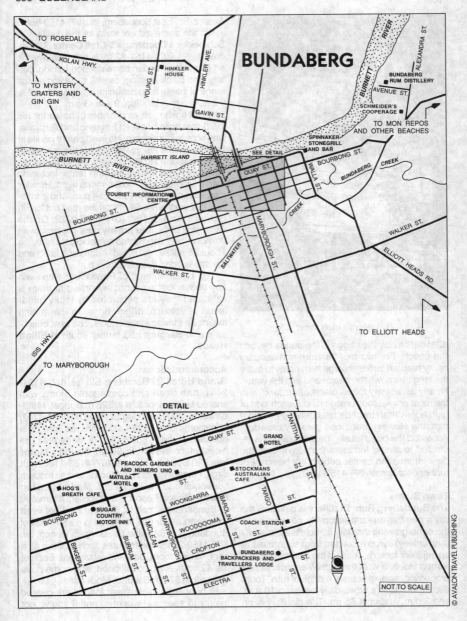

TO ROSEDALE

KOLAN HWY.

TO MYSTERY
CRATERS AND
GIN GIN

YOUNG ST.

HINKLER
HOUSE

HINKLER AVE.

GAVIN ST.

BUNDABERG

BURNETT RIVER

ALEXANDRA ST.

BUNDABERG
RUM DISTILLERY

AVENUE ST.

SCHMEIDER'S
COOPERAGE

TO MON REPOS
AND OTHER BEACHES

BURNETT RIVER

HARRIETT ISLAND

SEE DETAIL

SPINNAKER
STONEGRILL
AND BAR

QUAY ST.

BOURBONG ST.

WALLA ST.

BUNDABERG CREEK

TOURIST INFORMATION
CENTRE

CREEK

BOURBONG ST.

WALKER ST.

MARYBOROUGH ST.

SALTWATER

WALKER ST.

ELLIOTT HEADS RD.

TO ELLIOTT HEADS

ISIS HWY.

TO MARYBOROUGH

DETAIL

QUAY ST.

TANTITHA

GRAND
HOTEL

PEACOCK GARDEN
AND NUMERO UNO

MATILDA
MOTEL

HOG'S
BREATH CAFE

SUGAR
COUNTRY
MOTOR INN

BOURBONG

ST.

ST.

ST.

WOONGARRA

BAROLIN

MCLEAN

MARYBOROUGH

WOODOOOMA

BURRUM ST.

CROFTON

BINGERA ST.

ELECTRA

ST.

ST.

ST.

STOCKMANS
AUSTRALIAN
CAFE

TARGO

ST.

ST.

COACH STATION

BUNDABERG
BACKPACKERS AND
TRAVELLERS LODGE

ST.

ST.

NOON

NOT TO SCALE

the correct visas, lodge staff will help you find work fruit-picking (Oct.-July). The pick of the bunch is **Bundaberg Backpackers and Travellers Lodge,** corner Targo and Crofton Streets, tel. (07) 4152-2080, right opposite the bus depot, is modern, and being purpose-built has all the usual facilities, including a pleasant outdoor barbecue area. All beds are $15 pp, including transportation to crop farms.

Turtle Sands Tourist Park, Mon Repos Beach, tel. (07) 4159-2340, is right on the beach, within walking distance of the turtle rookery and home to many native birds. Sites are $15-16 per night, self-contained units go for $50, and deluxe villas with ocean views are $57.

Food

Stockmans Australian Cafe, 142 Bourbong St., tel. (07) 4153-4774, serves Australian-style meals, including hearty breakfasts with damper bread from $6.50. The rest of the day, it's damper and meat pies. For counter meals, head to the Grand Hotel, at 89 Bourbong St., where lunchtime specials are just $3 and meals in the beer garden are $6-10. **Peacock Garden,** 161 Bourbong St., tel. (07) 4152-5588, is a popular Chinese joint, and a door away is **Numero Uno,** 167 Bourbong St., tel. (07) 4151-3666, a rowdy Italian restaurant where large servings of pasta are $12-15. The **Hog's Breath Cafe,** 66 Quay St., tel. (07) 4153-5777, may be American, but its setting in Bundaberg is true-blue Australian—a restored Queenslander overlooking the Burnett River. The food's not cheap, around $14-20 for a main dish, but the atmosphere is great; open daily for lunch and dinner. The **Spinnaker Stonegrill and Bar,** Quay St., tel. (07) 4152-8033, specializes in local seafood, and prices are reasonable, with the outdoor tables having panoramic river views.

A local institution is Sunday lunch at **Bucca Hotel,** 30 km north of Bundaberg on the road out to Rosedale, tel. (07) 4157-8171. The barbecue costs just $3, including all the salad you can eat, and kicks off at 1 p.m.

Transportation, Services, and Information

All northbound trains from Brisbane make stops at Bundaberg. The railway station is on McLean St., close to downtown. Buses terminate at the Coach Station on Targo Street. All major bus lines stop at Bundaberg. To make onward travel arrangements or book local tours, head to **Stewart and Sons Travel,** in the Coach Station, tel. (07) 4152-9700. All major car rental companies have offices in Bundaberg, or try **Can Do Car Rentals,** tel. (07) 4151-7933, which rents cars from $45 per day including insurance and unlimited km.

The **Tourist Information Centre** is on the main highway into town from the south and is open daily 9 a.m.-5 p.m., tel. (07) 4152-2333 or (1800) 06-0499. The **Department of Environment** is at 46 Quay St., tel. (07) 4153-8620; open Mon.-Fri. 9 a.m.-5 p.m.

BUNDABERG TO GLADSTONE

Inland Route

A sealed road leading west from Bundaberg to **Gin Gin** on the Bruce Highway is the quickest route north. Southwest of Gin Gin is **Goodnight Scrub National Park,** protecting stands of hoop pine that escaped early logging.

The only worthwhile detour between Gin Gin and Gladstone, 160 km to the north, is **Mount Colosseum National Park,** east of Miriam Vale. This park is mostly undeveloped, with a trail leading to a summit from where the coastline and offshore islands can be seen in all their glory.

Cania Gorge National Park, on the Burnett Highway 123 km west of Gin Gin and 26 km north of Monto, is named for spectacular sandstone cliffs and deep gullies filled with tree ferns and piccabeen palms. Look for platypuses at dawn and dusk along Three Moon Creek. The park has no campgrounds. **Cania Gorge Tourist Park,** north of the national park, tel. (07) 4167-8188, has camping, cabins, and bunk beds.

Coastal Route

The coast north of Bundaberg is most appealing for its lack of development. A road north from Bundaberg, sealed to Rosedale, has numerous spurs leading to picturesque coastal communities such as **Miara, Norval Park,** and **Rules Beach.** Farther north is **Agnes Water** and **Town of 1770,** named for the year Captain Cook sighted the mainland. The beaches

Town of 1770 is a sleepy village overlooking a protected inlet.

here are the best between the Sunshine Coast and Gladstone, and the view from Round Hill Head is excellent.

North of Agnes Water is 7,830-hectare **Eurimbula National Park,** protecting vegetation that ranges from coastal heath to subtropical rainforests. A primitive campground is located at Bustard Beach, but the access road may be impassable after rain, and you must bring drinking water.

CAPRICORN COAST AND CENTRAL HIGHLANDS

Named for the tropic of Capricorn, the Capricorn Coast extends between the cities of Gladstone and Rockhampton. For those traveling north it marks the beginning of the 2,000-km **Great Barrier Reef**. Gladstone certainly isn't the most beautiful city in the world, but it is gateway to some of the reef's most beautiful islands, including Heron Island, one of the reef's few coral cays with a resort. A short trip up the Bruce Highway from Gladstone is the tropical city of Rockhampton, gateway to Great Keppel Island, easily accessible to day trippers and boasting a range of accommodations for all budgets.

West of Rockhampton is the central highlands, a 400-km-long plateau abreast the Great Dividing Range. The main route west is the Capricorn Highway, which passes through the mining towns of Blackwater and Emerald before descending into Queensland's vast Outback. South of this highway is spectacular Carnarvon National Park, dissected by a spectacular 30-km gorge.

GLADSTONE

This city of 23,500, 550 km north of Brisbane, is the mainland gateway for islands of the Capricorn Group, among the most beautiful of all Great Barrier Reef islands. When the giant Comalco company descended on the prosperous provincial town in the 1960s to build the world's largest alumina (aluminum oxide) smelter, Gladstone grew quickly to become an important industrial center and one of Australia's busiest ports. The smelter refines bauxite mined from Weipa, on Cape York Peninsula. To the south of Gladstone, on Boyne Island, the alumina is converted to aluminum. These industries, along with Queensland's biggest power station and the country's sixth busiest port, have transformed Gladstone's coastline into an industrial wasteland.

Auckland Hill provides a good view of the city and ocean panorama. From a waterfall at its base, which is floodlit at night, stairs lead up to a viewing platform. Access is from Flinders Parade. **Curtis** and **Facing Islands** lie close to the mainland, linked to Gladstone by a weekend ferry service. Both have campgrounds with limited facilities and at Connor Bluff, a two-km walk from the Curtis Island jetty, is a large rookery where turtles nest Nov.-March.

Practicalities

Rusty Anchor Motor Inn, 167 Goondoon St., tel. (07) 4972-2099, has decent rooms for $42 s, $48 d. Inexpensive. The **Country Club Motor Inn,** corner Far St. and Dawson Hwy., tel. (07) 4972-4322, is the flashiest place in town with rooms for $80 s, $90 d. Moderate.

Sunstate, tel. (13) 1313, flies between Gladstone and Brisbane daily. Gladstone is on the main rail line north, and all major bus companies stop in town.

The **Gladstone Visitor Information Centre** is at the marina along Bryan Jordan Dr., tel. (07) 4972-9922; open daily 9 a.m.-5 p.m. The **Department of Environment and Heritage** is in the Centrepoint Building on Goondoon St., tel. (07) 4972-6055.

THE BUNKER AND CAPRICORN ISLAND GROUPS

This string of islands lying between 70 and 100 km from the mainland form the southern extent of the Great Barrier Reef. They differ from many of the resort islands farther north, including all the Whitsunday Group, in that they are coral cays, made up entirely of reef debris that has washed up on top of the living reef. Over eons the cays have become vegetated, providing nesting areas for large populations of muttonbirds, black noddy terns, and turtles. Vegetation on all the cays is similar, with the shingly shoreline dominated by the creeper goatsfoot, easily recognizable by its light purple flowers. Higher up the beach, pisonia, she-oak, and pandanus dominate. But it's what's *underwater* that attracts the majority of visitors.

Whereas most resort islands to the north are a two-hour trip away from the reef, the Bunker and Capricorn Groups are right on its doorstep, with the colorful coral and profusion of reef fish a short dive away.

Two of the islands have resorts (because the islands are small, the resorts are low-key, with the emphasis on the natural surroundings), four are open to campers, and six remain uninhabited except for thousands of seabirds.

Lady Elliot Island

One of the reef's three coral cays with a resort, this 42-hectare island at the extreme southern end of the reef is surrounded by a magnificent lagoon. Guano was mined on the island last century, stripping much of the vegetation, and in 1873 a lighthouse, which still stands, was built on the island's west shore to aid northbound ships navigating the beginning of the reef's treacherous

inside channels. Goats, once bred on the island as a source of food for shipwreck survivors, have been eradicated, and apart from the scar of an airstrip, the island has returned to its original state. Between October and April tens of thousands of seabirds congregate on the island to raise newly hatched chicks, and humpback whales pass close by on migration routes.

Lady Elliot Island Reef Resort is fairly low-key, with rooms furnished for practicality rather than luxury and the emphasis on the island's natural wonders and surrounding reef. Diving around the island is among the best and most accessible on the entire reef. Shore dives are free February, May, and June, and $30-45 pp per dive at other times of the year. Tent Cabins (very basic, bunk beds; $175 s, $230 d), Lodge Cabins (basic, share facilities; $175 s, $230 d), Reef Units (private facilities, veranda; $210 s, $300 d), and Island Suites (secluded, lagoon views; $230

ISLANDS OF THE GREAT BARRIER REEF

Bedarra
86-hectare continental; go for exclusive yet relaxed atmosphere; resort accommodations; no day trips; reached from Mission Beach by boat

Brampton
464-hectare continental; go to relax and for resort activities; resort accommodations; day trips from $50; reached from Mackay by boat

Daydream
16-hectare continental; go for resort activities; resort accommodations; day trips from $24; reached from Airlie Beach by boat

Dunk
890-hectare continental; go for resort activities; resort accommodations; day trips from $22; reached from Mission Beach by boat

Fitzroy
324-hectare continental; go for fishing and diving; lodge accommodations; day trips from $30; reached from Cairns by boat

Frankland Islands
78-hectare continental; go for snorkeling and deserted beaches; camping; day trips from $125; reached from Cairns by boat

Great Keppel
1,480-hectare continental; go for hiking, beaches, resort activities; all types of accommodations available; day trips from $27; reached from Rockhampton by boat or plane

Green
12-hectare coral cay; go for snorkeling; resort accommodations; day trips from $40; reached from Cairns by boat

Hamilton
611-hectare continental; go for resort activities; resort accommodations; day trips from $37; reached from Airlie Beach by boat

Hayman
322-hectare continental; go to be pampered; resort accommodations; no day trips; reached from Airlie Beach by boat

Heron
16-acre coral cay; go for diving and snorkeling; resort accommodations; no day trips; reached from Gladstone by boat

Hinchinbrook
39,350-hectare continental; go for the hiking; accommodations include resort and camping; day trips from $69; reached from Cardwell by boat

s, $340 d), in total accommodate a maximum of 140 guests. All rates include organized activities and three meals daily. Standby rates are 80% of the full price, giving you a bed and hot meals from less than $100 pp per night (must be booked less than 48 hours prior to arrival). The only way to get to the island is by air. The main departure point for the island is Bundaberg ($130 pp roundtrip), but transfers can also be made from Hervey Bay. For resort and transfer bookings call (07) 4125-5344 or (1800) 07-2200.

It's possible for day trippers to visit Lady Elliot Island, but as you must fly in, it's not cheap. The cost from Hervey Bay or Bundaberg, including snorkeling gear, a guided walk, and a buffet lunch, is $140. Book through the resort.

Lady Musgrave Island

Just 20 hectares in area, this tiny coral cay is a small part of a massive lagoon, protected from the surrounding ocean by a platform reef exposed only at low tide. The island itself is encircled by a beach of broken coral that rises to thickly vegetated cover of pisonia. Like Lady Elliot Island to the south, Lady Musgrave was mined for guano and once had a high population of goats but is now totally deserted, save for day trippers and campers. For those visiting the island, the lagoon is center of most activity, with snorkeling and diving the main attractions; it also provides a safe anchorage for yachties.

Camping on a remote tropical island is many people's idea of the ideal holiday, and Lady Musgrave is the most accessible of the Great Barrier Reef cays for such an adventure, but you'll need to be totally self-sufficient (bring drinking water) and willing to forgo luxuries for a few days, or weeks, or even months if you so choose. Campers require a national parks permit ($3.50 pp per night), and as numbers are limited (a max-

---

Hook
5,180-hectare continental; go for snorkeling and diving; accommodations include a lodge and camping; day trips range $45-55; reached from Airlie Beach by boat

Lady Elliot
42-hectare coral cay; go for diving and snorkeling; resort accommodations; day trips from $140; reached from Bundaberg by plane

Lady Musgrave
20-hectare coral cay; go for snorkeling and beaches; camping; day trips range $108-165; reached from Bundaberg or Town of 1770 by boat or plane

Lindeman
790-hectare continental; go for resort activities; resort accommodations; day trips from $100-130; reached from Airlie Beach by boat or plane

Lizard
1,012-hectare continental; go for diving and beaches; accommodations include resort and camping; day trips from $195; reached from Cairns/Cooktown by plane

Long
1,215-hectare continental; go for resort activities and relaxation; three resorts provide accommodations; day trips from $24; reached from Airlie Beach by boat

Magnetic
5,030-hectare continental; go for water sports and hiking; all types of accommodation available; day trips from $24; reached from Townsville by ferry

Newry
44-hectare continental; go for low-key, relaxing atmosphere; camping and cabins; day trips from $15; reached from Seaforth by boat

Orpheus
1,376-hectare continental; go for informal yet stylish atmosphere, snorkeling; resort accommodations; no day trips; reached from Townsville/Lucinda by boat

Pumpkin
6-hectare continental; go for solitude; cabins; no day trips; reached from Rockhampton

South Molle
420-hectare continental; go for resort activities and hiking; resort accommodations; day trips $28; reached from Airlie Beach by boat

Whitsunday
10,800-hectare continental; go for Whitehaven Beach; camping; day trips from $49; reached from Airlie Beach by boat or yacht

imum of 50 campers per night) advance bookings are required; for permits call the Department of Environment in Gladstone, tel. (07) 4972-6055.

Captain Cook Great Barrier Reef Cruises, tel. (07) 4974-9077, offers camper drop-offs and pickups Thursday and Sunday from Town of 1770, north of Bundaberg. The fare is $205 pp roundtrip. As well as transfers, this company can organize camping equipment, water containers, and dinghies (great for fishing and snorkeling around the lagoon's outer reaches). **Lady Musgrave Barrier Reef Cruises,** tel. (07) 4152-9011 or (1800) 07-2110, offers transfers from Bundaberg for $205 roundtrip.

Captain Cook Great Barrier Reef Cruises makes day trips to the island Saturday and Sunday departing Town of 1770 at 8 a.m.; $108 pp. Lady Musgrave Barrier Reef Cruises operates day tours departing Port Bundaberg, 18 km east of Bundaberg, Mon.-Thurs. and Saturday at 8:30 a.m. returning at 6 p.m. The fare is adult $108 pp, which includes a buffet lunch, snorkeling equipment, glass-bottomed boat tour, and access to an underwater observatory. The trip to the island takes less time from Town of 1770 and more time is spent ashore. Either way, if seas are rough, the journey over will be unpleasant, and it may be better paying the extra for a day trip with **Bundaberg Seaplane Tours,** tel. (07) 4155-2068. The flight takes 30 minutes each way; $165 pp includes accommodation transfers in Bundaberg and a light lunch on the island.

Heron Island

A paradise for nature lovers and those who want to escape the regimented formula of other reef resorts, 16-hectare Heron Island is one of the reef's three coral cays with resorts.

Lying in the middle of the Capricorn Group, 80 km northeast of Gladstone and just 30 km from the Continental Shelf, Heron Island sits on the northwest corner of a platform reef nearly 10 km long. The island itself is oval shaped, and just under one km long, but there's enough room for a couple of hundred thousand sea birds as well as a high population of white and gray herons, for which the island is named. Between November and March sea turtles lay their eggs on island, but these animals were not always afforded the security they now enjoy—for much of the 1920s a turtle soup factory operated on the is-

land. The waters around the island are considered among the finest on the entire reef for diving, with the best dive sites in the immediate vicinity of the island. Diving costs $120 pp per day.

Heron Island Resort sprawls over most of the northwestern end of the island, spread among pisonia trees and around two pools, a tennis court, and restaurant complex. Accommodation is inclusive of meals and includes many activities. The resort atmosphere is definitely casual and relaxed, but the standard of all facilities and lodging is high. Breakfast and lunch are buffet style, while dinner is à la carte. Rates in the Turtle Cabins (bunk beds, shared bathroom) are $140 pp; Reef Units (private bathroom) are $289 s, $448 d. Heron Units (private bathroom) are $311 s, $492 d. Point Units are isolated from the rest of the resort and have a terrific beachfront location; $371 s, $612 d. Transfers between Gladstone and the island by the *Reef Adventurer* catamaran take around two hours each way; $150 roundtrip. Helicopter transfers from Gladstone are $240 pp one way. When available, standby rates on Heron Island offer considerable savings (usually around $200 pp per day inclusive of transfers). For resort and transfer bookings call (07-4978-1488 or 13-2469. In North America call (800) 225-9849. It is not possible to visit Heron Island for just the day.

Masthead Island

Unlike other cays at the southern end of the reef, this 65-hectare island was never mined and has had no goats to destroy the native vegetation. Closest of the Capricorn Group to the mainland, it lies 60 km northeast of Gladstone. It sits at the northwestern end of a platform reef forming a large lagoon but, unlike Lady Elliot, there is no navigitable break in the reef, making boat landings difficult in rough weather and anchorage unsafe. Between October and April thousands of seabirds nest on the island and Nov.-Jan. loggerhead turtles clamber up the beach to lay their eggs.

Camping on the island is limited to 50 people (30 during bird-nesting periods) at any one time, and with no scheduled boat service you'll need to have a flexible schedule to fit in with other campers (usually groups of 10-20) for transportation. A number of charter boats go out to the island, but the best chance of getting in with a group is on the *Reef Adventurer,* which also transfers guests out to Heron Island. Fares to Masthead are $220 pp roundtrip. For bookings call (07) 4972-5166. For permits, call the Department of Environment in Gladstone, tel. (07) 4972-6055.

North West Island

Northwest of Heron Island and 83 km northeast of Gladstone, this 150-hectare coral cay is the largest island of the Capricorn Group and has been protected as a national park since 1980. In the past it has been mined for guano and, like Heron Island, had a turtle soup factory. Although various signs of human history remain, the island provides an excellent opportunity to escape to a deserted tropical isle. Like other islands of the Bunker and Capricorn groups, it's an important nesting site for seabirds and has a large green turtle nesting area.

For camping permits, contact the Department of Environment in Gladstone, tel. (07) 4972-6055. Boat transfers can be arranged on *Reef Adventurer* through Heron Island Resort, tel. (07) 4972-7166; $240 pp from Gladstone.

Tryon Island

Just 12 hectares in area, Tryon Island sits on the edge of a massive platform reef a couple of km beyond North West Island. The island is fringed by a shingle beach, and at high tide it takes just 15 minutes to walk around it. Between October and May the island is home to thousands of very noisy muttonbirds who come ashore to raise chicks. The same camping permit and transportation applies to Tryon as to North West Island, although at press time the island was closed to all visitors until the completion of a regeneration program.

ROCKHAMPTON

Best known as "Rocky," this historic city of 61,000 sits on the Fitzroy River 640 km north of Brisbane and is the gateway to Great Keppel Island. The area's first settlers arrived in 1853, and a gold rush 60 km north in 1858 furthered the influx of Europeans. The actual town was established as a river port for the transportation of coal and cattle. Today, Rocky claims to be the Beef Capital of Australia, and with Aus-

tralia's largest abattoirs on the city's outskirts and one-third of the state's cattle grazing in the region, it's probably true.

Sights

As you enter town from the south, it's impossible to miss The Spire, marking the tropic of Capricorn (23°26'30"s), the border between temperate and tropical zones south of the equator. Many of Rocky's historic buildings are on Quay St.; *Driving Tour* and *Heritage Walk* brochures detail each and its significance. **Rockhampton City Art Gallery,** Victoria Parade, tel. (07) 4931-1248, is regarded as one of the state's best provincial galleries; open Mon.-Fri. 10 a.m.-4 p.m., Sat.-Sun. 11:30-4:30 p.m.

On the city's southern outskirts is a **botanic garden** and **zoo.** Established more than 120 years ago, the garden covers 40 hectares and includes a display of palms. Within the botanic garden is a small zoo featuring koalas, kangaroos, crocodiles, cassowaries, emus, and other native animals; no admission charge. To get there, take the first left north of the information center and follow the signs. The grounds are open daily 8 a.m.-5 p.m.

Most attractions lie north of city limits. Northeast of downtown **Mt. Archer** rises to an elevation of 604 meters, providing an excellent view of the city and mountains beyond. Frenchville Rd. leads right to the summit. The **Dreamtime Cultural Centre,** tel. (07) 4936-1655, seven km north of the city at the Yeppoon turnoff, sprawls over 12 hectares of land significant to the local Durambal tribe. The center features a museum, displays of Torres Strait Islander culture, boomerang throwing demonstrations, and explanations of native plant use. Admission is adult $11, child $5, which includes a guided tour at 11 a.m. Open daily 10 a.m.-5 p.m.

Continuing north, and just beyond the signed turnoff to Yeppoon, is the **Heritage Village Museum,** tel. (07) 4934-2827, a "living" village encompassing the decades between 1850 and 1950. Admission is $10. Open daily 10 a.m.-5:30 p.m. Farther north still are a number of limestone cave systems, of which two are open to the public. **Cammoo Caves,** tel. (07) 4934-2774, are open daily for self-guided tours while **Capricorn Caverns,** tel. (07) 4934-2883, are accessible only on a guided tour ($25 pp).

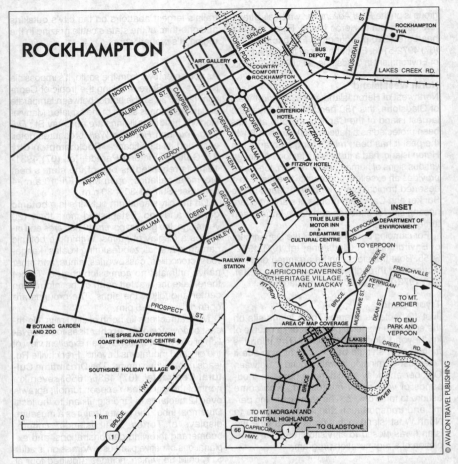

ROCKHAMPTON

NORTH ST.
ALBERT ST.
CAMPBELL ST.
CAMBRIDGE
FITZROY
ARCHER ST.
DENISON ST.
KENT ST.
BOLSOVER ST.
ALMA ST.
QUAY ST.
EAST ST.
VICTORIA PDE.
BRUCE HWY.

ART GALLERY
COUNTRY COMFORT ROCKHAMPTON
CRITERION HOTEL
FITZROY HOTEL

BUS DEPOT
MUSGRAVE ST.
LAKES CREEK RD.
ROCKHAMPTON YHA

FITZROY RIVER

WILLIAM ST.
DERBY ST.
STANLEY ST.
GEORGE ST.

RAILWAY STATION

PROSPECT ST.

BOTANIC GARDEN AND ZOO

THE SPIRE AND CAPRICORN COAST INFORMATION CENTRE

SOUTHSIDE HOLIDAY VILLAGE

BRUCE HWY.

TO MT. MORGAN AND CENTRAL HIGHLANDS

CAPRICORN HWY. 66

INSET

TRUE BLUE MOTOR INN
DREAMTIME CULTURAL CENTRE

YEPPOON RD.
DEPARTMENT OF ENVIRONMENT
TO YEPPOON

TO CAMMOO CAVES, CAPRICORN CAVERNS, HERITAGE VILLAGE, AND MACKAY

MOORES CREEK RD.
KERRIGAN ST.
FRENCHVILLE RD.
TO MT. ARCHER
DEAN ST.
TO EMU PARK AND YEPPOON

AREA OF MAP COVERAGE
LAKES CREEK RD.
BRUCE HWY.
MUSGRAVE ST.
YAMBA
FITZROY RIVER

TO GLADSTONE

0   1 km

© AVALON TRAVEL PUBLISHING

Accommodations and Food

One of Rocky's most distinctive buildings is the historic **Criterion Hotel** on Quay St. opposite the river, tel. (07) 4922-1225. Basic rooms above the bar are $22 s, $32 d, while four motel rooms out back are $45 s, $50 d. Inexpensive. Motels line the highway north and south of the city. The least expensive are in the suburb of Parkhurst, just north of Yeppoon turnoff. **True Blue Motor Inn,** Bruce Hwy., Parkhurst, tel. (07) 4936-1777, has large, clean rooms, a pool, and laundry; $40 s, $48 d. Inexpensive. Back in the heart of town

is the nine-story **Country Comfort Rockhampton,** 86 Victoria Parade, tel. (07) 4927-9933 or (1800) 06-5064, where rooms are air-conditioned and have private balconies; other facilities include a restaurant, bar, and laundry; $92 s or d. Expensive.

Rockhampton YHA is on the north side of the river at 60 MacFarlane St., tel. (07) 4927-5288. This large hostel has modern facilities and bike rentals (biking is a great way to get around the city). Dorm beds are $15, while the few doubles are $18 pp.

North of the Yeppoon turnoff is a rest area where camping is permitted. For more facilities stay at **Southside Holiday Caravan Village,** on the Bruce Hwy. opposite the information center, tel. (07) 4927-3013. Facilities are excellent and include a pool, kitchen, and tennis court. Unpowered sites are $13, powered sites $17, on-site vans $31, and cabins $45. Budget-Inexpensive.

Without a doubt, the best place to go for a counter lunch is the **Fitzroy Hotel,** 366 East St., where a rump steak with vegetables is just $5 at lunch. Or try the **Criterion Hotel** on the corner of Quay and Fitzroy Streets.

Transportation, Services, and Information
Ansett Australia, tel. (13) 1300, and **Qantas,** tel. (13) 1313, fly daily between Brisbane and Rocky, with a cab from the airport to downtown running $8-9.

Rockhampton is the terminus of **Queensland Rail's** TiltTrain, a luxurious train that reaches speeds of 170 km/hour on the journey up the coast from Brisbane. The other service, the Spirit of Capricorn, runs daily between Brisbane and Rocky, taking around 10 hours each way. For bookings call (13) 2232. All major bus companies stop in town with fares similar to rail.

Capricorn Coast Information Centre is on the Bruce Hwy. right on the tropic of Capricorn. It's open daily 9 a.m.-5 p.m., tel. (07) 4927-2055. For information on nearby national parks, including those of the central highlands, head to the **Department of Environment,** on Yeppoon Rd. just off the Bruce Hwy., tel. (07) 4936-0511.

YEPPOON AND VICINITY

Yeppoon, 40 km northeast of Rockhampton, may be the largest town on the Capricorn Coast, but it's still a sleepy seaside resort town. It lies at the north end of a 35-km stretch of coast, which attracts mainly fishers and families content to enjoy a relaxed holiday away from the hustle and bustle of the more commercial coastal areas. The main road out to the coast is Yeppoon Rd., which begins five km north of downtown Rocky; an alternative is to take Lakes Creek Rd. out of Rocky to **Emu Park,** a small coastal settlement spread over undulating hills overlooking a wide sandy beach. On the headland is the **Singing Ship,** a 40-meter-high monument to Captain Cook. Representing a mast and sail, the hollow pipes are pierced to create a musical noise when the wind blows. From Emu Park, the road hugs the coast, passing the community of **Mulambin Beach** and the turnoff to **Rosslyn Bay,** gateway to Great Keppel Island, before ending at Yeppoon. The effects of the tide at Yeppoon are amazing; as it ebbs, large pools of water are left on the gently sloping beach, and boats moored in Fig Tree Creek are left lying on dry mudflats, only to float again as the tide floods the wide creek bed a few hours later. South of Yeppoon is **Wreck Point** and a lookout affording panoramic views over the Keppel Group.

Practicalities
In 1972 Japanese businessman Yohachiro Iwasaki purchased 8,500 hectares of prime oceanfront land immediately north of Yeppoon. His plans for an international-standard resort were marred with a decade of controversy, but, finally, **Capricorn International Resort** is now operational, providing accommodation for 800 guests and a myriad of activities, including two 18-hole championship golf courses. The resort is contained on only a small section of the 8,500 hectares, with the rest remaining in its natural state and open for guests to explore on 4WD safaris, nature walks, or on horseback. Originally aimed at the Asian market, many Australians take advantage of package deals and high-standard facilities. Standard rate is $175 s, $220 d, while self-contained suites are $240-260, but you'd be crazy to pay these prices. Two-night packages, including airfare from Sydney, start at less than $300 pp; call **Ansett Australia,** tel. (13) 1300, or **Qantas,** tel. (13) 1313, for details. For direct reservations call (07) 4939-5111 or (1800) 07-5902. Luxury.

Yeppoon has a number of motels, with **Driftwood Motel,** 7 Todd Ave., tel. (07) 4939-2446, being right on the beach; $50 s, $55 d. Inexpensive. **Barrier Reef Backpackers,** 30 Queen St., tel. (07) 4939-4702, is an old Queenslander with dorm beds for $12 pp and a few doubles for $26. Staff will pick up in Rocky and will also drop guests at Rosslyn Bay Harbour.

Capricorn Coast Information Centre is beside the big roundabout by Ross Creek, tel. (07) 4939-4888.

GREAT KEPPEL ISLAND

Great Keppel is a large continental island of 1,480 hectares surrounded by beautiful white beaches and a fringing reef of coral. Most of the island is covered in a forest of eucalypts, with casuarinas fringing the beaches and a large area of low-lying wetland on the north side. Not only does ease of access make the island popular, it also has one of the reef's largest and most popular resorts, made famous by the long-running "Get Wrecked on Great Keppel" advertising campaign. If resort-style living isn't your idea of fun, there's also camping in safari-style tents and a backpacker lodge, or just come over for the day.

Recreation

Hiking is one of Great Keppel's main attractions. The most used trail is the Yellow Brick Road, which runs from the spit where the ferry docks one km south to Great! Keppel Resort. From the

north end of an airstrip (behind the resort), a one-km trail climbs to a lookout with spectacular views extending to other islands of the Keppel Group. From the lookout it is two km to the summit of Mt. Wyndham, from where Long Beach can be seen far below and Halfway and Humpy Islands lie immediately south. Other trails lead from the lookout to an old shearing shed and homestead, to **Leeke's Beach, Wreck Beach,** and a lighthouse on the island's remote and rugged west coast.

The island's best snorkeling spot is **Monkey Beach,** reached by continuing south beyond the main resort. Snorkeling gear can be rented from the island's dive shop, tel. (07) 4939-5022. The shop also rents diving gear and charges $55 per dive.

Accommodations

Set behind a sparkling white palm-fringed beach **Great! Keppel** is a fun-oriented resort with more activities on offer than any other resort on the Great Barrier Reef—tennis, squash, golf, archery,

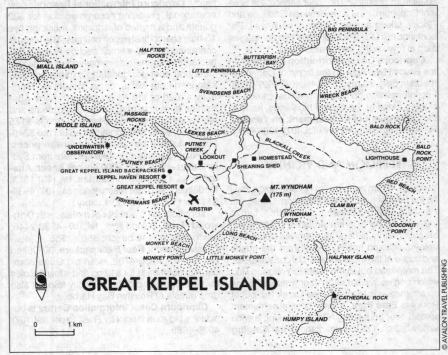

GREAT KEPPEL ISLAND

© AVALON TRAVEL PUBLISHING

Long Beach, Great
Keppel Island

basketball, tandem, skydiving, aqua bikes, scuba diving, snorkeling, reef trips, parasailing, tandem skydiving, and dancing the night away at a disco—you name it, the resort has it. Fairly recently, the resort underwent a $14-million facelift, which included the construction of 60 new units. Facilities now include five pools, a café, store, hairdresser, and restaurants. Rooms are all basically the same with Garden Units at $280 s or d; Beachfront Units $320 s or d; and the new Hillside Villas, offering panoramic views, also $398 s or d. These rates include breakfast, all nonmotorized activities and, if you've got any energy left after the sun has set, free admission to the nightclub. Package deals through Qantas, tel. (13) 1313, offer massive savings; at last report you could fly between Sydney and the island and enjoy three nights' accommodation for just over $300 pp. To call the resort direct (ask about standby deals), phone (07) 4939-5044. Luxury.

Between Fishermans and Putney Beaches is **Keppel Haven Resort** (formerly Wapparaburra Haven), offering a Tent Village ($25 s or d), and spacious cabins with kitchenettes ($110). The Tent Village is a series of canvas "tents," each with four bunk beds. Guests have use of a communal kitchen. This complex also has a small grocery store, café, and restaurant. For bookings call (07) 4939-1907. Budget. Next door is **Great Keppel Island Backpackers,** tel. (07) 4939-8655, which organizes many activities at a much cheaper rate than the main resort. Dorm beds are $15 pp. Budget. In the same

vicinity is the new **Great Keppel Island Village,** tel. (07) 4927-5288, a YHA-affiliated accommodation offering three-bed dorms for $15 pp, and doubles and twins for $18 pp. Budget.

Food
The best way to eat cheap on the island is to bring your own food (Rosslyn Bay Co-op, a five-minute walk from the mainland ferry terminal, offers a great selection of fresh and precooked seafood). Aside from the resort restaurants (nonguests welcome), there's a pizza joint and a small café selling Devonshire teas and light meals throughout the day.

Transportation
Sunstate, tel. (13) 1313, flies daily between Rockhampton, with a same-day roundtrip standby fare for $60, less than the standard one-way fare. From Rosslyn Bay Harbour, south of Yeppoon, **Keppel Tourist Services,** tel. (07) 4933-6744, has a ferry service over to the island departing daily at 7:30 a.m., 9:15 a.m., 11:30 a.m., and 3:30 p.m., returning at 8:15 a.m., 2 p.m., and 4:30 p.m.; $27 roundtrip, and for an extra $12, you can either go boomnetting and snorkeling or visit the underwater observatory on Middle Island.

Keppel Tourist Services also operates a high-speed catamaran, *Reefseeker,* to the outer reef Tuesday and Thursday. Inclusive of lunch, snorkeling, and a glass-bottomed boat ride, the fare is adult $105, child $60.

Other Islands of Keppel Bay

Great Keppel is the largest of 19 islands in Keppel Bay. On **Middle Island** is an underwater observatory. Keppel Tourist Services runs over to the observatory from Great Keppel Island for $12.

North of Great Keppel Island, six-hectare **Pumpkin Island** has five cabins (sleeping up to six), complete with drinking water, solar, power, and basic cooking facilities, for $130 per night. For bookings and transportation details call (07) 4939-2431. Camping is permitted on **North Keppel, Miall,** and **Humpy Islands.** You'll need a permit from the Department of Environment in Rockhampton, tel. (07) 4936-0511, for camping on any of these islands. Inquire at Keppel Tourist Services, tel. (07) 4933-6744, or Keppel Bay Marina, tel. (07) 4933-6244, for island transfers.

WEST FROM ROCKHAMPTON

The Capricorn Highway runs west from Rockhampton to the mining towns of **Blackwater** and **Emerald,** continuing to Longreach in Queensland's vast Outback. The highway also runs past Carnarvon National Park, south of Emerald, one of Australia's most spectacular inland parks.

Mount Morgan

Tourism is about all that keeps this historic gold-mining town, 38 km southwest of Rockhampton, alive. Gold was first discovered in the area in 1882, turning out to be among the richest lodes in the world, with Mt. Morgan Gold Mining Company extracting more than 35 million ounces of gold in its hundred years of operation. After the mine closed in the late 1980s, most residents left town, but it's still an interesting place to visit. The streets are lined with buildings hinting at the town's prosperous past. **Mount Morgan Museum,** 87 Morgan St., tel. (07) 4938-2312, features a good collection of mining memorabilia, historic photos, and samples of minerals extracted from the mine. It's open Mon.-Sat. 10 a.m.-1 p.m., Sunday 10 a.m.-4 p.m.; admission $4.

Blackdown Tableland National Park

This 23,000-hectare park encompasses a large portion of a plateau rising 600 meters above the surrounding plains of the central highlands. Millions of years ago massive forces below the earth's surface pushed up layers of sedimentary rock, forming a rolling plateau of sandstone. Over eons, erosion has carved deep gorges, caves, and crevices along the plateau's escarpment. The plateau is covered in forests of eucalypt, including towering Blackdown stringybark. Where soil is shallow, low heaths dominate, and in spring these areas come alive with color when a profusion of wildflowers bloom.

The plateau was inaccessible until a logging road was cut up its steep slopes in 1971, and a decade later a large part of it was declared a national park. Just beyond the park entrance, trails lead to **Peregrine Lookout** (1.4 km one-way), where views extend for many kilometers north, and **Two Mile Falls** (1.5 km one-way). At **Mimosa Creek** another couple of short trails lead through a deep gorge, and at the end of the access road a five-km trail leads to the rim of a spectacular sandstone gorge.

Mimosa Creek Camping Area has toilets and drinking water; for bookings call the ranger at (079) 86-1964. The park turnoff is 11 km west of Dingo.

The Gemfields

Around 200 km west of Rocky, and just west of Emerald, is the world's most productive sapphire-mining area. Other gems found are amethyst, gold, rubies, diamonds, and zircon. Large companies do a lot of the mining, but during winter months hundreds of amateurs descend on the area, hoping to strike it rich. Most don't, but everyone comes away with a gem of some standard. Before digging, a fossicking license is needed; these are available from the Emerald courthouse. The gemfields are scattered around the towns of **Anakie, Willows, Sapphire,** and **Rubyvale. Gemfields Information Centre,** in Anakie, tel. (07) 4985-4525, has maps of the region and friendly staff to guide you to the most productive areas. All gemfields towns have caravan parks, each with on-site vans or cabins.

Clermont, 110 km northwest of Emerald, is Queensland's oldest inland tropical town. It exists only to serve workers at **Blair Athol Mine,** a massive open-cut mining operation on the world's largest steaming coal seam.

CARNARVON NATIONAL PARK

A bone-shaking 100 km from the nearest sealed road, and 400 km west of Rockhampton, this park encompasses 251,000 hectares of a plateau rising high above the surrounding plains. Remarkable **Carnarvon Gorge** is the park's major attraction. Almost 30 km long, 250 meters deep, and with innumerable arms, the gorge area is a dramatic landscape of sheer-sided cliffs, natural bridges, and caves. The gorge has been created by **Carnarvon Creek,** little more than a babbling stream most of the year, but a raging torrent during the Wet. Thousands of years of water erosion have eaten into the multicolored sandstone layers deposited on the bottom of an ocean many millions of years ago.

The creek flows year-round, supporting an oasis of ferns and mosses that thrive in an otherwise desolate landscape and attract a surprisingly large number of animals. Forests of dry eucalypt dominate higher elevations, while the lush vegetation of the gorge is mainly tree ferns, cabbage tree palms, orchids, and, along the creek bed, moss-covered boulders.

The gorge's first human visitors were Aboriginals, who used the many caves as ceremonial places, burying their dead among the rocky caves. **Kenniff Cave** is adorned with early rock art; stencil paintings depict animals and people with boomerangs and shields.

Hiking

The road into the park ends at the entrance to the gorge, leaving exploring on foot the only option. The main trail leads 9.3 km to **Cathedral Cave,** its lower walls covered in ancient art. Along the route side tracks lead to the aptly named **Art Gallery** and the park's most magnificent feature, the **Amphitheatre,** five km from the visitor center. The final approach is up a steel ladder and through a one-meter gap into a chasm surrounded by sheer sandstone walls towering more than 100 meters high. An easy walk from the visitor center leads to the **Moss Garden** in Violet Gorge. Here, lush palms, mosses, and ferns thrive on the small creek that tumbles down a long ravine.

Practicalities

The campground by the visitor center has toilets, drinking water, and cold showers; bookings are essential during holiday periods, tel. (07) 4984-4505. Just outside the park entrance is **Oasis Lodge,** consisting of individual cabins spread around native bushland. Each has a bathroom, fridge, tea- and coffee-making facilities, and a veranda. They also have a lounge, library, and a packed program of activities and guided walks (April-Jan. only). Rates, inclusive of all meals, are $150 pp per night; the low season (Dec.-March) rates drop to $96 pp per night. **Flight West** offers a package, including flights between Brisbane and Roma, charter flights between Roma and the lodge, and all-inclusive accommodations for three nights for $859 in high season, tel. (1800) 77-7879. For reservations call (07) 4984-4503 or (1800) 64-4150.

rock art, Carnarvon Gorge

WHITSUNDAY COAST AND ISLANDS

Between Mackay and Bowen lie the Whitsunday Islands, the single most popular destination on the entire reef. Rising magnificently from the turquoise waters that are protected from ocean swells by the outer reef, they are a watery playground for divers and sailors, or those who want to relax at an island resort. They are not true coral islands, but are continental in origin, linked geologically to the mainland.

The Whitsundays are unashamedly tourism oriented, but offer something to suit everyone, whether you want to spend your day hiking along a deserted beach, snorkeling and scuba diving, or participating in resort-style activities (islands close to the mainland are affected by box jellyfish Nov.-March). Of the main group of islands, seven have resorts, with accommodations ranging from rustic lodges to five-star resorts, or you could always camp on an uninhabited island. Day trips to the resort islands start at $20 and many excellent standby deals make island accommodation an excellent value for late arrivals. The islands are the perfect domain for yachties, with many bareboat charter operators renting yachts, or you can sail aboard one of the many maxi-yachts that have retired to islands.

The cane-growing town of Mackay is southern gateway to the Whitsundays and departure point for cruises to Brampton Island. To the north, and east of Proserpine, is Airlie Beach, which exists only to serve tourists heading to the islands. Shute Harbour, 16 km east of Airlie Beach, is the main departure point for island-bound cruise boats.

Cape Palmerston National Park

Accessible only by 4WD, this 7,200-hectare park encompasses an undeveloped stretch of coastline 100 km south of Mackay. The landscape is dominated by long stretches of sandy beach separated by grassy headlands and backed by low-lying areas of mangroves and swamps. The park is accessed at Ilbilbie, on the Bruce Highway, where a rough track parallels the coast past possible campsites on Coconut Beach and ends at the cape itself. Campers must be totally self-sufficient. For road conditions call (07) 4957-6292.

MACKAY

Promoting itself as Sugar Capital of Australia, this pleasant tropical city of 42,000 is gateway to the southern islands of the Whitsundays and Eungella National Park. Around seven million tons of cane are grown and processed in the Mackay region annually. As early as 1875, Mackay had 20 sugar mills crushing cane for transportation to southern ports. The Pioneer River, which flows through town, functioned as a port until the modern **Port of Mackay** was constructed. At the port is the world's largest sugar terminal, capable of holding 670,000 tons of cane at any one time.

Sights and Beaches

Mackay sprawls south and north of the Pioneer River, with commercial center being along the river's south bank. **Victoria Street,** the heart of the city, is a wide boulevard divided by a landscaped medium strip dominated by towering palms. Many historic buildings dot this part of the city, including the courthouse (1880) and police station (1885); *A Heritage Walk in Mackay,* available at the Tourist Information Centre, details the history of these and other buildings around town. Guided tours of the sugar terminal are offered weekdays at 10:15 a.m., and a few of the sugar mills offer tours during harvest season (July-Nov.); for details and all bookings contact the Tourist Information Centre, tel. (07) 4952-2677.

West of Mackay along the road to Eungella National Park (see below) is **Illawong Sanctuary,** tel. (07) 4959-1777, one of many wildlife parks along the Queensland coast. It features all the usual native animals, including crocodiles, fed daily at 2:30 p.m., and koalas, fed daily at 10 a.m. and 4:30 p.m. Guided park tours leave from the ticket office daily at 3:30 p.m. Admission is adult $10, child $5, or take a day tour from Mackay for $40 pp. Open daily 9:30 a.m.-5 p.m.

Mackay's best beaches are north of the city, but **Illawong Beach,** at the eastern end of Bridge St., is worth seeing at low tide, when it extends nearly two km out to sea. **Harbour Beach,** immediately south of Port of Mackay, has a surf club and palm-filled picnic area with barbecues. Farther north, **Slade Point** and **Eimeo** have reasonable beaches.

Accommodations and Food

Most motels are strung along Nebo Rd. (a continuation of the Bruce Hwy.) south of downtown. **Golden Reef Motel,** 164 Nebo Rd., tel. (07) 4957-6572, is one of the least expensive, with rooms at $36 s, $44 d. Inexpensive. Closer to the city, and within walking distance of downtown, is **Paradise Lodge Motel,** 19 Peel St., tel. (07) 4951-3644, opposite the bus terminal; $48 s, $52 d. Inexpensive. The excellent **Mackay Motor Inn,** 208 Nebo Rd., tel. (07) 4952-2822, has large rooms with comfortable beds, as well as barbecues, laundry, and pool; $60-68 s or d. Moderate. **Larrikin Lodge,** 32 Peel St., tel. (07) 4951-3728, an associate hostel of the YHA, is just 100 meters from the bus terminal. Facilities in this old timber house include a small pool and a barbecue area; dorm beds are $15, doubles $34. Budget.

If you'd prefer a beachfront location, consider **Illawong Lakes Resort,** Illawong Dr., Far Beach, tel. (07) 4957-8427 or (1800) 65-6944. It comprises 37 modern and simply furnished self-contained villas spread along the oceanfront, as well a tennis court, swimming pool, and restaurant. Rates range $110-125, which includes transfers from Mackay. Expensive. Also on the beach at Illawong is **Beach Tourist Park,** Petrie St., tel. (07) 4957-4021, with a large kitchen area, barbecue, pool, and kiosk. Unpowered sites are $14, powered sites $18, on-site vans $32, and cabins $44-52. Budget-Inexpensive.

Most of Mackay's cafés and restaurants are strung along Victoria St., as are a handful of hotels, many serving counter meals. **Wilkinson's Tavern,** tel. (07) 4957-2241, serves meals noon-2 p.m. and 6-9 p.m.; most are less than $10. Upstairs is a restaurant, with main dishes $9-14. The **Spotted Dick,** Sydney St., tel. (07) 4957-2368, is an old pub that has been converted into a trendy restaurant featuring live music on the weekend. One of the city's finer dining establishments is **Sundays Restaurant,** in a restored church at 15 Palmer St., North Mackay, tel. (07) 4957-6775. It's open for dinner Tues.-Sat. and for a popular brunch at 10 a.m. on Sunday. For something more casual, try **Billy Baxter's Cafe** in the Mt. Pleasant Shopping Centre on Phillip Street.

Transportation, Services, and Information

Ansett, tel. (13) 1300, flies nonstop between Brisbane and Mackay, as does **Qantas,** tel. (13) 1313. **Sunstate,** tel. (13) 1313, links Mackay to Townsville, Rockhampton, and Gladstone. The airport is on Mackay's southern outskirts, a $10 cab ride from downtown. **Queensland Rail,** tel. (13) 2232, operates services along the coast. The railway station is on Boddington Street. All major bus lines stop at **Mackay Bus Terminal,** 500 meters from downtown on Milton St., tel.

Mackay

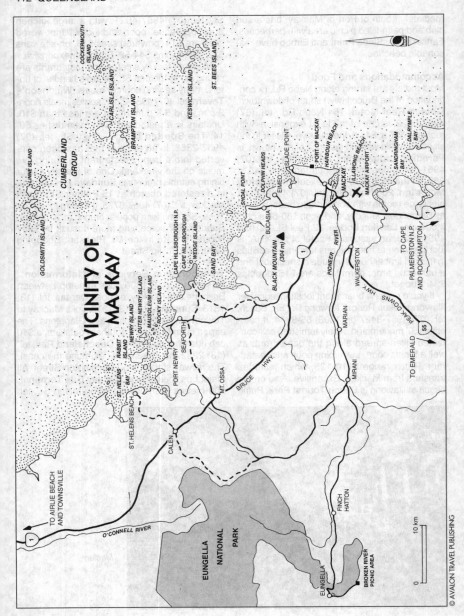

VICINITY OF MACKAY

CUMBERLAND GROUP

GOLDSMITH ISLAND
LINNE ISLAND
COCKERMOUTH ISLAND
CARLISLE ISLAND
ST. BEES ISLAND
KESWICK ISLAND
BRAMPTON ISLAND

TO AIRLIE BEACH AND TOWNSVILLE

O'CONNELL RIVER

ST. HELENS BEACH
ST. HELENS BAY
RABBIT ISLAND
NEWRY ISLAND
OUTER NEWRY ISLAND
MAUSOLEUM ISLAND
ROCKY ISLAND
WEDGE ISLAND
CAPE HILLSBOROUGH
CAPE HILLSBOROUGH N.P.
SAND BAY
SHOAL POINT
DOLPHIN HEADS
EIMEO   SLADE POINT
PORT OF MACKAY
HARBOUR BEACH
ILLAWONG BEACH
MACKAY AIRPORT
SANDRINGHAM BAY
DALRYMPLE BAY

PORT NEWRY
SEAFORTH
BUCASIA
MACKAY
SANDRINGHAM BAY

CALEN
MT. OSSA
BLACK MOUNTAIN (304 m)
PIONEER RIVER
WALKERSTON

EUNGELLA NATIONAL PARK

FINCH HATTON
MIRANI
MARIAN
BRUCE HWY.
PEAK DOWNS HWY.

TO PALMERSTON N.P. AND ROCKHAMPTON

TO CAPE

1

55

EUNGELLA
BROKEN RIVER PICNIC AREA

TO EMERALD

0   10 Km

© AVALON TRAVEL PUBLISHING

(07) 4951-3088. **Avis, Budget,** and **Hertz** have outlets at the airport.

The **Tourist Information Centre** is three km south of town on the Bruce Hwy., tel. (07) 4952-2677. It's open Mon.-Fri. 8:30 a.m.-5 p.m., Sat.-Sun. 9 a.m.-4 p.m.

ISLANDS OFF MACKAY

Off the coast of Mackay lie 17 islands, part of the Cumberland Islands. Officially they are known as the Cumberland Group, one of four groups making up the Cumberland Islands, better known as the Whitsundays. Like the rest of the Whitsundays, islands of the Cumberland Group are continental in origin and were once part of the mainland. The actual Great Barrier Reef lies well beyond the islands and about 100 km from the coast. Apart from Brampton Island, which has an elegant resort, the islands are either privately owned or protected as national parks.

Brampton Island

Brampton, a rugged continental island of 464 hectares, features a deeply indented coastline with seven pretty beaches, each with a fringing coral reef (the best of these are on the island's south side), while the hilly interior consists of an open forest where gray kangaroos, goannas, and ever-present scrub turkeys can be seen. A seven-km trail encircles the island, with a two km spur ascending to the summit of 219-meter Brampton Peak.

The Busuttin family, which originally ran sheep on nearby St. Bees Island, planted coconut palms and developed a small resort on a flat section of the island in 1933. It's now owned by Australian Resort Companies, who rebuilt the resort in 1985. The emphasis is on rest and relaxation, with no televisions or phones. The beach is right at the resort's doorstep, offering all the usual water sports. The resort caters for 216 people in air-conditioned units. Rates are $300-370 s or d, with the meal package an additional $64 pp per day. Package deals offered by Ansett and Qantas make staying on the island much more affordable. For bookings call (07) 4951-4499.

Roylen Cruises, tel. (07) 4955-3066 or (1800) 07-5032, provides transportation between Mackay and the island for overnight guests as well

as day trippers; $50 roundtrip. The services depart Port of Mackay daily at 9 a.m. It is also possible to reach the island on daily flights with Sunstate, tel. (13) 1313; $80 one-way.

Monday, Wednesday, and Friday, Roylen Cruises continues from Brampton Island to Credlin Reef on the outer reef, where a pontoon is located. The pontoon has a small underwater observatory and provides a base for snorkeling, scuba diving, and swimming. The outer reef trip is $110 from Mackay, which includes a buffet lunch.

Carlisle Island

At low tide a sand bar joins Carlisle Island to Brampton. Protected as a national park, Carlisle is uninhabited, and no tracks delve into its rugged interior. The island has some good beaches and a colorful fringing reef. On the west coast is the hull of *Geelong,* which wrecked in 1888. A small camping area at Southern Bay overlooks the resort on Brampton Island. Campers must be totally self-sufficient and bring their own drinking water. For permits contact the Department of Environment on the corner of Wood and River Streets, Mackay, tel. (07) 4951-8788.

EUNGELLA NATIONAL PARK

An area of rainforest isolated by climatic changes at the end of the last ice age and now supporting species of plants found nowhere else in the country, 50,800-hectare Eungella (YOUNG-gulla) is a world away from the coastal plains immediately to the east. Platypuses are the park's biggest attraction, and it's probably the best place in mainland Australia to view these unique critters.

Access from Mackay, 80 km to the east, along a road that parallels the Pioneer River up an ever-narrowing valley before climbing steeply to the plateau on which the park lies. From the village of Eungella it's six km south to the Park Information Centre, two campgrounds, and a platypus viewing area. These facilities are contained in a small corner of the park; the rest, north of Eungella, is inaccessible, rising to 1,280 meters at Mt. Dalrymple.

Around 10,000 years ago, at the end of the last ice age, the climate became warmer and drier, and areas of rainforest retreated to higher elevations. Eungella is one such area, now surrounded by open forests of eucalypt. Trees typical of subtropical rainforest—tulip oak, beech, silver quandong, curtain figs, palms, and ferns—all thrive in the environment.

The **platypuses** of Eungella live in the Broken River. They are most active just after dawn and before dusk and best viewed from a platform adjacent to the picnic area. The park boasts many other species of mammals as well as a reported 100 species of birds. One of the park's most interesting animals is the Eungella gastric brooding frog. Eggs are incubated in its stomach, before spitting out the young.

From the Broken River picnic area, the one-km Rainforest Discovery walk passes through typical rainforest environment. The Broken River track branches off this trail, following the river through rainforest to Crediton Creek. Another slightly longer hike is the **Palm Walk Track,** which follows the rim of the escarpment from just south of Eungella township to Broken River (8.3 km one-way.)

Practicalities

The park has two camping areas; both are on the Broken River. Each has toilets, showers, and picnic tables. Open fires are not encouraged; $7.50 per night. For bookings call (079) 58-4552.

Also on the river is **Broken River Mountain Retreat,** tel. (07) 4958-4528, with self-contained cabins in a setting of native bushland; $58 s or d. Inexpensive. **Eungella Chalet,** in Eungella township, tel. (07) 4958-4509, is an older establishment perched on the top of the range, with views all the way down the Pioneer Valley. Rooms with a view and shared facilities are $25 s, $40 d, rooms with private facilities are $60, and self-contained one-bedroom cabins are $80 s or d. A large grassed beer garden offers tremendous views, as does the restaurant. Inexpensive.

No public transportation is available to the park. Tours are offered by a number of operators, including **Reeforest Safaris,** tel. (07) 4952-2677. The $75 pp fare includes transport from Mackay, guided walks, and lunch.

The **Park Information Centre** is beside the Broken River, tel. (07) 4958-4552. It's open daily 7-8 a.m., 11 a.m.-noon, and 3-3:30 p.m.

NORTH FROM MACKAY

Cape Hillsborough National Park

The diverse habitat and long stretches of beach of this 816-hectare park, 45 km north of Mackay, make it a worthwhile detour from the Bruce Highway. The park access road traverses a large wetland area of mangroves, ending at a beach flanked to the north by a high, rugged headland dropping straight into the ocean. Behind the beach is the visitor center and a grassed picnic area where wallabies feed under the shade of eucalypts. At the very end of the access road is the trailhead for 1.4-km **Juipera Plant Trail,** passing through littoral rainforest with many palms. At regular intervals, interpretive boards describe the flora and its one-time significance to the Aboriginal diet. At low tide it's possible to walk to **Wedge Island,** off the southern end of the beach. As the park access road enters the park, a six-km (one-way) trail climbs northward over an isthmus to Smalleys Beach.

Behind the beach is a small campground (no showers); $7.50 per night. At the end of the access road is **Cape Hillsborough Tourist Park,** tel. (07) 4959-0152. Facilities include a pool, café, and laundromat. Unpowered sites are $10, powered sites $15, and cabins $45.

Newry Island Group

Newry Island, with a low-key resort, is part of a group of six continental islands that make up **Newry Island Group National Park,** lying close to the mainland around 50 km northwest of Mackay. Each island is rugged and covered in open forests of eucalypts. Koalas (introduced), possums, echidnas, and bandicoots inhabit the islands.

Newry Island Resort, tel. (07) 4959-0214, is spread along a palm-fringed beach facing Rabbit Island. Walking, fishing, and snorkeling (except Oct.-May, when stingers are present) are all popular activities. Accommodation is in self-contained cabins ($20 pp per night), each with a kitchen and bathroom. The resort has a restaurant and bar, but you'll need supplies from the mainland to be self-sufficient.

Camping is possible on Rabbit, Outer Newry, Mausoleum, and Rocky Islands, but you'll need to be self-sufficient. To camp, permits from the

Department of Environment in Mackay, tel. (07) 4951-8788, are required.

Newry Island Resort provides transfers between the island and Port Newry (a rather fancy name for what is no more than boat ramp), four km north of Seaforth; $15 roundtrip. With advance reservations it's possible to make a day trip to the island or arrange drop-offs to other islands of the group.

AIRLIE BEACH AND VICINITY

Airlie (Air-LEE) Beach (pop. 2,700), gateway to the Whitsundays, is a bustling resort town 26 km east of Proserpine and 1,130 km north of Brisbane. The town is misnamed—there is no beach to speak of, and even the actual departure point for cruises is 15 km beyond the town at **Shute Harbour.** But Airlie Beach is a hive of activity year-round, existing only to serve tourists—both those passing through on their way to an island holiday or those based in town and making day trips to the islands. The short main street is crammed with budget accommodations, restaurants, boutiques, and booking agents, but somehow, through all the commercialism and crowds, a relaxed atmosphere prevails.

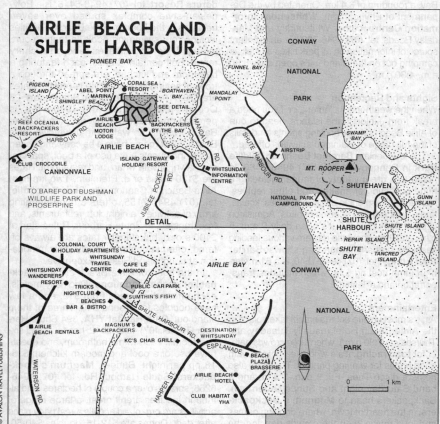

© AVALON TRAVEL PUBLISHING

Conway National Park

This 23,800-hectare park extends south from Airlie Beach to Cape Conway, taking in 50 km of rugged and inaccessible coastline as well as a group of small islands near Shute Harbour. The park is cloaked in subtropical rainforest running right down to the coast, with an extensive swamp of mangroves around the back of Repulse Bay. The road between Airlie Beach and Shute Harbour passes through the park's northern section. From the campground along this road a trail branches north to **Mt. Rooper,** from where the Whitsunday Islands and Passage provide a spectacular panorama, continuing to Swamp Bay, a roundtrip of 6.4 km. Operated by the Department of Environment, **Whitsunday Information Centre,** corner Whitsunday and Mandalay Roads, tel. (07) 4946-7022, is an excellent source of information on all park hikes as well as camping out on the islands. It's open daily 8:30 a.m.-4:30 p.m.

Sights and Recreation

When the weather is inclement, or if you need a break from exploring the islands, head to one of Airlie Beach's many booking agents for details of the full range of mainland activities offered.

The four-hectare **Barefoot Bushman Wildlife Park** in Cannonvale, tel. (07) 4946-1480, is home to a great variety of fauna, including a huge collection of snakes and other reptiles, kangaroos, Tasmanian devils, crocodiles, koalas, and a hundred-odd species of birds. Admission is adult $15, child $7. It's open daily 9 a.m.-5 p.m., and throughout the day are various feeding sessions and snake-handling shows. **Barrier Reef Bungy,** tel. (07) 4946-1540, is a 61-meter-high jump costing $70, which includes transportation and a T-shirt.

Entertainment

Airlie's most unique entertainment takes place in the Airlie Beach Hotel (usually Tuesday and Thursday at 7:30 p.m.), when large crowds gather for **toad racing.** It's a whole load of fun, with good prizes for winning punters. The hotel also hosts a disco Tues.-Fri. 9 p.m.-3 a.m. and a band Saturday night and Sunday afternoon. Backpackers head to **Magnum's Backpackers,** in the heart of town, where drinking games and loud music keep the crowds dancing the night away. Another nightclub is **Tricks,** at 352 Shute Harbour Rd., tel. (07) 4946-6465.

Accommodations

Right in the heart of town is **Airlie Beach Hotel,** 16 Esplanade, tel. (07) 4946-6233, with basic small rooms for $40 s, $50 d. Inexpensive. Also central is **Colonial Court Holiday Apartments,** corner Shute Harbour Rd. and Broadwater Ave., tel. (07) 4946-6180, featuring self-contained units for $55 s or d. Inexpensive. **Airlie Beach Motor Lodge,** 6 Lamond St., tel. (07) 4946-6418, is another central option, with rooms for $62 s, $70 d. Moderate. **Whitsunday Wanderers Resort,** tel. (07) 4946-6446, is a Polynesian-style complex spread over seven hectares in the heart of Airlie Beach. Facilities include four swimming pools, a tennis court, mini-golf, aerobic classes, and an archery range. Self-contained units, each featuring a bathroom and kitchen, are spread through a tropical setting where birdlife is prolific. Rates are $79-119. Moderate. **Coral Sea Resort,** 25 Ocean View Ave., tel. (07) 4946-6458, is perched on a headland overlooking Pioneer Bay, a five-minute walk from downtown Airlie Beach. Most rooms have a balcony and ocean views and guests have use of a pool, spa, croquet lawn, private wharf, and restaurant. Rates are $130-200 s or d. Premium. Two km from Airlie Beach in Cannonvale, **Club Crocodile,** tel. (07) 4946-7155, offers a mind-boggling array of activities, a nightclub, restaurants, and free transfers to Shute Harbour. Rates start at $100 s or d, but standby rates are always offered, often in conjunction with accommodation at Long Island Resort. Expensive.

In the heart of Airlie Beach are five **backpacker accommodations.** Originally motels, each offers dorm beds from $12, and a few have doubles for around $40. Three of them stand out. **Club Habitat YHA,** 394 Shute Harbour Rd., tel. (07) 4946-6312, has four- and six-bed rooms, each with a bathroom, and guests have use of a pool and modern kitchen; $15-18 pp per night. Budget. **Magnum's Backpackers,** Shute Harbour Rd., tel. (07) 4946-6266, sprawls over a couple of hectares, and although facilities aren't great, a large range of activities are organized and it's a real party place after dark. Dorms are $12-15, doubles $40-50.

Budget. **Backpackers by the Bay,** Hermitage Dr., tel. (07) 4946-7267, is a small hostel and much quieter than those in town. Dorms are $14, doubles $32. Budget. The pick of Airlie's backpacker accommodations is **Reef Oceania Backpackers Resort,** 147 Shute Harbour Rd., Cannonvale, tel. (07) 4946-6137 or (1800) 80-0795. Set on a 15-hectare beachfront property, it features all the usual facilities (including a large pool), and each dorm room has a TV and fridge. A regular shuttle service links the resort to downtown Airlie. Rates are $16 pp for a dorm bed or $39 s or d in a private room. Inexpensive.

If you're looking for **campgrounds,** three excellent caravan parks are scattered along the road between Airlie Beach and Shute Harbour, but the least expensive place to camp is in Conway National Park, 12 km from Airlie Beach and four km from Shute Harbour. The campground is small and fills up fast. Sites are $3.50 pp and there are no hot showers. **Island Gateway Holiday Resort,** two km from Airlie Beach toward Shute Harbour, tel. (07) 4946-6228, has modern bathrooms, a covered kitchen area with basic cooking equipment, a pool, mini-golf, half-court tennis, and movies shown nightly. Unpowered sites are $14, powered sites $17, safari tents $20, on-site vans $30, and cabins $39.

Food
Cafe le Mignon, tel. (07) 4946-7459, beside the parking lot off Shute Harbour Rd., is open daily from 7:30 a.m. with delicious croissants from $4 and healthy sandwiches $3.50-7. For the best fish and chips in town, head to **Sumthin's Fishy,** beside the supermarket. On Shute Harbour Rd., **Beaches Bar & Bistro,** tel. (07) 4946-6244, has a popular bar and inexpensive meals, such as hamburgers and Mexican dishes for $5. **KC's Char Grill,** at the top end of Shute Harbour Rd., tel. (07) 4946-6320, is a casual eatery with wooden booths, ceiling fans, and greenery giving it a real tropical ambience. Most meals are charbroiled, with choices including steak, chops, prawns, and delicious racks of lamb; prices range $15-22. Meals are served daily 6 p.m.-2 a.m., and it also opens for Sunday lunch. Away from the crowds of Shute Harbour Rd. is the large **Beach Plaza Brasserie,** a casual place on the Esplanade and overlooking the bay, tel. (07) 4946-7448.

Transportation, Services, and Information
The closest airport to Airlie Beach is in Proserpine. **Qantas,** tel. (13) 1313, flies in daily from Brisbane and Sydney. If you plan to stay on one of the islands, flying directly to Hamilton Island with **Ansett Australia,** tel. (13) 1300, and catching a water taxi to your final destination is less hassle. **Sampson's,** tel. (1300) 65-5449, meets all Qantas flights and provides bus transfers to Airlie Beach ($12 one-way) and Shute Harbour ($16).

All major bus companies, including **Greyhound Pioneer,** tel. (13) 2030, and **McCafferty's,** tel. (13) 1499, detour from the Bruce Highway to Airlie Beach, terminating in the public carpark off Shute Harbour Road. From Brisbane, the trip takes 15 hours. Townsville is four hours north.

Sampson's, tel. (1300) 65-5449, runs a regular bus service between Proserpine and Shute Harbour, picking up at accommodations en route (when booking day trips to the islands, inquire about free transfers from Airlie Beach accommodations to Shute Harbour).

Between Airlie Beach and Shute Harbour is a short airstrip. It receives no scheduled flights, but a variety of chartered flights leave here for destinations throughout the islands. **Island Air Taxis,** tel. (07) 4946-9933, offers flightseeing trips around the islands (from $75 pp) and to the outer reef ($125). **Helireef,** tel. (07) 4946-9102, offers a variety of helicopter joy flights, ranging from a 15-minute flight over a couple of islands ($125 pp) to a three-hour flight to a pontoon on the outer reef ($375).

Avis, Budget, and **National** all have outlets on Shute Harbour Road. Another option for a rental car is **Airlie Beach Rentals,** on Waterson Rd., tel. (07) 4946-6110; rates start at $45 half day, $60 full day. For a cab call **Whitsunday Taxi** at 13-1008.

Airlie Beach has no official information center, just a dozen-odd booking agents vying for your business. As each one is a commercial operation, getting general information on the Whitsundays is difficult. **Destination Whitsunday,** corner Shute Harbour Rd. and the Esplanade, tel. (07) 4948-0200 or (1800) 64-4563, has helpful staff who actually find out what you're interested in doing before flogging tours, as well as Internet access for $10 per hour; open daily 7:30

a.m.-6:30 p.m. **Whitsunday Travel Centre** is a good source of information on onward bus, rail, and air transportation. It's at 265 Shute Harbour Rd., tel. (07) 4946-6224. The Department of Environment runs the **Whitsunday Information Centre,** corner Whitsunday and Mandalay Roads, tel. (07) 4946-7022. Head here for park and camping details for the entire Whitsundays; open daily 8:30 a.m.-4:30 p.m.

WHITSUNDAY ISLANDS

When Capt. James Cook sailed through this area on Whit Sunday, the seventh Sunday after Easter, 1770, he must have been in awe at the beauty of the 74 islands crammed within just one degree of latitude. It's the east coast's greatest concentration of islands, each flanked by sandy beaches and fringing coral reefs and rising from magnificent turquoise-colored water. The seven resort islands cater to all budgets, many not as expensive as you'd think, while the rest are uninhabited and protected as national parks. Regular motor launch services link Shute Harbour to the island resorts, and a couple of days a week, links can also be made from Mackay.

The least-expensive way to book an island holiday in advance is through a travel agent. The packages offered through Ansett Australia, tel. (13) 1344, start at $679 for five nights accommodation and return airfares from Sydney. Only during peak holiday periods are resorts running at full occupancy; to fill empty rooms, **standby rates** are offered, generally two to three days before the empty rooms become available. Savings can be quite considerable, so always ask when making bookings direct through the resort.

The most respected guidebook to the Whitsundays, and definitive reading for yachties, is David Colfelt's *100 Magic Miles of the Great Barrier Reef.*

Long Island

Closest of the resort islands to the mainland, 1,215-hectare Long Island is aptly described by its name. It lies just six km southeast of Shute Harbour, and regular water taxi service links two of the island's three resorts to the mainland, making a pleasant day trip over smooth waters. Apart from the area immediately around the resorts, the island is all national park, with 13 km of trails leading to high lookouts and secluded coves.

Club Crocodile Long Island Resort, tel. (07) 4946-9400 or (1800) 07-5125, is a budget-oriented resort geared toward those looking for action-packed days and to drink and dance the night away. Operated as Happy Bay Resort for 50 years, it was rebuilt in 1984 and has seen various owners and name changes in the time since. Spread around a palm-fringed beach, the large resort is well set up with a wide range of activities offered, a variety of eateries, an outdoor bar, nightclub, and boutique shops. If you don't mind hearing the activities program blasted over the loudspeaker system all day, it's an enjoyable place to spend a couple of days. Lodge units, with shared bathrooms, are $55 pp per night; Garden units, with private bathrooms, are $75 pp, and Beachfront units are $95 pp. Rates include breakfast and island transfers. No discount is offered for late bookings; instead, if rooms are available, a second night is offered for free. This is currently the Whitsunday's best standby deal, and as there always seems to be vacant rooms, it should be available most of the time.

A 20-minute walk south from Long Island Resort is **Palm Bay Hideaway,** tel. (07) 4946-9233 or (1800) 77-7760, a low-key resort of just 16 freestanding units and eight basic cabins spread around a pleasant beach area. The relaxed atmosphere appeals to those who want to get away from it all. Water sport equipment, such as catamarans, sailboards, paddle skis, and snorkeling gear, is provided, and there's a small pool, but, for the most part, the guests attracted here spend their days lazing around the beach or relaxing on the hammock and outdoor furniture outside each unit. Rates range $146 s, $224 d plus meals, or stay in the cabins from $40 pp. Standby rates are often as low as $75 pp per night.

Whitsunday All Over, tel. (1300) 36-6494, offers transfers for guests and day trippers to the above resorts for $24 roundtrip, which includes bus transfers between Airlie Beach accommodations and Shute Harbour. Departures from Shute Harbour are at 9:15 a.m., returning at 4:15 p.m.

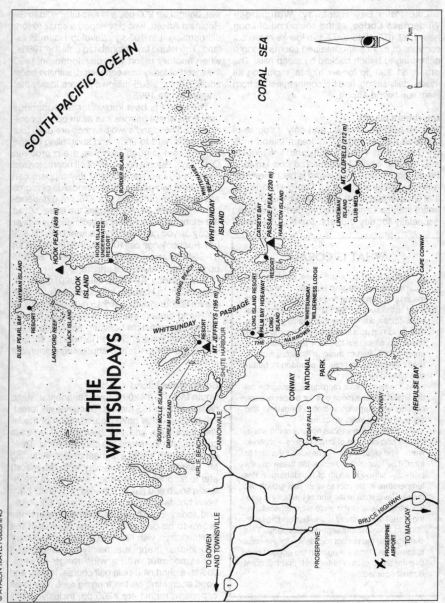

© AVALON TRAVEL PUBLISHING

Like Palm Bay Hideaway, **Whitsunday Wilderness Lodge,** at the south end of Long Island, tel. (07) 4946-9777, is a low-key resort. It consists of eight self-contained cabins along a palm-fringed beach backed by steep hills. The rate is $1,390 pp for six nights, including all meals, daily sailing, and helicopter transfers from Hamilton Island Airport.

Daydream Island

Just 16 hectares in area and only a couple of hundred meters wide, Daydream Island (officially known as West Molle Island) lies four km northeast of Shute Harbour and one km from South Molle Island. The island is best known for a large, moderately priced family-style resort that sprawls over most of the island, including the entire southern end, which has been developed especially for day trippers. In 1933 the island

---

WHAT IS CORAL?

Coral is a polyp, of the same family as the sea anemone and jellyfish. The reef is made up of **hard coral** and **soft coral.** The hard coral is the reef builder. The polyp secretes a hard, calcareous coating that begins as a base, then builds up as a limestone casing into which the polyp can draw itself for protection. The polyp is only two to three millimeters wide; it feeds by capturing floating plankton in tentacles around its mouth.

As the hard corals reproduce, they grow on the limestone skeletons of their predecessors, binding together with secreted limestone and algae to form a solid structure.

Coral is found in various oceans of the world, but the combination of three factors—shallow, warm, and clear water—is needed for a reef to form. The Queensland coast fits these criteria perfectly, although south of Bundaberg, water temperature is too cool to allow reef growth. As the sea level rose at the end of the last ice age, low-lying coastal plains were submerged, forming a shallow continental shelf extending up to 300 km from the present-day coastline. This shelf formed the perfect foundation for the coral to form a reef, and it is right on the edge of continental shelf, on the outer reef, that the coral is most spectacular.

---

was bought for 200 pounds and later sold to Sir Reginald Ansett, who developed a small resort, dismantling it in 1953 to develop Hayman Island. The island lay uninhabited until the 1960s, when another resort was developed. In 1990 the resort of today was completed, with the latest addition being a $25-million childcare facility that opened in late 1998.

The resort is best known for an enormous pool from where patrons can swim up to a poolside bar. The island's two beaches are okay (but solitude is hard to find), and snorkeling on the fringing reef is good (stingers are a problem Oct.-May). Guests have use of all nonmotorized water sports equipment, and day trippers can use one of two pools. Three standards of rooms are available, ranging $175-275 s or d depending on the view. Meal packages are extra, but as the island offers a variety of eateries, it is easier to pay as you go (the nightly dinner buffet is $28 pp). For bookings call (07) 4948-8488 or (1800) 07-5040. Standby rates, when offered, are $85 pp per night inclusive of transfers.

Whitsunday All Over, tel. (1300) 36-6494, departs Shute Harbour four times daily for Daydream Island, including a 5:15 p.m. departure for an island dinner; the fare of $24 roundtrip includes bus transfers between Airlie Beach accommodations and Shute Harbour, or for $37 you'll also get lunch and snorkeling equipment to rent.

South Molle Island

South Molle is a 420-hectare continental island rising gently to 195 meters. Once heavily forested, grazing cattle have cleared much of the island's southern end, but the many hiking trails crisscrossing the island are still interesting. Trails lead to all the island's highest peaks, including Mt. Jeffreys (four km one-way from the resort) and to a couple of secluded beaches at the island's south end (six km one-way). Tourists have been holidaying on South Molle for 60 years, and today **South Molle Island Resort** has grown to be one of the largest resorts of the Whitsundays, with nearly 200 rooms of six configurations. It appeals mainly to families and honeymooners, with a wide range of water sports, a short nine-hole golf course, tennis, and good snorkeling on the fringing reef. The least expensive rooms are $205 pp, inclusive of all meals, activities, and transfers from Hamilton Island or Proserpine Airports. Worth the extra few dollars are the Whitsunday rooms, with ocean views and private balconies for $235 pp. The standby rate (book within 48 hours) is $120 pp. For all bookings call (07) 4946-9433 or (1800) 07-5080.

Whitsunday All Over, tel. (1300) 36-6494, transfers resort guests from the mainland, as well as taking day trippers over; departures are daily at 10 a.m. returning at 5 p.m.; $28 roundtrip. **Seatrek,** tel. (07) 4946-5255, offers a similar service, or a stop at South Molle can be made as part of a three-island cruise (Daydream and Hook Islands are the others) for $50 pp, including snorkeling, lunch, and a submarine ride.

Lindeman Island

Home to Australia's first **Club Med** resort, this 790-hectare island lies at the southern end of the Whitsundays, well away from other resort islands. Half the island is protected as a national park, with the resort and airstrip at the south end and thickly forested ridges dominating the north. Extensive grasslands around the island's eastern slopes and 212-meter summit of Mt. Oldfield allow unimpeded views of the beaches below.

Tourists have been coming to the island since the late 1920s, but it wasn't until 1992 that Club Med opened, offering the all-inclusive activity-oriented style that the resort company is known for. Lots of water activities are offered, as well as a large beachfront pool, golf, and tennis. Rates start at $199 pp per night, including all meals, beer and wine, and activities. This rate doesn't include the one-time $50 Club Med membership. For reservations call (079) 46-9333 or (1800) 80-7973. From North America call (800) 258-2633.

If you would like to come over to Lindeman Island for just the day, there are three options, but being so far from mainland gateways, it's not cheap. From Shute Harbour, **Whitsunday All Over,** tel. (1300) 36-6494, departs daily at 7 a.m.; the cost is $108, which includes all resort activities and a buffet lunch. From Mackay, **Roylen Cruises,** tel. (07) 4955-3066, departs Saturday and Sunday at 9 a.m.; inclusive of meals and booze it's $100 pp. The third alternative is to fly over from Proserpine, Shute Har-

bour, or Hamilton Island; from $65 one-way. Resort guests can use any of the above services, or pay $50 roundtrip for a water taxi from Hamilton Island Airport.

Hamilton Island

Hamilton lies in the middle of the Whitsunday Islands, 18 km southeast of Shute Harbour. It's the most developed of the islands, more like a small town than a resort, with high-rise accommodation towers, a 400-berth marina, an endless array of activities, and an international airport capable of handling Boeing 767s. The development of the island was the vision of just one man, Keith Williams (when Williams was at the helm, the resort was known as Williamstown), whose hands-on approach and determination to build a resort like no other in the Whitsundays has become part of Queensland folklore. In the 1970s and '80s when Queensland was ruled by the National Party, changing Hamilton's long-term farming lease to a tourism zoning and getting a megaresort approved in the middle of an UNESCO World Heritage area was met with little opposition. As the high-rise accommodations grew, a bay was dredged for a marina and a whole hillside dynamited with little government intervention.

Development is on the north end of the island, with the main resort facing Catseye Bay and sprawling over a low ridge to an artificial harbor on the island's west side. The island's south end is scarred by the runway, but the wide eastern peninsula is interesting to explore, with a 15-km hiking trail leading to Passage Peak and a lookout above the resort.

The island can accommodate more than 2,000 guests in multistory towers, low-rise beachfront lodges, and a couple of super-luxurious private residences (up to $1,500 per night). Rooms at the Beach Club stand out. Each of the 60 spacious rooms overlooks the pool, with guests arriving at a unique poolside check-in. The rooms are named after Whitsunday beaches, each featuring a painting of its namesake. Beach Club rooms are $300 s or d, while rates through the rest of the resort start at $200, rising to $350 for a room with a view. Standby rates are $80 pp. The resort itself is very activity-oriented, but almost everything is additional to accommodation cost. All manner of water-oriented activities are based at the marina, which is surrounded by a boardwalk dotted with boutiques, cafés, and restaurants. For bookings call (07) 4946-9999 or (1800) 07-5110.

Until the construction of the island's airport, Proserpine was the gateway to the Whitsundays. Nowadays **Ansett Australia,** tel. (13) 1300, flies directly from Brisbane, Sydney, Melbourne, and Cairns to the island. For guests of the resorts on Long, Daydream, and South Molle islands, **Whitsunday All Over,** tel. (1300) 36-6494, provides transfers from Hamilton Island Airport for $37 roundtrip. Lindeman and Hayman Islands operate their own water taxi services. From the Airlie Beach airstrip, **Island Air Taxis,** tel. (07) 4946-9933 or (1800) 64-6933, offers charter flights to Hamilton for $40 pp one-way. **Fantasea Cruises,** tel. (07) 4946-5111 or (1800) 65-0851, offers boat transfers between the island and Shute Harbour; adult $40, child $20. Boats depart Shute Harbour daily at 8:30 a.m. For $49 (child $24.50), island transfers can be combined with a trip to Whitehaven Beach on Whitsunday Island (Tuesday, Thursday, and Sunday only). From Port of Mackay **Roylen Cruises,** tel. (07) 4955-3066, heads to Hamilton Island Saturday and Sunday departing 9 a.m.; $55 roundtrip (a stop is made at Lindeman Island en route).

Whitsunday Island

Largest of the Whitsundays, this 10,800-hectare island is undeveloped and uninhabited. It's most popular with day trippers who flock to six-km **Whitehaven Beach** on the island's east coast, the longest beach in the group (its pure white sand is almost 99% silica). Rugged topography and long inlets that almost divide it make Whitsunday Island an interesting place to explore. Until the arrival of Europeans in the late 1800s, Aboriginals lived permanently on the island. A sawmill operated at Cid Harbour for many years, but today the entire island is protected as a national park.

Camping is permitted at the south end of Whitehaven Beach, but as there are no facilities or drinking water, you'll need to be totally self-sufficient. A better option for campers is one of three campgrounds on Cid Harbour (a personal favorite is Dugong Beach), where there are toilets, showers, drinking water, and gas barbecues. Most cruise boats do camper drop-offs, with **Island Camping Connection,** tel. (07) 4946-5255, a specialist; $35 pp.

Fantasea, tel. (07) 4946-5111, departs Shute Harbour Tuesday, Thursday, and Sunday at 8:30 a.m. on a cruise taking in Whitehaven Beach and Hamilton Island for $45 pp. For more personal service and an informative commentary, *Reef Express,* tel. (07) 4946-6675, is ideal. This boat departs Abel Point Marina daily at 9 a.m. for Whitehaven Beach, continuing to Hook Island for snorkeling, then returning to Airlie Beach around 5 p.m. This trip is a great value at adult $55 pp.

Hook Island

Rugged and remote, 5,180-hectare Hook Island lies 30 km northeast of Shute Harbour and is separated from Whitsunday Island by a narrow channel. The island's fringing reef provides the best diving and snorkeling of all Whitsunday Islands, providing an alternative to more-expensive outer reef diving trips. A small resort and underwater observatory on the southeast coast are the only development on this otherwise uninhabited island.

Hook Island Underwater Resort, tel. (07) 4946-9380 or (1800) 07-5080, is a low-key place where the emphasis is on diving. It has basic but adequate accommodations and the only commercial camping on any of the Whitsunday Islands. Snorkeling and scuba diving is good in front of the resort (although visibility can be poor during spring tides), and the resort's dive boat heads out to the reef three times weekly. The resort dive shop rents gear, fills tanks, and operates PADI dive courses. Around a headland from the lodge is an underwater observatory (admission $10), surf-skis for guest use, and basic groceries for sale. Dorm beds are $20 pp; campsites are $13 pp, and cabins are $60 s or d. At last report, two nights' accommodation and transfers was $44 and five nights' accommodation plus a PADI dive course was $320 pp. Lodge guests and campers may dine in the restaurant (open for breakfast, lunch, and dinner) or cook their own meals in the communal kitchen.

Seatrek, tel. (07) 4946-5255, provides transfers to the resort from Abel Point Marina, departing daily at 9 a.m. The cost is $35 roundtrip, but the fare is often incorporated as an accommodation package. **Whitsunday All Over,** tel. (1300) 36-

6494, visits Hook Island Underwater Observatory as part of a three-island day cruise; $55 pp.

Off Hook Island's northwest coast is **Langford Reef,** a popular destination for divers, and **Black Island** (often called Bali Ha'i), where Whitsunday All Over, tel. (1300) 36-6494, operates a small submarine giving passengers a chance to view a coral reef without getting wet; adult $67, child $35 includes lunch and an hour on Daydream Island.

Hayman Island

Guests at 322-hectare Hayman Island enjoy the absolute best of everything at a resort generally regarded as one of the world's most luxurious, while also surrounded by the beauty of one of the best fringing reefs in the Whitsundays. While emphasis at other upmarket island resorts is on natural surroundings, Hayman flatters its guests with facilities and accommodations equal in standard to any of the world's greatest resorts.

In 1985 a planned $25-million facelift turned into a two-year $300 million redevelopment with no expense spared. Highlights include a one-hectare pool featuring both fresh- and saltwater sections separated by narrow walkways, an elegant bar styled on an English gentleman's club, a collection of antiques and artworks, traditional Japanese Garden, palm trees, and 60,000 tons of imported sand that's smoothed over at the end of each day.

The island has excellent scuba diving facilities, including a school, shop, and boat, as well the following guest activities: windsurfing, sailing, waterskiing, parasailing, tennis, squash, aerobics, and mini-golf. The *Reef Goddess* heads out from the resort each morning, taking guests to either Whitehaven Beach or the outer reef. All guest rooms have water views, many with marble bathrooms and air-conditioning. All rates are room-only; transfers, meals, and select activities are extra. Rates start at $460 s or d, rooms along the beachfront start at $680, and suites range $1,030-1,240. Guests have the choice of dining in one of six restaurants, including the elegant La Fontaine, and enjoying nightly entertainment such as cabaret shows. Access to the island is aboard one of three luxurious motor yachts from Hamilton Island Airport ($320 roundtrip). For bookings and package deals call (079) 40-1234 or (1800) 07-5175. From North America call (800) 366-1300.

DAY TRIPS TO THE OUTER REEF

The Whitsundays are Queenland's best known island group, but they lie close to the mainland and well away from actual reef. The closest reefs, which lie 63 km from Shute Harbour, include Bait, Hook, Line, and Sinker (look at a chart to see how they were named). These platform reefs sit at and below water level. There are no islands to explore, no resorts, just a few pontoons moored in strategic positions for the use of day trippers who come to dive and snorkel at one of the world's great dive sites. Only high-speed motor cruisers can make it from the mainland to the outer reef and back in one day. **Fantasea Cruises,** tel. (07) 4946-5111, departs Shute Harbour daily at 8:30 a.m. for **Reefworld,** a large pontoon on the outer reef. The pontoon has an underwater observatory, sundeck, restaurant, showers, and plenty of good snorkeling; cost of the cruise is adult $120, senior $90, child $60. Certified divers pay $155, including gear rental. **Helireef,** tel. (07) 4946-9102, flies out to Reefworld from Airlie Beach, with snorkeling and lunch for $215 pp. **Air Whitsunday Seaplanes,** tel. (07) 4946-9111, offers the least expensive way to see the outer reef, with a one-hour flight over Hayman Island and the reef for $80 pp.

Island resorts offering guests day trips to the outer reef include: Hook, Hayman, Hamilton, Lindeman, and South Molle.

SCUBA DIVING IN THE WHITSUNDAYS

The suspended sediment that gives the waters of the Whitsundays a magnificent color inhibits visibility for divers, so serious divers will want to head to the outer reef. That said, the diversity of coral and fishlife around the islands will not disappoint, and with the islands' fringing reefs protected from the full brunt of the ocean by the outer reef, the waters are relatively calm.

Each of the island resorts caters to divers, with Hook Island Underwater Resort being especially good for keen divers and those planning to complete a dive course (package deals offered here are less expensive than staying on the mainland). For those not staying out on the islands, organizing a diving holiday can be problematic. The best diving is on the outer reef, but being more than 60 km from Airlie Beach, it makes for a long and expensive day diving. Numerous operators run to the outer reef, but few cater specifically to divers. **Fantasea Cruises,** tel. (07) 4946-5111, runs out to Reefworld, on the outer reef, for $155 including lunch, one dive, and equipment. **Whitsunday Diver,** tel. (07) 4946-5366, charges $130 pp for a day trip, enough time for two dives.

Airlie Beach holds a profusion of dive operators, most of which offer learn-to-dive PADI certification courses. **Rum Runner Adventures,** tel. (07) 4946-6508 or (1800) 07-5120, is one such company. They offer a three-day diving package including transfers to the outer reef, almost unlimited dives, all meals, and accommodation on board their boat for $415 pp. This is also a good company to learn to dive with; the basic PADI course is $325 over three days. Experienced divers should consider **Anaconda III,** operated by Oceania Dive, tel. (07) 4946-6032 or (1800) 07-5035, which regularly sails out on a three-day trip beyond the outer reef for diving in the Coral Sea; $420 pp.

CRUISING THE WHITSUNDAYS

Calm waters, sheltered anchorages, uninhabited islands, and an ideal climate make the Whitsundays the prime destination for a sailing holiday, but it is only in the last 15 years that the opportunity to experience the Whitsundays under sail became possible for those without a yacht. The options are a day trip on one of the many racing maxi-yachts that have retired to the Whitsundays, or on a bareboat charter. "Bareboat" is a seafaring term for skippering a rented yacht, and so long as at least one member of the crew can sail it is the perfect way to explore the Whitsundays.

A Day under Sail
Australia's strong ocean-racing traditions date back several decades, and many of the country's fastest yachts spend their retirement days sailing around the Whitsundays with their decks full of tourists. Some examples are **Gretel,** tel. (07) 4946-4999, a 20.8-meter maxi that challenged for the America's Cup in the early 1970s; **Apollo,** tel. (07) 4946-7122, which won just about

every race in the South Pacific including a Sydney-Hobart; and **Ragamuffin,** tel. (07) 4946-7777, which won the Sydney-Hobart race three times. These and other yachts depart Shute Harbour daily 8:30-9 a.m., sailing out to Langford Reef (not on the outer reef) or Whitehaven Beach for snorkeling or scuba diving ($40-50 extra) and returning 4-4:30 p.m. Prices range $65-75. Sailing isn't restricted to ex-champions; **On the Edge** is a high-speed catamaran (meaning more time at the destination) sailing to Whitehaven Beach (Monday, Wednesday, and Saturday) and Hook Island (Tuesday, Thursday, Friday, and Sunday); departures are from Abel Point Marina at 9 a.m. The cost is $63 pp; for bookings call (07) 4946-5433.

Some operators offer overnight sailing cruises, typically departing 9 a.m. and returning 4 p.m. two nights and three days later, with price inclusive of accommodation on board, all meals, and snorkeling equipment for $250-300 pp. Try: **Waltzing Matilda,** tel. (07) 4946-4782, a 20-meter ketch; **Prosail Whitsunday,** tel. (07) 4946-7533, which has a large fleet and caters to under-35s (bring your own booze); and **Providence,** tel. (1800) 07-5111, a timber replica of a gaffed-rigged schooner.

Bareboat Charters
Chartering your own yacht is the ultimate way to enjoy the Whitsundays, although it's not particularly cheap and you'll need at least one crew member proficient at handling the size yacht you intend renting. Local weather and navigational considerations to be taken into effect will be explained before heading out. Most yachts have a hot shower, kitchen, barbecue, music system, and a whole range of other luxuries. Yachts range in size from seven to 15 meters. Each has a recommended crew number, but these are really a maximum—try to crew the boat at least two less. Rates start at $250 per day for the smallest yachts. A 12-meter yacht, perfect for a crew of four, runs $320-400 per day, with discounts for weekly rentals. Most charter operators offer food packs, and although convenient, they can really add up ($25-30 pp per day). Two of the most experienced operators are **Queensland Yacht Charters,** tel. (07) 4946-7400 or (1800) 07-5013, and **Whitsunday Rent-a-Yacht,** tel. (07) 4946-9232 or (1800) 07-5111.

THE WHITSUNDAYS TO CAIRNS

Once you've managed to drag yourself away from the Whitsundays, it's an easy day's drive 600 km north to Cairns, but along the way are enough distractions to make the trip last at least a few days. This region is the heart of tropical Queensland, dominated by miles of rugged coastline, stately colonial-style buildings, and streets lined with colorful bougainvilleas. The first major center north of Proserpine is Townsville, home to the excellent Great Barrier Reef Wonderland, a living coral reef transposed to the heart of the city. Offshore is Magnetic Island, easily accessible for day trippers. The reef may be Queensland's favorite holiday destination, but Hinchinbrook Island, halfway between Townsville and Cairns, is another amazing place you shouldn't miss. Lying close to the mainland, it's the world's largest island national park. For the best mainland beaches north of the Sunshine Coast, head to the string of communities along Mission Beach and overlooking Dunk Island.

Bowen
Founded in 1861 and north Queensland's oldest town, this farming and fishing center of 8,600 features wide palm-lined streets dotted with colonial buildings. Salt production is also a part of the local economy, with almost 10,000 tons produced annually. Murals along Powell and Williams Streets depict scenes from the town's past, and **Bowen Historical Museum,** 22 Gordon St., tel. (07) 4786-2035, displays hundreds of artifacts dating from pre-European days to modern industries. The museum is open Mon.-Fri. 10:30 a.m.-4 p.m., Sunday 10:30 a.m.-12:30 p.m. East of the main street is the coal-loading terminal of **Port Denison** and **Bowen Boat Harbour,** protected from the elements by North Head and an artificial sea wall. Immediately north of Bowen is the long expanse of Queens Beach and rocky **Cape Edgecombe,** indented on its eastern flanks by pretty **Horseshoe Bay,** a narrow cove of sand surrounded by rugged outcrops of granite. At the back of the bay a short trail leads to a lookout high above the beach.

Right downtown, **North Australian Hotel,** 55 Herbert St., tel. (07) 4786-1244, has good pub-style rooms with shared bathrooms for $38 s, $45 d. Inexpensive. Another inexpensive place to stay is **Barnacles Backpackers,** 16 Gordon St., tel. (07) 4786-4400, geared mainly for fruit-pickers. Dorms are $12 pp and doubles are $28. Budget. Out at Horseshoe Bay is **Whitsunday Sands Resort,** tel. (07) 4786-3333. Rooms are fairly basic, and the whole place has seen better days, but the resort has an excellent beachfront location and the price is right; $55 s, $60 d for a self-contained unit. Inexpensive. **Horseshoe Bay Resort,** tel. (07) 4786-2564, on the same beach, features a heated pool, barbecue area, and kiosk; sites are $12-16, on-site vans $24, and cabins from $30. Budget.

Bowen Tourism operates a small **information center** downtown at 34 Williams St., tel. (4786) 4494; open daily 9 a.m.-5 p.m. South of town, in a rest area on the east side of the road, is an information booth manned by friendly volunteers offering coffee and coconuts to passersby.

Ayr
This town of 8,500 sits on the north bank of the **Burdekin River,** one of Queensland's largest rivers. This is sugarcane country, with one million tons of raw sugar produced annually. **Ayr Nature Display,** corner Wilmington and McKenzie Streets, tel. (07) 4783-2189, houses 60,000 specimens of small Australian fauna. Admission $2.50; open daily 8 a.m.-4 p.m.

Bowling Green Bay National Park
Straddling the highway between Ayr and Townsville, this 55,400-hectare park has two distinct sections. East of the highway is Bowling Green Bay, a low-lying area of mangroves protected from prevailing winds and currents by Cape Bowling Green, a long crescent of land. But it is west of the highway, in a mountainous area dominated by 1,342-meter **Mt. Elliot,** that you'll find the park's accessible attractions. This section of the park protects the southern extent of tropical rainforest in Australia. The high peaks are the source of many watersheds that flow in an easterly direction over granite outcrops and through lushly vegetated gorges. The main access road spurs

west from the Bruce Highway 60 km northwest of Ayr and 30 km south of Townsville. The facility area at the end of this road is the trailhead for paths leading up the lower slopes of Mt. Elliot; one, along **Cockatoo Creek,** is eight km one-way (three hours); the other, to **Alligator Falls,** is 17 km one-way (five hours). A campground area has toilets, showers, and barbecues; for bookings call (07) 4778-8203.

TOWNSVILLE

Largest tropical city in Australia and Queensland's third-largest city, Townsville (pop. 100,000) lies 1,370 km north of Brisbane and 340 km south of Cairns. It may not be the prettiest place on the coast, but it's home to the excellent Great Barrier Reef Wonderland and is the gateway to Magnetic Island. Townsville was the original capital of reef tourism, especially for North Americans, but the construction of Cairns International Airport changed all that, and today, although areas of downtown look a bit rough around the edges, much is being done to spruce the place up. The city sprawls over the delta of the Ross River, with the city center spread along Ross Creek and nestled in the shadow of Castle Hill, a granite massif rising 286 meters from the surrounding plains.

Established by a Sydney businessman in 1864 to serve vast pastoral leases, Townsville grew as a beef and wool center. A rail line completed between Brisbane and Townsville in 1877 and the construction of a line to Mt. Isa in 1929 saw Townsville grow to be Queensland's busiest port.

Great Barrier Reef Wonderland

The Great Barrier Reef may lie 70 km off Townsville's coastline, but modern technology has brought the reef to the mainland by re-creating its form under artificial conditions. The complex comprises the **Great Barrier Reef Aquarium, Omnimax Theatre,** and a Museum of Tropical Queensland display devoted to the **Pandora,** and serves as the departure point for ferries to Magnetic Island. Without a doubt, the aquarium is the highlight of a visit to Townsville. It holds a living reef contained in a tank 38 meters long, 17 meters wide, and 4.6 meters deep. All reef conditions are artificially maintained to keep the reef alive. Wave motion, tidal movement, and a farm of algae combine to maintain the natural balance of nutrients while replenishing oxygen within the tank. The aquarium is home to 150 species of coral and 200 species of fish. A transparent walk-through tunnel winds through the main aquarium, allowing visitors to experience life underwater without getting wet. Within the aquarium complex is an interactive display and audiovisual, and information on reef protection. Admission is adult $14.50, child $10. Open daily 9 a.m.-5 p.m. For further information call (07) 4750-0800 or visit the website www.aquarium.org.au.

The **Museum of Tropical Queensland,** tel. (07) 4721-1662, a branch of the Queensland Museum, has an excellent new display in the wonderland complex. Known as **Pandora,** it catalogues the history of the HMS *Pandora,* an integral part of one of the world's best-known seafaring stories—the mutiny on the *Bounty.* After the mutiny and Captain Bligh's incredible return to Great Britain, the *Pandora* was sent in search of his boat, the *Bounty.* After capturing a small part of the mutinous crew in Tahiti, the *Pandora* hit the Great Barrier Reef off Cape York. The captain managed to float his ship free of the reef before it sank on a sandy seabed and lay undisturbed for 186 years, until its discovery in 1977. In the ensuing years, many artifacts have been recovered from the wreck, forming an evolving exhibition due for completion by 2001. Other museum displays include those dedicated to the Koori, dinosaurs, and tropical flora and fauna. Admission is $5. It's currently open daily 9 a.m.-5 p.m.

Another part of Wonderland is the Omnimax Theatre, tel. (07) 4721-1481, a cavernous auditorium with a domed roof and seats tilted back for comfortable viewing. For extra clarity, underwater images are shot on film 10 times the normal size; combined with a screen 180-degrees wide, the show gives viewers an awesome experience. The documentary *Living Sea* is shown continuously between 10 a.m. and 5:30 p.m.; $9.

Other Sights

Flinders St. Mall, the commercial center of Townsville, buzzes with activity on weekdays and houses a popular market Sunday. At the east end of the mall is **Flinders St. East,** a strip of historic buildings overlooking Ross Creek.

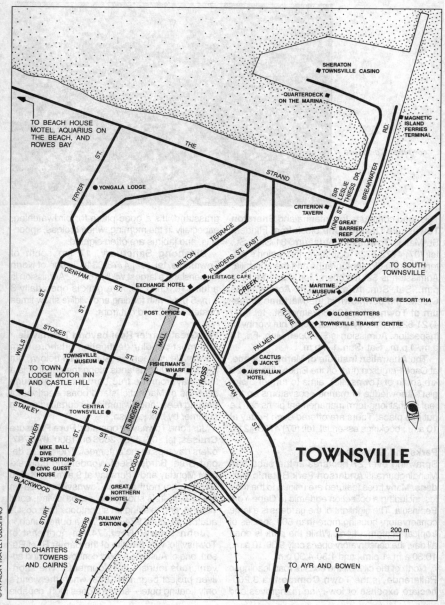

SHERATON
TOWNSVILLE CASINO

QUARTERDECK
ON THE MARINA

MAGNETIC
ISLAND
FERRIES
TERMINAL

TO BEACH HOUSE
MOTEL, AQUARIUS ON
THE BEACH, AND
ROWES BAY

THE

STRAND

FRYER ST.

YONGALA LODGE

SIR LESLIE THIESS DR.

BREAKWATER RD.

CRITERION
TAVERN

KING ST.

GREAT
BARRIER
REEF
WONDERLAND

MELTON TERRACE

FLINDERS ST. EAST

CREEK

TO SOUTH
TOWNSVILLE

DENHAM ST.

EXCHANGE HOTEL

HERITAGE CAFE

MARITIME
MUSEUM

ADVENTURERS RESORT YHA

STOKES ST.

POST OFFICE

PLUME ST.

GLOBETROTTERS

TOWNSVILLE TRANSIT CENTRE

WILLS ST.

TOWNSVILLE
MUSEUM

MALL

ST.

FISHERMAN'S
WHARF

ROSS

DEAN ST.

PALMER ST.

CACTUS
JACK'S

AUSTRALIAN
HOTEL

TO TOWN
LODGE MOTOR INN
AND CASTLE HILL

STANLEY ST.

CENTRA
TOWNSVILLE

FLINDERS ST.

WALKER ST.

MIKE BALL
DIVE
EXPEDITIONS

CIVIC GUEST
HOUSE

BLACKWOOD ST.

OGDEN ST.

TOWNSVILLE

STURT ST.

GREAT
NORTHERN
HOTEL

FLINDERS ST.

RAILWAY
STATION

TO CHARTERS
TOWERS
AND CAIRNS

0   200 m

TO AYR AND BOWEN

downtown Townsville

This road continues to a marina and **Sheraton Townsville Casino.** One block from Flinders St. Mall is **Townsville Museum,** 81 Sturt St., tel. (07) 4772-5725, displaying the region's history through old photographs and memorabilia. Admission is $2. It's open Mon.-Fri. 10 a.m.-3 p.m., Sat.-Sun. 10 a.m.-1 p.m. Across Ross Creek from downtown is the **Maritime Museum of Townsville,** 42-68 Palmer St., tel. (07) 4721-5251. It's only a small facility but worthy of inspection. Admission is $2. Open Mon.-Fri. 10 a.m.-4 p.m., Sat.-Sun. 1-4 p.m.

The **Australian Institute of Marine Science,** at Cape Ferguson (turn off the Bruce Highway 30 km south of Townsville), aims to further biologist's knowledge of marine ecosystems on the reef so that long-term management plans can be put into place. Tours are offered each Friday at 10 a.m.; bookings essential, tel. (07) 4753-4211.

Parks and Gardens
Sprawling over 27 hectares in the suburb of Mundingburra is **Anderson Park Botanic Gardens.** Many trees featured are unique to the tropics, including a collection endemic to Cape York Peninsula. The highlight of the gardens is a large conservatory housing more than 500 species of tropical rainforest flora. While the park is open all day, the conservatory opens only 9:30-10 a.m., 10:30 a.m.-1 p.m., and 1:30-4:30 p.m.

North of the city, off the coastal road leading to Pallarenda, is the **Town Common,** a 3,200-hectare expanse of low-lying mangroves and grassland. It's a good place for birdwatching, especially in the morning, when brolgas, spoonbills, and jabirus are often sighted.

Billabong Sanctuary, 17 km south of Townsville, tel. (07) 4778-8344, is one of North Queensland's largest wildlife parks. Admission is adult $16, child $8. The park is open daily 8 a.m.-5 p.m., with feeding and wildlife show times posted on a board out front.

The Great Barrier Reef beyond Townsville
The most popular destination offshore from Townsville is Magnetic Island (see below), but like a majority of islands along the coast, it is a long way from the true barrier reef (although sections of Magnetic Island boast sections of fringing reef), and swimming is curtailed during summer by box jellyfish.

Just one Townsville operator, **Pure Pleasure Cruises,** tel. (07) 4721-3666 or (1800) 07-9797, offers day trips to the outer reef. Their boats depart Great Barrier Reef Wonderland daily except Monday and Thursday at 9 a.m. for **Kelso Reef** 90 km northeast of Townsville. Once on the reef, there's snorkeling, scuba diving, coral viewing, and relaxing on a pontoon. Tour cost is adult $124, child $74 including a buffet lunch.

John Brewer Reef, 74 km northeast of Townsville, was the site of the Barrier Reef Resort, one of Australia's most controversial and adventurous tourism developments. The short-lived project began in 1988, when the world's only floating hotel—seven stories high, capable of accommodating 400 guests, and complete with restaurants, spas, a tennis court, and a nightclub—was towed into a lagoon on the outer reef. The second part of the project, **Fantasy Island,** featuring a restaurant, outdoor lounge area, movie theater, and palm-fringed swimming pool, was towed into place two months later. Fantasy Island lasted all of 10 days before a storm sent it to Davy Jones's locker. Barrier Reef Resort lasted a little longer; wracked by monetary problems and low occupancy rates, it was last seen being towed north to Ho Chi Minh City.

Mike Ball Dive Expeditions

One of Australia's premier dive operations, Mike Ball Dive Expeditions is based at 252 Walker St., Townsville, tel. (07) 4772-3022. The two most popular destinations for dive trips from Townsville are **John Brewer Reef** and the wreck of the *Yongala,* a passenger ship that sank off Cape Bowling Green in 1911 with the loss of 122 lives. Three-day, two-night expeditions out to the *Yongala* depart every Tuesday and Friday at 8 p.m. The tour cost, inclusive of accommodation on board *Watersport,* all meals, and diving, is $466-546 pp. (In bad weather diving the *Yongala* is substituted for John Brewer Reef). A unique feature of Mike Ball's dive program are trips well beyond the outer reef to remote coral reefs where visibility can reach 50 meters. Rates for these seven-day trips start at $2,100 pp.

At the company's Townsville headquarters is a large and unique complex, with the dive shop built into the side of a training pool. Rates for an open-water PADI course range $399-485.

Arts and Entertainment

The **Criterion Tavern,** corner Strand and King St., tel. (07) 4771-2271, comprises a beer garden and nightclub, with bands performing most nights. On Flinders St. East, the wine bar in the Exchange Hotel is a good place for a quiet drink, as is **Quarterdeck on the Marina,** with live music Wed.-Sun. evenings.

Townsville Civic Theatre, 41 Boundary St., tel. (07) 4772-2677, hosts performing arts, including drama, orchestral concerts, musicals, and dance. Tickets range $12-40.

Sheraton Townsville Casino, tel. (07) 4722-2333, is built on a breakwall that wraps around the harbor. Games offered include roulette,

blackjack, craps, keno, and Australia's own two-up. The casino has two bars, a number of eateries, and live jazz Fri.-Sat. nights; open daily 10 a.m.-3 a.m.

Accommodations

Yongala Lodge, 11 Fryer St., tel. (07) 4772-4633, a two-story timber building dating from 1884, is named for the *Yongala,* which sank off Townsville in 1911 killing more than 100 people, including the lodge's original owners. Rooms in the main house have been restored while out back are modern motel units. Rates range $79-95 s or d. Moderate. The **Great Northern Hotel,** 496 Flinders St., tel. (07) 4776-6191, has typical pub-style rooms with shared facilities and a bar downstairs; $24 s, $36 d. Inexpensive.

Town Lodge Motor Inn, 15 Victoria St., tel. (07) 4771-2164, is one of the least expensive motels within walking distance of downtown. Facilities include a pool, barbecue, and laundry, and many rooms have a kitchen; $56 s, $64 d. Moderate. Close to the waterfront is **Beach House Motel,** 66 The Strand, tel. (07) 4721-1333, a little worse for wear but reasonably priced at $62 s, $68 d. Moderate. Also on The Strand, at no. 75, is the 14-story **Aquarius on the Beach,** tel. (07) 4772-4255. All rooms are large and have a kitchen and private balcony with ocean views; $110-120 s or d. Expensive. In the same expensive category is the **Mercure Inn,** Woolcock St., tel. (07) 4725-2222 or (1800) 64-2244, which features 200 rooms, a massive saltwater lagoon-style pool, and two tennis courts, all set among four lush hectares of tropical plants; from $115 s or d.

Budget travelers have a few choices. **Adventurers Resort YHA,** 79 Palmer St., tel. (07) 4721-1522, is a huge hostel with excellent facilities, including a pool and restaurant; dorm beds are $13-14, while private rooms are $20-22 s, $28-30 d. Budget. Another good choice is **Globetrotters,** 45 Palmer St., tel. (07) 4771-3242, where a bed in a six-share dorm is $14, singles are $26, and twins are $34. Budget. Closer to the city center, and next door to Mike Ball Dive Expeditions, is **Civic Guest House,** 262 Walker St., tel. (07) 4771-5381; dorm beds are $15-16 and large doubles are $38. Budget. **Rowes Bay Caravan Park,** Heatley Parade, tel. (07) 4771-3576, right opposite the beach, features a pool, barbecue area, and kiosk. Un-powered sites are $13, powered sites $17.50, and cabins range $42-55 per night. Budget-Inexpensive.

Food
Townsville may be a big city, but, as always, head to the pubs for hearty and inexpensive meals; try **Great Northern Hotel,** 500 Flinders St., or **Australian Hotel,** on Palmer St., which has a good beer garden. If Townsville can be said to have a trendy street, it would be Flinders St. East, where many of the historic buildings have been converted to restaurants. The **Heritage Café,** 137 Flinders St., is a popular little coffeehouse oozing atmosphere. The menu is mostly health-oriented, but Thursday night the diet goes out the window when a bucket of prawns and a beer is just $7.50. Downstairs in the **Exchange Hotel** is a wine bar with cheese plates and light snacks offered, while upstairs is **The Balcony,** tel. (07) 4771-3335, a stylish restaurant with tables inside and out.

Cactus Jack's, on the south side of Ross Creek, 21 Palmer St., tel. (07) 4721-1478, is one of Townsville's most popular restaurants. Featuring all the usual Mexican fare, dishes are large and authentic, ranging $8-14 for a main dish, and Margaritas are just $2.50 nightly 5-7 p.m.

Quarterdeck on the Marina, opposite the casino, tel. (07) 4722-2324, has seating inside or out on a covered deck over the water. Meals are well-priced with an outside barbecue $7.50-11 each evening. Meals are served daily noon-2 p.m., 6-9 p.m. For a splurge, head to **Melton's,** in the casino, tel. (07) 4722-2333, featuring a beef and seafood-inspired menu; from $22 for a main.

Transportation
Ansett Australia, tel. (13) 1300, and **Qantas,** tel. (13) 1313, fly into Townsville from Brisbane, Sydney, and Cairns as well as other centers such as Darwin and Alice Springs. **Sunstate,** tel. (13) 1313, flies along the Queensland coast and out to Dunk Island. **Flightwest,** tel. (13) 2392, operates from Townsville to inland destinations such as Mt. Isa and Longreach. A cab between the airport, seven km southwest of the city, and downtown runs about $10, or catch the shuttle bus, tel. (07) 4721-3660, for $5 one-way, $8 roundtrip.

Queensland Rail, tel. (13) 2232, serves Brisbane and Cairns, stopping at Townsville. From Brisbane, you can choose the Sunlander or the more luxurious Queenslander. Twice weekly the Inlander runs between Townsville and Mt. Isa, an eight-hour journey.

Greyhound Pioneer, tel. (13) 2030, and **McCafferty's,** tel. (13) 1499, have regular services between Townsville and all Queensland's coastal towns. Regular services also head inland to Mt. Isa, from where connections can be made through to Darwin and Alice Springs. All buses arrive and depart from **Townsville Transit Centre,** Palmer St., where you'll find accommodation booking agents, lockers, and a restaurant.

Relatively flat Townsville has some great cycling paths running along the oceanfront. Rent bikes from $15 per day at **City Cycles,** 251 Charters Towers Rd., tel. (07) 4775-1686. The following car rentals are available in the city, and all have desks at the airport (but call ahead): **Avis,** tel. (07) 4721-2688; **Budget,** tel. (07) 4725-2344; **Hertz,** tel. (07) 4779-9022; and **National,** tel. (07) 4722-5133. For a taxi call **Standard White Cabs,** tel. (13) 1008.

Services and Information
Clothes can be washed at **Southside Laundromat,** 115 Boundary, South Townsville. **Townsville General Hospital** is on Eyre St., tel. (07) 4781-9211.

In the middle of Flinders St. Mall is a **tourist information booth,** tel. (07) 4721-3660, with friendly staff and handy information sheets detailing attractions, accommodations, dining, and Magnetic Island practicalities. It's open Mon.-Sat. 9 a.m.-5 p.m., Sunday 9 a.m.-1:30 p.m. The main **Tourist Information Centre** is on the Bruce Hwy. eight km south of the city (not very convenient if you're arriving from the north or by public transportation), tel. (07) 4778-3555. It's open daily 9 a.m.-5 p.m. The **Department of Environment** has an information center in Great Barrier Reef Wonderland, tel. (07) 4721-2399; it's open Mon.-Sat. 9 a.m.-5 p.m. The Wonderland complex also houses the headquarters of the **Great Barrier Reef Marine Park Authority,** tel. (07) 4750-0801, caretaker of the reef. The authority maintains an excellent library of marine-related literature. It's open Mon.-Tues. and Thurs.-Fri. 10 a.m.-noon and 2-4 p.m.

MAGNETIC ISLAND

A large continental island lying eight km off Townsville, 5,030-hectare Magnetic Island features white sandy beaches and good bushwalking. The atmosphere on the island is relaxed and informal; it's more like an outer suburb of Townsville than a resort island. The island's population is 2,500, most of whom reside in settlements along the east coast. Southernmost of these is Picnic Bay, where ferries from the mainland dock hourly.

Roughly triangular in shape, the island rises to 497 meters at **Mt. Cook** and extends 11 km at its widest point. About half the island is protected by **Magnetic Island National Park.** The park's thickly forested slopes are punctuated with gran-

ite outcrops, while granite boulders flank many beaches. Birdlife is prolific and similar to that found on coastal mainland of a similar latitude. Rock wallabies are common (look for them on Bright Point), as are koalas (look for them on the Forts hiking trail).

Around the Island
Passenger ferries arrive at **Picnic Bay,** the island's largest town, where you'll find shops and restaurants, car rental outlets, and accommodations. The beach at Picnic Bay has the island's only stinger-free enclosure. To the east, around Hawkings Point, a steep trail descends to **Rocky Bay** and a small secluded beach.

Immediately north of Picnic Bay is **Nelly Bay,** with a number of budget accommodations and residential houses scattered around a low-lying

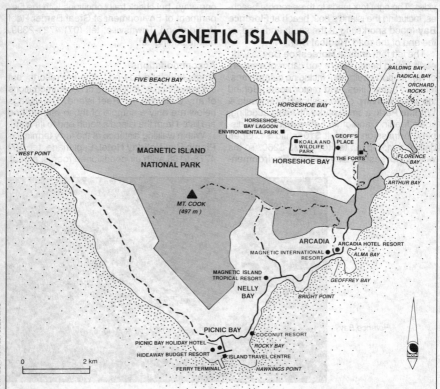

MAGNETIC ISLAND

FIVE BEACH BAY

BALDING BAY
RADICAL BAY
ORCHARD ROCKS

HORSESHOE BAY

HORSESHOE BAY LAGOON ENVIRONMENTAL PARK

KOALA AND WILDLIFE PARK

GEOFF'S PLACE

THE FORTS

FLORENCE BAY

WEST POINT

MAGNETIC ISLAND NATIONAL PARK

HORSESHOE BAY

ARTHUR BAY

MT. COOK (497 m)

ARCADIA
ARCADIA HOTEL RESORT

MAGNETIC INTERNATIONAL RESORT

ALMA BAY

MAGNETIC ISLAND TROPICAL RESORT

GEOFFREY BAY

NELLY BAY

BRIGHT POINT

PICNIC BAY

COCONUT RESORT

PICNIC BAY HOLIDAY HOTEL

ROCKY BAY

HIDEAWAY BUDGET RESORT

ISLAND TRAVEL CENTRE

FERRY TERMINAL

HAWKINGS POINT

0   2 km

N

© AVALON TRAVEL PUBLISHING

area in the shadow of Mt. Cook. Along the bay is a long beach, scarred at the north end by an ambitious marina development that never came to fruition.

Over the northern headland is **Arcadia,** a small village overlooking two good beaches. Geoffrey Bay, south of the headland, is good for snorkeling on the fringing reef, and at low tide it's possible to take a self-guided walk over the exposed coral. To the north is Alma Bay and a small but picturesque beach. The island's biggest dive operator, **Pleasure Divers,** tel. (07) 4778-5788, is based in Arcadia Hotel Resort. As well as renting snorkeling equipment ($6 half-day), they offer certified divers the opportunity to explore various island dive sites ($50-80) and operate PADI open-water dive courses ($249).

Near the north end of the island, the road divides. The right fork leads to three remote beaches, including the island's best beach at **Florence Bay** (good snorkeling at the south end) and, at the end of the road, **Radical Bay.**

The left fork ends at **Horseshoe Bay,** a wide north-facing beach where you can rent a variety of water sport equipment including catamarans, jet skis, aqua bikes, and motor boats. Behind the small township of Horseshoe Bay is **Koala & Wildlife Park,** a small park with koala cuddling, koala feeding, and other native animals on display. Admission is adult $10, child $4. Open daily 9 a.m.-5 p.m., tel. (07) 4778-5260. To the west is **Horseshoe Bay Lagoon Environmental Park,** a good area for viewing abundant and varied birdlife.

Hiking

Trails lead to the island's rugged interior from the east coast, but most are ill-defined and, for some strange reason, traversing them is not encouraged. An easy-to-reach lookout is **The Forts.** The trail begins at the Radical Bay turnoff, climbing steadily to an area of massive granite outcrops inlayed with command posts, lookouts, and gun emplacements used during WW II. The trail is 1.3 km one-way. From the east end of the beach at Horseshoe Bay, a trail climbs through a forest of dry eucalypt to lovely Balding Bay and Radical Bay. Longer walks are from Nelly Bay to Arcadia Bay (six km one-way) and Nelly Bay to the summit of Mt. Cook (five km one-way), but check trail conditions with the Department of Environment at Great Barrier Reef Wonderland, Townsville, tel. (07) 4721-2399, before setting out.

Accommodations

Magnetic Island has no upmarket resorts, but still boasts the widest range of accommodations of any Great Barrier Reef island. The listings below are only a sample of those offered and are listed from the island's south end to its north.

Within walking distance of the ferry terminal is **Picnic Bay Holiday Hotel,** Esplanade, tel. (07) 4778-5166, with air-conditioned rooms, a pool,

Florence Bay

and beer garden; $45 s or d or $65 with a kitchen. Inexpensive. For backpackers, **Hideaway Budget Resort,** 32 Picnic St., Picnic Bay, tel. (07) 4778-5110, offers two-bed dorms for $14 pp, singles for $22, and doubles for $32. Each room is fan-cooled and guests have use of a kitchen, barbecue, and pool. Budget.

Descending into Nelly Bay, the first accommodation you'll pass is **Coconuts Resort,** tel. (07) 4778-5777 or (1800) 06-5696, with tent sites for $8 pp, and four- and eight-berth cabins for $14-16 pp. Right on the beach, this place has a communal kitchen, laundry, pool, bar, and restaurant and offers a variety of water sports. Budget. In the same price range is **Magnetic Island Tropical Resort,** 56 Yates St., Nelly Bay, tel. (07) 4778-5955, a sprawling complex set among native bushland with a pool, spa, bar, game area, and free transport to the ferry terminal. Beds in a six-bed dorm are $16 pp and comfortable doubles are $45. Inexpensive. The island's premier accommodation is **Magnetic International Resort,** Mandalay Ave., Nelly Bay, tel. (07) 4778-5200, which has a pool, tennis court, and dive center; $140-170 s or d. Premium.

Arcadia Hotel Resort, Arcadia, tel. (07) 4778-5177, has motel-style units, each with a kitchen, set around a landscaped pool; $60-75 s or d. Moderate.

Geoff's Place, Horseshoe Bay Rd., Horseshoe Bay, tel. (07) 4778-5577, is well suited for budget travelers, with many planned activities and a party atmosphere. Camping is $6 pp, dorm beds $14 pp, and doubles $34. Transfers to Picnic Bay are complimentary.

Food

Restaurants and cafés are scattered throughout the island and each settlement has a grocery store. In Picnic Bay Mall, **Green Frog Cafe** has views over the bay and is open for breakfast and lunch. The hotel in Picnic Bay serves inexpensive counter meals.

Over in Nelly Bay, the bistro in **Magnetic Island Tropical Resort,** 56 Yates St., tel. (07) 4778-5955, serves large portions and is open daily 8 a.m.-8:30 p.m., with all main meals less than $12 and a $11 roast served Sunday 6:30-8:30 p.m. Dishing up good-quality meals at very reasonable prices is **Mexican Munchies** at 37 Warboys St., Nelly Bay, tel. (07) 4778-5658.

Banister's Seafood, 22 McCabe Crescent, Arcadia, tel. (07) 4778-5700, has the best fish and chips on the island, either takeaway ($4-6) or eat-in ($9-10); it's open daily 9 a.m.-8:30 p.m. **Blue Waters Café Gallery,** in Arcadia Shopping Centre, tel. (07) 4778-5645, is a casual restaurant with tables set among a pleasant garden; open daily from 6 a.m.

Cotter's on the Beach, in Horseshoe Bay, specializes in seafood but also offers beef and chicken dishes ranging $14-16; call (07) 4778-5786 for reservations.

Transportation and Tours

Magnetic Island Ferries, tel. (07) 4772-7122, departs 13 times daily from a terminal on Townsville's breakwater for Picnic Bay. The first departure is 6:05 a.m. From 8:20 a.m. pickups are also made at Great Barrier Reef Wonderland. The last departure from Picnic Bay is 7:15 p.m., with later services Friday and Saturday nights. The roundtrip fare from Townsville to the island is adult $24, child $12. Pickups and dropoffs at Townsville accommodations are complimentary. **Magnetic Island Car Ferry** runs two to four times daily between the island and a boat ramp on Ross St., South Townsville; $98 per vehicle includes passengers. For bookings call (07) 4772-5422.

Magnetic Island Bus Service, tel. (07) 4778-5130, meets all ferries and runs the length of the island; $9 for an all-day pass, $10 for a two-day pass or $1.50-3.60 per sector. **Magnetic Moke,** Esplanade, Picnic Bay, tel. (07) 4778-5377, rents mokes (jeeps) for $35 pp per day including petrol.

Services and Information

The tourist information booth in Townsville's Flinders St. Mall has all the information you'll need on the island. Once ashore, head to the **Island Travel Centre,** on the foreshore at Picnic Bay, tel. (07) 4778-5155; open daily 9 a.m.-5 p.m.

PALM ISLANDS

Located north of Townsville, these 11 continental islands are secluded and, apart from one island resort, rarely visited by outsiders. Named by Captain Cook for palm-fringed beaches, the group has been inhabited by Aborigines for generations and today all but two of the islands are Aboriginal reserves, including the largest, 5,666-hectare Great Palm Island, which has a population of 1,400. Those not designated as reserves are Orpheus Island, second-largest of the group and site of an upmarket resort, and Pelorus Island, protected as a national park.

Orpheus Island

A long and narrow continental island of 1,376 hectares, Orpheus is rugged and rocky but also boasts excellent beaches and undisturbed fringing reefs. For the most part, the island is forested and supports a diverse array of birdlife. James Cook University maintains a small research station at Pioneer Bay.

On the island's west coast, behind a white sandy beach on Hazard Bay is **Orpheus Island Resort.** Geared for those who want to escape (no television or newspapers), the resort is elegant without being pretentious. Accommodation for 74 guests is in stylish beachfront units or six Mediterranean-style villas set on the hillside. Each unit has a queen-size bed and comfortable sitting area. Rates are $490-580 s, $780-1,100 d per night inclusive of meals. For reservations call (07) 4777-7377 or (1800) 07-7167. Transportation to the resort is by floatplane from either Townsville ($290 roundtrip) or Cairns ($460); book through the resort.

On the island's west coast are two campgrounds. Campers must be totally self-sufficient and have no access to the resort. Like all other national park islands, permits are required to camp; obtain these from the Department of Environment at Great Barrier Reef Wonderland, Townsville, tel. (07) 4721-2399. For campers, the only transportation is aboard the *Scuba Doo*, tel. (07) 4777-8220, from Lucinda; $150 pp roundtrip.

WEST FROM TOWNSVILLE

The most direct route between Townsville and Outback Queensland is along the **Flinders Highway**, which leads southwest from Townsville to the historic mining town of Charters Towers, then west through a dry and desolate piece of country to Mt. Isa, 890 km from the Pacific Ocean.

Ravenswood

Between Charters Towers and Townsville a narrow road leads 40 km south to the once-booming mining town of Ravenswood. Gold was found in the area in 1868 and by the end of the following year a rush was on. Company mining soon took over; equipment capable of crushing huge amounts of ore was brought in, and the town prospered. For a while anyway. The quality of gold was poorer than first thought and in 1912 the original company mine closed. In ensuing years, many companies invested heavily in the area, the most recent in 1994, but today the town is a shadow of its former self. Abandoned mine shafts, equipment and machinery, and a few remaining buildings provide a glimpse of past glories. A small museum in the courthouse is open Wed.-Mon. 10 a.m.-3 p.m.

Charters Towers

This historic town of 9,000, in the Leichhardt Range 140 km inland from Townsville, was once Queensland's second-largest city, with a population exceeding 30,000. Things are a lot quieter in Charters Towers today, but streets lined with historic buildings and a cool climate make a detour from the coastal highway worthwhile.

Gold was discovered late last century at nearby Towers Hill by an Aboriginal boy named Jupiter Mosman, who, ironically, was accompanying a group of prospectors. By 1900 the town's population had peaked. By the 1920s, the richest lodes of gold had been extracted and the beef industry came to prominence. Modern technology made gold mining economical in the 1980s.

Charters Towers' one-time importance is reflected in downtown civic buildings, including an impressive city hall and stock exchange. The 1897 **Stock Exchange Arcade**, on Mosman St., has been restored and now houses a small mining museum; it's open Mon.-Fri. 8:30 a.m.-1 p.m. and 2-4 p.m.; admission $5. Farther along Mosman St. is **Zara Clark Folk & Military Museum**, housing artifacts and photos from the town's earliest days. Open daily 10 a.m.-3 p.m., admission $3. It's at 36 Mosman St., tel. (07) 4787-4161. **Venus Battery**, five km east of town on Millchester Rd., was one of dozens of mills used to crush ore during the town's boom period. The battery has been restored and is open for inspection daily 9 a.m.-3 p.m. with tours at 10 a.m. and 2 p.m.; $3 pp.

Where the Flinders Highway enters town from the northeast is **Park Motel,** 1 Mosman St., tel. (07) 4787-1022, built as a hotel in 1888. Rooms in the original hotel have been beautifully restored, including brass beds and bathtubs; $70 s, $85 d. Out back, and spread around a pool, is a string of motel units; $60 s, $68 d. Moderate. North of town is **Dalrymple Tourist Van Park,** tel. (07) 4787-1121, with good facilities and a saltwater pool. Sites are $10-12. Budget.

All the pubs serve counter meals, with **Court House Hotel,** 120 Gill St., offering $4-6 lunches and $6-9 dinners. In the historic Stock Exchange Arcade is **Ye Olde Coffee Shoppe,** serving sandwiches and light meals as well as Devonshire teas; open daily 8:30 a.m.-5 p.m. The **RSL Club** on Prior St. dishes up a dinner buffet Saturday and Sunday night. For something more fancy, try **Lissner's** in the Park Motel, tel. (07) 4787-1022. Main dishes range $11-20.

Further information on the town is available at the **National Trust of Queensland** office in the Stock Exchange Arcade on Mosman St., tel. (07) 4787-2374.

Great Basalt Wall
This geological wonder northwest of Charters Towers formed around three million years ago, when a huge lava flow from violent volcanic explosions cooled to form a "wall" of basalt. Gregory Developmental Rd., linking Charters Towers to the Gulf Developmental Rd., crosses the ancient lava flow 44 km north of Charters Towers. The western end of the flow is protected by 30,500-hectare **Great Basalt Wall National Park,** accessible along a rough track spurring off the Gregory Developmental Rd., 39 km north of Charters Towers.

Porcupine Gorge National Park
The rolling hills around **Hughenden** seem never-ending, and the land is so harsh that graziers are only able to graze one sheep for every three hectares, but 45 km north of the highway is Porcupine Gorge, an oasis of lush vegetation supported by a creek flowing year-round. The gravel access road ends suddenly, right on the rim of the park's main feature, where sheer walls drop vertically 120 meters. Seeing the creek in the dry season, it's hard to comprehend the quantity of water that flows during the Wet, and its

power to carve the canyon in the soft sandstone. A couple of lookouts lie along the gorge rim, but to get into the gorge continue north to **The Pyramid,** an isolated outcrop of rock, and descend into the valley from the parking area. This area is outside the park boundary. Camp here. For park information, call the ranger at (07) 4741-1113.

TOWNSVILLE TO CARDWELL

From Townsville, it's 110 km north to Ingham, then 52 km farther to Cardwell, gateway to Hinchinbrook Island. Between Townsville and Ingham you'll find two national parks worthy of a short detour. They protect much of the Paluma Range, a mist-laden rainforest of palms, fig trees, umbrella trees, and abundant small creatures. Southernmost is 10,600-hectare **Mt. Spec National Park,** accessed from the highway 66 km north of Townsville. Camping is permitted at Big Crystal Creek, west of Paluma township, while at the top of the range is McClelland's Lookout and a couple of short hiking trails.

North of Paluma is the turnoff to **Paluma Range National Park,** six km west of the Bruce Highway. The park's main feature is **Jourama Falls,** which cascades down a massive face of granite, 1.5 km from the facility area.

Ingham and Vicinity
The cane-growing town Ingham, 110 km north of Townsville, holds little of interest, but to the east and west are interesting detours. To the east is **Lucinda,** where shallow waters forced the construction of a six-km-long pier to load bulk sugar carriers.

West of Ingham is massive 124,000-hectare **Lumholtz National Park,** best known for 300-meter-high **Wallaman Falls,** one of Australia's highest. The section of the park holding the falls is south of the main park and can be accessed by following a road 52 km west from Ingham. Camp downstream of the falls, on the bank of Stony Creek.

Cardwell and Vicinity
Along the entire 1,700 km between Brisbane and Cairns, Cardwell is the only place where the Bruce Highway runs right along the coastline, and even then, it's only for a couple of km. Card-

well holds little of interest, but as gateway to Hinchinbrook Island, staying in town is often a necessity. **Cardwell Forest Drive** is a 26-km circuit that begins in town and winds through native forests to a panoramic lookout, a picnic area, numerous swimming holes, and the trailhead for a couple of short hikes. North of Cardwell is 6,950-hectare **Edmund Kennedy National Park**, named for the explorer whose ill-fated expedition was the first to traverse Cape York. The park protects an area of coastal habitat featuring rainforest, swamps, and long deserted beaches. Even if you aren't heading out to Hinchinbrook Island, the **Rainforest and Reef Centre**, by the jetty at 142 Victoria St., tel. (07) 4066-8601, is worth a visit. This Department of Environment facility features interesting interpretive displays, including a simulated boardwalk complete with the sights and sounds of the island environment. It's open Mon.-Fri. 8 a.m.-4:30 p.m., Sat.-Sun. 8 a.m.-noon.

Cardwell has a couple of motels, including **Lyndoch Motor Inn,** 215 Victoria St., tel. (07) 4066-8500, which charges $35 s, $50 d. Inexpensive. But the best place to stay is **Kookaburra Caravan Park,** 175 Bruce Hwy., tel. (07) 4066-8648, which has excellent facilities including a pool and laundry and free use of golf clubs (greens fees are $8 on the local course), tennis rackets, bikes, and fishing gear. Camping, on a shaded grassy area with access to undercover cooking facilities, is $12-15, on-site vans are $28, cabins are $40, and fully self-contained villas are $50-70. Dorm beds (YHA affiliated) are $15 pp and doubles are $36. Budget-Inexpensive.

The enormous red crab in front of **Muddies,** Victoria St., tel. (07) 4066-8907, makes this popular seafood restaurant difficult to miss. Dinner mains average $14-18. Open daily 11 a.m.-9 p.m.

HINCHINBROOK ISLAND

Separated from the mainland by mangrove-choked Hinchinbrook Channel, this magnificent wilderness island rises from the water to more than 1,000 meters. The island's west coast is dominated by mangrove flats while on the east coast are 50 km of rugged headlands, secluded

bays, and a white sandy beach stretching eight km along Ramsey Bay. Hiking the Thorsborne Trail is the island's biggest attraction, but day trips are also popular and there's a low-key resort at Cape Richards.

The Land

All of the island's 39,350 hectares are protected as a national park. It was once part of the mainland, but after the last ice age, when sea levels rose, a high coastal ridge remained as an island. The island's highest peak is **Mt. Bowen** (1,142 meters), Queensland's third highest point, part of a massive spine of granite extending the length of the island. On the western slopes, where rainfall is high, a canopy of tropical rainforest protects palms, ferns, vines, and figs that extend to mangrove swamps at sea level. East of the ridge line, where rainfall is lower and slopes are exposed to high winds, dry forests of eucalypt dominate, with patches of rainforest thriving in the gullies. From the middle of the island, a wide, flat peninsula branches northward. On the ocean side is a magnificent stretch of beach backed by six km of mangrove forests dissected by a maze of shallow channels.

From a visitor's point of view, the most important living creatures to know about are sand flies, march flies and mosquitoes, all of which can be unbearable. All the usual crocodile and stinger warnings are relevant to the island, so beware.

Thorsborne Trail

Formerly known as the East Coast Trail, this three- to five-day 30-km bushwalk is one of Australia's premier overnight hikes. The going can be tough, especially after rain when the trail gets very slippery. The trail begins at Ramsey Bay (it's most often hiked from north to south), accessed along a one-km boardwalk from where shallow-draft boats tie up in the mangroves of Missionary Bay. Ramsey Bay itself is a magnificent stretch of sand (good views from Nina Peak), but scenery improves farther south where the trail hugs the coastline, meanders along sandy beaches, crosses creeks, passes through rainforest, and climbs to various viewpoints. Apart from caution at creek crossings and the incessant nuisance of insects, the trail should pose few problems for experienced hikers.

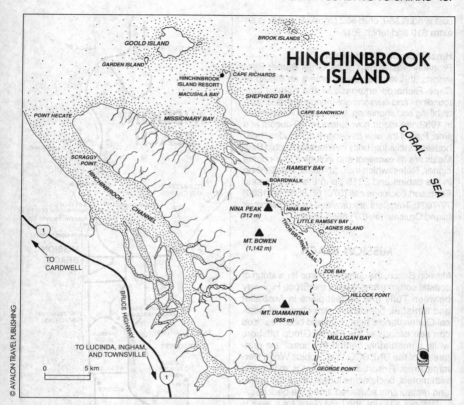

The only way to get on the trail is with a permit; $3.50 pp per night. For these write: Department of Environment, P.O. Box 1293, Ingham, QLD 4850, tel. (07) 4776-1700. Permits can also be purchased at the department's Cardwell office at 142 Victoria St., tel. (07) 4066-8601, but mostly they are snapped up months in advance. If a full quota of hikers (40 per day) is booked on the Thorsborne Trail, inquire about permits for travel on only the north section of the trail or camping at Macushla Bay or Goold Island, to the north of Hinchinbrook.

Transportation to the northern trailhead is made easy by two Cardwell companies who offer a drop-off at the trail's north end for $45 pp one-way, $69 roundtrip. They are **Hinchinbrook Adventures,** tel. (07) 4066-8270, and

Hinchinbrook Island Cruises, tel. (07) 4066-8539. Both have offices on Cardwell's main street. Both companies can also provide roundtrip transfers to the northern trailhead, Macushla Bay, and Goold Island. They can also arrange boat pickup from the trail's southern end to Lucinda, and coach transfers up the Bruce Highway to Cardwell, for an additional $45 pp.

Day Trips to the Island
Hinchinbrook Adventures, tel. (07) 4066-8270, and **Hinchinbrook Island Cruises,** tel. (07) 4066-8539, depart daily for the everglades of Missionary Bay, from where it's a short hike along a boardwalk to the sandy beaches of Ramsey Bay. Time is also spent sunbaking and snorkeling at the nearby Brook Islands. Tour

cost is adult $69, child $32 (snorkeling gear is an extra $10 and lunch $8).

Hinchinbrook Island Resort
Probably least known of the Great Barrier Reef resorts, this low-key development on the tip of Cape Richards emphasizes the natural surroundings and environment-friendly activities such as hiking and snorkeling. Upgraded and expanded in 1989, the resort now caters for 50 guests at a time. Part of the new development includes "treehouses," individual units overlooking Orchid Bay. Meals are all excellent and include a four-course dinner. Rates, which include meals, are $228 pp in the cabins and $315 pp in the Treehouses. For resort bookings call (070) 66-8585 or (1800) 77-7021. Transfers are provided by Hinchinbrook Island Cruises, tel. (07) 4066-8539.

MISSION BEACH

Mission Beach, the collective name for a string of coastal communities east of the Bruce Highway between **Tully** (the wettest place in Australia) and **Innisfail,** boasts a 10-km stretch of tropical Queensland's best mainland beaches. You can see islands of the Family Group offshore while immediately behind the coast are rainforests of the UNESCO Wet Tropics World Heritage Area. Resort development is extensive, with motels, backpacker lodges, caravan parks, and restaurants scattered along the beaches.

Without a doubt, the best place for a walk is along the palm-fringed beaches, but inland, in **Tam O'Shanter State Forest,** other opportunities present themselves. Head to Licuala facility area, where a 1.3-km trail leads to an area of rainforest featuring licuala palms; you'll find it on the road linking Tully to the coast. At the north end of the forest, at Lacey Creek, is short trail through an area inhabited by cassowaries.

Visiting the Outer Reef from Mission Beach
Two operators run to the outer reef from Clump Point, at the north end of Mission Beach. **Friendship Cruises** departs daily at 8:30 a.m., and at $64 pp it's one of the cheapest ways to get to the outer reef anywhere along the coast. But, of course, there's a downside—it's a slow boat,

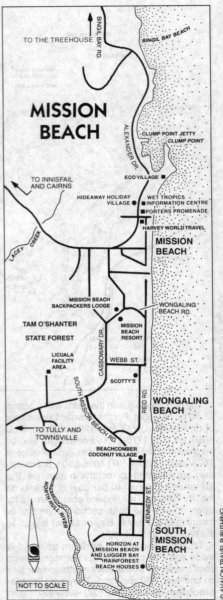

taking more than two hours to get to the reef. Once on the reef, there's snorkeling, a glass-bottomed boat, and a coral cay to sunbake on. For bookings call (07) 4068-7262. The other option is aboard *Quick Cat,* tel. (07) 4068-7289, which departs Clump Point Jetty at 10 a.m. ($122 adult, $61 child). Six hours are spent on the outer reef, with the fare including snorkeling, lunch, and a glass-bottomed boat tour. Diving is an extra $55 pp.

Budget Accommodations

Mission Beach has a ton of budget accommodations and a few upmarket resorts but no midrange places—it's either a cheap dorm bed or a $100-a-night room.

Surrounded by lush rainforest, three km west of Bingil Bay Beach, is **The Treehouse** on Bingil Bay Rd., tel. (07) 4068-7137. This YHA complex has 60 beds, a pool, large deck area, lounge, and kitchen. Rates are $16-20 pp and camping is $10 pp. Inexpensive. **Mission Beach Back-**

licuala fan palms, Tam O'Shanter State Forest

packers Lodge, 28 Wongaling Beach Rd., tel. (07) 4068-8317, just 200 meters from the beach, is central to the shops and restaurants of Mission Beach, and has kitchen and laundry facilities, along with meals in an inexpensive café. Rates in dorms are $15 pp, in doubles $19 pp. Budget. **Scotty's Mission Beach House** is a family-run backpacker lodge across the road from a great beach. It has a large pool, shaded verandas, and modern facilities. Dorms are $15 pp, doubles $35, and a few rooms have private bathrooms and air-conditioning for $45. It's at 167 Reid Rd., Wongaling Beach, tel. (07) 4068-8676. Budget.

Hideaway Holiday Village, Porters Promenade, Mission Beach, tel. (07) 4068-7104, has great facilities and is only a short walk from the beach. Sites range $15-17 while cabins are $44-60. Budget-Inexpensive. **Beachcomber Coconut Village,** South Mission Beach, tel. (07) 4068-8129, equals any caravan park in the state, with a wide variety of activities and a beachfront location. Shaded sites are $15.50-17.50, cabins $43-62, and fully self-contained villas $53-69. Budget-Inexpensive.

Resort Accommodations

The following accommodations are listed from north to south. Surrounded by rainforest and a short walk through bushland to the beach is the **Eco Village,** Clump Point Rd., tel. (07) 4068-7534. Each freestanding bungalow is fully self-contained, with a large kitchen, king-size bed, air-conditioning, and a television. They are built around a beautifully landscaped pool area and linked to the main restaurant/guest lounge building by paths winding through palm-filled gardens. Rates are very reasonable at $98-118. Some units feature a private spa. Expensive.

Mission Beach Resort is set among 18 hectares of rainforest three blocks from the beach. Take advantage of the wide range of sporting activities and the pleasant, landscaped pool area. The resort also has four restaurants, three bars, and live entertainment most nights. Rates are $80 s, $90 d; units with kitchenettes are $90 s, $100 d (also inquire about standby rates). It's on Wongaling Beach Rd., tel. (07) 4068-8288. Expensive.

For more upscale lodging, check out the resorts at South Mission Beach. **Horizon at Mission Beach,** tel. (07) 4068-8154, overlooks Dunk

and Bedarra Islands and has a large pool and
balcony area scattered with palms and seating.
All units have ocean views and are of the highest
standard; $160 s or d. Luxury. **Lugger Bay Rain-
forest Beach Houses,** tel. (07) 4068-8400, is
much the same setup, but on a smaller, more intimate scale, with elegant log units built on poles
and catching ocean views. Each has a kitchen,
outdoor eating area, spa, and separate sleeping
quarters; $250-360 per night. Luxury.

Food

A cluster of shops on Porter's Promenade in Mission Beach includes good cafés and restaurants.
For healthy meals to go, search out the deli; a
picnic hamper for two is $25. Also on the prome-
nade is a takeout with well-priced seafood; a slab
of delicious barramundi, chips, and salad is $9.
Next door, **Friends,** tel. (07) 4068-7107, is a classy
seafood restaurant serving meals from $18.

Transportation

All long-distance bus companies stop at Mission Beach (Greyhound at Mission Beach Resort
and McCafferty's at Harvey World Travel, Mission Beach), with four or five services daily making the detour from the Bruce Highway.

Mission Beach Bus Service, tel. (07) 4068-
7400, runs between the communities of Mission
Beach six to eight times daily.

Information

Mission Beach Tourist Information Centre is
in Porters Promenade, Mission Beach, tel. (07)
4068-7099. It's open Mon.-Sat. 9 a.m.-5 p.m.,
Sunday 9 a.m.-4 p.m. Next door is the **Wet Tropics Information Centre,** tel. (07) 4068-7179,
run by the Department of Environment.

ISLANDS OFF MISSION BEACH

Lying off Mission Beach are 14 islands of the
Family Group. Most are protected as national
parks, and a couple are privately owned. Two of
the islands have resorts, including the largest,
Dunk, and Bedarra.

Dunk Island

Immortalized by E.J. Banfield in four books, including his best-known work *Confessions of a*
Beachcomber, more has been written about
Dunk than any other island on the reef. Banfield
lived on the island for more than 25 years, until
his death in 1923. His lyrical description of Dunk's
flora and fauna and his relationship with the island have attracted many to the South Pacific.

The island is five km from the mainland and
about 30 km from the outer reef. It is 890
hectares in area, rising steeply to 271-meter Mt.
Kootaloo. Apart from a resort, the island has
many beaches; the best are on a low-lying spit of
sand extending west from the center of the island. Low-lying areas have been cleared, but
the island is mostly rugged, and vegetation remains in its natural state, cloaked in a thick cover
of tropical rainforest extending right down to the
rocky shoreline. Birdlife is prolific.

Walking is one of the island's most popular
activities; 13 km of trails crisscross the island
including one to the summit of Mt. Kootaloo (1.5
km one-way) and to Coconut Beach (five km
one-way), home to a colony of artists. Water
sports equipment is available from a kiosk at
the beach, but the resort and its facilities are
off-limits to day trippers.

Dunk Island Resort attracts a variety of holidaymakers but is best suited to those keen to
keep active; guests enjoy the two pools, tennis,
six holes of golf, archery, trap shooting, horseback riding, and squash as well as all the usual
water sports. The resort caters for nearly 400
guests. Rooms set in landscaped gardens are
$340-410 s or d, while those along the beach-
front start at $480 s or d. The meal package is
$75 pp extra. Children are well looked after, with
a petting farm and camping trips offered. For
reservations call (07) 4068-8199; for packages
deals call Qantas, tel. (13) 1415. From North
America call (800) 227-4411.

Most resort guests arrive on package tours,
with flights included. Otherwise the flight to Dunk
Island from Townsville or Cairns is $125 one-
way. If you plan to stay at Mission Beach resorts, fly into Dunk Island and catch a water taxi
to the mainland.

At last count, three operators ran water taxis
between Mission Beach communities and Dunk
Island. The trip over takes 10-15 minutes, and all
operators charge $22 roundtrip. The most fre-
quent service is with **Dunk Island Express,** tel.
(07) 4068-8310, which runs seven times daily

from Wongaling Beach (expect to get your feet wet—passengers load from the beach). The *Quick Cat,* tel. (07) 4068-7289, runs once daily from Clump Point. **Dunk Island Cruises,** tel. (07) 4068-7211, runs the MV *Lawrence Kavanagh* daily from Clump Point. Combined with snorkeling and boomnetting around Bedarra Island, the cost on this vessel is $49, or pay $22 for just the island transfer.

Bedarra Island

Lying six km south of Dunk, this 86-hectare island is home to one of the reef's most exclusive resorts. It's one of the few Queensland islands best known by its Aboriginal name, although marine charts denote it as Richards Island. The island features great beaches and also has a fine fringing reef. At **Bedarra Island Resort** guests are guaranteed privacy and solitude in settings that blend into surrounding rainforest. The Dunk Island Resort mentioned above and the Bedarra Island Resort are owned by Australian Resorts, but the similarities end there. It features 16 split-level villas with sunken baths and private balconies, a stylish landscaped pool area, and a wide range of activities such as tennis, fishing, and sailing. Rates are all-inclusive (including alcohol—Bedarra is the only reef resort with an open bar); $1,000 s, $1,290 d per night. For reservations call (07) 4068-8233. Within North America call (800) 227-4411. Transport to the island is provided for guests by launch from either Mission Beach or the airport on Dunk Island. Day-trippers are not permitted.

MISSION BEACH TO CAIRNS

Innisfail, at the confluence of the North and South Johnstone Rivers, is the heart of a rich cane-growing area. The **Australian Sugar Industry Museum,** at Mourilyan, south of Innisfail, tel. (07) 4063-2306, depicts the industry and has an old steam engine out back. Admission $4; open daily 9 a.m.-4:30 p.m.

Wooroonooran National Park

Dozens of creeks, waterfalls, lookouts, and hiking trails are features of this little-known park protecting land west of the Bruce Highway be-

tween Innisfail and Cairns. The Palmerston Section is accessed from Innisfail along the Palmerston Highway, which climbs up the Atherton Tableland. This section of the park straddles the highway with two seven-km circuits taking in all the best natural features. Camping is at Henrietta Creek. In the park's northern section is **The Boulders** (six km west of Babinda), starting point for a number of short trails including one to a lookout above Boulders Gorge and a two-km rainforest circuit. The Boulders picnic area is also the start of the **Goldfield Trail,** cut through the Bellenden Ker Range by diggers on their way to a short-lived gold rush. The trail leads 19 km into the Goldsborough Valley, climbing over the range and descending to the East Mulgrave River (11 km one-way) and continuing eight km downstream to a campground accessible by car off the Gillies Highway.

South of Babinda, a road leads eight km west to **Josephine Falls.** West of the falls is 1,622-meter **Mt. Bartle Frere,** Queensland's highest peak. **Bartle Frere Summit Trail** is 7.5 km one-way, a strenuous but rewarding full-day hike that should be attempted only by the fit. A softer option is the climb to Broken Nose (970 meters); four km each way.

Frankland Islands

This beautiful group of continental islands lies 10 km from the coast midway between Innisfail and Cairns. The combined area of the five islands is less than 80 hectares, and each features rainforests of casuarinas and sandy beaches fringed by undisturbed coral reef. Camping is permitted on **Russell Island,** but you must be totally self-sufficient and obtain permits from the Department of Environment in Cairns.

The *Frankland Islander II,* tel. (1800) 07-9039, heads out to the Frankland Islands daily for five hours of snorkeling, swimming, and sunbaking (usually to Normanby Island). Coaches pick up passengers from Cairns daily at 8 a.m. for transfers to the boat, which departs from Deeral Landing on the Mulgrave River 45 km south of Cairns. The fare of $125 pp includes all transfers as well as snorkeling equipment, morning and afternoon tea, and a buffet lunch. For campers, the roundtrip fare to Russell Island is $140 pp.

CAIRNS

Sandwiched between the clear waters of the Great Barrier Reef and lush rainforests of the Atherton Tableland lies Cairns (CANS), tourist capital of far north Queensland and gateway to a myriad of natural wonders. Founded in 1876 as a gateway to western goldfields and growing to become a major sugar port, Cairns (pop. 92,000) has been Australia's fastest-growing resort city for the last 15 years. Wide palm-lined streets, groves of bougainvilleas scattered through parks, and raised whitewashed buildings give Cairns an authentic tropical atmosphere, belying the hustle and bustle of the thriving tourism industry, contained on just a few streets along the bay.

Long a holiday destination for budget-conscious Australians, the construction of five-star resorts, a casino, an international airport, and championship golf courses has broadened the city's appeal. Apart from local fishers, plantation owners, and Koori, the blend of the international jetsetters, backpackers, four-wheel drive enthusiasts, honeymooners, and holidaying families adds to Cairns unique atmosphere.

Although Cairns is the tourist capital of the far north, it's not the city itself that attracts the visitors, but the proximity to a great variety of natural attractions in the immediate vicinity, including beautiful islands, the outer reef, Atherton Tableland, Port Douglas, the Daintree Rainforest, and Cape Tribulation.

SIGHTS AND RECREATION

Town Sights

The Esplanade, which runs along the shore of Trinity Bay, is the center of the action in Cairns. On one side is a long strip of palm-fringed park overlooking the calm waters of the bay and on the other a mass of booking agents, cafés, and budget accommodations. At the south end of the Esplanade is **Pier Marketplace,** a large shopping plaza with boutiques, restaurants with ocean views, a marina, and markets Saturday and Sunday. Also in the complex is **Undersea World Aquarium,** tel. (07) 4041-1777. It may not be as extensive as Townsville's Great Barrier

Reef Wonderland, but tanks display many hundreds of reef creatures, including coral, and a diver feeds the fish at regular intervals throughout the day. Admission is adult $12, child $7. Open daily 8 a.m.-8 p.m. Pier Marketplace also serves as a departure point for many island and reef trips.

Pier Marketplace is at the mouth of **Trinity Inlet,** a shallow body of water extending three km into wetlands. Along the mouth of this waterway are various cruise-departure jetties and Trinity Wharf, the main coach terminal. *Louisa* is a small paddlewheeler that departs daily at 10 a.m. and 1 p.m. for a two-and-a-half hour cruise through the inlet and around Admiralty Island; adult $18, child $7 includes morning or afternoon tea. For bookings, call (07) 4054-1145.

At City Place, on Lake Street, is **Cairns Museum,** tel. (07) 4051-5582, displaying Aboriginal artifacts, goldfields memorabilia, photographs from the city's earliest days, and an interesting exhibit on the building of the Skyrail. Admission is $3. Open Mon.-Sat. 10 a.m.-3 p.m.

The **Royal Flying Doctor Service** has a base in Cairns, serving patients around Queensland's far north, including Cape York. A visitor center at the base, open for hourlong tours 9 a.m.-4:30 p.m. ($5 pp), features a documentary on some of the more memorable rescues performed by the service. It's at 1 Junction St., Edge Hill, tel. (07) 4053-5687.

Tjapukai Aboriginal Cultural Park

An hour-long Tjapukai (JAB-a-guy) Aboriginal dance performance on Kuranda market days (see below) proved so popular that the concept was expanded into a cultural theme park and relocated to Caravonica Lakes, 15 km northwest of Cairns at the base of the Skyrail base station. The dance, which tells the story of Aboriginal myths and customs, is still the major attraction, but other aspects of Koori culture can be experienced here. A slide show at the History Theatre tells the story of the Aboriginal people since European contact, and another theater presents the story of the creation of the Tjapukai people through a stunning laser and holograph-

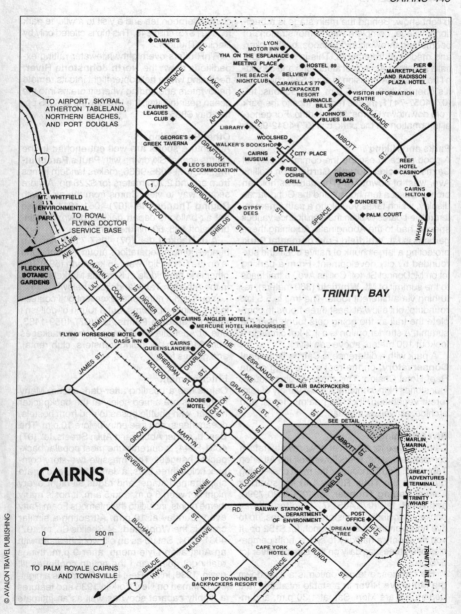

DETAIL

DAMARI'S

LYON MOTOR INN
YHA ON THE ESPLANADE
MEETING PLACE
THE BEACH NIGHTCLUB
HOSTEL 89
BELLVIEW
CARAVELLA'S 77 BACKPACKER RESORT
BARNACLE BILL'S

PIER MARKETPLACE AND RADISSON PLAZA HOTEL
VISITOR INFORMATION CENTRE

CAIRNS LEAGUES CLUB
LIBRARY
GEORGE'S GREEK TAVERNA
WOOLSHED
WALKER'S BOOKSHOP
CAIRNS MUSEUM
CITY PLACE
LEO'S BUDGET ACCOMMODATION
RED OCHRE GRILL

JOHNO'S BLUES BAR

ORCHID PLAZA

REEF HOTEL CASINO
CAIRNS HILTON

GYPSY DEES
DUNDEE'S
PALM COURT

FLORENCE ST.
LAKE ST.
APLIN ST.
GRAFTON ST.
SHERIDAN ST.
MCLEOD ST.
SHIELDS ST.
SPENCE ST.
ABBOTT ST.
THE ESPLANADE
WHARF ST.

TO AIRPORT, SKYRAIL, ATHERTON TABLELAND, NORTHERN BEACHES, AND PORT DOUGLAS

MT. WHITFIELD ENVIRONMENTAL PARK
TO ROYAL FLYING DOCTOR SERVICE BASE

FLECKER BOTANIC GARDENS

COLLINS AVE.
CAPTAIN COOK HWY.
LILY ST.
SMITH ST.
COOK ST.
DIGGER ST.
McKENZIE ST.

TRINITY BAY

CAIRNS ANGLER MOTEL
MERCURE HOTEL HARBOURSIDE
FLYING HORSESHOE MOTEL
OASIS INN
CAIRNS QUEENSLANDER

SHERIDAN ST.
CHARLES ST.
THE ESPLANADE
LAKE ST.
GRAFTON ST.

JAMES ST.
MCLEOD ST.

BEL-AIR BACKPACKERS

ADOBE MOTEL

GROVE ST.
MARTYN ST.
SEVERIN ST.
LIPWARD ST.
MINNIE ST.
GATTON ST.
FLORENCE ST.

SEE DETAIL

ABBOTT ST.
SHIELDS ST.

MARLIN MARINA
GREAT ADVENTURES TERMINAL
TRINITY WHARF

CAIRNS

0   500 m

BUCHAN ST.
MULGRAVE ST.
BRUCE HWY.

RD.
RAILWAY STATION
DEPARTMENT OF ENVIRONMENT
POST OFFICE
DREAM TREE
CAPE YORK HOTEL
HARTLEY ST.
BUNDA ST.
SPENCE ST.

UPTOP DOWNUNDER BACKPACKERS RESORT

TO PALM ROYALE CAIRNS AND TOWNSVILLE

TRINITY INLET

ic light show. Behind the main stage is a traditional village, complete with demonstrations of boomerang throwing, didgeridoos, bush tucker, and medicinal treatments. This is one of Australia's premier Aboriginal attractions and shouldn't be missed. Admission is adult $24, child $12. It's open daily 9 a.m.-5 p.m. The Sunbus, tel. (07) 4057-7411, makes regular trips to the park from downtown Cairns; $9 roundtrip. For general information on the park, call (07) 4042-9999.

Parks and Hiking

A good place to escape the commercialism of Cairns is **Flecker Botanic Gardens** on Collins Ave. west of downtown. The gardens hold an orchid house, a fern house, and the Gondwanan display, which takes you along a path where interpretive boards explain the significance various species had to the Aboriginals. Adjoining these gardens is **Mt. Whitfield Environmental Park,** protecting a large chunk of native bushland surrounded by city development. From a parking lot on McDonnel St. (off Collins Ave.) a trail leads to the summit of **Mt. Whitfield** (360 meters), returning via a different route. The trail is 5.5 km roundtrip, but allow at least three hours to complete the trail as the going gets tough near the summit. A shorter option is a 1.3-km circuit to a lookout 100 meters above sea level.

A park with a difference is **Cairns Botanical Conservatory,** on the roof of the wing of the Reef Hotel Casino. This massive glasshouse, four stories high, contains a great variety of rainforest vegetation, including palms, ferns, and orchids, as well as a restaurant.

River Running

Cairns is base for a number of whitewater rafting companies that run rivers flowing off the Atherton Tableland. You'll encounter the most challenging rapids on the **Tully River,** 140 km south of Cairns; **Raging Thunder,** tel. (07) 4030-7990, and **R'nR,** tel. (07) 4051-7777, offer full-day packages including transfers from Cairns, up to five hours on the river, and lunch for $132 pp. If you have only a half day to spare, both companies offer three trips daily on the **Barron River** for $75 pp.

For families, a tamer option is a float down the **Mulgrave River** in a stable inflatable raft; departures are Mon.-Sat. at 1:30 p.m. and include afternoon tea and a visit to a wildlife park for adult $75, child $48. This trip is offered only by Raging Thunder.

R'nR offers overnight whitewater rafting expeditions down the **North Johnstone River,** beginning with a helicopter flight into its remote headwaters and ending where it drains into the ocean near Innisfail; the two-day trip is $385 pp, five-day $835.

Other Recreation

Adventure sports are well entrenched in the Cairns scene. Skydiving with **Paul's Parachuting,** tel. (07) 4035-9666, makes tandem jumps from around 2,700 meters for $228 pp. A more sedate way to view Cairns from the air is with **Raging Thunder,** tel. (07) 4051-4911, whose hot-air balloons depart daily at dawn; 30 minutes aloft $98, 60 minutes for $160.

A.J. Hackett, tel. (07) 4057-7188, has two bungee jumping operations around Cairns. One is on the Cook Highway, 15 km north ($95); the other is in the middle of Kuranda Markets ($39), in the Atherton Tablelands (see below).

You'll find a number of excellent golf courses in the vicinity of Cairns, but a round of golf isn't cheap. **Paradise Palms,** tel. (07) 4059-1433, one of Australia's top courses, has packages from $190 pp, including transfers, club rental, and greens fees.

Entertainment

Cairns has a bustling after-dark scene. Many nightclubs are aimed solely at the backpacker market, with shuttle buses to and from hostels, cheap meals, and free entry before 10 p.m. **The Beach,** corner Abbott and Aplin Streets, tel. (07) 4031-3944, is currently the most popular backpacker hangout. This massive two-story complex holds three bars, a dance floor, and pirate ship-themed stage, and rages all night every night between 6 p.m. and 5 a.m. It hosts many theme nights, including the infamous Foam Party every Sunday at 10 p.m. Attracting a similar crowd is the **Woolshed,** 24 Sheilds St., tel. (07) 4031-6304. Set up as an old woolshed and with an Australian-style menu, after 9 p.m. things really get going, and the action continues till dawn. **1936,** in the Reef Hotel Casino, is a nightclub themed on New York in 1936 and features a nightly cabaret show as well as an intimate dance floor and separate bar and lounge areas.

Johno's Blues Bar, above McDonald's along the Esplanade, tel. (07) 4031-5008, features live blues and rock nightly; the cover charge varies with the band.

The Pier Marketplace holds two good bars: the **Pier Tavern,** tel. (07) 4031-4677, overlooking the marina and attracting the local yachtie crowd, and **Gilhooley's,** tel. (07) 4051-3063, an Irish pub where the Guinness flows freely.

The opening of the $210-million **Reef Hotel Casino,** tel. (07) 4030-8888, in the heart of the city has seen Cairns shed its image as a haven for the budget-conscious once and for all. Gaming rooms sprawl over two floors, each catering to different levels of gambler, with the majority of first-time punters heading to the Main Casino.

HOTEL AND MOTEL ACCOMMODATIONS

A string of backpacker lodges lines Cairns's main commercial strip, the Esplanade, which runs along the edge of Trinity Bay. To the south are high-rise hotels, with most charging well over $100 per night. Sheridan St., running north from Cairns, has a two-km strip of moderately priced motels ($60-90). If being close to the main cruise and tour departure points isn't a priority, head to the northern beaches for accommodations.

Lost among the outdoor tables and booking agents of the Esplanade is the **Bellview,** 85 Esplanade, tel. (07) 4031-4377, a cheap motel with a pool, laundry, and air-conditioning. Rooms are basic; those with shared bathrooms are $27 s, $36 d; private bathrooms $49 d. Inexpensive. **Leo's Budget Accommodation,** 100 Sheridan St., tel. (07) 4051-1264, a few blocks from the waterfront, has rooms with shared bathrooms and a communal kitchen; $38 s, $45 d. Inexpensive. Farther out is the old **Cape York Hotel,** corner Spence and Bunda Streets, tel. (07) 4051-2008, which charges $30 s, $40 d for a basic room with shared facilities. If you're staying in Cairns for more than a few days and the backpacker scene doesn't appeal to you, the weekly rate is a steal at $190 d including breakfast. Inexpensive.

Across from Trinity Bay and along the busy Esplanade at Aplin St. is the **Lyon Motor Inn,** tel.

(07) 4051-2311 or (1800) 07-9025. The rooms are basic, but each has a fridge. You're really only paying for position here; $55-80 s or d. Moderate. **Adobe Motel,** 191 Sheridan St., tel. (07) 4051-5511, located in the middle of a long stretch of motels, has basic but clean rooms for a reasonable $60 s, $75 d. Moderate. **Flying Horseshoe Motel,** 285 Sheridan St., tel. (07) 4051-3022, is a friendly place with free airport shuttles and a pool; $79 s, $89 d. Moderate. **Oasis Inn,** 276 Sheridan St., tel. (07) 4051-8111, is a newer accommodation; each room is air-conditioned and features a shower, bath, small kitchenette, and balcony overlooking a large pool area. Rates are $85-105 s or d. Moderate.

Cairns Queenslander, 22 Digger St., tel. (07) 4051-0122, is a similar setup (although the pool is smaller). Each balcony has a table setting and kitchens are well equipped. One-bedroom units are $110, and two-bedroom units $155, making them a good deal for families or small groups. Expensive.

Away from the hustle and bustle of downtown Cairns is **Palm Royale Cairns,** 7-11 Chester Court, tel. (07) 4032-2700, set on one hectare. The 150 rooms surround a large pool area, landscaped to feel like a private beach resort with an outdoor café, three pools (one for dive training), and a spa. Each room has a private balcony with views over the pool area and is air-conditioned with king-size beds, bath and shower, tea- and coffee-making supplies. At the far end of the complex is Colossus, an indoor/outdoor restaurant open nightly for dinner. Shuttles run into Cairns every two hours. Rates are $150-180 s or d, plus $30 for an extra couple. Premium.

Mercure Hotel Harbourside, 209 Esplanade, tel. (07) 4051-8999, is an eight-story hostelry overlooking Trinity Bay; each modern room has a balcony with views; $150 s or d, $160 with a kitchenette. Luxury. **Cairns Hilton,** Wharf St., tel. (07) 4052-1599, is of the high standard associated with this worldwide chain, and every room has water views; from $230 s or d. Luxury. **Radisson Plaza Hotel,** tel. (07) 4031-1411, is part of the Pier Marketplace complex, right on the waterfront and departure point for many day cruises. For guest use only are an outdoor pool, gym, spa, and sauna. Rooms start at $275-320 s or d. (Even if you're not staying here, check out the amazing rainforest setting in the lobby.) Luxury.

More expensive still is Cairns's newest hotel, the five-star **Reef Hotel Casino,** tel. (07) 4030-8888 or (1800) 80-8883. Each of the 128 rooms is luxuriously appointed and features a spa, interactive entertainment system, and a private balcony. Other hotel facilities include the casino, a rooftop conservatory filled with plants of the rainforest, a stylish nightclub, restaurants, and bars. Rates start at $310 and go all the way up to $2,500 per night. Luxury.

Northern Beaches
On the northern beaches, **Agincourt Beachfront Apartments,** Clifton Beach, tel. (07) 4055-3500, has huge units, each with a bedroom, large living area, private balcony, and kitchen. Rooms with garden views are $98 per night; those facing the beach are $118 per night, with a minimum wintertime stay of three nights and discounts Nov.-May. Expensive. For those in the know, one of North Queensland's favorite hideaways is **Reef House,** 99 Williams Esplanade, Palm Cove, tel. (07) 4055-3633. Secluded from the outside world and featuring Cairns's best beach across the road, tropical surroundings, casual yet elegant rooms, and unrivaled service, it's a relatively good value at $240 s or d. Luxury.

BUDGET ACCOMMODATIONS

Backpacker Accommodations
The largest concentration of backpacker places is along the Esplanade, a location handy to downtown, cafés and restaurants, and Pier Marketplace. Most lodges are old motels, with as many beds in each room as possible. **YHA on the Esplanade,** 93 Esplanade, tel. (07) 4031-1919, is one of the better ones, with five-bed dorms, each with a bathroom. Beds are $17-18, with small double rooms for $40. Inexpensive. Next door is **Hostel 89,** 89 Esplanade, tel. (07) 4031-7477; each room is air-conditioned and dorms have a maximum of four beds; $15 pp. Budget. **Caravella's 77 Backpacker Resort,** 77 Esplanade, tel. (07) 4051-2159, is a large complex with clean and comfortable air-conditioned dorms for $16 pp and doubles with private bathroom for $40. Inexpensive.

A few blocks north of the hostels listed above is another bunch, still within easy walking distance of everything. **Bel-air Backpackers,** in an old Queenslander at 157 Esplanade, tel. (07) 4031-4790, has good facilities; dorms are $16 and doubles a reasonable $34. Inexpensive.

The pick of Cairns's budget accommodations is **Dreamtime,** away from the waterfront but still very central at 4 Terminus St., tel. (07) 4031-6753. As the name suggests, it's a tropical paradise in the heart of the city, with a pool, barbecue area, great tour booking service, and friendly Irish owners who somehow seem to remember everyone by name. There are no bunk beds; share rooms are $15 pp, doubles and twins are $35, which includes tea and coffee. Inexpensive. **Uptop Downunder Backpackers Resort,** 164 Spence St., tel. (07) 4051-3636, is a friendly place, just over one km from downtown. The kitchen is well equipped and there are two TV rooms, a lounge area, pool, and pool table; dorms $15, doubles $32. Inexpensive.

Campgrounds
Cairns has no downtown campgrounds. Closest to the action is **Coles Villa & Leisure Park,** 28 Pease St., tel. (07) 4053-7133. All facilities here are of the highest standard; unpowered sites $16, powered sites $18. Also here are large cabins and villas for $50-75. Budget-Inexpensive. **Cairns Coconut Caravan Village,** on the Bruce Highway eight km south of downtown, tel. (07) 4054-6644, also has excellent facilities including a tennis court and saltwater pool; sites are $18.50-21, self-contained cabins are $50, and luxurious villas are $95. Budget-Inexpensive. **Ellis Beach Caravan Park** is 32 km north of Cairns, tel. (07) 4055-3538, and has a great beachfront location.

FOOD

Breakfast
Without a doubt, the best place to head for breakfast is the **Beach Hut,** tel. (07) 4031-2133, in Pier Marketplace. Its upstairs location allows panoramic views across Trinity Bay. A huge buffet offers plenty of fresh fruit, breakfast cereals, bacon, eggs, some Chinese dishes, and tea and coffee, all for just $7.50; served daily 7-11 a.m. On the Esplanade, the same money will get you bacon and eggs or a croissant and coffee at one

of the many sidewalk cafés. **Pacific Flavours Brasserie,** in the Reef Hotel Casino, is open daily 24 hours and offers a great variety of breakfast choices.

Cheap Eats

The Esplanade, between Shields and Aplin Streets, is a continuous strip of cafés and takeaways, many with tables strung out along the footpath. Just around the corner, on Aplin St., is **Meeting Place,** a small food court with a variety of Asian outlets. One block back from the Esplanade, the local art gallery, on the corner of Abbot and Sheilds Streets, holds a great little café with ocean views. On the second floor of Pier Marketplace, and overlooking the marina, is a large food court and a variety of inexpensive restaurants, including the **Beach Hut,** which has a buffet lunch ($13.50) and dinner ($24 or $18 before 7 p.m.). Escape the tourist crowds at **Cairns Leagues Club,** 139 Grafton St., tel. (07) 4031-1079, where you'll find a casual bistro serving lunch or dinner for less than $10.

Australian

With a large proportion of tourists to Cairns coming from overseas, Australian-style restaurants are very popular. The most unique of these is **Red Ochre Grill,** 43 Shields St., tel. (07) 4051-0100, where all dishes are inspired by Aboriginal food, combining bush tucker with modern cooking styles in a casual atmosphere. **Dundee's,** 29 Spence St., tel. (07) 4051-0399, features a menu packed with Australian cuisine, including emu, crocodile, buffalo, and plenty of local seafood; open daily from 6 p.m. A more casual Australian-style restaurant, with prices to match, is the **Woolshed,** offering Stockmen's Pie for $7 and Shearers Delight (rack of lamb) for $10. It's at 24 Shields St., tel. (07) 4031-6304. At the opposite end of the price range is **Sirocco,** with water views from the Radisson Plaza Hotel, tel. (07) 4031-1411. The elegant setting and dishes featuring local mainland produce and reef seafood combine to create one of Cairns's best dining experiences.

Other Restaurants

As you can gather from the name, **Barnacle Bill's,** 65 Esplanade, tel. (07) 4051-2241, at the marina end of the Esplanade, specializes in seafood, with prawns, lobster, crab, barramundi, and crocodile all available. Eating here isn't particularly cheap (main dishes $18-27), but a 30% discount is offered on orders taken before 6 p.m.; open daily from 5 p.m. **George's Greek Taverna,** 16 Aplin St., tel. (07) 4041-1500, is a stylish place with good food. **Fiesta Cantina,** 96 Lake St., tel. (07) 4041-2412, is a trendy Mexican place with most main dishes less than $15.

Gypsy Dee's, 41 Shields St., tel. (07) 4051-5530, is surely one of Cairns's most unique restaurants. Styled on the exotic gypsy lifestyle, colored lighting, cane chairs, fake chandeliers, a complete gypsy wagon, and live music add to the atmosphere. As an added gimmick, the entire front end of the restaurant collapses to the sidewalk, revealing a plant-filled terrace. The menu is fairly standard, with mains ranging $10-18 and plenty of vegetarian choices. It's open daily 6 p.m.-2 a.m. **Damari's,** 171 Lake St., tel. (07) 4031-2155, is typically Italian, decorated in red, green, and white, with tables close together and plenty of greenery. Most pizza and pasta dishes are $12-18, with steak and seafood dishes more expensive.

TRANSPORTATION

Getting There

Cairns International Airport is off Captain Cook Dr. north of the city. As well as being served by Australia's national carrier, **Qantas,** tel. (13) 1313, it is served by the following international airlines: **Air New Zealand,** tel. (1800) 06-1253; **Air Niugini,** tel. (13) 1380; **Cathay Pacific,** tel. (13) 1747; **Garuda,** tel. (1800) 80-0873; **Japan Air Lines,** tel. (07) 4031-2700; **Malaysian,** tel. (13) 2627; and **Singapore Airlines,** tel. (07) 4031-7538. Qantas has direct flights between Cairns and the west coast of the United States. Facilities at the international terminal include car rental outlets, lockers ($2 per day), shops, showers, a café and restaurant, currency exchange, and a tourist information booth. The domestic terminal, a 200-meter walk from international (or a $1 shuttle ride), has similar facilities (no currency exchange) and is served by the following domestic airlines: **Ansett Australia,** tel. (13) 1300; **Qantas,** tel. (13) 1313; **Sunstate,** tel. (13) 1313; and **Flightwest,** tel. (13) 2392.

The **Airporter** runs between both terminals and downtown; $4.50 one-way, tel. (07) 4031-3555. A cab between either terminal and downtown runs $12-15. **Coral Coaches,** tel. (07) 4031-7577, runs north from the airport to Palm Cove, Port Douglas, Mossman, and beyond.

The railway station is located on McLeod St. at Shields St., a part of downtown earmarked for continuing development. The Sunlander and Queenslander all make the 32-hour journey between Brisbane and Cairns. The Queenslander is more luxurious than other services and has a bar, lounge, and restaurant. The fare to Cairns on this service is $532 one-way including meals. It departs Brisbane Sunday 10 a.m. The best rail deal is the East Coast Discover Pass, which allows unlimited stops between Sydney and Cairns for $200. For information on all these services, call (13) 2232, or if you're in Brisbane, drop by **Brisbane Travel Centre** at 305 Edward Street.

All long-distance buses operate from Trinity Wharf, with both major operators, **Greyhound Pioneer,** tel. (13) 2030, and **McCafferty's,** tel. (13) 1499, running five services daily between Brisbane and Cairns. This trip takes 30 hours.

Getting Around
Local bus companies serve all suburbs of Cairns, with schedules posted at Lake Street Transit on City Place. The most useful of these is the **Sunbus,** tel. (07) 4057-7411. This service runs regularly between downtown Cairns and the northern beaches as far as Ellis Beach ($1-4 per sector or $9 to ride all day). It stops at all beaches on route, including Palm Cove. The **Cairns Explorer,** tel. (07) 4033-5244, also operates from Lake Street Transit, stopping at eight tourist spots in the vicinity of Cairns. A commentary is given along the way and you may alight and re-board anywhere. Cost is adult $25, child $12.50.

Major car rental companies are: **Avis,** tel. (07) 4051-5911; **Budget,** tel. (07) 4051-9222; **Hertz,** tel. (13) 3039; and **National,** tel. (07) 4051-4600. **Cairns Rent-a-car,** tel. (07) 4051-6077 or (1800) 64-0404, has cars for $60 per day, including unlimited kilometers. The smallest

four-wheel drives are $120, with the rate dropping to $90 per day for a week.

For a cab call **Black and White Taxis,** tel. (13) 1008, or **Taxis Australia, tel. (13) 2227.**

Tours
The most popular tours from Cairns take in the reef, the hinterland, and rainforest (see below). The major tour companies are **Australian Pacific Tours,** tel. (13) 1304; **Cairns Scenic Tours,** tel. (07) 4032-1381; **Down Under Tours,** tel. (1800) 07-9119; and **Tropic Wings,** tel. (07) 4035-3555.

SERVICES AND INFORMATION

The **post office** is on the corner of Grafton and Hartley Streets. For foreign exchange transactions, head to the **American Express** office in Orchid Plaza at 79 Abbott St., tel. (07) 4031-2871. **Walker's Bookshop** is at 96 Lake St., tel. (07) 4051-2410. **Proudmans,** another good bookshop, is in Pier Marketplace. **Cairns City Public Library,** 177 Lake St., tel. (07) 4050-2404, is open Monday 10 a.m.-6 p.m., Tues.-Fri. 10 a.m.-7 p.m., Saturday 10 a.m.-4 p.m.

Cairns has no official information center, but **Tourism Tropical North Queensland** has a Visitor Information Centre along the Esplanade opposite the end of Shields St., tel. (07) 4051-3588, website: www.tnq.org.au, which is a good source of information on Cairns and surrounding destinations; open daily 9:30 a.m.-5:30 p.m. The dozen-odd booking agents, most along the Esplanade, offer limited amounts of information, but are really in business to make commissions off booking tours. The **Traveller's Contact Centre,** 13 Shields St., tel. (07) 4051-4777, is one of the better ones and has e-mail access for $10 an hour. The **RACQ,** a good source of maps for travel in the far north, is at 138 McLeod St., tel. (07) 4051-6543. For information on the many surrounding national parks and road conditions around the cape, head to the **Department of Environment** at 10 McLeod St., tel. (07) 4052-3096; open weekdays 8:30 a.m.-4:30 p.m.

VICINITY OF CAIRNS

Cairns is an excellent base for day trips to a number of different areas. A great variety of cruises depart daily from Pier Marketplace for Green and Fitzroy Islands, giving day trippers the chance to experience tropical islands for a reasonable price, as well as to the outer reef. West of Cairns is Atherton Tableland, part of the Wet Tropics World Heritage area, and the small village Kuranda. Along the Captain Cook Highway north of Cairns is Port Douglas, smaller than Cairns, but with its own unique charm and a good access point to the outer reef. North of Port Douglas is the spectacular Daintree Rainforest and, farther north, Cape Tribulation, where rainforest descends right to the ocean.

GREAT BARRIER REEF

Green Island

The appeal of this small 12-hectare island is twofold—it's a coral cay (one of the reef's three true coral islands with resorts), and its location is prime, just 27 km from Cairns. Ringed by a shingle beach of broken coral, the island's interior is thickly vegetated, rising less than two meters above high-tide level. Declared a national park in 1937 to protect its fragile environment, the island is now, ironically, the most visited site on the entire reef (because of its size there's no escaping the crowds). As well as snorkeling, swimming, and sunbaking, visitors can ride in a semi-submersible or glass-bottomed boat and view the aquariums of Marineland Melanesia.

A hotel was first built on the island in the mid-1960s, but the island didn't come to prominence until August 1994, when five-star **Green Island Resort** opened for business. Although accommodations and facilities are of the highest standard, the unpretentious development blends into the island environment. Rates at the resort are among the most expensive on the reef, and with the amount of day trippers, solitude can only be found within the resort complex. That said, the pool area is a delightful place to relax and no expense has been spared in furnishing the rooms. Rates of $640 s, $780 d are inclusive of meals. For reservations call (07) 4031-3300 or (1800) 67-3366.

The best deal for day trippers heading over to Green Island is aboard the **Big Cat,** tel. (07) 4051-0444, which departs Marlin Marina daily at 9 a.m. The trip over takes 80 minutes, with five hours spent on the island; $42 pp includes lunch and either snorkeling gear or a glass-bottomed boat trip. **Great Adventures,** tel. (07) 4051-0455 or (1800) 07-9080, runs out to the island on a high-speed catamaran for $40, with snorkeling equipment an extra $10. Other packages offered by this company include a two-hour stop on the island and a trip to the outer reef for $126 plus entry to all island attractions and lunch for $78. Departures are from Great Adventures terminal daily at 8:30 a.m. and 10:30 a.m. Return flights with **Aquaflight Airways,** tel. (07) 4031-4307, are $100 pp.

Fitzroy Island

This 324-hectare continental island, 23 km east of Cairns, features an inexpensive resort and makes an ideal day trip from Cairns. The beaches are made up of broken coral, making sunbaking unpleasant, but snorkeling on fringing reefs is excellent. Hiking trails lead to Nudie Beach (good snorkeling) and a lookout on the island's eastern extremity, six km from the resort.

Fitzroy Island Resort is on Welcome Bay, a long stretch of beach flanked by outcrops of large granite boulders. Because of limited resort activities, scuba diving and PADI dive courses attract the most people. Three distinct levels of accommodation are offered, making it one of the few island resorts appealing to all budgets. Beach Bunkhouses have four bunk beds with a shower block and communal kitchen; $28 pp (discounts for YHA members) or $95 for the entire room. Each of the eight Beach Cabins has two rooms, a bathroom, a balcony, and ceiling fan; $240 s, $340 d includes breakfast and dinner. Campsites are $15 (book through the local council at 07-4051-0455), and unless eating in the resort restaurant, you need to be self-sufficient. For bookings call (07) 4051-9588 or (1800) 07-9080.

VICINITY OF CAIRNS

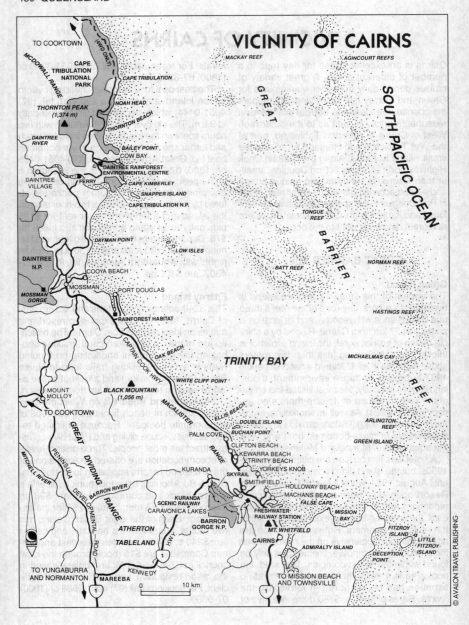

TO COOKTOWN
(4WD ONLY)

MCDOWALL RANGE

CAPE TRIBULATION NATIONAL PARK

THORNTON PEAK
(1,374 m)

CAPE TRIBULATION

NOAH HEAD

THORNTON BEACH

DAINTREE RIVER

BAILEY POINT

COW BAY

DAINTREE RAINFOREST
ENVIRONMENTAL CENTRE

DAINTREE VILLAGE

FERRY

CAPE KIMBERLEY

SNAPPER ISLAND

CAPE TRIBULATION N.P.

DAINTREE N.P.

DAYMAN POINT

LOW ISLES

MOSSMAN GORGE

COOYA BEACH

MOSSMAN

PORT DOUGLAS

RAINFOREST HABITAT

OAK BEACH

WHITE CLIFF POINT

CAPTAIN COOK HWY

MOUNT MOLLOY

BLACK MOUNTAIN
(1,056 m)

TO COOKTOWN

ELLIS BEACH

DOUBLE ISLAND

PALM COVE

BUCHAN POINT

CLIFTON BEACH

KEWARRA BEACH

TRINITY BEACH

YORKEYS KNOB

KURANDA

SKYRAIL

SMITHFIELD

HOLLOWAY BEACH

MACHANS BEACH

FALSE CAPE

KURANDA SCENIC RAILWAY

CARAVONICA LAKES

FRESHWATER RAILWAY STATION

BARRON GORGE N.P.

MT. WHITFIELD

MISSION BAY

GREAT DIVIDING RANGE

MACALISTER RANGE

PENINSULA DEVELOPMENTAL ROAD

MITCHELL RIVER

BARRON RIVER

ATHERTON TABLELAND

CAIRNS

ADMIRALTY ISLAND

DECEPTION POINT

FITZROY ISLAND

LITTLE FITZROY ISLAND

TO YUNGABURRA
AND NORMANTON

MAREEBA

KENNEDY HWY

TO MISSION BEACH
AND TOWNSVILLE

TRINITY BAY

SOUTH PACIFIC OCEAN

GREAT BARRIER REEF

MACKAY REEF

AGINCOURT REEFS

TONGUE REEF

BATT REEF

NORMAN REEF

HASTINGS REEF

MICHAELMAS CAY

ARLINGTON REEF

GREEN ISLAND

0   10 km

© AVALON TRAVEL PUBLISHING

Sunlover Cruises, tel. (07) 4031-1055, departs Trinity Wharf daily at 9 a.m. for Fitzroy Island, returning at 4:30 p.m.; $30 roundtrip. **Great Adventures,** tel. (07) 4051-0455, departs the terminal beside Trinity Wharf daily at 8:30 a.m. and 10:30 a.m. for $30 with optional extras of snorkeling and scuba diving.

Lizard Island

Northernmost of the resort islands, 1,012-hectare Lizard Island is surrounded by beautiful fringing reefs and some of the best beaches to be found on the entire reef, its upmarket resort a popular spot for divers and game fishing enthusiasts chasing black marlin (Sept.-Nov.). In front of the resort a fringing reef beckons snorkelers, but, immediately south, a platform reef provides a greater array of life. But it's the shoals of the inner reef that scuba divers head to Lizard Island for, including one particular site, the **Cod Hole,** famous for giant potato cod that grow to a length of two meters. For resort guests a day's diving is $110-150 and equipment rental is another $50. Although the island is just seven km long, there are some good hiking opportunities, including to the summit of **Cook's Look** (259 meters), from where Captain Cook searched out a northward passage in 1770. Views from this summit are tremendous, extending 360 degrees.

Lizard Island Lodge is on Anchor Bay, a small cove fronted by a wide sandy beach. The 40 units are very comfortable, with the emphasis on solitude and service, and each is air-conditioned. Food of the highest standard is served in a dining area that sprawls along the veranda with spectacular ocean views. Rates are $860 s, $1,040 d inclusive of meals. For bookings call (07) 4060-3999; from North America, call (800) 227-4411.

Sheltered in the northern corner of Mrs Watson's Beach is a national park campground with toilets, barbecues, and drinking water; $5 per night, book through the Department of Environment in Cairns, tel. (07) 4052-3096. Campers must be self-sufficient as they are denied access to the resort.

The only scheduled transport to Lizard Island is from Cairns flying **Sunstate,** tel. (13) 1313; $400 roundtrip. **Marine Air,** tel. (07) 4069-5915, offers a day trip to the island from Cooktown for $195 pp, or transfers for up to four people for $400 one-way.

Outer Reef Cruises

One of Cairns's most appealing features is its proximity to the outer reef, which is closer to the mainland off Cairns than at any point farther south.

The least expensive way to get to the outer reef is aboard *Seastar II,* an 18-meter cruiser that holds 40 passengers. Hastings Reef, 52 km northeast of Cairns, is the final destination, but a stop is also made at Michaelmas Cay; $50 pp includes snorkeling and lunch. Departures are from Marlin Marina daily at 7:15 a.m., tel. (07) 4033-0333.

Great Adventures, tel. (07) 4051-0455 or (1800) 07-9080, offers the widest variety of outer reef cruises, all departing from their own terminal on Wharf Street. The most popular departs at 8:30 a.m., with two hours spent on Green Island before speeding out to Norman Reef, 59 km northeast of Cairns, where the company has a pontoon, and snorkeling, glass-bottomed boat rides, and lunch are included for $135 pp. The 10:30 a.m. departure is a few dollars cheaper, but no stop on Green Island is made. This company also offers a cruise to Moore Reef, 49 km east of Cairns, with a stop at Fitzroy Island and the same inclusions for $95 pp. In both cases, kids are half price.

Sunlover Cruises, tel. (07) 4031-1055, has a full-day cruise out to Arlington Reef in a large high-speed catamaran. At the reef is a large pontoon from where submarine tours, glass-bottomed boat cruises, snorkeling, and a buffet lunch are offered; adult $112, child $60. This company also combines a stopover on Fitzroy Island with a trip out to Moore Reef with all the above inclusions for adult $130, child $65. Both cruises depart Trinity Wharf daily at 9 a.m.

Ocean Spirit, tel. (07) 4031-2920, a luxurious 32-meter sailing catamaran, departs from Marlin Marina daily at 9 a.m. for Michaelmas Cay, a low coral cay 42 km northeast of Cairns. Once on the island, which is a bird sanctuary, you can snorkel, sunbake, or ride a semi-submersible boat. The fare is adult $130, which includes a buffet lunch, pickups, and all activities (except scuba diving).

The largest operator of reef trips is **Quicksilver,** tel. (07) 4031-4299, which operates out of Port Douglas. For Cairns-based tourists, connections to Port Douglas with Quicksilver depart Marlin Marina daily at 8 a.m. (see below).

Scuba Diving

All the above operators offer scuba diving as an extra, generally $40-65 for certified divers and $50-75 pp for uncertified divers. Diving is also offered at the three island resorts off Cairns (see above). At least five Cairns-based companies offer diving certification courses, but it really pays to shop around. You should allow at least four days and budget $300 for the course. **Reef Teach** is a super-popular two-hour program presented by marine biologist Paddy Codwell encompassing the story of the reef's formation and its inhabitants. It takes place at 14 Spence St., tel. (07) 4051-6882, Mon.-Sat. at 6:15 p.m. The cost is a worthwhile $10 pp.

Tusa Dive, tel. (07) 4031-1248, is one of the few operators running day trips to the outer reef specifically for divers. Trips depart Marlin Marina at 8 a.m. Cost is $155 pp for two dives and equipment rental ($95 for non-divers. **Down Under Dive,** tel. (07) 4031-1288, runs an old sailing ship out to the inner reef on a two-day, one-night trip for a reasonable $255 pp ($180 for nondivers). **Pro-dive,** tel. (07) 4031-5255, has a three-day, two-night outer reef trip, including 11 dives, for $420. Their PADI certification course, spread over five days, is $510.

One of the Great Barrier Reef's most spectacular dive sites is the **Cod Hole,** east of Lizard Island. Officially known as Cormorant Pass, the resident populations of potato cod—which grow up to two meters in length— moray eels, wrasses, and coral trout are all semi-tame and waiting to be fed. **Mike Ball Dive Expeditions,** tel. (07) 4031-5484, departs Cairns Friday and Monday at 7:30 a.m. for a three-day trip out to the Cod Hole on *Supersport,* a luxurious 30-meter catamaran. All-inclusive fare, including flights from Cairns to Lizard Island, starts at $845 pp.

figure from Aboriginal shield design

Flightseeing

Viewing the reef from the air is an unforgettable experience, and in some cases can be combined with a few hours spent lazing on an island. **Aquaflight Airways,** tel. (07) 4031-4307, combines flightseeing with reef landings, allowing time to swim and snorkel. Prices range from $100 pp to Green Island, $160 pp to Hastings Reef. Departures are from Marlin Marina. **Jayrow,** tel. (07) 4035-9999, offers helicopter flights, including 40 minutes over the reef for $245 pp. A one-way flight to Norman Reef, lunch, glass-bottomed boat tour, snorkeling, and return by high-speed catamaran is $275 pp.

ATHERTON TABLELAND

This plateau west of Cairns, part of the UNESCO Wet Tropics World Heritage Area, features lush rainforests, waterfalls, and picturesque lakes, away from the crowds and waiting for those who drag themselves from the reef. Kuranda is as far onto the plateau as many people travel, but it extends 100 km farther south and is all worthy of exploration.

Skyrail and the Kuranda Scenic Railway

From Caravonica Lakes and the Tjapukai Aboriginal Cultural Park (see above), 15 km northwest of Cairns, these two forms of transportation provide a unique way to reach the Atherton Tableland.

The railway, tel. (07) 4052-6249, was completed in 1891, taking five years, and winds from the eastern seaboard up the steep escarpment of the plateau to Kuranda with 15 tunnels and 100 curves in 35 km; the final 20 km gains more than 200 meters in elevation and passes through 15 tunnels. A highlight is a photo stop at spectacular Barron Falls. The rail trip begins at Freshwater Railway Station, at Caravonica Lakes. The fare is $25 one-way, $40 roundtrip, but packages are available that include transportation from Cairns.

Skyrail Rainforest Cableway, tel. (07) 4038-1555, the world's longest gondola, begins its 7.5-km journey adjacent to the railway, and also ends in Kuranda. It traverses virgin rainforest for much of the way above the canopy, allowing views of the sea of green below and the ocean beyond. Along the route are several stations; Red Peak, on the edge of the tableland, offers spectacular views across to the Coral Sea; at Barron Falls the mighty Barron River descends into a deep gorge. Also at Barron Falls, the Rainforest Interpretive Centre describes the surrounding environment. The fare is $27 one-way, $45 roundtrip.

Kuranda

The small mountain town of Kuranda, 20 km west of Cairns, is accessed along a winding road, Skyrail, or the scenic railway (see above). Its tree-lined streets shade open-air cafés, boutiques specializing in Australiana, and a few commercial attractions. But it's markets for which Kuranda is best known. Held Wed.-Fri. and Sunday, the markets have some great arts and crafts and fresh produce (and also a lot of junk). The markets are spread around Therwine St., but crowds fill the entire town. A good way to escape the market-day masses is to head into **Jumrum Creek Environmental Park,** on the south side of town, or follow Barron Falls Rd. to a spectacular lookout perched on the rim of the Atherton Tableland.

In the middle of the markets is the **Australian Butterfly Sanctuary,** tel. (07) 4093-7575. The sanctuary has a large outdoor display area, as well as an enclosed aviary. It's open daily 10 a.m.-3 p.m. Admission adult $10.50, child $6. Also with the market grounds is **Sky Screamers Bungy,** tel. (07) 4041-3280, costing $39 per jump. On Coondoo St. is **Kuranda Wildlife Noctarium,** tel. (07) 4093-7334, where day and night have been artificially reversed for viewing Australia's many nocturnal animals. Admission is adult $9, child $4.50. Open daily 10 a.m.-4 p.m., with feeding times at 10:30 a.m., 11:30 a.m., 1:15 p.m., and 2:30 p.m.

The only accommodation right in town is **Kuranda Backpacker Hostel,** 6 Arara St., tel. (07) 4093-7355, an old place that has recently seen extensive renovations. It has a real tropical feel, with extensive gardens holding a pool and barbecue area, and dozens of colorful rainbow lorikeets that come in to feed every morning. Dorm beds go for $14 pp and a couple of doubles for

$32. Budget. The other choice for budget travelers is **Kuranda Caravan Park,** Myola Rd., tel. (07) 4093-7316, where campsites are $13-15 and cabins are $35. Just out of town on the road to Mareeba, and a pleasant five-minute walk from Kuranda, is **Kuranda Rainforest Resort,** tel. (07) 4093-7555 or (1800) 80-6996. Set among tropical rainforest, the resort rings a magnificent landscaped pool area. Other facilities include a tennis court, large gym, restaurant, bar, and laundry. Each unit has a balcony and is well furnished; $138 s or d. Scattered around the property are a number of freestanding cedar cabins, each with two bedrooms and a private balcony; $225. Transfers from Cairns Airport are complimentary. Premium.

One of many eateries on Coondoo St. is **Frogs Restaurant,** tel. (07) 4093-7405, a bright and breezy place with old wooden floors, plenty of greenery, and a few tables on a veranda out back. As well as all the usual café fare, seafood is well priced at $10-15 for main dishes.

The most popular way to get to Kuranda from Cairns is aboard **Skyrail** or the **scenic railway** (see above), but this is not the cheapest way. You can also jump aboard one of **Whitecar Coaches** thrice-daily buses from Tropical Paradise Travel, 44 Spence St.; $12 one-way, tel. (07) 4051-9533.

Yungaburra and Vicinity

Yungaburra sits in the center of Atherton Tableland, 13 km east of Atherton and 65 km southwest of Cairns. Only 900 people live in Yungaburra, but it has the tableland's best choice of accommodations and restaurants, and is a great base for exploring surrounding sights. Definitely worth the effort to find is the **curtain fig,** a particularly enormous example of a tree that is typical in tropical rainforests. This one is more than 15 meters high, having grown along an ancient tree that had fallen against another. After the fallen tree rotted, the curtain fig remained, forming a "sail" of hanging vines. To get there follow the road out of Yungaburra toward Atherton for one km, then head two km south toward Malanda.

East of Yungaburra are two interesting lakes filling the craters of a volcano that erupted 95,000 years ago. **Lake Eacham,** the smaller of the two, has no rivers flowing into it, so it's filled with

curtain fig

Lake Eacham Hotel, tel. (07) 4095-3515, a classic country pub, serves lunch and dinner. Across the road is Burra Inn, tel. (07) 4095-3657, a more formal eatery with large servings for $16-24.

South from Yungaburra

Malanda, 12 km south of Yungaburra, is home to a large dairy that supplies towns with milk throughout the far north and as far away as Darwin. Right by the road on the town's western outskirts is Malanda Falls, the start of a couple of short hikes and site of a shaded picnic area. Malanda Falls Caravan Park, between town and the falls, tel. (07) 4096-5314, has tent sites for $15, bunk beds for $15 pp, and cabins for $35-50. Budget.

Waterfalls tumble off the tableland's higher elevations south of Malanda, and although none are breathtakingly spectacular, each has its own charm, and, chances are, crowds will be minimal. The best are on the Waterfall Route, a 24-km drive east of Millaa Millaa.

From Millaa Millaa, the Palmerston Highway leads east to Innisfail, 88 km south of Cairns, and the Kennedy Highway leads southwest to the Gulf Developmental Rd., the most direct road link between Cairns and Normanton.

only rainwater, making it crystal clear. It is encircled by a four-km trail (slippery after rain) and is also good for swimming. Lake Barrine has a six-km trail around its circumference and a restaurant overlooking its calm waters. North of Yungaburra is Lake Tinaroo, a reservoir that's part of the Barron River hydroelectric power scheme. To drive around the lake takes at least an hour (60 km) with many rough sections. Along the route are campgrounds (free) and a short nature walk around Lake Euramoo.

In Yungaburra, stay at Yungaburra Park Motel, Atherton Rd., tel. (07) 4095-3211, where rooms are modern and there's a pleasant outdoor area with barbecue; $55 s or d. Inexpensive. For backpackers, On the Wallaby, 37 Eacham Rd., tel. (07) 4095-2031, provides comfortable accommodation in rustic surroundings. Dorm beds are $15 pp, doubles $35, and transportation from Cairns is offered for $15 pp one-way. Budget. At Lake Eacham is a caravan park, tel. (07) 4095-3730.

PORT DOUGLAS AND VICINITY

As a sister resort town to Cairns, Port Douglas (pop. 2,400) couldn't be more different. Located on a low spit of land flanked to the east by the magnificent golden sands of Four Mile Beach, the town has one short strip of boutiques, cafés, and restaurants surrounded by a few blocks of residential housing. The four-km road into town from the Captain Cook Highway is lined with palm trees, a subtle sign of the transformation Port Douglas has undergone in the last decade.

Founded in 1877 as a gateway to Hodgkinson goldfields, the town's population peaked late last century at 12,000, but by 1911, after Cairns was chosen as a railhead and tropical cyclones had destroyed most buildings, Port Douglas's short-term destiny was sealed. Things began changing in the mid-1980s, when new resorts, trendy shops, and a million-dollar marina complex breathed life into the sleepy village. Today

Port Douglas is a good choice as an alternative to Cairns, retaining its sleepy reputation while providing accommodations for all budgets, having a relaxed tropical feel, and providing easy access to reef destinations.

Sights and Recreation

At the west end of Macrossan St. are the sheltered waters of **Dickson Inlet.** Home to a small fleet of motley-colored fishing vessels just 10 short years ago, the waterway has been transformed by **Marina Mirage,** chock-full of luxurious motor cruisers, where restaurants serve cuisine from around the world, and shops brim with brand names that seem more at home in Paris or New York. The paddlewheeler *Lady Douglas* departs twice daily for a relaxing cruise around Dickson Inlet; $25 pp, which includes a light seafood snack. For bookings call (07) 4099-5051. Toward the mouth of the inlet is **Shipwreck Museum,** tel. (07) 4099-5858, put together by Ben Cropp from the 100 shipwrecks he has discovered off the Australian coastline. Admission is adult $5, child $2; open daily 9 a.m.-5 p.m.

Four Mile Beach is a magnificent stretch of sand extending south from Island Point in one unbroken arc. Hidden from the beach by casuarina trees is **Mirage Country Club,** a world-class 18-hole golf course. Greens fees are $120; for bookings call (07) 4099-5537. The aptly named resort rises like a mirage from a two-hectare swimming pool that surrounds most of the main complex.

On the Port Douglas access road is **Rainforest Habitat,** tel. (07) 4099-3235, a re-creation of typical rainforest complete with more than 150 species of creatures you may or may not see in the wild, including crocodiles, cassowaries, and koalas. Entry to the park is steep at adult $16, child $8. Breakfast with the Birds, including admission and a lavish hot buffet complete with champagne (from 8 a.m.), is adult $30, child $15; park hours are daily 8 a.m.-5:30 p.m.

Reef Cruises

Port Douglas is home base for **Quicksilver,** tel. (07) 4099-5500, a large operation with day trips to destinations off Port Douglas, with transfers offered to those based at Cairns. A 37-meter wavepiercer makes daily excursions to **Agincourt Reefs,** a string of reef considered among the most beautiful of those accessible by day trippers. At the reef is a two-story pontoon, the base for snorkeling, a semi-submersible ride, scuba diving (two dives; $90 extra), and helicopter flightseeing ($85). From Port Douglas the fare is $135 (10 a.m. departure), from Cairns $145 (8 a.m. departure).

A more personalized way to view the outer reef is aboard *Aristocat,* a 16-meter high-speed catamaran carrying just 25 passengers. The itinerary includes visiting two reefs, snorkeling, a reef ecology presentation, buffet lunch, morning and afternoon tea, and accommodation pickups. Departures are from Marina Mirage Tuesday, Thursday, and Saturday at 8:30 a.m.; adult $124, child $68. On Monday, Wednesday, Friday, and Sunday the itinerary is a little different, with less time spent on the reef to allow time for fishing and boomnetting (being pulled behind the boat in a net); adult $124, child $64. For bookings call (07) 4099-4727.

About halfway between Port Douglas and the outer reef is **Low Isles,** a small coral cay with shingle beaches and a great fringing reef for snorkeling. The cay is thickly vegetated and forms an important bird-breeding area. A lighthouse has operated on the island since 1878. Quicksilver's *Wavedancer,* a 30-meter sailing catamaran, cruises out to Low Isles from Port Douglas daily at 10 a.m. (departures from Cairns at 8 a.m.), with lunch, an informative reef presentation, snorkeling, and a glass-bottomed boat tour included in the fare of adult $89, child $44.50.

Accommodations

Although Port Douglas is best known for its top-end resorts, there are some options for budget travelers, including a few caravan parks and a backpacker lodge. Of the motels, least expensive is **Coconut Grove Motel,** 58 Macrossan St., tel. (07) 4099-5124, a friendly place within walking distance of the beach, restaurants, and marina. Facilities include a pool and popular bar/restaurant. Rooms are $60 s or d, a little higher with air-conditioning. Moderate. **Lazy Lizard Motor Inn,** 121 Davidson St., tel. (07) 4099-5900, is a step up in quality and just over one km from downtown; from $85 s or d. Moderate. On the road into town are a few expensive hotels including **Radisson Reef Resort,** tel. (07) 4099-5577 or (1800) 33-3333, a great value for those who prefer luxurious accommodations; rates start at $155 s or d, and a few rooms cater to physically challenged travelers. Luxury. As famous for its exiled ex-owner Christopher Skase as its unequaled luxury, **Sheraton Mirage Port Douglas,** tel. (07) 4099-5888 or (1800) 22-2229, features an 18-hole golf course, 10 tennis courts, and a two-hectare pool. Rates start at $490 per night. Premium.

Port o' Call Lodge, Port St., tel. (07) 4099-5422, an associate YHA of the highest standard, has a pool, bike rentals, and a restaurant. Each four-bed dorm has a bathroom ($19 pp) and there are also a few doubles ($55-85 s or d). Transfers from Cairns are complimentary. Inexpensive.

Four Mile Beach Caravan Park, Barrier St., tel. (07) 4098-5281, a pleasant four-km walk from town along the beach, has good facilities; unpowered sites $15, powered sites $17, on-site vans $35, and cabins $55-70. Budget-Inexpensive. If this park is full, try those on Davidson St., closer to town but away from the beach.

Food

For a town of less than 2,500 residents, Port Douglas has a fabulous array of dining options—60 at last count—most of which are on Macrossan Street. **Cafe Macrossan,** 42 Macrossan St., tel. (07) 4099-4372, opens at 9 a.m., and although there's no official breakfast menu, the light meals offered are a great start to the day, especially when enjoyed in the outdoor dining section. Lunch is inexpensive ($6-9) and dinner features local produce, including delicious coral trout. Another good little breakfast spot, **Wharf St. Café Bar,** corner Macrossan and Wharf Streets, opens daily at 8 a.m.

Popular for dinner is the restaurant in Coconut Grove Motel, 58 Macrossan St., tel. (07) 4099-5124, where three-course meals are less than $20 and the small bar has a real tropical ambience. In Marina Mirage, **Fiorelli's,** tel. (07) 4099-5201, has an extensive menu of classical Italian dishes ranging $14.50-24 and a well-priced lunchtime blackboard menu. **On the Inlet,** 3 Inlet St., tel. (07) 4099-5255, is tucked away down a laneway beside Marina Mirage but has a great outdoor deck overlooking the water. The seafood-oriented menu features prawns, calamari, crab, and a variety of reef fish, but is a

best value between 4-6 p.m., when a beer and a bucket of prawns cost just $10. The most elegant of Port Douglas's eateries is **Nautilus Restaurant,** 17 Murphy St., tel. (07) 4099-5330, set in a dense rainforest with no walls and a canopy of greenery for a roof. This restaurant, legendary for its mud crab caught daily ($25-40), has a set menu featuring other seafood such as tiger prawns, mud crab, and coral trout.

Transportation

Cairns, and the closest airport, are 60 km south from town, but regular bus and boat connections make travel to Port Douglas easy. **Coral Coaches,** tel. (07) 4099-5351, operates between Cairns and Port Douglas 10-15 times daily ($32 round-trip), continuing north along the coast to Cooktown. The fare between Cairns and Cooktown is $92 roundtrip, with stops in Port Douglas permitted. Tours from Cairns into the Daintree include a stop at Port Douglas on the itinerary.

Quicksilver, tel. (07) 4099-5500, departs Marlin Marina, Cairns, daily at 8 a.m. in high-speed catamarans, and also pick up passengers in Palm Cove. Primarily designed for day trippers heading to the outer reef, this service can be used as a transfer to Port Douglas ($20 one-way, $30 roundtrip), allowing an inexpensive day trip from Cairns.

Major car rental agencies in Port Douglas include **Avis, Budget,** and **National. Crocodile Car Rentals,** tel. (07) 4099-5555, has four-wheel drives from $69 per day. Port Douglas is relatively flat, so biking is a good way to get around; **Aussie Bike Hire,** 79 Davidson St., tel. (07) 4099-4444, has mountain bikes for $15 per day.

Information

Commercial information centers that are primarily booking agents line the streets of Port Douglas. The local **visitors bureau** operates almost entirely over the Internet (www.portdouglas.com), but it can also be reached by calling (07) 4099-4644.

DAINTREE AND CAPE TRIBULATION

Part of the Wet Tropics World Heritage Area, Daintree and Cape Tribulation National Parks contain an amazing variety of flora and fauna

Daintree ferry crossing

and are among the most beautiful areas of Queensland. Cape Tribulation adjoins the Great Barrier Reef, giving the region the distinction of being the only place on the planet where two UNESCO World Heritage Areas sit side by side. The small sugarcane-growing town of Mossman is gateway to the area. Farther north, a ferry crosses the crocodile-infested Daintree River leading to Cape Tribulation National Park, forested coastline with long stretches of golden beaches. North of the cape, the road is unsealed and passable only in a four-wheel drive.

Mossman and Vicinity

Historic Mossman, 75 km north of Cairns, is Australia's northernmost sugar town. The Mossman River winds through town, emptying into the ocean three km east. On the south side of the river mouth is **Cooya Beach,** where at low tide the beach is more than half a km wide. West of Mossman is 56,550-hectare **Daintree National Park,** an area of jagged mountains, steep escarpments, and impenetrable rainforest. Only the park's extreme southern end, where the Mossman River has carved a wide, deep gorge through the rainforest, is accessible. A 2.7-km trail leads along the river, past picnic tables and swimming holes, over a couple of photogenic creeks, and climbs through a section of lush rainforest before returning to the trailhead.

In Mossman, **Exchange Hotel,** 2 Front St., tel. (07) 4098-1410, has basic rooms for $15 pp. Budget. One km north of town is **Mossman**

Caravan Park, Foxton Ave., tel. (07) 4098-1922, with sites for $11-12 and on-site vans $25. Budget. Out by the gorge is **Silky Oaks Lodge,** tel. (07) 4098-1666, surrounded by virgin rainforest and home to a variety of orphaned animals. Refurbished in 1997, 60 luxurious safari-style bungalows sit throughout the property, each with a tropical ambience and private bathroom, and many have kitchenettes. Rates are $375 per bungalow. Luxury. The restaurant here opens to the rainforest and serves breakfast, lunch, and dinner. Nonguests are welcome.

Daintree River

For most of the 1980s the Daintree was the focus of international attention as protesters and developers clashed over the fate of rainforest that had changed little since dinosaurs roamed the earth. In 1988 a win for the environmentalists saw the forests incorporated into the Wet Tropics World Heritage Area.

A cruise is the best way to experience the river, and with more than a dozen operators, choices are plenty. A variety of wildlife is seen, but crocodiles are the highlight (most often sighted in the winter months). The pick of the bunch is **Daintree Connections,** tel. (07) 4098-6120 or (1800) 65-8833. They offer regular river cruises, departing four times daily from Daintree Village. One-hour cruises are adult $15, child $5. This company also operates dawn and dusk cruises (on demand) for small groups, where wildlife viewing is more productive.

The tiny settlement of **Daintree Village,** the only community between Mossman and Cape Tribulation, lies beside the river a few km upstream of the ferry crossing. The short main street is a concentration of tourist shops. The least expensive place to stay is **Daintree River View Caravan Park,** right in the center of town, tel. (07) 4098-6119. Sites are $12-15, and a few on-site vans are $35 s or d. Budget-Inexpensive. Bed and breakfast **Red Mill House,** Stewart St., tel. (07) 4098-6169, has three rooms that share a bathroom. The gardens are immaculate and there's a pool and spa; $50 s, $60 d includes breakfast. Inexpensive. On the road into the village is **Daintree Eco Lodge,** tel. (07) 4098-6100 or (1800) 80-8010. Freestanding bungalows are scattered around the property, each with a balcony boasting spectacular views of surrounding rainforest. All aspects of the construction and day-to-day lodge operation revolve around the natural surroundings, including a unique restaurant built over a creek and around a tree. Rates are $308 s, $330 d, which includes breakfast and transfers from Cairns for those who require them. Luxury.

Cape Tribulation National Park
This long and narrow 16,959-hectare park extends between the Daintree and Bloomfield Rivers and from the coastline west to the high peaks of the McDowall Range, rising to 1,374 meters at Thornton Peak. Except after heavy rains, two-wheel-drive vehicles can negotiate the 34 km from Daintree River ferry to Cape Tribulation itself (although many car rental companies prohibit their conventional vehicles traveling north of the Daintree River), but travel north of the cape is four-wheel-drive territory only.

Crossing the Daintree River is made easy by a regular ferry service running every 10 minutes between 6 a.m. and midnight. Ferry charges are car (with passengers) $7 one-way, motor bike $3, pedestrian $1.

Before the road climbs the Alexandra Range, a turnoff to the east leads six km to **Cape Kimberley** and a short beach. From the cape **Snapper Island** is easily identified. In the lee of the cape is **Club Daintree,** tel. (07) 4090-7500, a campground with a kitchen area, pool, and restaurant. Camping is $8 pp, on-site tents $15 pp, deluxe cabins are $98 s or d. Budget-Expensive.

Farther north is **Daintree Rainforest Environmental Centre,** tel. (07) 4098-9171. Admission may seem a little steep (adult $10, child $5), but the self-guided interpretive trail along a raised boardwalk, the chance to ascend a 25-meter-high tower into the rainforest canopy, audiovisual, and other displays will expand your understanding of the surrounding rainforest no end; open daily 9 a.m.-5 p.m.

At the turnoff to Cow Bay is the modern **Cow Bay Hotel,** tel. (07) 4098-9011, with motel units for $68 s, $82 d including a cooked breakfast. Moderate. Across the road is **Rainforest Retreat,** tel. (07) 4098-9101, with dorm beds for $15 and a few basic motel rooms with kitchenettes for $45 s, $70 d. Budget-Moderate. Along the road out to Cow Bay is **Crocodylus Village,** tel. (07) 4098-9166, a YHA hostel set among tropical rainforest filled with hundreds of colorful (and raucous) birds. Accommodation is in large canvas cabins, while the main complex has a restaurant, bar, and swimming pool. Beds are $16 or, if you'd prefer some privacy, a few doubles go for $55. Inexpensive.

The only national park campground is at **Noah Head,** five km north of the Oliver Creek crossing. Facilities are limited to toilets and drinking water, but the location is magnificent, tucked behind a stretch of golden sand and surrounded by dense rainforest; $5 per site. For bookings call the Department of Environment in Mossman, tel. (07) 4052-3096.

Beyond the campground and two km from Cape Tribulation is **Coconut Beach Rainforest Retreat,** tel. (07) 4098-0033 or (1800) 81-6525. This upmarket resort, a two-minute walk from the beach, features 67 wooden villas set among a dense rainforest of palms, ferns, and figs. The centerpiece is the grand Long House, which overlooks the large landscaped pool area. Rates are $215-315 s or d. Luxury.

At the cape itself, a 400-meter boardwalk leads through the rainforest to an elevated lookout where views extend across the beach and bays beyond. Another trail leads over the headland to Myall Beach.

Transportation and Tours
Coral Coaches, tel. (07) 4099-5351, operates a scheduled bus service between Cairns and Cooktown. Stops are permitted along the route, providing the perfect opportunity to explore the

cape without your own vehicle. Three days a week the service travels the coastal route (Tuesday, Thursday, and Saturday) or the inland route (Wednesday, Friday, and Sunday). From Cairns, the one-way fare to Cape Tribulation is $28 and to Cooktown via the coastal route $52. Transport and accommodation packages offered by Coral Coaches are good value, including one night at Rainforest Retreat, one night at Cooktown Motor Inn, and transport from Cairns for $150 pp.

Jungle Tours, tel. (07) 4031-1110, operates a four-wheel-drive tour from Cairns taking in Cape Tribulation National Park, a Daintree River cruise, a guided bush walk, Mossman Gorge, and a quick stop in Port Douglas; $85. Departures are daily 7:30 a.m. A similar tour, but with a larger group, is offered by **Tropic Wings,** tel. (07) 4035-3555, with time also spent at Rainforest Habitat and a barramundi lunch included in the fare of $108 pp.

CAPE YORK PENINSULA

As the population of Australia's east coast continues to mushroom, Cape York Peninsula remains wild and unsettled, one of the world's last great wildernesses. In the Wet (Nov.-April) surface travel is impossible north of Cooktown, but for the rest of the year the Cape is a mecca for four-wheel-drive enthusiasts who trek north for the region's great beauty, the fishing, the adventure, and for the achievement of reaching Australia's northernmost point.

The peninsula extends more than 600 km, forming an apex at Cape York and flanked to the east by the Great Barrier Reef and Coral Sea, to the west by the Gulf of Carpentaria, and to the north by Torres Strait. Unchanged for millions of years, the landscape is one of forests, swamps, plains, and rivers, cursed by early explorers and still challenging adventurers today. The Great Dividing Range is the cape's dominant geological feature; on its eastern flanks, rainforests descend right to the ocean, while to the west, swamps and alluvial plains dominate. During the Wet, dozens of rivers flow westward, including the Jardine, just 80 km from the cape, which has the greatest year-round water volume of any Queensland river.

The population of the entire cape is about 20,000. The largest town is Cooktown, 130 km north of Cairns; other major settlements are Coen, halfway up the Cape, Weipa, a bauxite mining center on the gulf, and Bamaga, just south of Cape York.

Organized Tours

Overland tours from Cairns take about seven days to reach Cape York, with the option of returning along the same route, by air, or by sea.

One of the well-established operators is **Heritage 4WD Tours,** tel. (07) 4038-2628. Their 12-day trip includes Cape Tribulation, Quinkan rock art, crossing the Jardine River, time at the actual cape, the opportunity to visit Thursday Island, and overland back to Cairns. Rates of $1,450 pp include lodge accommodation combined with bush camping, meals, and all transfers. Departures are late May through mid-October. A shorter option is the six-day trip that combines the overland journey with a flight; $1,300 pp. Another established operator is **Oz Tours Safaris,** tel. (07) 4055-9535 or (1800) 07-9006, which offers a seven-day four-wheel-drive safari to Cape York with a flight back to Cairns for a similar price.

Two companies offer cruises along Cape York Peninsula. **Jardine Shipping,** tel. (07) 4035-1900, operates the *Cairns Express,* a 50-meter barge, between Cairns and Thursday Island. Primarily for transporting supplies and vehicles (good for those who only want to drive one-way up the cape), the barge has accommodation for 12 passengers. The boat departs Cairns Monday 4 p.m., arriving Horn Island Wednesday 10 a.m. and Thursday Island a few hours later, returning to Cairns that same day. The barge is too big to dock at the mainland port of Seisia, and transport must be arranged separately through Seisia Village Campground, tel. (07) 4069-3243, for transport to Horn Island. The Cairns-Horn Island fare is $250 pp one-way, $400 roundtrip, including meals. Vehicles cost $750 one-way. The more luxurious option is aboard *Kangaroo Explorer,* tel. (07) 4032-4000 or (1800) 07-9141, a 25-meter motorized catamaran designed specially for task. The five-day cruise between Cairns and

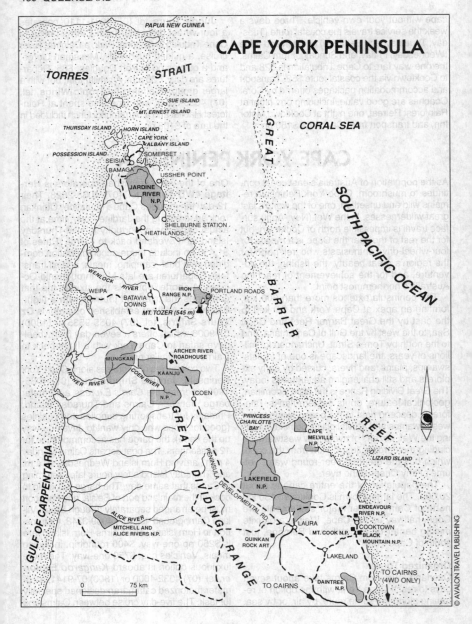

CAPE YORK PENINSULA

PAPUA NEW GUINEA

TORRES   STRAIT

SUE ISLAND

MT. ERNEST ISLAND

THURSDAY ISLAND   HORN ISLAND
CAPE YORK
ALBANY ISLAND
POSSESSION ISLAND   SOMERSET
SEISIA
BAMAGA   USSHER POINT
JARDINE
RIVER
N.P.
SHELBURNE STATION
HEATHLANDS

CORAL SEA

GREAT

SOUTH PACIFIC OCEAN

WENLOCK   RIVER
WEIPA   IRON RANGE N.P.   PORTLAND ROADS
BATAVIA
DOWNS   MT. TOZER (545 m)

BARRIER

MUNGKAN   ARCHER RIVER
ROADHOUSE
ARCHER   RIVER   KAANJU
COEN RIVER   N.P.
COEN

REEF

PRINCESS
CHARLOTTE
BAY   CAPE
MELVILLE
N.P.

LIZARD ISLAND

GREAT

GULF OF CARPENTARIA

DIVIDING

LAKEFIELD
N.P.

PENINSULA DEVELOPMENTAL RD.

ENDEAVOUR
RIVER N.P.

ALICE RIVER   LAURA   COOKTOWN
MITCHELL AND   MT. COOK N.P.   BLACK
ALICE RIVERS N.P.   MOUNTAIN N.P.
QUINKAN   LAKELAND
ROCK ART

RANGE

TO CAIRNS
(4WD ONLY)

TO CAIRNS   DAINTREE
N.P.

0   75 km

© AVALON TRAVEL PUBLISHING

Thursday Island stops at Cooktown, the Cod Hole, Lizard Island, and Forbes Island with many snorkeling opportunities en route. All rooms feature twin beds, but these can be converted to sleep four. Rates are $1868-2403 June through mid-Oct. ($400 cheaper the rest of the year). Rates include all meals and a one-way flight between Thursday Island and Cairns.

Sunstate, tel. (13) 1313, and **Flightwest,** tel. (13) 2392, fly between Cairns and Bamaga and Thursday Island. Most operators include these flights in tour prices. **Cape York Air Services,** tel. (07) 4035-9399, operators of the world's longest mail run, flies to remote cattle stations and communities throughout the peninsula. Routes vary every day, stopping up to a dozen times. The cost is $195-300 pp, and if there's a group of five, a charter flight up the coast to Cape York and lunch on Horn Island costs $550 pp.

COOKTOWN

A small town (pop. 1,500) at the mouth of the Endeavour River, Cooktown's claim to fame as Australia's first European settlement is the main reason for its existence. This frontier town has a real tropical feel, and its many sites of historical significance alone make it a worthwhile destination. It's possible to visit Cooktown and return to Cairns in just one day, but to do the place justice, you should plan to stay overnight.

History
A small cairn beside the Endeavour River and opposite the police station marks the site where Captain Cook and his crew set up camp for seven weeks in 1770, repairing the *Endeavour,* which had been holed on an offshore reef. "Cook's Town" was officially founded 100 years later as a gateway to the Palmer River goldfields, 140 km southwest. Within weeks of the start of the rush, a main street lined with banks, brothels, and hotels had taken shape. Within a year, the population peaked at 30,000, and the settlement had grown to become Queensland's second-largest town. About half the residents were Chinese, and although racial tensions led to rioting, the malaria, typhoid, and dysentery were more deadly. When the gold rush ended, a mass

---

VISITING CAPE YORK ON YOUR OWN

Monsoonal rains make the peninsula inaccessible by road for at least six months of the year, but June-Oct. hundreds of 4WD enthusiasts head up the unsealed **Peninsula Developmental Rd.** with Cape York in their sights. This long and rough trip requires much advance preparation. For road conditions, contact the RACQ in Cairns, tel. (07) 4051-6543. For general touring information, contact **Tourism Tropical North Queensland,** corner Fogarty Rd. and the Esplanade, Cairns, tel. (07) 4051-3588, website: www.tnq.org.au. It is also important to carry a high-frequency radio; to obtain a frequency listing, contact the Royal Flying Doctor Service, tel. (07) 4053-1952. For travel north of the Jardine River, permits are necessary because the road passes through Aboriginalowned land. For permits, write: Chairman, Injinoo Aboriginal Council, Injinoo, QLD 4876, tel. (07) 4069-3252.

---

exodus took place. A cyclone in 1907 and the scare of Japanese invasion during WW II just about finished off the town. But in 1970, the bicentenary of Cook's landing saw the quasi ghost town become focus of national media attention, and its future as a tourist destination was assured through the opening of the James Cook Historical Museum.

Town Sights
James Cook Historical Museum, Helen St., tel. (07) 4069-5386, provides glimpses of early life in far north Queensland. One room is devoted to Cook and his exploration of the area, while other sections are dedicated to the Aborigines, the gold rush, and European and Chinese settlers. The museum is open daily 10 a.m.-4 p.m. and admission is $5.

A few monuments around town are worth visiting for their historical significance, including those to Captain Cook and Edmund Kennedy on the road out to the wharf. In the cemetery, at the west end of town, are the graves of many early miners; also buried here is Mary Watson, who was attacked by Aborigines in 1881 while living on Lizard Island. She managed to escape, going to sea in a metal pot and drifting north with her son and a servant. They all died of thirst.

Nearby National Parks
Three very different national parks lie in the vicinity of Cooktown. The closest is **Mt. Cook National Park,** on the southwest outskirts of town; a trail at the end of May St. leads to the 430-meter summit for which the park is named.

Across the river from town is **Endeavour River National Park,** accessible only by boat. This park preserves an area of wetland and riverside dunes, unchanged since the botanist on Cook's ship, Joseph Banks, collected plant specimens here in 1770. **Cooktown Cruises,** tel. (07) 4069-5712, has a two-hour boat trip through the park for $18 pp. It departs from the wharf on Webber St. daily at 2 p.m.

South of Cooktown, at the junction of the inland and coastal routes, is **Black Mountain National Park,** protecting a small mountain of granite boulders, the black color coming from a dark green algae that covers them.

Accommodations and Food
The **Sovereign Resort,** Charlotte St., tel. (07) 4069-5400, is an old two-story hotel that was renovated in 1997. It has a range of rooms; the most basic share facilities; $38 s, $50 d. Inexpensive. Apartments with kitchens are $105 s, $116 d. Expensive. **Cooktown's River of Gold Motel,** corner Hope and Walker Streets, tel. (07) 4069-5222, has basic but large rooms and a pool and restaurant; $60-68 s or d. Moderate.

Pam's Place, three blocks from the center of town on Charlotte St., tel. (07) 4069-5166, is a YHA-associate hostel that features a pool, modern kitchen, and large gardens; rates are $16 pp in the dorm and $29 s, $40 d in private rooms. Inexpensive.

On McIvor Rd., a couple of blocks out of town, is **Cooktown Tropical Breeze Caravan Park,** tel. (07) 4069-5417. Sites are $12-15, on-site vans $30, and air-conditioned units $50-64. Budget-Inexpensive.

The **Sovereign Resort,** Charlotte St., tel. (07) 4069-5400, has inexpensive counter meals and, for something a bit more formal, upstairs is a small restaurant with tables along the balcony; main dishes here range $8.50-17. For the best fish and chips in town (and an owner that's a

wealth of information on the region), head to **Endeavour Farms Trading Post,** 12 Charlotte St., tel. (07) 4069-5723. Another place for takeout is the **Reef Café,** also on Charlotte Street.

Transportation and Tours
Flightwest, tel. (13) 2392, flies between Cairns and Cooktown daily; $97 one-way. **Marine Air,** tel. (07) 4069-5915, offers flightseeing tours of the area, including a day trip out Lizard Island for $195 pp.

Coral Coaches, tel. (07) 4098-2600, departs once daily from Trinity Wharf, Cairns, for Cooktown, traveling the inland and coastal routes on alternate days. The fare is $47 one-way on the inland route and $52 one-way on the coastal route, but accommodation packages, such as transportation and two nights' accommodation in Cooktown from $125 pp, are excellent deals.

From Cairns, most day tours to Cooktown incorporate a four-wheel-drive trip through Cape Tribulation National Park with a scenic flight, cutting down on travel time considerably. **Oz Tours Safaris,** tel. (07) 4055-9535, offers the choice of traveling either the inland or coastal route, a town tour, lunch, and one-way air transfers for $220 pp. Two-day tours, taking in both overland routes, range $245-370 depending on the Cooktown accommodation chosen. If you're on a tight budget, **Strikies Safaris,** tel. (07) 4099-5599, offers the same sort of tour, but travel is by four-wheel drive in both directions.

COOKTOWN TO THE CAPE

The only road to Cape York is the 4WD-only 750-km **Peninsula Developmental Road,** which begins 85 km southwest of Cooktown at the small service town of **Lakeland.**

Quinkan Rock Art
Sprinkled around sandstone escarpments southwest of Laura (turn off 48 km north of Lakeland) are one of the world's largest concentrations of primitive rock art, with hundreds of "galleries" scattered around the area. Of the four galleries open to the public, **Split Rock,** a 400-meter walk from the parking area, is most accessible while **Guguyalangi** lies 1.2 km farther north along an escarpment. Several pieces of rock art date back

10,000 years, but it's thought that Aborigines inhabited the area much earlier than this. The art depicts mostly animals, painted in colorful ochre colors, along with figures of their religious beliefs. Before entering the sites, you must obtain a permit from the ranger's office in Laura, tel. (07) 4060-3260. Entry is $3 pp. With care, two-wheel drives can make it to the site. **Trezise Bush Guides,** tel. (07) 4060-3236, has a longtime association with the rock art and has been instrumental in cataloging and protecting the sites. They offer a full-day guided walk of the site for $60 pp. They also offer a variety of land-based, multiday safaris from Cairns.

Laura

Laura, a small community 64 km north of Lakeland, has all necessary services (having a beer under the mango trees outside the pub is almost compulsory). On the last weekend in June Aboriginals from around the cape congregate in town for the **Laura Aboriginal Dance Festival.**

West of town is **Jowalbinna Bush Camp,** tel. (07) 4060-3236, or in Cairns call (07) 4051-4777, operated by the Trezise brothers, who helped catalog the nearby Quinkan rock art. They offer a variety of all-inclusive tours to the camp from Cairns, with the emphasis on hiking, swimming, and Aboriginal art. The two-night safari is $355 pp, which includes transportation, accommodations, guided walks, and all meals. You can also camp here for $5 or stay in a cabin for $30. Budget. An alternative accommodation is the **Quinkan Hotel,** back in Laura, tel. (07) 4060-3255, which charges $20 for a bed or $5 to camp. Budget.

Lakefield National Park

Immediately north of Laura is the access road to 537,000-hectare Lakefield National Park, most accessible of all the cape's parks and second largest in Queensland. Comprising mostly savannah grasses and open woodlands, the park

Quinkan rock art

also encompasses a 35-km stretch of coast along Princess Charlotte Bay where salt marshes and mangroves dominate. Through the park flow three major rivers—the Laura, Kennedy, and Normanby—but during the Wet, vast low-lying areas are underwater. In parts of the park this water remains year-round, providing ideal habitat for millions of waterbirds, including storks, jabirus, brolgas, spoonbills, and other species such as black cockatoos and the extremely rare golden-shouldered parrot. More than 18 species of mammals have been recorded in the park; the most commonly sighted are wallabies and kangaroos (look for them grazing in open grassland). Like on the rest of the cape, both species of crocodiles are present, so don't go swimming in deep or murky rivers.

The Peninsula Developmental Rd. skirts the southwest corner of the park, but a much longer, more rugged track heads north from Laura straight through the heart of the park. Campgrounds are scattered throughout the park and permits are required; call the ranger, tel. (07) 4060-3271, for these and to check road conditions.

Cape Melville National Park

Accessible only by boat, this 42,000-hectare park sits on a remote headland at the northern tip of land extending far east from the peninsula. The park features long sandy beaches linking rocky headlands, and in the west of the park, behind Bathurst Bay, are extensive salt marshes that end abruptly at the Melville Range, similar in composition to Black Mountain, near Cooktown.

To the west, between Bathurst and Princess Charlotte Bays, is the **Flinders Island Group,** comprising several continental islands, including Flinders, Stanley, and Denham, which feature short stretches of sandy beach. Camping on the islands or Cape Melville is by permit only; for these contact the Department of Environment in Cairns, tel. (07) 4052-3096.

Coen

Located on the Coen River and surrounded by rolling hills 245 km north of Laura, this small town is the largest settlement between Cooktown and Cape York. The highlight of Coen's social calendar is the **Annual Picnic Races,** run on a bush racing track each August. Services on the main street include a grocery store, two petrol stations, mechanic, post office, and pub (rooms are $25 s, $35 d. Inexpensive), tel. (07) 4060-1133, while on the riverbank north of town are a few campsites.

Mungkan Kaanju National Park

This remote 291,000-hectare park comprises the former Rokeby and Archer Bend National Parks. It extends from the Peninsula Developmental Rd. between the Coen and Archer Rivers west to the Archer River watershed. Large elevation changes within the park support many vegetation types, ranging from dense tropical rainforests of the McIlwraith Range to open woodlands of melaleucas on the alluvial plains farther west. The headwaters of the Archer River are in the McIlwraith Range, near the east coast, from where it flows across almost the entire peninsula. The river is lined with a luxuriant growth of vine forests and flanked by alluvial plains dotted with swamps and lagoons.

The park actually straddles the Peninsula Developmental Rd., but the only access to the park proper is just north of Coen Airstrip, extending 70 km west to the ranger station at Rokeby; call (07) 4060-3256 for more information and road-access details. The park's western section remains inaccessible to all but the most experienced off-road drivers.

The first services north of Coen are at the **Archer River Roadhouse,** on the south side of the Archer River, 65 km to the north. Here you'll find fuel, food, and basic rooms for $30 s, $40 d. Inexpensive.

EDMUND KENNEDY: FIRST MAN ACROSS THE PENINSULA

The travels of Edmund Kennedy may not be as well documented as those of Burke and Wills, but his tragic last journey was just as extraordinary, and while Burke and Wills' own ignorance brought about their tragic downfall, it was pen-pushing planners who killed Kennedy. With no experience in tropical travel, Kennedy was placed in charge of an expedition that would become the first to traverse the rugged and inhospitable Cape York Peninsula. On 21 May 1848, Kennedy and his men were put ashore at Rockingham Bay, 900 km from Cape York itself. Although Aboriginals had inhabited the Cape for thousands of years, and passing ships had anchored at various points along the coast, no white man had ever penetrated the region. Things started badly for the Kennedy party—from the landing site they were hemmed in by a maze of rivers and swamps, and it immediately became obvious to Kennedy that the journey had been planned by officials totally ignorant of the type of country to be traversed. The expedition headed west, to the higher ground of the Great Dividing Range, before any northward progress could be made.

After five months' travel in hellish conditions, and with the Wet upon them, the party stumbled off the Great Dividing Range into Weymouth Bay, three-quarters of the way to their final destination. Inadequate supplies and fatigue led Kennedy to split the party, leaving nine men and most of the horses at the bay. The party split again farther north, leaving just Kennedy and his Aboriginal tracker, Jackey Jackey, to make for the Cape. By mid-December, Kennedy was very ill, exhausted, and on the point of starvation, leaning on Jackey Jackey for support and stumbling at every step. Descending to the final river before the rendezvous point with a supply ship, the two realized the severity of their predicament, for the river mouth described on marine charts as having an "inviting shoreline" was in fact the outlet of a swamp many hundreds of square kilometers in area.

Aboriginals had been following the two men for many weeks, and although friendly at times, they were simply biding their time. While resting beside a stream, Kennedy was killed by a hail of spears. Using bush skills, Jackey Jackey slunk off, traveling through the dangers of the swamp to the waiting *Ariel.* Sailing south, no sign was found of the second group left behind, and by the time the ship reached Weymouth Bay, just two of the nine men there remained alive.

Iron Range National Park

This 34,600-hectare park, protecting the largest remaining area of tropical lowland rainforest in Australia, extends west from the shoreline of Weymouth Bay to 545-meter Mt. Tozer, the highest point along a ridge of jagged granite summits. Many plant species present in this park are found nowhere else in Australia, yet are common in Papua New Guinea. Much of the park's birdlife is also endemic, including palm cockatoos, green-backed honey eaters, and eclectus parrots.

Access to the park is along a rough 150-km track that spurs off the Peninsula Developmental Rd. 20 km north of the Archer River Crossing. At the end of the road is the small settlement of **Portland Roads** (no services), consisting of a few houses around a palm-fringed beach. A campground is south of Portland Roads. To contact the ranger call (07) 4060-7170.

Weipa

Located on the Gulf of Carpentaria and originally the site of an Aboriginal mission established in 1898, Weipa is now a company town of 2,200, existing only to mine the world's largest deposit of bauxite. The mineral occurs around Weipa as red-colored pebbles in layers of clay up to 10 meters deep. Although Dutch explorers were the first to record the red coloring, the true wealth wasn't recognized until the 1950s. After extraction, the bauxite is washed and crushed, then shipped to Gladstone, where it is refined into alumina for use in aluminum products. Since mining began, 130 million tons of bauxite have been mined, but with reserves of 2,000 million tons remaining under lease, Weipa will continue to thrive well into the next century.

There's not really a great deal to do in town. Take to the water at Evan's Landing in a rented boat from **Weipa Boat Hire,** tel. (07) 4069-7495. Inquire here about chartered fishing trips—this the heart of barramundi territory.

The town has all the services of a similarly sized town, including a supermarket, library, cinema, tennis court, golf course, and swimming pool.

Paxhaven Camping Ground is southwest of Rocky Point, behind Nanum Shopping Centre, tel. (07) 4069-7871. Facilities include a laundry, hot showers, and barbecue; unpowered sites are $14, powered sites $16.

Flightwest, tel. (13) 2392, flies daily between Weipa and Cairns.

Jardine River National Park

Before reaching this magnificent park at the tip of the continent, you must negotiate the **Wenlock River,** 170 km north of the Archer River Roadhouse. The crossing is difficult not only for the river's depth but for its steep banks.

The Jardine River, 155 km north of the Wenlock River, flows year-round from a catchment area of 2,500 square km. Most of its watershed is protected by 237,000-hectare Jardine River National Park, extending east from the Peninsula Developmental Rd. to the Coral Sea and encompassing the northernmost extent of the Great Dividing Range.

In the mid-1980s, a barge service across the Jardine made crossing the cape's most daunting river a whole lot easier; $80 roundtrip. (To the east of the barge is the old crossing point; the river here is one meter deep and 150 meters wide.)

Access to the east coast of the park is possible at a couple of points, through a landscape of wetlands where insectivorous plants such as sundews and pitcher plants thrive. Access to the east coast is 109 km north of the Wenlock River along a track leading to **Shelburne Station** and an area of coast dominated by white silica sand dunes. The other access is 10 km north of the Jardine River to **Ussher Point.** The ranger station is at Heathlands, tel. (07) 4060-3241.

Bamaga and the Cape

Bamaga (pop. 900), Australia's northernmost settlement, is 35 km north of the Jardine River and just 30 km from Cape York. On the approach into town, just south of the airport, a sign marks the resting place of a DC3 that crashed while attempting to land at Bamaga airstrip during WW II. The town itself has a motel, post office, grocery store, petrol station (closed most weekends), and hospital.

To the north of Bamaga is 510-hectare **Possession Island,** where Captain Cook landed in 1770 and planted a second British flag (the other was at Botany Bay) to complete his goal: "possession of the whole east coast."

Halfway between Bamaga and the cape, a road spurs east to the coast and the site of **Som-**

erset, one of Australia's most remote outposts. It was established in 1864, both as a sign of British occupancy and as a safe haven for sailors shipwrecked in the treacherous Torres Strait. The first posting was given to John Jardine, but it was his son, Frank, who had the most impact on the cape. Placed in charge in 1866, Frank stayed on after the post officially closed 10 years later to marry a Samoan princess, operate a pearling boat, grow coconuts, and even drive a herd of cattle up the cape from Rockhampton. He died in 1919, his wife followed a few years later, and today all that remains of Somerset are their graves, a few coconut trees, and the foundations of a jetty.

If you arrive at the cape on an organized tour, accommodations will have been prebooked and you'll return to Cairns by air from nearby Horn Island, return overland to Weipa for a southern flight, or make the return trip by cruise boat. Having traveled this far north, you may want to spend more time in the area and take a trip over to Thursday Island (see below), but to do so, you'll need to book the following accommodations well in advance. Punsand Bay Safari Lodge, 28 km north of Bamaga, tel. (07) 4069-1722, has safari-style tents for $25 pp and allows camping. Budget-Inexpensive. Just 400 meters from the cape itself is Pajinka Wilderness Lodge, tel. (07) 4069-2100 or (1800) 80-2968. Each of the 24 cabins has a bathroom and private balcony. Since the lodge's purchase by local Aborigines in 1993, the Injinoo culture has become part of the activities program, with field trips offered and boats with fishing gear for guest use. Rates are $250 s, $460 d, which includes all meals. Luxury. A campground has been developed at Seisia, north of Bamaga, tel. (07) 4069-3243; sites are $14-17.

Jacky Jacky Airport, nine km southeast of Bamaga, was built during WW II and is now served by Sunstate, tel. (13) 1313, and Flightwest, tel. (13) 2392. Book transport to Thursday Island by boat through Seisia Village Campground, tel. (07) 4069-3243.

ISLANDS OF THE TORRES STRAIT

The Torres Strait is a shallow but treacherous body of water between Cape York Peninsula and Papua New Guinea. Until 15,000 years ago, the two pieces of land were joined, but as the last ice age ended, the sea level rose. Many of the 70-odd islands that dot the strait were the peaks of mountains along the land bridge, while others, to the east, are sandy cays of the Great Barrier Reef. Of the 17 inhabited islands, **Thursday Island,** part of a rugged group of islands northwest of Cape York, has the largest population.

El-Torito, operated by Jardine Shipping, tel. (07) 4035-1900, departs Thursday Island every Wednesday on a four-day cruise. The itinerary includes Possession Island, Punsand Bay, historic Somerset, Albany Island (a bastion of Torres Strait heritage and home to a pearl farm), snorkeling on uninhabited Sue Island, and hiking on Mt. Ernest Island. The cost, $1,440 pp, includes accommodations and all meals.

History

Torres Strait Islanders are descendants of people who migrated from Polynesia and Melanesia around 2,000 years ago, and are unrelated to the Aborigines of mainland Australia. Violence between tribes dominated the islanders' pre-European lifestyle, when headhunting and cannibalism were rife.

In 1877 the Australian government moved its official northern residence from Somerset to Thursday Island, where pearling had become a major industry, employing up to 1,500 men. In the following years the introduction of Christianity, Japanese bombing raids, and an influx of European bureaucrats caused drastic changes in the islands, and many islanders moved to mainland Australia.

Thursday Island

Rugged Thursday Island (best known as T.I.), just 534 hectares in area and 35 km from Cape York, is no beautiful tropical island, but its interesting history and a laid-back atmosphere make it an appealing, if little-visited, destination. At one time a major pearling center, the island now has a population of 3,200, most of whom live around **Kennedy Bay,** filled with a colorful array of old wooden pearling luggers, aluminum dinghies, yachts, and barges. You'll find most services (a motel, hotels, banks, a supermarket, hospital, post office, motorboat rentals, and a swimming pool) on the island along Douglas St., lined with mango trees. On Green Hill, overlooking town, a fort built in 1891 to repel an envisaged Russian invasion, now holds a small museum. The local cemetery has some interesting graves, including many hundreds of pearl divers.

Jardine Motel, Victoria Parade, tel. (07) 4069-1555, is a two-story building across a road from the bay and just 200 meters from the ferry wharf. Rooms have private bathrooms and are air-conditioned; rates are $130 s, $160 d. Luxury. The only other option is **Gateway Torres Island Resort,** a rather grandly named motel on neighboring Horn Island, tel. (07) 4069-2222. Rates here are $96 s, $122 d, which includes transfers from the airport, seven km distant.

Building an airstrip on rugged Thursday Island was never practical, so neighboring Horn Island is used, with ferries meeting all flights; $30 roundtrip (if you're not an airline passenger the fare is more reasonable at $5 each way). **Flightwest,** tel. (13) 2392, and **Sunstate,** tel. (13) 1313, have regular flights to Cairns. **Peddell's Ferry and Tour Bus Service,** tel. (07) 4069-1551, runs tours around the island and a ferry service to Seisia on the mainland; $40 one-way.

GULF COUNTRY

Queensland's Gulf Country is a remote region of low-lying coastal plains extending hundreds of kilometers inland from the Gulf of Carpentaria. During the Wet, the entire region becomes one huge flooded swamp as a maze of river channels and basins fill with water. The actual coastline is ill-defined, made up of impenetrable tidal flats, mangrove swamps, and, near the Northern Territory border, salt pans. Karumba, on a firm chunk of ground at the mouth of the Norman River, is the only town right on the gulf, with the region's only other settlements being Normanton and Burketown, the former linked to Cloncurry by sealed road and to Cairns by the 700-km unsealed (but passable in two-wheel drive) Gulf Developmental Road. The alternate route west from Cairns is the much longer **Burke Developmental Road** (4WD only), which provides access to Staaten River National Park.

CAIRNS TO NORMANTON VIA THE GULF DEVELOPMENTAL ROAD

Undara Lava Tubes
These fascinating geological features snake for almost 100 km through high country 210 km west of Cairns. They were formed around 190,000 years ago when a stream of lava from a nearby volcano flowed along a dry riverbed. As the outer layer of lava cooled quickly, a molten mass of rock continued flowing underneath. In the time since, layers of sediment, washed off the Great Dividing Range, have covered the tube, and in areas the tube's roof (up to 15 meters high) has collapsed, allowing access, creating pockets of lush vegetation, and dividing the tube into a row of smaller ones. The tubes are mostly protected by **Undara Volcanic National Park,** but the main center of activity is **Undara Lava Lodge,** which lies at the park's northern boundary 15 km south of Gulf Developmental Rd., tel. (07) 4097-1411. From here, Savannah Guides leads daily tours. Cost for a basic two-hour tour is $26 pp, and a half-day tour with lunch is $68. The tubes are only a small part of the area's attractions; there's also bushwalking, birdwatching,

and flightseeing, and Australia's hottest hot springs are a short drive away.

The lodge comprises a series of railway carriages restored to provide small but comfortable accommodations; there's also a dining car, lounge car, and reading car. Nightly rates are $109 pp, including breakfast and dinner. Camping is $16 per site, or stay in Swags Tent Village, part of the same complex, for $20 pp (less for YHA members). The lodge also runs a number of packages from Cairns under the name **Undara Experience,** tel. (07) 4031-7933; one such package features transportation, tours, one night's accommodation, and all meals for $297 pp.

The Savannahlander
Forsayth, 40 km south of Georgetown, is the railhead for a line built to Cairns earlier this century. A section of rail, between Mt. Surprise and Forsayth, is now used by the Savannahlander, a tourist train operated by Queensland Rail. The trip takes five to six hours and is $38 one-way (departs Mt. Surprise Monday and Thursday 12:30 p.m.). For package-tour information, call Queensland Rail, tel. (13) 2232.

Cobbold Gorge
Set among the sparsely vegetated gulf savannah, and surrounded by an area rich in gems, this spectacular gorge was discovered by the property owners as recently as 1993. The gorge holds water year-round, its craggy walls shaped by thousands of years of water erosion. A half-day tour, which includes a boat trip into the gorge, and a visit to the station and sites of historical significance, is adult $50, child $25. The gorge cuts through a property 75 km south of Georgetown; for tour bookings, call (07) 4062-5470. You can camp for $5 pp.

CAIRNS TO NORMANTON VIA THE BURKE DEVELOPMENTAL ROAD

This route is rough in places and should only be attempted by those in four-wheel drives (conventional vehicles can only make it from Cairns as far west as Chillagoe).

Chillagoe-Mungana Caves National Parks

Late last century, Chillagoe, 235 km west of Cairns, was one of Queensland's most productive mining towns, with copper, lead, silver, and gold extracted. Major mining operations ceased in the mid-1940s, but signs of early activity remain, including the ruins of a large smelter. But the highlight of the area is a string of limestone caves protected by small national parks. The caves are part of a complex geographical structure that also includes limestone pinnacles rising 70 meters. High rainfall has dissolved the limestone surface, and where water has seeped underground extensive cave systems have formed. Five caves are open to the public; Archway and Pompey caves can be explored independently, while three others, including the most impressive—Royal Arch Cave—can only be visited with a guide. Ranger-led hikes are led into the caves daily, with one cave visited each day. Tours range $5-7.50 pp. To contact the ranger call (07) 4094-7163.

Chillagoe Caves Lodge, King St., tel. (07) 4094-7106, is a small motel where rooms with shared bathrooms are $25 s, $30 d, and rooms with private bathrooms are $45 s, $55 d. You can also camp here for $8-10. Budget-Inexpensive.

Staaten River National Park

This large park south of the Burke Developmental Rd. encompasses 470,000 hectares of open woodland, typical of gulf savannah country, as well as a 120-km stretch of the Staaten River. Termite mounds are one of the most distinctive features of the landscape, some up to three meters high, each aligned north-south to minimize heat absorption.

The park has no formed roads, making access difficult. Conceivably, and with permission, you can enter the park through Bulimba or Highbury Stations to the east, or Dorunda Station, which borders the park to the west.

Mitchell and Alice Rivers National Park

Named for the two rivers bordering it, this remote park lies 80 km northwest of Dunbar on the Burke Developmental Road. It features open woodland with small areas of rainforest along

permanent rivers. Birdlife is prolific, especially early in the dry season, when large lagoons of water remain. Freshwater and saltwater crocodiles are common, as are feral pigs.

NORMANTON AND VICINITY

With a population of 1,200, Normanton is the largest town in the 120,000-square-km Gulf Country. From Cairns, access is along the Gulf Developmental Rd.; from the south, access is from Cloncurry. By river, the actual gulf lies 40 km beyond Normanton, and 69 km by road. Established in 1867, Normanton grew as a port for copper fields around Cloncurry and, later, as gateway to the Croydon goldfields.

The foot of the gulf is impenetrable, a maze of mangrove swamps, mudflats, and river mouths, but at the mouth of the Norman River is a rare piece of firm ground where the community of **Karumba** has been established. It is an important fishing town, a base for prawn and barramundi boats, as well as for holidaying anglers.

The Gulflander

Originally conceived as a way of transporting cattle from Cloncurry to the Gulf, the discovery of gold at Croydon saw the Gulflander rail line diverted in the opposite direction. Although the gold rush was short-lived and Croydon's population has dwindled to less than 200 residents, the Gulflander still operates and is one of the Gulf's main tourist attractions. The train rolls out of its impressive Normanton terminus on Wednesday at 8:30 a.m., arriving in Croydon four hours later ($64 pp roundtrip), just in time for lunch at the Croydon Club Hotel, better known as the "Purple Pub," and departing Croydon for the return journey the following morning. The hotel, tel. (07) 4745-6184, has rooms for $35 s, $50 d. Inexpensive. Nearby, the **Croydon Gold Caravan Park,** tel. (07) 4745-6238, has campsites for $12 and six on-sites vans for $40. Budget-Inexpensive.

Croydon offers a few things to do the afternoon that the train rolls in—the streets are lined with many historic buildings, including the general store, which is more than 100 years old. Plus there's always cold beer back at the pub. Through winter, the train heads out from Normanton every Saturday at 9:30 a.m. on a two-hour trip for $26, which includes a light snack. For all reservations call (07) 4745-1391.

Practicalities

Accommodation in Normanton is at the **Albion Hotel,** Haig St., tel. (07) 4745-1218, where rooms with private facilities are $55 s, $60 d. Inexpensive. **Karumba Lodge Hotel,** Yappar St., Karumba, tel. (07) 4745-9121, has similarly priced rooms and meals served Tues.-Saturday. Inexpensive. You can camp free at Walker's Creek, halfway between the two towns, or at **Normanton Caravan Park** on Brown St., tel. (07) 4745-1121; sites cost $10-12, and there are hot showers, a laundry, and barbecue. Budget.

Flightwest, tel. (13) 2392, flies between Normanton and Cairns, continuing to Karumba and Mornington Island. If you're in Cairns and want to visit the gulf in just one day, contact **Cape York Air Services,** tel. (07) 4035-9399, which makes a mail run to Normanton every Friday; $275 pp roundtrip. **Oz Tours Safaris,** tel. (07) 4055-9535 or (1800) 07-9006, offers a seven-day overland safari from Cairns, taking in all sights along the Gulf Developmental Rd. as well as Lawn Hill Gorge and Burketown, ending at Normanton for a flight back to Cairns. Tours run late April-Oct. and are $1,295 pp if camping and $1,595 in motels.

BURKETOWN AND VICINITY

The other gulf community worthy of a detour is Burketown, 269 km northeast of the Burke and Wills Roadhouse. In the Wet, Burketown can be isolated for weeks as the surrounding salt pans and savannah grasslands become flooded from inland rainfall. The township has a pub on one side of the road (call 07-4745-5104 to book a room) and a few shops on the other.

Lawn Hill National Park

Aboriginals have been coming to Lawn Hill Gorge for at least 20,000 years, and little has changed in this time. It's a magical place, a lush oasis surrounded for hundreds of kilometers by a dry, harsh landscape. The gorge itself is only a small part of the 262,000-hectare park. Water from artesian springs to the west, on the Barkly Tableland, created the gorge and allows tropical vegetation such as palms, ferns, and figs to thrive. Lawn Hill Creek is home to freshwater crocodiles and turtles, and a variety of small mammals and marsupials come from afar to drink its waters. The park's Riversleigh section, straddling the Gregory River in the south of the park and accessible only by four-wheel drive, is the site of important fossil discoveries, some of which are displayed in Mt. Isa.

The park is 400 km from Mt. Isa. To get there, turn off the Barkly Highway 120 km west of Mt. Isa and follow the Burketown Rd. north for 180 km to **Gregory Downs,** tel. (07) 4748-5566; rooms, petrol, and food), then cross the Gregory River and head west for 100 km. A primitive camping area has been developed beside Lawn Hill Creek and at **Adel's Grove,** at the park entrance, you'll find a campground with hot showers, barbecues, and basic supplies, tel. (07) 4748-5502. To contact the park ranger call (07) 4748-5572.

OUTBACK QUEENSLAND

While most visitors to Queensland dive on the reef and sun themselves on the beaches, a few venture over the Great Dividing Range and across the tablelands to the Outback, an area of endless plains and red-soil desert where towns lie hundreds of kilometers apart, existing only as service centers for road-weary travelers and vast cattle stations. Among this desolate landscape are many surprises—pleasant country towns where hospitality is second nature, and huge national parks protecting all the best natural features.

Outback Queensland is generally regarded as everything west of the **Matilda Highway,** a collection of highways 1,700 km long, passing through areas of interest to travelers and also of historical importance. The highway begins on the NSW/Queensland border, about 700 km inland, and makes a long arc around the eastern edge of the Outback to Mt. Isa and the Queensland/Northern Territory border. Highways lead westward from the coastal cities of Brisbane (Warrego Highway), Rockhampton (Capricorn

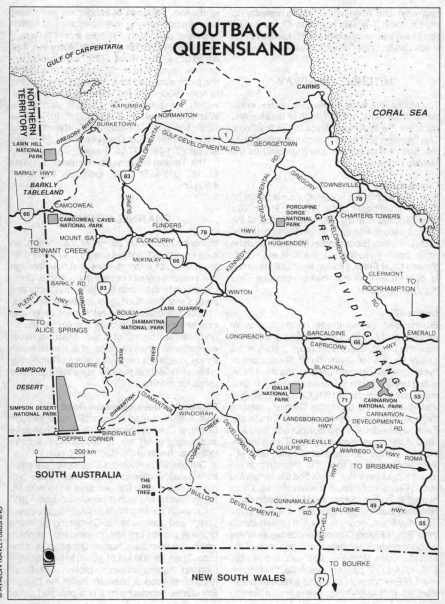

OUTBACK
QUEENSLAND

GULF OF CARPENTARIA

CORAL SEA

NORTHERN
TERRITORY

KARUMBA

NORMANTON

APR.

CAIRNS

GREGORY RIVER

BURKETOWN

GULF DEVELOPMENTAL RD.

GEORGETOWN

1

LAWN HILL
NATIONAL
PARK

BARKLY HWY.

BARKLY
TABLELAND

66

CAMOOWEAL

CAMOOWEAL CAVES
NATIONAL PARK

MOUNT ISA

83

BURKE

DEVELOPMENTAL

FLINDERS

78

CLONCURRY

McKINLAY

66

TO
TENNANT CREEK

BARKLY RD.

GEORGINA

DEVELOPMENTAL

GREGORY

TOWNSVILLE

78

PORCUPINE
GORGE
NATIONAL
PARK

CHARTERS TOWERS

1

HWY.

HUGHENDEN

KENNEDY

DEVELOPMENTAL

GREAT

CLERMONT

TO
ROCKHAMPTON

PLENTY

HWY.

83

GEORGINA

RIVER

BOULIA

WINTON

LARK QUARRY

TO
ALICE SPRINGS

BEDOURIE

DIAMANTINA
NATIONAL PARK

LONGREACH

BARCALDINE

66

DIVIDING

CAPRICORN

HWY.

EMERALD

SIMPSON

DESERT

RIVER

DIAMANTINA

RIVER

DIAMANTINA

BLACKALL

71

IDALIA
NATIONAL
PARK

CARNARVON
NATIONAL PARK

55

RANGE

SIMPSON DESERT
NATIONAL PARK

DIAMANTINA

WINDORAH

CARNARVON
DEVELOPMENTAL
RD.

POEPPEL CORNER

BIRDSVILLE

0   200 km

COOPER

CREEK

DEVELOPMENTAL

LANDSBOROUGH
HWY.

RD.

CHARLEVILLE
QUILPIE

WARREGO

54

HWY.

ROMA

SOUTH AUSTRALIA

THE
DIG
TREE

BULLOO

DEVELOPMENTAL

RD.

HWY.

TO BRISBANE

CUNNAMULLA

49

BALONNE

HWY.

55

MITCHELL

TO BOURKE

NEW SOUTH WALES

71

Highway), and Townsville (Flinders Highway) to the Outback. Travel is best May-October. The rest of the year is stifling hot, and during the Wet roads can be under water for weeks.

MITCHELL HIGHWAY

The Mitchell Highway enters Queensland in the south of the state, 138 km north of Bourke, and parallels the **Warrego River** to Cunnamulla. This highway, and those that continue through to the Gulf of Carpentaria, are promoted as the Matilda Highway.

Cunnamulla
First town north of the border, Cunnamulla sits on the tree-lined banks of the Warrego River. This town of 1,500 is at the western terminus of the rail line used to transport sheep to eastern markets. The small **Bicentennial Museum** on John St. is worth investigating, but little else is. At **Yowah Opal Field,** 165 km west of Cunnamulla, opal nuts—opal in a shell of ironstone—are highly sought after.

Charleville
Surrounded by hundreds of thousands of hectares of sheep and cattle stations and 800 km from the coast, Charleville (pop. 3,800) is the hub of southwest Queensland. Reminders of the town's earliest days abound, the most interesting being a Stiger Vortex rainmaker gun. During a terrible drought in 1902 Clement L. Wagge imported six of the guns from Germany, setting them at strategic locations around Charleville. Each was loaded with gunpowder and fired skyward in the hope of creating rain. Two guns imploded, a few horses stampeded, and Mr. Wagge rode out of town the following day— under a cloudless sky. You'll find the remaining gun in Centennial Park, just south of town. Other highlights in town include the 1881 **Queensland National Bank** (open Mon.-Fri. 9 a.m.-4 p.m., Saturday 9 a.m.-noon) and one of Queensland's three **Royal Flying Doctor Service** bases where a visitor center describes the importance of the service; open Mon.-Fri. 8:30 a.m.-5 p.m., tel. (07) 4654-1233. East of Charleville, the Department of Environment operates a **research station,** tel. (07) 4654-1255, where you're likely to

spot various species of kangaroos and wallabies grazing among three hectares of native bushland; open Mon.-Fri. 8:30 a.m.-4:30 p.m.

Charleville Waltzing Matilda Motor Inn, 125 Alfred St., tel. (07) 4654-1720, has the least expensive rooms in town; $38 s, $45 d (the roof of this place was used as a helipad during flooding in April 1990 when the entire town was underwater). Inexpensive. Of a higher standard is **Warrego Motel,** 75 Wills St., tel. (07) 4654-1299, $55 s, $65 d. Moderate. Campers should head to **Bailey Bar Caravan Park,** 196 King St., tel. (07) 4654-1744. Budget.

The **Tourist Information Centre** is on Wills St., tel. (07) 4654-3057; open daily 9:30 a.m.-4:30 p.m.

CHANNEL COUNTRY

In the southwestern corner of the state is an area known as Channel Country, so named for the mosaic of watercourses that flow through it. It's either very wet or very dry out here. Summer rains to the north fill the many rivers and creeks that flow southwest toward Lake Eyre. The watercourses divide, rejoin each other, and eventually dissipate into the soft soils of the far northeastern corner of South Australia. After exceptionally heavy rains, the whole basin floods, creating a massive system of temporary lakes that isolate remote stations and flood roads for months.

Diamantina Developmental Road
This 1,350-km road is the main route through Channel Country, heading west at Charleville and ending at Mt. Isa. It also provides access to the north end of the Birdsville Track.

Quilpie, 210 km west of Charleville, is a cattle transportation railhead surrounded by many productive opal mines. The next town en route to Mt. Isa is **Windorah,** with a population under 100 but enough passing trade to justify a pub, petrol pump, and general store. Continuing west, the highway passes brilliantly colored red sandhills, which rise from the Channel Country like a mirage. Then it's 500 km of gravel to Boulia. It's a long trip, the arid landscape broken occasionally by an outcrop of sandstone and the town of **Bedourie,** consisting of just a pub and petrol pump. A track heading south from Bedourie leads to Birdsville. After crossing the Georgina River and passing the small town of Boulia, the land becomes rocky, changing subtly, as the road climbs the Isa Highlands to Mt. Isa.

Birdsville

Famous for its pub, this, Queensland's most remote town, lies at the northern end of the famous Birdsville Track just 12 km north of the South Australia border and 1,570 km west of Brisbane. It grew from a store established on the Diamantina River in 1872, the last stop for stockmen driving cattle southward through the Simpson Desert to Adelaide. Named by a settler's wife for the profusion of birdlife on the river, Birdsville boasted three hotels, a couple of shops, and dozens of houses in its heyday. Today, the population is less than 100, but on the first weekend of each September, more than 5,000 punters descend on the town for the annual **Birdsville Races,** a colorful celebration of everything that Outback Australia stands for. Needless to say, an amazing amount of beer is consumed over the weekend, much of it in and around the **Birdsville Hotel,** right by the airport. Dating from 1884, it features sandstone walls, a slate floor, and exposed timber roof beams—a classic Outback pub in all regards. Small air-conditioned rooms are $50 s, $70 d, tel. (07) 4656-3244. Moderate.

Simpson Desert National Park

In the extreme west of the state, and accessible only by four-wheel drive, is the enormous one-million-hectare Simpson Desert National Park. It encompasses just the northeast corner of a 20-million-hectare desert for which the park is named. The landscape is barren, featuring waves of sand dunes, gibber flats, and large areas of clay plains. The extensive dune system spreads through much of the park, typified by dunes up to 25 meters high, spaced 300-400 meters apart, and running parallel for up to 70 km. A surprisingly large number of life-forms exist in the park—a few species of spinifex, wattle, grevilleas, snakes, lizards, marsupials, and birds of prey all thrive in this harsh, waterless environment.

Permits are required before entering the park, available from the Department of Environment in Longreach, tel. (07) 4658-1761, or Charleville, tel. (07) 4654-1255, and you must also register with the police in Birdsville. The park has no established camping area, but as the only formed road leads from Birdsville to Poeppel Corner (150 km) most people camp somewhere en route.

CHARLEVILLE TO LONGREACH

Blackall

In 1892, gun-shearer Jack Howe set a new world record, shearing 321 sheep in less than eight hours. For blade shearing, the record stands to this day, and it took until 1950 for a machine shearer to equal it. A statue of the great man stands in the main street of Blackall, a pleasant Outback town 300 km north of Charleville.

Blackall Historical Woolscour, four km north of town, was where wool was washed and dried, then sorted, pressed, and transported to eastern ports. Much of the plant remains as the day it closed in 1978, allowing an authentic glimpse at the industry upon which Outback Australia was built. The complex is open daily 8 a.m.-4 p.m.; admission is adult $5, child $2. Like many Outback towns, Blackall's drinking water is from artesian bores, and one is located at the woolscour.

The **Barcoo Hotel,** 95 Shamrock St., tel. (07) 4657-4197, is right in the center of town and has rooms with shared facilities for $38 s, $54 d, which includes a cooked breakfast. Inexpensive. Lunches at the bar are $5-8, and Friday and Saturday nights there's a barbecue in the beer garden. **Blackall Motel,** also on Shamrock St., tel. (07) 4657-4491 or (1800) 35-7367, has standard rooms for $45 s, $55 d. Inexpensive. **Blackall Caravan Park,** 53 Garden St., tel. (07) 4657-4816, has unpowered sites for $10, powered sites $12, on-site vans $22-25, and cabins $30-42. The Outback-style communal kitchen features a wood-fired camp oven.

Avington Outback Holiday Station, tel. (07) 4657-5952, allows guests to enjoy life on a working cattle station; you can ride horses, round up sheep, and watch shearers at work, not to mention cruise on the Barcoo River, golf on a unique nine-hole course, and play tennis. Rooms, large and air-conditioned but with shared bathrooms, cost $50 s, $95 d, including meals. To get there, head north out of Blackall for 18 km, then take Avington Rd. for 57 km northwest to the homestead. Expensive.

Idalia National Park

Located 100 km southwest of Blackall, deep in the Gowan Ranges that form the eastern boundary of Channel Country, is this new 144,000-hectare park. It encompasses the headwaters of the Bulloo River, and although the river is dry for most of the year, a variety of vegetation thrives, including stands of river red gums around low-lying areas. Access is by four-wheel drive only and camping is permitted at Monk's Tank. To contact the ranger, call (07) 4657-5033.

Barcaldine

The pleasant town of Barcaldine lies at the junction of the Capricorn and Landsborough Highways, 580 km west of Rockhampton. In 1891 more than 1,000 striking shearers converged on the town, meeting under a big ghost gum outside the railway station to demand higher wages and better working conditions. The following year, union leaders endorsed a candidate for parliament, under the same tree, beginning the formation of the Australian Labor Party. The tree stands today, in mute testimony to the shearers' resolve. The role played by ordinary working Australians, such as shearers, in the development of the country is celebrated at the **Australian Workers Heritage Centre,** which opened in May 1991 on the centenary of the strike. The large complex features a museum, interactive displays, films, historic buildings transported to the site, a seven-story theater where the Australian tribute *Celebration of a Nation* is shown, and extensive landscaped gardens complete with a billabong. Admission is $7. Open Mon.-Sat. 9 a.m.-5 p.m., Sunday 10 a.m.-5 p.m. On Ash St., tel. (07) 4651-1422.

Barcaldine Motel, on the main drag through town, tel. (07) 4651-1244, has basic rooms for $40 s, $50 d. Inexpensive. With nicer rooms and a laundry and pool is **Landsborough Lodge,** also on the highway, tel. (07) 4651-1100; $55 s, $70 d. Moderate. **Homestead Caravan Park,** Blackall Rd., tel. (07) 4651-1308, has shady sites, a barbecue area where camper meals (with bush tucker) are cooked nightly, and friendly hosts who organize tours to anywhere in the

region. Sites are $10-12, on-site vans $30, and small cabins $35-50. Budget.

The **Barcaldine Tourist Information Centre** is on Oak St., tel. (07) 4651-1724; it's open daily 9 a.m.-5 p.m. but closes for lunch.

LONGREACH

Home to the Australian Stockman's Hall of Fame, Longreach (pop. 4,200) is the largest town in the central west. From Brisbane, it lies 1,232 km to the northwest—a sealed highway spans the whole distance—or 24 hours away on Queensland Rail's Spirit of the Outback.

Longreach began life as a campground for shearers, receiving a boost when a rail line was completed from Rockhampton in 1892. **Qantas** (Queensland and Northern Territory Aerial Services) was born in Longreach. The airline's first flight was made in 1922, and for seven years it was headquartered in Longreach.

Australian Stockman's Hall of Fame and Outback Heritage Centre

No one could begrudge the stockmen and others who developed the Outback a tribute to their pioneering spirit and never-say-die attitude. And this is it, a magnificent museum dedicated to everything the Outback stands for. It opened in 1988, amid much fanfare; even the Queen of England made it to town for the occasion. The architects have combined traditional Outback materials with modern design concepts to create a distinct building. The complex comprises a series of corrugated iron half-pipes, overlapping to form one long roof. Individual exhibits are dedicated to shearers, miners, traveling salesmen, women of the Outback, Aboriginals, and other topics. One display provokes much comment—an 1860s settler's hut. The hut is the size of an average bedroom, but it served as a home for one woman and three children, with a stove crammed in one corner and beds taking up most of the rest of the dirt floor. Historical displays are only a part of the Hall of Fame; computers and audiovisual programs help bring the history of the Outback to life. The complex also has a gift shop and café. Open daily 9 a.m.-5 p.m. Admission is a worthwhile $15 adult, $7 child, family $35. For further information call (07) 4658-

2166 or surf the Web to www.outbackher-itage.com.au. Allow at least half a day here.

Other Sights
Out at the airport, plans to build the **Qantas Founders Outback Museum,** tel. (07) 4658-3737, a museum dedicated to the history of the airline, are well underway. At the moment, the original Qantas hangar holds the displays, including a replica of an Avro 504K, the airline's first plane. Admission is $6. Open daily 9 a.m.-5 p.m.

The **Powerhouse Museum** is on the site of an old power station and remains as it was built in 1921 with many working exhibits. Power was produced by enormous generators, whose engines were cooled by artesian-bore water; open April-Oct. daily 2-5 p.m.

On the Landsborough Highway, east of town, is **Longreach School of Distance Education,** tel. (07) 4658-4222. Pupils throughout central Queensland attend lessons broadcast over UHF radios, sending homework by mail and getting together a few times a year. Tours are offered weekdays at 9 a.m. and 10 a.m.

Entertainment and Events
Most afternoons, the pioneering spirit of the Outback comes alive at **Banjo's Outback Theatre and Pioneer Shearing Shed,** at the end of Stork Rd., tel. (07) 4658-2379. Demonstrations of wool shearing, pressing, classing, and spinning take place, with everyone invited to try their hand. A whole lot of bush poetry is read, yarns spun, and light snacks served at the end of it all; $10 pp. Performances are Mon.-Thurs. and Saturday at 2:30 p.m.

The **Longreach Show** brings together stockmen from throughout the Outback for the **Thomson River Campdraft,** and while the old-timers spend the weekend drinking, spinning yarns, bronco-branding, and rough-riding, unique Outback sports keep the city slickers occupied. All the action takes place in May. On the third weekend of July **The Diamond Shears,** Australia's most prestigious shearing event, takes place.

Accommodations and Food
Welcome Home Hotel, 128 Eagle St., tel. (07) 4658-1361, has air-conditioned rooms with shared bathrooms for $25 s, $40 d. Inexpensive. Similarly priced is the **Royal Hotel,** 111 Eagle St., tel. (07) 4658-2118. Inexpensive. **Jumbuck Motel,** Landsborough Hwy., tel. (07) 4658-1799 or (1800) 06-1573, has a pool, air-conditioned rooms, and a good restaurant; $55 s, $65 d. Moderate. The best place in town is **Albert Park Motel,** Landsborough Hwy., tel. (07) 4658-2411, with a covered pool, sundeck area, and large modern rooms; $59 s, $69 d. Moderate. The above motels are within 500 meters of both the airport and Hall of Fame. **Gunnadoo Caravan Park,** 12 Thrush Rd., tel. (07) 4658-1781, has a pool, barbecue area, and laundry. Sites are $12-14, cabins $50 d. Budget-Inexpensive.

Along Eagle St. is **Merino Bakery** and a number of cafés open breakfast through dinner. For lunch, all the hotels serve counter meals for less than $7. The **R.S.L. Club,** on Duck St., is another option for an inexpensive meal. The Jumbuck Motel also has a restaurant.

Transportation and Tours
Flightwest, tel. (13) 2392, serves 36 western Queensland towns, with Longreach the central-western hub. Flights depart Brisbane and Townsville daily for Longreach.

A favorite and traditional way to reach Longreach is aboard **Spirit of the Outback,** a twice-weekly rail service between Brisbane and Longreach via Rockhampton. The train departs Brisbane Tuesday and Friday at 7 p.m., with the less-interesting scenery traversed at night and the climb through the Drummond Ranges west of Rockhampton taking place during daylight hours. The train features a themed dining car and bar, and seating to suit all budgets. (It is part of Australian folklore that in 1859, when Queensland was granted statehood, it could only afford a three-foot six-inch gauge rail line, the narrowest in Australia—and you'll come to realize its downside when eating and drinking.) For bookings call **Queensland Rail,** tel. (13) 2232.

Greyhound Pioneer and **McCafferty's** serve Brisbane daily (16 hours one-way) and Mt. Isa (eight and a half hours), with McCafferty's also running to Rockhampton thrice weekly (nine hours). All buses stop at Outback Travel Centre, 115 Eagle St., tel. (07) 4658-1776.

The major car rental companies with offices in Longreach are **Avis,** tel. (07) 4658-1799, and **Hertz,** tel. (07) 4658-1155. For a cab call **A 1 Taxi Service** at (07) 4658-3446.

Outback Aussie Tours, tel. (1300) 787-890, offers a great variety of day and overnight tours. They run at least one tour a day, including the Longreach Lookabout, which takes in everything there is to do and see in town, including the Stockman's Hall of Fame; $69 pp. An afternoon cruise on the Thomson River costs $25.

Services and Information

The **post office** is at 100 Eagle Street. For the hospital call (076) 58-1133.

The **Tourist Information Centre** is housed in a replica of the first Qantas booking office in Qantas Park, tel. (07) 4658-3555; it's open Mon.-Fri. 9 a.m.-5 p.m., Sat.-Sun. 9 a.m.-1 p.m.

LONGREACH TO MOUNT ISA

Winton

Winton may not have a Stockman's Hall of Fame to draw the tourists, but its close ties to the legendary Australian bush poet Banjo Patterson provide the basis for a thriving tourist industry. The town began its life as Pelican Waterhole, with one main street lined with pubs and the usual array of Outback businesses. In 1895 Patterson wrote *Waltzing Matilda* after hearing stationhands' recollections of a swagman's suicide in a local billabong. The station owner's wife, Christina MacPherson, sang the words in the North Gregory Hotel on 6 April 1895. Its appeal was immediate, and it soon became Australia's favorite song, recited with pride around the country. The original North Gregory Hotel is long gone. Its replacement, a jewel of 1950s architecture, sits on the main street, and a statue of a not-so-jolly-looking Jolly Swagman stands opposite the pool.

The **Waltzing Matilda Centre,** a short walk from the Gregory Hotel on Elderslie St., tel.

(07) 4657-1466, is the only museum in the world dedicated to a song. "The Home of the Legend" is a sound and light show telling the story of the song and its associated legend, while another section is dedicated to the people of the Outback. The center also holds an art gallery and a café. Admission is $10. Open daily 9 a.m.-5 p.m. For those interested, Combo Waterhole, where the swagman took his fatal plunge, is 170 km northwest of Winton, then five km out of Kynuna. Inside a circus tent beside the Kynuna Hotel is **Kynuna's Swagman Hall of Fame,** which catalogs the history of the song. Richard Magoffin, the bloke who runs the place, will let you in for free, but it costs $4 to view the words to the song; for $10 he'll sing the tune for anyone who so desires.

North Gregory Hotel, 67 Elderslie St., tel. (07) 4657-1375, has rooms with shared bathrooms for $25 pp. Inexpensive. Another choice is the **Matilda Motel,** 20 Oondooroo St., tel. (07)

WALTZING MATILDA

Oh! There once was a swagman camped in a billabong,
Under the shade of a coolabah tree;
And he sang as he looked at his old billy boiling,
"Who'll come a-waltzing, Matilda, with me?
Who'll come a-waltzing, Matilda, my darling,
Who'll come a-waltzing, Matilda, with me?
Waltzing Matilda and leading a water bag—
Who'll come a-waltzing, Matilda, with me?"

Down came a jumbuck to drink at the waterhole,
Up jumped the swagman and grabbed him in glee;
And he sang as he stowed him away in his tucker-bag,
"You'll come a-waltzing, Matilda, with me."

Down came the squatter a-riding his thoroughbred;
Down came policemen—one, two, three.
"Whose is the jumbuck you've got in the tucker-bag?
You'll come a-waltzing, Matilda, with me."

But the swagman, he up and he jumped in the waterhole,
Drowning himself by the coolabah tree;
And his ghost may be heard as it sings in the billabong
"Who'll come a-waltzing, Matilda, with me?"

4657-1433, which has small but comfortable rooms for $45 s, $50 d. Inexpensive. Campers should head to **Matilda Country Caravan Park,** on Chirnside St., tel. (07) 4657-1607. Budget.

Lark Quarry

While Winton and Longreach provide tourists with a glimpse of the past 100 years, a dry rocky area 115 km southwest of Winton provides a look much further back in our history. It's Lark Quarry, site of a dinosaur stampede some 95 million years ago. Today's rocky outcrops and spinifex-studded gullies are much different than they were then, when the landscape was flat and high rainfall ensured lush vegetation. A carnosaur (flesh-eating lizard) walking along a riverbed disrupted a herd of about 200 much smaller animals drinking from a lake and, panic-stricken, they stampeded across an area of thick mud. Paleontologists are able to re-create the events of that day incredibly accurately, right down to the fact that the stampeding dinosaurs were moving at 15-30 kph. Three areas have been excavated; the largest, covered from the elements, is about 20 meters long, with interpretive boards along its length revealing further details. The site is accessible by two-wheel drive, except after rain. **Diamantina Outback Tours,** tel. (07) 4657-1514 or (1800) 62-5828, departs Winton daily at 8 a.m. for the quarry and other natural features en route; $80 pp includes lunch.

Diamantina National Park

The road from Winton out to Lark Quarry continues in a southerly direction for 270 km to Windorah, on the Diamantina Developmental Road. Thirty km beyond Lark Quarry, a rough track leads west to Diamantina National Park, encompassing 716,000 hectares of Channel Country on either side of the Diamantina River. Except during the Wet, the river is dry, with just billabongs remaining along its bed. The only vegetation is spinifex and stunted eucalypts. The park has no facilities and if planning a trip seek advice from the Department of Environment in Longreach, tel. (07) 4658-1761.

McKinlay

Anyone who has seen the movie *Crocodile Dundee* will want to stop at this small town of 20, halfway between Winton and Cloncurry. The small pub here was featured as **Walkabout Creek Hotel** in the movie, and although you're unlikely to see anyone wrestling crocodiles, it's a pleasant place to stop for a beer and meal. The hotel has rooms for $38 s, $46 d, and a few campsites out back, tel. (07) 4746-8424. Budget-Inexpensive.

Cloncurry

Large lodes of copper were discovered in the hills around Cloncurry in the 1860s and by WW I the town was Australia's largest copper producer. As the mineral-rich Isa Highlands to the west were developed, interest in Cloncurry waned. Today abandoned mining claims surround this town of 2,500. The town's main claim to fame is as the birthplace of the **Royal Flying Doctor Service.** The service was started by John Flynn (featured on the new $20 note) in 1927, when aircraft were still a novelty and wireless transmissions through the Outback were unheard of. Qantas built him an aircraft, and a Melbourne businessman helped fund the wireless transmission sets. **John Flynn Place,** tel. (07) 4742-1251, is a modern complex comprising a museum dedicated to Flynn, an art gallery, and theater; open Mon.-Fri. 7 a.m.-4 p.m., Sat.-Sun. 9 a.m.-3 p.m. Admission is $3 pp.

On the east side of town is **Mary Kathleen Memorial Park.** It's home to a couple of civic buildings transported from the uranium-mining town of Mary Kathleen, halfway between Cloncurry and Mt. Isa. The uranium mine was worked 1958-63, when atomic-hungry scientists searched the world for a reliable source of the mineral. After the mine closed, the town stood empty for many years and was then dismantled. The park's museum houses a mineral collection and other historic memorabilia, including from the ill-fated Burke and Wills Expedition; open Mon.-Fri. 7 a.m.-4 p.m., Sat.-Sun. 9 a.m.-3 p.m., tel. (07) 4742-1361.

Cloncurry also holds the record for the highest temperature ever recorded in Australia. In 1889 the thermometer reached 53.1° C (127.6° F).

North from Cloncurry

Cloncurry marks the end of the Landsborough Highway and the beginning of the Burke Developmental Rd., linking Cloncurry to the Gulf of Carpentaria (450 km one-way).

Quamby, the first settlement north of Cloncurry, consists of just a hotel, dominated by a large water tank painted as a can of Fosters.

Northwest of Cloncurry is the Selwyn Range, once home to the fierce Kalkadoon tribe, combatants in the bloodiest battle ever fought on Australian soil. During the 1880s, as Europeans settled on traditional hunting grounds, there were many clashes between the two groups. In 1884, a police cavalry charge saw most of the tribe's male population massacred on Battle Mountain. The hotel in Kajabbi (pop. 20), 26 km northwest of the Burke Developmental Rd., is named for the tribe. On Saturday night the publican puts on a barbecue, inevitably followed by a singalong. The hotel also has rooms, or you can camp, tel. (07) 4742-5979.

MOUNT ISA AND VICINITY

Best known as The Isa, this Outback city of 24,000 is one of the country's great mining towns. Although artesian-bore water allows many gardens to thrive, the city is basically unappealing, its skyline dominated by the mine and a 270-meter lead-smelter stack. Mount Isa does have one claim to fame: it's the world's largest city in area, at 40,978 square km—and it's in the Guinness Book of Records to prove it. The city exists only because of the mine, but also plays a vital role in reducing the isolation of the Outback. It is the world's largest single-mine producer of lead and silver (150,000 tons of lead and 30 tons of silver are extracted annually) and the world's largest underground mine. It is also Australia's largest copper producer, yielding 155,000 tons annually. More than 200,000 tons of zinc are also produced here each year.

Mount Isa dates from 1923, when John Campbell Miles, an old-time prospector, found an ore outcrop in an area known as the Isa Highlands, the eastern end of a mineral-rich belt that rises 400 meters above the surrounding landscape. The area may be desolate and uninviting, but it holds untold wealth. Many millions of years ago, as great forces pushed the land upward, molten intrusions impregnated the sedimentary rock, cooling to form the rich seams of minerals upon which the city grew.

Those who invested in the copper mines around Cloncurry had always banked on a port

being established on the Gulf of Carpentaria. But one never eventuated, and by the 1920s, when a rail line was built from Townsville, interest in copper had waned. Up until this time, only small mines were operating farther west. But in 1924 Mount Isa Mines moved into the area, investing enormous sums of money to make mineral extraction viable.

Sights

Mount Isa Mines is across the Leichhardt River from downtown. Touring the mining operation is Mount Isa's main attraction. The three-hour **Underground Mine Tour** requires reservations well in advance. Before heading into the 500 km of tunnels, you are fitted with a hard hat, miner's light, overalls, and boots. These three-hour tours depart Mon.-Tues. and Thursday 7:30 a.m., 11:30 a.m., and 2:45 p.m.; $35 pp. Book well ahead by calling (07) 4749-1555. The two-hour **Surface Tour** departs daily April-Sept.; $15. **Campbell's Coaches,** tel. (07) 4743-2006, takes bookings for this tour.

John Middlin Mining Display, on Church St., tel. (07) 4749-1429, has an underground mine mock-up, mineral displays, and large pieces of mining equipment. It's open Mon.-Fri. 9 a.m.-4 p.m. Also displaying mining exhibits is **Frank Aston Underground Museum** on Shackleton Street. As well as mining equipment, there's a replica of a native Kilkadoon camp. It's open March-Nov. 10 a.m.-3 p.m.; $4 admission.

Riversleigh Fossils Centre, in Centenary Park on Marian St., tel. (07) 4749-1555, contains displays from Riversleigh, 300 km north of the city. Riversleigh, where limestone beds contain a variety of skeletons, is one of Australia's most important fossil sites. Admission $5; open Mon.-Fri. 9 a.m.-4:30 p.m., Sat.-Sun. 9:30 a.m.-2:30 p.m. Also in Centenary Park is the **Kalkadoon Tribal Centre,** tel. (07) 4749-1435. The local Kalkadoon tribe was among the fiercest of all the Aboriginals and resisted European settlement until 1884, when they were nearly wiped out in a bloody confrontation with troopers, The center tells their story. It's open weekdays 9 a.m.-5 p.m. Across Marian St. from the park, Hilary St. leads to a lookout affording views across the city and to the mining operations to the west. Dating from the 1930s, **Tent House,** on 4th Ave., is one of the few remaining examples of early mine-company housing; open

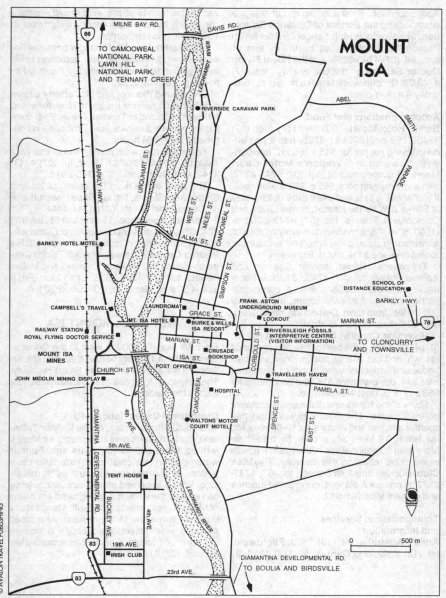

MOUNT ISA

MILNE BAY RD.

DAVIS RD.

66

TO CAMOOWEAL
NATIONAL PARK,
LAWN HILL
NATIONAL PARK,
AND TENNANT CREEK

LEICHHARDT RIVER

ABEL

SMITH PARADE

URQUHART ST.

BARKLY HWY.

● Riverside Caravan Park

WEST ST.

MILES ST.

CAMOOWEAL ST.

ALMA ST.

SIMPSON ST.

● Barkly Hotel Motel

SCHOOL OF
DISTANCE EDUCATION

BARKLY HWY.

78

● Laundromat

CAMPBELL'S TRAVEL ●

MT. ISA HOTEL ●

GRACE ST.

FRANK ASTON
UNDERGROUND MUSEUM

● Lookout

MARIAN ST.

● BURKE & WILLS
ISA RESORT

RIVERSLEIGH FOSSILS
INTERPRETIVE CENTRE
(VISITOR INFORMATION)

CORBOULD ST.

RAILWAY STATION
ROYAL FLYING DOCTOR SERVICE

MARIAN ST.

ISA ST.

● CRUSADE
BOOKSHOP

TO CLONCURRY
AND TOWNSVILLE

MOUNT ISA
MINES

CHURCH ST.

POST OFFICE

● TRAVELLERS HAVEN

JOHN MIDDLIN MINING DISPLAY ●

CAMOOWEAL

● HOSPITAL

SPENCE ST.

PAMELA ST.

EAST ST.

DIAMANTINA DEVELOPMENTAL RD.

4th AVE.

● WALTONS MOTOR
COURT MOTEL

5th AVE.

TENT HOUSE ■

BUCKLEY AVE.

4th AVE.

83

19th AVE.

IRISH CLUB ■

23rd AVE.

0   500 m

DIAMANTINA DEVELOPMENTAL RD.
TO BOULIA AND BIRDSVILLE

83

© AVALON TRAVEL PUBLISHING

April-Sept. Mon.-Fri. 9 a.m.-3 p.m. Other sights worth visiting are **School of Distance Education,** at Kalkadoon High School on Abel Smith Parade (tours schooldays at 10 a.m. and 11 a.m., tel. (07) 4743-0255, and the **Royal Flying Doctor Service** on the Barkly Hwy., tel. (07) 4743-2800; open weekdays 9 a.m.-5 p.m., Saturday 9 a.m.-1 p.m.

Accommodations and Food

Barkly Hotel/Motel, 55 Barkly Hwy., tel. (07) 4743-2988 or (1800) 81-4795, has a few air-conditioned rooms for $45 s, $55 d. Inexpensive. Also central is **Walton's Motor Court Motel,** 23 Camooweal St., tel. (07) 4743-2377, with a laundry and pool; $55 s, $65 d. Moderate. If you're willing to spend a few extra dollars, stay at **Burke & Wills Isa Resort,** corner Grace and Camooweal Streets, tel. (07) 4743-8000 or (1800) 67-9178, a modern, two-story motel with a swimming pool, gym, spa, and restaurant; rooms here are $110 s or d. Expensive.

Travellers Haven, corner Spence and Pamela Streets, tel. (07) 4743-0313, has backpacker accommodations with a communal kitchen, pool, and air-conditioning. It's also only 500 meters from town. Dorm beds are $14, singles $26, doubles $34. Budget.

Riverside Caravan Park, 195 West St., tel. (07) 4743-3904, is the best of four campgrounds in town, and has a large pool, kitchen with barbecue and refrigerator, and laundry. Unpowered sites $14, powered sites $16, and new cabins for $55 s or d. Budget-Inexpensive.

Many of the hotels and clubs serve excellent no-frills meals. The Barkly Hotel/Motel has counter lunches and dinners for $5-8, while **Mt. Isa Hotel,** 19 Miles St., is open for breakfast. More than 60 nationalities converge in Isa, with many clubs reflecting this diversity. The **Irish Club,** Buckley and 19th Streets, tel. (07) 4743-2577, is one such place, serving buffet lunches and dinners less than $12.

Transportation, Services, and Information

Ansett Australia, tel. (13) 1300, **Flightwest,** tel. (13) 2392, and **Qantas,** tel. (13) 1313, fly into Mt. Isa from Brisbane, with Ansett Australia continuing to Alice Springs and Flightwest to Townsville and Normanton.

The **Queensland Rail** Inlander operates between Townsville and Mt. Isa, departing twice weekly (Sunday and Wednesday 6 p.m.). For bookings call (13) 2232.

Greyhound Pioneer and **McCafferty's** have a daily coach service between Townsville and Mt. Isa, continuing to Tennant Creek. Both companies operate a service from Brisbane via Longreach, taking 24 hours.

The major car rental companies in town are **Avis,** tel. (07) 4743-3733; **Hertz,** tel. (07) 4743-4142; and **Thrifty,** tel. (07) 4743-2911.

The **post office** is on the corner of Isa and Camooweal Streets. **Mt. Isa Base Hospital** is at 30 Camooweal St., tel. (07) 4744-4444.

Crusade Bookshop, 11 Simpson St., tel. (07) 4743-3880, carries a good selection of Outback literature and a range of topographic maps. **Mt. Isa Visitors Centre** is in the Riversleigh Fossils Centre on Marian St., between Corbould and Mullan Streets, tel. (07) 4749-1555. Open Mon.-Fri. 9 a.m.-4:30 p.m., Sat.-Sun. 9:30 a.m.-2:30 p.m.

WEST FROM MOUNT ISA

From Mt. Isa, it's 200 km west to the Queensland/Northern Territory border, then 460 km farther to Tennant Creek, on the Stuart Highway. The only town to speak of is **Camooweal,** just east of the border.

Camooweal Caves National Park

This 13,800-hectare park, on the Barkley Tableland north of Camooweal, protects sinkholes formed about 500 million years ago. Further water erosion has created an extensive cave system, with several caves more than 200 meters long. With a torch and sturdy footwear anyone can explore the system. Aboveground are plains of Mitchell grass interspersed with stands of dry eucalypt extending to the horizon. At a small billabong, which attracts lots of birdlife, is a camping area with toilets. Check road access after rain, tel. (07) 4743-2055.

SOUTH AUSTRALIA

License plates proclaim it "The Festival State." Fact decrees it the driest state in Australia. And the Tourism Commission banners it—most accurately—"The State of Surprise." The surprises are many, for, dry as most of its 984,200 square km may be, South Australia is definitely not dull.

Flanked by Victoria and New South Wales on the east, by Western Australia on the west, and neatly tucked beneath the Northern Territory, this land has almost as many ripe attractions to pick from as it does grapes growing on its famous vines. Most people have heard about the Barossa and Clare Valleys, famous for fine wines and the warm feelings that go with them; and about Adelaide, the "pretty" capital city, where nearly two-thirds of the state's 1.4 million inhabitants live from one festival to the next-and, without a doubt, the mere mention of the huge Outback part of the state sends shivers down the spines of those who dream of scorching in their boots. Coober Pedy, the opal-mining town so hot that homes and shops are built underground, has also received its share of publicity (though it's often depicted as the end of the earth).

Not so popularized by films, jewels, or wine labels are South Australia's lesser-known gems:

Hahndorf, a German settlement where you can pick up streusel on the corner instead of meat pie; Burra, an exquisitely preserved copper center with miners' dugouts, Cornish cottages, and the "monster mine"; Kangaroo Island, abundant in 'roos and other wild-and-woollies, with picnic areas that keep the humans fenced in so the animals can watch *them* eat and perform; the Flinders Ranges, spectacular multicolored rock formations, about 1.6 billion years old, with deep gorges and endlessly changing vistas; the Blue Lake, which is actually gray but turns bright blue at the exact same time each year; Lake Eyre, a (usually) dry salt pan that is Australia's largest lake; and the mighty Murray, the country's most important river, which stretches more than 2,000 km from the Snowy Mountains to Lake Alexandrina.

These, of course, are just a few tidbits to whet your appetite. You will also discover heritage towns with exquisitely crafted sandstone buildings, little sleepy fishing villages, bustling beach resorts, reputed UFO landing sites, and Outback tracks to test the heartiest, nerviest, and possibly craziest souls. Naturally, there are some dry spots, but think of them as crackers to clear your palate between sips (or gulps) of the sweetest wine.

Most places are easily accessible by a variety of transportation. Hop a vintage tram to the beach or catch the Ghan and train it up to the Red Centre. To get around cities, between towns, or across the Nullarbor Plain, hire an air-conditioned luxury car, a 4WD jeep, or use your thumb and feet. Float along the Murray in your own houseboat, or sign up for a paddle steamer cruise. (Incidentally, some of the gurgly ferries-'cross-the-Murray will pang the nostalgic hearts of early '70s travelers who once clutched tattered copies of *Siddhartha* against their searching breasts.)

CLIMATE

There is good reason why more than 99% of the state's population lives south of the 32nd parallel—it is the only part that isn't hot, harsh, and desolate.

Adelaide is frequently described as having a "Mediterranean-like" climate. The short, mild winters (June-Aug.) average 17° C (62° F). Even with occasional downpours and some very chilly nights, most days are bathed in plenty of sunshine. Summers (Dec.-Feb.) are very dry and range from a

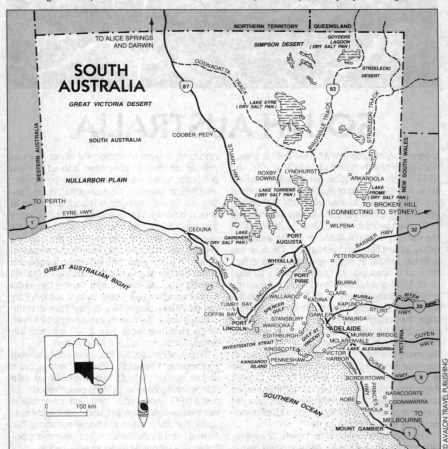

© AVALON TRAVEL PUBLISHING

warm 29° C (87° F) to a downright hot 38° C (100° F). Autumn (March-May) and especially the spring months (Sept.-Nov.) are delightful times to visit the wine country or plan a bushwalk.

Adelaide's surrounding hills and vineyards are fertile and well irrigated. The southeast corner of the state and Kangaroo Island are cooler and greener yet. And, though snow is a rarity in South Australia, an occasional spatter of white has been sighted atop the Mt. Lofty Ranges.

The Outback, which makes up most of the state's northern region, blisters in summer. Searing temperatures of 51° C (132° F) have been recorded in the Oodnadatta area—and that was in the *shade*. The yearly rainfall is less than 25 cm, but an occasional fierce storm can prompt sudden, violent downpours.

In 1989, the Nullarbor Plain actually flooded, even halting the fabled Indian Pacific train in its tracks! Several months after the rains, there were so many pools of water and bits of scrub popping up out of the normally cracked, parched, and stark earth that it seemed like hallucinations of multiple oases. Lake Eyre, normally a huge salt pan, has also been getting its fill. For world weather-watchers, these unusual occurrences probably seem all too usual.

HISTORY

There was life before Light—Colonel William Light, that is, the British surveyor general who laid out the site for the capital city.

Thousands of years prior to Britain's colonization of South Australia, small tribes of Aboriginal hunters and gatherers lived a nomadic lifestyle in the environs of what is now Adelaide. Part of the coastline was charted as early as 1627 by Dutch explorer Peter Nuyts, but it was British navigator Matthew Flinders who in 1802 actually became the first white man to fully explore the coast. (Amazingly, American sealers, who established a base on nearby Kangaroo Island only one year later, stayed right where they were and minded their own business.)

Meanwhile, Charles Sturt, a hotshot who'd been exploring the country's interior, began making his way south along the Murray River, being spit out of its mouth at Lake Alexandrina in 1830. The London tabloids reported the exciting news of his discovery—a rich, fertile riverland. This inspired a fellow named Edward Gibbon Wakefield to come up with a great idea for reducing Britain's unemployment crisis: colonize this bountiful new land and raise much-needed money by selling off parcels. In other words—move in, run out the natives, and start subdividing. Sound familiar? Best yet, they would not need any of those nasty convicts because the settlers, having the "pride of ownership" carrot dangling over their noses, would be motivated to do their own hard labor. To this day, South Australians are pretty haughty about the fact that theirs is the only state in the country that was not begun as a convict colony.

In 1836 the British established their settlement, naming Captain John Hindmarsh as its first governor. Colonel William Light, responsible for laying out the capital city, called it Adelaide, in honor of King William IV's wife.

The new settlers were supposed to be religious, morally upright, and hardworking. However, as soon as they arrived in "their" new land, the Aboriginal population quickly dwindled. Many were killed by the white men, others died from the diseases the settlers brought, and the remainder were forced out to the hostile territory up north. There were the inevitable squabbles, bickering, red tape, and claims of incompetent government. There was a shortage of labor; bankruptcy loomed. Then in 1842 rich copper deposits were discovered, and South Australia quickly bounced back. Besides the mining boom, crops flourished. Soon Adelaide became an agricultural mecca for wheat, fruits, and wool. Shortly after, European refugees settled in the Barossa Valley, bringing with them their considerable talent for winemaking. Though the state's economy is still based mainly on its agricultural products—wine, citrus fruit, merino wool, wheat, barley, and fishing—other important industries include shipbuilding and automobile manufacturing.

A Crown colony in 1842, with its own legislative assembly elected by ballot in 1856, South Australia was made a state of the Commonwealth of Australia in 1901.

The state's staid image has greatly diminished since the advent of the Adelaide Festival of the Arts in 1960, not to mention some rather liberal legislation in the areas of homosexuality, marijuana usage, and Aboriginal land rights.

ADELAIDE

Colonel William Light has practically been beatified for his foresight in planning South Australia's capital city (pop. 1.1 million). The man loved straight lines and broad boulevards. He wanted Adelaide to reflect both simplicity and elegance, and he had a magnificent site on which to realize his vision: a flat plain, centrally located on the southern coastline, with the glorious backdrop of rolling hills and dales and the Mt. Lofty Ranges.

Light designed a one-square-mile central business district composed of grid-patterned streets bisecting at right angles and five perfect city squares interspersed at regular intervals. One of these, Victoria Square, is the designated heart of the city (you'll find the general post office

---

Approaching Adelaide from Melbourne, we left the train and were driven in an open carriage over the hills and along their slopes to the city. It was an excursion of an hour or two and the charm of it could not be overstated.

The road wound through gaps and gorges and offered all variety of scenery and prospect—color, color everywhere and the air fine and fresh, the skies blue and not a shred of cloud to mar the downpour of the brilliant sunshine.

And finally the mountain gateway opened, and the immense plain spread out below, stretching away into the dim distance on every hand, soft and delicate and dainty and beautiful.

On its near edge reposed the city; with wide streets compactly built; with fine houses everywhere, embowered in foliage and flowers and with imposing masses of public buildings nobly grouped and architecturally beautiful.

—MARK TWAIN

---

across the street and the central bus station about a block away). Gouger St., on one perimeter, has not only the bounty-filled Central Market but a bevy of international cuisines and a mini-Chinatown.

Running north and south, skirting around Victoria Square, is King William St., the center for business and commerce and supposedly the widest city street in any Australian capital. (Light named the main thoroughfare after his king, but it was his Queen Adelaide who took the whole city and, eventually, a wine label as well.)

Heading north up King William St., you'll come to the intersection of Hindley St. on the west and Rundle Mall on the east—same street, but it changes names. Hindley St. is lined with restaurants, discos, and nightclubs, a couple of strip joints, and an adult bookshop or two. This is Adelaide's "racy" quarter, if the occasional street brawl, broken beer bottle, or risqué book jacket justify the term.

Rundle Mall is the no-cars-allowed main shopping promenade that sports arcades with specialty shops, art galleries, department stores, outdoor cafés, occasional street vendors and buskers, and the much-debated stainless-steel sculpture of an enormous pair of balls. One block farther up King William St., on your right, is the **South Australian Tourism Commission Travel Centre.**

Rundle St. East, an "add-on" of Rundle Mall, is the student sector, replete with grunge and retro shops, alternative everything, the fabulously funky East End Market, and an energetic street scene with many outdoor cafés at which to hide behind a tattered copy of Kerouac or Proust.

The city center is bounded in a neat little parcel by broad tree-lined terraces, aptly named North, South, East, and West Terrace. North Terrace, just another block up from the Travel Centre, is where you'll find most of the city's architectural and cultural attractions—Parliament House, the museums, Festival Arts Centre, University of Adelaide, and such. The terraces, in turn, are bordered by expansive parklands with lovely greenbelts, towering eucalyptus trees, picnic areas, and recreation facilities.

The River Torrens, navigated by rowboats, motor launches, and a variety of other putt-putts, separates the business district from North Adelaide, one of the oldest sections of the city. North Adelaide is yet another of Colonel Light's babies—the Chosen Suburb, an exclusive residential grid built around a perfectly regular town square, surrounded by lots of greenery. Melbourne St., part of the plot, is famed for its too-chic-to-be-believed boutiques and eateries.

Now, don't start thinking that all these well-organized grids and squares mean this is a metropolis full of unimaginative boxes. The architecture is *brilliant*—at least most of it—splendid stone churches, ornate and filigreed mansions, superb colonial buildings. As in most big cities, however, the old and beautiful structures do sometimes sit beside new and tasteless office blocks. But Adelaide has attentively tried to preserve as much of the original architecture as possible, or at least to keep the original facades.

Because of its compactness and methodical layout, Adelaide is easy to explore on foot. And, though it lacks the street action of many major cities, the small-town atmosphere and almost pastoral spaciousness make this state capital unique.

You're likely to hear a string of adjectives rattled off whenever Adelaide is mentioned—"calm," "stately," and, occasionally, "staid." The slightly more than one million residents like to think of themselves as sophisticated and infinitely more cultured than those inhabiting the rest of the country. In Adelaide they drink fine wines, follow the cricket matches, attend the theater, and put on a world-class Festival of the Arts.

Calm, stately, staid? In 1988, Mick Jagger opened his solo world concert tour in Adelaide. Let someone try to grid and square *that* one.

ON THE TERRACE

North Terrace, wedged between the city hustle-bustle and the gentle River Torrens, is Adelaide's historic and cultural heart. This easy walk begins at the corner of West Terrace and North Terrace and ends at the corner of East Terrace. Conveniently, you start off at the **Newmarket Hotel** and finish up at the **Botanic Hotel,** two of Adelaide's most sumptuous pubs, which date back to the late 19th century.

Lion Arts Centre
Many of the Adelaide Arts Festival fringe events are held in this old Lions Club building at the corner of Morphett St.. Performance stages, galleries, arts and crafts workshops, and casual eating areas are the core of this vibrantly renovated factory. It is usually open during the daytime for a wander or coffee and a sandwich, otherwise hours depend on scheduled events. For more information, phone (08) 8231-7760.

Holy Trinity Church
The foundation stone for the state's oldest Anglican church, beside the Morphett St. bridge, was laid by Governor Hindmarsh himself in 1838. The present building is actually about 50 years newer, but the original clock still remains.

Adelaide Casino
You can bet that more people cross the threshold of the swanky casino than of the church across the street! Built atop the classic sandstone railway station with its majestic colonnades and balconies (still used by commuters), the casino offers two floors of gaming tables— roulette, craps, blackjack, baccarat—plus keno, a money wheel, and two-up. For those of you who prefer one-armed bandits, you're already out of luck: you'll find no poker or slot machines here. High rollers, however, can try to get a pass into the exclusive International Room. Even if you don't gamble, this is a good spot to people-watch. Also, there are five bars and two restaurants, the **Pullman** and the less formal **Carvery.**

Security is tight—photography is not allowed. In addition, a dress code is enforced; dressy or "smart casual." Guards will scrutinize you from head to toe as you cross the marble hall to the entrance.

The casino is part of Adelaide Plaza, which also houses the Adelaide Convention Centre and Festival Centre, as well as the Hyatt Regency Hotel. It is open Mon.-Thurs., Fri.-Sun. 24 hours, closed Christmas Day and Good Friday (when you can probably lay odds that more people are over at the church). Automatic teller machines are on the premises, and visitors under 18 are *not.* For more information, phone (08) 8212-2811.

State History Centre

Sandwiched between the casino and the new Parliament House, South Australia's original Parliament House is one of the state's oldest and most historic buildings. In 1855 it was home to the first Legislative Council. Painstaking renovations were completed in 1980, and it is now the **Constitutional Museum,** which presents audiovisual displays and exhibits depicting the state's history, from Dreamtime to the present. The museum's **House of Assembly** is reputedly the world's oldest surviving chamber of democracy. A bookshop specializes in South Australian history, and there's a relaxing restaurant in the garden courtyard.

New Parliament House, next door, was a 56-year-long construction project, begun in 1883

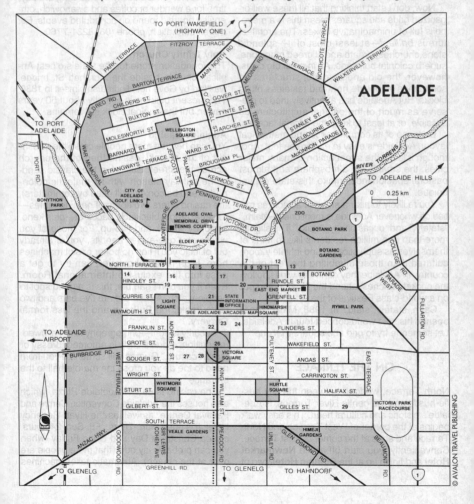

ADELAIDE

© AVALON TRAVEL PUBLISHING

and completed in 1939. Built out of gray Kapunda marble with high Corinthian columns in neoclassical style, it is a sharp contrast to its simpler predecessor. The public is invited to watch proceedings when Parliament is sitting, and tours are available at various times. For more information, phone (08) 8237-9100.

The State History Centre is open Mon.-Fri. and public holidays 10 a.m.-5 p.m., Sat.-Sun. noon-5 p.m., closed Christmas Day and Good Friday. Admission is $6. For more information, phone (08) 8207-1077.

The Adelaide Festival Centre

On King William St., just behind the houses of Parliament and banking the River Torrens, the Adelaide Festival Centre, built in 1972, is home to the three-week Adelaide Festival of Arts, held in March of even-numbered years. Ranked as one of the world's top international multi-arts festivals, it draws diverse and big-name talents like Muddy Waters, Placido Domingo, the Royal Shakespeare Company, Japan's Kabuki Theatre, Twyla Tharp, and Mick Jagger. In addition, the Fringe Festival, which takes place simultaneously, presents innovative theatrical productions, performance events, poetry readings, art exhibitions, and a writers' week. Fringe events are held at the Lion Arts Centre and a host of other venues around town. The local newspapers' daily listings will keep you informed of when and where.

The Adelaide Festival Centre comprises a 2,000-seat multipurpose theater and concert hall, a drama theater (home to the South Australian Theatre Company), an additional flexible performance space, an open-air amphitheater, a piano bar, and two restaurants. A variety of entertainment is presented year-round, including professional productions of successful musicals like *Cats* and *Evita,* chamber orchestra symphonies, and an informal late-night cabaret.

You can tour the Festival Centre Mon.-Fri. 10 a.m.-5 p.m., Saturday 1-5 p.m. Tours depart hourly and the cost is $5, payable at the enquiry counter in the foyer. For more information, phone (08) 8216-8600.

Government House

Back on North Terrace and east across King William St. is the Regency-style official residence of South Australia's governor. The first governor, John Hindmarsh, lived on the same site in 1836, but not in the same house. Governor Hindmarsh lived in a mud hut. It was George Gawler, the second governor (1838-41), who decided it was time to build a more suitable residence and, in 1839, began construction of the east wing. The midsection was added in 1855, and by 1878 the house as you see it was completed.

On either side of Government House are two **war memorials:** to the west is a bronze infantryman, commemorating South Australians who died in the Boer War; to the east is the National War Memorial, honoring those who died in WW I; plaques along the wall of Government House pay tribute to the dead of WW II.

Royal Society of the Arts

Across Kintore St., the Society, founded in 1856, exhibits at least six major members' works per year, its own permanent collection, and works of various individual artists. The archives and reference library are available for research. Hours are Mon.-Fri. 11 a.m.-5 p.m., Sat.-Sun. 2-5 p.m.,

1. St. Peter's Cathedral
2. Light's Vision
3. Adelaide Festival Centre
4. Convention Centre
5. Adelaide Casino (and Railway Station)
6. Parliament House
7. Migration and Settlement Museum
8. State Library
9. Mortlock Library
10. South Australian Museum
11. Art Gallery of South Australia
12. University of Adelaide
13. Royal Adelaide Hospital
14. New Market Hotel
15. Lion Arts Centre
16. Qantas Airways
17. South Australian Tourism Commission Travel Centre
18. Ayers House
19. Hindley St. Restaurant and Entertainment Area
20. Rundle Mall Shopping Area
21. Edmund Wright House
22. General Post Office
23. Adelaide Town Hall
24. YMCA
25. central bus station
26. Glenelg Tram Terminal
27. Central Market
28. Hilton International Hotel
29. Adelaide Youth Hostel

closed Christmas, New Year's Day, and Easter weekend. Admission is free. For information, phone (08) 8223-4704.

State Library
This place is just a bit confusing: the State Library, which was originally in the old wing, is now in the Angaston white marble building next door; the **Mortlock Library,** restored to Victorian grandeur, is actually the original state library. To put it another way: the State Library carries all the regular books and overseas newspapers; the Mortlock has all the special collections—memorabilia relating to South Australia, a Historic Treasures Room with Colonel Light's surveying equipment on display, a family history research library, and a cricketing memorabilia collection. Both libraries are open Mon.-Fri. 9:30 a.m.-6 p.m., Wednesday and Friday until 8 p.m., Sat.-Sun. noon-5 p.m., closed public holidays. For information, phone (08) 8207-7200.

Migration Museum
Next to the State Library, on Kintore Ave., is Australia's first multicultural museum. The building itself is Adelaide's restored Destitute Asylum. Exhibits and an audiovisual program give a realistic picture of what life was like for the early settlers. You can even visit the dark cells built back in the 1870s after a riot. The bookshop specializes in South Australian history. **Mrs. Gifford's** is a café in the courtyard. The museum is open Mon.-Fri. 10 a.m.-5 p.m., Sat.-Sun. and public holidays 1-5 p.m. Closed Good Friday and Christmas Day. Except for special traveling exhibits, admission is free. Guided tours are available. For information, phone (08) 8207-7580.

Police Barracks and Armory
Tucked in a courtyard, near the Migration and Settlement Museum, the small **South Australian Police Museum** displays 1860s law enforcement memorabilia. Open Sat.-Sun. and public holidays 1-5 p.m., closed Christmas Day and Good Friday. Donations are requested. For information, phone (08) 8218-1228.

South Australian Museum
A distinctive North Terrace landmark, with whale skeletons in the front window, this museum is especially noteworthy for its extensive collec-

tions of Aboriginal, New Guinean, and Melanesian native artifacts. The museum shop stocks natural history and anthropology books, as well as related gift items. The museum is open daily 10 a.m.-5 p.m., closed Good Friday and Christmas Day. Except for special exhibitions, admission is free. For information, phone (08) 8207-7500.

Art Gallery of South Australia
Next door to the museum, a comprehensive collection of Australian, European, and Asian art is housed in two wings of the gallery. Highlights include examples of Australian impressionists, colonial works (including furniture, silver, and other decorative arts), 20th-century works by important painters like Arthur Boyd, Sir Sidney Nolan, and Russell Drysdale, recent Aboriginal landscapes, and an interesting collection of Southeast Asian ceramics. Changing exhibitions of contemporary art and Australian and international touring shows are also on display. The bookshop has a good collection of art books, periodicals, cards, some jewelry, and other related items. A relaxing coffee shop in the rear sells small cakes and sandwiches. The gallery is open daily 10 a.m.-5 p.m., closed Good Friday and Christmas Day. Admission is free, but there is often a charge for special exhibitions. Tours are available. For information, phone (08) 8207-7000.

Museum of Classical Archaeology
The Mitchell Building, a striking Gothic edifice on the **University of Adelaide** campus, is a fitting site for this collection of Greek, Egyptian, and Etruscan relics—some more than 5,000 years old. The museum, on the first floor, is open Mon.-Fri. noon-3 p.m., closed for two weeks at Christmas. Admission is free. For information, phone (08) 8303-5226. (There are many fine examples of 19th-century architecture on this 10-hectare campus. Of particular interest is castle-like Bonython Hall.)

Ayers House
Across Frome Rd. and opposite the Royal Adelaide Hospital, this former residence of Sir Henry Ayers, former premier of South Australia, is now headquarters of the **National Trust.** Construction on the elegant bluestone manor was begun in 1846 and took 30 years to complete. Carefully

preserved and refurnished, Ayers House is a lovely specimen of gracious Victorian living, with special displays of fine silver, crystal, nursery toys, and an early kitchen. You can inspect the house Tues.-Fri. 10 a.m.-4 p.m., Sat.-Sun. and holidays 1-4 p.m., closed Good Friday and Christmas Day. Admission is $5. For information, phone (08) 8223-1234.

OTHER CITY SIGHTS

King William Street
You'll find several more noteworthy attractions as you stroll along King William St., between North Terrace and Victoria Square.

Edmund Wright House, 59 King William St., was built in 1876 for the bishop of South Australia. These days the ornate Renaissance-style residence is used for government offices and official functions. Take a peek inside during normal business hours. Free lunchtime music performances are held here every Wednesday during autumn and spring.

The **Telecommunications Museum,** in Electra House at 131 King William St., features working displays and original equipment that trace South Australia's technology from past to present. Open Sun.-Fri. 10:30 a.m.-3:30 p.m., closed Saturday. Admission is free. For information, phone (08) 8225-6601.

Approaching Victoria Square, on the opposite side of the street is **Adelaide Town Hall.** Built in 1863, the freestone facade is carved with the faces of Queen Victoria and Prince Albert. There's a free one-hour guided tour on Tuesday and Wednesday 2:30 p.m., Thursday at 10:30 a.m. and 2:30 p.m. A two-week advance booking is requested. For information, phone (08) 8203-7777.

The post office, across the street, is another fine example of stately colonial architecture. For postal history buffs, the **Postal Museum** next door (on the Franklin St. side) has a reconstructed turn-of-the-century post office, as well as archival philatelic displays. Open Mon.-Fri. 11 a.m.-2 p.m. Admission is free. For information, phone (13) 1318.

More Museums and Manors
You can view historic transport vehicles as well as ride on restored trams at the **Australian Elec-**

trical **Transport Museum** in St. Kilda (about 30 km northwest of the city center). Open Sunday and Wednesday during school holidays, closed Good Friday and Christmas Day. Admission is $6. For information, phone (08) 8261-9110.

Carrick Hill, 46 Carrick Hill Dr., Springfield (a 10-minute drive from the city), was built in 1939 in the fashion of a late Elizabethan-era English manor house. Set on nearly 39 hectares of English gardens and surrounded by native Australian bush, the estate features a superb collection of Australian, English, and French paintings, as well as silver, pewter, and English oak furniture. The grounds also include a sculpture park and picnic area. The tearooms serve Devonshire tea. The home and grounds are open Wed.-Sun. and public holidays 10 a.m.-5 p.m., closed the month of July. Tours are available several times each day. Admission is $8. For information, phone (08) 8379-3886.

Botanic Gardens
The Botanic Gardens sit on 16 hectares near the junction of North and East Terraces. Besides the usual and unusual Australian and exotic species, the Adelaide gardens house Australia's only **Museum of Economic Botany** and the **Bicentennial Conservatory,** the largest conservatory in the Southern Hemisphere. The museum, housed inside a Grecian-style heritage building, exhibits an array of plants used for commercial, medicinal, and artistic purposes. The conservatory, built with the help of NASA technology, has been designed to address ecological imbalance and the importance of preserving the rainforests. Built of steel and lens-shaped glass, the building—measuring 100 meters long, 45 meters wide, and 27 meters high—encompasses rainforest plants from Australia, Indonesia, Papua New Guinea, and other nearby Pacific islands. Gardeners will not disturb the growth of any plants, allowing leaves and bits of bark to fall and heap on the ground. The workings of a tropical rainforest are clearly explained at two information centers within the conservatory.

The Botanic Gardens are open Mon.-Fri. 7 a.m.-sunset., Sat.-Sun. and public holidays 9 a.m.-sunset. Guided tours leave from the kiosk on Tuesday and Friday at 10:30 a.m. Admission is free. The conservatory is open daily 10 a.m.-4 p.m. (admission is $2.50). The garden

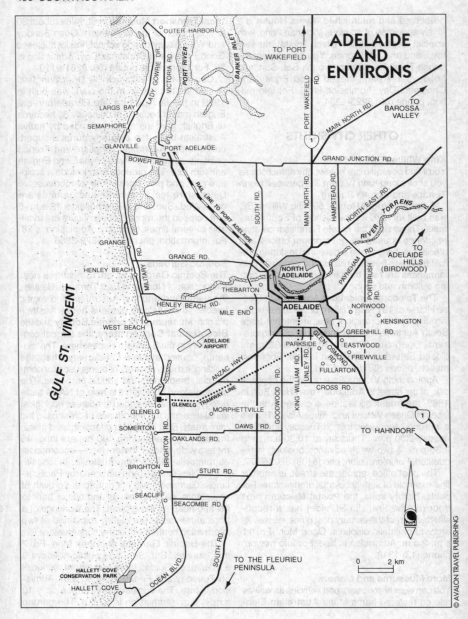

ADELAIDE AND ENVIRONS

TO PORT WAKEFIELD

TO BAROSSA VALLEY

TO ADELAIDE HILLS (BIRDWOOD)

TO HAHNDORF

TO THE FLEURIEU PENINSULA

OUTER HARBOR

BARKER INLET

PORT RIVER

LARGS BAY

SEMAPHORE

GLANVILLE

PORT ADELAIDE

LADY GOWRIE DR.

VICTORIA RD.

PORT WAKEFIELD RD.

MAIN NORTH RD.

MAIN NORTH RD.

GRAND JUNCTION RD.

BOWER RD.

GRANGE

HENLEY BEACH

GRANGE RD.

MILITARY RD.

SOUTH RD.

HAMPSTEAD RD.

NORTH EAST RD.

TORRENS RIVER

PAYNEHAM RD.

PORTRUSH RD.

NORTH ADELAIDE

THEBARTON

ADELAIDE

NORWOOD

KENSINGTON

GREENHILL RD.

GULF ST. VINCENT

HENLEY BEACH RD.

MILE END

WEST BEACH

ADELAIDE AIRPORT

ANZAC HWY.

GOODWOOD RD.

PARKSIDE

GLEN OSMOND RD.

UNLEY RD.

KING WILLIAM RD.

EASTWOOD

FREWVILLE

FULLARTON

CROSS RD.

GLENELG

GLENELG TRAMWAY LINE

MORPHETTVILLE

DAWS RD.

BRIGHTON RD.

GOODWOOD RD.

SOMERTON

OAKLANDS RD.

BRIGHTON

STURT RD.

SEACLIFF

SEACOMBE RD.

SOUTH RD.

OCEAN BLVD.

HALLETT COVE CONSERVATION PARK

HALLETT COVE

RAIL LINE TO PORT ADELAIDE

0   2 km

© AVALON TRAVEL PUBLISHING

complex also features a book and gift shop, and a lovely lakeside restaurant. For information, phone (08) 8228-2311.

Adelaide Zoo

On Frome Rd., next to the Botanic Gardens, the Adelaide Zoo is one of Australia's oldest zoos. Set on the banks of the River Torrens, the animals, birds, and reptiles are contained in grassy moat enclosures, walk-through aviaries (with 1,200 birds), and nocturnal and reptile houses. The zoo is acclaimed for its exhibitions of infrequently seen native animals, such as the yellow-footed rock wallaby (native of the Flinders Ranges), and for its breeding programs of rare species like the Persian leopard, red panda, Prezewalski's horse, ctontop tamarin, pygmy hippopotamus, and other roll-off-your-tongue types. The zoo is open daily 9:30 a.m.-5 p.m., closed Christmas Day. Admission is $9.50. For information, phone (08) 8267-3255 (ask what the feeding times are for the big cats, seals, bears, penguins, and pelicans).

Other Parks and Gardens

It would be impossible not to stumble onto the many expansive parks that virtually surround this city. **Elder Park,** which fronts the River Torrens, deserves a special mention within this section because it is the departure point for the *Popeye* motor launch, an alternate and cheap ($2) way of traveling between the Festival Centre and the zoo. Departures are Mon.-Fri. hourly 11:25 a.m.-3:25 p.m., Sat.-Sun. every 20 minutes 11 a.m.-5 p.m.

A short ride away aboard the Glenelg tram is **Veale Gardens,** a portion of the South Parklands with lovely flower beds, meandering streams, fountains, and a conservatory. Following the terrace east will bring you to **Himeji Gardens,** a traditional Japanese garden honoring Adelaide's sister city.

Wittunga Botanic Garden, Shepherds Hill Rd., in Blackwood, 14 km southeast of the city center, and dating from 1901, offers 15 hectares of flowering South Australian, Australian, and African plants, accessed via meandering pathways. Open daily 9 a.m.-5 p.m. For information, phone (08) 8228-2311. **Gamble Cottage Garden,** 296 Main Rd., also in Blackwood, intersperses heritage roses with old-fashioned peren-

nials and flowering plants and shrubs. The rear lawn is a delightful picnic area.

North Adelaide

Outstanding architecture and ritzy shops are the focal points of this exclusive suburb. Like everywhere else in the city, it's easy to get to—just continue north up King William St., a nice walk across Adelaide Bridge and the River Torrens (or you can walk up Frome Rd., from the zoo).

If you're coming up King William St., the first place you'll notice is **St. Peter's Cathedral,** at the corner of Pennington Terrace. It is one of the few churches in the country with twin spires, and though the church building itself was built between 1868 and 1876, the spires and towers were not erected until 1902. And here's a fun fact for your almanac—St. Peter's has the finest and heaviest bells in the Southern Hemisphere.

Continue west to Montefiore Rd., where atop Montefiore Hill stands **Light's Vision.** A statue marks the spot where Colonel William Light purportedly started blueprinting his plans for the city. Here you can see his beatific vision through your own eyes.

Walking about the North Adelaide "grid," you'll view many architectural wonders with their grand and fascinating touches. The pricey bluestone mansions are well kept, and most are quite ornate with eye-catching roof lines, iron lace verandas, towers, and filigree. Melbourne and O'-Connell Streets are the "smart" shopping districts, with equally pricey boutiques, restaurants, and hairdressing salons, along with some interesting little pubs peppered in between. Many of the commercial buildings are renovated Victorian workers' cottages.

Port Adelaide

Port Adelaide, about 25 minutes from the city center (buses leave from North Terrace), is South Australia's first heritage area. The 19th-century wharf district, an important hub for coastal steamers until World War II, has been preserved as the **South Australian Maritime Museum,** spread over seven historic sites. Main display galleries are inside the **Bond** (1854) and **Free** (1857) stores; **Weman's Building** (1864) is the old sailmaker's shop; the **Lighthouse** (1869), first erected at the entrance to the Port River, was shifted over to South Neptune Island in

1901, then, in 1986, re-sited to its present location. The **Customs House, police station,** and **courthouse** complete the museum buildings. You'll soak up lots of atmosphere just wandering the streets. Many of the facades, ranging from modest houses to ornate banks (particularly those along Lipson St.), have been restored to old port-days splendor. At **No. 1 Wharf** you can hop aboard the *Nelcebee* (1883), an old coastal ketch, or the *Yelta* (1949), the last tug to steam in the port. The museum buildings are open Tues.-Sun. 10 a.m.-5 p.m. Admission is $8. For information, phone (08) 8207-6255.

Port Dock Station Railway Museum, also on Lipson St., has one of the country's largest collections of locomotives and carriages, as well as lots of memorabilia, an audiovisual theaterette, and model railways. Go on the weekend when you can take a ride on one of two different steam trains. A railway cafeteria car houses tearooms. Open daily 10 a.m.-5 p.m. Admission is $6. For information, phone (08) 8341-1690.

Rather planes than trains? The **Historical Aviation Museum,** Ocean Steamers Rd., exhibits various aircraft as well as engines and aero-memorabilia. Open Sat.-Sun. and public holidays 10 a.m.-5 p.m. Admission is $3. For information, phone (08) 8240-1230.

If you're there on Sunday, be sure to visit **Fisherman's Wharf Market** in a huge warehouse on Queens Wharf. Junk, junque, and Asian foodstalls are among the offerings. Open Sunday 8 a.m.-5 p.m.

Got your sea legs and find the salt air flaring your nostrils? Check at the dock for available cruises.

Glenelg

This is the most popular of Adelaide's suburban beaches. Though not equal to the famed beauties on the east and west coasts, there's water (sometimes blue), sand (at low tide), shark netting (to keep out South Australia's deadly white pointer), a water slide, amusement park, pie carts, and wienie wagons. What more do you want? History? Then you've come to the right place—Glenelg is where South Australia began, the landing place of Governor Hindmarsh and the first settlers back in 1836. Over at the **Patawalonga Boat Haven,** you can climb aboard a replica of the HMS *Buffalo,* from which Captain

Hindmarsh stepped ashore and proclaimed South Australia a colony. (Unlike the original, however, this buffalo is fitted with a restaurant, bar, and small museum.) Open daily 10 a.m.-5 p.m. For information, phone (08) 8294-7000.

The **Old Gum Tree,** on MacFarlane St., marks the exact spot where the Union Jack was raised. You can witness a reenactment each year on Proclamation Day, 28 December.

A large shell display, including circa-1930s shell art and crafts, is on exhibit at **Shell Land,** 17 Mary Street. Open Tues.-Sun. 10:30 a.m.-noon and 1-4:30 p.m. For information, phone (08) 8294-5837.

The **Tourist Information Centre,** 10 Grenfell St., tel. (13) 1801, provides walking and cycling maps. Open daily, weather permitting, 9 a.m.-5 p.m.

Adelaide's only tram makes a sentimental journey from Victoria Square directly to Jetty Rd., Glenelg's main street, taking approximately 30 minutes. Cost is $2.70 one-way.

Other Options

Favorite local beaches north of Glenelg are West Beach, Henley Beach, Grange, West Lakes, Glanville, Semaphore, and Largs Bay; south of Glenelg (where the surf is decent) are Somerton, Brighton, and Seacliff. Nude bathing is allowed at Maslin Beach, about 40 km south of the city. Between Seacliff and Maslin is **Hallett Cove Conservation Reserve,** where the landscape has been fabulously molded and colored by a glacial movement some 270 million years ago.

At Grange, you can visit **Sturt's Cottage,** where the famous explorer, Captain Charles Sturt, lived between 1840 and 1853 (when he was home, that is). The house contains his family memorabilia and is furnished in that period's style. Sturt's Murray River campsite has been re-created on the grounds—in case you need some pointers. The home is open Wed.-Sun. and public holidays 1-5 p.m. Admission is $3. For information, phone (08) 8356-8185.

Fort Glanville, in Semaphore, was built in 1878 and restored in the 1980s. You can blast your ears out on the third Sunday of each month, 1-5 p.m., when reenactments of rifle drills and cannon firings (two 64-pounders!) are staged. Admission is $3. For information, phone (08) 8281-4022.

For a gentler pursuit, visit **Bower Cottages**, 200 Bower Rd., where you can watch local craftspeople and their works-in-progress. The cottages were built in 1897 to commemorate Queen Victoria's Diamond Jubilee. Open Wed.-Fri. noon-4 p.m., and tours are available. For information, phone (08) 8449-2959.

ACCOMMODATIONS

As in most large cities, accommodations in Adelaide run the spectrum from cheap and basic to ritzy and plush—except here, quite often, the two ends sit side by side and back to back. It's usually easy to find a room unless you arrive at festival time. Keep in mind that the Adelaide Festival of the Arts (three weeks in late February or early March, in even-numbered years) and the spillover from the Barossa Valley Vintage Festival (Easter week, in odd-numbered years) are peak periods. If you plan to attend any of these events, or to be in the Adelaide area at those times, you'd be well advised to book a room *way* in advance.

In the City

Words of caution: If you or your traveling companions are unaccustomed to city noises, you may not want to bed down on occasionally rowdy Hindley Street. Prices in Adelaide, as might be expected, run somewhat higher than in rural areas.

The **Metropolitan Hotel**, 46 Grote St., tel. (08) 8231-5471, near Victoria Square, has basic accommodations with shared facilities. Inexpensive. The **Austral Hotel**, 205 Rundle St., tel. (08) 8223-4660, has clean and simple pub accommodations with shared facilities. Inexpensive. At the corner of Gawler Place and Flinders St., the **Earl of Zetland Hotel**, tel. (08) 8223-5500, offers good value in pub accommodations. Rooms are air-conditioned and have private showers and toilets. The pub downstairs puts out a decent buffet spread at lunch (about $6) and a selection of more than 200 malt whiskeys. Inexpensive. The **Clarice**, 220 Hutt St., tel. (08) 8223-3560, is both a hotel and motel, near the East Terrace side of town. Rooms with shared facilities start low. It'll cost you $10-20 more to stay in the newer motel wing, with your own shower and toilet. Inexpensive.

Accommodations at **City Central Motel**, 23 Hindley St., tel. (08) 8231-4049, have private facilities and include continental breakfast. Moderate. **Directors Studio Suites**, 259 Gouger St., tel. (08) 8231-3572, offers roomy apartment-style digs close to the Central Market. Moderate. Near the Festival Centre and casino, try the **Festival Lodge Motel**, 140 North Terrace, tel. (08) 8212-7877, or **The Strathmore**, 129 North Terrace, tel. (08) 8212-6911. Both are well located and have all the modern amenities. Moderate.

The **Grosvenor Vista Hotel**, 125 North Terrace, tel. (08) 8407-8888, is another proeprty close to the Festival Centre and casino action. Deluxe rooms at this former grand dame hotel are comfortable and comforting, with TVs, room service, and good perks for the money. Expensive. **The Mansions**, 21 Pulteney St., tel. (08) 8232-0033, is a really good deal, especially if you're sharing. Spacious studios or one-bedroom apartments in this circa 1910 building feature cooking facilities as well as a rooftop spa and sauna. Premium.

If you're a big spender (or you've just hit it big at the casino), Adelaide's luxury high-rise hotels are: the **Hilton International**, 233 Victoria Square, tel. (08) 8217-0711, peacefully situated over the center city square; the super-glitzy **Hyatt Regency**, tel. (08) 8231-1234, on North Terrace, smack dab in the middle of the fun side; and **Stamford Plaza**, tel. (08) 8217-7552, a glamorous, contemporary hotel with all the expected top-notch perks, also on North Terrace. Basic doubles at either hotel cost around $200, and go way up. Luxury.

On the Outskirts

If you've got your heart set on staying in lovely North Adelaide, the moderately priced **Princes Lodge Motel**, 73 Lefevre Terrace, tel. (08) 8267-5566, on the outer edge of the suburban grid, is your best bet ($35 including continental breakfast). Inexpensive. If you like to spread out, **Greenways Apartments**, 45 King William Rd., tel. (08) 8267-5903, offers one-, two-, and three-bedroom flats with cooking facilities and parking. Moderate. The more deluxe **Adelaide Meridien**, 21 Melbourne St., tel. (08) 8267-3033, sits on North Adelaide's prestigious shopping street. Expensive. **Adelaide Heritage Apartments**, tel. (08) 8272-1355, can book you in a lovely heritage apartment or cottage—all fully equipped, many with fireplaces or spas. Rates are expensive if you're alone, a great deal if you're with one or more companions. Inexpensive-Expensive.

If you're coming in from the southeast, Glen Osmond Rd., which heads straight into the city, is Adelaide's motel row. Some good choices include **Princes Highway Motel,** 199 Glen Osmond Rd., Frewville, tel. (08) 8379-9253; **Fullarton Motor Lodge,** 284 Glen Osmond Rd., Fullarton, tel. (08) 8379-9797; **Sands Motel,** 198 Glen Osmond Rd., Fullarton, tel. (08) 8379-0066; and **Powell's Court,** 2 Glen Osmond Rd., Parkside, tel. (08) 8271-7033. (Don't be confused—the suburbs change names frequently along this thoroughfare.) All of these motels are in the moderate range. Powell's Court has cooking facilities. Just two km from the city, **Parkway Motor Inn,** 204 Greenhill Rd., Eastwood, tel. (08) 8271-0451, is well located, has a pool and restaurant, and costs slightly more than the others. Moderate-Expensive.

Glenelg and the Beaches

Glenelg has lots of places to stay, most at reasonable prices—particularly during off seasons, when many of the holiday flats offer attractive weekly rates. The tourist office on the foreshore can provide a list of available flats.

St. Vincent Hotel, 28 Jetty Rd., tel. (08) 8294-4377, a cozy, locally popular establishment, has rates of $35-50 per room, which includes continental breakfast. Inexpensive. **Colley Motel Apartments,** 22 Colley Terrace, tel. (08) 8295-7535, and the **South Pacific,** 16 Colley Terrace, tel. (08) 8194-1352, both opposite Colley Reserve, are good midrange choices for holiday flats. Moderate. Priced slightly higher, but still excellent value for two or more traveling together, are the holiday flats at **Seawall Apartments,** South Esplanade, tel. (08) 8295-1197. Moderate-Expensive. The big ticket in town is the beachfront **Stamford Grand Adelaide,** Moseley Square, tel. (1800) 88-2777, a high-priced high-rise with highfalutin frills. Luxury.

In Glenelg South, the **Bay Hotel Motel,** 58 Broadway, tel. (08) 8294-4244, not far from the beach, has rooms with color television and private facilities, as does the **Norfolk Motor Inn,** 71 Broadway, tel. (08) 8295-6354. Prices at both are moderate.

West Beach and Henley Beach are also packed with holiday flats. In West Beach, try **Cootura Holiday Flats,** 8 West Beach Rd., tel. (08) 8271-2415, **Marineland Village Holiday Villas,** Military Rd., tel. (08) 8353-2655, or **Tuileries Holiday Apartments,** 13 Military Rd., tel. (08) 8353-3874. Inexpensive-Moderate. A best bet in Henley Beach is **Meleden Villa,** 268 Seaview Rd., tel. (08) 8235-0577, a seafront bed and breakfast with a lot of atmosphere. Inexpensive-Moderate. Down the way, **Allenby Court,** 405 Seaview Rd., tel. (08) 8235-0445, offers fully equipped, two-bedroom holiday flats. Moderate. Keep in mind that holiday flats are moderately priced but often require minimum stays of two or more nights. Farther north in Semaphore, the **Semaphore Hotel,** 17 Semaphore Rd., tel. (08) 8449-4662, is your *very* basic pub with shared facilities. Inexpensive. A better choice is a few doors away at the **Federal Hotel,** 25 Semaphore Rd., tel. (08) 8449-6866. Moderate.

Hostels

Adelaide's hostels, like everything else in the city, are centrally located and easy to find. Three of the hostels are in the South Terrace district and can be reached by foot or by bus from Pulteney Street). The 50-bed **Adelaide YHA Hostel,** 290 Gilles St., tel. (08) 8223-6007, has a friendly atmosphere and helpful staff. The office is closed Mon.-Sat. 10 a.m.-1 p.m., Sunday 10 a.m.-5:30 p.m., but hostel guests have 24-hour access. Dorm beds run $16. The 40-bed **Adelaide Backpackers Hostel,** nearby at 263 Gilles St., tel. (08) 8223-5680, is the oldest hostel in the city, with a homey atmosphere and $12 dorm beds. Both of these hostels have kitchen facilities and lounges where you can meet up with other travelers.

Another hostel, closer to the center of town, is **Adelaide Backpackers Inn,** 112 Carrington St., tel. (08) 8223-6635. This former pub offers both dorm beds ($15) and double rooms ($40), in either the main building or the newer annex. **Adelaide Rucksackers,** next door at 257 Gilles St., tel. (08) 8232-0823, is a renovated Victorian with $12 dorm beds that caters primarily to cyclists.

Backpack Australia Hostel, 128 Grote St., tel. (08) 8231-0639—known as "party central"—makes up for the small dorms with friendly atmosphere, a bar, and inexpensive meals. **East**

Park Lodge, 341 Angas St., tel. (08) 8223-1228, is a private family-run hostel, also near the city center. Dorm beds ($13), double rooms, and some meals are available.

Both men and women are welcome at the **YMCA,** 76 Flinders St., tel. (08) 8223-6007, conveniently near Victoria Square and the central bus station. Dorm beds run $12, singles are $22, doubles are priced at $34. Gym access is available for another few bucks.

In Glenelg, **Glenelg Backpackers Resort,** 7 Mosely St., tel. (1800) 066-422, offers homestyle accommodations in a heritage building with kitchen, laundry, and even car rental facilities. Dorm beds ($14) and some single and double ($22-34) rooms are available.

Homestays

The **South Australian Tourism Commission Travel Centre,** 1 King William St., Adelaide 5000, tel. (08) 8303-2070, will provide you with a list of homestay properties, which include city homes, historic cottages, health resorts, villas, and farms. Prices range from budget to luxury.

Camping

South Australia has a large number of camping facilities, though some accept only caravans, not tents. Tent sites run about $10, $5 more for powered sites, caravans for two range $25-40. Most provide a number of powered and unpowered sites, as well as on-site cabins and vans. The state's caravan parks are generally of a very high standard—clean and comfortable. Many have swimming pools, game rooms, and tennis courts. The South Australian Tourism Commission Travel Centre can provide maps and brochures and assist with bookings. The following is a sampling of some of the more convenient and interesting locales.

Adelaide Caravan Park, Bruny St., Hackney, tel. (08) 8363-1566, is the nearest park to city attractions. **Brownhill Creek Caravan Park,** Brownhill Creek Rd., Mitcham, tel. (08) 8271-4824, set in 120 acres of bushland, is only seven km from Adelaide. **Belair Caravan Park,** Belair National Park, tel. (08) 8278-3540, is just 11 km from the city center.

West Beach Caravan Park, Military Rd., West Beach, tel. (08) 8356-7654, sits on a good swimming beach and is surrounded by playing fields and golf courses. And, for those of you who want to be near Fort Glanville's big cannons, there's **Adelaide Beachfront Van and Tourist Park,** 349 Military Rd., Semaphore Park, tel. (08) 8449-7726, also on the beach.

FOOD

Adelaide does not have the "foodie" scene so prevalent in its sister capital cities, Melbourne and Sydney. Though there are some "nouvelle" gourmet establishments sprinkled about, the emphasis here is on casual, outdoor dining—a terrace restaurant along the river, a picnic in the park, takeaways to eat in one of the city squares. Many of the restaurants are licensed, no doubt to keep those famous South Australian wines flowing. Adventurous eaters will often find dishes made from kangaroo meat on the menu—so if you want to try it in some form other than an old Jumbo Jack, keep your eyes peeled. If you prefer to pass on the braised 'roo, you'll find plenty of fresh fish and seafood. Especially commendable are King George whiting and the local crayfish (sometimes called lobster).

Most of the ethnic restaurants are on Gouger Street, also home to the Central Market and Chinatown. Noisier dining can be had on Hindley Street, lodged above, between, or beneath the strip joints and sex shops and their accompanying sounds. Rundle Street East is where the fashionable avant garde dine indoors or out in chichi, trendy, and tony establishments; the fashionable old guard usually hang out on North Adelaide's Melbourne Street. Outdoor cafés on Rundle Mall can fix you up with a caffeine buzz so you don't drop before you shop. Many Adelaide restaurants are closed on Sunday, so plan accordingly.

Center City

The **Adelaide University** campus has two informal eating places that are popular with students, faculty, and travel types. Both are in the Union Building. The cafeteria, on the ground floor, serves all the typical "uni" fare—sandwiches, apples, weak coffee, a few miscellaneous hot meals ($2-6). The **Bistro** offers better quality at higher prices, about $5-9 for main dishes. The cafeteria has the customary casual class-in class-out hours; the Bistro is open Mon.-

Fri. noon-2:30 p.m. for lunch, 5:30-8:30 p.m. for dinner.

Marcellina Pizza Bar, 273 Hindley St., serves delicious pizzas ($6-12) all night, every night except Sunday. **Al Frescoes,** 260 Rundle St., is a superb late-night café, usually packed with Italians eating the Italian food—always a good sign. Pastas range $7-14. Ciao down on inexpensive designer pizzas ($8-12) and foccacia ($5-7) at **Scoozi,** 272 Rundle Street.

Vegetarian travelers will be happy at **Vego and Lovin' It,** 240 Rundle St., an inexpensive café with freshly prepared vegan and vegetarian dishes ($7-10). The veg set mainstay **Govinda's Hare Krishna Food for Life,** 79 Hindley St., puts out its renowned buffet for lunch Mon.-Fri. ($4-6).

Noodles, 119 Gouger St., tel. (08) 8231-8177, offers oodles of the stuff. Choose your shape, color, size, and sauce, and you'll be presented with a generous heap at reasonable cost ($6-12).

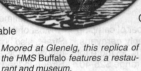

Moored at Glenelg, this replica of the HMS Buffalo *features a restaurant and museum.*

The **Red Ochre Grill,** 129 Gouger St., tel. (08) 8212-7266, is the buzz of the town with its unlikely, but nonetheless successful, marriage of typical Outback bush tucker with anything-but-typical gourmet flair. Diners can eat in the swank restaurant, café, or outdoors under the vines. Main courses run $13-18. Open Mon.-Fri. lunch, Mon.-Sat. dinner; the café is open daily.

Jasmin Indian Restaurant, 31 Hindmarsh Square, tel. (08) 8223-7837, has terrific North Indian dishes for about $14. Specialties include tandoori oven dishes and biryani rice plates. Open Tues.-Fri. lunch, Tues.-Sat. dinner.

Fifties-style **Ruby's Café,** 255B Rundle St., tel. (08) 8224-0365, with changing art exhibitions and a cocktail bar, is famed for its all-day Sunday breakfasts ($5-9). Chicken dishes and kangaroo fillet will set you back $12-14.

The popular and casual **Boltz Café,** 286 Rundle St., tel. (08) 8232-5234, offers everything the youngish trendsetters could ask for: pseudo-industrial styling, a menu to please most ap-

petites (pizzas, focaccias, curries, salads—in the $10-12 range), live music, and late hours. Open Mon.-Sat. lunch and dinner.

Nediz Tu, 170 Hutt St., tel. (08) 8223-2618, creates exotic and sublime Vietnamese delicacies, in a purifying white room filled with glorious floral arrangements—a sacred environment for the almost prayer-inducing cuisine. Dinner is approximately $40 pp. Open Tues.-Sat. dinner.

For fabulous—and fabulously expensive—hotel restaurants, try **The Grange Restaurant and Brasserie,** at the Hilton International, tel. (08) 8217-0711, or **Blake's,** at the Hyatt Regency, tel. (08) 8238-2381. Prepare to fork out $18-30 for entrees at either.

Don't forget about the cafés at the historic sites on **North Terrace.** You can get snacks and simple meals at the Botanic Gardens, Art Gallery, State History Centre, and the Lion Arts Centre.

North Adelaide

The **Oxford,** 101 O'Connell St., tel. (08) 8267-2652, has been running strong since the 1980s and continues to win awards. The fetching cuisine is created from the best and freshest ingredients. The service is dependable, the wine list is outstanding, and the meals are surprisingly inexpensive ($12-18). Open Tues.-Sat. lunch and dinner.

The **Magic Flute,** 109 Melbourne St., tel. (08) 8267-3172, is another old-time bastion of elegance, serving divine continental fare in a lovely room with enclosed courtyard. If you can't afford the main dining room ($28-36), try the attached café, which has a changing blackboard menu with entrees at about half the price. Open Mon.-Sat. dinner; café is open Mon.-Fri. lunch and Mon.-Sat. dinner.

The French Splurge

Head directly for **Chloe's,** 36 College Rd., Kent Town, tel. (08) 8363-1001, composed of several grandly furnished dining rooms within a stunning restored villa. Classic French food and a superb wine list (choose from a 20,000-bottle cellar!) are standout features here. Without wine, you can expect to pay about $50 pp. Book ahead for Mon.-Fri. lunch, Mon.-Sat. dinner.

Pub Meals

You can get a plain, simple **counter meal** at pubs throughout the city. Usually there's a blackboard outside the door that states meal times (around noon-2 p.m.) and prices (as low as $3-7). Menus are often bland and occasionally heavy on the grease. Typical choices are fish and chips, chicken schnitzel, and gravy-covered beef and lamb. Some Adelaide pubs now offer more "nouvelle" and international cuisine (which also boosts the prices). Some best bets include: **Old Queen's Arms,** 88 Wright St.; **Hotel Franklin,** 92 Franklin St.; **Austral Hotel,** 205 Rundle St.; and the **Griffin's Head Tavern,** Hindmarsh Square, at Grenfell Street.

Students and grungers tend to adore **Exeter Hotel,** 246 Rundle St., for both its good-value prices and wine list.

Food Halls and Markets

Pick and choose from some of the city's international food centers, where different eateries are positioned around one central dining area. You can mix and match Indian, Thai, Chinese, Australian, and other cuisines for about $5 (more if you get carried away). Centrally positioned food centers are: **Hawker's Corner,** corner of Wright St. and West Terrace; **City Cross Arcade,** off Grenfell St.; **Gallerie of International Cuisine,** Renaissance Tower Center, Rundle Mall; **The Food Affair,** basement level, Gallerie Shopping Centre (between North Terrace and Gawler Place); and the **International Food Plaza,** on Moonta St. next to the Central Market. Most of the foodstalls stay open during shopping hours.

The **Central Market,** between Grote and Gouger Streets (near Victoria Square), is a great spot to put together a meal or a picnic. The many colorful stalls in this historic old building feature fresh fruit and vegetables, meat, bread, cheese, and a variety of other foods. Or you can get a ready-made cheap (under $6) meal at **Malacca Corner,** a restaurant housed inside the market. Market hours are Tuesday 7 a.m.-5:30 p.m.,

Thursday 11 a.m.-5:30 p.m., Friday 7 a.m.-9 p.m., and Saturday 7 a.m.-5 p.m.

East End Market, on Rundle St., redeveloped at the site of the original old market, features a huge central food court with stalls selling a delectable array of Asian and continental cuisine, and seating for 200. Fruit, vegetables, meats, cakes, nuts, breads, and other tasty treats are also on sale. Hours are Fri.-Sun. 9 a.m.-6 p.m.

Late-Night Eats

It's slim pickings for late-night refrigerator raiders. If you're desperate you might try the **pie carts,** which set up outside the post office on Franklin Street and at The Parade, Norwood, every night from 6 p.m. until the wee hours. They sell that infamous Adelaide gastronomic *specialité,* the "floater"—an Australian meat pie floating (sort of like a rock) inside a bowl of thick green pea soup, topped with tomato sauce (catsup).

Maybe you'd prefer some harmless pancakes. The **Pancake Kitchen,** 13 Gilbert Place, tel. (08) 8211-7912, on the South Terrace side of the city grid, is open every day, 24 hours ($4-9 for a stack). Also, don't forget **Marcellina Pizza Bar** on Hindley St. (see above). And, if you're dressed "correctly," there's always the casino.

For late-night food you're probably best off tucking some tucker in your backpack, satchel, or motel fridge to tide you over until morning.

ENTERTAINMENT AND EVENTS

Adelaide has all the usual amusements of a city its size—cinemas, art galleries, discos, pubs and clubs with live music, theater and concert performances, plus a couple of extras—the hustle-bustle casino and a really special festival of the arts. Newspapers, particularly Thursday's *Advertiser,* provide up-to-date information. Another good source is the monthly *Adelaide Review,* with lots of reviews and announcements of literary, arts, and theatrical happenings. *Rip It Up,* a free local zine, can be picked up at pubs, clubs, and record stores. For info on the gay scene, consult *Gay Times,* available at record stores, bookshops, and the Adelaide University Union on North Terrace. You can also call in at the South Australian Tourism Commission Travel Centre, on King William St., tel. (08) 8303-

2070, for current entertainment listings and booking assistance. And don't forget about Adelaide University where, during school sessions, there's always something on.

Cinemas

If you're looking for commercial cinema (with releases that are ordinarily three to six months behind the U.S.), the four-, six- and eight-plexes are scattered around Hindmarsh Square, Hindley St., and Rundle Mall, and on Jetty Rd. in Glenelg. And now Oaklands Park, in suburban Adelaide, is home to a 5,500-seat 30-plex in Marion Shopping Centre. For artier films, try: **The Capri,** 141 Goodwood Rd., Goodwood, tel. (08) 8272-1177; **The Track,** 375 Greenhill Rd., Toorak Gardens, tel. (08) 8332-8020; **The Palace,** Rundle St., tel. (08) 8232-3434; **NOVA,** Rundle St., tel. (08) 8223-6333; **The Piccadilly,** O'Connell St., North Adelaide, tel. (08) 8267-1500; or Adelaide University. Tuesday is the usual discount night for Adelaide cinemas.

Or curl up in front of the telly and watch some really terrific classic, contemporary, and cutting-edge films on SBS. Check the newspaper for times.

Pubs and Clubs

You can do an easy—albeit tacky—pub crawl along **Hindley Street,** between King William Street and West Terrace.

City pubs that regularly feature music are: the **Austral Hotel,** 205 Rundle St.; the **Earl of Aberdeen,** Hindmarsh Square; **Seven Stars Hotel,** 187 Angas St., promising "no renovations, no bullshit"; and the **Exeter Hotel,** 246 Rundle Street. Both the Austral and Exeter hotels are popular with students and the artsy crowd.

A few of Adelaide's trendiest upmarket musical pubs are **Bull and Bear Ale House,** 91 King William St.; **The Oxford,** 101 O'Connell St., North Adelaide; and, on Melbourne St., also in North Adelaide, the **Old Lion Hotel.** Still trendier are the bars and discos housed inside the **Hilton International, Stamford Plaza,** and **Hyatt Regency** hotels.

You'll pay a cover charge of $4-8 to hear music in the city pubs; about $12-16 at the big hotels.

Too-hip-to-be-believed (mainly) dance clubs are: **Cargo Club,** 213 Hindley St.; **Cue,** 274 Rundle St.; and **The Synagogue,** Synagogue Place, off Rundle Street.

The young, energetic Lycra set sizzles over at **Heaven II,** 7 West Terrace, in New Market Hotel, and **The Planet,** 77 Pine St., while serious partiers hang at **The Big Ticket,** 128 Hindley Street.

Edinburgh Castle, 233 Currie St., is a pub-like spot catering mainly to gay males, while **Bean's Bar,** 258a Hindley St., welcomes a mixture of gay men and lesbians. Also popular is the perennial **Mars Bar,** 120 Gouger St., with weekend drag shows.

Serious **winetasters** should not miss the stylish **Universal Wine Bar,** 285 Rundle St., which offers not only an extensive wine list (including many wines-by-the-glass), but winetastings and workshops. **Mecca,** 290 Rundle St., also draws tasters to its bar and bistro.

Beer lovers can sample house-made brews at **Earl of Aberdeen,** Hindmarsh Square; **Old Lion Hotel,** North Adelaide; and **Port Dock Brewery Hotel,** Port Adelaide.

Theater and Concerts

The **Adelaide Festival Centre** is the city's major venue for theater, stage musicals, opera, concerts, and most other performing arts. For information, phone the box office at (08) 8216-8600, Mon.-Sat. 9:30 a.m.-8:30 p.m.; for credit card bookings, phone BASS at (13) 1246 in South Australia. Free and casual jazz as well as classical and chamber music performances are often held on Sunday afternoon in the Festival Theatre Foyer.

The **Adelaide Symphony Orchestra** and **Australian Chamber Orchestra** perform at the old Adelaide Town Hall on King William Street. For information, phone BASS at the numbers above. BASS also handles bookings for many other events, including Baroque and Renaissance music concerts at St. Peter's Cathedral.

Adelaide has a very active performance and contemporary theater scene. If you don't find what you're looking for at the Festival Centre, check with the Lion Arts Centre, tel. (08) 8231-7760. Other good tries are **Red Shed Theatre Company,** 255 Angas St., tel. (08) 8232-2075, and **Vitalstatistix Theatre Company,** Nile St., Port Adelaide, tel. (08) 8447-6211, which showcase experimental works. **Little Theatre,** Victoria Drive, University of Adelaide, tel. (08) 8303-5401, is where you'll see student productions, while **Her Majesty's Theatre,** 58 Grote St., tel. (08) 8216-8600, is the venue for big names and traditional works.

Events

The **Adelaide Festival of the Arts,** the oldest in Australia and one of the best in the world, attracts top international talent. During the first three weeks of March, in even-numbered years, the festival brews such mixes as Shakespearean tragedies with avant-garde performances, Beethoven symphonies with fusion jazz, Placido Domingo with Mick Jagger.

The **Fringe Festival,** which is often even more exciting, coincides with the main event. During festival time, the city is agog over theater, dance, music, and art. Writers' Week attracts a wide array of poets, novelists, playwrights, and journalists to swig and tipple as they excerpt and expound. Make bookings for the festival well in advance by writing Adelaide Festival, G.P.O. Box 1269, Adelaide, SA 5001, tel. (08) 8226-8111.

Late February or early March, in odd-numbered years, Adelaide hosts the **WOMAD** (World Music and Dance) festival, a three-day extravaganza of local, national, and international performers. Stages are erected in the Botanic Gardens, drawing about 60,000 world music-loving fans.

For information on the **Barossa Classic Gourmet Festival,** contact Barossa Wine and Tourism Association, tel. (08) 8563-0600. For information on the **McLaren Vale Bushing Festival,** phone (08) 8323-9455.

SPORTS AND RECREATION

Locals take advantage of the mild weather, gorgeous parklands, and nearby beaches, and spend a lot of time outdoors—if not participating in something themselves, then watching others who are. The parklands, particularly, are full of recreational areas. Meander too long in one grassy spot and you'll probably be commandeered into a game of soccer or cricket. Walkers and joggers will take happily to the many park pathways with their peaceful vistas and gentle climbs. Those of you who are more interested in a hike or bushwalk,

see below. For useful info on almost every activity, contact the **Department of Sport and Recreation,** 11 Hindmarsh Square, tel. (08) 8226-7301.

Cycling

Cycling about this nitty-gritty city, and the nine tracks that surround the parklands, is smooth and trouble-free. Rent bikes from **Super Elliotts,** 200 Rundle St., tel. (08) 8223-3969; **Ace Cycle Tours and Hire,** 101 Hindley St., tel. (08) 8212-7800; or **Pulteney Street Cycles,** 309 Pulteney St., tel. (08) 8223-6380. All are open Mon.-Saturday. In Glenelg, contact **Holdfast Cycles,** 768 Anzac Hwy., tel. (08) 8294-4537.

Scuba Diving

Diving is best off Kangaroo Island and the Yorke Peninsula, but boat diving isn't bad at Port Noarlunga Reef Marine Reserve, 18 km south of Adelaide, or Aldinga, 43 km south. You'll need proof of diving experience before you can rent equipment. For information, contact the **Scuba Divers Federation of South Australia,** 1 Sturt St., tel. (13) 0666.

Swimming

Swim along the beaches of Gulf St. Vincent, or dip into the **Adelaide Aquatic Centre,** Jeffcott Rd., North Adelaide, tel. (08) 8344-4411, in the north parklands. The pool's open daily 9 a.m.-5 p.m. A gym, sauna, and spa are also available.

Tennis

Both grass and hard courts, as well as tennis rackets, are available for rent at **Memorial Drive Tennis Club,** War Memorial Dr., North Adelaide, tel. (08) 8231-4371, and **Roseland's Tennis World,** 323 Sturt Rd., Bedford Park, tel. (08) 8276-9229. **Adelaide City Courts** are in the parklands.

Golf

Guests are welcome to tee off at **City of Adelaide Golf Links,** War Memorial Dr., North Adelaide, tel. (08) 8261-2171. Equipment is available for hire.

Sailing

Adelaide's shoreline is fine for sailing. All the city beaches have yacht clubs, and most welcome casual visitors.

Skating and Skiing

You can ice skate 'round the rink, on either a beginner- or Olympic-size arena, or ski down the 12-meter-high indoor slope (covered in Permasnow, a real snow-like Australian product), at **Mt. Thebarton Ice Arena,** 23 East Terrace, Thebarton, tel. (08) 8352-7977. Cost is $10, including skate hire, and both ski and skating instruction is available. Hours are Mon.-Fri. 9:30 a.m.-4:30 p.m., Wednesday and Friday 7-11 p.m., Sat.-Sun. 12:30-4 p.m. and 7:30-11 p.m.

Spectator Sports

Adelaide Oval, north of the city on King William St., is the main location for **cricket** matches, the country's favorite summer sport. International and interstate test matches are played Oct.-March. For information, phone (08) 8231-3759.

The big winter sport, **Australian rules football,** is played—usually on weekends—at both Adelaide Oval and Football Park, West Lakes. Soccer, rugby, and rugby union are also played during the April-Sept. season. For information, phone (08) 8268-2088.

You can play the ponies or the pups year-round. The **South Australian Jockey Club** conducts meetings at Victoria Park, Morphettville, and Cheltenham; **Adelaide Greyhound Racing Club** is the venue for those flying dogs. Check local newspapers for meeting times.

SHOPPING

It's doubtful you'll ever "shop 'til you drop" in this city, but you will find the basics, maybe a few bargains, and possibly some baubles. **Warning:** Be especially careful when purchasing opals—take your time and shop around for reputable dealers. City shopping hours are generally Mon.-Fri. 8:30 a.m.-5:30 p.m., Saturday 8:30 a.m.-noon, late-night trading Friday until 9 p.m. (late-night trading is held on Thursday in the suburbs). A small smattering of shops, mostly in the city center, are open on Sunday.

Rundle Mall, with its branches of arcades, offers standard mall-isms—department stores, specialty shops that are really nothing special, a handful of commercial art galleries, a cinema complex, photo developers, jewelry stores, sandwich shops, a few buskers, and flower carts. **Run-**

dle Street East is far more exciting, with retro shops, alternative clothing and jewelry, New Age trinkets and nose rings, and black, black, and more black. For bookstores, see below.

For more chic and boutiques, North Adelaide's exclusive **Melbourne Street** will fill your Louis Vuitton luggage until you make it back to Rodeo Drive.

Markets

For far less sterile shopping, **Central Market** has colorful stalls stocked with food, produce, flowers, and bazaar items. The **East End Market** has the same plus bizarre items. **Orange Lane Market,** off The Parade in nearby Norwood, is open Sat.-Sun. for seekers of imported fabrics, retro clothing, antiques, and full-body massages.

The **Brickworks Market,** 36 South Rd., Torrensville, is about three km from the city center. Hundreds of stalls sell everything from food and clothing to arts and crafts to junk and junque. Take the bus from Grenfell and Currie Streets in the city. The market is open Fri.-Sun. 9 a.m.-5 p.m.

Good markets to hit during cold or rainy weather are **Fisherman's Wharf Market,** Port Adelaide (open Sunday 8 a.m.-5 p.m.), and **Junction Market,** corner of Grand Junction and Prospect Rd. (open Fri.-Sun. 9 a.m.-5 p.m.). Both are housed indoors and feature a broad range of market wares.

Arts and Crafts

Local craftspeople create and sell jewelry, fabric, leather, glass, wood, ceramics, and other handmade wares at the **Jam Factory Craft and Design Centre,** 19 Morphett St., tel. (08) 8410-0727. The gallery features monthly changing exhibitions. Open Mon.-Fri. 9 a.m.-5:30 p.m., Sat.-Sun. and public holidays 10 a.m.-5 p.m.

Contemporary and traditional Aboriginal arts and crafts are sold and displayed at **Tandanya Aboriginal Cultural Institute,** 253 Grenfell St., tel. (08) 8223-2467. The institute, representing 50 traditional Aboriginal groups of South Australia, also sponsors performing and visual arts and houses a museum. Items for sale include Aboriginal artifacts, T-shirts, backpacks, and books. Open daily 10 a.m.-5 p.m. Admission is $4. **Adella Gallery,** 12 Hindley St., tel. (08) 8212-2171, features a good range of authentic Aboriginal arts and crafts. Open Mon.-Fri. 10 a.m.-5 p.m.

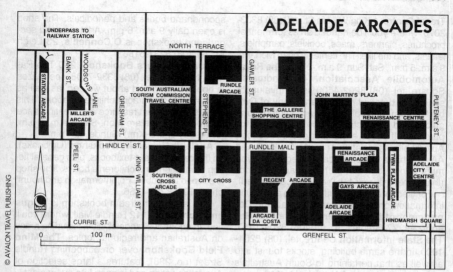

ADELAIDE ARCADES

UNDERPASS TO RAILWAY STATION

NORTH TERRACE

STATION ARCADE

BANK ST.

WOODSON'S LANE

MILLER'S ARCADE

GRESHAM ST.

SOUTH AUSTRALIAN TOURISM COMMISSION TRAVEL CENTRE

STEPHENS PL.

RUNDLE ARCADE

GAWLER ST.

THE GALLERIE SHOPPING CENTRE

JOHN MARTIN'S PLAZA

RENAISSANCE CENTRE

PULTENEY ST.

HINDLEY ST.

PEEL ST.

KING WILLIAM ST.

SOUTHERN CROSS ARCADE

CITY CROSS

RUNDLE MALL

REGENT ARCADE

RENAISSANCE ARCADE

GAYS ARCADE

ADELAIDE ARCADE

TWIN PLAZA ARCADE

ADELAIDE CITY CENTRE

CURRIE ST.

ARCADE DA COSTA

GRENFELL ST.

HINDMARSH SQUARE

0   100 m

© AVALON TRAVEL PUBLISHING

See a broad spectrum of postmodern exhibitions by local and interstate artists, changing every few weeks, at **Union Gallery,** Level 6, Union Building, Adelaide University, tel. (08) 8228-5013. Open Mon.-Fri. 10 a.m.-5 p.m.

Chic rustic kitchen accessories made from recycled wood and environmentally friendly Kangaroo Island swamp gums can be purchased at **D.Lux Homewares,** 238A Rundle St., while **Bimbo Productions,** a few doors away at 279 Rundle St., offers pickings for metal- and wire-lovers.

SERVICES

King William Street is lined with **banks** and other financial institutions. Business hours are Mon.-Thurs. 9:30 a.m.-4 p.m., Friday 9:30 a.m.-5 p.m. When changing traveler's checks, be sure to carry your passport or driver's license for identification. Many city and suburban banking facilities have automatic teller machines that accept international credit cards.

Change money at Thomas Cook, 45 Grenfell St., tel. (08) 8212-3354, or American Express, 13 Grenfell St., tel. (08) 8212-7099.

The **general post office,** 141 King William St., provides the full range of postal services,

including a philatelic bureau. Another convenient branch of Australia Post is in Rundle Mall. Hours of operation are Mon.-Fri. 8 a.m.-6 p.m., Saturday 8:30 a.m.-noon.

Just about every hotel, motel, and hostel provides **laundry facilities** for guests. Launderettes are dispersed around the city and suburbs. **Adelaide Launderette,** 152 Sturt St., is open daily 7 a.m.-8 p.m., and provides wash and iron service Mon.-Sat. 8 a.m.-5 p.m.

Stow your bags at any of the hostels, the YMCA residence hotel, the railway station, or central bus station—but not at the airport. The small fee will vary according to how many bags you stash and how long they're left.

Fruit pickers should have luck finding **casual labor** (during harvest time). Check at wineries in the Barossa and Clare Valleys, as well as the Southern Vales, Riverland, and Coonawarra. The Murray River fruit-bearing districts of Berri, Renmark, and Loxton may also yield seasonal work.

INFORMATION

Bring an extra suitcase for all the literature you're sure to accumulate. Your first stop should be at the **South Australian Tourism Commission**

Travel Centre, 1 King William St., tel. (08) 8303-2070, where you'll be handed an assortment of brochures, planners, maps, booklets, pamphlets, leaflets, and the like. The center is open Mon.-Fri. 9 a.m.-5 p.m., Sat.-Sun. 9 a.m.-2 p.m. The Royal Automobile Association, 41 Hindmarsh Square, tel. (08) 8202-4500, is an invaluable source for detailed maps (particularly of Outback areas). They also have accommodations guides and a selection of books available for purchase. If you're a member of the American Automobile Association or the U.K.'s RAC and AA, you have full reciprocal privileges, but you must show your membership card as proof (that's what they say, but I've never been asked).

For literature, maps, and camping and hiking information on specific parks, contact the Department of Environment and Natural Resources, 77 Grenfell St., tel. (08) 8204-1910. The State Information Centre, tel. (08) 8204-1900, in the same building, stocks tourist info as well as that pertaining to South Australia's government, state and Aboriginal history.

The Disability Information Centre, 195 Gilles St., tel. (08) 8223-7522, is open Mon-Fri. 9 a.m.-5 p.m.

Adelaide's YHA offices are at at 38 Sturt St., tel. (08) 8231-5583, and 290 Gilles St., tel. (08) 8223-6007. Hours are Mon.-Fri. 9:30 a.m.-5:30 p.m.

Emergencies

Dial 000 to contact the police, fire brigade, or ambulance. Royal Adelaide Hospital, corner North Terrace and Frome Rd., tel. (08) 8223-0230, is a full-service facility with 24-hour emergency services. Also on Frome Rd. is Adelaide Dental Hospital, tel. (08) 8222-8222. Burden Chemist, 62 King William St., tel. (08) 8231-4701, is open daily 8 a.m.-midnight for your pharmaceutical needs.

Bookstores, Newspapers, and Other Sources

Read all about it on North Terrace. The Mortlock Library and bookshops in the museums, historic sights, and Adelaide University can provide inquiring minds with all they want to know about South Australian history, anthropology, archaeology, art, botany, and politics past and present.

The Readers Bookshop, 88 Pirie St., tel. (08) 8223-7355, is crammed with all subjects of secondhand books and periodicals. The shop is open daily 9 a.m.-6 p.m. Another good secondhand bookshop is O'Connell's, 23 Leigh St., tel. (08) 8231-5188.

Murphy Sisters Bookshop, 240 The Parade, Norwood, tel. (08) 8332-7508, specializes in books by, for, and about women, as well as nonsexist and nonracist children's books. This shop is an excellent resource and meeting place for women. Hours are Mon.-Sat. 9 a.m.-5 p.m. (Thursday until 8 p.m.), Sunday 1-4 p.m.

Adelaide University Bookshop (Unibooks), on the campus, sells textbooks, plus general fiction, nonfiction, and children's books. The shop is open to the public. For information and hours, phone (08) 8223-4366.

The large mainstream bookshop is Angus and Robertson, 112 Rundle Mall, where you'll find an enormous range of titles, including many on Australian and regional topics. The Mind Field Bookshop, over on happening Rundle Street (no. 238), features a large selection of Australian fiction and is open late every night.

Psychic sciences, astrology, women's spirituality, health, and healing are some of the selections at Quantum, The Metaphysical Bookshop, 113 Melbourne St., North Adelaide. You can also pick up quartz crystals and relaxation music. Hours are Mon.-Fri. 9 a.m.-6 p.m. (Thursday until 9 p.m.), Saturday 9:30 a.m.-5 p.m., Sunday 1-5 p.m.

If your map collection is still lacking, try The Map Shop, 16a Peel St., tel. (08) 8231-2033, or Mapland, 282 Richmond St., Netley, tel. (08) 8226-4946.

The coffee-and-newspaper crowd sips lattes over the morning Advertiser or Australian.

The Wilderness Society is an Australian conservation group dedicated to addressing important and timely issues, such as preservation of rainforests, harmful effects of logging, and other environmental concerns. They also operate wilderness shops in each state, which sell books, T-shirts, badges, and other "collectibles." In Adelaide, you'll find the office at 116 Grote St., tel. (08) 8231-6586, and the shop at Victoria Square Arcade, tel. (08) 8231-0625. The Conservation Council of South Australia, 120 Wakefield St., tel. (08) 8232-2566, is another clearinghouse for eco-info and has a bookshop, notice board, and library.

For **women,** the Murphy Sisters Bookshop (see above) is an excellent contact spot. Other resources include: the **Women's Information Switchboard,** tel. (08) 8223-1244; the **Women's Studies Resource Centre,** 64 Pennington Terrace, North Adelaide, tel. (08) 8267-3633; and **Dale Street Women's Health Centre,** Dale St., North Adelaide, tel. (08) 8447-7033.

South Australia, being the first state to legalize homosexuality, offers a range of hassle-free services. Pick up a copy of the *Gay Times* for news on current events, resources, and the club scene. **Gayline,** tel. (08) 8362-3223, can also provide help and information.

TRANSPORTATION

Getting There by Air
Qantas, 144 North Terrace, tel. (08) 8208-8877 or (13) 1313, is the only international airline that flies into Adelaide from North America (and that's with a change of aircraft in Sydney). Other internatianal carriers include **Singapore Airlines, Japan Airlines,** and **British Airways.**

The two major domestic airlines, **Ansett,** 205 Greenhill Rd., Eastwood, tel. (08) 8208-4101 or (13) 1300, and **Qantas,** 144 North Terrace, tel. (08) 8208-8877 or (13) 1313, provide daily direct and connecting service from all major Australian cities. Sample fares to or from Adelaide are: Melbourne, $175; Sydney, $260; Brisbane, $320; Perth, $380; Alice Springs, $285; Darwin, $365. These prices reflect the 40% discount accorded international ticket holders, but you can get about the same fare by going standby. There are other passes and discounts available depending upon your route and length of time traveling. **STA Travel,** 235 Rundle St., tel. (08) 8223-2426 or (13) 1776, is your best source for info and bargains.

Getting There by Train
Keswick Railway Terminal, on Railway Terrace, near the city center, is the arrival and departure point for interstate trains. The **Indian Pacific,** between Sydney and Perth, passes through both Adelaide and Broken Hill on its twice-weekly run. From Sydney to Adelaide, the 25-hour journey costs $148 economy, $271 economy sleeper without meals, or $414 first-class sleeper with meals. From Perth to Ade-

laide (38 hours), the fare range is $230 economy, $492 economy sleeper without meals, or $758 first-class sleeper with meals. An alternative from Sydney to Adelaide is the **Speedlink**—an XPT train from Sydney to Albury, a deluxe V-line coach from Albury to Adelaide. Economy sitting is $105 and first class is $135. The Speedlink is about six hours faster than the train.

From Melbourne, the **Overland** departs nightly for the 12-hour overnight journey to Adelaide. Fares are $56 economy sitting or $178 first-class sleeper.

The **Ghan** travels once a week between Alice Springs and Adelaide (twice weekly April-Jan.). The 20-hour journey costs $150 economy sitting, $325 economy sleeper without meals, or $524 first-class sleeper with meals. Though the refurbished Ghan is not nearly as magical as the original, the trek along the historic Afghan camel-driving route is still quite spine-tingling.

For rail information, phone (08) 8217-4111 or (13) 2232.

Getting There by Bus
Greyhound Pioneer, tel. (13) 2030, and **McCafferty's,** tel. (13) 1499, operate coach services between Adelaide, the other capital cities, and most of the rest of Australia. Major services that operate daily are: Sydney-Adelaide (22 hours), $96; Melbourne-Adelaide (10 hours), $50; Alice Springs-Adelaide (19 hours), $135; Perth-Adelaide (35 hours), $214; and Brisbane-Adelaide (38 hours), $150. A number of bus passes are available, allowing unlimited travel for a specified number of days. Some passes need to be purchased outside Australia; others can be issued by STA Travel, YHA Travel, the South Australian Tourism Commission Travel Centre, or the coach company. The **central bus station** is at 111 Franklin St., near Victoria Square. For information, phone (08) 8415-5533.

Getting There by Car
If you're coming to Adelaide by road, the major routes are the coastal **Princes Highway** from Melbourne (929 km), the inland **Western** and **Dukes** Highways from Melbourne (731 km), **Mid-Western** Highway from Sydney (1,414 km), **Sturt Highway** from Sydney (1,418 km), **Barrier Highway** from Sydney (1,666 km), **Stuart Highway** from Darwin (3,026 km), and **Eyre**

ADELAIDE SUBURBAN RAIL

OUTER HARBOUR
- NORTH HAVEN
- OSBORNE
- MIDLUNGA
- TAPEROO
- DRAPER
- LARGS NORTH
- LARGS
- PETERHEAD
- **GLANVILLE**

ETHELTON
PORT ADELAIDE
- ALBERTON
- CHELTENHAM
- CHELTENHAM RACECOURSE
- HOLDENS
- ALBERT PARK
- SEATON PARK
- EAST GRANGE

ROSEWATER
JUNCTION ROAD
EASTERN PARADE
NORTH ARM ROAD
WINGFIELD
GREENFIELDS

GRANGE

WOODVILLE
WOODVILLE PARK
KILKENNY
WEST CROYDON
CROYDON
BOWDEN

GLENELG
GLENELG TRAMWAY

- CLARENCE PARK
- EMERSON
- EDWARDSTOWN
- **WOODLANDS PARK**
- ASCOT PARK
- MARION
- OAKLANDS
- WARRADALE
- HOVE
- **BRIGHTON**
  - SEACLIFF
  - MARINO
  - MARINO ROCKS
  - HALLETT COVE
  - HALLETT COVE BEACH
  - **LONSDALE**
  - CHRISTIE DOWNS
  - **NOARLUNGA CENTRE**

MITCHELL PARK
CHRYSLER PARK
TONSLEY

TUBE MILLS
KILBURN
ISLINGTON
DUDLEY PARK
OVINGHAM
NORTH ADELAIDE
ADELAIDE
MILE END
MILE END GOODS
KESWICK
GOODWOOD
MILLSWOOD
UNLEY PARK
HAWTHORN
MITCHAM
TORRENS PARK
CLAPHAM
LYNTON
EDEN HILLS
COROMANDEL
BLACKWOOD

DRY CREEK
CAVAN
POORAKA
NORTHFIELD
CHIDDA
PARAFIELD
PARAFIELD GARDENS

SALISBURY
NURLUTTA
HILRA
GMH ELIZABETH
ELIZABETH SOUTH
WOMMA
BROADMEADOWS
SMITHFIELD
MUNNO PARA
KUDLA
TAMBELIN
EVANSTON
GAWLER
GAWLER OVAL
GAWLER CENTRAL

ELIZABETH
PENFIELD

BRIDGEWATER
- CARRIPOOK
- JIBILLA
- ALDGATE
- MADURTA
- HEATHFIELD
- MOUNT LOFTY
- UPPER STURT
- LONG GULLY
- NATIONAL PARK
- **BELAIR**
  - PINERA
  - GLENALTA

Highway from Perth (2,691 km). Allow *plenty* of time if you're driving; except for Melbourne, these Outback stretches can be risky business for inexperienced motorists.

Getting Around

Warning: Trains, especially late at night, are hotbeds of violence for violent hotheads—it's best to stick to buses or taxis at night.

The **Transit Bus,** tel. (08) 8381-5311, will whisk you from the airport to center city (six km) every half-hour Mon.-Fri. 7 a.m.-9 p.m. (hourly on weekends and holidays) for $6, and stops at major hotels and hostels. Taxis charge about $15 for the 25-minute ride.

Adelaide's **TransAdelaide** operates the city's buses, the suburban trains, and its one tram, and prices cover the entire transportation system. Buses run between city and suburbs daily 6 a.m.-11:30 p.m., but there is no service on Sunday morning. Suburban trains serving Glenelg, Port Adelaide, several coastal points, and the Adelaide Hills depart Adelaide Railway Station, North Terrace, daily 5:30 a.m.-midnight. Free **City Loop** buses (all wheelchair accessible) make some 30 stops in downtown and at major tourist attractions Mon.-Thurs. 8:30 a.m.-6 p.m., Friday 8:30 a.m.-9 p.m., and Saturday 9 a.m.-5 p.m. The free **Beeline** bus cruises along King William St., from Victoria Square to the North Terrace Railway Station, every five minutes Mon.-Thurs. 9 a.m.-6 p.m., every 15 minutes Friday 9 a.m.-7 p.m. and Saturday 8 a.m.-5 p.m. Tickets ($1.60-2.70), priced according to zones, are good for up to two hours on all modes of transportation. The **Day Tripper** ticket costs $5.10 and allows unlimited travel within the entire system Mon.-Fri. after 9 a.m., Sat.-Sun. all day. Another money-saver is the **Multitrip** ticket, which gives you 10 two-hour tickets for $10-17. Buy tickets and pick up transport maps and timetables at the TransAdelaide Information Centre, corner of King William and Currie Streets, tel. (08) 8210-1000, Mon.-Fri. 9 a.m.-5 p.m., Saturday 9 a.m.-noon.

Taxis are plentiful and can be hired at the airport, railway stations, city center taxi stands, or by phoning direct. Companies include **Adelaide Independent,** tel. (08) 8234-6000; **Suburban,** tel. (08) 8211-8888; and **Des's Cabs,** tel. (13) 1323. For wheelchair-accessible taxis, contact **Access Cabs,** tel. (08) 8234-6444.

All the big-name car rental firms are represented in Adelaide, with offices at the airport, the major hotels, and along North Terrace. A couple of lesser-known and cheaper firms are **Action Rent-a-Car,** tel. (08) 8352-7044; **Rent-a-Bug,** tel. (08) 8234-0655; and **Delta,** tel. (13) 1390. For moped and bicycle rentals, see above. Mopeds will run about $34 per day, $15 per hour (be prepared to pay a $50 deposit). Mountain bikes average $25 per day, while 10-speeds are in the $15-20 bracket.

The **Adelaide Explorer Bus,** tel. (08) 8364-1933, departs from 14 King William St. several times daily (except Christmas Day and Good Friday) for two-hour sightseeing trips to eight popular city spots, including Glenelg. One $22 ticket permits you to get on and off at will, so if one place strikes your fancy, you can spend as much time there as you like, reboarding the bus next time around. Many tour operators offer City Sights, Adelaide Hills, Mt. Lofty Ranges, and Adelaide by Night junkets. Check with the tourist office for the current list of contenders.

Getting Away

Intrastate air carriers include **Kendell Airlines, Augusta Airways, Air Kangaroo Island, Eyre Commuter, Emu Airways,** and **O'Conner** airlines. The smaller carriers will take you to communities such as Ceduna, Mount Gambier, Port Lincoln, Whyalla, Coober Pedy, Broken Hill, Olympic Dam, Woomera, American River, Kingscote, Parndana, Wudinna, Cummins, Tumby Bay, Port Lincoln, Renmark, and Mildura. Make bookings through Ansett or Qantas, or contact the South Australian Tourism Commission Travel Centre, tel. (08) 8212-1505.

The **MV** *Philanderer III* and **MV** *Island Navigator,* tel. (13) 1301, passenger ferries operate service from Cape Jervis to Penneshaw, Kangaroo Island. Fares are $32 per person and $60 per vehicle, one-way for the one-hour journey. The **MV** *Island Seaway,* tel. (08) 8447-5577, ferries between Port Adelaide and Kingscote (seven hours) for $25 per person, $62 per vehicle.

Country trains depart Keswick Railway Terminal for Peterborough, Port Pirie, and Mt. Gambier. For information, phone (13) 2232.

Aside from Greyhound Pioneer and McCafferty's, several smaller bus companies service the state's country towns, coastal villages, and remote stations. Inquire at the **Central Bus Station,** 101 Franklin Street. For information, phone (08) 8415-5533.

Wayward Bus, tel. (1800) 882-823, a private operator, packages trips from Adelaide to Alice Springs via the Flinders Ranges and Uluru (Ayers Rock). Cost runs around $600, including meals, accommodations, and a seat on the bus.

HILLS AND VALES

Less than half an hour's drive from grid-and-square Adelaide are rambling hills and rolling vales, secluded hollows and hideaway valleys, nook-and-cranny villages and lush green terrain smothered in wildflowers, delicate orchids, and bold yellow wattle, and bathed in the fragrance of almond, apple, pear, and cherry orchards, and strawberry patches. Euphoric names such as Happy Valley, Tea Tree Gully, Basket Range, Mount Pleasant, and Chain of Ponds will ring in your ears with the distant echo of a near-forgotten, favorite fairy tale.

Adelaide is the perfect base for short excursions into the hills; or do the reverse—nestle into some cozy dell and day trip down to the city.

ADELAIDE HILLS

The hills, part of the Mt. Lofty Ranges (or, Urebilla-its Aboriginal name), can be explored by a number of meandering scenic routes. There's something for everyone—endless vistas for tourists in buses, scads of secluded picnic spots for lovers and loners, 1,000 km of walking tracks for hikers. One exceptionally pretty itinerary that leads you around and through conservation parks and lookout spots with a bird's-eye view of the city begins at **Windy Point** on Belair Rd. (reached from the city via Fullarton Rd.). Skirt around Upper Sturt Rd. to **Belair National Park,** one of the world's oldest national parks (established 1891). Facilities include tennis courts, football ovals, cricket pitches, a popular golf course, bushwalking tracks, and camping sites. Admission is $3 per vehicle. For information, phone (08) 8278-5477.

Continue along Upper Sturt Rd., cross the South Eastern Freeway, and you'll be on Summit Road. Take the turnoff to **Mt. Lofty,** the ranges' highest point (771 meters). At road's end, a monument pays tribute to Colonel Matthew Flinders,

and a large lookout area affords a panoramic view of Adelaide and the surrounding hills and plains. Near the summit, **Mt. Lofty Botanic Gardens** covers more than 42 hectares with exotic cool and subalpine plants. The gardens are closed in winter and are most colorful in autumn. For information, phone (08) 8228-2311.

Cleland Conservation Park, on the slopes of Mt. Lofty, features koalas (cuddling daily 2-4 p.m.), emus, kangaroos, native birds, and other wildlife, as well as many enticing walking tracks along its 972 hectares of bushland. For information, phone (08) 8339-2444.

Back on Summit Rd., you'll pass pear and apple orchards until you reach **Norton Summit,** where there's a restaurant and yet another view.

Turning toward the city will bring you into **Morialta Conservation Park,** noted for its waterfalls, deep gorge, and excellent bushwalking. Trails lead to the gorge and several waterfalls (and some pretty spectacular views), as well as points like Pretty Corner, Kookaburra Rock, and the Giant's Cave. For information, phone (08) 8365-2599.

Magill Rd. runs into Payneham Rd., which leads back to Adelaide. An alternate route is Marble Hill Rd. (turn off before Norton Summit) to Montacute, toward the city through Morialta and the **Black Hill** Conservation Parks, then to Payneham Road.

Para Wirra Recreational Park, 40 km northeast of Adelaide, is a wooded plateau with steep gullies, kangaroos, birds, spring wildflowers, and more good walking trails and picnic areas. Admission is $3 per vehicle. For information, phone (08) 8280-7048.

Accommodations and Food

See the Adelaide **YHA** for information on its five limited-access hostels in the Mt. Lofty Ranges. Advance bookings are required. Budget.

Belair National Park, tel. (08) 8278-3540, rents campsites, on-site vans, and cabins with cooking facilities. Budget-Inexpensive. Guestrooms at **Drysdale Cottage,** Debneys Rd., Norton Summit, tel. (08) 8390-1652, include breakfast. Moderate-Expensive. **Hoppy's Nest,** Summit Rd., Mt. Lofty, tel. (08) 8370-9767, opposite the entrance to Cleland Conservation Park, is a cozy bed and breakfast. Moderate.

If you feel like doing a little work in exchange for cheap keep, try out **Fuzzie's Farm,** Colonial Dr., Norton Summit, tel. (08) 8390-1111. In exchange for $10 per day and a variety of chores,

you'll get meals and a bed in one of the cabins overlooking Morialta Conservation Park.

Really big spenders and splurgers should consider a stay at **Mt. Lofty House,** 74 Summit Rd., Crafers, tel. (08) 8339-6777. The exquisitely furnished house, built between 1852 and 1858, has sumptuous bedrooms, sitting rooms, and two luscious restaurants. Prices are hefty—$215-430 per double—and the breakfast is light. Luxury.

You'll find tearooms and pubs tucked cozily away in the hills and valleys. Luxury. At Norton

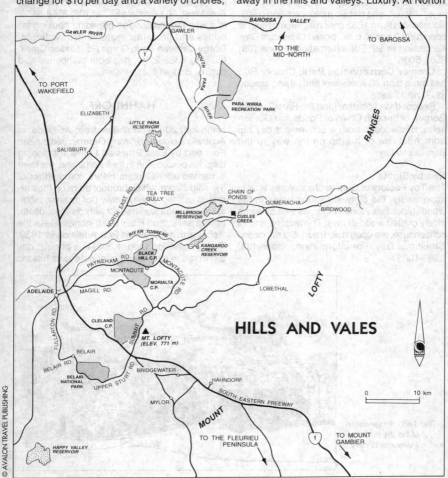

Summit, the **Scenic Hotel,** hanging onto the hill, is a thrill for meals (entrees $12-18) and drinks.

BIRDWOOD

Once upon a time Birdwood, less than 50 km northeast from Adelaide, was a gold-mining center. Today its claim to fame is the **National Motor Museum,** which displays more than 300 vintage, veteran, and classic motor cars and bikes. Housed inside an 1852 flour mill, the museum is open daily 9 a.m.-5 p.m., closed Christmas Day. Admission is $9. For information, phone (08) 8568-5006.

Cromer Conservation Park, Cromer Rd., has more than 70 species of birds flying around its 50 hectares.

Reached via Lobethal (and the River Torrens Gorge), or through Chain of Ponds and Gumeracha, Birdwood is both a convenient day trip from Adelaide or a stop on the way to the Barossa Valley.

Nearby Sights
The **Toy Factory** of Gumeracha features what is supposedly "the biggest rocking horse in the world" (about six stories high), as well as some nicely crafted wooden toys. The factory, and its coffeehouse, are open daily 9 a.m.-5 p.m., closed Christmas Day. For information, phone (08) 8389-1085.

Cudlee Creek Gorge Wildlife Park, Cudlee Creek (a short detour from Chain of Ponds), boasts a large, privately owned wildlife collection, with koalas just dying to be cuddled. The park is open daily 8 a.m.-5 p.m. Admission is $6. For information, phone (08) 8389-2206.

Accommodations
The **Gumeracha Hotel,** Albert St., Gumeracha, tel. (08) 8389-1001, has the cheapest rooms. Inexpensive. In Birdwood, **Birdwood Bed and Breakfast,** 38 Olivedale St., tel. (08) 8568-5444, is a well-tended cottage providing cooking facilities and breakfast ingredients. Moderate. **Gorge Caravan Park,** Gorge Rd., Cudlee Creek, tel. (08) 8389-2270, has both campsites and cabins. Budget-Inexpensive.

HAHNDORF

Hahndorf, 20 km southeast from Adelaide, is Australia's oldest surviving German settlement. Founded by East Prussian Lutherans fleeing religious persecution in their homeland, the town is named after Captain Hahn, commander of the ship *Zebra,* which brought them on their arduous journey. The typically (for its time) nightmarish voyage was fraught with disease, death, ripped sails, and killer heat; nonetheless the *Zebra* arrived safely at Port Adelaide in 1839. Today Hahndorf (pop. 1,300) is a popular day trip from the city, drawing tourists to its historic

This 1860 Bridgewater Mill is the home of Petaluma Winery.

KAREN McKINLEY

buildings and well-preserved town to buy slices of *streuselkuchen* and examples of *typische* folk crafts or just partake of some old-world charm (albeit on the cutesy side). Stop by for a cuppa *kaffee,* and you're apt to be greeted with a *"Guten Tag,* mate."

Sights
Hahndorf Academy, 68 Main St., established in 1857 as an educational facility, now functions as the town museum and a showcase for landscape paintings by Sir Hans Heysen, a Hahndorf favorite son. The museum is open daily 10 a.m.-5 p.m., closed Christmas Day. Admission is $5. For information, phone (08) 8388-7250.

View elaborate timepieces, a gigantic cuckoo clock, and buy your own authentic Black Forest cuckoo at the **Antique Clock Museum,** 91 Main Street. Open daily 9 a.m.-5:30 p.m. Admission is $3. For information, phone (08) 8388-7349.

German Model Train Land, 47 Main St., features intricately pieced, imported-from-Germany model trains and villages. Open daily 9 a.m.-5 p.m., closed Christmas Day and Good Friday. Admission is $3. For information, phone (08) 8388-7953.

Nearby Sights
Detour on Mt. Barker Rd. before you get to Hahndorf for an inspection of the 1860 stone **Bridgewater Mill,** restored and transformed into **Petaluma Winery.** View the huge waterwheel, taste the cabernet sauvignon and chardonnay, and have lunch in the cavernous **Granary Restaurant.** Open Wed.-Mon. 11 a.m.-5 p.m. (dinner is not served). For information, phone (08) 8339-3422.

Warrawong Sanctuary, Williams Rd., Mylor, is another sidetrack to Hahndorf. See rare and endangered animals on organized dawn, daytime, and nocturnal walks. The property also has a nocturnal observatory and craft and coffee shops. Open by reservation only. Dawn and

evening walks are $15. For information, phone (08) 8370-9422.

Accommodations and Food
Hochstens, 145 Main St., tel. (08) 8388-7361, has a wide range of accommodations, from on-site caravans to luxury motel units and private chalets. Prices vary from budget to expensive. **Hahndorf Old Mill Motel and Restaurant,** 98 Main St., tel. (08) 8388-7888, has pleasing rooms with all the creature comforts. Moderate. **Elderberry,** Old Mt. Barker Rd., tel. (08) 8388-7997, is a one-bedroom cottage with cooking facilities and a wood-burning fireplace. Moderate-Expensive.

You can get stick-to-your-bones German food all over town. The **German Arms Hotel,** 50 Main St., dating from 1834, serves pub meals ($4-8) in historic surroundings. Along Main St., **Otto's Bakery, Karl's German Coffee House, Gretchen's Coffee Shop,** and **The German Cake Shop** will keep you going with good coffees and fresh cakes.

Do-it-yourselfers will want to pack the best of the wurst at shops and takeaways around town, and pick the homegrown berries at either the **Berry Farm** on Tischer Rd., tel. (08) 8388-7071, or **Beerenberg Strawberry Farm,** Mt. Barker Rd., tel. (08) 8388-7272.

Events
Hahndorf's big event is the annual mid-January **Schutzenfest,** a traditional shooting festival with German folk dancing, entertainment, cuisine, and beer—*lots* of beer.

Transportation and Information
A number of public buses travel between the city and **Adelaide Hills.** For information and schedules, phone (08) 8210-1000.

For information on all areas of the Hills and Vales, contact **Adelaide Hills Tourist Information Centre,** 64 Main St., Hahndorf, tel. (08) 8388-1185.

THE BAROSSA VALLEY

South Australia's most famous wine district lies in a shallow valley just 29 km long and eight km wide, amid gently rounded hills, icy-cold brooks, neat-as-a-pin grape-staked fields, pseudo chateaux and castles, and authentic Lutheran churches.

Less than an hour's drive north of Adelaide, most of the 50 or so wineries are situated in the 20-km span from Lyndoch to Nuriootpa, with the town of Tanunda in between. Serious connoisseurs or occasional tipplers can follow their noses or their whims to both commercial megacomplexes and family-run boutique wineries for a gargle or a swallow of full-bodied reds, crisp whites, sherries, ports, and sparkling wines.

Two routes will get you to the Barossa—a rather boring, but quicker and more direct road through Gawler, or the longer, winding, picture-postcard way via Birdwood and Torrens Gorge. Assuming that you'll start off on the scenic route and by day's end be wishing for the straight highway with the dividing lines, the following towns have been geographically arranged to reflect that. Also, not all of the wineries have been listed below, only some of the most historical and interesting. Well-placed signposts will lead you to others off the beaten path—it's fun to make a wrong turn here or there, up or down, to make your own vintage discoveries.

You can do the Barossa in a day trip from Adelaide, but if your feet get a little wobbly—or you haven't had your fill—consider bedding down for the night at a hostel, guesthouse, or motel along the way.

History

The Barossa was settled in 1842 by the same persecuted East Prussian Lutherans who arrived on the good ship *Zebra* with Captain Hahn. Their expedition had been funded by Englishman George Fife Angas, one of the original colonizers, in the hopes he was snagging good, hardworking folk whose skills would benefit South Australia. The new arrivals who didn't go to Hahndorf followed their pastor, August Kavel, to the Barossa Valley and put down roots in Lyndoch, Tanunda, Angaston, and Bethany. A few years earlier, the same region had been explored by Silesian mineralogist Johannes Menge, who passed the word that the area, similar to parts of Poland, was a grape-grower's heaven. By the late 1840s the new settlers had planted their vines and were soon turning out vintages ambrosial enough to knock their lederhosen off. At the same time they constructed beautiful stone churches, cottages, and town buildings, which you'll see on your tour of the valley.

1. Twin Valley Estate
2. Wards Gateway Cellar
3. Chateau Yaldara Estate
4. Charles Cimicky Wines
5. Burge Family Winemakers
6. Kies Estate Cellars
7. Barossa Settlers
8. Kellermeister Wines
9. Jenke Vineyard
10. Rovalley Estate
11. Orlando Winery
12. Grant Burge Wines
13. Charles Melton Wines
14. Krondorf Wines
15. Rockford Wines
16. Bethany Wines
17. St. Hallett Wines
18. High Wycombe Wines
19. Turkey Flat Vineyard
20. Lanzerac
21. Basedow Wines
22. Tarchalice Wine Co.
23. Old Barn Winery
24. Hardy's Siegersdorf
25. Peter Lehmann Wines
26. Richmond Grove
27. Veritas Winery
28. BernKastel Wines
29. Chateau Dorien Wines
30. Tolle Pedare Winery
31. Tarac Distillers
32. Heritage Wines
33. Seppeltsfield Winery
34. Greenlock Creek Cellars—
   Near town of Greenock
35. Gnadenfrei Estate
36. Penfolds Winery
37. Kaesler Wines
38. Elderton Wines
39. The Willow Vineyard
40. Wolf Blass Wines
41. Saltram Winery
42. Yalumba Winery
43. Henschke Wines

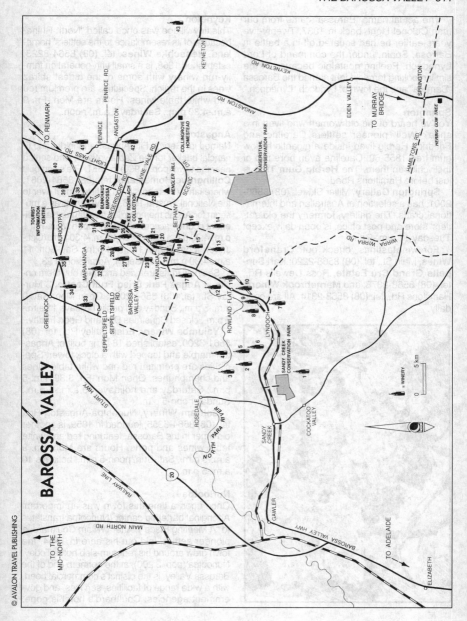

BAROSSA VALLEY

© AVALON TRAVEL PUBLISHING

The actual name "Barossa" came from our man Colonel Light, back in 1837. Twenty-five years earlier he had squared off in a battle in Barrosa, Spain, under the command of Lord Lynedoch. Feeling nostalgic because of the similar-looking terrain, Light named the Barossa "Barrosa" and the town of Lyndoch "Lynedoch."

Springton

You've heard of the old woman who lived in a shoe? Well, pioneer settlers Caroline and Friedrich Herbig lived inside a gigantic hollow gum tree 1855-60. Caroline even bore two of their children there. The **Herbig Gum Tree** is just before Hamiltons Road.

Springton Gallery, Miller St., tel. (08) 8568-2001, has a selection of Australian and international crafts. The gallery, formerly the old settlers' store and post office, is open daily except Tuesday 11 a.m.-5 p.m.

For winetastings, check out: **Craneford Wines,** Main St., tel. (08) 8568-2220; **Karl Seppelts Grand Cru Estate,** Ross Dewells Rd., tel. (08) 8568-2378; and **Marnebrook Winery,** Hamiltons Rd., tel. (08) 8568-2314. All are open daily.

Keyneton

This tiny village was once called "North Rhine" because of its resemblance to the settlers' homeland. **Henschke Wines,** tel. (08) 8564-8223, established 1868, is a small fifth-generation family-run winery with some of the oldest shiraz vines in the region. Specialties are premium red and white table wines. Hours are Mon.-Fri. 9 a.m.-4:30 p.m., Saturday 9 a.m.-noon.

Angaston

Named for George Fife Angas, landholder and financial backer for the *Zebra* voyage, who settled near the town (pop. 1,950) in 1851. Fife's son built **Collingrove Homestead,** tel. (08) 8564-2061, where family members lived until turning it over to the National Trust in 1976. It now serves as a museum for Angas memorabilia, a restaurant, and elegant country accommodation. Open Mon.-Fri. 1 p.m.-4:30 p.m., Sat.-Sun. 11 a.m.-4:30 p.m. (Oct.-June); Mon.-Thurs. 1 p.m.-4 p.m., Sat.-Sun. 11 a.m.-4:30 p.m. (July-Sept.). Admission is $3.

See how fruits are dried and then buy them onsite at **Angas Park Dried Fruit Centre,** 3 Murray St., tel. (08) 8564-2052. Open Mon.-Sat. 9 a.m.-5 p.m., Sunday and public holidays 11 a.m.-5 p.m., closed Christmas Day and Good Friday.

Yalumba Winery, Eden Valley Rd., tel. (08) 8561-3200, established 1849, is built of Angaston marble and topped with a clock tower. Specialties are premium red and white table wines and champagnes. Open Mon.-Fri. 8:30 a.m.-5 p.m., Saturday and holidays 10 a.m.-5 p.m., Sunday noon-5 p.m.

Saltram Winery, Nuriootpa-Angaston Rd., tel. (08) 8564-3355, founded in 1859, is another old-timer in the Barossa, featuring red and white table wines and ports. Hours are Mon.-Fri. 9 a.m.-5 p.m., Sat.-Sun. noon-5 p.m., holidays 10 a.m.-5 p.m.

Nuriootpa

Once upon a time this town was an important Aboriginal bartering center (Nuriootpa translates to "A Meeting Place"). After William Coulthard, a pioneer settler, laid out his acre in 1854, the town grew around his red-gum-slab hotel. Today, Nuriootpa (pop. 3,200), at the northern end of the Barossa Valley, is the district's commercial heart, with a wide range of facilities, services, and government agencies. Coulthard's hotel is gone, but his home has been preserved and serves as the main information center for the Barossa Valley. Aside from the many clusters of wineries, Nuriootpa has some lovely parks and picnic grounds banking the North Para River, which meanders through town.

Buildings to take note of along Light Pass Rd., are **Immanuel Lutheran Church** (1886), **Luhr's Pioneer German Cottage** (1841), and **Strait Gate Lutheran Church** (1861).

Penfolds Wines, Tanunda Rd., tel. (08) 8560-9408, established in 1812, is a huge commercial complex (particularly after merging with Kaiser Stuhl) specializing in a full range of red and white table wines and fortified wines. This property can store more than 22 million liters of wine! Hours are Mon.-Fri. 9 a.m.-5 p.m., Saturday and holidays 10 a.m.-5 p.m., Sunday 1-5 p.m. Admission is $4.

ballooning over Barossa Valley vineyards

Elderton Wines, 3 Tanunda Rd., tel. (08) 8562-1058, established 1906, has red and white table wines, sparkling wines, *and* bicycles and mokes for hire. Hours are Mon.-Fri. 8:30 a.m.-5 p.m., Sat.-Sun. 11 a.m.-4 p.m.

Wolf Blass Wines, tel. (08) 8562-1955, along the Sturt Highway, was only established in 1973, yet practically started out winning Australia's most coveted red-wine prize three years in a row. Specialties are premium red and white table wines and champagne. Hours are Mon.-Fri. 9:15 a.m.-4:30 p.m., Sat.-Sun. and holidays 10 a.m.-4:30 p.m.

Bored with wine? Check out **Tarac Distillers,** Tanunda Rd., tel. (08) 8562-1522, for brandy, rum, gin, bourbon, vodka, whiskey, and tequila. Hours are Mon.-Fri. 8:30 a.m.-4:30 p.m.

Marananga
Gnadenfrei ("Freed by the grace of God") was the original name given to this little town by its settlers in the 1840s. In 1918, when Germanic names were being changed, it was christened Marananga, Aboriginal for "My Hands."

It's worth making the turn off the main road to see the old schoolhouse, cottages, and splendid **Gnadenfrei Church,** begun in 1857, with additions in 1873 and 1913.

Heritage Wines, tel. (08) 8562-2880, is small and newish (established 1984), with interesting dry red and white table wines. Hours are daily 11 a.m.-5 p.m.

Seppeltsfield
Take the out-of-place-looking, date-palm-fringed road from Marananga to Seppeltsfield, founded by Silesian migrant Joseph Seppelt in 1851. Seppelt, who started off as a tobacco farmer, discovered that his crop was too rank for sale. He experimented with winemaking, and the rest, as they say, is history. And history, as reported in the 1892 *London Gazette,* called Seppelt's cellars and stores "the most modern in the world." Those "modern" buildings have been carefully preserved and make for an interesting tour between sips of red and white table wines, fortified wines, and champagnes. Hours are Mon.-Fri. 8:30 a.m.-5 p.m., Saturday 10:30 a.m.-4:30 p.m., Sunday 11 a.m.-4 p.m. For information, phone (08) 8562-8028.

Barossa Valley Way
It only takes about five minutes to get from Nuriootpa to Tanunda along this stretch of road, but you'll probably get hung up for hours if you stop at the **Kev Rohrlach Collection,** tel. (08) 8563-3407, a private museum of science, transport, and technology. More than 3,000 mechanical exhibits collected by Mr. Rohrlach (a builder) from all over South Australia will amaze, amuse, confound, and confuse you. The transport collection alone includes a maharaja's barouche and the 1955 Australian Grand Prix-winning car. Hours are daily 10 a.m.-5 p.m. Admission charge is $6.

Tanunda
Established in 1843, Tanunda (pop. 2,860) was the second German settlement in the valley. Many of the traditional early stone buildings line

the main avenue, as well as **Langmeil Road,** one of the backstreets. **Goat Square,** site of the first town market, is bordered by original cottages, preserved and classified by the National Trust.

Tanunda is home to four of the valley's most exquisite Lutheran churches: **Langmeil Church,** on the main drag, has Pastor Kavel's remains buried in the adjacent cemetery; **St. John's,** Jane St., is home to life-size wooden statues of Jesus, Moses, and selected apostles; **Tabor Lutheran Church,** north end of Murray St., is notable for its orb-topped spire; **St. Paul's,** corner Murray St. and Basedow Rd., features fine stained glass.

Brauer Biotherapies, 1 Para Rd., tel. (08) 8563-2932, welcomes visitors to its laboratories where homeopathic medicines are concocted. Hours are Mon.-Fri. 8:30 a.m.-4 p.m., with guided tours at 2 p.m.

Rather watch performing dogs? You can watch 25 trained canines at **Norm's Coolie Sheep Dog Performance,** Gomersal Rd., tel. (08) 8563-2198. Show times are Monday, Wednesday, and Saturday 2 p.m. Admission is $7.

The numerous wineries in this area should obliterate both homeopathic remedies and bad dog memories.

Bethany

Bethany was the first German settlement in the Barossa, founded in 1842 by a group of Silesian families. This peaceful, pretty village is still home to old stone houses, cottage gardens, and farmlets, as well as Australia's smallest hotel. The old village common has been transformed into **Bethany Reserve,** a haven for picnickers along bubbling Bethany Creek. The church bells still ring at dusk on Saturday to signal the end of the work week in case anyone forgets. The **Landhaus,** on Bethany Rd. near the railway tracks, claims to be Australia's smallest licensed motel.

Opposite Bethany Reserve, **Bethany Art & Craft Gallery,** tel. (08) 8564-3344, is an outlet for handmade textiles, pottery, glass, and wooden wares. The gallery is open daily 10 a.m.-5 p.m.

Rowland Flat

Commercial winemaking began at Jacobs Creek in 1847 when Johann Gramp planted his first vines. Nowadays the **Orlando Winery,** which dominates the town, pays its tribute by carrying an excellent claret with the Jacobs Creek label. The complex is enormous and pretty sterile, but it does offer a very good, educational $2 winery tour. If you visit February through April you'll get to view the grape-crushing process. Red and white table wines and champagnes are the specialties. Hours are Mon.-Fri. 9:30 a.m.-5 p.m., Sat.-Sun. and holidays 10 a.m.-4 p.m. For information, phone (08) 8521-3111.

Rockford Wines, tel. (08) 8563-2720, is on Krondorf Rd., about three km from Rowland Flat. If you've just been to Orlando, this tiny establishment, with its tasting room inside a former stable, may underwhelm you—but the spectacular vintages won't. Specialties are traditional full-bodied Australian wine styles (premium regional wines). Hours are daily 11 a.m.-5 p.m.

Lyndoch

Lyndoch (pop. 705), at the southern edge of the valley, was originally settled in 1839 as a farming community; the first winery was installed in 1896 in a converted flour mill. All of the 10 or so wineries in this district are family-owned. The largest is **Chateau Yaldara,** Gomersal Rd., tel. (08) 8524-4200, established in 1947 on the remains of that same converted flour mill. Besides red and white table wines, sparkling wines, and port, the "chateau" displays a collection of porcelain and antiques. Hours are daily 9 a.m.-5 p.m.

Along the Barossa Highway, the **South Australian Museum of Mechanical Music,** tel. (08) 8524-4014, features antique music boxes, automatic accordions, barrel pianos, player organs, an 1840s musical church, and singing birds. The museum is open daily 9 a.m.-5 p.m., closed Christmas Day. Admission is $5.

Cockatoo Valley

Detouring off the Barossa Highway, you'll pass through this small village with a general store (for petrol and provisions), remnants of goldfields, and an 1870s miner's cottage (converted to accommodations). The big attraction, down the road, is Barossa Reservoir (built in 1898) and its famed **Whispering Wall,** a retaining wall with peculiar acoustics that enable you to stand on one side and hear whispers all the way from the opposite side of the dam.

Gawler

Gawler (pop. 15,000), founded in 1839, was South Australia's second country town after Port Adelaide. Superb bluestone architecture, dating from the late 19th and early 20th centuries, is reflected in the town hall, post office, and various churches. Other fine buildings are the **Old Telegraph Station** (home of the National Trust), constructed of One Tree Hill sandstone, and homes and fences crafted from local limestone.

PRACTICALITIES

Accommodations

Angaston: Barossa Valley Hotel, 41 Murray St., tel. (08) 8564-2014, has both a cozy dining room and a saloon bar. Budget-inexpensive rates include continental breakfast. Historic **Angaston Hotel,** 59 Murray St., tel. (08) 8564-2428, is known for the Bacchus mural in its lounge. Inexpensive. **Collingrove Homestead,** Eden Valley Rd., tel. (08) 8564-2061, is the Angas family ancestral home where guests can spend the night in converted servants' quarters. Moderate-expensive rates include continental breakfast.

Nuriootpa: Barossa Gateway Motel, Kalimna Rd., tel. (08) 8562-1033, has plain, inexpensive rooms, and a bed in the hostel section only costs $10. **Karawatha Guest House,** Greenock Rd., tel. (08) 8562-1746, is a much homier environment. Moderate prices include breakfast. The modern **Vine Inn Hotel/Motel,** 14 Murray St., tel. (08) 8562-2133, is in the center of town. Moderate-expensive rates include continental breakfast.

Marananga: The **Hermitage of Marananga,** corner Seppeltsfield and Stonewell Roads, tel. (08) 8562-2722, features spacious suites overlooking the property's vineyards. Rates include breakfast in the popular country restaurant. Expensive-Luxury.

Seppeltsfield: You have your choice between the comfy, modern, and moderately priced **Holiday Cabins,** Seppeltsfield Rd., tel. (08) 8562-8240, for $55-70 double, or the sumptuous **Lodge,** Main Rd., tel. (08) 8562-8277, where for about $290 you can live in the old Seppelt family digs. (A room with all meals will set you back $395.) Moderate-Luxury.

Barossa Way: Barossa Bunkhaus Travellers Hostel, Barossa Hwy., tel. (08) 8562-2260, is a friendly backpackers' hostel with kitchen facilities, TV room, swimming pool, and bicycle rental. Dorm beds cost $11 per night, and a cottage with cooking facilities and fireplace is $30 for two. Budget. **Barossa Junction Resort,** Barossa Hwy., tel. (08) 8563-3400, offers motel-style accommodations inside converted railway cars, including lounge and dining carriages. Rates, with continental breakfast, are inexpensive to moderate.

Tanunda: Tanunda Hotel, 51 Murray St., tel. (08) 8563-2030, with shared facilities, has a restaurant and swimming pool. Inexpensive. **Weintal Hotel Motel,** Murray St., tel. (08) 8563-2303, with bars, a bistro, restaurant, underground cellar, tennis courts, swimming pool, and sauna. Moderate. An interesting choice is rural **Lawley Farm,** Krondorf Rd., tel. (08) 8563-2141, where the farm cottage and barn have been converted into lovely country rooms. Expensive rates include breakfast.

Bethany: The **Landhaus,** Bethany Rd., tel. (08) 8563-2191, may be Australia's smallest licensed motel, but the price is a big $125, including breakfast. Premium.

Lyndoch: Chateau Yaldara Estate, Barossa Valley Hwy., tel. (08) 8524-4268, has a restaurant, swimming pool, and wine country ambience. Expensive-Premium.

Cockatoo Valley: The old 1870 **Miner's Cottage,** Goldfields Rd., tel. (08) 8524-6213, has private accommodations comprised of living room with open fireplace, bedroom, and bathroom. Expensive rates include continental breakfast.

Gawler: Prasad's Gawler Motel, 1 Main North Rd., tel. (08) 8522-5900, features good rooms, a swimming pool, spa, and sauna. Moderate (luxury during festival season). **Gawler Arms Hotel,** 102 Murray St., tel. (08) 8522-1856, doesn't have all the fancy amenities, but the prices are steady. Moderate.

Camping

Barossa Valley Tourist Park, Penrice Rd., Nuriootpa, tel. (08) 8562-1404, is a very large park with swimming pool, barbecue, playground, tennis courts, a recreation lake, and reserve. **Tanunda Caravan Park,** Barossa Valley Way, Tanunda, tel. (08) 8563-2784, features full-service grass sites in a sheltered setting. **Barossa Caravan Park,** Barossa Valley Hwy., Lyndoch, tel. (08) 8524-4262, is fairly plain, but near the Whispering Wall and other hot spots. **Gawler Caravan Park,** Main North Rd., Gawler, tel. (08) 8522-3805, has a quiet rural setting, with swimming pool, playground, sheltered picnic and barbecue areas.

Most of the caravan parks offer campsites, on-site vans, and cabins. Campsites are budget priced; vans and cabins are inexpensive-moderate.

Food

You mean you want something besides bread and cheese? You'll easily find tearooms, coffee shops, pub meals, bakeries, and takeaways, as well as some gourmet restaurants with food to match the local wines.

Angaston: Angas Park Dried Fruit Centre, 3 Murray St., tel. (08) 8564-2052, has a wide selection of dried fruit and nuts for your picnic basket. The **Angaston Hotel,** 59 Murray St., tel. (08) 8564-2428, is a favorite for counter meals as well as more expensive à la carte dining. **Barossa Bistro,** 37 Murray St., tel. (08) 8564-2361, is a best bet for upmarket bush tucker ($16-22 for eclectic entrees). **The Vintners Bar and Grill,** corner Nuriootpa and Stockwell Roads, tel. (08) 8564-2488, is another expensive choice ($50 pp, sans wine), popular with winemakers so you can be sure of a good menu and exceptional wine list.

Nuriootpa: Family-owned **Linke's Bakery and Tearoom,** 40 Murray St., tel. (08) 8562-1129, has been turning out cakes and breads for more than 50 years. The tearooms serve sandwiches and other lunch items ($5-8). The dining room at the **Vine Inn Hotel/Motel,** 14 Murray St., tel. (08) 8562-2133, serves standard bistro fare ($8-12 entrees) as well as cheap counter meals ($4-9). Big splurgers should book a table at **The Wild Olive Restaurant,** Pheasant Farm Rd., tel. (08) 8562-1286, with its fine dining, equally fine wines, and a changing menu of contemporary Australian dishes ($16-18 for entrees)-served in a setting overlooking the lake. The restaurant is closed during February.

Tanunda: Stock up on delicious bakery items any day but Sunday at **Apex Bakery,** Elizabeth St., tel. (08) 8563-2483. **Zinfandel Tearooms,** 58 Murray St., tel. (08) 8563-2822, features inexpensive light lunches ($5-11) and cakes. Moderately priced German cuisine (entrees $8-12) is the specialty at **Die Gallerie Stonegrill,** 66 Murray St., tel. (08) 8563-2303, where you eat in the courtyard when it's warm, or next to the open fire when it's cold. **Tanunda Hotel,** 51 Murray St., tel. (08) 8563-2030, serves hearty counter meals at reasonable prices ($7-12). The stylish **1918 Bistro and Grill,** 94 Murray St., tel. (08) 8563-0405, housed in a villa, is known for its regional cuisine and superb wines ($16-22 for countrified entrees).

Lyndoch: Get your counter meals ($4-9) at **Lyndoch Hotel,** Gilbert St., tel. (08) 8524-4211. **Lyndoch Bakery,** on Barossa Valley Hwy., tel. (08) 8524-4422, offers terrific baked goodies, plus good, moderately priced meals ($9-14 for hot entrees) in the adjoining restaurant.

Events

With all that wine around, you can well imagine that denizens of the Barossa Valley are ready to party at the drop of a grape.

Other prominent annual events include January's **Oom Pah Festival** in Tanunda, the March **Essenfest** in Tanunda, **Barossa Balloon Regatta** in May, **Barossa Classic Gourmet Weekend** in August, and the **Barossa Music Festival,** also in August. Needless to say, all of these events feature *a lot* of food and grog!

Information

Barossa Wine and Tourism Association, 66 Murray St., Tanunda, tel. (08) 8563-0600, is the regional information hub for the entire Barossa Valley. You can pick up maps to the vineyards, inquire about guided tours, etc., Mon.-Fri. 9 a.m.-5 p.m., Sat.-Sun. and holidays 10 a.m.-4 p.m. The **Gawler Tourist Association,** Murray St., tel. (08) 8522-6814, is open daily 10 a.m.-4 p.m. (Heritage bus tours of Gawler leave from the tourist office at 10 a.m. every Tuesday.)

For police, medical, and fire **emergencies,** dial 000. **Hospitals** are located at Angaston, tel. (08) 8564-2062; Tanunda, tel. (08) 8563-2398; and Gawler, tel. (08) 8521-2000. **Police stations** are at 61 Murray St., Nuriootpa, tel. (08) 8568-6020, and 23 Cowan St., Gawler, tel. (08) 8522-1088.

Transportation

If you're driving, the scenic route can be reached via Chain of Ponds, through Birdwood, to Springton. The direct route is straight up Main North Rd. from Adelaide, through Elizabeth, to Gawler.

Barossa Adelaide Passenger Service, tel. (08) 8564-3022, leaves Adelaide's central bus station for Lyndoch, Tanunda, Nuriootpa, and Angaston. Service runs three times Mon.-Fri., twice on Saturday, and one time only on Sunday. The fares range $8-12 one-way.

Rent bicycles by the day or the hour from the

Barossa Bunkhaus, corner Barossa Valley Hwy. and Nuraip Rd., Nuriootpa, tel. (08) 8562-260; **Elderton Winery,** Nuriootpa, tel. (08) 8562-1058; or **Zinfandel Tea Rooms,** Tanunda, tel. (08) 8563-2822.

Cars can be rented from **BP Service Station,** 8 Murray St., Nuriootpa, tel. (08) 8562-3022, or Elderton Winery, Tanunda Rd., Nuriootpa, tel. (08) 8562-1058. Rent mopeds at **Caltex Service Station,** Murray St., Tanunda, tel. (08) 8563-2677. Elderton Winery also rents mini-mokes.

FLEURIEU PENINSULA

The Fleurieu bills itself "South Australia's Holiday Playground." Like the Adelaide Hills and the Barossa Valley, the Fleurieu is easy day-tripping distance south of the city center. Aside from rolling hills, clustered vineyards, and pastoral farmlands, there are beaches—lots of beaches—from the Gulf St. Vincent, around Cape Jervis, along the pounding Southern Ocean, to Encounter Bay and the mouth of the Murray River—beaches to surf at, fish from, swim off, jog along, glide above, sail aside, and sun worship on.

Bushwalkers and nature lovers can explore more than 20 coastal, wetland, and woodland parks inhabited by native birds and animals. Hiking trails are plentiful, particularly within Deep Creek Conservation Park between Cape Jervis and Victor Harbor, where super-adventurous hikers can hit the Heysen Trail and follow it all the way to the Flinders Ranges. Cape Jervis is also the jumping-off spot for Kangaroo Island, or you can island-hop to Granite Island off Victor Harbor for a glimpse of the fairy penguins, or to Hindmarsh Island, off Goolwa, to boat, fish, or water-ski.

Less sporty travelers will enjoy tasting and tippling at the Wine Coast vineyards (especially noteworthy for reds), admiring early buildings, browsing the many antique shops and crafts cottages, holing up in a secluded cove, or maybe taking the plunge at clothing-optional Maslin Beach.

History

All the big-name explorers—Sturt, Light, Barker—traversed the Fleurieu, but it was French explorer Nicholas Baudin who, in 1802, named

the area for Napoleon's Minister of the Navy, Charles Pierre Claret Comte de Fleurieu. In the same year, Baudin "encountered" rival Matthew Flinders at a site that was appropriately named Encounter Bay—the Encounter Coast becoming a natural tangent thereof. Interestingly, neither Baudin nor Flinders spotted the sand-covered mouth of the Murray, Australia's largest river, a stone's throw away.

It was at Encounter Bay, in 1837, that South Australia's first whaling station (and first successful industry) was created.

THE WINE COAST

About 20 km south of Adelaide, the Wine Coast stretches from old Reynella, home of Cellar Number One, to Old Willunga, with its own share of historic buildings.

Most of the Fleurieu wineries sprouted in the 1850s, when individual farmers harvested small vineyards for their personal use. It was Thomas Hardy who, in 1876, put the area on the map with his purchase of Tintara Vineyards (which subsequently evolved into a dynasty) in McLaren Vale. In the early 1900s, after the all-important London market accepted the Australian wines into their cellars and down their gullets, the local vintners began growing vines with a more serious bent. In 1973, the first annual bushing festival, celebrating the release of the year's vintage, furthered the Wine Coast's popularity. Today the district is comprised of about 50 (mostly family-owned) wineries.

THE FLEURIEU PENINSULA

© AVALON TRAVEL PUBLISHING

Reynella

Old Reynella, at the turnoff from Main South Rd., marks the start of the Wine Drive.

This is the town where John Reynell, South Australia's first commercial winegrower, planted his vines in 1839 and created Cellar Number One (also known as the Old Cave Cellar). See Reynell's original cellar and his home, Chateau Reynell, on the grounds of **Hardy's Reynella Winery,** Reynell Rd., tel. (08) 8392-2222. The winery, established in 1853, is open daily 10 a.m.-4:30 p.m., except Christmas Day and Good Friday.

Reynella's first school, erected in 1858 and since renovated, is on Peach Street.

Morphett Vale

South Australia's first Roman Catholic church, St. Mary's, was built here in 1846. If you'd like to view other historic buildings, turn off of Main South Rd., at the Noarlunga turnoff, for **Pioneer Village** at Hackham, where they've built a rather hokey re-creation of other old structures, furnished in period style. Hours are Wed.-Sun. 10 a.m.-5 p.m., including public holidays. Admission is $4.

Lakeside Leisure Park, Main South and Brodie Roads, Hackham West, is a 14-hectare hillside park with two lakes, a 700-meter tobaggan track, a water slide, horseback riding, and—in mini form—railways, miniature golf, and dune buggy rides. Admission is free. Hours are daily 10 a.m.-dusk. For information, phone (08) 8326-0200.

Onkaparinga River Recreation Park, Piggott Range Rd., tel. (08) 8278-5477, is open daily for birdwatching, gum-viewing, and bushwalking (check in with rangers first—some trails are very steep, and flash floods are another potential hazard).

Eat a pork pie, plum pudding, or traditional plowman's lunch at **James Craig Inn,** Main South Rd., Hackham, tel. (08) 8384-6944.

Old Noarlunga

This was the oldest concentrated settlement in the southern part of the state. Some of the heritage buildings that remain are **Horseshoe Hotel** (1840), the **market square** (1841), **Horseshoe Mill** (1844), **Church of St. Philip and St. James** (1850), and **Jolly Miller Hotel** (1850).

McLaren Vale

Explore the many surrounding wineries, but pay a special visit to **Hardy's Wines,** Main Rd., tel. (08) 8323-9185, whose purchase by Thomas Hardy in 1876 changed the course of Wine Coast winemaking. (Author's favorite is Hardy's black bottle, pot-still brandy.) Hardy's is open daily 10 a.m.-4:30 p.m.

Andrew Garrett Wines, Kangarilla Rd., tel. (08) 8323-8853, is a large, popular operation with a large selection of reds and whites, and a lovely lake setting. Open Mon.-Fri. 9 a.m.-5 p.m., Sat.-Sun. 10 a.m.-4 p.m.

Chapel Hill Winery, Chapel Hill Rd., tel. (08) 8323-8429, formerly the Sir Samuel Way church and school, has a superb stained-glass window, plus excellent dry red and white wines and ports. Open Mon.-Fri. 9 a.m.-5 p.m., Sat.-Sun. 11 a.m.-5 p.m.

Wirra Wirra Vineyards, McMurtrie Rd., tel. (08) 8323-8414, dating from 1894, offers hearth-warming ambience to go with some wondrous shiraz, cabernet sauvignon, and riesling delights. The "Church Block Red" is a must-taste. Open Mon.-Fri. 9 a.m.-5 p.m., Sat.-Sun. 11 a.m.-5 p.m. Even more historic **Seaview Winery,** Chaffey's Rd., tel. (08) 8323-8250, produces notable sparkling wines and a variety of whites. Open Mon.-Fri. 9 a.m.-5 p.m., Saturday 10 a.m.-5 p.m., Sunday 11 a.m.-4 p.m.

Luong Rice Winery, Main St., tel. (08) 8323-8156, is Australia's first Chinese rice-winery. **Dennis Wines,** Kangarilla Rd., tel. (08) 8323-8665, produces both wine and mead (or honey wine). Both wineries are open daily 10 a.m.-5 p.m.

Shotesbrooke Vineyards, Bagshaws Rd., off Kangarilla Rd., tel. (08) 8383-0002, is a small family operation that produces a handful of divine reds and whites. Hours are daily 10 a.m.-5 p.m.

The **World Thru Dolls,** Chalk Hill Rd., tel. (08) 8323-8624, displays antique dolls, portrait figures, nursery rhymes, fairy tales, Bible stories, and other toys and dollies. Open Wed.-Fri. 1-4 p.m.; Saturday, Sunday, and holidays 1-5 p.m. Admission is $3.50.

You'll need an appointment to visit **Camelot Carriage Complex,** 8 Pethick Rd., tel. (08) 8323-8225, where 40-or-so horsedrawn carriages and related memorabilia (like harnesses and whips) are displayed on a rural property. Admission is $4.

McLaren Vale Motel, Caffrey St., tel. (8323) 8265, has a swimming pool and spa. Moderate. Bed and breakfasts include: **McLaren Vale,** 56 Valleyview Dr., tel. (08) 8323-9351; **Southern Vales,** 13 Chalk Hill Rd., tel. (08) 8323-8144; and **Samarkand,** Branson Rd., tel. (08) 8323-8756. All are moderate-expensive.

Lakeside Caravan Park, Field St., tel. (08) 8323-9255, provides campsites, on-site vans, and several cabins. Budget-Inexpensive.

Quite a few wineries have picnic and barbecue areas, as well as restaurants that feature a wine-taster's lunch. **James Haselgrove Wines,** Foggo Rd., tel. (08) 8323-8706, has good meals ($9-18 entrees), as does **Oliverhill Winery,** Seaview Rd., tel. (08) 8323-8922, featuring an Italian wine-maker and homemade pasta ($8-14).

McLaren Vale Bushing Festival, celebrating the release of a new vintage, occurs for several days over the last weekend in October. Activities include tastings, tours, a ball, fairs, toasting and crowning of the Bushing King and Queen, and an Elizabethan feast. **McLaren Vale's Sea and Vines Festival,** held around the beginning of June, features fine wine and seafood, as well as live music hosted by participating wineries. Early October brings **The Continuous Picnic,** a "progressive" sip and sup between wineries (a shuttle does the designated driving).

Obtain winery maps and other local info at the **McLaren Vale and Fleurieu Visitor Center,** Main Rd., tel. (08) 8323-9455.

For help, dial 000; **McLaren Vale Hospital,** tel. (08) 8323-8606; or **police,** tel. (08) 8323-8330.

Willunga
Willunga, derived from Willa-unga, Aboriginal for "Place of the Green Trees," was first laid out in 1839. These days the town is one of Australia's most important almond-growing regions, with 4,500 acres planted. Several old bluestone buildings preserved by the National Trust include the courthouse and police station, dating from 1855. Many of the roof slates have been quarried locally.

View approximately 1,000 different rose varieties (when in season), all clearly labeled, at the **Rose Display Garden,** St. Andrews Terrace, tel. (08) 8556-2555. Hours are daily during daylight, and tours can be arranged.

Vanessa's Restaurant Motel, 27 High St., tel. (08) 8556-2379, has comfortable rooms with continental breakfast included. Moderate. The motel restaurant, with entrees ranging $16 and up, is on the expensive side. **Willunga House,** 1 St. Peters Terrace, tel. (08) 8556-2467, offers B&B accommodations (some with fireplaces). Moderate-Expensive.

Rosella Café, Upper High St., tel. (08) 8556-258, serves light lunches ($6-10) and home-made European cakes. The **Salopain Inn,** on Old Willunga Rd. before town, tel. (08) 8323-8769, features daily lunch ($8-14) in a restored 1861 hotel.

In late July, Willunga celebrates the start of spring with an **Almond Blossom Festival.**

Conservation Parks
South of Willunga, take the Hope Forest turnoff to **Kyeema Conservation Park,** which has an active bird population and walking trails, including a special trail that explores park animals' homes.

Also southeast of Willunga, the Yundi turnoff will lead you to **Mt. Magnificent Conservation Park,** where a portion of the Heysen Trail ascends steeply to the top of the mount.

GULF ST. VINCENT BEACHES

Heading south of Adelaide, past Hallet Cove, the first beach you come to is **O'Sullivan's,** with its breakwater-protected swimming and boating facilities. Next is **Christies Beach,** a popular family resort with safe swimming, sailing, and reef fishing. **Port Noarlunga,** circled by steep cliffs and sandhills, features a lovely reef (at low tide), fishing jetty, and the **Onkaparinga River Recreation Park,** a natural aquatic reserve with many types of water birds.

A favorite with surfers is **Moana,** where you can drive (cautiously!) onto the beach. **Moana Beach Tourist Park,** on the Esplanade, tel. (08) 8327-0677, has on-site vans and campsites. The park has a boat ramp, tennis courts, gymnasium, sauna, and spa. Budget-Moderate.

Maslin Beach, South Australia's first legal nude beach, is exceptionally popular for its, er, scenery and bodysurfing. Be aware that only the 1.5-km southern strip of the beach is clothing-optional (*trust* me). **Maslin Beach Caravan and Camping Ground,** 2 Tuit Rd., tel. (08) 8556-6113, rents campsites and on-site vans. Features include swimming pool, tennis court, coin-operated barbecue, and laundry facilities. Budget-Inexpensive.

Port Willunga is a historic spot with offshore reefs, occasional good surf, scuba diving to the shipwrecked *Star of Greece,* swimming, and sandy beaches.

Aldinga Beach also has good scuba diving, swimming, and sometimes surfing. Remnant plains scrub, wildflowers, and birdlife are features of **Aldinga Scrub Conservation Park,** off Cox Road. Walk through the scrub to the beach at **Aldinga Holiday Park,** Cox Rd., tel. (08) 8556-3444. On-site vans and campsites are available, and there are also five yurtlike cottages and a swimming pool. Budget-Moderate.

There's good fishing from offshore boats at **Silver Sands,** swimming at **Sellicks Beach,** and decent surf at sheltered **Myponga Beach.** Three conservation parks near the town of Myponga are **Myponga,** nine km southwest; **Spring Mount,** 13 km southeast; and **Nixon-Skinner,** behind Myponga Reservoir.

Be careful of the rips at **Carrickalinga.** A better choice is **Normanville,** which has excellent swimming, both jetty and boat fishing, snorkeling on the offshore reef, and paraflying during the summer. A river runs through the **Normanville Beach Caravan Park,** Jetty Rd., tel. (08) 8558-2038. Rent an on-site van or campsite there, or at **Beachside Caravan Park,** Willis Dr., tel. (08) 8558-2458. Budget-Inexpensive.

High Country Trails, Cape Jervis Rd., Normanville, tel. (08) 8558-2507, organizes horseback rides, from an hour's trot along the beach to three-day pack trips, for learners or experienced riders.

The beaches get pretty rocky from here on out. Try **Lady Bay** for snorkeling, **Second Valley** for boat and jetty fishing, and **Rapid Bay** for excellent scuba diving. (Colonel Light first landed in Rapid Bay.) In Second Valley, **Leonard's Mill,** tel. (08) 8598-4184, a restored 1849 stone mill, is open daily for à la carte meals (entrees $10-16), light snacks, and drinks at indoor or outdoor courtyard bars.

The tiny town of **Delamere,** inland along Main South Rd., has a number of historical buildings, including the Uniting Church (1858), rural school (1861), St. James Church (1871), and council offices (1878).

CAPE JERVIS TO VICTOR HARBOR

Rounding the cape, the coast becomes more rugged as the waves of the Southern Ocean pound the shores, and branch roads lead through weathered terrain to isolated and occasionally ferocious beaches below.

At the tip of the peninsula, **Cape Jervis** is both the jumping-off point to Kangaroo Island, 13 km across the Backstairs Passage, and the Heysen Trail, which passes through many different conservation parks on its faraway way to the Flinders Ranges. The coastal waters are noted for jetty and deep-sea fishing as well as scuba diving, and the tall cliffs and powerful breezes make it an ideal base for hang gliding. The **Cape Jervis Lighthouse** was in operation from 1871 to 1972. **Old Cape Jervis Station Homestead,** Main Rd. 9, tel. (08) 8598-0233, offers B&B accommodations, cheap bunkhouse beds, and a tennis court. Budget-Inexpensive. **Cape Jervis Tavern Motel,** Main Rd., tel. (08) 8598-0276, has modern rooms and rates that include continental breakfast. Moderate.

Back on Range Rd., turn into **Talisker Conservation Park,** where you can fossick about the 1862 silver and lead mine. You'll pass through the old mining town of **Silverton** on your way to the park. **Warning:** Watch out for those mine shafts!

Deep Creek Conservation Park is nothing short of spectacular—rugged cliffs form sheer drops downward to the raging sea, profusions of delicate orchids and luxuriant ferns tangle along cool running streams, native birds and wildlife sweep from steep terrain to secluded coves. Accessed from Range Rd., Deep Creek offers a number of exciting trails for hikers—everything from casual strolls to challenging bushwalks. It is essential that you check in at Park Headquarters before embarking on any of the walks, particularly the strenuous, long-distance Heysen Trail, which is closed outside the conservation parks in summer. You can also pick up trail maps, camping permits, and other detailed information from the park headquarters, or phone (08) 8598-0263.

Due to powerful rips and changing currents, only very experienced surfers and strong swimmers should tempt their fate at isolated **Parsons** and **Waitpinga** Beaches, both part of **Newland Head Conservation Park,** reached from Range Road. The park also has walking trails and camping facilities. **Rosetta Harbor,** on the northern side of the Bluff in Encounter Bay, has good snorkeling and scuba diving.

VICTOR HARBOR

Situated on the shores of Encounter Bay, Victor Harbor (pop. 5,300) is the largest town on the Fleurieu Peninsula. Being a close 83 km from Adelaide makes it exceptionally popular with city folk, who invade the town during summer and school holidays. Two unique natural formations are the Bluff, a 100-meter-high headland, and—protecting the bay from the Southern Ocean's wild surf—Granite Island, connected by causeway to the shore.

History

Victor Harbor's whaling stations bustled with activity from 1837 (when the first station was established) until 1869, attracting both small and large vessels to its port, making it one of the state's most important export terminals. Assuming that Victor Harbor would not only become *the* river port, but possibly the state capital, a railway was built in 1864, linking the town to Goolwa, at the mouth of the Murray River. Unfortunately, big ship owners, scared off by the Southern Ocean's erratic and stormy seas, searched for safer spots to drop anchor, and the port soon became obsolete.

Sights

The **Museum of Historical Art,** Yankalilla Rd., three km from Victor Harbor, tel. (08) 8552-1546, has a large private collection of shells, rocks, coins, medals, firearms, and miniature cars. Open Sundays and school holidays 1-5 p.m. Admission is $3.

Historic buildings include the **Railway Station, Telegraph Station** (1867), **Newland Memorial Congregational Church** on Victoria St. (1869), and **St. Augustine's Church of England** on Burke St. (1869).

If you climb to the top of the rather steep **Bluff,** you'll get a stupendous view of the bay where Baudin and Flinders had their famous meeting in 1802, and below to Rosetta Bay and Whale Haven, where the whaling stations operated.

Ride to **Granite Island** on Australia's only horse-drawn tram. Gentle giant Clydesdales commute from Victor Harbor to the island daily 10 a.m.-4 p.m. Fare is $3 one-way. Buy tickets at the causeway on the Victor Harbor foreshore. During South Australian school holidays and good-weather weekends, chairlifts operate to the top of the peak for expansive views of the town and bay. Summertime visitors to the island might spy fairy penguins as they waddle toward their rocky homes each night after dusk. You can also walk to the island (it takes about 20 minutes) for free from the causeway entrance.

Urimbirra Wildlife Park, Adelaide Rd., five km from Victor Harbor, tel. (08) 8554-6554, is a 16-hectare open-range park with dingoes, crocs (there's one named Aunty Jack), koalas, kangaroos, bats, wombats, bettongs, bandicoots, snakes, eels, and a nocturnal house. Hours are daily 9 a.m.-5 p.m. Admission is $7.

The **South Australian Whale Centre,** 2 Railway Terrace, tel. (08) 8552-5644, features displays and exhibits relating to this great ocean mammal, as well as a concise history of the local whaling industry. Seals, dolphins, and penguins co-exist in the three-story interpretive center. Hours are daily 9 a.m.-5 p.m. Admission is $6.

Opposite Urimbirra, the one-hectare **Nagawooka Flora Reserve** is planted with almost 1,000 named trees, shrubs, and groundcovers from all over Australia. The park is open daily during daylight hours.

Safe swimming beaches are on either side of the Causeway to Granite Island, good snorkeling at **Oliver's Reef,** and bodysurfing at **Chiton Rocks,** between Victor Harbor and Port Elliot.

Accommodations

You have a choice of simple guesthouses, motel rooms, or fully equipped holiday flats. Check with the tourist office for long-term selections. If you're visiting during peak periods, book far in advance, and expect rates to increase (and often double).

Anchorage Guest House, 21 Flinders Parade, tel. (08) 8552-5970, is a nearly century-old traditional establishment, set right on the sea with terrific views. Inexpensive rates include breakfast. Both the **Grosvenor Junction,** Ocean St., tel. (08) 8552-1011, and **The Clifton Lodge,** 39 Torrens St., tel. (08) 8552-1062, have well-kept rooms and traveler-friendly ambience. Inexpensive-Moderate. **Villa Victor,** 59 Victoria St., tel. (08) 8552-4258, charges $55 single, including full breakfast. Inexpensive. More luxurious (and expensive) is centrally located **Apollon Motor Inn,** 15 Torrens St., tel. (08) 8552-2777, with quality rooms and the usual perks. Moderate-Expensive. **Kerjancia Motor Lodge,** 141 Hindmarsh Rd., tel. (08) 8552-2900, also more upmarket, offers self-contained apartments with a solar pool and spa. Expensive.

Victor Harbor Holiday Centre, Bay Rd., tel. (08) 8552-1949, has on-site vans, cabins, and campsites, as well as moderately priced motel units with cooking facilities. Budget-Moderate.

Food
You'll find the usual resort town takeaways. Stop for breads, cakes, and pastries at **Bourman's Bakery,** Victoria St., or **Ocean Street Bakehouse,** Ocean Street. The **Sub Station,** Ocean St., is another good sandwich-maker ($4-8 per sub), and **South Coast Fish Café,** also on Ocean St., is a good spot for fresh catches ($6-12 for fish and chips). **Café Bavaria,** Albert Place, cooks up German-Aussie rib-stickers for around $8-12. **Anchorage Guest House** serves moderately priced home-style meals (entrees $8-12) in historic surroundings. The **Hotel Crown,** Ocean St., is the cheap pub-meal stop ($3-7). For finer and costlier meals, try the restaurants at **Apollon Motor Inn, Bayview Motel, Ocean Crest Motel, Hotel Victor,** or **Whalers Inn.** Their entrees will set you back around $9-16.

Information
The **Victor Harbor Tourist Information Centre,** 10 Railway Terrace, tel. (08) 8552-4255, provides maps, directions, and other assistance. Open daily 10 a.m.-4 p.m.

Dial 000 for emergencies. **South Coast District Hospital,** tel. (08) 8552-1066, and **police,** tel. (08) 8552-2088, serve the immediate area. For maps and other road information, contact the **Royal Automobile Association,** 59 Maude St., tel. (08) 8552-1033.

PORT ELLIOT

Farther along the Encounter Coast, on Horseshoe Bay, the historic township of Port Elliot (pop. 1,050) attracts body and board surfers to its fabled beaches and tourists to its picturesque shores with views of the Murray mouth and Coorong National Park.

History
Proclaimed a town in 1854—with the opening of South Australia's first iron railway on its inaugural Port Elliot-to-Goolwa link—Port Elliot was named by Governor Young after his buddy, Sir Charles Elliot. Like neighboring Victor Harbor, Port Elliot did not fare very well as a port. Though the first ship anchored in 1851, and traffic grew to a busy 85 arrivals in 1855, by 1864 seven ships had been sunk and strewn about the bay. So much for Port Elliot—in that same year, another railway link was built to Victor Harbor, and for a short time traffic was redirected.

Sights
Historic structures lining **The Strand** include the **police station** (1853), **courthouse** (1866), **council chamber** (1879), and nearby **St. Jude's Church** (1854). The National Trust has set up a historical display in the **Port Elliot Railway Station,** built in 1911.

For excellent **coastal views,** take the scenic walk from just above Horseshoe Bay and follow the cliffs to Knight's Beach, or look out from **Freeman Knob,** along The Strand at the main Victor Harbor-Goolwa Rd. junction.

West of town, **Boomer Beach** is where experienced bodysurfers come for large, dumping waves. Small, sheltered **Green Bay,** on Freeman Knob, is good for sunbathing, but swimming is dangerous in the rocky bay with its strong riptides. Swimmers will find very good facilities at **Horseshoe Bay,** with small surf at the Commodore Point end. **Middleton Beach,** on the way to Goolwa, is one of the best surfing beaches on the Encounter Coast. **Big Surf Australia,** Main Rd., Middleton, tel. (08) 8554-2399, sells bodyboards, swimwear, and accessories, rents quality gear, and is open daily. Flagstaff Hill Rd. leads from central Middleton to another inspiration point, a winery, and a mushroom farm.

Accommodations

Royal Family Hotel, 32 North Terrace, tel. (08) 8554-2219, has simple rooms with shared facilities. Inexpensive. **Hotel Elliot,** on The Strand by the railway station, tel. (08) 8554-2218, has more of a family-type atmosphere. Inexpensive. At **Cavalier Inn Motel,** The Strand, tel. (08) 8554-2067, you'll find good views and a swimming pool. Moderate. **Thomas Henry's Country Inn,** 8 Charteris St., tel. (08) 8554-3388, offers 1930s-style B&B accommodation. Moderate-Expensive. If you're staying put, the following spots can set you up in a holiday unit with weekly rates: **Lifeplan Holiday Units,** 4 The Strand, tel. (08) 8554-2772; and **Dolphins Court,** Strangways Terrace, Horseshoe Bay, tel. (08) 8554-2029. Inexpensive-Moderate.

Port Elliot Caravan Park, Horseshoe Bay, tel. (08) 8554-2134, has on-site vans, campsites, and moderately priced cottages. Budget-Moderate. **Middleton Caravan Park,** Middleton, tel. (08) 8554-2383, rents on-site vans and campsites. Budget-Inexpensive.

Food

Royal Family Hotel and **Hotel Elliot** both serve inexpensive counter meals ($3-8). **Sitar Indian Restaurant,** The Strand, tel. (08) 8554-2144, has moderately priced Indian meals and takeaways (curries range $8-12). For moderately priced meals ($9-14 for entrees), a cut above the usual counter fare, try **The Middleton Bistro,** Main Rd., tel. (08) 8554-3230, or **Old Registry Restaurant,** The Strand, tel. (08) 8554-3366.

You'll pay dearly for the beautiful continental cuisine at **Thomas Hardy's Restaurant,** tel. (08) 8554-3388, where well-presented seafood and meat dishes run $22-40.

Middleton Seafoods, tel. (08) 8554-2988, and **Middleton General Store and Post Office,** tel. (08) 8554-2064, are both open daily for takeaway food and snacks.

GOOLWA

Situated where the Murray River meets the great Southern Ocean, Goolwa (pop. 2,360) draws railway buffs and river rats who come to ride Australia's first iron public railway, to cruise up and down the Murray or around Lake Alexand-

rina, or to laze away the days by the historic old wharf. Hindmarsh Island, a ferry ride away, sits between the mighty mouth and the entrance to Lake Alexandrina.

History

Prosperous paddle steamer trade along the Murray River made Goolwa an important port from the mid- to late 1800s. The opening of the railway line to Port Elliot gave the town true, though short-lived, notoriety. Alas, a new line extending all the way to Adelaide and built in the 1880s caused Goolwa's final fizzle as port extraordinaire.

Over on Hindmarsh Island, an obelisk marks the place where Charles Sturt, in 1830, squinted past the sand hills and into the Murray mouth, as did Captain Collett Barker, another explorer, who must have opened *his* eyes a little too wide before he got speared to death by the natives.

Sights

The **Goolwa Hotel** (1853), Cadell St.; **post office** (1857), Cadell St.; **Corio Hotel** (1857), Railway Terrace; and **police station** (1859), Goolwa Terrace, are some of the old buildings still in use today. (The Goolwa Hotel has a figurehead from the wrecked ship *Mozambique* on its parapet.)

Other historic sights are the **Railway Superintendent's House** (1852), **Railway Horse Stables** (1853), the **Saddlery** (1867), **Town Mechanics Institute** (1868), and **Church of England** (1867), all on Cadell Street.

The **Goolwa National Trust Museum** (1870), Porter St., is housed inside a former blacksmith shop. The museum has many exhibits focusing on Goolwa's early beginnings, including a "Port of Goolwa" room. Hours are Tues.-Thurs., Sat.-Sun., school and public holidays 2-5 p.m. Admission is $2.

Signal Point, The Wharf, tel. (08) 8555-3488, opened in 1988 by the illustrious Prince of Wales, is the River Murray Interpretive Center. High-tech computerized displays show what the river was like before the Europeans came as well as the impact of modern industry and development on the important waterway. Climb aboard *Oscar W,* a restored paddle wheeler built in 1908, which sits alongside the wharf. Hours are daily 10 a.m.-5 p.m., except Christmas Day. Admission is $5.

The only way to get to **Hindmarsh Island** is

by the free 24-hour ferry near the wharf. Walking trails and lookouts enable you to see the Murray mouth on one side and Lake Alexandrina on the other. The Sturt Memorial granite obelisk is about three km from the ferry landing, on the right side of the main road. Boat ramps on the island will launch you into salt or fresh water.

Built between 1935 and 1940, **Goolwa Barrage**, an enormous concrete structure atop a multitude of wooden piles pounded into the riverbed, crosses the lower Murray—from Hindmarsh Island to Sir Richard Peninsula—and separates the salty sea from the fresh river water. A bird blind, off Barrage Rd., lets watchers view the area birdlife.

Currency Creek, an eight-km drive up Cadell St., has an Aboriginal canoe tree alongside the road, picnic areas, and a walking trail that will take you to a waterfall, old copper mine, and short detour to the cemetery.

Goolwa Beach often has big surf, crosscurrents, and some rips—recommended for experienced swimmers only.

Accommodations

Two of the town's oldest buildings, **Goolwa Hotel,** Cadell St., tel. (08) 8555-2012, and **Corio Hotel,** Railway Terrace, tel. (08) 8555-2011, offer basic rooms with shared facilities. Inexpensive. For cheap home-style accommodations, try **Graham's Castle,** corner Castle Ave. and Bradford Rd., tel. (08) 8555-2182. Inexpensive.

South Lakes Motel, Barrage Rd., tel. (08) 8555-2194, features modern rooms with kitchenettes, swimming area, and adjacent golf course. Moderate. For motel-style accommodations, try **Goolwa Central,** 30 Cadell St., tel. (08) 8555-1155, where rates include continental breakfast, a pool, spa, and rec room. Moderate.

Narnu Pioneer Holiday Farm, Monument Rd., Hindmarsh Island, tel. (08) 8555-2002, features self-contained cottages in a rural setting for $50-60 per double, with horse riding and aquatic equipment available. Inexpensive-Moderate.

On-site vans and campsites are available at **Goolwa Camping and Tourist Park,** Kessell Rd., tel. (08) 8555-2144, and campsites only at **Hindmarsh Island Caravan Park,** Madsen St., Hindmarsh Island, tel. (08) 8555-2234. Budget-Inexpensive.

Food

Counter meals ($4-7) and à la carte fare ($7-11) are served daily at both the **Goolwa** and **Corio** hotels. A coffee shop at **Signal Point** serves light lunches ($6-9), snacks, and cakes. **South Lakes Motel** has a comparatively pricey restaurant at the water's edge ($10-16 for seafood entrees). Otherwise, it's the usual takeaways, chicken joints, and a Chinese restaurant.

Information

The **Goolwa Tourist and Information Centre,** Cadell St., tel. (08) 8555-1144, provides information on all area facilities, as well as maps for historic walking tours. Hours are daily 10 a.m.-4 p.m., closed Christmas Day and Good Friday.

For assistance, contact the **police,** tel. (08) 8555-2018; **ambulance,** tel. (08) 8552-2111; or **fire brigade,** tel. (08) 8555-2000. The **Royal Automobile Association,** tel. (08) 8555-2009, will assist with maps and driving-related questions.

STRATHALBYN

Approximately 30 km north of Goolwa, beautiful Strathalbyn (pop. 1,925), a designated heritage township, was settled by Scottish immigrants in 1839. Examples of architecture that reflect Scottish influence are the **Angus Flour Mill** (1852), **20 High Street Crafts** (1854), **London House** (1867), and **Argus House** (1868). **Saint Andrew's Church** (1848), overlooking the river, is one of Australia's most fabled country churches.

The River Angus, which flows through town, is bordered by **Soldiers Memorial Gardens,** a peaceful setting for picnicking, duck-feeding, swan-songing, and gentle strolls. Several Aboriginal canoe trees line the water's edge, and gum trees hover above lush lawns and rambling bridges.

Many arts and crafts, antique, and second-hand shops are scattered about the town. A walking-tour book ($1) to Strathalbyn's two shopping areas is available at many locations.

Milang, 20 km southeast of Strathalbyn, is another former river port, now used as a launching point for boating, windsurfing, and water-skiing on Lake Alexandrina. **Langhorne Creek,** 60 km northeast from Milang, is a grape- and almond-growing district on the way to **Wellington,** farther east yet, on the banks of the Murray

River. Don't miss a ride on the 24-hour free ferry, operating since 1839 (when it was the only access across the river between South Australia and the eastern states).

Accommodations
Two fine old pubs are **Robin Hood Hotel,** 18 High St., tel. (08) 8536-2608, and the **Terminus Hotel,** 17 Rankine St., tel. (08) 8536-2026. Both offer the usual basic rooms with shared facilities. Inexpensive.

Strathalbyn Caravan Park, Coronation Rd., tel. (08) 8536-3681, has on-site vans and campsites. Budget-Inexpensive.

Food
Both the Robin Hood and Terminus Hotels have reasonably priced counter meals ($5-7). **Café Ruffino's,** High St., tel. (08) 8536-2355, dishes up pizza, pasta, salads, and sandwiches ($6-14). **Albyn Riverside Chinese and Asian Restaurant,** Albyn Terrace, tel. (08) 8536-3744, features all your favorite Asian delights ($6-12).

Events
The **Penny Farthing Challenge Cup,** held annually in March, is an international event in which more than 30 riders race through the township on pennyfarthings and other vintage bicycles. Accompanying hoopla consists of parades, band performances, barbecues, a pancake brekky, arts and crafts displays, and Scottish street entertainment.

Information
Pick up info at the **Tourist Information Centre,** 20 South Terrace, in the old railway station,

tel. (08) 8536-3212. Open Mon.-Sat. 9:30 a.m.-4 p.m., Sunday 11 a.m.-4 p.m.

For **emergencies,** dial 000. For other assistance, contact the **police,** tel. (08) 8536-2044; **ambulance,** tel. (08) 8536-2333; or local **Royal Automobile Association,** tel. (08) 8536-2066.

TRANSPORTATION

Stateliner, tel. (08) 8415-5555, travels the Adelaide-Willunga-Victor Harbor route daily. Fare to Victor Harbor is about $14 one-way. **Kangaroo Island Connection,** tel. (08) 8231-5959, departs twice daily for Cape Jervis. Fare is $30 one-way. **TransAdelaide,** tel. (08) 8210-1000, serves outer suburbs within the Fleurieu area.

Railway buffs should board the steam-powered **Cockle Train,** which follows the historic Victor Harbor-Goolwa route at least three times daily on school holidays, long weekends, and Sundays. The one-hour-and-45-minute roundtrip costs about $12. For information, phone (08) 8231-1707.

The MV *Philanderer III,* tel. (13) 1301, provides ferry service from Cape Jervis to Kangaroo Island up to five times daily for $30 one-way.

Huck Finn-ers and river queens can choose from a variety of Murray River cruises departing from Goolwa. **PS *Mundoo*** makes daily half- and full-day paddle steamer cruises to the Mundoo Channel, Currency Creek, Narnu Bay, and Goose and Goat Islands. Fares range $15-30. **MV *Aroona*** has a luncheon cruise downstream to the Murray mouth, as well as a pelican-feeding excursion. Fares range $12-30. For information, phone (08) 8555-3488.

KANGAROO ISLAND

After Tasmania and Melville (off Darwin's coast), Kangaroo Island (pop. 4,000), approximately 145 km by 60 km, is Australia's third largest island. Though the climate is temperate, with only rare frosts and highs not usually exceeding 38° C, the island is at its best (and most crowded) during the summer months.

Dramatic cliffs, sheltered beaches, untamed coastline, untouched scenery, and flourishing wildlife lure tourists to this popular holiday resort, a relatively close 113 km southwest of Adelaide and just a short hop off the Fleurieu Peninsula. Families enjoy swimming and sunning, camping and hiking in their choice of 16 conservation parks. Divers have a grand time exploring the 40-plus ships reported wrecked around the coastal waters, beginning with the *William,* in 1847. Anglers drop their lines from jetties, rocks, and boats, into surf, rivers, and the deep blue sea. Naturalists are enthralled by the plentiful wildlife—kangaroos (natch), plus koalas, seals, fairy penguins, emus, sea lions, echidnas, possums, and an occasional platypus—unscathed by such predators as foxes or dingoes, which are nonexistent on the island. On the western side, you can still see the kin of wild pigs, reputedly set ashore by French explorer Nicholas Baudin as feed for shipwrecked sailors. Besides all the critters, you can tiptoe through more than 700 native wildflower species, and about 150 others brought in from elsewhere in the world. *And,* if you're into the birds and the bees, keep your eyes and ears perked for crimson rosellas, purple-gaped honeyeaters, ospreys, sea eagles, the rare glossy black cockatoo, and the unique Ligurian honeybee.

Kingscote, on Nepean Bay, is the island's commercial center and the city nearest the airport. Other communities with holiday facilities are American River, Penneshaw, and Parndana. The north coast flaunts calmer waters, with stretches of beach for swimming, sunning, and lazy-day fishing. Dudley Peninsula, along the Backstairs Passage, boasts fairy penguins, pelicans, stunning views, and the Cornwall-style village of Penneshaw. The south coast is the wild side, with sand dunes, crashing waves, and three conservation parks. And Flinders Chase National Park, on the south and west coasts, is Kangaroo Island's spectacular wildlife sanctuary.

History

Not much is known about the Aboriginals who originally inhabited the island; stone tools thought to be more than 10,000 years old are about the only sign of their presence. Anyway, they were long gone by 1802, when Matthew Flinders, voyaging on the *Investigator,* "discovered" Kangaroo Island for himself (and his king). But French explorer Nicholas Baudin was also nosing about, doing some circumnavigating of his own. By the time the two sailors faced off shortly afterward in Encounter Bay, Flinders had named the island—this time in tribute to the many kangaroos he'd seen, instead of for a compatriot—while Baudin had christened the places *he'd* charted *en français.* Consequently, you'll find French names attached to many island sights, reflecting the French vs. English "tug-of-words."

The island has an American influence also. In 1803, one year after Matthew Flinders had taken the island, a group of American sealers arrived at a site eventually named "American River." Using native pine, they built the *Independence,* South Australia's first boat.

It wasn't until 1836 that the first 400 settlers, sponsored by the South Australian Company, arrived from England aboard the *Duke of York* to formally establish a township at Reeves Point, north of Kingscote. The lack of fresh water kept this from being a viable colonial settlement and, by 1840, except for a few lingering souls, most of the population had shifted over to the mainland. The fact is, though, that Reeves Point was South Australia's first official European settlement, and the present inhabitants are tremendously proud of that bit of history.

Early industries on the island were yacca gum production, salt mining, and eucalyptus oil distilling (eucalyptus oil was Australia's first export product). Agriculture, however, was in a slump until the 1930s, when cobalt and copper were added to the soil. After that, crops flourished and, before long, one-half the island had be-

KANGAROO ISLAND

FLEURIEU PENINSULA

INVESTIGATOR STRAIT

BACKSTAIRS PASSAGE

SOUTHERN OCEAN

© AVALON TRAVEL PUBLISHING

= SHIPWRECK

0   10 Km

KONA (1916)
WILLIAM (1847)
CAPE JERVIS
PASSAGE
PENNESHAW
FRENCHMAN'S ROCK
CHAPMAN RIVER
ANTECHAMBER BAY
CAPE WILLOUGHBY
CAPE HART
CAPE HART C.P.
DUDLEY C.P.

FANNY (1885)
BIRD PROTECTION DIST.
ROBERT BURNS (1906)
GOLDEN HOPE (1885)
GEM (1915)
REDEN BAY
WESTERN COVE
AMERICAN RIVER
KINGSCOTE
BROWNLOW
EMU BAY
PELICAN LAGOON C.P.
PENNINGTON BAY
WANDERER (1906)
YOU YANGS (1890)
OSMANLI (1853)
MURRAY'S LAGOON
CAPE GANTHEAUME C.P.
CAPE GANTHEAUME

FAIRFIELD (1874)
BROTHERS (1916)
AIRPORT
PARNDANA
SOUTH COAST RD
SEAL BAY C.P.
SEAL BAY
VIVONNE BAY C.P.
VIVONNE BAY

MINOSA (1884)
STOKES BAY
NORTH COAST RD
COAST RD
PLAYFORD HWY
LITTLE SAHARA
MONTEBELLO (1905)
CAPE YOUNGHUSBAND

TASMAN (1877)
SNELLINGS BEACH
WESTERN RIVER COVE
WESTERN RIVER C.P.
CAPE TORRENS C.P.
KELLY HILL CAVES
KELLY HILL C.P.
DUNCON (1897)

TREASURE (TROVE)
CAPE TORRENS
HARVEY'S RETURN
CAPE BORDA
MERMAID (1905)
FIDES (1860)
LOCH VENNACHAR (1905)
WEST END HWY
SHACKLE RD
LARRIKIN LAGOON
FLINDERS CHASE NATIONAL PARK
ROCKY RIVER HEADQUARTERS
REMARKABLE ROCKS
CAPE DU COUEDIC
MAIRS (1855)
EMILY SMITH (1877)
LOCH SLOY (1899)
PORTLAND MARU (1935)
BIRD SANCTUARY

come productive farmland. Today Kangaroo Island's most vital industries are agriculture, fishing, and tourism.

KINGSCOTE

On the shores of Nepean Bay, Kingscote (pop. 1,450) blends its historical significance with modern-day necessities. Sheer cliffs to the north afford terrific views of the harbor and Western Cove, while cliffs to the south provide a languid drop to the Cygnet River swamp and bird lands. Kingscote is the island's major shipping port and trade center.

Sights
Reeves Point Historic Site is where the *Duke of York* anchored in 1836 and South Australia officially began. You'll find remnants of the first post office, the state's oldest cemetery and, farther north, the state's oldest introduced tree—a mulberry, planted around 1836, that still bears edible fruit! (You can buy jam made from the berries.)

Hope Cottage, the National Trust Museum, on Centenary Ave., is housed in an 1850s building built by two pioneering brothers. Displays include working exhibits, maritime history, family histories, photographs, and early newspapers. Open daily 2-4 p.m., closed mid-July through August. Admission is $4. For information, phone (08) 8553-2656.

St. Alban's Church, built in 1884, is Kingscote's oldest public building. Stained-glass windows, memorials to pioneer families, and graffiti from when the church was used as a schoolroom are worth seeing.

Memorial Park, on the seafront close to the town center, has memorials to Flinders and the war dead, as well as barbecue and picnic areas for when your nostalgia gives way to hunger pangs.

Fairy penguins parade to their homes at dusk on most nights. Best viewing places are between the swimming pool and jetty, or among rocks near the jetty. At **Bay of Shoals,** see pelicans and other birds fed daily at 4 p.m.

Heritage Walking Trails explore Kingscote's natural history and heritage sights. Pick up maps at the Tourist Information Centre on Dauncey Street. For information, phone (08) 8553-2165.

Family **beaches** with shallow swimming and wading facilities can be found in front of the Ozone Hotel and at Little Brownlow Beach, in front of the Yacht Club. Another spot for safe swimming is the rockbound **seawater pool.**

Accommodations
Be sure to book ahead, especially during school holiday periods. **Kangaroo Island Central Backpackers,** 19 Murray St., tel. (08) 8553-2787, several blocks from the coast, offers a lounge, kitchen, bicycle rentals, and dorm beds for $13.

Kangaroo Island Holiday Village, 9 Dauncey St., tel. (08) 8553-2225, has self-contained family units with kitchens. Moderate. **Parade Units,** adjacent to Brownlow Beach, tel. (08) 8553-2394, is another decent choice with kitchen facilities. Moderate.

Slightly higher-priced are the **Island Resort,** Telegraph Rd., tel. (08) 8553-2100, with an indoor heated pool, sauna, and spa, and **Ellison's Seaview Motel,** Chapman Terrace, tel. (08) 8553-2030, featuring seafront motel units and guesthouse rooms. **Ozone Seafront Hotel,** the foreshore, tel. (08) 8553-2011, has comfortable rooms and great views. Moderate-Expensive.

Both **Nepean Bay Caravan Park,** the foreshore, Brownlow Beach, tel. (08) 8553-2394, and **Emu Bay Caravan Park,** on the Esplanade, tel. (08) 8553-2325, rent campsites, on-site vans, and cabins. Budget-Inexpensive.

Food
Good takeaways are **Pelican Pete's Takeaway Eats,** Main St., tel. (08) 8553-2138, and **Rick's Seaview Takeaway,** 3 Kingscote Terrace, tel. (08) 8553-2585. **Port of Call Restaurant,** the foreshore, tel. (08) 8553-2834, serves seafood, steak, and pasta ($9-16 for entrees) in an intimate setting overlooking Nepean Bay. The **Ozone Seafront Hotel** features an à la carte dining room, bistro, and informal coffee shop with meals at all prices. **Ellison's Seaview Motel Restaurant,** Chapman Terrace, tel. (08) 8553-2030, is another choice for sit-down dining on decent meals ($8-14 entrees). **Blue Gum Café,** on Dauncy St., between Commercial and Murray Streets, is your sandwich ($4-7) and cappuccino stop. **Roger's Deli and Café,** also on Dauncey St., tel. (08) 8553-2053, makes up satisfying sandwiches, salads, and hot and cold drinks (about $6-8 for sandwich and side salad).

DUDLEY PENINSULA

Kangaroo Island's eastern tip, the Dudley Peninsula, starts as a narrow neck at Pelican Lagoon Conservation Park and white-sand beaches, then rounds northeast to Cornish-influenced Penneshaw, over to rugged Cape Willoughby, south to Cape Hart, and then west to Dudley Conservation Park.

American River

This tiny village, midway between Kingscote and Penneshaw, is named for the American sealers who lived here for four months in 1803. It's a favorite spot for fishers, who come not only for a fresh catch-of-the-day, but for the scenic beauty of gum and she-oak forested hills as they dip to meet the calm waters of Eastern Cove. Try to arrive at the end of August, when the freesias cover every knoll, dell, and pathway with brilliant blossoms.

The nearby aquatic reserve, Pelican Lagoon Conservation Park, is abundant with pelicans, swans, and Cape Barren geese.

Linnetts Island Club Resort, tel. (08) 8553-7053, has a choice of rooms, suites, villas, or holiday flats, ranging in price from inexpensive to expensive. **Yantoowarra Resort Motel,** Wattle Ave., tel. (08) 8553-7044, overlooks the American River and has a pool, spa, and sauna. Continental breakfast is included in the deal. Moderate-Expensive. Bucolic **Wanderers Rest,** corner Government and Bayview Roads, tel. (08) 8553-7140, is a guesthouse on a hillside with sweeping views of American River. Expensive. All of these accommodations have restaurants or dining rooms.

Pennington Bay

Just one km off the Kingscote-to-Penneshaw Road, very near American River, Pennington Bay is a popular swimming and surfing beach—but only for the experienced. Otherwise, you can take a hike (more of a climb, actually) to the top of Mt. Thisby for views of both Pelican and Pennington Bays.

Dudley Conservation Park, near Pennington Bay, is one of the island's many wildlife havens where you may see the dama wallaby, Kangaroo Island kangaroo, purple-gaped honeyeater, echidna, and fairy wren.

Penneshaw

Passing along the sandy-white Island and American Beaches, you'll come to Cornish-like hamlet Penneshaw, only 16 km across the Backstairs Passage from mainland South Australia. Tourists are drawn here for the safe bathing beach, excellent fishing off Hog Bay Jetty, and the parade of fairy penguins nesting (returning home each evening) in the cliffs and sand hills near town.

In 1802, Captain Flinders landed near **Christmas Cove,** also known as "The Basin." The granite boulders there had a slightly earlier arrival than the good captain—they were deposited by a glacier more than 200 million years ago.

Frenchman's Rock, at Hog Bay, marks the spot where, in 1803, Captain Baudin, who'd just "encountered" Captain Flinders, came ashore to fill his empty water casks. The two seamen, unaware that their respective countries were waging war, unwittingly became water brothers.

Penneshaw Museum, housed inside the 1922 school, features maritime and other historic and folk exhibits. Hours are Monday, Wednesday, and Saturday 3-5 p.m., daily in January and during Easter. Admission is $2.50. For information, phone (08) 8553-1108.

Hog Bag Jetty, built 1902-09, is not only a famous fishing locale, but home port for the MV *Philanderer III.*

Bookings are essential at **Penneshaw Youth Hostel,** 43 North Terrace, tel. (08) 8553-1284 or (1800) 01-8258, where dorm beds cost $14 per night. Facilities include scooter, bicycle, and boat rentals; kitchen facilities; launderette; swimming beach; nature walks; slide and video presentations; and a range of organized tours of the island. Budget. **Penguin Walk Hostel,** corner of Middle and Bay terraces, tel. (08) 8553-1233, offers dorm beds for $12, a number of private bathrooms, and an adjacent pizza parlor. Budget.

Tandarra Holiday Units, 33 Middle Terrace, tel. (08) 8553-1233, offers moderately priced holiday flats and a bunkhouse with $13 beds. Budget-Moderate. **Seaview Lodge,** Willoughby Rd., tel. (08) 8553-1132, is a comfortable bed and breakfast with friendly hosts and decent prices. Inexpensive-Moderate. **Sorrento Resort,** North Terrace, tel. (08) 8553-1028, features modern motel suites, cottages with kitchenettes, and alpine chalets with kitchenettes. The resort, set on two acres of seafront gardens, has a safe swimming beach, swimming pool, poolside bar, half-court tennis facilities, spa, and sauna, and offers a variety of island tours. Moderate-Expensive.

Penneshaw Caravan Park, Talinga Terrace, tel. (08) 8553-1075, with campsites and on-site vans, is opposite a safe beach and close to town. Budget-Inexpensive.

Sharpy's Cafe, North Terrace and Third St., tel. (08) 8553-1151, serves breakfast, chicken, chips, salads, sandwiches, and good cappuccinos ($5 for chicken and chips). Penneshaw Pizzas, Bay Terrace, tel. (08) 8553-1110, offers a delicious assortment of toppings for your pie ($8-14). The Old Post Office Restaurant, tel. (08) 8553-1063, in one of Penneshaw's oldest commercial buildings, on the first corner away from the ferry, gives you a choice of à la carte dining ($11-16 entrees) or more relaxed (and inexpensive) bistro meals ($6-10 entrees) in the enclosed courtyard. It's open every night except Monday.

Antechamber Bay

This long, sweeping stretch of beach meets the ocean, backdropped by the mainland and bisected by Chapman River as it runs into Lashmar Lagoon. Though this area is famous for canoeing and bream fishing, you'll also find hiking tracks leading to bushland, sandhills, and lagoons.

Cape Willoughby

The first flicker of light was emitted from Cape Willoughby Lighthouse (South Australia's first) in 1852. Built of local limestone, the tower measures 27 meters high and sits 73 meters above sea level. Just below the lighthouse, the rocky, wild, crashing coastline is aptly named Devil's Kitchen. The lighthouse is open to visitors daily 10 a.m.-4 p.m. For information, phone (08) 8553-1191.

Cape Hart Conservation Park, four km southwest of Cape Willoughby, sports massive granite boulders and sandstone cliffs with drops to the Southern Ocean.

THE SOUTH COAST ROAD

From Kingscote to Flinders Chase National Park, ride the wild side in search of shells, shipwrecks, seals, and scenery, scenery, scenery.

Murray's Lagoon

Kangaroo Island's largest freshwater lagoon is encompassed by Cape Gantheaume Conservation Park, a favorite spot for birders. At D'Estrees Bay, on the east side of the park, you can catch fish or collect shells—both line the shores.

Seal Bay

Take the turnoff from South Coast Rd. to Seal Bay Conservation Park, a famous breeding colony of rare sea lions whose ancestors escaped the early sealers. Guided tours, led by the National Parks and Wildlife Service, will take you within a few meters of sunbathing sea lions. Tours run regularly year-round, and times are posted just off the road. The visitors' center is a great stop for gifts, snacks, and general information. For information, phone (08) 8559-4207.

Little Sahara

Back on South Coast Rd., the first road on the left (immediately before the bridge) will take you down to Little Sahara desert, where ridge upon ridge of bleached white dunes blend into the surrounding bushland.

Vivonne Bay

The only safe harbor on this side of the coast, Vivonne Bay has a long, curvy beach with dazzling scenery and a variety of activities—beach, boat, and jetty fishing; beachcombing; swimming; and picnicking. Make inquiries before you take a dip. Normally, safe swimming areas are near the jetty, boat ramp, and Harriet River—other parts of the bay have an undertow.

Kelly Hill Conservation Park

The Kelly Hill Conservation Park has an vast network of limestone ridges, dense mallee, and a coastal trail that winds its way seaward. Kelly Hill shelters sinkholes, caverns, and caves molded from ornately shaped calcite that casts eerie shadows in the tricky light. The largest cave is open to visitors. For information, phone (08) 8559-7231.

At the park's western boundary and sheltered on each side by ocean reefs and rocky headlands, Hanson Bay is another top spot for swimming and fishing.

Continuing along South Coast Rd., you'll soon approach Rocky River Headquarters in Flinders Chase National Park.

FLINDERS CHASE NATIONAL PARK

South Australia's largest national park consists of 73,662 hectares of sanctuary for Kangaroo Island's rare and opulent wildlife. Taking up the entire western end of the island, Flinders Chase is a mecca of unspoiled wilderness for friendly kangaroos (the distinctive Kangaroo Island kangaroo has dark, sooty brown fur), emus, Cape Barren geese, koalas, glossy black cockatoos, and possums riding piggy on their mother's back. The natives are so plentiful and friendly that at Rocky River, humans picnic in enclosed areas while the animals scratch their chins and ogle at *them*.

South of Rocky River Headquarters you can reach the huge, oddly sculpted **Remarkable Rocks,** not to mention **Admiral's Arch,** another intriguing formation, and **Cape du Couëdic Lighthouse,** an "automatic" opened in 1906. (The island's largest shipwreck, that of the *Portland Maru,* occurred near the cape in 1935.)

On the north side of the park, **Cape Borda Lighthouse,** tel. (08) 8559-3257, opened in 1858, stands 155 meters above the sea. Before radio communication, the nearby cannon was used to signal ships of impending dangers. These days the meteorological station, nearby, is a quieter guide—and, no doubt, preferred by the wildlife inhabitants.

The **Rocky River Headquarters,** tel. (08) 8559-7235, will provide you with maps, necessary permits, and all the information you require for your park visit. Be sure to check in with the rangers before embarking on any lengthy hikes along isolated trails. Camping in the park is permitted, and, if you like, you can spend a night or two at the Cape du Couëdic and Cape Borda Lighthouses (for a moderate fee). Admission to the park is $6.50 per vehicle.

THE NORTH COAST ROAD

The West End Highway, which borders the eastern edge of Flinders Chase National Park, will take you to the Playford Highway, a smooth run through grazing country back to Kingscote. The North Coast Rd. leaps and jogs off the beaten path to smooth beaches, rocky points, snug coves, and more stunning scenery.

Harvey's Return

This rugged, rocky cove, east of Cape Borda, was once a camp for American sealers. Later, after the lighthouse was built, it was used as a drop-off point for supplies. You can visit the graves of shipwrecked sailors and lighthouse keepers at the nearby cemetery.

Cape Torrens Conservation Park

Towering cliffs hanging more than 200 meters above the sea make this a dazzling spot for bushwalkers who like trails with drop-dead views, or for birders in search of the rare glossy black cockatoo. Be sure to check in with the rangers at Rocky River Headquarters before setting out.

Western River Cove

This popular swimming and fishing beach, at the mouth of the Western River, is a steep descent from **Western River Conservation Park.** If you don't feel like hitting the beach, the park is full of stringy bark forests, wildlife, and excellent gorge, water, and valley views from its many high cliffs.

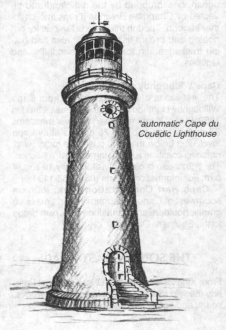

"automatic" Cape du Couëdic Lighthouse

Snellings Beach

Swim, surf, dive, or fish at this peaceful protected bay, situated at the mouth of the Middle River (but be careful of the river's hidden snags and weeds). **Constitution Hill,** above the beach, affords great views of the area.

Accommodations at **Middle River Homestead,** tel. (08) 8559-2278, and **Donanda Hills Cottage,** tel. (08) 8553-9019, are comfy and homelike. Inexpensive-Moderate (the cottage is cheap if you're with several other travelers).

Stokes Bay

Farther east along the coast road, this white sandy beach draws families to its secluded shores, reached by walking through a tunnel within enormous limestone boulders. Though Stokes Bay is an excellent surf spot and fishing hole, its special feature is the large rock-enclosed pool, which provides a safe swimming area.

Paul's Place, between Stokes Bay and Amen Corner, has horse riding, a large aviary (on the off-chance you haven't seen enough birds in the wild), and a glass-fronted beehive where you can get a close-up look at the island's special Ligurian honeybee.

Stokes Bay Holiday House, tel. (08) 8559-6977, provides unpretentious accommodations. Moderate.

Parndana

You have to head inland, back to the Playford Hwy., to visit this little farming community.

Though an experimental farm had been set up in 1938, development was hindered when the area became a soldiers' settlement during World War II. Eventually, 174 soldier-settlement farms were established, and, in 1950, a government research center was set up on the experimental property. Today, the area is used mainly for sheep and cattle grazing.

For holiday house accommodations, try **Kelly's Pioneer Bend Homestead,** Pioneer Bend Rd., tel. (08) 8559-2256, or **Coora Cottage,** Wetheralls Rd., tel. (08) 8559-6027. Moderate. **Gum Valley Resort,** tel. (08) 8559-3207, is a good choice for B&B lovers. Expensive.

Emu Bay

In the early 1900s (and up until the 1970s), this town was named Maxwell. Once it was discovered that the bay was both too shallow and too exposed, the port was moved over to Kingscote. Emu Bay is now a top-notch spot for safe swimming and boat or jetty fishing.

INFORMATION

The island's main tourist information office is the **Kangaroo Island Gateway Visitors Centre,** near the ferry terminal, in Penneshaw, tel. (08) 8553-1185, where you can get all the help you need with tours, trails, and treks, as well as directions to dive shops and bait stores. Be sure to pick up maps that detail the roads branching off main highways. Open Mon.-Fri. 9 a.m.-5 p.m., Sat.-Sun. 10 a.m.-4 p.m. In Kingscote, you can pick up info at **Kingscote Gift Shop,** Dauncey and Commercial Streets, tel. (08) 8553-2165. Open Mon.-Fri. 10 a.m.-5 p.m., Saturday 10 a.m.-2 p.m.

The information office can also provide brochures, issue permits, and arrange guided tours of the island's many conservation parks. Or, contact the **Department of Environment and Natural Resources,** 27 Dauncey St., Kingscote, tel. (08) 8552-2381. Open Mon.-Fri. 9 a.m.- 5 p.m. Regional branches are: at Murray's Lagoon Headquarters, tel. (08) 8553-8233; Seal Bay Conservation Park, tel. (08) 8559-4207; Rocky River Headquarters, tel. (08) 8559-7235; Kelly Hill Conservation Park, tel. (08) 8559-7231; and Cape Borda, tel. (08) 8559-3257. Be sure to pick up a copy of the national park code, and follow all rules to protect the island's sacred wildlife.

Do not fish without first finding out regulations and acquiring the necessary licenses. The Tourist Information Centre can help with these, as well as recommend and organize fishing expeditions. For more information, phone the **Fisheries Officers** at tel. (08) 8553-2130. At no time is fishing, or *any* disturbance of the seabed, permitted at the Pelican Lagoon and Seal Bay aquatic reserves.

Most of the island's emergency facilities are based in Kingscote, though park rangers provide assistance within their jurisdiction. In the case of an emergency, call the local ranger station, dial 000, or, in Kingscote, call the **ambulance,** tel. (08) 8553-2028, or **police,** tel. (08) 8553-2018.

TRANSPORTATION

For information on getting to Kangaroo Island by plane or ferry, see "Getting Away" in the "Adelaide" section.

Getting Around

Airport Coach Service, tel. (08) 8553-2390, operates a shuttle from the Kingscote airport into town for $10, each way. **Kangaroo Island Sealink,** 7 North Terrace Rd., Penneshaw, tel. (08) 8553-1122 or (13) 1301, runs buses between Penneshaw, American River, and Kingscote, to connect with ferry departures. The Penneshaw Penguin Walk and Kangaroo Island youth hostels also provide some airport/ferry pickup and some shuttle services for guests.

If you don't bring a car over with you on the ferry, you can rent one when you arrive. The Kangaroo Island Gateway Visitors Centre or your accommodation hosts can help you; otherwise, try **Kangaroo Island Car Hire,** corner Telegraph and Franklin Streets, tel. (08) 8553-2390, or **Budget,** 76 Dauncey St., Kingscote, tel. (08) 8553-3133. Expect to pay $75 and up per day (weekly deals are cheaper). Again, advance bookings are strongly recommended.

Rent bicycles at **Condon's Takeaway** (home of the rooburger), Penneshaw, tel. (08) 8553-7173; Penneshaw's **Penguin Walk Hostel,** tel. (08) 8553-1233; Kingscote's **Kangaroo Island Backpackers,** tel. (08) 8553-2787; or **Wisteria**

Lodge Motel, Kingscote, tel. (08) 8553-2707. Rent **scooters** at either Country Cottage, Centenary Ave. Kingscote, tel. (08) 8553-2148, or Penneshaw's Penguin Walk Hostel.

With nearly 1,600 km of roads on the island, only the major highways are sealed. The extensive maze of off-the-beaten-paths range from bush tracks to gravel roads. The combination of dust and gravel makes driving at high speeds very hazardous. Even experienced cyclists can find road conditions exhausting. Allow plenty of time to cover the distance you expect to travel. Except during peak holiday periods, the roads have very little traffic, so don't depend on catching a lift. If you're driving, keep your petrol tank full (fill it at Kingscote, American River, Penneshaw, Parndana, and Vivonne Bay, year-round). Bushwalkers must inform rangers before embarking on remote or dangerous trails. And whether driving, hiking, or cycling, carry plenty of water.

For those who'd rather sit back and relax, sign up for an organized coach tour through the visitor center or hotels and motels. Most of the hostels offer an interesting selection of one- and two-day jaunts. **Penguin Tours,** tel. (08) 8553-2844, departs nightly from Penneshaw and Kingscote for ranger-led observations of penguin lifestyles. Cost is $6. **Kangaroo Island Sealink,** tel. (08) 8553-1122 or (13) 1301, offers a one-day coach tour of the island. Divers, kayakers, climbers, and fishers might want to sign up for a one day or longer tour through **Adventure Charters,** tel. (08) 8552-9119.

THE SOUTHEAST

On the map, South Australia's southeast region doesn't appear to be more than a couple of major highways along the Adelaide-Melbourne route. Those "in the know" read between the thick black lines and head straight for the juicy parts—swamplands and wetlands, bird sanctuaries and wildlife preserves, sandy dunes and beaches, yawn-away fishing ports (including one marked by a giant walk-in lobster, named Larry), thick-as-thieves pine forests, pastoral farmland, weathered limestone caves, volcanic lakes and craters, a right-regular share of "ye olde" buildings, and some downright extraordinary red wines.

Aside from bountiful fishing (especially Oct.-April, when it's lobster season) and delectable wines produced from rich *terra rossa* soil, this area also sustains timber and farming industries. Good annual rainfalls yield lush landscapes and, combined with neighboring western Victoria, this district is known as the Green Triangle.

TAILEM BEND

Both the Dukes and Princes Highways, principal routes between Adelaide and Melbourne, converge at Tailem Bend, along with the less-traveled Ouyen Highway. The inland Dukes Highway (which becomes Western Highway at Victoria's border) passes through a lot of flat farmland and is often referred to as the "boring road." The Princes Highway, running along the coast, is the preferred passage, as coastal roads usually are. If you're not in a rush to get to Melbourne, or if you're not going there at all, you can make a complete tour of the southeast by taking Princes Highway from Tailem Bend to Mt. Gambier; then, detouring north through wine and cave country, join up with the Dukes Highway at Keith and loop back to Tailem Bend.

Sights
Tailem Bend's most noteworthy attraction is **Old Tailem Town,** another one of those authentic turn-of-the-century villages. The township, five km north of Tailem Bend, features the usual pioneering cottages, butcher, barber, and bootmaker shops, emporium, church, one-room schoolhouse, and "real" general store. Old Tailem Town is open daily 10 a.m.-5 p.m. Admission is $5. For information, phone (08) 8572-3838.

Accommodations
If you need more time to decide which road to take, **River Bend Motel,** 110 Princes Hwy., tel. (08) 8572-3633, will put you up for the night. Inexpensive. **Westbrook Park River Resort,** Princes Hwy., tel. (08) 8572-3794, on the banks of the Murray, has campsites, cabins, and on-site

SOUTH AUSTRALIA ~ THE SOUTHEAST

© AVALON TRAVEL PUBLISHING

vans. Budget-Inexpensive. **Rivers Edge Caravan and Tourist Park,** Princes Hwy., tel. (08) 8572-3307, also on the Murray, features a boat ramp and canoes for hire. Budget-Inexpensive.

MENINGIE

At the northern edge of the Coorong National Park, and the southern side of Lake Albert, Meningie (pop. 900) offers water sports, birdwatching, and easy access to the Coorong. The town is nothing special, but it is a decent place to overnight and stock up on provisions for your Coorong exploration. From Trigg Hill you can look out on Lakes Albert and Alexandrina, which comprise 746 square km of fresh water. **Melaleuca Nursery,** 76 Princes Hwy., displays a variety of flowers and plants, and also serves as the Tourist Information Centre. Hours are Mon.-Fri. 9 a.m.-5 p.m., Saturday 9 a.m.-12:30 p.m., Sunday and public holidays 11 a.m.-3 p.m. For information, phone (08) 8575-1259.

Accommodations
The motels along Princes Highway are all in the inexpensive to low-moderate range. **Lake Albert Caravan Park,** Narrung Rd., tel. (08) 8575-1411, offers bike, canoe, and sailboard hire, and a nice lakeside location.

THE COORONG

If you've seen the film *Storm Boy,* the poignant tale of a boy and his pelican, then you should have no trouble visualizing the Coorong, for it was filmed here. If you missed the flick, well, imagine a long, narrow, and shallow saltwater lagoon stretching 132 km from the Murray mouth to that big lobster Larry's mouth, just north of Kingston. Separated from the Southern Ocean by the shimmering sand dunes on Younghusband Peninsula (an average of two km wide), the Coorong is a haven for approximately 400 species of birds, including cormorants, terns, shags, ducks, swans, and pelicans. You can get from the Coorong across to the peninsula at Salt Creek during summer months; otherwise there's a year-round road about 75 km south, toward Kingston.

Pelicans and hundreds of other bird species find sanctuary in The Coorong.

KAREN McKINLEY

A large Aboriginal tribe lived on the Coorong for thousands of years (the name is derived from "Kurangh," Aboriginal for "Long Neck of Water"), subsisting on fish, seafood, reptiles, birds, kangaroos, and wombats. You'll also come across wells built in the 1800s by Chinese immigrants who landed in Robe and, instead of joining their compatriots who headed for Victoria's goldfields, strayed northward to Adelaide. Australia's first oil well was drilled near Salt Creek in the 1890s, after Coorongite (a derivative of surface algae) was discovered.

In 1966, the Coorong was designated a national park, and since then the National Parks and Wildlife Service has been responsible for its 43,500 hectares, as well as for **Messent Conservation Park,** six km northeast of Salt Creek.

The Coorong is an ideal location for fishing, boating, and hiking. Walking trails are marked throughout the park (try the three-km Lakes Nature Trail at Salt Creek), and during Easter, Christmas, and New Year's holidays, rangers lead informative walks. Camping is permitted in the park, but you're required to obtain a permit first. The **Department of Environment and Natural Resources** has offices at Salt Creek, tel. (08) 8575-7014, and Noonameena, tel. (08) 8575-1200.

KINGSTON

When you come upon a 17-meter-tall, four-ton, pre-fab lobster named Larry, you've arrived in Kingston (pop. 1,370), "Gateway to the Southern Ports." Larry, presumably the "World's Biggest [fake] Lobster," stands watch over the entrance to this popular fishing port and beach resort. The town was established in 1856 by the Cooke brothers, who had procured government land grants near Maria Creek (so named for the vessel *Maria,* which wrecked near the Cape Jaffa Lighthouse in 1840; the crew and the passengers survived the shipwreck, only to be massacred by Aboriginals after they went ashore). The original jetty was too short and too shallow to make it useful for loading goods and, in 1876, was replaced by another—much longer, sitting in much deeper water—but even that one ceased being practical with the advent of modern roads and railways.

Sights

The **National Trust Museum,** 15 Cooke St., originally a timber mill built in 1872, presents items of local interest, including nautical memorabilia. Hours are daily 3-4 p.m. during school and public holidays. Admission is $3. For information, phone (08) 8767-2050.

Cape Jaffa Lighthouse, moved from its 100-year-old post on Margaret Brock Reef, has been reerected nearby on Marine Parade and is open to visitors. Other historic buildings are the post office, courthouse, and police station (now an antique shop). Hours are daily 2-5 p.m. during school and public holidays. Admission is $4. For information, phone (08) 8767-2050.

Aside from the Coorong to the north, Kingston is near three other national parks: **Butchers Gap Conservation Park,** six km southwest, off Wyomi Rd., is another natural bird sanctuary where coastal vegetation thrives in the wetlands; part of a former coastal dune, **Mt. Scott Conservation Park,** 20 km east of Kingston, on Keith Rd., has good bushwalks through stringybark forest inhabited by mallee fowl, sugar gliders, and wombats; and **Jip Jip Conservation Park,** 50 km northeast of Kingston, features a variety of wildlife amid big exotically shaped granite boulders. You can also see unusual rock formations much closer to town at the **Granites,** off the highway north of Kingston, along the beach.

The fish are jumping in Kingston; anglers can cast lines from beach, boat, or jetty, either at Kingston or Cape Jaffa, a wee fishing village to the south. The foreshore and Wyomi and Pinks Beaches provide safe swimming, while Lacepede Bay is popular for sailing.

Accommodations

Crown Inn Hotel, Agnes St., tel. (08) 8767-2005, has simple, pub-style rooms. Inexpensive. More modern **Kingston Beehive Motor Inn,** Marine Parade, tel. (08) 8767-2444, is near the jetty on the foreshore. Moderate. **Kingston Caravan Park,** Marine Parade, tel. (08) 8767-2050, is situated on a sand beach. The usual range of campsites, on-site vans, and cabins are offered. Budget-Inexpensive.

Events

If you're visiting the area in January, you can catch the annual **Yachting Carnival** and Cape Jaffa-to-Kingston race.

Information

Larry, the Big Lobster, tel. (08) 8767-2555, is not just another pretty face, but a tourist complex with a bistro, cafeteria, takeaways, souvenir and bottle shops, *and* tourist information. You can also pick up tourist info at **Wood Hut Craft Shop,** Kingston District Hall, Agnes St., tel. (08) 8767-2151. Both places are open daily.

ROBE

In 1802, French explorer Nicholas Baudin cruised this area and bestowed Guichen Bay with its name. The town of Robe (pop. 740) was officially established in 1847, growing to be South Australia's third major port (before the downfall of shipping in 1864). It was used for exporting wool and horses and importing about 15,000 Chinese immigrants. The Chinese, on their way to Victoria's goldfields, had found an ingeniously simple way to avoid the £10-per-head poll tax charged by Victorian officials—they landed in South Australia and quietly made their way across the state line.

Sights

Robe is a peaceful and picturesque village with many historic buildings. The **National Trust Museum,** in the old Customs House (1863), will tell you of the town's early history. Hours are Tues.-Sat. 2-4 p.m. Admission is $3. For information, phone (08) 8768-2419.

From **Beacon Hill,** you can get a great view of Robe, Guichen Bay, and the Southern Ocean. Or look out from the **obelisk,** right or left, to shimmering expanses of coastline.

Little Dip Conservation Park, four km south of Robe, comprises sand dunes, coastal strips, and salt lakes, through which waterbirds and wildlife roam, as can you—along the bushwalking tracks, that is. Rangers lead guided walks during the summer months.

Long Beach, a 17-km stretch of calm white sand along Guichen Bay, is noted for excellent swimming and windsurfing (the National Championships were held here in 1989). In the summer, you can drive along the beach and discover your own nook and cranny. Guichen Bay is also popular for sailing.

Anglers can get a bite just about anywhere. Crayfish lovers should visit Oct.-April, when the fleet brings in a fresh catch each day.

Events

The Sunday before 1 October is the annual **Blessing of the Fleet.** Afterward, local fishers invite tourists to join them for a jaunt around the bay.

Accommodations

You'll find all kinds of atmospherey accommodations in and around Robe. **Bushland Cabins,** Nora Criena Rd., tel. (08) 8768-2386, has well-equipped units with kitchen facilities. Moderate. The **Caledonian Inn,** Victoria St., tel. (08) 8768-2029, built in 1858, offers newer cottages and cheaper motel rooms in the restored original section. Inexpensive-Moderate. **Flinders Rest Holiday Units,** Powell Ave., tel. (08) 8725-2086, in the Long Beach area, rents fully equipped two-bedroom cottages with open fires. Moderate.

Or, choose from three caravan parks in the area. **Lakeside Tourist Caravan Park,** Main Rd., tel. (08) 8768-2193, is on a safe swimming lake. **Long Beach Tourist Park,** the Esplanade, tel. (08) 8768-2237, is just 200 meters from the

Long Beach water sporting area. **Sea-Vu Caravan Park,** Squire Dr., tel. (08) 8768-2273, is near beaches and attractions. All have campsites, onsite vans, and cabins. Budget-Inexpensive.

Information

Robe Historical Interpretation Centre, in the library building on Smillie St., tel. (08) 8768-2465, can provide additional tourist information. Hours are Tues.-Fri. 10 a.m.-5 p.m., Saturday 8:30 a.m.-12:30 p.m.

BEACHPORT

Beachport (pop. 410) is another seaside lobster, crayfish, and one-time hustle-bustle port. Set at the northern edge of Rivoli Bay, this former whaling station, established by the Henty brothers in the 1830s, became a township in 1878, the same year a Beachport-Mt. Gambier railway line was built, instantly turning the town into a train-trip-away holiday resort. And, though the trains no longer run, Beachport is still a desirable destination for family excursions.

Sights

If you're coming from Robe, follow the detour to impressive **Woakwine Cutting,** a drainage project constructed by one farmer and his helper in less than three years. You can *ooh* and *aah* from the specially built viewing platform.

See fishing, farming, and whaling displays, as well as local relics, at the **National Trust Museum,** inside the old wool and grain store on Railway Terrace. Hours are Sunday 2-4 p.m. Admission is $3. For information, phone (08) 8735-8013.

Bowman's Scenic Drive, from Foster St. to Wooleys Rocks, takes in terrific views of the town and Lake George on one side, the ocean on the other. You'll find lookout points at Backlers Lookout and Salmon Hole.

If you've got a 4WD vehicle you can drive past Wooleys Rocks, along sand dunes, and into **Beachport Conservation Park;** otherwise access is from Railway Terrace North. The park includes tracks through sand dunes and coastal vegetation, and around Wooleys Lake. The eight km drift, accessible only by four-wheelers or two feet, offers safe sailing and windsurfing.

Swimmers will do well around the jetty, scuba divers enjoy the **Back Beach** reef areas, and surfers like a spot known as the **Blowhole.** The **Pool of Siloam,** a very salty (six times more than the sea) lake near Beachport, is thought to be therapeutic.

Accommodations
Beachport Hotel, Railway Terrace, tel. (08) 8735-8003, has basic pub accommodations. Inexpensive. **Beachport Motor Inn,** Railway Terrace, tel. (08) 8735-8070, offers more contemporary digs. Moderate. Try the Beachport **YHA Hostel,** Beach Rd., tel. (08) 8735-8197, for dorm beds at $8 per night.

Beachport Caravan Park, Beach Rd., tel. (08) 8735-8128, with cabins and on-site vans, is situated on the foreshore with a jetty. Budget-Inexpensive. **Southern Ocean Tourist Park,** Somerville St., tel. (08) 8735-8153, is close to the beach. It has open fireplaces, cabins, and campsites. This park is also the local Tourist Information Centre. Budget-Inexpensive.

MILLICENT

Bordered on the north and southeast by thick, fragrant pine forests, Millicent (pop. 5,075) is big timber country. From Kingston to Millicent, coastal travel is along Alternate Highway 1; it reconnects with the main highway here.

This mini-city, begun in 1870 as a rural community, shifted to a timber center after pines were cultivated in nearby ranges. Sawmills and paper mills soon moved in, and were followed by a steady stream of workers (including a large European population).

Sights
Millicent Museum, 1 Mt. Gambier Rd., tel. (08) 8733-3205, is one of the region's most extensive facilities, with natural history and Aboriginal displays, restored horse-drawn vehicles, farm implements, tools, machinery, and a coin-operated waterwheel. The museum also houses **Admella Gallery,** which exhibits and sells local arts and crafts, and which also serves as the tourist information office. Hours are Mon.-Sat. 10 a.m.-4 p.m., Sunday 1-4 p.m. Museum admission is $2.50.

Tantanoola Caves, on Princes Hwy., 21 km from Millicent, are inside a dolomite marine cliff beside the highway. Take one of the hourly guided tours of the single chamber ($6), or sign up for a "wild cave tour" that explores the underground system (by appointment). At the nearby town of Tantanoola, you can view the stuffed carcass of *the* Tantanoola tiger, at—where else?—the **Tantanoola Tiger Hotel.** Load up on brew to go along with all the bull you'll hear about this legendary beast.

If you'd rather climb than cave, coastal **Canunda National Park,** beginning at Southend, 27 km west of Millicent, has a system of huge, wondrous sand dunes for you to sink your feet into. You can also camp here and, in the summer, take informative ranger-guided walks.

Accommodations
Grand Hotel, 55 George St., tel. (08) 8733-2242, has no-frills rooms with shared facilities. Inexpensive. Other unexciting motels are **Diplomat Motel,** 51 Mt. Gambier Rd., tel. (08) 8733-2211; **Millicent Motel,** 82 Mt. Gambier Rd., tel. (08) 8733-2655; and **Somerset Hotel Motel,** 2 George St., tel. (08) 8733-2888. Inexpensive-Moderate.

Hillview Caravan Park, Dalton St., tel. (08) 8733-2806, with campsites and cabins, is less than two km from the town center. Budget-Inexpensive. **Millicent Lakeside Caravan Park,** Park Terrace, tel. (08) 8733-3947, also has on-site vans, a deli, and is adjacent to a swimming lake. Budget-Inexpensive.

Information
Millicent Tourist Information Centre is in the Millicent Museum, or on George St., tel. (08) 8733-2177. For information on Canunda National Park, contact the **Department of Environment and Natural Resources** at Southend, tel. (08) 8735-6053. To sign up for cave walks at **Tantanoola Caves Conservation Park,** phone the park office at (08) 8734-4153.

MOUNT GAMBIER

The volcano has been extinct for 5,000 years, but the city of Mt. Gambier (pop. 20,815), built upon the volcano's slopes and situated about halfway between Adelaide and Melbourne, is a busy commercial center, regarded as the capital of the southeast. The city's big attractions are the many crater lakes. Of these, mysterious **Blue Lake** is the largest, with a circumference of five km. It's so famous that Mt. Gambier is often called the "Blue Lake City." The lake, which is actually gray, mysteriously changes, almost overnight, into an extraordinary blue each and every November, staying that color until late March, when it gradually reverts to gray. Long believed to be "bottomless," echo-sounding equipment has dispelled that myth by measuring an 80-meter maximum depth. Blue Lake also supplies Mt. Gambier with its domestic water.

In 1800, Lieutenant James Grant, in the HMS *Lady Nelson,* was sailing along the coast when he sighted two peaks. He named them Mt. Schank (after Admiral Schank, who had invented the *Lady Nelson*'s centerboard keel) and Mt. Gambier (for Lord Gambier of the Royal Navy). Mount Gambier developed as an agricultural township in 1841, when Stephen Henty and his companions, enticed by the rich volcanic soil and appreciable annual rainfalls, built their cottages between Valley and Brownes Lakes and brought their stock to graze on the fertile farmlands. Though agriculture is still important, now the city's major source of employment is the forest industry and the area's six large sawmills.

Sights

Besides Blue Lake, Mt. Gambier's other unique feature is **Cave Park,** an open cave in the city center, surrounded by lovely rose gardens. In complete defiance of Mt. Gambier's southern latitude, two banana trees rise from the cave and stretch toward the light. Other caves are **Umpherston Cave,** with terraced gardens and picnic grounds, and water-filled **Engelbrecht Cave,** a popular diving spot. Other diving locations are **Little Blue Lake, Ewens Ponds, Picaninnie Ponds, Three Sisters,** and **Hell Hole.**

Historic buildings near Cave Park are the **post office, town hall,** and **Jens Hotel. Old Courthouse Museum,** Bay Rd., operated by the National Trust, displays the original courthouse furnishings and other local historic items. Hours are Mon.-Fri. noon-4 p.m., Sat.-Sun. 10 a.m.-4 p.m. Admission is $3. For information, phone (08) 8724-1730.

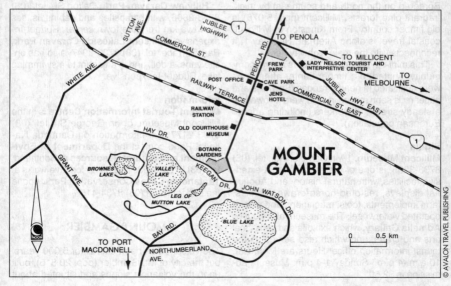

Lewis' Museum, Pick Ave. (across from the showgrounds), is jam-packed with more than 30,000 Aboriginal, mechanical, industrial, and historical artifacts. Hours are daily 8 a.m.-4 p.m. Admission is $6. For information, phone (08) 8725-1381.

Accommodations
About 30 motels and hotels and six caravan parks are sprawled around the town. Prices for double rooms range from moderate to expensive, but none of the accommodations are exceptional. In this town, a room at the cheap end should do you just fine.

The **Jens Hotel,** 40 Commercial St. East, tel. (08) 8725-0188, is a beautiful heritage property with days-of-yore rooms and shared facilities. Inexpensive. **Federal Hotel Motel,** 112 Commercial St. East, tel. (08) 8723-1099, is another historic spot, sans private facilities. Inexpensive.

Caravan parks with campsites, on-site vans, and cabins, include: **Blue Lake City Caravan Park,** Bay Rd., tel. (08) 8725-9856 or (1800) 67-6028; **Mt. Gambier Central Caravan Park,** 6 Krummel St., tel. (08) 8725-4427; and **Pine Country Caravan Park,** corner Bay and Klisby Roads, tel. (08) 8725-1899. Budget-Inexpensive.

Information
The **Lady Nelson Tourist and Interpretive Centre,** Jubilee Hwy. East, near the city center, tel. (08) 8724-9750 or (1800) 087-187, is a treasure trove of information. Besides the usual brochures and such, the center arranges all types of accommodations, tours (to sawmills, pumping stations, and dairies), and provides everything you want to know about the lakes area (including issuing diving permits). It will even prepare a customized itinerary. While there, you can view a full-size replica of HMS *Lady Nelson,* hear Lieutenant Grant (another replica, and *no* competition for Madame Tussaud!) give his spiel, and watch the volcano erupt in a blaze of neon! The center is open daily 9 a.m.-5 p.m., closed Christmas Day.

For emergencies, dial 000; the **police,** tel. (08) 8735-1020; or **Mt. Gambier Hospital,** tel. (08) 8721-1200. For road mishaps or info, contact the **Royal Automobile Association,** tel. (08) 8725-6267.

PORT MacDONNELL

South Australia's southernmost port and crayfish center is Port MacDonnell, 28 km south of Mt. Gambier. Once a bustling shipping center for freight being hauled between Adelaide and Melbourne, Port MacDonnell (pop. 650) these days is a quaint fishing village. On the way to Port MacDonnell, climb Mount Schank. Follow walking tracks both inside and outside the crater or just sit back and check out the grandiose view.

Sights
To the west of town, **Cape Northumberland Lighthouse,** reached by traveling through a petrified forest, affords a towering view of the rugged coastline below.

Dingley Dell Conservation Park, two km west of Port MacDonnell, is the restored 1860s home of horsey Scottish poet Adam Lindsay Gordon (he was South Australia's big-time bard). Picnic on the grounds and soak up some of Gordon's inspiration.

The large **Old Customs House,** on the foreshore, was built in 1860 to accommodate the sizable freight loads of the time.

Accommodations
Get a pub room with shared facilities at **Victoria Hotel,** 40 Meylin St., tel. (08) 8738-2213. Inexpensive. Or anything from on-site vans to fully equipped holiday flats at **Sea View Motel,** 77 Sea Parade, tel. (08) 8738-2243. Budget-Moderate.

Information
Gather tourist information at **Port MacDonnell District Council,** Charles St., tel. (08) 8721-0444.

For emergencies, dial 000; the **police,** tel. (08) 8738-2216; or the **Royal Automobile Association,** tel. (08) 8738-2238.

PENOLA

North of Mt. Gambier, venture through the pine-forested communities of Tarpeena and Nangwarry to this tiny heritage town noted for its beautiful buildings and churches. Penola is also the gateway to the southeastern wine region.

Sights

Many 1850s cottages, built by the town's first settlers, still stand. The **Penola Heritage Walk,** which departs from the Tourist Information Centre, takes in nearly 30 historic sites around Penola. **Petticoat Lane,** a sort of open-air museum of Penola's early architecture, features a number of traditional buildings, including the former Anglican rectory. Arts and crafts hounds will find galleries and gift shops inside many of the historic sites.

Mary Mackillop Interpretive Centre, Portland St., pays tribute to the town's heritage and its most prominent citizens (including John Riddoch). Hours are daily 10 a.m.-4 p.m. For information, phone (08) 8737-2092.

Yallum Park, Old Millicent Rd., Riddoch's personal mansion, built in 1880, depicts the grand style of the upper crust. Hours are by appointment. Admission is $4. For information, phone (08) 8737-2435.

Penola Conservation Park, 10 km west of town, features a signposted interpretive trail into this swampy wildlife sanctuary.

Accommodations

Haywards Royal Oak Hotel, 31 Church St., tel. (08) 8737-2322, offers pub rooms with shared facilities. Inexpensive. Book a variety of heritage accommodations through **Australian Country Cottages,** 33 Riddoch St., tel. (1800) 62-6844. Moderate-Expensive.

Information

Penola **tourist information** is available at Wattle Range District Council, 42 Church St., tel. (08) 8737-2391. A **Tourist Information Centre,** inside the Mary Mackillop Interpretive Centre, provides maps for scenic drives and heritage walks, and other local information. Hours are daily 10 a.m.-4 p.m., closed Christmas Day and Good Friday. For information, phone (08) 8737-2092.

In emergencies, dial 000; the **police,** tel. (08) 8737-2315; the **hospital,** tel. (08) 8737-2199; or the **Royal Automobile Association,** tel. (13) 1111.

COONAWARRA

It was John Riddoch, Penola mogul, who liked the looks of the grapevines in his Coonawarra Fruit Colony and, subsequently, established the

district's first winery. Though the vines of Riddoch's winery, built in 1893, thrived, demand was low. It wasn't until the 1960s that the industry really took off. Today, about 15 wineries in the district, which runs for 16 km north of Penola, are famous for the bold reds produced from the rich *terra rossa* soil.

Accommodations

Coonawarra offers nothing in the inexpensive category. The cheapest cottage accommodations are **Skinner, Redman,** and **The Pickers Hut,** tel. (08) 8736-3304 for all three. Moderate-Expensive.

Chardonnay Lodge, Penola Rd., tel. (08) 8736-3309, is a deluxe motel with an art gallery, swimming pool, good restaurant, and complimentary continental breakfast. Expensive.

Information

For tourist info, see the Penola Tourist Information Centre, above.

NARACOORTE

Proclaimed a town in 1870 (though the first hotel and store were erected in the 1840s), Naracoorte (pop. 4,640) functions mainly as a regional service and commercial center, with lovely old dwellings scattered all about.

Sights

The **Sheeps Back Museum,** tel. (08) 8762-1518, in the old flour mill on MacDonnell St. and run by the National Trust, traces the history of the wool industry. Hours are daily 10 a.m.-4 p.m. Admission is $2.

More interesting is the **Naracoorte Museum and Snake Pit,** Smith St., tel. (08) 8762-2059, where more than 100 collections of gemstones, clocks, weapons, butterflies, and other artifacts commingle with venomous snakes and other reptiles lounging about rocks and cacti. Hours are Mon.-Thurs. 10 a.m.-5 p.m., Sat.-Sun. 2-5 p.m., closed mid-July through August and on Christmas Day. Admission is $6.

Take a look at **Padthaway Estate,** about 41 km north of Naracoorte, a gracious country mansion built in 1882. **Padthaway Conservation Park** boasts stringybark and red gum forests where you can bushwalk or picnic.

Naracoorte Caves Conservation Park, 12 km southeast of town, features about 69 caves along a 25-km expanse of range. Daily tours explore Alexandra, Blanche, and Victoria Fossil caves (on the World Heritage list), and during holiday periods, you can sign up for special wild-caving tours into undeveloped areas (be prepared to climb and crawl). For information and tour bookings, phone (08) 8762-2340.

Bool Lagoon, a bit farther south, is a vast and diverse wetland where you can see about 75 species of birds and other wildlife. Self-guided and organized walking tracks are available. A bird blind and boardwalks, built over the lagoon, allow for excellent birdwatching. For information, phone (08) 8764-7541.

Mary Seymour Conservation Park, near Bool Lagoon, is another sanctuary for breeding birds.

Accommodations

Naracoorte Hotel Motel, 73 Ormerod St., tel. (08) 8762-2400, has inexpensive rooms with shared facilities in the older hotel; or, for $20 more, you can stay in the updated motel section. Inexpensive-Moderate. **Country Roads Motor Inn,** 28 Smith St., tel. (1800) 08-8363, is more posh, with larger and better quality rooms. Moderate. Big splurgers can spring for elegant accommodations at the historic **Padthaway Estate,** tel. (08) 8765-5039, where doubles run about $130, including breakfast. Premium.

Naracoorte Caravan Park, 81 Park Terrace, tel. (08) 8762-2128, is close to the town center and has campsites, on-site vans, and cabins. Budget-Inexpensive. Camping is permitted at both **Naracoorte Caves,** tel. (08) 8762-2340, and **Bool Lagoon,** tel. (08) 8764-7541.

Information

The **tourist information office** is at Sheeps Back Museum. In an emergency, dial 000; the **police,** tel. (08) 8762-0466; the **hospital,** tel. (08) 8762-8100; or the trusty **Royal Automobile Association,** tel. (08) 8762-2247.

BORDERTOWN

Situated 42 km northeast of Padthaway, along the Dukes Highway, Bordertown (pop. 2,320) isn't on but is near the Victorian border, 20 km away. Settled in 1852, along the route of the gold escort from Victoria to Adelaide, the area's rich farmlands produce wine grapes, small seeds, cereals, wool, meat, and vegetable crops. Also the former Australian Prime Minister Bob Hawke spent his early childhood here. His home has been renovated, and his bust has been bronzed.

Adjacent to Dukes Highway, **Bordertown Wildlife Park** is home to, besides the usual native birds and animals, four specially bred pure white kangaroos.

Accommodations

Several good motels with inexpensive to low-moderate prices line Dukes Highway. **Bordertown Caravan Park,** Penny Terrace, tel. (08) 8752-1752, near the town center, is another place to rest your head. Inexpensive.

Events

The annual **Camel Racing Festival,** held each November, features camel and donkey races, parachute jumping, various other antics, and camels from every state and territory in Australia.

Information

For tourist information, contact **Bordertown Council Office,** 43 Woolshed St., tel. (08) 8752-1044. For emergency assistance, dial 000; the **police,** tel. (08) 8752-1355; the **hospital,** tel. (08) 8752-1166; or the **Royal Automobile Association,** tel. (08) 8752-1270.

KEITH

Keith (pop. 1,190), 46 km northwest of Bordertown, was proclaimed a township in 1889. At one time the region was part of a 90-mile desert, but after zinc and copper were added to the soil, it became profitable grazing and farm land. Most of the old buildings sit along Heritage St., facing the Dukes Highway.

Sights

Peek into the foyer of the **Congregational Church,** on Heritage Street. The 1910 building features four interesting stained-glass windows, made by locals, depicting the pioneering era. Hours are daily 9 a.m.-5 p.m.

Mount Monster Conservation Park, 10 km south of Keith, boasts spectacular views from the lookout (a signposted walk will guide you) and a wide variety of vegetation, birds, and wildlife. Mount Monster and others in a chain of granite outcrops, were islands about 40 million years ago.

Ngarkat Conservation Park, northeast of Keith, is perfect for bushwalks. The 262,700-hectare park is full of native animals and abundant in flora. **Warning:** There are a large number of beehives in this park. **Note:** At writing, a week-long bush fire had burned more than 100,000 hectares (or approximately one-third) of this park.

Situated in the southwest corner 20 km north of Keith, **Mount Rescue Conservation Park** has 28,385 hectares of sand plains and dunes containing rare species of birds and plants.

Accommodations
Keith Hotel Motel, Makin St., tel. (08) 8755-1122, offers the only beds in town at about $50 for a double. Inexpensive. **Keith Caravan Park,** Naracoorte Rd., tel. (08) 8755-1957, has campsites and on-site vans. Budget-Inexpensive.

Information
The **Tourist Information Centre** is inside the old Congregational Church, on Heritage Street. Hours are daily 9 a.m.-5 p.m. For information, phone (08) 8755-1584.

In emergencies, dial 000; the **police,** tel. (08) 8755-1211; the **hospital,** tel. (08) 8755-1555; or the **Royal Automobile Association,** tel. (13) 1111.

BACK TO TAILEM BEND

Heading back to Tailem Bend, you'll pass through more grazing land. Stop by **Tintara,** 38 km northwest of Keith, which has a nice old post office and homestead (10 km west of town on Woods Well Rd.).

Mount Boothby Conservation Park, 20 km northwest of Tintara, features 4,045 hectares of heath, mallee, pink gum forest, and granite outcrops, where you can picnic or stretch your legs, between farmland scenes.

Watch for **Coonalpyn,** the last dot on the map before Tailem Bend.

TRANSPORTATION

Kendell Airlines, tel. (08) 8231-9567, Adelaide (or book through Ansett), makes the 50-minute flight from Adelaide to Mt. Gambier, and on to Melbourne, several days a week. **O'Connor Airlines,** tel. (08) 8723-0666, Mt. Gambier (or book through Qantas), makes daily flights from Mt. Gambier to either Adelaide or Melbourne.

Catch **Mt. Gambier Motor Services,** tel. (08) 8231-9090, from Adelaide's central bus station to Kingston, Robe, Millicent, or Mt. Gambier, or travel **Greyhound Pioneer,** tel. (13) 2030, along Princes Highway to Mt. Gambier.

THE MURRAY RIVER

In these parts it's called the "Mighty Murray," and it conjures up all the romantic images a mighty river should—paddle steamers plying their trade, floating casinos and riverboat gamblers, dashing gents and bawdy women, a host of rascals, scoundrels, ne'er-do-wells, and free spirits, runaways aboard makeshift rafts, and secret trysts along the banks.

Beginning in the Snowy Mountains, traveling along the border between New South Wales and Victoria, the river gains momentum as it reaches South Australia, makes a sharp turn seaward at Northwest Bend, and eventually empties into Lake Alexandrina, where its mighty mouth meets the great Southern Ocean. And, though the Murray has often been called the "Mississippi of Australia," and the flavor is much the same, this river—at 2,575 km from source to mouth—is less than half the length of its American counterpart.

Within South Australia's 640-km section, the Murray is divided into two districts—the River-

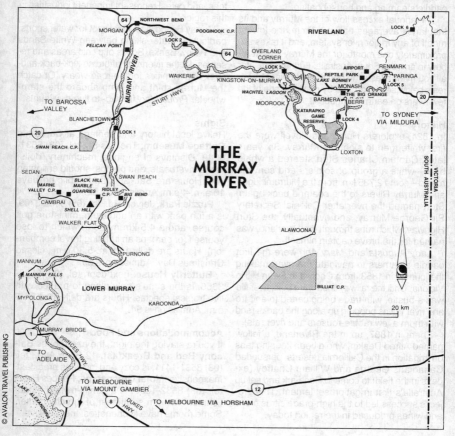

land and the Lower Murray. The Riverland includes the Murray's six locks, bountiful citrus groves, 17,000 hectares of vineyards, and the towns from Renmark to Blanchetown. This, in fact, is Australia's biggest wine-producing region (yes, *more* than the Barossa, Clare, and Coonawarra, and even the Hunter Valley, in New South Wales), noted for high-quality table wines and a variety of other products. The Lower Murray spans from below Blanchetown to Murray Bridge, where you'll encounter more orchards, large granite outcrops, waterfalls, lagoons, and phenomenal birdlife. Throughout the entire Murray area, you'll enjoy abundant sunshine with good fishing, swimming, water-skiing, and boating—including both paddle steaming and houseboating.

The annual excess flow of the Murray and its tributaries averages only 12.7 mm, the lowest runoff of any major river system, and it takes approximately one month for the Murray flow at Albury to arrive at South Australia. Furthermore—for all you riverphiles—the bed of the Lower Murray rests below sea level, thereby making it one of the few rivers on earth to run uphill!

History
In 1824, explorers Hume and Hovell were the first white men to sight the Murray. Six years later, Captain Charles Sturt steered a whale boat—while a group of soldiers and convicts rowed—some 2,735 km, from the Murrumbidgee and Murray Rivers to the sea and back again. Sturt named the river after Colonial Secretary Sir George Murray, and eventually, the Sturt Highway, which runs through the Riverland, was named for the brave captain himself.

Lady Augusta and *Mary Ann* were the first paddle steamers to navigate the river, making the journey in 1853, from Goolwa to Swan Hill in Victoria. Until the railway lines were built, river life was a-bustle, with trade being carted to and fro and river towns popping up along the banks (and with them a few rabble-rousers and river rats).

Then, in 1887, up in the Riverland, a fellow named Alfred Deakin, who'd been keeping tabs on irrigation in the California deserts, persuaded Canadians George and William Chaffey (experts in the field) to come to Renmark and set up Australia's first irrigation settlement. This project's success led to the high-grade citrus crops and wines produced in the region today.

MURRAY BRIDGE

Situated approximately 80 km from Adelaide, Murray Bridge (pop. 16,250) is the state's largest river town. This city should really be called Murray *Bridges,* since three of them cross the river here. Originally named "Edwards Crossing," the calm waters made this a favored spot for early settlers crossing the river—though at first they floated their wagons from shore to shore atop beer kegs! The road bridge was opened in 1879, followed by the rail bridge in 1927, and the Swanport Bridge—South Australia's longest—in 1979. Dairy farming, chickens, pigs, glasshouse tomatoes, and cereal represent important industries in this region.

Murray Bridge is an ideal spot for water sports, particularly water-skiing between White Sands and Willow Banks. Scads of picnic areas and reserves dot the riverfront, affording kick-back-and-relax opportunities for the road-weary. Or catch the Murray spirit and jump aboard the stern-wheeler *Proud Mary* for two- to five-day jaunts.

Sights
Relive local history and heritage at **Captain's Cottage Museum,** Thomas St., tel. (08) 8531-0049. Displays of engines, machinery, dolls, model riverboats, and photos, should enlighten you. Hours are Sat.-Sun. and public holidays 10 a.m.-4 p.m. Admission is $2.

Puzzle Park, Jervois Rd., tel. (08) 8532-3709, is a fun park with an aquarium, miniature golf course, and a 4.5-km maze in which to lose yourself (or perhaps an irritating travel companion). Hours are daily 10 a.m.-5:30 p.m., closed Christmas Day. Admission is $9.

Butterfly House, next door, tel. (08) 8532-3666, is the state's only place to prance with live tropical species. Hours are daily 10 a.m.-5 p.m. Admission is $4.

Accommodations and Food
If you're staying the night, the bare-bones **Balcony Bed and Breakfast,** 12 Sixth Ave., tel. (08) 8531-1411, is cozy and includes breakfast. Inexpensive. **Motel Greenacres,** Princes Hwy., tel. (08) 8532-1090, is a family-owned establishment five km southeast of the city center. Some rooms have kitchenettes. Inexpensive.

Avoca Dell Caravan Park, Loddon Rd., tel. (08) 8532-2095, on the Murray, has cabins, on-site vans, and campsites, as does **White Sands Riverfront Caravan Park,** Jervois Rd., tel. (08) 8532-1421. Budget-Inexpensive.

Many **houseboats** are available for weekly rentals; inquire at the Tourist Information Centre.

Pick up natural foods, vitamins, herbal teas, and grains at **Murray Bridge Health Foods,** corner of Seventh and Fourth Streets, tel. (08) 8532-4383. **Cockatoo Haven Diner,** Jervois Rd., tel. (08) 8532-3666, offers cheap, plentiful meals ($5-9 for meat or veg entrees). Favorite takeaways are **Danny's Diner** and **Chick 'N' Spuds,** both on Bridge St., and **Quick Chick,** over on Adelaide Road.

Information
Stop by the **Murray Bridge Community Information and Tourist Centre,** 3 South Terrace, tel. (08) 8532-6660. Hours are Mon.-Fri. 8:30 a.m.-4 p.m., Saturday 10 a.m.-3:30 p.m., Sunday and public holidays 10 a.m.-2 p.m., closed Christmas Day.

For emergencies, dial 000; the **police,** tel. (08) 8535-6020; or **ambulance,** tel. (8532) 1271. The local branch of the **Royal Automobile Association** is on Railway Terrace, tel. (08) 8532-2022, and the **hospital,** tel. (08) 8535-6725, is at the corner of Swanport Rd. and Monash Terrace.

Transportation
A local bus service operates Mon.-Saturday. For information, phone **Murray Bridge Passenger Service,** tel. (08) 8532-2633. The daily bus to Adelaide costs about $12 one-way. There's a **taxi** stand off Bridge St., or phone (08) 8531-0555.

MANNUM

On your way to Mannum, stop at Mypolonga, eight km north of Murray Bridge on Mannum Road. It's a small farming community comprising both highlands and swamplands. Noted for its well-irrigated orange, apricot, peach, and pear orchards, Mypolonga is another water sport and houseboat haven.

Mannum (pop. 2,000), a wide spot in the river 21 km north of Murray Bridge, is the birth-place of Australia's paddle steamers. In 1853, Captain W.R. Randell (who had settled in the district some 10 years earlier) constructed *Mary Ann,* the first steamboat, and the following year sailed it up to Swan Hill in Victoria. In 1854, the busy captain also built Mannum's first house, which, over time, was bought, sold, and transformed into the Mannum Hotel. Subsequent to the *Mary Ann*'s inaugural voyage, Mannum became a busy shipbuilding center. Today Mannum is a peaceful community, known for its scenic beauty, rich heritage, and water activities, as well as its designation as home port for the *Murray Princess.*

Sights
Recreation Reserve (called the "Rec" by locals) lines the banks of the Murray with 350 meters of grassy picnic and barbecue areas, a boat ramp, and scenic lookouts to town, river, and valley.

The National Trust operates **Mannum Museum,** tel. (08) 8569-1303, inside the restored 1896 paddle steamer *Marion.* Moored at Randell's original wharf at Arnold Park, the floating museum contains river relics and other memorabilia. The museum is open daily 9 a.m.-4 p.m., closed Christmas Day. Admission is $2.

The **Bird Sanctuary,** on Halidon Rd., is home to ducks, swans, pelicans, and other beautiful waterbirds. Have a look.

Mannum Waterfalls Reserve, 20 km south of town, offers picnic spots and walking tracks, but if you want to see the falls be aware that they flow mainly in the winter.

Accommodations and Food
Stay at Captain Randell's homestead-turned-**Mannum Hotel,** 15 Randell St., tel. (08) 8569-1008, with shared facilities. Inexpensive. **Mannum House,** 33 River Lane, tel. (08) 8569-2631, offers bed and breakfast accommodations in an 1883 homestead. Moderate. **Mannum Motel,** 76 Cliff St., tel. (08) 8569-1808, is the top choice for standard motel amenities. Expensive.

Mannum Caravan Park, Purnong Rd., tel. (08) 8569-1402, adjacent to the Bird Sanctuary, has campsites and cabins. Budget-Moderate.

Stroll over to **Kia Marina,** on Younghusband Rd., to check out weekly deals on the many **houseboats** for rent.

Café De Jour, 96c Randell St., tel. (08) 8569-1354, is open daily for cappuccino, croissants, cakes, and light meals ($6-10). For heartier fare and good seafood ($14-18), try **Captain Randell's Restaurant,** 76 Cliff St., tel. (08) 8569-1808.

THE MID MURRAYLANDS

The Mid Murraylands comprise the area from Bow Hill in the south (32 km from Mannum) to Swan Reach in the north, from Nildottie in the east to Sedan in the west. Just a 90-minute drive from Adelaide, this district offers lovely scenery and not-so-touristy river action where you can fish and boat in peace or just sit on the banks and float twigs downstream.

There's a stunning **scenic drive** along Younghusband Rd., on the way to Purnong, that takes in lagoons, lakes, stone quarries, and stupendous bird life. **Bow Hill,** before Purnong, is a popular water-skiing spot. **Purnong** is a slow-going holiday village, but a barrage of river craft float past just the same. Great views can be enjoyed at **Caurnamont Landing,** a base for houseboat rentals. **Walker Flat,** sheltered by tall cliffs, is another location sought out by both water-skiers and waterbirds. Small, rural **Nildottie,** once an old paddle steamer landing, now bears citrus fruit and vegetable crops. **Big Bend** boasts big river red gums and sandstone cliffs that draw vast numbers of cockatoos to nest.

Surveyed in 1839, **Swan Reach** (pop. 200) is the Mid Murraylands' largest town and halfway

---

RULES FOR THE MURRAYLANDS

As part of a "Don't Muck up the Murray" campaign, aimed at preserving the river environment, the South Australia Department of Environment and Planning asks that visitors adhere to the following rules:

Protect Water Supplies

- Do not bury excrement within 50 meters of the Murray.
- Do not use pollutants, like soap, anywhere near the water.
- Do not wash plates or utensils within 50 meters of the river.
- Camp away from the river bank. Avoid blocking the access of stock or wildlife to the water; they need their water to live.

Respect Farmers, Their Property, and Their Stock

- Leave machinery alone. Windmills, pumps, tractors, and generators are important for a farm's survival. Your interference could cause costly or ruinous breakdowns.
- Do not frighten or disturb stock. Farm animals are valuable and easily disturbed, and some can injure you. They could be lambing or calving, so keep away.

- Camp away from windmills and pumps, and don't interfere with farm water supplies, except in an emergency.
- Report vandalism. If you see any acts of vandalism, notify the landowner.

Respect and Keep to Roads and Tracks

- Fences, gates, roads, and tracks represent important investments to farmers and property owners, so while you're a guest on their land, be considerate of your responsibilities.
  - Leave gates as you found them.
  - Avoid damaging fences; use gates and stiles where they are provided.
- Keep to existing roads and tracks, and do not widen them.
- Contact the landowner if you propose to drive off a track or travel across his property.
- Avoid vehicle travel when roads are wet.

Report Polluters

- If you see persons violating or polluting the river, you are asked to phone **River Watch,** the Murray's 24-hour watchdog, at (085) 82-2700.

DON'T MUCK UP THE MURRAY

point between the Barossa Valley and the Riverland. It's another holiday and water sport mecca. **Punuelroo,** seven km south, is a longtime holiday hot spot, and *not* the place to hit if you want peace and quiet. **Ridley Conservation Park,** five km south of Swan Reach, is where you might glimpse hairy-nosed wombats and the rare striped honeyeater bird. **Swan Reach Conservation Park,** 11 km northwest of Swan Reach, is 1,900 hectares of grasslands, thick mallee, false sandalwood, open woodland, and roaming wildlife, including emus and western gray kangaroos.

Sedan, about 16 km west from Swan Reach Conservation Park, provides facilities for the surrounding farm community. Established in the late 1890s, the town has preserved many of its old buildings. From Sedan, you can take a number of scenic drives. Best is the route that winds from Cambrai through the Marne River Valley—taking in huge river red gums, a granite quarry, a pinnacle of fossils, and a myriad of wildlife—then swings north to Ridley Conservation Park and back to Swan Reach.

Accommodations
Pub-style rooms are available at **Swan Reach Hotel,** tel. (08) 8570-2003. Inexpensive. **Yookamurra Sanctuary,** Pipeline Rd., Sedan, tel. (08) 8562-5011, offers bunkhouse accommodations within its delicate woodlands. All meals are included in the rates. Moderate.

Punyelroo Caravan Park, on the riverbanks, tel. (08) 8570-2021, has campsites and on-site vans. Budget-Moderate.

BLANCHETOWN

This popular holiday resort—which begins the Riverland—sits 28 km north of Swan Reach and 134 km northeast of Adelaide, along the Sturt Highway. Governor R.G. MacDonnell named this town for his wife, Lady Blanche. There were high hopes for Blanchetown, begun in 1855 as an important commercial center and established as a port in 1863, but they fizzled after northerly neighbor Morgan won the much-sought-after railway line. In 1922, construction began here on the complex system of locks and weirs created to control fluctuations of the river's water level. If you stand atop Blanchetown Bridge, you might see a houseboat passing through Lock Number One.

Sights
Brookfield Conservation Park, 11 km west of Blanchetown, features 6,332 hectares of open scrub mallee, mallee box, and yorrell, through which wander red kangaroos, hairy-nosed wombats, fat-tailed dunnarts, and a variety of birds. Don't veer off marked walking trails without checking with the ranger station (three km inside the entrance); some areas are closed due to scientific research on the hairy-nosed wombat.

Trenetas, Old Ferry Landing, tel. (08) 8540-5071, a floating sand gallery overlooking the river, exhibits and sells arts and crafts with a sand motif, and also houses a coffee shop. Hours are Tues.-Sat. and public holidays 10 a.m.-8 p.m.

Accommodations
Riverside Caravan and Camping Park, Sanders St., tel. (08) 8540-5070. is a quiet riverfront park with a beach, offering campsites, on-site vans, cabins, and canoe-hire. Budget-Moderate.

For **houseboats,** inquire at Blanchetown or Kayandee Moorings.

Information
In an emergency, dial 000; the **police,** tel. (08) 8540-5013; or the local **Royal Automobile Club,** tel. (08) 8541-2600.

MORGAN

At one time Morgan (pop. 1,265) was South Australia's second busiest port (Port Adelaide ranked first). Originally known as "Northwest Bend," "Great Bend," and the "Great Elbow" (this is where the Murray makes its sharp turn), Morgan was officially named after Sir William Morgan by Governor Musgrave in 1878, the same year a railway line was opened. In the good old days Morgan used to have a veritable traffic jam of steamers and barges unloading cargo, which was then transferred by rail to Port Adelaide.

Sights
Reminders of the town's formidable history include the huge wharf, built in 1878, and the heritage buildings along Railway Terrace. **Port of**

Morgan Historic Museum, on Railway Terrace, displays original river charts and trading-days artifacts. The 1940s **Pumping Station and Water Filtration Plant,** on Renmark Rd., can be toured on Tuesday 1-3 p.m.

Cross the river by ferry to **White Dam Conservation Park,** in the northwest bend, to view waterbirds in the wetlands or picnic under towering red gums.

Accommodations

Both the **Commercial Hotel,** tel. (08) 8540-2107, and **Terminus Hotel Motel,** tel. (08) 8540-2006, on historic Railway Terrace, have simple but adequate accommodations. Inexpensive. **Morgan Riverside Caravan Park,** tel. (08) 8540-2207, has on-site vans and cabins, with air-conditioning and telly. Budget-Moderate.

Look for **houseboat rentals** along the riverfront.

WAIKERIE

Waikerie (pop. 1,700), reached from Blanchetown along the Sturt Highway, or from Morgan (passing Lock Number Two), is the "Citrus Center of Australia." Founded in 1880 by the Shepherd Brothers, the name "Waikerie" is a derivative of an Aboriginal word meaning "many wings or birds," no doubt because of the abundant colorful birds (and, nowadays, the gliders) hanging around the district's lagoons and riverbanks.

Mild sunny winters and hot temperate summers, combined with modern irrigation, have turned this former desert into a citrus-fruit oasis of more than one million bountiful trees, planted on over 5,000 acres (try to visit in Sept.-Oct. when they're in bloom).

Sights

In the center of town is **Waikerie Producers Packing House,** the largest of its kind in Australia. Arrange a tour by calling (08) 8541-2244.

Pooginook Conservation Park, 12 km northeast of Waikerie, is home to a variety of animal and bird life, in environs ranging from open to dense mallee. **Terrigal Fauna Park,** tel. (08) 8541-3414, and **Waikerie Fauna Park,** tel. (08) 8541-2077, also afford peeks at local critters. Or, catch your view from atop **Clifftop Lookout,** a short walk from the town center, along Goodchild Street.

Accommodations and Food

The centrally located **Waikerie Hotel Motel,** McCoy St., tel. (08) 8541-2999, has down-to-basic older rooms and nicer motel-style digs, depending on which section you stay in. The restaurant offers both counter meals and à la carte dining. Inexpenisve-Moderate. Air-conditioned on-site vans and cabins are available at **Waikerie Caravan Park,** Peake Terrace, tel. (08) 8541-2651. Inexpensive-Moderate.

Purchase local citrus, dried, and glacé fruits, honey, juices, and nonalcoholic wines at **The Orange Tree,** on Sturt Hwy., tel. (08) 8541-2332. A viewing platform looks out over the river and town. Hours are daily 9 a.m.-5 p.m.

Sports and Recreation

Waikerie, sight of the 1974 World Gliding Championships, is the perfect place to soar and spiral the skies. **Waikerie Gliding Club,** tel. (08) 8541-2644, offers glider joy flights (about \$50 for 20 minutes), as well as instruction.

Information

The **Tourist Information Centre,** 20 McCoy St., tel. (08) 8541-2183, can help with juice queries and other needs. Hours are Mon.-Fri. 8:30 a.m.-5:30 p.m., Saturday 8:30-11:30 a.m., closed public holidays.

In emergencies, dial 000; the **police,** tel. (08) 8541-2888; or **ambulance,** tel. (08) 8541-2878. For road service, phone the **Royal Automobile Association,** tel. (08) 8541-2600. Waikerie Hospital, tel. (08) 8541-2300, is located on Laurie Terrace.

BARMERA

Traveling 48 km east of Waikerie, past rural Kingston-on-Murray and the bird refuge at Wachtel Lagoon (part of the Moorook Game Reserve), the Sturt Highway enters Barmera (pop. 1,900), dubbed the Murray's "aquatic playground." Set on the shores of freshwater Lake Bonney, this town draws like flies those who take to the water like fish. Joseph Hawdon discovered the lake while hauling stock overland from New South

Wales to Adelaide and named it after his pal Charles Bonney, who was with him. Originally called Barmera by local Aboriginals, the lake's title was transferred to the new township. Besides being a holiday resort, Barmera grows citrus and stone fruits, grapes, and vegetables.

Lake Bonney offers all types of water sports—swimming, fishing, windsurfing, yachting, water-skiing, and speed boating. (In 1964, Englishman Donald Campbell tried to break the world water speed record here.) Or you can picnic, barbecue, and laze around on one of the sandy beaches (Pelican Point, on the western shore, is a nude beach).

Sights

Built in 1859, the **Overland Corner Hotel Museum,** 19 km from Barmera on Old Coach Road, was one of the Riverland's first stone buildings. This was where the weary overlanders and cattle drovers rested themselves and their bullock teams. Restored and run by the National Trust, the museum features pioneer exhibits and area artifacts. Hours are sporadic at the museum, but the pub sticks to its normal schedule. For information, phone (08) 8588-7021.

Country-music fans can view memorabilia at **Rocky's Country Music Hall of Fame,** Monash Bypass Rd., tel. (08) 8588-3035. Hours are daily 9-11 a.m. and 2-4 p.m. Admission is $2.

At **Cobdogla,** five km west of town, you can see the world's only operating Humphrey Pump and other historical displays at **Cobdogla Irrigation Museum,** Trussel Avenue. Admission is $4. For information, phone (08) 8588-2289.

On the other side of Lake Bonney's Nappers Bridge, **Loch Luna Game Reserve,** set on 1,905 hectares, is another favorite fishing, canoeing, and waterfowl-breeding haunt. There's a picnic area at Lock Number Three, a few km west of the reserve, where you can watch the action.

Accommodations

For lakeshore accommodations, **Lake Bonney Caravan and Holiday Park,** Lakeside Dr., tel. (08) 8588-2234, has everything from on-site vans to holiday flats, in a range of prices. This is a huge family-oriented complex, complete with a gym, sauna, and squash courts. Inexpensive-Moderate. For more resortlike lodging, head to **Barmera Country Club,** Hawdon St., tel. (08)

8588-2888, or **The Lake Resort,** Lakeside Dr., tel. (08) 8588-2555. Expensive.

Camping is permitted at the Pelican Point nude bathing beach, but there are no facilities. To reach the beach, go three km along Morgan Rd., turn right onto Ireland Road.

Recreation and Events

Lake Bonney Aquatic Centre, Lakeside Dr., tel. (08) 8588-2679, rents paddleboats, canoes, windsurfers, catamarans, and single and tandem bicycles. The center is open during school holidays, and weekends from Sept.-May.

Catch the **South Australian Country Music Awards,** each June on the Queen's birthday weekend, at the old Bonney Theatre.

Information

For tourist information, drop by **Barmera Travel Centre,** Barwell Ave., tel. (08) 8588-2289. Hours are Mon.-Fri. 8:30 a.m.-5:30 p.m., Saturday 9-11:30 a.m., Sunday 9 a.m.-4:30 p.m., closed Good Friday.

For emergencies, dial 000; the **police,** tel. (08) 8588-2122; **ambulance,** tel. (08) 8588-1275; or the **Royal Automobile Association,** tel. (08) 8582-1644. **Barmera Hospital,** tel. (08) 8588-2006, is on Hawdon Street.

BERRI

The name is certainly appropriate for this wine and citrus growing district; however, it does not stem from "berry," but from *"berri berri,"* Aboriginal for "wide bend in the river." Established about 1870 as a riverboat refueling stop, Berri (pop. 3,500) is *still* a refueling stop—for wines and juices. The town also sports the customary riverfront parks and water activities. Get your bearings at the lookout tower on Fiedler Street. And, if you're into bronco bulls, pay a visit on Easter Monday for the annual **Berri Rodeo.**

Sights

Berri Estates Winery, Sturt Hwy., is reputedly the largest single winery-distillery in Australia—if not the entire Southern Hemisphere; anyway, it's big enough to produce annually seven million liters of varietals, bulk, cask, and fortified wines, as well as brandies. The winery is open for tastings Mon.-Fri. 9 a.m.-5:30 p.m., Saturday 9 a.m.-5 p.m. For information, phone (08) 8582-0300.

When you're finished with the hard stuff, **Berrivale Orchards,** on McKay Rd., sells fruit juices, canned fruits, almonds, and gherkins, and presents a 10-minute video about the canning and juicing business. Hours are Mon.-Fri. 8:30 a.m.-4:30 p.m., Saturday 9 a.m.-noon, closed on major holidays. For information, phone (08) 8582-1455.

MURRAY RIVER SAFETY TIPS

The Department of Environment and Planning has issued the following warnings to Murray River users:

• On the Murray, it's important to have consideration for other river users, so please observe all boating and fishing regulations. This includes bag limits and closures, because these are in force to prevent the depletion of fish.

• Before boating or swimming, get to know the waters. And watch out for snags.

WHEN SWIMMING

• Wear a buoyancy vest. It might look funny, but it could save your life.

• Don't even think about swimming the width of the Murray. Currents, snags, and powerboats make it quite hazardous.

• Dive as shallowly as possible, especially if you're not certain of the depth. Steep dives have resulted in back or neck injuries.

• Keep clear of busy boating areas. There's a chance the skippers might not see you.

WHEN BOATING

• Carry all the required safety equipment on board.

• Give a wide berth to other boats when overtaking.

• Take care when turning, and don't turn across the bow of another vessel.

• Don't drink and drive. Swimming or driving a motorboat, when drunk, is setting a sure course for disaster. Alcohol, petrol, and water do not mix.

Grant's Super Playground, in the nearby community of Monash, houses more than 180 amusements for kids of all ages. Equipment includes roller coasters, flying foxes, earthmovers, multiple slides, and rotary cones. The park is always open and *free,* though donations are accepted.

The Riverland Big Orange, corner Sturt Hwy. and the Monash bypass, is billed—in the spirit of Larry the Kingston Lobster—as the "Largest [fake] Orange in the World." You can pick up a bag of oranges and get freshly squeezed juice. There's a small admission fee to the panoramic lookout. Hours are daily 9 a.m.-5 p.m. For information, phone (08) 8582-2999.

Riverland Display Centre, adjacent to the Big Orange, houses a collection of vintage and classic cars, large-scale model airplanes, antique toys and dolls, as well as gem, mineral, and Aboriginal culture displays. Its hours are the same as the Big Orange's. Admission is $2. For information, phone (08) 8582-2325.

A Special Place for Jimmy James is a commemorative riverfront walking trail and engraved granite slab dedicated to the esteemed Aborigine. The polished slab contains images of Jimmy's spirit world, and nearby are bronze plaques with statements from admirers.

Accommodations and Food

Rooms at the **Berri Resort Hotel,** Riverview Dr., tel. (08) 8582-1411, are an eclectic mix of basic to contemporary, and the pub serves cheap counter meals. Inexpensive-Moderate. **Berri River Motor Inn,** Sturt Hwy., tel. (08) 8582-2688, offers modern rooms and a convenient location. Inexpensive-Moderate. You can get a campsite, or on-site vans and cabins with air-conditioning and television, at **Berri Riverside Caravan Park,** Riverview Dr., tel. (08) 8582-3723. Budget-Moderate.

If you enjoy fruit, you won't go hungry in these parts. Sturt Highway is lined with fruit berry growers and juice processors. Pick up fresh and dried fruits, nuts, jams, and honey at stands along the way.

Information

Berri Tourist and Travel Centre, Vaughan Terrace, tel. (08) 8582-1655, can arrange accommodations, and provide winery maps and general information. Hours are Mon.-Fri. 9 a.m.-5 p.m., Saturday 9-11:30 a.m., closed Christmas Day and Good Friday.

In an emergency, dial 000; the **police,** tel. (08) 8595-2020; **ambulance,** tel. (08) 8582-1078; or the **Royal Automobile Association,** tel. (08) 8582-3644. Riverland Regional Hospital, tel. (08) 8580-2400, is located on Maddern Street.

LOXTON

Berri's twin ferries, the main link to Loxton, will whisk you across the river in one and a half minutes; from there you pass around Lock Number Four and Katarapko Island and head into town. Settled in the 1890s and established in 1907, Loxton (pop. 7,288) is a picture-postcard township overlooking both the Murray and a game reserve. Named for William Charles Loxton, a boundary rider who worked on the original station property, irrigation methods turned the area into the same rich grounds as the rest of the Riverland.

Sights

Loxton's most famous attraction is the **Historical Village,** a riverfront collection of 25 fully furnished early buildings, including a replica of William Charles Loxton's pine and pug hut. Early farm equipment and machinery are also on exhibit. Hours are Mon.-Fri. 10 a.m.-4 p.m., Sat.-Sun. 10 a.m.-5 p.m. Admission is $5. For information, phone (08) 8584-7194.

Magill Estate Winery, Penfold Rd., Magill, tel. (08) 8301-5569, specializes in de-alcoholized wines. Hours for sales and tastings are Mon.-Sat. 10 a.m.-5 p.m.

For easeful entertainment you can check flood levels on the trunk of **The Tree of Knowledge,** in Lions Park, on the riverfront.

Murray River National Park is home to almost 150 species of birds. You can camp, fish, or bushwalk through red gum floodplain, explore horseshoe lagoons and gentle backwaters. **Kai Kai Nature Trail,** beginning at campsite 20, is a 40-minute walk encompassing a wide variety of Katarapko Creek birdlife and natural habitat.

Alawoona, 35 km south of Loxton, is the entry point for mallee country. The 36,815-hectare **Billiatt Conservation Park** is home to the western gray kangaroo, hopping mouse, pygmy possum, and many mallee birds, including the endangered mallee fowl and red-lored whistler.

Accommodations and Food

Loxton Hotel Motel, East Terrace, tel. (08) 8584-7266, has both old pub rooms ($35) and newer riverview motel suites. Inexpensive-Moderate. The restaurant serves counter meals ($4-7) and offers an à la carte menu (entrees $7-12). **Loxton Riverfront Caravan Park,** tel. (08) 8584-7862, on the Murray, has campsites and on-site vans, plus bicycle and canoe rentals. A 48-bed hostel is also available. Budget-Moderate. At **Nadia Host Farm,** tel. 085-87-4362, 20 minutes from Loxton, you can experience life on a wheat and sheep farm. Its moderate rates include breakfast.

East Terrace has a variety of decent cafés, as well as a Chinese restaurant. **Medea Cottage Fruit and Veg,** Bookpurnong Rd., tel. (08) 8584-5993, is the place to buy homemade jams, nuts, and both fresh and dried fruits. Hours are daily 10:30 a.m.-5:30 p.m.

Information

Loxton Tourist and Art Centre, Bookpurnong Terrace, tel. (08) 8584-7919, will assist you with accommodations and tours, as well as canoe, bicycle, or houseboat rentals. Hours are Mon.-Fri. 9 a.m.-5 p.m., Saturday during school holidays 9-11:30 a.m.

For emergency services, dial 000; the **police,** tel. (08) 8584-7283; **ambulance,** tel. (08) 8584-7876; or the **Royal Automobile Association,** tel. (08) 8584-6797. Find the hospital on Drabsch St., tel. (08) 8584-7201.

Getting Around

Rent **trail bikes** from Loxton Motorcycle Centre, 10 Bookpurnong Terrace, tel. (08) 8584-7698.

RENMARK

Renmark (pop. 4,256) sits on a willow-lined Murray River bend, 255 km northeast of Adelaide and very near the Victoria border. Founded in 1887, Renmark is Australia's oldest irrigation district—thanks to Alfred Deakin's idea and the Canadian Chaffey brothers' expertise, the system spurred the Riverland's thriving citrus and wine industry. Ironically, the Chaffey brothers inserted a prohibition clause in their plans for the town's development. In 1897, the British Commonwealth erected the Renmark Hotel, the first hotel to challenge the clause. And we know who won!

Today Renmark is a busy commercial and holiday center, with plenty of wine to taste, houseboats to rent, and arts and crafts galleries to browse.

Paringa, four km east from Renmark, is the location of **Lock Number Five,** and nearby lie the quite wonderful **Headings Cliffs Lookout Tower,** the quite interesting **Lyrup Village** communal growing settlement (dating from 1894), and the quite dumb **Big Tyre.**

Sights

The **PS *Industry,*** built in 1911, serves as historical museum. Through a coin-in-the-slot operation, you can see how paddle wheels and other engine parts function. Moored on the Murray, between 9th and 10th Streets, the museum is open daily 9 a.m.-5 p.m. Admission is $2. For information, phone (08) 8586-6704.

Olivewood Homestead, Renmark Ave. and 21st St., the original home of Charles Chaffey, now operates as a National Trust museum. Hours are Thurs.-Mon. 10 a.m.-4 p.m. Admission is $3.50. For information, phone (08) 8586-6175.

Bredl's Reptile Park and Zoo, on the Sturt Hwy., five km from town, has pythons, taipans, cobras, boa constrictors, rare yellow anacondas, lizards, alligators, crocs, and other reptiles. Hours are daily 8 a.m.-6 p.m. in summer, 9 a.m.-5:30 p.m. in winter, and there are special snake feedings Sunday 2-3 p.m. Admission is $7. For information, phone (08) 8595-1431.

Accommodations and Food

The historic **Renmark Hotel,** Murray Ave., tel. (08) 8586-6755, has decent rooms with shared facilities, as well as motel units. The hotel features both a bistro and dining room. Inexpensive-Moderate. At **Renmark Country Club,** Sturt Hwy., tel. (08) 8595-1401, guests are privy to the tennis court, swimming pool, spa, and 18-hole grass golf course. Moderate-Expensive.

Riverbend Caravan Park, Sturt Hwy., tel. (08) 8595-5131, and **Renmark Caravan Park,**

Sturt Hwy., tel. (08) 8586-6315, are situated on the riverfront. Both have campsites, on-site vans, and cabins for rent. Budget-Moderate.

Rivergrowers Ark Kiosk, Renmark Ave., tel. (08) 8586-6705, sells a variety of juices, nuts, honey, jams, chocolates, and fresh and dried fruits—most processed in the factory next door. Hours are Mon.-Fri. 10 a.m.-4 p.m., Saturday 9 a.m.-noon.

Sports and Recreation

Facilities at **Renmark Health and Fitness Centre** include indoor tennis, indoor swimming pool, squash courts, weight-training equipment, spa and sauna, a suntan unit, and large multipurpose stadium for cricket, soccer, netball, badminton, volleyball, basketball, and roller skating. For information, phone (08) 8586-6072.

Shopping

Most of the arts and crafts galleries are situated on or near Renmark Avenue. **Ozone Art and Craft Gallery,** Ral Ral Ave., is one of the more interesting spots for local creative wares.

Pick up camping equipment at **Cole and Woodham,** Renmark Ave., tel. (08) 8586-6731.

Information

The **Tourist Information Centre,** Murray Ave., tel. (08) 8586-6704, distributes info and rents tandem or single bicycles (there's a good cycling track to Paringa). Hours are Mon.-Fri. 9 a.m.-5 p.m., Saturday 9 a.m.-4 p.m., Sunday and public holidays 12 p.m.-4 p.m., closed Christmas Day.

TRANSPORTATION

Getting There

Local airlines fly daily from Adelaide to Renmark and on to Mildura. Book through Ansett or Qantas.

Murray Bridge Passenger Service, tel. (08) 8532-2633, operates daily coaches between Murray Bridge and Adelaide's Franklin Street depot for about $12 one-way. **Stateliner,** tel. (08) 8415-5555, has daily coaches from Adelaide to Blanchetown, Waikerie, Barmera, Berri, Loxton, and Renmark. Many interstate coaches also serve the Lower Murray and Riverland.

River Cruising

Why not feel the river rush through your veins by traveling *on* the Murray, instead of along it? In the Lower Murray, you can rent **houseboats** at Murray Bridge, Mannum, Younghusband, and Purnong; in the Riverland, houseboats are based at Morgan, Waikerie, Loxton, Berri, Paringa, and Renmark. Houseboats are completely self-contained, accommodate four to 10 people, and are capable of traveling six to eight knots. Rental prices depend upon the size of boat, length of rental, and the season you rent it in—typically about $1,200 per week (you can get them as low as $600). However, keep in mind that this takes care of both transport and accommodations, as well as cooking facilities—and, if you share the cost with others, it even becomes cheap. At any rate, it will be a delightful and memorable experience, floating along the Murray, in comfort, and at will. Use a little imagination and you may run into Tom Sawyer, Matthew

Flinders, or Mr. Lucky. Rent a fully equipped luxury houseboat from **Swan Houseboats**, tel. (08) 8582-3663 in Berri or (1800) 08-3183.

Book houseboats (*well* in advance) at any South Australian Tourism Commission Travel Centre, or through local Tourist Information Centres. You won't need a boat operator's license, but a driver's license is required.

Or, leave the navigating to someone else. The 18-cabin *Proud Mary* luxury boat departs Murray Bridge for two- to five-day cruises. Cost is $550-850 pp. For information, phone (08) 8231-9472. The 60-cabin paddle steamer *Murray Princess* departs Mannum for two- or five-day Riverland cruises, at $400-850 pp. For information, phone (08) 8569-2511 or (1800) 80-4843. All of the above prices include accommodations and meals.

Get a quick taste of the Murray on a lunch, dinner, or other short sail. Check in with the various tourist offices for a list of local operators.

THE MID-NORTH

South Australia's Mid-North lies north of the Barossa Valley, west of the Riverland, east of Yorke Peninsula, and just south of the Flinders Ranges. And it is special—touristed, but not *touristy*.

The Mid-North is a wonderful part of the state. Burra, the historic copper mining town, is marvelous, and then there's Mintaro, a truly gorgeous heritage town. Down the road is Martindale Hall, a very chic B&B where *Picnic at Hanging Rock* was filmed.

Farther north is Peterborough, a railway junction, where train buffs—with hearts that chug instead of beat—can all-aboard a narrow-gauge steam train through the Mid-North countryside. Port Pirie, along the Spencer Gulf, is a mixture of heritage town, busy seaport, and commercial center.

You have a variety of options for exploring the Mid-North. The Clare Valley is a 135-km zip north of Adelaide, along Main North Road.

From Adelaide, the Barrier Highway will lead you (with a couple of detours) to Burra and Peterborough. From Peterborough, you turn westward to Jamestown, Gladstone, and Port Pirie, or continue north to the Flinders Ranges. At the junction of the Barrier and Sturt Highways, be

sure to take the Kapunda turnoff. The back road, through Hamilton, Marrabel, and Saddleworth—where you'll reconnect with the Barrier Highway—is a favorite day-in-the-country drive.

Highway 1, also from Adelaide, travels to Port Wakefield (where you can cut over to Balaklava), up to Snowtown, Crystal Brook, and Port Pirie, then on to Port Augusta and the Eyre Peninsula, or across the Nullarbor to Western Australia.

Whichever road you follow, every once in a while veer off the beaten path—this territory is full of little surprises, marked by hand-lettered signposts, European-style back roads, an ornery cow, a stubborn mule, and unusual gusto in the breeze.

KAPUNDA

Located at the northern edge of the Barossa Valley, 75 km from Adelaide, Kapunda (pop. 1,620) was the location of South Australia's first significant copper find. An accidental discovery of green copper ore prompted the opening of one of the world's richest copper mines on 32 hectares owned by the Dutton and Bagott fami-

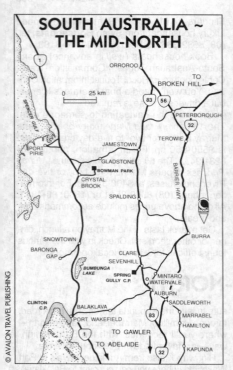

SOUTH AUSTRALIA ~ THE MID-NORTH

0   25 km

ORROROO
TO BROKEN HILL
PETERBOROUGH
TEROWIE
JAMESTOWN
GLADSTONE
BOWMAN PARK
CRYSTAL BROOK
SPALDING
PORT PIRIE
SPENCER GULF
BARRIER HWY
BURRA
SNOWTOWN
BARONGA GAP
CLARE
SEVENHILL
BUMBUNGA LAKE
SPRING GULLY C.P.
MINTARO
WATERVALE
AUBURN
CLINTON C.P.
BALAKLAVA
SADDLEWORTH
MARRABEL
HAMILTON
PORT WAKEFIELD
TO GAWLER
TO ADELAIDE
KAPUNDA
GULF ST. VINCENT

© AVALON TRAVEL PUBLISHING

lies. The mine operated 1844-1912, turning out approximately 14,000 tons of copper, and Kapunda soon grew into the state's largest country town. Though the community now lives off agricultural rather than mining products, many historic buildings, cottages, and churches still stand, and the town retains a lot of its original charm. Particularly stunning is the decorative iron lacework, known as "Kapunda lace," made locally at the turn of the century.

Sights and Events

Kapunda Historical Museum, tel. (08) 8566-2657, is in the former Baptist church on Hill Street. Historical exhibits include colonial artifacts, memorabilia, and archival recordings. Hours are Sat.-Thurs. Sept.-May, and weekends June-Aug. 1-4 p.m.

The eight-meter-tall bronze sculpture of *Map Kernow* (Cornish for "Son of Cornwall"), at the south end of town, pays tribute to early Cornish miners.

Take the **Old Kapunda Copper Mine and Walking Trail,** an easy 1.5-km hike through the old mine, for close-up investigation of shafts, tunnels, the open cut area, the mine chimney, and an early miner's cottage.

The **Heritage Trail** leads to 42 historical buildings along a 10-km route.

The **Celtic Festival,** held the first weekend in April, fills the town's pubs with Celtic, bush, and folk bands and fans.

Accommodations and Food

Sir John Franklin Hotel, Main St., tel. (08) 8566-3233, has large pub-style rooms with shared facilities. Inexpensive. Across the street, **Ford House,** tel. (08) 8566-2280, is a beautifully renovated B&B with prices to match ($10 less without breakfast). Excellent à la carte dinners ($8-14 for beef or chicken entrees) are served at both accommodations, and Sir John Franklin's lively pub also has inexpensive counter meals ($5-9).

Dutton Park Caravan Park, Montefiore St., tel.08-8566-2094, rents campsites, and has a tennis court and playground. Budget-Inexpensive.

Information

Get maps for both walking trails mentioned above, as well as other information, from **Kapunda Tourist Centre,** on Main Street. The tourist center is open daily 10 a.m.-1 p.m., closed Christmas Day and Good Friday. For information, phone (08) 8566-2902.

MINTARO

The entire tiny township of Mintaro (pop. 80) is on the heritage list. Of course, you'll find only a handful of streets, but they're lined with 1850s slate, stone, and wooden colonial structures—influenced by Italian, English, and German hands—constructed of such diverse materials as Baltic pine and Indian cedar. Most buildings incorporate the locally produced fine slate—a specialty of this district—in walls, floors, or fences, and many of the old cottages have been converted into accommodation houses. The town is thought to have been named by Uruguayan mule drivers who stopped there while carting copper ore between Port Wakefield and Burra.

Mintaro sits 130 km from Adelaide and about 14 km from Clare, burrowed among gentle hills and rolling pastures. It is a gorgeous, quiet country village. Go there!

Sights

Robinson's Cottage, tel. (08) 8843-9029, a museum inside an original 1851 settler's cottage, features fire engine displays, fire appliances and memorabilia, classic and vintage cars, and other early equipment. Hours are daily 9 a.m.-4:30 p.m., closed Christmas Day.

Reilly's Cottage Gallery, tel. (08) 8843-9013, exhibits local and national arts and crafts in a cottage more than 120 years old. Hours are Wed.-Sun. 10 a.m.-5 p.m.

Martindale Hall, on the outskirts of Mintaro, is the positively splendid Georgian mansion portrayed as "Appleyard College" in the film *Picnic at Hanging Rock.* A bachelor named Edmund Bowen had the house built in 1879 in an attempt to win the hand of a spoiled rich girl, who promised to marry him if he built her a house as nice as her father's. Martindale Hall (which, in those days, cost the dear sum of £36,000) apparently wasn't up to snuff, for Edmund built the house but then lost the girl! The mansion is open for inspection daily 1-4 p.m., closed Christmas Day. It costs $5 admission, but you can visit the grounds for free. For information, phone (08) 8843-9088.

Accommodations

All Mintaro accommodations are in converted historic digs going for prices that probably have the original inhabitants rolling over in their historic graves. **Pay Office Cottages,** Hill St., tel. (08) 8843-9026, once the cheapest, is now way up there. Expensive. **Mintaro Hideaway,** tel. (08) 8843-9011, and **The Teapot Inn,** tel. (08) 8843-9037, both include breakfast. Expensive. **Mintaro Mews,** tel. (08) 8843-9011, offers two (yes, pricey) deluxe cottages with breakfast included. Expensive. And, if you're a romantic or film-crazy, you'll want to stay at the house Edmund built; **Martindale Hall,** tel. (08) 8843-9088, will give you a scrumptious room, pamper you with attention, and feed you delectable candlelight dinners. Oddly, this once really expensive spot is

now one of the cheapest if you just want a room with breakfast—toss in dinner and the rates double. Expensive-Luxury.

THE CLARE VALLEY

The Clare Valley, famous for winemaking since 1851, is a 30-km stretch, 135 km north of Adelaide, nestled within the northern Mount Lofty Ranges. Comprising the surrounding communities of Auburn, Watervale, Sevenhill, and Penwortham, about 20 wineries—ranging from small boutiques to nationally known brands—take advantage of the district's high rainfall and rich soil to create premium products.

Edward Burton Gleeson founded Clare in 1840, naming the settlement for his native County Clare, Ireland. Only one year later the Hawker brothers set up Bungaree Station, one of Australia's best-known sheep stud farms. The winemaking didn't get going until 1848, when the Jesuits planted vines to produce altar wine, which Sevenhill Cellars still turns out, along with other fine vintages.

You'll find historic buildings, serene roadways, and picturesque scenery throughout the Clare Valley towns, all dating back to the early 1800s—and it's a lot less touristy than the Barossa.

Sights

Historic buildings in **Auburn** include: Miss Mabel Cottage Living (1859), Mechanics Institute (1859), Police Station and Courtroom (1860), St. John's Anglican Church (1862), post office (1862), Stonehurst Gallery and Library (1866), and Council Chambers (1879).

Stanley Grammar School, Uniting Church of Australia, Watervale Primary School, and the Methodist Church are National Trust buildings in **Watervale.**

Run by the National Trust, the **Old Police Station Museum** (1850), corner Victoria Rd. and West Terrace in Clare, tel. (08) 8842-2376, was the valley's first courthouse and police station. Hours are Saturday 10 a.m.-noon, 2-4 p.m., Sunday 2-4 p.m. Admission is $2.

Take a tour of **Bungaree Station,** dating from 1841, when the Hawkers established the famous merino stud farm, and still run by their grandsons! The self-sufficient community has a church, council chambers, school, blacksmith shop, as well as wool shed, stable yard, and shearers quarters, that are still in use. One- to two-hour conducted tours are arranged by appointment only, as the station is still going full-stud. Original knitting patterns and woolen yarns are sold on the premises. For information, phone (08) 8842-2677.

Saint Aloysius Church and Sevenhill Cellars, College Rd., Sevenhill, tel. (08) 8843-4222, is where the valley's first vines were planted. Father Aloysius Kranewitter, a young Jesuit priest, chose the site (patterned after the seven hills of Rome) as a cellar for his altar wines. Saint Aloysius Church was begun in 1856 and consecrated in 1875. Besides altar wines, Sevenhill specializes in dry red and white wines, and liqueur Tokay. Hours are Mon.-Fri. 8:30 a.m.-4:30 p.m., Saturday and holidays 9 a.m.-4 p.m., closed Sunday, Christmas Day, New Year's Day, and Good Friday (you know where you can get their wine on *those* days).

Wolta Wolta Homestead, tel. (08) 8842-3656, was one of the earliest settler's cottages. Unfortunately, it burned down in 1983's devastating Ash Wednesday fire. The homestead, now restored, features antiques, artwork, history, and memorabilia relating to the Hope family, owners of the property for four generations. Tours are conducted Sat.-Sun. 10 a.m.-4:30 p.m. Admission is $3.

Accommodations and Food

If you're not fussy, you can stay cheaply in the shearers' bunkhouse at **Bungaree Station,** Port Pirie/Port Augusta Rd., tel. (08) 8842-2677. Facilities include a large dining hall and modern kitchen. Budget. **Clare Valley Cabins,** Hubbe Rd., tel. (08) 8842-1155, offers seven two-bedroom self-contained cottages on a large property five km north of Clare. Inexpensive-Moderate. **Bentley's Hotel Motel,** 191 Main North Rd., tel. (08) 8842-1700, rents well-kept rooms in both units. Moderate. **Clare Central Motel,** 325 Main North Rd., tel. (08) 8842-2277, is down the street and runs about $20 more than Bentley's. Moderate-Expensive. **Trestrail Cottage,** tel. (08) 8842-3794, in Sevenhill, is more upmarket and tosses in breakfast ingredients. Moderate-Expensive.

Clare Caravan Park, Main North Rd., tel. (08) 8842-2724, near Clare, has campsites and on-site vans. Budget-Inexpensive.

Cheap eats on the main drag are **Clare Valley Café, Beba's Coffee Lounge,** and **Pantry Plus Coffee Shop,** where sandwich/salad-type meals run $4-8. **Bentley's Hotel** serves country-style meals at moderate prices ($9-14 for large entree portions). And more country cookin' is dished up at **Chaffmill Country Restaurant,** Main North Rd., tel. (08) 8842-3055, for Mon.-Sat. lunch and dinner ($8-13 for entrees). **Clare Dragon Restaurant,** 308 Main North Rd., tel. (08) 8842-3644, is both a moderately priced licensed restaurant ($8-13 for Asian delights) and an inexpensive takeaway. For curries and other Indian specialties ($8-14 for curries), book a table at **Clare Valley Motel and Indian Restaurant,** Main North Rd., tel. (08) 8842-2799.

Pick up fresh-from-the-oven breads, pastries, and cakes at **Clare Valley Bakery,** 292 Main North Rd., tel. (08) 8842-3523.

Events

Similar to the Barossa event, Clare Valley's **Gourmet Weekend,** held every May, is when connoisseurs sip and sample, and the hungry pig out on a progressive lunch at area wineries.

Information

Clare Valley Tourist Information Centre, 229 Main North Rd., Clare, tel. (08) 8842-2131, has maps of Clare Valley wineries and other local information. Hours are daily 9 a.m.-4 p.m., closed Christmas Day.

BURRA

With the feel and flavor of a down under Bisbee, Arizona, Burra (pop. 2,225) is one of South Australia's most enchanting towns.

Originally, the community was a sheep-grazing area on the brink of bankruptcy. But in 1845, after shepherd William Streair discovered copper, followed by Thomas Pickett's find, the "Monster Mine" was created and Burra blossomed with prosperity. Named "Burra Burra" (Hindi for "Great Great") by Indian coolie shepherds, the district was collectively called "The Burra," and embraced several townships, all named according to their inhabitants' origins—thus Kooringa (Aboriginal), Redruth (Cornish), Aberdeen (Scottish), Hampton (English), and Llwychrr (Welsh).

Though the mine was one rich mother lode, operations ceased in 1877 when it dried up. Agriculture (Burra was declared "Merino Capital of the World" in 1988) and tourism are the local revenue-takers these days. A leisurely 156-km drive from Adelaide, Burra draws visitors to its fascinating streets and dwellings to follow in historic footsteps along the copper trail.

Sights

Just about the whole town can be classified a sight, but you'll need a passport to cross many thresholds. The **Burra Passport** is a rental key, available from the tourist office, that allows you entrance to **Burra Creek Miner's Dugouts, Burra Open Air Museum, Redruth Gaol, Police Lock-up and Stables,** and **Unicorn Brewery Stables.** Cost of the passport is $20 per family or vehicle, plus a $5 deposit.

Also included in the passport's attractions is **Morphett's Enginehouse.** Built in 1858 and reconstructed in 1986, it helped to pump water from the mine. A 30-meter entry tunnel enables visitors to walk into the shaft to view original pump pipes.

Bon Accord Museum, on the site of the original Bon Accord Mine, serves as an interpretive center, with a working forge, five- by six-meter model of the Monster Mine, and tours of the old mine shaft. Hours are Mon.-Fri. 12:30-2:30 p.m., Sat.-Sun. and public holidays 12:30-3:30 p.m. Admission is $3. For information, phone (08) 8892-2056.

Paxton Square Cottages is three rows of 1850s miners' cottages overlooking Burra Creek. The cottages are now visitor accommodations, but **Malowen Lowarth,** furnished as a mine captain's cottage, is open for inspection Saturday 1-3 p.m., Sunday 10:30 a.m.-12:30 p.m. Admission is $3.

If you're into cemeteries, old **Burra Cemetery** is especially nice. If you're into diseases, it will be of interest that most causes of death at the time were typhoid, diphtheria, measles, and consumption.

Market Square Museum, operated by the National Trust, consists of a general store, post office, and private home, built 1870-1915. Nearby is the 13-meter ironbark and blue gum **Jinker,** which toted the huge Schneider's engine-house cylinder from Port Adelaide to Burra Mine in

1852. Hours are Saturday 2-4 p.m., Sunday 1-3 p.m., or by arrangement. For information, phone (08) 8892-2154.

Burra Gorge, 18 km east of town, has good walking trails through river gum forests and other scenic bushland.

Accommodations and Food

You can check into a pub for the night, but it's certainly more fun to stay in one of Burra's seeping-with-history heritage dwellings. The tourist center has all the info on these accommodations. The exquisite **Paxton Square Cottages,** Kingston St., tel. (08) 8892-2622, with fully equipped kitchens, are a very reasonable $40-55 double (plus $10 for linen and $5 per load of firewood). Inexpensive-Moderate. **Bon Accord Cottage,** West St., tel. (08) 8892-2519, the preserved mine manager's residence, can be had for about twice the price. Expensive. **Saffron Downs,** Morgan Rd., tel. (08) 8892-2012, is a picture-pretty B&B with old-mining-town hospitality. Moderate. Book all accommodations (especially Paxton Cottages) well in advance.

Reasonably priced places to fill your belly are **Polly's Tearooms,** tel. (08) 8892-2544, **Pantry Plus,** tel. (08) 8842-3544, and the counters at **Burra Hotel,** tel. (08) 8892-2389, and **Kooringa Hotel,** tel. (08) 8892-2013. **Price's,** in Market Square, is your stop for homemade soups and fabulous wieners ($3-5). **Jumbuck's Restaurant,** Market St., tel. (08) 8892-2777, serves pastas, and chicken and beef dishes ($14-18).

Information

Apply for cottage "passports" and load up on brochures at **Burra Tourist Centre,** Market Square, tel. (08) 8892-2154. Hours are daily 10 a.m.-4 p.m., closed Christmas Day.

A number of historical books on the area are also sold here (*Discovering Burra* is included with your passport).

TEROWIE

Continuing up the Barrier Highway (be careful of kangaroos) for 63 km north of Burra brings you to Terowie, another historic town and a prominent part of the 1880s railway network. Horse and bullock teams from the surrounding country stations kept up a steady rush hour while loading or unloading produce, supplies, and stock. And, history buffs, get this: Terowie, site of a World War II army bivouac camp, was where General Douglas MacArthur, fresh from his Philippines escape, made his famous "I came out of Bataan and I shall return" statement.

It's a good wander down Main St., where the original century-old shopfronts reflect times past. **Arid Lands Botanic Garden**, also on Main St., features a large assortment of Australian arid-zone plants and is open daily.

Accommodations and Food
Terowie Hotel, on Main St., tel. (08) 8659-1012, offers pub rooms with breakfast included. Inexpensive. **Terowie Roadhouse and Motel**, Barrier Hwy., tel. (08) 8659-1082, is not much classier than the pub, but is air-conditioned. Inexpensive. Chow on nouveau pub ($3-7) at **Terowie Hotel**, and grab snacks over at the roadhouse.

Information and Services
Terowie Information and Souvenir Shop, Main St., tel. (08) 8659-1087, will organize visits to the Terowie Pioneer Gallery and Museum, as well as conducted tours of the town and buildings. Hours are daily 9:30 a.m.-5:30 p.m.

For emergencies, dial 000. The local **RAA** branch is on East Terrace, tel. (08) 8659-1082.

PETERBOROUGH

Turn off the Barrier Highway at Terowie for the 23-km ride into Peterborough—frontier town, historic railway depot, and gateway to the Flinders Ranges. Railway aficionados will thrill to find that Peterborough is one of the world's two known towns where three different rail gauges converge. This is still an important rail center on the Port Pirie-Broken Hill-Sydney main line. Get a good peek at the town (and the tracks) from **Tank Hill Lookout**, at the end of Government Road.

Sights
Don't miss a ride on the steam passenger train, along the narrow-gauge line, from Peterborough to Orroroo (about 38 km). The tourist center has schedules.

Round House Exchange, a unique railway turntable used for rerouting rolling stock, displays historic rail equipment.

Saint Cecelia, the former bishop's residence, is palatially furnished with paintings, antique pianos, polished mahogany, and stained-glass windows within its parlors, ballroom, 10 bedrooms, and library. The coach house now functions as an art center. Moderately priced accommodations are available in the main house, converted stables, coachman's room, or attached artist's studio, and include breakfast. Daily tours 1-4 p.m. are arranged through the tourist center. For information, phone (08) 8651-2654.

The **Gold Battery** once extracted gold from locally mined crushed ore. Guided tours can be arranged. For information, phone (08) 8651-2708.

Information
You can't miss the **Peterborough Tourist Centre**, tel. (08) 8651-2708—it's in a railway carriage along Main Street. Get your steam train tickets here, and if you're headed to the Flinders Ranges, inquire about roads and routes. Hours are daily 9 a.m.-4 p.m., closed Christmas Day, New Year's Day, and Good Friday.

TO PORT PIRIE

Traveling coastward, the back road southwest of Peterborough hooks up with Route 83. At Jamestown, it starts east leaving Route 83, drops a bit southward at Gladstone, then curves northward, merging with Highway 1, heading to Port Pirie and beyond.

Jamestown
This wool-, wheat-, and barley-producing agricultural community, 44 km from Peterborough, originated back in the 1870s. Its **National Trust Museum**, Mannanarie Rd., tel. (08) 8664-0026, houses a collection of early memorabilia and historical relics. Hours are Mon.-Sat. 10 a.m.-5 p.m., Sunday 2-4 p.m. Admission is $2.

South Australia's first government forest plantation, **Bundaleer Forest Reserve**, nine km south of Jamestown, affords refreshing walks and picnics. Climb up to the lookout tower and you'll see Mt. Remarkable in the distance.

Gladstone

This pastoral and grazing community, 28 km southwest of Jamestown and adjacent to the Rocky River, also dates back to the 1870s. In 1877, after the railway connected Gladstone to Port Pirie, the community became an important grain collection center. Eventually it became home to South Australia's largest inland silo (which now contains 82,500 tons of grain). At the Gladstone railway yards, you can view one of the world's few places where narrow, standard, and broad gauges are interlaid in one siding.

Experience conditions withstood by "inebriates, debtors, and other prisoners" at century-old **Gladstone Gaol,** Ward St., tel. (08) 8662-2200. (Some of the "other prisoners" included Italians and Germans interned there during WW II.) Hours are Monday, Tuesday, and Friday 1-4 p.m., Sat.-Sun. and school holidays 10 a.m.-4 p.m. Admission is $4.

PORT PIRIE

Port Pirie (pop. 15,114), 210 km from Adelaide, is well positioned on the eastern side and northern end of Spencer Gulf, shadowed by the Flinders Ranges. As the Mid-North's largest center, Port Pirie (named after the colonial workhorse windjammer *John Pirie*) is notable for its enormous lead smeltery, capable of producing 280,000 kg of silver, 250,000 tons of refined lead, 90,000 tons of sulphuric acid, 45,000 tons of electrolytic zinc, as well as gold, cadmium, copper matte, and antimonial lead alloys—the annual turnout from rich Broken Hill mines.

As the closest port to Broken Hill, the precious metal is railed in and treated at the smeltery or exported internationally. Other products shipped from the port are large quantities of wheat and barley.

Obviously, industry and shipping get top billing at Port Pirie, yet you'll also discover intriguing old buildings, excellent sports facilities, and a surprising variety of entertainment.

Sights

Port Pirie National Trust Museum, Old Ellen St., tel. (08) 8632-1080, is comprised of the railway station, customs house, and police station. Displays include historical exhibits, a scale model

of the smelters, railway and shipping exhibits, 10,000- to 20,000-year-old diprotodon bones, and a former shunting engine. Hours are Mon.-Sat. 10 a.m.-4 p.m., Sunday 1-4 p.m., closed Christmas Day. Admission is $3.

The historical home **Carn Brae,** 32 Florence St., tel. (08) 8632-1314, belonged to the pioneering Moyles, soft-drink moguls. Aside from fine architecture, collections include turn-of-the-century furnishings, paintings, glassware, and porcelain, as well as more than 2,500 antique and contemporary dolls. Hours are daily 10 a.m.-4 p.m., closed Christmas Day. Admission is $5.

Fishermen's Jetty, with fishing and boat-launching ramps, is either busy or tranquil, depending on the tide. **Solomontown Jetty** provides a safe swimming beach, children's playground along the reserve, and sunbathing area. **Port Davis,** 15 km south of Port Pirie off Port Broughton Rd., has both jetty fishing and a boat launch.

Accommodations and Food

Rooms are unremarkable, but accordingly priced, at **International Hotel Motel,** 40 Ellen St., tel. (08) 8632-2422. Inexpensive. **Flinders Range Motor Inn,** 151 Main Rd., tel. (08) 8632-3555, offers videos, room service, beer garden, swimming pool, tennis court, and a Saturday night dinner dance. Moderate. **John Pirie Motor Inn,** Main Rd., tel. (08) 8632-4200, features a swimming pool and room service. Moderate-Expensive. Both **Port Pirie Caravan Park,** Beach Rd., tel. (08) 8632-4275, and **Rangeview Caravan Park,** Hwy. 1, tel. (08) 8634-4221, have campsites and on-site vans. Budget-Inexpensive.

Hungry? Hope you like Chinese food and fish 'n' chips!

Entertainment and Events

Northern Festival Centre, at Memorial Park, is patterned after the Adelaide Centre. Theater, films, exhibitions, and performances by both visiting and local entertainers are scheduled regularly.

Information

Local details are provided by **Port Pirie Regional Tourism and Arts Centre,** 3 Mary Elie St., tel. (08) 8633-0439. Hours are Mon.-Fri. 9 a.m.-5 p.m., Sat.-Sun. 1-4 p.m.

ALONG HIGHWAY ONE

Up Highway 1, beyond Gawler, the coastal road passes picturesque parklands, old copper ports, salty lakes, and sculptural rock formations.

Balaklava
A short 26-km detour east from Port Wakefield, Balaklava (pop. 1,365) was once a rest stop for bullock teams hauling copper ore from Burra to Port Wakefield. Nearby **Rocks Reserve,** with interesting rock formations, is a good spot to stop in for a picnic.

Port Wakefield
Port Wakefield, top of the Gulf St. Vincent, is a one-time copper and wool port with a lovely old wharf. Go bush at **Clinton Conservation Park,** just north of town. Back on Highway 1 and another 30 km north is **Bumbunga Lake,** a huge salt pan covering 3,530 acres. The lake changes color according to the weather—the weather's good if it's blue and unsettled if it's pink. You can tour the processing plant. The scenic drive along Lochiel-Ninnes Rd. affords a superb view of the inland lakes and countryside.

Snowtown
This primo sheep- and cattle-breeding township, 49 km north of Port Wakefield, was established in the 1840s by early settlers seeking greener pastures. These days, Snowtown provides services for surrounding rural communities.

See what's left of **Burunga Gap Township,** 10 km west of Snowtown, established in 1873.

Crystal Brook
Scenic Crystal Brook (pop. 2,100), 52 km north of Snowtown, was declared a township in 1873, though it was named in 1839 by early explorer Edward John Eyre. It's a lovely town with tall river gums, picnic parks, water ponds, and of course, the crystal brook, which runs from the lower Flinders Ranges to the River Broughton.

Bowman Park Homestead, five km east of Crystal Brook, is a peaceful parkland for picnics and play, as well as a Mid-North point for the Heysen Trail. The Native Fauna Zone houses crocodiles, koalas, kangaroos, waterfowl, goannas, pythons, eagles, and other critters. Hours are daily 10 a.m.-4 p.m. Admission is $6. For information, phone (08) 8636-2116.

Make camp at either **Crystal Brook Caravan Park,** tel. (08) 8636-2640, or the 22-bed lodge and tent sites for Heysen Trail trekkers (contact park manager at 08-8636-2116). Budget.

TRANSPORTATION

Contact the **Central Bus Station** in Adelaide for coaches to Kapunda, Burra, Peterborough, and Port Pirie. For information, phone (08) 8415-5533.

The major transcontinental rail lines stop at Port Pirie and Peterborough on journeys between Adelaide and Perth, Alice Springs and Sydney. For information, phone (08) 8231-7699 or (13) 2232.

Or *walk!* **The Heysen Trail** passes from Tanunda (in the Barossa), through Burra, Mt. Bryan, Spalding, and Crystal Brook, in the Mid-North.

YORKE PENINSULA

Rich fields of golden wheat and barley, moody beaches and sandy coves, wildlife peeking from the bush, fluttering birds, cotton-puff skies, sparkling blue seas, spring wildflower blankets, and Cornish mining settlements, combined with close proximity to Adelaide, make the Yorke Peninsula an attractive holiday getaway. (Either that or travelers miss it altogether, ending up on the Eyre Highway and headed for Western Australia, having lost the whole Yorke in one blink!)

Set between Spencer Gulf and the Gulf St. Vincent, most of the peninsula's parks, beaches, and towns are not more than a two- or three-hour drive from Adelaide. The two sealed highways follow the east coast and midsection of the peninsula, converge at Warooka, and end at Stenhouse Bay in Innes National Park (near the Park Headquarters). Gravel roads and dirt tracks spur off from the main highways, leading to hideaway beaches, rural communities, and patchwork farmlands. Yet, even on the inland route, you're never more than 25 km from the coast, with beaches to please anglers, divers, surfers, and sunners. So, if you're seeking a destination that lacks in the typical tourist trappings, is user-friendly rather than hard-sell, the Yorke offers a laid-back environment where you can set your own sights. The fishing is good year-round, but it's the spring months (Sept.-Nov.)—when the wildflowers serve up a visual feast of daisies, wattles, orchids, and red flame bush—that are exceptional.

Detour off Highway 1, north of Port Wakefield (about 100 km from Adelaide), along the eastern coast, through the ports of Androssan and Edithburgh, down to Innes National Park, where the emus and kangaroos play. Take the scenic drive around Corny Point, meet the sealed highway at Warooka, pass through the "inland" communities of Minlaton and Maitland, up to the historic Copper Triangle towns of Moonta, Kadina, and Wallaroo, to Port Broughton, the seaside resort at the Yorke's northern tip.

History

Captain Matthew Flinders first sighted the Yorke Peninsula in 1802, the year he was exploring South Australia's coastline. Sheep farmers, looking for greener pastures for their stock, settled the region in the 1830s, but it was the 1859 discovery of copper at Kadina that made the Yorke prosper, plus provided a much-needed boost to South Australia's precarious economy. By 1861, extensive deposits were uncovered at Wallaroo and Moonta, and the copper rush was on. Cornish (and some Welsh) miners flocked to the Yorke, bringing their picks and shovels, and leaving their heritage and pasties behind. Thus, the Copper Triangle towns of Kadina, Wallaroo, and Moonta also became known as "Little Cornwall." A bienniel festival pays tribute to the area's rich Cornish heritage.

The Yorke's copper mines operated up until the 1920s, when declining prices, combined with increased labor expenses and international competition, prompted closure (Poona Mine, at Moonta, reopened in 1988). Mines closed or not, the Yorke was hardly dried up. The flat plains of Australia's granary are considered one of the world's richest wheat and barley regions.

Information

For more information on the Yorke Peninsula, contact any South Australian Tourism Commission Travel Centre.

THE COPPER TRIANGLE

The historic Cornish townships of Kadina, Wallaroo, and Moonta are easily reached via the Kadina turnoff from Highway 1, three km north of Port Wakefield. Otherwise, if you're exploring the entire Yorke Peninsula, you'll catch these towns on your way up the west coast. Most of the artsy-craftsy galleries are in that "tri-city" area, so if you're dying for a locally painted landscape, you'll probably find it there.

Kadina

This is the Yorke Peninsula's largest town. As one-time center of the copper action, Kadina (pop. 3,500) has a distinctively Cornish atmosphere, reflected in many of the old buildings.

YORKE PENINSULA

TO ADELAIDE

WALLAROO

KADINA

TO PORT AUGUSTA

CLINTON C.P.

PORT WAKEFIELD

MOONTA BAY

MOONTA

PORT CLINTON

MOONTA BAY

PRICE

SALT EVAPORATION PANS

TIDDY WIDDY BEACH

WIDDY BEACH

ARDROSSAN

MAITLAND

ROGUES POINT

BLACK POINT

GULF ST. VINCENT

PINE POINT

WARDANG ISLAND

URANIA

PORT VICTORIA

PORT JULIA

PORT VINCENT

SPENCER GULF

MINLATON

BRENTWOOD

STANSBURY

WOOL BAY

HARDWICKE BAY

PORT GILES

COOBOWIE

POINT TURTON

WAROOKA

YORKETOWN

EDITHBURGH

LAKE FOWLER

CORNY POINT

LIGHTHOUSE

TROUBRIDGE ISLAND C.P.

STURT BAY

DALY HEAD

FORMBY BAY

WARRENBEN C.P.

FOUL BAY

BROWNS BEACH

BUTLERS BEACH

MARION BAY

MARION BAY

INNES NATIONAL PARK

NATIONAL PARK HEADQUARTERS

INVESTIGATOR STRAIT

ETHEL M.

CAPE SPENCER

LIGHTHOUSE

0   10 km

1 DEEP LAKE
2 MARION LAKE
3 SNOW LAKE
4 CHAIN OF LAKES

© AVALON TRAVEL PUBLISHING

THE CORNISH PASTY

The pasty was a traditional meal for the miners. Sometimes meat and veggies were placed at one end, fruit at the other. In all cases, there was crimping along the top. The crimping acted as a handle, so the men—hands filthy from work—could eat their meal and toss away the "handle." These days the crimped edge is devoured along with the contents.

The Original Cornish Pasty Recipe

Pasty rolled out like a plate, filled with turmut, tates an' mait. Doubled up an' baked like fate. Tha's a Pasty.

Matta House Museum, 1.5 km south of Kadina off Moonta Rd., contains many relics and exhibits pertaining to the good old Matta Matta mining days, housed in the former mine manager's home. Hours are Wednesday, Saturday, Sunday, and holidays 2-4:30 p.m. Admission is $2.

The **Banking and Currency Museum,** 3 Graves St., tel. (08) 8821-2906, displays every type of Australian currency ever issued, as well as other banking exhibits. The museum also buys and sells coins, notes, and medals. Hours are Sun.-Thurs. 10 a.m.-5 p.m.; closed Good Friday, Christmas Day, and the month of June. Admission is $3.

A heritage drive leads to **Wallaroo Mines,** one km west of Kadina, on Wallaroo Road. Signposts lead you on a walking tour of the old site, where you'll see ruins of the two-story-high engine building and visit places named Jericho and Jerusalem.

Wombat Hotel, 19 Taylor St., tel. (08) 8821-1108, has pub-style accommodations. Inexpensive. **Kadina Village Motel,** 28 Port Rd., tel. (08) 8821-1920, has slightly higher rates, but includes breakfast. **Kadina Caravan Park,** Lindsay Terrace, tel. (08) 8821-2259, has campsites and on-site vans, and is close to all facilities. Budget-Inexpensive.

Food? This is Cornish pasty country—they'll stick to your ribs but won't shrink your pocketbook. Buy 'em anywhere! Try **Cross's Cornish Bakeshop,** 20 Graves St., or **Price's Heritage Bakery,** 5 Digby Street. **Dynasty Room,** 4 Goyder St., tel. (08) 8821-3829, offers Chinese, Thai, and Australian cuisine ($5-9 for Asian specialties) at moderate prices.

For local info, contact the **Tourist Information Centre,** Victoria Square, tel. (08) 8821-2093. Hours are Mon.-Fri. 10 a.m.-2 p.m., Sat.-Sun. 9:30 a.m.-1:30 p.m.

In emergencies, dial 000; the **police,** tel. (08) 8828-1100; **ambulance,** tel. (08) 8821-1078; or the **Royal Automobile Association,** tel. (08) 8821-1111.

Wallaroo

Wheat and barley are shipped from this busy port (pop. 2,225), but it still doesn't equal the millions of tons of copper ore once trafficked over the jetty to destinations overseas.

Situated 10 km west of Kadina, Wallaroo was originally settled by the Welsh. The **Welsh Chimney Stack,** a Wallaroo landmark, contains 300,000 bricks in its huge square structure. For some reason, Welsh masons built square chimney stacks and the Cornish masons made theirs round.

See an extensive pictorial display of sailing ships, exhibits related to the smelting industry, and postal and sporting relics at **Wallaroo Nautical Museum,** Jetty Rd., in the old post office, tel. (08) 8823-2843. Hours are Wednesday 10:30 a.m.-4 p.m., Saturday, Sunday, and public and school holidays 2-4 p.m. Admission is $3.

Other heritage buildings include **Harvey's Pumping Station,** the **Institute, General Store,** old **Methodist Church,** and original **Wesleyan Chapel.**

You can safely swim at Wallaroo's sandy beaches. The boating and jetty angling are excellent as well.

Wallaroo Hotel, 26 Alexander St., tel. (08) 8823-2444, is pretty basic, but rooms are only about $30 per double. Inexpensive. **Sonbern Lodge Motel,** 18 John Terrace, tel. (08) 8823-2291, has heritage accommodations, with rooms in the motel section costing $10 more. Moderate. **Riley Village,** Woodfoorde Dr., tel. (08) 8823-2057, offers two-bedroom holiday units with cooking facilities. Moderate-Expensive.

Campsites and on-site vans are available at both **Wallaroo North Beach Caravan Park,** North Beach, tel. (08) 8823-2531, and **Office Beach Holiday Flats and Caravan Park,** Office Beach, tel. (08) 8823-2722. Budget-Inexpensive.

Dine on moderately priced ($8-14) local

seafood at **Wallaroo Café,** tel. (08) 8823-2420, or **Wallaroo Chicken and Seafood,** tel. (08) 8823-2920, both on Hughes Street.

Moonta

The third point in the Copper Triangle, Moonta (pop. 2,200) lies 10 km south of Wallaroo. Moonta is the nicest of the three mining towns—maybe because it was the richest. The dignified architecture, from tiny miners' cottages to the Gothic-esque Uniting Church, is a splendid reminder of times past.

After you've explored around town, head for the nearby mine site to investigate the old buildings and relics. The former schoolhouse, now **Moonta Mines Museum,** is a living history exhibit where you can experience what conditions were like for the miners, many of whom worked the 767-meter-deep Taylor Shaft. The museum provides a self-guiding map. **Miner's Cottage,** adjacent to the museum, is a restored Cornish dwelling, open for public viewing. On weekends you can ride a narrow-gauge tourist railway around the mine's complex. Hours are Wednesday, Sat.-Sun., public and school holidays 1:30-4 p.m. Admission is $1. For information, phone (08) 8825-3422.

Both the **Royal Hotel,** 2 Ryan St., tel. (08) 8825-2108, and the **Cornwall Hotel,** 20 Ryan St., tel. (08) 8825-2304, have basic pub accommodations. Inexpensive. **Moonta Bay Caravan Park,** Tossell St., tel. (08) 8825-2406, on the foreshore, offers campsites and cabins. Budget-Inexpensive.

For your Cornish pasty fix, go to **Moonta Bakery and Coffee Lounge,** 8 George St., tel. (08) 8825-2115, or **The Cornish Kitchen,** 14 Ellen St., tel. (08) 8825-3030. The historic **Cornwall Hotel** serves homestyle Australian meals ($7-11 for basic meaty entrees), and the **Shaft Steak House,** Ellen St., tel. (08) 8825-2981, specializes, obviously, in slabs of beef ($8-12 for a generous cut).

Events

Kerneweck Lowender, held in May of every odd-numbered year, is a festival commemorating the Copper Triangle's Cornish heritage. Activities include "A Golya," a Cornish feast with dancing and drinking, "A Fer Tref," all the fun of a village green fair, "A Fer Kernewek," a

Cornish fair with traditional sports and the crowning of "Cousin Jack" and "Cousin Jenny," and the Gorseth ceremony, a gathering of bands from Cornwall and Australia. Aside from Cornish pasties, revelers can sip on Swanky, a specially brewed ale.

THE EAST COAST

A sealed thoroughfare follows the coast to Edithburgh, where you either cut inland to Yorketown, Warooka, and Innes National Park, or continue along the coast on mix-or-match gravel and dirt roads.

Port Clinton to Ardrossan

Port Clinton, the east coast's northernmost seaside resort, has good crabbing beaches and is a seashell's throw from Clinton Conservation Park. **Port Clinton Caravan Park,** on the foreshore, tel. (08) 8837-7003, has campsites and on-site vans.

Tiddy Widdy Beach is a good spot for sunning and swimming. **Price Beach** is near a large salt refinery, harvesting from a vast area of pans pumped full of Gulf St. Vincent seawater.

Ardrossan, about 150 km from Adelaide, is not just the largest east coast port, with bulk grain-handling facilities; it's also home of the stump-jump plough. This particular tool, invented by Clarence Smith in 1876, enabled mallee scrubland to be turned into golden wheatfields all across the country. The folks over at the **Ardrossan District Historical Museum,** on Fifth St., will be delighted to fill you in on more of the town's history. Hours are Sunday 2:30-4:30 p.m. Admission is $2. For information, phone (08) 8837-3213.

You can catch a scenic view of Gulf St. Vincent from the **BHP lookout** or trap some crabs at the jetty.

Royal House Hotel Motel, 1 Fifth St., tel. (08) 8837-3007, is a deal in the older hotel section, $20 more for motel rooms. Inexpensive. **Ardrossan Caravan Park,** Park Terrace, tel. (08) 8837-3262, offers campsites, cabins, and on-site vans. Budget-Inexpensive.

For emergencies, dial 000; the **police,** tel. (08) 8837-3017; **ambulance,** tel. (08) 8837-3204; or the local **hospital,** tel. (08) 8837-3021.

TO EDITHBURGH AND BEYOND

Continuing south, along the coast, you'll pass the fishing "villagettes" of **Rogues Point, Pine Point, Black Point,** and **Port Julia.** Divers will want to check out the shipwrecked *Zanoni,* about 15 km southeast of Ardrossan.

Port Vincent, set on a sweeping bay 46 km south of Ardrossan, is an old ketch-landing place, and a popular swimming, yachting, and water-skiing resort. The **Port Vincent Fisherman's Retreat,** corner Parson and Kemp Streets, tel. (08) 8853-7057, offers moderately priced holiday flats. **Seaside Flats and Caravan Park,** Minlacowie Rd., tel. (08) 8853-7011, rents inexpensive flats as well as campsites and cabins.

Stansbury, 16 km away, is another sought-after holiday resort. Originally known as "Oyster Bay," it still offers some of the state's best oyster beds. Jetty fishing is also excellent here, and you'll find a decent selection of tourist facilities. The units at **Stansbury Villas,** Adelaide Rd., tel. (08) 8852-4282, are fully equipped, self-contained holiday flats. Moderate. **Stansbury Holiday Motel,** Adelaide Rd., tel. (08) 8852-4455, is on the deluxe side, with sea views from every room. Moderate-Expensive. Campsites, cabins, and vans are available at **Stansbury Caravan Park,** on the foreshore, tel. (08) 8852-4171. Budget-Inexpensive.

Past Wool Bay, Port Giles, and Coobowie lies picturesque **Edithburgh.** A former salt-producing township (and the first proclaimed settlement on southern Yorke Peninsula), Edithburgh is celebrated by divers drawn to the many shipwrecks along its coastline. If you take the scenic drive up to Troubridge Hill, you'll be able to see part of the shipwreck *Clan Ronald.*

Swimmers will find a rock pool set into a small cove, while the jetty provides ideal conditions for anglers. The small **Edithburgh Museum** features maritime displays and artifacts. Hours are Sunday and public and school holidays 2-4 p.m. Admission is $1.

Take a guided day tour over to **Troubridge Island,** to view fairy penguins and other birds contained within the 14-hectare conservation park. For information, contact the **District Council,** tel. (08) 8852-1433.

Motel accommodations in Edithburgh are moderately priced. If you plan to stay awhile,

you can get a self-contained unit for $160-245 per week at **Ocean View Holiday Flats,** O'Halloran Parade, tel. (08) 8852-6029. Budget-Inexpensive. **Edithburgh House,** Edith St., tel. (08) 8852-6373, offers old-fashioned seaside guesthouse rooms, and rates include breakfast and dinner. Moderate-Expensive. **Edithburgh Caravan Park,** corner South Terrace and O'Halloran Parade, tel. (08) 8852-6056, situated on the foreshore, offers campsites, on-site vans, and cabins. Budget-Inexpensive.

Venture inland from Edithburgh 16 km to **Yorketown,** one of the peninsula's earliest pastoral settlements. Surrounded by salt lakes where crystal formations decorate the shores, several of the lakes are pink and worth watching at sunset. You'll find unremarkable accommodations at **Melville Hotel Motel,** 1 Minlaton Rd., tel. (08) 8852-1019, or at **Yorke Hotel,** 1 Warooka Rd., tel. (08) 8852-1221, but neither place is really comfy. The motel section at the Melville is probably your best bet. Inexpensive. Camping and on-site vans are available at **Yorketown Caravan Park,** Memorial Dr., tel. (08) 8852-1563. Budget-Inexpensive.

Beyond Edithburgh, the coast road turns to gravel (and occasionally to dirt) as it travels a sparsely populated route along scenic beaches and secluded bays, merging with the sealed highway about 10 km north of Innes National Park.

Hillocks Drive, 16 km east of Marion Bay, is a scenic road leading to **Butlers Beach,** set on a seven-km sea frontage. Privately run by the Butler family, the property has two surf beaches, a number of fishing spots, camping facilities, and a small general store. The property is closed mid-June through mid-August. For information, phone (08) 8854-4002.

INNES NATIONAL PARK

The main entrance to Innes National Park is four km southwest of Marion Bay. Situated at the southernmost tip of the Yorke Peninsula, this spectacular coastal park's 9,232 hectares stretch from Stenhouse Bay on the east coast, around Cape Spencer, to Browns Beach on the west coast. Just a three-hour drive from Adelaide, the park is a favorite with city dwellers who come to surf, fish, dive, and bushwalk.

Big sightseeing attractions are the shipwreck *Ethel M,* run aground in 1904 and now disintegrating near an isolated cove called The Gap, and the old ghost town at **Inneston** (follow the historical markers past the Cape Spencer turnoff).

Clean beaches, crystal-clear water, and colorful marinelife create a delightful environment for aquatic activities. There's good fishing at Chinaman's Beach, Salmon Hole, Pondalowie Bay, Browns Beach (terrific for year-round salmon fishing), Little Browns Beach, Cape Spencer, and a host of rock fishing spots between Pondalowie and Stenhouse Bays (be careful of those wet rocks!).

Bushwalkers can choose from a variety of tracks leading through such diverse terrain as low scrub, salt lake flats, coastal dunes, and rugged cliffs—with a good probability of running into a friendly emu or kangaroo!

Camping is permitted within the park at several different areas. The main camping area is at Pondalowie Bay, where facilities were recently upgraded.

During Christmas holidays, park rangers conduct guided activities for children and young adults. For camping permits and other information, contact **Park Headquarters,** Stenhouse Bay, tel. (08) 8854-4040 or (08) 8854-4066.

UP THE PENINSULA

Going northward from Innes National Park, the sealed road brushes by **Warrenben Conservation Park,** 4,061 hectares of dense mallee, dryland tea-tree vegetation, and native pines. The gravel road from Marion Bay sort of winds around the coast, with other gravel or dirt paths branching out to the beaches. **Daly Head** is yet another special fishing hole, as is **Corny Point** at the northwestern tip. Corny Point also has a lighthouse and camping facilities.

At Point Turton, you can either continue zigzagging the beachy back roads to the top of the peninsula or turn onto the seven-km sealed stretch that leads back to the main highway at Warooka.

In the tiny township of **Brentwood,** 17 km north of Warooka, visit **Brentwood Pottery,** tel. (08)

8853-4255, in the old general store/post office. Rent a **gypsy wagon,** pulled by a gentle Clydesdale, for overnight camping by the sea or for a longer and leisurely ride around southern Yorke Peninsula. Rates run about $125 per day, with a three-day minimum. For information, contact Stansbury Holiday Motel, tel. (08) 8852-4455.

Minlaton (pop. 900), about 14 km north of Yorketown, is referred to as the "Barley Capital of the World." It's also the home of Captain Harry Butler's *Red Devil,* a 1916 monoplane flown by the pioneering aviator during World War I. Ostensibly, this is the world's only remaining Bristol fighter plane, and lucky you can see it at the glass-fronted **Harry Butler Hangar/Museum,** near the town center. Nearby, on Main St., the **National Trust Museum,** tel. (08) 8853-2127, exhibits photos, memorabilia, and farming implements, and at the corner of Bluff and Maitland Roads, **Jolly's Museum,** tel. (08) 8853-4306, features restored tractors and other machinery.

Rooms are offered at the convenient **Minlaton Hotel Motel,** 26 Main Rd., tel. (08) 8853-2014. Moderate. Rent campsites or on-site vans at **Minlaton Caravan Park,** corner of Bluff and Maitland Roads, tel. (08) 8853-2435. Budget-Inexpensive

For Minlaton emergencies, dial 000; the **police,** tel. (08) 8853-2100; **ambulance,** tel. (08) 8853-2050; and the **Royal Automobile Association,** tel. (08) 8853-2243.

Turn off at Urania for **Port Victoria,** "last of the windjammer ports" and now a busy little fishing resort. Sailing and water-skiing are popular around Wardang Island. See relics and curios of the nautical past at **Port Victoria Maritime Museum,** tel. (08) 8834-2057. Hours are Sunday and school holidays 2-4 p.m. Admission is $1.

Bayview Holiday Flats, 29 Davies Terrace, tel. (08) 8834-2082, offers fully self-contained units, and rates depend upon the season. Inexpensive-Moderate. Beachfront **Port Victoria Caravan Park,** tel. (08) 8834-2001, has campsites and on-site vans. Budget-Inexpensive.

Maitland, the heart of Yorke Peninsula, is Colonel Light's vision at work again—a modern agricultural center well laid out and surrounded by parklands. View agricultural artifacts and brush up on local history at **Maitland Museum,**

corner Gardiner and Kikerran Streets, tel. (08) 8832-2220. Hours are Sunday and public holidays 2-4 p.m. Admission is $2.

Maitland Hotel, 33 Robert St., tel. (08) 8832-2431, "where the beer is cold and the welcome warm," has basic rooms. Inexpensive. The pub serves good, home-cooked meals ($7-10). **Eothen Farmhouse,** tel. (08) 8836-3210, near beaches and bush, is a fully equipped separate home, with kitchen, lounge, and open fires. Moderate-Expensive.

For Maitland emergencies, dial 000; the **police,** tel. (08) 8832-2621; or **ambulance** and local **hospital,** tel. (08) 8832-2626. Contact the local **RAA** at (08) 8832-2601.

A 20-km jaunt westward from Maitland brings you to **Balgowan,** a century-old landing place for ketches making pickups and deliveries for local farmers. Today it serves as a serene retreat for fishers.

Back on the main highway, it's a 35-km drive to Moonta, lower edge of the Copper Triangle, then about 60 km more through Kadina to **Port Broughton,** a seaside resort at the tippy-top of the peninsula, where there's a safe swimming beach for children and a good fishing jetty for anglers.

Spend the night at **Port Broughton Hotel,** on the foreshore, tel. (08) 8635-2004. Built in 1888, this family-style establishment has spacious rooms, with breakfast included. Other facilities include a main bar, saloon bar, beer garden, large dining room, à la carte dining room, and bottle shop. Inexpensive-Moderate. **Main Park,** 2 Broughton St., tel. (08) 8635-2188, has campsites, on-site vans, and cabins. Budget-Inexpensive.

Port Broughton Charter Boats, 19 Harvey St., tel. (08) 8635-2466, offers fishing trips ($30-80) or pleasure cruises ($10, for one hour) in the Spencer Gulf.

For Port Broughton emergencies, dial 000; the **police,** tel. (08) 8635-2255; **ambulance,** tel. (08) 8635-2853; the local **hospital,** tel. (08) 8635-2200; or **Royal Automobile Association,** tel. (08) 8635-2522.

TRANSPORTATION

Stateliner Roadlines, tel. (08) 8415-5555, operates daily service from Adelaide to Kadina, Wallaroo, Moonta, Port Hughes, and Moonta Bay.

Yorke Peninsula Passenger Service, tel. (08) 8823-2375 in Wallaroo or (1800) 625-099, travels daily from Adelaide to Ardrossan, Port Vincent, Edithburgh, and Yorketown.

There is no public transport south of Warooka, and if you're hitching, road traffic is minimal.

EYRE PENINSULA

Wild coastlines with stupendous surf and isolated beaches, round-the-clock steel mills and busy grain terminals, phenomenal rock formations and ancient ranges, gentle sea lion colonies and great white shark breeding grounds are some of the Eyre Peninsula attractions that keep travelers coming (and going).

The peninsula is *wide,* stretching 469 km from Port Augusta in the east, across the Eyre Highway, past the Gawler Ranges, to Ceduna, the last ample outpost before the Nullarbor Plain. Alternate Route 1 (called Lincoln Highway from Port Augusta to Port Lincoln, and Flinders Highway from Port Lincoln to Ceduna) traverses the peninsula, hugging the coast—and its bays, beaches, ports, and parks—along sheltered Spencer Gulf on the east, round the pounding Southern Ocean and the Great Australian Bight. The distance from Port Augusta back up to Ceduna is 668 km. Another option that enables you to see a sizable chunk of this region is to follow the Eyre Highway. If you take this route you can journey into the Gawler Ranges to the north and explore famed Mt. Wudinna Rock along the way, and cut through the center of the peninsula along the Tod Highway (258 km of sheep and cereal scenery) down to Port Lincoln, the adjacent national parks, and the offshore islands. From there, depending on which way you're headed, you can either follow the east coast up to Whyalla (and back to Adelaide or onward to the Northern Territory) or take the west side, skirting round the sea-lion colony, passing through Streaky Bay to Ceduna and the great beyond.

EYRE PENINSULA

© AVALON TRAVEL PUBLISHING

History

By now you've surely guessed that super-sailor Capt. Matthew Flinders charted the Eyre Peninsula during his 1802 mega-voyage aboard the *Investigator*. He was not using his own charts, however, but those of Dutch explorer Peter Nuyts, who in 1627, sailed his *Gulden Zeepaard* ("Golden Seahorse") as far as Streaky Bay. Nuyts, more inclined toward trade than homesteading, turned back when he got to the offshore islands now named Nuyts Archipelago.

By the time Flinders arrived, Abel Tasman and Captain Cook had already been there, Tasman circling the country and Cook glimpsing the peninsula's east coast. Flinders did a more thorough examination of the coastline, naming the majority of features after crew and family members, as well

as locales around his hometown of Lincolnshire. The peninsula itself was named by Governor Gawler for Edward John Eyre, the explorer who in 1839-40 made a series of frustrating obstacle-fraught overland expeditions, culminating in the first east-west crossing of Australia.

Bountiful golden-grain harvests, iron ore deposits, a thriving steel industry, and an ocean bounty that makes this one of the country's largest commercial fisheries are the region's money-makers. Port Lincoln and Thevenard, the two biggest seaports—both with road and railway connections—ship a steady flow of cargo worldwide.

Apropos of fish, the white pointer shark breeds around Dangerous Reef, off Port Lincoln's shores, and the underwater scenes in *Jaws* were filmed here.

PORT AUGUSTA

At the head of the Spencer Gulf, bustling Port Augusta (pop. 15,300) is the town at which Highway 1, the Eyre Highway (actually Highway 1 with a change of name and direction), and the Stuart Highway all converge. From this crossroads, travelers scurry and scamper north to the Flinders Ranges, south to Adelaide, east to Sydney, and west across the Nullarbor, or slightly southwest to the Lincoln Highway and the Eyre Peninsula coast. Besides that, it's on the main railway line used by the Ghan and the Indian Pacific.

Established in 1852, Port Augusta served as a wool port for nearly a century. Today its major functions are transporting goods to and from the isolated Outback and generating electricity for much of South Australia.

Sights

Wadlata Outback Centre, 41 Flinders Terrace, tel. (08) 8642-4511, features displays, videos, and models depicting Aboriginal Dreamtime (including a big fiberglass serpent storyteller). Other exhibits highlight the early explorers and the history of electricity and communications. Hours are Mon.-Fri. 9 a.m.-5:30 p.m., Sat.-Sun. 10 a.m.-4 p.m. Admission is $6.

Homestead Park Pioneer Museum, Elsie St., tel. (08) 8642-2035, displays pioneer artifacts and machinery. Hours are daily 10 a.m.-5 p.m., closed Christmas Day.

ETSA (Electricity Trust of South Australia) Northern Power Station, tel. (08) 8642-0521, conducts one-hour behind-the-scenes tours of its $500 million coal-fired power plant Mon.-Fri. 11 a.m. and 1 p.m. (Strong footwear is advised.) Turn off Highway 1 at Andy's Truck Stop, 2.5 km east of Port Augusta.

Royal Flying Doctor Service, 4 Vincent St., tel. (08) 8642-2044, provides medical care to Outback residents. The center is open for tours Mon.-Fri. 10 a.m.-3 p.m.

School of the Air, 59 Power Corners, tel. (08) 8642-2077, offers educational programs to children residing in the Outback. Facilities are at Central Primary School at the southern end of Commercial Rd., and tours are conducted Mon.-Fri. 10 a.m., except holidays. Admission is $2.

Accommodations and Food

Port August Backpackers Hostel, 17 Trent Rd., tel. (08) 8641-1063, offers kitchen facilities and $14 dorm beds. **Augusta Hotel,** 1 Loudon Rd., tel. (08) 8642-2701, has plain pub rooms. Inexpensive. **Myoora Motor Inn,** Eyre Hwy., tel. (08) 8642-3622, and **Port Augusta East Motel,** Hwy. 1, tel. (08) 8642-2555, both offer comfy rooms at wallet-friendly rates. Moderate. Also well priced is centrally located **Flinders Hotel Motel,** 39 Commercial Rd., tel. (08) 8642-2544, with modern conveniences, family units, and good home cookin'. Moderate.

Both **Shoreline Caravan Park,** Gardiner Ave., tel. (08) 8642-2965, situated on the gulf, and **Big 4 Fauna Caravan Park,** corner of Hwy. 1 and Stokes Terrace, tel. (08) 8642-2974, set amidst peacocks and other birds, rent campsites and on-site vans. Budget-Inexpensive.

Eat at the pubs, where you'll probably catch a live band or DJ disco on weekends. **Ozzie's Coffee Lounge,** 22 Commercial Rd., tel. (08) 8642-4028, in the Port Augusta Mall, serves coffee, croissants, pâté, quiches, and sandwiches ($3-7). A branch of the **Barnacle Bill Fish 'n' Chippery** sits at 60 Victoria Parade, tel. (08) 8641-0000, where fish and chips run $4-8. **Basic Food Discovery,** Commercial St., tel. (08) 8642-2271, prepares vegetarian meals ($4-9). For that 24-hour truckin' experience, stop at **Andy's Truckstop,** Hwy. 1, tel. (08) 8641-0700, 2.5 km east of Port Augusta, where you'll find home-style meals, showers, and a laundromat.

Information

Wadlata Outback Centre, 41 Flinders Terrace, tel. (08) 8642-4511, is also home to Port Augusta's Tourist Information Centre. Hours are daily 9 a.m.-5:30 p.m. The North District Office of the **National Parks and Wildlife Service** can be reached at (08) 8548-5300.

For emergencies, dial 000. Other contacts are **Port Augusta Hospital,** tel. (08) 8648-5500; the **police,** tel. (08) 8648-5020; and the **Royal Automobile Association,** tel. (08) 8642-4357.

Transportation

Both the *Ghan* and *Indian Pacific* stop in Port Augusta on their rail routes. For information, phone (13) 2232.

A variety of vehicles can be rented from **Budget,** 16 Young St., tel. (08) 8642-6040, and **Complete Ute and Van Hire,** tel. (08) 8642-6688. Check with the Tourist Information Centre for a variety of reputable operators who can lead you in (and out) of the Outback in air-conditioned 4WD vehicles.

WHYALLA

A big-time shipbuilding port until 1978, Whyalla (pop. 26,900) survives today on its round-the-clock steel production and shipments of ore from nearby Iron Knob and Iron Baron. As South Australia's largest provincial city—with a sunny, Mediterranean-style climate—facilities are good, and "pass-through" tourism gives yet another economic boost.

Originally called Hummock Hill by Captain Flinders, the township developed around 1901, after iron ore was discovered at Iron Knob. Trammed from mine to town, the ore was then barged over to the Port Pirie smelters. The flourishing community was renamed in 1914.

Whyalla had two major boom periods—the first in 1938 with the establishment of a blast furnace, and the second in 1958 when BHP Company confirmed plans for building its completely integrated steelworks. In between was the creation of a deep-water port and successful shipyard, memorable days that still tug the hearts of the local old salts.

Sights

Whyalla Maritime Museum, Lincoln Hwy., tel. (08) 8645-8900, is where you can climb aboard Australia's largest landlocked ship, the 650-ton corvette *Whyalla* (a.k.a. HMA *Whyalla* and the *Rip*). Displays inside the Tanderra Building include shipping memorabilia, valuable BHP models, and one of the country's largest model railways. Hours are daily 10 a.m.-4 p.m. Ship tours leave hourly 11 a.m.-3 p.m. (closed footwear mandatory). Admission is $5.

Mount Laura Homestead Museum, Ekblom St., behind Westland Shopping Centre, tel. (08) 8645-9319, is the place to brush up on town history and view restored buildings and machinery. Hours are Sunday, Monday, and Wednesday 2-4 p.m., Friday 10 a.m.-noon. Admission is $2.

BHP Steelworks offers guided tours of their operations, including the blast furnace, steelmaking plant, coke ovens, railway line, and one-km-long rolling mill. Tours last two hours or so and depart from Whyalla Tourist Centre Monday, Wednesday, and Saturday 9:30 a.m. Be sure to wear closed footwear. Admission is $8. For information and bookings, phone the tourist office at (08) 8645-7900.

Hummock Hill Lookout, site of a World War II gun battery, affords a dynamite view of Whyalla, the foreshore, upper Spencer Gulf, Port Bonython, Point Lowly, and the Middleback Ranges. Follow the brown and white "Route 61" (Whyalla Tourist Drive) signs.

Whyalla Wildlife and Reptile Sanctuary, Lincoln Hwy., across from the airport, tel. (08) 8645-7044, features koalas, wombats, dingoes, 'roos, emus, deadly snakes, and a walk-through aviary in natural bushland. Hours are daily 10 a.m.-6 p.m. (Nov.-April), 10 a.m.-4:30 p.m. (other months). Admission is $5.

Port Bonython, about 10 km north of Whyalla, off the Lincoln Hwy., is the site of the massive SANTOS plant, which distills liquid hydrocarbons that have passed from Moomba through a 659-km underground pipeline. Though you can't tour the facility, you can get a view of operations from along the roadway or shore.

Port Lowly, two km beyond SANTOS, offers beautiful gulf views, a popular summer beach, and the Port Lowly Lighthouse (more than 110 years old), which looks out upon playful dolphins that often swim by.

The **Scenic Coastal Drive** is a 20-km combination sealed and gravel road along Spencer Gulf, from Fitzgerald Bay to Point Douglas. Take the marked turnoff before Port Bonython.

The **Whyalla Foreshore** redevelopment provides excellent swimming, jetty fishing, windsurfing, and picnicking. **Whyalla Marina** has a four-lane launching ramp for all boating activities.

Murrippi Beach, off Eight Mile Creek Rd., 12 km south of Whyalla, is a legal nude beach (no facilities).

Accommodations and Food

As with most cities this size, you'll find pubs, motels, restaurants, and takeaways—all pretty standard. Most accommodations have their own dining facilities.

Pub rooms are available at **Lord Gowrie Hotel,** Gowrie Ave., tel. (08) 8645-8955. Inexpensive. **Airport Whyalla Motel,** Lincoln Hwy., tel. (08) 8645-2122, and **Sundowner Hotel Motel,** Lincoln Hwy., tel. (08) 8645-7688, both offer comfortable rooms. Moderate. Campsites, cabins, and on-site vans are available at **Foreshore Caravan Park,** Broadbent Terrace, tel. (08) 8645-7474. Budget-Inexpensive.

Recreation

Whyalla Recreation and Leisure Centre, off Racecourse Rd. near the junction of Nicolson Ave., tel. (08) 8645-5488, welcomes visitors to use the heated indoor swimming pool, squash courts, gymnasium, weightlifting equipment, sweat track, and volleyball and tennis courts. Equipment is available for rental.

Information

Whyalla Tourist Centre, tel. (08) 8645-7900 or (1800) 088-589, next to the steelworks on Lincoln Hwy., provides maps, tour bookings, and info on the local bus service (weekdays and Saturday mornings). Hours are Mon.-Fri. 9 a.m.-5 p.m., Saturday 9 a.m.-4 p.m., Sunday and public holidays 10 a.m.-4 p.m. Closed Christmas Day and Good Friday.

For emergencies, dial 000. The **Royal Automobile Association** can be reached at (08) 8645-757.

TO PORT LINCOLN

From Whyalla, the Lincoln Highway makes a slight inland jag, traveling for a short distance along the iron-ore-rich Middleback Ranges, angling back to the coast (in about 111 km) at Cowell.

Cowell

Set on scenic Franklin Harbour, a protected bay noted for calm waters and great fishing, Cowell (pop. 692) is also famous for its huge jade deposits, discovered in the nearby Minbrie Ranges in 1965, as well as some interesting marble uncovered along with the jade boulders. The area is thought to be the world's largest producer of green and black jade.

Several operators offer mine tours, or you can visit the factory and showroom of **Gem-**

stone Corporation of Australia, Second St., tel. (08) 8629-2111.

Other attractions include the **Franklin Harbour Historical Museum,** in the old post office, and the **Agricultural Museum,** on Lincoln Highway. Both are open by appointment. For information, phone (08) 8629-2032.

Lucky Bay, 16 km north of town, is a popular beach resort with safe swimming, good fishing, and a boat ramp. **Poverty Beach,** just south of town, has good surfing.

Rooms are spartan but clean at the **Franklin Harbour Hotel,** 1 Main St., tel. (08) 8629-2015. Inexpensive. **Shultz Farm,** Smith Rd., tel. (08) 8629-2194, offers home-style accommodations on a sheep and grain property overlooking the coast, and breakfast is included. Moderate. **Cowell Foreshore Caravan Park,** the Esplanade, tel. (08) 8629-2307, has campsites, cabins, and on-site vans. Don't miss a taste of the delicious locally harvested oysters. Budget-Inexpensive.

Obtain local **tourist information** at District Council of Franklin Harbour, 6 Main St., tel. (08) 8629-2019.

Cowell District Hospital, tel. (08) 8629-2001, is located on South Terrace.

Continuing Southward

From Cowell, you can cut inland 42 km to the rural community of Cleve. The scenic Cleve-Cowell Hills drive provides great views of the countryside and Spencer Gulf. From Cleve, you can cut southeast 25 km back to the coast at Arno Bay. Or stick to the coastal road and pass along the wide, lovely beaches at **The Knob, Port Gibbon,** and **Point Price Sandhills.**

Arno Bay, halfway point between Whyalla and Port Lincoln, is a tranquil fishing village in winter and a tourist mecca in summer. **Redbanks,** six km north of town, is a designated geological monument of rock pools and just-as-rocky cliffs. **Arno Hotel,** tel. (08) 8628-0001, near the beach, has country-style rooms with breakfast included in the rates. Inexpensive.

Port Neill, 33 km south from Arno Bay and two km off the main highway, is another attractive, clean, safe water sports haven. Check out the blue water and the rolling hills from **Port Neill Lookout,** one km north of town. **Fauser's Museum,** opposite the caravan park, tel. (08)

8688-9041, is a private collection of steam and stationary engines, motorcycles, vintage autos, and other relics. Hours are daily 10 a.m.-4 p.m.

Port Neill Hotel, Peake Terrace, tel. (08) 8688-9006, has basic pub-style rooms. Inexpensive. **Henley's Holiday Flats,** Gill St., tel. (08) 8688-9001, are fully self-contained units. Inexpensive. **Port Neill Caravan Park,** Peake Terrace, tel. (08) 8688-9067, rents campsites and on-site vans. Budget-Inexpensive.

If you wait until low tide to visit **Lipson Cove,** another 20 km south, you can walk across to **Lipson Island,** a coastal bird sanctuary.

Tumby Bay shelters fishing and boating waters and is also service center for the surrounding rural townships. **C.L. Alexander National Trust Museum,** corner West Terrace and Lipson Rd., tel. (08) 8688-2574, features local memorabilia in an original wooden schoolhouse. Hours are Friday and Sunday 2:30-4:30 p.m. Admission is $2.

Head to **Island Lookout** to catch a good view of town, bay, and the **Sir Joseph Banks Group of Islands,** 15 km offshore. Named by Captain Flinders for the renowned English botanist, the islands are bird sanctuaries for Cape Barren geese, pied cormorants, eastern reef egrets, crested terns, and many other species. If you don't have your own boat, sign on for a half- or full-day tour. For information, phone (08) 8629-2019.

Seabreeze Hotel, Tumby Terrace, tel. (08) 8688-2362, rents simple rooms. Inexpensive. **Tumby Bay Motel,** Berryman St., tel. (08) 8688-2311, near the beach, has a swimming pool. Moderate. Campsites, cabins, and on-site vans are available at **Tumby Bay Caravan Park,** Tumby Terrace, tel. (08) 8688-2208, along the foreshore. Budget-Inexpensive.

If you don't think you can live without another display of vintage implements, machinery, and artifacts (or if you just want to explore the hill country between Tumby Bay and Port Lincoln), take the 40-km detour to Koppio and the **Koppio Smithy Museum.** Try to get there for the annual Open Day, when all the machinery is turned on and huffs, puffs, toots, and honks in unison. Hours are Tues.-Sun. 10 a.m.-5 p.m. For information, phone (08) 8684-4243.

Back on the coast, **North Shields,** just 11 km north of Port Lincoln, is home of the **Karlinda Collection,** an amazing amassment of more than 10,000 shells, rocks, minerals, fossils, and other marine curios. It's all housed in the building next to the post office on Dorward Street. Hours are daily 9 a.m.-9 p.m. Admission is $2. For information, phone (08) 8684-3500.

You can live cheaply and simply at the historic 1868 **Wheatsheaf Hotel,** Dorward St., tel. (08) 8684-3531, where rates include continental breakfast. Inexpensive. The Wheatsheaf serves counter meals ($3-6) in the pub and à la carte in the dining room (entrees $6-11) overlooking Boston Bay.

Heading into Port Lincoln, you will pass through one of the country's more recent wine-growing regions (vines planted in 1984, first harvest in 1987), and the cellars of **Boston Bay Wines.** Specializing in red and white table wines, the vineyard is open Sat.-Sun. and public holidays 11:30 a.m.-4:30 p.m., daily December and January. For information, phone (08) 8684-3600.

PORT LINCOLN

At the Eyre Peninsula's southern edge, Port Lincoln (pop. 12,550) is often referred to as "blue water paradise." Paradise? Not quite, but there *is* plenty of blue water. Boston Bay, stretching from Point Boston to the tip of Port Lincoln National Park, is three times larger than Sydney Harbour. Mild winters and comfortable summers, combined with ideal conditions for boating, fishing, skin diving, and windsurfing (and great white shark breeding!) keep the tourists coming.

Named by Captain Flinders after his home county of Lincolnshire, Port Lincoln was originally set to be South Australia's state capital. A lack of freshwater, along with Colonel Light's decided bent toward Adelaide, caused that plan to be withdrawn. The city didn't fare badly, though. Aside from a healthy tourist industry, Port Lincoln is home to Australia's largest commercial tuna fishing fleet and one of the country's busiest grain terminals.

Sights
Axel Stenross Maritime Museum, Lincoln Hwy. near Shaen St., tel. (08) 8682-3624, features memorabilia from windjammer days, as well as early photos, a working slipway, and a blacksmith shop. Hours are Tuesday, Thursday, Sat.-Sun., and public holidays 1-5 p.m. Admission is $2.

A short distance from the maritime museum is the **First Landing Site.** See the freshwater spring that lured the early settlers—it's still bubbling and gurgling through the sand.

Mill Cottage, tel. (08) 8682-4650, and **Settler's Cottage** museums, located on the grounds of Flinders Park (at Lincoln and Flinders Highways), both display artifacts and historical exhibits of Port Lincoln's early beginnings. Hours for Mill Cottage are Tues.-Sun. 2-4:30 p.m. Admission is $2. Contact Port Lincoln Library to arrange entrance to Settler's Cottage.

Nearby, **Rose-Wal Memorial Shell Museum,** tel. (08) 8682-1868, on the grounds of the Old Folks' Home, displays a large and valuable collection of shells and sealife. Hours are daily 2-4:30 p.m. Admission is $2.

Apex Wheelhouse, Hindmarsh St., tel. (08) 8682-2537, across from the caravan park, is a restored tuna boat wheelhouse and interpretive center. Photos, charts, and a color video will brief you on the fishing industry. Hours are daily 9 a.m.-5 p.m.

You'll find excellent **lookout points** at: **Winter's Hill,** five km northeast of town on Flinders Hwy.; **Puckridge Park,** on Angas St.; and the **Old Mill,** Dorset Pl., an 1846 flour mill (historic both because it's old and because it was never operated).

A popular day trip is the cruise to **Boston Island,** a working sheep station, discovered and named by Captain Flinders. Select either the Boston Island Safari (a trip to the island, sightseeing, and historical commentary) or Bay Island Cruise (usually run only if a landing on the island is not possible). Departures are from the jetty at Tasman Terrace. Tours can be booked at the tourist office or Kirton Point Caravan Park.

More daring souls, who'd rather eyeball sharks instead of sheep, can journey to **Dangerous Reef,** "home of the great white shark" and locale for underwater scenes in *Jaws.* You can take a diving charter (good luck) or the *Dangerous Reef Explorer,* a high-speed commuter vessel (travel time about 40 minutes). A safer option for those who left their diving gear at home is a 30- by 12-meter underwater viewing platform with observatory and aquarium (and a dive cage). A large sea lion colony also lives on the reef. For info and bookings, contact the tourist office.

Accommodations and Food

If you plan to stay in a pub, seek out the old Wheatsheaf in North Shields (see above). Most of the motels are on Lincoln Highway or Tasman Terrace. **First Landing Motel,** 11 Shaen St. near the maritime museum, tel. (08) 8682-2344, has rooms with four-poster beds. Moderate. **Westward Ho Holiday Flats,** 112 London St., tel. (08) 8682-2425, are fully self-contained units. Moderate. **San Pan Windinna,** 34 Lincoln Hwy., tel. (08) 8682-1513, is a fully equipped beachfront cottage. Expensive. You can rent a cabin or campsite at **Kirton Point Caravan Park,** Hindmarsh St., tel. (08) 8682-2537. Inexpensive. And, if you've got the bucks ($200 per week, per person, with a minimum of five people and maximum of 12), you can rent all of Boston Island. Tariff includes a six-bedroom home, fishing dinghies, tractor, and trailer. No linen, though—you must bring your own or pay an extra fee. Budget-Inexpensive. For information, contact the Port Lincoln Visitor Information Centre or South Australian Tourism Commission Travel Centre.

Tasman Mall has the best cheap eats in town. Aside from that, look to the local pubs for meals and nightlife.

Information

Port Lincoln Visitor Information Centre, 66 Tasman Terrace, tel. (08) 8683-3544 or (1800) 62-9911, books tours and accommodations, and provides info on bicycle rentals, boat charters, and local coach service. Hours are daily 9 a.m.-5 p.m. For park and camping information, contact the Eyre District Office of the **National Parks and Wildlife Service,** 75 Liverpool St., tel. (08) 8688-3111.

In an emergency, dial 000; the **hospital,** tel. (08) 8683-2200; the **police,** tel. (08) 8688-3020; or the **Royal Automobile Association,** tel. (08) 8682-3501.

Events

Port Lincoln's big blowout is the annual **Tunarama Festival,** held each January. Festivities include parades, cavalcades, roving musicians, a variety of competitions, firework displays, rock concerts, dinner dances, and the crowning of Miss Tunarama.

TIP OF THE EYRE

The southernmost edge of the Eyre Peninsula stretches from Lincoln National Park, leaning on Spencer Gulf, to Coffin Bay National Park, jutting into the Great Australian Bight.

Lincoln National Park, 20 km south of Port Lincoln, recently expanded, now covering 29,060 hectares with open spaces, rugged cliffs, and peaceful bays, plus a nearby 308-hectare conservation reserve. Catch panoramic views of park and town from Stamford Hill. Conventional vehicles can access scenic spots like Surfleet Point, Spalding Cove, Old Donington House, Cape Donington Lighthouse, and Taylor's Landing, but you'll need a 4WD to reach wilderness areas like Memory Cove and Cape Catastrophe. Check with the park service, tel. (08) 8688-3111, for camping information and road conditions.

You'll need a key and permit ($20 plus $5 deposit) to enter privately owned **Whaler's Way,** a dynamically scenic cliff-top drive at the very tip of the peninsula. Magnificent lookouts, blowholes, caves, sparkling beaches, and roaring surf—as well as a wildlife and bird sanctuary—are some of the features. Get yet another special permit to camp at the Redbanks area. On the road to Whaler's Way, you'll pass **Mikkira Station,** an 1840s sheep station. Pick up keys and permits at Port Lincoln Tourist Office or at service stations. Visits are limited to Sunday and school and public holidays.

Continuing along Flinders Highway, you'll pass **Port Lincoln Fauna Park, Little Swamp, Big Swamp,** and **Wanilla Forest.** Turn off toward Coffin Bay, through **Kellidie Bay Conservation Park** and the **Coffin Bay Lookout,** through the township, and straight into the national park.

Coffin Bay National Park, 46 km from Port Lincoln, is a massive 28,106 hectares of wilderness area, much of it accessible only to bushwalkers and those in four-wheel drives (there are some sealed roads for conventional vehicles). Hike the 25-km **Yangie Trail** to Almonta Beach, Avoid Bay, and Yangie Bay—be careful if swimming; **sharks are common.** The park is particularly spectacular early spring to early summer, when gorgeous wildflowers bloom. Inquire

about road conditions and pick up camping permits at the ranger's headquarters, near the park's entrance.

The town of **Coffin Bay** is literally surrounded by parks and offers sheltered waters for fishing, boating, swimming, skin diving, and windsurfing. Normally a teeny township of 350 residents, the population leaps to nearly 10 times that in summer. Oysters cultivated here are renowned across Australia. Pay a visit to **Coffin Bay Oyster Farm,** where the motto is, "Eat fish and live longer, eat Coffin Bay Oysters and love longer."

Holiday flats, ranging from inexpensive to moderately priced, line the Esplanade. **Coffin Bay Caravan Park,** tel. (08) 8685-4170, has campsites, cabins, and on-site vans. Budget-Moderate.

Pick up **tourist info,** bus tickets, postage stamps, fishing tackle, and hot roasted chicken at Beachcomber Agencies, the Esplanade, tel. (08) 8685-4057.

UP FLINDERS HIGHWAY

Climbing up the peninsula, the highway makes gentle jags inward to pastoral land and country townships, then teases you back to sparkling bays and beaches along the Great Australian Bight.

Turn off at Wangary, 29 km north of Coffin Bay, to **Farm Beach** and Anzac Cove (sometimes called Gallipoli Beach), where the movie *Gallipoli* was filmed. You'll pass Mt. Dutton on the way, a good climb, but get permission first, as the land is privately owned.

Back on Flinders Highway, it's mostly sheep and farm country. At **Coulta,** you can experience farm life for $35 at **Wepowie Farm,** Edelillie Rd., tel. (08) 8687-2063. One- or two-day horseback trips and packhorse treks are offered, as well as customary farm activities (with plenty of emus and ostriches). Close by is salty Lake Greenly, with hang gliding at Mt. Greenly, and good surfing at Greenly Beach.

Elliston, 100 km from Coulta, is a small fishing village on Waterloo Bay, where the scenic coastline jumps from rugged cliffs to sheltered inlets. Here you'll find "clogs," fossilized cocoons of the *Leptopius duponti* weevil thought to be nearly 100,000 years old. **Ellen Liston Motel and**

Holiday Flats, Beach Terrace, tel. (08) 8687-9028, offers various accommodations in motel rooms or fully equipped units. Inexpensive-Moderate. Both **Elliston Caravan Park,** Flinders Hwy., tel. (08) 8687-9061, and **Waterloo Bay Caravan Park,** Beach Terrace, tel. (08) 8687-9076, have campsites, cabins, and on-site vans. Budget-Moderate.

Flinders Island, 35 km off the coast of Elliston, is a 3,700-hectare getaway with swimming beaches and picturesque views. Accommodations in either a renovated cottage or shearer's quarters cost about $340 double, with a four-night minimum stay. Luxury. For bookings and air charters ($150 roundtrip), contact Flinders Island Holidays, tel. (08) 8626-1403.

Talia Caves, 40 km north of Elliston, has wonderful limestone caves, gnarly rock formations, and bleached sand dunes to explore. **Venus Bay,** another 22 km north, is a small township popular with small boat and jetty anglers and, increasingly, with surfers. **Needle Eye Lookout** gives a great view of the pounding sea, intriguing rocks and arches, and towering cliffs. Turn off at **Point Labatt,** a designated national park, to view Australia's only permanent mainland colony of sea lions.

Back on Flinders Highway, east of Point Labatt, you'll be able to glimpse **Murphy's Haystacks,** sculptured rock formations rising out of the wheatfields. These huge granite *inselbergs* are reputedly more than 1.5 billion years old.

Streaky Bay, 85 km north of Venus Bay (first sighted in 1627 by Dutch explorer Peter Nuyts), was named by Captain Flinders because of the seaweed streaks coloring the bay. This township (pop. 1,200), another of the myriad picturesque fishing villages, is also a service center for the local agricultural communities. Historical buildings of interest are the **School and Kelsh Pioneer Museum,** full of local artifacts, and **Hospital Cottage,** built in 1864. On Alfred Terrace, the **Restored Engine Centre** features a collection of some 60-odd engines, some dating back to the early 1900s. All of the museums are open Tuesday and Friday 2-4 p.m.

Koolangatta Farm, via Piednippie Rd. 25 km from town, tel. (08) 8626-1174, offers country accommodations that include breakfast ingredients. Inexpensive. Just as cheap is **Mulgunyah,** Poochera Rd., tel. (08) 8626-1236, also a

cottage on a farm. Breakfast not included but farm activities are. Inexpensive. **Streaky Bay Motel,** 7 Alfred Terrace, tel. (08) 8626-1126, features self-contained units with cooking facilities. Moderate. Rent a campsite or a cabin at **Streaky Bay Foreshore Tourist Park,** Wells St., tel. (08) 8626-1666. Budget-Inexpensive.

Sheltered **Smoky Bay,** about midway between Streaky Bay and Ceduna, is a teeny villagette, best known for its annual Easter rodeo.

For **tourist information,** contact the Streaky Bay District Council, 29 Alfred Terrace, Streaky Bay, tel. (08) 8626-1001.

THE EYRE HIGHWAY

From Port Augusta to Ceduna, the Eyre Highway (Highway 1) spans 469 km of industrial sights, wheat belts, wilderness, and geological wonders.

Iron Knob, 68 km west of Port Augusta, is the birthplace of Australia's steel industry. Iron ore, discovered here in 1894, is quarried and shipped to the Whyalla Steelworks, along with supplies from the neighboring mines of Iron Monarch, Iron Baron, Iron Prince, Iron Queen, and Iron Duke (only Iron Knob is open to visitors). Tours are available Mon.-Fri. at 10 a.m. and 2 p.m., Saturday at 2 p.m. Cost is $4. For information, phone (08) 8646-2129.

Iron Knob Mineral & Shell Display, 266 Gill St., tel. (08) 8646-2130, features more than 2,000 crystals from all over the world and ore specimens from Iron Monarch mine. Hours are daily 10 a.m.-4 p.m. Admission is $1.

Rooms are available at either **Iron Knob Hotel,** Main St., tel. (08) 8646-2013, or **Iron Knob Motel Roadhouse,** Eyre Hwy., tel. (08) 8646-2058. Inexpensive.

Kimba, 89 km from Iron Knob, is the "Gateway to the Gawler Ranges" and, really, not much else. If you need a rest, **Kimba Community Hotel Motel,** High St., tel. (08) 8627-2007, has reasonable rooms ($20 higher in the motel section) and a bar, bistro, beer garden, and dining room. Inexpensive.

At Kimba, turn off onto the winding gravel road that leads through the Gawler Ranges, where you'll see gentle hills with unique rock formations, varied bird and animal life, and glorious spring wildflowers such as Sturt's desert pea, the state flower, which was first sighted here in 1839 by Eyre. You can camp at **Mt. Ive Station,** tel. (08) 8648-1817, near Lake Gairdner, in a range of very inexpensive facilities. A large part of the district is privately run, so visitors are asked to stick to the public roads, obtain permission before camping or hiking, leave all flora and fauna alone, and take all rubbish with them. Conventional vehicles can access much of the area, but, as in all wilderness and isolated regions, check the weather and road conditions regularly. A number of experienced tour operators offer two- to four-day 4WD safaris into the region (check with any South Australian Government Travel Centre).

Kyancutta, 89 km from Kimba, sits at the junction of the Eyre and Tod Highways. **Wudinna,** 13 km farther, is the service center for the surrounding rural community, and the airstrip is used for regular service to and from Adelaide. Travelers stop here en route to see Australia's second largest granite outcrop, **Mt. Wudinna Rock** (261 meters high), 10 km northeast of town. Other weathered masses in this group are **Polda, Turtle,** and **Little Wudinna Rocks.**

If you need a place to stay in the area, **Gawler Ranges Motel,** Eyre Hwy., tel. (08) 8680-2090, has both modern rooms and a caravan park with campsites and on-site vans. Budget-Moderate.

The **Minnipa** area, 38 km northwest of Wudinna, has more granite outcrops. There you'll find the Minnipa-Yardea road, another route into the Gawler Ranges. As you head farther east on the Eyre Highway, you'll pass through plains-and-grains country, the townships of **Poochera** and **Wirrulla,** and finally into Ceduna.

CEDUNA

On the shores of Murat Bay, and at the junction of the Eyre and Flinders Highways, Ceduna (pop. 2,880) is the last full-service town before the vast reaches of the Nullarbor Plain. As such, its name was quite aptly derived from *chedoona,* Aboriginal for "a resting place."

Established as a town in 1901, Ceduna is the business hub of the far west coast and an important regional cereal-growing center (with an

airport and regular service to Adelaide). The community began originally at Denial Bay, about 12 km to the west, where cargo ships pulled up close to shore, waited until low tide, then loaded wagons with provisions for the settlers. You can still see the ruins at **McKenzie Landing,** on the road to Davenport Creek. More recently, Thevenard (four km from Ceduna) serves as deep-sea port for the area, transporting grain, salt, and gypsum worldwide. (An interesting aside: According to map references in *Gulliver's Travels,* Gulliver encountered those little people of Lilliput on St. Peter and St. Francis Islands, off the coast of Thevenard.)

Aside from being a supply and rest stop for travelers, Ceduna boasts a variety of local beaches for fishing, swimming, boating, and surfing.

Sights

The **Old Schoolhouse National Trust Museum,** Park Terrace, tel. (08) 8625-2210, displays historic relics of Ceduna's early days. The **Telecommunication Earth Station** (OTC), 37 km northwest of town, is a global satellite system that channels approximately half of Australia's daily telecommunications with Asia, Africa, and Europe via Indian Ocean satellites. Guided tours of the facility are offered Mon.-Fri. 11 a.m. and 2 p.m. For information, phone (08) 8625-2505.

Accommodations and Food

The hotel section in **Ceduna Community Hotel Motel,** O'Loughlin Terrace, tel. (08) 8625-2008, overlooking Murat Bay, is the only inexpensive accommodation choice. Other motels, mostly along Eyre Highway, range from moderate to expensive. (There's not a lot of choice way out here.) Campsites, cabins, and on-site vans are available at **Ceduna Foreshore Caravan Park,** 5 South Terrace, tel. (08) 8625-2290. Budget-Moderate.

Meals are at the pubs, motel dining rooms, coffee lounges, and takeaways, or make your own from the supermarket.

Information

Stop in at **Ceduna Gateway Tourist Centre,** 46 Poynton St., tel. (08) 8625-2780, for local and Eyre Peninsula information. Hours are Mon.-Fri. 9 a.m.-5:30 p.m., Saturday 9 a.m.-2 p.m.

TRANSPORTATION

For air services operating to and about the Eyre Peninsula, contact: **Ansett Australia,** tel. (13) 1300; **Qantas Airways,** tel. (13) 1313; **Kendell Airlines,** tel. (08) 8231-9567, in Adelaide; or **Lincoln Airlines,** tel. (08) 8682-5688 or (1800) 018-234.

Greyhound Pioneer operates daily coach service along the Eyre Highway on the Adelaide-Perth route, with stop-offs at Iron Knob, Kimba, Wudinna, Minnipa, Ceduna, and the Nullarbor. Coaches depart Adelaide's central bus station. For information and bookings, phone (13) 2030. **Stateliner** coaches serve all west coast towns—on the peninsula and along the highway—from Adelaide. For information and bookings, phone (08) 8415-5555 in Adelaide, or (08) 8625-2115 in Ceduna.

CROSSING THE NULLARBOR

Now that the road is sealed, this isn't *quite* the adventure it used to be (we'll get to the authentic Outback later). But, sealed highway or not, it is still a long, lonesome (and, sometimes, loathsome) trek across the Nullarbor Plain into Western Australia—480 km from Ceduna to the state line, and another 725 km to Norseman, end of the Eyre Highway, where you either take the high road or the low road another 725 km to Perth.

Nullarbor is Latin for "No Trees," but you'll see some timber, a few saplings, and a bit of scrub along the coastal part of the highway, particularly if you travel after the winter rains. It's the transcontinental railway line, several hundred km north, that traverses the really plain Plains, a span 692 km long and 402 km wide. (By the way, that 478-km chunk of single track is the world's longest stretch of straight railway.)

The usual Outback driving rules apply (review the tips in this book). Also, you'll encounter quarantine stations at Ceduna, in South Australia, and Norseman, in Western Australia. Either have a picnic before reaching those two checkpoints or be prepared to surrender plants, fruits, veggies, nuts, grains, wool, animal skins, honey, soil, and even used containers that held these products.

Another thing to remember (or discount altogether) is the time change between Balladonia and Nullarbor. Put your watch back 45 minutes at the border, unless it's daylight saving time—then it increases to three hours. But, all in all, three hours either way are pretty insignificant when you're smack in the middle of nowhere!

See above for information on traversing the plain.

History

The Eyre Highway was named for Edward John Eyre, who in 1841, became the first fellow to cross the country from east to west—an agonizing five-month journey in which Eyre's buddy, John Baxter, bit the Nullarbor dust. Following Eyre's dusty footsteps came John and Alexander Forrest, brothers who mapped out much of the overland telegraph route that would connect Perth with Adelaide. In 1877, the eastern and western sections of the telegraph line were linked up at Eucla, and in the 1890s those same bullock and camel tracks that helped build the line were followed by miners on their arduous trip to Western Australia's goldfields. After that, the Nullarbor was crossed by a succession of odd transport—camels, cycles, a 10-horsepower Brush car, a Citroen. In 1941, with the advent of World War II, army engineers commenced construction of the Eyre Highway. Cross-country traffic, at first a trickle in the 1950s, grew (thanks to the Commonwealth Games in Perth) to more than 30 vehicles a day in 1962. The Western Australia section of the highway was sealed in 1969, and the South Australia portion was surfaced seven years later.

Ceduna to Border Village

Penong, 73 km west from Ceduna, is the "Town of 100 Windmills" and a good place to stop for petrol and supplies. Rooms are available at **Penong Hotel,** tel. (08) 8625-1050. Inexpensive.

Cactus Beach, 21 km south of Penong, is famous worldwide for its three perfect surfing breaks, "Castles," "Cactus," and "Caves," with both left and right breaks for serious surfers. Other

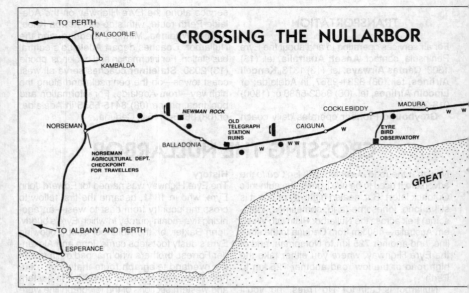

CROSSING THE NULLARBOR

nearby attractions are **Point Sinclair** and **Pink Lake. Fowlers Bay,** on the turnoff to **Nundroo,** is a great fishing hole. **Scott's Bay, Mexican Hat,** and **Cabot's Beach** are popular camel-trekking points. The **Nundroo Hotel Motel,** tel. (08) 8625-6120, features varied take-a-load-off rooms. Inexpensive-Moderate. You can buy locally made Aboriginal artifacts at **Yalata Roadhouse,** tel. (08) 8625-6990, a tourist complex another 51 km along, run by the Yalata Aboriginal Community. Accommodations and campsites are also available. Budget-Inexpensive.

From June through October, **southern right whales** can be seen during their annual breeding migration along the coastline between Yalata and the border. In 1989, the largest group of these whales to visit the country's shores was spotted just off Yalata Reserve. Obtain permits to enter the land at Yalata Roadhouse.

From Nullarbor to the border, you'll pass along sheer coastal cliffs with plunging views of the rugged terrain and the Great Australian Bight. **Nullarbor,** 94 km from Yalata, is adjacent to the original **Nullarbor Homestead.** Rooms in **Nullarbor Hotel-Motel,** tel. (08) 8625-6271, are welcoming. Moderate. The Eyre Highway tran-

sects **Nullarbor National Park,** where signs point the way to spectacular lookouts over the Bunda Cliffs, a 200-km stretch from the Head of the Bight almost to the Western Australia border. The area around the Nullarbor is cave land, but recommended for experienced cavers only. **Koonalda Cave** features a collection of Australia's earliest rock engravings. For information and camping permits, phone the South Australia National Parks and Wildlife Service, Ceduna (08) 8625-3144. Permits to enter the area must be obtained from Yalata Roadhouse.

You'll know you've reached **WA/SA Border Village,** 184 km from Nullarbor, when you spot **Rooey II,** a hideous five-meter-tall fiberglass kangaroo. (Climb inside Rooey II's pouch if you're in need of a photo op.) The signpost with distances to international locales like Paris, London, New York, etc., is another visited site. Rooms are moderate-expensive and campsites are cheap at **WA/SA Border Village,** tel. (08) 9039-3474.

To Norseman
In 1887, historic **Eucla,** only 13 km from Border Village, served as an important communications link. Visit the old telegraph station ruins (closed

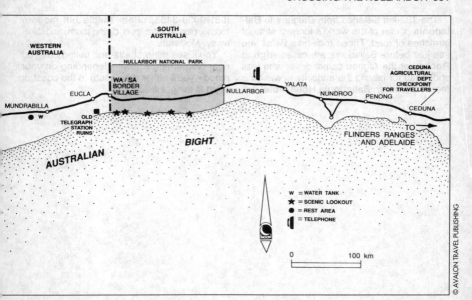

in 1924—the new line runs along the rail line), the town jetty, as well as the nearby cliffs, caves, and blowholes, and the sandhills at Eucla Pass. View gold rush relics at the old **School of Mines,** Mon.-Fri. 10 a.m.-4 p.m. Admission is $3.

Sixty-six km west from Eucla, **Mundrabilla** is a tiny township with an animal and bird sanctuary along the highway. Rooms at **Mundrabilla Motor Hotel,** tel. (08) 9039-3465, are a welcome sight, but the adjacent caravan park also has campsites and cabins. Budget-Moderate.

Ninety-one km along the way, **Madura** once served as a breeding spot for the Indian Army horses. You can still view ruins of the old Madura Roadhouse, located along a track several km from the "new" roadhouse. Comfortable rooms are available at **Madura Pass Oasis Inn,** tel. (08) 9039-3464, and the adjacent caravan park has campsites. Budget-Expensive.

You can still see the stone ruins of an Aboriginal mission at **Cocklebiddy,** 66 km from Madura. In 1983, a team of French explorers set a world depth record at nearby Cocklebiddy Cave. If you have a four-wheel-drive, take the 32-km coastward detour before "town" to **Eyre**

Bird Observatory (established in 1977), part of Nuytsland Nature Reserve. Housed inside the 1897 Eyre Telegraph Station, the observatory studies a variety of birds, flora, and other fauna. A small museum features old telegraph memorabilia. The observatory also houses a library donated by deceased American millionaire Harold Anderson, who believed a forthcoming nuclear disaster would spare this isolated spot. If you book in advance, you can overnight at the observatory for about $60 (cheaper if you stay longer or have a YHA card) including room and full board. Roundtrip transport from Cocklebiddy is about $30. For advance bookings (mandatory), phone (08) 9039-3450. In Cocklebiddy, **Wedgetail Inn,** tel. (08) 9039-3462, has a lounge, pub, dining room, and takeaway. Moderate-Expensive.

It's another 66 km to **Caiguna,** with service facilities as well as an airstrip used both by charter planes and the Royal Flying Doctors. About 10 km south is the memorial to Eyre's buddy, Baxter, killed in 1841 by angry natives. **John Eyre Motel,** tel. (08) 9039-3459, has modern, air-conditioned rooms. Moderate-Expensive.

The 182-km distance from Caiguna to **Balladonia** is one of the world's longest straight stretches of road. Those rock-hole dams you see just before Balladonia are called **Afghan Rocks,** for the Afghan camel driver who was shot dead for having the audacity to wash his feet in the water. **Balladonia Hotel Motel,** tel. (08) 9039-3453, offers simple but modern rooms, plus a bistro, pub, dining room, and takeaway. Moderate.

You'll see mine shafts and tailings as you near Norseman, where—depending on your mood—you'll either drop south to the coast or north to the goldfields.

THE FLINDERS RANGES

Photographers, painters, bushwalkers, and nature lovers travel to these desert range rock formations for hot shots, divine inspiration, colorful adventure, and a breath of fresh air.

The Flinders Ranges—broken into southern, central, and northern sections—begin to jut between Crystal Brook and Peterborough (about 250 km north of Adelaide), then sweep and arc northward to a point 160 km east of Marree at the edge of the Outback.

Thrust up from the sea about 1.6 billion or so years ago, these bent, twisted, buckled, and gorged ranges are best described as earth sculptures. Minerals embedded in the ancient plains and cliffs chameleon along with the sun or moon, the time of year, a turn of your head into delicate pink, salmon, mauve, purple, angry red, and sunshine yellow. These ranges aren't high, but they'll surely make you feel that way!

The scenery varies from woodsy slopes in the temperate south to rugged peaks in the dry north, with Wilpena Pound, the great natural amphitheater in the central region, ranking as the highlight of the Flinders Ranges. Wildflowers (including South Australia's state flower, Sturt's desert pea), wildlife, and birds can be seen throughout the area. In fact, you're likely to spot lots of interesting vegetation and pretty posies, but please help preserve this fragile and beautiful region by leaving your finds intact. As requested by the Royal Automobile Association: "If you must take something home—make it a photograph."

The most popular time to visit is April through October. Summer months are usually very hot and very cold. Rain, at any time of year, can cause flash flooding and render roads impassable. Be sure to follow Outback driving regulations and inquire about road and weather conditions along your journey. It is imperative that bushwalkers obtain detailed maps and information from park rangers or Tourist Information Centres before embarking on either a short trail or lengthy trek. Those taking the Heysen Trail should note that the Flinders section is closed 1 Nov.-30 April because of fire restrictions.

The easiest way to reach the Flinders Ranges is via Highway 47 from Port Augusta. The road is sealed to Wilpena Pound, and also up to Lyndhurst (junction of the Strzelecki Track). After that it becomes gravel, dirt, and indescribable. A popular "circle tour" is to start at Port Augusta, pass through Quorn and Hawker to Wilpena, continue northward through Flinders Ranges National Park up to Blinman, swing west to Parachilna, then south back to Hawker.

History

This region is older than the hills—literally.

Captain Matthew Flinders undoubtedly thought he discovered the place when he visited in 1802—after all it was later named after him. Well, try telling that to the Aboriginals. Though you won't find too many of them around anymore. You will find their paintings and rock carvings, some known to be 12,000 years old, scattered about the ranges. (*Please* do not tamper with paintings, carvings, or relics.)

There are a number of historical sites in and around the ranges, mostly old copper- and gold-mining towns, homesteads that served as resting spots for overland teams. They're remnants of the late-1800s wheat farming boom, nipped in the sheaf by bad weather, plagues, and hunger.

SOUTHERN FLINDERS RANGES

You can travel any of several sealed roads from the Mid-North to tour the relatively gentler and more accessible southern region.

Telowie Gorge

Located 25 km northeast of Port Pirie, with access off Highway 1, Telowie Gorge (1,946 hectares) is the southernmost park of the Flinders Ranges. Steep red cliffs, open woodlands, spring wattle blossoms, yellow-footed rock wallabies, and prolific birdlife are the main features. There are no facilities and limited camping sites.

Melrose

This one-time copper town, situated at the foot of Mt. Remarkable, is the Flinders Ranges' oldest settlement. These days it's a grazing and wheat-

and barley-growing community and a good base for exploring Mt. Remarkable National Park. In fact, a walking trail leads from town all the way to the top of Mt. Remarkable (956 meters). Good views can be had from either the **War Memorial** or **Lookout Hill.**

Historic buildings include the old **Police Station and Courthouse** (now a National Trust museum, open daily 2-5 p.m.), **post office, Jacka's Brewery,** and **Melrose Inn.** Two other oldies, built in the 1850s, are **North Star Hotel,** Nott St., tel. (08) 8666-2110, and **Mt. Remarkable Hotel Motel,** Stuart St., tel. (08) 8666-2119. Both offer inexpensive pub-type accommodations. **Melrose Caravan Park,** Joes Rd., tel. (08) 8666-2060, rents campsites, cabins, and on-site vans. Budget-Inexpensive.

Mt. Remarkable National Park
Wedged between the Melrose-Wilmington road and the Port Pirie-Port Augusta highway, Mt. Remarkable National Park (8,649 hectares) is known for its dramatic scenery and diverse plant and animal life. The three best places to explore are the somewhat separate Mt. Remarkable (behind Melrose), the narrow Alligator Gorge (accessed one km south of Wilmington), and red gum-lined Mambray Creek (accessed from a branch road about 45 km north of Port Pirie, off Highway 1). Walking trails with plenty of signposts lead to panoramic lookouts and isolated gorges from both Alligator Gorge and Mambrey Creek. Mambray Creek campground is open, except during fire-ban days; bush camping is permitted in some

areas. Admission is $5 per vehicle. For information, phone (08) 8666-2014. Backpacker accommodations are available at **Mt. Remarkable Hut,** tel. (08) 8666-2060. Budget.

Nearby points of interest are: **Hancock's Lookout,** north of the park, at the top of Horrocks Pass; the ghost towns of **Hammond** and **Bruce,** northeast of Wilmington; and, for all you rodeophiles, **Carrieton,** about 25 km northeast of the ghost towns, hosts a nationally known rodeo every October.

Quorn
From 1917 until 1937, Quorn (pop. 1,080) served as an important railway junction on both east-west and north-south transcontinental routes. Not so after a new standard gauge line was built to Marree in 1956, leaving the town to fend for itself. In 1974, after part of the old line was restored to accommodate a steam-powered tourist train, Quorn was back in business—not as the big-time rail depot it used to be but with travelers who want to putt-putt through Pichi Richi Pass. Billed as the "Gateway to the Flinders Ranges," Quorn is about 40 km from Wilmington and a bit farther from Port Augusta.

The **Pichi Richi Railway** departs from old Quorn Railway Station for a picturesque two-hour-and-45-minute roundtrip journey (about $19) into Pichi Richi Pass, rolling over bridges, along the Pichi Richi River, and through the long-abandoned Pichi Richi township. The train only runs during school holidays and long weekends. Check at the tourist information office or phone

Quorn's Pichi Richi Railway takes tourists on a sentimental journey.

MIKE WELLINS

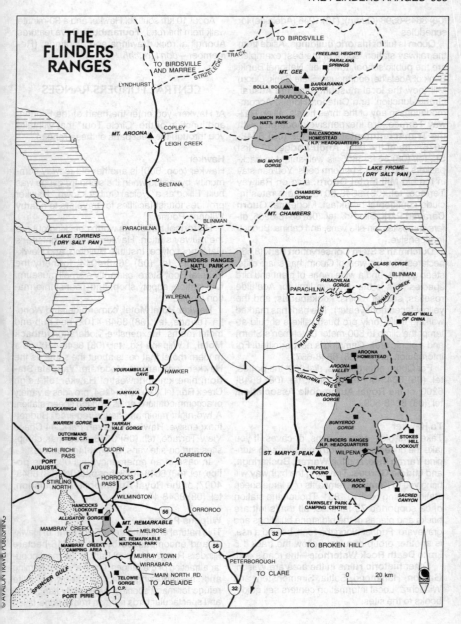

THE
FLINDERS
RANGES

TO BIRDSVILLE
AND MARREE

LYNDHURST

TO BIRDSVILLE

STRZELECKI TRACK

FREELING HEIGHTS
PARALANA
SPRINGS
MT. GEE
BARRARANNA
GORGE
BOLLA BOLLANA
ARKAROOLA
GAMMON RANGES
NAT'L PARK

MT. AROONA
COPLEY
LEIGH CREEK

BALCANOONA
HOMESTEAD
(N.P. HEADQUARTERS)

BELTANA

BIG MORO
GORGE

LAKE FROME—
(DRY SALT PAN)

LAKE TORRENS
(DRY SALT PAN)

PARACHILNA

BLINMAN

CHAMBERS
GORGE

MT. CHAMBERS

FLINDERS RANGES
NAT'L PARK

WILPENA

GLASS GORGE

PARACHILNA
GORGE

BLINMAN

PARACHILNA

BLINMAN CREEK

GREAT WALL
OF CHINA

YOURAMBULLA
CAVE

HAWKER

47

KANYAKA

MIDDLE GORGE
BUCKARINGA GORGE

WARREN GORGE

DUTCHMANS
STERN C.P.

YARRAH
VALE GORGE

QUORN

AROONA
HOMESTEAD

AROONA
VALLEY

BRACHINA CREEK

BRACHINA
GORGE

BUNYEROO
GORGE

ST. MARY'S PEAK

FLINDERS RANGES
N.P. HEADQUARTERS

WILPENA

STOKES
HILL
LOOKOUT

PORT
AUGUSTA

PICHI RICHI
PASS

47

STIRLING
NORTH

CARRIETON

HORROCK'S
PASS

WILMINGTON

HANCOCKS
LOOKOUT

ALLIGATOR GORGE

MAMBRAY CREEK

MAMBRAY CREEK
CAMPING AREA

MT. REMARKABLE

MT. REMARKABLE
NATIONAL PARK

MT. REMARKABLE

MURRAY TOWN
WIRRABARA

MELROSE

56

ORROROO

56

PETERBOROUGH

32

TO BROKEN HILL

TO CLARE

WILPENA
POUND

ARKAROO
ROCK

RAWNSLEY PARK
CAMPING CENTRE

SACRED
CANYON

SPENCER GULF

TELOWIE GORGE
C.P.

MAIN NORTH RD.
TO ADELAIDE

1

PORT PIRIE

0   20 km

N

© AVALON TRAVEL PUBLISHING

(08) 8648-6598 (Quorn), (13) 1246 (Adelaide) for schedules.

Quorn is full of **historic buildings.** Aside from the railway station, some of the best examples are the public school, town hall, National Bank, Bank of Adelaide, courthouse, State Bank, Quorn Mill (now the local museum), and the Austral, Grand Junction, and Criterion Hotels. Accommodations in any of the three hotels, all on Railway Terrace, are inexpensive-moderate, with the **Transcontinental Hotel,** tel. (08) 8648-6076, one of the best. **Andu Lodge,** 12 First St., tel. (08) 8648-6655, is well-suited to backpackers and offers $14 dorm beds. You can stay in the old **Mill Motel Quorn,** also on Railway Terrace, tel. (08) 8648-6016, where rates include continental breakfast. Moderate. **Quorn Caravan Park,** Silo Rd., tel. (08) 8648-6206, offers campsites, on-site vans, and cabins. Budget-Inexpensive.

Dutchman's Stern Conservation Park (3,532 hectares), five km west of Quorn, has sharp cliffs, steep gorges, and a wide range of plant and bird species (this is the northern limit for Adelaide rosellas, scarlet robins, kookaburras, and the yellow-faced honeyeater). The park has marked walking trails (only pro bushwalkers should attempt the climb to 800-meter Dutchman's Stern) and a picnic area. Camping is not permitted. For information, phone (08) 8648-6571.

For Quorn emergencies, dial 000; the **police,** tel. (08) 8648-6060; **hospital,** tel. (08) 8648-6200; or the **Royal Automobile Association,** tel. (08) 8648-6093.

To Hawker

Take your pick: gorges, ruins, or caves. If you take the unsealed road, you'll pass through stunning **Yarrah Vale,** and the **Warren, Buckaringa,** and **Middle Gorges.** Traveling the highway will bring you to **Kanyaka,** remnants of a large sheep station dating back to 1851. Though the station once supported 70 families, all that's left are bricks and pieces of the old stone buildings and graveyard. Farther along the road, behind a rise, is another group of ruins. Follow the track 1.5 km to **Death Rock Waterhole**—the road's end.

Other **historic ruins** in the area are Wilson, Gordon, Hammond, Saltia, Simmonston, and Willochra. Local information centers sell guidebooks to the sites.

About 10 km south of Hawker and a 30-minute walk from the road, **Yourambulla Cave** features Aboriginal rock drawings and paintings. (Remember—*don't touch!*)

CENTRAL FLINDERS RANGES

At Hawker, you enter the heart of the Flinders and junction of the "Circle Tour" that will take you through the best parts of these ranges.

Hawker

Hawker (pop. 300) is another old railway community, bypassed when the standard gauge was built. Billed as a "typical Outback town," Hawker provides tourist facilities for travelers to nearby Wilpena Pound.

Historical buildings worth checking out are the railway station, Hawker Hotel, Sightseer's Café, post office, Institute Building, and Hawker Motors, tel. (08) 8648-4014, formerly the Federal Boot Store, currently a small museum, fuel station, supply shop, and Tourist Information Centre.

Hawker Hotel Motel, corner Elder and Wonoka Terrace, tel. (08) 8648-4102, has pub and motel rooms. Inexpensive-Moderate. **Outback Motel,** 1 Wilpena Rd., tel. (08) 8648-4100, is a modern motel that costs about the same as the Hawker. Inexpensive-Moderate. **Yappala Station,** nine km northwest of Hawker, off Leigh Creek Rd., tel. (08) 8648-4164, provides a variety of accommodations on its working sheep station. A two-night minimum stay is required. Budget-Inexpensive. **Hawker Caravan Park,** 44 Chace View Terrace, tel. (08) 8648-4006, has campsites and on-site vans. Budget-Inexpensive.

In case of an emergency, dial 000; the **police,** tel. (08) 8648-4028; **hospital,** tel. (08) 8648-4007; or the **Royal Automobile Association,** tel. (08) 8648-4014.

Wilpena Pound

This natural amphitheater, 55 km north of Hawker and encompassed by the 92,746-hectare Flinders Ranges National Park, is the most popular attraction of the ranges. Once a wheat-farming and sheep-grazing area, this is now a wildlife refuge for many species, particularly kangaroos and spectacular birds ranging from wedge-tailed eagles to colorful parrots. The basin is a grandiose 80 square km, surrounded by a circle of sheer, splintered, multicolored cliffs (the highest point is 1,190-meter **St. Mary's Peak**). Within the circle, however, gentle slopes lead into the vast central plain. Wilpena Pound is a bushwalker's heaven. Myriad trails guide you along everything from a casual one-hour stroll to a full-day's steep and stony climb. (Be sure to complete a log sheet at the park office, open 24 hours, before embarking on extended walks.) The only access into the pound is through the narrow gorge above **Sliding Rock,** near Wilpena Pound Motel.

The Pound is important in the Aboriginal mythology of the Flinders Ranges (*wilpena* means "a kangaroo skin curled up on its edges"). Tribal drawings, paintings, and carvings can be seen at **Arkaroo Rock,** near Moonarie Gap, and at **Sacred Canyon.** Both areas are about 19 km south of Wilpena (though on different roads).

Other points of interest within Flinders Ranges National Park are the **Bunyeroo** and **Brachina Gorges** and the **Aroona Valley,** where you can see ruins of the old homestead.

The only motel accommodations at the Pound are at **Wilpena Pound Resort,** tel. (08) 8648-0004, with pool, bar, and dining room. Expensive. Tent camping is permitted near the entrance to the Pound for about $10 per night. **Arkaba Station,** 35 km east of the Pound, tel. (08) 8648-4195, offers fully equipped cottage accommodations. Moderate-Expensive. **Rawnsley Park Camping Centre,** tel. (08) 8648-0030, 20 km south of Wilpena, offers campsites, on-site vans, and holiday units. Budget-Expensive. For camping within the park, see below.

To and from Blinman

You'll be traveling on gravel once you leave the Pound. Engaging spots along the 59-km drive to Blinman are **Stokes Hill Lookout** and a long, ironstone-topped rock formation called the **Great Wall of China.**

Blinman (pop. 98), at the northern edge of Flinders Ranges National Park, was a hustle-bustle copper mining town from 1862 until 1890. Old mine machinery and relics are still in evidence, as are a few historic buildings. You can overnight at the 1869 **Blinman Hotel,** tel. (08) 8648-4867, with a pool and hotel or motel sections, as you like. Inexpensive. **The Captain's**

Cottage, Mine Rd., tel. (08) 8648-4895, is a fully equipped three-bedroom cottage with fireplace. Expensive. **Blinman Caravan Park,** Mine Rd., tel. (08) 8648-4867, offers campsites. Budget.

Heading west to circle back to Hawker, two routes will get you to the highway junction at Parachilna: **Glass Gorge** is slightly out of the way along a dirt road, but the views are terrific, especially when the wild hops are in bloom; the gravel road goes through **Parachilna Gorge,** a tourist village at **Angorichina,** and the spring-fed **Blinman Pools** (near Angorichina, reached from the Parachilna and Blinman Creeks). **Angorichina Tourist Village,** tel. (08) 8648-4842, rents campsites, cabins, and cottages. Budget-Expensive.

Experience life on a working sheep station, bunk in the shearers' quarters, and fall asleep counting at **Gum Creek Station,** tel. (08) 8648-4883, or **Angorichina Station,** tel. (08) 8648-4863. You'll pay about $16 for a bunk but must also supply your own bedding and food. Budget.

Rejoin the main highway at **Parachilna,** and either go north 70 km to Leigh Creek or south 89 km to Hawker. **Prairie Hotel,** in Parachilna, tel. (08) 8648-4895, a "typical bush pub," has rooms with or without breakfast included. Moderate.

About 70 km east of Blinman, along one route to the Northern Flinders Ranges, **Chambers Gorge** features 100 meters of Aboriginal rock carvings on its left wall. **Mount Chambers** (409 meters) provides dynamic views of Lake Frome on one side, Wilpena on the other.

NORTHERN FLINDERS RANGES

Rugged, arid, remote, and exquisite, the northern ranges are reached from either Leigh Creek or the Chambers Gorge road.

Leigh Creek

Leigh Creek (pop. 1,635) used to be 13 km north of where it is now. That's right—the whole town just up and moved when the original site was needed for additional coal mining. Beat that for town spirit! Leigh Creek South reopened in 1981 and grass (the kind you mow) has been banned. Like it or not, this is your northern ranges oasis, with shopping facilities, bank, post office, hospital, fuel, auto mechanic, as well as a regional office of the Department of Environment and

Natural Resources. **Aroona Dam,** four km west of town, is a popular picnic area.

If you're a coal enthusiast, you'll enjoy looking down at some of the mine workings from the visitor's viewing area, about three km from the turnoff to Leigh Creek Coalfields, on the Hawker-to-Marree highway. Free public tours are given March-Oct. and school holidays.

In emergencies, dial 000; the **police,** tel. (08) 8675-2004; or **hospital,** tel. (08) 8675-2100.

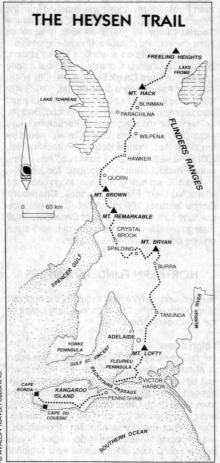

THE HEYSEN TRAIL

FREELING HEIGHTS
LAKE FROME
MT. HACK
BLINMAN
LAKE TORRENS
PARACHILNA
WILPENA
HAWKER
FLINDERS RANGES
QUORN
MT. BROWN
MT. REMARKABLE
0   60 km
CRYSTAL BROOK
MT. BRYAN
SPALDING
BURRA
SPENCER GULF
TANUNDA
MURRAY RIVER
ADELAIDE
YORKE PENINSULA
MT. LOFTY
GULF ST. VINCENT
FLEURIEU PENINSULA
BACKSTAIRS PASSAGE
CAPE BORDA
KANGAROO ISLAND
VICTOR HARBOR
PENNESHAW
CAPE DU COUEDIC
SOUTHERN OCEAN

© AVALON TRAVEL PUBLISHING

Arkaroola

Despite the harsh, occasionally hostile environment, Arkaroola's 60,000-hectare sanctuary harbors a large variety of plants and wildlife. This former mining area was only established as a privately run reserve in 1968. Since then it's been the buzz of naturalists, adventurers, and travel guides.

At Arkaroola, see the art gallery, mineral and fossil museum, pioneer cottage, outdoor pastoral museum, and astronomical observatory, tel. (08) 8212-1366; viewing is subject to light and weather conditions. Nearby points of interest are the Cornish smelters at **Bolla Bollana,** the dazzling view from **Mt. Painter** (790 meters), waterholes at **Barraranna** and **Nooldoonooldoona,** and **Sitting Bull, Spriggs Nob,** and **The Pinnacles** mountaintops. Radioactive **Paralana Hot Springs,** 27 km north of Arkaroola, is thought to be Australia's last site of volcanic activity, and is also an Aboriginal ceremonial spot.

Gammon Ranges National Park (128,228 hectares) is extremely rugged and isolated territory, accessed only by 4WD vehicles, except for the park headquarters area. Walking trails are not marked, and only very experienced and well-equipped bushwalkers should trek this area. Be sure to notify park rangers of your proposed route. For camping in the park, see below.

Don't miss **Mt. Gee,** sitting between Mt. Painter and Freeling Heights. It's a crystal mountain, one gigantic mass of crystallized quartz.

Three different motels make up **Arkaroola Tourist Village,** and campsites cost about $15 per night. For information and bookings, phone the village direct at (08) 8648-4848, or (1800) 676-042. Inexpensive-Expensive.

Even if you're on a tight budget, spring $65 for the 4WD **Ridgetop Tour,** a four-hour adventure up, over, and around absolutely astounding scenery. Book through Arkaroola Tourist Village.

SERVICES AND INFORMATION

Fuel and **public telephones** are available at the following Flinders Ranges locations: Arkaroola, Beltana, Blinman, Carrieton, Copley, Hawker, Leigh Creek, Mambray Creek, Melrose, Morchard, Murray Town, Orroroo, Parachilna, Peterborough, Port Augusta, Port Germein, Quorn, Rawnsley Park, Wilmington, Wilpena, Wirrabara, and Yunta.

For comprehensive information, contact **Flinders Outback Tourism,** GPO Box 666, Adelaide, SA 5001, tel. (08) 8373-3430 or (1800) 633-060. This agency also sells detailed maps of the Flinders Ranges and the Outback.

Other **regional information centers** are: Flinders Ranges Council Office, Seventh St., Quorn, tel. (08) 8648-6419 in Quorn or (08) 8648-4011, Hawker; Peterborough District Council, Main St., Peterborough, tel. (08) 8651-3566; and Port Augusta Tourist Information Centre, 41 Flinders Terrace, Port Augusta, tel. (08) 8642-4511. Most motels, caravan parks, and road-houses also carry tourist information.

Information and **camping permits** for the national and conservation parks within the Flinders Ranges can be obtained from the **Department of Environment and Natural Resources,** Far North Region, in Hawker, tel. (08) 8648-4244.

Contact **park rangers** at Flinders Ranges National Park, tel. (08) 8648-0048; Wilpena, tel. (08) 8648-0048; Oraparinna, tel. (08) 8648-0017; Balcanoona Homestead, tel. (08) 8648-4829; and Mambray Creek, tel. (08) 86-34-7068.

Obtain detailed maps of the **Heysen Trail,** produced by the Department of Recreation and Sport, from Flinders' area shops, as well as map- and bookstores throughout Australia. Also collect maps and other motoring tips from RAA branches.

Northern Roads Condition Hotline, tel. (11) 6333, provides up-to-date info on Flinders and Outback road conditions.

TRANSPORTATION

Augusta Airways, tel. (08) 8642-3100, operates scheduled air service between Port Augusta, Adelaide, and Leigh Creek, as well as scenic and charter flights to Outback areas.

Stateliner, tel. (08) 8415-5555 in Adelaide or (08) 8625-2115 in Ceduna, provides coach service to Arkaroola, Beltana, Booleroo Centre, Copley, Hawker, Leigh Creek, Melrose, Murray Town, Mambray Creek, Parachilna, Port Augusta, Port Germein, Peterborough, Quorn, Wilmington, Wilpena, Wirrabara, and Yunta. **Greyhound Pioneer,** tel. (13) 2030, offers a Port Augusta-Hawker-Leigh Creek service. Fare between Port Augusta and Wilpena Pound runs around $70 roundtrip.

Bushwalkers *must* carry detailed trail maps and adhere to all warnings. It is mandatory that you check in with park rangers before starting off. Heed rules for Outback travel and safety.

Organized Tours

For travelers who'd rather leave rules and regulations in the hands of experienced guides, a wide variety of Flinders Ranges tours are available. Sightsee by air, coach, four-wheel-drive, horse, or camel. Any Tourist Information Centre can provide a list of recommended operators. Also inquire locally—often a shopkeeper or motel manager has a tour-guide relative. **Wilpena Pound Resort** and **Rawnsley Park Camping Centre,** at Wilpena Pound, offer many different excursions.

For an Aboriginal-eye view of the Flinders Ranges, sign up with **Aboriginal Cultural Tours,** tel. (08) 8395-0885. They offer three- to four-day adventures, led by Yarluyandi Aboriginals, that include art, culture, and dreaming stories.

Butler's Outback Safaris, tel. (08) 8642-2188, is a well-established company that operates a range of 4WD tours, as does **Intrepid Tours,** tel. (08) 8648-6277. **Arkaba Station,** tel. (08) 8648-4195 or (1800) 805-802, conducts 4WD tag-along tours, as well as nature walks and retreats. **Ecotrek,** tel. (08) 8383-7198, and **Exploranges,** tel. (08) 8294-6530, also offer eco-walks and tours.

Or ride a **camel** (Bush Safari Outback Camel Co., tel. 08-8543-2280) or a **horse** (Flinders Rides, tel. 08-8528-2132).

INTO THE OUTBACK

This region may be as close as you'll ever come to feeling like you're on another planet—one reason being that it's not particularly well suited to human life.

In 1845, explorer Charles Sturt described the Outback as "a country I firmly believe has no parallel on earth's surface" (then he died). And that is precisely why 99% of the state's population lives south of the 32nd parallel. Much of this area is no man's (or woman's) land. Peaceful, open space contrasts with harsh terrain, stony deserts, enormous salt pans, and eerie desolation. Then again, the challenge of surviving the elements is often what attracts travelers in the first place—that and thousands of native birds, fish jumpin' out of desert waterholes, the search for fiery opals, dry salt lakes, artesian springs, the odd spaceship, and a bunch of odd, spaced-out characters.

Encompassing about 60 million hectares, the Outback presents a massive frontier to pioneering spirits, some pretty hazardous odds to those who gamble with nature, and breathing space galore for incurable claustrophobics. But pay attention to whose land you're on; vast areas are administered by the Department of Environment and Natural Resources, and others are Aboriginal reserves or part of the military's Woomera Prohibited Area. (Though *you* may feel free out here, the *land* is not!)

Choose from four Outback routes. The **Stuart Highway,** the sealed road connecting Port Augusta with Alice Springs, passes through the Woomera missile test site, Coober Pedy, and the opal-mining district. **Oodnadatta Track** is the old dirt road that follows the path of the old Ghan railway and overland telegraph lines, eventually meeting up with the Stuart Highway at Marla. Both the **Birdsville** and **Strzelecki Tracks** are long, hard treks through remote desert into remote Queensland. Whichever route you take, at some point you'll cross the Dingo Fence, a protective wire stretching more than 3,000 km across central Australia to keep those wild dogs from entering southern pastoral lands. Exceptionally adventurous souls—with a lot of time, money, and energy—might want to tackle

the various "bomb roads" or the Canning Stock Route.

The best time of year for Outback travel is April to September, when the weather is usually mild and dry, though early mornings can be frosty (camping June-Oct. can be very cold and uncomfortable). Summers, as you'd expect, are scorching infernos when you can indeed fry your eggs (and seated body parts) atop any rock in this hard place. Rains, though infrequent, should be taken quite seriously, particularly if you're off the sealed highway. Dirt tracks can be washed away suddenly, leaving you stranded for what could be a deadly long time. But the Outback is exquisite after a rainfall, carpeted with wildflowers and exotic plants.

Make certain both you and your vehicle are well prepared for your journey. Follow Outback driving rules, inquire about road conditions, carry detailed maps, keep your car full of petrol and your body full of water.

The first vehicle crossing from Adelaide to Darwin was made in 1908. Since then, historic journeys, in a wide assortment of transport, are still being made. Yours could be next!

ALONG THE STUART HIGHWAY

Woomera and Vicinity

Unless you're desperate for petrol or a quick snack, pass by the ugly little town of **Pimba,** 173 km northwest of Port Augusta. In the 1950s and '60s, Woomera, off the highway a few km from Pimba, was a test site for British experimental rockets. The most famous launching was that of the *Europa,* 1964-70. About those same years NASA ran a deep-space tracking station at nearby Island Lagoon. The testing range and "Narrungar" (the communications station) are controlled by the Australian Defence Department. Woomera still serves as a military base, and U.S. personnel continue to be stationed here (and what *stories* people tell about what goes on at this place—spooky doings about spies, satellites, and alien spaceships!). Rumor now has it that Woomera will be used as a U.S. testing site.

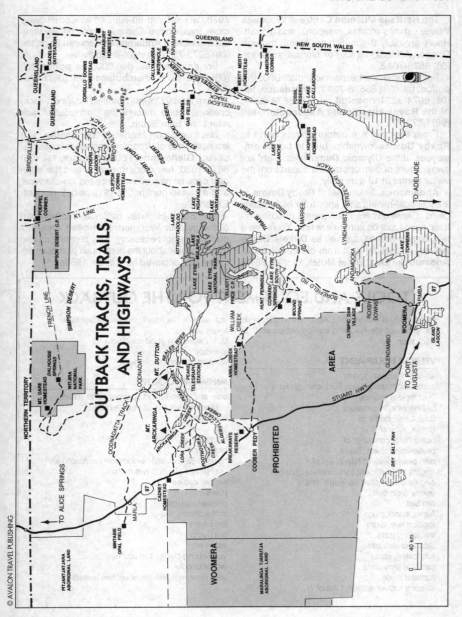

OUTBACK TRACKS, TRAILS, AND HIGHWAYS

© AVALON TRAVEL PUBLISHING

The **Heritage Museum Centre** at Woomera Village exhibits rockets, weapons, and aircraft. Hours are daily 9 a.m.-5 p.m., March through October. Admission is $3. For information, phone (08) 8673-7042.

For Woomera emergencies, dial: 000; the **police,** tel. (08) 86673-7244; **ambulance,** tel. (08) 8674-3234; **hospital,** tel. (08) 8674-3294; or the **Royal Automobile Association,** tel. (08) 8673-7715.

From Woomera, a detour travels north to **Roxby Downs** township, built to house employees at the **Olympic Dam** mines, eight km away. Tours of dam operations depart from the visitor center at 10 a.m. daily.

Andamooka, 30 km east of Roxby Downs, is a small opal-mining site, known for high-quality gems. Claim owners often permit noodling on their claims, but be sure to ask first. You'll see a few dugout homes, as well as **Duke's Bottle House,** a dwelling built from old beer bottles. **Andamooka Opal Hotel Motel,** tel. (08) 8672-7078, will set you up with an air-conditioned room. Inexpensive. Campsites and on-site vans are available at **Andamooka Caravan Park,** tel. (08) 8672-7117. Budget-Inexpensive.

For emergencies, dial 000; the **police,** tel. (08) 8672-7072; or **ambulance,** tel. (08) 8672-7087.

From Roxby Downs, Borefield Rd. (a dirt track) continues north, meeting the Oodnadatta Track near Lake Eyre South.

Back on Stuart Highway, **Glendambo,** 113 km northwest of Woomera, provides tourist facilities. **Glendambo Tourist Centre,** tel. (08) 8672-1030, has modern rooms, and the adjacent caravan park offers campsites, on-site vans, and a cheap bunkhouse ($12 beds). Budget-Expensive.

The Stuart Highway continues through part of the gigantic Woomera Prohibited Area, but permits are not necessary. Stay on the road and try not to think about the hush-hush plutonium accident that occurred here in the 1950s.

TOOLS AND EQUIPMENT FOR THE OUTBACK

The Royal Automobile Association suggests you take the following equipment on an Outback tour:

VEHICLE EQUIPMENT

air-filter element, spare
automatic transmission fluid, enough for a
    complete change
bailing wire, two meters
Bars-Leak, bottle of
Bostik, tube of
brake fluid, container of
brake-lining rivets, brass
disc brake pads (if fitted), set of
engine oil (sufficient for complete change)
engine oil/fuel filter cartridge, spare
epoxy resin putty
fan belt
fuses, spark plugs
ignition key, extra
insulating tape
jack and jack base
lubricating spray
petrol in jerry cans
radiator hose
silicone rubber gasket, tube of

spare bulbs (for headlights and taillights)
spare tire
spare wheel (in good condition)
tow rope
welding wire or copper wire

MINIMUM TOOL KIT

box- and open-ended spanners and socket
    spanner, set to suit your vehicle
cold chisel
file
hacksaw
hammer
hose (6.35-mm-inside-diameter reinforced fuel-
    resistant plastic), two meters
jumper cables
pliers
pressure gauge
screwdrivers, set of
tire levers
tire pump
valve key
vulcanizing clamp and patches
wheel chocks
wire (four-mm, low tension), two meters

Coober Pedy

Coober Pedy (pop. 2,800), one of the world's leading opal-mining centers, was established in 1915 after a teenage boy discovered a gem while gold prospecting with his father. It's so oppressively hot and dusty that most of the town works, lives, and prays in dugout dwellings underground. (Appropriately, the name Coober Pedy is derived from Aboriginal words that, put together, mean "White Man in a Hole.") Lying 254 km northwest of Glendambo, it's a good pit stop (literally); otherwise, this town is better suited to miners (about 40 different nationalities), ants, and movie companies who choose this locale for lunar shots (*Mad Max III*) or drag-queen spectacles (*Priscilla, Queen of the Desert*).

The best spot to noodle (pick through old diggings) is in the "jeweler's shop" mining area, on the edge of town. You don't need a permit unless you're on a pegged claim, and you can't use any sort of digging device—otherwise, you must obtain a permit from the Department of Mines and Energy in Adelaide.

If you're in the market to buy, beware and shop around (there are more than 30 dealers in town). Highly regarded though expensive outlets are those at the Opal Inn and Desert Cave motels. You'll find scads of tours to dugout homes and opal outlets (it should be noted that some tour guides double as opal salespeople). Worth investigating are **Old Timer's Mine,** tel. (08) 8672-5555; **Umoona Opal Mine and Museum,** tel. (08) 8672-5288; and **Crocodile Harry's Underground Home,** on 17 Mile Road.

Radeka's Backpacker's Inn, corner Hutchinson and Oliver Streets, tel. (08) 8672-5223, has $14 dorm beds in its "cave maze" and an in-house dungeon. **Joe's Backpacker's,** also on Hutchinson St., tel. (08) 8672-5613, features $14 dorm beds and more comfortable rooms in the adjoining motel. Budget-Inexpensive.

Opal Inn, Hutchison St., tel. (08) 8672-5054, offers a range of accommodations, from basic motel rooms to deluxe suites. Inexpensive-Expensive.

City Gate Motel, Wright Rd., tel. (08) 8672-3125, and **Look Out Cave Motel,** McKenzie Circle, tel. (08) 8672-5118, offer nicely appointed motel rooms. Moderate-Expensive. The **Underground Motel,** Catacomb Rd., tel. (08) 8672-5324, with similar amenities, includes breakfast.

Moderate. Deluxe digs draw groups and desert wimps to the $100-plus at the **Desert Cave Motel,** Hutchinson St., tel. (08) 8672-5688, a more "hotel-ish" experience. Expensive-Luxury. Claustrophobics with cash might opt for **Coober Pedy Opal Fields Motel,** St. Nicholas St., tel. (08) 8672-3003, where the building is constructed of rammed earth. Guest rooms as well as apartments go for top prices. Expensive-Luxury.

Rent campsites, on-site vans, or bunkhouse beds at **Oasis Caravan Park,** Hutchison St., tel. (08) 8672-5169, or **Stuart Range Caravan Park,** Hutchison St. and Stuart Hwy., tel. (08) 8672-5179. Budget-Moderate.

Because of Coober Pedy's multinational population, you'll find a wide range of ethnic eating spots. Pub-crawling, as you might imagine, can be rough here—as can some of the miners. Women should be particularly cautious.

For emergencies, dial 000; the **police,** tel. (08) 8672-5056; hospital, tel. (08) 8672-5009; or the **Royal Automobile Association,** tel. (08) 8672-5030.

Breakaways Reserve, 28 km north of Coober Pedy, is a 40-square-km block of low hills featuring a continually changing color landscape, unique flora and fauna, and walking trails.

Marla and Vicinity

The drive to **Cadney Homestead,** tel. (08) 8670-7994, 153 km north of Coober Pedy, is fairly dreary, but the place has expensive homestead accommodations, moderate bunkhouse beds, and cheap campsites. Refuel yourself and your vehicle, and either cut east through Arckaringa Hills, Copper Hills, and the Painted Desert to Oodnadatta (160 km), or continue north on the Stuart Highway.

Another featureless 81-km drive brings you to Marla (pop. 240), established in 1978 as a tourist service center. The highway meets the Ghan railway line here. Rooms at **Marla Travellers Rest,** tel. (08) 8670-7001, are moderate to expensive; campsites at the caravan park are cheap.

The opal fields at **Mintabie,** 50 km west of Marla (along a gravel road), have proved to be richer than those at Coober Pedy. It's another 165 km to the Northern Territory border, 185 km to teensy Kulgera township, and 464 km to Alice Springs.

ALONG THE OODNADATTA TRACK

Marree to William Creek

Marree (pop. 380), 379 km north of Port Augusta, is the beginning (and ending) point for both the Oodnadatta and Birdsville Tracks. During the 1880s, this mini-town was a big depot for camel drivers transporting goods to the Outback. (You can still see a couple of leftover date palms and a few Afghani names as reminders.) Between 1960 and 1980, it was the changing-gauge station for the old Ghan, choo-chooing to Alice Springs. **Marree Great Northern Hotel,** Main St., tel. (08) 8675-8344, has simple pub rooms. Inexpensive. Campsites and on-site vans are available at **Marree Caravan and Camper's Park,** tel. (08) 8675-8371. Budget.

It's 210 km from Marree to William Creek. The track edges along **Lake Eyre South,** where two lookouts adjacent to the roadway afford views of this salt pan, which stretches 185 km north. (This is a baby compared with Lake Eyre North.) A rough piece of track leads to the lakeshore.

At **Stuart Creek** you can view a six-km piece of the original Ghan line, as well as a few preserved sheds, fettler's cottages, and a water tank. The oasis at **Coward Springs,** about 35 km farther north, includes railway ruins, an old plantation (now a bird refuge), some old date palms, and a warm, bubbling pond.

Bubbler and **Blanchecup** are mound springs, six km south of the track (you'll see fences around them), adjacent to Coward Springs. Bubbler is a bubbling pool of fine sand. Blanchecup is deceptively clear and clean-looking, but you have to dip in and out through a muddy, weedy stench. Either of the springs should open every pore in your body; stick your head in and you won't need a facial—or maybe even a shampoo—for years! (You'd pay a fortune for this in Europe!)

Other points of interest are the old **Beresford** railway siding and flowing bore (artesian well), 24 km north of Coward Springs, and, 11 km farther, **Strangways,** the old Overland Telegraph repeater, where there's also a flowing bore (a bare water pipe).

William Creek to Oodnadatta

William Creek, 45 km north of Strangways, is touted as South Australia's (some say the world's) smallest town that lies within one of the state's (if not the world's) largest cattle stations—30,027-square-km Anna Creek. The big thing to do here is hang around the pub, soaking up local color and lore, or gawking at other travelers, usually crowded around the pay phone. Basic accommodations at that same **William Creek Hotel,** tel. (08) 8670-7880, and campsites cost just $5 pp. Budget-Inexpensive.

It's 206 km to Oodnadatta, a journey through gibber (Aboriginal for "stone") plains, ranging in color from sand to charcoal, and in size from pebbles to Frisbees. The gibbers also have a strange reflective quality. Sights along this section of track are **Edwards Creek** ruins and bore (you can take a shower here, but your hair will turn to Brillo), **Warrina Siding** ruin, a memorial to explorer Ernest Giles (in 1876 he crossed from Geraldton, Western Australia, to Peake Telegraph Station, east of the memorial), the **Algebuckina** siding ruin, one of the best old **Ghan railway bridges,** and **Mt. Dutton.**

Oodnadatta (pop. 230) sprang into being in 1891 with the arrival of the railway and then, in the 1980s, came close to fading back out of existence when the rail line was moved and the Stuart Highway was sealed. This true Outback town (whose Aboriginal name translates to "flower of the mulga") has turned its old railway station into a museum, but the real attraction here is the **Pink Roadhouse,** which serves as social center, petrol stop, supermarket, "Oodnaburger" supplier, mechanic's garage, caravan park, info provider, tour organizer, and travelers' clearinghouse and meeting place. Both campsites and on-site vans are available. Budget-Inexpensive. The roadhouse is open daily. For information, phone (08) 8670-7822.

Rooms at **Transcontinental Hotel,** tel. (08) 8670-7804, are also available, and facilities are shared. Inexpensive. **Oodnadatta Caravan Park,** tel. (08) 8670-7822, offers campsites, on-site vans, and a rather pricey bunkhaus. Budget-Inexpensive.

For emergencies, dial 000 or the **police,** tel. (08) 8670-7805.

The Oodnadatta Track continues northwest for 118 km, then turns west. From this junction, it's about 100 km to Marla and the Stuart Highway.

THE BIRDSVILLE TRACK

In the 1880s, the Birdsville Track was created so that stockmen could drive their cattle from the grazing grounds in southwest Queensland to the rail station at Marree, where they were loaded onto a train. This border community kept busy during the days when interstate customs were charged. In 1901, after free trade was instigated, they began to ship the cattle by truck along different routes.

The 517 km from Marree to Birdsville (in Queensland) pass by deserted homesteads and mission ruins, scalding bores and welcoming waterholes, not to mention phenomenal amounts of sandy dunes and rocky plains at the Tirari, Simpson, Sturt Stony, and Strzelecki Deserts. At **Clifton Hills Homestead** the road splits: the inside track, which crosses **Goyder Lagoon,** is closed; the Birdsville goes around it. Seek advice before picking your fork—a wrong decision could be fatal. Also keep in mind that the lagoon is a breeding ground for snakes.

Birdsville, 12 km across the Queensland border, was established in 1882 to serve stockmen headed down the Birdsville Track. Today it caters to travelers following in the stockmen's tracks. Original buildings are the old pub and mission hospital. Even though this is a remote outpost town, after an arduous Outback trek Birdsville's simple tourist facilities seem like a limo ride down Rodeo Drive.

This route is for very well-prepared vehicles and bodies. Check in with police at either Marree or Birdsville, and follow all Outback driving rules and local advice.

THE STRZELECKI TRACK

For those with more larceny than cow pie in their souls, who'd rather follow in the bootsteps of outlaws than stockmen, the background on this route has a bit more juice to it.

The Strzelecki Track came into being in 1871 when bushman Henry Radford (a.k.a. Captain Starlight) used it to drive his herds of stolen cattle from Queensland down to the Adelaide markets. (Strzelecki Creek had been named earlier by Charles Sturt, for his fellow explorer Count Strzelecki.) Other drovers, legitimate and otherwise, used the track also, alternating the route a bit around Cooper Creek where there were more watering holes. The track fell into disuse for many years until the Moomba gas fields southwest of Innamincka were established. The Moomba section of this track (from Strzelecki Crossing to Innamincka) is better kept, but the original bit will appeal more to wanna-be rustlers.

Lyndhurst to Innamincka

Starting at Lyndhurst, 193 km north of Hawker and 79 km south of Marree, the Strzelecki Track wends 459 km northeasterly to Innamincka, a tiny service town, then cuts north for 305 km, turning west in Queensland for the 110-km portion that leads into Birdsville. It's also possible to cross into Queensland from Innamincka and the Arrabury Homestead junction, and to travel 53 km east to Betoota and beyond, instead of going west to Birdsville (just keep in mind, you're still a long, long way from "civilization").

Pick up any necessary provisions at Lyndhurst; this is your last fuel stop until Innamincka (don't expect a petrol pump at the Moomba gas fields).

Following the northern edge of the Flinders Ranges, you'll pass ruins of several old homesteads, cruise through the Cobbler Desert between Lakes Blanche and Callabonna (incidentally, **Lake Callabonna** is the site of the fossilized diprotodon, the largest known marsupial), finally crossing Strzelecki Creek about 85 km north of Mt. Hopeless Homestead. From the creek crossing, you must choose either the track that passes the **Moomba gas fields** (no tourist facilities except a telephone at the security gate) or the old road that goes through **Merty Merty Homestead,** where if you're one of those people who likes to sprawl across different sides of borders at the same time (and have a photo taken!), you can drive 109 km southeast to **Cameron Corner,** a coming-together of South Australia, Queensland, and New South Wales.

Innamincka and Beyond

Innamincka, another outpost town à la Birdsville, is also the place where explorers Burke and Wills bit the dust (you can see their legendary **Dig Tree** along Cooper Creek, about 42 km east of the post office). Several historic spots are dotted

BOMB ROADS

Bomb roads—offspring of the 1950s and brain-children of surveyor Len Beadell—were constructed during the Woomera rocket- and Emu A-bomb-tests era. Beadell and his "Gunbarrel Road Construction Party" went to work. The Gunbarrel Highway, Len's first and best-known feat, was completed in 1958. More than 6,000 km of "road" (really desert tracks—and *really* a rocket range) span western South Australia and a chunk of neighboring Western Australia, north of the intercontinental railway line. Some of the roads run east-west, joining up at points with various north-south stretches. Outback adventurers with 4WD vehicles love this desert grid. These are difficult roads. As with all remote Outback travel, make sure that your body is healthy, your vehicle in excellent condition, and you are well-equipped for breakdowns and emergencies. You will need to carry quite a bit of extra petrol, and permits are required for many of the roads. (Also, be prepared to run into "radioactivity warning" signs.) Detailed information can be obtained from Royal Automobile Club offices.

Gunbarrel Highway: The original Gunbarrel is a very rough, rugged, and desolate stretch running from Victory Downs Homestead, near the junction of the Stuart Highway and Northern Territory and South Australia borders, to Carnegie Homestead (349 km east of Wiluna). Other than the turnoff beyond Giles Meteorological Station to Docker River Aboriginal Community, the Gunbarrel leads to plenty of nothing. "Fake imitations," such as the Laverton-Warburton Road and a more "improved" version of the Gunbarrel, will get you from Uluru (Ayers Rock) to Wiluna or Leonora in Western Australia; obtain permits from Central Land Council, Alice Springs (for the Northern Territory section), and Aboriginal Affairs Planning Authority, Perth (for the Western Australia section).

Anne Beadell Highway: Coober Pedy west to Emu (watch the radioactivity warning signs!), across the South Australia/Western Australia border, crossing Connie Sue Highway, to Laverton; obtain permits from Defence Support Center (P.O. Box 157, Woomera, SA 5720, tel. 086-74-3370), Maralinga-Tjarutja Council, or Maralinga Land Council.

Connie Sue Highway: North from Rawlinna railway siding, past Anne Beadell Highway and the Laverton-Warburton Road, to Gunbarrel Highway; obtain permits from Aboriginal Affairs Planning Authority, Perth.

Gary Highway: North from the Gunbarrel Highway (known as Everard Junction) to Canning Stock Route at Well 35—from there heading west, on a mostly unused track, northwest to the Indian Ocean, north of Marble Bar; no permits necessary.

Sandy Blight Junction Road: Between the Gunbarrel Highway, west of Docker River Aboriginal Community, and Sandy Blight Junction, near Kintore Aboriginal Community; obtain permits from Central Land Council, Alice Springs.

Canning-Papunya Road: Alice Springs west, through Papunya, Sandy Blight, and Gary junctions, to Canning Stock Route at Well 35; obtain permits from Central Land Council, Alice Springs.

Talawana Track-Windy Corner Road: West on Windy Corner Road at Gary Junction, crossing Canning Stock Route near Well 24, becoming Talawana Track, continuing into Pilbara Region (WA), south of Marble Bar; no permits necessary.

about this bitsy service town, most of them memorials to the exploring dead—places where bodies were found, moved to, finally buried, where rescue parties set up camp, where the sole survivor was discovered by Aborigines, etc. On Cooper Creek, rock carvings by the Yantrwantas Aboriginal tribe can be seen at the eastern end of Cullyamurra waterhole. Fish can be found inside that very same waterhole as well as the waterholes along the northwest branch of Cooper Creek.

Find basic accommodations at **Innamincka Trading Post,** tel. (08) 8675-9900. Inexpensive. Barbecues, dances, and other raves with locals are usually held weekends at the "upmarket" **Innamincka Hotel,** tel. (08) 8675-9901.

The **Coongie Lakes,** 112 km northeast of Innamincka, a bird and wildlife refuge, also offers excellent fishing opportunities. It's a long, rough drive from Innamincka to Birdsville, past Cordillo Downs and Arrabury Homesteads (no facilities) and the ruins of Cadelga Outstation, used in the 1930s by the Royal Geographic Society to observe the transit of Venus.

Again, this is not an out-for-a-Sunday-drive road. Make sure that you are well prepared, and check in with police at Lyndhurst.

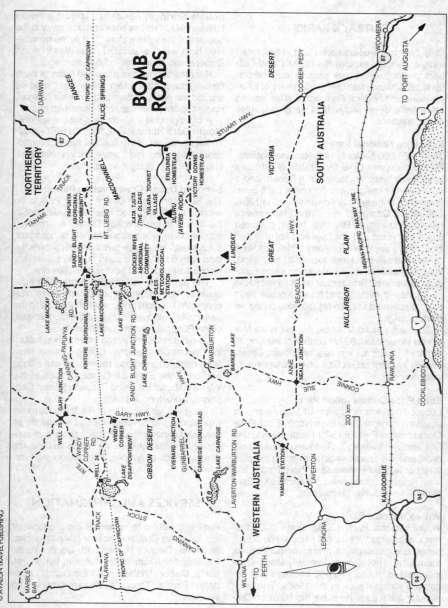

BOMB ROADS

© AVALON TRAVEL PUBLISHING

0   200 km

OUTBACK PARKS

Only the most well-equipped and preinformed travelers should explore the remote, arid Outback parks. Desert park passes must be obtained in advance from the Department of Environment and Natural Resources. The issuing office will provide you with all necessary rules and regulations.

Lake Eyre National Park
The 1,228,000 hectares of Lake Eyre National Park encompass Lake Eyre North (Australia's largest salt lake), adjacent Tirari Desert, and a desert wilderness conservation area. Lake Eyre, normally a huge dry salt pan, is where, in 1964, Sir Donald Campbell set a world land-speed record (640 kph) in Bluebird, his jet-powered car; a few years ago, the lake was full of water! Reaching a depth of 16 meters below sea level (where the salt crust measures 230 mm thick), the lake has filled only a few times since European settlement. Smaller salt lakes lie within the duney desert section, and fossil deposits have been discovered at Lake Ngapakaldi, on the far eastern edge.

The park has no facilities. Access is via Muloorina Homestead, 90 km north of Marree or, alternately, travel six km east of William Creek, then 51 km east to Belt Bay, on the lake's southwest corner.

Elliot Price Conservation Park
Located 105 km northwest of Marree on the southern edge of Lake Eyre North, Elliot Price Conservation Park (64,570 hectares) was the first arid zone reserve. Red kangaroos, grass owls, and low sparse vegetation make the park their home. Hunt Peninsula, within the park, is a long limestone arm reaching into Lake Eyre North. The park has no facilities.

Witjira National Park
Witjira National Park, 120 km north of Oodnadatta, comprises flat hills, salt pans, sandy dunes, desert and gibber plains, and numerous mound, thermal, and hot springs. Formerly Mount Dare Homestead, these 776,900 hectares just became a national park in the 1980s. The most popular attractions here are the 80 or so **Dalhousie Springs,** Australia's largest artesian baths, in which visitors soak and laze away in the bubbles of the tepid waters. This same mineralized bath water originated as rainfall in north Queensland about four million years ago!

Near the springs are ruins and relics of early farming days. After a rain, wildflowers spurt up around the pools. Native birds include brolgas, darters, gibbers, thrush, and cinnamon quail.

A campground is available near the springs. **Mount Dare Homestead,** tel. (08) 8670-7835, 70 km northwest of the springs, has accommodations, camping, food, emergency repairs, fuel, and an airstrip. Budget-Inexpensive.

Simpson Desert Conservation Park
The Simpson Desert Conservation Park is an enormous (692,680 hectares) arid wilderness in the middle of the Simpson Desert. A large bird population, including zebra finches, budgerigars, black kites, and wedge-tailed eagles, shares the land with parallel red sand dunes, salt lakes, gidgi woodlands, and post-rain wildflowers.

The park has no facilities. More-than-adequate provisions, proper equipment, and a first-class 4WD vehicle are essential. Access to the park is via Dalhousie Springs from Oodnadatta, or via Poeppel Corner from Birdsville.

Large areas surrounding Innamincka, including Cooper Creek and the Coongie Lakes, have been declared a regional reserve, as has a huge portion of the Simpson Desert outside of the Witjira National Park and Simpson Desert Conservation Park boundaries.

Travelers who wish to make the hazardous trek across the Simpson Desert should do so only with experienced Outback drivers, in top-condition 4WD vehicles, with massive amounts of equipment, provisions, information, and stamina.

SERVICES AND INFORMATION

Fuel and **public telephones** are available at the following Outback locations: Andamooka, Birdsville, Cadney Homestead, Coober Pedy, Glendambo, Innamincka, Kulgera, Lyndhurst, Marla, Marree, Mintabie, Olympic Dam, Oodnadatta, Pimba, Tarcoola, William Creek, and Woomera.

For tourist information, see above. Also obtain information at **Coober Pedy Tourist Information Centre,** Hutchison St., tel. (08) 8672-3474. Purchase cards, maps, local-interest publications, and a surprisingly eclectic range of fiction at **Underground Books and Gallery,** Post Office Hill Rd., tel. (08) 8672-5558, in Coober Pedy. Additionally, most pubs, motels, caravan parks, and roadhouses (particularly the Pink Roadhouse) carry information.

For information on **Desert Park Passes,** about $60 per vehicle, contact the **Department of Environment and Natural Resources,** P.O. Box 78, Port Augusta, SA 5710, tel. (08) 8648-5300 or (1800) 816-078. Passes can also be purchased at various shops in the area.

TRANSPORTATION

Augusta Airways, tel. (08) 8642-3100, operates a "Channel Mail Run" between Port Augusta and Mount Isa (Queensland), with stops in Innamincka and Birdsville on the weekend, though it's not cheap (about $700, just for the air portion). This company also offers charter and scenic flights.

For commercial flights between Adelaide, Woomera, Olympic Dam, and Coober Pedy, contact **Ansett Australia,** tel. (13) 1300; **Qantas,** tel. (13) 1313; or **Kendell Airlines,** tel. (08) 8231-9567 in Adelaide or (08) 8673-7688 in Woomera.

Stateliner, tel. (08) 8415-5555 in Adelaide or

(08) 8625-2115 in Ceduna, operates frequent coach service from Adelaide and some Flinders Ranges communities to Andamooka, Cadney Homestead, Coober Pedy, Glendambo, Lyndhurst, Marla, Marree, Olympic Dam, Pimba, Roxby Downs, Woomera, and on to Alice Springs. **Greyhound Pioneer Australia,** tel. (13) 2030, provides service to some of the communities via its express routes.

For **organized tours,** see above. Arrangements can be made for fishing and cruising trips along **Cooper Creek,** as well as other Innamincka area tours. For more information, contact **Innamincka Trading Post,** tel. (08) 8675-9900.

One top-favorite Outback tour is the **Coober Pedy-to-Oodnadatta Mail Run,** a 12-hour, 372-mile odyssey in which you tag along with the postman as he drops letters and bills to residents of enormous cattle stations and teensy settlements ($60-90 pp). For information, phone (08) 8672-5558 or (1800) 069-911.

TASMANIA

INTRODUCTION

Tasmania (pop. 472,000), Australia's only island state, is separated from the mainland by the wild waters of Bass Strait. The island's landscape has few similarities to the rest of Australia and because of its greenery and mountains is often compared to New Zealand. Although small in area, the island is sparsely populated, leaving vast tracts of wilderness. This is Tasmania's greatest attraction, and much of the island has been dedicated as national park, including 20% of the island protected as the Tasmanian Wilderness World Heritage Area. All sorts of outdoor recreation is possible, but it is the unparalleled opportunity for long-distance hiking and whitewater rafting that attracts the hard-core adventurers. Tasmania's history is the most colorful but tragic of all states, and while on the mainland progress has meant the demolition of many historic buildings, the slower pace of development in Tasmania has seen dozens of colonial-era buildings saved, many of which have been converted to B&Bs, arts and crafts galleries, and restaurants.

THE LAND

Tasmania may not have the size of Western Australia, the diverse landscapes of Victoria, or the beaches of Queensland, but what it does have is sandwiched on an island where no point is more than 120 km from the ocean, and yet much of the island is wilderness and seemingly remote. Most of the population lives along the east and north coasts, with Hobart, the state's capital, in the southeast. Water dominates Hobart's layout, and while there are a few high-rise developments, the many colonial-era buildings give the city its character. Some of Tasmania's best-known attractions are on Hobart's doorstep, including the delightful Huon Valley and the unspoilt beaches of Bruny Island immediately to the south. East of Hobart is the Tasman Peninsula and Port Arthur, site of Australia's harshest penal settlement and now the state's number-one tourist attraction. Along the east coast are beautiful beaches as

TASMANIA

KING
ISLAND

CURRIE

FLINDERS
ISLAND

WHITEMARK

STRZELECKI
NATIONAL PARK

CAPE BARREN
ISLAND

THREE
HUMMOCK
ISLAND

HUNTER
ISLAND

BASS   STRAIT

ROBBINS ISLAND

CAPE PORTLAND

STANLEY

ROCKY CAPE
NATIONAL PARK

SMITHTON

MARRAWAH

ARTHUR
RIVER

WYNYARD

BURNIE

PENGUIN

ULVERSTONE

DEVONPORT

LATROBE

ASBESTOS RANGE
NATIONAL PARK

GEORGE TOWN

BRIDPORT

DERBY

SCOTTSDALE

MOUNT WILLIAM
NATIONAL PARK

TAMAR RIVER

ST. HELENS

SAVAGE RIVER

SHEFFIELD

DELORAINE

MOLE CREEK

LAUNCESTON

LONGFORD

BEN LOMOND
NATIONAL
PARK

SCAMANDER

ST. MARYS

CORINNA

CRADLE VALLEY

ROSEBERY

LAKE
PIEMAN

CRADLE MOUNTAIN-
LAKE ST. CLAIR
NATIONAL PARK

WALLS OF
JERUSALEM
NATIONAL
PARK

DOUGLAS - APSLEY
NATIONAL PARK

BICHENO

ZEEHAN

QUEENSTOWN

STRAHAN

CAPE SORELL

MACQUARIE
HARBOUR

RIVER

LAKE
GORDON

FRANKLIN-GORDON
WILD RIVERS

NATIONAL PARK

STRATHGORDON

SOUTHWEST

FRANKLIN

GORDON RIVER

DERWENT
BRIDGE

CAMPBELL TOWN

ROSS

SWANSEA

GREAT
OYSTER
BAY

FREYCINET
NATIONAL
PARK

OATLANDS

BOTHWELL

OUSE

HAMILTON

DERWENT RIVER

TRIABUNNA

ORFORD

MARIA
ISLAND

MARIA ISLAND
NATIONAL PARK

MOUNT FIELD
NATIONAL
PARK

NATIONAL PARK

BRIDGEWATER

RICHMOND

COPPING

FORESTIER
PENINSULA

NEW NORFOLK

GLENORCHY

HOBART

KINGSTON

HUONVILLE

GEEVESTON

PIRATES BAY

TASMAN
PENINSULA

PORT ARTHUR

LAKE
PEDDER

NATIONAL

PARK

HARTZ
MOUNTAINS
NATIONAL PARK

DOVER

HASTINGS CAVES
STATE RESERVE

SOUTHPORT

BRUNY
ISLAND

BATHURST
HARBOUR

SOUTH WEST
CAPE

SOUTH EAST
CAPE

0   100 km

© AVALON TRAVEL PUBLISHING

TASMANIAN TIGER (THYLACINE)

This large carnivorous marsupial, once widespread throughout Tasmania, has been *officially* extinct since 1936, when the last remaining example of the species died in Hobart Zoo. The demise of the species came about almost entirely through man's doing after the Van Diemen's Land Company put a bounty on the unfortunate animal when its predatory habits were seriously affecting sheep numbers in the northwest of the state. Speculation and debate as to whether the Tasmanian tiger still exists continues to this day. It has been more than 65 years since the last wild one was seen (and shot), but the distinctively striped marsupial just may be lurking out there somewhere.

well as a number of national parks, including Maria Island and Freycinet, both with excellent hiking opportunities. The southwest of the state is all wilderness and mostly inaccessible. Its gateway is Mount Field National Park, which provides day-hikers the chance to experience the alpine environment. To the northwest is Franklin-Gordon Wild Rivers National Park, scene of a lengthy battle in which conservationists blocked the construction of a hydroelectric scheme that would have caused the Gordon River to flood. Strahan, the only town on the entire west coast with ocean access, is the departure point for a variety of river cruises. Best known of Tasmania's national parks is Cradle Mountain-Lake St. Clair, in the state's north-central region, which protects a high alpine area of deep glacial lakes and rugged peaks. The north coast comprises a string of towns and small cities, including Tasmania's second-largest city, historic Launceston, at the headwaters of the Tamar River. The Bass Strait is a treacherous stretch of water that has claimed hundreds of lives, many on board ships that have crashed into the many islands dotting the strait. Two of these, King and Flinders, are populated by a resilient band of Tasmanians who welcome travelers with open arms.

Climate

During winter, Tasmania's southern latitude sees temperatures drop considerably with snowfalls on the higher peaks. Daily maximum tempera-

tures in July are around 10° C (50° F). Summer is more pleasant, with temperatures in the capital averaging about 20° C (68 ° F). Rainfall along the east and north coasts is fairly consistent year-round, with each month averaging 5.5 cm of precipitation. The interior and west coast are a different story, with some areas receiving more than three meters of rain annually.

HISTORY

The first European to sight Tasmania was Dutchman Abel Tasman, who sailed by in 1642, naming the island **Van Diemen's Land.** In the next 140 years a string of European sailors visited Van Diemen's Land, including Capt. James Cook and William Bligh, but all assumed it was part of the mainland. After settlement at Sydney Cove in 1788, shipping in the region became more frequent, with ships sailing between England and Sydney Cove taking a route around the southern tip of Van Diemen's Land. In 1798 Matthew Flinders, captain of the small sloop *Norfolk,* became the first person to circumnavigate Van Diemen's Land, proving that it was in fact an island. He named Bass Strait after fellow explorer and the ship's surgeon George Bass.

Late in the 1790s, with the population of Sydney Town overflowing, it was decided to establish a second settlement. The site, at the mouth of the Derwent River, Van Diemen's Land, was decided upon in 1804. It wasn't until 1821 that a penal colony was established on the island, first on the west coast, then on Maria Island, and finally, in 1832, at notorious Port Arthur on the Tasman Peninsula. Only the very worst convicts, or those who re-offended once in Australia, were sent to Van Diemen's Land, and the island's notorious reputation grew rapidly. Transportation of convicts was abolished in 1856, and to distance the island from its past, its name was changed to Tasmania, for its European discoverer.

The Aborigines

European treatment of Aborigines during the last 200 years has been grossly unjust, but it was in Tasmania during the first 30 years of European settlement that the Aboriginals' plight was the most tragic. European settlers fenced off all the best land for farms, and as they encroached upon traditional hunting grounds, the Aboriginals began fighting back. In turn, the settlers hunted and shot down the Aboriginal men as they would animals, kidnapped native children to use as slave labor, and raped and tortured the women. In 1828 Governor Arthur proclaimed a law that gave police the right to shoot Aboriginals on sight. Within a couple of years the entire population had been flushed out from settled districts, and over the following five years the remaining stragglers, numbering less than 200, were transported to Flinders Island to be converted to Christians.

TRANSPORTATION

Getting to Tasmania requires a simple choice—to travel by sea or air. For those with a vehicle, there is the choice between the *Spirit of Tasmania,* a large ferry service operating between Melbourne and Devonport, and the *Devil Cat,* a high-speed catamaran operating between Melbourne and Georgetown. Flying is the best option for those with a limited amount of time, and can be inexpensive if booked as part of a package offered by the major airlines.

Getting There by Air

The main gateways are Launceston and Hobart, with most flights originating in Melbourne and Sydney. **Ansett Australia,** tel. (13) 1300, and **Qantas,** tel. (13) 1313, have regular flights

to Tasmania from major mainland cities. Some sample fares to Hobart are: from Melbourne ($258 one-way), Sydney ($290), and Brisbane ($389). Roundtrip fares are much cheaper, especially if purchased 14 days in advance. Both major carriers offer inexpensive packages, such as $299-359 (depending on the season) for airfares from Sydney and three nights' accommodations. **Island Airlines,** tel. (1800) 81-8455, flies from Melbourne and Traralgon, in Victoria's Gippsland, to Launceston and Hobart ($230) via Flinders Island. Their five-night packages are also a good deal, including airfares from the mainland, a two-night stop on Flinders Island, mainland Tasmania accommodations, and a rental car, all from $580 pp. **Kendell,** tel. (1800) 33-8894, flies between Melbourne and Devonport ($206 one-way) and Burnie ($192). This company also offers packages.

Getting There by Ferry

The *Spirit of Tasmania* is a large vehicular ferry operating a regular service across Bass Strait. The ship is modern and comfortable, able to accommodate 1,290 passengers and transport 320 vehicles. More like a cruise ship than a ferry, the ship boasts 10 levels, with three decks of public space that include a variety of restaurants and bars, a swimming pool, sauna, fitness room, nightclub, video arcade, casino, and visitor center. The *Spirit of Tasmania* departs Port Melbourne every Monday, Wednesday, and Friday at 6 p.m., arriving Devonport 8:30 a.m. the following morning. Return sailings depart Devonport Tuesday, Thursday, and Saturday at 6 p.m., arriving back in Melbourne at 8:30 a.m. the following morning. As the ferry always sails overnight, all fares include air-conditioned accommodations, as well as a buffet dinner and light breakfast. Check-in for passengers with a vehicle is up to four hours prior to departure, while walk-on passengers can board three hours before departure.

The *Devil Cat* is a summer-only service. This futuristic, high-speed catamaran cruises across the strait at up to 42 knots and makes the crossing between Melbourne and George Town in around six hours. The *Devil Cat* departs Port Melbourne four times daily Dec.-March at 7:30 a.m., arriving in George Town at 1:30 p.m. that same afternoon. Return sailings depart George

SPIRIT OF TASMANIA AND DEVIL CAT FARES

ADULTS (CHILDREN UNDER 16 TRAVEL FOR HALF FARE)

Peak: (mid-Dec.-late Jan.): $132 hostel/$176-308 pp cabin (dbl.)

Shoulder: (late Jan.-mid-April, late Sept.-mid-Dec.): $110 hostel/$160-246 pp cabin (dbl.)

Off-peak: (mid-April-late Sept.): $103 hostel/$151-225 pp cabin (dbl.)

VEHICLES

Peak: $40 under five meters; $149 under six meters; $30 motorcycle; $25 bicycle

Shoulder: $30 under five meters; $149 under six meters; $25 motorcycle; $20 bicycle

Off-peak: $30 under five meters; $74 under six meters; $25 motorcycle; $20 bicycle

- All fares quoted are one-way; roundtrip fares are double (slight discounts for students and seniors).

- "Hostel" accommodations separate males and females.

- Surcharge applies for Sole Use of a cabin.

- Five- and six-meter vehicle fares adhere to Bass Strait Passenger Vehicle Equalization Scheme.

- Book all classes of travel well in advance by calling (13) 2010 from Australia, (800) 551-2012 from North America.

Town at 4 p.m., arriving back in Melbourne at 10 p.m.

Crossing Bass Strait with a vehicle has become an enticing proposition with the imple-mentation of the government-funded **Bass Strait Passenger Vehicle Equalization Scheme,** introduced to encourage tourism to the island state. It provides a savings of between $100 and $150 per vehicle each way.

See the chart *"Spirit of Tasmania* and *Devil Cat* Fares" for fares. Both vessels are operated by the TT-Line, tel. (13) 2010, website: www.tt-line.com.au.

Getting Around

Tasair, tel. (1800) 06-2900, and **Aus-Air,** tel. (1800) 33-1256, operate scheduled flights to all major centers as well as King and Flinders Islands.

Transportation around the island's road system is provided by two bus companies. **Tasmanian Wilderness Travel,** tel. (03) 6334-4442, website: www.tassie.net.au/wildtour, has an extensive timetable, with service to all cities and major towns as well as the most popular national parks. Some routes are served daily, others less regularly and with a limited number of runs April-October. Fares are reasonable with a Wilderness Pass, ranging from a pass valid for five days' travel in seven days for $100 to a pass valid for 30 days' travel in 40 days for $220. **Tasmanian Redline Coaches,** tel. (03) 6331-3233, offers more daily runs but to fewer destinations, and offers similar passes.

NATIONAL PARK ENTRANCE FEES

Entry to all Tasmanian national parks requires paying a fee. A day pass is $9 per vehicle or $3 pp for those on foot. A better value is the two-month pass, valid for entry to all parks. This pass costs $20 per vehicle or $12 pp for those on foot. For those planning longer trips to Tasmania, the Annual Pass is $40 per vehicle.

HOBART

Hobart (pop. 130,000), the capital of Tasmania, lies at the mouth of the Derwent River on the island-state's southeast coast. Of Australia's state capitals, only Sydney rivals Hobart for surrounding natural beauty, for behind the city Mt. Wellington, snowcapped during the winter months, rises sharply to an elevation of 1,270 meters, sandwiching the city between the mountains and the water. With less pressure for expansion than other capitals, Hobart has retained its colonial charm and also has an English feel, not unlike the city of Victoria on Canada's Vancouver Island.

Downtown Hobart surrounds Sullivans Cove, a protected body of water on the Derwent River that is a continuous buzz of activity, from cruise liners to fishing trawlers to, around the New Year, dozens of yachts sailing into the cove

upon completion of the Sydney-Hobart Yacht Race. Surrounding the waterfront are dozens of convict-era sandstone buildings, many on Salamanca Place, where a bustling market is held each Saturday.

The Tasman Bridge, spanning the Derwent River north of downtown, links residential suburbs of Rosny, Bellerive, and Howrah to the city center, and also leads northeast to the Tasman Peninsula.

History

With the population of Sydney Town overflowing, the colonial government decided to establish a new settlement in Van Diemen's Land. A settlement was first established at Ridson Cove and a year later, in 1804, moved by decision of the colony's Lieutenant Governor David Collins 10

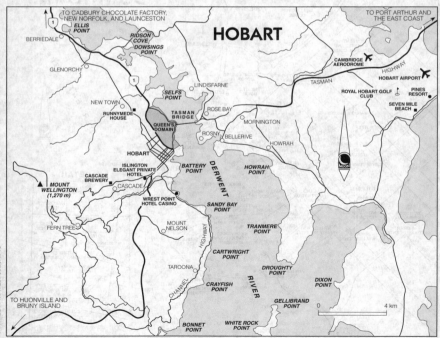

© AVALON TRAVEL PUBLISHING

km downstream. The new site was more suitable than Ridson Cove; it was sheltered and had deepwater access, and rainfall was plentiful. A townsite was quickly surveyed, many stone structures built, and in 1812 Hobart Town, with a population of 1,000, was declared the capital of Van Diemen's Land. The settlement continued to prosper through the early 1800s, becoming an important shipbuilding and whaling port and by the 1850s rivaling Sydney for commercial importance.

Progress stagnated with the discovery of gold on the mainland, but the 20th century has seen Hobart expand greatly, first to the south and north, then, with the completion of the **Tasman Bridge** in 1964, along the eastern bank of the Derwent River. Just 11 years after the completion of the Tasman Bridge, tragedy struck when the iron ore bulk carrier *Lake Illawarra*

plowed into the bridge, collapsing two of its massive support columns, killing 12 people, and sinking under the weight of the collapsed bridge. It took construction crews two years to rebuild the shattered bridge, during which time commuters from the east were forced to either travel across the river by ferry or take a roundabout inland route.

DOWNTOWN SIGHTS

The best way to discover Hobart's past is with **Hobart Historic Walks,** tel. (03) 6230-8233, which takes in historic sites around the cove, such as the City Hall, the notorious dockside suburb of Wapping, the laneways off Hunter St., reclaimed Hunter Island, the cellars of the old Customs House (now Parliament House), St.

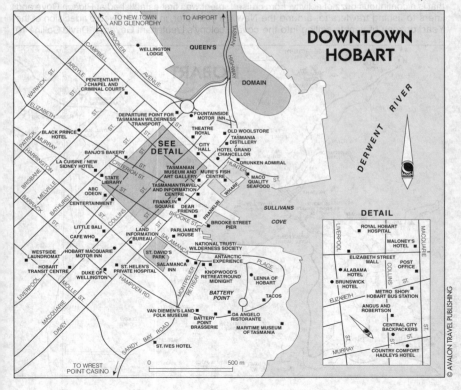

David's Park cemetery, and the site of Hobart's first jail. Tours depart the Tasmanian Travel and Information Centre daily at 10 a.m.; adult $15, children under 12 free.

Tasmanian Museum and Art Gallery

First-floor displays of this fascinating museum feature Tasmanian fauna, a mineral and gemstone display, sealife found around the Tasmanian coast, and 20th-century Australian art. Displays on the second floor include the story of Tasmanian Aboriginals, a coin collection, "People of the Pacific," the state's maritime history, convict history, and early Australian art. The complex is open daily 10 a.m.-5 p.m. Admission is free. It's at 40 Macquarie St., tel. (03) 6235-0777.

Penitentiary Chapel and Criminal Courts

These attractive redbrick buildings on the corner of Brisbane and Campbell Streets are among the oldest remaining structures in Tasmania. The Penitentiary Chapel, completed in 1835, was used by convicts and warders for compulsory Sunday church services. In 1858 additions were made to the building, and the whole place was converted to criminal courts. The National Trust, tel. (03) 6231-0911, offers tours of the chapel, courtrooms, underground passages, graffiti-covered jail cells (the last man hanged in Australia, in 1968, autographed the wall), solitary cells, and the outdoor execution yard. Tour cost is adult $5, child $2.50. They operate daily 10 a.m.-2 p.m.

Sullivans Cove

Hobart's main thoroughfare, Elizabeth St., ends to the east at **Franklin Wharf** on Sullivans Cove. The wharf, lined with boats of all sizes and colors, has been Hobart's main tie-up point for shipping since the first settlers arrived in 1804. In the 1800s up to 600 internationally registered ships would visit annually. In times gone by it was the haunt of thirsty seamen, English aristocracy, traveling missionaries, and rowdy whalers, but today things are much quieter. The land around the back of the cove is mostly reclaimed; steps linking Davey and Brooke Streets mark the original extent of water and of the cliff that once surrounded the cove. While commercial use of the cove has changed considerably, it's still a hive of activity with cruise liners, cargo ships, and yachts. In Gasorks Village is the **Tas-**

mania Distillery, 2 Macquarie St., tel. (03) 6231-0588, easily recognized by a 38-meter-high chimney stack. It has been distilling spirits since 1822, and today produces whiskey, brandy, vodka, gin, and a variety of liqueurs. It holds a small museum and is open for free tastings daily 9 a.m.-7 p.m.

On Brooke Street Pier is **Franklin Wharf Cruise Centre,** operator of a ferry between Sullivans Cove and Bellerive, across the Derwent River from downtown. Ferries operate weekdays only and are $1.20 each way.

BATTERY POINT SIGHTS

This area, a maze of narrow and one-way streets immediately south of downtown, is a great place to wander around exploring one of Australia's greatest concentrations of convict-era architecture. The best source of Battery Point information is the National Trust Shop at 33 Salamanca Place, tel. (03) 6223-7371.

Salamanca Place

This cobbled street lined with Georgian-era sandstone warehouses and bondstores is one of Hobart's best-known landmarks. Built in the 1830s, when Hobart was one of the world's great whaling ports, today the buildings contain arts and crafts shops, art galleries, cafés, and restaurants. Each Saturday between 9 a.m. and 3 p.m. the street comes alive with the sights and smells of bustling **Salamanca Market,** where everything from handcarved Huon pine to candles is sold from colorful streetside stalls while buskers perform up and down the street. The **National Trust,** preserver of Australia's historic buildings, has its Tasmanian headquarters at 33 Salamanca Place, tel. (03) 6223-7371. It's open to the public, with a small gift shop and lots of information on Hobart's oldest buildings. Open Mon.-Fri. 9:30 a.m.-5 p.m., Saturday 9:30 a.m.-1 p.m. Each Saturday at 9:30 a.m. the Trust offers a walking tour of Salamanca Place and Battery Point, ending with a morning tea; $10 pp.

Antarctic Adventure

Hobart is home to the headquarters of the Australian Antarctic Division and the base for a growing Antarctic tourism industry. The actual operation is based in Kingston, south of Hobart, but the newly opened Antarctic Adventure, right downtown on Salamanca Square, tel. (03) 6220-8220 or (1800) 35-0028, is, short of visiting the continent itself, the best place to experience Antarctica. Exhibits cover every aspect of life at the end of the earth—the flora and fauna, geology, climate, and history—presented in a way that will keep you entertained for hours. You can visit an authentic field camp, experience subzero temperatures in the cold room (extra clothing is provided), ski through a blizzard, and watch the goings-on at the Australian Antarctic base via the Internet. A world globe, 10 meters in diameter, gives a unique perspective of the earth, a theater shows stunning audiovisuals, and a number of computers are loaded with Antarctic-based games. Admission is adult $16, child $13. It's open daily 10 a.m.-5 p.m. Don't miss it.

Van Diemen's Land Museum

Housed in **Narryna,** a stately old mansion built in 1836, this museum contains a fascinating collection of household memorabilia dating from the convict era. Each room is authentically decorated, while in the courtyard is the original Hobart Town coat of arms, relics from the whaling era, some old brewing equipment, an anchor salvaged from an 1858 shipwreck, and some horse-drawn buggies. Admission is adult $5, child $2. Open Mon.-Fri. 10 a.m.-5 p.m., Sat.-Sun. 2-5 p.m. It's at 103 Hampden Rd., tel. (03) 6234-2791.

Maritime Museum of Tasmania

This museum is in Secheron House, built in 1831 and considered one of Hobart's finest examples of Georgian architecture. The house contains a large collection of maritime memorabilia, including paintings, photographs, whaling relics, a couple of figureheads, models, and other artifacts from Tasmania's colorful maritime history. Admission is $4. Open daily 10 a.m.-4:30 p.m. Located at the end of Secheron Rd., tel. (03) 6223-5082.

SIGHTS IN OTHER PARTS OF THE CITY

Runnymede House

Built in 1844 for Robert Pitcairn, Hobart Town's first lawyer, this sandstone home has been painstakingly restored and is now surrounded by colorful flower gardens. Later owners, such as Capt. Charles Bayley, who renamed the residence after his ship, made additions, but the house manages to retain its original colonial charm. Admission is adult $6, child $3. Open Mon.-Fri. 10 a.m.-4:30 p.m., Sat.-Sun. noon-4:30 p.m. The house is at 61 Bay Rd., New Town, tel. (03) 6278-1269.

Cascade Brewery

This, Australia's oldest brewery, is an impressive building standing southwest of downtown at 140 Cascade Rd., Cascade, tel. (03) 6221-8300. Tours take in all elements of the brewing process and include viewing of a small museum. Tours depart Mon.-Fri. at 9:30 a.m. and 1 p.m. (booking essential). The cost is adult $7.50, child $5.

Taroona

The highlight of Taroona, on the Channel Hwy. 10 km south from downtown, is **Taroona Shot Tower,** the world's only remaining circular sandstone shot tower. Shot was produced by dropping lumps of molten lead from the top of the 48-meter-high tower; on the way down it would form a sphere, then hit the water and cool. The tower, which operated between 1870 and 1904, produced award-winning shot. Visitors view a short video, then climb 259 stairs to the top of the tower. Admission is adult $3, child $1.50. Open daily 9 a.m.-5 p.m.

Cadbury Chocolate Factory

Sprawling over 15 hectares, this factory, established in 1921, is Australia's largest confectionery manufacturing plant. Tours are offered Mon.-Fri. at regular intervals between 9 a.m. and 5 p.m.

The tour begins with an audiovisual of Cadbury's history, then it's on to the good stuff—viewing the various chocolate-making processes and doing a bit of quality control. Admission is adult $10, child $5. And, yes, free samples are included in the tour cost. The factory is in the suburb of Claremont 12 km north of downtown. To book a tour, call (1800) 62-7367; to inquire about employment, call (03) 6249-0111.

Another way to visit the factory is aboard *Derwent Explorer,* tel. (03) 6234-9294, on a four-hour cruise departing Brooke Street Pier Mon.-

Fri. (departure times vary; call ahead); adult $30, child $14.

west coast for $160 pp, which includes a cruise on Bathurst Harbour.

PARKS, GARDENS, AND VIEWPOINTS

The **Royal Tasmanian Botanical Gardens** are incorporated in Queen's Domain, on the northern outskirts of downtown. Established in 1818, the gardens feature a large collection of native Australian species and are noted for colorful floral displays each spring. A conservatory (admission $1 pp) allows a year-round display of some flowering species, and a small kiosk/restaurant provides meals. The gardens are open daily between 8 a.m. and dusk.

The best city and river views are from the summit of **Mt. Wellington,** which rises immediately west of the city to a lofty elevation of 1,270 meters. A 22-km road passing through the outer suburbs of Cascade and Fern Tree leads right to the summit.

OUTDOOR ACTIVITIES

Biking
If screaming down Mt. Wellington on a mountain bike sounds like fun, **Brake Out Cycle Tours,** tel. (03) 6239-1080, offers a 21-km, three-hour-long Summit to Sea downhill experience for $30 pp. Departures are daily and they offer transfers from Hobart accommodations.

Golfing
Royal Hobart Golf Club, at Seven Mile Beach east of the city, is open to members of overseas golf clubs Mon.-Fri. only. Greens fees are $35, and club rentals are available. For tee times call (03) 6248-6108.

Wilderness Flightseeing
Two companies offer flightseeing trips from Cambridge Aerodrome, northeast of downtown on the Tasman Highway. **Tas Air,** tel. (03) 6248-5088, has a 30-minute flight over Hobart and the Derwent River Estuary for $55 pp (minimum two) and a two-and-a-half-hour flight over Southwest National Park for $155 pp. **Par Avion Wilderness Tours,** tel. (1800) 64-6411, has longer tours, including a four-hour trip to the

ARTS AND ENTERTAINMENT

The best sources of arts and entertainment information are the Friday and Saturday entertainment sections of Hobart's *Mercury* newspaper, where festivals and events, movies, and live music venues are listed. The main booking agent for major shows and events is **Centertainment,** 134 Liverpool St., tel. (03) 6234-5998.

Theater and Music
Theatre Royal, Australia's oldest theater, is a striking sandstone building that hosts Australian and international productions as well as performances by local theater and musical groups. Ticket prices range $10-32. The theater booking office, at 29 Campbell St., tel. (03) 6233-2299, is open Mon.-Fri. 10 a.m.-5 p.m., or book through Centertainment.

For information on the **Tasmanian Symphony Orchestra** (TSO), call (03) 6235-3633. Most performances are at the ABC Odeon, 167 Liverpool Street.

Cinemas
Village 7 Cinema Complex, 181 Collins St., tel. (03) 6234-7288, is the city's largest cinema center and has double features Friday and Saturday nights starting at 9 p.m.; adult $10. The Australian Film Institute screens locally made films at the **State-A.F.I. Cinema,** 373 Elizabeth St., tel. (03) 6234-6318. Admission to most films is $10.

Casino
Wrest Point Casino, 410 Sandy Bay Rd., Sandy Bay, tel. (03) 6225-0112 or (1800) 03-0611, was Australia's first (legal) casino; its distinctive white tower overlooking the Derwent River is a city landmark. Gaming facilities are open Mon.-Thurs. 1 p.m.-3 a.m., Fri.-Sat. 1 p.m.-4 a.m., and Sunday noon-3 a.m. Games include roulette, blackjack, poker variations, two-up, keno, and baccarat. As well as providing accommodations and offering many eateries, the casino has a number of bars, nightly live entertainment, and a nightclub.

Hotels, Bars, and Nightclubs

One of the best places in Hobart to enjoy a drink while soaking up some colonial atmosphere is **Knopwood's Retreat,** at 39 Salamanca Place, tel. (03) 6223-5808. Located in the heart of Hobart's historic precinct, this bar with its casual Victorian atmosphere attracts an eclectic array of patrons, who range from visiting dignitaries to local artisans. Opened in 1829 as a drinking hole for thirsty seamen, the bar has come a long way in the time since, now offering more than 100 beers and a great variety of Tasmanian wines.

St. Ives Hotel, 86 Sandy Bay Rd., Sandy Bay, tel. (03) 6223-3655, has bands playing Wed.-Sun. nights; it's usually rock and roll or blues. Other pubs with live entertainment include the **Theatre Royal Hotel,** 31 Campbell St., tel. (03) 6234-6925, and the **New Sydney Hotel,** 87 Bathurst St., tel. (03) 6234-4516, a popular Irish pub. **Café Who,** 251 Liverpool St., tel. (03) 6231-2744, is a trendy little café serving meals until 10 p.m., followed by live jazz most nights.

The two most popular nightclubs for dancing the night away are **'Round Midnight,** above Knopwood's Retreat at 39 Salamanca Place, tel. (03) 6223-2491, and **Club Surreal,** in the St. Ives Hotel at 86 Sandy Bay Rd., Sandy Bay, tel. (03) 6223-3655. **Wrest Point Casino** has a number of different bars and a stylish nightclub.

SHOPPING

Most downtown shops are open Mon.-Fri. 9 a.m.-5 p.m. (until 9 p.m. Friday), Saturday 9 a.m.-noon. The main shopping precinct is Elizabeth Street Mall, in the heart of downtown, but for the most interesting selection of Tasmanian arts and crafts head to **Salamanca Place** on Battery Point. Some of the best shopping experiences on Salamanca Place can be had at the **Handmark Galleries, Spinning Wheel, National Trust Shop,** and **Wilderness Society Shop.** Don't miss **Salamanca Market** each Saturday morning, when an amazing array of items are on offer at more than 200 colorful stalls set along the street.

FESTIVALS AND EVENTS

Sullivans Cove is busy year-round, but for the finish of the **Sydney-Hobart Yacht Race,** between 28 December and 2 January, the harbor, and in fact the whole city, buzzes, as hundreds of yachties celebrate the completion of Australia's most famous yacht race. In conjunction with the race, the city hosts the **Hobart Summer Festival,** with events throughout the city, including **Taste of Tasmania,** when an area of waterfront in front of Salamanca Place is chockablock with stalls of samplings from local cafés, restaurants, and wineries.

Between mid-April and early May, the **Tasmanian Heritage Festival,** hosted by the National Trust, offers the opportunity to visit many of the state's historic buildings at a reduced cost, with tours and daily entertainment at some venues.

ACCOMMODATIONS

Downtown Hotels and Motels

Downtown Hobart has a number of cheap hotels, but most have seen better days. Pick of the bunch is **Alabama Hotel,** 72 Liverpool St., tel. (03) 6234-3737; $28 s, $44 d. Inexpensive. In the same general area is **Brunswick Hotel,** 67 Liverpool St., tel. (03) 6234-4981, with rooms for $35 s, $50 d. Inexpensive. The **Black Prince Hotel,** 145 Elizabeth St., tel. (03) 6234-3501, one km north of downtown, has clean and comfortable rooms with shared facilities for $45 s, $60 d, including a light breakfast. Inexpensive.

Good value among downtown motels is **Fountainside Motor Inn,** corner Brooker Ave. and Liverpool St., tel. (03) 6234-2911, which has large, well-equipped rooms from $75 s or d. Moderate. **Hobart Macquarie Motor Inn,** 167 Macquarie St., tel. (03) 6234-4422 or (1800) 80-2090, has rooms of a good standard, as well as a heated pool, spa, and laundry, for $75 s, $80 d. Moderate. More central, and a little more expensive, is **Country Comfort Hadleys Hotel,** 34 Murray St., tel. (03) 6223-4355, where rooms start at $89 s or d. Moderate.

The **Salamanca Inn,** 10 Gladstone St., tel. (03) 6223-3300, comprises one-bedroom self-contained apartments 200 meters from Salamanca Place. Each apartment is well appointed and has a full kitchen and in-house movies, while guests have use of a laundry service, indoor pool, and restaurant. Rates are $140-248 s or d. Premium. On Battery Point, and just around the corner from Salamanca Place, is **Lenna of Hobart,** 20 Runnymede St., tel. (03) 6232-3900 or (1800) 03-0633, a grand old sandstone mansion dating from 1874. Rooms are spacious and elegantly furnished, and each has a private bathroom. Rooms with mountain views are $160 s or d; those with harbor views are $180. Luxury. **Hotel Grand Chancellor,** 1 Davey St., tel. (03) 6235-4535, overlooking the harbor, is Hobart's most prestigious accommodation. Many rooms have water views, and all are luxuriously equipped. Guest facilities include a heated indoor pool, health club, restaurant, bistro, and bar. Rates start at $230 s or d. Luxury.

Hotels and Motels
in Other Parts of the City
Staying at **Wrest Point Hotel Casino,** 410 Sandy Bay Rd., tel. (03) 6225-0112 or (1800) 03-0611, south of downtown, isn't cheap, but there are a few price options. Most rooms are in the tower. These feature panoramic views, tea- and coffee-making facilities, fridge, large lounge area, and a spacious bedroom with king-size bed. Rates range $220-280 s or d, depending on the view. Luxury. Motor Inn rooms, with river or garden views, are older and start at $115 s or d. Expensive. In the same part of the city is **Regent Park Apartments,** 17 Regent St., Sandy Bay, tel. (03) 6223-3200. These luxurious units, each with a well-equipped kitchen and laundry facilities, are great value at $99-124 s, $109-149 d. Expensive.

In New Town, a few km north of downtown along Hwy. 1, the best-value choice of accommodations is **Hobart Tower Motel,** 300 Park St., tel. (03) 6228-0166, where clean and comfortable rooms are $58 s, $62 d. Moderate. Farther north, six km northwest of downtown, is **Martin Cash Motor Lodge,** 238 Main Rd., Glenorchy, tel. (03) 6272-5044, featuring rooms of a good standard for $80-90 s or d. Moderate.

Across the Tasman Bridge from Hobart, motels are scattered through most suburbs, and although they are less expensive than those downtown, you'll need your own transportation. A good choice on this side of the bridge is **Lindisfarne Motor Inn,** 103 East Derwent Hwy., Lindisfarne, tel. (03) 6243-8666; $55 s, $65 d. Moderate.

Pines Resort, 20 km east of Hobart on Seven Mile Beach, tel. (03) 6248-6222, is a good choice for those who have their own transportation and want to be on the beach. The resort comprises self-contained two-bedroom units spread around sprawling grounds; $120-130 s or d. Premium.

Bed and Breakfasts
Wellington Lodge, 7 Scott St., Glebe, tel. (03) 6231-0614, is a restored Victorian-era house one km north of downtown. Five guest rooms are offered; one has a private bathroom while the others have shared facilities. Rates are $65-75 s, $75-95 d. Moderate.

The luxurious **Islington Private Hotel,** built in 1845, is a beautiful old colonial home in a quiet residential area two km southwest of downtown at 321 Davey St., tel. (03) 6223-3900. Each of the eight rooms is spacious and tastefully decorated. Guests relax in a large downstairs lounge area, and large French doors open to a garden. A continental breakfast is served in a bright sunny room overlooking the swimming pool. Rates are $75 pp for a standard room and $175 s or d for a Grand Room. Luxury. **Corinda,** 17 Glebe St., Glebe, tel. (03) 6234-1590, is a restored 1880 Victorian mansion with mountain and city views. Accommodation is in an upstairs attic room or in a couple of 1850s cottages out back that were formerly servants' quarters. Rates start at $150 s or d. Luxury.

In Taroona, along the coastal highway between downtown and Kingston, is **Hillgrove Colonial Accommodation,** 269 Channel Hwy., tel. (03) 6227-9043, in a stunning location across from the Shot Tower. The original Georgian-era cottage has been greatly expanded, and the entire lower floor has been converted to a suite with stunning river views from the balcony. The suite has a kitchen and breakfast provisions are included in the rate of $75 s, $95 d. Expensive.

Backpacker Lodges
Hobart's main YHA accommodation is **Adelphi Court,** three km north of downtown at 17 Stoke St., New Town, tel. (03) 6228-4829. It's a large complex centered around a courtyard. Facilities include a communal kitchen, dining room, laundry, lounge, outdoor barbecue area, and bike rentals (half day $12, full day $20). Members of the YHA pay $14 pp for a dorm bed, $18 pp twin, $24 pp d and $45 for sole use of a room.

Nonmembers pay around $3 pp extra per night. The Airport Shuttle offers a discounted fare of $6 pp to the hostel. Budget.

Central City Backpackers, 138 Collins St., tel. (03) 6224-2404, is right downtown in the Imperial Mansions (enter from the Imperial Arcade). This friendly place features a modern kitchen and comfortable lounge area. Rates are $15-17 pp in a dormitory and $20 pp in a twin or double room. Budget. Also central is **Transit Centre Backpackers,** 199 Collins St., tel. (03) 6231-2400, above the Transit Centre. Dorm beds are $13 pp, and there are a few double rooms for $35. Budget.

Campgrounds
The closest camping to the city center is **Sandy Bay Caravan Park,** 1 Peel St., Sandy Bay, tel. (03) 6225-1264, on a hillside overlooking the Derwent River four km south of downtown. Facilities include hot showers, a kitchen, and a laundry. Unpowered sites are $14, powered sites $16, self-contained on-site vans $35, and cabins start at $55. Budget-Inexpensive.

On the opposite side of the city, nine km north of downtown, is **Treasure Island Caravan Park,** 671 Main Rd., Berriedale, tel. (03) 6249-2379. All facilities are of the highest standard and there are cooking facilities for campers. Sites are $12-15, on-site vans $32, and cabins $48-55. To get to the park from the highway, take the Berriedale East exit. Budget-Inexpensive.

FOOD

Cheap Eats
Elizabeth Street boasts a number of inexpensive eateries, including many in the **Cat and Fiddle Arcade** food court, where you'll find pasta, seafood, souvlaki, pizza, fruit salad, and baked goods. Like most of Hobart, it's closed Sunday. Also on Elizabeth St. is **Banjo's Bakery,** 103 Elizabeth St., serving an array of delicious breads, pastries, rolls, and Devonshire teas. **Lipscombe Larder City,** at the north end of Elizabeth St. Mall, offers gourmet sandwiches and hot foods to eat in-house or take away. **La Cuisine,** 85 Bathurst St., is a trendy little café offering healthy lunches for about $5-7.

For a pub meal, head to **New Sydney Hotel,** 87 Bathurst St., where daily lunch specials average $6 and dinner $8.

Seafood
Hunter St., running along the waterfront on the opposite side of Sullivans Cove to Salamanca Place, is home to the **Drunken Admiral,** 17 Hunter St., tel. (03) 6234-1903, decorated with maritime memorabilia and renowned for a wide variety of seafood. Start with oysters, cooked four different ways, or the legendary Fish Market Chowder ($8), then dive into the fish stew, made with everything available at the markets that morning ($18.50). Open daily for dinner only, 6-11 p.m. Also on Hunter St. is **Maco Quality Seafood Takeaway,** offering fresh seafood cooked to order; a juicy chunk of Australia's trevally is $4 and a large serving of hot chips is $1.50. They have a few tables, but if the sun's out, you're better off finding a spot along the waterfront.

On the docks in front of downtown is three-story **Mures Fish Centre,** with eateries to suit all budgets: **Fishmongers,** selling fresh fish, shellfish, and smoked fish (perfect if you have cooking facilities at your accommodation); the **Lower Deck Restaurant,** serving seafood dishes for around $10; the **Upper Deck Restaurant,** tel. (03) 6231-1999, featuring great harbor views and offering a three-course lunch for $19.50 pp and dinner for $28; and the sushi bar **Orizuru,** tel. (03) 6231-1790.

Asian and European Restaurants
Little Bali, 84A Harrington St., tel. (03) 6234-3426, is a small place offering inexpensive Indonesian dishes weekdays at lunch and weekends for dinner. Most main meals are less than $10 and you'd be doing well to spend $20 pp for three courses. Most of the other Asian restaurants are at the north end of downtown along Elizabeth Street. One of these is **Vanidol's,** 353 Elizabeth St., tel. (03) 6234-9307, which specializes in Indian and Thai food; most main dishes are less than $14.

For excellent Italian food and a buzzing atmosphere, try **Marti Zucco,** 364 Elizabeth St., tel. (03) 6234-9611, featuring freshly prepared pizza and pastas for $10.50-17.50.

Upmarket

In recent years **Dear Friends,** 8 Brooke St., tel. (03) 6223-2646, has been consistently voted Tasmania's best restaurant. The setting is elegant, and the walls are adorned with stylish works by Tasmanian artists. The chef is best known for his preparation of local produce, with salmon and King Island beef the favorite choices. Main courses range $19-27. It's open Mon.-Fri. for lunch and Mon.-Sat. for dinner. In Hobart's best accommodation, the Grand Chancellor Hotel, at 1 Davey St., is **Meehan's,** tel. (03) 6235-4535, offering an intimate setting and fabulous harbor views.

Salamanca Place

Delicious food can be found at most times of the day and during the early evening hours at one of the many interesting eateries lining Salamanca Place, immediately south of the city center. One of the most unusual places is **Mr. Wooby's,** behind 65 Salamanca Place, tel. (03) 6234-3466, named for an early Hobart merchant who late last century ran a sweets stall on the wharf. The food offered is hearty and inexpensive (less than $15 for three courses), but it's the homey atmosphere that attracts most visitors, many of whom come only to sip coffee. It's closed Sunday. The **Cove Food Hall,** 27 Salamanca Place, with dining inside and out, has an array of delicious deli-style foods and daily specials served 7:30 a.m.-6 p.m. (until 4 p.m. on Sunday). **Tea House Restaurant,** 33 Salamanca Place, tel. (03) 6224-8700, offers the cuisine of Malaysia, Singapore, Thailand, Indonesia, and China in a smart Oriental atmosphere. All main dishes are less than $16. Open Wed.-Sun. for lunch and Tues.-Sunday for dinner.

The first warehouse built on Salamanca Place, and still with bare sandstone walls, is now the **Ball and Chain Restaurant,** 87 Salamanca Place, tel. (03) 6223-2655. Charcoal-grilled steak from $18.50 is the specialty, but those who don't eat beef have plenty to choose from. It's open Mon.-Sat. for lunch and daily for dinner. Next door, at no. 89, is one of Salamanca Place's trendiest eateries, **Panache Cafe Restaurant,** tel. (03) 6224-2929, attracting a well-dressed clientele that comes for freshly prepared pasta dishes.

Other Battery Point Restaurants

Also on Battery Point is **Tacos,** 41 Hampden Rd., tel. (03) 6223-5297, a stylish Mexican joint with authentic southern dishes at reasonable prices; most main dishes are $12-16. In an old post office a little farther along the same road is **Battery Point Brasserie,** 59 Hampden Rd., tel. (03) 6223-3186. Local game is featured heavily on the menu, and for these you pay a reasonable $12-18. It's open Mon.-Sat. 6:30 p.m.-midnight. **Da Angelo Ristorante,** 47 Hampden Rd., tel. (03) 6223-7011, has delicious pizza from $6.50 and daily blackboard pasta specials for $10-12. This place is extremely popular, both for the food and the great atmosphere, so advance bookings are necessary.

Wrest Point Casino

The casino, at 410 Sandy Bay Rd., Sandy Bay, tel. (03) 6225-0112, has three eateries. The 24-hour **Coffee Shop** offers a lot more than coffee, with a daily breakfast buffet ($13.50 pp), a lunch buffet Mon.-Sat. ($18.50; $27 for Sunday brunch), and a daily dinner buffet ($28.50). The **Asian Restaurant** is open for dinner Tues.-Sat. with main meals from $13.50 and desserts from $5.50. Atop the casino tower is **Wrest Point Revolving Restaurant,** offering 360-degree views of Hobart and surrounds from every table (a full revolution takes one hour). At lunch, appetizers are $7, main meals $15, and desserts $5.50. Dinner is more formal; a set four-course meal costs $52, seafood and local game selections from the à la carte menu range $24-32. On Sunday, a buffet breakfast is offered for $17.95 pp.

Moorilla Estate Wine Centre

On the Derwent River nine km north of downtown, this complex comprises a winetasting room and restaurant. The restaurant, open for lunch daily noon-2:30 p.m., has seating indoors and out (most tables have views of the vineyard) and a menu that changes with the season. Appetizers are $4-6 and main meals range $15-18.50. Try the Grapepickers Lunch, a sample of many local produces, for $19.50. Tasting the latest wine releases costs $5, which includes a sampling of Tasmanian cheeses. Open daily 9 a.m.-5 p.m. It's at 655 Main Rd., Berriedale, tel. (03) 6249-2949.

TRANSPORTATION

Getting to Hobart from mainland Australia means flying with **Ansett Australia,** tel. (13) 1300, or **Qantas,** tel. (13) 1313, or taking the *Spirit of Tasmania* or *Devil Cat,* tel. (13) 2010, across Bass Strait and connecting with an across-island bus service. For details on all the above services, as well as air and bus services throughout the state, see above.

Air

Hobart Airport is on the Tasman Hwy. 19 km northeast of downtown. Within the main terminal is a café, information boards, Ansett Australia and Qantas reservation desks, and Avis, Budget, and Thrifty car rental desks. Tasmanian Redline Coaches, tel. (03) 6231-3233, operates an **airport shuttle** that meets all incoming flights and leaves the city one hour prior to most departures. The fare is $7 each way. A cab between the airport and downtown runs about $24-27. Parking at the airport is a reasonable $6 per day.

From Hobart by Coach

Hobart Transit Centre, at 199 Collins St., is the terminus of all buses operated by **Tasmanian Redline Coaches,** tel. (03) 6231-3233. This company offers scheduled services throughout the state, sightseeing tours, and an airport shuttle. The other major carrier, with services to all major national parks and most tourist centers, is **Tasmanian Wilderness Travel,** tel. (03) 6334-4442, also with departures from the transit centre. Their booking office is at 103 George Street.

Getting around Hobart by Bus

City buses go just about everywhere throughout the city; services to suburbs in the south and west depart from Franklin Square while those to the north and east depart from Hobart Bus Station at the corner of Macquarie and Elizabeth Streets. Fares are $1.50 per ride, but the best value is a Day Rover ticket, which allows unlimited bus travel for a day 9 a.m.-4:30 p.m. and after 6 p.m. weekdays and all weekend. For all public bus information, head to the **Metro Shop,** in the Hobart Bus Station, tel. (13) 2201. It's

open Mon.-Fri. 8 a.m.-5:15 p.m., Saturday 8:30 a.m.-12:30 p.m.

Taxi

Hobart's two main cab companies are **Taxi Combined Services,** tel. (13) 2227, and **City Cabs,** tel. (03) 6334-3573. A cab anywhere around downtown is less than $5; from downtown to the casino will run about $8, and to the airport ranges $24-27, depending on the traffic.

Car Rental

All major car rental companies have offices in Hobart, including **Avis,** tel. (1800) 22-5533; **Budget,** tel. (13) 2727; **Hertz,** tel. (13) 3039; and **Thrifty,** tel. (1300) 36-7227. There is much competition for business, with vouchers in many tourist brochures, standby rates, and lots of drop-off locations. Independent agencies will offer better rates, but cars are often older models. These agencies include **Advance,** tel. (1800) 03-0118; **Bargain Car Rentals,** tel. (03) 6234-6959; **Drive Time,** tel. (03) 6224-8999; **Metro Auto Rentals,** tel. (03) 6234-3717; and **U-Drive Rentals,** tel. (03) 6231-1077.

For small motorhomes, call **Tasmanian Camper Van Hire,** tel. (03) 6248-9623 or (1800) 80-7119.

City Tours

Half-day tours of the city and to the summit of Mt. Wellington are offered by **Hobart Sightseeing Tours,** tel. (03) 6231-3511; adult $28, child $18. Similarly priced are tours offered by **Hobart Coaches,** tel. (03) 6234-4077, and **Tigerline,** tel. (1300) 65-3633.

SERVICES

The **general post office** is right in the heart of downtown on the corner of Elizabeth and Macquarie Streets. Traveler's checks can be cashed at banks and most major hotels; for checks not in Australian currency a fee or commission will be charged. Automatic teller machines are located at most Hobart banks, but once you're outside the capital these machines become few and far between, so plan ahead.

Most central of Hobart's laundromats is **Westside Laundromat,** on the corner of Goulburn and Molle Streets; open daily.

Emergencies

For medical emergencies, dial 000 or one of the following hospitals: **Royal Hobart Hospital,** 48 Liverpool St., tel. (03) 6238-8308, or **St. Helen's Private Hospital,** 186 Macquarie St., tel. (03) 6221-6444.

INFORMATION

The **State Library of Tasmania** is at 91 Murray St., tel. (03) 6233-7481. One whole section is devoted to "Tasmaniana." The library is open Mon.-Fri. 9:30 a.m.-5 p.m. For a large selection of books, including many Australian travel guides, head to **Angus and Robertson,** 98 Collins St., tel. (03) 6234-4288. The **Government Info Bookshop** is at 31 Criterion St., opposite YHA Tasmania, tel. (03) 6234-1403. Another good spot for Tasmanian literature is the **Wilderness Society Shop** at 130 Davey St., tel. (03) 6234-9366.

The **Tasmanian Travel and Information Centre,** at 20 Davey St., tel. (03) 6230-8233, provides information on the city as well as the rest of the state. Staff can make transportation and accommodation bookings throughout Tasmania. It's open Mon.-Fri. 8:30 a.m.-5:15 p.m., Sat.-Sun. 9 a.m.-4 p.m.

Land Information Services, operated by the Department of Environment and Land Management, caretaker of Tasmania's parks, is at 134 Macquarie St., tel. (03) 6233-3382.

Pick up road touring information and maps from the **Royal Automobile Club of Tasmania,** corner Murray and Patrick Streets, tel. (13) 1111.

SOUTH FROM HOBART

Before setting out north from Hobart to Port Arthur and the famous national parks, consider spending a day or two exploring the rugged landscape south of the capital, driving through the apple orchards of the Huon Valley to Cockle Creek, gateway to the vast wilderness of Southwest National Park, or traveling by ferry over to Bruny Island, a sparsely populated island with ample opportunities for exploration.

Kingston

The most direct route south from Hobart is the Huon Highway, but if you're heading out to Bruny Island take the Channel Highway through Kingston to Kettering. The highlight of Kingston is the headquarters of the **Australia Antarctic Division,** on the Channel Hwy., tel. (03) 6232-3209. This center is the base for Australian expeditions heading to Antarctica and provides support services for field stations. Within the complex, a display room open to the public features the history of Australian involvement in Antarctica through photos, maps, and relics. Admission is free and it's open daily 9 a.m.-5 p.m.

BRUNY ISLAND

Lying off the coast immediately south of Hobart, and separated from the mainland by D'Entre-casteaux Channel, this elongated island is almost cut in two by a long isthmus of sand. The island's two halves are very different. In the north, where the passenger-and-vehicle ferry from Kettering docks, the landscape is relatively flat, while in the south the terrain is hilly and almost mountainous with long stretches of beach and rugged headlands along the coast. In 1642 Abel Tasman became the first European to record the island, but it wasn't until 1792, when French Admiral Bruny D'Entrecasteaux charted Tasmania's southwest coast, that it was named. Today, the island's main drawcards are long stretches of golden sand, opportunities for hiking along the beaches and headlands, and abundant birdlife.

Island Sights

Heading south from the ferry terminal, the island's main road passes **Camel Tracks,** tel. (03) 6260-6335, which offers camel rides out to Big Lagoon (one hour; $28 pp) and along the beach (2.5 hours; $45). From Great Bay, the road south traverses a narrow isthmus and **Bruny Island Neck Game Reserve.** Within the reserve is a platform to view the prolific birdlife, including muttonbirds (Sept.-April) and fairy penguins (Sept.-February). Beyond the isthmus are the island's two main communities, **Alonnah** and **Lunawanna.** From Lunawanna, an unsealed road continues south to **Labillardiere State Reserve,** on Great Taylors Bay, where there are a number of short walks. Facing the wild Tasman Sea, on the southern shore of Adventure Bay, is the **Bligh Museum,** tel. (03) 6293-1117, named for Captain Bligh of *Bounty* fame, who visited the island in the 1788. Constructed of bricks salvaged from a nearby convict-built church, this small museum catalogs the island's history. Admission is $3. Open daily 10 a.m.-3 p.m.

Accommodations
Many privately owned cottages can be rented by the night; one of the most comfortable is **St. Clairs,** near Lunawanna, tel. (03) 6293-1300. While only a small, one-bedroom place, it's very comfortable and well equipped; $125 per night. Premium. At the southern end of Adventure Bay are two caravan parks. Best of these is **Adventure Bay Holiday Village,** tel. (03) 6293-1270, with sites for $10-13 and on-site vans and cabins for $40-60. Budget-Inexpensive. Camping is also possible at Neck Beach, on the isthmus, and in the south at Cloudy Bay and Jetty Beach.

Transportation
Ferries to Bruny Island depart Kettering 10 times daily between 7:15 a.m. and 6:30 p.m. The crossing takes 15 minutes. The fare for a vehicle under five meters is $18 roundtrip ($23 on Friday afternoon, Saturday, Sunday, and all public holidays. Bicycles are $3 roundtrip. Foot passengers travel free of charge. For more information, call Bruny Island Ferry Service at (03) 6273-6725.

HUON VALLEY TO THE END OF THE ROAD

The lush Huon Valley, south of Hobart, is dominated by apple orchards. To find out more about the industry, stop by the **Huon Valley Apple and Heritage Museum,** near Grove, tel. (03) 6266-4345, which displays 500 different types of apples—all grown in a nearby orchard—along with an antique apple corer and peeler, apple-picking equipment and graders, and other apple-growing memorabilia. Admission is adult $3, child $1.50. Open daily 9 a.m.-5 p.m. (closed July).

Huonville
This picturesque town (pop. 1,600) on the Huon River 48 km south of Hobart is the hub of the Huon Valley. The river, discovered by Bruny D'Entrecasteaux in 1792, was to provide easy access to the valley, which was blessed with large supplies of Huon pine, a softwood good for construction. The most popular form of recreation in Huonville is the 40-minute jet-boat ride with **Huon Jet,** tel. (03) 6264-1838, which runs over four sets of exciting rapids; adult $40, child $24.

Accommodation in Huonville is limited. The ugly **Grand Hotel,** right downtown at 2 Main Rd., tel. (03) 6264-1004, has rooms with shared facilities for $25 s, $35 d. Budget. With river views, **Huon Manor Restaurant,** corner of Main Rd. and Short St., tel. (03) 6264-1311, is one of the better places in town for a meal. The menu is varied and wine can be ordered by the glass. At lunch, when eating at the outdoor tables is popular, main meals start at $6.50, while in the evening they range $11-16.50. It's open daily for lunch and dinner Mon.-Tues. and Thurs.-Saturday.

Geeveston
South of Huonville is Geeveston, center of a large timber industry and gateway to the rugged Hartz Mountains to the west. A highlight of a visit to town is the **Forest and Heritage Centre,** on Church St., tel. (03) 6297-1836. Displays incorporate the entire history of southwestern Tasmania's forestry through to modern management techniques. Admission is adult $4, child $2.50. In the same complex is an information center (with maps of surrounding forest drives) and an arts and crafts outlet. Hiking trails leading from the information center take you through various forest environments and to a lookout high above the rainforest canopy. Open daily 10 a.m.-4:30 p.m.

The Glades, Church St., tel. (03) 6297-1834, offers a range of delicious meals in a delightful atmosphere; on colder days the staff will stoke the fireplace. Open daily for lunch and dinner.

Hartz Mountains National Park
Making up only a tiny portion of the Tasmanian Wilderness World Heritage Area, and adjacent to the vast wilderness of Southwest National Park, this small 7,226-hectare park 25 km west of

Geeveston boasts many good hikes and, unlike most of the World Heritage Area, is easily accessible. The park's rugged landscape was carved by glaciers, with extremes in weather finishing the job. The rugged snowcapped peaks rise above deep gorges and plateaus of alpine heathland. Within the park are short but strenuous hikes, the most spectacular ending atop mountain ridges. All hiking trails are well defined and geographical features signposted. The most popular trail leads to the 1,255-meter summit of **Hartz Peak.** From the trailhead to the summit takes about two hours each way, but there are many tempting detours to be made, including to **Lakes Esperance, Osborne,** and **Hartz.**

The park's only facility area is at **Waratah Lookout,** where there are picnic facilities. The park has no campground. For further information, contact the ranger at (03) 6298-1577.

Dover

The small port of Dover, on the Huon Hwy. 25 km south of Geeveston, developed around the logging of Huon pine, which was processed in town, then transported to East Asian and European markets. Today, the town's main industry is the farming of Atlantic salmon.

As Dover is a popular tourist spot, there are a number of accommodations. Pick of the bunch is **Driftwood Holiday Cottages,** Bay View Rd., tel. (03) 6298-1441, with outstanding views of Esperance Bay. The units are modern, each featuring interior furnishings in a different native timber. Rates are $100 s, $120 d. Expensive. On Main Rd., and also overlooking Esperance Bay, is **Dover Hotel,** tel. (03) 6298-1210. Rooms are basic, and many share bathrooms, but the location is right and within the complex is a bar and restaurant. Rates, with breakfast included, start at $30 pp. Inexpensive. **Dover Beachside Caravan Park,** tel. (03) 6298-1301, has an absolute waterfront location and a good grassed area set aside for tent campers. Sites range $8-10, onsite vans are $30, and cabins are $52. Budget.

Hastings Caves and Vicinity

South of Dover and 10 km west of the Huon Highway is Hastings Caves State Reserve, tel.

(03) 6298-3209, which protects a number of caves including the magnificent **Newdegate Cave,** alive with formations that have evolved through thousands of years of water seeping through the dolomite bedrock. Tours of this cave (45 minutes) are offered four to six times daily; adult $10, child $5.

On the road leading to the caves are thermal springs that bubble out of the ground at about 28° C (82° F). A pool area has been developed around them. Admission is adult $2.50, child $1.50. The pool is open daily 10 a.m.-4 p.m., until 6 p.m. in summer.

Continuing South

Beyond **Southport** the road turns to gravel and makes a detour around Southport Bay to Lune River and ends 30 km farther south at Cockle Creek, Australia's southernmost point accessible by vehicle.

The 16-km **Ida Bay Railway,** tel. (03) 6298-3110, departs Lune River every Sunday at 10:30 a.m., noon, 1:30 p.m., and 3 p.m. (additional trips are made in summer on Wednesday and Saturday) for Deep Hole Bay and a delightful little beach. The roundtrip fare is adult $10, child $5. Immediately south of town is **Lune River Cottage,** tel. (03) 6298-3107, offering comfortable accommodations in five rooms; $35 s, $62 d, includes breakfast. Inexpensive. Lune River also has a YHA hostel, tel. (03) 6298-3163, but it's a bit rough around the edges. Camping free of charge is possible at **Gilliams** and **Finns Beaches,** farther south.

Walking opportunities present themselves at Cockle Creek. One of the shorter trails leads to Fishers Point, northeast of Cockle Creek and an easy 40-minute walk from the end of the road. Hiking along the final section of the 170-km South West Track is also rewarding, with the first section, to South Cape Bay (seven km oneway), taking about two hours.

Southwest National Park

The massive wilderness protected by this 605,000-hectare park is accessible on foot from Cockle Creek or by road west from Hobart. For further information on the park, see below.

TASMANIA'S EAST COAST AND THE MIDLANDS

Tasmania's east coast is blessed with some of the state's best beaches, but before rushing north for swimming and sunbaking, plan to make a detour to Tasmania's most-visited attraction, Port Arthur, on the Tasman Peninsula, site of a penal colony built to contain convicts who had re-offended upon arriving in Australia. The road north from the Tasman Peninsula makes a wide loop inland before passing offshore Maria Island, also formerly penal settlement. One of Tasmania's premier natural features is the Freycinet Peninsula, protected as a national park and accessible only on foot. North of the peninsula is a string of seaside resort towns, including Bicheno, and a great inland wilderness. For those with limited time, the inland route between Hobart and Launceston, through the midlands, is interesting for some of Tasmania's best-preserved historic towns.

HOBART TO PORT ARTHUR

The main highway along the east coast, the Tasman Highway, begins in downtown Hobart, crosses the Tasman Bridge and continues past the airport to a long causeway spanning the wide mouth of the Coal River. The causeway, built in 1866, shortened the trip along the coast considerably, cutting out a long inland detour through Richmond. At the end of the causeway is **Sorell**, an agricultural service center of 3,000. From Sorell, it's 42 km along the Arthur Highway to Dunalley, gateway to the Forestier and Tasman Peninsulas. An alternate route east follows the coastline of Frederick Henry Bay through Dodges Ferry and along the mouth of the Carlton River. A side road over the river leads eight km to **Primrose Sands Coastal Reserve.** From the top of the protected dune system, the panorama extends along a magnificent beach and over Frederick Henry Bay to Green Head on the Tasman Peninsula.

Copping
If you are traveling to the Tasman Peninsula along the more direct Tasman Highway, take time to stop at the **Colonial and Convict Exhibition,** in Copping, tel. (03) 6253-5373, featuring an eclectic collection of convict-era relics, much of it from the Tasman Peninsula. Admission $6. Open daily 9 a.m.-5 p.m.

Forestier Peninsula
This wide peninsula is more like an island, joined to the mainland by an isthmus at Dunalley. The Tasman Highway runs across the peninsula, under the shadow of 319-meter Mt. Forestier, and over **Eaglehawk Neck,** a narrow isthmus linking the peninsula to Tasman Peninsula. The seaward side of this link is the long curve of **Pirates Bay.** At the bay's northern end is the **Tessellated Pavement,** a stretch of vertically cracked sandstone beds that have further eroded to form an intriguing natural mosaic. Search out the abundant marinelife in adjacent rock pools at low tide. **Eaglehawk Neck Backpackers,** tel. (03) 6250-3248, is a great little place featuring two cabins, each with a kitchen and living room. The friendly owners are a great source of information on outdoor recreation in the region. Beds are $14 pp per night. Budget.

Pirates Bay to Port Arthur
Over the narrow bridge linking the two peninsulas a road spurs southeast to a number of natural geologic formations, the result of relentless wave action into the soft sandstone. From north to south, they are: **Tasman Blowhole, Tasman Arch,** and **Devil's Kitchen.**

The first town beyond Eaglehawk Neck is **Taranna,** terminus of Australia's first railway. The railway was built to transport convicts and supplies across the peninsula to Port Arthur, saving a hazardous journey by ship around the coast. **Tasmanian Devil Park,** tel. (03) 6250-3230, on the site of an old Aboriginal camp site, features Tasmanian animals, including the park's namesake, kangaroos, wallabies, and wombats, and a variety of birds. Admission is a bit steep at adult $10, child $5, especially if you miss feeding time (daily 10 and 11 a.m.). Open daily 9 a.m.-5 p.m. **Norfolk**

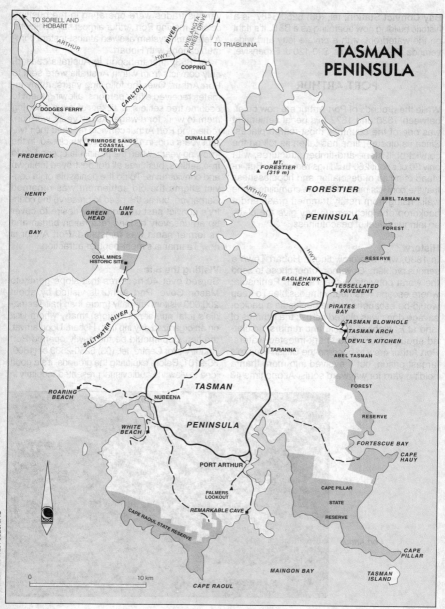

TASMAN PENINSULA

TO SORELL AND HOBART

ARTHUR HWY

IWELANGTA FOREST DRIVE

RIVER

TO TRIABUNNA

COPPING

DODGES FERRY

CARLTON

DUNALLEY

FREDERICK

PRIMROSE SANDS COASTAL RESERVE

MT. FORESTIER (319 m)

HENRY

ARTHUR HWY

FORESTIER PENINSULA

ABEL TASMAN FOREST

BAY

GREEN HEAD

LIME BAY

COAL MINES HISTORIC SITE

SALTWATER RIVER

ABEL TASMAN FOREST

RESERVE

EAGLEHAWK NECK

TESSELLATED PAVEMENT

PIRATES BAY

TASMAN BLOWHOLE

TASMAN ARCH

DEVIL'S KITCHEN

TARANNA

ROARING BEACH

NUBEENA

TASMAN

PENINSULA

WHITE BEACH

FORTESCUE BAY

CAPE HAUY

RESERVE

PORT ARTHUR

PALMERS LOOKOUT

REMARKABLE CAVE

CAPE RAOUL STATE RESERVE

CAPE PILLAR STATE RESERVE

MAINGON BAY

CAPE RAOUL

TASMAN ISLAND

CAPE PILLAR

0   10 km

MOON

© AVALON TRAVEL PUBLISHING

Bay Convict Station, tel. (03) 6250-3487, is a historic building now operating as a B&B. It's right on the waterfront, with a private jetty and wide veranda. Rates are $70 s, $90-120 d. Expensive.

PORT ARTHUR

While the grounds of Port Arthur are now quiet, between 1830 and 1877 this penal settlement was one of the country's most-feared places. Since its closure, time has taken its toll on the convict-built stone-and-timber structures, with only 30 of about 260 buildings remaining. But, instead of an air of desolation and hopelessness that the convicts must of felt, the crumbling stone walls rising from neatly trimmed grass and a backdrop of a picturesque bay give the place an intriguing feel of peacefulness.

History

In 1830, with overcrowding in Hobart Town a serious problem, Governor Arthur chose to send the worst convicts to the Tasman Peninsula, where escape was nearly impossible. To keep would-be escapees on the peninsula a pack of savage dogs was placed across the isthmus of land at Eaglehawk Neck, and rumors circulated about surrounding shark-infested waters. Port Arthur grew to become the British Empire's largest prison, but it evolved into more than a holding yard for wayward souls. At one time 43

various trades were operating in the bustling colony, making Port Arthur almost self-sufficient. A telegraph system allowed almost-instant communications with Hobart.

In 1853, after transport to Australia ceased, only convicts from within Australia were sent to Port Arthur. Over the following years, many inmates received either pardons, allowing them to become free settlers, or tickets of leave, allowing them to work for a wage. As the years wore on, remaining Port Arthur convicts reached their twilight years and, in 1877, Port Arthur closed. In the following years, when the peninsula opened up to free settlers, bushfires all but destroyed the town and convict ruins. To rid the peninsula of its convict stigma the old settlement was renamed Carnarvon, but as the need to preserve the country's convict past overtook any desire to cover up an unsavory history, restoration began and its former name was reinstated. Port Arthur is now Tasmania's most-popular attraction.

Visiting the Site

Spread over 40 hectares that slope gently to Mason Cove, Port Arthur is visited by about 200,000 visitors annually (more than half Tasmania's total number of visitors), many whom visit on an organized day trip from Hobart. Upon arrival, the first stop should be the newly opened Port Arthur Visitor Centre, tel. (03) 6250-2539 or (1800) 65-9101. Before exploring the grounds, it's a good idea to view the audiovisual presented regularly in

Port Arthur

JANE KING

the Asylum, built for the mentally ill in 1867 and now also containing a museum. Take one of the guided tours (free with admission) that depart regularly through the day or wander around at your own pace with one of the many information sheets available. Admission is adult $16, child $8. The site is open daily 9 a.m.-5 p.m. After hours, no admission is charged, but there is no access to the many buildings open through daylight hours. Within the grounds are cafés and restaurants as well as souvenir shops and a couple of outlets selling the works of local artisans.

Port Arthur Penal Settlement

Isle of the Dead, a small offshore island, was the burial grounds for convicts and free settlers of Port Arthur. Cruises out to the island depart the wharf immediately east of the Information Office daily at noon and 4:30 p.m.

PORT ARTHUR'S "MODEL PRISON"

In the half-century that Port Arthur served as a penal settlement, about 12,500 of Australia's worst convicts served time at the prison. Those sent to Port Arthur were generally hardened criminals who had re-offended upon arriving in Australia. The worst of these convicts spent their days in chains, building stone structures and roads. Until 1848, those who offended *again* were subjected to a flogging. These took place on Sunday, after a compulsory church service, and with the other convicts watching.

After flogging was abolished, in 1848, a new form of punishment was devised: solitary confinement in the Model Prison. Convicts feared it more than a good flogging. Upon being sent to the Model Prison, convicts were stripped of their identities, their names replaced by numbers. They were confined to a tiny cell 23 hours of every day, permitted one hour of exercise daily in the confines of a walled yard while wearing a head mask, banned from talking, and fed a diet of bread and water.

The cost of this cruise is included in the general admission.

Entertainment

Not all the action at Port Arthur takes place during the hours of daylight. In the years since the penal colony closed, many ghostly apparitions have been reported around the grounds. **Historic Ghost Tours,** departing nightly at 8:30 p.m. (9:30 p.m. during daylight saving) from the Information Office, allow you the opportunity to, maybe, view the apparitions. Adult $12, child $8. Make bookings at the Information Office or by calling (03) 6250-2539.

Another form of entertainment is to view the original 1926 version of *For the Term of his Natural Life,* based on convict life at Port Arthur and filmed on location. The film is shown throughout the day in the museum. Admission is $5. The film is also screened on in-house televisions for guests of the Port Arthur Motor Inn.

Accommodations

Port Arthur is an easy day trip from Hobart, but the Tasman Peninsula has enough attractions to keep you busy for two or even three days. A few peninsula townships have accommodations, and right at Port Arthur there are a couple of choices. Closest to the historic site is **Port Arthur Motor Inn,** on a high ridge overlooking the site, tel. (03) 6250-2101. Rooms are pricey, at $100 s, $110 d, but comfortable, and there's a restaurant. Expensive.

The grandly named **Port Arthur Holiday World,** about 700 meters from the historic site, tel. (03) 6250-2262, overlooks delightful Stewarts Bay. Accommodations are in attractive self-contained log cabins scattered through native bush. Rates are a reasonable $90-120 per night depending on cabin size. These cabins are a great deal and therefore advance reservations will be needed. Expensive. **Fox & Hounds Resort,** two km north of Port Arthur, tel. (03) 6250-2217, has motel rooms for $80-90 and self-contained villas with cooking facilities from $110. Moderate.

On the same road as Port Arthur Motor Inn, and overlooking the historic site, is **Port Arthur YHA,** tel. (03) 6250-2311, a mustard-colored two-story historic building complete with creaking hallways and steep stairwells leading to dark rooms. Rates are $12 pp. Budget.

The expansive **Port Arthur Caravan and Cabin Park** is out on Garden Pt., two km from Port Arthur, tel. (03) 6250-2340. The park is well maintained, and facilities, including two kitchens, barbecues, kiosk, and laundry, are excellent. Tent sites are $11, powered sites $12 ($18 with private bathroom), and cabins $50. Also offered are dorm beds for $13 pp. Budget. A coastal walking track links the campground to Port Arthur Historic Site; 40 minutes each way.

Food
Within the historic site are a number of eateries, including **Frances Langford Tearooms,** in a stone structure built originally as policemen's living quarters. Light lunches and Devonshire teas are served daily 10 a.m.-5 p.m. **Kelley's,** at Port Arthur Holiday World, tel. (03) 6250-2666, is in a spectacular log building with seating indoors or out on a covered deck. Tasmanian seafood is the specialty, with main dishes starting at $17, which includes salad, chips, and freshly baked bread. The restaurant in the **Port Arthur Motor Inn,** tel. (03) 6250-2101, has expansive views across the historic site and a typical motel restaurant-style menu, and is priced accordingly. Dinner plates average $18. The motor inn pub also serves meals; they are less expensive than the restaurant's and the views are better.

Transportation
The only way to visit Port Arthur from Hobart and return the same day is on an organized tour. The best of these are run by **Hobart Sightseeing Tours,** tel. (03) 6231-3511, and **Tigerline,** tel. (1300) 65-3633. Tours cost $38-60 depending on inclusions, and pickups at Hobart accommodations are complimentary. **Hobart Coaches,** tel. (03) 6234-4077, runs once a day Mon.-Fri. between Hobart and Port Arthur. **Peninsula Coach Service,** tel. (03) 6250-3186, runs from the Hobart Transit Centre to Port Arthur and also makes drops at the hostel.

OTHER SIGHTS ON THE TASMAN PENINSULA

Fortescue Bay and Vicinity
This deep coastal indent lies on the east coast of an arm of the Tasman Peninsula 20 km east of Port Arthur. It's a beautiful place: clear water lapping against a beach of golden sand and backed by towering eucalypts. A campground lies in the bay's protected southern corner; cost is $6 pp, which includes one wheelbarrow filled with firewood. **Cape Hauy** is a pleasant walk from the campground; allow two hours each way. South of the bay is **Cape Pillar State Reserve,** a tract of wilderness reached only on foot. The track out to Cape Pillar is 16 km each way, too far to return in one day, but perfect for an overnight hike.

Remarkable Cave
South from Port Arthur, the main road passes a golf course, then skirts the shore of Safety Bay before cutting across a narrow neck of land to scenic Basket Bay, where sheer cliffs drop into the ocean. A steep path leads down to sea level where at low tide Remarkable Cave is exposed. From the road into the cave, a two-km side road leads to **Palmers Lookout,** comprising well-manicured gardens and a barbecue area. Views from the lookout extend to Port Arthur, the Isle of the Dead, and across Maingon Bay to Tasman Island Lighthouse.

Port Arthur to Saltwater River
From Port Arthur, the road westbound cuts across a wide section of the peninsula to **Nubeena.** Coastal access is possible along hiking trails in **Cape Raoul State Reserve** and at **White Beach,** where there's a caravan park, tel. (03) 6250-2142, fronting a nice sandy beach. Beyond Nubeena a gravel road leads to **Roaring Beach,** a windswept stretch of sand that catches all the swell.

When Port Arthur was a penal colony many other convict outposts were scattered around the Tasman Peninsula. The most important of these was beyond Saltwater River at Plunkett Point, where coal was discovered in 1833. It's now preserved as 214-hectare **Coal Mines His-**

toric Site. In typical colonial fashion, when a coal deposit was discovered, Governor Arthur requested that a convict with coal-mining experience examine the site for its mining potential. Deeming it good, gangs of convicts were sent to begin mining. At peak production, around 50 tons of coal were excavated daily and loaded directly onto ships bound for Hobart Town. Like Port Arthur, fire and vandalism have taken their toll on the site.

At **Lime Bay,** beyond the mining area, is a pleasant campground set behind a sandy beach and among boulders and trees.

TASMAN PENINSULA TO TRIABUNNA

To continue north from the Tasman Peninsula along sealed road entails a detour inland, back through Sorell. The alternative is **Wielangta Forest Drive,** a winding gravel road spurring off the main highway west of Copping. First stop should be the **Wielangta Forest,** where a one-km (roundtrip) trail leads through a forest of towering eucalypts. The trailhead is south of Robertson Bridge, one of the state's longest log bridges. As the road climbs from the forest, the panorama of the coastline and offshore Maria Island come into view. After crossing Sandspit River, the road forks. Take the eastern option, which parallels the coast and passes access tracks to numerous beaches. **Spring Beach** is particularly scenic and is a popular surfing spot.

Triabunna

On the far reaches of Spring Bay, this small village was established in the 1800s as a mainland base for shipping supplies and convicts to offshore Maria Island (see below), and is today home to a small fleet of cray, abalone, and scallop boats.

Surrounded by pastureland, **Triabunna YHA,** Spencer St., tel. (03) 6257-3439, across Maclaines Creek from the center of town, is picturesque. Facilities are basic but comfortable. Dorm and twin beds are $10-14 pp. Budget. **Tandara Motor Inn,** on the north side of town, tel. (03) 6257-3333, has a pool, barbecue, and laundry; $55 s, $65 d. Moderate.

MARIA ISLAND NATIONAL PARK

This hourglass-shaped island, 15 km east of the mainland, is protected as national park. The island is much altered from its original state and has seen a tumultuous history, but, still, it remains an excellent destination ideal for exploration on foot. The island can be visited as a day trip or an overnight excursion for those prepared to camp or stay in rustic dorm-style accommodations. Transport to the island is on a ferry (foot passengers only) that departs regularly from south of Triabunna.

The island is 20 km from north to south and about 13 km at its widest point. A narrow isthmus of sand, pushed above sea level by wind and wave action, is the island's most interesting natural feature. This narrow strip of sand links what around 10,000 years ago would have been two separate islands, which in turn were part of mainland Tasmania many millions of years ago.

convict-built barn, Maria Island

While some species of larger mammals such as wombats, echidnas, and pademelons are native to the island, others such as the Forester kangaroo and Bennett's wallaby were introduced in the 1960s when the island was first declared a wildlife reserve. Maria Island is good for birdwatching enthusiasts; some of the more interesting species present include the albatross, gannet, muttonbird, and Japanese snipe. Like the mammal population, some bird species have been introduced, including the Cape Barren goose, first introduced to the island in 1968.

History

Maria Island was the site of Tasmania's second penal colony, established in 1825 at Darlington, on a bay in the northwest. The settlement was short-lived, closing seven years later, then reopening for a few years in the 1840s. In 1884 Italian entrepreneur Diego Bernacchi arrived on the island, setting up winegrowing and silk industries. He renovated many of the deserted convict buildings, and with grand expectations renamed the settlement San Diego. Business for Bernacchi started well enough, but by the end of the century he left the island, returning after WW I to use the island's abundant limestone deposits to establish a cement works. A wildlife reserve was first established in the 1960s, and in 1972 the entire 9,672-hectare island was declared a national park.

Buildings from the convict era remain in varying states of disrepair, some having been restored as accommodations and to serve park staff.

Hiking

The island offers many hiking opportunities, and those staying on the island overnight have the chance to explore farther afield. One of the most popular short hikes is to the **Fossil Cliffs** (two km each way), where hundreds of ancient shell fragments are embedded in a cliff face. A hike of a similar distance is to the **Painted Cliffs,** a sandstone headland sharply eroded and covered in colorful patterns left by iron and magnesium oxides.

Beyond the Fossil Cliffs, a moderately steep trail continues a farther steep two km to the summit of **Bishop and Clerk Mountain,** at the north end of a high ridge. From this peak, views extend north to the Freycinet Peninsula. Farther south along this ridge is the island's highest peak, **Mt.**

Maria (709 meters). From Darlington, this peak is eight km each way (allow five to six hours for the roundtrip), with the final ascent up a scree slope. The walk to the sandy isthmus is 12 km each way, making the return trip to Darlington a long day hike. At the isthmus are two campgrounds; these provide a good base for exploring the island's southern reaches.

Accommodations

Accommodation on the island is in convict-built structures converted to bunkhouses. These are often booked out by groups, so call ahead to reserve a bed. Bunk beds are $8 pp per night. All rooms are sparse; you must bring your own linen or sleeping bag, lantern or flashlight (no electricity), and cooking utensils and camp stove. Budget. A nearby campground has toilets, fresh water, and gas barbecues (bring change for these); sites are $6 pp. No supplies are available on the island. For all bookings and further information call the park ranger at (03) 6257-1420.

If you'd prefer to stay on the mainland, visiting the island for just the day, consider staying at **Eastcoaster Resort,** tel. (03) 6257-1172, right at the ferry terminal. This large holiday resort features indoor and outdoor pools, a tennis court, squash, golf, spa and sauna, bar, and restaurant. Standard rooms, each with a kitchen and comfortable furnishings, are $95 s or d (less in the off season). Expensive.

Transportation, Services, and Information

The 15-km crossing of the Mercury Passage takes about 20 minutes aboard the *Eastcoaster Express,* tel. (03) 6257-1172, operated by the Eastcoaster Resort. The roundtrip fare is adult $20, kids $13. A bike or kayak is an additional $3. Departure times vary with the season and weather conditions, but there are generally at least four sailings daily; call ahead for details of the current timetable.

Built in 1825, the sturdy **Commissariat Store** now serves as a **park information center.** The center features a large relief map of the island and a photography display of island highlights. Between December and Easter the center is open daily 9:30 a.m.-4:30 p.m. At other times of the year, it's open weekends only. To contact the ranger call (03) 6257-1420.

SWANSEA

The small town of Swansea (pop. 550) overlooks the protected waters of Great Oyster Bay 140 km north of Hobart. It's along a stretch of coast popular with holidaymakers. The area was first settled in 1821, and Swansea grew as a rural service center. The oldest remaining building in Swansea is Morris Store, built in 1834. The highlight of a visit to town is **Swansea Bark Mill,** on the Tasman Hwy. north of town, tel. (03) 6257-8382. Built in 1885, the mill crushed bark to extract the tannic acid that was then used in the tanning of leather. Admission adult $5, child $2.75. Open daily 9 a.m.-5 p.m. In the same complex is **Swansea Wine and Wool Centre,** selling wine and sheepskin products, and a small café open daily for lunch. A **museum** is housed in the 1860 Swansea School House, on Franklin Street. It features many relics from the town's past, but the highlight is an oversized billiards table dating from 1860 ($2 a game). Admission to the museum is $5.

Accommodations and Food

Although Swansea has a couple of motels, a better choice would be to stay in one of the many historic accommodations. **Oyster Bay Guest House,** 10 Franklin St., tel. (03) 6257-8110, dating from 1836, is one of Swansea's oldest buildings. Guests have a choice of 10 simple but well-furnished rooms, while downstairs there's a small guest lounge with fireplace, and a popular restaurant. Rates start at $50 s with shared facilities, and the double rooms, which open to a veranda and spectacular views, are $90. All rates include a cooked breakfast. Moderate. Another good choice is two-story **Schouten House,** 1 Waterloo Rd., tel. (03) 6257-8564, which offers spacious rooms with private bathrooms for $126 s or d, including a cooked breakfast. Premium. **Central Swansea Backpackers,** 20 Franklin St., tel. (03) 6257-8399, is a rambling old house that dates from 1860. Views from the wide front veranda extend across the bay, and inside there are a number of comfortable living areas. Rates start at $12 pp per night. Budget. Also overlooking the bay is **Swansea Caravan Park and Holiday Village,** Shaw St., tel. (03) 6257-8177, with a beach frontage. Facilities include a heated pool, lounge room, kitchen, barbecue area, and laundry. Tent sites, right on the beach, are $12, powered sites are $15, and cabins range $40-70. Budget-Inexpensive.

For its size, Swansea has a surprising number of eateries. One of the most popular is **Maggie's,** on Franklin Street. The **Old Swan Inn,** 1 Franklin St., offers counter meals Mon.-Sat. noon-2 p.m. and daily 6:15-8:15 p.m. **Shy Albatross Restaurant,** in the Oyster Bay Guest House at 10 Franklin St., tel. (03) 6257-8110, is open daily for dinner. The menu features mostly pasta ($8-12), with daily specials, usually steak, chicken, and seafood dishes ($16-19).

FREYCINET NATIONAL PARK

This magnificent park protects an elongated peninsula that juts southward from Tasmania's east coast. The park is undeveloped and penetrated only partway by road. This leaves the rest of the park to be explored on foot, including famous **Wineglass Bay,** a stretch of golden sand flanked by rugged peaks of granite. The park encompasses 10,100 hectares, extending the length of the peninsula from the small town of **Coles Bay,** 205 km north of Hobart. In the north is the Hazards, a steep rocky ridge. This part of the park is separated from the southern end of the peninsula by a isthmus flanked by Wineglass Bay in the east and Hazards Beach in the west. Across the isthmus is another range of mountains, dominated by 620-meter **Mt. Freycinet.** Off the peninsula's southern extremity is **Schouten Island,** also part of the park.

Around 50 million years ago massive forces deep below the earth's surface thrust sections of Tasmania skyward. One section was the Freycinet Peninsula. In the time that has elapsed since, erosion has worn the mountaintops to their present level. When sea levels rose around 10,000 years ago they cut the peninsula in two places, creating two islands. Sand has since built up south of the Hazards, forming a peninsula, but Schouten Island remains separated.

The park features diverse habitats, ranging from low shrublands in exposed areas to forests of eucalypt and profusions of orchids in protected gullies. Wildlife is plentiful throughout the park, with dawn and dusk the best times for

FREYCINET NATIONAL PARK

© AVALON TRAVEL PUBLISHING

turous, it's possible to climb 331-meter **Mt. Parsons** in about an hour.

Freycinet's best-known feature, **Wineglass Bay,** is a popular destination with day-hikers. The hike starts with a gentle climb to a low pass of the Hazards, where the panorama of the bay unfolds in all its glory. From the lookout, the trail descends to the golden sands of the bay, perfect for a day's sunbaking and swimming. At the beach's southern end are the remains of a cutter that wrecked on the peninsula in 1885. The trek between the parking lot and Wineglass Bay takes 60-90 minutes each way. A good alternative to returning along the same route is taking the Isthmus Track from Wineglass Bay across to Hazards Bay, returning to the parking lot on the Hazards Beach Track. The entire circuit is just over nine km; allow three hours without stops. For experienced hikers, it is possible to complete the **Peninsula Track** in one long day, but most will find it more comfortable to extend the trip to two days, camping at Cooks Beach. The high point of this trek is 579-meter Mt. Graham, from where views extend west across Great Oyster Bay and south to Schouten Island.

Freycinet Experience, tel. (03) 6223-7565 or (1800) 50-6003, offers an excellent four-day hiking trip through the park. Hikers stay the first two nights in comfortable tent camps and the last in an attractive, environmentally friendly lodge overlooking Friendly Beaches. The trip costs $1,095 pp all-inclusive, including transfers from Hobart.

Accommodations and Food
A campground is on the park access road, and six other backcountry campgrounds are scattered through the park. **Freycinet Lodge,** tel. (03) 6257-0101, comprises 60 comfortable cabins (30 with kitchen facilities and some with spa baths) designed to blend into the environment. Guests have use of a tennis court, recreation room, and laundry. Rates range $155-200 s or d, and include use of all facilities and the services of a naturalist who leads short interpretive hikes in the vicinity of the lodge.

Coles Bay has no motels, but **Coles Bay Caravan Park,** tel. (03) 6257-0100, has backpacker beds for $15 pp and a few on-site vans for $30. Campsites here are $11-13. Budget. Also in Coles Bay is a general store selling basic groceries and

viewing resident fauna. Commonly sighted are a variety of possums, Tasmanian devils, pademelons, Bennett's wallabies, wombats, sugar-gliders, and quolls.

Sights and Hikes
The park's only access road ends at Parsons Cove, five km south of Coles Bay. This road passes a couple of beautiful spots including **Honeymoon Bay,** a sandy beach flanked by rocky headlands. The road out to Cape Tourville skirts **Sleepy Bay,** a pleasant stretch of sand with rock ledges at either end that are perfect for exploration at low tide. For the more adven-

camping supplies. The only places open for regular meals are the bistro and restaurant in **Freycinet Lodge,** where main dishes range $13-22.

Transportation, Services, and Information

Getting to the park by public transport is possible but time-consuming. From Hobart, you'll need to get yourself to Bicheno aboard either a **Tasmanian Redline Coaches** or **Hobart Coaches** service, then jump aboard one of the **Bicheno Coach Services** buses, tel. (03) 6357-0293, with two daily connections to Coles Bay. Between Monday and Friday this company offers transport (on demand) between Coles Bay (departs 9:40 a.m.) and the national park; book ahead. **Freycinet Air,** tel. (03) 6375-1694, offers scenic flights over the park, such as a 30-minute flight over Wineglass Bay for $70 pp.

The **ranger station,** at the park entrance, is open in summer daily 8:30 a.m.-5 p.m. and the rest of the year daily 9 a.m.-noon. Park entry is $9 per vehicle. Available at the ranger station is *Freycinet Map and Notes,* good for those planning extensive hiking. To contact the ranger or any of his friendly staff call (03) 6257-0107.

BICHENO

As early as 1800, sealers and whalers used the natural harbor around which Bicheno now lies as shelter from rough seas. No permanent settlement was established until 1854, when the bay was used as a port for loading coal mined nearby. In the time since, Bicheno (pop. 700) has grown to become one of Tasmania's busiest holiday towns, with tourism, along with fishing, most important to the local economy.

Sights

One of the greatest joys in Bicheno is exploring the town's natural surroundings, walking along the waterfront south to a blowhole and to Courlands Bay. From **Freycinet Lookout,** west of town, views extend south to the high peaks of Freycinet National Park. At low tide it's possible to walk over to **Diamond Island** where a colony of fairy penguins have their burrows. Back in town is the **Sea Life Centre,** tel. (03) 6375-1121, with a motley collection of marinelife, including cray-

fish and seahorses. Also on display is a restored ketch. Admission is a bit steep at $4.50. Open daily 9 a.m.-5 p.m.

Bicheno Penguin and Adventure Tours, tel. (03) 6375-1333, offers a variety of activities in the area, including a nightly Penguin Walk ($12 pp), horseback riding, game fishing in season, and flightseeing.

Accommodations and Food

Accommodation outside of the caravan parks is limited to a few motels. Pick of the bunch is the **Wintersun Gardens Motel,** 35 Gordon St., tel. (03) 6375-1225, north of downtown, which has standard rooms for $45 s, $60 d. Inexpensive. Closer to the center of town is **Silver Sands Resort,** Burgess St., tel. (03) 6375-1266, with basic but clean and comfortable rooms, many with ocean views, for $65 s, $75 d. Moderate. **Bicheno Cabins and Tourist Park,** 4 Champ St., tel. (03) 6375-1117 or (1800) 30-2075, is a large campground with sites for $11-13 and good cabins for $50-75. Budget-Inexpensive.

NORTH FROM BICHENO

Douglas-Apsley National Park

North of Bicheno the Tasman Highway closely follows the coastline, with 16,080-hectare Douglas-Apsley National Park, a vast tract of undisturbed forest, west of the highway. The park only came into being in 1989, and hiking and camping facilities are limited. The park is named for two main watersheds that rise in the west of the park, flowing eastward through deep gorges where pockets of rainforest thrive. Access at the Douglas River includes a couple of short trails, including one leading to a deep aqua-colored waterhole. Above the main waterhole are smaller pools and good views of the Douglas River Valley. Near the trailhead is a campground with basic facilities. The other park access is along a gravel road north of Seymour.

St. Marys

At the headwaters of the South Esk River system and 10 km inland is St. Marys, lying in the shadow of the Mt. Nicholas Range.

The town developed as the eastern terminus of a rail line and is still today an important transportation hub, as it lies at the intersection of the Tasman Highway and the A4, which follows the South Esk River to **Fingal,** a coal-mining town, and links up to the busy Midlands Highway.

St. Marys Hotel, Main St., tel. (03) 6372-2181, has rooms from $25 s, $40 d and serves good pub-style counter meals. Budget. The other accommodation option is **Seaview Farm Lodge,** a backpackers on German Town Rd. eight km north of town, tel. (03) 6372-2341. The location, on a sheep farm with panoramic coastal views, is magnificent. Dorm beds are $11 pp, and there are a few units for $22 s, $37 d. Budget-Inexpensive.

Scamander

This small resort town at the mouth of the Scamander River halfway between St. Marys and St. Helens is on a picturesque stretch of coast. The town features many delightful beaches and bream fishing in the river. A good place to stay is **Scamander Kookaburra Caravan Park,** right on the beach one km north of town, tel. (03) 6372-5121. Sites are $10 and the few basic on-site vans are $28. Budget. **Scamander Beach Resort,** tel. (03) 6372-5255, is beside the mouth of the Scamander River, making it a good base for walking, river and beach swimming, or fishing. Rates are $75-85 s or d, but standby rates can be as low as $60. Moderate.

St. Helens and Vicinity

Although away from the ocean beaches, St. Helens (pop. 1,200) is a popular coastal resort at the head of narrow Georges Bay. Established as a whaling station in the 1830s, the local economy still relies heavily on the ocean's renewable resources, and today St. Helens boasts the state's largest fishing fleet. The town itself has little of interest, and the best beaches are east of town along Georges Bay. **St. Helen's History Room,** 59 Cecilia St., tel. (03) 6376-1744, features the local history with lots of photos and an audiovisual. Admission is adult $4, child $2. It's open Mon.-Fri. 9 a.m.-4 p.m., Saturday 9 a.m.-1 p.m. South of town, the road continues beyond the airport to **St. Helen's Point,** winding past some decent sandy beaches and the massive Peron Dunes. From the end of the road a short trail leads past a rocky point to **Beerbarrel Beach.** The road along the north side of Georges

Bay leads to **Humbug Point State Recreation Area,** passing good beaches at Binalong Bay. Within the recreation area are many good day-use areas and beachfront camping at Dora Point and Moulting Bay (bring drinking water from St. Helens). The coastline within the recreation area comprises many short stretches of pristine beach as well as protected coves perfect for exploring on foot.

St. Helens has a variety of inexpensive lodgings, and although there is a caravan park, campers should head out to Humbug Point (described above). The least expensive place to stay in town is **St. Helens Hotel/Motel,** 49 Cecilia St., tel. (03) 6376-1133, where rooms start at $25 s, $45 d. Inexpensive. Also central is the comfortable **Artnor Lodge** at 71 Cecilia St., tel. (03) 6376-1234. Rooms with shared facilities are $40 s, $50 d; private facilities $50 s, $60-70 d. Inexpensive. All rates include breakfast. **Warrawee,** tel. (03) 6376-1987, is an old guesthouse on a few hectares overlooking Georges Bay south of town. Rates start at $65 s, $90 d, including a cooked breakfast. Moderate. For a feed of locally caught seafood, head to **Tidal Water Restaurant,** on the corner of the main highway and Jason St., tel. (03) 6376-1100; it's open for dinner from 6 p.m.

West from St. Helens

From St. Helens the highway veers inland, following the George River through rolling hills to a high pass before descending to plains that slope gently to Bass Strait. In **Pyengana,** just off the highway 24 km west of St. Helens, is **Healey's Pyengana Cheese Factory,** tel. (03) 6373-6157, a great spot for cheese lovers to sample delicious cheddar cheeses made the traditional way from pasteurized milk and salt. The factory is open daily 9 a.m.-6 p.m. The last edition mentioned the picturesque **Pub in the Paddock,** tel. (03) 6373-6121, and its resident beer-drinking pig. The pig has passed on and is buried by the front drive, but the pub lives on, serving up cold beer and hearty counter meals, and providing inexpensive accommodations ($30 s, $40-50 d). Beyond Pyengana is 90-meter-high **St. Columbia Falls,** with a flow of 200,000 liters per minute in the Wet. The falls can be seen from the road, but from the parking lot a short trail leads to the valley floor for a different angle of the falls.

At **Weldborough Pass Scenic Reserve** is a 20-minute rainforest walk, with interpretive boards describing common species of the local flora and fauna communities. To the north, in Weldborough itself, is the whitewashed **Weldborough Hotel,** tel. (03) 6354-2223, proclaiming itself "the worst pub in Tasmania."

Derby

Sandwiched between a steep hill and the Cascade River, Derby, in the far northeast of the state, flourished after the discovery of tin in 1874. Today, much of the architecture from the mining era remains, with rows of miner's cottages surrounded by well-kept gardens. Payable tin had been found throughout the northeast, with many leases taken up by the Briseis Tin and General Mining Company. At the time, the Briseis Mine was the Southern Hemisphere's largest open-cut tin mine, with 120 tons of the mineral extracted each month. On 4 April 1929, after 30 years of production, heavy rainfalls collapsed a dam wall at the mine workings, releasing 3,000 million liters of water into the already flooded Cascade River. The disaster destroyed much of the mine workings and part of Derby, leaving 14 dead. The mine reopened a few years later, but never at its former capacity, and in 1948 it closed for good.

Derby Tin Mine Centre, in an old schoolhouse, tel. (03) 6354-2262, catalogs the history of local mining, including the famous Briseis Mine, through relics, historical records, and photographs. Within the grounds is a re-creation of a shantytown featuring old Derby buildings such as a cottage, store, butcher shop, mines office, the original blacksmith's shop, and jail. You can also pan for tin and gemstones and feed rainbow trout. Admission is a worthwhile $4. The center is open in summer daily 9 a.m.-5 p.m., the rest of the year daily 10 a.m.-4 p.m. A popular annual event is the **Derby River Derby,** held on the third Saturday of every October. The event attracts hundreds of competitors to run a five-km route down the river on homemade watercraft. Many competitors never reach the finish line, but those who do can win prizes in a multitude of divisions, including one class for boats holding up to 24 people.

Mt. William National Park

This spectacular coastal park of 13,899 hectares lies in the far northeastern corner of the state. It protects long stretches of unspoilt beach rising to a low mountain range that forms the park's western border. The park provides an important sanctuary for the Forester kangaroo, Tasmania's largest mammal. Their preferred habitat is open areas of high grasses, and for this reason several large areas of developed pasture have been incorporated into the park and are maintained in this condition to support the species. Also present in the park are Bennett's wallabies, wombats, and echidnas. More than 100 species of birds are also present, including kookaburras and honeyeaters.

Southern access to the park is along a road that traverses some spectacular scenery, passing beautiful **Picnic Point Beach** and ending at **Eddystone Point Lighthouse,** from where views extend north along the park's best beaches to the Furneaux Group islands. Northern access to the park is along a 23-km road east from Gladstone. Within the park, this road forks. The right fork leads to a great campground at **Stumpy's Bay.** Also along this road, south of the bay, is a short trail to the summit of 216-meter **Mount William.** Views from this peak, the park's highest point, are panoramic, extending across the park and the entire northeastern corner of Tasmania. The left fork leads you to a group of holiday shacks and a campground at **Musselroe Bay** at the park's northern tip.

The nearest services are in **Ansons Bay,** a small village south of the park with petrol and a general store selling groceries, fishing tackle, and hot food. Gladstone, in the north, has similar services. To contact the park ranger call (03) 6357-2108.

THE MIDLANDS: HOBART TO LAUNCESTON

The 200-km route between Tasmania's two largest cities was established in 1825, before which all supplies between the two centers had been transported by sea. In the early days of the overland route, with bushrangers roaming the bush robbing travelers, garrison stations were established to protect travelers. Many of these stations grew into townships, and today they boast an amazing array of historic buildings. What's more, early settlers planted English trees to ease homesickness, giving the midlands a distinctive English feel.

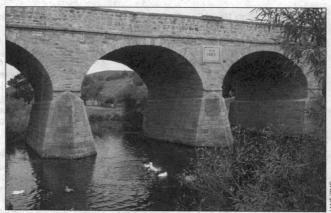

Richmond Bridge

JANE KING

Richmond

With more than 50 buildings dating from the first half of last century, Richmond, 30 km north of Hobart, is a classic example of an 1800s town. As the population of Hobart Town expanded, exploration inland commenced, and one of the first spots chosen for settlement was Richmond, in the Coal River Valley, on the route between Hobart and Port Arthur. Today, Richmond's best-known feature is a convict-built bridge dating from 1823. **Richmond Gaol,** tel. (03) 6260-2127, built about the same time, housed convicts engaged in local construction projects. Within the solid structure are displays of convicts and the penal system under which they were held. Admission is $2.50. It's open daily 9 a.m.-5 p.m. Other historic landmarks include the 1834 **St. John's Church,** Australia's oldest Catholic church; the 1825 **courthouse;** and **Richmond Arms Hotel,** built in 1888. **Old Hobart Town,** on Bridge St., tel. (03) 6262-2502, is a scaled down model of Hobart, built from the original plans. Admission adult $4.50, child $2.50. Open daily 9 a.m.-5 p.m.

Richmond is an easy day trip from Hobart, and many tour operators head out there. The other public transportation option is with **Hobart Coaches,** tel. (03) 6234-4077, which runs out to Richmond four times daily (except Sat.-Sun.).

Oatlands

Of all Tasmania's historic townships, none has the concentration of convict-built, Georgian-era buildings that Oatlands does. The town straddles the Jordan River, 85 km north of Hobart, and was established as a garrison station on the route between Hobart and Launceston. Many historically important buildings have plaques detailing their history and past tenants. Along the main street alone sit 87 historic sandstone buildings, including many dating from the 1820s. The town's dominant structure is **Callington Mill,** a steam-powered windmill built in 1837. The craftsmanship is amazing. The tower is 15 meters high, each sandstone block cut to a different size to create a conical taper. The building fell into disrepair at the turn of the century, but at peak production it was capable of grinding enough wheat to produce up to a ton of flour per hour. Admission to the mill and an adjacent cottage and stables is $2. It's open daily 9 a.m.-5 p.m. For information call (03) 6254-1525.

Midlands Hotel, 91 High St., tel. (03) 6254-1103, has basic but spotlessly clean rooms with shared facilities for $35 s, $45 d. Inexpensive. Opposite is **Oatlands Lodge,** 92 High St., tel. (03) 6254-1444, a rambling old sandstone guesthouse built by convicts in 1837. It features four guest rooms of a high standard for $65 s, $85 d, inclusive of a cooked breakfast. Moderate. South of Oatlands on a picturesque creek is **Commandant's Cottage,** Jericho, tel. (03) 6254-4115, built in 1839 to house the superintendent of a road-building gang. Today it provides accommodation for travelers. Each room in the cottage has its own charming character, with slate floors, comfortable beds, and a fully-equipped kitchen with breakfast provisions. Nearby is a creek where platypuses are sometimes sighted. The cottage takes only one booking per night, so if you're a couple or family, you get the whole place to yourselves; $90 d, $20 each extra person. Moderate.

The **Midlands Hotel** serves good counter meals daily noon-1:30 p.m. and 6-7:30 p.m. **Blossom's of Oatlands**, 116 High St., tel. (03) 6254-1516, features a menu of Tasmanian-inspired dishes, including trout. Interesting in itself is the building, constructed of bricks made by convicts and with the original wooden floors.

Ross

Established in 1812 to protect travelers from bushrangers, this picturesque town on the Macquarie River 120 km north of Hobart is one of Tasmania's rural gems. The tree-lined streets are dotted with beautiful old buildings (the best way to get around is on foot). The dominant feature of Ross is the convict-built bridge spanning the Macquarie River. A convict stonemason, Daniel Herbert, left his mark on the bridge by way of more than 150 carvings, and in return he was granted a pardon. The bridge, along with three historic churches, is floodlit at night. One of the most colorful features of Australia's convict past is the many Female Factories, where settlers were encouraged to use the labor of female convicts for household chores and pardoned convicts were able to choose a wife. The **Female Factory** in Ross operated between 1847 and 1855. It was destroyed soon after, but foundations and the original staff quarters remain. To get there take Church St. out of town, turn left onto Bridge St., then right onto Bond Street. Across the road from the site, and along the gravel path following the old stone wall, is **Ross Original Cemetery**, with readable gravestones dating from 1840. The **Tasmanian Wool Centre**, on Church St., tel. (03) 6381-5466, has interesting displays on the Tasmanian wool industry and woolen articles (not cheap) for sale. Within the center is a small museum cataloging the history of Ross and the importance of the wool industry in the town's growth; museum admission is $4. If you want to know more about Ross and, in particular, the carvings on Ross Bridge, contact Tim Johnson who, dressed in appropriate period costume complete with top hat, operates a guided tour around the village, tel. (03) 6381-5354.

Least expensive of the town's accommodations is **Ross Caravan Park**, Bridge St., tel. (03) 6381-5462, in a beautiful shaded spot beside Ross Bridge. Park facilities are adequate. The park has resident possums and ducks, and if you're lucky, you'll see the platypuses in the river. Tent sites are $10 and powered sites $12. Also within the park are five small cabins (supply your own linen) with limited cooking facilities for $25. Budget. Local Tim Johnson has restored four cottages scattered around town. Each has its own charm and contains an album telling the story of the cottage and its restoration. Typical is **Captain Samuel's Cottage**, built in 1830. It features a large living area and bathroom, modern kitchen (breakfast provisions are provided), and opens to a veranda and a garden that extends down to the river; $70 s, $120 d. Expensive. Call ahead for reservations and directions at (03) 6381-5354. The other accommodation is **Man-O-Ross Hotel**, on the corner of Church and Bridge Streets, tel. (03) 6381-5240; $40 s, $60 d. Inexpensive.

As well as providing accommodations, Man-O-Ross Hotel has a delightful shaded beer garden and restaurant. Prices start at $9 for main meals, and on Sunday night there's a barbecue for adult $12, child $6. This hotel also serves cooked breakfasts 8-9:30 a.m. **Old Ross General Store** has a variety of light snacks, an in-house bakery, and a small tearoom out the back.

Campbell Town and Vicinity

Like Ross, 12 km to the south, this picturesque village was established as a garrison station in the early 1820s. The highway runs right through the center of town and over a fine old bridge across the Elizabeth River. One of the town's oldest and most attractive buildings is **Fox Hunters Return**, built as an inn in 1829. Accommodations in town include **Powells Hotel**, 118 High St., tel. (03) 6381-1161, with basic rooms for $30 s, $40 d (Inexpensive), and **The Gables**, 35 High St., tel. (03) 6381-1347, with comfortable rooms with shared facilities for $65 s, $85 d. Moderate.

East of Campbell Town, about halfway out to the coast, is **Lake Leake**, a popular trout-fishing and boating spot. **Lake Leake Chalet**, tel. (03) 6381-1329, has basic rooms with shared facilities for $25 s, $40 d, which includes a light breakfast. Inexpensive. Counter meals in the bar are $8-12. On the lakeshore is a primitive campground; $5 per night.

Longford

First settled in 1813, Longford, 28 km south of Launceston, is one of northern Tasmania's oldest towns. The main street is lined with Georgian-era buildings. The historic property **Woolmers** has been in the same family for seven generations, with the main house having been lived in since 1819. Typical of the era is the exposed timber framework filled in with bricks and white-washed. The interior is complete with furnishings from around the turn of the century, including shutters to keep bushrangers out. In the grounds is an old timber windmill, pumphouse, the original cottage, stables and barns, blacksmith's shop, a barn full of antique cars and machinery, and a superb little church with its original Huon pine pews. Woolmers is open daily 10 a.m.-4:30 p.m. for two-hour tours throughout the day ($10 pp); for bookings call (03) 6391-2230.

Brickendon, Wellington St., tel. (03) 6391-1251, is an 1830s house with two historic cottages renovated to accommodate visitors. The cottages are spacious and feature a kitchen, separate bedrooms, private garden, and a living area with fireplace. Both are $120 per night. Expensive. The **Servant's Kitchen,** at Woolmers, is open for light meals throughout the day. If you're looking for a counter meal, head to the bistro at the **Country Club Hotel** on Wellington Street. For about $9-12 you can choose from a blackboard menu with a large variety of main dishes. Also in Longford is **James Service Store,** a delightful old-fashioned store with some tempting gourmet fare.

SOUTHWESTERN TASMANIA

This region is accessed from the **Lyell Highway,** which follows the Derwent River from Hobart then crosses a mountainous region to end on the west coast. It's a stretch of highway just 300 km long, but it provides various access points to the Tasmanian Wilderness World Heritage Area, worthy of as much time as you can afford. The World Heritage Area encompasses five national parks, of which three are accessed along the Lyell Highway. Closest to Hobart is Mt. Field National Park, a highland area of mountains with one of Tasmania's two downhill ski resorts (no accommodations). Farther west is Southwest National Park, a massive expanse of wilderness that extends from the mountainous area around Lake Pedder to the inhospitable coastline of the state's extreme south. Adjacent and to the north is Franklin-Gordon Wild Rivers National Park, a wilderness area best known for its narrow escape from flooding that would have been caused by a proposed hydroelectric scheme in the late 1970s.

NEW NORFOLK

This historic town of 6,300, on the Derwent River 34 km west of Hobart, was named for the area's earliest settlers, who were relocated from Norfolk Island in 1807. The first party comprised 34 islanders, and in the following year another 500 arrived, leaving Norfolk Island uninhabited. By the 1860s many local farmers were growing hops—the flavoring and preservative used in beer—an industry that continued for most of this century. Hop-growing has been phased out in the valley, but many signs of the industry remain, including distinctive rows of stately poplars, planted as windbreaks to protect the hops from wind damage.

Sights and Recreation
One of Tasmania's oldest buildings, **Old Colony Inn,** was built of brick and mud in 1815 to store hops. In later years a second story was added, and it was converted to a residence. Today, the ground floor is an intriguing museum storing enormous bellows, assorted balls and chains, horse-

shoes, old bicycles, a collection of lamps, and all sorts of interesting historical items. Admission $1.50. It's at 21 Montagu St., tel. (03) 6261-2731.

Behind Old Colony Inn a trail leads along the Derwent River to the confluence with the Lachlan River. Across the Lachlan River is **Oast House,** tel. (03) 6261-1030, part of the former Tynwald hop-growing property. Built as a hop-drying kiln, the Oast House is now a museum dedicated to the industry, with walk-in kilns, some great old photos, and hop-growing implements on display. An interesting art gallery is upstairs. Admission is $3.50. It's open Wed.-Sun. 9 a.m.-5 p.m. Back in the center of town are many other historic buildings, including **St. Matthew's Church of England** (1823), one of Australia's oldest churches; **Willow Court** (1830), once a hospital for convicts; and Old Watch House Gaol (1838), built of locally quarried sandstone.

On 21 April 1864 a container of trout roe arrived in Tasmania after a 90-day journey from London. The hatchlings formed the breeding stock for the first trout released in streams across southern Australia and New Zealand. The **Salmon Ponds,** 11 km west of New Norfolk, tel. (03) 6261-1614, the site of the original breeding program, has been developed into a museum displaying the process. Admission is $3.50 and it's open daily 9 a.m.-5 p.m.

The **Devil Jet,** tel. (03) 6261-3460, is a jet-boat that offers a thrill-seeking ride along the Derwent River at speeds up to 80 kph, traveling across shallow rapids and performing 360-degree spins. Departures are from behind the Bush Inn, Montagu Street. Adult $48, child $24.

Accommodations
Bush Inn, 49 Montagu St., tel. (03) 6261-2011, has the cheapest rooms in town, and has been serving travelers since way back in 1815. Rates are $30 s, $50 d, which includes breakfast. Inexpensive. At the **Old Colony Inn,** on Montagu St., tel. (03) 6261-2731, accommodation is offered in a small cottage with a private balcony overlooking the inner courtyard; $80 s or d, includes a full breakfast. Moderate. Dating from the 1830s, **Tynwald-Willow Bend Estate,** Lyell

Hwy., tel. (03) 6261-2667, is a stunning building that was built for a local hop farmer. The home is magnificent, featuring wrought-iron lacework and surrounded by well-manicured gardens. Five rooms have been restored for guests, and each is furnished with antiques. A pool, tennis court, old-fashioned lounge room, laundry, and restaurant are other features. Rates are $110-142 s or d, including breakfast. Also on the grounds is The Granary, a self-contained cottage dating from 1822; $136 per night. Premium.

New Norfolk Caravan Park, the Esplanade, tel. (03) 6261-1268, on the river and a short walk from the center of town, has good facilities (coin-operated showers). Sites are $8-12, on-site vans $30, and cabins $40. Budget-Inexpensive.

Food

Bush Inn, 49 Montagu St., tel. (03) 6261-1075, has a dining room out back with river views. Prices are a little higher than your average pub meal, but quality is good. Main dishes range $9.50-12. It's open daily for lunch and dinner. For an English-style meal head to **Old Colony Inn,** also on Montagu St., tel. (03) 6261-2731.

MOUNT FIELD NATIONAL PARK

Jagged peaks, a string of glacial lakes, lush rainforests, and one of the state's two downhill ski areas are features of this 16,265-hectare park 73 km west of Hobart. Its proximity to the capital makes the park a popular day trip, but some day hikes and a range of accommodations make an overnight stay almost compulsory.

The Land

The land encompassed by the park is generally of a high elevation. The lowest elevations are around the facility area, which is only 180 meters above sea level. The park's central section is a high plateau, flanked by high peaks, including 1,434-meter **Mt. Field West.** The central plateau is dotted with deep lakes of glacial origin. In fact, most of the park's dominant features are glacial in origin. Ice covered this region as recently as 15,000 years ago and upon retreating left a variety of easy-to-recognize scars. Broad River Valley is typical; as a glacier flowed down the valley, then retreated as temperatures warmed,

it ground away the valley walls, scraping away protruding ridges and forming a U-shaped valley. At the head of the valley is Lake Seal, a massive basin carved by the same glacier. Glaciers have long since melted, but erosion continues. Russell Falls, near the park entrance, is a good example of the process. Water rushing down Russell Falls Creek has carved steep walls into the mudstone behind the falls, washing the sediment downstream to build up somewhere else.

Like all of Tasmania's mountain parks, weather conditions in Mt. Field are very dynamic, and the old cliche of four seasons in one day is very apt. Snow and sleet can fall at any time of year, and the park experiences more overcast than clear days.

Flora and Fauna

As the park is near the center of the state, it has flora from both the east and west side of the island. As well, abrupt elevation changes make defining the various vegetation zones easy. At lower elevations, such as around the facility area, are forests of eucalypt with swamp gum, which grows up to 100 meters high. Also dogwood, stringybarks, and white gums grow in the area. In gullies and other sheltered areas grow Antarctic beech and sassafras. Subalpine forests, dominated by colorful snow gums and areas of low heath, grow up to an elevation of 800 meters. On the plateau, where drainage is poor, dead and dying plant matter has formed extensive bogs, which, after time, have become overgrown with low-growing heath plants. The only larger species at high elevations are conifers, generally twisted and stunted by harsh weather conditions.

The variety of habitat provides a home for diverse species of fauna, but few larger mammals are within the park. The marsupials, such as Bennett's wallabies and pademelons, feed at dawn and dusk while bandicoots and potoroos only feed at night. Possums are widespread through the park, but again, they are only active at night. Echidnas and platypuses are also present; look for the latter at dusk in quiet reaches of Russell Falls Creek.

Sights and Hikes

Little exertion is needed to reach **Russell Falls.** Just a couple hundred meters from the facility area (the trail begins opposite park headquarters), they are one of the most beautiful waterfalls in Tasmania. The trail to the falls passes through a variety of lush vegetation, emerging at the falls, which cascade over five tiers before plunging 40 meters into a fern-lined pool below.

From the facility area on the park's eastern boundary, a winding road climbs steadily through an ever-changing forest to the central plateau and ends at **Lake Dobson,** the trailhead for a number of challenging hikes. The first hike along the road, five km from the facility area, is **Lyrebird Nature Walk,** just 15 minutes roundtrip. The forested landscape changes dramatically as the road ascends over a ridge and onto the plateau, almost treeless and strewn with moss-covered boulders. Immediately to the right upon reaching the plateau is a parking lot for a number of trails, including to **Seagar's Lookout** (1.7 km; allow 30 minutes each way) and the summit of 1,270-meter **Mt. Field East** (four km; allow two hours each way), along a trail that passes two alpine lakes. Back on the road, beyond these trailheads, is **Lake Fenton,** encircled by stunted eucalypts. At Lake Dobson is a map of all trails and a self-registration booth. **Pandani Grove Nature Walk** (2.4 km; 40 minutes roundtrip) leads around picturesque Lake Dobson and through a stand of ancient pencil pine. Most serious hikers will want to head farther afield to destinations such as **Twisted Tarn** (six km; two and a half hours each way). The ascent of the park's highest peak, 1,434-meter **Mt. Field West** (10 km; four hours each way), should only be attempted on a clear day. The going can be tough.

Mount Mawson Ski Area

Although Tasmania's southern latitude should mean ample snowfall, that is not the case, and when it does snow, conditions are often atrocious. That said, Tasmanian skiers are a hardy bunch, and as the closest downhill skiing to Hobart, this small ski area overlooking Lake Dobson is very popular. The area has three tows, ski rental, and instructors. From the Lake Dobson parking lot to the lifts is a 30-minute walk. For ski conditions, call (03) 6288-1319.

As well as downhill skiers, wintertime attracts those keen on cross-country skiing, tobogganing, snow trekking, and ice skating.

Accommodations

Russell Falls Holiday Cottages, just beyond the park gate, tel. (03) 6288-1198, comprises rustic but spacious four- and six-berth cabins with a kitchen in each. Rates are a reasonable $40 s, $50 d; advance bookings are a good idea. Inexpensive. Each of the three **Lake Dobson Cabins,** 15 km beyond the park gate, has six bunks, a wood heater, running water, toilets, and firewood (bring your own stove). The cost is $20 pp. Budget. Book through the park ranger, tel. (03) 6288-1149, and collect the key from him upon arrival at the park entrance.

Outside the park, in the small village of **National Park,** are two more options. **National Park Hotel,** tel. (03) 6288-1103, has basic rooms with shared facilities for $35 s, $55 d, including breakfast. Inexpensive. Across the road is **National Park YHA Hostel,** tel. (03) 6288-1369, where dorm beds are $12 (members only). Budget.

The **campground,** close to the park entrance, has a variety of sites, including some right by the river. Facilities include hot showers, laundry, and a cooking shelter with two barbecues. Firewood is supplied, but you're better off with your own stove. Nonpowered sites are $5 pp and powered sites are an extra $2 pp. No bookings are taken for holiday periods; the rest of the year call (03) 6288-1477 to reserve a site. During the night, nocturnal wildlife abounds around the campground, so zip up your tent and seal all food containers.

Other Practicalities

Tasmanian Wilderness Travel, tel. (03) 6334-4442, operates a bus service between the park (the pickup point is outside the kiosk) and Hobart. In summer buses depart Hobart daily at 8:30 a.m., with service Monday, Wednesday, and Saturday the rest of the year.

Basic groceries and hot food are available at the **Park Kiosk** (open daily 8:30 a.m.-6 p.m.), but it's best to stock up on supplies before heading to the park. **National Park Hotel** serves meals but closes early. At Westerway, four km east of the park entrance, tire chains can be rented from the service station, while other shops sell groceries, stove fuel, and takeaway food.

The **Visitor Centre,** at the park entrance, has displays of the park's natural history and information sheets on the most popular hikes. It's open daily 8:30 a.m.-5 p.m. To contact the ranger, call (03) 6288-1149. A 1:50,000 topographical map is available from the Visitor Centre.

SOUTHWEST NATIONAL PARK

Encompassing the entire southwestern corner of Tasmania, this 605,000-hectare park is a vast wilderness of mountain ranges and river systems along an almost-inaccessible stretch of coast. And while Mt. Field and Cradle Mountain-Lake St. Clair National Parks may have a concentration of natural wonders, the joy of this park comes from the opportunity to experience a real wilderness area and, for those experienced in back-country travel, attempt long-distance hikes. The park also makes up a significant section of the Tasmanian Wilderness World Heritage Area, which includes Franklin-Gordon Wild Rivers National Park immediately to the north. The main park access is 42 km west of the Mt. Field National Park turnoff. From this point Scotts Peak Rd. leads south along **Lake Pedder** to campgrounds and trailheads for a variety of hikes, while Gordon River Rd. leads west to **Strathgordon.** Apart from the motel at Strathgordon the park has no services. Maydena is the last fuel stop.

Scotts Peak Road
This gravel road leads south from Junction Hill and ends at the southern reaches of Lake Pedder, where there are camping and hiking opportunities. Near the beginning of the road on the right is **Creepy Crawly Nature Trail,** a one-km (20-minute) circuit through rainforest. Around 10 km south is the trailhead for a seven-km (one-way) trek to the summit of 1,425-meter **Mt. Anne;** allow 10 hours for the roundtrip.

At earth-filled Edgar Dam, a farther 10 km south and past a fantastic lookout, is **Edgar Campground,** while a farther four km is **Huon Campground.** Both campgrounds have toilets, drinking water, and firewood. The road dead-ends at **Red Knoll Lookout,** where views extend north across the lake and south to the jagged Arthur Range.

Port Davey/South Coast Tracks
Southwest National Park is best known for its longer hikes, including the combination of these two trails, which link the shore of Lake Pedder to the southern tip of Tasmania, a 170-km trek that takes 10-18 days, depending on how many side trips you make. It's possible to walk each trail separately, but this requires an air charter through Melaleuca. **Par Avion,** tel. (03) 6248-5390, and **Tasair,** tel. (03) 6248-5088, provide this service and can also fly in food drops for those attempting the complete hike.

The trails can be hiked in either direction, but the most popular section is the South Coast Track from Melaleuca to Cockle Creek. The Port Davey Track, which begins from Huon Campground at the end of Scotts Peak Rd., traverses a remote valley along the back of the jagged

taking in the remote southern coastline along the South Coast Track

DONNALEE YOUNG

Arthur Range to Lost World Plateau before descending along Spring Creek to Bathurst Narrows, 62 km from the trailhead. This deep channel is the outlet for Bathurst Harbour. On each side of the crossing point is a small dinghy. It is imperative to leave one on each side after crossing (which will entail multiple crossings and some simple common sense). From Joan Point, on the south side of the narrows, it's 14 km to Melaleuca, site of a small mining operation, an airstrip, and the only huts along the track. From Melaleuca, the coast is an easy day's hike through open plains of buttongrass. The trail then parallels the coast, descending to sandy bays, heading inland to cross the larger rivers, and climbing to a number of lookouts before ending at Cockle Creek, 87 km from Melaleuca.

Hikers do not need permits but should check trail conditions with the ranger, tel. (03) 6288-1283, and register with the Tasmanian police.

Strathgordon
Established to serve workers on a nearby hydroelectric scheme, Strathgordon is a good base when visiting nearby Gordon Dam and trout fishing in the area. The dam is part of the Gordon River Power Development, which encompasses Australia's largest storage area of fresh water. Strathgordon itself lies on an isthmus of land between Lake Gordon and Lake Pedder in the north of the park, and 33 km west of Junction Hill. Accommodation is provided at **Lake Pedder Motor Inn,** tel. (03) 6280-1166, a large complex of 75 rooms right on the lake. Rooms are only basic (they originally housed workers) but have bathrooms. Guest facilities include heated indoor pool, sports center, tennis courts, squash, sauna, boat rental, barbecue area, laundry, restaurant, and bar. Rates range $55-95 s or d, depending on the season. Moderate.

Beyond Strathgordon, the road ends at **Gordon Dam Lookout,** where there's a visitor center and picnic area.

LAKE COUNTRY AND VICINITY

Lake Country, the southern section of Tasmania's central plateau, forms the headwaters for dozens of rivers that flow in a southwesterly direction to the Derwent River. The vast volume of water flowing through these watersheds is harnessed by a string of hydroelectric projects that supply just under 10% of Australia's total electricity demands.

Hamilton
The rural town of Hamilton lies on the River Clyde 70 km northwest of Hobart. The area was settled soon after New Norfolk had been established and was destined to become Tasmania's capital—except barges were unable to travel far enough up the Derwent River. So, instead, the village became a transportation hub for the rich agricultural districts of the central plateau. Many convict-built structures remain, including **Glen Clyde House,** built as a private residence in 1840 and now an excellent gallery, full of Tasmanian arts and crafts. It's on Grace St., tel. (03) 6286-3276, and is open daily 9:30 a.m.-5 p.m.

The **Old School House,** Lyell Hwy., tel. (03) 6286-3292, was built in 1856 for the town's ever-growing population of school-age children. After being saved from bulldozers in the 1970s, it's been restored and converted to a comfortable accommodation. It features three double rooms, each furnished with antiques, while in the garden is a self-contained cottage. All are $110 per night, including breakfast. Expensive.

Bothwell
Bothwell is on the east bank of the River Clyde 30 km upstream of Hamilton. Once an important cattle and sheep center, the town is now a sleepy center of 500. The earliest settlers were Scottish, and their legacy is excellent trout fishing in the surrounding streams and rivers. For trout fishing gear and hints on all the best spots, head to **Crown Tackle Shop,** tel. (03) 6259-5508. They can also arrange guides. More than 50 historic buildings line Bothwell's wide streets. The best way to appreciate them is by following the *Let's Browse Bothwell* brochure, available at the council building. Built in 1887, the sandstone schoolhouse on Market Place houses the **Australasian Golf Museum,** tel. (03) 6259-4033, a collection of golf memorabilia owned by a former Australian amateur champion, Peter Toogood. It's open Tues.-Sun. 10 a.m.-4 p.m. Bothwell also boasts Australia's oldest golf course, with unique fenced-off greens to prevent grazing sheep from spoiling the grass.

Bothwell Grange, Alexander St., tel. (03) 6259-5556, is a large two-story sandstone building dating from 1836. It has seven guest rooms, each with a bathroom. Rates are a reasonable $72 s, $92 d. Expensive. **Bothwell Camping Ground** is just a small grassed area behind the public toilet building on Market Place, but it's peaceful and pleasant, and costs only $6 for powered sites. Budget. Dating from 1829, the **Castle Hotel,** Patrick St., serves lunch daily, dinner Friday and Saturday, and cold beer all the time.

Hamilton to Derwent Bridge

This 100-km stretch of the Lyell Highway parallels the Derwent River and passes through small towns and by many river access points. Along this section of the river are seven large power stations.

North of **Ouse** and at the north end of Wayatinah Lagoon is **Wayatinah Power Station,** and off an access road beyond the power station is a campground with tennis, pool, and a golf course. Sites are $7. The next town north is **Tarraleah,** built for hydroelectric workers. Visitors are welcome at the power station; it's north of town and very ugly.

A signposted road 19 km from Tarraleah spurs northeast from the highway to a private road that leads to **London Lakes Fly-Fishing Lodge,** tel. (03) 6289-1159. The lodge caters specifically to fly-fishing enthusiasts (it hosted the 1988 World Fly-fishing Championships), but its remote setting on a private estate of 2,000 hectares appeals to varying interests. The lodge is rustic but comfortable, and with only five rooms, service is personal. Rates include accommodations, three excellent meals, and use of all lodge facilities. Fully guided, the rate ranges $500-720 pp per night, depending on the season (Nov.-March is high season); nonguided, but with all equipment provided, rates range $270-370. Nonanglers pay $205-285. Luxury.

Derwent Bridge

This small service center, 165 km northwest of Hobart, is the southern gateway to Cradle Mountain-Lake St. Clair National Park. Although the park's most famous features are accessed from the north, Lake St. Clair is just up the road from Derwent Bridge. A cruise boat operates on the lake, accessing easy day hikes and picking up adventurers who have completed the Overland Track from Cradle Valley.

Immediately west of the Lake St. Clair turnoff is **Derwent Bridge Wilderness Hotel,** tel. (03) 6289-1144, a large wooden complex with rooms, a restaurant, and bar. Rooms are basic but comfortable. Rates are $45-55 s, $75-85 d, depending on facilities. Moderate. Backpacker accommodation is $20 pp. None of the rooms have cooking facilities, but the restaurant is inexpensive and open for all meals.

FRANKLIN-GORDON WILD RIVERS NATIONAL PARK

Declared in 1981, this 440,000-hectare park protects the entire watershed of the untamed Franklin River. On the western side of the park tributaries flow south into the Franklin from the Cheyne Range, 1,400 meters above sea level and running along the southern boundary of

Nelson Falls, Franklin-Gordon Wild Rivers National Park

PETE UNGARD

adventurous hikers on the summit of Frenchman's Cap, Franklin-Gordon Wild Rivers National Park

Cradle Mountain-Lake St. Clair National Park. Fed by a heavy annual rainfall of more than 300 cm, the river is in turn the major tributary of the mighty Gordon River, Tasmania's largest river. The river parallels a 20-km stretch of the Lyell Highway, but for the most part it flows through a wild and totally inaccessible region of the state. The Lyell Highway is the only road to traverse the park, offering you a chance to experience a dramatic mountain landscape dominated by rugged peaks and valleys of ancient forest.

The 1981 discovery of stone tools in a cave on the Lower Franklin confirmed a long-held theory that during the last ice age Tasmania was the earth's most southerly point of human occupation. Escaped convicts from a penal colony on Macquarie Harbour were the first Europeans to venture into the area. The first recorded crossing between Hobart and the west coast was in 1840, but it wasn't until 1932 that a road was completed, and as recently as 1974 that it was sealed. The 1970s brought worldwide attention to the Franklin River with conservationists fighting to save it from flooding from the construction of the Gordon-Lower Franklin Dam. They eventually won, having the park declared in 1981 and incorporated in the Tasmanian Wilderness World Heritage Area two years later.

Park Highlights

The park's eastern boundary is eight km west of Derwent Bridge and beyond Lake King William. Just inside the park boundary is 800-meter-high King William Saddle, marking the divide of the Derwent and Gordon river systems, which flow to the east and west coasts respectively. Continuing west, the road passes through open fields of buttongrass before a sudden change of scenery sees the road enter the dense rainforest of the Surprise Valley. In this valley is **Franklin River Nature Trail,** where an information board details attractions along the Lyell Highway. The one-km (25 minutes roundtrip) nature trail follows the banks of the Franklin and Surprise Rivers. Although it's only a short trail, the feeling is one of total wilderness, and the roar of the river drowns out any traffic noise.

Frenchman's Cap, an impressive massif of quartzite, is visible from several lookouts along the Lyell Highway, but to reach its summit entails a three- to five-day trek. From the highway, it's 27 km to the summit and an elevation gain of just over 1,000 meters, with some sections of muddy plains and others of rough slopes of scree. The most exciting section of the entire hike is crossing the Franklin River aboard either a swing bridge or flying fox. From the highway, the river is an easy 15-minute walk.

Donnaghy's Hill, six km west of the trailhead for Frenchman's Cap Walking Track, is 400 meters from the highway (40 minutes roundtrip) and provides panoramic views of the wilderness to the south. A farther four km west, the highway crosses the **Collingwood River,** put-in point for Franklin River rafters. Continuing west, the highway passes through a picturesque valley backed by the rugged Raglan Range to the south. **Nelson Falls** is an easy 10-minute (each way) walk from the highway. The trail passes through a rainforest of lush ferns and colorful leatherwood trees before emerging at the falls, a spectacular cascade of water over a sandstone ledge.

The park has no information center and the only facility is primitive camping by the Collingwood River. To contact the ranger, call (03) 6471-7122.

Running the Franklin River

Symbolizing a victory for conservationists against the overwhelming tide of human encroachment, this wild river is Australia's premier whitewater rafting destination. But it certainly isn't a trip for the fainthearted. The 10- to 14-day trip entails wilderness travel and should only be attempted by experienced rafters or under the leadership of a qualified guide.

The river's headwaters are shallow, so the preferred put-in point is where the Lyell Highway crosses the Collingwood River. Most of the fearsome rapids—including Churn, Cauldron, and Thunderush—are on the upper half of the river. Once beyond Frenchman's Cap, the river is quieter and passes alongside some Aboriginal caves before it drains into the Gordon River, just over 120 km from the Lyell Highway.

Peregrine, tel. (03) 9662-2800, operates a variety of trips down the river. These range from a five-day easy float starting halfway down the river (from $1,100 pp) to running the entire river in 11 days ($1,750). Trips run Nov.-April. If you plan to run the river independently, contact the **Department of Parks, Wildlife, and Heritage** in Hobart, tel. (03) 6233-6391. From Heritage Landing, on the Lower Gordon River, arrange pickups with **Gordon River Cruises,** tel. (03) 6471-7317, or **Wilderness Air,** tel. (03) 6471-7280.

TASMANIA'S REMOTE WEST COAST

Tasmania's west coast is dominated by wilderness. Steep mountains rise from deep gorges, rainforests descend to raging rivers, and the coastline itself is accessible in only a couple of spots. But it's also a region of stark contrasts, one that boasts the wonders of the UNESCO Tasmanian Wilderness World Heritage Area alongside a bizarre landscape resulting from years of humanity's exploitative use of the environment's natural resources.

QUEENSTOWN

The mining town of Queenstown (pop. 2,600) lies on the Queen River, 260 km west of Hobart. Surrounding the town is a landscape like no other place in the country. But the panorama is certainly no natural beauty—it's all humanity's doing (or undoing). The barren but colorful surroundings are due to a combination of factors, but all relate directly to the town's famous **Mt. Lyell Copper Mine.** Over a period of 73 years smelters from the mine gave off dense clouds of sulphur-laden smoke. Rich in mineral content, the clouds settled on the surrounding hills, destroying vegetation for kilometers in all direc-

tions. It was a vicious cycle—as new growth on the land cleared to feed the smelters was killed off by the sulphurous clouds, soil was washed away by heavy rainfall, leaving surrounding hills barren and impregnated with sulphur. During this same period about 1.5 million tons of mine tailings were dumped into the Queen River annually and washed into the King River, eventually draining into Macquarie Harbour. Consequently, the lower King River is ecologically dead, and a two-km-square delta is a solid mass of gray sludge. All the doom and gloom aside, a visit to Queenstown is fascinating, for it gives visitors the chance to understand humanity's ever-changing attitude to the environment. The best way to get an overview of the entire area, including the bare hills and township, is by catching a chairlift that ends at a viewpoint high above an old silica quarry; $6 roundtrip.

Sights

Don't miss **Galley Museum,** on the corner of Driffield and Sticht Streets, tel. (03) 6471-14830, which gives an insight to Queenstown's industrial past. Originally the Imperial Hotel, it contains an eclectic collection of local memorabilia spread over two floors. Displays include the story of Abo-

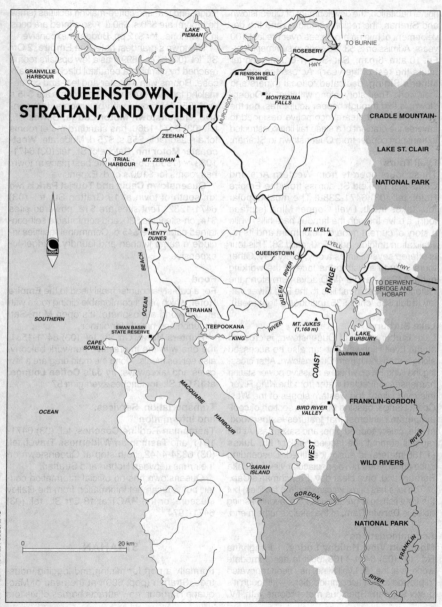

QUEENSTOWN, STRAHAN, AND VICINITY

riginal habitation, the development of Queenstown and Strahan, the region's geology, and the development of mining processes over the last 100 years. Admission is $3. It's open in summer Mon.-Fri. 10 a.m.-6 p.m., Sat.-Sun. 1-6 p.m. (shorter hours the rest of the year). Across the road is **Miner's Siding,** dedicated to local miners and their work. Their story, along with that of Queenstown, is told through copper sculptures, but the centerpiece is a steam locomotive designed to traverse the gradient of a steep rail line constructed to transport copper from Queenstown to Strahan.

Lyell Tours
These tours operate from Western Arts and Crafts at 1 Driffield St. across from the Empire Hotel, tel. (03) 6471-2388. The most popular tour takes in Mt. Lyell Copper Mine (surface tour), a drive through the famous bare hills, while a story of current mine development and its revitalization unfolds; adult $10, child $6. This tour is offered several times a day, every day. Other tours include a visit to the face of the working mine ($40 pp) and a 4WD adventure along the historic Kelly Basin rail line to the Bird River Valley (adult $55, child $35, includes a light meal).

Lake Burbury
Lake Burbury, east of Queenstown, is crossed by the Lyell Highway but can also be accessed along a road south from Queenstown. After crossing the King River, where a massive power station harnesses redirected water from the King River, this road climbs the western slopes of the West Coast Range, passing through a section of cool-temperate rainforest that features leatherwood, myrtle, celery-topped pine, and sassafras. At the range's summit, the jagged peak of **Mt. Jukes** (1,168 meters) is easily identified. Descending once again, you'll have spectacular views of Lake Burbury and, on a clear day, Frenchman's Cap.

The lake has primitive camping (no facilities) but the trout fishing is great; one of the favorite fishing holes is **Darwin Dam,** at the lake's southern end.

Accommodations
Mountain View Holiday Lodge, 1 Penghana Rd., tel. (03) 6471-1163, built to accommodate workers at the Mt. Lyell Mine, has been renovated to provide tourist accommodations—although it's pretty spartan. Spacious motel rooms with TV, fridge, and tea- and coffee-making facilities (small bathroom) are $50 s, $60 d. Also offered are beds in dormitories for $12 pp. Budget-Inexpensive.

The town's grandest hotel, the **Empire,** 2 Orr St., tel. (03) 6471-1699, has a few upstairs rooms reached by climbing a beautiful blackwood staircase. Rooms with a heater and tea- and coffee-making facilities but shared bathrooms are $45 s or d, $55 for rooms with bathrooms. Inexpensive. **Queenstown Motor Lodge,** Bowes St., tel. (03) 6471-1866, has standard motel rooms for a reasonable $55 s, $75 d. Moderate. **Westcoaster Motor Inn,** Batchelor St., tel. (03) 6471-1033 or (1800) 06-0957, the best place in town, has rooms for $100 s or d. Expensive.

Queenstown Cabin and Tourist Park is two km south of town at 19 Grafton St., tel. (03) 6471-1332. Tent sites are $12, powered sites $14, on-site vans $30, and comfortable self-contained cabins are $45 d. Communal facilities include a camp kitchen and laundry. Budget-Inexpensive.

Food
For a pub-style counter meal head to the **Empire Hotel,** which has a comfortable dining room with an old-world atmosphere. It's open Mon.-Sat. for lunch and nightly for dinner.

Hunters Hotel, Orr St., tel. (03) 6471-1531, the one with the impressive ironwork balcony, also serves meals. Along the main drag are a few cafés and takeaways: try **JJ's Coffee Lounge,** at 13 Orr St., for lunches averaging $7.

Transportation, Services, and Information
Tasmanian Redline Coaches, tel. (03) 6471-1011, and **Tasmanian Wilderness Travel,** tel. (03) 6334-4442, both stop at Queenstown on their runs between Hobart and Strahan.

Queenstown has no official information center, but you can get information from the Galley Museum, or the RACT at 18 Orr St., tel. (03) 6471-1974.

STRAHAN

Formally a port for mining and logging industries, Strahan (pop. 600), at the head of Macquarie Harbour, now attracts hordes of visitors who come to cruise the lower reaches of the Gordon River. For the first decade of settlement, Strahan was little more than a supply base for prospectors. As larger mineral deposits—such as at Mt. Lyell, Zeehan, Dundas, and Mt. Reid—were developed, Strahan grew to become one of Tasmania's busiest ports. The population quickly reached 1,500; the town then boasted two railway stations, impressive civic buildings, Union Steamship Company offices, a hospital, and a sawmilling operation. Since the beginning of this decade, with mining and logging operations along the west coast in decline, Strahan has grown rapidly as a tourist center. What was, until a few short years ago, a sleepy fishing village is now a bustling town, overflowing with visitors in summer, yet, somehow, managing to retain a relaxing seaside atmosphere. With recreation on most visitors' minds, the region offers the opportunity to go fishing in the harbor, swimming at West Strahan Beach, or surfing at Ocean Beach.

Strahan Wharf Centre

Overlooking Macquarie Harbour, this intriguing timber-and-glass building should be the first stop for all visitors to town. Its unusual form, described as the world's first "magical realist building," includes one entire wall of multiple-paned glass supported by roughly hewn poles of celery-topped pine, a wood featured throughout the interior. In the foyer, where a massive Huon pine desk is located, are seven mural scenes describing western Tasmania's human history. Beyond the information desk is a museum cataloging southwestern Tasmania's entire natural and human history. From the sounds and sight of a rushing waterfall upon entering the museum, to the lifestyle of Aboriginals, to the story of conflicts between conservationists and developers, the complex gives an excellent overview of the west coast. Admission to the exhibition section of the center is a worthwhile adult $4.50, child $3. The complex is open Nov.-March daily 10 a.m.-8 p.m. and April-Oct. daily 10 a.m.-6 p.m.

Adjoining the complex is an outdoor amphitheater where the play *The Ship that Never Was*, detailing the plight of Sarah Island convicts, is performed throughout summer; adult $10, child $5. For more information call (03) 6471-7622.

Scenic Drives

Teepookana, on the King River south of Strahan, was the site of a thriving logging industry early this century. From Strahan, the road south out to Teepookana passes Lettes Bay, where the Mt. Lyell Company built a small holiday village for workers, and passes through paddocks that once supported the dairy herds that provided the mining communities with fresh milk. At Teepookana, a rusting iron bridge is the major remnant of this once-bustling township.

A gravel track off the road out to Ocean Beach heads south through **Swan Basin State Reserve,** where a steep trail to a lookout and picturesque picnic area are located. From here the road continues south through a lush forest of pine plantations to **Macquarie Head Camping Ground;** $5 per night. Budget. Beyond the campground is a long sandy beach, with views across the narrow mouth of Macquarie Harbour to the white, cross-topped lighthouse on Cape Sorell. From this point you can continue on foot to the southern end of Ocean Beach. At the end of the access road to Ocean Beach, west of Strahan, is a muttonbird colony that comes alive Nov.-April when thousands of birds return to their burrows from a day's feeding at sea.

Between Strahan and Zeehan lie the **Henty Dunes.** An access road in their midst leads to a picnic area, where you can scramble up the dunes to the 360-degree views on the highest ridges.

Gordon River Cruises

Strahan has two companies competing for your cruising dollars. The main destination for both is the lower reaches of the Gordon River, part of the Tasmanian Wilderness World Heritage Area, but both companies include interesting stops en route. One of these is Sarah Island, site of a remote and brutal penal settlement at the beginning of the 1800s. Another interesting stop is made at Heritage Landing, where a raised boardwalk leads through coastal rainforest. **Gordon River Cruises,** tel. (03) 6471-7187, has a full-day cruise departing Strahan Wharf daily at 9 a.m. for $65 and a half-day cruise for $45 (includes meals). Run by seven generations of the Grining family, **World Heritage Cruises,** tel. (03) 6471-7174, is a smaller and more personal operation. Their cruises aboard the *Wanderer II* run daily 9 a.m.-3:30 p.m.; adult $44, child $20 (no meals included).

Wild Rivers Jet, tel. (03) 6471-7174 (book at the office on Strahan Wharf), operates 50-minute jet-boat rides up the King River for $40 pp. **Wilderness Air,** tel. (03) 6471-7280, has a 90-minute flightseeing trip taking in the Gordon and Franklin Rivers and Frenchman's Cap for $99 pp.

Accommodations
Right downtown is **Hamers Hotel,** tel. (03) 6471-7191, part of a complex that includes a bakery, café, restaurant, bar, and laundry. Upstairs rooms are basic and have shared facilities, but views across Macquarie Harbour are good; from $45 s, $68 d, which includes breakfast at the bakery. Moderate. The hotel also operates **Strahan Village Cottages,** nearby. Cottages are small but well furnished. Rates are $99-155 s or d. Expensive. On the northwest outskirts of town is **Strahan Wilderness Lodge,** Harvey St., tel. (03) 6471-7142, a simple yet comfortable accommodation. Rooms have shared facilities, and there's a spa, barbecue area, and indoor pool; $30 s, $50 d. Inexpensive. Strahan's most luxurious accommodation is **Franklin Manor,** on the Esplanade, tel. (03) 6471-7311. Built in 1889, the mansion has 18 guest rooms, each with bathroom, and a few have private spas. Guests have use of a comfortable lounge with a large fireplace. Rates of $90-200 s, $110-210 d include breakfast, and an extra $38 pp will get you a three-course dinner. Expensive.

Near the turnoff to Ocean Beach, and a 10-minute walk from town, is **Strahan YHA,** tel. (03) 6471-7255. Beds in the dormitories and twin rooms are $13-18 pp. Budget.

West Strahan Caravan Park, west of town on Innes St., tel. (03) 6471-7239, is across the road from the beach. Grassy tent sites are $10, powered sites $12. Budget. Between this park and downtown is **Strahan Cabin Park,** tel. (03) 6471-7442, providing self-contained cabins with cooking facilities for $48-73. Inexpensive.

Food
If you feel like fish and chips, there's no option but **West Coast Fishmobile,** beside the wharf. Their takeaway meals include locally caught fish, salmon burgers, crayfish salad, scallops (in season—April), and fish fingers for the kids. Prices range $2.50-8.50, open daily until 8:30 p.m. Another place for an inexpensive feed is **Strahan**

Bakery, the Esplanade, offering pies, pastries, and sandwiches along with freshly brewed coffee. Between 6 and 9 p.m. pizza and pasta are also offered. The restaurant in **Hamers Hotel** features Tasmanian specialties such as crayfish, scallops, and oysters. Lunch prices start at $4.50, rising to $25 for a crayfish salad, the house specialty. Dinner is more of the same, but a little more expensive. **Regatta Point Tavern,** tel. (03) 6471-7103, is another popular spot for a casual meal.

Transportation, Services, and Information
Tasmanian Wilderness Travel, tel. (03) 6334-4442, departs Hobart every Saturday at 8:30 a.m. for Strahan, with a one-hour stopover at Lake St. Clair. This company also offers a service between Strahan and north coast towns each Saturday, departing Launceston at 8:30 a.m. and Devonport at 10:30 a.m. **Tasmanian Redline Coaches,** tel. (03) 6431-3233, operates a direct service between Hobart and Strahan Mon.-Sat. (departs Hobart 8:30 a.m.) for a similar price.

The old Customs House Building contains the **post office,** a **Commonwealth Bank** agency, and **Department of Parks, Wildlife, and Heritage** office, tel. (03) 6471-7122, which incorporates a World Heritage Area Visitors Centre. The latter is open daily 8 a.m.-5 p.m. A board outside lists all local activities. **Strahan Visitor Centre** is on The Esplanade, tel. (03) 6471-7622.

ZEEHAN AND VICINITY

Sailing along Tasmania's west coast in 1642, Abel Tasman recorded a peak he named for his ship, *Zeehan.* More than 200 years later, with the discovery of a silver and lead deposit immediately north, a township developed. The mineral wealth attracted thousands of workers, and in 1910 Zeehan's population peaked at 10,000. From this time onward the town's fortunes took a nosedive, and it wasn't until the 1970s and the re-opening of the Renison Bell Tin Mine that the economy stabilized.

Zeehan's main street is lined with turn-of-the-century buildings. One of these, the 1902 School of Mines building, is now **West Coast Pioneers Memorial Museum,** tel. (03) 6471-6225. Browsing through the museum's many galleries, which include a large mineral collection, historic photos, the re-creation of an underground mine, old maps, and relics from the west coast penal colonies, can easily take a couple of hours. The museum is open daily 8:30 a.m.-5 p.m., and don't forget to drop a $2 donation for admission into the miner's wheelbarrow (made from Huon pine).

Tasmania's west coast is remote in the truest sense of the word, with only a half dozen access points along its entire length. Two of these, **Trial Harbour** and **Granville Harbour,** are west of Zeehan; neither has services.

Practicalities
The town's best-value accommodation is **Treasure Island West Coast Caravan Park,** on Hurst St. one km northeast of town, tel. (03) 6471-6633. Small caravans with cooking facilities and bathrooms are $40, while cabins range $55-60. For campers, pitching a tent will cost $14 and powered sites are $16. Budget-Inexpensive. Right downtown is **Hotel Cecil,** tel. (03) 6471-6221, where rooms have shared facilities and are $40 s, $65 d. Moderate. On the south side of town is **Heemskirk Motor Hotel,** tel. (03) 6471-6107, with a high standard of rooms for $75. Moderate. This hotel is the place to grab a counter meal; lunches are about $6 and dinners range $7-12.50.

Tasmanian Redline Coaches stops in Zeehan Mon.-Sat. on the route between Strahan and Devonport.

NORTHWESTERN TASMANIA

While most of Tasmania's best-known sights are bunched around Hobart and scattered through the interior, northwestern Tasmania, facing the wild waters of Bass Strait, is also worth exploring. The main routes through the area are the Murchison Highway and the Bass Highway, which follows the coast closely for more than 80 km. Bass Highway's western terminus is the west coast, where a couple of small communities cling to the rugged coastline. Westernmost of the towns facing Bass Strait is Stanley, nestled below a distinctive lump of land known as the Nut, and port for the surrounding rural area. East of Stanley are Wynyard, Burnie, and Penguin, which are great bases for exploring the more remote areas of coastline or just relaxing on the beaches. Largest of the north coast towns is Devonport, where the passenger and vehicle ferry *Spirit of Tasmania* from mainland Australia docks. From Devonport you can reach **Cradle Mountain-Lake St. Clair National Park,** 161,000 hectares of stunning topography.

MURCHISON HIGHWAY AND VICINITY

This highway links Tasmania's west and north coasts, although access to the actual ocean is limited. Northeast of Zeehan the Murchison Highway passes Renison Bell Tin Mine and the trailhead for a five-km hike to **Montezuma Falls,** considered one of Tasmania's most photogenic waterfalls. Farther east, on an arm of manmade Lake Pieman, is **Rosebery,** an old mining town with a tumultuous history. Although the town has little of interest the surrounding landscape of rolling hills and forests of leatherwood is picturesque. **Tullah,** north of Rosebery, was established as a mining town and now functions as a service center for workers on nearby hydroelectric schemes.

To the West Coast
Halfway between Rosebery and Wynyard a road branches west, dead ending at Corinna on the Pieman River. The first town along this route is **Waratah,** founded in 1871 after the discovery of a rich tin deposit on the slopes of nearby 784-meter Mt. Bischoff. Mining began in earnest in 1888, and for a time it was the world's richest tin mine. Some turn-of-the-century buildings remain along the main street, including the courthouse, which now houses a museum. Adjacent to the museum is a replica of an old miner's hut.

West of Waratah the road passes two mining towns, each existing to serve mine workers and their families, before turning to gravel and ending at **Corinna** on the Pieman River. It was the discovery of gold in 1881 that first brought settlers to this remote part of the state, and although the rush was shortlived, it was particularly rich, with the largest nugget found weighing 243 ounces.

The area's only formal tourist activity is a cruise along the Pieman River aboard *Arcadia II*. Departures are daily at 10:30 a.m. Accommodation in town is at **Pieman Retreat,** tel. (03) 6446-1170, which has cabins for $60-100 per night (supply your own linen) and tent sites for $6 pp. Moderate.

Hellyer Gorge

Carved by the Hellyer River, this impressive gorge is accessed by a one-km trail (15 minutes each way) that starts on the west side of the highway where it crosses the river. The trail passes through a lush rainforest of ferns, sassafras, giant myrtle, blackwood, and leatherwood. Across the road from the trailhead is a great little picnic area.

STANLEY

In 1825 the Van Diemen's Land Company was granted a large tract of land in northwestern Tasmania, establishing its headquarters at Highfield and developing a port facility at nearby Stanley. As the importance of Highfield diminished, Stanley grew in stature. Today the town boasts a population of about 600. Stanley is nestled in the shadow of a massive knob of basalt that rises from the ocean. Geologists think it formed about 12 million years ago when a mass of molten rock spewed from a crack in the earth's surface, cooling to form basalt. Named Circular Head by early explorers, the landmark is better known today as, simply, the **Nut.** Along the Nut's southern flanks is a large port facility and a breakwall that protects a colorful fleet of fishing vessels. At the base of the Nut (on Browns Rd.) is a parking lot from where a trail leads up to the summit, 143 meters above sea level. Another option for reaching the summit is to ride the **chairlift,** which operates daily 10 a.m.-5 p.m.; adult $6, child $4. Once at the top, there's a three-km circuit trail dotted with interpretive signs. One of the trail highlights is a rookery of shearwaters that nest Nov.-March. The extremely rare peregrine falcon is occasionally sighted on the Nut. A buggy ride around the trail costs $5 pp.

Town Sights

Plough Inn, 35 Church St., tel. (03) 6458-1226, dating from 1840, was a licensed hotel for a cou-

ple of decades in the mid-1800s. A few rooms have been restored, each decorated with furnishings you'd expect in an inn from this period. Admission is $4.50. Open daily 9:30 a.m.-5 p.m. Also on Church St. is the **Discovery Museum,** tel. (03) 6458-1286, cataloging Stanley's early history through photographs as well as having relics from shipwrecks and mineral and shell displays. Admission is $3, and it's open daily 10 a.m.-4 p.m. (closed in winter). Those interested in the history of Australian politics may want to visit **Lyon's Cottage,** a bluestone building preserved as the birthplace of Joseph A. Lyons, prime minister of Australia between 1932 and his death in 1939. Open for inspection daily 10 a.m.-4 p.m.

Highfield Historic Site

At Greenhills, six km from Stanley, is Highfield, the original Tasmanian headquarters of the Van Diemen's Land Company. Granted 250,000 acres, this British stock company was instrumental in the northwest's settlement. The company's massive business empire functioned almost as a separate colony, with ships sailing directly between England and Highfield and developing whole towns to service their workers. The Highfield property remains much as it would have looked in the mid-1800s, with many original buildings still standing and an interesting array of farm machinery scattered around the grounds. The main residence has been extensively restored, and a self-guided tour takes you through each room, with detailed descriptions of all displays. Admission to the site is $5 pp. Open daily 10 a.m.-5 p.m. For information call (03) 6458-1100.

Arts and Crafts

Stanley boasts a number of good arts and crafts shops. Housed in a sandstone inn dating from the 1850s, **Stanley Craft Centre,** 35 Church St., tel. (03) 6458-1226, holds only Tasmanian-crafted items. Also check out nearby **Touchwood Craft Shop** at 31 Church St., tel. (03) 6458-1348.

Accommodations

The **Stanley Motel,** Dovecote Rd., tel. (03) 6458-1300 or (1800) 06-2298, is one km west of town. Basic motel rooms start at $75 d, those with spas are $100. Also offered are self-contained units. These are older, but have great ocean views, making them a good value at $80-95. Moderate. Across from Highfield Historic Site is **Anthony's at Highfield,** tel. (03) 6458-1245, a spacious accommodation with clean and bright rooms, ocean views, and a kitchen stocked with breakfast provisions. Rooms start at $80 d. Moderate. Dating from about 1860, **Bayside Colonial Cottage,** 4 Alexander Terrace, tel. (03) 6458-1209, is a comfortable three-bedroom house with views extending across the beach to the ocean. Rates are $90-120 s or d, which includes the use of a kitchen stocked with breakfast provisions. Expensive.

Stanley Caravan Park, right at the waterfront on Wharf Rd., tel. (03) 6458-1266, is a large place with plenty of good campsites and cabins with water views. The camper kitchen features stoves and a fridge. Tent sites are $12, powered sites $13, on-site vans $30, and cabins $50. Book ahead in summer. Budget-Inexpensive. Within this caravan park is **Stanley YHA,** which has all the usual facilities; $12 pp. Budget.

Food

Stanley has a few good restaurants specializing in local seafood. **Hursey Seafoods,** 2 Alexander Terrace, contains a number of eating options, including a café, bakery, seafood outlet, and restaurant. The seafood outlet features two massive tanks, one filled with a variety of fish, the other with crays. They sell fresh seafood, perfect if you have access to a kitchen. Upstairs is the restaurant **Julie and Patrick's,** tel. (03) 6458-1103, featuring oysters, crayfish, and seafood crepes. Main dishes average $16.50. For a filling counter meal, head to the popular **Union Hotel** on Church Street. This places really comes alive on Friday night when bands crank up the pace and seemingly half the town crams in.

THE REMOTE NORTHWEST CORNER

The Bass Highway extends 65 km west from Stanley to a remote stretch of coast accessible in only a couple of spots. Just out of Stanley is **Smithton,** an administrative center for the surrounding farming region. South of Smithton, on the road to Edith Creek, is **Allendale Gardens,** featuring two hectares of pleasant gardens criss-crossed with walking trails. Admission $5. Open Sept. to mid-May 9 a.m.-5 p.m.

Marrawah

This small seaside community at the end of the Bass Highway is Tasmania's westernmost town. It comprises little more than a hotel and general store, but beyond is **Green Point,** one of Tasmania's premier surfing spots.

Arthur Pieman Protected Area

The small community of **Arthur River,** 14 km south of Marrawah, lies at the north end of 100,000-hectare Arthur Pieman Protected Area. Between Marrawah and Arthur River are various access points to the wild coastline, but access roads are rough. The protected area encompasses a 90-km stretch of the coast and features a diverse landscape of rocky headlands, dune systems, and rivers rolling down westward from the Norfolk Range. The best way to explore the river is on an **Arthur River Cruise** aboard a beautiful old timber boat. The cruise penetrates around 14 km upstream, passing rainforest to Turk's Landing where a barbecue lunch is served. The trip lasts about five hours and is a reasonable adult $40, child $20. For bookings, call (03) 6457-1158. The coastal scenery out by Gardiner Point, at the mouth of the Arthur River, is quite spectacular, with water from the river flowing headlong into the ocean. From Arthur River, a road continues south, with many sidetracks leading to the ocean. Around Couta Rocks, 18 km south of Arthur River, the scenery is especially spectacular. Farther south are the remains of **Balfour,** a once-thriving copper-mining town that slid into oblivion after the mine closed in 1916.

The best-value accommodation in the area is **Arthur River Holiday Units,** tel. (03) 6457-1288, comprising comfortable self-contained units for $60-70 s or d. Moderate.

STANLEY TO BURNIE

Rocky Cape National Park

Protecting a rugged stretch of coastline where the Bass Highway makes an inland detour east of Stanley, this 3,064-hectare park features sheltered beaches flanked by rocky headlands. The main entry is from the east, but another access road dead-ends out on Rocky Cape, the park's westernmost point. From the end of this road a short trail descends to **North Cave**, once used by Aboriginals as shelter.

Access west from Boat Harbour leads to the golden sands of **Sisters Beach.** Near the end of the road is a fork. The road to the left leads to 10-hectare **Birdland Nature Park,** where a short hiking trail passes through various local habitats to a lookout where views extend over Sisters Beach. Admission is $2.50. Open daily 9 a.m.-5 p.m. Several trails begin from the end of the sealed road. The most enjoyable is east along the beach, returning via an inland trail; allow 90 minutes roundtrip. Another trail (two km roundtrip) leads through a dense grove of coastal banksia. The Anniversary Bay Circuit, taking about two and a half hours to complete, heads to a hidden coastal beach, with sidetracks to a lookout and waterfall. The trail between Sisters Beach and Rocky Cape is 11 km each way (allow three and a half hours each way), with the option to return along an inland route. Beyond the trailheads for the above hikes a rough gravel road continues west, providing access to the beach at various points. The park has no campgrounds; the only facilities are at a shaded picnic area beside Sisters Creek.

Boat Harbour Beach
Along the main road into Rocky Cape National Park the road branches right to Boat Harbour Beach, one of Tasmania's most beautiful stretches of sand. Behind the beach is a pleasant holiday village with all facilities. **Boat Harbour Beach Resort,** Esplanade, tel. (03) 6445-1107, with coastal and ocean views, a pool, spa, and sauna, has rooms for $65 s, $85 d. Moderate. **Country Garden Cottages,** tel. (03) 6445-1233, comprises cozy timber cottages surrounded by well-manicured gardens. Each has a separate bedroom, kitchen, and living area. Rates are $75-85 per cottage, with breakfast hampers extra. Moderate. A short walk from the beach is **Boat Harbour Beach Backpackers,** Strawberry Lane, tel. (03) 6445-1273, with a communal lounge room, barbecue area, and laundry. Dorm beds are $14 pp, doubles $32-40. Budget-Inexpensive. **Harbour Restaurant,** tel. (03) 6445-1371, specializes in seafood, with dinners

averaging $18. Open Tues.-Sat. for lunch and dinner. Next door is **Harbour Shoppe,** a takeaway joint serving great hamburgers.

Wynyard and Vicinity
Although Wynyard itself has little of interest, this commercial center of 4,700 is a good base for exploring the surrounding coastal habitats. Immediately west of town is **Table Cape,** a magnificent plateau of green fields that drop dramatically into the ocean. On the cape itself is **Fossil Bluff,** best viewed at low tide. Also out on the cape is a lighthouse dating from 1888 and a lookout with views extending back to Wynyard and the valley in which it lies.

Leisure Ville Caravan Park, 145 Scenic Drive, tel. (03) 6442-2291, three km west of town, is a great place to stay, with a shell-covered beach across the road and views of Table Cape. Facilities include an indoor heated pool, spa, barbecues, and laundry. Sites are $11-15, on-site vans $36, and cabins $50-80. Budget-Inexpensive. **Wynyard YHA,** 36 Dodgin St., tel. (03) 6442-2013, is a small house one block from downtown. Beds are $13-16 pp per night. Budget. For a little more style, there's **Alexandria Guesthouse,** an old homestead out on Table Cape that dates from 1908. Each of the four rooms has a bathroom while guests have use of a pool, barbecue, and laundry. Rates of $75 s, $95 d include a cooked breakfast. For bookings call (03) 6442-4411.

Grab a meal at the **Federal Hotel,** 82 Goldie St., tel. (03) 6442-2056, open daily for lunch and dinner; main dishes average $10. The **Seaward Inn,** 59 Old Bass Hwy., tel. (03) 6442-4009, is a casual restaurant featuring mostly local seafood and produce.

BURNIE

Burnie (pop. 21,500) is a bustling service and tourist center on the shore of Emu Bay 20 km east of Wynyard and 326 km northwest of Hobart. It is an important industrial center, with Amcor, Australia's largest papermaker, having a mill in town. The town's port is an intregral part of all local industry. Constructed as a single wharf in 1827 to move ore from Waratah onto ships bound for the mainland, it has grown to be Australia's fifth-largest containerport.

Sights

On Wilmot St., one block from the Bass Hwy., the **Civic Centre Precinct** features the Pioneer Village Museum, an information center, a library, and an art gallery. **Pioneer Village Museum,** tel. (03) 6430-5746, is a replica of an 1890s street, complete with a blacksmith's shop, printer, bakery, and bootmaker. Also part of the museum is a collection of historic wedding gowns and photography and map displays. Admission is adult $4.50, child $2.50. Open Mon.-Fri. 9 a.m.-5 p.m., Sat.-Sun. 1:30-4:30 p.m. In the same complex is the **Regional Art Gallery;** open the same hours as the museum and with free admission.

Burnie Park, along Shorewell Creek off North Terrace, is a pleasant spread of parkland with a few caged native birds and animals. Also within the park is **Burnie Inn.** This small inn, Burnie's oldest building, dates from 1847 and is open daily except Tuesday 10:30 a.m.-3:30 p.m.

Lactos Cheese Tasting and Sales Centre, in the Lactos Cheese Factory on Old Surrey Rd., off Bass Hwy. east of downtown, tel. (03) 6432-1588, has a tasting room open Mon.-Fri. 9 a.m.-5 p.m., Sat.-Sun. 10 a.m.-4 p.m. Meals served here are remarkably inexpensive, with a filling Farmer's Lunch only $6 and a chunk of delicious cheesecake a tempting $2.50.

Accommodations and Food

In summer, finding somewhere to stay in Burnie can be difficult; even the caravan parks require advance bookings. Best value of all accommodations is **Treasure Island Caravan Park,** on the Bass Hwy. three km west of town, tel. (03) 6431-1925. On-site vans are $40, cabins start at $44, and campsites range $10-14. Budget-Inexpensive. Otherwise try the very basic **Hillside Motor Inn,** 20 Edwards St., tel. (03) 6431-3222, southeast of downtown; $40 s, $60 d. Inexpensive. The flashiest place in town, and priced accordingly, is **Beachfront Voyager Motor Inn,** 9 North Terrace, tel. (03) 6431-4866 or (1800) 35-5090; $100-140 s or d. Expensive.

Rose's on the Park Cafe, in the historic Burnie Inn (Burnie Park), is open for morning and afternoon teas and lunch. For a good quality counter meal, head to the **Beach Hotel,** on the corner of Wilson St. and North Terrace. The seafood here is delicious; daily specials are about $13. Across

the road, in the Beachfront Voyager Motor Inn, is **Terrace Cafe,** with water views and main meals from as little as $8.50. For a more formal meal, **Wellers Inn,** 36 Queens St., tel. (03) 6431-1088, is the place to go. This restaurant specializes in seafood (from $17), but chicken and beef dishes are also offered. **Rialto Restaurant,** Wilmot St., tel. (03) 6431-7718, has a wide range of Italian dishes, with meals averaging around $12. Open Mon.-Sat. for lunch and dinner.

Transportation, Services, and Information

Burnie Airport is a $22 cab fare west of town at Wynyard. This is the closest Tasmanian airport to the mainland (apart, of course, from those on King and Flinders Islands). **Kendell,** tel. (13) 1300, flies this route (to Melbourne) daily. **Aus-Air,** tel. (1800) 33-1256, and **Tasair,** tel. (1800) 06-2900, fly to other state centers. **Tasmanian Redline Coaches,** tel. (03) 6331-3233, has regular services between Burnie and Devonport, continuing two days a week to Stanley.

The **Tasmanian Travel and Information Centre,** right downtown in the Civic Centre Precinct, tel. (03) 6434-6111, has information on not only Burnie but the entire northwest, and staff will help find overnight accommodations. The center is open Mon.-Fri. 9 a.m.-5 p.m., Saturday 9 a.m.-noon.

BURNIE TO DEVONPORT

Penguin

Named for the colonies of fairy penguins that were once common along the north coast, this small town of 3,000 is spread along picturesque bays and backed by rolling hills of forest. The penguin population has all but been wiped out in the immediate vicinity of town, but Nov.-March, if you're lucky, you may sight the odd bird at dusk near the caravan park. Organized penguin viewing is at Penguin Point at dusk; adult $5, child $2. Call ahead at (03) 6437-2590.

The two-story **Beachfront Lodge,** 64 Main St., tel. (03) 6437-2672, right in the center of town and opposite the beach, has four high-standard rooms from $55 s, $65 d, including a light breakfast. Moderate.

Penguin to Ulverstone
via the Inland Route

The coastal townships of Penguin and Ulverstone lie 12 km apart via a coastal road, but a far more interesting route detours inland through the Gunns Plains, passing many hop farms

At the end of a beautiful valley southwest of Gunns Plains, **Gunns Plains State Reserve** protects a small system of limestone caverns. Tours of the caves depart daily 10 a.m.-4 p.m. on the hour; adult $6, child $3. For details call (03) 6429-1388.

Beyond Gunns Plains and alongside the Leven River is 40-hectare **Wings Farm Park,** Winduss Rd., tel. (03) 6429-1335. This large campground is in a great rural location with camping on a grassed area or in shade along the river. Tent sites are a bargain at $7, powered sites are $9.50, and self-contained cabins with river views are $50-60. Budget-Inexpensive.

Ulverstone

Straddling the wide mouth of the Leven River, this bustling town of 10,000 is in the heart of a rich agricultural district. Like Penguin to the west, the town is a popular holiday spot with loads of facilities and many nearby beaches and headlands to explore. The life of local pioneers is catalogued at the **Local History Museum,** 50 Main St., tel. (03) 6425-6270. Admission is $3. Open Tues.-Sun. 1:30-4:30 p.m.

The aptly named **Ocean View Guest House,** 1 Victoria St., tel. (03) 6425-5401, is in a great location right across from the beach. Rooms are clean and comfortable, each with a bathroom; $60 s, $80 d includes breakfast. Moderate. Another option is **Ulverstone Motor Lodge,** 2 Tasman Parade, tel. (03) 6425-1599, west of downtown, where rooms range $50-80 s or d. Moderate.

DEVONPORT

In 1890 settlements on the east and west banks of the Mersey River united to become the town of Devonport. Today this industrial town is a port for the mainland ferry, *Spirit of Tasmania,* and with a population of 25,000 is northwestern Tasmania's largest town. Devonport's main attractions are all within walking distance of each other,

with a hiking trail following the west bank of the Mersey River from downtown to the river mouth and out to Mersey Bluff.

Mersey Bluff

On this magnificent headland immediately north of downtown is Devonport's top attraction, **Tiagarra,** an Aboriginal culture and arts center. The entire history of Tasmanian Aboriginals, from 23,000 years ago when they crossed a land bridge from mainland Australia and developed their own unique culture, to their undignified fate 150 years ago, is detailed. From the center, a trail leads along the coast to Tasmania's most accessible concentration of native rock art, with about 240 engravings. Admission is adult $3, child $2. Open daily 9 a.m.-5 p.m. For more information call (03) 6424-8250.

Other Sights

The **Tasmanian Maritime and Folk Museum,** at the north end of Victoria Parade, tel. (03) 6424-7100, is open daily except Monday 1-4 p.m. (shorter hours in winter). It contains a collection of maritime memorabilia, including model ships, a Lloyd's Register of Ships, relics from the whaling era, a historical display of the Bass Strait Ferry, old diving gear, and a full listing of all the wretched souls deported on the First and Second Fleets. Admission is a worthwhile $2.

In the old Baptist Church at 45-47 Stewart St., tel. (03) 6424-8296, is **Devonport Gallery and Art Centre,** featuring works by Tasmanian artists. Open Mon.-Sat. 10 a.m.-5 p.m., Sunday 2-5 p.m.

Home Hill, 77 Middle Rd., tel. (03) 6424-3028, a large whitewashed home, was built in 1916 for former prime minister Joseph A. Lyons, who ran Australia between 1932 and 1939. A guided tour of the property is $6. Farther west, where the Bass Hwy. crosses the Don River, is **Don River Railway,** tel. (03) 6424-6335, holding Tasmania's largest collection of steam locomotives and carriages. Don't miss riding on the old train, which operates daily 10 a.m.-4 p.m.; adult $7, child $4.

Accommodations

The most popular travelers' accommodation in Devonport is **River View Lodge,** 18 Victoria Parade, tel. (03) 6424-7357, across the road from the Mersey River and a short walk from downtown. Each room is well decorated and has a

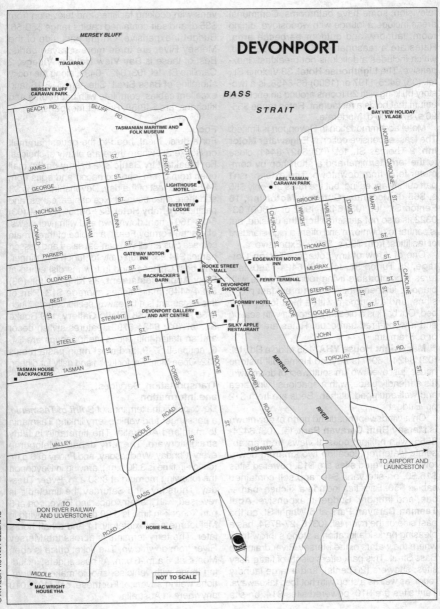

DEVONPORT

MERSEY BLUFF

TIAGARRA

MERSEY BLUFF
CARAVAN PARK

BASS

STRAIT

BEACH RD.

BLUFF RD.

BAY VIEW HOLIDAY
VILAGE

TASMANIAN MARITIME AND
FOLK MUSEUM

VICTORIA

FENTON

NORTH

CAROLINE

ST.

ST.

ST.

JAMES

ST.

GEORGE

ST.

LIGHTHOUSE
MOTEL

RIVER VIEW
LODGE

ABEL TASMAN
CARAVAN PARK

BROOKE

WRIGHT

TARLETON

DAVID

MARY

ST.

NICHOLLS

GUNN

PARADE

CHURCH

ST.

RONALD

WILLIAM

ST.

THOMAS

PARKER

GATEWAY MOTOR
INN

ST.

EDGEWATER MOTOR
INN

MURRAY

ST.

OLDAKER

ROOKE STREET
MALL

ROOKE

FERRY TERMINAL

STEPHEN

ST.

ST.

ST.

CAROLINE

BACKPACKER'S
BARN

DEVONPORT
SHOWCASE

ESPLANADE

BEST

ST.

FORMBY HOTEL

DOUGLAS

ST.

STEWART

DEVONPORT GALLERY
AND ART CENTRE

ST.

JOHN

ST.

STEELE

SILKY APPLE
RESTAURANT

TORQUAY

RD.

ST.

TASMAN HOUSE
BACKPACKERS

TASMAN

FORBES

ROOKE

MERSEY

FORMBY

RIVER

MIDDLE

ROAD

ST.

ROAD

VALLEY

HIGHWAY

TO AIRPORT AND
LAUNCESTON

BASS

TO
DON RIVER RAILWAY
AND ULVERSTONE

ROAD

HOME HILL

MIDDLE

MAC WRIGHT
HOUSE YHA

MOON

NOT TO SCALE

© AVALON TRAVEL PUBLISHING

television; some have bathrooms. Communal areas include a lounge with woodstove, dining room, laundry, and outdoor barbecue area. Rates are a reasonable $45-55 s, $55-70 d, which includes a delicious hot breakfast. Inexpensive. The **Lighthouse Hotel,** 33 Victoria St., tel. (03) 6425-1197 or (1800) 65-8458, is a two-story building with 29 rooms around an enclosed atrium that holds a restaurant. Rates range $55-90 s, $70-100 d. Moderate.

Motel accommodation in Devonport is limited. The least expensive option is **Edgewater Motor Inn,** 2 Thomas St., tel. (03) 6427-8441, close to the ferry terminal and a short hop by commuter ferry from downtown. The exterior isn't particularly appealing, but the rates are only $55 s, $65 d. Moderate. **Gateway Motor Inn,** 16 Fenton St., tel. (03) 6424-4922 or (1800) 03-0322, is also not attractive from the outside, but is central to downtown and offers a high standard of facilities; from $90 s, $98 d. Expensive.

One of a row of tiny cottages, **Turton Cottage,** 28 Turton St., tel. (03) 6424-1560, features a comfortable living room complete with piano, a kitchen stocked with breakfast provisions, and a bedroom with a high four-poster bed. Out back is a pleasant veranda with seating and a wood-fired barbecue. Rates are $130 s or d. Premium.

MacWright House YHA, 155 Middle Rd., tel. (03) 6424-5696, is beyond Home Hill historic house, just over two km southwest of downtown. It's a friendly place, with a spacious living area and well-equipped kitchen. Beds are from $12 pp. Budget.

On a windswept headland north of downtown is **Mersey Bluff Caravan Park,** tel. (03) 6424-8655, with brilliant coastal views from an absolute waterfront location two km from downtown. Unpowered sites are $13, powered sites $15.50, on-site vans $40, and self-contained cabins $50. Facilities include a kitchen, barbecue, and laundry. Budget-Inexpensive. **Abel Tasman Caravan Park** at 6 Wright St. on the east side of the river, tel. (03) 6427-8794, has a pleasing parkside location a stone's throw from where the waters of the Mersey River drain into Bass Strait. This park offers plenty of flat grassy sites, showers (20 cents), and a large laundry room, as well as a shop with hot food takeaways. Tent sites are $10, powered sites $14, on-site

vans with cooking facilities and television from $35 d, and self-contained cabins range $50-56. Budget-Inexpensive. On the east side of the Mersey River are three more caravan parks. Best of these is **Bay View Holiday Village,** 2 Caroline St., tel. (03) 6427-0499, along the rocky shoreline of Bass Strait. Sites are $12-16, and excellent cabins, complete with bathrooms and kitchens, are $48-58. Budget-Inexpensive.

Food
For a quick meal, head to the pedestrian mall on Rooke St., where there are plenty of choices. For breakfast try **Banjo's,** a bakery on the mall open from 6 a.m. serving bacon and eggs from $4.50. The rest of the day, Devonshire tea is $3 and there's the usual choice of pies, cakes, and pastries. **Formby Hotel,** 82 Formby Rd., tel. (03) 6424-1601, right downtown and with river views, offers the Formby Feast, a choice of three main courses plus an all-you-can-eat salad and dessert bar for $14.95. Open daily for lunch and dinner. The best Chinese food in town is dished up at **Silky Apple Restaurant,** 33 King St., tel. (03) 6424-4148; main dishes average $13. Part of this restaurant is a takeaway section where lunch is $5 and dinner $8. **Rialto Gallery,** 159 Rooke St., tel. (03) 6424-6793, features stylish decor and an Italian-influenced menu; soups are $4-6, antipasti $7-9, and most main pasta meals $12. Open Mon.-Fri. for lunch and daily for dinner.

Transportation, Services, and Information
Devonport is the terminus of *Spirit of Tasmania,* a passenger and vehicle ferry linking Tasmania to mainland Australia. The timetable is fairly straightforward. The ferry departs Melbourne every Monday, Wednesday, and Friday at 6 p.m. (check-in time is 3:30 p.m.), arriving in Devonport the following morning at 8:30 a.m. Every Tuesday, Thursday, and Saturday the timetable is reversed, with the ferry departing Devonport at 6 p.m. (check-in time is 3:30 p.m.) and arriving in Melbourne approximately 14 and a half hours later. The ferry terminal is across the Mersey River from downtown. The ticket office is open Mon.-Sat. 8 a.m.-6 p.m. All passengers, including those with vehicles, should make reservations well in advance. For these, call (13) 2010 anywhere in Australia.

For those who arrive in Devonport without transportation, there are a few options. The easiest way to travel between the terminal and downtown is aboard a small commuter ferry that crosses the Mersey River every 15 minutes; $1.50 each way. A shuttle bus also runs into town from the terminal. On the upstairs level of the terminal are desks for the following car rental agencies: Avis, Budget, Colonial, Hertz, and Thrifty. Cars should reserved well in advance; book through any mainland office.

Tasmanian Wilderness Travel, tel. (03) 6334-4442, and **Tasmanian Redline Coaches,** tel. (03) 6331-3233, depart the terminal for destinations throughout the state soon after the ferry arrives.

Devonport's **Pardoe Airport** is seven km east of town on the road out to Port Sorell. It is served by **Kendell,** tel. (13) 1300; **Southern Australia Airlines,** tel. (13) 1313; and **Tasair,** tel. (1800) 06-2900. An airport shuttle, tel. (03) 6424-9112, meets all flights; $5 each way. At the airport are a few car rental desks, but again, reserve a car well in advance. **Bass Flight Services,** tel. (03) 6427-9777, offers flightseeing starting at $50 pp for a quick run along the coast, but the opportunities are unlimited, with flights also over Cradle Mountain and along the remote west coast.

Backpacker's Barn, 10 Edwards St., tel. (03) 6424-3628, has a good range of camping and backcountry equipment. It's open Mon.-Fri. and Saturday morning. The **Tasmanian Travel and Information Centre** is in Devonport Showcase at 5 Best St., tel. (03) 6424-8176; open Mon.-Fri. 9 a.m.-5 p.m., Sat.-Sun. 9 a.m.-4 p.m.

DEVONPORT TO CRADLE MOUNTAIN

Sheffield

Founded in 1886 after gold was discovered in the area, Sheffield nestles among rolling hills blanketed in lush green farmland with the southern horizon dominated by 1,231-meter Mt. Roland. Since 1986 Sheffield has become known as "Town of Murals," and you'll see why cruising down the main street (even the local toilet block is decorated). The town has 33 murals in total, most created by local artists and depicting the

history, geography, wildlife, and people of north-central Tasmania. An audiovisual screened Mon.-Fri. 8:30 a.m.-5:30 p.m., Sat. 10 a.m.-5:30 p.m. at **Diversity Murals Theatrette,** 34 Main St., tel. (03) 6491-1613, describes the meaning of each mural. This is also the local information center. The **Kentish Museum,** 93 Main St., tel. (03) 6491-1180, with displays on the nearby Mersey-Forth hydroelectric scheme and the world's first self-serve petrol pump, is open Mon.-Fri. 1-3 p.m. and in summer Sat.-Sun. 2-4 p.m. Admission by donation. Pottery shoppers shouldn't miss **No Where Else Pottery,** also on the main street, tel. (03) 6491-1952, which sells a great variety of unusual pieces.

The best-value accommodation in the Sheffield area is **Paradise Cottage,** on Jeffrey's Rd. five km south of town, tel. (03) 6491-1626. It's on a 30-hectare farm in the shadow of towering Mt. Roland. The cottage is divided into two rooms; both are spacious and open to an outdoor area with stunning views. Rates are $45-60 s or d. Inexpensive. Another bed and breakfast-style accommodation is **Tanglewood,** 25 High St., tel. (03) 6491-1854, just west of the post office. The comfortable rooms here are $72 s, $100 d per night. Expensive. The other option is **Sheffield Caravan Park** at 63 High St., tel. (03) 6491-1366, where sites are $8-10 and basic on-site vans are $25 (coin-operated showers). Budget.

Best of the bunch of cafés along the main street is **Red Rose Cafe,** open daily from 7:30 a.m. Across the road is **High Country Bakehouse,** which has delicious bread rolls and a choice of fillings for less than $3.

Silver Ridge Retreat

This magnificent accommodation is on Rysavy Rd. 11 km south of Sheffield, tel. (03) 6491-1727. It comprises self-contained, fully equipped, two-bedroom timber cottages, each with a log fire and comfortable lounge area. The property overlooks a working farm with the distinct Mt. Roland as a backdrop. Other features include an indoor heated swimming pool, a resident family of platypuses, lounge bar, and a restaurant serving delicious home-style meals. Cottages are $140 d, or $160 d for the luxury of a private spa with mountain views. Premium.

Gowrie Park

Gowrie Park was established as the construction base for the massive Mersey-Forth hydroelectric scheme, which was completed in 1973. The development comprises seven power stations, seven large dams, and three major tunnels, all of which combine to harness power from the flow of four rivers over an area of 2,070 square km. At the time of construction 2,500 workers were accommodated in the settlement, but upon completion, most buildings were removed, leaving only an assortment of structures to house administrative and mechanical concerns. Hiking trails allow you the opportunity to explore the natural surroundings, although most people will want to push on farther into the mountains. One hike worth considering is to the summit of Mt. Roland, a leisurely six-hour roundtrip. The best sources of trail information are the hosts of the backpacker lodge (see below) or the book *Family Walks in Northwest Tasmania* by Jan Hardy and Bert Elfin.

Part of the remaining workers' quarters has been converted to **Mt. Roland Budget Backpackers Rooms,** tel. (03) 6491-1385, with spacious communal facilities including a kitchen, dining room, living room, and laundry; from $12 pp. Budget. Also in the complex is **Weindorfer's Restaurant.** The menu features something to suit every appetite, with main meals starting at around $9. It's open Oct.-May daily from 10 a.m., but you'll need reservations for dinner.

CRADLE MOUNTAIN-LAKE ST. CLAIR NATIONAL PARK

Of Tasmania's many wilderness areas, the mountainous terrain encompassed by this 161,000-hectare park is generally accepted as the most spectacular, while also being relatively accessible. Not only is the region protected as a national park, but it's also an integral part of the Tasmanian Wilderness World Heritage Area. Park topography is varied and complex but can be basically divided into three regions. In the north is a high treeless plateau broken by deep glacial lakes and the ridge upon which 1,545-meter Cradle Mountain sits. The park's central portion is also high, an area of heathland surrounded by jagged peaks, including Tasmania's highest peak,

1,617-meter **Mt. Ossa.** In the south is the Du Cane Range, whose watershed flows eastward to **Lake St. Clair.**

The park's main facility area is the Cradle Valley, in the north of the park. By road, this valley is 85 km south of Devonport and 284 km northwest of Hobart.

The Land

Present park landforms are a result of glacial activity some 20,000 years ago, but it was many millions of years before that the mountains themselves were formed. Ice was first involved in the mountain-making process 290 million years ago when the region was covered in a sheet of ice, which, when melted, exposed a massive river plain upon which layers of sediment were deposited over time. Massive upward thrusts around 160 million years ago formed a mountain range that subsequent ice ages and wind and water erosion have sculpted to its present form. Glaciation in Tasmania ended 14,000 years ago. In the 10,000 years preceding that time, vast areas of the state's western portion were covered in a sheet of ice. As the ice retreated to high valleys, it gouged massive U-shaped valleys, rounded off mountaintops, and left moraines of rock to form natural dams.

Weather conditions within the park are unpredictable; even the most beautiful sunny morning can turn into a howling gale and driving sleet within hours. Almost three meters of precipitation falls annually, and the park averages rain on 275 days of every year. This figure doesn't take into account overcast days; these account for another two out of every 10 days. On average just 32 days a year are sunny.

Flora and Fauna

Due to extreme elevation differences within the park, you'll encounter a great variety of plant species. In the valleys cool-temperate rainforest thrives. These areas are dominated by Antarctic beech with an understory of mosses, ferns, and lichens. Eucalypts are found away from the damp valley floors, but it's above the treeline that the real survivors of the plant kingdom are found. At higher elevations glacial forces have scraped the bedrock almost bare of soil while freezing winds and heavy winter snows prohibit growth more than a meter or so above the ground.

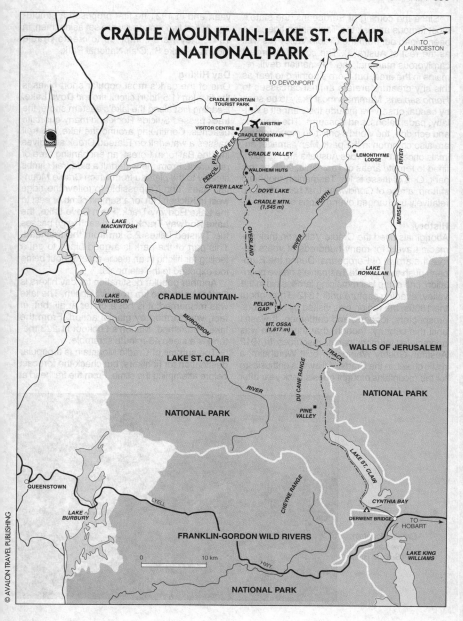

CRADLE MOUNTAIN-LAKE ST. CLAIR NATIONAL PARK

TO LAUNCESTON

TO DEVONPORT

CRADLE MOUNTAIN TOURIST PARK

VISITOR CENTRE

AIRSTRIP

CRADLE MOUNTAIN LODGE

PENCIL PINE CREEK

CRADLE VALLEY

WALDHEIM HUTS

LEMONTHYME LODGE

CRATER LAKE

DOVE LAKE

CRADLE MTN. (1,545 m)

FORTH RIVER

MERSEY RIVER

LAKE MACKINTOSH

OVERLAND

RIVER

LAKE ROWALLAN

LAKE MURCHISON

CRADLE MOUNTAIN-

PELION GAP

MT. OSSA (1,617 m)

WALLS OF JERUSALEM

MURCHISON

LAKE ST. CLAIR

DU CANE RANGE

TRACK

NATIONAL PARK

RIVER

NATIONAL PARK

PINE VALLEY

QUEENSTOWN

CHEYNE RANGE

LAKE ST. CLAIR

CYNTHIA BAY

LYELL

LAKE BURBURY

DERWENT BRIDGE

TO HOBART

FRANKLIN-GORDON WILD RIVERS

LAKE KING WILLIAMS

HWY

0   10 km

NATIONAL PARK

© AVALON TRAVEL PUBLISHING

Since the coming of Europeans, the state's most famous animal, the Tasmanian tiger, has been wiped out from the Cradle Valley (as well as the rest of Australia). The country's largest carnivorous mammal, the Tasmanian devil, remains in the area, but there's nothing to fear as this shy creature prefers animal carcasses to *Homo sapiens.* Mammals most likely to be seen by casual observers include the Bennett's wallaby, pademelons, and possums. The platypus and echidna, the world's only two monotremes, are also common in the park. Many smaller animals once prolific across Australia are now confined to remote areas of Tasmania, such as this park. One of these is the Tasmanian mountain shrimp, a relic of Gondwana that has remained relatively unchanged over millions of years.

History

Aboriginals used the Cradle Valley on their nomadic travels for many hundreds of years before the arrival of Europeans. During the European push to eradicate Tasmania's native population, one of the last remaining families hid in the valley, evading capture until 1842. Throughout the 1800s, the region was visited by surveyors, prospectors, loggers, and cattlemen. It wasn't until this century, though, that the region was appreciated for more than its resources. In 1912 Austrian Gustav Weindorfer built Waldheim, a rustic chalet, in the Cradle Valley. His enthusiasm for the mountains brought guests back year after

year, and in 1921 he first proposed a sanctuary. At first two reserves were set aside, then, in 1947, they were combined to create Cradle Mountain-Lake St. Clair National Park.

Day Hiking

One of the park's most popular short hikes is the five-km (1.5-hour) circuit around **Dove Lake.** Heading first along the lake's eastern shore, the track passes Suicide Rock and many quartzite beaches. Continuing around the lake, the trail passes a waterfall on Plateau Creek and dives into the Ballroom Forest, an enchanting area of rainforest. From the waterfall a side trail climbs steeply to the plateau from which Cradle Mountain rises, and it's possible to follow the ridge west to Kitchen Hut for a summit climb or east to the Lake Rodway Track. From Dove Lake, the **Lake Rodway Track** (six km each way) passes the Twisted Lakes 2.5 km from the trailhead. This part of the park is a good place to get a feeling for hiking in an alpine area without being too exposed to the elements.

Another popular destination for day hikers is **Crater Lake,** two km from Waldheim. The lake was misnamed; it is not a crater at all, but, in fact, was formed by glacial action. From the lake's boatshed, Marion's Lookout (1,223 meters) is a steep 45-minute scramble.

The summit of Cradle Mountain is a popular destination for fit hikers, but check the forecast before attempting the climb. From the trailhead at

Cradle Mountain,
Dove Lake, and
Suicide Rock

Waldheim, the track gains around 700 meters in elevation, following the Overland Track to Kitchen Hut (five km) before making the final leg-burning ascent to the 1,545-meter summit (a farther 1.3 km). Allow six hours for the roundtrip.

Overland Track

One of Australia's most famous hikes, this 85-km five- to eight-day trail traverses a great variety of terrain to link Cradle Valley to Cynthia Bay on the shore of Lake St. Clair. It can be completed by anyone of a reasonable level of fitness—if you don't feel competent attempting the trip by yourself, a number of companies offer fully guided adventures. It can be hiked in either direction, but north to south is most popular.

The track officially begins at Waldheim, then passes Crater Lake before ascending to an exposed plateau and the beautiful Waterfall Valley, a good overnight stop. From there the trail continues through an area of heathland exposed to the elements, then climbs to a ridge before descending to deep blue Lake Windermere, another overnight stop. Continuing south, the trail passes through a forest of eucalypt, re-emerging into open heathland, then, after two km, descends to Frog Flats and the Forth River, which is crossed via a bridge. The next overnight stop is Pelion Hut, a basic accommodation 2.4 km beyond the bridge. Some of the track's most spectacular vistas are at Pelion Gap, 2.8 km beyond the hut. From this pass, it is possible to climb 1,617-meter **Mt. Ossa,** Tasmania's highest point (five km each way; allow three hours roundtrip). From Pelion Gap, the main track descends to Pinestone Creek and Kia-ora Hut. Along the Overland Track 2.8 km south of this hut is a 500-meter trail to Hartnett Falls, where the Mersey River plunges over a rocky ledge into a deep pool below. From the Mersey River Valley, the main track climbs steadily to Du Cane Gap before descending two km to Windy Ridge Hut. From this hut it's only 12 km to Lake St. Clair, but most hikers make the overnight detour up Pine Valley, where there's an array of unusual geological features, such as the Acropolis, a ridge of intriguing columns, and the Labyrinth, a high plateau of small lakes. From Pine Valley Hut, Lake St. Clair is a soggy nine km south. From the hut at Narcissus Bay, the *Idaclair,* tel. (03) 6289-1137, transports hikers out to

civilization at Cynthia Bay. The trip is made twice daily, with times posted on the hut wall. The trip is $15 one-way. To continue on foot to Cynthia Bay is a farther 19 km.

Weather conditions in the mountains can deteriorate quickly, but the region is less prone to unpleasant weather in summer. Still, being an alpine area, the weather is unpredictable year-round. Although the huts en route are open to anyone, they fill early, so it is imperative to bring a tent and sleeping bag. Warm clothing, hiking boots, and a cooking stove are also necessary. A 1:100,000 scale topographical map has been produced especially for the Overland Track; it can be purchased at most outdoor shops or at Cradle Mountain Lodge. All hikers attempting the Overland Track must register with a park ranger. Huts along the trail cost $15 pp per night. To contact the ranger in advance, call (03) 6492-1133.

Craclair Tours, tel. (03) 6424-7833, operates an eight-day guided hike along the Overland Track. The pace is leisurely, with the option of climbing peaks en route or resting. Rates range $1,100-1,400, which includes camping equipment, all meals, and transportation to and from Devonport. These tours run Oct.-April.

The more luxurious option is with **Cradle Mountain Huts,** tel. (03) 6331-2006. This company operates the same style of trip but with overnight accommodations in magnificent timber huts, each with hot showers, hot meals, comfortable beds, and a relaxing lounge area. This trek includes a boat trip across Cynthia Lake, shortening the trail by 20 km. Cost of the six-day trip is $1,550 pp, which includes transportation to and from Launceston.

Cradle Mountain Lodge and other Accommodations

For those who want to experience the beauty of the Tasmanian wilderness while staying in a luxurious accommodation, you can't go past this stately two-story lodge surrounded by magnificent mountain scenery. The most popular rooms are the Pencil Pine Cabins, each with a potbelly stove, bath, and shower; $166 s or d, $216 with a private spa. Luxury. Upstairs in the main lodge are basic rooms, each with two bunk beds and a double bed, tea- and coffee-making facilities, and shared bathrooms. These rooms are $95 s or d. Expensive. Facilities in the lodge include a large comfortable lounge, two bars, and a dining room open for all meals (reservations necessary for dinner). For accommodation bookings, call (03) 6492-1303 or (1800) 03-0377.

The least expensive place to stay in the area is **Cradle Mountain Tourist Park,** two km north of the Visitor Centre and a 40-minute walk to Cradle Mountain Lodge. The campground is large, and sites have lots of privacy. Facilities include showers, toilets, laundry sinks, covered cooking shelter, and kiosk. Camping fees are $5-8 pp per night. Within the campground are bunkhouses with bunk beds and heaters (no cooking facilities). Guests must also supply their own linen. Rates are $22 pp. Budget. The campground office is open in summer 8:30-11:30 a.m. and 12:30-7 p.m. Only during holidays and summer weekends are reservations necessary, tel. (03) 6492-1133. Within the park, eight km south of the Visitor Centre, are the **Waldheim Cabins,** tel. (03) 6492-1110. The huts sleep four to eight people and are fairly basic; each has a gas stove, cooking utensils, cutlery, crockery, table, and heater, but no linen. Facilities are shared. Rates per cabin are $55-75; book through the Visitor Centre. Inexpensive.

Outside the park, off the road to Launceston, is remote **Lemonthyme Lodge,** tel. (03) 6492-1112, a wilderness retreat set on 43 hectares. The main lodge is a stunning log structure with four adjacent self-contained cabins nestled among the trees. Rooms in the main lodge are rustic and have shared facilities; $85 s or d. Moderate. The cabins are spacious and more comfortable. Each has a separate bedroom, large living area with a log fire, and kitchen. These are $175 s or d. In the main lodge is a cavernous dining area with timber tables and chairs, comfortable lounge area with a fireplace, bar, barbecue area, and large deck with bush views. All meals are available and are reasonably priced. As well as for guests, 7 p.m. is feeding time for local wildlife, which congregates outside the lodge.

Transportation, Services, and Information
Tasmanian Wilderness Travel, tel. (03) 6334-4442, operates a daily bus service (May-Oct. Tuesday, Thursday, and Saturday only) to the park from Devonport and Launceston. Three times weekly the service continues from the Cradle Valley to Strahan. Between December and Easter, Tasmanian Wilderness Travel operates a shuttle bus along the Cradle Valley and to Dove Lake. From Cynthia Bay, at the south end of the Overland Track, Tasmanian Wilderness Travel runs to Hobart, Launceston, and Devonport daily during summer.

Maxwell's, tel. (03) 6292-1400, runs a taxi between Derwent Bridge and Cynthia Bay.

Viewing the park's rugged topography from above is an awesome experience. Flightseeing with **Seair Adventure Charters,** tel. (03) 6492-1132, is $75 pp for 25 minutes and $115 for 50 minutes.

Cradle Mountain Visitor Centre, tel. (03) 6492-1110, is just inside the park boundary, in an area of lush rainforest above Pencil Pine Creek. Inside the attractive building are displays well worth viewing, including a three-dimensional model of the park, a photographic display, and an audiovisual. It's open year-round daily 8 a.m.-5 p.m. From the center, a 500-meter boardwalk leads through rainforest to Pencil Pine Falls.

The **ranger station** at Cynthia Bay, tel. (03) 6289-1172, is another source of information.

CRADLE MOUNTAIN TO LAUNCESTON

To get to Launceston from Cradle Valley, take the first turnoff at Moina. The winding eastward road skirts the base of the great central plateau upon which Walls of Jerusalem National Park lies. The road has spectacular views of the Great Western Tiers and descends through the lush Mersey River Valley and an area of farmland to the plains, beyond which lies Launceston.

Walls of Jerusalem National Park
When talking of north-central Tasmania, it is Cradle Mountain-Lake St. Clair National Park that is thought of, but immediately east, and part of the Tasmania Wilderness World Heritage Area, is the fabulous and remote scenery of 51,800-hectare Walls of Jerusalem National Park. The park is part of the central plateau, dotted with a maze of shallow lakes and surrounded by a natural amphitheater of rugged peaks rising to 1,500

meters. Access is from the north, along an unsealed road that hugs the eastern bank of Lake Rowallan. The road ends at the park boundary. From this point a few trails begin, but most serious hikers will want to explore their own routes and ascend surrounding mountain ranges. There are no designated campgrounds within the park. For further park information, call (03) 6363-5182. **Tasmanian Wilderness Travel,** tel. (03) 6334-4442, departs Launceston daily (except Friday and Sunday) at 9:30 a.m. for the park.

Mersey River Cave Systems

Along the Mersey River and its tributaries west of Mole Creek is extensive karst terrain, which comprises a limestone bedrock that has been eroded by underground waterflow to create complex cave systems extending many kilometers. Two caves are open to the public. Westernmost is **King Solomon Caves,** part of a state reserve on the road to Liena. Tours of this cave system depart from the ticket office, a five-minute walk from the road, six times daily between 10:30 a.m. and 4 p.m. The tour costs adult $8, child $4. Equally spectacular, **Marakoopa Caves,** nine km from the King Solomon turnoff, is known for its glowworms. Tour times and costs are the same as for King Solomon Cave. If you plan on visiting both, buy a combined ticket for adult $12, child $6.

Halfway between the caves and Mole Creek is **Mole Creek Camping Ground,** tel. (03) 6363-1150. Facilities are basic, but it's in a great little spot, spread along Sassafras Creek and surrounded by forested hills. Sites are $5-8. Budget.

Mole Creek

Lying in the shadow of the Great Western Tiers, Mole Creek has a picturesque location and some good accommodations. Important to the local economy is leatherwood honey. The leatherwood tree is confined to damp areas of the state, and here in the Mersey River Valley it thrives. The honey is produced Jan.-April, and during these months you can watch the extraction and bottling processes at the **Tasmanian Honey** factory, Main Rd., tel. (03) 6363-1170; open Mon.-Fri. 8 a.m.-4 p.m.

Mole Creek's biggest attraction is the large **Trowunna Wildlife Park,** several km east of town, tel. (03) 6363-6162. It features a range of

native animals, including many species casual observers are unlikely to see in the wild. Featured are the koalas (not native to Tasmania), waterfowl, raptors, lizards, wombats, tiger snakes, Tasmanian devils, and potoroos. The noctarium contains those animals most active at night, such as possums, Eastern bettongs, spotted-tail quolls, and sugar gliders. Kangaroos and wallabies hop throughout the park and raucous cockatoos make themselves known among the trees. Also at the park are a restaurant serving typical Aussie fare, like damper and billy tea ($7), and a shop selling some interesting pieces of pottery. Admission to the park is adult $7.50, child $3.50. It's open daily 9 a.m.-5 p.m.

Rooms at **Mole Creek Hotel,** tel. (03) 6363-1102, have shared facilities and are $30 s, $55 d. Inexpensive. Breakfast is a few dollars extra. **Mole Creek Guest House,** a few hundred meters west of the hotel, tel. (03) 6363-1399, has five tastefully decorated rooms, which although basic are comfortable; $55 s, $70 d ($80 with bathroom), including breakfast provisions. Moderate. Downstairs is **Laurelberry Tearooms,** a pleasant place for a meal, with lunch specials for about $7.50 and dinner $10-12.50. Meals are also available at Mole Creek Hotel, but no orders are taken after 7:30 p.m.

Deloraine

Midway between Devonport and Launceston, Deloraine features many buildings from the mid-1800s and a fabulous backdrop of the Great Western Tiers. The town has a wide range of accommodations, making it a good base for exploring nearby natural attractions. Worth visiting, **Bowerbank Mill,** two km east of town, tel. (03) 6362-2628, houses a gallery chock-full of art from all mediums. It's open daily 10 a.m.-5:30 p.m.

Originally a hospital, the atmosphere at Victorian-style **Arcoona,** East Barrack St., tel. (03) 6362-3443, couldn't be more different today. It's been restored to an upmarket B&B, with six spacious and comfortable rooms, each with king-size bed and private bathroom. Also available for guest use is a laundry, barbecue area, and dining room. Rates are $85 s, $140-150 d, including breakfast. Premium. Another good option for those who enjoy historic accommodations are the two cottages at **Bowerbank Mill,** two km east of town, tel. (03) 6362-2628; $110-130 s or d. Expensive. An inexpensive option is **Highview Lodge YHA,** at 8 Blake St., tel. (03) 6362-2996. Facilities are clean and modern, and a spacious deck takes full advantage of the mountain vista. Dorm beds are $13-16. Budget. **Deloraine Apex Caravan Park,** 51 West Parade, tel. (03) 6362-2345, has riverside sites for $10-13 but no vans or cabins. Budget.

Deloraine Hotel, Emu Bay Rd., tel. (03) 6362-2022, serves meals for $7-12. **Sullivans Takeaway Restaurant,** 17 West Parade, tel. (03) 6362-3264, is a popular local hangout dishing up no-frills meals at good prices; open daily from 8 a.m. Next door to the Deloraine Hotel is **Bonney's Inn,** tel. (03) 6362-2122, built in 1830, open for morning tea ($3-6.50), lunch ($4.50-11), and dinner ($11-14.50). Closed Sunday and Monday.

Deloraine Visitor Information Centre, 29 West Church St., tel. (03) 6362-2046, is open daily 7 a.m.-6 p.m.

Westbury

With grand plans for a city, this historic town was first settled in 1828. Many original buildings remain, including **White House,** on the corner of Adelaide and King Streets, tel. (03) 6393-1171, which dates from 1841. The main house contains a collection of 17th- and 18th-century furniture and other artifacts from the era. Around the inner courtyard are several restored buildings, including a bakehouse (which features an enormous wood-fired, cast-iron oven—selling breads and cakes, the bakery is open to the public Wed.-Sun. 9 a.m.-5 p.m.), stables, and a garage full of vintage cars, horse-drawn carriages, and a collection of 1860s bicycles. The complex is open Tues.-Sun. 10 a.m.-4 p.m. (closed winter); admission is $6. Also in town is **Pearn's Steam World,** tel. (03) 6397-3313, a collection of steam-powered farm machinery. Admission is $3. Open daily 9 a.m.-5 p.m.

Egmont, 922 Birralee Rd., tel. (03) 6393-1164, in the same family since 1838, is a historic home renovated to a guesthouse. Surrounded in gardens, the house features a large fireplace, country kitchen and dining area, and plenty of rooms and halls to explore. Rates for the entire house are a reasonable $80, which includes breakfast provisions. Moderate.

LAUNCESTON AND VICINITY

Launceston, a small city 200 km north of Hobart, lies at the head of the **Tamar River,** a tidal waterway extending 50 km from Bass Strait. The city sprawls around the confluence of two rivers, the North Esk and South Esk, which merge to form the Tamar River. From this confluence, and the city of Launceston, the river flows northwestward to Bass Strait through the wide, hospitable Tamar Valley, dotted with orchards, wineries, and various accommodations. Flanking the river mouth are rugged Asbestos Range National Park and historic George Town, settled in 1804.

Launceston was founded in 1805, making it Australia's third-oldest city. Earlier attempts at settlement along the Tamar River had proved unsuccessful, but the ideal location, along with rich mineral deposits farther inland, saw the settlement grow to become one of Australia's wealthiest mining towns and to develop as Tasmania's major industrial center. Today, the city has a population of 67,000, making it Tasmania's second-largest city.

LAUNCESTON SIGHTS

Launceston is a colorful city, featuring many gardens, a friendly atmosphere, and a compact downtown core that allows plenty of opportunities for exploring on foot.

Cataract Gorge

This spectacular gorge on Launceston's western outskirts was formed through a combination of a powerful earthquake 40 million years ago and erosion caused by the flow of the South Esk River. The gorge is protected by a reserve through which many hiking trails have been cut, but the gorge itself is most spectacular. From Kings Bridge, trails lead along both sides of the gorge to First Basin, a deep pool of water, where you'll find the **Interpretation Centre** (open Mon.-Fri. 9 a.m.-4 p.m., Sat.-Sun. till 4:40 p.m.), a swimming pool, tearooms, and a restaurant. A 300-meter-long chairlift spans the gorge, ending at an area called **Cliff Grounds,** which is alive with trees, ferns, exotic plants, and grassy lawns. Tickets for the chairlift are adult $5, child $3. One of the best ways to escape the crowds is to head out along the 2.3-km trail along the south side of the gorge to **Duck Reach,** site of an old power station.

Off Gorge Rd., which leads into the reserve's north end, is a road leading to **Freelands Lookout Reserve,** which has a good view of the Tamar River and surrounding landscape.

Penny Royal World

This large complex, beside Kings Bridge and opposite the north end of Cataract Gorge, recreates life in the mid-1800s through working displays, a watermill, gunpowder museum, cornmill, and candy factory. Other action is on the water, including an old sloop, barges, and *Lady Stelfox,* a paddlesteamer that cruises along the Tamar River. Admission is a steep $19.50, child $9.50, but it's possible to take the river cruise only for about $6.50. Also on-site is a café, restaurant, and gift shop. The park is open daily 9 a.m.-4:30 p.m. For more information call (03) 6331-6699. Show your admission tickets at the adjacent Penny Royal Watermill Motel for a 25% accommodation discount.

Other Town Sights

Downtown Launceston features many historic buildings and areas of parkland, and a **tram tour,** with an informative commentary, is the best way to view them; $23 pp.

The main displays at **Queen Victoria Museum and Art Gallery,** housed in a large building on Wellington St., tel. (03) 6331-6777, include Tasmania's all-important mineral deposits, Launceston's interesting geology, the state's unique flora and fauna, and a collection of Chinese treasures. The Art Gallery contains a fabulous collection of colonial art. Admission to both is free. They are open Mon.-Sat. 10 a.m.-5 p.m., Sunday 2 p.m.-5 p.m. Within the same complex is **Launceston Planetarium,** featuring astronomical displays and a changing program of events. It's open Tues.-Sat. at 2 p.m. and 3 p.m.; admission is adult $3, child $2. If you're interested in

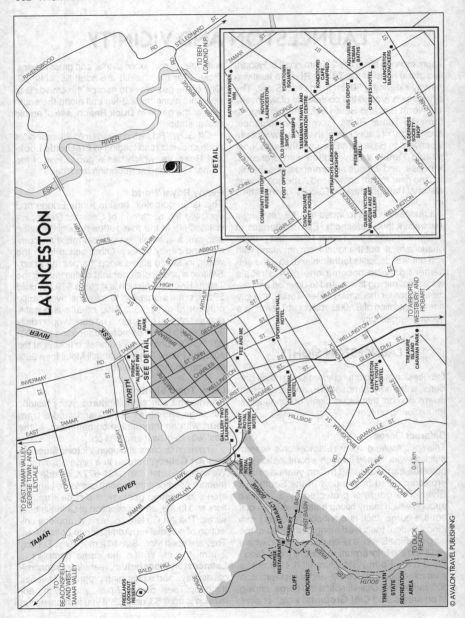

LAUNCESTON

TO BEN
LOMOND N.P.

ST. LEONARD
ST.

RD

RD

TAMAR

RAVENSWOOD

HOBART ESK. BRIDGE

ESK

RIVER

ST

ESK

CRES

ELPHIN

RACECOURSE
ST

ABBOTT
ST.

CLARENCE ST.

HIGH
ST.

ARTHUR
ST.

MARY
ST.

MULGRAVE
ST.

RD

INVERMAY

ESK

RIVER

TAMAR

NORTH

PRINCE
ALBERT INN

CITY
PARK

SEE DETAIL

YORK

ST.

GEORGE
ST.

ST.

ST.

FEE AND ME

SPORTSMAN'S HALL
HOTEL

WELLINGTON
ST.

HOWICK

ST.

TO AIRPORT,
WESTBURY, AND
HOBART

RD

TAMAR
HWY

LINDSAY
ST

FORSTER
ST

EAST
TAMAR

HWY

BRISBANE
ST

ST. JOHN

CHARLES

WELLINGTON

BATHURST

MARGARET
ST.

CRES

THISTLE
ST.

GLEN
ST.

DHU
ST.

TREASURE
ISLAND
CARAVAN PARK

LAUNCESTON
CITY YOUTH
HOSTEL

TO EAST TAMAR VALLEY,
GEORGE TOWN, AND
LILYDALE

TAMAR

RIVER

WEST
TAMAR
RD

TREVALLYN
RD

GALLERY TWO
LAUNCESTON

PENNY
ROYAL
WATERMILL
MOTEL

PENNY
ROYAL
WORLD

HILLSIDE

CENTENNIAL
MOTEL

BROUGHAM
ST.

GRANVILLE
ST.

WILHELMINA AVE.

BROUGHAM ST.

TO
BEACONSFIELD
AND WEST
TAMAR VALLEY

BALD
HILL
RD

FREELANDS
LOOKOUT
RESERVE

GORGE
RD

GORGE
RESTAURANT

CLIFF
GROUNDS

CATARACT

CHARLFUT

GORGE

FIRST BASIN

TREVALLYN
STATE
RECREATION
AREA

RIVER

ESK

SOUTH

TO DUCK
REACH

0.4 km

© AVALON TRAVEL PUBLISHING

DETAIL

ST. LEONARD
ST

TAMAR
ST

ST

BATMAN FAWKNER
INN

NOVOTEL
LAUNCESTON

YORKTOWN
SQUARE

GEORGE

KONDITOREI
CAFE
MANFRED

AQUARIUS
ROMAN
BATHS

LAUNCESTON
BACKPACKERS

CAMERON

CIMITIERE

CHARLES

ST. JOHN

OLD UMBRELLA
SHOP

SHRIMPS

BUS DEPOT

O'KEEFES HOTEL

TASMANIAN TRAVEL AND
INFORMATION CENTRE

WILDERNESS
SOCIETY
SHOP

PEDESTRIAN
MALL

ELIZABETH
ST

COMMUNITY HISTORY
MUSEUM

POST OFFICE

PETRARCH'S LAUNCESTON
BOOKSHOP

CIVIC SQUARE /
HENTY HOUSE

QUEEN VICTORIA
MUSEUM AND ART
GALLERY

PATERSON
ST

BRISBANE
ST

YORK
ST

WELLINGTON

ST

local history, the **Community History Museum,** corner Cimitiere and St. John Streets, tel. (03) 6337-1391, is the place to head. It's in a building built back in 1842 and formerly used as a trading center for grains, wine, and spirits. Admission is free. It's open Mon.-Fri. 10 a.m.-4 p.m.

The **Old Umbrella Shop,** 60 George St., tel. (03) 6331-9248, in the business of selling umbrellas since the 1860s, has been owned by the same family since 1900. The building and shop is now preserved by the National Trust, with umbrellas from the last 100 years on display. It's open Mon.-Fri. 9 a.m.-5 p.m., Saturday 9 a.m.-noon.

Housed in another historic building is **Gallery Two Launceston,** at 2 Bridge Rd., tel. (03) 6331-2339. Originally a mill, it now houses galleries and studios and a great little café. It's open daily 11 a.m.-5 p.m.

Recreation

Trevallyn State Recreation Area is a heavily forested 400-hectare park immediately west of downtown is bordered on three sides by the Esk River, and is most easily accessed from the Tamar Highway. Beyond the park gate (locked nightly at 8:30 p.m.) is an information center, the starting point for several short walks, including to a lookout (100 meters) and to Trevallyn Dam (1.3 km). The dam is a popular windsurfing spot, while within the park you can go horseback riding and hang gliding down a 200-meter-long cable ($10 per ride; daily 10 a.m.-5 p.m.).

Complete with marble-like columns and classic statues, the **Aquarius Roman Baths,** 127-133 George St., tel. (03) 6331-2255, are Roman-style baths, of varying temperatures: the Tepidarium is warm while the Caldarium is much hotter. There are also a number of spa baths and massages and beauty treatments are offered. Admission is $18 for one person or $25 per couple. It's open Mon.-Fri. 8 a.m.-10 p.m., Sat.-Sun. 9 a.m.-6 p.m.

PRACTICALITIES

Accommodations

Sportsman's Hall Hotel, 252 Charles St., tel. (03) 6331-3968, is a historic pub in a quiet area a few blocks from downtown. Rates are $30 s,

$45 d, which includes breakfast. Inexpensive. **Batman Fawkner Inn,** 35 Cameron St., tel. (03) 6331-7222, dates from 1822 and oozes colonial charm. (Check out the prints in the lobby, including those of the hotel's namesakes, John Batman, founder of Melbourne, and John Pascoe Fawkner, the hotel's original landlord). Rates range $40-50 s, $70-80 d, and for a few bucks extra you'll get a light breakfast. Moderate.

Penny Royal Watermill Motel, 147 Paterson St., tel. (03) 6331-6699 or (1800) 06-0954, is in a historic watermill building dating from 1825. Rooms are decorated in old-English style; $130 s, $140 d including breakfast. Premium. The six-story **Novotel Launceston,** 29 Cameron St., tel. (03) 6334-3434, right downtown, is one of the city's tallest buildings and also its finest hotel. For the standard of rooms, the rates of $140 s or d are reasonable. Premium. On the city's outskirts, eight km southwest of downtown, is the **Country Club Casino,** tel. (03) 6335-5777 or (1800) 03-0211. It features a luxurious country club atmosphere, with one of Tasmania's best golf courses, tennis courts, squash, horseback riding, an indoor pool, and a fitness room. Rates start at $235 s or d for a standard room. Luxury.

Alices Cottages, at 129 Balfour St., tel. (03) 6334-2231, is one section of various historic accommodations that share a lovely garden. The Shambles is a row of small, comfortable, attached cottages, each individually decorated with huge old fireplaces, high four-poster beds, claw-footed baths, lots of intriguing objects from the past, and theme-related curios and knick-knacks, yet all the modern conveniences you'd expect. Ample breakfast provisions are included in the price of $140 s or d. Premium.

Launceston City Youth Hostel (not a YHA), a large backpacker accommodation with 100 beds, is at 36 Thistle St., two km south of downtown, tel. (03) 6344-9779. The hostel is not particularly inviting, but it offers a wide range of guest facilities, including a spacious living area, fully equipped kitchen, lockers, and bathrooms with coin-operated showers. Dorm beds are $12 pp, with discounts for stays over three nights. Budget. The owners have backpacking equipment and mountain bikes for rent (10- and 12-speed bikes are $12-18 per day or $65-95 per week). Another inexpensive choice is **Launceston City Backpackers,** 139 George St., tel.

(03) 6334-2327. Dorms are $14 and there are a few doubles for $30. Budget.

Launceston has one campground, **Treasure Island Caravan Park,** 94 Glen Dhu St., tel. (03) 6344-2600, a noisy place right beside the main route into town from the south and two km from downtown. Sites are $12-15, on-site vans $32, and cabins with good cooking facilities $50-60. Budget.

Food

Banjo's, Yorktown Square, is a local bakery with a wide selection of breads, pastries, and pizza. **Konditorei Cafe Manfred,** 95 George St., has German-style cakes and pastries, including excellent apple strudel. **Posh Nosh,** 127 St. John St., is a busy weekday lunchtime hangout. Everything is prepared on the premises, from simple healthy sandwiches to a King Island Platter of cheeses and smoked beef. For a casual snack or meal with water views, you can't go past **Ripples** in Gallery Two Launceston on Bridge Road. Meals, including delicious fluffy pancakes, start at $4.50, and the coffee isn't bad either.

In historic Albert Hall in City Park is **Victoria's Tassie Fare,** 72 George St., tel. (03) 6334-0534, featuring a menu of strictly Tasmanian produce and game. Lunch is a casual affair, while in the evening, starched-white tablecloths and silvery cutlery make for a more formal setting. Dinner mains average $17-18.

O'Keefes Hotel, 124 George St., tel. (03) 6331-4015, is a popular local hangout offering an inexpensive blackboard menu that includes delicious beer-battered fish ($8). Open daily for lunch and dinner. Another place for a pub meal, if you don't mind the stuffed animals overhead, is **Centennial Hotel,** corner Balfour and Bathurst Streets, tel. (03) 6331-2184. The daily two-course special is a good value at $7.

Owl's Nest Restaurant, 147 Paterson St., tel. (03) 6331-6699, part of Penny Royal Watermill Motel, is a cozy restaurant with old stone walls and dark timber furniture, giving it a real colonial atmosphere. Local produce is featured on the menu, where main dishes range $14.50-16.50. On the same property is an English-style pub. The **Gorge Restaurant,** on the northwest side of Cataract Gorge, tel. (03) 6331-3330, takes advantage of the surrounding natural beauty with outdoor seating (and peacocks). It's open

for lunch and dinner Tues.-Sat. and for lunch on Sunday only.

For a Chinese buffet, try the **Golden Sea Dragon** on the corner of Bathurst and Canning Streets, tel. (03) 6331-7728; $16.50.

In a convict-built structure, right downtown at 72 George St., tel. (03) 6334-0584, is **Shrimps,** Launceston's finest seafood restaurant. With an intimate atmosphere and a menu featuring Tasmanian seafood delicacies, this is the place for a special night out. **Fee and Me,** on the city's outskirts at 190 Charles St., tel. (03) 6331-3195, is an upmarket restaurant housed in a grand mansion dating from 1835. The menu is Mediterranean-influenced and the dress code is semiformal.

Transportation, Services, and Information

Launceston is a major gateway for airlines from mainland Australia, while **Aus-Air,** tel. (1800) 33-1256, and **Island Airlines,** tel. (1800) 81-8455, link the city to other state centers, such as Hobart. **Tasmanian Redline Coaches** operates an airport shuttle for $6 each way. To book this service call (03) 6331-3900. A cab between the airport and downtown runs about $22. Tasmanian Redline Coaches also operates bus services between Launceston and Devonport, Burnie, St. Marys, and Hobart. The depot is at 112 George St., tel. (03) 6331-3233. To top the monopoly off, Tasmanian Redline Coaches also offers tours of the city for $25 pp; for these, call (03) 6331-9177. The other bus company serving the city is **Tasmanian Wilderness Travel,** tel. (03) 6334-4442, which links Launceston to Cradle Mountain National Park and the west coast towns of Strahan and Queenstown.

Metro, tel. (13) 2201, runs a local bus service, with a $3 day pass for unlimited travel Mon.-Fri. 9 a.m.-4:30 p.m., after 6 p.m., and all weekend. All major car rental companies have outlets in Launceston, including **Avis,** tel. (03) 6391-8314, and **Budget,** tel. (03) 6334-0099, but for something cheaper call **Apple Car Rentals,** tel. (03) 6343-3780. **Rent-a-cycle,** at Launceston City Youth Hostel, tel. (03) 6344-9779, has mountain bikes for $12-18 per day.

The **post office,** on St. John Street opposite Civic Square, is a grand old building. **Petrarch's Launceston Bookshop** is in Quadrant Mall on Brisbane St., tel. (03) 6331-8837. The best source of local and state information is **Tasmanian Travel and Information Centre,** corner St. John and Paterson Streets, tel. (03) 6336-3122. For accommodation bookings, call this office at (03) 6336-3133. It's open Mon.-Fri. 9 a.m.-5 p.m., Saturday 9 a.m.-noon. For adventure travel information, head to the **Wilderness Society Shop,** 174 Charles St., tel. (03) 6334-2499.

TAMAR VALLEY

The wide Tamar River extends over 60 km inland from Bass Strait to Launceston. It is crossed by a bridge in just one place, 20 km from the mouth, making a roundtrip along both sides of the valley possible with a short detour to wild Asbestos National Park. The valley is Tasmania's premier wine-producing area, with vineyards on both sides of the river. Many roadside stalls sell local produce, and arts-and-crafts outlets abound.

Launceston to Beaconsfield

From Launceston the highway through West Tamar passes open farmland with plenty of river views. The first township north of Launceston is **Legana.** A good alternative to staying in the city, **Launceston Holiday Park Legana,** tel. (03) 6330-1714, has a large grassed area for tents, and clean, modern facilities. Sites range $10-12, and there are a few cabins for $38-58. Inexpensive. North of Legana is **Grindelwald,** a Swiss-style residential and resort complex complete with a manmade lake, golf course, accommodations, and restaurants. Accommodation in self-contained chalets is $140, while motel rooms are slightly less expensive. For bookings, call (03) 6330-0400. Premium.

Beyond this complex is **Strathlynn Wine Centre,** part of Pipers Brook Vineyard. It's open for tastings daily 10 a.m.-5 p.m. Also nearby is **St. Matthias Vineyard,** with tastings also and similar hours.

Waterbird Haven Trust, 17 km from Launceston, is a marshy area along the Tamar River protected as a bird sanctuary. Within the reserve is a massive walk-through aviary, a display of geese, and a variety of other caged birds. Admission is $4. It's open daily between 9 a.m. and dusk. To book a guided tour, call ahead, tel. (03) 6394-4087.

The next stop heading north should be **Rosevears Waterfront Tavern,** tel. (03) 6394-4074, a historic hotel and microbrewery first licensed in 1831 (look for original brickwork in the public bar). Meals are served at lunch and dinner, but don't expect any bargains; most start at $10.

Back out on the main road is **Brady's Lookout,** a vantage point used by the bushranger Matthew Brady. For many years, this area was the haunt of Brady and his gang. They also evaded capture in remote **Notley Gorge State Reserve,** accessed from southwest of Exeter. The reserve escaped logging because of its inaccessibility, the same reason Brady found it an excellent hideout.

The area surrounding the village of **Deviot** is dotted with more vineyards while to the north is **Batman Bridge,** the only span across the Tamar River. It is a cable-stayed bridge, dominated by a 100-meter-high steel-frame tower.

Beaconsfield and Farther North

Founded to serve a nearby gold mine, this small town is best known for **Grubb Shaft Gold and Heritage Museum,** tel. (03) 6383-1473, on the site of Tasmania's largest gold mine, from which 849,913 ounces of the precious metal were extracted before its closure in 1914. Today it's a tourist attraction, with working models, exhibits and photographic displays, domestic displays, and a re-created mine office depicting life at the turn of the century. Admission is a worthy $4. Open daily 10 a.m.-4 p.m.

North of Beaconsfield is the aptly named **Beauty Point,** a great little spot overlooking the Tamar River. Stay at **Astra Motel,** tel. (03) 6383-4375, with river views and an extensive rose garden. Rates are a great value at $45 s, $55 d. Inexpensive.

To the north is **Greens Beach,** a typically picturesque end-of-the-road village with a great stretch of sandy beach, golf course, tennis, and a variety of accommodations. **Greens Beach Caravan Park,** a stone's throw from the beach, tel. (03) 6383-9222, has tent sites for $9-12. Budget.

Asbestos Range National Park

This 4,349-hectare park extends along the coast between Greens Beach, at the mouth of the

Tamar River, and beautiful Bakers Beach, opposite Port Sorell. It features long sandy beaches and rocky headlands backed by extensive dune and lagoon systems. Behind these is the Asbestos Range, providing challenging hiking and some spectacular lookouts. The park was declared as recently as 1976, and yet wildlife populations are high and the magical feeling of an unspoilt wilderness area prevails.

The park's main feature, its namesake, was thrust skyward around 600 million years ago and slowly eroded to its present height of about 400 meters since. Between the range and Bass Strait are layers of gravel and sand, pushed inland by wind and water to form the low coastal topography. The park's flora is extremely hardy. Climatic extremes, a lack of fresh water and decent soil, and salt-laden winds allow only a few species to survive. Early settlers drained swampland behind the dune systems to create pastures for grazing cattle. The introduced species are long gone, native species abound. The best time for viewing park wildlife is dusk; species you'll most likely spot are brush-tailed possums, pademelons, Bennett's wallabies, wombats, and Tasmanian devils.

Access to the park is from Beaconsfield, with the road joining the coast at **Badger Beach.** The beach is a beautiful golden-yellow color and is deserted at all but the busiest times of year. Along this beach after heavy storms, sand is often washed away, revealing the roots of ancient she-oaks dating from the last ice age when Tasmania was linked to the mainland. Farther west, around Badger Head, is Bakers Beach and the main facility areas.

Starting at the park information center, the Springlawn Nature Walk leads along the edge of a lagoon (where towering melaleucas sit with their roots submerged in the water), through typical coastal heathland, and past various water ecosystems that attract abundant waterbirds. A more challenging trail is to **Archer's Knob** (two km each way), with its panoramic coastal vistas.

Within the park are three campgrounds; each has pit toilets, bore water, and a limited amount of firewood. All sites are $4 pp. The small information center features a three-dimensional model of the park and boards detailing ranger-led activities. It's open daily 9 a.m.-5 p.m., tel. (03) 6428-6277.

George Town

In 1804 Col. William Paterson came ashore with 180 convicts to found George Town, northern Tasmania's first settlement. Today the town has a population of about 5,600, and although the streets are lined with many historic buildings, most local attractions lie farther north, toward Low Head. George Town is also the terminus of the *Devil Cat* from mainland Australia. In town is **The Grove,** 25 Cimitiere St., tel. (03) 6482-1336, an elegant stone house dating from 1829. It's open daily 9 a.m.-5:30 p.m., with regular (and short) tours for $3 pp and lunch available in a small restaurant. **Mount George Scenic Lookout,** accessed along a road spurring west from the information center, allows views over the entire area. **Seal and Sea Adventure Tours,** tel. (0419) 35708, heads out onto the bay's quiet waters in search of seals, with the option of donning a wetsuit and joining these fun-loving creatures in the water; $100 pp.

The least-expensive place to stay in town is the **Travellers YHA Hostel,** 4 Elizabeth St., tel. (03) 6382-1399, across from the Pier Hotel and bus depot. All the usual facilities are provided; rates are $14-17 pp. Budget. Another inexpensive option is **Nanna's Cottage,** a small, cozy, self-contained cottage in the grounds of The Grove at 25 Cimitiere St., tel. (03) 6382-1336. Rates are $65-75 s or d. Moderate. **Central Court Apartments,** Main Rd., tel. (03) 6382-2155, has basic self-contained units from $65. Moderate. More expensive, but of a higher standard and with river views, is **The Pier** at 5 Elizabeth St., tel. (03) 6382-1300. Facilities at this hotel are clean and modern, and each of the eight rooms has basic cooking facilities; $118 s or d. Expensive. This hotel also has an excellent restaurant with a casual and friendly atmosphere.

Entering George Town from the south, you'll pass a small **information center,** tel. (03) 6382-1700, run by friendly volunteers who seem to know everything that's happening in town. It's open daily 11 a.m.-4 p.m.

Low Head and Vicinity

Low Head is a narrow finger of land at the mouth of the Tamar River. On the river side of the headland is **Port of Launceston Authority's Pilot Station,** manned since 1805, and although operation equipment has changed considerably in that time, its function is basically the same—to guide shipping through the treacherous mouth of the Tamar River. Within the complex is a variety of buildings, including some convict-built structures dating from 1835. One of the oldest buildings on the site, originally built as accommodation for the pilots, now houses an interesting collection of maritime memorabilia, including old navigational lights, compasses, barometers, maps, historic prints, and a collection of 19th-century log books. Admission is $3. Open daily 8 a.m.-6 p.m., tel. (03) 6382-1143.

Toward Low Head itself, past a row of stately colonial-era houses, is a **penguin walk** at **Low Head Coastal Reserve.** The track is open year-round, but the birds are most active Oct.-Jan. at dusk. At the end of the road is **Low Head Lighthouse,** built in 1888, and stunning river and ocean views.

Beach Pines Holiday Village, in a protected hollow on the ocean side of Low Head, tel. (03) 6382-2602, is a short walk from the beach and features a good range of facilities. Tent sites are $10-16 and self-contained timber cabins start at $58. Budget-Inexpensive.

NORTHEAST OF LAUNCESTON

From Launceston two roads lead through hilly terrain to **Scottsdale,** an agriculture center and the gateway to the remote northeast tip of Tasmania. The longer of the two routes passes through **Lilydale** on the way. Just north of this town, Lilydale Falls Reserve has a short trail leading to the falls, a picnic area with barbecues, and free camping.

Bridestowe Estate Lavender Farm

The bright purple fields of this farm, north of Nabowla on the road between Lilydale and Scottsdale, are in stark contrast to the surrounding native bush. You can tour the farm and buy an assortment of lavender products and souvenirs. Admission is $3 during the flowering season (January), and it's open daily 9 a.m.-5 p.m. (closed in winter). Call (03) 6352-8182 for more details.

Scottsdale

Surrounded by rolling hills and backed by a remote mountainous wilderness, this town is an agricultural center of 2,000. The main street is lined with buildings dating from the turn of the century. At 46 King St. is **Anabel's of Scottsdale,** tel. (03) 6352-3277, with five rooms for overnight accommodation. Each room has a bathroom and limited cooking facilities. Rates are $95 s or d. Expensive. In the same complex is a tastefully decorated restaurant open for dinner daily from 6:30 p.m.

Bridport and Farther East

This popular seaside holiday village lies on Anderson Bay, 20 km north of Scottsdale. The road into town follows the foreshore, passing a jetty and a colorful assortment of fishing boats. There's not much to see, but it's a relaxing place to hangout when visiting the couple of wildlife reserves in the area.

The least expensive place to stay is **Bridport Seaside Resort,** across the road from the estuary at 47 Main St., tel. (03) 6356-1585. Single rooms are $20 and doubles $32-42. Facilities include a kitchen with water views and a laundry. Inexpensive. **Bridairre Bed and Breakfast,** Frances St., tel. (03) 6356-1438, offers small, clean rooms on the lower floor of a home. Communal bathrooms and living room; $60 s, $70 d. Moderate. A little farther out of town, on Ada St., tel. (03) 6356-1873, is **Platypus Park Farm Chalets,** surrounded by open fields and native bushland. The rooms are self-contained and quite comfortable. Rates are $95-106 s or d.

East of Bridport, a sealed road leads 65 km to **Tomahawk,** a remote village on **Ringarooma Bay.** The bay's eastern arm is protected by a narrow reserve. Access is only possible at a few spots, including the outlet of Ringarooma River. Accommodation is at **Tomahawk Caravan Park,** tel. (03) 6355-2268. Budget.

BEN LOMOND NATIONAL PARK

Located 50 km southeast of Launceston, this 16,527-hectare park encompasses the magnificent Ben Lomond Range, which rises dramatically to a height of 1,573 meters at Legges Tor. The park is best known for its ski slopes, but in summer the scenery is equally spectacular, especially along the hiking trail to the summit of Legges Tor. The display of alpine wildflowers each spring is magnificent, while at lower elevations forests of eucalypt dominate.

From the turnoff at the North Esk River it's eight km to the park gate and 18 km to the end of the road. The road is unsealed and all uphill, getting progressively steeper as you ascend. The summit track is four km each way (allow three hours roundtrip) but is ill-defined in places. Another track leads across the lunar-like landscape to **Ladder Lookout** for views to the valley below. The park has no official trails, but on the back of the park map are distances between prominent landmarks.

In the village is **Ben Lomond Creek Inn,** tel. (03) 6372-2444, offering accommodations year-round, meals in a cozy restaurant, and drinks at the bar. Rooms are sparse and rates aren't cheap at $105 s, $120 d and up to $200 d in winter, including breakfast. In winter, dorm accommodation in an attached chalet is $30 pp. The park has no campgrounds (see below for an alternative). For park information, call the ranger at (03) 6390-6279. For ski area information, call **Ben Lomond Ski Rentals,** tel. (03) 6331-1312. When the ski area is open, day tickets are $36 pp and **Tasmanian Wilderness Travel,** tel. (03) 6334-4442, operates transfers from Paddy Palin, at 59 Brisbane St., Launceston, to the mountain.

From the turnoff to the park, the road continues eastward to the coast. Near Upper Blessington are great views of Ben Lomond Range to the south. Farther east is **Griffin Camping Area,** a pleasant grassed area beside the South Esk River where views extend west to the Ben Lomond Range.

BASS STRAIT ISLANDS

About 12,000 years ago, as the sea level rose at the end of the last ice age, the land link between Tasmania and mainland Australia was broken, leaving the high peaks of the link as rugged islands dotted through the waters of Bass Strait. Of the strait's 120 islands, most of which are barren outcrops of rock, just two—King and Flinders— are populated. King and Flinders Islands are magical places, with rugged headlands separated by unspoilt beaches and coastlines alive with large populations of marine mammals and sea birds, and, in the case of Flinders Island, opportunities for hiking the high peaks of Strzelecki National Park. The two islands are very different. King Island is dominated by lush green farmland and renowned for culinary delights such as cheese, seafood, and honey. Flinders is renowned for its adventure opportunities and long beaches. Both are delightful destinations, different from anywhere else in the country, and little known, even to mainland Australians.

Both islands are well equipped for travelers, with a range of accommodations and restaurants, air links to both Tasmania and the mainland, and rental cars. The least-expensive way to visit them is on an all-inclusive package with **Aus-Air,** tel. (1800) 33-1256; **Island Airlines,** tel. (1800) 81-8455; **Kendell,** tel. (1800) 33-8894; or **Tasair,** tel. (1800) 06-2900.

History
The idyllic lifestyle of today's Bass Strait islanders belies a wild and bloody history of shipwrecks, kidnapping, and the massacre of almost all the islands' seals. George Bass, who became the first European to record the fact that Tasmania was separated from mainland Australia, told of an abundance of seals in the strait. Sealers descended on the area in the hundreds. Dumped on the islands by unscrupulous employers, they lived in temporary camps with often-inadequate provisions and worked long hours in the harshest weather conditions. Seal oil and skins were to become Australia's first export; by 1800 25,000 skins a year were being transported to England. As seal numbers declined, most sealers moved back to the mainland; those remaining on the islands lived a rough and reckless life, a lifestyle that attracted many escaped convicts and rogues.

The discovery of Bass Strait had cut 1,000 km from the main shipping route between England and Sydney, but the advantages of the shorter journey were overshadowed by Bass Strait's treacherous waters. *Sydney Cove,* bound for Sydney Town with 7,000 gallons of spirits, became the first ship to be wrecked when it went aground in 1797 en route from England. During one month in 1835, Bass Strait claimed 358 lives when the convict ships *George III* and *Neva* wrecked (in a cruel twist of fate, some survivors from the *Neva* died of alcohol poisoning after salvaging pans of whisky). The region's worst disaster occurred a decade later when the *Catargui,* filled with British immigrants, crashed into a reef on King Island's west coast, killing all but nine of the 425 people aboard. Shipwrecks were so much a part of life in Bass Strait that the islanders came to rely on their cargo for survival.

The islands entered this century much different from the last. Residents now live a more sedate lifestyle, relying heavily on high rainfalls to keep agriculture concerns profitable. Until 1990, scheelite, a tungsten-bearing ore used for hardening steel, was mined on King Island.

KING ISLAND

Lying off the northwestern tip of Tasmania, rugged King Island has been the setting for some of Australia's most tragic maritime disasters, but today it's best known for gourmet foods such as creamy brie cheese, fresh seafood, and juicy beef. The island is 55 km long and 22 km wide, but its contrasts are staggering, ranging from long sandy beaches flanked by rugged headlands to lush fields filled with herds of dairy cows. **Currie,** on the west coast and with a population of 900 (more than half the island's total), is the island's main settlement. At **Surprise Bay,** south of Currie, is a forest of calcified plantlife. On the southeast coast is **Grassy Harbour,** which has undergone major upheaval since the scheelite mine, the only reason for the town's existence, closed in 1990. Formerly known as Grassy, the settlement was built purely to serve miners and their families. The mine had a turbulent history, its fortunes fluctuating with world tungsten prices. After its closure most miners and their families moved from the island, leaving a town complete with swimming pool, tennis courts, and golf course, deserted. Recently, a group of local businessmen banded together and bought the whole town, securing its future against demolition. Look for the penguin rookery at the end of the town's breakwall. To the north, past a honey farm, is the small east coast community of **Naracoopa,** on beautiful Sea Elephant Bay. The north end of the island is more remote, with a narrow road leading to **Cape Wickham,** where a lighthouse

has been guiding ships since 1861. Other roads from Currie end at secluded bays, such as Yellow Rock Beach, where a wreck is visible.

Accommodations and Food
King Island Colonial Lodge, 13 Main St., tel. (03) 6462-1066, right in the heart of Currie, has six rooms with shared facilities and a laundry. It is also the departure point for island tours. Rates are $60 s, $70 d, which includes a light breakfast. Moderate. Also right in town is **Parer's King Island Hotel,** Main St., tel. (03) 6462-1633, a mod-

ern place where rooms have bathrooms. A bar, bistro, and restaurant are on the premises; $65 s, $95 d. Expensive. A rental car makes access to other accommodations possible, including **King Island Gem Hotel,** two km north of Currie, tel. (03) 6462-1260. Two-story A-frame units ($80-100 s or d) are self-contained, allowing you to sample home-cooked King Island produce without the cost of eating at a restaurant. Moderate. Also here are a few motel units for $60 s, $80 d. Over at Naracoopa is **Rocky Glen Retreat,** tel. (03) 6461-1103, a series of chalets set among landscaped gardens and right by a long stretch of beautiful beach; $70 s, $85 d. Moderate.

For many, a highlight of a visit to King Island will be sampling the local fare. The best place to start a culinary tour is **King Island Dairy,** north of Currie, tel. (03) 6462-1348, for creamy brie cheeses. In Currie, **King Island Seafoods,** tel. (03) 6461-1528, has crayfish in season. For Devonshire tea, a light meal, or just coffee and home-cooked cakes, head to **Nautilus Coffee Lounge,** on Edward St., Currie, tel. (03) 6462-1868. For the best range of local produce, try the following restaurants: **Fishbowl Restaurant,** tel. (03) 6462-1288, overlooking the ocean at Boomerang by the Sea Motel, open nightly from 6 p.m.; one of the three eateries in Parer's King Island Hotel; or, over in Naracoopa, **King Island Bay View Restaurant,** Lovers Lane, tel. (03) 6461-1103.

Transportation, Services, and Information

Aus-Air, tel. (1800) 33-1256, and **Tasair,** tel. (1800) 06-2900, fly from various points in Tasmania to King Island, including Launceston, Burnie, and Devonport. Both airlines offer packages from Launceston for $299 pp, inclusive of return flight, two nights' accommodation, and car rental. From mainland Australia, **Kendell Airlines,** tel. (1800) 33-8894, flies daily from the domestic terminal at Melbourne Airport to King Island. The regular one-way fare is $172, advance purchase fares start at $224 roundtrip, but, again, a package is the way to go—from $399 pp for flights, three nights' accommodation, most meals, and three-day tours.

If a rental car isn't included in your package, **Howell's Auto Rent,** tel. (03) 6462-1282, has small sedans for $65-75 per day including unlimited km. **Top Tours,** tel. (03) 6462-1245, of-fers three different day tours, each taking in a different part of the island; each costs $55 pp and includes lunch.

King Island Tourist and Information Centre is at 13 Main Rd., Currie, tel. (03) 6462-1245.

FLINDERS ISLAND

Flinders Island is the largest of the **Furneaux Archipelago,** a group of 55 islands that lie off Tasmania's northeastern tip. This island has less than one-half of King Island's population and is better suited to those looking for a more active holiday, with camping, birdwatching, hiking, fishing, and scuba diving all possible. This island also features endless stretches of unspoilt beach and a national park.

The final chapter of one of Australia's most appalling events, the massacre of Tasmania's Aborigines, took place on Flinders Island. Between 1829 and 1934 George Robinson brought the few Aborigines who had survived Tasmanian massacres to the island and established **Wybalenna,** a community where they were to be trained in the ways of Christianity. Within a few years, more than half died, unable to cope with the ways of the white settlers and losing the will to live. All that remains of the community is a chapel, the only building in Tasmania associated with early Aborigines, and a cemetery. The site is Settlement Point, halfway up the west coast and north of the airport. Also on the point is a **muttonbird rookery,** with an observation platform for easy viewing. To the west is **Emita Museum,** chock-full of relics from the strait's early history, including many items salvaged from shipwrecks. It's open Sat.-Sun. and daily during holidays 1-5 p.m. Farther north is **Killiecrankie Bay** where Killiecrankie diamonds (clear topaz) are occasionally found.

Whitemark, south of the airstrip, is the commercial center of the island and has all services. At Adelaide Bay, on the south coast, is **Lady Barron,** the island's only other settlement and home to a fleet of fishing vessels. The island's southern peaks are protected by 4,215-hectare **Strzelecki National Park,** which also encompasses a pristine stretch of coastline. The hike to the summit of 756-meter Mt. Strzelecki is seven km each way (allow four to five hours roundtrip).

FLINDERS ISLAND

STANLEY POINT

FURNEAUX

KILLIECRANKIE BAY

CAPE FRANKLAND

0   20 km

MARSHALL BAY

BABEL ISLAND

SELLARS POINT

EMITA
WYBALENNA

SETTLEMENT POINT

PRIME SEAL ISLAND

ARCHIPELAGO

WHITEMARK
PARRYS BAY

MT. STRZELECKI
(756 m)
STRZELECKI NATIONAL PARK

LADY BARRON

POT BOIL POINT

TROUSERS POINT

ADELAIDE BAY

BADGER ISLAND

ANDERSON ISLAND

CAPE   BARREN   ISLAND

© AVALON TRAVEL PUBLISHING

Accommodations and Food

As with King Island, most visitors to Flinders Island arrive as part of an all-inclusive package tour, which will include options for the many cottages scattered around the island. On Bluff Rd., Whitemark, is **Flinders Park Units,** tel. (03) 6359-2188, where self-contained cabins are $55 s or d. Inexpensive. At Emita is **Greenglades Host Farm,** Fairhaven Rd., tel. (03) 6359-8506, a small guesthouse with two rooms, a lounge,

and laundry; rates here are $60 pp, which includes meals. The island's largest accommodation is **Flinders Island Lodge,** in Lady Barron, tel. (03) 6359-3521 or (1800) 81-8826. Rooms here are $70 s, $95 d, which includes a continental buffet breakfast. Expensive. At **Trousers Point,** beside Strzelecki National Park, is a picturesque campground under a stand of she-oaks. Facilities include toilets, fireplaces, and drinking water. It's possible to camp elsewhere on the island, including Stanley Point on the north tip.

Whitemark and Lady Barron have shops selling groceries. Otherwise eat at the restaurant in **Flinders Island Lodge,** tel. (03) 6359-3521, where views extend over Adelaide Bay.

Transportation and Tours
Island Airlines, tel. (1800) 81-8455, provides flights between Flinders Island and Launceston. Flights to Flinders Island also originate from Traralgon, in Victoria's Gippsland, and Melbourne. To save up to 50% on one-way fares, book a roundtrip flight more than 14 days in advance. Packages offered include airfares from Melbourne and two nights' cottage accommodations for $309 pp. **Aus-Air,** tel. (1800) 33-1256, flies to the island from Launceston and Moorabbin.

Rental cars are available from **Bowman Transport,** tel. (03) 6359-2019, and **Flinders Island Car Rentals,** tel. (03) 6359-2168; expect to pay from $70 per day.

Strait Lady is a 10-meter motor cat that cruises to uninhabited islands of the Furneaux Archipelago for wildlife viewing, fishing, and diving; call Flinders Island Adventures at (03) 6359-4507 for details.

VICTORIA

THE LAND

Occupying just three percent of Australia (similar in size to Great Britain) and smallest of the mainland states, Victoria is a package of welcome surprises. To the north, separated by the Murray River, is New South Wales; to the west is South Australia; and to the south is 1,300 km of rugged coastline, which gets the full brunt of unpredictable weather from Bass Strait and the Southern Ocean. Victoria has the most diverse landscape of any state; within the confines of these borders are wild ocean beaches, a desert-like landscape in the west, snow-covered peaks in the east, forests filled with unique Australian flora and fauna, and cities steeped in gold-rush history.

Regions

Melbourne is very central to the state's attractions; all parts of the state can be reached within a day's drive. Immediately north of the capital are the goldfield towns of Ballarat and Bendigo.

The Great Ocean Road, which follows the coastline southwest of Melbourne, is one of the world's great ocean drives. In the west of the state are the Grampians, a spectacular outcrop of mountains with some of the state's best hiking and wildlife-viewing. The mighty Murray River originates in the east of the state and flows westward; along its banks are the charming towns of Mildura, Swan Hill, and Echuca, which originated as inland ports. Some of Victoria's most spectacular scenery is found in the High Country, the southern extent of the Great Dividing Range. These mountains are protected by Alpine National Park and provide endless opportunity for exploration, whether on foot, horseback, or a 4WD day trip. And yes, Australia *does* have snow; this part of the state is dotted with ski resorts. The coastal Princes Highway provides an alternative route between Melbourne and Sydney and detours can easily be made to Phillip Island, home to a large population of penguins, and Wilsons Promontory, southernmost point of mainland Australia.

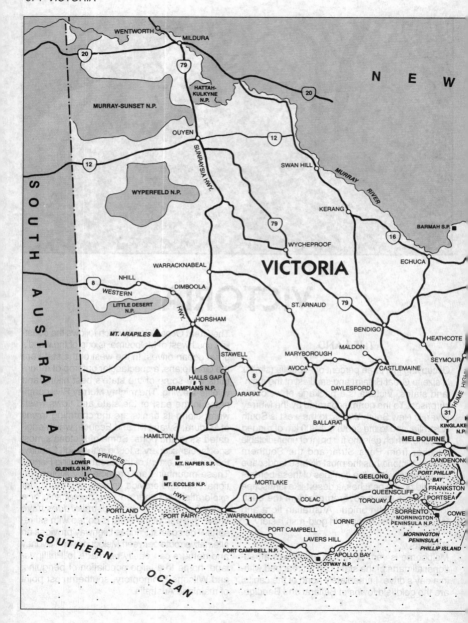

S O U T H   W A L E S

GREAT   DIVIDING   RANGE

MURRAY   RIVER

39

16

COBRAM

YARRAWONGA

RUTHERGLEN

ALBURY

WODONGA

TALLANGATTA

CORRYONG

BURROWA-PINE
MOUNTAIN N.P.

41

31

16

SHEPPARTON

WANGARATTA

BEECHWORTH

BENALLA

GLENROWAN

MT. BUFFALO
N.P.

MT. BOGONG

GOULBURN VALLEY

31

EILDON

CATHEDRAL
RANGE S.P.

MARYSVILLE

HEALESVILLE

ALPINE N.P.

GREAT

OMEO

ALPINE N.P.

SNOWY
RIVER
N.P.

COOPRACAMBRA
N.P.

ERRINUNDRA
N.P.

CANN RIVER

1

MT. BAW BAW

BAW BAW N.P.

ERICA

MITCHELL
RIVER
N.P.

PRINCES   HWY.

ORBOST

CANN RIVER

CROAJINGOLONG N.P.

MALLACOOTA

1

WARRAGUL

MOE

WESTERN PORT

MORWELL

TRARALGON

SALE

BAIRNSDALE

1

PAYNESVILLE

LAKES ENTRANCE

METUNG

THE LAKES N.P.

GIPPSLAND LAKES
COASTAL PARK

FRENCH ISLAND

SOUTH GIPPSLAND HWY.

WONTHAGGI

FOSTER

PORT WELSHPOOL

WILSONS
PROMONTORY N.P.

B A S S   S T R A I T

0   50 km

© AVALON TRAVEL PUBLISHING

Climate

Victoria, and Melbourne in particular, has a reputation among those living in the northern states for inclement weather, namely overcast skies and drizzling rain. But this isn't the case, or so the statisticians claim. Their records prove, much to the delight of southerners, that Sydney receives twice the annual rainfall of Melbourne, but, whereas Sydney has short bursts of heavy rain, Melbourne can be overcast for days. Weather in the rest of the state is very dynamic; cold fronts can whip across the Southern Ocean from Antarctica any month of the year. In the High Country, snow falls June-Sept. and often flurries occur a month either side (snow also falls as far west as the Grampians and, on occasion, in downtown Melbourne). Rainfall throughout the state is not particularly high, but is more frequent in coastal areas. In the far northwest of the state, the desert-like landscape is drastically affected by rainfall. As the Murray River, to the north, floods, it flows through a series of floodplains.

Climate should play a role in choosing the time of year to visit Victoria but is not as important a factor as in other parts of the country. (You should avoid summer school holidays—mid-Dec. to Jan.—as everywhere is crowded.) Summer (Dec.-Feb.) is the only season when ocean swimming and sunbaking are pleasant. Spring (Sept.-Nov.) and autumn (March-May) are good times for touring and walking. Winter (June-Aug.) sees the crowds head to High Country ski resorts, but, compared to North America, winters are mild and there is no better time explore the goldfields or experience the culinary delights of Melbourne.

HISTORY

European Settlement

For 40,000 years Aboriginals, known also as Koori, lived freely throughout Australia; those in the southeast lived a seminomadic lifestyle throughout what would become Victoria, but within 50 years of the arrival of Europeans, only 500 Aboriginals in Victoria survived. At the beginning of the 1800s, with Sydney Town's population overflowing and the French sending ships to explore the Australian coast, the British sent a small party of convicts to establish a colony in Port Phillip Bay. Within a year, due to a lack of

fresh water, they abandoned the settlement and sailed for Van Diemen's Land, now known as Tasmania. In 1835 a Tasmanian, John Batman, sailed into Port Phillip Bay searching for land suitable for grazing and agriculture. For a few blankets, knives, and trinkets, he bought 250,000 hectares of land from local Koori and established a settlement on the Yarra River.

Gold

Ten thousand people were living in the vicinity of Melbourne by 1840. Towns had been established along the coastline, including Portland and Port Fairy, and a few remote sheep stations were scattered across the interior. Gold rushes west of Sydney drew many people from the fledgling colony of Victoria. Wanting to avoid a collapse of the city, a group of businessmen posted a reward to anyone who found gold within 100 miles of Melbourne. Within weeks gold had been discovered at Warrandyte, northwest of Melbourne, and by the end of that year, 1851, massive gold strikes had been made throughout central Victoria and tens of thousands of hopeful diggers had flocked to the goldfields. Immigrants from around the world arrived in the colony; Melbourne boomed, and what had begun as rough shanty towns grew to become permanent settlements. About this time, Melbourne businessmen set about separating from New South Wales, and in 1851 a new colony, named for the Queen of England, was proclaimed. By 1860 the biggest of the gold rushes was over and the colony's population stabilized, with 600,000 people living in Melbourne alone.

20th Century

On 1 January 1901 Australia was federated, and Victoria became a state. Apart from the 1920s, during the Great Depression, Victoria continued to boom, especially in times of high wool prices. For most of this century, immigration policies topped up the population; after WW II, immigrants arrived from Europe and in the 1970s from Southeast Asia. Property prices shot skyward in the 1980s, but by 1990 the economy recessed and Victoria was hit particularly hard. A change of government in the early 1990s brought a breath of fresh air to the state. Through cost-cutting measures and aggressive marketing, the state has managed a turnaround and is prospering once again.

MELBOURNE

A blend of impressive Victorian-era buildings, modern skyscrapers, tree-lined avenues, large areas of parkland, and trams trundling the streets of downtown combine to make Melbourne (MEL-bun) one of the world's great cities to visit (a 1990 U.S. survey declared Melbourne to be the "world's most livable city"). Sydneysiders see their southern relatives as conservative and dull, while Melburnians see themselves as refined and culturally inclined. Indeed, Melbourne is often called "The Least Australian City."

Melbourne is the capital of Victoria, and with a population of 2.9 million, it is Australia's second largest city. In area, Melbourne is one of the world's largest cities, extending 100 km from north to south and 80 km from east to west. It sprawls over coastal plains around Port Phillip Bay, a massive body of water indented into the coastline of Victoria. Whereas Sydney lies around a beautiful natural harbor, Melbourne has no such natural feature, just the sluggish Yarra River winding through it. Its dirty brown color is not man's doing, but due to suspended clay sediment.

Downtown Melbourne is spread along the Yarra River a couple of km from Port Phillip Bay. North of the river are, traditionally, working-class suburbs such as Richmond and Collingwood, while to the south are middle- and upper-class suburbs such as South Yarra, Kew, and, on an elevated area west of downtown, Toorak, one of Australia's most expensive addresses and *definitely* the most expensive away from water.

The city boasts an air of distinctive tradition, making it hard to believe that just 150 years ago it was an expanse of savannah grassland. Through a short, nonconvict past, Melbourne flourished as a cultural center, supportive of music and the performing arts, as well as being the home of many distinguished artists, sophisticated shopping precincts, and fine dining restaurants. Not all Melbourne's culture revolves around the visual and performing arts. There's also sporting culture. One of the world's great sporting venues, the **Melbourne Cricket Ground**, is the scene of cricket matches all summer. Few cities have proclaimed a public holiday for a three-minute horse race, in this case the **Melbourne Cup.** But it is Victoria's own code of football, **Aussie Rules,** that has the most fanatical following.

History

The European history of Melbourne began in 1835 when John Batman and a group of pastoralists from northern Tasmania established a settlement beside the Yarra River. For the first 50 years, Melbourne's only link to the outside world was by sea, and in 1883 a rail link was completed with Sydney.

Upon separation from New South Wales in 1851, Melbourne was declared capital of the newly named Victoria. That same year, gold was discovered in Victoria and the city boomed, its population doubling to 46,000 within 12 months, and, by the end of the decade, its population had eclipsed that of Sydney. The gold rush attracted businesses that based themselves in the gateway city, and by the 1880s Melbourne had become the financial capital of Australia. As the gold rush ended, public land was set aside for diggers, encouraging them to remain in the Melbourne district. By late last century Melbourne's economy had become strongly linked to Victoria's pastoral hinterland, where sheep and cattle stations had been established. The large population in Melbourne formed a base for the business and manufacturing industry that continues to thrive today. It was during this period that much of Melbourne's impressive architecture dates, a time when Melbourne was the South Pacific's most important city, attracting travelers, writers, and adventurous aristocrats from around the world.

In 1901, when the Australian colonies were federated, Melbourne was proclaimed the seat of federal parliament and remained temporary capital until 1927 when parliament moved to Canberra. After WW II, Melbourne's British origins were slowly diluted as immigration policies changed, bringing large numbers of Italians, Greeks, Turks, and other Europeans into Australia. To this day, Melbourne remains the world's second-largest Greek city and has the largest population of Italians outside Italy.

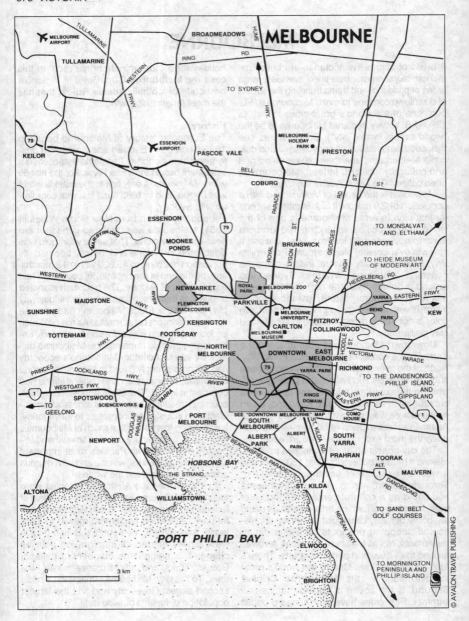

MELBOURNE

DOWNTOWN SIGHTS

Swanston Street

A ferry service that once connected Swanston St. to the south side of the Yarra River saw this street become downtown's main thoroughfare, with many historic buildings constructed along its length. The street is now closed to vehicular traffic—only trams and pedestrians travel the route. At the Yarra River-end of the street is **Flinders St. Railway Station,** a long domed building that has been the transportation hub of Melbourne for most of this century. Diagonally opposite is **St. Paul's Cathedral,** sections of which date from 1880; open daily 7 a.m.-6 p.m. Across the road is **Young and Jackson's Hotel.** Built in 1861, the hotel is best known for *Chloe,* a painting of a nude woman, which hung in the public bar for 80 years before being moved to the upstairs restaurant. One block north is **City Square,** currently undergoing redevelopment and home to a statue of the hapless Burke and Wills. Diagonally opposite is the 1932 **Manchester Unity Building,** one of Melbourne's first high-rise buildings and home to the city's oldest escalator. Next to the Manchester Unity Building is the **Capitol Building,** designed by Walter Burley Griffin. The original facade has been replaced, but, inside,

---

RULES OF THE ROAD: CARS AND TRAMS

Traveling by tram is one of the true joys of Melbourne, but sharing the roads with them when you're driving is a different matter. Remember that trams can only be overtaken on the *left.* Also, you must always stop behind a tram when it stops.

A special road rule, known as the "Hook Turn," has been developed to allow trams to travel more freely through the city. It may seem straightforward if you've lived all your life in Melbourne, but to visiting drivers it can be confusing. It applies at any intersection marked with a black-and-white sign hanging from cables. When turning *right,* you must pull to the *left* and wait for the lights of the street you're turning *into* to turn green.

---

the Capitol Theatre is considered one of the world's greatest theaters (now showing Chinese language films only). Opposite is **Town Hall,** built in 1870 and restored in the mid-1990s. The interior walls are decorated by the work of some of Australia's best-known artists, and the highlight is a massive organ, made up of 6,000 pipes.

Four blocks north, two very different buildings face each other. On the east side of Swanston St. is the **State Library,** sections of which date from 1854. Its classical facade leads into a cavernous foyer and the famous domed reading room. Opposite the library is **Melbourne Central,** an ultramodern retail complex and 55-story office tower. The central atrium, topped by a massive cone-shaped glass ceiling, protects a historic brick shot tower, which itself is 20 stories high.

Collins Street

Prestigious Collins St. is lined with 19th-century buildings housing some of Melbourne's most exclusive shops as well as restaurants and cafés, interspersed with modern buildings such as 35-story Regent Melbourne. The street's east end has the fashionable boutiques while west of Swanston St. is home to bankers and stockbrokers. Between Exhibition and Swanston Streets are three historic churches; the oldest, **Collins St. Baptist Church,** dates from 1862 (open Mon.-Fri. 11 a.m.-2 p.m.). At 162 Collins St. is **Georges,** Melbourne's most exclusive department store. Between Swanston and Elizabeth Streets is **Block Arcade,** a stylish arcade of shops built in 1892 and styled on the Galleria Viltorio Emmanuel in Milan, Italy. It features shopfronts with high windows, mosaic floors, marble columns, and high vaulted ceilings.

The many historic buildings of the financial district are dwarfed by **Rialto Tower,** a modern 55-story office tower (tallest building in the Southern Hemisphere). On the top floor is a viewing deck; open daily Mon.-Fri. 11 a.m.-11 p.m., Sat.-Sun. 10 a.m.-11 p.m. Admission is adult $7.50, child $5, which includes a 38-second lift ride, use of telescopes, entry to a historic display, and viewing of the wide-screen audiovisual "Melbourne the Living City."

Chinatown

The colorful sights and aromatic smells of Chinatown are marked by an ornate gateway across

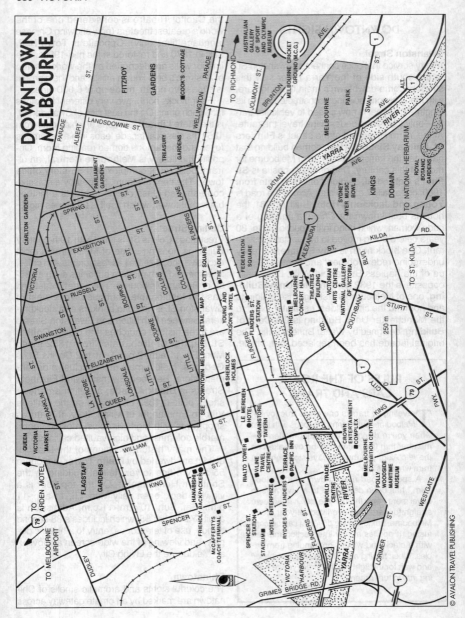

DOWNTOWN MELBOURNE

© AVALON TRAVEL PUBLISHING

Little Bourke St. at Swanston Street. This part of town was a focus for the Chinese since the gold rush, and the streetscape has changed little since. The **Chinese Museum,** in Cohen Place, tel. (03) 9662-2888, depicts the history of Chinese in Australia and the racism and persecution they encountered on the goldfields. Admission is $6. Open Sun.-Fri. 10 a.m.-4:30 p.m., Saturday noon-4:30 p.m.

Parliament House

One of Melbourne's oldest buildings, Parliament House lies in an area known as the Parliamentary Precinct, set aside by early town planners for various civic buildings, parks, and a treasury. The precinct is located east of Spring St., with the impressive facade of Parliament House facing Spring Street. Construction started in 1856, at a time when the gold rush was injecting untold wealth into the colony of Victoria. Various additions were made to the building during its early years, but a dome that was part of the original

Parliament House

plan still hasn't been completed. The interior of the building is also impressive, and on days when parliament isn't sitting tours are offered hourly 10 a.m.-3 p.m.; call (03) 9651-8568 for bookings.

Behind Parliament House are a few blocks of historic buildings, including churches and the **Commonwealth Building,** used 1901-27 when Melbourne was the temporary national capital. Beside Parliament House is the **Old Treasury,** tel. (03) 9651-2233, its size and formidable appearance testimony to the vast wealth the goldfields produced. Permanent exhibitions tell of the journey that the gold followed after being mined, from the convoys that brought it to Melbourne to ships that transported it to London. Admission is adult $5, child $3. It's open daily 9 a.m.-5 p.m.

Windsor Hotel

Across from Parliament House is Australia's only remaining Victorian-era hotel. Built in 1883, it features a distinctive facade, and in the foyer, all the opulence you'd expect, with the original elevators now serving as phone booths.

National Philatelic Centre

Within this large complex at 321 Exhibition St., tel. (03) 9204-5021, is the **Post Master Gallery,** displaying every stamp ever issued in Australia. Displays also catalogue the history of stamps and stamp collecting as well as the design process. It's open Sat.-Mon. noon-5 p.m., Tues.-Fri. 10 a.m.-5 p.m.

Old Melbourne Gaol

When troopers finally captured Australia's most infamous bushranger Ned Kelly, it was in this jail that he was held and hanged. It was completed in 1858, and in its 90-year history, more than 130 souls were hanged. Today, it's open to the public, a good place for those with a fascination with Australia's convict history to view morbid relics such as death masks and gallows. Other displays include documents cataloging the small crimes that condemned people to a life in a penal colony and a grim collection of memorabilia that allows a glimpse at life behind bars. The platform from where Ned and others were hanged is on display, as is his bullet-dented armor and death mask. Admission is $7 adult, $4 child. Open daily 9:30 a.m.-4:30 p.m. On Wednesday and Sunday at 7:30 p.m., you can

THERRY ST.

HOTEL Y

MAC'S HOTEL

MELBOURNE TRANSIT CENTRE

FRANKLIN

HOTEL BAKPAK

TOAD HALL

OLD MELBOURNE GAOL

RUSSELL ST.

SWANSTON

ELIZABETH ST.

QUEEN ST.

LITTLE LA TROBE ST.

INDIA HOUSE

ST.

MUSEUM RAILWAY STATION

STATE LIBRARY

LA TROBE

MELBOURNE CENTRAL

ST.

DOWNTOWN MELBOURNE DETAIL

LONSDALE

FLIGHT CENTRE

RUBY RED

TSINDOS THE GREEK'S RESTAURANT

KING'S WOK

SUPPER INN

LITTLE

ST.

THE LOUNGE

KUN MING

LONSDALE

MYER DEPARTMENT STORE

ONG INTERNATIONAL FOOD COURT

SWANSTON

HORSE & HOUND TAVERN

BOWYANGS TRAVEL BOOKS

BOURKE

TRAVELLER'S MEDICAL CLINIC

GENERAL POST OFFICE

INFORMATION BOOTH

LITTLE

CAMPARI BISTRO

TRAVELLERS CONTACT POINT

ST.

QUEEN

ST.

DAVID JONES

GOPAL'S

ABORIGINAL HANDCRAFTS

ELIZABETH

BOURKE

0   100 m

ST.

COLLINS

ST.

BLOCK ARCADE

CITY SQUARE MOTEL

LITTLE

MET SHOP

ST.

COLLINS

BACKPACKERS TRAVEL CENTRE

NOON

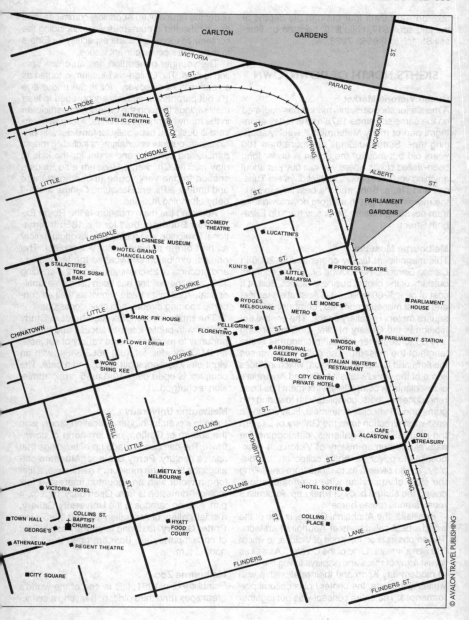

take an After Dark tour through the depths of the jail; adult $17, child $10. Located on Russell St., tel. (03) 9663-7228.

SIGHTS NORTH OF DOWNTOWN

Queen Victoria Market

A mecca for shoppers, this market has operated on the same site since 1878 and is today an integral part of many Melburnians' weekly shopping trips. Some buildings are more than 100 years old but most of the action is under long open-walled sheds where you can buy just about anything you'll ever need. Market days are Tuesday and Thurs.-Sun., and the best time to go is the morning. To get there from downtown take tram no. 55 up William St. or any tram up Elizabeth Street

Melbourne Museum

This magnificent facility opens in July 2000 in Carlton Gardens, Rathdowne St., on the northern outskirts of the central business district. Built at a cost of over $260 million, it is Australia's largest and finest museum complex, comprising 7,000 square meters of gallery space. The central exhibition is the Gallery of Life, a 55-meter-long and up to 30-meter-tall hall running the entire length of the museum. The gallery showcases the flora and fauna of the region, which includes some of the world's tallest trees and Australia's oldest plants. A complete environment has been reproduced indoors, complete with towering red gums and 25 species of animals. Running in an east-west direction from the Gallery of Life are the main exhibition galleries, cataloguing the natural and human history of Victoria. It is impossible to cover the entire collection, but displays are so diverse as to range from one telling the story of Australian wine to another showcasing the stuffed body of Phar Lap, Australia's most famous racing horse.

Bunjilaka, the Aboriginal Centre, is one of the world's best collections of Aboriginal artifacts. The emphasis is on the Koori of Victoria, to whom "Bunjilaka" meant "Land of the Creator." As well as a vast array of relics and displays telling the story of modern day Koori and their relationship with white Australians, the center hosts cultural performances. The entire concept was put together under the advice of an Aboriginal committee, and this is reflected in numerous ways, including the conference rooms set aside especially for Elders to meet and discuss current issues.

The younger generation has an entire section to itself. The Children's Museum is touted as a "pathway of discovery" for those under age 10, but parents are actively encouraged to lead their siblings through the gallery and participate in the many organized activities. An open courtyard is designed especially for families, with picnic tables; outdoor entertainment including music, dance, and comedy; and water for the kids to play in. The Children's Museum also holds a section for the very young (those aged three and under), a Parent Resource Centre, and full baby-changing facilities.

Adjoining the main museum is the **Royal Exhibition Building,** built for the 1880 International Exhibition and restored to its original glory as part of the museum complex project. The original exhibition showcased the technology and products of 25 countries, and in the ensuing 120 years the building has been used on a smaller scale for similar trade shows as well as concerts, sporting events, and civic occasions.

The museum complex also holds a Study Centre with public Internet access and the opportunity to research a wide variety of subjects, an IMAX theater, tel. (03) 9663-5454, with an eight-story screen, a gift shop, and a café. The complex is open daily 10 a.m.-5 p.m.; admission is charged.

Melbourne University

Victoria's premier higher education facility is in the suburb of Carlton, one km north of downtown. The campus is made up of buildings that span a century. **Percy Grainger Museum** catalogs the life of the museum's namesake, a lifelong traveler with an eccentric interest in folk music. Admission is free. Open daily 10 a.m.-4 p.m. Also on campus is the **University Gallery,** a small gallery of Australian art, and the **Sir Ian Potter Gallery,** featuring temporary exhibitions of contemporary art. Both are open Wed.-Sat. noon-5 p.m.

Melbourne Zoo

Established in 1861, this is one of the world's great zoos (and third oldest), boasting a collection of 3,000 animals in "natural" surroundings. And, as far as zoos go, cages are spacious and viewing easy. The collection of Australian fauna is extensive and includes a platypusary, where one of the world's most unusual animals is on display, and underwater viewing of fur seals. Other highlights include gorillas in a rainforest setting as well as bears and snow leopards. The zoo has a good souvenir shop, two restaurants, and a café. Admission is adult $13, child $7. Open daily 9 a.m.-5 p.m. with free guided tours offered throughout the day. Located on Elliot Ave., Parkville, tel. (03) 9285-9300. To get there by tram, take no. 55 or 56 north on William St., or on Sunday no. 68 on Elizabeth Street.

Heide Museum of Modern Art
Set among parkland extending to the banks of the Yarra River, this place was originally the home of John and Sunday Reed, whose 1930s patronage of famous Australian artists such as Sir Sidney Nolan and Albert Tucker, combined with a web of sexual intrigue between the artists and patrons, saw the house become the scene of change in Australian contemporary art. It now houses a large collection of art from that era and is surrounded by an expansive sculpture park. It's open Tues.-Fri. 10 a.m.-5 p.m., Sat.-Sun. noon-5 p.m. Admission $2. It is located at 7 Templestowe Rd., Bulleen, tel. (03) 9850-1500. Take bus no. 203 to get there.

SIGHTS SOUTH
OF THE YARRA RIVER

From downtown, continue south along Swanston St. and over the Princes Bridge to access the following sights.

Victorian Arts Centre
This complex comprises two main buildings, the distinctive circular **Melbourne Concert Hall** and the **Theatres Building,** which are linked by landscaped walkways. The Concert Hall hosts major events year-round, while the Theatres Building holds the **Performing Arts Museum,** tel. (03) 9684-8263. Exhibitions change regularly but feature all aspects of the arts. Open Mon.-Sat. 11 a.m.-5 p.m., Sunday 10 a.m.-5

p.m. Tours of the center depart weekdays at 10 a.m. and 2:30 p.m., and cost $12 pp. Contact the booking office on Level 5, tel. (03) 9281-8000, for the details.

National Gallery of Victoria
This, Australia's premier art gallery, will be closed until early 2001 for extensive renovations, with a small percentage of its works displayed at the State Library and other temporary locations through the city. For details and progress reports, check out the website: www. ngv.vic.gov. au. When open, this facility displays about 70,000 works of art from around the world. It was built in the late 1960s, part of an arts precinct that includes the Victorian Arts Centre and Victorian College of Arts. Out front is *Angel,* a colorful and distinctive sculpture by Deborah Halpern. The gallery has collections of art from all eras of Australian history, including works by prominent Aboriginal artists, Arthur Streeton, Tom Roberts, Arthur Boyd, and Sir Sidney Nolan. Picasso, Monet, Rembrandt, and Turner are featured in international galleries, while in the courtyard are works by sculptor Henry Moore. The gallery is open daily 10 a.m.-5 p.m. Admission is free to the permanent gallery, while temporary exhibitions charge up to $10 pp.

Southgate
This riverfront complex, tel. (03) 9690-9800, sits on the Yarra River opposite Flinders St. Station and beside Melbourne Concert Hall and is linked to downtown by a footbridge across the river. Three-story Southgate houses a food court, restaurants, and boutiques. On the first floor is **AustraliaGate SensorVision Theatre,** a unique complex where the movie *Experience Australia* is screened with the help of a huge video screen, the latest audio technology, a range of smells piped into the theater, and computer-controlled temperature and humidity changes. The idea is to experience as many aspects of life in Australia as possible, including the Dreamtime, a convict ship, early settlers, the goldfields, bushfire, rainforest, life on a beach, and Australians at war. The show runs 50 minutes, running hourly 11:30 a.m.-4:30 p.m. Tickets are a worthwhile $7.50 adult, $4.50 child.

Polly Woodside Maritime Museum

Polly Woodside, an Irish-built ship dating from 1885, spent her working life sailing between Europe and South America before ending her working life as a coal hulk in Port of Melbourne. Restoration began in 1972, and she now sits in dry dock on the south side of the Yarra River, downstream from Southgate. One of only six ships worldwide to be awarded an International Heritage Medal for excellence in restoration, it is part of an ever-growing museum with a small lighthouse, an old pumphouse, and other maritime memorabilia. Admission is adult $7, child $4. Open daily 10 a.m.-4 p.m., tel. (03) 9699-9760.

Como Historic House

Built in 1840, Como House overlooks the Yarra River in South Yarra. The original house was a single-story residence, with later owners expanding it to the grandeur evident today. Landscaped gardens and interior restoration make this house one of the finest places to view early Melbourne life. Open daily 10 a.m.-5 p.m.; admission is adult $8, child $5.50. To get there from downtown, take tram no. 80 to stop 33 and walk down Como Avenue.

St. Kilda

Late last century, St. Kilda, south of downtown on Port Phillip Bay, was a seaside resort popular with day trippers wanting to escape the crowded streets of downtown Melbourne. First they came by horse and cart, then a tram line was built, opening the suburb up to everyone. People would flock to the beach, the swimming baths, the foreshore fun parks, and the hotels and restaurants. By the turn of the century, St. Kilda was home to many of Melbourne's wealthiest citizens. For most of this century, though, the suburb was in decline, but has undergone a dramatic facelift in the last 15 years, its brothels and drug dens replaced with fashionable boutiques, stylish cafés, and many fine restaurants. Most of the action is on Fitzroy St., which ends at the foreshore, at a large strip of coastal park where **St. Kilda Pier** juts into the bay. South of the pier is the familiar laughing face of **Luna Park,** a fun park dating from 1912. It's free to wander around the park, but the many rides cost $1-3 each. Call (03) 9525-5033 for hours.

PARKS AND GARDENS

Kings Domain

Bordered by the Yarra River, St. Kilda Rd., Domain Rd., and Anderson St., Kings Domain is one of Melbourne's finest chunks of parkland. The southeast corner is the **Royal Botanic Gardens,** encompassing 36 hectares and containing more than 11,000 plants from Australia and around the world. It is a peaceful place to spend an hour or so, with many lakes attracting waterfowl and a lakeside café serving Devonshire teas (daily 9 a.m.-5 p.m.). A visitor center is in the **National Herbarium,** on Birdwood Avenue. The herbarium was established in 1853 to help the general public with plant identification. Open daily 10 a.m.-5 p.m., tel. (03) 9252-2300. Toward the city is the **Shrine of Remembrance,** built for the memory of Victorians killed in WW I; from its lofty perch views extend to the city. Built in 1839, **Governor La Trobe's Cottage,** on Birdwood Ave., is the original governor's residence, and is open to the public Monday and Wednesday 11 a.m.-4 p.m. and Sat.-Sun. 11 a.m.-4 p.m. Admission is adult $2, child $1. The cottage is a far cry from the new Government House, built in 1872 in the center of the gardens and open for tours Monday, Wednesday, and Saturday; $8 pp. Bookings are essential; call the National Trust at (03) 9654-4711 for times.

Carlton Gardens

These gardens are on the northeast corner of downtown, encompassing the **Royal Exhibition Building,** built for the 1880 Great Exhibition and still in use today. The gardens are also home to the spectacular new Melbourne Museum.

Fitzroy Gardens

Fitzroy Gardens date from 1857, and are laid out in the design of Great Britain's flag, the Union Jack. They feature tree-lined avenues, colorful flower displays, and a fern-filled gully. **Cook's Cottage,** in a corner of the park, was the English home of Capt. James Cook's parents. It was dismantled and rebuilt in the gardens in 1934. The interior is furnished with period antiques, and a small part of the cottage is devoted to the life of their famous son. Admission is $3. Open daily 9 a.m.-5 p.m.

Yarra Park and the Melbourne Cricket Ground

Yarra Park, a sprawling area east of downtown, is home to the Melbourne Cricket Ground (M.C.G.), one of the world's great sporting fields; **Melbourne Park,** home to the Australian Tennis Open; and a variety of other sporting fields. The M.C.G. oozes tradition; its cavernous hallways lead to rooms full of sporting relics. In 1858 the first official game of Australian Rules Football was played on a field where the carpark now stands, and in 1877 Australia met England in the first test match between the two countries. The 90,000-seat stadium was built to host athletic events of the 1956 Summer Olympic Games.

At the main entrance to the M.C.G., off Wellington Parade, is the **Australian Gallery of Sport and Olympic Museum,** dedicated to sport-loving Australians. It has three levels chock-full of memorabilia, including the original Australian Rules Football rules and displays cataloging the history of 10 sports. Other areas of the M.C.G. are open to the public, but you must take a tour to view them, including change rooms, Members Hall, Long Room, and a hallway filled with paintings of various sporting scenes. A combined ticket is adult $10, child $6. Open daily 9:30 a.m.-4:30 p.m., with tours on the hour. For further details call (03) 9657-8879. The M.C.G. is a 10-minute walk from Flinders St. Station, or jump aboard tram no. 48 or 75.

Linked by a footbridge to the M.C.G., Melbourne Park (formerly known as the National Tennis Centre) was built in 1988 and is the premier tennis facility in the country, with an enormous retractable roof. April-Sept. tours are offered Wed.-Fri. at 11 a.m., noon, and 1:30 p.m. Tour cost is $5 adult, $2.50 child. For bookings call (03) 9655-1234.

Yarra Bend Park

The Yarra River flows through Melbourne's northeast suburbs and for much of the way is lined by parkland and golf courses. Yarra Bend Park, in the suburb of Collingwood, is one of the most popular expanses, home to a variety of birds, with a large area of native bushland. Also in the park is **Riverside Boathouse,** with canoes for rent and light snacks served in an 1860s building.

THE DANDENONGS

When Melburnians want to escape from the rat race, this is where they come, a world away from the city, but just 40 km east of downtown. Early settlers cleared large tracts of the Dandenongs, and although hordes of visitors flock to the many parks and villages, the area has managed to retain its original charm. Early settlers established many gardens, planting English trees to make them feel at home, building stone churches, and, in later years, developing guesthouses. Access is easiest with your own transport (take South Eastern Frwy., turning north on Ferntree Gully Rd. in the suburb of Notting Hill), or take the train to Belgrave Station. From Upper Ferntree Gully, **Mount Dandenong Tourist Rd.** winds through the center of the range, passing quaint villages and public gardens, including the **Rhododendron Gardens** in Olinda, tel. (03) 9751-1980. This 40-hectare garden features thousands of rhododendrons and azaleas, with a three-km path leading through the colorful gardens (best Sept.-Dec.). Admission is adult $6.50, kids free. Open daily 10 a.m.-4:30 p.m. Take a train to Upper Ferntree Gully, then bus no. 698.

William Ricketts Sanctuary, in Mt. Dandenong, is an amazing collection of clay sculptures inspired by the Koori of central Australia. Sculptures are spread throughout the six-hectare property, among towering mountain ash, fern-filled gullies, and waterfalls. Admission is $6, and it's open daily 10 a.m.-4:30 p.m.

Dandenong Ranges National Park

Since 1882, the Victorian government has been buying back land in the Dandenongs and protecting it as a national park. Currently, the park encompasses 3,100 hectares in three distinct sections. The Mt. Dandenong Tourist Rd. provides access to the park's many picnic areas, lookouts, and hiking trails. The Ferntree Gully section is accessed from the beginning of the Mt. Dandenong Tourist Rd., from where a three-km hiking trail leads into the park. East of the tourist road is Sherwood Forest Section, home to a population of lyrebirds. For information call Parks Victoria, tel. (13) 1963.

Puffing Billy

A restored steam train, Puffing Billy has been chugging along a scenic 13 km of track between Belgrave and Emerald Lake for 90 years. Originally built to provide a link between Melbourne and the mountains, it is now run for the tourists, with open-sided carriages allowing views of the lush forest. The roundtrip takes a little more than two hours, but allow time at the lake, which has a picnic area, paddle boats, and a model railway. The fare is adult $17.50, child $12. To get to Belgrave, take a train from Flinders St. Station. Call (03) 9754-6800 for the Puffing Billy timetable.

WILLIAMSTOWN AND VICINITY

South of where the Yarra River drains slowly into Port Phillip Bay is the suburb of Williamstown, Victoria's first port and at one time destined to become state capital. Until the Yarra

This bluestone lighthouse dates to the days when Willimastown was an important port.

River was dredged and the Port of Melbourne developed, it was Melbourne's major port, the base for Victorian customs and immigration, and had large dockyards extending to the mouth of the river. **Nelson Place** is the main road through Williamstown, running along the foreshore and lined on one side with historic buildings, many constructed of locally quarried bluestone. Restaurants, cafés, and antique shops line the street and at 5 Electra St. is a small museum of maritime relics and artifacts from Williamstown's earliest days; open Sunday 2-5 p.m. At Gem Pier **HMAS Castlemaine,** a mine sweeper built at Williamstown in 1842, now operates as a museum; open Sat.-Sun. noon-5 p.m. Admission adult $4, child $2, tel. (03) 9397-2363.

Williamstown is a 20-minute drive from downtown, or take a ferry from Southgate; $10 one-way, $18 return; call (03) 9506-4144 for times.

Scienceworks

This museum combines science and technology with a hands-on approach. Kids love it, but all ages can enjoy the old machinery, displays explaining the principles of light, sound, movement, and centrifugal force, interactive exhibits, a planetarium, and other temporary displays. To get there by public transport, take the train to Spotswood Station, then walk 700 meters down Craig Street. It's at 2 Booker St., tel. (03) 9392-4800. Admission is adult $8, child $4. Open daily 10 a.m.-4:30 p.m.

OUTDOOR ACTIVITIES AND SPECTATOR SPORTS

Canoeing and Boating

The Yarra River certainly isn't one of the world's most beautiful waterways, but many sections are good for flatwater canoeing. For something more adventurous than a river cruise, canoes and small boats can be rented at **Riverside Boathouse,** in Yarra Bend Park northeast of the city, tel. (03) 9853-8707. Boats can also be rented at **St. Kilda Boat Hire,** on the pier at St. Kilda, tel. (03) 9534-2491; **Fairfield Boathouse,** Fairfield Park Dr., Fairfield, tel. (03) 9486-1501; and **Williamstown Boat Hire,** tel. (03) 9397-7312. **Note:** Check weather forecasts before heading out on Port Phillip Bay.

Swimming
Melbourne City Baths, corner Swanston St. and Victoria Parade, tel. (03) 9663-5888, at the top end of downtown, has a 25-meter indoor pool and other facilities including a gym, spas, and saunas. Admission is $5. Open Mon.-Fri. 6:15 a.m.-10 p.m., Sat.-Sun. 8 a.m.-6 p.m.

Golfing
Melbourne is blessed with a number of Australia's top golf courses along a strip southeast of the city known as the "sand belt." They include **Huntingdale, Kingston Heath, Metropolitan,** and **Royal Melbourne,** ranked as the world's sixth-best course by *Golf* magazine. All these courses are private, and unless you're a member of an equally prestigious club, getting a game is difficult.

Melbourne has around 100 other courses, with **Yarra Bend,** tel. (03) 9481-3729, considered one of the country's finest public courses. Closer to the city, you'll find courses in Royal Park, tel. (03) 9387-1326, and Albert Park, tel. (03) 9510-5588. Greens fees at these courses average $15-25, and all have club rentals.

The **Australian Masters,** held each February at Huntingdale, is a permanent fixture on the calendar of many of the world's top golfers. For tickets call (03) 9696-2022.

Tennis
Except when major tournaments are in progress the public can rent courts Mon.-Fri. 7 a.m.-11 p.m., Sat.-Sun. 9 a.m.-6 p.m., at the **Melbourne Park,** in Flinders Park, southeast of downtown off Batman Avenue. Court charges range $14-32 per hour, or for $75 per hour you can play on Court One; call (03) 9655-1244 for bookings. For information on the many other courts around Melbourne, call the Victorian Tennis Association, tel. (03) 9286-1285.

The **Australian Open,** one of the tennis world's four Grand Slam tournaments, attracts the world's best male and female players each January. For tickets call Ticketek, tel. (13) 2849.

Australian Rules
Best known as Aussie Rules, this unique sport has a fanatical following in Melbourne, which is both the birthplace and center of the sport. The game combines kicking with running, marking (catching the ball, often by leaping in the air), and passing. Each team has 18 men, with the ultimate goal to kick the ball through the opposing team's goal posts. Six points are awarded for a goal kicked through the central posts and one point through posts either side. Because of its pace, and often rough tactics, Aussie Rules is a great game to watch, especially when surrounded by 40,000 fanatical fans. The season runs early March through September, with the Grand Final held on the last Saturday of September at the M.C.G. in front of a crowd of 100,000.

Cricket
Each summer, cricket can be seen on parks and grounds throughout the city, but the biggest crowds are drawn to the Melbourne Cricket Ground where international tests and one-day matches are held among the world's leading cricket nations. For dates and ticket prices call (03) 9650-3001.

Horse Racing
On the first Tuesday in November the entire country stops for the **Melbourne Cup,** Australia's richest horse race. For many Australians it is the only day of the year they make a wager, and then for a few minutes they crowd around radios and television sets for the famous two-mile race. It is held at Flemington Racecourse and is part of the monthlong Spring Racing Carnival. For ticketing details call (03) 9376-4100. For information on horse racing throughout the city call **Racing Victoria,** tel. (03) 9258-4763 or (1800) 35-2229.

ARTS AND ENTERTAINMENT

The best source of information on what's happening in Melbourne is the **EG** lift-out in Friday's *Melbourne Age* or the **Hit** lift-out in Thursday's *Herald Sun.* Or pick up a copy of *Melbourne Events* from the information center, or the free entertainment guides *Inpress* and *Beat* distributed weekly throughout the city.

Half Tix, tel. (03) 9650-9420, offers all theater tickets at half price the day of the performance. They operate from a small booth on Bourke St. Mall and are open Monday 10 a.m.-2 p.m., Tues.-Fri. 11 a.m.-6 p.m., Saturday 10 a.m.-2 p.m. For advance tickets call **Ticketek,** tel. (13) 2849, or **Bass,** tel. (11) 500.

Art Galleries

The National Gallery of Victoria in the Victorian Arts Centre (see above) is the city's premier gallery, but there are many commercial galleries open to the public. One of the most interesting is **Montsalvat,** an artist's colony established by Justus Jorgensen in the 1930s on Hillcrest Ave., Eltham, tel. (03) 9439-8771. The grounds are interesting, with work in a variety of mediums for view and sale. Open daily 9 a.m.-5 p.m.; admission is adult $2, child 50 cents. **Metro Craft Centre,** 42 Courtney St., North Melbourne, tel. (03) 9329-9966, is a former meat market converted for craftspeople to work and display their wares. Materials worked with include wood, clay, metal, textiles, leather, and glass. The market is open Tues.-Sun., but the craftspeople only work weekdays.

Theater

The cultural center of the city is the **Victorian Arts Centre,** on St. Kilda Rd. south of downtown. It comprises three theaters—State, Playhouse, and George Fairfax—and the Melbourne Concert Hall. The State Theatre seats more than 2,000 people on three levels and is capable of staging opera, ballet, and musical comedy productions. The Playhouse seats 888 and is home to the Melbourne Theatre Company. Ticket prices depend on the production, ranging $32-78. "An Evening at the Victorian Arts Centre" includes a show, dinner, and tour of the center; cost starts at $82 pp. For bookings call (03) 9684-8484.

Built in 1886, **Princess Theatre,** 163 Spring St., tel. (03) 9229-9850, is Melbourne's oldest theater; its impressive marble staircase and intricate plaster ceiling signify days gone by. It was restored for the opening of *Les Miserables,* and today offers short runs of big musicals; ticket prices range $25-70. The **Regent Theatre,** 191 Collins St., tel. (13) 2849, is another grand old theater building that has recently undergone renovations—$35 million in this case—and features mainstream productions. Another historic theater is the **Athenaeum,** 188 Collins St., tel. (03) 9650-1500, built in 1884 and opened as a theater in 1924. Performances vary greatly, but are often Shakespeare; tickets are $16-40. The **Comedy Theatre,** 240 Exhibition St., tel. (03) 9209-9000, opened as a comedy venue but is now home to musicals and plays. Tickets range $30-44. The **Malthouse,** 113 Sturt St., South Melbourne, tel. (03) 9685-5111, is a new complex featuring Australian contemporary theater performed by the Playbox Theatre Centre. Tickets range $9-34. **La Mama,** 205 Faraday St., Carlton, tel. (03) 9347-6142, is a tiny theater company performing new and innovative works by Australian writers.

Music and Dance

The **Australian Opera Company,** tel. (03) 9684-8198, performs at the State Theatre in the Victorian Arts Centre on St. Kilda Road. Tickets start at $40. The State Theatre is also home to the **Victoria State Opera** and the **Australian Ballet Company.**

The 2,677-seat **Melbourne Concert Hall,** part of the Victorian Arts Centre, is home to both the **Melbourne Symphony Orchestra** and **State Orchestra of Victoria.** This venue is renowned for excellent acoustics, aided by massive glass shells suspended above the stage. Tickets are $40-55. The **Sidney Myer Music Bowl,** Kings Domain, tel. (03) 9684-8360, is used for opera, jazz, and ballet performances in the summer months.

Cinemas

The city's largest cinemas are around the intersection of Bourke and Russell Streets. They include a **Greater Union, Hoyts,** and **Village.** Carlton has a few cinemas, such as **Nova,** 380 Lygon St., tel. (03) 9347-5331, and **Carlton Moviehouse,** 235 Faraday St., tel. (03) 9347-8909, that feature alternative and foreign films. Back downtown, **Kino Cinema,** 45 Collins St., tel. (03) 9650-2100, has more of the same, as does the **Astor,** corner Chapel St. and Dandenong Rd., St. Kilda, tel. (03) 9510-1414.

An **IMAX** theater, tel. (03) 9663-5454, is part of the Melbourne Museum Complex on Rathdowne St., Carlton. Its eight-story-high screen makes it the world's largest. The latest IMAX films cost from $12 each and are screened daily 10 a.m.-11 p.m.

Casino

After spending a few years in a temporary location in the World Trade Centre, the **Crown Entertainment Complex** moved directly across the Yarra River to its permanent site at 8 White-man St., South Melbourne, tel. (03) 9292-8888, in 1997. Australia's largest casino, it contains all the usual glitzy gaming facilities (including 2,500 slot machines) open 24 hours. It also features dozens of upmarket shops, 28 restaurants, 14 bars, a nightclub, and Crown Towers, one of Australia's largest hotels, where rates start at $490 per night.

Pubs, Bars, and Taverns

Built in 1853, **Young and Jackson's Hotel,** corner Flinders and Swanston Streets, tel. (03) 9650-3884, is one of the city's oldest pubs. The much-admired *Chloe,* a painting of a nude woman, adorned the walls of the bar for 100 years before being moved upstairs, but the public bar is still a good place to have a beer. **Mac's Hotel,** 34 Franklin St., tel. (03) 9663-6855, dates from the same year and was originally the terminus for gold escorts, with a special lockup provided for the gold.

For an English atmosphere head to **Horse & Hound Tavern,** 221 Queen St., tel. (03) 9670-8488, or **Sherlock Holmes,** 415 Collins St., tel. (03) 9629-1146, both popular lunchtime hangouts and open daily till midnight. Many of the better downtown hotels have elegant bars. The **Cricketers Bar,** in the Windsor Hotel on Spring St., combines the feel of an elegant English pub with cricketing memorabilia. If you can afford a $5 beer, head to the 35th floor bar in the **Hotel Sofitel,** 25 Collins St., for stunning city views. **Le Monde** is a trendy bar/café that stays open 24 hours; it's at 18 Bourke St., tel. (03) 9663-7804.

The old **Esplanade Hotel** (the "Espy"), overlooking Port Phillip Bay in St. Kilda, is beginning to look out of place as the suburb goes upmarket, but it is one of the city's best live music venues, with bands performing nightly. North of downtown, **Jimmy Watson's,** Lygon St., Carlton, is a wine bar that has been around for years. In neighboring Fitzroy, the **Pumphouse Hotel,** 128 Nicholson St., is done up in art deco and features a relaxing atmosphere, with jazz musicians entertaining drinkers on Sunday afternoons. The **Great Britain Hotel,** 447 Church St., Richmond, has comfortable couches on the inside and a plant-filled courtyard beer garden. The **Glasshouse Hotel,** 51 Gipps St., is an interesting place to stop by.

Nightclubs

Melbourne boasts the largest number of nightclubs of any Australian city. The **Metro,** 20 Bourke St., tel. (03) 9663-4288, is a three-level nightclub in an old theater building. It has eight bars and is the largest nightclub in the Southern Hemisphere. Two of downtown's trendiest dance clubs, **Dream,** 229 Queensberry St., and **The Lounge,** 243 Swanston St., feature DJs spinning everything from indie to pop discs until the wee hours of the morning. The **Mansion** is in fact an old mansion, but with a modern club atmosphere. It's at 83 Queens Road. **Monsoon's,** in the Grand Hyatt Melbourne at 123 Collins St., tel. (03) 9657-1234, attracts an older crowd, but in a more intimate atmosphere. Cover charge is $8-15, and a strict dress code is enforced. The vibes are similar at **Heat,** the Crown Casino nightclub.

The inner suburbs hold many nightclubs. **Night Cat,** 141 Johnson St., Fitzroy, features a funky 1970s-style atmosphere, offering a mix of jazz, funk, and fusion music. Many pubs and clubs line the streets of South Yarra and adjacent Prahran. **Chasers,** 386 Chapel St., South Yarra, has been around since the 1980s and continues to be one of the city's most popular dance clubs. A newer venue, **Revolver,** 229 Chapel St., Prahran, hosts everything from cutting-edge performing arts, to local bands, to DJ-inspired dance nights.

Jazz, Folk, and Comedy

Limerick Arms Hotel, 364 Clarendon St., South Melbourne, tel. (03) 9690-0995, has live jazz on Thursday and Sunday nights; cover charge $5-10. Downtown, **Ruby Red** (9 Drewery Lane) is a popular jazz venue, and on Sunday afternoons **Beaconsfield Hotel,** 341 Beaconsfield Parade, St. Kilda, has live jazz, as does **Bennetts Lane Jazz Club,** 25 Bennetts Lane. If you're around in January, the **Montsalvat Jazz Festival,** at an artist's colony northeast of downtown, shouldn't be missed.

The Melbourne Folk Club hosts performances at **Brunswick East Hotel,** Lygon St., Brunswick. Closer to town, in North Melbourne, **Dan O'Connell Hotel,** 225 Canning St., has live folk music Wed.-Sat. nights (no cover charge).

Besides the **International Comedy Festival,** Melbourne offers many comedy options. The **Last Laugh,** 64 Smith St., Collingwood, tel. (03)

9419-8600, has local and international acts nightly. Generally, dinner is served 7:30 p.m., and the show commences at 9 p.m. Tickets for the dinner and show range $24-48; for the show only, from $14. The **Comedy Cafe,** 177 Brunswick St., Fitzroy, tel. (03) 9348-1622, is a favorite spot for the country's best-known comedians. The **Gershwin Room** in the Esplanade Hotel, St. Kilda, is another comedy venue; performances take place Sunday afternoon and Tuesday night.

SHOPPING

The main shopping area is right downtown, with the best places to browse and buy being the large department stores and plazas. **Myer** is the

world's fifth largest department store, with 12 floors of shopping pleasures, including a great Food Emporium on the ground floor; the main entrance faces Bourke St. Mall. **Daimaru,** Australia's only international department store, is part of **Melbourne Central** shopping complex on La Trobe Street. Other large department stores are **David Jones** at 310 Bourke St., spanning two blocks, and **George's,** 162 Collins St., for old-fashioned luxury.

Block Arcade is a stylish shopping arcade running between Collins and Little Collins Streets. Farther up the hill, **Royal Arcade** links Little Collins and Bourke Streets. **Australia on Collins** is a modern, stylish arcade.

Many of the inner suburbs provide a fantastic way to immerse yourself in the local culture, and each provides a unique shopping experience.

MELBOURNE FESTIVALS AND EVENTS

Summer

Christmas is celebrated with **Carols by Candlelight** at the Myer Music Bowl, when 30,000 people sing their hearts out along with some of the country's top entertainers. For tickets, call BASS, tel. (03) 9529-3544. The **New Year** is ushered in with partying on the streets and, the following day, an international cricket test match at the Melbourne Cricket Ground. **Chinese New Year Festival** sees celebrations through Chinatown. **St. Kilda Festival,** a week-long celebration of food, music, sports, and art displays, takes place through St. Kilda. In the last two weeks of January, Melbourne hosts the **Australian Open,** which brings together the world's best male and female tennis players for the year's first Grand Slam event. During that same period, the **Melbourne International Jazz Festival** plays at venues throughout the city.

Autumn

Autumn kicks off with a bang when the **Australian Formula One Grand Prix** starts following a public road circuit around Albert Park the first weekend of March. **Moomba,** supposedly meaning "Getting Together and Having Fun," features 10 days of events through downtown Melbourne, with an amusement park and displays set up along the Yarra Valley. The finale is Sunday. The **Dragon Boat Festival** on the Yarra River commemorates the death of Qu Yuan, a Chinese poet who threw

himself into a river as a protest against political corruption, and his friends, who set out in boats, thrashing the water with oars and beating drums to keep away the monsters. The city's largest ethnic gathering is the **Antipodes Festival,** in late March, promoting the culture of Greece through art, music, and food. April brings the **International Comedy Festival,** with performances by acts from around the world at all the city's comedy venues.

Winter

The only event of note in winter is the **Melbourne International Film Festival,** held each July. It has been part of the calendar for nearly 50 years and screens some of the world's most innovative contemporary films.

Spring

In September, the country comes to the city for the **Royal Melbourne Show,** a large agricultural fair with wood chopping, show jumping, and equestrian events. The **Melbourne Festival,** in October, is a 17-day extravaganza of performing arts featuring writers, artists, singers, musicians, and dancing from around the world. In October, at the Royal Melbourne Showgrounds, **Oktoberfest** is held in the tradition of its famous Bavarian origins. During that same month, **food and wine** festivals are held in suburban Carlton as well as along Brunswick and Chapel Streets.

Dragon Boat Races, Moomba Festival

Getting there is made simple by tram or bus, then you can spend hours browsing around, people watching, or just hanging out at the local cafés, which reflect the surrounding ambience. Starting north of downtown, head to **Brunswick St.,** Fitzroy, for a bohemian atmosphere and shops selling handmade arts and crafts, secondhand books, and clothing by up-and-coming designers; **Bridge Rd.,** Richmond, for secondhand stores, cheap clothing, and Asian produce; **Chapel St.,** South Yarra, for trendy clothes shopping; **Chapel** and **Greville Streets,** Prahran, for alternative clothing and secondhand stores; and **Toorak Rd.,** Toorak, for the glamour and glitz of the world's leading fashion labels.

Markets

The city's largest, with 1,000 stalls, is **Queen Victoria Market,** between Elizabeth and William Streets north of downtown. It encompasses a few blocks, offering rows and rows of just about everything imaginable, including food from around the country, furniture, clothing, giftware, kitchenware, and souvenirs. The market is open Tuesday and Thursday 6 a.m.-2 p.m., Friday 6 a.m.-6 p.m., Saturday 6 a.m.-3 p.m., and Sunday 9 a.m.-4 p.m. Other major markets, all held on Sunday, include those on **St. Kilda Esplanade, Greville St. Sunday Market** in Prahran, and **St. Andrews Market** in Healesville.

Australiana

Aboriginal Handcrafts, 9th Floor, 125-133 Swanston St., tel. (03) 9650-4717, sells authentic Aboriginal art, but it's not cheap. Artifacts include bark paintings, carvings, boomerangs, woomeras, and didgeridoos; open Mon.-Friday. **Aboriginal Gallery of Dreamings,** 73-77 Bourke St., is another good place to check out. **Yarrandoo Souvenirs and Native Art,** at 131 Exhibition St., has a huge range of Australiana souvenirs, although most of the less-expensive Aboriginal work isn't authentic. Across the road, opal dealer **Altmann & Cherny,** 120 Exhibition St., tel. (03) 9650-9685, holds the world's largest and most valuable opal, valued at $1.8 million.

Thomas Cook, 60 Hoddle St., Abbotsford, tel. (03) 9417-7555, is the place to head for Australian clothing such as an Akubra hat or a Drizabone coat.

HOTEL AND MOTEL ACCOMMODATIONS

Downtown

Many of the oldest downtown hotels have been refurbished (or demolished) in recent years, so finding a cheapie is difficult. If you're on a budget, consider staying at a backpacker lodge (see below) or outside the city center, as public transport to downtown is efficient.

Most central of the budget hotels is **Victoria Hotel,** half a block from Swanston Walk at 215 Little Collins St., tel. (03) 9653-0441 or (1800) 33-1147. This rambling old place contains more than 500 rooms. Those with shared facilities are $42 s, $58 d; those with bathrooms are of a much higher standard and cost $85 s, $120 d. Inexpensive-Expensive. **City Centre Private Hotel,** 22 Little Collins St., tel. (03) 9654-5401, looks dowdy from the street, but the rooms are clean, and each floor has a communal kitchen;

$45 s, $60 d. Moderate. Rooms with shared facilities at **Hotel Enterprize,** 44 Spencer St., tel. (03) 9629-6991, are similarly priced, and rates include breakfast and parking. Nicer rooms here, with private facilities, are $90 s or d. Moderate. **City Square Motel,** 67 Swanston St., tel. (03) 9654-7011, just a block from Flinders St. Station and right on the main shopping strip, features ordinary rooms that cost $69 s, $89 d. Moderate.

A little farther out, but a good value, is **Arden Motel,** 15 Arden St., tel. (03) 9329-7211, which has large, basic rooms for $73 s, $82 d. Moderate. **Terrace Pacific Inn,** 16 Spencer St., tel. (03) 9621-3333, is a new hotel across from Spencer St. Railway Station and the casino, and is a 10-minute walk to downtown. Rooms with private facilities are $109 s or d. Expensive. Once one of Melbourne's grand hotels, **Hotel Grand Chancellor,** 131 Lonsdale St., tel. (03) 9663-3161, is slowly losing its stars, but rates are coming down accordingly, and it's a good value now at $115 s, $120 d. Rooms are large, each has a balcony, and the place has all the services of the more expensive places. Parking is $10 per day. Expensive.

Melbourne has a good choice of international-class accommodations downtown. While most are fully booked during the week, when the businesspeople have gone home for the weekend, rooms are easy to come by and rates go down, often drastically.

The grand lady of Melbourne is the **Windsor Hotel,** 103 Spring St., tel. (03) 9633-6000, one of Australia's grandest hostelries. Built in 1883, the imposing Victorian facade, complete with top-hatted doormen, is a Melbourne institution. Inside, the foyer and Grand Dining Room exude opulence of a bygone era, with marble floors and mahogany furniture. Standard rooms are $450 s or d, while suites, much larger and with balconies, start at $650 s or d. Luxury.

On the corner of Spencer St. and Flinders Lane is **Rydges on Flinders,** tel. (03) 9629-4111, recently restored and as friendly as any of the downtown accommodations. Facilities include a pool, sauna, gym, restaurant, bar, and laundry. Rates are $165-210 s or d. Luxury. **The Adelphi,** 187 Flinders Lane, tel. (07) 9650-7555, a small boutique hotel housed in a converted warehouse, uses a contemporary geometrical design throughout. Its most unique feature is a 25-meter-long glass-bottomed swimming pool that extends beyond the edge of the building. The 24 rooms are simply but luxuriously furnished, and each has a king-size futon bed; $185 s or d. Luxury. In the same price range, **Rydges Melbourne,** 186 Exhibition St., tel. (03) 9662-0511, has well-decorated rooms, each with a view, as well as an outdoor pool; $220 s or d. Luxury.

If you're into paying top price for a room, the **Hotel Sofitel,** 25 Collins St., tel. (03) 9653-0000, makes a good candidate. The lobby is behind an elegant shopping mall, away from the street, and the hotel takes up the top 15 floors of a 50-story building, ensuring excellent views. Room furnishings are of the highest standards. A restaurant and café are on the 35th floor, as is a gym, spa, and sauna. Rates are from $385 s or d, with weekend packages considerably lower. Luxury.

North Melbourne and Carlton

North of the city center, the suburbs of North Melbourne and Carlton have a wide range of accommodations, with plenty of public transport running downtown. One of the closest to city center, **Chifley on Flemington,** 5-17 Flemington Rd., tel. (03) 9329-9344 or (1800) 06-5064, is a large hostelry built around a courtyard. Rooms have recently been renovated and facilities include a pool, restaurant, and bar; rooms start at $146-156 s or d. Luxury. Continuing north, **Marco Polo Inn,** corner Flemington Rd. and Harker St., tel. (03) 9329-1788, has spacious rooms, a laundry, and pool; $90 s, $108 d. Expensive. Farther up Flemington Rd., at no. 94, is **Park Squire Motor Inn,** tel. (03) 9329-6077, within walking distance of the zoo and a good value at $72-85 s or d. **City Gardens Holiday Apartments,** 335 Abbotsford St., tel. (03) 9320-6600, are spread over one hectare, made up of two-story townhouses. All rooms are fully self-contained; many even have dishwashers, and rooms are serviced weekly. The smallest studios are $124, one-bedroom units $150, and two-bedroom units $185. Premium.

Downtowner on Lygon Motel, 66 Lygon St., tel. (03) 9663-5555, is in the suburb of Carlton and has decent-sized rooms for $119 s or d. Expensive. Of a slightly higher standard is **Rydges Carlton,** 701 Swanston St., tel. (03) 9347-7811, a modern five-story place with a rooftop pool and sauna; $125-155 s or d. Premium. **Lygon Quest Lodgings,** 700 Lygon St., tel. (03) 9345-3888, is made up of 30 self-contained apartments, each with laundry and cooking facilities. They range $130-170, depending on size. Premium.

Around the junction of Royal Parade and Park St. is another group of motels. The best value is **Princes Park Motor Inn,** right at this junction, tel. (03) 9388-1000, where each room has a balcony; $82 s, $92 d. Expensive.

East Melbourne

Georgian Court Guest House, 21 George St., tel. (03) 9419-6353, built in 1870, has an authentic historic atmosphere, with antiques scattered throughout. Rooms are fairly basic, but each has a TV and tea- and coffee-making facilities. Rates in rooms with shared facilities are $60 s, $70 d, with larger rooms going for $80 s, $90 d. All rates include breakfast. Moderate. Another option is **Magnolia Court,** 101 Powlett St., tel. (03) 9419-4222, located on a quiet street among other historic terraces. Part of the property dates from 1858 and has been restored to its former glory. These rooms are $135 s, $155 d, while rooms in the newer wing are less expensive. Breakfast is the only meal served here, and the managers enjoy helping guests organize itineraries. Luxury.

South Yarra

South Yarra is a stylish suburb where many of the original buildings have been restored and boutiques and cafés line the streets. It's also only a five-minute train or tram trip to downtown. **Domain Motel,** 52 Darling St., tel. (03) 9866-3701, is a short walk to public transportation and has rooms of a reasonable standard for $64 s, $72 d. Moderate. **Tilba Hotel,** 30 West Toorak Rd., tel. (03) 9867-8844, was once a private residence, and a bit of refurbishment has transformed it into a stylish and elegant accommodation that attracts an eclectic collection of guests. Rooms are decorated with antiques, and each has a bathtub. The hotel's many alcoves have lounge chairs, while classical music is piped in throughout the hotel. Rates are $135-190 s or d and include breakfast. Book well in advance. Premium.

Hotel Como, 630 Chapel St., tel. (03) 9824-0400, features the best of everything. Even the

standard rooms are huge, and each features ultramodern furnishings, a large bathtub, and a king-size bed; most have views. Downstairs is Maxim's, one of Melbourne's best restaurants. Rates start at $275 s or d (weekend packages provide a better deal). Luxury.

St. Kilda and Other Bayside Suburbs

The bayside suburb of St. Kilda has Melbourne's best range of backpacker accommodations, but also boasts a wide range of motels, including many cheapies not quite up to scratch. **Cabana Court Motel,** 46 Park St., tel. (03) 9534-0771, provides the best value, especially considering that each room has a small kitchen; $80 s, $95 d. Expensive. **Novotel Bayside Melbourne,** 16 the Esplanade, tel. (03) 9525-5522, a modern and luxurious hotel, overlooks Port Phillip Bay. Rates are $140 s or d, and rooms with kitchens are $200. Premium. Opposite the beach, **Warwick Beachside Apartments,** 363 Beaconsfield Parade, tel. (07) 9525-4800 or (1800) 33-8134, has 64 basic self-contained apartments, each with a small kitchen; $65-95 per unit. Moderate.

To the west of St. Kilda is Albert Park and a number of good accommodation choices. Built in 1888, **Hotel Victoria,** 123 Beaconsfield Parade, tel. (03) 9690-3666, is a classic Victorian building with unbroken views across Port Phillip Bay. The hotel has only 30 rooms, 20 with shared facilities ($45 s, $60 d), and 10 spacious corner rooms with fantastic views and private bathrooms ($150 s or d). Inexpensive/Premium.

On the other side of Albert Park is the recently renovated **St. Kilda Road Travelodge,** corner St. Kilda Rd. and Park St., tel. (03) 9209-9888, where rooms range $130-190. Premium.

BACKPACKER ACCOMMODATIONS

Most of the best backpacker lodges are in St. Kilda, while Melbourne's two YHAs are in North Melbourne. Right downtown are a few possibilities, but their standards are generally not as high as in the suburbs.

Downtown

One block from Spencer St. Station, the **Friendly Backpacker,** 197 King St., tel. (07) 9670-1111 or (1800) 67-1115, is the best accommodation choice for budget travelers who want to be right downtown. It is indeed a friendly place, with dorm beds spread over four floors in rooms holding four to 16 beds. All beds are $15 pp. Budget.

Other choices, on the northern outskirts of downtown, are still an easy walk from all the major attractions, bus terminals, and Museum Station. **Hotel Bakpak,** 167 Franklin St., tel. (07) 9329-7525, is a cavernous complex with 500 beds spread over six floors. Facilities include numerous lounges, a fitness room, small cinema, employment center, travel agency, bar and café, and Internet access. Dorm beds are $16-18, private rooms are $45 s, $50 d or twin. Inexpensive. Around the corner in a restored Victorian-era residence is the much smaller and quieter **Toad Hall,** 441 Elizabeth St., tel. (03) 9600-9010. It has all the usual facilities, as well as a courtyard with barbecue. Beds in the dormitory are $17, singles $30, doubles $50. Inexpensive.

One block north is the **Hotel Y,** 489 Elizabeth St., tel. (03) 9329-5188, part of a YWCA complex where guests have use of a pool, gym, and fitness classes. Dorm beds are $25 pp and private rooms are $70 s, $80 d. Moderate.

On the south side of the river, but still an easy walk from everything, is **Nomads Market Inn,** 115 Cecil St., tel. (07) 9690-2220 or (1800) 24-1445. Upon arrival, you'll be greeted with a free beer or coffee, which sets the trend for this excellent accommodation. The rooms are large and comfortable, Internet access is $5 per hour, and a downstairs bar serves cheap drinks. Also, guests have free use of bikes, there's a barbecue every Sunday, and breakfast comes with the rate of $12-20 pp ($40-60 for private rooms). Budget-Inexpensive.

North of Downtown
Queensberry Hill YHA, 78 Howard St., North Melbourne, tel. (03) 9329-8599, is as good as any city backpacker accommodation you're likely to find. It opened in August 1991, everything is new, and the kitchens are large and modern, and many rooms have private bathrooms. On the roof is a large patio with city views. The hostel is very safety-conscious, with security parking and a small locker beside every bed. Other facilities include a currency exchange, laundry, and travel agency, and guests have free use of bikes. A cafeteria serves meals all day, with

breakfast around $5 and dinners less than $10. Rates are $16 for members ($4 extra for nonmembers). Singles are $45-52, doubles $52-58. The hostel is one km from North Melbourne Station and about 1.5 km from downtown. Inexpensive. A bit farther out is the much smaller **Chapman Gardens YHA,** 76 Chapman St., tel. (03) 9328-3595, also affiliated with the YHA. It is older, with dorms $14 and twin beds $17.50 pp. Budget.

St. Kilda
This suburb, south of downtown and on Port Phillip Bay, has the city's largest concentration of backpacker accommodations, many located within a block of busy Fitzroy Street. Most popular is **Enfield House,** 2 Enfield St., tel. (03) 9534-8159, an old boardinghouse with 20 four-bed dorms ($16) and a few twins ($28 pp). Inexpensive. Within 200 meters of Enfield House is a cluster of five hostels; none are particularly good, but beds are generally $15 pp, or less, per night. Try similarly priced **Coffee Palace Backpackers,** 24 Grey St., tel. (03) 9534-5283, and **Kookaburra Backpackers,** 56 Jackson St., tel. (03) 9534-5457. Budget.

Olembia Beachside, 700 meters from Fitzroy St., 96 Barkly St., tel. (03) 9537-1412, has a relaxed atmosphere and friendly staff. Rooms are okay, but all communal facilities are excellent. Dorms are $17, and the few singles and doubles are $35 and $50 respectively. Inexpensive.

CAMPGROUNDS

North
The closest campground to the city center is the excellent **Melbourne Holiday Park,** 265 Elizabeth St., tel. (03) 9354-3533, nine km north in the suburb of Coburg East. The tenting area is shaded and grassy, with a covered kitchen. Other facilities include a large pool, recreation room, and laundry. Unpowered sites are $14, powered sites $16.50, sites with a bathroom $21, small on-site vans $34, and self-contained cabins $39.50-52. Northeast of the city, in the suburb of Doncaster, is **Crystal Brook Holiday Centre,** 182 Warrandyte Rd., tel. (03) 9844-3637, not really suited to tent camping. Sites are $16, on-site vans $30, and well-equipped cabins $45-60.

Southeast

Heading toward Phillip Island, the closest campground to downtown is in Chelsea Heights, 32 km southeast of downtown, where you'll find **Blue Gum Caravan Park,** Wells Rd., tel. (03) 9772-8436. It has excellent facilities including a pool, tennis court, and barbecues; tent sites $10, powered sites $12, cabins $26-48. A farther 15 km toward Phillip Island, in the small town of Beaconsfield, is **Blue Gum Eastside Caravan Park,** Brunt Rd., tel. (03) 9707-2753, which has basic facilities and a few powered sites for $12.

West

Coming into Melbourne from Ballarat, **Bacchus Marsh Caravan Park,** 54 km west of the city, is just off the main freeway and has sites for $10-12 and cabins for $30-45, tel. (03) 5367-2775. South of Bacchus Marsh is Brisbane Ranges National Park, which has a basic campground.

DOWNTOWN DINING

Melbourne is regarded as Australia's culinary capital, and with more than 3,000 restaurants featuring food from 70 countries, it would be hard for anyone to disagree. Melburnians take their dining seriously; at least a dozen food and wine festivals are scattered through the year, and, at last count, there were three books guiding diners to the best restaurants on offer.

Cafés and Food Courts

Melbourne has literally hundreds of cafés, and while some come and go, the reputations of many have remained high for years. **Pellegrini's,** 66 Bourke St., has been wooing coffee lovers for decades. The clientele may have changed looks over the years, but they still come, drinking espresso coffee and enjoying inexpensive Italian meals, such as pasta from $6; open daily 8 a.m.-11:30 p.m. In the same part of town, toward Parliament House, is **Le Monde,** 18 Bourke St., a trendy café attracting an eclectic mix of patrons, especially during the early hours of the morning. They also offer light Italian meals and a selection of delicious cakes. Downtown also has a few upmarket cafés, including **Cafe Rialto,** in Le Meridien Hotel at 495 Collins St., and **Cafe Alcaston** in a historic building at 2 Collins Street. At

the **Lounge,** in the Windsor Hotel, 103 Spring St., tel. (03) 9653-0653, a grand afternoon tea is served Mon.-Sat. 3:15-5:30 p.m.; $24 pp.

Many downtown shopping plazas have a food court on the ground floor, featuring cuisine from all parts of the world for $5-8. The **Hyatt Food Court,** 127 Collins St., has the widest variety of choices, is open 7:30 a.m.-midnight, and has a certain amount of class. Under the Myer Department Store is **Myer's Wonderful World of Food,** on Little Bourke St., with an eclectic mix of foods from around the world.

Chinese

Chinatown is centered along Little Bourke St., between Spring and Swanston Streets. **Kun Ming,** 212 Little Bourke St., tel. (03) 9663-1851, won't win any interior design awards, but the food is delicious, and with soups less than $2.50 and main dishes from $5.50 you can't go wrong; open Mon.-Sat. noon-3 p.m., 5-10 p.m., and Sunday 5-9 p.m. Moving up the street, **Supper**

Chinatown, on Little Bourke St., is a good place to head for a cheap meal.

Inn, 15 Celestial Ave., tel. (03) 9663-4759, upstairs along a narrow alleyway (and easy to miss), has an extensive menu and large servings that will satisfy everyone's Chinese cravings. It's open until 2:30 a.m. **Shark Fin House,** 131 Little Bourke St., tel. (03) 9663-1555, is one of the few restaurants featuring *yum cha* during the week. It's a huge place, three stories of trolley-wheeling waiters offering around 50 dishes; open daily 11:30 a.m.-3 p.m., 5:30-11 p.m. The **Flower Drum,** 17 Market Lane, tel. (03) 9662-3655, is generally considered to be Australia's finest Chinese restaurant. The elegant atmosphere, efficient servers, and well-presented dishes make the prices easier to handle; expect to pay around $50 pp for three courses. It's open for lunch and dinner, but closed Sunday.

Some Chinatown restaurants don't open for lunch, but instead stay open all hours of the night. Off Little Bourke St. is **Happy World,** 141 Russell St., tel. (03) 9663-3341, a little worse for wear but with excellent food. **Wong Shing Kee,** 166 Russell St., tel. (03) 9663-1346, is a casual place with more of the same.

Other Asian Restaurants

Gopal's, 139 Swanston St., tel. (03) 9650-1578, by Little Collins St., is a small vegetarian café operated by the Hare Krishna. Servings aren't enormous, but most dishes are less than $4, with some main dishes as low as $1.50. A three-course meal, with a drink, is $6. **India House,** 433 Elizabeth St., tel. (03) 9663-5858, is another cheapie. The atmosphere is quiet and relaxed and most dishes are less than $7. At the top end of Chinatown is **Little Malaysia,** 26 Liverpool St., tel. (03) 9662-1678, a large place where service is fast and efficient and a three-course meal is less than $20 per head. **Ong International Food Court** is good for a lunchtime meal, with cuisine from throughout Asia; it's at 265 Little Bourke Street.

Japanese restaurants are, on the whole, more expensive than other Asian places, but a few inexpensive options are scattered around downtown. Immediately east of Chinatown, **Kuni's,** 56 Little Bourke St., tel. (03) 9663-7243, is a no-frills restaurant that has been a long-time favorite for Melburnians from all walks of life. And with good reason—the sushi is delicious, and you'd be doing well to spend $30 pp for dinner. **Hanabishi,** 187 King St., tel. (03) 9670-1167,

is a stylish restaurant, popular with the lunchtime crowd for sushi; closed Sunday.

Greek

Lonsdale St. is the Greek center of downtown, and as Melbourne is the world's third-largest Greek city, naturally there are lots of Greek dining choices. **Tsindos the Greek's Restaurant,** 197 Lonsdale St., tel. (03) 9663-3194, features a variety of grills (from $9) and mezze platters to start, a plate full of dips, cheeses, and cold vegetables. On Friday and Saturday nights after 8:30 p.m., they have live entertainment. **Stalactites,** 177 Lonsdale St., tel. (03) 9663-3316, has an offering of basic Greek dishes in a bland setting, but the price is right, the portions good, and it's open daily 24 hours.

Italian

Campari Bistro, 25 Hardware St., tel. (03) 9670-3813, is a typical Italian restaurant—always busy and great for people watching. Pasta, starting at $10 for a main dish, is cooked to perfection. **Italian Waiters' Restaurant,** 20 Meyers Place, tel. (03) 9650-1508, is noted among Melburnians for exceptional food, good prices (all main dishes are less than $15), and healthy portions; open Mon.-Sat. until midnight. **Amiconi,** 359 Victoria St., tel. (03) 9328-3710, is a classy yet inexpensive Italian bistro about one km west of downtown. **Florentino,** 80 Bourke St., tel. (03) 9662-1811, looks more expensive than it actually is, with the building divided into a bistro, restaurant, and cellar bar. Each section has its own character and menu, with daily lunchtime specials in the bistro for $7.50 and dinner $12-18. **Lucattini's,** 22 Punch Lane, tel. (03) 9662-2883, is at the Parliament House end of Chinatown and features traditional Italian dishes ranging $14-20 (less at lunch); closed Sunday.

French

Mietta's of Melbourne, 7 Alfred Place, tel. (03) 9654-2366, located just off Collins St., is one of Melbourne's finest restaurants. The building has been restored to its Victorian glory and is furnished with period antiques. Food is of the highest standard, averaging $25 for main dishes. Of note is the fixed-price lunch, good value at $21 pp; closed Sunday. Downstairs is a lounge that stays open till 3 a.m., and light meals range $10-

18. Le Restaurant, 25 Collins St., tel. (03) 9653-0000, on the 35th floor of the Hotel Sofitel, is one of the city's most renowned upmarket restaurants. The views are fabulous, service excellent, ambience sophisticated, and, it goes without saying, expensive.

Colonial Tramcar Restaurant
In this unique restaurant, housed in one of Melbourne's familiar trams, diners are whisked around the streets while enjoying fine food in an elegant atmosphere. The tram was built in 1927 and has since been restored to the height of luxury with comfortable velvet seating, brass lamps, and silver service. The menu changes regularly, but is generally five courses, with a choice of main dishes. Lunch (1-3 p.m.) is $65, early dinner (5:45-7:15 p.m.) $55, and dinner (8:35-11:30 p.m.) $80 Sun.-Thurs., $90 Fri.-Saturday. Departures are from the National Gallery of Victoria, Southbank Boulevard just off St. Kilda Rd.; for reservations, call (03) 9696-4000.

Other Downtown Restaurants
Crystal chandeliers, marble floors, and imposing stained-glass domes create an atmosphere of absolute Victorian luxury in the **Grand Dining Room** of the Windsor Hotel, 103 Spring St., tel. (03) 9653-0653. The service is impeccable, with white-gloved waiters tending to your every need and serving food of the highest quality. The fixed-price dinner is $65.

Southgate, on the south side of the Yarra River, has a wide range of eateries, including a large food court. Many of the restaurants in the complex overlook the river and have tables inside and out. A good choice is **Akvavit,** tel. (03) 9699-9947, serving a lunch buffet for $18 and dinner buffet for $32. **Walter's Wine Bar,** tel. (03) 9690-9211, has light meals from $6 to accompany a huge variety of wines by the glass, while the more substantial dishes run $16-19. Dining is indoors and out, with lunchtime particularly busy.

DINING IN THE SUBURBS

Carlton
Carlton has been home to a large population of Italians since late last century, with many using

their cooking expertise to operate restaurants. The restaurants were centered along Lygon St., and although the style of them has changed considerably, Carlton is still the center of Italian culture in Melbourne, with many Italian-style coffee shops and pasta houses.

Toto's, 101 Lygon St., tel. (03) 9347-1630, is a legendary pizza place that claims to be Australia's original pizzeria (operating since the mid-1960s). It's always busy, and noisy, but the pizza is great and priced right. Open daily noon-1 a.m. **Pasta Veloce,** 181 Lygon St., tel. (03) 9347-4273, is a no-frills pasta house where everything is cooked to perfection. Huge plates of pasta start at $11, with meat or seafood sauces $15; open daily noon-midnight. A couple of doors away, **Nyonya,** 191 Lygon St., tel. (03) 9347-8511, serves inexpensive Malaysian meals in a bright and airy atmosphere, not unlike the Italian restaurants that surround it. Curries start at $6.50, while most other main dishes cost less than $10. **La Spaghettata,** 238 Lygon St., tel. (03) 9663-6102, is a casual eatery with tables inside and out. All pasta is made on the premises, with a blackboard menu offering choices less than $15 and mouthwatering Italian desserts for about $5; open daily noon-3 p.m., 5-11 p.m. **Papa Gino's,** 221 Lygon St., tel. (03) 9347-5758, is the place to head for gigantic servings at reasonable prices (pastas average $12-17). Between Lygon and Rathdowne Streets is **Toofey's,** 162 Elgin St., tel. (03) 9347-9838, a fine seafood restaurant. The menu changes daily, depending solely on what the markets have to offer. There is always a choice of at least three types of grilled fish, which generally cost from $22.

Farther north, on Rathdowne St., are many more choices. At **Carlton Curry House,** 206 Rathdowne St., tel. (03) 9347-9632, a favorite of students, takeaway is the main trade, but there are a few worn-looking tables in the back. **La Porchetta,** 392 Rathdowne St., tel. (03) 9347-8906, is one of Carlton's least expensive restaurants, with nothing over $10, including the large pizzas. This, naturally, attracts droves of students from the nearby university.

The majority of Carlton's restaurants are within two km of downtown; take tram no. 1, 15, 21, or 22 north along Swanston Street.

Fitzroy

While Carlton is predominantly Italian, Fitzroy, immediately to the east, features cuisine from around the world. Dozens of trendy restaurants are interspersed with shops selling weird and wonderful gifts, retro clothing, antiques, books, and crystal balls. In just three blocks of Brunswick St., you'll find cuisine ranging from African to Caribbean, while Johnston St. has a concentration of Spanish restaurants.

The **Gypsy Bar,** 334 Brunswick St., is a popular local breakfast hangout. A cooked breakfast, complete with hash browns and avocado, is $10.50. A few doors further from downtown, **Black Cat Café,** 252 Brunswick St., is one of the older, more popular cafés. It offers a light menu, but most of the regulars just come to gossip and take in the eclectic atmosphere while sipping a coffee.

In a renovated warehouse at 380 Brunswick St., you'll find the **Vegie Bar,** tel. (03) 9417-6935, where most of the vegetarian and vegan dishes are less than $10. **Thai Thani,** 293 Brunswick St., tel. (03) 9419-6463, is a small, dimly lit restaurant where diners have the choice of eating Thai-style, sitting on the floor, or at a table. Appetizers range $4.50-8 and all main meals are less than $16. Open Mon.-Sat. 6 p.m.-midnight.

Along Johnston St. the tastes of Spain dominate. The pick of the bunch is **Carmen,** 74 Johnston St., tel. (03) 9417-4794, always packed to the rafters, usually by Spanish locals. Outside is a cook-your-own barbecue, and most nights flamenco is performed. Open Tues.-Sat. from 6 p.m. until late.

Back on Brunswick St. **Rhumbaralla's,** 342 Brunswick St., tel. (03) 9417-5652, is a microcosm of Fitzroy, attracting an eclectic array of patrons with a varied and inexpensive menu. **Baker's Cafe,** 384 Brunswick St., tel. (03) 9419-7437, is much more intimate but attracts the same sort of crowd. Pastas cost about $9, and coffee and cake is less than $6; open daily 7 a.m.-10 p.m.

Richmond

East of downtown, this suburb has always been a bastion of Greek culture, but in recent years, as new Australians arrive from Southeast Asia, Victoria St. has turned into a Vietnamese shopping area, gaining the nickname "Little Saigon" along the way. In most cases, emphasis in Vietnamese restaurants isn't on decor, but for an adventurous meal at an affordable price, Victoria St. is a good place to head. **Thy Thy,** upstairs at 142 Victoria St., tel. (03) 9429-1104, is legendary. All dishes are less than $10 and many less than $5, including the huge bowls of soup. On the downside, it's always crowded, and the decor is plain, to say the least. One small step up in style is **Thy Thy 2,** a few doors down Victoria St. at No. 116, tel. (03) 9428-5914.

Rajdoot, 142 Bridge Rd., tel. (03) 9427-1118, is a small, inexpensive Indian restaurant with a large tandoor oven churning out delicious dishes (most less than $12); open for lunch Tues.-Fri. and daily for dinner. Also serving Asian cuisine, in this case Thai food, is **Palm Sugar,** 282 Bridge Rd., tel. (03) 9429-9649. Simply furnished and always busy, the menu is standard Thai, with the curries (from $7) the best deal.

Vlado's, 61 Bridge Rd., tel. (03) 9428-5833, is one of Melbourne's premier steakhouses, with mouthwatering cuts of beef grilled to perfection. The three-course set menu is $52 pp; closed Sunday. This is the perfect place for a splurge if you're staying at nearby Georgian Court Guest House.

Running parallel to Bridge Rd., and to the south, is Swan St., with distinctive-sounding Greek music wafting from the restaurants. **Salona,** 260 Swan St., tel. (03) 9429-1460, is a good place to head for fresh seafood cooked Greek-style, for $16. Most other dishes are around $10.

South Yarra, Toorak, and Prahran

Toorak Rd. and Chapel St. are the two main shopping and dining strips in South Yarra, offering restaurants with a wide variety of cuisine and the chance to mix a shopping expedition with lunch. From South Yarra, Toorak Rd. continues east to the stylish suburb of Toorak, which boasts many elegant bistros, while Chapel St. leads south to more restaurants and the excellent **Prahran Markets,** a great place to stock up on fresh fruit and vegetables.

Barolo Bistro, 74 Toorak Rd., tel. (03) 9866-2744, which has a large courtyard, is enjoyable on a sunny day or clear summer night. Pastas average $10; open daily 9 a.m.-midnight. Of the dozen or so Italian restaurants and bistros along this strip, try **Tamani,** 156 Toorak Rd., tel. (03) 9866-2575, for pasta cooked to perfection for less than $15. **Pieroni,** 172 Toorak Rd., tel. (03) 9827-7833, is the place for a splurge.

Up in Toorak, **Minootz,** 436 Toorak Rd., tel. (03) 9826-9121, looks a lot more expensive than it is. Cuisine is Italian and less than $10 for lunch main dishes, or just relax with a coffee and enjoy the stylish ambience.

The first stop walking down Chapel St. from Toorak Rd. should be at **Caffe e Cucina,** 581 Chapel St., tel. (03) 9827-4139—if you can get a table, that is (expect a wait at lunch). Most main dishes are less than $16, with pastas around $11. The wine and beer are also reasonably priced. **Ankara,** 310 Chapel St., tel. (03) 9529-4940, is one of Melbourne's few Turkish restaurants. All the entree dips are around $5 and no main dish is more than $12, including combination kabob and grill.

St. Kilda and Other Bayside Suburbs

Melbourne's lively seaside suburb of St. Kilda has an eclectic mix of eateries spread along fashionable Fitzroy St., which links St. Kilda Rd. to the bay. Most cafés and trendy bars are at the bay end of the street. **Topolino's,** 87 Fitzroy St., tel. (03) 9534-4856, has legendary pasta (from $8) and pizza (from $6) and is busiest early in the evening. Continuing down Fitzroy, **Chichio's,** 109 Fitzroy St., tel. (03) 9534-9439, offers a huge variety of Italian dishes, with a special backpackers menu, where most pizza and salad dishes are just $5.

Circa, The Prince, at a street level corner in the Prince of Wales Hotel at 2 Acland St., tel. (03) 9534-5033, opened in 1998 and has quickly become one of St. Kilda's most popular restaurants. The decor is elegant yet simple, but it is the food that stands out, with an eclectic menu featuring everything from lamb to barramundi. Mains range $20-32. **Scheherezade,** 99 Acland St., tel. (03) 9534-2722, is typical of many Acland St. restaurants: well priced, serving healthy portions, and low-key—a world away from busy Fitzroy Street. In the same vicinity but known for cheap and greasy breakfasts and burgers is **Greasy Joe's,** at 68 Acland Street.

GETTING THERE

Air

Melbourne Airport is 20 km northwest of downtown in the suburb of Tullamarine. It serves both international and domestic flights, and after a $190 million redevelopment project completed early in 1996, it's Australia's most modern and efficient airport. Around 11 million travelers pass through the airport annually, of which about 17% are traveling internationally. On the arrivals level there is no real information center, but a few motels have courtesy phones. The major car rental companies have service desks, there's a currency exchange, and lockers are $5 per day. **Sky Plaza,** on the departures level, has a food court, bar, restaurant, a variety of touristy shops, a post office, and the ubiquitous duty-free shop for international travelers, who must also pay departure tax of $27. Around 20 international airlines fly into Melbourne, including **Qantas,** tel. (13) 1313; **United Airlines,** tel. (13) 1777; **Air New Zealand,** tel. (13) 2476; and **British Airways,** tel. (13) 1223. The domestic airlines that fly to Melbourne are **Ansett Australia,** tel. (13) 1300; **Eastern,** tel. (13) 1313; **Kendell,** tel. (13) 1300; and **Southern Australian,** tel. (13) 1313.

Transfers between the airport and downtown are offered by **Skybus,** tel. (03) 9335-2811, which runs half-hourly, daily 6 a.m.-7:30 p.m. The main downtown drop-off is Bay 30 in the coach terminal at Spencer St. Station. The fare is $9 one-way, $16 roundtrip. A cab between the airport and downtown runs about $30-35, depending on the traffic. A less expensive option is bus 478 or 479, which depart hourly from the arrivals terminal for Moonee Ponds Junction, from where you transfer to a tram for downtown; $3.80 one-way.

Rail

The main interstate services are the XPT from Sydney and the Overland from Adelaide. **V/Line** operates all rail services throughout the state and offers regular service between Melbourne and Ballarat, Warrnambool, Mildura, and Albury. All long-distance trains arrive and depart from Spencer St. Station. Special fares are offered year-round, including the Super Saver, a saving of 40% for travel Tues.-Thursday. For all bookings call (13) 2232 or drop by the **V/Line Travel Centre,** in the Spencer St. Station concourse, tel. (03) 9619-8080.

Bus

Melbourne has two long-distance bus terminals. **Greyhound Pioneer,** tel. (13) 2030, arrives and departs from the Melbourne Transit Centre at 58 Franklin St., while **McCafferty's,** tel. (13) 1499, uses a terminal beside Spencer St. Station. Competition between the major companies is fierce; the best deals are the various travel passes offered by each.

Ferry

Port Melbourne is the main departure point for ferries between mainland Australia and Tasmania. For details see "Transportation" in the "Introduction" of the Tasmania chapter.

GETTING AROUND

The Met

Known collectively as the Met, trams, trains, and buses make up an excellent system of public transportation from throughout the inner city to all major sights and outlying suburbs. One ticket covers all three forms of transportation, which have three fare zones. Most of the city falls within Zone 1: $2.30 for two hours of unlimited travel, $4.40 for an all-day ticket, and $19.10 for a

weekly ticket. An all-day ticket for the entire network costs $9.50. The **City Met Shop** is at 103 Elizabeth St., tel. (13) 1638.

Tram routes cover the inner city, with many heading into the suburbs; all lines are served every eight to 15 minutes. The CircleTram route is for tourists (the tram is a distinctive burgundy and cream color). It runs along Flinders, Spring, and Nicholson Streets, Victoria Parade, La Trobe St., and Spencer St. with the driver giving a running commentary. It runs daily 10 a.m.-6 p.m., in both directions, every 10 minutes. Best of all, it's free.

Flinders St. Station, on the City Loop rail line that encircles downtown, is the main city terminal. Trains service the outlying suburbs and places such as the Dandenong Ranges.

Taxi

Cab prices in Melbourne are comparable to those in other Australian cities, and the cabs are particularly useful after midnight when all public transportation stops. The flag charge is $2.60, then 96 cents per km. Midnight to 6 a.m., the flag charge is $3.60 and the km rate is $1.16. A good place to look for taxis is outside Flinders St. or Spencer St. Stations. The main companies are **Arrow,** tel. (13) 2211; **Black Cabs,** tel. (13) 2227; **Embassy,** tel. (13) 1755; and **Silver Top,** tel. (13) 1008.

Car

There are three very good reasons for not driving in downtown Melbourne: high parking charges, a strange road rule, and the biggest obstacle,

Trams make travel through the city enjoyable.

trams. Parking charges average $4 per hour, with all-day rates offered before 9 a.m.

If the above hasn't dissuaded you from city driving, or you need a car to explore outlying areas, expect to pay from $40 per day to rent an older car and from $75 per day to rent from the larger car rental chains. Main companies are **Avis,** tel. (1800) 22-5533; **Budget,** tel. (13) 2727; **Dollar,** tel. (1800) 65-8658; **Hertz,** tel. (13) 1918; **National,** tel. (03) 9329-5000; and **Thrifty,** tel. (03) 9663-5200. **Backpacker Car Rental,** tel. (03) 9329-4411, offers vehicles from $120 per week as well as a buy-back scheme for long-term travel.

Bicycle
Bike paths wind through much of the city, including along the Yarra River, around Port Phillip Bay, and along Moonee Ponds Creek. The **City of Melbourne Bike Map,** available from information centers, covers these as well as points of interest along the routes and handy inclusions such as bike stands and drinking fountains. **Fitzroy Cycles,** 224 Swanston St., tel. (03) 9639-3511, rents mountain bikes for $12 per hour and $32 per day. **St. Kilda Cycles,** 11 Carlisle St., tel. (03) 9534-3074, is similarly priced.

Ferry
The bayside suburb of Williamstown is linked by ferry to downtown Melbourne and St. Kilda on Saturday and Sunday. The boat leaves the World Trade Centre, downtown Melbourne, at 10 a.m. for Williamstown, and for the rest of the day runs between St. Kilda and Williamstown. The fare from either departure point is $10 return. For information call (03) 9397-2255.

Passengers with Disabilities
The **Travellers Aid Disability Access Service,** 169 Swanston St., tel. (03) 9654-7690, offers support and information for disabled persons and publishes a CBD Mobility map. Another handy source of information for wheelchair-bound visitors is the website: www.access-melbourne.vic.gov.au.

Tours
City Explorer, tel. (03) 9563-9788, is a double-decker bus that makes a continuous loop starting from Flinders St. Station, stopping at all major tourist sights. It runs on the hour 10 a.m.-4 p.m.; adult $20, child $10. Several companies offer sightseeing tours of Melbourne, including **Grayline,** tel. (03) 9663-4455, and **Great Sights,** tel. (03) 9639-2211. Typically, they pick up passengers at major hotels. The tours usually include downtown sights, the Dandenong Ranges, and a cruise on the Yarra River. Each company has a basic three- to four-hour tour for $45-50, with a river cruise included for around $60, and a full-day tour taking in city sights and Penguin Parade on Phillip Island for $85-100. **Melbourne River Tours,** tel. (03) 9629-7233, departs regularly from Princes Bridge (on the river's north side) for a cruise along the Yarra River ranging $15-28.

SERVICES

The **general post office** is on the corner of Bourke and Elizabeth Streets and is open Mon.-Fri. 8:15 a.m.-5:30 p.m., Saturday 10 a.m.-1 p.m. Traveler's checks can be cashed at all banks and major hotels, but remember, if your checks aren't in Australian currency, you'll be charged a fee or commission. **Thomas Cook Foreign Exchange** is at 261 Bourke St., tel. (03) 9654-4222.

Kodak, 1-19 Hoddle St., tel. (03) 9483-1011, processes slide film in 24 hours.

Get onto the Internet at **Melbourne Central Internet Café,** in the Melbourne Central shopping center, 300 Lonsdale St., tel. (03) 9663-8410; **Cosmos Internet Services,** 247 Flinders Lane, tel. (03) 9650-4776; or at the **State Library** (see below). As well as offering Internet access, **Hello International,** 22 Fitzroy St., St. Kilda, tel. (03) 9534-9535, provides long-distance telephone calls at reduced rates.

The **Flight Centre,** 317 Swanston St., tel. (03) 9663-1304, is the place to start looking for onward airline tickets. Also check the travel section in Saturday's *Age* newspaper.

Downtown has no self-service laundromats, but most hostels and hotels offer a laundry service. **Brown Gouge Dry Cleaners** is on the 5th floor of the Myer Centre on Lonsdale St., tel. (03) 9661-2639.

Emergency and Support Services

For medical emergencies, dial 000 or one of the following hospitals: **Royal Melbourne Hospital,** Grattan St., Parkville, tel. (03) 9342-7000; **St. Vincents Hospital,** Victoria Parade, Fitzroy, tel. (03) 9288-2211; **Alfred Hospital,** Commercial Rd., Prahran, tel. (03) 9276-2000; or **Royal Women's Hospital,** Grattan St., Carlton, tel. (03) 9344-2000. Private medical clinics are an alternative for nonemergency cases. A good option is **Fitzroy Central Clinic,** 117 Brunswick St., Fitzroy, tel. (03) 9419-3488. **Traveller's Aid Society,** 169 Swanston St., tel. (03) 9654-2081, assists travelers with nonmedical problems, offering advice, showers, toilets, and light snacks. For onward travel **Traveller's Medical Clinic,** 2nd Floor, 393 Little Bourke St., tel. (03) 9602-5788, advises on vaccinations and infectious diseases, and sells medical kits; open Mon.-Fri. 8:30 a.m.-5:30 p.m.

INFORMATION

Libraries

The **State Library,** much of which dates from the last century and former home of the Museum of Victoria, is an impressive domed building at 328 Swanston St., tel. (03) 9669-9888. The cavernous **reading room** makes for a great rainy day hangout. It's open Monday 1-9 p.m., Tuesday 10 a.m.-6 p.m., Wednesday 10 a.m.-9 p.m., and Thurs.-Sun. 10 a.m.-6 p.m.

Bookstores

The main bookshop chains—**Collins, Angus and Robertson,** and **Dymocks**—all have outlets

scattered throughout downtown and in major shopping centers. **Bowyangs Travel Books,** 372 Little Bourke St., tel. (03) 9670-4383, specializes in travel books as well as a variety of accessories such as maps.

Information Centers

The **Melbourne Visitors Centre** is in the Town Hall complex on Swanston St. and Little Collins St., tel. (03) 9658-9036, website: www.melbourne.org. As well as being the best source of city information, the center is home to the **Melbourne Greeter Service,** which links visitors with local volunteers for a free three- to four-hour tour of the city. Tours can be arranged by filling out a form three days in advance, by calling (03) 9658-9524, or by e-mailing greeter@melbourne.vic.gov.au. Also within the visitors center is the **City Experience Centre,** featuring historical displays and interactive city tours via computer. The complex is open Mon.-Fri. 8:30 a.m.-5:30 p.m., Sat.-Sun. 9 a.m.-5 p.m. Small **information booths** can be found in the Bourke St. Mall, Flinders St. Station, and Queen Victoria Market.

Early in 2000, Melbourne's main information center was relocated to **Federation Square,** a three-hectare civic and cultural facility that has been a decade in the planning and construction. The square will also hold a civic plaza, a courtyard designed for cultural festivals, botanic gardens, a cinema complex, and restaurants. Federation Square replaces the old Gas and Fuel Towers at a prime downtown location, right on the river beside the Flinders St. Bridge, and is part of an even larger long-term redevelopment project—the Jolimont Railyards, which currently extend all the way to Melbourne Park.

GOLDFIELDS

In early 1851, when gold was discovered near Bathurst, New South Wales, people from around the country and as far away as California descended on the area. For the newly established city of Melbourne, the exodus of people from Victoria caused a massive problem, and so a handsome reward was offered to anyone who found gold within 100 miles of Melbourne. Within weeks, gold had been discovered at Warrandyte near Clunes, and with thousands of dig-

gers swarming over every river and stream in the region, many more strikes occurred. The most important strike was made in September 1851, near Ballarat, which grew to become inland Victoria's largest city and one of the world's richest gold-bearing areas. Town populations grew quickly, with often as many as 30,000 diggers living in deplorable conditions in cities of canvas. Ballarat and Bendigo are gracious reminders of this prosperous past, and still thrive today while other towns, such as Maldon, Clunes, Talbot, and Moliagul are a shadow of their former selves and diggings such as Amherst have slipped into oblivion, completely.

MELBOURNE TO THE GOLDFIELDS

Organ Pipes National Park
A few years ago the main feature of this 85-hectare park, 25 km northwest of Melbourne along the Calder Highway, was part of a privately owned farm and overgrown with noxious weeds. When the weeds were killed a group of 20-meter basalt columns were exposed. They formed when lava from a volcano cooled quickly upon coming into contact with an ancient river. Native vegetation has been restored and

today the park is a pleasant place for a short walk and picnic lunch. The **Park Information Centre,** tel. (03) 9651-3038, is open daily 8:30 a.m.-4:30 p.m. (the park is locked outside these hours).

Sunbury
Sunbury, originally a stopping point for those heading to the goldfields, is the birthplace of cricket's best-known trophy. **Rupertswood,** a 50-room mansion on the outskirts of town, was the scene of a social cricket match held in late 1882 between a team of touring English cricketers and a motley bunch of locals—who apparently got thrashed. As a joke, the locals burnt part of the cricket stumps and presented the ashes in an urn to the captain of the English team. Today **The Ashes** is a five-match series

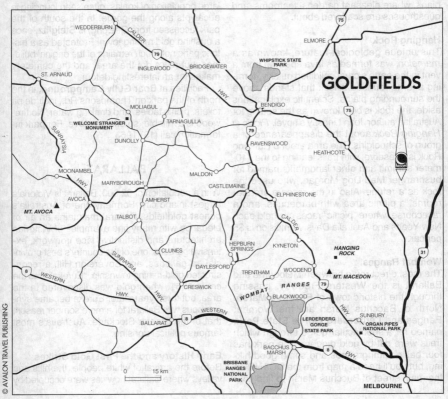

GOLDFIELDS

between Australia and England, and the original ashes are presented to the winner.

On the main road through town in a restored courthouse is **Sunbury Tourist Information Centre,** tel. (03) 9744-2291; open daily 9 a.m.- 5 p.m. In the grounds of the police station, next door, is a relocated jail, dating from the gold rush.

Macedon Ranges

The Macedon Ranges rise to the northeast of the Calder Highway, around 65 km from Melbourne. The highest peak is **Mount Macedon** (1,013 meters), an extinct volcano. A road leads right to the summit, where views extend southeast to Melbourne. The surrounding area, serviced by the small townships of **Macedon** and **Mt. Macedon,** is a popular retreat for Melburnians, where pleasant gardens, tearooms, and guesthouses are scattered about.

Hanging Rock

This unique geological feature, known as a *mamelon,* was formed as lava spewing from a vent in the earth's crust solidified quickly, forming a large rounded hillock that stands above the surrounding plains. Scientific explanations aside, the rock is best known as the setting for Australian author Joan Lindsay's novel, *Picnic at Hanging Rock* about the disappearance of a group of schoolgirls. The area around Hanging Rock is a reserve, with trails leading to the 710-meter summit and other landmarks named for bushranger Mad Dog Morgan, who used the rock as a refuge. Also in the reserve are tearooms, a picnic area with barbecues, and a racecourse, where "picnic" races are held each New Year's and Australia Days. Admission is $5 per car.

Wombat Ranges

The most direct route between Melbourne and Ballarat is the Western Freeway, passing through the historic town of **Bacchus Marsh.** North of Bacchus Marsh are the Wombat Ranges and **Lerderderg Gorge State Park,** named for a spectacular gorge through which trails were cut by gold diggers. The park has four basic campgrounds and some good hiking, but you'll need a map from the DC&NR on the main street of Bacchus Marsh to find your

way around. To the north and east of the park is **Wombat State Forest,** accessible through **Blackwood** and **Trentham.** The road through these towns from Bacchus Marsh continues north to Daylesford (see below).

Brisbane Ranges National Park

A springtime display of more than 400 different species of wildflowers is this park's main attraction. The 7,517-hectare park is not on the way to anywhere else, so a detour is required, either south from Bacchus Marsh or north from Geelong, to reach the facility area at **Anakie Gorge.** The gorge was created over millions of years, as water from Stony Creek eroded the soft sandstone and igneous bedrock. A hiking trail links two picnic areas (three km one-way), crossing Stony Creek a number of times. The park has a large population of koalas, often seen lounging in eucalypts along the gorge. In the south of the park (accessed from Geelong) is **Steiglitz,** once a bustling gold mining town. Protected as a historic park, not much remains of the original buildings, but relics dot the area, and the cemetery makes for an interesting detour.

Facilities at **Boar Gully Campground,** in the north of the park on Thompsons Rd., include pit toilets, picnic tables, and drinking water. No firewood is available, so bring a stove. For park information call (13) 1963.

BALLARAT

With a population of 82,000, Ballarat is Victoria's largest inland city. Formerly one of Australia's richest goldfields, Ballarat maintains an air of elegance with many fine examples of Victorian architecture and distinctive lace ironwork, extensive gardens, one of the country's best provincial art galleries, and Sovereign Hill, a reconstructed gold-mining township. "Eureka" was the cry in 1851, when gold was discovered in the area, but three years later Eureka became synonymous with Ballarat for a more somber reason, that of the Eureka Stockade, Australia's most famous political uprising.

Early History and the First Gold Strikes

Before the arrival of white people, the hills and valleys where Ballarat now lies were occupied by

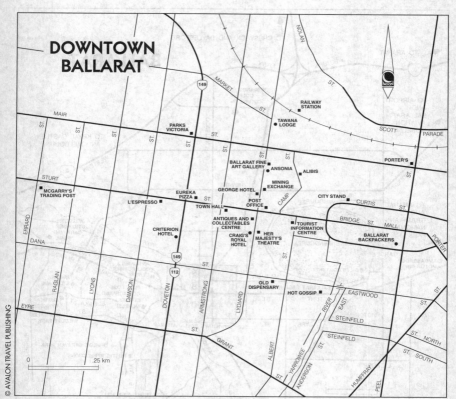

DOWNTOWN BALLARAT

MAIR ST.

PARKS VICTORIA

RAILWAY STATION

TAWANA LODGE

SCOTT PARADE

PORTER'S

STURT

MCGARRY'S TRADING POST

BALLARAT FINE ART GALLERY

ANSONIA

ALIBIS

MINING EXCHANGE

EUREKA PIZZA

GEORGE HOTEL

CITY STAND

CURTIS ST.

L'ESPRESSO

TOWN HALL

POST OFFICE

CAMP

BRIDGE ST.

MALL

ANTIQUES AND COLLECTABLES CENTRE

TOURIST INFORMATION CENTRE

CRITERION HOTEL

CRAIG'S ROYAL HOTEL

HER MAJESTY'S THEATRE

BALLARAT BACKPACKERS

PORTER

DANA

RAGLAN

LYONS

DAWSON

DOVETON

ARMSTRONG

LYDIARD

OLD DISPENSARY

HOT GOSSIP

EASTWOOD

EYRE

GRANT

ALBERT

RIVER

EAST

STEINFELD

STEINFELD

ST. NORTH

YARROWEE

ANDERSON

HUMFRAY

PEEL

ST. SOUTH

0   .25 km

the Wathurung tribe, who camped on the banks of Lake Wendouree (Ballarat is Aboriginal for "Resting Place"). When gold was first discovered there was no crazy rush, but within two years, in 1853, 20,000 miners from all parts of the world had converged on the shallow diggings. Within five years, 100 million ounces of gold had been extracted, including the **Welcome Nugget,** weighing 68,956 ounces, unearthed on Bakery Hill.

The Eureka Stockade

The goldfields were a great equalizer. No matter what a man's background or how wealthy he was, the amount of gold he found was dependent on how hard and long he toiled. As miner numbers swelled, the quantity of easily found al-

luvial gold began diminishing, and the inequality between the diggers and political powers widened. The miners had no powers to purchase crown land, nor could they vote, but their main grievance was the licensing system, whereby they paid 30 shillings per month for the right to dig for gold. Not only did they feel the fee was unnecessary, it was administered by the police, many of whom were exconvicts, and as they received half of each fine they were often brutal in their chase for licenses. The catalyst for the rebellion was when James Bently, owner of the Eureka Hotel, was honorably discharged on a murder charge against one of the diggers. On 17 October 1854, 5,000 miners gathered outside the hotel and burnt it down. Under the leadership of Peter Lalor they pro-

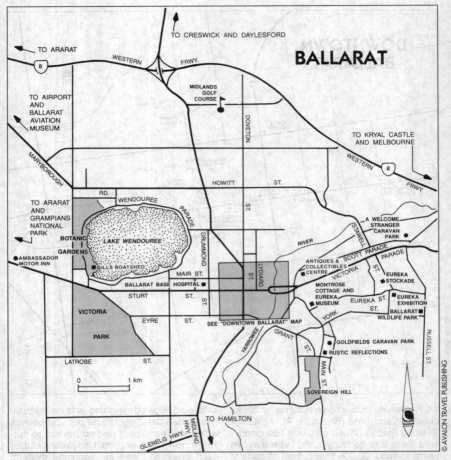

BALLARAT

TO CRESWICK AND DAYLESFORD

TO ARARAT

WESTERN FRWY.

MIDLANDS GOLF COURSE

TO AIRPORT AND BALLARAT AVIATION MUSEUM

MARYBOROUGH

DOVETON

TO KRYAL CASTLE AND MELBOURNE

WESTERN FRWY.

HOWITT ST.

ST.

WENDOUREE PARADE

RD.

TO ARARAT AND GRAMPIANS NATIONAL PARK

A WELCOME STRANGER CARAVAN PARK

STAWELL

DRUMMOND ST.

LAKE WENDOUREE

BOTANIC GARDENS

RIVER

SCOTT PARADE

PARADE

VICTORIA

ANTIQUES & COLLECTIBLES CENTRE

AMBASSADOR MOTOR INN

GILLS BOATSHED

LYDIARD ST.

EUREKA STOCKADE

MAIR ST.

MONTROSE COTTAGE AND EUREKA MUSEUM

EUREKA ST.

EUREKA EXHIBITION

BALLARAT BASE HOSPITAL

STURT ST.

BALLARAT WILDLIFE PARK

VICTORIA

EYRE ST.

SEE "DOWNTOWN BALLARAT" MAP

YORK ST.

GOLDFIELDS CARAVAN PARK

PARK

LATROBE ST.

YARROWEE

GRANT ST.

MAIN ST.

RUSSELL ST.

RUSTIC REFLECTIONS

0   1 km

SOVEREIGN HILL

TO HAMILTON

MIDLAND HWY.

GLENELG HWY.

© AVALON TRAVEL PUBLISHING

ceeded to burn all the licenses, then stood under a blue flag adorned with the Southern Cross and pledged to fight their arrest. A rough-and-ready stockade was built around the Eureka Claim. Early on 3 December 1854, more than 300 police charged the compound, quickly over-powering the undisciplined diggers and killing 25 of them in the process. The diggers had paid a price, but ultimately they achieved their goal—the aftermath was a Miner's Right (license), costing one pound a year and allowing diggers to cultivate their own land and vote for mem-bers of the Legislative Assembly. All rebels were acquitted, except the editor of the *Ballarat Times,* whose articles on police brutality led to a six-month jail term.

But the diggers' joy was shortlived. As alluvial deposits dried out, larger companies, capable of extracting lodes of gold deep below the sur-face, moved in. The last of the company mines closed in 1918, but the city has continued to prosper as the center of a large merino wool district, by the farming of a variety of crops, and as an important inland transportation hub.

Sovereign Hill

Sovereign Hill, once one of Victoria's richest goldfields, is now a 25-hectare reconstructed gold-mining village where visitors can wander through period buildings, watch working exhibits, and observe craftsmen at work. It is one of the best such historical parks in Australia, and it's easy to spend at least five or six hours wandering through. Along the township's main street is a hotel, blacksmith's shop, bank, bakery, and a variety of other businesses, all with workers dressed in period costume and acting out their parts. At the back of the main street is Red Hill Gully diggings, site of the original claim. Most of the equipment is original, right down to the mine shaft, and for a small fee you can pan for your own gold. Also represented are the Chinese who lived in a tent village on a slight rise behind Red Hill Gully diggings. The period 1860-1918, when large companies dominated the local mining industry, is displayed through a mine tour, associated buildings, and a museum. Guided tours are offered of the museum, diggings, and Chinese Village, while a shuttle bus tour (small fee) takes in the diggings and township.

Many shops are open for business, selling the goods they did in the 1850s—the post office handles mail, Waterloo Store sells gold, drinks, and snacks, and meals are available at stores throughout the grounds.

The park is open daily 10 a.m.-5 p.m., and admission is adult $17.50, child $13. For more information call (03) 5331-1944. Ballarat Transit's route 9 and 10 depart Curtis St. twice an hour for Sovereign Hill.

Blood on the Southern Cross is a nightly spectacular of light and sound that re-creates events that led to the Eureka Stockade. It takes place across the entire park and definitely shouldn't be missed. Showtimes vary, but it's usually an hour after dusk. Tickets are adult $25, child $14, but packages are available that include dinner, accommodation, or daytime park admission.

Museums

Across the road from the entrance to Sovereign Hill is the **Gold Museum**, tel. (07) 5331-1944, built on the mullock heaps of early mining activity. The museum features imaginative displays, including one on the Eureka Stockade, as well as some gold nuggets. Admission is included in the Sovereign Hill ticket or separate admission is adult $3.50, child $1.50.

The **Eureka Exhibition** is on Eureka St., opposite the site where all the action took place. Here, details of the rebellion, its causes, and its aftermath are displayed. For what it is, admission is steep—adult $4, child $2. Open daily 9 a.m.-5 p.m., tel. (03) 5331-5822.

Eureka Museum is contained in the 1856 **Montrose Cottage,** Ballarat's only remaining bluestone miner's cottage. It is meticulously furnished in the period style and has extensive gardens, great for relaxing when the sun's out. Ad-

Lydiard Street is lined with historic buildings, some of which still serve their original purposes. At the Mining Exchange, 8 Lydiard St., gold is bought and sold, and you can buy nuggets and gold jewelry such as earrings, chains, and pins. It's open daily 10 a.m.-5 p.m.

mission is adult $5, child $2.50. Open daily 9 a.m.-5 p.m. Located at 111 Eureka St., tel. (03) 5332-2554.

The only non-gold-related museum in town is **Ballarat Aviation Museum,** at the municipal airport northwest of town on the Sunraysia Hwy., tel. (03) 5339-5016. The museum houses a collection of vintage aircraft and is open Sat.-Sun. 1-5 p.m. Admission is adult $5, child $2.

Lydiard Street

Lydiard St., which crosses Ballarat's main drag (Sturt St.) just west of the information center, has been designated a historic precinct, thereby protecting the many fine Victorian buildings along its length. Many buildings function today as they did when first built, including the **George Hotel, Ballarat Fine Art Gallery,** the **Mining Exchange,** and **Her Majesty's Theatre.** Just off Lydiard St., on Sturt St., is the magnificent **Town Hall,** built in 1870.

The Ballarat Fine Art Gallery is one of Australia's premier provincial galleries. Most work is Australian, including paintings by artists Sir Sidney Nolan, Russell Drysdale, and Tom Roberts. One room is devoted to the works of the Lindsay family, who once lived just north of Ballarat. Also on display is the original Eureka flag, or at least remnants of it. Admission is adult $4, child $2. Open daily 10:30 a.m.-5 p.m. Located at 40 Lydiard St., tel. (03) 5331-5622.

Commercial Attractions

Kryal Castle, a replica of a medieval castle, is the most popular of Ballarat's commercial attractions. Features include jousting, hangings, and medieval reenactments. Admission is adult $14, child $10. The castle is on Forbes Rd., eight km southeast of Ballarat, tel. (03) 5334-7388, and is open daily 9:30 a.m.-5 p.m.

Ballarat Wildlife and Reptile Park is on York St., East Ballarat, tel. (03) 5333-5933. Highlights include the Tropical Reptile House, a tour of the grounds at 11 a.m., and Tasmanian devil feeding at 2:30 p.m. Admission is adult $10, child $4. Open daily 9 a.m.-5:30 p.m.

Recreation

Originally a large swamp, **Lake Wendouree,** near the center of town, and its surrounding parks and gardens are popular with joggers and cyclists. The 40-hectare **Botanic Gardens,** on the western shore, were first planted in the 1850s and are well maintained. Within the grounds is the cottage of poet Adam Lindsay Gorden. **Wendouree Parade** encircles the lake and features many Victorian buildings. **Midlands Golf Club** has an 18-hole championship golf course open to the public; located on Heinz Lane, tel. (03) 5332-6965.

Festivals and Events

Ballarat Rainbow Festival, held the last weekend of January in the School of Mines building, features workshops and displays aimed at improving lifestyles through alternative methods. Ballarat's largest celebration is the **Begonia Festival,** in early March. Many thousands of people converge on the Botanic Gardens for 10 days of floral displays, arts and crafts stalls, music, and a street parade. Later that same month is the **Eureka Jazz Festival.** There's an agricultural show in November and **Eureka Commemorations** in December. Call the Ballarat Tourist Information Centre for dates, tel. (03) 5332-2694.

Antiques and Galleries

Ballarat has an astonishing number of antique emporiums and art galleries. Many of the pieces for sale were brought to the area by those on the goldfields who struck it rich, and it is these items that command the highest prices. The **Antiques and Collectables Centre,** 9 Humffray St., tel. (03) 5331-7996, is the largest, boasting more than 40 stands. **McGarry's Trading Post,** at 809 Sturt St., has a good selection of unrestored pieces and some great examples of early Australian furniture.

Accommodations

Unfortunately, the grand old hotels that feature so prominently in most country towns are often not so grand on the inside. But here in Ballarat a number have been restored to their former glory, offering guests a taste of the luxury afforded to those who struck it rich during the gold rush. **Craig's Royal Hotel,** 10 Lydiard St., tel. (03) 5331-1377, is the best of these. Rooms of varying standards are available; the most basic, with shared facilities, are $50 s, $55 d, while those with private bathrooms start at $90 s or d. Inexpensive. A cheaper option is the **Criterion Hotel,** 18 Doveton St., tel. (03) 5331-1451, where rates are $30 s, $45 d, which includes a light breakfast. Inexpensive.

Ambassador Motor Inn, 1759 Sturt St., tel. (03) 5334-1505, is a good-value motel with lots of facilities and large rooms for $62 s, $74 d. Moderate.

One of the most impressive accommodations is **Ansonia,** 32 Lydiard St., tel. (03) 5332-8296, in the heart of Ballarat's historic precinct. Built as offices in the 1870s and converted to a boutique hotel, each of the 21 rooms is comfortable and well furnished. In four configurations, rates range $90-160 s or d. Expensive.

Sovereign Hill Lodge allows you to stay within the grounds of the park, but it is a long way from the city. Rates for members of Hostelling International are $16 pp, a few bucks extra for non-members, with motel-style rooms also available. For bookings call (03) 5333-3409. Inexpensive.

The closest campground to the center of town is **Goldfields Caravan Park** on Clayton St., tel. (03) 5332-7888. Sites are $14-17 and on-site vans start at $35. Budget-Inexpensive. Of the half-dozen other parks, **A Welcome Stranger Caravan Park,** east of town at 263 Scott Parade, tel. (03) 5332-6818, has the best facilities.

Food and Entertainment

L'Espresso, 417 Sturt St., is one of many cafés in downtown Ballarat; it has a good range of coffees and a few outdoor tables. If you have your own transportation, head out to **Gills Boatshed,** on the southwest corner of Lake Wendouree, for a relaxing atmosphere and parklike surroundings. Full meals are offered, but no one seems to mind if you just stop by for a coffee. Head to **Eureka Pizza,** at 316 Sturt St., tel. (03) 5331-3682, for plenty of pastas and pizza; most dishes are less than $10. **Rustic Reflections,** 429 Main Rd., tel. (03) 5332-4922, at Sovereign Hill, is a bit corny, as you'll gather from the swagman out front; they have Aussie-style meals for around $10. For an inexpensive pub meal, head to the Criterion Hotel at Doveton Street. **Porter's,** corner Mair and Peel Streets, tel. (03) 5331-4320, is an old pub that has been renovated into a restaurant. The menu is varied, diners have a choice of two sizes of main meals, and

service is excellent. Open for lunch Tues.-Fri., dinner Tues.-Saturday.

One of Ballarat's better upmarket restaurants is **Alibis,** 10 Camp St., tel. (03) 5331-6680, open for dinner only Tues.-Saturday. It is housed in a bluestone building dating from the 1850s and has a small but varied menu, including mouth-watering rack of lamb.

George Hotel, 27 Lydiard St., is a popular student drinking hole, and **Hot Gossip,** 102 Dana St., is the hottest nightclub in town.

Transportation, Services, and Information

The railway station is on Lydiard St., tel. (13) 2232. **V/Line** trains run daily between Ballarat and Melbourne and west to Stawell and Mildura. V/Line buses leave from the railway station for Geelong, Hamilton, and Bendigo. **Ballarat Coachlines,** tel. (03) 5333-4660, operates a shuttle service between Ballarat and Melbourne International Airport three to five times daily; $20 one-way. The depot is at 202 Lydiard St., right beside the railway station.

Ballarat Transit has two terminals on Bridge St. Mall and routes that take in all major sights, tel. (03) 5331-7777. For **Ballarat Taxis** call (13) 1008.

The **post office** is on the corner of Sturt and Lydiard Streets. **Parks Victoria** has an office on the corner of Doveton and Mair Streets, tel. (03) 5333-6584. **Ballarat Base Hospital** is on Sturt St., tel. (03) 5320-4000.

Ballarat Tourist Information Centre is right in the heart of town at 39 Sturt St., tel. (03) 5332-2694 or (1800) 64-8450; open daily 9 a.m.-5 p.m.

NORTH OF BALLARAT

The area north of Ballarat is rich with gold-mining history, and, although the populations have dwindled, the area's towns retain elegant buildings and historic charm.

Creswick

At one time Creswick, 18 km north of Ballarat, had a population of more than 25,000 diggers, most attracted by the discovery of gold in 1852. Today Creswick is a quiet highway town of 2,500 with many historic buildings lining the main street and evidence of diggings all around. On Albert

St. is a small **historical museum,** open Sunday 1:30-4:30 p.m., and two km north along the road to Clunes is **Australasian Mines,** site of what was, at the time, Australia's worst mine disaster—Mine No. 2 flooded, killing 22 men.

Since the 1880s, Creswick has been the center of a large forest industry, with the **School of Forestry,** tel. (03) 5345-2100, working toward re-establishing the area's natural vegetation.

Clunes

Clunes, 20 km northwest of Creswick, was the site of one of Victoria's first gold rushes. When gold was first discovered a few thousand diggers pitched their tents on the banks of Creswick's Creek, but their interests were soon diverted. The gold that was in the area lay in quartz reefs, deep below the surface, and required large operations to successfully extract it. So in 1856 the Port Phillip Company set up a large-scale operation. By the 1860s and 1870s many impressive buildings had been constructed along **Fraser St.,** including the **Town Hall** (1873) and the **Post and Telegraph Office** (1879), and on other streets bluestone churches began to appear. **Clunes Museum,** 36 Fraser St., tel. (03) 5345-3592, is the best place to begin your visit; open daily during school holidays 11 a.m.-4:30 p.m., and at other times during the year, Saturday only 10 a.m.-4:30 p.m. Walking tour brochures to Clunes (40 cents) and the many other towns dotting the area are available there.

Keebles of Clunes, 114 Bailey St., tel. (03) 5345-3220, was built as the Telegraph Hotel in 1863 and has been restored to provide six comfortable rooms, each with private bathrooms. Other facilities include a guest lounge with log fire, game room, and library. Rates start $90 s, $130 for bed and breakfast; dinner is also available. Premium.

Tuki Trout Fishing Complex

East of Clunes and eight km north of Smeaton is Tuki Trout Farm, tel. (03) 5345-6233, where you can go trout fishing in an artificial reservoir, then have your catch filleted and served up with a delicious array of salads for $18 pp.

Talbot and Vicinity

With a population optimistically stated as 350, Talbot's deserted streets and surrounding open fields seem a world away from Ballarat, yet during the height of the gold rush 30,000 diggers lived in a city of canvas tents around workings along Back Creek.

Permanent buildings, constructed in the 1860s, still exist in varying states of disrepair, providing a glimpse into life on the goldfields. One that has been restored is the **Bull and Mouth Hotel,** tel. (03) 5463-2325, which has been converted to a stylish restaurant. It's open for dinner Thurs.-Sun. and serves a variety of country-style meals; main dishes start at $17.

Amherst was a thriving center during the gold rush, but the years have taken their toll—many buildings have been taken apart for their materials and bushfires in 1985 destroyed most of those that were left. The town's streets are still discernible, many with extensive basalt culverts, as are some foundations. But the best way to appreciate the town's one-time importance is by walking through the cemetery—it's huge. Amherst is four km northwest of Talbot on the road to Avoca.

Maryborough

Maryborough, 10 km north from Amherst, is a thriving agricultural center of 8,000 on the Pyrenees Highway. Gold was discovered in the nearby White Hills in 1854, and within six months 25,000 diggers had converged on the area. Fine examples of Victorian architecture are a legacy of the town's one-time prosperity, including the railway station (some say it was designed for Melbourne but somehow was built in Maryborough), Bull and Mouth Hotel, and Town Hall. If you're in the area during the Sept.-Oct. school holidays, don't miss the **Golden Wattle Festival,** where highlights include the Australian Gum-leaf Playing Championship and a birdcalling competition.

Wattle Grove Motel, 65 Derby Rd., tel. (03) 5461-1877, is the least expensive motel in town at $38 s, $44 d. Inexpensive. **Eany Farm** is more comfortable, and rates of $30-50 pp include a hearty country-style breakfast. It's 10 km southeast of Maryborough, tel. (03) 5464-7267. Moderate. **Golden Country Caratel,** 134 Park Rd., tel. (03) 5461-2344, has a number of self-contained units for $42-52, and 26 campsites, all with power and a private bathroom, for $26. Budget-Inexpensive.

The old lantern room on the platform of the Maryborough railway station is now **Twains,** tel. (03) 5460-4062, a delightful little restaurant, where main meals range $8-13.

Maryborough Tourist Information Centre is on the corner of Tuaggra and Alma Streets, tel. (03) 5461-2643; open daily 10 a.m.-5 p.m.

Avoca and Nearby Wineries

Avoca is a small agricultural center at the junction of the Sunraysia and Pyrenees Highways, 70 km northwest of Ballarat. To the west is the spectacular Pyrenees Range, named by Major Thomas Mitchell in 1836 for the Pyrenees Mountains in western Europe, but they bear little resemblance to them—the highest point is **Mt. Avoca,** just 762 meters high. Still, the area has strong connections to France through a number of renowned vineyards. In the early 1960s, Remy Martin, famed for its brandy, established Chateau Remy Winery seven km west of Avoca and produces sparkling wines. Chateau Remy has extensive gardens and is open to the public for tasting, tel. (03) 5465-3202. Just to the south of Chateau Remy is **Mt. Avoca Vineyard,** which produces some of the region's most successful wines; open daily 10 a.m.-5 p.m., tel. (03) 5465-3282.

Warrenmang is best known for its red wines but also boasts a renowned restaurant and 14 colonial-style timber cottages dotted among towering eucalypts. Its bed and breakfast is $99 d ($189 d Sat.-Sun. dinner included). Expensive. The elegant restaurant has impressive views over the surrounding vineyards to the mountains beyond. To get there, take the Sunraysia Highway northwest from Avoca and turn off to Moonambel and follow the Warrenmang signs, tel. (03) 5467-2233. Back in town, **Avoca Caravan Park,** Liebig St., tel. (03) 5465-3073, has a tranquil setting by the river; $10 for tents, and on-site vans are $28 d. Budget.

The Golden Triangle

Within the area bounded by Inglewood, Wedderburn, and Dunolly, 90% of the world's largest gold nuggets have been found, including the 2,293-ounce **Welcome Stranger,** the largest chunk of gold ever found. The Welcome Stranger was found by John Deason and Richard Oates in 1869 near the small hamlet of Moliagul; now a cairn marks the site of the find. **Dunolly,** south of

Moliagul, has a small museum full of gold-mining memorabilia including the anvil on which the Welcome Stranger was unceremoniously cut up—so that it would fit on the scales! The museum is open 1:30-5 p.m., daily during school holidays, and Sunday only the rest of the year.

From Dunolly, the most interesting route to the northern tip of the Golden Triangle is northeast through almost-a-ghost-town **Wanyarra,** to **Tarnagulla,** which boasts some fine examples of Victorian architecture, then onto **Bridgewater,** a town of 1,500 on the Calder Highway.

Just northwest is **Inglewood,** center of a large eucalyptus oil industry that started shortly after the gold rush ended. That's not to say there's no gold left—in 1980 a 952-ounce nugget was found in the old schoolyard. West of Inglewood is **Kooyoora State Park** (3,500 hectares), where Captain Melville, the gentleman bushranger, had a hideout, living in a series of large overhangs and using a rocky ledge as a lookout point to detect troopers.

SPA COUNTRY

The twin towns of Daylesford and Hepburn Springs are surrounded by Australia's largest concentration of mineral springs. Signs of the prosperity bought by the gold rush are abundantly clear, but it is the springs themselves that are the main attraction.

Daylesford

The Wombat Flat Diggings grew around Lake Daylesford after the discovery of gold there by John Egan in August 1851. The tent city gradually grew more permanent and underwent a name change from Wombat to Daylesford. As the gold rush ended, the soothing qualities of the mineral springs grew in reputation, attracting the wealthy from Melbourne, creating a need for grand guesthouses and other facilities that the wealthy demanded. Today the town has a population of 2,500, many of whom are Melburnians who have escaped to the idyllic lifestyle the town provides.

Apart from wandering along the main street and admiring the many arts-and-crafts shops, you can head to **Wombat Hill Botanic Garden,** off Central Springs Road. Formerly a nunnery, the **Convent Gallery,** Daly St., tel. (03)

5348-3211, holds an eclectic collection of local art, including paintings, sculptures, and jewelry. Also, **Central Highlands Tourist Railway** operates between the station on Fraser St. and the small community of Musk. The self-propelled diesel passenger cars are restored versions of those used earlier this century. Trains depart Sunday on the hour 10 a.m.-3 p.m. Roundtrip tickets cost adult $6, child $4. For details call (03) 5348-3927.

As has been the tradition for more than 100 years, the most popular accommodations in Daylesford are self-contained cottages. **Possum Cottage,** 33 Leggatt St., tel. (03) 5348-3173, is a large lakefront cottage with three bedrooms, a colonial-style kitchen, and a log fire. It costs $150 per night. Luxury. Also overlooking Lake Daylesford is **Ambleside Bed and Breakfast,** 15 Leggatt St., tel. (03) 5348-2691, a historic house carefully renovated to retain a Victorian ambience; rates are $95 s, $120 d. Premium. **Jubilee Lake Caravan Park,** tel. (03) 5348-2186, is on the shores of the eponymous lake, three km south of town. Sites are $10-12 and cabins start at $50. Budget-Inexpensive.

Daylesford boasts a number of gourmet eateries and delis—one that shouldn't be missed for fine chocolates and a delicious array of light meals is **Sweet Decadence,** on Vincent Street. At 77 Vincent Street is **The Food Gallery,** tel. (03) 5348-1677, a French-Italian bistro dishing up homemade meals and picnic hampers to go; open daily 9 a.m.-6 p.m. **Lake House** is regarded as one of country-Victoria's finest weekend getaways. The luxurious accommodation here may be a little more than most budgets allow ($180-300 d, includes dinner, bed, and breakfast), but the licensed restaurant overlooking Lake Daylesford is open to the public and features continental cuisine starting at $20 for main dishes and a three-course dinner on Saturday night for $60 pp. The lodge is on King St., tel. (03) 5348-3329.

The closest railway station to Daylesford is Woodend. Buses connect the two villages, departing and arriving from a garage at 45 Vincent Street.

Daylesford Information Centre is at 49 Vincent St., tel. (03) 5348-1339; open daily 9 a.m.-4 p.m.

Hepburn Springs

Diggers who came to the Hepburn Springs area were predominantly of Swiss-Italian descent and, as the gold began running out, they saw value in the mineral springs. **Hepburn Springs Reserve** was established in 1865, and soon after a pavilion for bathers was constructed. Today the reserve is an idyllic place to relax; each of four main springs contains water of a different chemical composition—magnesium, soda, iron, and sulphur—and each is obtainable from iron hand-pumps scattered throughout the reserve. Also in the reserve is **Hepburn Spa Resort,** where the health-giving properties of the water have attracted generations of Melburnians. Admission to the pool and indoor spa is $9, 20 minutes in a spa is $21, and massages are also available; open Mon.-Fri. 10 a.m.-8 p.m., Sat.-Sun. 9 a.m.-8 p.m., tel. (03) 5348-2034.

Numerous hiking trails crisscross the area around Hepburn Springs, including one that begins at the end of Blowhole Rd. and follows Sailors Creek though **Brace's Flat** to the Mistletoe Mine and **Tipperary Spring.**

For accommodation, **Liberty House,** 20 Mineral Springs Crescent, tel. (03) 5348-2809, opposite Mineral Springs Reserve, provides comfortable rooms for $40 s, $80 d. Moderate. The upmarket **Perini Country House,** 4 8th St., tel. (03) 5348-2579, is an English-style house set in extensive and well-manicured gardens overlooking Doctor's Gully. Each of the three guest rooms has a private bathroom and possesses distinctive charm. Rates start at $85 s, $125 d, which includes a sumptuous breakfast. Premium. At the other end of the scale is **Springs Caravan Park,** Forest Ave., tel. (03) 5348-3161, where tent sites are $10 and on-site vans $28. Budget.

Cosy Corner Cafe, 10th St., is the only casual dining in Hepburn Springs, although many of the guesthouses offer formal dinners with advance bookings.

A shuttle bus runs four times a day (weekdays only) between Daylesford and Hepburn Springs.

Trentham and Vicinity

Trentham is a picturesque hamlet nestled in the middle of the densely forested Wombat Ranges east of Daylesford. Although many buildings lining

Trentham's main street date from the gold rush, it is the surrounding bush that's the drawcard here. Casual prospectors still find gold in the surrounding hills, and many trails used by the old diggers are today used as hiking tracks. The 50-km **Wombat Forest Drive** is a scenic route through the hills with many lookouts, mineral springs, and other points of interest. It starts in Daylesford and heads east through Lyonville and Trentham, then south to Blackwood, where a renowned four-hectare botanic garden is located. North of Trentham, you'll find **Trentham Falls** cascading over a wide rock ledge into a deep pool below.

Kyneton

Kyneton's main street is one of the best-preserved examples of a Victorian streetscape in the country. Today many of the buildings house specialty shops. There's a small Russian museum in Walkden's General Store and a collection of old brewing equipment in the Royal George Hotel. An old bank, at 67 Piper St., houses **Kyneton Museum,** tel. (03) 5422-1228, which has been renovated and features a replica of a settler's cottage and a vast collection of colonial memorabilia. Open Wed.-Sun. 11 a.m.-4 p.m.

CASTLEMAINE AND VICINITY

While Bendigo and Ballarat survived and thrived on company mining, Castlemaine was less fortunate. Gold was discovered in the area in late 1851, and subsequent diggings became known as Mt. Alexander. At first, the promise of gold produced the largest of the early rushes, and as the wealth continued Castlemaine saw itself as a sister city to Bendigo. Businessmen built accordingly. By the time alluvial gold began running out, streets had been laid out and a large market building, banks, civic buildings, and a theater had been constructed.

Today, the city of 7,600, 119 km northwest of Melbourne, is the center of a fruit-growing and farming district, its excellent examples of Victorian architecture a lasting legacy of the short-lived gold rush.

One of Australia's favorite beers, Castlemaine XXXX, was first brewed here in 1859, but the brewery moved to Queensland in 1887 and is now the preferred *drop* in that northern state.

Sights

Castlemaine Market, built in 1862, is now a museum with mining artifacts and an audiovisual display of the town's history; open daily 10 a.m.-5 p.m. Dignified homes from last century are scattered throughout town, but one of special note is **Buda Historic Home,** built by local silversmith Ernest Leviny. The house and surrounding gardens are open daily 9:30 a.m.-5 p.m., and admission is adult $5, child $2.50; located at 42 Hunter St., tel. (03) 5472-1032. Other worthy sights are botanic gardens (one of the state's oldest), on Walker St., and **Castlemaine Art Gallery,** on Lyttleton St., which boasts a fine collection of colonial paintings.

Accommodations and Food

You don't need to break the law to spend a night in the Castlemaine jail. Between 1861 and 1990, prisoners were the only guests at **Old Castlemaine Gaol,** Bowden St., tel. (03) 5470-5311, but today travelers can pay for the privilege of being incarcerated for the night. The cells remain pretty much as they were through the last 100 years, although the whole place has been carpeted and the beds replaced. It's only open on weekends, and the cost is $65 pp for bed, breakfast, and dinner. Moderate. Built in 1854, **Broadoaks,** 31 Gingell St., tel. (03) 5470-5827, was the last home of Robert O'Hara Burke, of Burke and Wills fame. The home features antique brass beds and a comfortable lounge with log fire, and a hearty country-style breakfast is served each morning. Rooms begin at $75. Moderate. **Botanic Gardens Caravan Park,** Walker St., tel. (03) 5472-1125, beside the botanic gardens, has tent sites from $10 and on-site vans for $26-32. Budget.

Theatre Royal, 28 Hargreaves St., tel. (03) 5472-1196, is a historic theater that functions as a cinema and restaurant. Meals average about $15, but three-course meal-and-movie deals are often offered weeknights. For a casual meal or light snack, **Tog's Place,** 58 Lyttleton St., has a unique style and serves delicious gourmet sandwiches. The **Cumberland Hotel,** 191 Barker St., offers more traditional Australian fare, such as steak sandwiches for $6.

Transportation and Information

The railway station is on Kennedy St., tel. (03) 5472-4205. **V/Line** trains run daily to Melbourne and Bendigo, while buses depart from the station for Ballarat.

Castlemaine Tourist Information Centre, tel. (03) 5470-6200, is on the main route into town from Melbourne (Pyrenees Hwy.); open school holidays and weekends only, 10 a.m.-4 p.m.

Maldon

Of all the goldfields' towns, Maldon, 20 km northwest of Castlemaine, remains as well preserved an example of a gold-rush town as any other. At one time 20,000 diggers lived in and around Maldon; now the population is less than 2,000, but the hotels, theaters, and civic buildings remain. In fact virtually every building on the main street is recognized by the National Trust as being of "historical importance." Many of the shops now house specialty gift shops and antique emporiums—adding to the old-world charm.

Off Parkin's Reef Rd., two km south of town, is **Carman's Tunnel,** a 600-meter-long tunnel cut through solid rock over a period of two years in the 1880s. The result of this immense effort was a paltry $300 worth of gold. Tunnel tours take place Sat.-Sun., daily during school holidays, 1:30-4 p.m.; $2.50. For bookings, call (03) 5472-2656. To the north of the tunnel is **Mt. Tarrengower,** where a lookout gives you tremendous views of the surrounding countryside.

BENDIGO

Like Ballarat, Bendigo (pop. 70,000), 140 km north of Melbourne, is a grand and prosperous city founded on the wealth of gold. The mines around Bendigo were among the richest in Australia; their legacy is streets lined with extravagant Victorian-era architecture.

History

In 1851 gold was discovered at Ravenswood. The tens of thousands who descended on the diggings spread out over claims that totaled 360 square km. With so much activity, alluvial gold quickly ran out and the diggers moved to a newly discovered field, **Sandhurst,** as Bendigo was then known. As surface gold ran out, companies moved in to extract gold located in reefs of quartz. By the mid-1860s reef mining was in full swing, and it is from this period that Bendigo's more impressive buildings date.

Sights

Named for the gold-bearing reef of quartz that it was sunk to mine, 500-meter-deep **Central Deborah Gold Mine** was the last on the Bendigo field to close. It reopened in 1972, this time for tourists. The mine remains much as it was when it closed, although a replacement poppet head from the rich Sheepshead Line Mine is now in place. A tour takes in displays of mining memorabilia and a talk, then it's on with a hard hat and light to descend 60 meters underground and experience what life as a miner was like and how the gold was extracted. Open daily 9 a.m.-5 p.m.; tour cost adult $15, child $7. The mine is at 76 Violet St., tel. (03) 5443-8322. At the mine site is a café and information center. It's also the terminus for **Bendigo Talking Tram,** a vintage tram that runs through town to all the sights. Trams run hourly 9:30 a.m.-5:30 p.m. The fare is $7.50 pp, which includes admission to a tramway museum along the route.

The Bendigo diggings attracted a large contingent of Chinese diggers, whose hard work often yielded better results than other diggers, causing widespread resentment. Bridge St. was the original **China Town,** and a few reminders of their colorful culture remain. **Golden Dragon Museum,** 9 Bridge St., tel. (03) 5441-5044, has a large collection of Chinese artifacts in a modern setting with the highlight being 100-meter-long **Sun Loong,** the world's longest ceremonial dragon. Admission is adult $6, child $3. Open daily 9:30 a.m.-5:30 p.m.

The **Joss House,** one of four Chinese places of worship that once dotted Bendigo, was built in 1864. It's painted bright red, a traditional Chinese color, and the front entrance is guarded by a pair of mythical beasts. Inside are a variety of paintings, embroidered banners, and Chinese lanterns. Admission is adult $4, child $2. Open daily 10 a.m.-5 p.m.; on Finn St., north of the rail line. **White Hills Cemetery,** farther along Finn St., has a Chinese section with a traditional prayer oven where mourners burnt money in respect for the deceased.

Pall Mall, Bendigo's main street, is lined with impressive Victorian-era buildings that mirror the wealth the goldfields produced. Along View St. are the restored **Capitol Theatre, Dudley House,** home to the historical society, and **Bendigo Art Gallery.** At 42 View St., tel. (03) 5443-4991, the latter is one of the state's finest regional galleries (open daily 10 a.m.-5 p.m.), with an extensive collection of contemporary Australian art. Behind these buildings is **Rosalind Park,** site of some of Bendigo's later gold rushes. Sign of the actual mining has disappeared under landscaped gardens, but a few outcrops of quartz remain. At a high point of the park and surrounded by a mosaic is a poppet head, which once sat above the shaft of Bendigo's richest mine, Garden Gully United. Panoramic views from the tower extend 360 degrees. The **Shamrock Hotel,** corner of Pall Mall and Williamson St., is a classic example of elegant goldfields architecture. The structure is four stories high and has an impressive balcony lined with iron lace, a cavernous ballroom, and an elegant foyer. Tours of the hotel are offered Sat.-Sun. at 2:30 p.m. for $7.50 pp, which includes a Devonshire tea; for bookings call (03) 5447-1383. Rooms are available (see below), or drop by for a beer anytime the bar is open. **Sacred Heart Cathedral,** on the corner of Mackenzie and Wattle Streets, is one of many grand churches that dot the city. Parts of the sandstone and granite structure date from 1897 and its spire stands 86 meters tall.

BENDIGO

NOT TO SCALE

© AVALON TRAVEL PUBLISHING

Lansell's Fortuna, Chum St., tel. (03) 5442-0222, was the 1870s home of George Lansell, one of Bendigo's wealthiest residents. His mansion, at one time the largest in Australia, is open for tours Sunday at 1 p.m. The $8 pp cost includes afternoon tea.

Eaglehawk, seven km northwest of the city center, was the site of a gold rush in 1852. Now part of city sprawl, many buildings there date from the 1860s. Continuing in the same direction, **Victoria Hill** was the site of many rich mines (including George Lansell's). It's free to wander around, with interpretive boards showing points of historical interest.

Festivals and Events

Each year during **Easter Fair,** the dragon Sun Loong, all 100 meters of him, is paraded through the streets of Bendigo (with the help of 100 attendants). The parade takes place Easter Monday, but the preceding week is packed with events, including free street entertainment, theater, and kids' activities. The other major annual event, which, surprisingly, attracts just as many people, is the **Classic Cars—National Swap Meet,** when up to 30,000 enthusiasts descend on the showgrounds on the second weekend of November.

Accommodations

The grand five-story **Shamrock Hotel,** corner Pall Mall and Williamson St., tel. (03) 5443-0333, has rooms for travelers, and slowly they are being refurnished to their former glory. Rates start at $50 s, $90 d, with a number of suites going for $135 s or d. Moderate. **Old Crown Hotel,** 238 Hargreaves St., tel. (03) 5441-6888, has pub-style rooms of a reasonable standard for $30 s, $45 d, including breakfast. Inexpensive. A well-priced and central motel is **City Centre Motel,** 26 Forest St., tel. (03) 5443-2077, 200 meters northwest of Pall Mall; rates are $45 s, $55 d. Inexpensive. **Bendigo Central Motor Lodge,** 181 View St., tel. (03) 5443-9388, has good rooms, a pool, laundry, and barbecue area; $50 s, $65 d. Moderate. Opposite Lake Weeroona, on the Midland Highway, is a string of motels, including **Tea House Motor Inn,** tel. (03) 5441-7111, a good value at $49 s, $58 d (inexpensive), and **Julie-Anna Inn,** tel. (03) 5442-5855, which offers large, well-furnished rooms

set around a pool and landscaped courtyard for $90 s, $100 d (expensive).

Nanga Gnulle, east of downtown at 40 Harley St., tel. (03) 5443-7891, is a uniquely built bed and breakfast set among a hectare of landscaped gardens. It's built with mud bricks, recycled bricks, and railway sleepers, but still is stylish with two large, elegantly furnished guest rooms; $90 s, $120 d, including breakfast. Expensive.

Bendigo's best backpacker accommodation is **Central City Caravan Park,** 362 High St., tel. (03) 5443-6937, which has six bunk rooms of four beds for $12 pp. Although more than two km south of downtown, this park is closest to the attractions. Powered and unpowered sites are $12-14, on-site vans $30, and cabins $42-58. Budget-Inexpensive.

Food

Bendigo's hotels are the best place to head for an inexpensive meal. The restaurant in the **Shamrock Hotel,** corner of Pall Mall and Williamson St., opens early and closes late. This is a good bet before 10 a.m.—an extensive cold buffet breakfast is $8 pp. **City Family Hotel,** 41 High St., has decent-sized counter lunches for around $5. Try the **Metropolitan Hotel,** corner Bull and Hargreaves Streets for a bit more style. **Cafe Cumberland,** in the Cumberland Hotel, 56 Williamson St., has a pleasant setting overlooking the street from a second-story balcony. Sandwiches are $3-7, pasta is $7-10, or a huge serving of Nachos Supreme is just $7. You can also relax with just a coffee and cake or dessert. Open Tues.-Saturday.

Located in the 1887 National Bank building is **Mully's Cafe,** 32 Pall Mall, open for light, inexpensive meals, and with a gallery upstairs. Open daily 10 a.m.-5 p.m. **Clogs,** 106 Pall Mall, tel. (03) 5443-0077, is a modern bistro-style restaurant where you can stop for just coffee or a full meal. Pizza and pasta is around $8, with other main dishes $11-16.50. **The Match,** 58 Bull St., tel. (03) 5441-4403, is another centrally located, casual restaurant. Simply decorated and opening to a few outdoor tables, the pizza brings the locals to this popular eating place. **House of Khong,** 200 Hargreaves St., tel. (03) 5443-5656, is a good, inexpensive Chinese restaurant, with a buffet lunch weekdays for $10. At the other end of the scale is the **Jolly Puddler,** 101 Williamson St., tel. (03)

5443-9859, an intimate restaurant with main dishes from $17.

Transportation, Services, and Information

V/Line, tel. (13) 2232, has regular rail services between Melbourne and Bendigo. The station is on Railway Place, off Mitchell Street. V/Line buses from Bendigo head to Castlemaine, Ballarat, Echuca, and Mildura. **Bendigo Associated Taxis** can be contacted at (13) 1008.

The **post office** is on the corner of Williamson and Hargreaves Streets. **Bendigo Tourist Information Centre** has been recently moved to the grand old post office building at 51 Pall Mall, tel. (03) 5444-4445. Static displays and interactive computer terminals relate the city's history, making it a good place to start your exploration of Bendigo. Open daily 10 a.m.-5 p.m.

VICINITY OF BENDIGO

Whipstick State Park

Now protected as a state park, this area north of Bendigo saw its share of diggers, and still produces small amounts of alluvial gold to amateur prospectors who try their luck. The 2,300-hectare park was established to protect an area of whipstick mallee, a hardy and distinctive plant unique to the area. Near the park entrance is **Hartland's Eucalyptus Farm,** tel. (03) 5448-8270, which has been producing eucalyptus oil for more than 100 years. Open daily (tours Sunday only; $3) 10:30 a.m.-4 p.m.

Heathcote

Heathcote is a historic gold-mining town of 1,900, located 47 km east of Bendigo on the McIvor Highway, an alternate route between Melbourne and Bendigo. In 1853, at the height of the gold rush, 30,000 diggers lived in the town. Now a few old buildings remain along the main street. On the south side of town, to the west of the highway, is **Pink Cliffs Reserve,** an area of erosion caused by sluicing operations. On the east side of the highway, a 10-minute hike from the end of Barrack St. leads to a lookout with views across town. The area is noted for many fine wineries, including **Heathcote Winery,** 183 High St., tel. (03) 5433-2595, in a historic building right in the center of town.

GREAT OCEAN ROAD

"A tourist road comparable to that in California" was the claim when it was first proposed to carve a road into coastal cliffs between Torquay and Apollo Bay. And after driving the route, few would disagree with the comparison. Officially, the Great Ocean Road extends between Anglesea and Apollo Bay, but generally the entire coastal highway from Geelong to Warrnambool is considered part of the road. The road has three distinct sections—the **Surf Coast,** from Geelong to Apollo Bay, the lush, green world of the **Otway Ranges,** and the **Shipwreck Coast,** from Princetown to Warrnambool. The road's most famous landmarks are the spectacular rock formations, such as the Twelve Apostles, of **Port Campbell National Park,** but the entire road is a smorgasbord of history, scenery, surfing, and shipwrecks.

If you don't have a car, it's difficult to sample the entire smorgasbord. **V/Line** has no direct bus or train service along the Great Ocean Road, but V/Line trains run daily between Melbourne and Geelong and Melbourne and Warrnambool; V/Line buses run from Geelong to as far as Apollo Bay and, on Friday only, continue to Warrnambool.

Melbourne to Geelong

The easiest way to head southwest from downtown Melbourne is on the Westgate Frwy., which crosses the 2.7-km **Westgate Bridge** southwest of the city center and passes through 75 km of industrial sprawl, ending at Geelong. The only worthwhile detour is **You Yangs Regional Park,** a 2,025-hectare reserve surrounding volcanic intrusions (You Yangs translates from Koori to mean "Big Mountain in the Middle of the Plain"). The park's highest point is 348-meter **Flinders Peak,** accessible along a 1.6-km (one-way) trail. A longer trail circumnavigates the peak and provides more great views. A visitor center at the entrance is open daily 8:30 a.m.-4:30 p.m., tel. (03) 5282-3356.

GEELONG

With a population of 130,000, Geelong is Victoria's second-largest city. The Princes Highway bypasses the main commercial center, but if you have the time, some parts of what at first seems like just a massive industrial and residential sprawl are worth exploring.

The original settlement was established in the 1830s, mainly to service surrounding grazing land. The town boomed during the gold rushes of the 1850s, and as western Victoria was opened to settlers, Geelong's role as a major port for shipping grain and wheat increased.

National Wool Museum

This excellent museum is housed in the National Wool Centre, an 1855 bluestone building used as a woolstore for more than 100 years. Displays catalog the history of wool-growing, traditionally one of Australia's major industries,

National Wool Centre, Geelong

through a re-creation of a shearing shed. Other points of interest include displays showing the many breeds of sheep and the uses of each wool class, a short audiovisual in which shearers relate stories from the sheds, and a variety of machinery that classes, presses, and dispatches wool. The top floor was originally the sales room, and on display now are bales of wool ready for inspection by buyers. On the first floor, in the large foyer area, are shops selling wool and other Australiana products, and an information center. The complex is open daily 10 a.m.-5 p.m. with admission to the museum adult $7, child $3.50. Located at 26 Moorabool St., tel. (03) 5226-4660.

Other Sights

The city has more than 100 buildings classified by the National Trust, many of which are downtown and covered in the brochure *City of Geelong Heritage Trail,* available at local information centers. For a wide range of paintings (mostly Australian), head to **Geelong Art Gallery** at Little Malop St., tel. (03) 5229-3645. Works of many well-known Australian artists as well as touring exhibitions are its highlights. Admission adult $3, child $1. Open Tues.-Fri. 10 a.m.-5 p.m., Sat.-Sun. 1-5 p.m. The site of Australia's first naval college now houses the **Naval and Maritime Museum,** Swinburne St., North Geelong, tel. (03) 5227-0209, which tells the story of the Royal Australian Navy and the importance of Geelong to the maritime history of Port Phillip Bay. It's open 10 a.m.-4 p.m. (closed Tuesday and Thursday).

A small part of a larger reserve, **Geelong Botanic Gardens,** a few blocks from downtown, was first planted in 1850. Within the gardens is a timber cottage dating from 1838 and a tearoom open daily 11 a.m.-4 p.m. The main reserve extends to the shore of Corio Bay and **Eastern Beach,** a pleasant sandy area backed by formed gardens. Rent boats and aqua bikes in summer at the beach, tel. (03) 5243-4306.

Accommodations

Motels line the main routes into Geelong. One of the most central, **Kangaroo Motel,** 16 the Esplanade S, tel. (03) 5221-4022, also has a restaurant; $43 s, $53 d. Inexpensive. Northwest of downtown on Ballarat Rd. (Midland Hwy.) and

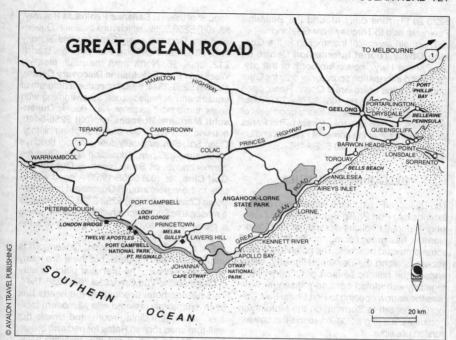

GREAT OCEAN ROAD

© AVALON TRAVEL PUBLISHING

right opposite Geelong Golf Club is **Parkwood Motel,** tel. (03) 5278-5477, where rooms are $45 s, $55 d. Inexpensive. A little more upmarket is **Lucas Innkeepers Motor Inn,** 9 Aberdeen St., tel. (03) 5221-2177, for $64 s, $72 d. Moderate.

On Barrabool Rd., alongside the Barwon River southwest of the city center, are three caravan parks.

Food

Inexpensive and casual eateries are spread along Little Malop and Moorabool Streets. If you've just spent a few hours in the National Wool Museum, **Lamby's Bar and Bistro,** in the National Wool Centre's basement, is an enjoyable place for a meal or just a drink. Roast of the day is $10, but a wide selection of other dishes and lighter meals start at $6.50. The National Wool Centre lies just one block from the waterfront, an area that has been the heart of a massive redevelopment program in recent years. Built over the harbor is Fishermen's Pier and a

number of cafés and restaurants, including the **Sailor's Rest Tavern,** tel. (03) 5222-4100, with alfresco seafood dining downstairs and a more formal restaurant upstairs. Immediately to the south, changing rooms have been converted to a casual café and an upstairs restaurant overlooking the promenade and harbor. The **Hill Grill,** 228 Moorabool St., tel. (03) 5221-3388, is another casual place, with most dishes $5-10, but it's very popular later in the evening and gets rather noisy. **Le Parisien,** 16 the Esplanade, tel. (03) 5229-3110, is a classy French restaurant with an extensive menu and many local wines. Another more formal establishment is **Tousson,** located in a two-story heritage building at 310 Moorabool St., tel. (03) 5221-1375.

Transportation, Services, and Information

V/Line operates hourly train services to Geelong from Melbourne; the station is on Fenwick St., tel. (13) 2232. **McHarry's Bus Line,** tel. (03)

5223-2111, runs daily around the Bellarine Peninsula and to Torquay from Geelong.

The main source of information is the **Geelong Otway Tourist Information Centre** on the Princes Hwy., seven km north of the city. It's a good information source, not only for Geelong, but for the entire Great Ocean Road; open daily 9 a.m.-5 p.m., tel. (03) 5275-5797. Also, the National Wool Museum has a good deal of brochures, as well as books for sale. The **Parks Victoria** office is at the corner of Fenwick and Little Malop Streets, tel. (03) 5226-4667.

BELLARINE PENINSULA

The Bellarine Peninsula, a wide thumb of land, extends into Port Phillip Bay southeast of Geelong. A popular holiday destination for Melburnians, it has great fishing, scuba diving, and some protected beaches. The peninsula's main access is along the Bellarine Highway, which ends at the historic seaport of Queenscliff. A regularly scheduled car and passenger ferry plies the narrow opening to Port Phillip Bay, linking Queenscliff to Sorrento on the Mornington Peninsula, making a 200-km round-the-bay excursion possible.

On the peninsula's northern tip is the small township of **Portarlington.** The massive three-story flour mill there dates from the 1850s and is open for inspection Sunday 2-5 p.m. **Portarlington Public Reserve** has the state's largest campground with 1,250 sites ranging $16-24, tel. (03) 5259-2764.

Queenscliff

The settlement of Queenscliff grew from a pilot station set up to guide ships heading through the treacherous waters between the Bellarine and Mornington Peninsulas. In the 1880s the town became popular with those who struck it rich on the goldfields. Many buildings from that era have been restored and the seaside holiday village atmosphere remains. A **fort,** built in 1870 to repel a perceived Russian invasion, overlooks the bay. It's open for tours Sat.-Sun. at 1 and 3 p.m. The tour cost of $2 also includes admission to Victoria's only black lighthouse.

During summer plenty of tourist-orientated activities happen in and around town. The most popular of these is **Bellarine Peninsula Railway,** tel. (03) 5258-2069, which runs between Queenscliff and Drysdale every Saturday and Sunday at 10:30 a.m. and 2:40 p.m. Roundtrip fare is adult $12, child $6. North from the main pier, on Weeroona Parade, is **Marine Discovery Centre,** tel. (03) 5258-3344, which operates a program of cruises and activities, such as swimming with seals, throughout summer. Next door is **Queenscliff Maritime Museum,** tel. (03) 5258-3440, housing displays of the area's shipping history. Open Sat.-Sun. and daily during school holidays 10:30 a.m.-4:30 p.m. Admission is $4. Over the narrow bridge, on Swan Island, is **Queenscliff Golf Club,** tel. (03) 5252-1951. A good way to take to the waters around Queenscliff is with **Impulse Charters,** tel. (03) 5258-3739. They charge a reasonable $80 pp for a half-day charter, which is plenty of time to combine swimming with the dolphins and a spot of fishing.

For a seaside holiday resort, Queenscliff is surprisingly free of motels, but there are many good alternatives. The grandest place to stay in Queenscliff is **Vue Grand,** tel. (03) 5258-1544. This historic hotel overlooking the heads has been extensively restored with all modern facilities, an elegant dining room, and simple but well-furnished rooms. Rates for bed and breakfast are $110 s, $180 d, but often midweek packages including dinner are offered. Luxury. In the same central area, and from the same era, is the large and recently renovated **Ozone Hotel,** tel. (03) 5258-1011, where rooms are $80 s, $120 d including breakfast. Expensive. **Queenscliff Inn,** 59 Hesse St., tel. (03) 5258-3737, is an Edwardian guesthouse with a relaxing atmosphere; private rooms are $45 s, $70-85 d (including breakfast). Moderate. The inn has recently become affiliated with the YHA and offers dorm beds to members for $15 pp. The closest camping to town is **Recreation Reserve Camping Area,** along the foreshore. Sites are $14-22. Budget. **Beacon Resort,** toward Point Lonsdale, tel. (03) 5258-1133, is more modern and has better facilities. Sites here are $17-25 and cabins are $48-58. Inexpensive.

Casual eateries are spread along Hesse Street. None stand out, although the **Ozone Hotel,** 42 Gellibrand St., tel. (03) 5258-1931, has good bar meals from $6 and a larger menu in the Boat Bar, decorated with historical photographs. More formal is **Miettas,** in the Queenscliff Hotel, tel. (03) 5258-1066, where diners choose between tables in a conservatory or courtyard, and the elegant dining room in Vue Grand.

McHarry's Bus Line, tel. (03) 5223-2111, has a regular service between Geelong and Queenscliff. The MV *Queenscliff,* tel. (03) 5258-3244, is a 60-meter-long car and passenger ferry making six to 12 trips daily from Queenscliff to Sorrento on the Mornington Peninsula. Fares vary with the season but are, in high season (summer), $34 for a car and $70 for the average motorhome. Adults are an extra $3, children $2 (double that for passengers without a car); no reservations taken.

Queenscliff to Torquay
Point Lonsdale, another popular summer resort, is linked to Queenscliff by a long sandy beach. From the lighthouse on the headland, views extend to Mornington Peninsula, and, if you're lucky, you'll be able to see ships negotiate the treacherous waters of "The Rip."

In 1835, when a group of Europeans, the first to visit the area in more than 30 years, were preparing to establish a settlement on Port Phillip Bay, they were amazed to come across a white man. He was William Buckley, an escaped convict who had spent 30 years in the area, much of this time in a cave below the lighthouse.

West of Point Lonsdale are the seaside resort communities of **Ocean Grove** and **Barwon Heads.** Both have good beaches, fishing, and scuba diving. Barwon Heads has a great golf course; call (03) 5254-2302 for tee times.

TORQUAY

Surf City
Outside of Hawaii, few towns in the world can claim surfing as their major industry. But Torquay (tor-KEY) can. With a population of 5,000, Torquay lies 90 km southwest of Melbourne. All the town's beaches and reefs have waves for all surfers, but it's **Bells Beach,** southwest of town, which is most famous. In 1949, when Vic Tantau and Owen Yateman first surfed the waves at Bells Beach, they would have had little idea that surfing would hold the key to Torquay's future. Its large swells from the Southern Ocean

and sandy shallows strewn with reefs form consistently perfect waves. Surfers from around the world gather here to ride the long right-handed wave at Bells and others further around the bight at nearby points such as **Winkipop.** But Eastertime's **Bells Surfing Classic,** the world's longest running professional surfing competition, draws the biggest crowd.

Surfing now plays an important role in Torquay's economy. Two surf-clothing companies, **Quiksilver** and **Rip Curl,** were started by local surfers and are today world leaders in innovative surfwear. Both have factory outlets in Torquay, along with a dozen other surf-related companies, in **Surf Coast Plaza,** on Surf Coast Highway. Also here is **Surfworld Australia,** tel. (03) 5261-4606, Australia's only surfing museum. Is the surf flat? Well, then, this is the place to spend a few hours. The museum delves into surfing's roots, from the styles and attitudes of Australia's earliest boardriders to today's top professionals, and from the very earliest Hawaiian surfboards to the cutting edge of the sport's technology, through audiovisuals and hands-on interactive displays. Open Mon.-Fri. 9 a.m.-5 p.m., Sat.-Sun. 10 a.m.-4 p.m.; admission adult $6, child $3.

If you feel like learning to surf, **Go Ride a Wave,** tel. (03) 5263-2111, charges $30 for a two-hour lesson.

Accommodations
Bells Beach Backpackers, 51 Surf Coast Hwy., tel. (03) 5261-7070, has that laid-back atmosphere that typifies the surfing lifestyle, making it a perfect place to bunk down for a few nights. This accommodation features all the usual backpacker facilities as well as a large collection of surfing videos and magazines. Dorm beds are $17 pp, while doubles go for $40. Inexpensive.

The best value of Torquay's three motels is **Surf City Motel,** 35 The Esplanade, tel. (03) 5261-3492, where the large rooms are loaded with modern facilities and the beach is only a short walk away; from $68 s, $79 d. Moderate.

Ocean Road Retreat is a more relaxing alternative, and well worth the extra dollars. Set among extensive gardens, it holds three comfortable and spacious rooms with floor-to-ceiling windows affording maximum views. Each well-appointed room features such extras as fluffy bathrobes and homemade chocolates on arrival. Tea, coffee, and cookies are always available in the large lounge area, along with many magazines and videos. Breakfast, served with the best silverware, comes with the rate of $100 s, $120 d ($150 s or d for the suite). It's located within walking distance of Bells Beach at 101 Sunset Strip, Jan Juc, tel. (03) 5261-2971. Expensive.

Bernell Caravan Park, Surf Coast Hwy., tel. (03) 5261-2493, is the pick of Torquay's four campgrounds; sites start at $17 and cabins are $49-83. Budget-Inexpensive.

Food

Gilbert St. is the main shopping strip, with a large supermarket, bakery, butcher, and a few cafés. **Yummy Yoghurt,** at the bottom end of Gilbert St., is a popular local hangout for light, healthy snacks, and, judging by the comments scribbled on the walls, many professional surfers think so too. **Tapas Café,** 14 Gilbert St., opens daily at 7:30 a.m. as a coffeehouse but is most crowded around lunchtime, when healthy sandwiches and various inexpensive hot dishes are offered. Because this is "Surf City," it is only fitting to include the staple of the surfers' diet—head to **Surfside Bakery,** in the small mall on Gilbert St., for a great variety of meat pies. Back on the highway, **Flippin' Fresh Seafoods,** 33 Surf Coast Hwy. (500 meters south of Surf Coast Plaza), offers fish and chips to go.

TORQUAY TO WARRNAMBOOL

Before a road connected the string of towns between Torquay and Apollo Bay, the only coastal access was rough tracks over the Otway Ranges from farmlands of southern Victoria. As servicemen returned from WW I, they were offered work constructing a coastal road. The vast undertaking commenced in 1919, taking three years to reach Eastern View, where the commemorative arch is located. It took another 10 years to complete, but was still only a rough and dusty one-way track between steep cliffs and the raging ocean. One journalist of the time noted that "it was beauty, but at present there is too much thrill in it." Over the years, the road has been sealed, and many of the more dangerous bends eliminated.

Anglesea

Point Roadknight juts into Bass Strait just south of Anglesea, protecting a long, curved bay where the holiday town of Anglesea lies. The town straddles **Anglesea River,** which cuts deeply through the hills of the hinterland. At the river's delta is **Coogoorah Nature Park,** an area offering nature walks, safe canoeing, fishing, barbecues, and an adventure playground. **Anglesea Golf Course** is home to a large population of kangaroos that freely roam the course. The course is open to the public and greens fees are $24; located on a hill above town off Noble St., tel. (03) 5263-1582. Even if you're a nongolfer, the kangaroos make for interesting viewing, and the clubhouse has a relaxing bar and bistro.

The 70-year-old timber **Debonair Motel Guesthouse,** Great Ocean Rd., tel. (03) 5263-1440, is the best value accommodation in town. It has a restaurant, pool, tennis court, and laundry; rooms are in the main building or in an adjacent motel; $48-85 s or d. Inexpensive. **Anglesea Family Caravan Park** is close to both the ocean and river mouth. It has sites for $15-21 and great little wooden cabins for $55 s or d. Located on Cameron Rd., tel. (03) 5263-1583. Budget-Inexpensive.

Diana's Riverbank Restaurant, 113 Great Ocean Rd., tel. (03) 5263-2500, in a small cottage by the river, has a small but varied menu; main meals start at $14. For bistro meals head to **Anglesea Hotel,** just off the main road at 1 Murch Crescent, tel. (03) 5263-1210.

Aireys Inlet

Aireys Inlet, a seaside holiday town, has the forest-covered hills of Angahook-Lorne State Park as a backdrop. The town grew as the turnaround point of Melbourne's Cobb & Co. coach service, and in later years, after **Split Point Lighthouse** was constructed in 1891, many wooden holiday cottages sprang up around the protected inlet. Most of the older houses were destroyed by ravaging Ash Wednesday bushfires in 1983, and the town has since been rebuilt. Although the lighthouse isn't open to the public, the point on which it sits is the start of many coastal walks. Behind the lighthouse is **Lighthouse Keepers Inn,** tel. (03) 5289-6306. These historic cottages are self-contained and spread through a well-manicured garden. All the old lighthouse out-buildings have been put to use—the old stone stables are now a café where lunch and after-noon teas are served daily 10 a.m.-6 p.m.

Lorne and Vicinity

For most of the year Lorne (pop. 1,200), at the mouth of the Erskine River, is a quiet seaside town, but each summer hordes of Melburnians descend on the town; accommodation is at a premium, the roads are jammed with cars, and the footpaths and beaches are crammed with people. The town developed early this centu-ry, housing timber cutters working in the sur-rounding forest, and has grown into a popular holiday getaway. On the main street, opposite the Commonwealth Bank, is a display of his-torical photos from the days of the Great Ocean Road's construction.

Behind town is **Angahook-Lorne State Park.** This hilly 22,000-hectare park traps a large amount of rainfall, which enables it to support lush forests of ferns and blue gums. Most of the park's 50 km of walking trails follow tramways built by timber cutters. From Lorne there are two main access roads into the park along which the network of walking trails begin. For details of these, picnic areas, and campgrounds head to the Department of Natural Resources and Envi-ronment office in Lorne, located at 56 Polwarth Rd., tel. (03) 5289-1732.

The **Pacific Hotel,** Great Ocean Rd., tel. (03) 5289-1609, may not be that grand anymore, but views from many of the rooms are stunning; from \$55 s, \$65 d. Moderate. **Motel Kalimna** is on the same high hill overlooking the ocean and has a tennis court, pool, restaurant, and bar. The rooms are plain but spacious and each has a balcony; \$64 s, \$74 d, tel. (03) 5289-1407. Moderate. **Erskine House,** at the other end of town, is a 1930s art deco guesthouse with rooms starting at \$65 s, \$95 d, including break-fast; located at 136 Mountjoy Parade, tel. (03) 5289-1209. Expensive. A short stroll from down-town and the beach, **Great Ocean Road Back-packers,** Erskine Ave., tel. (03) 5289-1809, is a number of modern timber cottages set among native bushland. Dorm beds are \$16-20 pp, but prices rise in summer. Inexpensive. **Erskine River Caravan Park** is located in town, right by the river, and has tent sites from \$15 and

cabins for \$55. Budget-Inexpensive. A lot qui-eter, but three km south of town, is **Cumber-land River Reserve,** in a pleasant bush set-ting. The Lorne Foreshore Committee, tel. (03) 5289-1382, takes booking for these camp-grounds, or you can stay in one of seven camp-ing areas in the surrounding state park.

Finding a place to eat in Lorne is easy enough; finding a table during summer is a dif-ferent matter. Some eateries, such as **The Arab,** a large café with plenty of outdoor tables, have been around for decades and have become in-stitutions, while others come and go with the summer crowds. The **Pier Seafood Restau-rant,** tel. (03) 5289-1119, below the Grand Pa-cific Hotel, has stunning views of the bay and forested hills beyond. This stylish eatery is fair-ly casual, but expensive; open daily for break-fast, lunch, and dinner. Also on the pier is a co-operative selling fresh seafood.

Lorne Visitor Information Centre, 144 Mountjoy Parade, tel. (03) 5289-1152, has a small amount of information on the town but mainly functions as a booking agency for ac-commodations; open daily 9 a.m.-5 p.m.

Lorne to Apollo Bay

Between these two townships, the Great Ocean Road is at its most spectacular as it hugs the ocean, backed by steep cliffs on one side and the powerful Southern Ocean on the other. Along the route are a number of small settlements, sandy beaches, gravel roads heading inland, and lookouts.

Just beyond Kennett River is **Whitecrest,** tel. (03) 5237-0228, a luxurious accommoda-tion on a gentle slope overlooking the ocean.

tree fern

Each unit is split-level, with a large dining, kitchen, and lounge area, opening to a private balcony on one level and the comfortable double bed on the other. Rates range $85-125 s or d. Moderate.

Apollo Bay

The long curving beach around Apollo Bay is the setting of a picturesque fishing town of the same name. The wide beach in front of the township is lined with cypress trees, and the bay's protected waters are perfect for swimming. The bay was named after the schooner *Apollo*, which carried wool from Port Fairy to Melbourne in the 1840s. In those days Point Bunbury, which protects the bay from heavy swells, was the site of a whaling station, a far cry from the grassy fairways of today's Apollo Bay Golf Course, one of the most picturesque courses in Victoria. The treacherous sea off Apollo Bay has claimed several large ships. Relics from these wrecks, as well as other local memorabilia, are housed in a

small museum located in an old cable station on the Great Ocean Rd.; open Sat.-Sun., and daily during school holidays, 2-5 p.m.

If you plan to spend around $100 on accommodation in Apollo Bay, don't think of staying anywhere but **Seafarers.** Set on eight hectares of land that slope gently to the ocean, it offers rooms with amazing ocean views, enjoyed from within glass-fronted ocean aspects and private balconies. Each has a kitchen and some have fireplaces. The property even boasts a trout pond—the perfect chance to catch dinner. Located four km northeast of town, tel. (03) 5237-6507. Expensive. Very central **Apollo Bay Motel,** Moore St., tel. (03) 5237-7577, has well-furnished rooms for $65 s, $75 d. Moderate. In front is **Apollo Bay Hotel,** tel. (03) 5237-6250, where motel-style rooms are slightly cheaper. Moderate. **Waratah Caravan Park,** 7 Noel St., tel. (03) 5237-6562, has reasonable campsites for $15 and basic on-site vans for $35, and cabins from $65. Budget-Inexpensive.

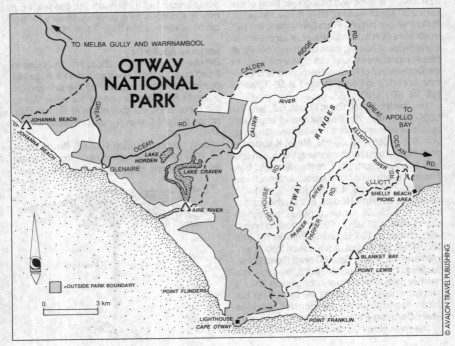

Otway National Park
The **Otway Ranges** rise west of Lorne and run parallel to the coast, branching south to Cape Otway and west to the vicinity of Lavers Hill. The 12,876-hectare Otway National Park protects the southern arm of the range, where it ends at a rugged peninsula of sandstone cliffs and sandy beaches. The backdrop for this spectacular coastline is of luxuriant blue gum, great gum, and towering mountain ash forests, which form a dense canopy protecting an understory of ferns and pockets of cool-temperate rainforest. More than 250 species of birds and 45 species of mammals have been recorded in the park. Of particular interest are the birds that visit the park while migrating, including the Japanese snipe and fluttering shearwater from Eurasia. The main access road into the park leads 15 km from the Great Ocean Rd. to Cape Otway.

Sailors kept well clear of the treacherous Cape Otway until 1848, when a lighthouse was built on the remote headland. The stone structure stands to this day, in testimony to the quality of convict labor. The lighthouse grounds are open daily 9:30 a.m.-4:30 p.m., with tours offered hourly; adult $6, child $3. At other times you can't get to the cape, but a track leads along the cliff to some impressive ocean views. The first turnoff from the Melbourne side of the park leads to **Shelly Beach Picnic Area** from where a trail leads down to the mouth of the Elliott River, providing access to the rugged coast.

Within the park are two campgrounds, each with basic facilities and fresh water. The one at Blanket Bay is sheltered from southerly winds and is near a sandy beach. For park information and to book camping sites call (13) 1963 or (03) 5237-6889. The only other accommodation on the cape is available in the assistant lightkeeper's sandstone cottages, built in the 1850s and still retaining their historic charm. Rates in the one-bedroom cottages are $50-60 during the week and $60-70 on weekends, while the entire four-bedroom house starts at $135 per night. For reservations call (03) 5237-9240. Moderate.

Johanna
Johanna is a windswept coastal community of holiday cottages spread haphazardly along the Johanna River and protected from the brunt of Southern Ocean storms by scrub-covered sand dunes. The shifting sand bars of Johanna's beach are famous among surfers for the heavy waves that consistently roll onto shore. You'll want to check the weather forecast before setting up camp at the semi-official campground behind the beach—it's unprotected from the wind.

Melba Gully
Located southwest of the hilltop community of Lavers Hill, this grove is part of a 65-hectare park that protects a temperate rainforest of lush tree ferns, covered by a canopy of myrtle, beech, and eucalypt. A short nature walk leads through this green wonderland to the cleverly named **Big Tree,** a 300-year-old messmate eucalypt measuring an incredible 27 meters in circumference. The park is also known for **glowworms,** best seen on tours offered by park staff each evening during summer school holidays.

Port Campbell National Park
From **Princetown** to Peterborough, at the mouth of the Curdies River, the Great Ocean Road passes through 1,750-hectare Port Campbell National Park, a narrow strip of coast that is among the most photographed in the country. The relentless power of the Southern Ocean has carved innumerable gorges, arches, caves,

THE WRECK OF THE *LOCH ARD*

On 1 March 1878, the clipper *Loch Ard* left England bound for Australia. She was carrying 54 passengers and a hold full of general cargo. Just 90 days later, at the entrance to Bass Strait, tragedy struck—the ship veered off course and smashed onto rocks off Mutton Bird Island, east of Warrnambool. Heavy seas took their toll on the crew and passengers; Tom Pearce and Eva Carmichael, both 18, were the only survivors. They were washed into the gorge that now bears the ship's name. Eva, a nonswimmer, was dragged from the ocean by Tom, who raised the alarm by heroically climbing the steep cliffs out of the gorge and stumbling across stockmen from nearby Glenample Station, where the two survivors subsequently recuperated.

Eva subsequently returned to Ireland and married someone else.

and a large number of offshore stacks along limestone cliffs rising from the ocean. Traveling from the east, the first of these dramatic formations is also the most photographed—the **Twelve Apostles.** The offshore stacks were once part of the headland, but as wave action eroded softer parts of the rock, they became separated from the mainland and, one day, will succumb completely to the power of the ocean. Just east of the Apostles is **Gibson's Steps,** cut into the cliffs by early settlers to provide access to the sandy beach below. At low tide, and when the sea is calm, it's possible to walk through to the beach behind the Twelve Apostles. A little farther along the coast, a side road leads to **Loch Ard Gorge.** Trails lead around the gorge to a small cemetery and then down to the beach.

Port Campbell
Port Campbell is a small township at the back of a protected harbor, the only spot along this stretch of coast where boats can be safely moored. The town was established as a base for sealers and whalers and has grown into a service center for the masses of tourists traveling the Great Ocean Road. Along Lord St., the main drag through town, are motels, cafés, takeaways, and other service shops. **Loch Ard Shipwreck Museum,** Lord St., tel. (03) 5598-6463, has an interesting array of treasures salvaged from shipwrecks along the coast and details of five major wrecks and subsequent salvage operations; open in summer daily 9 a.m.-5 p.m. Book through the museum for a variety of tours, including: along the coast ($30 pp), to a local wildlife park ($30), and an evening trip to the glowworms of Melba Gully ($20). From the beach at the back of the town, the 2.6-km **Discovery Walk** runs in a westerly direction to Two Mile Bay.

Port Campbell Hotel, tel. (03) 5598-6320, is cheapest of a cluster of accommodations that line the Great Ocean Road through town. Basic rooms with shared facilities are $28 pp, which includes breakfast. Inexpensive. Overlooking the harbor are **Loch Ard Motor Inn,** tel. (03) 5598-

6238, and **Southern Ocean Motor Inn,** tel. (03) 5598-6231, where rates for ocean-view rooms start at around $95. Expensive. **Port Campbell YHA,** 18 Tregea St., tel. (03) 5598-6305, is a recently renovated house 200 meters from the beach. Facilities are basic but adequate; members $12, nonmembers $15. Budget. Across from the hostel is **Port Campbell Caravan Park,** tel. (03) 5598-6492, which is spread along the river to the beach. Sites are $14-18. Budget.

Port Campbell Takeaway dishes up the best fish and chips in town ($5), and across the road is a grassy bank overlooking the harbor, the perfect place for eating lunch. At 25 Lord St., and looking a little out of place among other businesses, is **Emma's Tea Rooms,** tel. (03) 5598-6456, a small cottage with afternoon teas from $4.50 and main meals from $12 reservations essential in the evening. For finer dining, **Napier's,** tel. (03) 5598-6231, in the Southern Ocean Motor Inn, is recommended and overlooks the harbor.

The **Park Information Centre,** Morris St., tel. (03) 5598-6382, has displays on the park's famous natural features along with relics from various shipwrecks, including an anchor salvaged from the ill-fated *Loch Ard.* The 12-minute audiovisual is also worthwhile. Open daily 9 a.m.-5 p.m.

London Bridge and Vicinity
Another of Port Campbell National Park's famous natural features is **London Bridge,** west of Port Campbell. On 15 January 1990, the landward arch of London Bridge collapsed into the sea, forming another offshore stack and leaving two rather surprised tourists wondering how to get off. Just to the east is **The Arch** and to the west, **The Grotto** and **Bay of Islands.**

At the mouth of Curdies Inlet, and marking the western boundary of Port Campbell National Park, is the windswept fishing and holiday village of **Peterborough,** which has good fishing in a protected inlet, a nine-hole golf course along the cliff edge, and camping in a small reserve by the river.

VICTORIA'S SOUTHWEST COAST

For ships sailing between England and Australia in the 19th century, sailing along Victoria's southwest coast and negotiating Bass Strait was the first hazardous navigation they had to do after Cape Horn, and many wrecked. A lighthouse constructed on Cape Otway in 1848 did little to alleviate the problem—ships hugging the coast looking for the light more often than not ended up on the rocks. Although time has ravaged many of the wrecks, coastal communities still have strong ties to their maritime heritage. Warrnambool has the excellent Flagstaff Hill Maritime Village, and to the west is the quiet fishing town of Port Fairy. West of Port Fairy and the deepwater port city of Portland are the long sandy beaches of Discovery Bay, into which the Glenelg River flows, protected in its lower reaches by Lower Glenelg National Park, which offers the perfect opportunity for a wilderness canoe adventure.

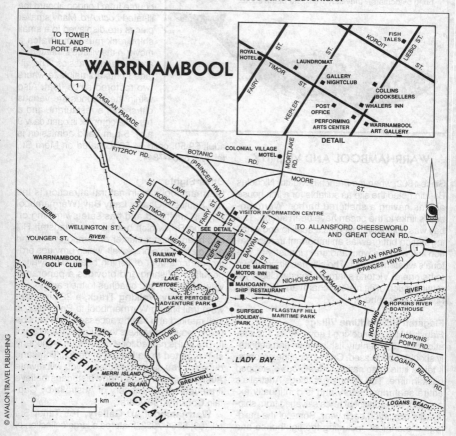

GLIMPSING THE SOUTHERN RIGHT WHALE

Five species of right whales (Balaenidae) are found in the world's oceans, but they were hunted to near-extinction last century. They were easy to hunt—slow swimmers, they preferred shallow water to breed, and were usually floating when killed—and had a high yield of baleen. Today, although the species has been protected for more than 60 years, fewer than 2,000 survive worldwide.

Although their population is not dramatically increasing, a small number migrate to the waters around Warrnambool to bear their young. They occasionally arrive as early as May but are most often seen July-October. At **Logans Beach,** across the Hopkins River from Warrnambool, a platform allows you to view the whales. But bring binoculars—they stay well clear of the shore.

WARRNAMBOOL AND VICINITY

Since 1802, when the French navigator Nicholas Baudin noted the site as suitable for a lighthouse and as having a sheltered harbor, Warrnambool's links to the ocean have been strong. The bay was originally settled as a sealing and whaling station but grew as an important transportation link with the wool and grain industry of Victoria's western district. The city has since grown to be one of Victoria's largest coastal cities, yet retains much of its historic charm and laid-back, holiday atmosphere.

Flagstaff Hill Maritime Village

Flagstaff Hill, overlooking Lady Bay, is a re-creation of a 19th-century fishing town and definitely shouldn't be missed. Once inside the grounds, it takes little imagination to feel you've stepped back in time. The complex catalogs Australia's entire seafaring history and is continually expanding, with additional relics salvaged from shipwrecks displayed each year. Some of the buildings are original, including the lighthouse and

lightkeeper's cottage. Fortifications and cannons, put in place in 1887 to fend off a perceived Russian invasion, are in their original position. The other buildings have been constructed using authentic materials and methods. Many of the shops and storehouses are open, and hundreds of items salvaged from shipwrecks are spread throughout the grounds, including a large and colorful porcelain peacock that was en route to Melbourne from London aboard the ill-fated Loch Ard. Many smaller pieces are displayed in a small shipwreck museum. Watch a movie in the village's theater; all are seafaring classics. The village fronts a small lake where two restored ships float. Also within the grounds are various gift shops, a restaurant, and a bar. The complex is open daily 9 a.m.-5 p.m., and admission is adult $9.50, child $4.50. Located on Merri St., tel. (03) 5564-7841.

Other Sights

Warrnambool's main natural attraction is the wild Southern Ocean. **Lady Bay** (Warrnambool Bay) is sheltered and has safe swimming off Pertobe Rd., which begins near Flagstaff Hill and heads past a cluster of campgrounds and picnic areas to a breakwall, which provides protection for a fleet of fishing boats. The wall is popular for fishing and provides a panoramic view of the city and beaches to the east.

Mahogany Walking Track, a 22-km (one-way) trail linking Warrnambool to Port Fairy, is well marked and can be accessed from various points, enabling walkers to do just one section of it. The trail is named for a mysterious mahogany ship reported to be hidden under shifting sand dunes. If you stumble across it, you will rewrite Australia's history, as many historians believe it predates the discovery of Australia by Captain Cook by 250 years.

Warrnambool Art Gallery, 165 Timor St., tel. (03) 5564-7832, features a large collection of

Australian works, from colonial to contemporary, including Thomas Clark's "The Mahogany Ship." Admission is $2.50. The gallery is open Tues.-Fri. 10 a.m.-4 p.m. and weekends noon-5 p.m.

Cheeseworld, at Allansford, 10 km east of Warrnambool, tel. (03) 5563-2130, is a large cheese-tasting and restaurant complex. The center is open Mon.-Fri. 8:30 a.m.-4:30 p.m., Saturday 9 a.m.-noon, and admission is free.

Recreation and Events

The 18-hole **Warrnambool Golf Course,** one of the state's better regional courses, is on Younger St., tel. (03) 5562-8528; greens fees are $17. **Lake Pertobe Adventure Park,** on Pertobe Rd., rents kayaks, canoes, and paddleboats, and has a maze, and small lakes stocked with fish; open holidays and weekends.

The **Wunta Fiesta,** held each February, celebrates the town's close ties to the ocean with a wine and seafood fair, whaleboat race, and music concert. The **May Racing Carnival** features Australia's longest horse race, a 5.5-km steeplechase.

Accommodations

None of the hotels in Warrnambool's downtown core are particularly appealing, but if you're looking for a cheap and central place to stay try **Royal Hotel,** corner Timor and Fairy Streets, tel. (03) 5562-2063, for $20 pp, including a self-serve breakfast. Inexpensive. The best of 20-odd motels is **Olde Maritime Motor Inn,** corner Banyan and Merri Streets, tel. (03) 5561-1415, which is very central, has large, well-furnished rooms and is a reasonable $75-150 s or d. Moderate. A good standby is **Colonial Village Motel,** 31 Mortlake Rd., tel. (03) 5562-1455, a couple of km from downtown. It has limited cooking facilities in each room and a tennis court, barbecue, and laundry; $40-65 s, $52-90 d. Inexpensive.

Surfside Holiday Park, tel. (03) 5561-2611, is a sprawling campground spread out behind the dunes of Lady Bay's main swimming beach and is one km from town. The park has all the usual facilities with sites $19 in summer and $14-17 during the rest of the year—a bit rich considering they also have coin-operated showers. The cab-

ins there are of a high quality and range $55-90. Budget-Inexpensive.

Food and Entertainment

A huge range of eateries is on Liebig St., between Koroit and Timor Streets. **Whalers Inn,** 53 Liebig St., is an old pub that has had its insides ripped out, literally, giving it a bright airy feeling around an indoor courtyard. At lunch and dinner, bistro-style meals start at $6, with the salad bar an extra $3. The **Royal Hotel,** corner of Timor and Fairy Streets, is another hotel with good meals—the buffet runs every lunch and dinner and costs $12 pp. **Fishtales,** 63 Leibig St., has the best takeout fish and chips in town. The **Mahogany Ship,** Merri St., tel. (03) 5561-1833, has tremendous views over Flagstaff Hill Maritime Village and Lady Bay. The bar serves light, simple meals for up to $10, while the more formal, pricier restaurant is renowned for its crayfish, fresh off the local fishing boats (closed Monday).

Gallery Nightclub, 214 Timor St., tel. (03) 5562-0741, is the town's only nightspot and hosts bands or a disco Wed.-Sunday. The beer garden there is popular on Sunday. The Mahogany Ship (see above) also has occasional live music but is a great place to have a drink at any time. Warrnambool also has a **performing arts center** on Timor St., tel. (03) 5564-7885.

Transportation, Services, and Information

Trains run daily between Melbourne and Warrnambool, terminating at the V/Line station on Merri St., tel. (13) 2232. From there, buses head west to Port Fairy, Portland, and into South Australia; north to Ballarat; and on Friday only, east along the coast to Apollo Bay. For a cab, call **Warrnambool Taxis,** tel. (03) 5561-1114.

At 234 Timor St. there's a **laundromat** open daily till 10 p.m. **Collins Booksellers,** 99 Liebig St., tel. (03) 5562-4272, has a large selection of Australiana literature, or for local material head to the gift shop at Flagstaff Hill.

Warrnambool Visitor Information Centre, 600 Raglan Parade, tel. (03) 5564-7837, is open in summer daily 9 a.m.-5 p.m., daily 10 a.m.-4 p.m. the rest of the year. Ask about their interesting audiovisual display on southern right whales. *Warrnambool Visitors Handbook* (free) is an excellent resource listing everything there is to do, see, and eat in town.

Tower Hill

Tower Hill, about midway between Warrnambool and Port Fairy, is Victoria's largest and most recent volcano. The rim of the crater is only slightly higher than the surrounding farmland, but inside is a system of lakes, wetlands, and plenty of native flora and fauna. Early settlers devastated the crater's vegetation and most animals within its walls. In 1961 the crater was declared a **state game reserve,** and since then 250,000 native trees have been planted and many native animals re-introduced. On the loop road that encircles one lake, you have a good chance of seeing emus, kangaroos, koalas, wombats, and echidnas. Along the way are many lookouts, a bird-hide, picnic areas, and the **Natural History Centre;** open daily 9:30 a.m.-12:30 p.m. and 1:30-4:30 p.m., tel. (03) 5565-9202.

PORT FAIRY

One of Victoria's oldest ports, Port Fairy is home to a large fishing fleet and maintains the historic atmosphere of an old seaport. Port Fairy originated as a whaling and sealing station in the 1830s, but as whale and seal numbers became depleted, the population turned to fishing and farming for a livelihood. By 1860 more than 2,000 people lived in the area, making the town one of the largest in rural Victoria.

Port Fairy's Victorian character has been preserved. More than 50 buildings date from that era, and seamen's bluestone cottages are scattered among veranda-fronted civic buildings. Many of the pubs still retain their charm, including the **Caledonian Hotel,** where the still-unfinished rooms show how workers there left for the goldfields in a great hurry.

Sights

Along the **Moyne River,** which separates the center of town from the beach, is a long boardwalk where fishing boats and pleasure cruisers tie up. An old wooden footbridge crosses the river farther upstream and leads to safe swimming at Port Fairy Beach. The **History Walk** passes many of the National Trust-classified buildings; on each a plaque provides a brief his-

tory; brochures available at the information center will get you on your way. One place open to the public is the historic **Mott's Cottage** at 5 Sackville Street. It was built as a boardinghouse and is now refurnished in the Victorian style; open Wednesday, Saturday, and Sunday 1-4 p.m. A small **museum** at 30 Gipps St. has a good collection of local seafaring memorabilia. Open daily during school holidays 2-5 p.m., Wednesday, Saturday, and Sunday only the rest of the year. At the south end of Port Fairy Bay is **Battery Hill,** where, like other coastal settlements, the town fortified itself against a Russian invasion; now only cannons remain.

Griffiths Island, across the Moyne River from Battery Hill, was once a whaling station but is now a wildlife reserve. The island is riddled with the nesting burrows of short-tailed shearwaters (commonly known as muttonbirds), which arrive to nest there in late September, lay eggs in January, and leave for Alaska in April. During their time on the island they feed in the ocean, returning in the evening and providing a spectacular sight best appreciated from the island's viewing platform.

Port Fairy Folk Festival

This is Australia's largest folk festival, attracting national and international acts and, of course, thousands of festival goers who descend on Port Fairy for the three-day Labour Day weekend in March. As well as musical performances, enjoy the food festival, craft fair, parade, buskers, and folk circus. For details and ticket reservations call (03) 5568-2227.

Accommodations

Of the 30-odd hotels that once graced Port Fairy's streets, only four of the originals remain. Each offers rooms of varying standards. **Star of the West Hotel,** Bank St., tel. (03) 5568-1715, has backpacker-style rooms for $16 pp. Inexpensive. Of a higher standard is **Caledonian Hotel,** Bank St., tel. (03) 5568-1044, where rooms are $55 s, $65 d. Moderate.

Many other historic buildings around town now take in guests. **Goble's Mill House,** 75 Gipps St., tel. (03) 5568-1118, was built as a riverside flour mill in 1865. It has been totally renovated and now holds six bedrooms, each furnished with antiques, and you can fish off the inn's private jetty. Bed and breakfast is $85 s, $100 d in a standard room, or splurge and stay in the third-floor suite for $150 s or d. Expensive. Across the road from the bustle of Moyne River is **Merrijig Inn,** 1 Campbell St., tel. (03) 5568-2324, built in 1842 to house the travelers of last century. Each of the five rooms is tastefully decorated and has a private bathroom. Downstairs is a large lounge area with log fires and a conservatory that opens to a garden. The inn also has a restaurant and cozy bar. Rooms are $70 s, $95 d. Expensive. **Hanley House,** 14 Sackville St., tel. (03) 5568-2709, is another historic home, this one built in the 1850s for the family of a local newspaper owner. The house has only three guest rooms, each with a log fire; $65 s, $95 d, which includes a cooked breakfast. Expensive. **Seacombe House Motor Inn,** 22 Sackville St., tel. (03) 5568-1082, was built in 1847 and has basic rooms from $30 s, $40 d. Some modern motel-style rooms are tacked onto the side for $90 s, $95 d, and scattered through the grounds are three bluestone cottages dating from 1853 for $150 s or d per night. Inexpensive-Premium.

Port Fairy YHA, 8 Cox St., tel. (03) 5568-2468, is in an 1844 building, with dorm beds in the main house and a more modern addition out back. The hostel also has bikes and canoes for rent; dorm beds are $13 for members, $16 for nonmembers (sleeping bags not allowed). Budget.

Gardens Caravan Park, 111 Griffiths St., tel. (03) 5568-1060, is the closest camping area to town and is only 100 meters from the beach. Tent sites are $14-18 and cabins start at $50. Budget-Inexpensive.

Food
Belfast Bakery, on Sackville St., bakes delicious pies, pastries, and cakes. It has a number of tables for sit-down meals; open Mon.-Sat. 8:30 a.m.-5:30 p.m. **Lunch Cafe,** 20 Bank St., is in the former town hall and serves simple bistro meals at reasonable prices as well as a few specialties, such as scrambled eggs with salmon. For bar meals try the **Caledonian Hotel** at 41 Bank Street. They have a wide selection of chicken and meat dishes starting at just $6, with soups for $2.50.

Merrijig Inn, 1 Campbell St., tel. (03) 5568-2324, has a great little restaurant furnished with Victorian-era antiques; main meals range $12-18. It's open daily in summer, and only on weekends the rest of the year, from 6 p.m. **Dublin House Inn,** 57 Bank St., tel. (03) 5568-1822, is

another historic building with a restaurant, although a little more formal than the Merrijig Inn.

Transportation, Services, and Information
V/Line buses run daily from Port Fairy to the rail station in Warrnambool, from where there are regular train connections to Melbourne. Buses also run west to Portland, continuing into South Australia.

The **Tourist Information Centre** is on Bank St., tel. (03) 5568-2682; open in summer daily 9 a.m.-4 p.m.

PORTLAND

This industrial city of 11,500 is south of the Princes Highway, 265 km west of Melbourne. It's on the leeward side of a massive peninsula along which breakwalls have been constructed, providing protection for shipping. **Portland Port,** the only deepwater port between Melbourne and Adelaide, and a $2-billion **aluminum smelter** dominate the landscape.

A shore-based whaling station was established here in 1828, but it wasn't until the Henty family came ashore in 1834 that a permanent settlement developed, one year before the official settlement of Melbourne, making Portland Victoria's first permanent settlement. Throughout the city's commercial and urban development, more than 200 National Trust-listed buildings have survived.

Town Sights
A walking trail brochure, available from the Tourist Information Centre, is the easiest way to discover the historic buildings scattered around the city center. One of the few open to the public is the **Steam Packet Inn,** at 33 Bentinck St., tel. (03) 5521-7496. Completed in 1841, it functioned as a hotel, often of ill-repute, for much of the last century and is now one of Victoria's oldest buildings. The inn is open Thursday and Sunday 2-4 p.m., and admission is $2. **Burswood,** 15 Cape Nelson Rd., tel. (03) 5523-4686, was built in 1850 for the city's first permanent resident, Edward Henty, and is surrounded by immaculate gardens, looking much as they did in Henty's days. The gardens are open daily 10 a.m.-5 p.m., and admission is $3.

On Cliff St. are **botanic gardens,** developed in the 1850s, with hundreds of species of trees and shrubs from throughout the world. Also here is a historic bluestone cottage (open Sunday 1:30-3:30 p.m.).

Other Sights

A redeeming feature of Portland's industrial sprawl is that the coastal foreshore south and west of the city is protected from development. At **Point Danger,** the site of the aluminum smelter, a 2.2-km wheelchair-accessible nature walk has been developed. Farther west, directly offshore, is **St. Lawrence Rock,** home to a colony of more than 5,000 Australasian gannets. Cape Nelson Rd. (Bentinck St. through town) leads to **Cape Nelson State Park,** where the lighthouse, built in 1883, is open for tours Tuesday and Thursday. Back at the intersection of Cape Nelson Rd. and Scenic Drive is the trailhead for a three-km walk through coastal scrub to a spectacular cliff lookout. Scenic Drive will take you to a number of barbecue areas and tracks that lead to the ocean.

Still farther west, along Bridgewater Rd., is the wide sandy beach of **Bridgewater Bay,** home to a colorful array of holiday cottages and the only surf club in the vicinity of Portland. At the beach's western end is the trailhead of a two-hour hike along the rocks and up a hill to a lookout, where seals and whales (Sept.-April) can be seen.

Bridgewater Rd. continues past the beach and climbs to a lookout where a short but rough trail leads to a **petrified forest.** The actual trees are long gone but a layer of stone formed around the trunks, slowly filling the trunks as the organic matter rotted, leaving "casts" of what scientists believe are moonah trees.

Accommodations

Hotel Bentinck, 41 Bentinck St., tel. (03) 5523-2188, is right downtown and has comfortable rooms in the main building for $85 s or d and motel-style units next door for $48 s, $55 d. Inexpensive-Moderate. **Portland Inn,** 4 Percy St., tel. (03) 5523-2985, a two-story timber house built in the 1840s, has well-appointed rooms for $85 s, $95 d, which includes a cooked breakfast and lunch. Expensive. **Burswood,** 15 Cape Nelson Rd., tel. (03) 5523-4686, is the homestead built for Portland's first settler, Edward Henty, but has been extensively refurbished (see above); $85 s, $105 d includes breakfast. Expensive.

Of Portland's six caravan parks, **Centenary Caravan Park** is most central; tent sites $14-16 and cabins $44-55. Budget-Inexpensive. **Henty Bay Caravan Park,** Dutton Way, tel. (03) 5523-3716, is just north of town but has an excellent location, and the tent sites are set among native bush.

Food

On Julia St., which links the main drag to the waterfront, are many eateries worth checking out. There's an excellent bakery on one side of the road and opposite is **Pino's Pizza House,** tel. (03) 5521-7388, which offers a wide selection of Italian dishes under $10. A little farther down the hill, upstairs in a historic commercial building, is the more formal **Old Bond Store,** tel. (03) 5523-3485. **Top of the Town** is a Lebanese restaurant on the corner of Julia and Percy Streets, tel. (03) 5521-7469. The atmosphere is casual and the food and service impeccable.

Transportation, Services, and Information

Buses to Portland stop at the corner of Henty and Percy Streets. They run daily to Port Fairy and Warrnambool and west to South Australia. For bookings call **V/Line** at (13) 2232.

The **Tourist Information Centre** is in a bluestone watchhouse built in 1850 on Cliff St., tel. (03) 5523-2671. Open Mon.-Fri. 9:30 a.m.-4:30 p.m., Sat.-Sun. 10 a.m.-3 p.m. The **Department of Natural Resources and Environment** is housed in offices on Julia St.; they have information on all state and national parks in this part of the state, tel. (03) 5523-3232.

FAR SOUTHWEST COAST

Mount Richmond National Park

Mount Richmond, 23 km west of Portland, is an extinct volcano that erupted around two million years ago. Over the years sand from Discovery Bay has blown in and around the crater, covering all evidence of volcanic activity. The major clue to the mountain's origin is the lack of creeks and lakes—as quickly as it falls, rain soaks into the sandy and porous ground, settling only in low areas where swamps are formed. The park may only be 1,700 hectares, but, still, 450 species of plants have been recorded, including 50 species of orchids. This varied vegetation provides an ideal habitat for a variety of mammals, including eastern gray kangaroos, koalas, red-necked wallabies, and the rare **southern potoroo,** one of the smallest members of the kangaroo family.

From the picnic area along the main access road, short trails traverse the park's varied topography. It's a very short walk to the summit of Mt. Richmond (229 meters), where there are 360-degree views of Lady Julia Percy Island, Discovery Bay, and the Grampians. The two-km **Benwerrin Nature Walk** is a self-guided walk through a variety of vegetation.

Discovery Bay Coastal Park

The beach, dune system, wetlands, and coastal heathlands between Cape Bridgewater and Nelson, on the South Australia border, are protected by this narrow strip of park. The park has no "sights" as such, but spending time walking along the totally deserted beach (especially during the all-too-frequent storms) or exploring the wetland communities behind the high dunes is an enchanting experience. For those with more time, and the experience, the **Great South West Walk** loop may be worth considering. It begins from the Tourist Information Centre in Portland and makes a 250-km circuit along the coast, through Lower Glenelg National Park to South Australia and back to Portland. Of course it's possible to do sections of the track but 12-15 days should be allowed for the entire length. Along the route are 16 campsites, each with fresh water, toilets, and fireplaces. Car access and camping is possible at **Swan Lake,** 34 km from Portland, where grassy sites are a short walk from the lake and beach. Farther west, at **Lake Mombeong,** is another camping area.

Lower Glenelg National Park

The deep gorges, lush forest, and spectacular limestone caves of this 27,300-hectare park are in stark contrast to the windswept beaches of Discovery Bay immediately to the south. The park protects the final 40 km of the **Glenelg River,** which begins its journey in the Grampians and drains into the ocean at Nelson, a small fishing and holiday village at the west end of Discovery Bay. The river meanders through the park carving a gorge up to 50 meters deep into the limestone bedrock. The park's highlight is **Princess Margaret Rose Cave,** one of 60 known caves within the park. The caves formed when rainwater drained through the soft rock, eating away at the limestone over tens of thousands of years. Tours of the Princess Margaret Rose Cave are offered at various intervals daily, except Friday, and admission is adult $5, child $3, tel. (03) 8738-4171. The short **River View Nature Walk** begins at the cave's entrance and winds through various sights relevant to the cave system before ending at a couple of lookouts high above the Glenelg River. The caves are only one small corner of the park; a network of unsealed roads both north and south of the river make exploration easy; on the south side, a road leads into the park from Nelson and follows the river for more than 15 km. Along this road are a number of established campgrounds and picnic facilities. Farther east, off the road to Dartmoor, is picturesque **Pritchards Campground.** The **Park Information Centre,** tel. (08) 8738-4051, is located at Princess Margaret Rose Caves; open daily except Tuesday 9 a.m.-4:30 p.m. The caves are a long way from the rest of the park, so pick up information if coming from the north or east from the Department of Natural Resources and Environment in Portland, tel. (03) 5523-3232.

Nelson

Nelson is a picturesque holiday and fishing village of 200 located at the mouth of the Glenelg River, just a few km east of the South Australia border. The main services overlook a sharp bend in the river, where a colorful array of boatsheds line up, fishers putter along in small aluminum boats, families picnic, and black swans feed among the river's reedy banks. From the west side of the river, the *Endeavour* cruises upriver into the national park and to Princess Margaret Rose Cave. Cruises depart daily at 9:30 a.m. and 1 p.m.; adult $15, child $7.50. For bookings call (08) 8738-4191. **Nelson Boat Hire,** just below the general store, tel. (08) 8738-4048, rents canoes ($10 per hour) and small motor boats ($30 per hour). A road through town leads along the shallow inlet to a carpark where trails lead to the estuary and across dunes to an ocean beach. Accommodation choices are both inexpensive. The **Nelson Hotel,** tel. (08) 8738-4011, has rooms for $20 s, $35 d, while the **Black Wattle Motel,** on the highway west of the Glenelg River, tel. (08) 8738-4008, charges $50 s, $55 d.

WESTERN VICTORIA

The ancient landscape of western Victoria is a world apart from the rest of the state. Parts of this arid land were settled as recently as the 1920s, and vast sections, set aside as national parks, will never be settled.

In the southwest is the city of Hamilton and the ancient volcanoes of Mt. Eccles and Mt. Napier, which have lava flows, lava caves, and craters for all to explore. The Grampians, north of Hamilton and rising more than 1,000 meters above the surrounding plains, are an oasis of lush forests, waterfalls, and spectacular rock formations and home to a staggering variety of flora and fauna. For rock climbers, Mt. Arapiles, west of Horsham, is a mecca. To the north is Little Desert National Park, home of the intriguing mallee fowl and a number of national parks protecting vast tracts of mallee scrub, a low-growing and hardy eucalypt that has frustrated settlers for generations. The state's northern border is the Murray River, one of Australia's largest rivers, lined with historic towns such as Mildura and Swan Hill.

HAMILTON AND VICINITY

Hamilton (pop. 10,500) lies 290 km west of Melbourne and 80 km north of the coastal city of Portland. It has grown as a service center for one of the world's richest wool-growing areas, surrounded to the south by distinct volcanic features and to the north by the Grampians.

Town Sights

Although the fiberglass **Big Woolbales** is a pretty tacky idea, displays within the gaudy exterior will give you a good idea of the wool-growing industry, the various strains of wool, how it is best preserved, and an insight into the quintessential Aussie working nomad—the shearer. The center is two km west of town along the road out to Coleraine, tel. (03) 5571-2810. Admission is adult $4, child $2. Open Mon.-Fri. 9 a.m.-4 p.m., Sat.-Sun. 10 a.m.-4 p.m. A lot less commercial are the expansive **botanical gardens,** on French St., which were first planted in 1870. **Hamilton Art Gallery,** Brown St., tel. (03)

5573-0460, is one of Victoria's premier provincial galleries, featuring 19th-century Australian paintings; closed Monday.

Hamilton was the birthplace of **Sir Reginald Ansett,** founder of one of Australia's most successful transportation empires. The company's first hangar is the base for **Sir Reginald Ansett Transport Museum,** a small showcase of company memorabilia, including a Fokker Universal, similar to the one used on Ansett's 1936 inaugural flight. Open daily 10 a.m.-4 p.m. Admission $2; located on Ballarat Rd., east of town, tel. (03) 5571-2767.

Accommodations and Food

For basic but adequate pub rooms, **Grand Central Hotel,** 141 Gray St., tel. (03) 5572-2899, should suffice; rates are $30 s, $40-50 d, which includes a light breakfast. Inexpensive. Of the motels, **Lenwin on the Lake Motor Inn,** 2 Riley St., tel. (03) 5571-2733, is one of the best priced; $45 s, $55 d. Inexpensive. **Goldsmith Motel,** 30 Goldsmith St., tel. (03) 5572-4347, has larger, more modern rooms for only $60 s, $68 d. Moderate.

Takeaways and restaurants are in Hamilton's main commercial center, along Gray and Thompson Streets. **Gilly's,** on Gray St., is a casual

---

HAMILTON'S $1-MILLION "GOLDEN BALE"

Hamilton's claim to the designation "Wool Capital of the World" may seem a little fanciful—especially to New Zealanders—but early in 1995, local grower Ian Appledore sold a bale of wool for more than $1 million (around $10,300 per kilogram), the most expensive bale of wool ever produced. Known as the "Golden Bale," it was transported under armed guard to a scouring plant in New South Wales before being whisked off to Japan for processing. Not every bale raises prices this high; this ultrafine wool, a specialty of the area, is garnered from sheep that are hand-fed, live indoors, and wear plastic coats.

restaurant serving up decent portions for $5-7 and is popular with the lunchtime business crowd. Sandwiched between fast-food joints on Coleraine Rd. is **Stirring Pot Restaurant,** 212 Coleraine Rd., tel. (03) 5572-2535, located in an 1880 residence with antique furnishings and an authentic colonial feel. Diners can choose from cozy rooms or, on summer evenings, a garden courtyard; main meals are $13.50-21.

Transportation, Services, and Information

Passenger trains no longer run to Hamilton, but the old station is the arrival and departure point for **V/Line,** tel. (13) 2232, buses to Melbourne and Mt. Gambier in South Australia.

Hamilton Visitor Information Centre is just off Thompson St. on Lonsdale St., tel. (03) 5572-3746 or (1800) 80-7056, and is open daily 9 a.m.-5 p.m. The **post office** is nearby in the commercial center along Gray and Thompson Streets.

Mount Napier State Park

Mount Napier, 15 km south of Hamilton, last erupted around 7,000 years ago. The summit of the cone is 447 meters above sea level, making it an easily identifiable landmark on the surrounding volcanic plain. A trail leads to the summit and into the shallow crater, but the most unique aspect of the area is **Byaduk Caves** (turn east off the Port Fairy Rd. 12 km south of Hamilton—just before the village of North Byaduk). These lava caves, or "tubes," were formed when molten lava from Mt. Napier cooled on the outside but continued to flow on the inside. The area is riddled with volcanic rock and is totally undeveloped (ask for a Caves Map at the Tourist Information Centre in Hamilton). The easiest cave to access is **Harman No. 1,** 200 meters south of the gate at the end of the road. This cave is about 70 meters long but is very dark and damp—you'll need a torch or lantern to get to the end. From this cave, the ancient lava flow zigzags toward the Mt. Napier, first to the east, to **Bridge Cave** (you'll need a rope to get into this one), then south to the large **Church Cave** and other smaller openings.

Mount Eccles National Park

West of the small town of MacArthur, this 5,470-hectare park protects a lava field where major eruptions occurred as recently as 7,000 years ago. Mount Eccles first erupted 20,000 years ago; this and two subsequent eruptions formed the three main craters that now hold the deep blue waters of **Lake Surprise.** Lava flowed from the volcano in all directions, with one canal flowing into the ocean and under the sea, forming flat-topped Lady Julia Percy Island. The two-km **Crater Rim Nature Walk** starts and ends at the main carpark and takes in most features of the area including a small lava cave, a lava canal, and views of the tranquil lake below. Another trail descends into the crater and circles the lake.

Near the main carpark is a **campground** with fireplaces, picnic tables, and toilets; $7 per night. Also here is an information center explaining the park's intriguing natural history, tel. (03) 5576-1014.

WESTERN HIGHWAY

The Western Highway is the quickest route between Melbourne and the Grampians and is also the main route between Melbourne and Adelaide. After passing through Ballarat (see above), it passes through an area known as the Wimmera, named by early explorer Major Thomas Mitchell, who misspelt woomera, a Koori implement designed for longer spear throwing.

Ararat and Vicinity

Named by the area's first permanent settler, who likened his journey out west to that of Noah and his ark, Ararat has grown into a thriving service center for the surrounding wheat, wool, and wine industries.

West of town is the abandoned **Lanton Lead Mine,** where displays relate the area's Chinese heritage. Behind the botanic garden on Vincent St. is a bluestone jail, which dates from 1858. It was used for more than 100 years, and at one time, **"J Ward"** was a home for the criminally insane. Admission is adult $5, child $2; open public holidays and every Sunday (tours at 11 a.m.). **Langi Ghiran State Park,** east of town, is an intriguing area of granite boulders scattered among a native forest, dominated by a 922-meter peak that the park is named for.

If you're looking for a place to stay, try **Chalambar Motel,** two km north of town, tel. (03)

5352-2430. It's pretty old, but rooms are only $36 s, $42 d. Inexpensive. Ararat also has a caravan park and the **Caffe Dominica,** 291 Barkly St., tel. (03) 5352-1002, an 1890s mansion converted into three eateries—a café, bistro, and formal dining room.

Ararat Visitor Information Centre, corner Vincent and Barkly Streets, tel. (03) 5352-2096, is open Mon.-Sat. 9 a.m.-5 p.m., Sunday 10:30 a.m.-3 p.m.

Great Western

Midway between Ararat and Stawell is the small town of Great Western, birthplace of Australian sparkling wine and home of **Seppelt Great Western,** established in the 1860s and now part of one of Australia's largest wine companies. The tradition of sparkling wine dates from the gold rush, when a French champagne maker was convinced by local businessmen to quit the goldfields and use his expertise to make wine. Tours of Seppelt's include descending to the "drives," underground tunnels dug by early miners and later used to store maturing wines. The winery is open daily 9 a.m.-5 p.m., with four tours daily, tel. (03) 5356-2202. Also known for sparkling wine is **Best's Wines Great Western,** tel. (03) 5356-2250, established in 1866. The tasting room here is a classic old stable built of red gum in 1870.

Stawell

Each Easter, Stawell's population of 6,500 swells to more than 20,000 for the running of the **Stawell Gift,** Australia's most prestigious, and the world's richest, professional running race. The beginnings of the event date from the gold rush, when diggers loved a bit of a wager and competition to get their minds off the toil of mining and breaking the land. The inaugural event was held in 1878; the original medal, photographs, video footage, and other memorabilia are housed in the **Hall of Fame** at Stawell Athletic Club on Main Street. The race meeting takes place over three days of Easter in Central Park, but it's the 120-meter handicapped dash on Easter Monday that is the big one.

Historic downtown Stawell has been bypassed by the highway, where a bunch of strip motels vie for business with advertised rates generally less than $50. For a bit of a splurge, stay at **Clovelly House,** a Victorian-era home built in 1872. The

house is surrounded by well-tended gardens and has been extensively restored, losing none of its original charm. Each of the two bedrooms has a log fire and private bathroom, and a delicious cooked breakfast is included in the rates; $90 s, $110 d. Expensive. Located at 7 Clifton Ave., tel. (03) 5358-2986. Expensive.

Stawell and Grampians Information Centre is on the Western Hwy., tel. (03) 5358-2314 or (1800) 24-6880, and can make accommodation bookings in the Grampians; open Mon.-Fri. 9 a.m.-5 p.m., Sat.-Sun. 10 a.m.-4 p.m.

GRAMPIANS NATIONAL PARK

The Grampians is a spectacular mountain range rising high above surrounding plains 260 km west of Melbourne. The 167,000 hectares protected as a national park encompass a spectacularly diverse landscape like no other in Victoria—one of lofty viewpoints, powerful waterfalls, lush valleys, and an amazing array of flora and fauna that includes more than 1,000 species of wildflowers. To Koori, the mountains were known as **Gariwerd,** a sacred place where many Dreamtime myths originated and ceremonial gatherings took place; more than 100 rock-art sites attest to these early human visitors. Today's visitors are a different breed of humans, and to cater to them hotels, restaurants, and souvenir shops have been developed, most at **Halls Gap,** on the park's eastern boundary.

The Land

The Grampians comprise four main ranges, each around 100 km long and running roughly north to south. Around 400 million years ago, tremendous upheavals forced layers of sandstone and granite upward, tilting great slabs to form parallel ridges, each with a steep cliff on one side and a gentle slope on the other. For millions of years the mountains were an island, surrounded by the raging waters of the Southern Ocean, which started the never-ending process of erosion. Since the water level dropped, wind and water have eroded the weaker rock, creating the weathered look of today.

The Grampians' combination of high mountains and long valleys surrounded by low plains creates a climate of its own. Rainfall in the

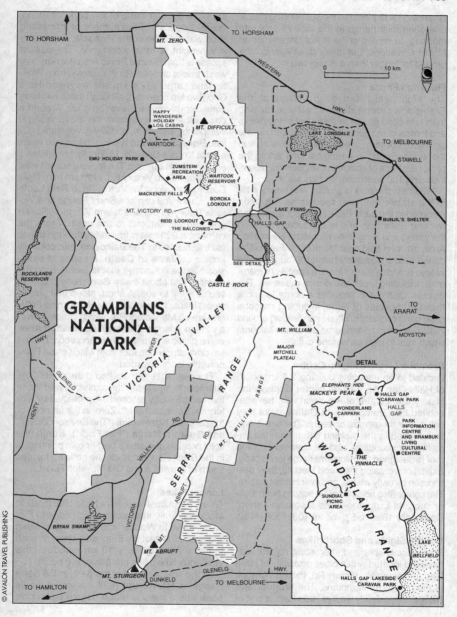

Grampians is higher than the surrounding plains, and often mist hangs in the valleys until late morning. In winter, snow is not uncommon at higher elevations, but rarely does it lie on the ground for longer than a day or two.

Flora and Fauna

The high peaks and deep valleys of the Grampians provide diverse habitats, ranging from fern-filled gullies to stands of stringybarks and forests of red gum. Some plants, such as the skeleton fork fern, are found nowhere else in the world. Spring is a magical time within the park; hundreds of species of wildflowers bloom, including 100 species of orchids alone.

Wildlife in the park is prolific, with nearly 40% of the state's mammal species having been recorded in the park. Easiest to spot are koalas (around Halls Gap and in tall eucalypts along the valley) and kangaroos (Zumstein Recreation Area, an open field near MacKenzie Falls). The dense native woodland habitat throughout the valleys provides shelter for rare species of mammals, including brush-tailed rock wallabies. The diverse habitat also provides a home for more than 200 species of birds, including raucous gang-gang cockatoos, often seen feeding around Halls Gap, and endangered peregrine falcons, which nest in high sandstone cliffs.

Brambuk Living Cultural Centre

Located in an intriguing building 2.6 km south of Halls Gap, the cultural center displays the history and culture of the Koori who have inhabited the Grampians—or Gariwerd, as they call it—for thousands of years. The stone and timber used in the building came from the immediate surroundings, and the distinctive curved roof is designed to complement the landscape. Exhibitions catalog the Koori lifestyle, their persecution by early whites, and their current culture. The center also holds a café—serving bush tucker such as kangaroo—and a souvenir shop. Open daily 10 a.m.-5 p.m., tel. (03) 5356-4452.

Natural Sights and Short Hikes

Easily accessible and interesting natural features are located within close proximity of Halls Gap and along Mt. Victory Rd. toward Wartook in the northern Grampians. The **Wonderland Range,** immediately west of Halls Gap, is one of the most popular parts of the park for hiking, mainly because of the number of interesting short walks. Of these, the **Pinnacle,** a panoramic viewpoint, is most worthwhile. The easiest access is from Sundial Picnic Area (two km one-way); tracks also lead to the summit from Wonderland carpark (2.6 km one-way) and Halls Gap (five km one-way), although these two have considerably more elevation gain. Around a dozen other hikes crisscross this area, leading to viewpoints, waterfalls, and lushly vegetated gullies. **Boroka Lookout** is a lofty perch with views across to Lake Bellfield, Major Mitchell Plateau, and the plains beyond. The lookout access road branches off Mt. Victory Rd. eight km from Halls Gap. Farther along Mt. Victory Rd. is **Reid Lookout,** where you can see Serra Range and Victoria Valley to the south and Wartook Reservoir and Mt. Difficult to the north. From the carpark, a 900-meter trail leads through dense tea tree bushes to **The Balconies,** also colorfully known as **Jaws of Death,** a series of sandstone ledges, a scene that is featured on the cover of just about every Grampians brochure you're likely to see. A short, steep trail (lots of steps) leads down to beautiful **MacKenzie Falls,** one km off Mt. Victory Rd., which cascade over a wide rock ledge. **Zumstein Recreation Area,** with a picnic area and lots of kangaroos, is three km downstream on foot from MacKenzie Falls, or a little longer by road.

Rock-art sites are scattered throughout the Grampians; many are inaccessible, and those that can be easily reached are protected by wire fences. Southeast of Mt. Zero, in the far north of the park, are **Ngamadjidj** ("The Cave of Ghosts") and **Gulgurn Manja** ("Flat Rock"). **Bunjil** (the spirit creator), the area's best known painting, is in the Black Range outside the park; it's located south of Stawell along Old Moyston Road.

Longer Hikes

An excellent bushwalk from Halls Gap leads to Mackeys Peak, then along a high ridge to Pinnacle, down to Wonderland carpark, and along Stoney Creek past the Elephants Hide, on back to town. Although only 10 km roundtrip, this strenuous hike takes more than five hours.

At the southern end of the park, in the Serra Range, is **Mt. Abrupt** (827 meters), a single peak where there is a 360-degree panoramic

Grampians National Park is full of pleasant surprises, including many small waterfalls.

view. The summit is accessible via a steep, winding track from Mt. Abrupt Road. Allow two hours one-way to complete this very steep hike.

Mt. Sturgeon (594 meters), a little farther south, is also climbable, with an easy gradient at first and most of the elevation gain being made in the final two km; 3.6 km one-way.

The park's most popular overnight hike is up to and across **Major Mitchell Plateau.** This two-day 28-km hike begins 21 km south of Halls Gap, at Stockyard Creek. The trail climbs onto the plateau, past various camping sites to the park's highest peak, Mt. William (1,167 meters), before following an old fire road back to the main road, six km from Stockyard Creek.

Check trail conditions with park staff before setting out on any hike, and, if you'll be around for a few days, grab a copy of *50 Walks in the Grampians,* available at the souvenir shop in Halls Gap.

Camping

Dotted around the park, and accessible by road, are 15 camping areas, each with drinking water, pit toilets, and fireplaces. Sites are first-come first-served and cost $8.50 per night.

Halls Gap Caravan Park, tel. (03) 5356-4251, is a commercial campground smack in the middle of Halls Gap. Sites are fairly close together, but the complex is surrounded by magnificent forests and is rarely full. Facilities include hot showers and a laundry. Sites are $14-16, on-site vans $38, cabins $45. Budget-Inexpensive. Similarly

priced is **Halls Gap Lakeside Caravan Park,** tel. (03) 5356-4281, south of Halls Gap.

Other Accommodations

Halls Gap Motel, tel. (03) 5356-4209, is close to the center of town and has basic rooms for $55 s, $65 d. Moderate. Behind the town's main group of shops is **Pinnacle Holiday Lodge,** tel. (03) 5356-4249, where some rooms have kitchenettes; from $70-110 s or d. Moderate. Of the self-contained holiday flats, **Kingsway,** one km south of town, tel. (03) 5356-4202, is the least expensive at $45-55 per unit. Inexpensive. Much nicer is **Grampians View Holiday Cottages,** tel. (03) 5356-4210. Each stone cottage has two bedrooms, kitchenette with microwave, washing machine, log fire, TV and video, and a veranda. They are great value at $63-80, but you'll need advance reservations. South of Wartook, in northern Grampians, is **Emu Holiday Park,** tel. (03) 5383-6304, situated on 16 hectares of natural bushland with a lake, golf driving range, bush tennis court, and some short nature walks; on-site vans ($32), cabins ($50-55), and two-bedroom cottages ($68). Inexpensive. **Happy Holiday Log Cabins,** tel. (03) 5383-6210, also in the northern Grampians, is a similar setup.

In the middle of Halls Gap is the old-fashioned **Mountain Grand Guest House,** tel. (03) 5356-4232. Established in 1945, the rambling building has many modern features, such as central heating, in each of the well-appointed rooms. A large lounge area overlooks the extensive gardens and beyond to the mountains. Bed and breakfast is $60-85 s, $85-95 d, with dinner packages around $18 extra pp. Moderate.

Halls Gap YHA is located in a bush setting one km north of town on Buckler Road. This small hostel has adequate cooking facilities and separate male and female dorms; members $13, nonmembers $16. The fee is collected nightly, or call (03) 5356-6221 for reservations.

Food
Along the main drag through Halls Gap are fast food eateries, restaurants, and a supermarket. In a tourist complex alongside Stony Creek is a butcher, bakery, ice creamery (serving large waffle cones), and the **Flying Emu,** a café overlooking the creek. Try the Flying Emu's big breakfasts, for $5-8 from 8:30 a.m. daily, or head to the bakery, grab a meat pie, cream bun, and flavored milk for less than $5, and sit on the grassy bank or in the small gazebo overlooking the creek. **Ralphy's** is a family restaurant in a basic, boring setting with main dishes averaging $10. The **Golden Phoenix,** a Chinese restaurant, is similarly priced.

For a great evening meal there is no real reason to eat anywhere but **Kookaburra Restaurant,** 200 meters south of the post office, tel. (03) 5356-4222. The building was once a cow shed, but has since been brick-veneered and decorated in a charming modern-colonial style with lace curtains and rustic furniture. Over the years the food here has gained a solid reputation, without being priced too high (main dishes are $11-18), using local game and produce. This place gets really busy so reserve in advance by phone or, as a message on the window says, slide a note under the door. Closed Monday. Across the road, in Mountain Grand Guest House, a casual bistro-style restaurant also serves excellent food.

Transportation, Services, and Information
The only public transportation into the park is the daily **V/Line** bus service between Stawell and Halls Gap. Stawell is on a main V/Line rail link to Melbourne. The YHA hostel offers guests a pickup service from Stawell on demand.

Sandlants operates coach service around the Wonderland Range loop road ($5-8, depending how far you go), dropping off and pick-

ing up at designated spots. Once a daily service, it now—at last report—runs only Wednesday and Sunday so call (03) 5356-9342 to confirm the latest timetable. From Melbourne, **Grayline,** tel. (03) 9663-4455, offers a day to the park ($85 pp), but if you really want to get to know the park, spend the day with **Grampian National Park Tours,** tel. (03) 5356-6221. These tours are also $85, but a full day is spent exploring the park's most remote sections. The **Centre for Activities,** in the Stony Creek shops, tel. (03) 5356-4556, also books tours.

Halls Gap has a petrol station, post office, cinema, and all the souvenir shops associated with tourist areas. In front of the Brambuk Living Culture Centre is the **Grampian National Park Visitor Centre,** with interesting displays on the park's natural and human history; a film is shown, and there's plenty of literature on the park. Open daily 9 a.m.-4:45 p.m., tel. (03) 5356-4381 or (13) 1963.

HORSHAM AND VICINITY

Horsham lies at the junction of the Henty, Western, and Wimmera Highways, 300 km northwest of Melbourne. The city itself doesn't have a great deal to offer tourists, but nearby are some interesting natural features, and the Grampians are only a one hour's drive south.

Horsham
This city of 13,000 began as a crossing point on the Wimmera River and has grown into the Wimmera's largest commercial center. At the southern end of Firebrace St. are **botanic gardens** and a trail that leads to a small river island. Also of interest in town is the **Wool Factory,** Golf Course Rd., tel. (03) 5382-0333, where ultrafine wool is processed. Tours of the complex are conducted four times daily; adult $4, child $2. **Horsham Art Gallery** houses a collection of Australian art bequeathed by Mack Jost, including works by Sir Sidney Nolan; located at 80 Wilson St., tel. (03) 5382-5575. Open Tues.-Fri. 10 a.m.-5 p.m. and Saturday 1-4:30 p.m.

Mark Twain once stayed at the **White Hart Hotel,** 55 Firebrace St., tel. (03) 5382-1231, where rates are $30 s, $40 d (inexpensive), but that doesn't really make it much better than the other hotels downtown or the scores of motels on all roads leading into the city. **Westlander Motor Inn** is three km south of town along the Western Hwy., tel. (03) 5382-0191; rooms are large and adequately furnished, and there's an indoor pool, laundry, and gymnasium; rates are $54 s, $62 d. Moderate. Still along the main highway, but on the north side of downtown, **Golden Grain Motor Inn,** 6 Dimboola Rd., tel. (03) 5382-4741, has the best rooms in town and also features an indoor pool; rates start at $79 s, $89 d. Moderate. Surrounded by parkland, **Horsham Caravan Park** has a good riverfront location at the end of Firebrace St. and has a ton of facilities including cooktops. Tent and powered sites are $10-12, on-site vans are $30, and cabins $40, tel. (03) 5382-3476. Budget.

Murtoa and Minyip
These two small towns are in the middle of an extremely rich grain-growing area northeast of Horsham. Murtoa's **Water Tower Museum** is located in a large, brick water tower and is open Sunday 2-5 p.m. The colonial streetscape of Minyip may be more recognizable to the English and Australians as **Coopers Crossing,** home of the television drama series *The Flying Doctors.*

Mount Arapiles
Rising abruptly from the plains west of Horsham, this 369-meter peak, within 5,060-hectare **Mt. Arapiles-Tooan State Park,** is one of Australia's few internationally renowned rock climbing sites. Rock climbing is only just beginning to gain wide appeal in the country, and with artificial climbing walls springing up everywhere, "the Piles," as it's known locally, is quickly becoming a hive of activity. The small town of **Natimuk,** eight km east of the mountain, has already become home to a number of hard-core climbers, fostering a climbing shop and a couple of guiding companies. Climbing takes place on the quartz and sandstone cliffs of Mt. Arapiles, two km along Centenary Park Road. More than 2,000 routes have been named and graded, ranging from beginner to expert.

For experienced climbers, all necessary gear and route information can be gained from **Arapiles Mountain Shop,** 69 Main St., tel. (03) 5387-1529. **The Climbing Company,** 117 Main St., tel. (03) 5387-1329, offers weekend instruction courses for beginners for $175 pp.

Mt. Arapiles is one of Australia's climbing hot spots.

At the base of the mountain, in Centenary Park, is a campground. All summer it is packed with a colorful array of climbers; if you don't know the difference between a cramp and a crampon, you probably won't fit in; $7 per night. Back in Natimuk, the **National Hotel,** tel. (03) 5387-1300, has basic rooms for $25 pp, including breakfast. Inexpensive. **Tim's Place YHA,** 18 km east on Asplins Rd., tel. (03) 5384-0236, features all the usual facilities as well as an outdoor gym and climbing wall. Dorm beds are $14 pp. Budget.

If climbing isn't your game, two very steep but short hiking trails lead to the summit ridge from Centenary Park, or you can drive to the summit along a sealed road from the Wimmera Highway.

Little Desert National Park
Little Desert isn't a desert at all, but 132,000 hectares of semi-arid land stretching from the Wimmera River to the South Australia border. Each spring many of the park's 650-plus species of native plants produce brilliantly colored wild-

flowers. In 1955 a small chunk of land was set aside to protect the rare **mallee fowl;** hectares have been added to it ever since, with today's park divided into three main "blocks." The central and western blocks are the most recent additions. These parts of the park are also the most remote, accessible only by 4WD, and have no facilities.

Camping is at **Horseshoe Bend,** on the western bank of the Wimmera River south from Dimboola, where the self-guided **Pomponderoo Hill Nature Walk** introduces hikers to the park's environment. South of Kiata, on the Western Highway, is another campground and nature walk (one km return). Both campgrounds have pit toilets, drinking water, fireplaces; $6 per night. For more information, or if you plan to explore the central and western blocks of the park, contact the Department of Natural Resources and Environment in Horsham, 21 McLachlan St., tel. (03) 5381-1255, or in Nhill, 6 Victoria St., tel. (03) 5391-1275.

THE MALLEE

Since the 1880s, when the first white settlers began arriving, the far northwestern corner of Victoria has been known as, simply, "the mallee." It is a semi-arid area, bounded to the north and east by the Murray River and to the west by the South Australian border, and is often described as "Victoria's Outback." Mallee is a hardy and squat eucalypt, with leathery leaves and gnarled, chunky root systems. Clearing mallee was a nightmare for early settlers, and inventions such as the stump-jump plough and the mallee scrub roller did little to make the job easier. Today, more than two-thirds of the land remains virgin mallee scrub, with the only cleared areas generally within 20 km of rail lines. To experience the real mallee, you'll need to leave the main highways and drive headlong into the national parks. From Melbourne, the most direct route into the mallee is the **Calder Highway,** which passes through Ouyen, the region's largest town, before ending at Mildura, on the Murray River.

Wyperfeld National Park

Wyperfeld, at 356,800 hectares, is the largest of the mallee parks and is also the most popular. The park's landscape is one of mallee scrub and open heathland, with a string of dry lakes lying along **Outlet Creek** and the southeast area of the park being the most accessible. Southeast of the park is Lake Albacutya. On the rare occasions that water from the Grampians fills this lake, Outlet Creek and its lakebeds act as an overflow. Only twice this century—the last time was in 1974—has this happened.

More than 450 species of plants are native to the park. In the lakebeds and sand dunes near of the campground distinct plant communities can be seen, including river red gums and, every spring, colorful displays of wildflowers. Fauna is plentiful, with western gray kangaroos and emus coming around the campgrounds. The park's birdlife is a major draw with an array of cockatoos, parrots, and galahs always in residence.

The facility area is centered around Outlet Creek (30 km west of Hopetoun, on the Henty Hwy., then 20 km north). The park information center, tel. (03) 5395-7221, has both literature on the mallee parks and displays detailing Outlet Creek's life-cycle. The 15-km Eastern Lookout Drive, beginning from the information center, provides an introduction to the park, and the lookout allows a good view of the mallee scrub. Of the many hiking trails around the Outlet Creek area (get details at the park information center), the **Desert Walk Circuit** is the most interesting because it traverses a variety of habitat and provides a good view of the system of dry lake beds. It begins 600 meters along Nine Mile Square Track, five km south of the campground (allow two hours roundtrip).

The campground has pit toilets, picnic tables, and fireplaces spread around a wide open area opposite the park information center. Water is not always available, so, to be safe, bring your own.

West of Outlet Creek the park is unaffected by humans. It is a vast area that extends west to Murrayville-Nhill Rd., with only the 4WD **Milmed Rock Track** penetrating the scrub. Between the Murrayville-Nhill Rd. and South Australia is an even more remote tract of land, 113,500 hectare **Big Desert Wilderness,** where the only access is on foot.

Ouyen

Sixty years ago, dozens of towns dotted the mallee. Today only a few remain; those that survive do so because of their position on a main highway. Ouyen (OY-en) is one such town. It's at the junction of the Mallee and Sunraysia Highways and is within an hour's drive of all three mallee parks. The town itself has little of interest, although walking down the main street is like stepping back in time (the bakery even still uses real cream).

On Rowe St., opposite the rail line, is **Victoria Hotel,** tel. (03) 5092-1550, a rambling old bush pub with small-town atmosphere. Rooms are basic, with shared facilities, and are $32 s, $46 d, which includes breakfast. Inexpensive. **Ouyen Motel,** on the Calder Hwy., tel. (03) 5092-1397, is another option; $54 s, $60 d. Inexpensive.

Murray-Sunset National Park

This 633,000-hectare park, northwest of Ouyen, extends to South Australia and is mostly undeveloped. The park was just dedicated in July 1991, so many maps still label the roadless tract of land as **Sunset Country.** Visitor facilities are at **Pink Lakes,** in the south of the park.

The "pink" of the four lakes is formed from an algae that secretes a reddish-orange pigment into the water. During summer, the water in the lakes often evaporates, leaving a thick crust of pink-colored salt behind. Salt was mined commercially at the lakes until the 1950s, but no signs of the small operation remain. The four Pink Lakes are close together and linked by walking trails.

A campground is at the southern end of Lake Crosbie, the perfect place to view a famous Pink Lakes' sunset. Facilities include picnic tables, pit toilets, and fireplaces. Drinking water is also available, but bring your own to be safe. Access to the Pink Lakes is north from Linga, 60 km west of Ouyen.

Lindsay Island is in the part of the park north of the Sturt Highway. This low-lying Murray River island is ringed by river red gums and hosts a wide variety of flora and fauna. A couple of areas have been set aside for camping, but there are no facilities. Access to the island is along a poorly marked road that branches north off the Sturt Highway around 40 km west of Cullulleraine. For park details call (03) 5092-1322.

Hattah-Kulkyne National Park

The Hattah Lakes, east of the Calder Highway, is a tranquil waterway lined with towering river red gums and an oasis to a variety of wildlife. For all intents and purposes, the park extends to the Murray River, for a total area just under 50,000 hectares, although officially a strip along the river is **Murray-Kulkyne Regional Park.** The significance of both parks was recognized by UNESCO, and in 1982 they were listed as a World Biosphere Reserve. The lakes are only filled when the Murray River floods, but, often, water remains for years. Official park literature states "western gray kangaroos are abundant." This is a bit of an Aussie understatement; in the 1980s 'roos were in plague proportions, degrading the land through sheer numbers. Old-timers call the park "The Kangaroo Paddock" and have done so for as long as anyone can remember. More than 200 bird species have been recorded in the park; naturally the best birdwatching area is around the lakes, where you can also see emus.

You can get to the park from a place marked on maps as Hattah, a once-thriving town, where just a roadhouse remains. **Hattah Nature Drive** begins from the Park Information Centre. Along the six-km route are numbered pegs corresponding to those in a brochure. Near the park entrance is a 1.2-km nature trail, but walking around any of the lakes is interesting.

A campground, just beyond the Park Information Centre, has basic facilities and drinking water is generally available. The Park Information Centre has some interesting boards describing the park's landscape; daily 8:30 a.m.-4:30 p.m., tel. (03) 5029-3253.

Red Cliffs

Red Cliffs is a northern mallee town on the Calder Highway 20 km south of Mildura. Opposite the Tourist Information Centre is **Big Lizzie,** a massive steam-powered tractor built in Melbourne in 1915. The original idea was to use it to transport wool from sheep stations in Outback NSW. With a top speed of just one mph, it took two years to reach the Murray River from Melbourne. Unfortunately, no one considered how Big Lizzie would cross the Murray River—and she never did. Big Lizzie was used for clearing mallee scrub for a few years, before finding its final resting place. **Lindemans,** Australia's largest winery, is located south of Red Cliffs along Karadul Rd.; tours aren't offered but the sheer size of the structure and surrounding vineyards is worth a look. The cellars are open daily 9 a.m.-5 p.m. Red cliffs, for which the town is named, stand east of town on the bank of the Murray River.

MILDURA AND VICINITY

In the far northwest corner of the state, on the southern bank of the Murray River, is Mildura, a surprisingly large city of 24,000—an oasis, surrounded in all directions by an arid, desert-like landscape. Mildura is primarily an agricultural town; complex irrigation systems support what seems like endless vineyards, fruit orchards, and olive groves. Two Canadians, the Chaffey brothers, developed an irrigation scheme on the river in the late 1880s, and it is from their foundations that the city prospers. Tourism is also a major part of the local economy. **Sunraysia,** as the area is known, promotes long sunny days and a ton of commercial attractions as a major drawcard.

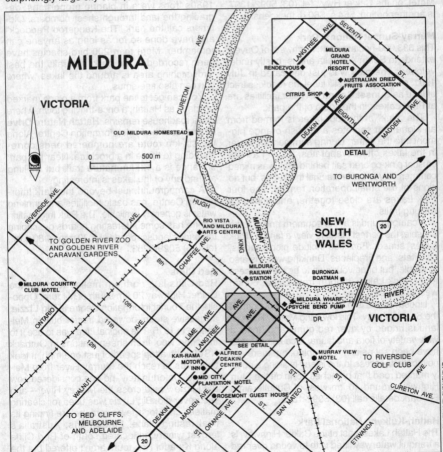

paddlesteamer, Mildura

River Cruises

Riverboat cruises are what will interest most people visiting Mildura. Each of the operating riverboats was used on the Murray when it served as a major transportation route. All cruises depart from Mildura Wharf at the end of Deakin Avenue. The *Melbourne* is the best known and departs daily except Saturday at 10:50 a.m. and 1:50 p.m. for a two- to four-hour river trip; adult $16, child $7. The faster *Rothbury,* operated by the same company, runs downstream to the zoo (adult $34, child $17) and upstream to Trentham Estate Winery (adult $36, child $18). For reservations on either of the above boats, call (03) 5023-2200. The *Avoca* operates a daily lunchtime cruise for adult $16, child $7; with lunch the fare is adult $25, child $12. On Thursday evening the same company has a Night Cruise and Carvery for adult $38, child $14. On Saturday evening the atmosphere is more formal, with a three-course dinner and dancing; adult $40, child $28. For bookings call (03) 5021-1166.

Town Sights

Along the riverfront is a stretch of parkland and pleasant picnic areas. Downstream from Mildura Wharf is **Old Mildura Homestead** and a small heritage park. The homestead, really just a cottage, was the first home of the town's founders, the Chaffeys. Admission is $2 and it's open daily 10 a.m.-4 p.m. On the riverbank, overlooking Mildura Wharf, is **Psyche Bend Pump,** an imposing brick building that was built by the Chaffey brothers to pump water into their irrigation system. Another legacy of the Chaffeys' is **Rio Vista,** once an imposing homestead, now a museum depicting the late 1800s through rooms set up as they would have been in that period. Open Mon.-Fri. 9 a.m.-5 p.m., Sat.-Sun. 1-5 p.m. Located at 199 Cureton Ave., tel. (03) 5023-3733. Adjoining the homestead is **Mildura Arts Centre,** boasting a fine collection of Australian works.

Commercial Attractions

Golden River Zoo, four km northwest of town on Flora Ave., tel. (03) 5023-5540, is mainly aimed at kids, with many hands-on animal feeding sessions throughout the day. Admission is adult $16, child $8, and it's open daily 9 a.m.-5 p.m. **Orange World,** tel. (03) 5023-5197, set on a working orchard, is eight km north of Mildura in Buronga. A one-hour tour on a tractor-led cart gives an interesting insight into the citrus industry. Tours depart daily at 10:30 a.m. and 2:30 p.m.; closed Saturday; admission $6 pp.

Recreation, Festivals, and Events

Buronga Boatman, opposite Mildura Wharf, tel. (03) 5023-5874, hires canoes and kayaks from $8 an hour; summer only. **Riverside Golf Club,** off Etiwanda Ave., tel. (03) 5023-1560, is a picturesque course alongside the Murray; club rentals are available and greens fees are $12. For a different perspective of town, **Cameron Balloon Flights,** 167 7th St., tel. (03) 5021-2876, has hot-air balloon flights for $100-120 pp.

Held in early January is **Siesta Fiesta,** which you'd probably have to live in town to appreciate; in April there are various skiing, rowing, and boating races on the river; July sees a hot-air ballooning championship; **Country Music Week** is held during September school holidays; and **Sunraysia Jazz and Wine Festival** takes place early October.

Accommodations

The only decent hotel in Mildura has recently been renovated to **Mildura Grand Hotel Resort,** 7th St., tel. (03) 5023-0511 or (1800) 03-4228. The resort first opened in 1890, under the name "Coffee Palace." The building itself is impressive—of a Spanish mission design and housing a casino. But the rooms are basic; $55 s, $77 d. Moderate. There are about 20 other motels in town, many well priced. The best value is **Murray View Motel,** corner Seventh and San Mateo Avenues, tel. (03) 5021-1200. As well as being centrally located, it features 10 modern air-conditioned rooms and a heated pool. Rates range $65-90 s or d. Moderate. Otherwise try **Kar-rama Motor Inn,** 153 Deakin Ave., tel. (03) 5023-4221, for rooms starting at $40 s, $47 d (inexpensive); **Mid City Plantation Motel,** 145 Deakin Ave., tel. (03) 5023-0317, which has large rooms and a nice pool area for $45 s, $52 d (inexpensive); or **Mildura Country Club Motel,** 12th St., tel. (03) 5023-3966, beside the golf course and with its own putting green; $75 s or d (moderate).

Staying in a houseboat is a unique and practical way to spend a couple of days in the Mildura area. More than 20 companies keep a whole range of boat sizes, and guests need no boating experience. Most boats have a minimum of three nights' rental and begin at $90 per day for a small two-bedroom boat. For details call **Rivermen Houseboat Holidays,** tel. (1800) 80-9152.

Rosemont Guest House, 154 Madden Ave., tel. (03) 5023-1535 or (1800) 62-1262, is an associate YHA, with clean kitchens, a good lounge area, and private rooms for $15-18 s, $42 d, including breakfast. Inexpensive.

Mildura has more than 20 caravan parks, of which three are clustered together southwest of city limits on the Calder Highway. Campgrounds on the river are nicer, but farther from Mildura; try **Golden River Caravan Gardens,** Flora Ave., tel. (03) 5021-2299, where sites are $15-18 and cabins $50-64. Budget-Inexpensive.

Food and Drink

Mildura is the perfect place to stock up on fresh fruit, wine, and dried fruit. Roadside stalls are the best places to pick up citrus fruits (oranges are generally around 10 cents each). On Deakin Ave. is the **Australian Dried Fruits Association,** which

has a large choice of dried fruits for sale as well as a café that serves Devonshire teas and healthy lunches. On the same street is the **Citrus Shop,** with samples and sales. Both are open Mon.-Fri. 9 a.m.-5:30 p.m., Saturday 9 a.m.-12 p.m.

In the city center, along a pedestrian mall on Langtree Ave., are many cafés and casual restaurants. **Rendezvous,** 34 Langtree Ave., tel. (03) 5023-1571, is a classy place that combines a café, bistro, and restaurant under one roof. The bistro is fairly casual and main dishes are $10-12, while the restaurant is only slightly more expensive; open for lunch Mon.-Fri. and for dinner Mon.-Saturday. Mildura Grand Hotel Resort, 7th St., tel. (03) 5023-0511, has four eateries, of which the **Grand Bistro** has the most variety.

Transportation, Services, and Information

Southern Australia, tel. (03) 5022-2444, flies daily between Mildura and Adelaide, Melbourne, and Broken Hill. The railway station is close to the center of town on 7th St., tel. (03) 5023-9001. **V/Line** trains run four times weekly between Melbourne and Mildura. V/Line buses run on days of no rail service and are the same price. The bus depot is at 100 7th Street. V/Line **Murraylink** buses run along the Murray River to Echuca and Albury-Wodonga. The three national bus lines pass through Mildura daily, heading to Melbourne, Adelaide, and Sydney. For a cab call **Mildura Taxis,** tel. (03) 5023-0033.

Mildura Visitor Information and Booking Centre, in the Alfred Deakin Centre, 41 Deakin Ave., tel. (03) 5021-4424 or (1800) 03-9043, website: www.mrt.org.au, can book accommodations and all tours. Open Mon.-Fri. 9 a.m.-5 p.m., Sat.-Sun. 10 a.m.-4 p.m. The Alfred Deakin Centre also holds the regional library, a small restaurant, and a swimming pool. The **Department of Natural Resources and Environment,** a good source of information on mallee national parks, is at 253 11th St., tel. (03) 5022-3000.

Wentworth

Wentworth is 30 km west of Mildura at the confluence of two of Australia's largest rivers—the Murray and Darling. The town may be smaller than Mildura, but more historic buildings remain, and it, favorably, lacks commercialism. Highlights of Wentworth are: **Perry Sandhills, Sun-**

raysia Oasis Botanical Gardens, Wentworth Gaol, and Australia's only monument to a tractor. The information center is in the craft shop on Adams St., tel. (03) 5027-3624.

Southwest to Swan Hill

Upstream of Mildura the Murray River winds its way through the mallee scrub, with the main road access being River Rd. in Hattah-Kulkyne National Park. The most direct route from Mildura to Swan Hill is through NSW to Robinvale, located on a long U-shaped curve in the river, then along the Murray Valley Highway.

SWAN HILL

The peaceful Murray River town of Swan Hill (pop. 9,500) is located halfway between Mildura and Echuca and is 365 km north of Melbourne. The town was named by Major Thomas Mitchell, who visited the area in 1836 and, so the story goes, couldn't get to sleep for the noise of swans. Although a couple of homesteads were established in the 1840s, it wasn't until 1853, when the first paddlesteamers arrived, that a town was established.

Sights

Swan Hill's major attraction is **Swan Hill Pioneer Settlement,** a re-creation of an 1800s river town. Once inside the impressive entrance—a large riverboat—you enter 4.8 hectares of living history. The main street is lined with businesses of the day—a general store, bakery, blacksmith, and so on, with workers plying their trades. Around the settlement are many horse-drawn carts and buggies, old cars, and farm machinery. The *Pyap* plies the river, departing from the park daily at 10:30 a.m. and 2:30 p.m. ($6). Admission is adult $12, child $6. Open daily 9 a.m.-5 p.m. One hour after sunset, the park reopens for a sound-and-light show; $8 pp. Located right in the middle of town, tel. (03) 5032-1093.

The two original homesteads still stand, and both are open to the public. **Murray Downs Homestead,** two km east of town, tel. (03) 5032-1225, is on a 4,000-hectare working farm. The mansion and English-style gardens have remained as they were when built in 1866, with much of the original furniture still in place. Also on

the property is a small animal park and tearooms. Admission is $6, which includes a one-hour tour. Open Tues.-Sun. 9 a.m.-4:30 p.m. The other homestead, **Tyntynder,** is 17 km north of town along the Murray Valley Hwy., tel. (03) 5037-6506. This property also has delightful gardens. The house itself is private property, but a small museum has many articles of interest. Admission is $6. Open Sat.-Sun. and school holidays 9:30 a.m.-4:30 p.m.

Opposite Settlement Park is **Swan Hill Regional Art Gallery,** tel. (03) 5032-9744, with mostly contemporary art. The only other point of interest in Swan Hill is the **Military Museum** at 400 Campbell St., tel. (03) 5032-4382. It contains a huge range of military memorabilia. Entry is $4.50 pp. Open Mon.-Sat. 9 a.m.-5 p.m., Sunday 9 a.m.-noon.

Accommodations

The **Commercial Hotel,** 91 Campbell St., tel. (03) 5032-1214, has basic, clean rooms with shared facilities for $25 pp, including breakfast. Inexpensive. **Paddlesteamer Holiday Resort,** Murray Valley Hwy., tel. (03) 5032-2151, is three km south of town; the older-style rooms are large and have many facilities. The resort also has a communal cooking area and pool. Rates are $45 s, $55 d. Inexpensive. **Swan Hill's Resort Motor Inn,** 405 Campbell St., tel. (03) 5032-2726 or (1800) 03-4220, has a great landscaped pool area, and the rooms are as modern as they come in Swan Hill; $79 s, $85 d. Moderate.

Riverside Caravan Park, Monash Dr., tel. (03) 5032-1494, has shaded sites and is right on the river central to town. Sites are $12-14, on-site vans are $28, and cabins start at $36. Budget.

Food

For good and inexpensive tucker, head for the **Commercial Hotel,** on Campbell St., where bistro meals are $3-6 at lunch and $5-9 at dinner; located at 91 Campbell Street. **Carriages,** at Pioneer Motor Inn, 421 Campbell St., tel. (03) 5032-2017, is located in a couple of old train carriages that have been converted to a restaurant. One carriage is formal, the other more casual, with prices to match. At Swan Hill Pioneer Settlement, *Gem,* the largest paddlesteamer ever to work the Murray, has been converted to a fun restaurant with a menu that features Aussie tucker such as witchetty grubs, kangaroo, yabbies, and Murray cod.

Transportation, Services, and Information
V/Line trains run daily between Melbourne and Swan Hill. The station is in the center of town on Curlewis Avenue. V/Line's Murraylink bus service runs daily to Mildura and Echuca.

Swan Hill Tourist Information Centre is at 306 Campbell St., tel. (03) 5032-3033 or (1800) 62-5373; open Mon.-Fri. 9 a.m.-5 p.m., Saturday 10 a.m.-1 p.m.

CENTRAL VICTORIA: MELBOURNE TO THE MURRAY

THE HUME HIGHWAY: MELBOURNE TO BENALLA

The Hume Highway, linking Melbourne and Sydney, is one of Australia's busiest highways. What was originally an 1850s wagon track between Sydney and the Victorian goldfields is today a four-lane divided freeway. The buses that link Melbourne and Sydney make stops in many of the towns in between.

Euroa
Euroa National Bank was held up by the Kelly Gang in December 1878, and that is Euroa's main claim to fame. The town is bypassed by the Hume Highway; roadhouses and petrol stations remain along the short access roads into town, and the main street is lined with many historic red brick buildings. **Farmers Arms Museum,** in an old hotel on Kirkland St., is open Sat.-Sun. 1-3:30 p.m.

Benalla
Benalla (pop. 9,000) straddles the Broken River, just off the Hume Hwy. 200 km northeast of Melbourne. Although many of the older buildings have been knocked down, the town retains much of its original character and is a pleasant stopover along the otherwise boring highway. Benalla grew from a crossing point on the Broken River, and as travelers moved between goldfields it grew in importance. In 1871, at just 16, Ned Kelly stood trial in Benalla court for assaulting and robbing a Chinese trader. Ned came back to Benalla in 1877, this time charged with riding a horse on the footpath and being drunk. He escaped temporarily but was recaptured, and fur-

ther charges were added. The **Costume and Pioneer Museum,** Mair St., tel. (03) 5762-1749, houses some pieces of Kelly memorabilia, including the witness box that Ned came to know so well. Also on display is the door of the Benalla lockup upon which Joe Byrne—a member of the Kelly Gang—had his dead body slung up and photographed. The museum also contains period costumes, underwear from the 1850s, and an 1870 artificial leg. Open daily 10 a.m.-5 p.m. The colorful **botanical gardens** and **Benalla Art Gallery,** tel. (03) 5762-3027, are together on the west bank of the river. The gallery houses an impressive collection of colonial and contemporary art in an equally impressive building overlooking Broken River. Admission is $2. Open daily 10 a.m.-5 p.m.

Broken River Hotel, 39 Bridge St., tel. (03) 5762-2014, has clean rooms for $25 s, $38 d, which includes do-it-yourself breakfast ingredients. Inexpensive. Of the many motels, **Rose City Motor Inn,** corner Midland Hwy. and Faithful St., tel. (03) 5762-2611, is a good cheapie; $39 s, $49 d. Inexpensive. More modern and with facilities such as a restaurant, pool, and larger rooms is **Glider City Motel,** corner Old Sydney Rd. and Witt St., tel. (03) 5762-3399, where rooms are a reasonable $55 s, $65 d. Moderate. **Benalla Motor Village Caravan Park,** tel. (03) 5762-3434, is on Winton Rd., three km northwest of town; campsites are $8-12 and cabins $38-42. Budget-Inexpensive.

Hide's Bakery, on Bridge St., serves a variety of delicious pies and pastries and has tables both inside and out. For something more substantial **Victoria Hotel,** 2 Carrier St., has counter meals from $5. **Georgina's,** 100 Bridge St., tel. (03) 5762-1334, is a small country-style restaurant in a building that dates from the 1880s; the menu is short and varied, with main dishes ranging $11-18. Open for dinner Tues.-Sun. 6-10 p.m.

The **Tourist Information Centre** is in the same complex as the museum on Mair St., tel. (03) 5762-1749; open daily 10 a.m.-5 p.m.

GLENROWAN

The sight of Ned Kelly suited in a coat of crude heavy armor fighting off police with all guns blazing is an image that has become part of Australia's folklore. That final showdown took place at Glenrowan, less than two hours on horseback from Kelly's childhood home of Greta. The small township seems to accept its place in Australia's history with a good deal of ambivalence; apart from Kelly commercialism along the old Hume Highway, there is little evidence of Glenrowan's most famous visitor. The Kelly Gang was the last of the real bushrangers, and as recently as the 1950s there were folks around town who could remember the gang's last stand. Many descendants of Kelly sympathizers still live in the area, but the only people who enjoy talking of the Kelly Gang are those who are cashing in on the name along the main drag.

Sights
Unfortunately all buildings relevant to the Kelly Gang's last stand have long since gone, including the Glenrowan Inn, which was destroyed on the night of the siege and never rebuilt. Six small stone obelisks provide the only reminders of that fateful night. Each is numbered, but to make searching them out more rewarding, you should read some Kelly Gang literature. On the main street is **Ned Kelly Memorial Museum,** which has various memorabilia in a small room and a replica of the Kelly homestead out back; admission $2. Open daily 9 a.m.-5 p.m. A little farther up the road, past a seven-meter statue of Ned, is **Glenrowan Tourist Centre,** tel. (03) 5766-2367, where *Ned Kelly's Last Stand,* a computerized audiovisual, is shown. The theater spans four rooms, each depicting a chapter in Ned's life. Through modern technology, the historic scenes are brought to life, but for adult $15 and child $8, it's a bit expensive. Each show lasts 40 minutes; screened daily 9:30 a.m.-4:30 p.m.

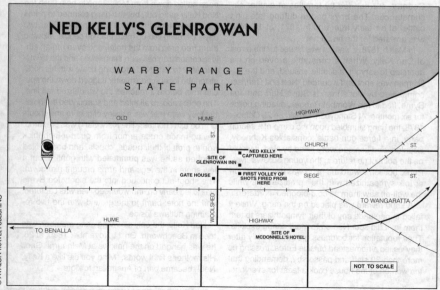

NED KELLY'S GLENROWAN

WARBY RANGE STATE PARK

Practicalities

The only place to stay in town is **Glenrowan Kelly Country Motel,** tel. (03) 5766-2202, where the rooms are $45 s, $53 d. Inexpensive. Over the rail line and two km north is **Glenrowan Bushland Caravan Park,** tel. (03) 5766-2288. It's in a natural bush setting with basic but adequate facilities. Sites are $11-12 and on-site

vans and small cabins a reasonable $28 s or d. Budget. **Glenrowan Hotel,** a pleasant escape from the busy main street, has good bar meals.

If you can get past the bushranger in front of **Billy Tea Rooms,** tel. (03) 5766-2496, you'll get some good tucker, such as the Ned Kelly pie and chips, or scones and endless coffee for $4.50. A three-course meal with damper is $12.95.

THE OUTLAW NED KELLY

A ustralian bushrangers were similar to the outlaws of the American West. But while Jesse James and his contemporaries held up banks and robbed trains, Australian bushrangers would capture whole towns, bail up the townsfolk, keep them amused with stories of life on the run, and force the local publican to supply free booze to all comers. *Then* they'd rob the local bank and ride out of town.

Australia's best-known bushranger, Ned Kelly, is also the country's greatest folk hero; his life on the run is retold in song, literature, and film. Ned Kelly was born to poor Irish parents who'd been transported to Australia in the 1840s. Ned, his brother Dan, and four sisters grew up in a rough slab hut near Greta in the foothills of the High Country, surrounded by families of similar circumstances. The boys began duffing (stealing cattle) at an early age, and in 1871, at 16, Ned was arrested for the first time.

In March 1878, a warrant was issued for the arrest of Dan Kelly. When a constable arrived on his doorstep to serve it, a scuffle ensued, and the policeman was shot and wounded. Ned and Dan, accompanied by close friends Steve Hart and Joe Byrne, fled to the Wombat Ranges, evading police for six months. At Stringybark Creek, on 25 October 1878, the gang stumbled upon the camp of a search party. In a fierce gun battle, constables Kennedy, Scanlon, and Lonigan were killed by Ned; it would be the point of no return in the young outlaws' lives. Public opinion toward the gang was divided—poorer folk sympathized with their predicament, while the well-off saw them as cold-blooded murderers.

A £500 reward was placed on the gang. While it failed to persuade any of their sympathizers to turn them in, it did spur Ned on to more daring exploits. Their reputation for boldness grew, especially after they visited a homestead outside Euroa, trussing up more than 30 staff and passersby, demanding that the women of the house cook a feast for everyone.

The following morning, they robbed the local bank.

The most daring escapade occurred just over the New South Wales border, in Jerilderie, in February 1879. After locking the town's policemen in their own cells, the gang spent the weekend living it up in town. They robbed the bank first thing Monday morning and left with a display of horseback-riding skills down the main street, much to the amusement of cheering townsfolk.

On 27 June 1880, the gang took over Glenrowan Inn. By this time, the reward for their capture had been increased to £8,000, an amazing amount of money for the time, and Joe Byrne had murdered his best friend, Aaron Sherritt, on the suspicion that he was a police informer. A detachment of police had been called down from Melbourne to help flush the Ned Kelly gang out, but the gang planned to derail the special train the police were riding. Over two days, the gang tied up more than 60 people, allowing them free grog from the hotel, and even ran an athletic competition between themselves and the townsfolk. After tricking Ned into going home with his "sick" sister, the local schoolmaster flagged down the special train before it reached the vandalized rail line. The police aboard alighted and surrounded the hotel, but they were met with a volley of gunfire and shouts of "You can't hurt us!" The Kelly Gang was prepared, having made crude armor from quarter-inch-thick iron to protect their heads, chests, and backs. Ned laughed as he was pummeled with gunfire, but a few shots in the legs and arms brought him down. The shoot-out continued into the night; Joe Byrne was killed early on, the wounded Ned was captured, and the hotel burnt to the ground with the two remaining outlaws inside.

Ned Kelly, the only surviving gang member, was tried in Beechworth. On 11 November 1880, at 26, he was hanged on the gallows at Melbourne Gaol. His mother's final words, "Mind you die like a Kelly, Ned!" became part of Australian folklore.

Also along the main street are several souvenir shops, a post office, and an antique shop.

Warby Range State Park

This park encompasses a low range of granite outcrops that extend for 30 km north from Glenrowan. The park's highest point, **Mt. Glenrowan** (410 meters), overlooks the town and would have provided a good lookout point for the Kelly Gang. A four-km (one-way) trail leads to the summit from Taminick Rd., five km beyond the caravan park. The north section of the park is best accessed from Wangandry Rd., 18 km north of Glenrowan. This area offers various hiking trails, a lookout, and camping under Mt. Warby.

WANGARATTA AND VICINITY

With a population of 17,000, Wangaratta, at the confluence of the Ovens and King Rivers, is the largest rural city along the Victorian section of the Hume Highway. It was established as a river crossing during the gold rush and grew into an important service center for the surrounding farmland. Agriculture is still an important factor in the local economy, with hops, tobacco, and various fruits contributing to it. Wangaratta has links to bushranging, with the Kelly Gang and Harry Power often visiting town, and Mad Dog Morgan's headless body is buried in the local cemetery.

Sights

Airworld, at the airport four km south of town, is Wangaratta's biggest tourist attraction. More than 40 aircraft are housed under one massive hangar; all are in working order and often appear in air shows around the country, but, for the most part, they remain here, offering a good opportunity for aircraft buffs to get a close-up view of the world's largest collection of operational civil aircraft. Open daily 9 a.m.-5 p.m. Admission is adult $6, child $4, tel. (03) 5721-8788.

Head to the information center, south of downtown on the Hume Highway, for a brochure describing the many buildings of historical importance along Faithfull, Reid, and Ford Streets, some of which date from the 1850s. A small museum is housed in the Old Fire Station on Ford St., but it's only open Sunday. Also at the information center is **House in Miniature,** a house built to one-sixth scale by a Mrs. Gay Stell, who spent 10 years on the project; she used only a Stanley knife, a small saw, and file. Admission is $2.

Accommodations

Pinsent Hotel, 30 Reid St., tel. (03) 5721-2183, is very central and has basic rooms with shared facilities for $38 s, $54 d, which includes a light breakfast. Inexpensive. Least expensive of the motels is **Billabong Motel,** 12 Chisholm St., tel. (03) 5721-2353, which has good-sized rooms for $40 s, $55 d. (Chisholm St. is at the southeast end of Reid Street.) Inexpensive. At the other end of the scale is **Advance Motel,** 55 Parfitt Rd., tel. (03) 5721-9100, just over one km north of town. All facilities are modern and, although the rooms aren't huge, they are well furnished. Basic rooms are $66 s, $77 d, with the suite at $110. Moderate.

Painter's Island Caravan Park, off Pinkerton Crescent, tel. (03) 5721-3380, is in a beautiful location alongside the Ovens River. Many sites are shaded, and there's a pleasant beach and sheltered barbecue area. Sites are $12 and onsite vans start at $28. Budget.

Food

Scribblers Cafe, 66 Reid St., tel. (03) 5721-3945, is a trendy little café with tables inside and out, decorated with scribblings by local literary people, local artwork, and photography. The menu, featuring dishes from a variety of cultures, is reasonably priced with lunches starting at $5. Open Mon.-Sat. 9 a.m.-5 p.m., and for dinner Thurs.-Sat. 6:30-9:30 p.m. **Peter's Cellar 47,** 54 Ryley St., tel. (03) 5721-6309, is a stylish restaurant with dinners averaging $18.

Transportation, Services, and Information

Trains run daily between Melbourne and Wangaratta ($27.20 one-way). The station is on Norton St., off Docker St., west of town, tel. (13) 2232. **V/Line** buses also use this station, running daily to Beechworth and Bright. **Avis** has an office at 46 Parfitt Rd., tel. (03) 5722-1223. For a cab call (03) 5721-8888.

Wangaratta Tourist Information Centre is on the Hume Hwy. at the corner of Handley St., on the south side of town, tel. (03) 5721-5711; open daily 9 a.m.-3 p.m.

Milawa

Milawa, 18 km southeast of Wangaratta, can be an expensive detour if you're a lover of gourmet foods. The small township is home to the famous **Brown Brothers Winery,** Milawa Cheese Co., a number of good restaurants, and an excellent bakery—all in a town where the population is 250. The Brown family has been producing wine at Milawa since 1889, and its operation has grown to become one of Australia's best-known and largest wineries. The large wine-tasting area has a huge range of wines (including some released only at the winery) and a small historical display. Winetasting is daily 9 a.m.-5 p.m., till 8 p.m. during the ski season. Also here is the **Epicurean Center,** an open, well-lit restaurant with a casual atmosphere; open daily 11 a.m.-3 p.m. Main dishes start at $10 and all are served with wine. For bookings call (03) 5720-5500. On the opposite side of Milawa is **Milawa Cheese Co.,** tel. (03) 5727-3588, producer of specialty cheeses. Tastings are held daily 9 a.m.-5 p.m. and the cheese is $32 a kilo.

Eldorado

The reefs of gold at Eldorado, 22 km east of Wangaratta, were 100 meters below the surface, needing larger-scale commercial operations to extract. In the 1930s, when a massive dredge was put in place, extraction became viable. Eventually mining costs overcame the company and, in 1955, it closed. The dredge remains in Eldorado, the largest such one in the Southern Hemisphere.

Eldorado Museum is open Sunday 2-5 p.m. Opposite the museum is **Gemstone Caravan Park,** tel. (03) 5725-1745, with sites $8-12, on-site vans for $25, and cabins from $38. Budget. **McEvoy Tavern,** tel. (03) 5725-1612, purported to be Victoria's smallest hotel, has information on the area and lots of good, cold beer.

East from Eldorado an unpaved road follows **Reedy Creek** to the charming town of Beechworth. This little-used stretch of road traverses an area known last century as **Woolshed Valley.** It was once home to many Kelly sympathizers and littered with caves used by the gang as hideouts; little has changed in the valley since those days. Trout fishing in Reedy Creek is good and there are places you could camp.

Chiltern

Gold was discovered in Chiltern in 1855 and mined with a varying degree of success until early this century. The streetscape of this small town, midway between Wangaratta and Albury, has changed little over the last 100 years and has been used as a set for a number of movies. The main street is lined with historical redbrick buildings, many protected by the National Trust. Some have been partly restored while others exist in varying states of disrepair. Some of the buildings are open to the public.

The **Athenaeum Library Museum** was built in 1866 and is nowadays open on weekends, as is **Dows Pharmacy,** the **Federal Standard Printing Works,** and **Lakeview House,** childhood home of Australian author Henry Handel Richardson. The **Famous Grapevine,** tel. (03) 5726-1395, is on the main street in the Star Hotel and Theatre. Part of the complex, the Grapevine Museum (open daily 9 a.m.-5 p.m.), has a display of antique furniture, but a grapevine growing in the courtyard is the highlight. It was planted in 1867 and now has a base circumference of 1.7 meters, with vines covering an area of 72 square meters.

Lake Anderson Caravan Park, tel. (03) 5726-1298, is located on the lake, only a short walk from town. Shady tent sites are $12, powered sites $14, and cabins $40. Budget-Inexpensive.

Along the main street are antique shops, tearooms, and the **Telegraph Hotel,** which serves bar meals daily noon-2 p.m. and 6-9 p.m. The **Mulberry Tree Restaurant,** 28 Conness St., tel. (03) 5726-1277, is in the Bank of Australia building. Lunch and afternoon tea are served daily and Thurs.-Sat. an a la carte dinner menu is offered.

Chiltern Regional Park

This 4,500-hectare park protects various areas of historical importance and one of Victoria's largest stands of box-ironbark. The park straddles the Hume Highway north and east of Chiltern. **Chiltern Historic Drive,** on the north side of the highway, begins on the road to Rutherglen. Along this well-signposted route are the remains of the **Indigo Goldfields,** once home to thousands of diggers. The Magenta Mine, farther along the route, is also interesting to explore.

SHEPPARTON AND THE GOULBURN VALLEY

Shepparton (pop. 26,000) is the largest town in the Goulburn Valley, the state's richest agricultural region. It's at the confluence of the Goulburn and Broken Rivers and is best known for its canneries, but also has a couple of good museums and galleries where the work of local artisans is displayed. **Shepparton Tourist Information Centre** is south of town on Wyndham St., tel. (03) 5831-4400 or (1800) 80-8839; open daily 9 a.m.-5 p.m.

Sights

Shepparton Art Gallery houses an ample collection of paintings, including works by two great Australian artists—Boyd and Streeton. It's beside Town Hall on Welsford St., tel. (03) 5832-9861; open Tues.-Fri. 10-5 p.m. and Sat.-Sun. 2-5 p.m. Also on Welsford St., at High St., is **Shepparton Historical Museum,** housed in the 1873 courthouse; open Sunday only, 1-4 p.m.

Accommodations and Food

The least expensive place to stay is **Victoria Hotel,** corner Fryers and Wyndham Streets, tel. (03) 5821-9955, where basic pub rooms are $25 s, $30 d, and the more-modern motel units are $35 s, $44 d. Inexpensive. **Shepparton Motel,** three km east of town, tel. (03) 5821-3866, is the least expensive of a dozen motels; $32 s, $40 d. **Shepparton Golf Club Motel,** Golf Links Dr., tel. (03) 5821-2155, is six km northwest of town. Rooms are basic and box-like but overlook a golf course; $48 s, $56 d. Inexpensive. **Belltower Motor Inn,** 587 Wyndham St., tel. (03) 5821-8755, is of a higher standard and is more central; $50 s, $62 d. Moderate. A little farther out is **Parklake Motor Inn,** 481 Wyndham St., tel. (03) 5821-5822, the classiest place in town, with an indoor pool, spa, gym, and restaurant; $85 s, $95 d. Expensive.

Victoria Lake Caravan Park, tel. (03) 5821-5431, is right beside the Tourist Information Centre and backs onto a lake. Sites are $12-15, on-site vans $30, and cabins $48. Budget.

Fryers Street Cafe, 127 Fryers St., has a country atmosphere, with no rush to move on. Breakfast and lunch menus are displayed on a blackboard, and the coffees are delicious; open Mon.-Sat. 9 a.m.-5 p.m. **Higgins Bakery** on Wyndham St. is also good.

Kyabram

This farming center of 6,000, 35 km west of Shepparton, is home to **Kyabram Fauna Park,** tel. (03) 5852-2883. The park houses Australian native fauna; many species wander around the grounds and are very tame. Admission is adult $7, child $3.50, and it's open daily 10 a.m.-6 p.m.

Murchison

This small town, southwest of Shepparton on the Goulburn River, was the impact point for a meteorite in 1969. The meteorite has long since gone but a **Meteorite Information Display** in town will tell you all about it.

Longleat Winery, south of Murchison, tel. (03) 5826-2294, has a pleasant barbecue area shaded by towering eucalypts—the perfect place for lunch with a bottle of their renowned red wine.

Rushworth and Whroo Historic Reserve

Rushworth, in the hills southwest of Murchison, was a resting place for diggers traveling between Bendigo and Beechworth, but by the mid-1880s gold had been found in many places around the settlement. The gold lasted only long enough for some classic bluestone buildings to be erected along the main street.

Alluvial gold was found south of Rushworth at Whroo (ROO), but it wasn't until large companies began mining quartz reefs that the settlement gained a permanent look. By the turn of this century gold began running out and today Whroo is a shadow of its former self. Most buildings have been dismantled, but the old mine shafts, some foundations, and a cemetery remain. A short trail leads into the open-cut Balaclava Mine where other relics lie.

ECHUCA

For 50 years Echuca (pop. 14,000) was the largest and most important of the Murray River towns, part of a transportation network that extended along the Murray to South Australia, the Darling River to Outback NSW, and rail to Melbourne.

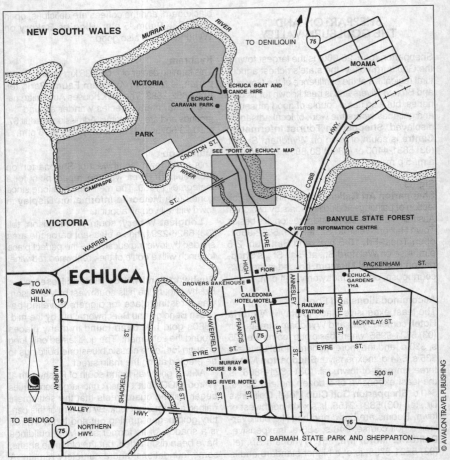

NEW SOUTH WALES

MURRAY RIVER

TO DENILIQUIN

75

MOAMA

VICTORIA

ECHUCA BOAT AND
CANOE HIRE

ECHUCA
CARAVAN PARK

PARK

CROFTON ST.

SEE "PORT OF ECHUCA" MAP

COBB HWY.

RIVER

CAMPASPE

VICTORIA

ST.

BANYULE STATE FOREST

VISITOR INFORMATION CENTRE

WARREN

ST.

ECHUCA

TO
SWAN
HILL

16

DROVERS BAKEHOUSE

HIGH

HARE

FIORI

PACKENHAM ST.

ANNESLEY

ECHUCA
GARDENS
YHA

HOWELL

CALEDONIA
HOTEL/MOTEL

RAILWAY
STATION

MCKINLAY ST.

HAVERFIELD

FRANCIS

ST.

ST.

75

ST.

EYRE ST.

EYRE

ST.

MURRAY

MCKENZIE ST.

SHACKELL

ST.

MURRAY
HOUSE B & B

BIG RIVER MOTEL

0   500 m

TO
BENDIGO

VALLEY HWY.

75

NORTHERN
HWY.

16

TO BARMAH STATE PARK AND SHEPPARTON

© AVALON TRAVEL PUBLISHING

The town of Echuca was founded in 1853 by exconvict Harry Hopwood, who settled in the area and started a ferry service across the river. With the gold rush in full swing, business thrived, so he built the Bridge Hotel. When he died, in 1869, Echuca had grown to become the largest inland port in the Southern Hemisphere and, in later years, a major railhead from Melbourne.

Port of Echuca

History lives on at Echuca; the riverfront area looks much the same as it did in the days of paddlesteamers. There may not be as many buildings along the riverfront as there once were, and the red gum wharf that stretched more than a kilometer has been partly dismantled, but everything is original, not set up like so many other historic parks. A "passport" (adult $7, child $5) allows entry to the Star and Bridge Hotels and the wharf. Tickets are available at the **Star Hotel,** where there's a paddlesteamer display and the exit is a tunnel under the hotel, dug in the days of prohibition. At the wharf, the railway station houses some large vehicles and the cargo shed has a display of life on the river. Moored alongside the wharf is PS *Pevensey* (used in the miniseries *All the Rivers Run*—in fact, most of the series was shot in and around the port area) and PS *Adelaide,* the world's oldest operating paddlesteamer. The **Bridge Hotel** has another historic display. This was the hotel built by the enterprising Harry Hopwood. Whenever trade at the bar was slow, his ferry service would close due to "mechanical problems." Open daily 9:15 a.m.-5 p.m., tel. (03) 5482-4248.

Other Sights

Downstream from the port is **Red Gum Works,** a historic working sawmill where woodturners and blacksmiths make traditional kitchen and household wares; open daily 9 a.m.-5 p.m., tel. (03) 5482-5711. Near the Star Hotel is **Sharp's Magic Movie House and Penny Arcade,** tel. (03) 5482-2361, Australia's largest collection of restored penny arcade machines. Admission is adult $10, child $5. Open daily 9 a.m.-5 p.m. Also near the riverfront, at 57 Murray Esplanade, is **Coach House Carriage Museum,** tel. (03) 5482-5244, exhibiting a large collection of horse-drawn vehicles and offering carriage rides around town (Sat.-Sun. only); admission adult $6, child $3.

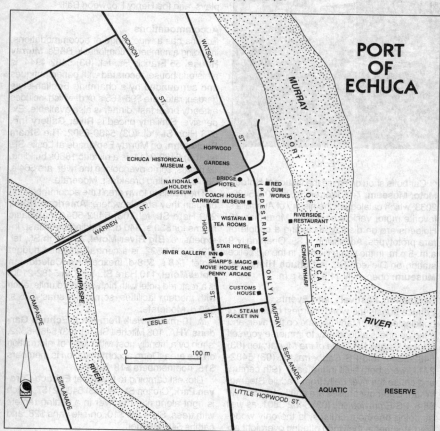

PORT OF ECHUCA

Port of Echuca

Car buffs shouldn't miss the **National Holden Motor Museum,** 7-11 Warren St., tel. (03) 5480-2033, which catalogues the history of Australia's favorite motor vehicle company. More than 40 Holdens are on display, including a couple of rare prototypes. Admission is $5. Open daily 9 a.m.-5 p.m. In the same vicinity, in the old police station on Dickson St., is **Echuca Historical Museum;** open daily 11 a.m.-3 p.m.

Recreation, Festivals, and Events
Echuca boasts the world's largest collection of paddlesteamers. Many operate on the river, and a trip on one is a good way to immerse yourself in local history. PS *Pride of the Murray,* tel. (03) 5482-5244, and PS *Canberra,* tel. (03) 5482-2711, were both built in the early 19th century and cruise the river daily from Paddle Steamer Wharf. One-hour cruises are adult $10-15, child $5-8. PS *Emmylou,* tel. (03) 5482-3801, as well as doing one-hour cruises, is the only wood-fired steamer in the world offering overnight ac-

commodation; two-night weekend cruises are $400 pp, including all meals.

Echuca Boat and Canoe Hire, tel. (03) 5480-6208, rents canoes ($15 an hour) and motor-boats ($28), and can provide transport upstream for full-day and overnight float trips; located at Victoria Park, downstream from Port of Echuca.

On the first weekend in June is a **Steam, Horse, and Vintage Rally** that brings together vintage and veteran cars, steam engines, and plenty of horse power. The year's other major event is the **Port of Echuca Heritage Festival,** held the third week of October; events include a parade of paddlesteamers, arts and crafts displays, and the Henry Hopwood Ball.

Accommodations
Echuca has a wide range of accommodations, including a number of comfortable B&Bs. **Murray House,** 55 Francis St., tel. (03) 5482-4944, is a historic house decorated with period antiques and surrounded by a charming English-style garden; rates are $95-165 s or d, which includes a hearty breakfast; dinner is also available. Expensive. Similarly priced is **River Gallery Inn,** 578 High St., tel. (03) 5480-6902. The **Steam Packet Inn,** on Murray Esplanade at Leslie St., tel. (03) 5482-3411, is a historic 1860s building. Its rooms, some overlooking the river, are $64 s, $87 d, including breakfast. Moderate.

The hotels in town aren't the accommodation bargain they are elsewhere; **American Hotel,** 239 Hare St., tel. (03) 5482-5044, has basic rooms for $30 s, $40 d, including breakfast. Inexpensive. **Big River Motel,** 317 High St., tel. (03) 5482-2522, is a centrally located budget motel; $48 s, $58 d. Inexpensive. **Caledonian Hotel/Motel,** 110 Hare St., tel. (03) 5482-2100, is a restored hotel with high-standard units, each with modern facilities, some with spas; $55 s, $80 d. Moderate.

A 10-minute walk from town, **Echuca Gardens YHA,** 103 Mitchell St., tel. (03) 5480-6522, is run by a friendly host with plenty of information on the area. Dorm accommodation is members $15, nonmembers $18. Budget.

Closest camping to town is at **Echuca Caravan Park,** Crofton St., tel. (03) 5482-2157, which is right alongside the river in a setting replete with trees. Sites are $10, on-site vans $28, and cabins $40. Budget.

Food

The **Drover's Bakehouse,** 513 High St., tel. (03) 5482-2528, is a large two-story complex that offers indoor and outdoor dining. A hot buffet breakfast is $10, with a great variety of gourmet sandwiches on offer throughout the day. A good place for lunch is **Wistaria Tea Rooms** at 51 Murray Esplanade. Built in the 1880s as a private residence, it is surrounded in colorful gardens. Light lunches are served, but the morning and afternoon teas are the specialty (from $4); open daily 10 a.m.-5 p.m. For more substantial meals, **Bridge Hotel,** Hopwood Place, tel. (03) 5482-2247, is a good choice. **Riverside Restaurant,** 101 Murray Esplanade, tel. (03) 5482-6951, overlooks the river and has a shaded veranda—perfect for lunch or dinner on those warmer evenings. The menu features mainly local game and produce with main dishes starting at around $12. **Fiori,** 554 High St., tel. (03) 5482-6688, is a casual yet stylish Italian restaurant that many locals swear by.

Transportation, Services, and Information

From Melbourne, **V/Line** operates trains as far north as Bendigo, from where buses continue to Echuca; the terminal is in the old railway station on Sturt St., tel. (13) 2232. From Echuca, buses run west to Swan Hill and Mildura, and east to Wodonga.

V/Line offers a variety of day trips to Echuca from Melbourne that include a cruise on a paddlesteamer. Call (03) 9619-5000 for details. Other companies offering Echuca day tours are: **Grayline,** tel. (03) 9663-4455, and **Australian Pacific Day Tours,** tel. (03) 9654-7700. Both charge $85 pp.

Housed in a historic pumphouse building is **Echuca-Moama Visitor Information Centre** at 2 Heygarth St., tel. (03) 5482-4525 or (1800) 80-4446; open Mon.-Fri. 9 a.m.-5 p.m., Sat.-Sun. 10 a.m.-4 p.m.

ALONG THE MURRAY FROM ECHUCA TO WODONGA

Barmah State Park

This 30,000-hectare park along a 100-km stretch of the Murray River contains the world's largest

and oldest red gum forest. The forest floor was once part of a vast inland lake and still today acts as a natural flood control for the river. Not just the number, but the sheer size of the red gums—as high as 40 meters—is staggering. Within the forest are many hiking trails, campgrounds, and wildlife such as kangaroos, koalas, and platypuses. During the Wet many trails are flooded, and the only way to get around is by canoe or boat. This is also the best time to view the 200 species of birds present. Tours through the park are offered on **Kingfisher,** tel. (03) 5869-3399, a flat-bottomed boat. The two-hour cruise leaves four times weekly and costs $16 pp.

The park's only facilities are a basic campground and **Dharnya Visitor Centre,** tel. (03) 5869-3302. Built of red gum, the latter houses artifacts relating to the local Yorta Yorta Koori and has general park information. Access to the forest is from the small town of Barmah, 32 km east of Echuca.

Ulpuna Island

East of Barmah State Park is **Barmah State Forest.** You can get there through the park, but it's easier to take the gravel road that lies one km west of **Strathmerton.** The sign says Ulpuna Island. Continue to the end of the road and take the left fork. Most of the island is cleared, but this section is home to a colony of koalas. They are hard to spot at first, but as your eyes become accustomed to spotting the furry little critters, their numbers become apparent. Although there are no facilities on the island, it's a wonderful spot to camp.

Cobram and Yarrawonga

Cobram and its NSW counterpart, Barooga, are the center of a stretch of the Murray River popular with families for the sandy beaches and tourist facilities that have sprung up around them.

Yarrawonga is on the banks of Lake Mulwala, an artificial lake used for irrigation. The **Lady Murray,** tel. (03) 5744-2005, cruises the river daily, with a lunchtime cruise for only $15. Built in 1842, **Byramine Homestead** was the home of the area's first white settlers. Admission is adult $5, child $2.50, and it's open Thurs.-Mon. 10 a.m.-4 p.m. Located 15 km west of Yarrawonga, tel. (03) 5748-4321.

Rutherglen

This small town of 2,000 people and many historic buildings, 46 km east of Yarrawonga and 40 km north of Wangaratta, is the hub of Victoria's best-known wine area. The Rutherglen region is renowned for its fortified wines, but each of the dozen-odd wineries has its own specialties.

Start your exploration of the area at **Rutherglen Tourist Information Centre,** Drummond St., tel. (02) 6032-9166 or (1800) 62-2871. The brochure *The Winemakers of Rutherglen* (available at all local wineries) covers all local wineries and makes it easy to decide which direction to head. One of the original wineries is **Fairfield Vineyard,** 13 km east of Rutherglen, tel. (02) 6032-9381. The original homestead, built in the 1880s, still stands and is open for tours. Best known for its reds, this winery still uses original equipment; open Mon.-Sat. 10 a.m.-5 p.m., Sunday noon-5 p.m. **Campbell's Winery,** two km west of Rutherglen, tel. (02) 6032-9458, is another well-established winery renowned for fortified wines. This place has a self-guided tour and small museum. Open daily 9 a.m.-5 p.m.

The classic old **Victoria Hotel,** 90 Main St., tel. (02) 6032-8610, was built in the days of the gold rush, and although the rooms haven't changed much since, they are clean and the beds comfortable; $24 s, $38 d. Inexpensive. **Mount Ophir** is the homestead of a former vineyard owner and has been refurnished to an excellent upmarket B&B. Rates are $75 s, $130 d, with din-

ner available. It's along Stillard's Lane, tel. (02) 6032-8920. Premium.

Both pubs in town serve good bar meals. The **Shamrock,** tel. (02) 6032-8439, is a historic two-story building on Main Street. The menu is small, but the chef does an excellent job, with daily specials usually being local game.

Wodonga

Wodonga is talked about in the same breath as Albury, its twin town on the NSW-side of the Murray River border. Wodonga, the smaller of the two with a population of around 28,000, has grown steadily since a rail line from Melbourne arrived in 1873. It has also had strong links to the military since 1943, including being home for a time to the famed Australian war heroes the Rats of Tobruk. The **Army Museum** is on the base, four km southeast of Wodonga, tel. (02) 6055-2525; open Sun.-Fri. 9:30 a.m.-4 p.m.

Two good sources of information are the **Department of Natural Resources and Environment** office, in the local TAFE College at 1 McKoy St., off Moorefield Park Dr., which is off Melbourne Dr., tel. (02) 6055-6111, and **Gateway Tourist Centre,** on the east side of the Hume Hwy., halfway between Wodonga and Albury. The latter has a ton of information on both Victoria and NSW destinations, and offers local arts and crafts for sale and a roaring log fire during winter. Open daily 9 a.m.-5 p.m., tel. (02) 6041-3875 or (1800) 80-0743.

flint pick

HIGH COUNTRY

In world terms, the Great Dividing Range isn't particularly high; in fact, no Victorian peak reaches more than 2,000 meters; but the High Country is spectacular, encompassing a vast section of northeastern Victoria that offers steep-sided valleys covered in forests of gnarled and stunted snow gums, cascading mountain streams, and high plateaus above the treeline with views extending many hundreds of kilometers.

Although most of the region is very remote, a number of roads penetrate the region, leading from the valley floor to ski villages perched among the mountain peaks. The most direct access is along the Hume Freeway, from where access roads spur east into the mountains. But a more picturesque alternative is through the Yarra Valley to Healesville and Marysville, from where it's only a short drive around massive Lake Eildon to Mansfield, a classic High Country town surrounded in rolling hills. East of Mansfield is Mt. Buller, one of four High Country ski resorts. The others are farther north: head to Mt. Buffalo for the relaxed atmosphere, Mt. Hotham for the expert skiing, and Falls Creek for all the style of an upmarket European resort. Another major gateway to the High Country is Beechworth, one of Australia's best-preserved gold-rush towns.

Alpine National Park
This 6,460-square-km park was proclaimed in 1989, providing an important advancement in the protection of Australia's alpine region. The park extends from the Latrobe Valley, in Gippsland, along the Great Dividing Range to the New South Wales border and Kosciusko National Park. The park provides opportunities for a great variety of recreational pursuits, including hiking, fishing, camping, horseback riding, and, in winter, downhill and cross-country skiing. The most spectacular part of the park is above the treeline, where views extend hundreds of kilometers. The main access to the park is east from Mansfield and south from Bright and Mount Beauty to the **Bogong High Plains.**

Alpine Walking Track
This 400-km trail was in place before proclamation of the park. It extends from Walhalla, near Baw Baw National Park, to Cowombat on the NSW border and can be walked in 30 days. Attempting the entire length of the trail requires much planning and backcountry experience, but many short sections can be hiked in a day, and as the trail crosses six highways, access is easy.

For details on the Alpine National Park and Alpine Walking Track, call (03) 5755-1577.

MELBOURNE TO THE HIGH COUNTRY VIA THE YARRA VALLEY

The most direct route to the High Country ski resorts and the towns of Mansfield, Beechworth, and Mt. Beauty is the Hume Freeway, but by detouring along the Yarra Valley you'll pass a number of interesting towns.

Healesville
Healesville, 61 km from Melbourne, is best known for **Healesville Wildlife Sanctuary,** one of the best showcases of Australian fauna in the country. The park grew from a plot of native bushland used for a study of Australian marsupials in 1929 and remains, for the most part, in its natural state—although the density of animals has increased. A trail winds its way through the sanctuary, passing wetlands, aviaries, various large enclosures, and a nocturnal creekside habitat. Park staff give informative talks and there are animal feeding sessions a couple of times a day. Other facilities include picnic tables, a barbecue area, café, and souvenir shop. Admission is adult $12, child $6. Open daily 9 a.m.-5 p.m. Located on Badger Creek Rd., tel. (03) 5962-4022.

Set in native bushland and within walking distance of the wildlife park is **Sanctuary House Motel,** Badger Creek Rd., tel. (03) 5962-5148. Rooms are fairly standard, but with many facilities, including an indoor pool and free laundry. Rates are $55 s, $70 d. Moderate. In the same vicinity is **Ashgrove Caravan Park,** tel. (03) 5962-4398. Budget-Inexpensive.

Yarra Valley-Healesville Tourist Information Centre is on the north side of Healesville at Kinglake Rd., tel. (03) 5962-2600; open daily 10 a.m.-5 p.m.

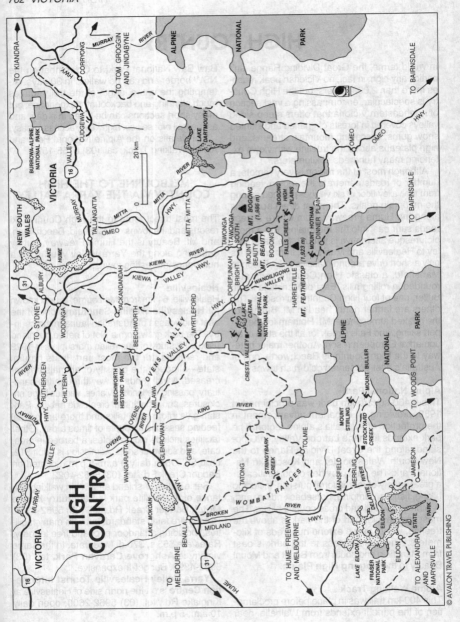

© AVALON TRAVEL PUBLISHING

Kinglake National Park and Vicinity

This 11,430-hectare park is made up of three separate sections of the Kinglake Ranges (an arm of the Great Dividing Range), each surrounded by cleared farmland. Central to the three sections is the small township of Kinglake, 33 km northwest of Healesville. In the park's western section, near Masons Falls, are short hikes and a park office, tel. (03) 5786-5328. Camping is at **The Gums,** in the northern section (accessible along Eucalyptus Rd., northeast of Kinglake). Sites are secluded and nearby trails lead along Hirts Creek and to the summit of Andrews Hill (661 meters), the park's highest peak.

Toolangi, 16 km east of Kinglake, along the road to Healesville, was once the home to poet C.J. Dennis, who wrote "The Sentimental Bloke." Gardens developed around his property, **Arden,** are open to the public daily except Friday, and Devonshire teas are served on weekends. Also in Toolangi is the **Forest Discovery Centre,** tel. (03) 5962-9214, a uniquely shaped building of Victorian timbers set among a towering eucalypts. Interpretive displays inside explain forest environments and humanity's role in protecting them, and trails lead through the forest to the Yea River and a lookout. Open daily 10 a.m.-5 p.m.; admission $2.

Marysville

For the early part of this century, when Melburnians went on their honeymoons, they went to Marysville. The many guesthouses, tearooms, and specialty shops remain, and it's still a popular spot for weekend getaways, surrounded by forested hills and with nearby gardens, valleys, and streams adding to the beauty. At 84 meters, **Steavenson Falls,** four km from town, is the highest of any waterfall in the state; it's floodlit daily until midnight. In winter Marysville is the gateway to **Lake Mountain,** an excellent cross-country skiing facility 21 km to the east.

Marylands Country House is one of the original guesthouses, having been completed in 1928, 27 years before the township got electricity. Everything about the original house was done on the grandest scale. Built as a country resort with all modern facilities, today it retains much of its original elegance. Rates are $150 s, $240 d, which includes breakfast and a three-course dinner; located on Falls Rd., tel. (03) 5963-3204. Luxury. In a more modern setting—

and with a swimming pool, spa, sauna, and large lounge area with library—is **Nanda Binya Lodge,** one km from the center of town along Woods Point Rd., tel. (03) 5963-3433. Rates are a reasonable $70-80 d, for bed and breakfast. Moderate. Marysville also has a couple of moderately priced motels, and a caravan park by the river, tel. (03) 5963-3443.

Cathedral Range State Park

North of Marysville is this 3,550-hectare park, named for the impressive cliffs that dominate the eastern skyline as you travel along the Maroondah Highway. Access is limited to gravel roads at the north and south ends of the park and a variety of signposted hiking trails heading of into the relatively remote wilderness. The park's five camping areas each have pit toilets, a water source, and not much else. Further information is available from the **Department of Environment and Natural Resources** on Lyell St. in Marysville, tel. (03) 5963-3379.

Lake Eildon

Water from this reservoir is used to irrigate surrounding farmland and the Goulburn Valley, but the lake itself offers many opportunities for water-based activities, which center mostly around the small town of **Eildon.** On the lake's western shore is **Fraser National Park,** 17 km beyond Alexandra. The park access road climbs a low, bare hill before descending into a native forest of eucalypts. The lakeshore isn't particularly pretty, but areas of the park once used for grazing are slowly being regenerated, providing the habitat for koalas, possums, wombats, and a large population of gray kangaroos. For birdwatching, the best part of the park is Candlebark Gully Nature Walk, beginning from Candlebark Campground. Scattered around the shoreline are three campgrounds with great facilities, including showers at Coller Bay and Candlebark; book in summer at (03) 5772-1293. Sites are $12 per night, and cabins range $35-70 s or d. Budget-Inexpensive. The park entrance fee is $5 per day.

Eildon grew from a settlement for hydroelectric workers and is now an accommodation center for holidayers. Worth stopping at is **Snobs Creek Fish Hatchery,** six km southwest of town, tel. (03) 5774-2208. A visitor center within this large hatchery complex has displays on the important role hatcheries have in maintaining stocks of

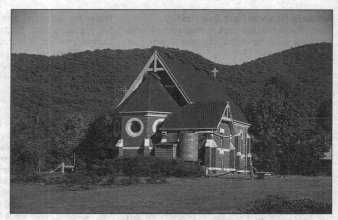

Jamieson church

rainbow trout, Murray cod, and golden perch throughout Victoria's inland waterways. Open daily 10 a.m.-4:30 p.m.

The shortest route from Eildon to Mansfield is around the lake's northwestern arm, but the eastern route is more interesting. That road, around 100 km to Mansfield, forms the southern boundary of **Eildon State Park,** which runs right down to Lake Eildon.

Jamieson and Woods Point Road
Only a short distance from the southeastern arm of Lake Eildon, the historic gold-mining town of Jamieson lies at the confluence of the Goulburn and Jamieson Rivers, surrounded by rolling hills. Decent gold strikes were made throughout the area, and many buildings from the gold-rush era remain, including a courthouse and church.

Southeast from Jamieson, an unsealed road winds its way through a valley littered with evidence of early mining operations to Woods Point, then spurs west to Marysville. If you've got a full tank of petrol, it is possible to continue south to the Latrobe Valley.

MANSFIELD AND VICINITY

Located 185 km northeast of Melbourne, Mansfield (pop. 2,500) is one of the main gateways to the High Country. As land in the Goulburn Valley was settled, graziers began looking farther afield, eventually setting up pastoral leases in the re-

mote valley in which Mansfield lies. There's not a lot to see and do in the actual town, but with plenty of tourist facilities it makes an excellent base for exploring the nearby alpine areas, and in winter at nearby Mt. Buller ski lifts crank up on some of Australia's best slopes.

Those interested in following the trail of the bushrangers may want to wander up to the cemetery at the end of Highett Street. While Ned and his gang were treated as folk heroes elsewhere in Victoria, the headstones on the graves of three murdered policemen here tell a different story. In the middle of the roundabout back in town is another memorial to the troopers.

Accommodations
The least expensive place to stay in town is **Mansfield Backpackers Inn,** 122 High St., tel. (03) 5775-1800, which offers good clean dorm accommodation (some double rooms) with a modern kitchen, laundry, and barbecue area. Rates are $17 pp ($25 pp in winter). Inexpensive. **Mansfield Hotel,** 86 High St., tel. (03) 5775-2101, has basic pub rooms, with breakfast thrown in for $28 pp. Inexpensive. If you're just after a standard motel room, a few places in Mansfield, Merrijig, and up at Mt. Buller are open year-round, but remember prices rise dramatically during the ski season (in winter make bookings through Mt. Buller Central Reservations, tel. (03) 9809-0291. **Alzburg Inn,** 39 Malcolm St., Mansfield, tel. (03) 5775-2367 or (1800) 03-3023, is spread out around a 100-year-old convent and has a large

pool, tennis court, and restaurant. Off-season rates (summer) start at $75 s or d. Moderate. Also in town, **Alpine Country Cottages,** 5 the Parade, tel. (03) 5775-1694, comprises small self-contained cottages set in pleasant gardens; rates are $125 per cottage. Premium. Toward Mt. Buller is the upmarket **Pinnacle Valley Resort,** tel. (03) 5777-5788 or (1800) 03-3214, spread out over a picturesque property with a small lake. Rooms are modern and facilities include a restaurant with stunning views, game room, gym, tennis courts, horse riding, and mountain bikes; from $130 s or d. Premium.

Food
Bon Appetit, 39 High St., tel. (03) 5775-2951, serves healthy breakfasts and deli-style lunches daily 7:30 a.m.-5 p.m. On either side are bakeries. Across the road is **Witch's Brew Cafe,** 28 High St., famous for its eerie decorations, or head to the light, bright **Collopy Street Cafe,** 26 High Street. **O'Malley's,** 147 High St., tel. (03) 5775-2296, is open daily from 6 p.m., serving up delicious pizza and pasta dishes at reasonable prices. Up on Mt. Buller, the **Arlberg Hotel** has an inexpensive bistro and a more formal restaurant, a couple of places that stay open year-round, tel. (03) 5777-6260.

Transportation, Services, and Information
Mansfield Bus Depot is in the center of town on High St., tel. (03) 5775-2606. **V/Line** operates daily services between Melbourne and Mansfield. **Benalla Bus Lines** links Mansfield with Benalla Monday and Thursday. Staff at the depot can organize transportation beyond Mansfield and tours into the High Country.

Mansfield Visitors Information Centre is in an old railway station on the Melbourne side of Mansfield; open daily 10 a.m.-5 p.m., tel. (03) 5775-1464 or (1800) 06-0686.

Merrijig and the Surrounding High Country
Beyond Mansfield, the highway passes through the small town of Merrijig, which hosts a big rodeo each Labour Day weekend (March), then parallels the Delatite River and climbs into the High Country. The ski resort of **Mt. Buller,** 47 km east of Mansfield, only opens lifts on special occasions in

summer, but with the newly opened Australian Alpine Institute attracting more summer visitors, the lifts may operate more frequently. The institute offers a variety of short courses that, although designed for learning, are a fantastic way to experience the High Country. For details call (03) 5777-6450. If you want to commune with nature, walking trails lie throughout the resort's village area, and the area around Mt. Stirling is less developed. Much of the movie *Man From Snowy River* was filmed up here, and **Craig's Hut,** part of the original set, is the destination of a popular four km (one-way) hike along a rough 4WD track. **Mountain Adventure Safaris,** tel. (018) 57-4746, offers 4WD tours from Mansfield up to the hut ($59 pp), as well as full-day and overnight tours (from $150 pp). For a horse-powered High Country expedition, **Watson's Mountain Country Trail Rides,** tel. (03) 5777-3552, offers a full-day ride into the wilderness for $85 pp, including lunch.

Stringybark Creek
This small creek flowing through an undistinguished valley of the Wombat Ranges north of Mansfield is synonymous with the Kelly Gang, claimed by some to be the place where Australia lost its innocence. On 25 October 1878 four troopers set off from Mansfield in search of the Kelly gang; through relatives and friends, the gang learned the whereabouts of troopers and stormed their camp, killing three officers, with the fourth managing to escape to raise the alarm. It didn't take long for Australia's biggest manhunt to get underway, concluding with a fiery showdown at Glenrowan. The massacre site is marked by a small plaque implanted in a large eucalypt. To get there from Mansfield, take the first left through town signposted to **Tolmie.** Beyond Tolmie, a gravel road spurs northwest (left) to Tatong (along this part of the route are two primitive campgrounds); the Kelly tree is signposted 11 km from Tolmie. Near the tree is a pleasant picnic area.

In Tolmie, the **Rose & Oak Inn,** tel. (03) 5776-2389, serves beer and bar meals and across the road is a petrol pump and general store with a hand-drawn map of the area.

The road out to Stringybark Creek continues north to Benalla, and the sealed road through Tolmie continues north to Wangaratta through the King Valley.

Headstones dotted around the High Country are about the only reminders of the days of bushrangers. This one, and two others in Mansfield Cemetery, mark the resting places of police shot by Ned Kelly at Stringybark Creek.

OVENS VALLEY

Gold diggers, then graziers and farmers, settled this wide valley through which the **Ovens River** flows in a northwesterly direction from Mt. Hotham through Wangaratta before it drains into the Murray River. Along the valley floor are the towns of Myrtleford and Bright, gateways, respectively, to the spectacular granite slabs of Mt. Buffalo National Park and, in winter, some of Australia's steepest ski slopes at Mt. Hotham.

Mount Buffalo National Park

Towering 1,000 meters above the surrounding plains, this 31,000-hectare park protects a plateau that, from a distance, early explorers likened to a buffalo. The impressive landscape of strange-looking granite tors alone makes the long and winding 30-km drive from the Ovens Valley worthwhile. The park also produces a dazzling display of wildflowers each spring and boasts impressive waterfalls, a picturesque lake, some of Australia's most challenging rock climbing, and, in winter, downhill skiing.

The plateau was formed around 300 million years ago when forces beneath the earth's crust pushed a molten mass through sedimentary rock, forming a plateau three times its present height. Through eons, wind and water have eroded the plateau to its present height. In many places the granite has cracked, with huge chunks falling away leaving the sheer cliffs.

Summer temperatures in the park average 10° C (about 20° F) cooler than the valley below. Only a few species of plants survive in this harsh subalpine environment; snow gum and alpine ash dominate, while areas with little soil and water support dry heath, grasses, and mosses. The presence of larger mammals is limited by surrounding cliffs, but the park does have populations of wombats and swamp wallabies. More than 100 species of reptiles and 130 species of birds have been recorded, including superb lyrebirds and a variety of cockatoos.

From **Porepunkah,** six km northwest of Bright, the access road passes the park gate ($10 per car) and climbs past scenic viewpoints to the plateau and **Lake Catani.** View Point Nature Walk begins from the lake and passes through a variety of plant communities (four km roundtrip). From the lake, the road continues climbing to Dingo Dell, a downhill and cross-country skiing area, past a field stacked with towering granite rock stacks, including the impressive Cathedral, and onto **Cresta Valley,** where the main skiing area and an information center are located.

The campground at Lake Catani has excellent facilities, including showers. Rates range $8.40-16. Budget. Reservations are needed only during public and school holidays, tel. (03) 5756-2328. Within the park are two guesthouses, both offering year-round accommodations. **Tatra Inn,** tel. (03) 5755-1988, is a modern lodge located at the end of the main access road, right by the main downhill skiing area. Off-season discounts aren't as steep here as other ski resorts, mainly because the area is so popular during summer. Dorm beds are $65 pp, double rooms $75 pp, rising to $85 and $115 pp respectively in the ski season. All rates include two cooked meals. Premium. Away from the action but with historic charm is **Mt. Buffalo Chalet,** tel. (03) 5755-1500. This grand old 1910 chalet overlooks a spectacular gorge, with the Buckland Valley far below and the horizon lined with Victoria's highest peaks. Rooms have recently been renovated, without losing any of their original charm. But with tennis, a swimming pool, cricket, croquet, a gym, and the wonders of the park, you won't want to spend long in your room. Rates start at $98 pp for rooms with shared facilities, and rooms with a view range $138-160 pp; all rates include a cooked breakfast, picnic lunch, and a three-course dinner in the Grand Dining Room. Nonguests can dine at the chalet with advance reservations. Luxury.

Park Headquarters, on the main access road, tel. (03) 5756-2328, is open daily 8:15-8:30 a.m. and 4-4:30 p.m.; at other times information is available at the Tatra Inn, where a booth is staffed daily 1:30-2:30 p.m.

Mount Buffalo National Park

Bright

This picturesque town of 2,000, spread out along the banks of the Ovens River, is at the crossroads of the High Country, a center of activities during summer and a good base for trips to the three major ski resorts in winter. After a gold rush in the nearby Buckland Valley, many diggers decided to settle in the area, and the town of Bright developed.

Lining the main thoroughfare are rows of elms, poplars, and chestnuts, which turn brilliant shades of orange and red each fall. Around town are a variety of walks, and a small museum is in the railway station (open Tuesday, Thursday, and Sunday 2-4 p.m.). **Wandiligong Valley,** immediately south of Bright, is today a far cry from the 1860s, when thousands of diggers lived in shanty towns along Morses Creek. Self-guided walks lead along the creek and through buildings that have survived the ravages of time.

Like all High Country towns, emphasis in Bright is on outdoor recreation. **Cyclepath,** 9 Camp St., tel. (03) 5750-1442, rents mountain bikes for $10 an hour or $30 a day. For guided horseback riding, **Freeburgh Trail Ride,** tel. (03) 5755-1370, has rides for all ability levels, including one-hour rides for $18 and overnight pub rides for around $100 pp per day. Mount Buffalo is a popular launch site for experienced hang gliders, but for first-timers, the **Eagle School of Hang Gliding,** tel. (03) 5750-1174, offers a two-day introductory course for $330 pp. **Alpine Paragliding,** tel. (03) 5755-1753, has tandem flights from $90 pp.

Bright Hikers Backpackers, 4 Ireland St., tel. (5750) 1244, is centrally located for all the outdoor recreational activities in the region. While a small facility, it features a games room, lounge room, modern kitchen and barbecue, and laundry. Dorm and double beds cost the same— $16 pp. Inexpensive. **Bright Alps Guesthouse,** 83 Delany Ave., tel. (03) 5755-1197, is another low-cost accommodation. Rooms have shared facilities, and there's also a lounge and dining area. Rates are $32 s, $58 d, including breakfast. Inexpensive. **Bright Central Motel,** 2 Ireland St., tel. (03) 5755-1074, has good, basic rooms from $45 s, $55 d, as does **Ovens Valley Motor Inn,** two km west of town, tel. (03) 5755-2022. Both are inexpensive. **Bright Caravan Park,** Cherry Ave., tel. (03) 5755-1141, spreads

VICTORIA SKI RESORTS

Victoria has five downhill ski resorts and three areas set aside for cross-country skiing. Each downhill resort has on-snow accommodation, and this should be booked well in advance. Roads to resorts are very steep, and chains must be carried at all times (grab them from all gateway towns). Although the resorts are owned privately, each is managed by the Alpine Resorts Commission (ARC), which collects a toll of $10-18 per *every* car using resort access roads (the fee increases in winter). This fee, plus chain hire ($15-20 per day), equipment hire ($25-45 per day), and lift tickets ($36-62 per day), makes for an expensive outing. But skiing above the treeline, among stunted snow gums and great outcrops of granite, is an experience that Northern Hemisphere skiers won't forget in a hurry. Ways to cut down costs are by taking an all-inclusive package from Melbourne, or staying off the mountain. For snow reports updated daily, call the **Victoria Snow Line**, tel. (13) 2842, for the cost of a local call anywhere within the state.

The closest snowfield to Melbourne is **Mt. Donna Buang**, near Healesville, where "Sightseeing Snow" is the main attraction.

Mount Baw Baw

This 25-hectare ski area with a vertical drop of 140 meters is located in Baw Baw National Park, 178 km east of Melbourne. It has eight lifts and is best suited to beginners and families. **Mt. Baw Baw YHA**, tel. (03) 5165-1129, is open daily during the season, and rates are $28 for members, $34 for nonmembers, with three meals an extra $14. Otherwise, call **Baw Baw Accommodations** at (03) 9764-9939 for other options and current transportation links. Lift tickets are adult $45, child $28, and the entry fee for cars is $16. For more information, call (03) 5165-1136 or, for a recorded message, call (03) 5165-1126.

On the southern end of the same plateau is **Mount St. Gwinear,** tel. (03) 5165-3481, a cross-country ski area with marked tracks, a kiosk, and ski rentals. Entry is $8 per car per day.

Lake Mountain

Australia's premier cross-country skiing area, Lake Mountain is 22 km west of Marysville at the top of the Yarra Valley and has more than 40 km of groomed trails. All trails are groomed daily and marked according to degree of difficulty. Facilities include ski hire, kiosk and café, information center, tel. (03) 5963-3288, and snow camping. You'll be charged $17 per car plus a trail fee of $6 pp. The closest accommodation is in Marysville, from where **Fallon's Bus Service,** tel. (03) 5772-1796, runs a weekend shuttle to the mountain.

Mount Buller

Victoria's largest ski resort, Mount Buller is located 240 km from Melbourne, 47 km beyond the town of Mansfield, which provides inexpensive accommodation alternatives to the mountain. This place gets busy on weekends but has an extensive snowmaking system, ensuring that most of the mountain remains open, even in years of poor snowfall. The resort covers 160 hectares and is served by 26 lifts. The village itself, with fantastic views across the High Country, has dozens of accommodations, an ice-skating rink, and night skiing on Wednesday and Saturday. Lift tickets are adult $62, child $38, and those under five and over 70 ski free. Gate entry fees are $17 per car. For accommodation, call Mt. Buller Central Reservations at (1800) 03-9049. The **Kooroora Hotel**, tel. (03) 5777-6050, is one of the mountain's least expensive places to stay at $65 pp, including breakfast. For resort information, call (03) 5777-6052, or for a snow report, call (03) 5777-6067. Transportation to the village is operated by **V/Line** from Melbourne. If you're only up for the day, there's no need to park near the village; lift tickets can be bought at the base of the Horse Hill chairlift.

Mount Stirling

This cross-country skiing area is 40 km from Mansfield along the same access road as Mt. Buller. It has 60 km of groomed trails, some through forests of snow gums, others above the treeline. After heavy snowfall, it's possible to ski between Mt. Stirling and Mt. Buller. Facilities include a ski school, rentals, café, and information center. The daily trail fee is $7 pp, and car entry fee is $12. For information and snow reports, call (03) 5777-5624.

Mount Buffalo

This resort may lack the hype of other areas, but the location, atop a massive plateau of granite surrounded by spectacular High Country scenery, makes up for a lack of challenging runs. Cresta Valley, with five lifts, is the main downhill area, with 27 hectares and a vertical drop of 157 meters. Throughout the park are some good cross-country skiing runs. Accommodation is at the on-slope **Tatra Inn,** tel. (03) 5755-1988, or **Mt. Buffalo Chalet,** tel. (03) 5755-1500. Lift tickets are adult $36, child $18, and gate entry fee is $10 per car. The area is not served by public transportation, but if you're booked at either of the lodges, transportation from Wangaratta can be arranged. For snow reports, call (03) 5755-1216.

Mount Hotham

The issue of which Australian ski resort has the most challenging slopes remains contentious, but Mount Hotham's name is always mentioned. The slopes are higher than others and more open to the elements, but at 1,750 meters, snowfall is high. The makeup of the resort is also different—the beginners area is around the summit of Mt. Hotham, while more difficult runs drop away from the village into a tree-filled valley. The resort has 10 lifts scattered over an area of 43 hectares and has a vertical drop of 428 meters. The village is tuned more to accommodating skiers rather than aprés-ski entertainment. Lift tickets are adult $54, child $29. The entry fee for cars is $17 per day. Accommodation in the village and nearby Dinner Plain can be booked through

Skicom, tel. (03) 5759-3522, or **Mt. Hotham-Falls Creek Reservation Centre,** tel. (1800) 35-4555. **Trekset Snow Services,** tel. (03) 9370-9055, offers a bus service from Melbourne each weekend and serves communities at the base of the mountain daily. For resort information, call (03) 5759-3508. For snow reports, call (0055) 32-002.

Falls Creek

A long 375-km drive from Melbourne, Falls Creek is one of Victoria's largest ski resorts. It is located on the Bogong High Plains, at the end of Kiewa Valley. Its 23 lifts are spread over two distinct areas, covering an area of 145 hectares; the vertical drop is 267 meters. The resort is the most upmarket in Victoria, and the village boasts a lively nightlife. Lift tickets are adult $59, child $33, and the entry fee is $15 per car. On-mountain accommodation starts at around $100 pp per night in the high season and can be booked through **Mt. Hotham-Falls Creek Reservation Centre,** tel. (1800) 35-4555. To lower costs, plan to stay at Mt. Beauty, on the valley floor. **Pyles Coaches,** tel. (03) 5754-4024, operates a Fri.-Sun. bus service between Melbourne and Falls Creek and a daily service from Albury. The bus line also operates a frequent shuttle from Mt. Beauty up to the slopes. For resort information, call (03) 5758-3280; for snow reports, call (0055) 32-003.

out along the banks of Morses Creek. Tent sites are $15, powered sites $18, and on-site vans $36. Within the grounds is **Bright Backpackers YHA,** a modern structure built especially for the World Hang Gliding Championships. Each dorm has four beds and a private bathroom, with rooms linked by a covered walkway to the main building, where a modern kitchen and comfortable lounge with an open fire are located. Rates are $15-18 pp. Budget-Inexpensive.

The Alpine Hotel, a restored pub on Anderson St., has an extensive bistro menu, available at the bar or in the lounge. For a more relaxed atmosphere, **Hummingbird Coffee Shop,** Starr Rd., is open daily 10 a.m.-5 p.m., serving healthy lunches and Devonshire teas. **Liquid Am-bar,** 8 Anderson St., tel. (03) 5755-2318, is a funky kind of place with all meals less than $10.

Bright Tourist Information Centre is on the main drag through town at Delaney Ave., tel. (03) 5756-2062. It's open daily 10 a.m.-4 p.m.

Harrietville to Hotham

Like Bright, Harrietville, 25 km to the southeast, is a gold-rush town. It is the gateway to Mt. Hotham ski area, a steep, 41-km drive away. East of Harrietville is **Mt. Feathertop;** at 1,923 meters it's Victoria's second-highest peak. It stands apart from the main range, making it all the more impressive. The hike to the summit is pretty steep, but is easy if tackled as an overnight trip. The trailhead is one km down a gravel road at the bridge just before town. From the carpark, it is nine km (four hours) to a hut and primitive campground. From there it's three steep km to the summit. You can return to the valley floor along the same route or by climbing the summit track for one km, then following a track that spurs left, passing another hut and ending on the Ovens Highway, four km north of Harrietville. A number of topographical maps cover the mountain; the best seems to be *Feathertop-Hotham Divide* (Algona Guides), available at outdoor shops in Bright and Harrietville.

Beyond Harrietville, the highway climbs steeply to a ridge above Mt. Hotham Ski Area. Not much happens up here in summer, although the road continues to the resort community of **Dinner Plain,** in Alpine National Park, and onto **Omeo** on the Omeo Highway.

MOUNT BEAUTY AND BEYOND

Nestled below **Mt. Bogong** (1,986 meters), the state's highest peak, the township of Mt. Beauty makes an excellent base for exploring the surrounding High Country. It lies at the end of the Kiewa Valley, separated from the Ovens Valley by a forested ridge and bounded to the south by Bogong High Plains. A winding 40-km road links Mt. Beauty to Bright, or the township can be approached from the north along the Kiewa Valley Highway. The town is relatively new, having been built in the 1940s for workers on the Kiewa Hydro Electric Scheme.

Bogong Horseback Adventures retains the original form of High Country transportation with half- and full-day rides starting from stables on Mountain Creek Rd. in Tawonga. December through April, overnight packhorse adventures are offered, starting at $450 for three days, tel. (03) 5754-4849. For the less energetic, greens fees at the short but challenging 18-hole **Mt. Beauty Golf Course** are $14; Snow Gum Motel, tel. (03) 5754-4508, has club rentals.

Mount Beauty Practicalities
The cheapest accommodations are in Mt. Beauty's twin town of Tawonga South and, farther north, in Tawonga. **Bogong Hotel,** in Tawonga, tel. (03) 5754-4482, has clean rooms for just $30 pp, including breakfast. Inexpensive. In Mt. Beauty itself **Snow Gum Motel,** on the Kiewa Valley Hwy., tel. (03) 5754-4508, has rooms of an excellent standard for $55 s, $65 d. Moderate. Between Mt. Beauty and Tawonga South is **Mt. Beauty Holiday Centre,** tel. (03) 5754-4396, offering camping sites for $12-21, self-contained cabins for $50-65 d, and European yurts from $85 per night. Budget-Inexpensive.

The main shopping precinct has a couple of supermarkets, but there's nowhere to recommend for a meal—try the golf club.

Pyle's Coaches operates a winter-only bus service from Albury and Melbourne to Falls Creek

and in summer offers a variety of 4WD trips onto the Bogong High Plains. Rates are $60-85 pp for a full-day tour, tel. (03) 5754-4024. This depot, on the main road into Mt. Beauty, is also the agent for Budget rental cars and the office of Falls Creek Chamber of Commerce; open daily 9 a.m.-4 p.m. The **Australian High Country Visitor Centre,** toward Mt. Beauty, is another source of information, tel. (03) 5754-3172.

Bogong
From Mt. Beauty, the road begins a steady ascent through a forest of eucalypt to the Bogong High Plains. En route is the small hamlet of Bogong, built to house workers on the nearby hydroelectric scheme. It is set around manmade **Lake Guy,** where canoes can be rented. The general store can arrange accommodations and has details of hiking in the area.

Falls Creek and Bogong High Plains
Falls Creek, as well as being one of Australia's top ski resorts, is a great summer destination with a variety of outdoor activities possible when it's not covered in snow (late Nov.-April). The village is located on Bogong High Plains, a plateau of low tussocky grasses, an alpine environment easily enjoyed by all levels of fitness. Surrounding the plains are steep-sided valleys filled with gnarled snow gums, and the odd isolated peak, such as Mt. Bogong, a huge chunk of granite separated from the main range. The village is the center of most organized outdoor recreation, but experienced bushwalkers will find plenty to do in the more remote areas of the High Plains. The 85-km (five- to six-day) **Bogong High Plains Circuit** takes in the best of the High Country; beginning and ending at the village of Bogong, it makes a wide circuit around Falls Creek village and includes a summit-climb of Mt. Bogong. It is also possible to walk only sections of this trail, including from above Falls Creek back to the village. Topographical maps and more details are available from the **Department of Environment and Natural Resources** on the Kiewa Valley Hwy. in Tawonga South, tel. (03) 5754-4693. Rangers operate various walks and talks in Alpine National Park through summer.

One of Falls Creek's chairlifts operates for sightseeing, Christmas through January and at Eastertime. It operates 11 a.m.-3 p.m. and costs

$14 for unlimited rides; call (03) 5758-3280 for details. During this same period **Bogong Horseback Adventures,** tel. (03) 5754-4849, operates horseback riding trips from corrals set up at the village. **Alpine Nature Rambles** has short guided hikes through the high country each afternoon, tel. (03) 5758-3492.

A few of the ski lodges are open through summer and offer some great accommodation deals. Best of the bunch is **Pretty Valley Alpine Lodge,** tel. (03) 5758-3210, where the rate of $75 pp per day includes three meals, use of mountain bikes, canoes, tennis facilities, and pool area. **Trackers Mountain Lodge,** tel. (03) 5758-3346, is also open year-round and is one of the best lodges on the mountain; rates there are $95 pp per day, including meals. **Snowland,** part of the base facilities, sells groceries and booze and has a small café open daily 10 a.m.-4 p.m.

BEECHWORTH

Of all historic gold-mining towns in the country, none are as well-preserved and picturesque as Beechworth, nestled in the foothills of the High Country, 37 km east of the Hume Highway and 270 km northeast of Melbourne. The wide tree-lined streets are dotted with National Trust-classified buildings, antique emporiums, excellent museums, good restaurants, and plenty of reasonably priced accommodations. Beechworth's attractions extend beyond town limits; in the sur-

rounding area are the remains of the various gold rushes.

Town Sights
Named for Capt. Robert O'Hara Burke, police superintendent of Beechworth until becoming lost on the ill-fated Burke and Wills expedition across Australia, the **Burke Museum** is a definite must-see while in Beechworth. Main features include a replica of an 1860s streetscape with 16 shops, a good collection of gold-rush-era photographs, and Kelly Gang memorabilia. Admission is adult $5, child $2.50. Open daily 10:30 a.m.-3:30 p.m. Located on Loch St. (access is easiest through the gardens of Shire Hall, tel. (03) 5728-1420.

Ford Street has the best examples of gold rush-era architecture with most buildings still in use. The **courthouse,** across from Town Hall, was where Ned Kelly made a court appearance for the triple murder at Stringybark Creek. The courthouse is open daily 10 a.m.-4 p.m., and admission is $3. Across the road, at the back of the Shire Hall, is the dingy cell in which Ned was held while awaiting trial. Beyond the courthouse is **Victoria Park** and **Beechworth Prison,** built in 1859. Farther along Ford St., **Gorge Rd.** leads off to the west, eventually looping back to town. The road has numerous scenic views, and the **powder magazine,** a stone building built to store blasting materials. **Historic Murray Breweries,** on the corner of William and Last Streets, tel. 035728-3233, is in a 100-year-old brewery. The cellar is

Beechworth

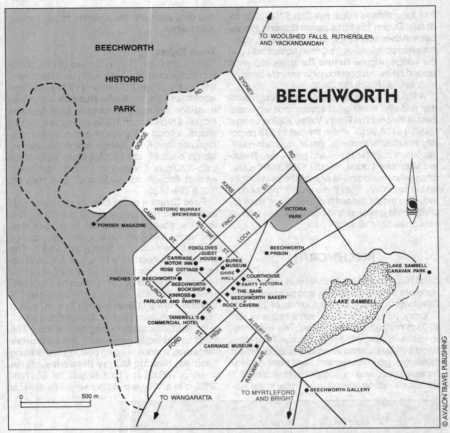

TO WOOLSHED FALLS, RUTHERGLEN, AND YACKANDANDAH

BEECHWORTH

BEECHWORTH HISTORIC PARK

POWDER MAGAZINE

HISTORIC MURRAY BREWERIES

FOXGLOVES GUEST HOUSE

CARRIAGE / MOTOR INN

ROSE COTTAGE

FINCHES OF BEECHWORTH

BEECHWORTH BOOKSHOP

KINROSS

PARLOUR AND PANTRY

TANSWELL'S COMMERCIAL HOTEL

BURKE MUSEUM

SHIRE HALL

PARTY VICTORIA

THE BANK

BEECHWORTH BAKERY

ROCK CAVERN

COURTHOUSE

BEECHWORTH PRISON

VICTORIA PARK

LAKE SAMBELL CARAVAN PARK

LAKE SAMBELL

CARRIAGE MUSEUM

TO WANGARATTA

TO MYRTLEFORD AND BRIGHT

BEECHWORTH GALLERY

0   500 m

© AVALON TRAVEL PUBLISHING

set up as a small brewing museum that includes a large collection of interesting bottles. Admission is $2. In the same complex, specialty old-style cordials are brewed and are available to the public for tasting and sales. The **Carriage Museum,** located in a goods shed on Railway Ave., houses about 20 horse-drawn carriages, buggies, and even an old bus. Open daily 10 a.m.-4 p.m. (closed noon-1 p.m.). Admission is $2.50.

Beechworth Historic Park

While buildings from the gold rush era line the streets of Beechworth, signs of the 15,000 diggers in the valleys below are just about non-existent.

Much of the activity, which followed the 1852 gold discovery in Spring Creek, took place directly below town, between Gorge Rd. and Woolshed Falls. The area has been declared a historic park and is crisscrossed with hiking trails. Along Gorge Rd. trails start from Ingram's Rock, One Tree Hill, and the powder magazine, dropping steeply into the valley below, but you really need the brochure *Discovering Beechworth Historic Park on Foot* ($1), from the Department of Environment and Natural Resources, to find your way around.

Woolshed Falls, five km north of town, is also part of the park. This was the hub of the goldfields, home to thousands of diggers, and a hive of activity for more than 20 years. Today, little evidence of this frenzied period remains. A 1.2-km trail loops around Spring Creek, along which many miners lived, ending back near the carpark at Woolshed Falls. It is also possible to walk from town to the falls (six km one-way), crossing Sheep Station Creek, where Aaron Sherritt, a police informer who brought about the downfall of the Kelly Gang, was gunned down by Joe Byrne, a member of the gang.

Accommodations

Tanswell's Commercial Hotel, 55 Ford St., tel. (03) 5728-1480, is a classic two-story pub built in the 1860s that has undergone extensive restorations, with the lounge area and dining room retaining their original grandeur; $40 s, $60 d includes breakfast. Inexpensive. Beechworth has a few decent motels, such as **Carriage Motor Inn,** corner Camp and Finch Streets, tel. (03) 5728-1830, with rooms for $66 s, $75 d, but you'd be better off staying in one of the many B&Bs, which have more character. **Rose Cottage,** 42 Camp St., tel. (03) 5728-1069, was built in 1876 and after being fully restored maintains an authentic atmosphere from the gold-rush era. Each room is decorated with antiques and has tea and coffee supplies, while the relaxing guest lounge has a log fire; $70 s, $95 d. Expensive. **Foxgloves Guest House,** 21 Loch St., tel. (03) 5728-1322, directly opposite the Burke Museum, is another restored cottage with rooms for $80 s, $110 d. Expensive. Moving up in price is **Kinross,** 34 Loch St., tel. (03) 5728-2351, built in 1858. This lodging is more luxurious than the others. Each room is large and has a fireplace and private bathroom; rates are $120 s, $148 d. Premium. **Finches of Beechworth,** 3 Finch St., tel. (03) 5728-2655, is another historic bed and breakfast—this one surrounded by an amazing garden. Rates are $180 d. Luxury.

Lake Sambell Caravan Park is a couple of km from town on Jarvis Rd., tel. (03) 5728-1421. Sites are $14 and on-site vans $31. Budget-Inexpensive.

Food

On Camp St., **Beechworth Bakery** is the center of much activity each morning. It has a great range of pies, pastries, and cakes to be consumed at tables inside, outside, upstairs, and downstairs. **Parlour & Pantry,** 69 Ford St., tel. (03) 5728-2575, has an old-world atmosphere. Within a historic shop, it houses a gourmet deli, coffee shop, and restaurant. You can also buy picnic hampers from $12 pp. Inexpensive bar meals are available from **Tanswell's Commercial Hotel,** on Ford Street. One of the few formal dining rooms in Beechworth is **The Bank,** at 56 Ford St., tel. (03) 5728-2223. The main foyer of this historic building has been converted to an upmarket dining room with a small but varied menu; main meals range $16-21.

Transportation, Services, and Information

Beechworth has no bus depot; buses stop outside the post office. Service between Beechworth and Wangaratta runs twice daily weekdays and once on Sunday.

Minibus tours of the town can be booked through Rock Cavern, corner Ford and Camp Streets, tel. (03) 5728-1374. They run around 90 minutes and depart daily 12:30 and 3:30 p.m.

Beechworth Bookshop, 31 Camp St., tel. (03) 5728-2611, carries a good range of new books, including many on the area's history, as well as a couple of shelves of secondhand literature.

The **Tourist Information Centre,** in the Shire Hall on Ford St., tel. (03) 5728-1374, is open daily 9 a.m.-5 p.m. The **Department of Environment and Natural Resources** has some excellent displays and literature on Beechworth Historic Park and some interesting maps of the area; on Ford Street, next to the courthouse; open Mon.-Thurs. 9 a.m.-12:45 p.m., Friday 8:30 a.m.-4:30 p.m., tel. (03) 5728-1501.

OMEO HIGHWAY AND THE NORTHERN HIGH COUNTRY

Yackandandah

Once on the main wagon route between Sydney and Melbourne, this well-preserved town looks much as it did in the days of the gold rush. In 1852 gold was discovered in a nearby creek, but, by the time a permanent settlement was established, the gold had run out. Today, along a street lined with deciduous trees, the sturdy redbrick civic buildings and original shopfronts remain, housing antique emporiums, tearooms, a bakery, and shops good for general browsing. The **Bank of Victoria Museum** houses displays focusing on the history of the town; open Sunday and daily during school holidays noon-4 p.m.

Star Hotel, tel. (03) 6027-1493, has rooms from $25 pp (inexpensive), and there's a caravan park down by the river, but most people visit the town as a day trip from Beechworth, 30 km away.

Tallangatta

Tallangatta is a small town that sits on the Murray Valley Highway, which parallels Lake Hume before traversing the remote northern corner of the state. The original townsite had to be moved when the Mitta Mitta River was dammed in the 1950s. The town's layout is very symmetrical, with shops and other services surrounding a semicircular park, all of which overlook the man-made lake. The streetscape of Old Tallangatta can be seen when water levels are low; located seven km east of town.

Omeo Highway

This is the major route through the High Country. It begins east of Tallangatta and winds its way south for 300 spectacular km to Bairnsdale on the Princes Highway. The first community along the route from Tallangatta is **Mitta Mitta,** a historic gold-mining center, from where a gravel road leads southeast to **Lake Dartmouth** in Alpine National Park.

Around 170 km from Tallangatta is the remote town of **Omeo** (pop. 580). The town has a wild history; when gold was discovered, diggers flocked to the region, and being so remote it took many years for the police to establish a post. Traces of gold can be found by panning in Livingstone Creek and a number of historic buildings remain in town. It's also a base for skiers heading to Mt. Hotham, one hour's drive west. The original courthouse and log jail still stand, and a small museum opens during school holidays. The **Golden Age Hotel,** tel. (03) 5159-1344, has basic rooms with shared bathrooms for $25 pp as well as more luxurious bed and breakfast rooms for $80 s, $125 d. Inexpensive-Premium. **Holston Tourist Park,** tel. (03) 5159-1351, has sites from $11 and on-site vans for $35. **Octagon Bookshop,** tel. (03) 5159-1411,

serves as an information center and is open Thurs.-Tues. 10 a.m.-5:30 p.m.

Burrowa-Pine Mountain National Park

Access to this remote 18,400-hectare park, located in the far northeastern corner of the state, is north from Cudgewa on the Murray Valley Highway between Tallangatta and Corryong. Two massive outcrops of volcanic rock are the park's main features, with Mount Burrowa rising to 1,300 meters. Along Falls Rd., near the park's entrance, is a picnic area from where a two-km (one-way) trail leads to Bluff Falls. Beyond the picnic area is a small campground. For further information on the park, call (03) 6055-6111.

Corryong

"In Memory of The Man From Snowy River Jack Riley Buried Here 16th July 1914." These simple words adorn the grave of Australia's most famous horseman, buried in the Corryong cemetery. The valleys and mountains around Corryong were the haunt of horsemen like Jack Riley, and many others, who earned a living using their skills to round up wild horses. Riley's fame grew from a poem written by Banjo Patterson, who stayed in his mountain hut and listened to him recall a ride down an impossibly steep slope near Tom Groggin. It was from this encounter that Patterson's immortal poem, "The Man From Snowy River," was written. It has since been made into one of Australia's most successful movies. The **Man From Snowy River Folk Museum,** Hansen St., tel. (03) 6076-1114, is about life in the High Country, rather than about Riley himself. It also displays an interesting collection of old snow skis. It's open daily 10 a.m.-noon and 2-4 p.m. (except June-Aug.) and admission is a worthy $2. **Corryong High Country Festival,** held each March, features a Stockman's Muster, poetry night, bush dancing, a market, and, the highlight, a horseback ride from Tom Groggin down into Corryong.

Alpine Gateway Lodge, 96 Hansen St., tel. (03) 6076-1269, has basic accommodations in a renovated house for $38 s, $56 d. Inexpensive. **Corryong Country Inn,** 7 Towong Rd., tel. (03) 6076-1333, is a little nicer and has the best restaurant in town; $64 s, $78 d. Moderate. At the west end of town, the caravan park, tel. (03)

6076-1152, has plenty of room for tents and vans, and on-site vans are only $25 d. Budget. Apart from the restaurant in Corryong Country Inn, there's a bakery on the main drag, and **Pio-** **neer Corner Cafe,** at the top end of town.

The news agency has some information on the area and the library has a large map on its side wall.

SOUTHEAST FROM MELBOURNE

MORNINGTON PENINSULA

Mornington Peninsula is a cusp of land extending south from Melbourne, around the eastern shore of Port Phillip Bay, and coming to an apex at Point Nepean, a couple of km from the Bellarine Peninsula on the opposite side of the bay. The bay side of the peninsula is lined with a string of holiday towns and safe sandy beaches. At the other extreme is the peninsula's southern coast, battered for eons by the wild Southern Ocean. The wave-eroded cliffs are dotted with sandy beaches. Many ships have wrecked along this stretch of coast, and the pounding surf has claimed many lives, including that of Australian prime minister Harold Holt, who drowned in 1967 while swimming at Cheviot Beach.

The peninsula has long been a favorite getaway for Victorian holidaymakers and towns such as Frankston and Mornington have become part of Melbourne's urban sprawl.

Arthur's Seat State Park
Arthur's Seat, the highest peak on the peninsula, is a granite massif that rises 305 meters. The surrounding park contains natural bushland and mature gardens. Near the summit is **Seawinds Botanical Garden,** from where views extend across Port Phillip Bay to Melbourne. A chairlift to the summit runs Sept.-April daily 11 a.m.-5 p.m. and weekends only the rest of the year, tel. (03) 5987-2565. The park is well signposted south of Dromana, off Morning Peninsula Freeway.

Sorrento
This historic port faces the quiet waters of Port Phillip Bay along the narrow western tip of Mornington Peninsula. It was the site of Victoria's first permanent European settlement, abandoned after just one year due to a lack of fresh water. All that remains are a few graves, but at the site of the settlement, east of Sorrento, just off Point

Nepean Rd., is a display center (open Sat.-Sun. and school holidays 1-4:30 p.m.). Sorrento itself has historic buildings dating from the 1870s and a small museum on Melbourne Rd. that's open weekends 1:30-4:30 p.m.

South Channel Fort, six km from Sorrento, is an island constructed in 1888 as a garrison to protect Melbourne from the threat of warships entering Port Phillip Bay. It was manned during the two world wars but is now in a state of disrepair, with the public only recently allowed access. The island has become a nesting ground for birds. Many tours are offered to the island, some of which include low-lying **Mud Island,** a wildlife reserve.

Carmel B&B, 142 Ocean Beach Rd., tel. (03) 5984-3512, is a classic limestone cottage in the center of town. The four rooms go for $100 s, $120 d. Expensive. **Motel Saltair,** corner Melbourne and Bowen Roads, tel. (03) 5984-1356, has rooms for $45 s, $55 d. Inexpensive. For backpackers, purpose-built **Sorrento Backpackers,** 3 Miranda St., tel. (03) 5984-4323, has modern facilities; $15-20 pp. Inexpensive. Campgrounds are spread along the entire length of the peninsula; closest to Sorrento is **Sorrento Foreshore Reserve,** west of town, tel. (03) 5984-2797, where sites are $12-18 per night (coin-operated showers). Budget.

Ocean Beach Rd. is lined with eateries, including two bakeries and a number of cafés. **Just Fine Food,** 23 Ocean Beach Rd., tel. (03) 5984-4666, open daily 7 a.m.-5 p.m., serves hearty breakfasts and healthy lunches. **Koonya Hotel,** 1 the Esplanade, tel. (03) 5984-2281, has the best bistro of three hotels, with views across the bay and an outdoor dining area. **Smokehouse,** 182 Ocean Beach Rd., tel. (03) 5984-1246, is a casual yet stylish pizza and pasta place—but you'll need a booking on weekends.

Trains from Melbourne run as far as Frankston, from where **Portsea Passenger Buses,** tel. (1800) 11-5666, runs every couple of hours to

Sorrento and onto Portsea. Sorrento is also the terminus of ferries from Queenscliff on the Bellarine Peninsula. Ferries run six times daily and cost $7 for adults and $36 for cars. For details call (03) 5258-3244.

Sorrento Tourist Information Centre is at 3183 Pt. Nepean Rd., tel. (03) 5984-5678 or (1800) 80-4009.

Portsea

Portsea, the westernmost community on the peninsula, has an air of elegance about it, with many large mansions overlooking the bay. The beach here is safe for swimming, and keen anglers stand shoulder to shoulder on the long wooden pier in the busy months of summer. Accommodation is more expensive here than the rest of the peninsula. **Delgany Country House Hotel,** Point Nepean Rd., tel. (03) 5984-4000, is one of the state's grandest and most luxurious accommodations. The main building is a turreted limestone castle set in more than five hectares of immaculately manicured gardens. Every last touch is aimed at making guests feel like king of the castle, and, if you drag yourself away from the award-winning restaurant, you'll find a large saltwater swimming pool and tennis courts. Weekday rates start at $225 d. Luxury. The restaurant here is open to nonguests, with the set two-course lunch a steal at $28 per head and dinner at $68. For something a little more casual and stunning water views, head to the **Portsea Hotel,** 3746 Pt. Nepean Road.

Mornington Peninsula National Park

More than 100 years of military occupation has been a blessing in disguise for the western portion of Mornington Peninsula. While the rest of the peninsula has been, for the most part, heavily developed, this area has remained relatively unscathed. When the army moved out in 1988, the Department of Environment and Natural Resources moved in, declaring the area a national park. The park extends from Pt. Nepean eastward along a narrow coastal strip to Cape Schanck. Entry to the western portion of the park is regulated, with this part open only weekends and school holidays, and only a certain number of people allowed in each of those days ($8.50 pp). Access to the many walks is by tractor-drawn trailers, which shuttle visitors to trailheads.

At the back of Portsea is a patrolled surf beach and, to the west, unusual rock formations such as Sphinx Rock and London Bridge. Access to the coastal strip of the park is unrestricted, with access roads leading through heath-covered dunes to the beach. Interconnecting trails lead along the coast and the entire strip of coast is 28 km. The southernmost tip of the park is **Cape Schanck,** where there's a lighthouse and walking track to **Bushranger Bay.** Access to this part of the park is south from Rosebud on Boneo Road. For park information call (13) 1963.

Western Port and French Island

The sheltered waters fringed by the mostly undeveloped coast of Western Port are a stark contrast to the frenzied activity a half-hour's drive away on the other side of Mornington Peninsula. With no reliable source of fresh water, settlement around this body of water was slow, although the towns of **Flinders, Somers,** and **Hastings** have grown to become popular seaside holiday towns. Flinders has a picturesque harbor, filled with fishing boats, pleasure crafts, and views extending to Phillip Island.

In the middle of Western Port is French Island, formerly a prison farm, and undeveloped except for a smattering of houses and shops around **Tankerton,** the island's only community. The 180-square-km island is low-lying; **Mt. Wellington** (96 meters) is the highest point. Half the island is a state park, in which koalas, potoroos, more than 200 species of birds, and 500 species of plants have been recorded. **Tortoise Head Lodge,** tel. (03) 5980-1234, is the island's only accommodation. Rates are $95 pp, including three meals. **French Island Ferry** runs from Stony Point, south of Hastings, across to Tankerton; $15.50 roundtrip, tel. (03) 9585-5730. Many of the island's attractions can be reached on foot, but a mountain bike is a good way to get around.

PHILLIP ISLAND

Linked to the mainland by bridge, this 10,000-hectare island is at the mouth of Western Port and 135 km by road from Melbourne. The island is one of Victoria's major tourist destinations, most famous for the nightly **Penguin Parade,** when thousands of fairy penguins march from the water and cross the sand to nesting grounds. Long sandy beaches, rugged coastal landscapes, large populations of koalas and seals, good fishing and surfing, and the sleepy towns of Cowes, Rhyll, and Newhaven also combine to make the island so popular.

Members of the Bunurong tribe lived on the island up to 40,000 years ago, but their nomadic lifestyle meant they lived on the island only seasonally. George Bass landed on the island's north shore in 1798, and sealers and whalers lived in shanties around the protected northern coastline for much of the early 1800s, but it wasn't until 1842, when the McHaffie family leased the entire island, that the first permanent settlement developed. The major crop was chicory, a beet-like vegetable that was ground to make a coffee substitute. A bridge to the mainland was constructed in 1940, creating a boom in tourism that continues to this day. Cowes, on the protected northern shore, is the island's largest town.

Newhaven and Vicinity

The motorist's gateway to Phillip Island is the small fishing town of Newhaven. Once on the island, the first stop should be **Phillip Island Information Centre,** one km west of the bridge; open

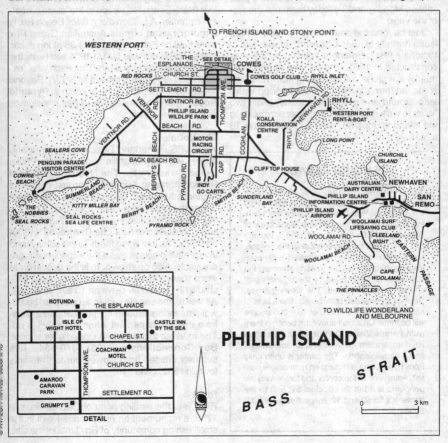

PHILLIP ISLAND

daily 10 a.m.-5 p.m., tel. (03) 5956-7447. The center is a complete source of island information, and staff can book various attractions (including the Penguin Parade) and accommodations.

Diagonally opposite the information center is the **Australian Dairy Centre**, tel. (03) 5956-7583, which houses the country's largest collection of dairy farming memorabilia as well as a realistic replica of an 1892 cheese factory, horse-drawn milk carts from various eras, some ice-cream-making equipment, and a small factory where specialty cheeses and candies are still being produced. Admission is adult $2.50, child $1. Open in summer daily 10 a.m.-6 p.m. (closed Monday and Tuesday mornings the rest of the year).

Just beyond the dairy center, a narrow road leads north to historic **Churchill Island,** site of Victoria's first permanent building, which was constructed in 1801. The building is gone, but nearby is a stone cottage dating from 1874 and some old farm machinery. Various short walks lead around and across the island; allow two hours to walk around the shoreline; admission to the island is adult $6, child $3. Open daily 10 a.m.-4.30 p.m.

PENGUIN PARADE

Like clockwork, shortly after sunset every night of the year, fairy penguins (also called little penguins) leave the water after a day's fishing and march to their burrows at the back of **Summerland Beach.** Their timing is incredible; as soon as the sun sets below the horizon, small groups that have congregated in the shallows head up the beach. In early summer, the spectacle is heightened by the squealing of chicks waiting to be fed. The viewing areas, reached by elevated boardwalks, line a strip of sand, and in peak season, up to 4,000 people will be there. On a bluff above the beach is **Penguin Parade Visitor Centre,** featuring a simulated underwater environment, an audiovisual, and a souvenir shop. The center is open daily from 10 a.m. and is busiest an hour before sunset. Admission to the center and for viewing the penguins is adult $9.50, child $7; just to the center it's $3.50 and $2, respectively, tel. (03) 5956-8300.

Cape Woolamai and Vicinity

At 109 meters above sea level, Cape Woolamai is a natural landmark on an island that is generally less than 30 meters above sea level. The cape is at the end of a narrow isthmus separating the surfing beach of **Woolamai** from the protected waters of **Cleeland Bight.** From **Woolamai Surf Lifesaving Club** a three-km (roundtrip) hiking trail leads to the summit of the cape and around cliffs where a number of muttonbird (short-tailed shearwater) rookeries are located.

Six km west of the Woolamai Rd. turnoff, Phillip Island Rd. divides; the right fork leads to the island's largest town, Cowes, and the left fork (Back Beach Rd.) leads to the island's western extremity. A few km along Back Beach Rd. is a **motor racing circuit.** Australian Grand Prix were held on Phillip Island 1928-35 along public roads. This circuit was built in 1956 and hosts the Australian Motorcycle Grand Prix each year (except 1991-95 when it moved to NSW). Beyond the circuit, Pyramid Rd. leads south to **Pyramid Rock,** where pyramid-shaped basalt columns rise from the ocean.

The Nobbies

West of Summerland Beach the rugged and deeply indented coastline continues to Phillip Island's western tip, The Nobbies, and **Seal Rocks,** home to Australia's largest colony of southern fur seals. Seal numbers are highest during the breeding season (Oct.-Dec.), but the colony is nearly two km offshore. Right on the cape, **Seal Rocks Sea Life Centre,** tel. (1300) 36-7325, has live video feeds to the colony, and interpretive displays make the experience more enjoyable. Also on show here is the largest great white shark ever caught. Admission is adult $15, child $12. Open daily between 10 a.m. and dusk. As well as the sea life center, an elevated boardwalk meanders around the point and to a blowhole that struts its stuff when the swell is up. The road out to the cape is closed after sunset. **Bay Connections,** tel. (03) 5678-5642, has summer cruises from Cowes out to the seals for adult $32, child $18.

Rhyll

Rhyll was the landing point of George Bass in 1798; a monument on Fishermans Point in the small fishing community of Rhyll marks the site.

Nobbies, Phillip Island

Along Rhyll Inlet are extensive mudflats that can be observed at low tide. In town is a small **Maritime Museum.**

Koala Conservation Centre

Although Phillip Island has always been considered a good place for viewing koalas, they are not native to the island, and until the development of this center, their population was in serious decline. They were introduced to the island in 1870, and by the 1930s only 1,000 remained in Victoria, most of which were on Phillip Island. Koalas can be seen in various reserves around Cowes, but this center has the highest density. It's open daily from 10 a.m. to sunset, and admission is adult $5, child $2. For more information call (03) 5956-8691.

Other Commercial Attractions

To appease the masses, a variety of attractions have been developed on the island. **Phillip Island Wildlife Park,** one km south of Cowes, tel. (03) 5952-2038, is the most worthwhile of these, with 16 hectares of native animals and birds. Admission is adult $7, child $3.50; open daily 9 a.m. to dusk. **Indy Go Carts,** tel. (03) 5952-3888, is out by the Motor Racing Circuit. **Grumpy's Waterslide and Crazy Golf,** tel. (03) 5952-3060, is in Cowes. Back on the mainland, just north of the Phillip Island bridge, is **Wildlife Wonderland,** tel. (03) 5678-2222, a first-class wildlife park. Many displays are indoors, making it an ideal rainy-day destination. Admission is adult $9, child $4.50.

Recreation and Tours

Boats can be rented from **Western Port Rent-a-boat,** opposite the boat ramp at 14 Beach St., Rhyll, tel. (03) 5956-9238. From Rhyll, many fishing spots along the island's north shore can be accessed by these boats—or just throw a line in from the many jetties and rock walls around the island.

The best surfing is at **Woolamai Beach,** where there's a surf shop with board rentals. **Cowes Golf Club** is an 18-hole course on Settlement Rd., just to the east of Cowes; for tee times call (03) 5952-2141.

Bay Connections offers a variety of cruises departing from Cowes Foreshore. In January cruises depart at least three times daily, with fewer sailings the rest of the year. The most popular trips are to Seal Rocks (adult $32, child $18) and French Island Tour (adult $35, child $22), and the Evening Shearwater Cruise (adult $25, child $15). From Cowes, they operate a drop-off service to French Island and Stony Point, on the mainland. For details, drop by the rotunda on the waterfront in Cowes, or call (03) 5678-5642.

Phillip Island Air, tel. (03) 5956-7316, offers tours ranging from a 10-minute flight around Cape Woolamai ($35 pp) to a 40-minute flight over Western Port ($85 pp). They also operate charters, including to King and Flinders Islands.

Accommodations

Even with more than 20 hotels and motels on the island, getting a room in summer entails booking well ahead. Phillip Island Information Centre, tel. (03) 5956-7447, can make advance bookings.

Isle of Wight Hotel, the Esplanade, tel. (03) 5952-2301, has a great location—right opposite the waterfront in downtown Cowes. Rooms in the hotel are $35 s, $45 d, and slightly higher in the motel out back. Inexpensive. With more facilities, including a heated pool, is **Coachman Motel,** 51 Chapel St., tel. (03) 5952-1098; $75 s or d. Moderate.

Castle Inn by the Sea, 7 Steele St., tel. (03) 5952-1228, is a luxurious B&B a short stroll from Cowes and the waterfront. Each room has a bathroom and private deck, and rates include a delicious three-course breakfast; $75 s, $100 d. Expensive. On the other side of the island is **Cliff Top Country House,** Marlin St., tel. (03) 5952-1033, which overlooks spectacular coastline and is only a short walk from sandy Smiths Beach. The house features well-appointed guest rooms, a lounge with fireplace, and a snooker room; $90 s, $140 d. Premium.

Amaroo Caravan Park, 97 Church St., Cowes, tel. (03) 5952-2548, is part of a large caravan park one block from the main street, with cooking facilities, well-priced meals, and a bar. The park also has a swimming pool, runs day trips, and organizes pickups from Melbourne. Tent sites are $14, powered sites $16, and on-site vans start at $38 d. Part of the same complex is a YHA hostel, with its own kitchen and communal areas; dorm beds are $17 pp, doubles $38. Budget-Inexpensive. The island holds more than a dozen other caravan parks, including **Anchor Belle Holiday Park,** 272 Church St., Cowes, tel. (03) 5952-2258, and **Koala World Caravan Park,** opposite the Koala Conservation Centre, tel. (03) 5952-2283.

Food

Most restaurants and takeaways are along Thompson Ave. and the Esplanade, both in Cowes. Many of these specialize in seafood, including **Fishbizz** on the Esplanade, which has takeout fish and chips from $4.50, and upmarket seafood restaurants such as **The Jetty,** also on the Esplanade, tel. (03) 5952-2060, which has a rustic atmosphere and sea views. Head to **Dutchies Stonegrill,** 1 Vista Place, Cape Woolamai, tel. (03) 5956-6000, for inexpensive dishes grilled on red-hot stones, served while still being cooked; open nightly Tues.-Sunday. Another elegant restaurant is **Banfields,** 192 Thompson Ave., Cowes, tel. (03) 5952-2088, furnished in a colonial-Australian style and specializing in seafood and steaks.

Transportation, Services, and Information

Scheduled flights between Phillip Island and the mainland ceased in early 1995, but it is possible they may recommence in the future; call **Phillip Island Air,** tel. (03) 5956-7316, to check.

From Melbourne, there is no direct bus or train transportation to the island. From Dandenong Station, a short train trip from Melbourne, **V/Line** buses run daily to Cowes. Amaroo Caravan Park offers complimentary shuttles twice a week for their guests from Queensberry Hill Hostel in Melbourne. By boat, **Bay Connections,** tel. (03) 5678-5642, links Cowes to San Remo and Stony Point on Mornington Peninsula.

Phillip Island Information Centre, tel. (03) 5956-7447 or (1300) 36-6422, website: www. phillipisland.com, is just over the bridge from the mainland and has a great deal of information on all attractions, sights, and accommodations; open daily 9 a.m.-5 p.m.

GIPPSLAND

Gippsland, southeast of Melbourne, extends from the rugged Great Dividing Range south to the wildly beautiful coastline of Bass Strait.

The **Princes Highway,** a coastal route between Melbourne and Sydney, passes through the Latrobe Valley, Victoria's industrial and farming heartland. An alternative route east is the longer **Bass Highway,** which takes you through coastal holiday towns. Both routes lead to Wilsons Promontory, a rugged peninsula surrounded by steep cliffs, white sandy beaches, and slabs of granite that rise many hundreds of meters above sea level.

For thousands of years, waves bending around Wilsons Promontory have deposited sand along the shore of East Gippsland, forming a beach 140 km long and enclosing a vast stretch of lagoons known as Gippsland Lakes, perfect for boating and fishing. This complex lake system is breached at only one place, the holiday playground of Lakes Entrance, 314 km from Melbourne.

WEST GIPPSLAND AND THE LATROBE VALLEY

The predominantly industrial Latrobe Valley has some of the world's largest known deposits of brown coal, the fuel for the power stations that supply most of Victoria's electricity. The main route through the valley is the Princes Highway. To the north and south of the route are areas of natural bushland and many small towns dotting the hills.

Warragul, Moe, and Erica

Westernmost town in the valley is Warragul, a center of 13,000 serving the surrounding dairy farms. South of Warragul are pick-your-own farms and villages filled with antique emporiums, arts and crafts shops, and tearooms.

With a population of 17,000, Moe is the largest of the Latrobe Valley towns and serves surrounding industrial and agricultural regions. **Old Gippstown Pioneer Township,** tel. (03) 5127-3082, is Moe's main attraction. It is a re-creation of a late-1800s Gippsland town. Most buildings are original

and have been moved to the park. The staff dresses in period costume and many of the "businesses" have working displays, giving the place an air of authenticity. The park is open daily 9 a.m.-5 p.m. and admission is adult $8, child $4. It's on the Princes Highway at the western end of town. **City of Moe Jazz Festival** is held each June long weekend and is one of Australia's largest provincial gatherings of jazz musicians and admirers.

Erica is a small timber milling town 26 km north of Moe. The local hotel has memorabilia from the town's earliest beginnings, and a small museum catalogs the history of a rail line that once ran between Erica and Walhalla.

Baw Baw National Park

This 13,300-hectare park encompasses a granite plateau extending south from the Great Dividing Range, its highest peak being **Mt. St. Phillack,** at 1,566 meters. The plateau's extensive subalpine vegetation comes alive with wildflowers each spring, and the steep-sided gullies running off the main plateau support Antarctic beech and stands of mountain ash at lower elevations.

The main access to the park is from the south, along a picturesque road extending 40 km north from Moe. This road traverses only a small part of the park, but from it gravel roads lead into more remote areas. The **Alpine Walking Track,** which begins in Walhalla (see below), follows the main plateau through the heart of the park and can be hiked in sections. From Mt. Erica carpark, **Beech Gully Nature Walk** (one km roundtrip) begins, as does a trail leading to the summit of Mt. Erica (four km one-way). Campgrounds are at Eastern Tyers and Aberfeldy River; both are well signposted. On the park's western boundary is a small downhill ski resort open late June-September. During summer, a hiking trail opens to Mt. St. Phillack and a hostel, tel. (03) 5165-1129, that's open weekends; $12-15 pp. Budget.

Walhalla

With a population of just 30, Walhalla may be West Gippsland's smallest town, but it is also the most interesting. It's 46 km north of Moe, along a road that winds through rolling hills and into the foothills of the Great Dividing Range. The 1880s saw Walhalla grow to become one of Victoria's richest gold-mining towns, and **Long Tunnel Mine** the most profitable mine in the state, producing nearly one million ounces of gold. At the mine entrance is a small museum open daily during school holidays and on weekends; tours of the mine shaft are offered at 1:30 p.m. and cost $5 pp, tel. (03) 5165-6242. Along the main street are a number of restored shops surrounded by hills dotted with timber miners' cottages, an interesting cemetery beside the creek, and an old cricket ground.

A rather unusual guesthouse is the **Old Hospital,** tel. (03) 5165-6246, which is exactly that. The rooms have shared facilities and are $60 s, $90 d, which includes a hot breakfast. Moderate. Otherwise, camp along the creek.

Morwell and Vicinity

Now a service town for a power station, pulp mills, and an open-cut coal mine, Morwell was originally little more than a supply point for diggers working goldfields to the north. **Power Works,** tel. (03) 5135-3415, has displays on the local nonrenewable resource industry. It's open Mon.-Fri. 9 a.m.-5 p.m., with tours of the power station and mine offered Thurs.-Sat. 6:30 p.m. On the same road as the Visitors Centre is **Latrobe Regional Gallery,** 138 Commercial Rd., tel. (03) 5134-1364; open Tues.-Fri. 10 a.m.-5 p.m., Sunday 1:30-4:30 p.m.

At just 480 hectares, **Morwell National Park** is only a remnant of the great forests that once covered the slopes of the **Strzelecki Ranges.** The mountain gray gum and blackwood eucalypt forests are best appreciated from Fosters Gully Nature Walk, which begins from the main facility area off Jumbuk Road. The park has a picnic area with drinking water, but no camping.

Traralgon, east of Morwell, is another industrial center, and is home to the Southern Hemisphere's largest power station, Loy Yang; worth driving through to appreciate its enormity. On Franklin St., **Ryans Hotel** has been extensively refurbished and serves tasty and inexpensive bar meals daily noon-2 p.m. and 6-9 p.m.

Sale

Sale is a modern town of 14,000 at the junction of the Princes and South Gippsland Highways, at the eastern end of the Latrobe Valley. The town developed through river links to the Gippsland Lakes and is now a service center for surrounding agricultural areas and offshore oil platforms. On the Princes Hwy. is **Central Gippsland Information Centre,** tel. (03) 5144-1108, with displays explaining the workings of oil rigs; open daily 9 a.m.-5 p.m.

SOUTH GIPPSLAND

The **Bass Highway** between Phillip Island and Wilsons Promontory is a scenic, but longer, alternative to the South Gippsland Highway to the north. The road follows an inland route, but you'll find many opportunities to head to the wild coastline of Bass Strait.

To the north of the highway are the **Strzelecki Ranges** and the scenic town of **Mirboo North,** home to Gippsland's only brewery. Mirboo is also a stopping point along the **Grand Ridge Road,** a spectacular 140-km mountain drive between the South Gippsland Highway, west of Korumburra, and Tarra-Bulga National Park.

Wonthaggi

Wonthaggi's main attraction is the **State Coal Mine,** southeast of town along Billson St., tel. (03) 5672-3053. The grounds are dotted with mine buildings and a small museum, but the highlight of a visit here is an underground tour, usually led by an ex-miner. Tours are conducted daily 10 a.m.-3:30 p.m.; adult $5, child $2.50. Also look for the enormous pair of whale jawbones outside the hotel on Murray Street.

Bunurong Marine Park

The most scenic route east from Wonthaggi is along the coast. From downtown Wonthaggi head southeast, past the State Coal Mine, to **Cape Paterson.** From here the road hugs 14 km of coastline, passing a number of sandy beaches, rocky headlands, caves, and intertidal rock platforms; there are plenty of opportunities for swimming, snorkeling, and walking.

Inverloch to Wilsons Promontory

Inverloch is a small seaside town at the eastern extremity of Bunurong Marine Park. Nearby beaches are somewhat protected from the elements by Cape Paterson to the west and Cape Liptrap to the east. To cater to the holiday rush, there's a number of caravan parks and motels.

East of Inverloch, the Bass Highway follows Anderson Inlet before heading inland and across to Fish Creek and onto Wilsons Promontory. An interesting detour is to head south to **Tarwin Lower,** popular with fishers for its location on the Tarwin River. Country music fans may want to check out Tarwin Lower Hotel, tel. (03) 5663-5211, on Sunday afternoon when local and interstate country music bands perform for free.

Venus Bay, on the seaward side of Anderson Inlet, is the starting point for a three-km (one-way) trek through low banksia heathland to Point Smythe, opposite Inverloch.

The road south from Tarwin Lower passes 138-hectare **Bald Hills Wetland Reserve,** where a short trail leads to a bird hide and ends at **Cape Liptrap Lighthouse.** From this cape, you can see Wilsons Promontory. In the right swell, the reef below the lighthouse is a legendary surf break.

East of the cape is **Waratah Bay,** a large body of water with a few small communities, each with a scattering of permanent residences and holiday cottages. **Walkerville North** and **Walkerville South** are both at the end of one-way roads and have protected sandy beaches, and a walking track links the two. The community of **Sandy Point** is farther around the bay and has a pleasant caravan park.

WILSONS PROMONTORY NATIONAL PARK

"The Prom," as it's best known, is a rugged peninsula whose coastline of spectacular granite outcrops and white sandy beaches juts into Bass Strait, forming the southernmost point of mainland Australia. The entire peninsula (49,000 hectares) was declared a national park in 1905; the signs of earlier attempts at settlement have all but disappeared. The park is one of the most popular in Australia, but the masses tend to congregate at **Tidal River,** where the park information center, all accommodations, and a café are located.

The Land

Wilsons Promontory is a massif of granite, formed around 350 million years ago as molten rock from deep below the earth's crust was pushed upward and, as it cooled, folded and wrinkled into the mountains and valleys that exist today. At that time, the promontory was part of a chain of mountains linking Tasmania to the mainland. Near the end of the last ice age, around 12,000 years ago, the link was severed, and what is now Wilsons Promontory became an island, similar in makeup to the rocky islands of Bass Strait. Over time, drifting sand filled the gap between the rocky outcrop and mainland, forming a low and narrow isthmus between the two. When the molten mass of rock originally cooled, it did so slowly, forming crystals such as garnets, rubies, and sapphires. Iron is also present; the iron-stained granite boulders that line Tidal River, in particular, are a photographer's delight.

Flora and Fauna

More than 700 species of plants have been recorded on the peninsula, many otherwise found only in Tasmania. Higher elevations are dominated by forests of eucalypt, with the protected, east-facing slopes interspersed with temperate rainforests and the more exposed slopes supporting only stunted eucalypt and banksia. Corner Inlet, in the north of the park, has the world's southernmost mangrove swamp.

Tidal River is well known for its population of rosellas, which seem to know just who has food scraps for the taking, foraging the grounds in front of the café and posing on visitors' shoulders for photographs. Possums and wallabies have also become tame around the campground area, while bandicoots, quolls, koalas, echidnas, and platypuses are sighted in more remote areas of the park.

Hiking

Many short trails lead from the park's main road to beautiful sandy beaches on the west coast. From the campground, a footbridge over Tidal River accesses easy trails to the north, including **Pillar Point** (1.6 km one-way), from where there are excellent coastal views, and **Squeaky Beach** (two km one-way). At the north end of Squeaky Beach, a trail continues through low heathland vegetation to Picnic and Whisky Bays.

About four km north of Tidal River, along the main road, is the trailhead for **Lilly Pilly Gully**

Nature Walk (five km roundtrip), which traverses heathland vegetation before suddenly descending into a temperate rainforest. From the cleared area above the rainforest, the trail climbs steeply, and a short spur leads to Mt. Bishop (319 meters), although returning along the original trail from the rainforest is much easier.

Of the few overnight hikes, the one to **South East Point** will bring the most satisfaction, as it is the southernmost point of land on mainland Australia. Along the most direct route, from the Mt. Oberon carpark, the point is 18.4 km one-way, but worthwhile options for the return trip are possible via Oberon or Waterloo Bays, where the white sand and deeply forested backdrop create a beautiful landscape.

Options for hiking in the north section of the park are less varied, but crowds are thinner. From the carpark at the end of Five Mile Rd., 21 km from Tidal River, a two-km track leads through groves of banksias to Millers Landing on Corner Inlet. Other trails from this carpark require an overnight stay at one of the many backcountry campgrounds.

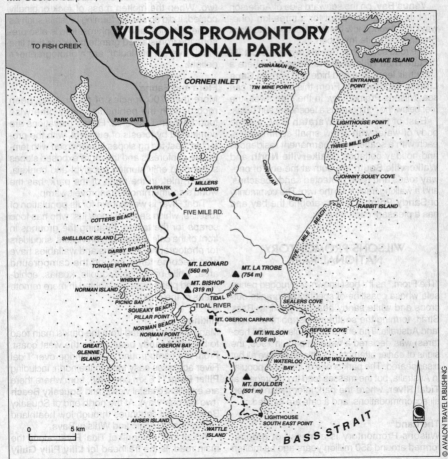

© AVALON TRAVEL PUBLISHING

These impressive boulders, beside Tidal River, mark the beginning of trails leading to some beautiful beaches.

Practicalities

All services are located at **Tidal River**, 30 km from the park gate (where national park staff issue park-use tickets; $7 per car). The large campground at Tidal River is excellent. Sites are well spaced, allowing a certain amount of privacy, especially on the Norman Beach side of the campground, and hot showers are available. All sites are $14.50 per night. Scattered throughout the Tidal River area are a number of different sized huts and cabins. Motor huts sleep two to six and have basic cooking facilities, but bathroom facilities are shared with campers; $60 s or d. The flats are larger and self-contained, with summer rates ranging $75-105. Minimum bookings are required in summer but not the rest of the year, when rates are also reduced. The Lighthouse Cottage provides accommodation for backpackers at $32 pp. Budget-Moderate. With 400,000 visitors a year, demand is high for all park ac-

commodations; chances of getting a hut or cabin without advance reservations are slim, but a number of campsites are reserved each day for out-of-state and overseas visitors. For all bookings call (03) 5680-9555 or (1800) 35-0552.

At the campground entrance is a café and grocery store with petrol. Also here is the **Park Information Centre,** tel. (03) 5680-9555. The excellent displays give an insight into the park's natural and human history, and the staff issue permits for camping at Tidal River and in the backcountry; open in summer Sun.-Thurs. 8 a.m.-9 p.m., Fri.-Sat. 8 a.m.-10 p.m., and the rest of the year 8:30 a.m.-4:30 p.m. Behind the store is a small cinema; tickets are $8.50.

TARRA TERRITORY

Foster and Vicinity

Foster, on the South Gippsland Highway, was established in the 1860s after gold was found in the surrounding hills. Today, this sleepy rural community of 1,000 is a major gateway to Wilsons Promontory and a pleasant stop for those traveling the Gippsland Highway. **Foster Museum,** open each Sunday and daily during school holidays 11 a.m.-4 p.m., is in an old post office and boasts a collection of relics from the gold-mining era. Across the road is Stockyard Creek and a shady park with barbecues.

Stockyard Creek Cottages, McGlead's Rd., tel. (03) 5682-2493, two km west of Foster, comprises two large, self-contained cottages on a small, self-sufficient farm. Each features two bedrooms, kitchen, laundry, log fire, and a veranda overlooking a lush valley, all from only $65 each per night. Moderate.

North of Wilsons Promontory and the South Gippsland Highway are the Strzelecki Ranges, rounded hills covered in a canopy of cool temperate rainforest. **Grand Ridge Road** traverses the ridge of the range, beginning between Warragul and Korumburra and ending east of Tarra-Bulga National Park, north of Yarram. For most of the way, this spectacular road is unsealed. It's well signposted.

Tarra-Bulga National Park

Beautiful Tarra-Bulga National Park is only 1,520 hectares, but within its boundaries are deep, fern-filled gorges, many stands of towering mountain ash, and a healthy population of lyrebirds. Two-km **Fern Gully Nature Walk** begins from the Park Information Centre, open Sat.-Sun. 10 a.m.-4 p.m., tel. (03) 5196-6166, in the north of the park, just off Grand Ridge Rd., and crosses a high suspension bridge. The park has no campgrounds.

Port Albert

As miners flooded the goldfields of Omeo and Walhalla it was through Port Albert that they arrived. Many buildings from this era remain, including **Port Albert Hotel,** which has held its liquor license for more than 150 years. The narrow spit of land on which the town sits is surrounded by protected waters, perfect for exploring in one of the boats for rent on the waterfront. In the maze of sandy-bottomed channels, fishing for snapper (Oct.-May), whiting, and flathead is excellent. On the road into town, west of the roundabout, is two-km **Old Port Trail,** which follows the shoreline, passing foundations of the town's bygone buildings.

Seabank Caravan Park, tel. (03) 5183-2315, is four km north of the town. Budget. In town, is **Port Albert Hotel,** tel. (03) 5183-2212, where motel-style units are $65 s or d (moderate), and meals at the bistro average $10.

GIPPSLAND LAKES

Gippsland Lakes is one of Australia's largest inland waterways. The three main lakes—King, Victoria, and Wellington—are fed by a number of High Country watersheds and drain into the ocean at the same place, Lakes Entrance.

Until 12,000 years ago, the entire area was a vast bay, then, as the sea level rose at the end of the last ice age, the land link between mainland Australia and Tasmania was broken. Prevailing wind and swell from the Southern Ocean deposited millions of tons of sediment east of Wilsons Promontory, forming a long ridge of sand and, eventually, enclosing the bay. Ninety Mile Beach separates these shallow lakes from the ocean and extends from the protected inlets north of Wilsons Promontory to Lakes Entrance. The lakes are undeveloped, although small fishing villages dot the shore of Lake King.

Ninety Mile Beach

This endless stretch of white sandy beach and scrub-covered sand dunes backed by shallow lakes is part of **Gippsland Lakes Coastal Park.** A 30-km stretch of road between **Seaspray** and **Golden Beach** provides the easiest access to the beach, ocean, and innumerable camping and beach-walking opportunities. The main access to the area is from Longford, south of Sale on the South Gippsland Highway. The small townships of Seaspray and Loch Sport have caravan parks and general stores.

The Lakes National Park

This 2,380-hectare park protects Sperm Bay Head Peninsula, a low-lying area of coastal heath, separated from Ninety Mile Beach by a shallow channel. To get there, take the access road from Golden Beach.

Since 1890, when a channel was dredged through Ninety Mile Beach to the ocean, the increased salinity of the water has killed vegetation along the lakeshore, but, inland, are well-preserved examples of coastal vegetation, and the area has a large wildlife population, including eastern gray kangaroos (look for them around the picnic area at Point Wilson), swamp wallabies, wombats, possums, sugar gliders, and echidnas.

Short walks begin and end at Point Wilson, including the Dolomite Walking Track, which passes through a dense forest of melaleucas to Pelican Point.

Rotamah Island, between Sperm Whale Head Peninsula and Ninety Mile Beach, is also part of the park. The Royal Australasian Ornithologists Union operates an observatory on the island. A converted old farmhouse has basic dorms and double rooms, with a kitchen, lounge, and library. Birdwatching is the island's main drawcard, but wildlife viewing, beachcombing, fishing, and hiking bring people out, too. The daily rate is $70 pp, which includes three meals. For further information, call Rotamah Island Bird Observatory, tel. (03) 5156-6398.

The national park's only other facilities for visitors are primitive campsites at Emu Bight (Loch Sport has the closest commercial campground) and a park information center at the park's entrance, tel. (03) 5146-0278; open Mon.-Fri. 8 a.m.-4 p.m.

Bairnsdale

Bairnsdale is a major agricultural service center of 11,000 located on the Mitchell River. A museum on MacArthur St., an interesting church beside McDonalds, and a boardwalk across a wetland reserve, just beyond the museum, are about the only sights in town, but Bairnsdale's location on the Princes Highway makes it an ideal spot to spend the night.

The **Commercial Hotel,** on Main St., tel. (03) 5152-3031, has basic rooms for only $18 pp, including breakfast. Inexpensive. **Bairnsdale Backpackers Hostel,** 119 Macleod St., tel. (03) 5152-5097, is one block from Main St. and a short walk from the railway station; beds are $15 pp. Budget. At the other end of the scale is **Riversleigh Country Hotel,** 1 Nicholson St., tel. (03) 5152-6966, a restored Victorian-era hotel with rooms for $78 s, $88 d. Moderate. This hotel also has a fine restaurant with main dishes beginning at $18.

Between McDonalds and St. Mary's Church, at 240 Main St., is an **information center,** tel. (03) 5152-3444; open daily 9 a.m.-5 p.m.

Mitchell River National Park

Located 42 km northwest of Bairnsdale, this 11,900-hectare park features spectacular Mitchell River Gorge and **Den of Nargun,** a small cave that Koori believed was home to a half-stone creature that dragged people to their deaths. Within the park are two distinct vegetation zones—the river gullies, home to warm-temperate rainforest, and the higher elevations, where vegetation is sparse. The gorge is popular with whitewater-rafting enthusiasts, and hiking and camping is also possible. For park information call (03) 5152-6277.

Paynesville

South of Bairnsdale, on the bank of a channel that links Lake King and Lake Victoria, is this small community of 1,800, with a commercial fishing fleet, holiday cottages, and a car and passenger ferry that plies the 200-meter-wide channel to **Raymond Island,** an isolated spot with a number of short walks.

North of Paynesville the silt-laden Mitchell River flows into Lake King. Over hundreds of years, the river's silt has been banked up at its mouth, forming twin fingers of land that protrude

more than nine km into Lake King. A gravel road extends along the southern finger all the way to the end, to a popular fishing spot.

LAKES ENTRANCE AND VICINITY

For 20 years people struggled to cut a permanent entrance to the ocean from the Gippsland Lakes, but it took a wild storm on 14 June 1889 to make the final break. When the area was first settled, a natural opening occurred east of the present entrance, but it was often unnavigable. Even today, the opening has to be continually dredged to make the often-rough crossing safe. Once fishers and coastal shipping had a permanent entrance, a community quickly grew. Today Lakes Entrance (pop. 5,500) has grown into a bustling holiday center on a spit of land between the Mitchell River's Cunningham and North Arms.

Sights and Recreation

Being one of Victoria's main holiday playgrounds, Lakes Entrance has a ton of tourist-oriented attractions, most of which are spread along the Esplanade.

For views of the lakes, town, and ocean, head to **Jemmy's Point Lookout,** at the west end of town over North Arm bridge. A footbridge opposite the end of Myer St. crosses Cunningham Arm, connecting the town to scrub-covered dunes and Ninety Mile Beach. From the bridge the lakes' entrance, for which the town is named, is 2.3 km (one-way) away.

The best way to explore the lake system is on a cruise operated by **Peels Tourist & Ferry Service,** based on Post Office Jetty, tel. (03) 5155-1246. Cruise timetables vary with the season. *Thunderbird* is their largest boat and is most popular for the longer cruises around Lake Victoria ($18-22). *Bluebird* does shorter trips to Metung ($15) and a lake fishing trip ($18). *Stormbird* does a luncheon cruise, allowing two hours at the small tourist town of Metung ($27.50, includes lunch). **Victor Hireboats,** based on Marine Parade, tel. (03) 5155-1888, has motor boats to rent from $18 per hour.

Boasting a collection of 90,000 shells, the **Sea Shell Museum,** 125 the Esplanade, tel. (03) 5155-1538, claims to be the largest of its

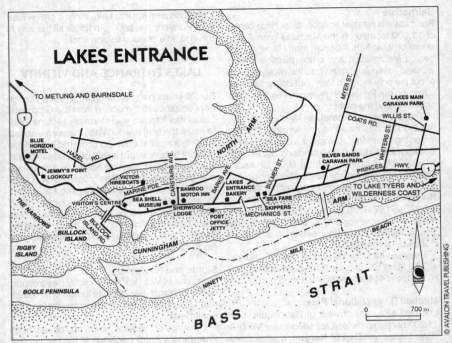

LAKES ENTRANCE

TO METUNG AND BAIRNSDALE

BLUE HORIZON MOTEL

JEMMY'S POINT LOOKOUT

THE NARROWS

BULLOCK ISLAND

RIGBY ISLAND

BOOLE PENINSULA

HAZEL RD.

VICTOR HIREBOATS

MARINE PDE.

VISITOR'S CENTRE

SEA SHELL MUSEUM

BULLOCK ISLAND RD.

CARSTAIRS AVE.

BARKS AVE.

BAMBOO MOTOR INN

SHERWOOD LODGE

POST OFFICE JETTY

LAKES ENTRANCE BAKERY

SKIPPERS

MECHANICS ST.

SEA FARE

BULMER ST.

CUNNINGHAM

NINETY

MILE

NORTH ARM

SOUTH ARM

MYER ST.

COATS RD.

WILLIS ST.

WHITERS ST.

PRINCES HWY.

LAKES MAIN CARAVAN PARK

SILVER SANDS CARAVAN PARK

TO LAKE TYERS AND WILDERNESS COAST

BEACH

BASS STRAIT

0   700 m

© AVALON TRAVEL PUBLISHING

type in Australia. Open in summer daily 9 a.m.-noon and 2-5 p.m.

Accommodations

There's certainly no lack of accommodations here, but finding a vacant room in January will pose a problem. **Blue Horizon Motel,** Princes Hwy., tel. (03) 5155-1216, has large modern rooms from $45 s, $55 d, but it's three km from the center of town. Inexpensive. More central, and more expensive, are **Sherwood Lodge,** 151 Esplanade, tel. (03) 5155-1444, with smart rooms, a pool, and laundry for $79 s or d, and **Bamboo Motor Inn,** 167 Esplanade, tel. (03) 5155-1551, for $85 s, $90 d. Both are moderately priced. In Metung, on Metung Rd., is **Terrazas del Lago,** tel. (03) 5156-2666, a series of two- to five-bedroom villas overlooking Bancroft Bay, with two heated pools and a spa. Each villa is totally self-contained and has a balcony with outdoor furniture and a barbecue. Rates start at $85 d. Moderate.

Affiliated with the YHA, **Riviera Backpackers** lies on Clarkes Rd. at the eastern end of town, tel. (03) 5155-2444. This accommodation features a swimming pool, modern facilities, and free linen, making it a good value at just $15 pp. Budget.

Of the 20 caravan parks in town, **Silver Sands Caravan Park,** 33 Myer St., tel. (03) 5155-2343, is most central and has the highest standard of facilities but also has crowded sites. Sites are $15-22, on-site vans start at $28, and cabins at $40. Budget. **Lakes Main Caravan Park,** 7 Willis St., tel. (03) 5155-2365, is similarly priced.

Food

Along the Esplanade is a profusion of pizzerias, fish and chips joints, and takeaways, but one place you shouldn't miss is **Lakes Entrance Bakery,** the best bakery in Victoria. Regular salad and meat rolls are huge ($4), but the foccacia bread topped with chicken, mango chutney, and delicious salad ($5.80) is better. Meat pies are also delicious and start at $2, but it's worth investing an extra 50 cents in the chunky beef. The best way to finish is with a splendid cream bun (real cream) and a cappuccino. Tables are inside or out, and it's open daily 7:30 a.m.-5 p.m. A little farther along the Esplanade is **Sea Fare,** a gourmet fish and chips shop with a large, brightly colored blackboard that makes decisions easier; expect to pay $4.50 for fish of the day and chips. Also serving fish, but at the expensive end of the scale, is **Skippers,** 481 Esplanade, tel. (03) 5155-3551, where main seafood dishes start at $16; open daily from 6 p.m. and for lunch during school holidays.

Fresh prawns are often sold directly from boats moored in the inlet (from $24 per kg), and a wide variety of seafood is sold at the co-op on Bullock Island.

Transportation, Services, and Information

Buses run daily between Lakes Entrance and Bairnsdale, where **V/Line** trains run to Melbourne. During school holidays and four days a week the rest of the year, buses continue east along the Princes Highway to Mallacoota and New South Wales.

Lakes Entrance Tourist Information Centre has a ton of information on the area and can book many of the accommodations and cruises. Its location, on the corner of the Princes Hwy. and Marine Parade, makes it a short walk from downtown, tel. (03) 5155-1966; open daily 9 a.m.-5 p.m.

Lake Tyers

Lake Tyers, 12 km east of Lakes Entrance, is a series of flooded valleys that extend far inland, unlike the lagoons to the west. The township is behind scrub-covered sand dunes, and access to the lake is nearby. The beaches at **Red Bluff** are popular with surfers, and fishing in the lake is excellent. The small settlement has three caravan parks, a couple of stores, and summer cruises on the lake.

WILDERNESS COAST

Traveling east from Lakes Entrance, the scenery changes dramatically. Gone are the farms and holiday townships of Gippsland; this is the remote corner of the state, a region never cleared for agriculture (although logging now plays an important role in the local economy), with vast tracts of forest and coastline preserved as national parks (here you'll find three of Victoria's least-visited national parks). The two most interesting coastal areas to explore are Cape Conran and Croajingolong National Park, both spectacular landscapes of beaches, inlets, rocky headlands, and some of the world's highest sand dunes.

LAKES ENTRANCE TO CANN RIVER

Orbost

Orbost is on the banks of the Snowy River, 50 km east of Lakes Entrance. It is mainly a service center for the local logging industry, but the excellent **Rainforest Centre,** 6 Browning St., tel. (03) 5161-1375, operated by Parks Victo-

ria, is definitely worth stopping for. The best-known rainforests are those in tropical and subtropical environments, but a large proportion of Australia's remaining rainforest is temperate, and is in Victoria. Three types of temperate rainforest—warm, cool, and dry—all thrive in the far east of the state. The center was developed to enhance understanding of these forests; this is done through displays, an audiovisual, and landscaped gardens established in an old quarry out back. The center also has information on Wilderness Coast national parks and is open weekdays 9 a.m.-5 p.m.

Across the road from the center is **Netherbyre Art and Gemstone Gallery,** tel. (03) 5154-2064. The operators are keen geologists who spend the winter months fossicking in various parts of Australia to add to their already impressive collection.

On the corner of Nicholson and Clarke Streets is **Slab Hut Information Centre,** tel. (03) 5154-2424. The structure was built in 1872 by an early settler on the Snowy River and moved to its present site 10 years ago.

Marlo

Watching the small fishing boats cruising around the quiet waters in front of Marlo, 15 km southeast of Orbost, it's hard to believe that 140 km upstream this body of water is a raging, ice-fed torrent whose main source is Mt. Kosciuszko, Australia's highest mountain. The river flows into a shallow lagoon, separated from the ocean by sand dunes, and breaks though at one place, a channel that is constantly moving. The Snowy Mountains Scheme, which channels the river into hydroelectric stations and then inland to the Murrumbidgee Irrigation Area, takes more than two trillion liters of water from the river annually, but this works in Marlo's favor—the low-lying areas around the river mouth are less prone to flooding and, as water flow is regulated, drought is also. The town's population is only slightly higher than 300, but that seems to be enough for a cinema and two caravan parks. Fishing in the river estuary is great, especially from the jetty. **French Narrows,** east of Marlo, has a large population of birdlife and a small footbridge providing access to ocean beaches.

Across the Snowy River from Marlo is **Corringle Slips Campground,** accessible from Newmerella, four km west of Orbost. The campground is spread out along the estuary, but getting to the ocean is easy. Facilities include pit toilets, barbecues, and a limited supply of drinking water (best to bring your own); $7.50 per night.

Cape Conran

From Marlo, the road continues east to Cape Conran, skirting a wide open beach with plenty of access points for swimming, surfing, and surf fishing. The cape is totally undeveloped, a delightful place to experience the remote coastal environment.

Cape Conran Nature Trail begins from the end of Cape Conran Rd. and traverses coastal vegetation of tree palms and banksias to **Joiners Channel** (2.5 km one-way). From the channel, it's an easy half-hour scramble around rocks to the cape itself. If you don't feel that energetic, West Cape Rd. leads to a point just before the cape. Some longer walks, including a 1.6-km track to Yeerung River Estuary, start on Yeerung Road. **Pearl Point** is 13 km past the river (allow eight hours roundtrip) and can be reached along the beach or an inland service road. A shorter

hiking option would be to **Dock Inlet,** seven km (one-way) from the Yeerung River, a landlocked lagoon of tannin-colored fresh water supporting a wide variety of waterfowl.

Banksia Bluff Camping Park, on Yeerung Rd., has more than 100 sites, each semiprivate and with easy access to East Cape Beach. Facilities include pit toilets, bush showers, and a few barbecues (bring drinking water). Sites are $7-15 depending on the season. Farther along Yeerung Rd. is a collection of cabins made from local timbers. Each self-contained cabin sleeps four to six in basic bunk accommodations. Rates vary with the season but are generally $50-65 per night. To book campsites or cabins call (03) 5154-8438. Budget-Inexpensive.

Lind National Park

This 1,365-hectare park between Orbost and Cann River protects one of Australia's few areas of warm-temperate rainforest and is home to a variety of interesting fauna, including wombats, possums, dingos, and lyrebirds. The park, for the most part, is undeveloped. Euchre Valley Nature Drive, part of the old Princes Highway, passes through the heart of the park and has a picnic area at Growlers Creek (listen for lyrebirds along the track that begins here).

Cann River and Vicinity

This small highway town at the junction of the Princes and Cann Valley Highways has a pub, petrol station, grocery store, and café—everything you'll need before heading into surrounding national parks. On the main road through town is a **Department of Environment and Natural Resources** office, tel. (03) 5158-6251, with tons of useful information on all Wilderness Coast parks and current road conditions posted out the front; open daily in summer 10 a.m.-4 p.m., the rest of the year Mon.-Fri. 10 a.m.-3 p.m.

Mountainous **Alfred National Park** is 20 km east of Cann River. The park protects areas of warm-temperate and subtropical rainforests but has no facilities or trails.

CROAJINGOLONG NATIONAL PARK

Beautiful unspoiled beaches, remnants of ancient forests, some of the world's highest sand

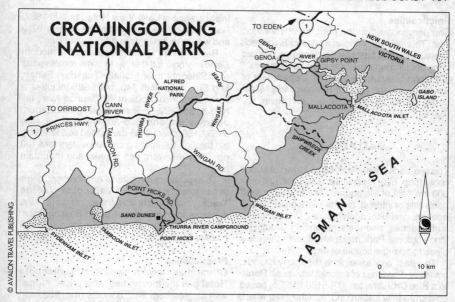

CROAJINGOLONG NATIONAL PARK

dunes, and Mallacoota Inlet make this 87,500-hectare park along a 100-km stretch of coastline one of Victoria's undiscovered jewels. The park's deeply indented coastline is a legacy of ancient river courses that changed with the onset of the ice age. Because of its undisturbed rivers, lakes, and inlets; the many rare plants species and endangered fauna; the varied vegetation, ranging from coastal heathland to rainforests; and its sand dunes, UNESCO designated the park a Biosphere Reserve in 1983. For further protection, as human encroachment continues, two adjacent chunks of land have been declared wilderness areas.

Birdlife throughout the park is prolific; more than 250 species have been recorded, including raucous black cockatoos, the rare ground parrot, colorful lyrebirds, and eagles and hawks. Of all the fauna, none is as unusual as the prehistoric-looking **lace monitor,** a member of the goanna family, which grows to lengths exceeding two meters.

Sights and Hikes

The conditions of access roads into the park vary greatly, from excellent to unpassable—the Department of Environment and Natural Re-

sources office in Cann River keeps updated bulletins on conditions (see above). From Cann River, Tamboon Rd., which becomes Pat Hicks Rd., leads to the mouth of the **Thurra River** and along the foreshore to **Point Hicks,** the first point of mainland Australia sighted by Captain Cook's 1770 expedition.

The park's sand dunes are the highest this side of Namibia, Africa. Two distinct types of dune occur—"relic" (well-vegetated and stable) and "mobile" (constantly moving and changing shape). From Thurra River Campground, a two-km trail leads through coastal banksia heathland to the dunes. To experience the most spectacular of the mobile dunes, hang a right where the trail first enters the dunes, traverse along a low ridge, and the panorama of dunes soon becomes apparent below.

Other access roads from the Princes Highway lead to **Sydenham Inlet** and **Wingan Inlet,** where there's a 30-minute self-guided nature walk. For experienced hikers, a coastal track leads 63 km from the township of Mallacoota to the Thurra River. The park also encompasses much of Mallacoota Inlet, considered one of Victoria's premier fishing grounds (see below).

Practicalities

Campgrounds within the park are at Tamboon Inlet, Thurra River, Wingan Inlet, and Shipwreck Creek; each has basic facilities, and you should bring drinking water. All sites are $8. Further information is available from the Department of Environment and Natural Resources in Mallacoota, tel. (03) 5158-0219, or Cann River, tel. (03) 5158-6351.

MALLACOOTA

The laid-back holiday and fishing town of Mallacoota (pop. 800) is on Mallacoota Inlet, just over 500 km east of Melbourne. The township itself holds little of interest, but the inlet's great fishing, boating, and birdwatching, its easy access to surf beaches, and the surrounding Croajingolong National Park make Mallacoota the ideal place to spend a couple of days.

The best way to explore the many islands, coves, and beaches of the inlet is by boat. **Rankin's Hire Cruisers,** tel. (03) 5158-0555, is based on a small jetty just around from the main wharf. A full-day hire is $50, plus $50 bond; this allows enough time to reach an eastern arm of the inlet, where an early settlement was located. Also on this side of the inlet, the **Spotted Dog Gold Mine** operated for 25 years, and although not much is left, the Department of Environment and Natural Resources has set up a self-guided interpretive walk around the site. Farther around

the shoreline is **Lake View Hotel,** built in 1882. Poet Henry Lawson stayed at the hotel in 1910 and was inspired to write "Mallacoota Bar."

Rankin's Hire Cruisers operates the modern *Discovery* on a full-day trip to some remote parts of Mallacoota Inlet (usually Tuesday, Friday, and Sunday); adult $40, child $28 includes a barbecue lunch. Book at 43 Maurice Ave., tel. (03) 5158-0555. For the more adventurous, **Journey Beyond Eco-adventures,** tel. (03) 5158-0166, offers a full-day guided sea-kayaking trip through the inlet's protected waters for $100 pp. They also rent sea kayaks and mountain bikes.

To experience the coastal environment, allow two to three hours for the **Mallacoota Walking Track,** which begins from the roundabout in the center of town and heads out to Bastion Point, along the beach, and back to town through coastal heathland.

Practicalities

Of the many accommodations, **Mallacoota Hotel** has the most reasonably priced rooms, with singles from $45, doubles from $55, and dorms for $16 pp. Budget-Inexpensive. **Adobe Mudbrick Flats,** 17 Karbeethong Hill Ave., tel. (03) 5158-0329, consisting of a collection of mud-brick one- and two-bedroom cottages scattered through a pleasant bush setting, is also home to a wide variety of animals. Summer rates start at $60 per night, but the rest of the year from $40. Inexpensive.

lace monitor

Mallacoota Hotel serves moderately priced meals noon-2 p.m. and 6-9 p.m. The other option is **Watt's Cooking at the Tide** on Maurice Ave., tel. (03) 5158-0100.

Note: What this place needs is a decent information center. The two places on the main street that have Information Centre signs out front seem more interested in selling real estate and boat trips; you may have more luck at the Department of Environment and Natural Resources office on the corner of Buckland St. and Allan Dr.; open weekdays 10:30 a.m.-3:30 p.m., tel. (03) 5158-0219.

THREE REMOTE NATIONAL PARKS

Snowy River National Park

Straddling the Snowy River, this 95,300-hectare park is a remote wilderness encompassing deep gorges, vast eucalypt forests, and spectacular waterfalls. The vegetation varies, with cool-temperate rainforests, stands of gray gum, alpine ash, native pine, and mallee scrub. Whitewater-rafting enthusiasts are drawn to the park for the challenge of tackling the Snowy River, especially the section between Mackillop's Bridge and a point to the east of Buchan. The four-day float is really an experts-only trip, but **Peregrine**, tel. (03) 9662-2700, and **World Expeditions**, tel. (03) 9670-8400, offer guided trips down the river for all levels of expertise.

Access to the park is along two main roads, both originating from Orbost; one passes through Buchan, the other is the Bonang Highway, to the east. Along the park's northern border, these roads are linked by **Mackillop's Rd.,** along which the park's limited camping and picnic facilities are located. At **Mackillop's Bridge,** a 250-meter span over Deddick River, are sandy beaches with good swimming, **Snowy River Nature Track,** which traverses a dry forest and flood plain, and a campground. West of the bridge is **Little River Gorge** and a lookout. For park information call (03) 5161-1375.

Errinundra National Park

This 25,400-hectare park encompasses Errinundra Plateau and protects Victoria's largest cool-temperate rainforest, a verdant place with trees up to 400 years old. Other parts of the park feature wet eucalypt forests of shining gum, which protects an understory for rainforest, creating an ideal habitat for a diverse variety of birds and mammals. Easiest access to the park is from 58 km east of Orbost at Lind National Park, but access is also possible from the Bonang Highway north of Orbost. The only official campground is at Frosty Hollow. For park information call (03) 5161-1375.

Coopracambra National Park

A rugged landscape, lack of facilities, and remote location make this 38,800-hectare park one of the state's least visited. It is located on the NSW border, east of the Cann Valley Highway. The park's most distinct feature is a spectacular sandstone gorge carved by the Genoa River. This is accessible along the only road that passes through the center of the park. The other dominant geological features are the granite peaks of **Mt. Kaye, Mt. Denmarsh,** and **Mt. Coopracambra,** all visible from the Cann Valley Highway. **Beehive Creek,** two km east of the highway, is a pleasant spot where water cascades into deep pools. The park has no official campgrounds; the closest accommodations are in Cann River or Genoa. For park information call (03) 5158-6351.

WESTERN AUSTRALIA

Western Australia, known for its rising pinnacles and deep cuts that come in all shapes and sizes; the fabulous sea with its ebb and flow of wave upon endless wave; and a riot of amazing wildflowers, blanketing the ground with their vibrant blooms. Fact is, W.A. (as the Aussies call it) can cause some downright fits of wanderlust.

THE LAND

Western Australia is not merely big, it is humongous. Its 2.5 million square km, taking up about one-third of the Australian continent and boasting an area more than triple the size of little ol' Texas, comprise the harsh, desolate expanses of the Great Sandy, Gibson, and Great Victoria Deserts, sandwiched like dry toast between the Kimberley Plateau and the Nullarbor Plain. Yet within all this space dwell a mere 1.7 million inhabitants (approximately 10% of the country's total population), most of them in or around Perth, the relaxed and youthful state capital, or along the southwest coastal sections.

Western Australia is divided into eight regions: the **south coast,** famed for its wineries, beach resorts, and surfer and sailor havens; the **southwest** (or Great Southern), boasting more swimming, surfing, and wave-pounded coastlines, as well as forests, wildflowers, coves, and capes; the **wheatlands,** notable not only for the obvious grain and wheat fields, but for its unusual rock formations; the **goldfields,** with its street of "sin" and "pound their chest" miners; the **midwest,** with more wildflowers, coastal hideaways, and the port city of Geraldton; the **Gascoyne,** with sights ranging from tame dolphins at Monkey Mia to relatively unknown Mount Augustus, the world's largest monocline; the **Pilbara,** famed for rich iron ore mines, stunning landscapes, fishing villages, and big-ship Port Hedland; and the remote **Kimberley,** a rugged land of cattle stations, eye-popping gorges, Wolfe Creek meteorite crater, the beehive-ish Bungle Bungle Ranges, and the old pearling port of Broome with its mini-Chinatown and maxi-dinosaur footprints.

It probably goes without saying that distances between Western Australia's sights and cities are vast and not always easily accessible, so plan your itinerary and your timetable carefully. However, it is this very remoteness and the consequent self-reliance of which Western Australians—particularly the residents of Perth—are so proud. Chances are, unless you are a surfer or a sailor, you didn't even know Western Australia existed until the Americans won back the America's Cup at Fremantle in 1987. The U.S. recaptured the cup, but W.A. managed to keep luring visitors not just to the site of the "victory" in Fremantle but also up the coast, down the coast, into the interior, and especially to the Kimberley, where adventurous and pioneering spirits can explore deserts, fertile plains, beehive mounds, and lots of gorges and chasms.

Wildflowers

An astounding 8,000 species of wildflowers burst from Western Australia's soil, many of them in and around Perth, from Kalbarri on the midwest coast to Albany in the southwest, and interspersed throughout the wheatlands. The "season" runs from early August into early November, following the rainy months of May, June, and July. Some of the more extraordinary flora include 150 types of ground orchids (including a fully underground orchid), the largest known mistletoe, grass trees ("blackboys"), several black-flower plants, trigger plants that have neuromuscular-type reflexes, and 80 different types of carnivorous plants.

CLIMATE

Perth reputedly has the best climate of any Australian city—"best" meaning sunny with mild temperatures and low humidity. Summer months (Dec.-Feb.) range from a low 17° C (63° F) to a high of 29° C (84° F). Winter (June-Aug.) sees lows of 9° C (48° F), highs of 18° C (65° F), and about 16.6 cm of rainfall per month.

The northern part of the state is similar in climate to the Northern Territory's Top End, experiencing both wet and dry seasons as well as intense heat and humidity. You will be more comfortable traveling this region in the winter months; besides, many areas are closed during the Wet due to impassable roads and other weather-provoked conditions. Winter is also the best time to traverse the state's desert areas.

Though nights can be freezing, it still beats the summertime average of 40° C (104° F).

Make sure when you're on those roads less traveled that you check with local police or the Automobile Association for the latest road and weather conditions, and that you and your vehicle are prepared for breakdowns and other emergencies. There will *not* be a McDonald's around the next bend.

HISTORY

In 1616 Dutchman Dirk Hartog and his fellow sailors rowed ashore from their vessel the *Eendracht,* making them the first acknowledged Europeans to land on Western Australia's coast. Between then and 1699 so many Dutchmen, traveling around South Africa on their way to Indonesia, sighted or alighted upon the shores that the region was dubbed "New Holland."

Buccaneer William Dampier landed near Broome in 1688, then again in 1699, but his findings went ignored by the British, who were none too impressed with his description of the area. Though Sydney was settled in 1788, the British showed little interest in extending their boundaries for another 38 years, when two important events took place: Matthew Flinders sailing 'round Australia in 1801 concluded that the east coast and New Holland were one and the same continent; and Britain got wind that the French, who'd been stirring about the local waters, might be planning to colonize. The usual barrage of dispatches, reports, and proposals were bandied about until, in 1826, Major Edmund Lockyer arrived from Sydney with a band of convicts and soldiers to settle a small penal colony at King George Sound (now Albany).

Shortly afterward, Captain James Stirling was dispatched by the governor of New South Wales to check out the Swan River region, already partially surveyed by the French, leading to the settlement of both Perth and Fremantle in 1829.

The new settlers soon became discouraged. The sandy soil rendered farming terrible and many of the newcomers scurried back to the east coast. Eventually the remaining colonists discovered fertile land at Guildford, between the Swan and Helena Rivers, and began planting crops and raising livestock. Aside from devastat-

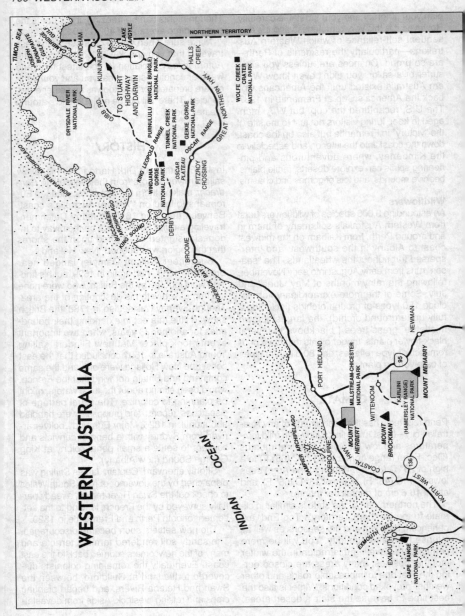

SOUTH AUSTRALIA

TO ADELAIDE

DOCKER RIVER
SETTLEMENT

TO
AYERS
ROCK AND
ALICE
SPRINGS

WARBURTON
COMMUNITY

NULLARBOR

EUCLA

COCKLEBIDDY

EYRE HWY.

GREAT AUSTRALIAN BIGHT

PLAIN

200 km

SOUTHERN OCEAN

CAPE ARID NATIONAL PARK

CAPE LE GRAND NATIONAL PARK

ESPERANCE

ARCHIPELAGO OF THE RECHERCHE

COAST HWY.

SOUTH

BREMER BAY

STIRLING RANGE NATIONAL PARK

PORONGURUP NATIONAL PARK

MOUNT BARKER

CRANBROOK

ALBANY

KING GEORGE SOUND

DENMARK

WALPOLE

TORBAY BAY

POINT D'ENTRECASTEAUX

KALGOORLIE

LAKE LEFROY

LAKE COWAN

NORSEMAN

COOLGARDIE

94

SOUTHERN CROSS

EASTERN HWY.

HYDEN

MERREDIN

GREAT SOUTHERN HWY.

94

NARROGIN

SOUTH WESTERN HWY.

ARTHUR R.

COLLIE R.

BRIDGETOWN

MANJIMUP

NANNUP

LEONORA

WILUNA

WARBURTON COMMUNITY RD.

MEEKATHARRA

GREAT NORTHERN HWY.

MOUNT MAGNET

95

TOODYAY

NORTHAM

YORK

PERTH

MIDLAND

FREMANTLE

GARDEN I.

ROTTNEST I.

30

YALGORUP NATIONAL PARK

BUNBURY

BUSSELTON

GEOGRAPHE BAY

MARGARET RIVER

BLACKWOOD R.

AUGUSTA

HAMELIN BAY

COLLIER RANGE NATIONAL PARK

GASCOYNE RIVER

MIDLANDS RD.

BRAND HWY.

WEST COAST HWY.

CERVANTES

JURIEN

YANCHEP

KALBARRI NATIONAL PARK

KALBARRI

GANTHEAUME BAY

GERALDTON

1

CARNARVON

SHARK BAY

MONKEY MIA

DENHAM

© AVALON TRAVEL PUBLISHING

ing floods and droughts, there were occasional face-offs with local Aborginals who, a mite miffed with the whites for stealing their traditional lands, murdering their kinfolk, and contaminating them with heretofore unknown diseases, directed an occasional spear and ripped off the odd beast.

In 1850, the settlers were given a new lease on life when those workhorse convicts were brought in to build roads and bridges that would create vital links and replace the ferries thus far used to transport goods to and from Guildford. By the 1870s the area north of Perth was opened to grazing, followed by the eastern wheatlands, and cattle ranching up in the Kimberley region, but it was the 1892 gold rushes at Coolgardie and Kalgoorlie that helped the colony finally prosper and increase its population.

Western Australia achieved self-government status in 1890 but was left to fall by the wayside by the rest of the country during the Depression. This prompted a move in 1933 to secede from Australia, an effort knocked down by the British Parliament, then laid to rest during the subsequent postwar Good Times, though rumblings and grumblings of secession are still occasionally heard. Today's Western Australia is the wealthiest state in the country, thriving on the Pilbara's incredibly rich iron-ore deposits, productive farm and winegrowing districts, and the tourism boom of Broome and the Kimberley.

PERTH

Isolated on the southwestern corner of the Australian continent, Perth is closer to Indonesia than to either Sydney or Melbourne. Nonetheless, this laid-back metropolis outdid its sister cities by once boasting the most millionaires in the country (though many of these are now bankrupt) as well as the fastest-growing population (in numbers, that is, not in age; approximately one-half of Perth's 1.5 million residents are under the age of 30).

As with the 1890s gold rush inland, the rich mineral deposits of the northern Pilbara region in the 1970s have filtered enormous wealth into the city, and this shows no evidence of slowing. Then, in the 1980s and '90s, local entrepreneurs (such as Alan Bond of America's Cup fame) managed to wheel and deal megabucks from the east coast and other sources, parlaying them into an incredible variety of national and international conglomerates, resorts, and other enterprises.

Sitting on the banks of the Swan River (named in 1697 by Dutch navigators for its resident black swans), Perth was settled by Captain James Stirling and his colonists in 1829 and declared a city in 1856. In 1962, Perth achieved worldwide attention when just about every light in town was turned on for orbiting astronaut John Glenn, thus tagging it the "city of lights." Perth was "put on the map" again in 1980, when America's Skylab satellite smashed to smithereens over the eastern desert and, of course, in 1987, when the America's Cup was held in neighboring Fremantle. And when Glenn returned to space in 1998, the city lit him an encore. Perth today is a relaxed, beach- and boat-loving center of commerce, surrounded by a gorgeous coastline, striking wildflower meadows, and fertile vineyards and farmlands, as well as a lot of youthful energy (albeit laid-back energy).

Compact and laid out in grids, Perth is a great city to get around in, particularly if you have no car—it's easy to walk just about anywhere. Both the bus and metropolitan railway stations are on Wellington St. just a few blocks from the city center, and the general post office and Tourist Information Centre are steps away. Parallel to Wellington St., heading south, are Murray and Hay Streets, the main shopping district; then comes St. George's Terrace, the major business street. Beyond St. George's Terrace is the Swan River and Barrack Street Jetty (with many of the big high-rise hotels sandwiched in between), and Kings Park sits at the west edge of town. North of the railway tracks is the suburb of Northbridge, home to many of the backpacker hostels, inexpensive ethnic eateries, chic cafés, and the Perth Cultural Centre.

Many books and brochures liken this city to California's San Diego or some place on the Mediterranean—the perfect blend of fast pace and relaxed ease.

ST. GEORGE'S TERRACE

This tour of the city's main business thoroughfare—a mix of glitzy modern banks and office buildings interspersed with historic structures—begins on the west side of Victoria Avenue and continues westward to Barracks Archway, then covers the north side of the street returning back to the government buildings.

Perth Concert Hall
Adjacent to Government House, this elaborate space with four foyers and two exhibition halls is the city's premier venue for folk music, orchestra recitals, and other year-round musical performances by both national and international artists. For information, phone (08) 9321-9900.

Government House
This Gothic-revival-style residence complete with turrets and arches (a la the Tower of London), built between 1859 and 1864 at a cost of $30,000, still serves as the official home to the governor of Western Australia, as well as to visiting royalty. The public is welcome to visit the surrounding expansive gardens during special celebrations.

Council House
On the other side of Government House, Perth's civic administration center, opened by HRH Queen Elizabeth in 1963, houses five levels of offices, a circular council chamber, councillors' dining room, a large reception area, and a free public library. Hours are Mon.-Fri. 9 a.m.-4 p.m. (ground floor only). Guided tours are available Mon.-Fri. at 10:30 a.m. and 2:30 p.m. Admission is free. For information, phone (08) 9425-3333.

The Supreme Court
Just below Government House, the Supreme Court complex (Francis Burt Law Centre) includes the **Old Court House,** one of the city's oldest surviving colonial buildings (erected in 1836 with a few rear additions made in 1905), with many original details still intact. Presently serving as a legal history museum, the Old Court House includes a replica of an early legal office and related objects. An audiovisual presentation depicts the history of the law and the W.A. legal

profession. The surrounding **Supreme Court Gardens,** sheltered by Norfolk Island pines, are a popular brown bag lunch spot for city workers. The **Barrack Street Jetty,** ferry and riverboat departure point, is just beyond the gardens.

The Old Court House hours are Tuesday and Thursday 10 a.m.-2 p.m. Admission is free. For information, phone (08) 9325-4787.

Alan Green Conservatory
Continuing west across Barrack St. along the green lawns of the Esplanade, you'll see this pyramid-shaped conservatory, which houses a wide range of exotic tropical and semitropical plants within its controlled environment. Hours are Mon.-Fri. 10 a.m.-5 p.m., Saturday 10 a.m.-4 p.m., Sunday and public holidays noon-4 p.m. Admission is free. For information, phone (08) 9265-3145.

Bankwest Tower
Head north on William St. back to St. George's Terrace. The Bankwest Tower, at the corner, is home to the beautifully restored, ornate old **Palace Hotel,** though it is currently used as banking chambers. Still, it will give you an idea of the type of architecture prevalent in late-19th century Perth.

Old Perth Boys' School
Pointing west again, and situated along St. George's Terrace between William and Mill Streets, this former government school (built in 1854) resembles a medieval church with its quarried limestone, steeply pitched gable roof, and Gothic windows. Several additions were constructed in 1860, 1865, and 1876. Hours are Mon.-Fri. 9 a.m.-5 p.m. Admission is free. For information, phone (08) 9321-6088.

Barracks Archway
At the western end of St. George's Terrace (where it branches off and becomes Malcolm Street), the three-story Tudor-style archway, built in 1863-66 of Flemish bond brickwork, stands as a memorial to W.A.'s early pioneers and is all that remains of the old Pensioners Barracks, which were demolished in 1966. The archway fronts **Parliament House,** which is open for conducted tours on weekdays. For information, phone (08) 9222-7222.

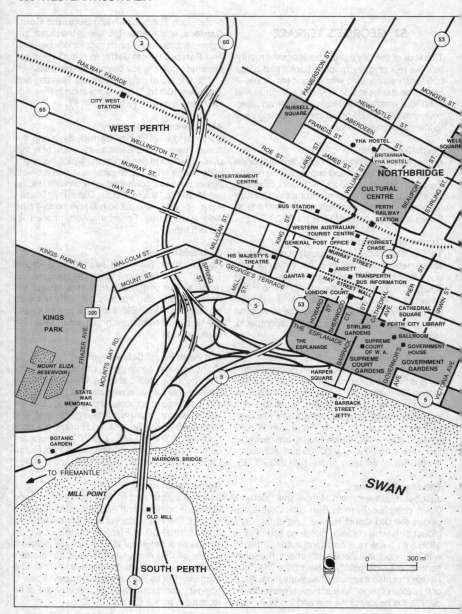

WEST PERTH

NORTHBRIDGE

KINGS PARK

MOUNT ELIZA
RESERVOIR

STATE
WAR
MEMORIAL

BOTANIC
GARDEN

SOUTH PERTH

SWAN

TO FREMANTLE

MILL POINT

NARROWS BRIDGE

OLD MILL

RAILWAY PARADE

CITY WEST
STATION

WELLINGTON ST.

MURRAY ST.

HAY ST.

ENTERTAINMENT
CENTRE

BUS STATION

KINGS PARK RD.

MALCOLM ST.

MOUNT ST.

ST. GEORGE'S TERRACE

FRAZER AVE.

MOUNTS BAY RD

MILL ST.

SPRING ST.

MILLIGAN ST.

ROE ST.

LAKE ST.

JAMES ST.

WILLIAM ST.

FRANCIS ST.

ABERDEEN ST.

NEWCASTLE ST.

PALMERSTON ST.

MONGER ST.

RUSSELL
SQUARE

WELL
SQUARE

YHA HOSTEL

BRITANNIA
YHA HOSTEL

CULTURAL
CENTRE

BEAUFORT ST.

STIRLING ST.

PERTH RAILWAY
STATION

WESTERN AUSTRALIAN
TOURIST CENTRE

GENERAL POST OFFICE

HIS MAJESTY'S
THEATRE

QANTAS

KING ST.

MURRAY STREET
MALL

HAY STREET MALL

ANSETT

TRANSPERTH
BUS INFORMATION

FORREST
CHASE

PIER ST.

IRWIN ST.

CATHEDRAL
AVE.

CATHEDRAL
SQUARE

PERTH CITY LIBRARY

LONDON COURT

HOWARD ST.

SHERWOOD CT.

BARRACK ST.

THE ESPLANADE

THE
ESPLANADE

STIRLING
GARDENS

SUPREME
COURT
OF W.A.

SUPREME
COURT
GARDENS

BALLROOM

GOVERNMENT
HOUSE

GOVERNMENT
GARDENS

GOVERNORS AVE.

VICTORIA AVE.

HARPER SQUARE

BARRACK
STREET
JETTY

0   300 m

PERTH

TO GUILDFORD ROAD

BULWER ST.

53

51

WEST PARADE

EAST PERTH
TERMINAL

SUMMERS ST.

EDWARD ST.

LORD ST.

PARRY ST.

PIER ST.

SHORT ST.

EAST PERTH

CLAISEBROOK
STATION

MOORE ST.

ROYAL PERTH
HOSPITAL

VICTORIA
SQUARE

WELLINGTON
SQUARE

HAIG PARK

YMCA JEWELL
HOUSE

PERTH MINT

GODERICH ST.

PLAIN ST.

WATERLOO CRESCENT

GLOUCESTER PARK
TROTTING GROUND

NELSON AVE.

HILL ST.

ROYAL
AUTOMOBILE
CLUB

BENNETT ST.

ADELAIDE TERRACE

QUEENS
GARDENS

W.A.C.A.
OVAL

LANGLEY
PARK

TERRACE RD.

65

TRANSPERTH
DEPOT

RIVERSIDE DR.

5

RIVER

CAUSEWAY

5

HEIRISSON

ISLAND

TO THE GREAT
EASTERN
HIGHWAY

TO
ALBANY HIGHWAY

© AVALON TRAVEL PUBLISHING

The Cloisters
Between King and Milligan Streets on the north side of St. George's Terrace, the snappy brick Cloisters, established in 1858, was W.A.'s first boys' secondary school.

His Majesty's Theatre
Turn north on King St. to see this restored Edwardian building—frequently referred to as "gracious"—a venue for ballet, opera, and theater performances. For information, phone (08) 9265-0999.

London Court
Back on St. George's Terrace, beyond William St., the London Court Arcade, built in 1937, is a great bit of Aussie kitsch. Running all the way to Hay Street Mall, the *very* mock-Tudor laneway, the brainchild of hit-it-rich gold miner Claude de Bernales, features sublimely silly details like medieval clocks with mechanical jousting knights. The clock at the Hay Street end is a mini-Big Ben.

Town Hall
Walk a short distance along the Mall to Barrack Street. Perth Town Hall, on the southeast corner, was constructed by convicts to resemble an English market. Check out the tower—still visible is a piece of hangman's rope carved in the stone. Another interesting feature are some of the tower windows built in the shape of reversed broad arrowheads—a symbol meaning "convict-built."

St. George's Cathedral
Reached from Cathedral Ave., off St. George's Terrace, this was the site of Perth's first church, constructed of timber and rush in 1829, then replaced by a stone building that served worshippers until 1841. The foundation stone for the present cathedral was laid in 1880.

The Deanery
At the corner of St. George's Terrace and Pier St., the Deanery, which currently functions as Anglican church offices, was built in the late 1850s as a residence for the first Anglican dean of Perth and ranks among W.A.'s few remaining houses from that period.

OTHER CITY SIGHTS

Perth Cultural Centre
Cross the railway tracks at Horseshoe Bridge to reach Northbridge, site of the Perth Cultural Centre, a "mall" comprised of several buildings, including the Art Gallery of Western Australia and the Western Australian Museum.

Closest to Horseshoe Bridge, the **Art Gallery of Western Australia** exhibits contemporary and traditional Australian and European paintings and sculpture, including a collection of Aboriginal paintings and crafts (with informative pamphlets). Hours are daily 10 a.m.-5 p.m., closed Good Friday and Christmas Day. Admission is free. Free guided tours are offered Tues.-Fri. at noon. For information, phone (08) 9328-7233.

On the corner of the Mall and Beaufort St., the **Western Australian Museum** is centered on the **Old Gaol,** a restored, convict-built Georgian stone courthouse and jail that served its purpose from 1856 to 1889 (the grounds were used for a number of public executions). Now serving as a museum, exhibitions feature W.A. historical and cultural memorabilia, including household items, political records, early mementos, a collection of meteorites (one weighs 11 tons!), a 25-meter blue whale skeleton, plus an outstanding Aboriginal gallery. Hours are Mon.-Fri. 10:30 a.m.-5 p.m., Sat.-Sun. 1-5 p.m., closed Christmas Day and Good Friday. Admission is free. For information, phone (08) 9328-4411.

More Museums
The **Mineral Museum of Western Australia,** 100 Plain St. East (in Mineral House), features rocks, minerals, and special displays related to mining and geology. Hours are Mon.-Fri. 8 a.m.-5 p.m. Admission is free. For information, phone (08) 9222-3333.

Perth's oldest **fire station,** corner Irwin and Murray Streets, serves as a museum that depicts W.A.'s firefighting techniques and machinery from 1901 to the present day. Hours are Mon.-Thurs. 10 a.m.-3 p.m. Admission is free. For information, phone (08) 9323-9468.

At the northeast edge of the city, at the junction of Lord and Bulwer Streets, the **Army Museum of Western Australia** houses uniforms, badges, medals, and other military items ranging from the colonial period to the present. Hours are Sunday and Thursday 1-4:30 p.m. A donation is requested. For information, phone (08) 9227-9269.

Scitech Discovery Centre
At the corner of Railway Parade and Sutherland St., Scitech features entertaining hands-on experiments (for kids of all ages) on a variety of high-tech equipment. Hours are daily 10 a.m.-5 p.m. Admission is $12. For information, phone (08) 9481-6295.

It's a Small World
See a huge museum collection of little things—miniature cars, rooms, trains, et cetera—located at 12 Parliament Place, West Perth. Hours are Sun.-Fri. 10 a.m.-5 p.m., Saturday 2-5 p.m. Admission is $5. For information, phone (08) 9322-2020.

Old Mill
Perth's first flour mill, built in 1835, is at the southern end of the Narrows Bridge and displays many pioneering relics. Hours are Monday, Wednesday, and Thursday 1-5 p.m., Sat.-Sun. noon-4 p.m. A donation is requested. For information, phone (08) 9367-5788.

Perth Mint
Dating from 1899, the mint still produces gold, silver, and platinum bullion coins. Displays include various coins, including a one-kg nugget coin. Located at 310 Hay Street. Hours are Mon.-Fri. 9 a.m.-4 p.m., Saturday 9 a.m.-1 p.m. Admission is free (no place to put any more coins?). For information, phone (08) 9421-7425.

Perth Zoo
Across the Swan River (and beyond the Old Mill), at 20 Labouchere Rd., South Perth, the zoo is easily reached by bus or ferry from the city center. Noteworthy attractions include the great ape complex, nocturnal house, wallaby park, great cat enclosure, gibbon lake, walk-through aviary, and the Conservation Discovery Centre. Hours are daily 10 a.m.-5 p.m. Admission is $7. For information, phone (08) 9367-7988.

Parks and Gardens
Kings Park, at the west edge of the city, is Perth's park supreme—even though bushfires in 1989 burned nearly half of it. A short drive or easy walk from city center, its nearly 400 hectares consist mostly of natural bushland as well as a five-hectare **botanic garden** (noted for its spring wildflowers), natural trails, picnic areas, and paths for walking, jogging, and cycling. You'll catch some terrific views of the city, river, and surrounding countryside from various perches and lookouts—especially from **Mount Eliza,** the park's most prominent knoll. Free guided tours are available. For information, phone (08) 9322-1456.

On the eastern edge of the city, **Queens Garden,** corner Hay and Plain Streets, is a quiet English-style park with a water garden. **Hyde Park,** corner William and Vincent Streets, North Perth, caters to families with its adventure playground and to birdwatchers with its ornamental lake. **Lake Monger,** in the close-by suburb of Wembley, is a popular spot for watching those enchanting black swans, as well as wild ducks and other birdlife.

Beaches
Pick and choose from any of Perth's well-known beaches. For calm, Swan River swimming beaches, try **Crawley, Peppermint Grove,** and **Como.** If you'd rather tackle the surf, head for the beaches along the Indian Ocean—best bets are **Cottesloe, City Beach** (site of many national surfing contests), **Scarborough,** and **Trigg Island. Leighton Beach** is the top choice for windsurfers and wave jumpers. If you're looking for surf *and* you forgot your bathers, **Swanbourne** (north of Cottesloe) is a popular nude beach. Almost all beaches can be easily reached by bus.

SUBURBAN SIGHTS

Claremont Museum
Housed within one of W.A.'s oldest buildings (constructed by convicts in 1861-62), the museum's displays depict early settlement, convict and farming life, as well as replicas of bootmaker and barber shops. Located at 66 Victoria Ave., Claremont. Hours are Tues.-Thurs. and Sunday 1-4 p.m., daily 2-5 p.m. during school holidays. Admission is $2. For information, phone (08) 9386-3352.

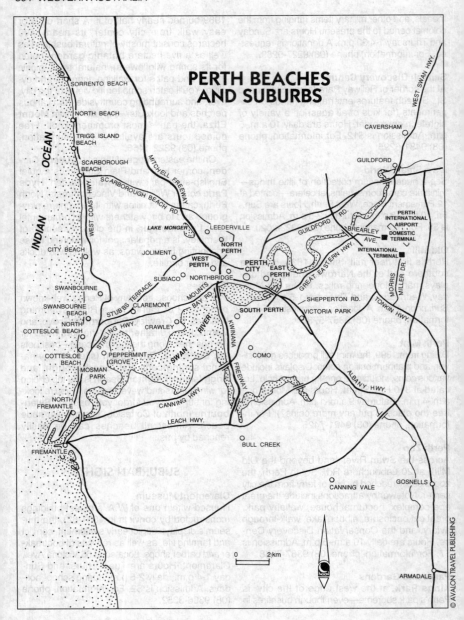

PERTH BEACHES AND SUBURBS

INDIAN OCEAN

SORRENTO BEACH

NORTH BEACH

TRIGG ISLAND BEACH

SCARBOROUGH BEACH

SCARBOROUGH BEACH RD.

MITCHELL FREEWAY

WEST COAST HWY.

WEST SWAN HWY.

CAVERSHAM

GUILDFORD

LEEDERVILLE

Lake Monger

NORTH PERTH

WEST PERTH

JOLIMENT

CITY BEACH

SUBIACO

NORTHBRIDGE

PERTH CITY

EAST PERTH

GUILDFORD RD.

BREARLEY AVE.

PERTH INTERNATIONAL AIRPORT

DOMESTIC TERMINAL

INTERNATIONAL TERMINAL

GREAT EASTERN HWY.

MORRIS MILLER DR.

TONKIN HWY.

SWANBOURNE

SWANBOURNE BEACH

STUBBS TERRACE

CLAREMONT

NORTH COTTESLOE BEACH

STIRLING HWY.

CRAWLEY

COTTESLOE BEACH

PEPPERMINT GROVE

MOSMAN PARK

MOUNTS BAY RD.

SWAN RIVER

KWINANA FREEWAY

SOUTH PERTH

SHEPPERTON RD.

VICTORIA PARK

COMO

ALBANY HWY.

NORTH FREMANTLE

CANNING HWY.

LEACH HWY.

FREMANTLE

BULL CREEK

GOSNELLS

CANNING VALE

0   2 km

© AVALON TRAVEL PUBLISHING

ARMADALE

Museum of W.A. Sport

Inside the Superdrome, trophies and other memorabilia recall the good and not-so-good moments of Western Australian sports figures. It's on Stephenson Ave. in Mt. Claremont. Hours are daily 8 a.m.-8 p.m. Admission is free. For information, phone (08) 9387-8542.

Museum of Childhood

Two buildings contain dolls (wax, wooden, and bisque), toys, photographs, literature, clothing, furniture, and other curios and playthings (almost 20,000 items) associated with W.A.'s pioneer children. Located at Edith Cowan University Campus, Bay Rd., Claremont. Hours are Tues.-Fri. and Sunday 10 a.m.-4 p.m., mid-December through mid-January. Admission is $3. For information, phone (08) 9442-1373.

Aviation Heritage Museum

Exhibits depicting the history of civil and military aviation from the origins up to the present (with an emphasis on W.A.) feature historic aircraft (such as the Lancaster heavy bomber and the Spitfire fighter), uniforms, medals, models, photos, and other aero-memorabilia. The museum is on Bullcreek Dr. in Bullcreek. Hours are daily 11 a.m.-4 p.m., closed Christmas Day and Good Friday. Admission is $5. For information, phone (08) 9311-4470.

Swan Brewery

Tour W.A.'s famed brewery and guzzle or sip some of the "homegrown" brews such as Swan Lager, Swan Draught, and Emu. Located at 25 Vaile Rd., Canning Vale. Tours last 90 minutes to two hours and are available Mon.-Thursday. Advance reservations are necessary. For information, phone (08) 9350-0222.

Cohunu Wildlife Park

Visit the Southern Hemisphere's largest aviary (on Mills Rd. in Martin) and see native animals in a "natural" environment. This is also the spot to have your photo taken with a koala. Hours are daily 10 a.m.-5 p.m. Admission is $12. For information, phone (08) 9390-6090.

Elizabethan Village

Full-size re-creations of Shakespeare's birthplace and Anne Hathaway's cottage are furnished with 500-year-old antiques. The village is on Canns Rd. in Armadale. Hours are Mon.-Fri. 10 a.m.-4 p.m., Sat.-Sun. 10 a.m.-5 p.m. Admission is $5. For information, phone (08) 9399-3166.

Pioneer Village

This working model of a 19th-century gold miners' village allows visitors to pan for their own gold nuggets, filings, and dust (30-minute limit). Other attractions include working craftsmen, sing-alongs, silent movies, vaudeville shows, and other entertainment. Located at junction of South West and Albany Highways, Armadale. Hours are daily 10 a.m.-5 p.m. Admission is $9. For information, phone (08) 9399-5322.

ACCOMMODATIONS

Perth's varied accommodations are as conveniently located as everything else in town. Older, cheaper hotels and some hostels are clustered in and around the city center, while others are just across the railway tracks in Northbridge. South Perth and several of the closer suburbs also provide motel and holiday-flat units. Big spenders will find no shortage of luxury hotels, most of which are between St. George's Terrace and the Swan River.

Optimism over Perth's tourism boom in conjunction with the America's Cup—and its accompanying groupies—saw upmarket accommodations increase by several thousand rooms. Many of these hotels have since experienced low occupancy, so it may be possible to strike a good deal on rates. Campgrounds and caravan parks are scattered 10-20 km from town.

As with all Australian cities and tourist centers, it's advisable to book rooms in advance. If you arrive without a reservation, contact the **Western Australia Tourist Centre,** Forrest Place, corner of Wellington St., tel. (08) 9483-1111.

City and Suburbs

The well-recommended **Downtowner Lodge,** 63 Hill St., tel. (08) 9325-6973, opposite the Perth Mint, has 12 clean, quiet rooms, plus TV lounge and laundry facilities. Inexpensive. The **Court Hotel,** 50 Beaufort St., tel. (08) 9328-5292, offers inexpensive rooms near the Perth Cultural Centre. Inexpensive.

Farther beyond the Cultural Centre, **Cheviot Lodge,** 30 Bulwer St., tel. (08) 9227-6817, features modern kitchen and bathroom facilities, TV and games room, a laundry room, and free pickup service from the bus station. Inexpensive. **Mountway Holiday Units,** 36 Mount St., tel. (08) 9321-8307, close to Kings Park, offers self-contained one-bedroom flats with cooking facilities, full-size bathtubs, and TVs. Inexpensive.

Make advance reservations for **The Adelphi,** 130A Mounts Bay Rd., tel. (08) 9322-4666, situated at the base of Kings Park bluff. Rooms are bright and cheery (upper levels feature Swan River views) and have air-conditioning, TVs, phones, and cooking facilities. Moderate. Another popular choice is **City Waters Lodge,** 118 Terrace Rd., tel. (08) 9325-1566, also with kitchens, phones, TVs, air-conditioning, and off-street parking. Moderate.

The **Wentworth Plaza,** 300 Murray St., tel. (08) 9481-1000, is a combination of the Federation-era Wentworth and Royal hotels, both decked out in period decor. If you stay in the Royal side, with shared facilities, the rates are moderate. The Wentworth portion, with private baths and larger rooms, edges its way into the expensive range. If you hang out at the happening bars downstairs, you probably won't care where your room is positioned. Moderate-Expensive.

Perth Riverview Holiday Apartments, 42 Mount St., tel. (08) 9321-8963, close to both Kings Park and city center, offers clean rooms in a good neighborhood, with all the conveniences of the other self-contained flats. Moderate.

Also on the "good side" of town, with Swan River views, is the **New Esplanade Hotel,** 18 the Esplanade, tel. (08) 9325-2000, with room service, restaurant, bar, and a less-expensive "travelers' wing." Expensive. **Miss Maud European Hotel,** 97 Murray St., tel. (1800) 99-8022, is a small, friendly, centrally located establishment with Scandinavian decor, and adjacent restaurant and bakery. Breakfast is included in the rates. Expensive.

Chateau Commodore, 417 Hay St., tel. (08) 9325-0461, one of the city's older hotels, is a local favorite, and cheaper than the name brands above. Though the decor is somewhat . . . robust, the rooms are large and some have balconies with views. The Chateau is also cheaper than the others in this range. Expensive.

As you might imagine, with all the millionaires and money around, the city suffers no shortage of luxury hotels. Most are centrally located (i.e., near the banks), and all have the customary amenities such as restaurants, bars, room service, shops, health clubs, and the like. The **Parmelia Hilton,** Mill St., tel. (08) 9322-3622, is considered one of the best. Public rooms are beautifully decorated with antiques and other artwork, and guest rooms have either river or city views. Luxury. The **Sheraton Perth,** 207 Adelaide Terrace, tel. (08) 9325-0501, is another hefty-price winner with terrific views, well-decorated guest rooms, and a superb formal dining room. Luxury.

For those who like their action packed, **Burswood International Resort Casino,** Great Eastern Hwy., Victoria Park, tel. (08) 9362-7777, has a full-on 24-hour casino (largest in the Southern Hemisphere), plus an 18-hole golf course and beautifully decorated rooms with city or river views. Luxury.

Hostels

Most of Perth's hostels and backpacker accommodations are easy walks from the bus and rail stations. Dorm beds average $12-14 per night.

The city's two **YHA hostels** are busy establishments, both situated in Northbridge. The closest hostel is the newly renovated 84-bed **Northbridge-Francis St. YHA Hostel,** 42 Francis St., tel. (08) 9328-7794, corner William and Francis Streets, past the Perth Cultural Centre. Around the corner, **Britannia YHA Hostel,** 253 William St., tel. (08) 9328-6121, offers 134 beds. Both sites have a communal kitchen, laundry, rec room, and bicycle hire.

Jewell House, 180 Goderich St., tel. (08) 9325-8488, is a YMCA-run establishment with clean, but basic, rooms. The reception office is open 24 hours, and guests have use of two TV rooms and a laundry room. Meals, weekly rates, and free baggage storage are available.

Rory's Backpackers Perth Inn, 194 Brisbane St., tel. (08) 9328-9958, has clean, spacious rooms in a renovated colonial house with gardens. **Budget Backpackers' International,** 342 Newcastle St., tel. (08) 9328-9468, and **North Lodge,** 225 Beaufort St., tel. (08) 9227-7588, are other choices with communal lounges and kitchens.

Other communal possibilities are: **Field Touring Hostel,** 74 Aberdeen St., tel. (08) 9328-4692, a quiet establishment catering mainly to hikers and cyclists who like to turn in early; **Globe Backpackers,** 479 Wellington St., tel. (08) 9321-4080, a large half-hostel/half-hotel; and **Backpackers International,** corner Aberdeen and Lake Streets, tel. (08) 9227-9977.

Camping

The following campgrounds and caravan parks fall within 20 km of the city and offer both on-site vans and campsites: **Central Caravan Park,** 38 Central Ave., Redcliffe, tel. (08) 9277-1704; **Kenlorn Caravan Park,** 229 Welshpool Rd., Queens Park, tel. (08) 9356-2380; **Starhaven Caravan Park,** 18 Pearl Parade, Scarborough, tel. (08) 9341-1770; **Perth International Tourist Park,** 319 Hale Rd., Forrestfield, tel. (08) 9453-6677; **Forrestfield Caravan Park,** 351 Hawtin Rd., Forrestfield, tel. (08) 9453-6378; **Guildford Caravan Park,** 372 West Swan Rd., Guildford, tel. (08) 9274-2828; and **Orange Grove Caravan Park,** 19 Kelvin Rd., Orange Grove, tel. (08) 9453-6226. Campsites range $5-10, about $5 more for powered sites; on-site vans run $25-50.

FOOD

Perth is hardly a culinary tour de force like Melbourne, but those millionaires do like to eat. About 700 restaurants dot the city, including many ethnic establishments along William St. in Northbridge, coffee shops and cafés in the city center, and high-priced gourmet dining rooms in hotels or spattered about the inner suburbs. Fresh, local seafood tops many of the menus.

Foodstalls and Halls

The cheapest—and perhaps tastiest—places to eat at are the foodstalls and halls, where you can do a budget-type graze of many different types of food for less than a greasy spoon takeaway. One of the best choices is **Down Under Food Hall,** near William St., downstairs in the Hay Street Mall. Select from a variety of ethnic goodies such as Indian, Indonesian, Chinese, and Mexican. Hours are Mon.-Wed. 8 a.m.-7 p.m., Thurs.-Sat. 8 a.m.-9 p.m. Nearby, but a bit more expensive, is **Carillon Food Hall,** in Carillon Arcade, also on Hay Street Mall. Hours are Mon.-Sat. 8 a.m.-9 p.m. In Northbridge, try

Northbridge Pavilion, corner Lake and James Streets, **Victoria Gardens,** on Aberdeen St. overlooking Russell Square, or the two Asian halls on James Street.

City Eats

Fast Eddy's, 471 Murray St., is a 24-hour burger joint. **Magic Apple,** 445 Hay St., features healthy salads, smoothies, and sandwiches. Another health-style lunch spot is called, not surprsingly, **Best Health Lunch Bar,** in City Arcade, with a good range of vegetarian selections ($7-12 for hot entrees). **Mr. Samurai,** 83 Barrack St., is a top choice for cheap Japanese specialties. And **Matsuri Sushi Bar,** 903 Hay St., tel. (08) 9324-2420, will also regale you with sushi, sashimi, tempura, and other presentations ($10-18).

Northbridge is packed with ethnic restaurants, many of them inexpensive. Take your tummy for a walk along William St. and you'll never go hungry—**Hare Krishna Food for Life** is just one of your options ($5, all you can eat).

In Northbridge, **Choi's Inn,** 68 Roe St., tel. (08) 9328-6350, is a friendly, casual Chinese establishment that serves traditional Cantonese and fiery Sichuan meals ($10-18 entrees). Advance orders are necessary for the beggar's chicken and Peking duck. Open daily for lunch and dinner.

Yen Do, 416 William St., Northbridge, tel. (08) 9227-8833, is a popular spot for Chinese, Vietnamese, and other Asian specialties. You can get excellent noodle dishes and spring rolls for less than $10.

For those not-to-be-missed yuppie lunches ($12-16 entrees), infiltrate **Moon and Sixpence Bar,** 300 Murray St., or **44 King St.,** around the corner. And don't miss the oh-so-cool **Frostbites Bar and Grill,** 397 Murray St. ($11-16).

Super Italian fare is served at **Romany,** 188 William St., tel. (08) 9328-8042, a fixture since 1940. Dishes like scallopino and parmigiana run $12-28, while hearty pasta dishes range $12-18.

Perugino, 77 Outram St., West Perth, tel. (08) 9321-5420, is considered Perth's best Italian restaurant. Regional specialties are prepared with fresh ingredients and fresh imagination ($14-22 entrees). The garden setting lures locals involved in romantic encounters, important business, or pure self-indulgence. Open Mon.-Fri. lunch, Mon.-Sat. dinner.

Fraser's, in Kings Park, tel. (08) 9481-7100, is a two-level, river- and city-view establishment, with fresh, flavorful contemporary cuisine and a daily-changing menu ($24-38). Open daily for lunch and dinner; outdoor dining available in good weather.

Suburbs

Searching for a top-notch, noisy, crowded, chic, imaginative, 24-hour brasserie with great cakes and a wonderful wine list? Choose from a cast of one: **Oriel,** 480 Hay St., Subiaco, tel. (08) 9382-1886.

And, for one of the best French restaurants, the prizewinner is **The Loose Box,** 6825 Great Eastern Hwy., Mundaring Weir, tel. (08) 9295-1787, about a 45-minute drive from the city. You'll pay dearly for classic French cuisine with Aussie accents in an elegant setting ($40-60), but it's worth every sous. The three-course prix-fixe Friday lunch is a steal at $30 per head. Open Sun.-Tues. and Friday for lunch, Wed.-Sat. for dinner. Inquire about dress codes and reserve tables well in advance, especially for weekends and holiday periods.

The **Witch's Cauldron,** 89 Rokeby St., Subiaco, casts its spell with killer garlic prawns and other potent concoctions ($12-20). **Mead's Fish Gallery,** 15 Johnson Parade, Mosman Park, tel. (08) 9383-3388, presents delectable seafood from salmon sashimi to king prawns to bay squid ($23-36) in a magnificent Swan River setting.

Suburban Leederville is yet another see-and-be-seen haunt. Cruise Oxford St., between Aberdeen and Vincent Streets, for everything from rock 'n' roll pizza to postwar Vietnamese.

A local favorite for beachside breakfast ($6-10) is **North Cott Café,** 149 Marine Parade, Cottlesloe. Down the street, **Indiana Tea House,** 99 Marine Parade, tel. (08) 9385-5005, is the place for those who want Indian, Malaysian, Thai, Chinese, and other Asian cuisines in a more elegant setting than the Northbridge eateries. All this ambience comes at considerably higher prices ($18-26).

ENTERTAINMENT AND EVENTS

Much of Perth's entertainment scene is geared toward its vibrant, young (or young at heart) res-idents, with Northbridge being the major gathering spot. Check local newspapers, particularly the Saturday edition of the *West Australian* newspaper for current listings of arts and cultural events. For gig info, pick up a copy of *X-Press,* the free weekly music mag, at any record shop and many other locations. The *Westside Observer,* free at Arcane Bookshop (212 William St.), has lists of gay and lesbian entertainment venues.

Cinemas

Perth has the usual round of commercial cinema complexes, with most of the flicks appearing months after their U.S. debut. Movie houses that show more arty and/or cerebral films are: the **Lumiere,** in the Perth Entertainment Centre; **Cinema Paradiso,** 164 James St., Northbridge; and the **Astor,** corner Beaufort and Walcott Streets, Mt. Lawley.

There's a two-level wraparound **Omni Theater** at the corner of Railway Parade and Sutherland St., West Perth, tel. (08) 9481-6481.

Pubs and Clubs

Plentiful clubs, pubs, and discos feature live music most nights of the week. Northbridge is the prime area for contemporary and casual venues ($5-8), while discos and nightclubs in the big hotels cater to the yup-and-coming ($10-17). Most of the discos and many bars impose a dress code—mainly no sneakers, jeans, or flannel shirts.

Catch live music in Northbridge at: **Brass Monkey Tavern,** 209 William St.; **Aberdeen Hotel,** 84 Aberdeen St.; and **The Lone Star,** corner Beaufort and Newcastle Streets. **Oriel Cafe,** 483 Hay St., Subiaco, is a favorite late-night spot, popular with the hip set. The even hipper crowd hang at the **Astoria,** 37 Bay View Terrace, Claremont. For pure dance, **The Globe,** 393 Murray St., features live bands and disco music. **Excapdade,** 187 Stirling St., Northbridge, is another happening dance club catering to the bebopping young crowd that dances on split levels to split styles.

Sophisticates sip their martinis and clink their cubes at **Club Bay View,** 20 St. Quentin's Ave., in suburban Claremont. Catch jazz and blues at the **Grosvenor Hotel,** 339 Hay St., **Charles Hotel,** 509 Charles St., North Perth, or **Hyde Park Hotel,** 331 Bulwer St., North Perth.

Perth has the usual round of hot discos with cold meat inspectors. Fashion victims might try **Margeaux's,** Mill St., in the Parmelia Hilton, or **Players,** 207 Adelaide Terrace, in the Sheraton Perth.

For good old drinkin' pubs, try **Sherwood's Tavern,** 77 St. George's Terrace; **Milligan's,** 205 James St.; and the **Northbridge Hotel,** 198 Brisbane Street.

The Casino
Burswood International Resort Casino, W.A.'s first casino, features more than 140 gaming tables, including roulette, baccarat, blackjack, craps, and Australia's own two-up. Restaurants, bars, and a cabaret are also part of this luxury resort complex on the banks of the Swan River, near the city. Open 24 hours a day except Christmas Day and Good Friday. For information, phone (08) 9362-7777.

Theater, Dance, and Concerts
The stunning **His Majesty's Theatre,** 825 Hay St., tel. (08) 9265-0999, is home not just to many of Perth's theatrical productions but also to the **West Australian Ballet Company** and the **West Australian Opera Company.** Modern and traditional ballets are performed in February, May, June, and October, while the operatic season (April, August, and November) features classical works and operettas.

The **Playhouse Theatre,** 3 Pier St., tel. (08) 9325-3344, is headquarters of the **Western Australian Theatre Company,** which uses the space to present a number of classical and contemporary plays throughout the year. Other good local theaters include: **Dolphin Theatre,** University of Western Australia, Crawley, tel. (08) 9380-2432; **Regal Theatre,** 474 Hay St., Subiaco, tel. (08) 9381-5522; **Subiaco** and **Hole in the Wall,** 180 Hamersley Rd., Subiaco, tel. (08) 9381-3694.

Perth Entertainment Centre, on Wellington near Milligan St., is where the big-name rock concerts and other major events are held. You can't miss the **Betts & Betts Walk of Fame** out front—a walkway of celebrities' autographed footprints. For information, phone (08) 9321-5432.

Folk music, orchestra recitals, and more "mellow" concerts are performed at **Perth Concert Hall,** 5 St. George's Terrace, tel. (08) 9321-9900.

In summer, the band shell in the **Supreme Court Gardens** presents a variety of live music.

Schedules for almost every entertainment event are advertised in the free weekly *X-Press* and in Saturday's *West Australian.*

BOCS is the state's major ticket booking agency for everything from concerts and ballet to theater and sporting events. For information, phone (08) 9484-1133, or stop by the outlet at the Western Australia Tourist Centre, on Forrest Place, tel. (08) 9483-1111.

Theme Parks
Adventure World, 179 Progress Dr., Bibra Lake, is a family-oriented entertainment complex with an amusement park, native animals, waterways, and parklands. Hours are daily, Sept.-May and school holidays, 10 a.m.-5 p.m. Admission is adult $20, child $17. For information, phone (08) 9417-9666.

Travel through an underground acrylic tunnel to view approximately 5,000 species of underwater life (such as starfish, crustaceans, and a small Port Jackson shark) at **Underwater World,** Hillary's Boat Harbour, West Coast Highway. Other attractions include Microworld, where you can watch sea horses, shellfish, and anemones through a video camera, and Touch Pool, where you can feel the creatures. There's also a gift shop, and an underwater café that looks out on the Indian Ocean. Hours are daily 9 a.m.-5 p.m. Admission is $16. For information, phone (08) 9447-7500.

Events
The city's big extravaganza is the annual **Festival of Perth** held in February and March. The festival showcases international and national big-name talents, as well as local joes, with a program roster that includes music, theater, dance, film, visual and literary arts, and a host of outdoor activities. For information, contact the University of Western Australia, Mounts Bay Rd., Crawley, tel. (08) 9386-7977.

SPORTS AND RECREATION

Great weather, great beaches, great park—it means Perth offers all types of land and water sports and year-round recreational opportunities. Call or drop by the **Western Australia Tourist Centre** on Forrest Place for information on spectator and participant sports throughout the state.

Diving

A few scattered, centuries-old shipwrecks offshore should make things interesting for divers. Contact **Neptune Scuba,** 379 Hay St., East Perth, tel. (08) 9221-5780, or the **Australasian Diving Centre,** 259 Stirling Hwy., Claremont, tel. (08) 9384-3966.

Fishing

You'll luck out on the catch of the day at many coastal ports, particularly Fremantle, as well as along the Swan River banks. The prized fish in these parts is the blue marlin. Charter boats are available (check the yellow pages).

Swimming Pools

Not happy with the ocean or the river? Try one or all three Olympic-size pools at **Challenge Stadium,** Stephenson Ave., Mt. Claremont, tel. (08) 9441-8222.

Sporting Facilities

Tennis: Fees are reasonable at public tennis courts within metropolitan and suburban parks. For sites and details, contact **Tennis West,** tel. (08) 9361-1112.

Golf: Select from one of the city's many public golf courses after consulting with the **Western Australia Golf Association,** tel. (08) 9474-1005, or the tourist office. Some of Perth's country clubs are on the snooty side.

Other Participant Sports

Yachties should head straight for the tourism office. **Catamarans** and **windsurfers** are available for hire at the Coode Street Jetty, South Perth, tel. (08) 9367-2988. They are popular on weekends and holidays, so book ahead. Depending on weather conditions, you can **parasail** on weekends at the South Perth foreshore. For information, contact **Flying High Parasailing,** tel. (08) 9313-3897.

Bushwalkers, cyclists, and **joggers** will find excellent trails throughout Kings Park and along the Swan River. The tourist office has maps and brochures.

Spectator Sports

Aussie Rules football is the prime winter spectator sport, with games played every weekend March through September at Subiaco Oval and at the Western Australia Cricket Association (WACA) grounds. For information, phone the **Western Australia Football Commission,** tel. (08) 9381-5599. In summer months, **cricket** is the buzz, with Sheffield Shield, Test, and one-day cricket played at the WACA grounds in Nelson Crescent, East Perth. For information, phone the (08) 9265-7222. Other spectator sports include **rugby, soccer, basketball, baseball,** and **hockey.** Watch for details of all matches and sporting events in the Sports section of the Friday and Saturday newspapers. **Racing** is a big-time favorite of Western Australians. For schedules and locales of **horse, trotting,** and **greyhound** racing, watch the Sports section of the morning newspapers. For **motor racing,** contact the W.A. Sporting Car Club, tel. (08) 9381-4432. For **motorcycle racing,** phone the Motorcycle Racing Club of W.A., tel. (08) 9409-1002. On Friday nights throughout spring and summer months, the **RAS Showground** in Claremont hosts thriller speedcar and motorcycle races. Look for details in Saturday's *West Australian.*

SHOPPING

Perth's main shopping district is the pedestrians-only Hay Street Mall and Murray Street Mall, both running parallel between William and Barrack Streets, and the many arcades that branch off to St. George's Terrace and Wellington Street. Major department stores such as Myer and Aherns are located here, as are scads of boutiques, specialty shops, bookshops, schlock and dime stores, cinemas, coffee lounges, and all kinds of general merchandise. King St., a few blocks away, within the past few years has nosed its way into the shopping mecca with some choice galleries and funky shops. Customary shopping hours are Mon.-Sat. 9 a.m.-6 p.m., Thursday until 9 p.m., and some of the larger shops are open on Sunday.

Markets

Colorful, bargain-filled markets offering a wide range of merchandise are: **Subiaco Market,** near Subiaco Railway Station, at Roberts and Rokeby Roads (Thurs.-Sun. 8 a.m.-6 p.m.); **Canning Vale Market,** corner of Bannister and Ranford Roads (Sunday 7 a.m.-4 p.m.); and **Midland Sunday Market,** 284 Great Eastern Hwy. (Sunday 8 a.m.-4 p.m.).

Crafts

For **Aboriginal handicrafts,** don't miss the **Creative Native,** 32 King St., tel. (08) 9322-3398, with its excellent range of traditional and contemporary handmade Aboriginal art, including carved emu eggs and boomerangs.

Indigenart, 115 Hay St., Subiaco, tel. (08) 9388-2899, exhibits and sells Aboriginal arts, crafts, and wearable arts, and also serves as a casual cultural center.

Pick up Australian items—from kitschy souvenirs to high-quality native crafts, at **Purely Australian** locations at City Arcade, London Court, and Hay Street Mall.

If you're heading into the Outback or just want to impress the folks back home, head over to **R.M. Williams** in Hay Street Mall's Carillon Arcade, tel. (08) 9321-7786. They'll fix you up head-to-toe, from an Akubra hat down to moleskin pants and heavy-duty tooled leather boots.

Other Shops

How about gems and money? See gems before they're turned into rings, pendants, and key chains at **Perth Lapidary Centre,** 58 Pier St., tel. (08) 9325-2954. Purchase proof-issue coins, commemoratives and bank notes, coin jewelry, and books related to coin collecting and Western Australia's pioneering prospectors at **The Perth Mint,** 310 Hay St., tel. (08) 9421-7425.

Record collectors and purveyors of the local *muso* scene will groove at **78 Records,** 884 Hay Street. On the way to or from, you'll be faced with enough retro and grunge wear for all your nights on this town.

SERVICES

Branches of all the major national **banks** are on or about St. George's Terrace, along with the ubiquitous automatic teller machines. You'll find **American Express** at 645 Hay St., in the Hay Street Mall, tel. (08) 9221-0777. Banking hours are Mon.-Thurs. 9:30 a.m.-4 p.m., Friday 9:30 a.m.-5 p.m.

The **general post office,** 3 Forrest Place, tel. (08) 9237-5460, between the railway station and Hay Street Mall, is open for all postal services Mon.-Fri. 8:30 a.m.-5 p.m., Saturday 9 a.m.-noon.

For migrant information (employment, permits, etc.), see the **Department of Immigration and Ethnic Affairs,** 1260 Hay St., West Perth, tel. (13) 1450. (Remember, it's illegal to work in Australia on a regular tourist visa.)

Some countries with Perth-based consulates are: **United States,** 16 St. George's Terrace, tel. (08) 9231-9400; **Canada,** 267 St. George's Terrace, tel. (08) 09322-7930; **United Kingdom,** 77 St. George's Terrace, tel. (08) 9221-5400; **New Zealand,** 16 St. George's Terrace, tel. (08) 9325-7877; and **Japan,** 221 St. George's Terrace, tel. (08) 9321-7816.

INFORMATION

As with all of Australia's capital cities, the state tourist office is chockablock with information, accommodations, and tour bookings. The **Western Australia Tourist Centre** (also known as WATC) is on Forrest Place, at the corner of Wellington Street and across from the railway station. Hours are Mon.-Thurs. 8:30 a.m.-6 p.m., Friday 8:30 a.m.-7 p.m., Saturday 8:30 a.m.-5 p.m., Sunday 10 a.m.-5 p.m. For information, phone (08) 9483-1111. A **Perth City Tourist Booth** is located along Hay Street Mall.

The **ACROD Access Committee,** 38 Short St., East Perth, tel. (08) 9221-9066, provides **disabled visitors** with helpful brochures and information on accommodations, restaurants, theaters, and recreational areas within the state.

To obtain maps and touring advice, call in at the **Royal Automobile Club of W.A.,** 228 Adelaide Terrace, tel. (08) 9421-4444. The bookshop has a good section of travel books, literature, and maps (many are free if you have proof of membership with a reciprocal club in another country). For an even broader range of maps, call into **The Perth Map Centre,** 891 Hay St., tel. (08) 9322-5733.

For information on Western Australia's national parks and conservation areas, contact the

Department of Conservation and Land Management (CALM), Hackett Dr., Crawley, tel. (08) 9442-0300 or (08) 9334-0333.

The **library** is at the Perth Cultural Centre, James St., tel. (08) 9427-3111. Hours are Mon.-Thurs. 9 a.m.-4:45 p.m., Friday 9 a.m.-5:30 p.m., Sat.-Sun. 10 a.m.-5:30 p.m. Internet access is available.

In an emergency, dial 000 to summon **fire, police,** and **ambulance** services. **Royal Perth Hospital,** Victoria Square, tel. (08) 9224-2244, maintains a 24-hour emergency room. For relief from killer toothaches, go to **Perth Dental Hospital,** 196 Goderich St., tel. (08) 9220-5777, or (08) 9325-3452 after-hours.

Angus and Robertson, 199 Murray St. and 625 Hay St., is the large commercial reading outlet. Another good shop is **Down to Earth Books,** 874 Hay Street. We love **Arcane Bookshop,** 212 William St., Northbridge (big selection of alternative literature, gay and lesbian sections, and poetry), and ditto for **New Editions,** South Terrace, Fremantle (with a café for real bookshop lovers).

The *West Australian* is the Monday through Saturday paper, while the *Sunday Times* finishes the weekend. **Plaza Newsagency,** in the Plaza Arcade off Hay Street Mall, sells national and international newspapers, as do some of the large hotels.

TRANSPORTATION

Getting There

By Air: If you're coming from Europe, Africa, or Southeast Asia, Perth will most likely be your Australian gateway city. **International carriers** include Qantas, Air New Zealand, United Airlines, British Airways, South African Airways, Garuda Indonesia, Malaysian Airlines, Thai Airways, Singapore Airlines, and Japan Airlines.

Domestic carriers that serve Perth from other Australian states are Ansett Australia, tel. (13) 1300, and Qantas, tel. (13) 1313. For up-to-date prices and cheapest deals, consult the **Britannia YHA,** 253 William St., Northbridge, tel. (08) 9328-6121, or **STA,** 100 James St., Northbridge, tel. (08) 9227-7299. Inquire into moneysaving **passes** before you leave home (or enter the country).

Sample airfares to domestic cities include: Adelaide ($380); Alice Springs ($485); Darwin ($490); Melbourne ($580); and Sydney ($590).

Perth International Airport is about 16 km northeast of the city center, and the separate **domestic terminal** is about 10 km closer. Moneychanging and other customary big-city facilities are available.

The privately operated **Perth Airport City Shuttle,** tel. (08) 9250-2838, meets all incoming flights and drops passengers off at city airline offices and major hotels. Fare is $9 international, $7 domestic. Several **Transperth** city buses operate between the domestic airport and city center. Services run daily, every 40-50 minutes 6 a.m.-10 p.m., less frequently on Saturday, not at all on Sunday. William St., between St. George's Terrace and the Esplanade, is the main pickup and drop-off spot. Fare is $4. **Taxis** are readily available and the 25-minute ride to city center should cost around $25.

By Train: Interstate trains arrive into and depart from the **East Perth Railway Terminal,** West Parade.

The fabled **Indian-Pacific** runs between Perth and Sydney. The 65-hour, three-night journey passes through Broken Hill and Adelaide and crosses the Nullarbor Plain on the world's longest straight stretch of railway line. Trains depart Sydney on Monday and Thursday, and Perth on Monday and Friday. One-way fares are: $1,172, first-class berth with meals; $763, economy berth with meals; and $378, economy seat. The Indian-Pacific is included in the **Austrailpass** (except the eight-day Austrail Flexi-Pass), which must be purchased outside the country.

For information and bookings, phone **Rail Australia,** tel. (13) 2232, or **Westrail,** tel. (08) 9326-2244 or (13) 1053.

Contact Westrail for bookings on the Prospector (daily Perth-Kalgoorlie, $58) and the Australind (daily Perth-Bunbury, $35). Intercity trains depart from East Perth Terminal, West Parade.

By Bus: Greyhound Pioneer, tel. (13) 2030, serves Perth daily from other Australian states. Routes from the east coast usually travel via Adelaide, while the Darwin-to-Perth coaches journey across the Top End and down the west coast. Sample fares are: Sydney-Adelaide-Perth (61 hours), $310; Adelaide-Perth (37 hours), $214; Darwin-Perth (59 hours), $415. Inquire about stopover privileges and special passes for overseas visitors.

By Car: Western Australia is long, far, and wide. Sealed roads, suitable for conventional vehicles, are: Eyre and Great Eastern Highways from Adelaide (2,697 km); Eyre, South Coast, and South Western Highways from Adelaide (3,212 km); Stuart, Victoria, Great Northern, North West Coastal, and Brand Highways from Darwin (4,379 km); and Stuart, Victoria, and Great Northern Highways from Darwin (4,253 km). Make sure your vehicle and body are prepared for the arduous trek.

Though roadhouse facilities are available along the major byways, distances between them can be vast. The road from Ayers Rock is unsealed all the way to the Goldfields region, where it connects with the big highways. Carry plenty of spare everything, even passengers to share the *very* long—and often boring—drive and expensive petrol costs.

Hitching

It's fairly cheap—and a lot less exhausting—to take the bus or share a ride (check the YHA bulletin boards). Plus, hitching in Australia is illegal and can be dangerous. Waits of several days are not uncommon, plus who knows where you'll be waiting. There are some creepy stories about hitchhiking out there! Some friends once picked up a haggard old guy—who looked as if he hadn't eaten for a year—from the edge of the Nullarbor and the middle of nowhere. He drove with them about 100 km even deeper into nowhere, said, "This is where I get out," and wandered off into the proverbial sunset. I'm sure that story has one of the better endings!

If you're dead set on thumbing it, hop a train to Midland if you're headed north or east, or Armadale if your direction is south. Women should be especially careful, and preferably travel with a male companion (or a pit bull).

Getting Around on Buses and Trains

Transperth, the metropolitan transit district, operates free Central Area Transit (CAT) buses approximately every 10 minutes, Mon.-Fri. 7 a.m.-6 p.m. Routes are color-coded and circle the city center, covering most tourist attractions. The blue CAT also runs a modified weekend service. Other buses connect the business center with suburban areas, and though not free, they're still good deals. Tickets, good for two hours from the time of issue, range $1.50-2.50, depending on the number of zones you travel (eight zones, in all). Going to Fremantle, for example, you'll go through only two zones and it's about 20 km away! Even sweeter, tickets are interchangeable on all Transperth buses, trains, and ferries.

If you're sticking around for a while, you might want to consider a **multirider ticket,** which gives you 10 trips for the price of nine, and a **day pass** only costs $6. Buses operate Mon.-Fri. 6 a.m.-11:30 p.m., less frequently on weekends and public holidays.

Obtain maps, schedules, tickets, and other information from Transperth Information Services, Perth Central Bus Station, Wellington St., tel. (13) 2213, or at the City Bus Port, Mounts Bay Rd., at the bottom of William Street. Even more convenient is the Transperth information office in the Plaza Arcade, off the Hay Street Mall. Hours are Mon.-Fri. 6:30 a.m.-8 p.m., Saturday 8 a.m.-5 p.m.

Taxis

Meter-operated taxis can be hailed on city streets, plucked from taxi ranks around the central business district and Fremantle, or hired by phoning **Swan Taxis,** tel. (08) 9444-4444, or **Black and White Taxis,** tel. (08) 9333-3333. Taxis for **disabled passengers** are available Mon.-Fri. 8 a.m.-4:30 p.m. For information, phone (08) 9333-3377. Cab fare begins at $2.50 plus $1 per km, rising to a base charge of $3.70 6 p.m.-6 a.m.

Car Rentals

The big-name rental car companies are located at both the domestic and international airports and in the city center. Charges range $65-90, depending on size—some include unlimited km while others give only the first 100-150 km for a free allowance. For information, contact **Avis,** tel. (08) 9325-7677; **Hertz,** tel. (08) 9321-7777; or **Budget,** tel. (08) 9322-1100.

Rent heartier vehicles for Outback travel from **South Perth 4WD Rentals,** 80 Canning Hwy., Victoria Park, tel. (08) 9362-5444.

Plenty of other companies are listed in the phone book, but be cautious: sometimes the bigger companies can afford to give the better deals, particularly if you book your car from outside Australia. Get tips from the YHA hostels or STA office in Northbridge.

Bicycles

Excellent trails and climate make Perth an ideal city for cycling. Rent bicycles for $10 per day from the YHA on Francis St. or, for about $16, from **About Bike Hire,** at Riverside Drive's southeastern end, tel. (08) 9221-2665. The Western Australian Tourism Centre provides trail maps and brochures to set you on your way.

Ferries

Transperth ferries depart from the Barrack Street Jetty to Mends Street Jetty, across the Swan River in South Perth, daily 6:45 a.m.-7:15 p.m. One-way fare is $1.50. Contact Transperth Information Services, Perth Central Bus Station, Wellington St., tel. (13) 2213, for details. (Don't forget—your two-hour bus ticket is good on this ferry.)

For **Rottnest Island** ferries, contact **Boat Torque,** tel. (08) 9221-5844, or from Fremantle, the **Rottnest Express,** tel. (08) 9335-6406.

Tours

The Western Australia Tourist Centre can help you plan and book organized tours within the city and state. Prices vary $20-120 and include such destinations as wildflower-viewing sites (Aug.-Nov.), Swan Valley, the Darling Ranges, Wave Rock, Monkey Mia, Mt. Augustus, and Yanchep National Park. Longer three- to four-day treks up and down the coast average $400-550. Again, first check with YHA and STA for the best deals with, possibly, more simpatico companions.

City Sights coach tours run about $22 for a half day, $12 for the **Perth Tram** (actually a bus in drag), which makes 90-minute commentator-assisted trips around the city sights. The tram operates daily 9:30 a.m.-6:30 p.m. Pickup point is at 124 Murray St. (near Barrack St.).

Free guided **walking tours** of Kings Park are available April-October. For information, phone

(08) 9321-4801. A three-hour **Perth and Beyond** tour takes in the city as well as the park. For information, phone (08) 9483-2601.

All **boat cruises** leave from Barrack Street Jetty. Both **Boat Torque,** tel. (08) 9221-5844, and **Captain Cook Cruises,** tel. (08) 9325-3341, operate a number of scenic cruises including Swan River journeys, winery visits, and lunch and dinner extravaganzas.

Whalewatching cruises are offered by various operators, including **Boat Torque,** tel. (08) 9221-5844, and **Mills Charters,** tel. (08) 9401-0833. The Western Australia Tourist Centre has a comprehensive list of tour operators.

Westrail offers a variety of rail excursions lasting from one day to one week, covering everything from coastal resorts and timber forests to wildflowers and goldfields. For information and bookings, contact the Western Australian Tourist Centre, or Westrail, tel. (08) 9326-2244.

And who would want to miss the free 90-minute tour of **Swan Brewery?** Tours depart Mon.-Wed. 10 a.m. and 2:30 p.m., Thursday 2:30 p.m. only. For bookings, phone (08) 9350-0220.

Getting Away

Ansett Australia, tel. (13) 1300, schedules regular services between Perth and many W.A. communities including Broome, Derby, Kununurra, Port Hedland, Newman, Exmouth, Carnarvon, Geraldton, and Kalgoorlie.

Skywest, tel. (08) 9334-2288 (or book through Ansett), flies from Perth to Albany, Esperance, Kalgoorlie, Geraldton, Cue, Meekatharra, Wiluna, and other communities. Qantas' **Airlink** connects Perth with Karratha, Tom Price, Port Hedland, Broome, and Kalgoorlie.

For Rottnest Island Service, contact **Rottnest Airlines,** tel. (08) 9478-1322.

Transperth, tel. (13) 2213, operates frequent "fastrack" rail service between the Wellington Street station and Fremantle, Midland, Armadale, and points in between. Trains run Mon.-Fri. 5:30 a.m.-11:30 p.m., with reduced schedules on weekends and public holidays.

VICINITY OF PERTH

Even though this mega-state spans a third of the continent, you can still manage to get to some pretty interesting places in the course of a day or two.

FREMANTLE

You've heard of Fremantle—site of the 1987 America's Cup race where Kevin Parry lost the yachties' prized petunia to San Diego's Dennis Connor. Believe it or not, Fremantle actually existed *before* then—and has continued since.

Perth's port district (pop. 27,000), called "Freo" by the locals, sits 19 km southwest of Perth, where the Swan River kisses the Indian Ocean. Founded along with Perth in 1829, the city was named for Captain Charles Howe Fremantle, who claimed Australia's west coast for the British Crown. The settlement was practically dormant until those hardworking convicts were brought in to construct many of the town's buildings—including their own jail.

Though Fremantle is a modern port, much of the old district with its 19th-century buildings and shop fronts has been preserved and—thanks to the Cup race—spruced up and painted,

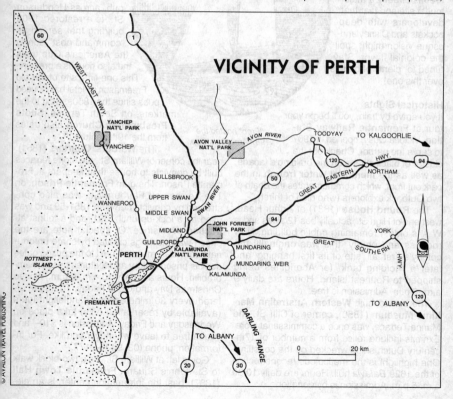

VICINITY OF PERTH

at least within the last decade. It's an easy stroll, a popular tourist town of historical sites, art galleries, and sidewalk cafés.

In 1998, a controversy began mounting in this otherwise low-key community. A "Master Plan" has been drafted that would call for a major development—referred to as the Maritime Precinct—to take place along Fremantle's treasured 19th-century Victoria Quay. The deal will include a multistory maritime museum, waterfront park and promenade, multiuse facilities, parking lots, new ferry port, and *plenty* of shops and restaurants. The point, of course, is to draw tourists (and their dollars). But many residents feel that Freo is *already* a major tourist site and fear that developers with deep pockets and Disneyland-esque vision might spoil the colonial flavor. Stay tuned for plenty of battles over this one!

Historical Sights

If you arrive by train, you'll begin your tour at **Fremantle Railway Station,** Victoria Quay, opened in 1907 to serve the harbor. Check out the cluster of black swans on the building's facade, as well as the **memorial water trough** in the park out front, which commemorates the death of two Outback explorers (who died of thirst).

The **Round House** (1831) at Arthur Head, west end of High St., actually has 12 sides and is W.A.'s oldest remaining public building. Now roofless and empty, this was originally the colony's first jail, site of its first hanging, and later a "holding tank" for Aborigines being shipped to Rottnest Island. Hours are daily 9 a.m.-6 p.m. Admission is free.

The convict-built **Western Australian Maritime Museum** (1850), corner of Cliff St. and Marine Terrace, was once a commissariat store. Exhibits include relics from a number of 17th-century Dutch ships wrecked off the coastline. One highlight is the meticulous reconstruction of the 1629 *Batavia* hull. Hours are daily 10:30 a.m.-5 p.m. Admission is by donation.

"Freo" hosted the 1987 America's Cup.

Following Marine Terrace back toward town, you'll pass the **Old Court House** on your left, and a statue of **C.Y. O'Connor** (he's the bloke who built the artificial harbor here in the 1860s) off to the right. Continue on Marine Terrace, turning left at Essex St., which, as you cross South Terrace, becomes Henderson Street.

Fremantle Markets, on the corner, date from 1897. Reactivated in the mid-1970s, this is still the area's most lively weekly market. Approximately 170 stalls offer fruit, veggies, arts, crafts, and other market kitsch, bargains, and buskers. Shopping hours are Friday 9 a.m.-9 p.m., Saturday 9 a.m.-5 p.m., Sunday and public holidays 10 a.m.-5 p.m.

The **Sail and Anchor** pub, across Henderson St., is a restored 1903 building that served as "command post" during the America's Cup trials and also houses a brewery. This one-time site of the old Freemason's Hotel has housed pubs since the 1850s. Next to the markets, on South Terrace, **Scots Presbyterian Church** also dates from the 19th century.

The **Warders' Quarters** (1851), near the corner of William St., are stone terraces built by convicts to house their keepers at Fremantle Prison. The grim **Fremantle Prison,** on The Terrace off Fairburn St., was also constructed by convicts between 1851-59 and was used as a lock-up until 1991, and a tourist attraction ever since. Of special note are the prison-wall drawings created by some unfortunate convict. A museum next to the prison gates depicts prison history and features prison memorabilia. Hours are daily 10 a.m.-6 p.m., closed Christmas Day and Good Friday. Tours are offered every 30 minutes, and candlelight tours (available by reservation only) take place on Wednesday and Friday. Admission is $10—and you're free to leave whenever you like. For information, phone (08) 9430-7177.

Going left at William St., it's a two-block walk to St. John's Square. **Fremantle Town Hall** (1887), past the information center, is an elegant structure opened in conjunction with Queen Victoria's Jubilee. Opposite the Town Hall, on William St., the **Federal Hotel** is another atmospheric pub that dates from 1887. **St. John's Anglican Church** (1881), next door, is a stone structure that took three years to complete.

Old **St. Patrick's Church** sits at the corner of Adelaide and Quarry Streets. **Proclamation Tree**, across Quarry St., is a Moreton Bay fig tree planted around the turn of the century. On the opposite side of Adelaide St., the **Old Fremantle Boys' School** used to be guess what.

Fremantle Museum and Arts Centre, corner of Ord and Finnerty Streets in Fremantle Park, served as the local lunatic asylum between 1861-65, a women's home in the early 1900s, and the 1942 headquarters for American Forces stationed in Western Australia. After a 13-year restoration, the Gothic-esque sandstone building reopened in 1972 as a museum and art center featuring changing exhibitions (with an emphasis on Western Australian artists), a museum wing with displays and mementos of Fremantle's history, a lecture room, and cloistered courtyard used for music and theatrical performances and crafts fairs. Hours are Mon.-Wed. 10:30 a.m.-5 p.m., Thurs.-Sun. 1-5 p.m. Sunday concerts are often performed in the courtyard. Admission to both wings is free. For information, phone (08) 9430-7966.

One block south, at the corner of Ord and Ellen Streets, **Samson House** (1888) was and still is associated with a prominent Fremantle family (name of Samson). Contained within are historic photographs, antique furnishings, and a 20-meter-deep, in-house well. Hours are Sunday and Thursday 1-5 p.m. Guided tours are available.

Other Sights

Down in the B Shed, at Victoria Quay, **Historic Boat Shed Museum** features a wide range of vessels, including the America's Cup winner *Australia II* and a full-size replica of the *Endeavour,* the ship in which Captain James Cook discovered Australia. Hours are daily 1-5 p.m. Admission is free.

Western Australia Maritime Museum, 1 Cliff St., tel. (08) 9431-8444, presents exhibits relating to W.A.'s sailfaring past, including marine archaeology, ship relics, and a photo gallery.

Hours are daily 10:30 a.m.-5 p.m. Admission is by donation.

Fremantle Wharves and Passenger Terminal, accessible by car, is usually filled with assorted ships from all over the world—free entertainment for boat lovers of all ages.

Up Mews Rd. toward the Esplanade, **Fremantle Crocodile Park** houses more than 200 fresh- and saltwater crocs, living as they might in their Kimberley homeland. Viewing is from the safety of a raised metal walkway, enclosed with a tall chain-link fence. Education tours and a film document crocodile history and explain how the Aussie crocs were saved from extinction. Hours are Mon.-Fri. 10 a.m.-4 p.m., Sat.-Sun. 10 a.m.-5 p.m. Feedings are daily at 2 p.m. Admission is $8. For information, phone (08) 9430-5388.

If you're into gas and electricity, you can study its local history at the **World of Energy Museum,** 12 Parry St., tel. (08) 9430-5655. Hours are Mon.-Fri. 12:30-4:30 p.m., Sat.-Sun. 1-4:30 p.m. Admission is free.

Arts and Crafts

Fremantle abounds with artisans, and their wares are on display and for sale in converted boat sheds, warehouses, and historic buildings and markets throughout town.

Bannister Street Craftworks, 8 Bannister St., is a converted warehouse that houses a variety of studios representing pottery, stained glass, fabric printing, leatherwork, woodwork, weaving, and gold- and silversmithing. Hours are Tues.-Sat. 10 a.m.-5 p.m., Sunday and public holidays 12:30-5:30 p.m.

Kidogo Arthouse, at the end of Marine Terrace, features the work of Western Australian artists, including renowned potter Joan Campbell. Hours are Mon.-Fri. 10 a.m.-5 p.m., Sat.-Sun. 11 a.m.-5 p.m.

J Shed, at Arthur's Head, houses the studio/workshop of renowned Australian sculptor Greg James. You've probably seen a number of his realistic-looking figures in public areas around the country. Hours are sporadic, dependent upon works in progress.

Accommodations

Simple pub accommodations are available at the **Newport Hotel,** 2 South Terrace, tel. (08) 9335-2428. Inexpensive. The **Norfolk Hotel,** 47

South Terrace, tel. (08) 9335-5405, and the **Fremantle Hotel,** 6 High St., tel. (08) 9430-4300, both historic beauties, are lovelier pub offerings. Moderate.

Studios and one-bedroom apartments are costly at the river-view **Tradewinds Hotel,** 66 Canning Hwy., East Fremantle, tel. (08) 9339-8188. Premium. The **Fremantle Esplanade,** 46 Marine Terrace, tel. (08) 9432-4000, represents the big splurge ($150-350 per night), with all the goodies that come with big bucks. Luxury.

For cozy, historic B&B accommodation, try **Moonrakers,** 79 South St., South Fremantle, tel. (08) 9336-2266, or **Fothergills,** 20 Ord St., tel. (08) 9335-6784. Both establishments will pamper you with luxurious surroundings, cloud-soft beds, and delectable breakfasts. Expensive. **Barbara's Cottages,** 26 Holdsworth St., Fremantle, tel. (08) 9430-8051, offers a beautiful two-bedroom heritage cottage with Victorian decor, open fireplace, stereo, and cloud-soft beds, or the less-costly rear-garden studio with bed-sitting room, loft area, and kitchenette. Moderate-Premium.

Dorm beds ($14) are available at **Backpackers Inn Freo,** 11 Pakenham St., tel. (08) 9431-7065. Ambiance is quiet, no locals are allowed, and the carved woodwork lends a bit of elegance. A kitchen, café, 24-hour check-in, and laundry facilities are extra perks, as is the YHA member discount. Budget. Another possibility is **Old Firestation Backpackers,** 18 Phillimore St., tel. (08) 996-6066, near the railway station. Dorm beds run $12, an adjacent Indian restaurant offers $5 curry dinners to guests, and there's an exclusive lounge just for women and couples. Budget.

Homestays can be arranged, at various rates. Contact the Fremantle Information Centre, tel. (08) 9430-2222, for a list of participants.

Food

You'll find plenty of reasonably priced pub meals and ethnic eateries in Fremantle, but fresh fish and seafood are the local specialties. **Lombardo's,** Mews Rd., Fishing Boat Harbour, is a waterfront complex with everything from takeaway fish and chips stalls and outdoor cafés to bistros and fine restaurants.

South Terrace is another popular area lined with cappuccino bars and sidewalk cafés. Not surprisingly, it's dubbed "Cappuccino Strip." One of Fremantle's ranking favorites is **Old Papa's,** 17 South Terrace, which serves coffee, cakes, and pasta dishes ($8-12) on a terrace overlooking the street. If there's a long wait, try the **Mexican Kitchen** next door. If you have your heart set on Italian, **Roma,** 9 High St., has been dishing up spaghetti and other inexpensive specialties ($8-16) for several decades. Other Italian favorites are **Luigi's** and **Pizza Bella Roma,** both on South Terrace (pastas at both range $10-16). And, at 64 South Terrace, the historic **Sail and Anchor Hotel** has an enjoyable brasserie ($8-14) and an even more enjoyable brewery (this was the first Australian on-site brewery, hopping the way for the boutique-beer industry).

The best breakfast is at the **Round House Café,** also on High St. ($6-10). **Vung Tau,** 19 High St., serves up Vietnamese and vegetarian dishes ($7-15). For Turkish specialties ($6-16) like yummy hummus, grilled lamb, flatbread, and baklava, head to **Istanbul,** 19-B Essex St., tel. (08) 9335-6068.

Granita's, 330 South Terrace, tel. (08) 9336-4660, specializes in seafood and pasta dishes at high prices ($16-27) in a trendy, upmarket spot in town. Sushi and teppanyaki lovers (preferably on expense accounts) will want to try posh **Chunagon,** 46 Mews Rd., tel. (08) 9336-1000, overlooking the harbor ($22-36).

Entertainment

High St. and South Terrace are where you'll find most of the live bands and a disco or two. Try the **Orient,** on High St., where bands blast at high volume. **Seaview Tavern** and **Newport Arms Hotel** are two front-runner band venues on South Terrace.

Catch live Irish music on weekends at the **National Hotel,** 98 High St., or **Rosie O'Grady's,** William St., across from the town hall. The smoke-free **Fly By Night Musicians Club,** Parry St., draws the local reggae, blues, and folk crowd.

Information and Services

Pick up info, brochures, and walking tour maps at the **Fremantle Information Centre,** Kings Square, in the Town Hall. Hours are Mon.-Fri. 9 a.m.-5 p.m., Saturday 9 a.m.-1 p.m., Sunday 10 a.m.-3 p.m. For information, phone (08) 9430-2222.

WA Naturally, 47 Henry St., Fremantle, tel. (08) 9430-8600, another branch of CALM, provides information and brochures on Western Australia's national parks and conservation reserves.

For emergencies, dial 000; the **police,** tel. (08) 9430-1222; or **Fremantle Hospital,** South Terrace and Alma St., tel. (08) 9431-3333.

Transportation

Frequent bus and train service connect Perth with Fremantle. **Transperth buses,** tel. (13) 2213, traveling various routes, depart from St. George's Terrace, while trains (traveling only one route) leave from Perth Central Station.

Captain Cook Cruises, tel. (08) 9325-3341, provides daily ferry service from Perth ($12). In addition, some Rottnest Island ferries stop at Fremantle. For information, phone **Boat Torque Cruises,** tel. (08) 9221-5844, or the **Rottnest Express,** tel. (08) 9335-6406.

For **bicycle rentals,** contact **Captain Munchies,** 2 Beach St., tel. (08) 9339-6633, or **Fleet Cycles,** tel. (08) 9430-5414. The **Fremantle Tram,** like the Perth Tram, makes frequent tours (with accompanying commentary) around the local sights. Cost is $9. A harbor tour ($10) and Top of the Port tour ($14) are also available. For information, phone (08) 9339-8719.

ROTTNEST ISLAND

This sandy island resort—affectionately known as "Rotto"—lies just 19 km off the Fremantle coast and is a favorite day excursion and holiday destination for Perth residents drawn to its bleached beaches, turquoise waters, and activities (or inactivity).

Rottnest translates to "Rat's Nest," a name bestowed upon it by Dutch mariner Willem de Vlamingh. Landing there in 1696, Willem mistook the native quokkas—a type of small marsupial—for a bunch of big, old rats. These days the quokkas are a protected species and one of the island's big tourist attractions.

Originally used as a prison settlement for mainland Aborigines back in 1838, the prison was vacated in 1903, and 14 years later it became a getaway spot for white society—which it

still is today. One of the few shady spots, Thomson Bay is the main resort area of this tiny 11-km-long, five-km-wide island. The rest of the landscape consists of sparse vegetation, a few low hills, some shallow salt lakes, plenty of white-sand beaches, and secluded rocky bays. Add to that the surrounding reef, protected lagoons, and some 12 shipwrecks to explore.

Sights

Get your bearings at **Rottnest Museum,** located at the main settlement. Exhibits and memorabilia cover convict history, wildlife, and shipwrecks. Walking-tour leaflets, including info and directions around the remaining convict-built structures, are available. Hours are daily 10 a.m.-1:30 p.m. and 2:30-4:30 p.m. Dec.-Feb., daily 11 a.m.-1:30 p.m. and 2:30-4 p.m. other months. For information, phone (08) 9372-9753.

Vlamingh Lookout, via Digby Dr., offers panoramic views of the island, surrounding ocean, and Gordon Lake. **Oliver Hill,** via Digby Dr., offers yet another dynamic island view and a leftover artillery battery.

Constructed of locally quarried limestone, **Rottnest Lighthouse,** Wadjemup Hill, in the center of the island, dates back to the mid-1800s. **Bathurst Lighthouse,** Gem Rd., Bathurst Point, the second of Rotto's lighthouses, was built in 1900.

Located in the island center east and northeast of the jetty are the small **salt lakes**—Government House, Serpentine, Herschell, Baghdad, Pink, and Garden Lakes. You'll see those quokkas (relatives of the wallaby) at the **Quokka Colony,** between Government House and Herschell Lakes. This lot—used to having their faces stuffed by tourists—is quite tame.

Best **swimming beaches** include **Parakeet Bay,** at the island's northernmost tip, and **The Basin,** north of the main settlement. **West End,** the island's westernmost point, is popular (and crowded) with hopeful **fishers. Shipwreck** sights are signposted along a marked trail around the island; however, snorkelers will need a boat to reach most of them. (Boats, as well as snorkeling and fishing gear, can be hired on the island.)

Accommodations and Food

If you want to make Rotto more than a day trip, keep in mind that accommodations must be booked way in advance, particularly during holidays and summer months when the Perthos descend en masse. For information on rates and bookings, phone **Rottnest Island Authority,** tel. (08) 9372-9752.

Accommodations are concentrated around the Thomson Bay settlement and comprise cabins, hotel and motel rooms, a hostel, and campground. Due to a water shortage, showers at Rotto accommodations are saltwater; bring saltwater shampoo and soap with you because it's more expensive on the island.

Overlooking the main beach, **Rottnest Hotel,** tel. (08) 9292-5011, is Rotto's gathering spot. Built in 1864 as the summer residence of Western Australian governors, it was reopened as a hotel in 1953. Moderate. **Rottnest Island Authority Cottages,** tel. (08) 9372-9729, sleep four to eight people, at a cost of $175-675 per week. Inexpensive-Moderate.

Rottnest Youth Hostel, tel. (08) 9372-9780, about one km from the ferry terminal, is in a former 1936 barracks and still looks the part. Facilities include a lounge and kitchen, but hot water is scarce. Beds cost $18.

Campsites, tents, and cabins are available at **Thomson Camping Areas,** tel. (08) 9372-9737. Budget-Moderate.

Food is relatively expensive, as on most tourist-type islands—even at the general store and fast-food center. **Rottnest Hotel** serves moderately priced steaks ($10-13) and salads in a casual environment, while another section offers fine dining. The **Rottnest Island Lodge** has a similar setup: the restaurant is à la carte and expensive; the bar section features inexpensive all-you-can-eat midweek meals ($8-12). Buy fresh bread and yummy baked goodies at the **Rottnest Island Bakery.**

Information

Tourist information along with walking and cycling maps are available at the **Tourist Information Centre,** at the end of the main jetty, tel. (08) 9372-9752. Hours are daily 9 a.m.-4 p.m.

Dial 000 to request **emergency assistance** or contact **Rottnest Nursing Post,** tel. (08) 9292-5030.

Transportation

Rottnest Airlines, tel. (08) 9478-1322, or (08) 9292-5027 in Rotto, flies daily from Perth for

about $65 roundtrip. A shuttle bus takes you from Rottnest Airport to the main wharf area.

Boat Torque Cruises operates a daily ferry service to the island aboard its *Star Flyte,* departing from Perth's Barrack Street Jetty and from Fremantle. Fare is $42 roundtrip from Perth, $30 roundtrip from Fremantle.

No cars are allowed on the island. Most visitors rely on bicycles—a round-the-island bike path covers 26 km. Bring your own cycle on the ferry (an extra $5) or rent one from **Rottnest Island Bike Hire,** behind the Rottnest Hotel, tel. (08) 9292-5105. Rates run $12-20 per day.

Bus service is available during summer months, bus tours around the island are available most months, and **Oliver Hill Railway** takes passengers along three-plus miles of reconstructed railway line into the heart of the island's gun batteries. Check with the tourist information office for schedules and bookings.

YANCHEP NATIONAL PARK

Only 51 km north of Perth, Yanchep National Park is a 2,799-hectare, family-oriented coastal wonderland with bushland, caves, walking trails, a wildlife sanctuary, boating lake, swimming pool, golf course, footie ovals (football fields), limestone gorges, fauna exhibits, aviaries, a beer garden, and a museum. Despite all these attractions, 90% of the park has been maintained in its natural state. The historic 1880s McNeese House, recently remodeled, is now an interpretive center providing information on park activities, history, flora, and fauna. The upper level houses an art gallery.

Of the numerous caves set in the limestone hills, **Crystal Cave,** open to the public, features an underground stream in the main grotto, good examples of stalactites and stalagmites, and "fantasy lighting." Guided tours are offered several times daily. **Yonderup Cave** has been upgraded and reopened, plus there are a variety of new walking trails, including the beginning point of a 100-km coastal plains trail walk.

Another favorite activity is the **Yanjidi Trail,** a 28-km walk through the Loch McNess wetlands, a refuge for waterfowl and other birds (and the Loch McNess monster?). Signs along the path—which follows the tracks used by the local Yaberoo Aborigines—explain the wetland ecology.

To reach Yanchep, follow the West Coast Highway north out of town, or catch a daily Transperth bus from Perth Central Bus Station. Admission is $5 per vehicle, or $2 per bus passenger.

Other Sights

Traveling the West Coast Highway from Perth, you'll pass through **Wanneroo,** another popular wine-producing area and a fast-growing artsy-craftsy-touristy center. The **Gumnut Factory,** 30 Prindiville Dr., Wangara Centre, tel. (08) 9409-6699, manufactures all types of gumnut creations, and you can watch it happen. Don't miss Gumnutland, a model village with more than 30 handcrafted buildings, working railways, roads, and mini gumnut people—all crafted from timber, flowers, and gumnuts. Open daily 9 a.m.-5 p.m. Admission is $2.

If you're passing through Wanneroo on the weekend, take time to stop at the **market** in the carpark at the corner of Prindiville Dr. and Ismail St., where 200 stalls offer a wide range of goods for sale.

Wineries offering tastings are **Faranda Wines,** 768 Wanneroo Rd., tel. (08) 9306-1174, and **Paul Conti Wines,** 529 Wanneroo Rd., tel. (08) 9409-9160.

And then there's **Wild Kingdom Wildlife Park,** Two Rocks Rd., tel. (08) 9561-1399, with wombats, dingoes, foxes, and other animals, as well as birdlife. Open daily 9:30 a.m.-5 p.m., closed Christmas Day. Admission is $5.

Accommodations

The **Yanchep Lagoon Lodge,** 11 Nautical Court, tel. (08) 9561-1033, at Yanchep Lagoon, has comfortable guesthouse accommodations. Moderate. **Club Capricorn,** Two Rocks Rd., tel. (08) 9561-2505, is a deluxe beachfront resort with lodge and chalet accommodations, plus a restaurant, swimming pools, and tennis courts. Expensive.

Information

For info on **Yanchep National Park,** phone (08) 9561-1004. In **Wanneroo,** the Tourist Information Centre is at 935 Wanneroo Rd., tel. (08) 9405-4678.

THE DARLING RANGE

This range, full of wooded hills, valleys, and dams, runs east of Perth and parallel to the coastline. It's a popular picnic, bushwalking, and weekend-away place for Perth dwellers, particularly from September to November, when an astounding assortment of more than 4,000 wildflower species are in bloom. You can take a number of different roads as far and flung as you like; one easy, close-to-Perth route is to catch Kalamunda Rd. from South Guildford, to Kalamunda sights, then pick up Mundaring Weir Rd., meeting the Great Eastern Highway back into Perth. Transperth buses journey to the range on a variety of routes.

Sights

For some great coastal plain and city lights views, negotiate three km of sharp hairpin and hair-raising turns on the one-way **Zig Zag Road** (formerly a railway line). Signs are posted off Kalamunda Rd., Gooseberry Hill. You can also reach steep, 33-hectare Gooseberry Hill via Gooseberry Hill Rd., Williams Rd., or Lascelles Parade.

Stirk Park and Cottage, 9A Headingly Rd., Kalamunda, is a restored 1881 cottage surrounded by a public reserve with scenic walks and waterways, an ornamental lake, model boat pond, and bowling greens. Hours are daily 9 a.m.-9 p.m. The cottage is open Sunday 1:30-4:30 p.m.

History Village, corner Railway and Williams Roads, Kalamunda, is a museum on the site of the old railway station, plus the original state school building, post office, and a settler's cottage, transported to the site. Memorabilia and displays illustrate the area's early history. Open Thurs.-Sat. 9 a.m.-noon, Sunday 2-4:30 p.m. Admission is $2.

Kalamunda National Park, via Kalamunda Rd., offers 375 hectares of forest scenery, granite boulder outcrops, seasonal wildflowers, wildlife, and birdlife. Visitors must carry their own water in hot weather.

Mundaring Weir, Mundaring Weir Rd., Mundaring, is the reservoir that provides water for the goldfields towns more than 500 km away. The **C.Y. O'Connor Museum,** named for the engineer who devised this system, features displays and exhibits relating to the complicated water system. Museum hours are Monday, Wednesday, Thursday, Friday, and public holidays 10:30 a.m.-3 p.m., Saturday 1-4 p.m., Sunday noon-5 p.m. Admission is $1.

John Forrest National Park, reached via the Great Eastern Highway, consists of 1,577 hectares of open forest and woodland, spring wildflowers, city and coastal views, and scenic walking trails. Western Australia's first national park was declared in 1895 and named for Lord John Forrest, the state's premier 1890-1901.

Accommodations
All Travellers Motel, 169 Great Eastern Hwy., Belmont, tel. (08) 9479-4060, offers motel rooms and is comfortable but not fancy. Moderate. **Mundaring Weir Hotel,** Mundaring Weir Rd., tel. (08) 9295-1106, is a popular getaway for Perth runaways. Expensive.

The YHA operates a **hostel** at Mundaring, on Mundaring Weir Rd., tel. (08) 9295-1809, offering dorm beds for $14 per night. **Campsites** are available at Mundaring Caravan Park, Great Eastern Hwy., tel. (08) 9295-1125. Budget.

SWAN VALLEY

The good news is that the scenic, fertile Swan Valley and its 20 or so wineries are a mere 20 km northeast of Perth—an easy car ride or river cruise away. The bad news is that the area is so close to the city, which is expanding so rapidly that many of the rural communities are blending into the urban area. The Swan River meanders the wide valley set at the foot of the Darling Range—a patchwork mix of small farms and award-winning wineries, stretching from Perth through historic Guildford to the Upper Swan, passing a number of interesting sights along the way.

Sights
The 1830 **Tranby House,** Johnson Rd., Maylands, is Western Australia's oldest inhabited property. Hours are Mon.-Sat. 2-5 p.m., Sunday 11 a.m.-1 p.m. and 2-5 p.m. Admission is $3.

View nearly 30 locomotives (including steam, diesel, and electric), antique carriages, and other railway memorabilia, photos, and artifacts at the **Rail Transport Museum,** 136 Railway Parade, Bassendean (300 meters east of Ashfield Railway Station). Steam train tours are available May-October. Hours are Sunday and public holidays 1-5 p.m., Wednesday 1-4 p.m. during school holidays. Admission is $4. For information, phone (08) 9279-7189.

In Guildford, situated at the rear of the historic 1840 Rose and Crown Hotel, 105 Swan St., the private **Hall Collection** consists of 40,000 antique and nostalgic artifacts, including porcelain, paintings, glass, copper work, cameras, musical instruments, toys, and kitchen items. Hours are Tues.-Sun. 10 a.m.-4:30 p.m. Admission is $3. For information, phone (08) 9279-8444.

Woodbridge House, Third Ave., Guildford, is the National Trust-restored 1885 residence of Perth personality extraordinaire Charles Harper. Hours are daily except Wednesday 1-4 p.m., Sunday 11 a.m.-1 p.m. and 2-5 p.m. Admission is $3. For information, phone (08) 9274-2432.

The **Historic Gaol and Settlers Cottage,** Meadow St., Guildford, exhibits period furnishings and clothing, blacksmithing tools and equipment, and bric-a-brac. Hours are 2-5 p.m. March to mid-December. Admission is $2. For information, phone (08) 9279-1248.

Other 19th-century Guildford buildings are **St. Matthew's Church,** in Stirling Square, and the jail, corner of Swan and Meadow Streets. See local pottery at **Guildford Potters,** 105 Swan Street. Hours are daily 10 a.m.-3 p.m.

Caversham Wildlife Park and Zoo, corner of Arthur Rd. and Cranleigh St., West Swan, is a wildlife park featuring Australian and imported animals and birds. Hours are daily 10 a.m.-5 p.m. Admission is $6. For information, phone (08) 9274-2202.

Gomboc Gallery and Sculpture Park, James Rd., Middle Swan, displays paintings, sculptures, and graphics by Western Australian artists. Hours are Wed.-Sun. and public holidays 10 a.m.-5 p.m. For information, phone (08) 9274-3996.

Wineries
Swan Valley vineyards are sprinkled along the river, from the Guildford area to Upper Swan. Though vines were first planted in the 1830s,

the Middle Swan district (with its more recent plantings) is responsible for much of the high production. Most of the wineries welcome visitors for divine tastings.

Olive Farm Winery, 77 Great Eastern Hwy., South Guildford, tel. (08) 9277-2989, named for the olive trees planted along with the vines, is the region's oldest winery. Hours are Mon.-Fri. 10 a.m.-5:30 p.m., Saturday and public holidays 9 a.m.-3 p.m.

Some of the valley's renowned wineries include: **Houghton Wines,** Dale Rd., Middle Swan, tel. (08) 9274-5100; **Jane Brook Estate Wines,** Toodyay Rd., tel. (08) 9274-1432; **Sandalford Wines,** corner West Swan and Middle Swan Roads, Caversham, tel. (08) 9274-5922; **Twin Hill Wines,** Great Northern Hwy., Baskerville, tel. (08) 9296-4272; and **Westfield Wines,** Memorial Ave., Baskerville, tel. (08) 9269-4356.

For maps and information about all of the wineries plus other Swan Valley attractions, stop into the Western Australia Tourist Centre in Perth or the **Swan Valley Tourism Association,** Great Eastern Hwy., Midland (under the Town Hall clocktower), or phone (08) 9274-1522.

Transportation

Transperth buses and trains depart regularly for the Swan Valley. Trains stop at Guildford, then go on to the valley's gateway town of Midland. Buses travel all the way to Upper Swan along Middle Swan Road. For information, phone Transperth, tel. (13) 2213.

If you're traveling by car (30-40 minutes' drive), take Guildford Road or the Great Eastern Highway to Midland, then turn onto the Great Northern Highway through the valley's center.

AVON VALLEY

Homesick English settlers fell in love with this lush, hilly valley, which reminded them of their very own Avon—hence the name. Rainfall-green in winter and parched-sun brown in summer, this rural land, settled only one year after Perth, follows the course of the Avon River (an east- and southward branch of the Swan), running through the historic towns of Toodyay, Northam, and York.

Toodyay

Say "Two Jay," otherwise you'll be ignored—or worse. The smallest of the river towns, Toodyay (pop. 560) sits at the bend where the Avon River turns from east to south. There was an earlier Toodyay settled in the 1830s, some eight km downstream; today's Toodyay—established in 1860 as Newcastle—was rechristened in 1910. The National Trust declared the town "historic" in 1980, and some 13 buildings have been classified as worthy of preservation.

Connors Mill, corner of Stirling Terrace and Piessa St., contains a steam engine, a 1941 generator, and the **Moondyne Gallery,** which recounts the story of infamous bushranger Joseph Bolitho Jones (a.k.a. Moondyne Joe). Hours are Mon.-Sat. 9 a.m.-5 p.m., Sunday and public holidays 10 a.m.-5 p.m. Admission is $1.

Trace the lives (and deaths) of 1800s pioneers and convicts at the **Old Gaol Museum and Police Station,** Clinton Street. The Old Gaol, an early stone and shingle-roofed structure, includes original cells. Hours are Mon.-Fri. 11 a.m.-3 p.m., Saturday 1-4 p.m., Sunday and public holidays 11 a.m.-4 p.m. Admission is $2.

White Gum Flower Farm, Sandplain Rd., features commercially grown wildflowers amid 283 hectares of white gum timberland. Hours are Wed.-Sun. 10 a.m.-4 p.m. Closed Christmas Day through March.

Avon Valley National Park, via Toodyay Rd. (make a left at Morangyup Rd. and follow posted signs), is a beautifully scenic 4,377-hectare park with valleys, slopes, woodlands, and open forest.

Northam

Believe it or not, Northam (pop. 6,800) is not only the largest Avon Valley town, but W.A.'s second-largest inland center (it's on the railway line to Kalgoorlie), notable for its black swans, white swans, and the whitewater Avon Descent Race.

See the **Avon Valley Arts Society,** 33 Wellington St., which comprises two historic structures—the Old Post Office (1892) and the Old Girls School (1877). The art center sells locally made arts and crafts. Hours are Tues.-Fri. 9 a.m.-4 p.m., Sat.-Mon. 10 a.m.-4 p.m. For information, phone (08) 9622-2245.

The **Old Railway Station,** Fitzgerald St. West, contains early 1900s appliances and railway relics, plus renovated carriages and an old steam train, and a tea garden. Hours are Sat.-Sun. 11 a.m.-4 p.m. Admission is $2.

Other historic sights are: **Pioneer Graves,** Goomalling Rd.; **Morby Cottage** (1836), Avon Dr.; the **police station** (1866) and **courthouse** (1896), both on Wellington St.; **St. John's Church** (1890), Wellington St.; **St. Saviour's Church** (1862), Toodyay Rd.; and **Presbyterian Church** (1908), Duke St. (present home of the Link Theatre).

Near Northam, at Irishtown, **Buckland House** (1874) is one of the state's most stately homes. The restoration, and collections of antique furnishings, paintings, and silver, are worth a peek. Hours are Mon.-Wed. and Sat.-Sun. 10 a.m.-5 p.m. Closed Christmas Day through February. Admission is $4. For information, phone (08) 9622-1130.

York

Settled in 1830, this one-time commercial center for the Avon Valley declined when the railway passed it by in 1894, and it reverted to an agricultural community. In the 1970s, York (pop. 1,140) was rediscovered for its architectural delights and reputedly has more original buildings than any other town in Western Australia.

Avon Terrace, the main street, features buildings reflecting architectural styles ranging from the 1860s to the turn of the century. The **Old Police Station** complex comprises the old courthouse, troopers' cottage, stables, and cell blocks. Hours are Mon.-Fri. 11 a.m.-3 p.m., Sat.-Sun. and public holidays 10 a.m.-4 p.m. Admission is $3. The **Post Office Museum** illustrates York's postal history beginning from 1840. Phone (08) 9641-1301 to arrange admittance. Car lovers can rev their engines at the **Motor Museum,** tel. (08) 9641-1288, where more than 100 veteran, vintage, classic, and racing vehicles are on display. Hours are daily 10 a.m.-5 p.m., closed Christmas Day and Good Friday. Admission is $7.

Trace printing history through commentary and demonstrations on a century-old letter press at **Sandalwood Press.** Hours are Tues.-Thurs. and Sat.-Sun. 1-3 p.m. For information, phone (08) 9641-1714.

The **Art Gallery,** Avon Terrace, exhibits locally crafted jarrah furniture, paintings, and stained glass. Hours are Sun.-Fri. 10 a.m.-4 p.m.,

Saturday 10 a.m.-1 p.m. The **Doll Museum,** also on Avon Terrace, features more than 1,000 doll babies representing all nationalities. Hours are Sat.-Sun. 10 a.m.-noon and 1-3 p.m.

One of York's oldest buildings is the **Residency Museum,** Brook Street. In a structure dating back to 1842, the museum displays photographs and artifacts of the town's early days. Hours are Tues.-Thurs. and school and public holidays 1-3 p.m., Sat.-Sun. 1-5 p.m. For information, phone (08) 9641-1751.

Balladong Farm, 5 Parker Rd., outside York on the way to Beverley, has been restored by the National Trust to show visitors what farm life was like in the 19th century. Displays include original breeds of stock and farm machinery, plus demonstrations of blacksmithing, milking, and wool spinning. Hours are Tues.-Sun. 10 a.m.-5 p.m. Guided tours can be arranged. For information, phone (08) 9641-1279. Admission is $6.

Accommodations

Toodyay: For typical pub rooms, try either the **Victoria Hotel,** tel. (08) 9574-2206, or the **Freemasons Hotel,** tel. (08) 9574-2201. Both are on Stirling Terrace. Inexpensive. **Appleton House,** Julimar Rd., tel. (08) 9574-2622, is a colonial-style B&B nestled in the hills. Moderate. Campsites and on-site vans are available at both **Toodyay Caravan Park,** Railway Rd., tel. (08) 9574-2612, and **Broadgrounds Park,** Racecourse Rd., tel. (08) 9574-2534. **Avon Valley National Park,** tel. (08) 9574-2540, 35 km west of Toodyay, has campsites with limited facilities. Budget-Inexpensive.

Northam: Find basic pub rooms at **Avon Bridge Hotel,** Fitzgerald St., tel. (08) 9622-1023, or the **Grand Hotel,** Fitzgerald St., tel. (08) 9622-5751. Inexpensive. **Buckland** country mansion, Buckland Rd., Irishtown, tel. (08) 9622-1130, offers stately—and costly—accommodations in two upstairs rooms. The mansion is closed Christmas Day through February. Expensive. **Mortlock Caravan Park,** Great Eastern Hwy., tel. (08) 9622-1620, has campsites and on-site vans. Budget-Inexpensive.

York: Opposite the railway station, the **YHA Hostel,** 3 Brook St., tel. (08) 9641-1372, features dorm beds in a converted hospital for $14 per night. The **Castle Hotel,** Avon Terrace, tel.

(08) 9641-1007, is the recommended pub. Inexpensive. **Hillside Homestead,** Forrest Rd., tel. (08) 9641-1065, a classified historic site, is an Edwardian residence with B&B accommodations, swimming pool, tennis court, and bicycles included in the price. Moderate. **Settlers' House,** on Avon Terrace, tel. (08) 9641-1096, offers elegant (albeit pricey) rooms with four-poster beds within its 1840s walls. Expensive. Campsites and on-site vans can be rented at **Mt. Bakewell Resort and Caravan Gardens,** Eighth Rd., tel. (08) 9641-1421. Budget-Moderate.

Events

Avon Valley holds about a dozen noteworthy events. Toodyay's **Moondyne Festival,** held annually in April, celebrates the colonial past, including mock shoot-'em-up holdups, jail breaks, coppers and convicts, plus an array of other fun sports and games.

The **Avon Descent Race,** begun at Northam each year on the first August weekend (when the river is full), features 800 or so canoeists in a fast-paced and furiously paddled whitewater race to Perth—a distance of 133 km. The cheering crowds partying on the banks are just as much fun to watch—and join.

Other popular draws are October's **Folk and** **Jazz Festival** and August's **Vintage and Veteran Car Race.**

Information

The **Avon Valley Tourism Association,** 2 Gray St., is open Mon.-Fri. 9 a.m.-5 p.m., Sat.-Sun. and public holidays 10 a.m.-4 p.m. For information, phone (08) 9622-2100. **York Tourist Bureau,** 81 Avon Terrace, is open Mon.-Fri. 9 a.m.-5 p.m., Sat.-Sun. 9 a.m.-4 p.m. For information, phone (08) 9641-1301.

Transportation

Westrail, tel. (13) 1053, operates buses to Northam and York, departing Perth every morning. Fare is about $15 one-way.

The Prospector rail service, also operated by Westrail, calls at Toodyay and Northam on its daily run to Kalgoorlie. Fares are a buck or two more than the bus. For information, schedules, and bookings, phone (08) 9326-2244 or (13) 1053.

It's about an hour-and-some's drive from Perth to any of the Avon Valley towns, and the distance between each of them averages 30 km. The two main valley roads branch from Midland. Choose either the Great Eastern Highway to Northam and York or the Toodyay Road to Toodyay. If you're returning to Perth, take one route going and the other coming back.

THE SOUTH COAST

Below Fremantle, the coastal road to Augusta, down in the southwest corner, passes nickel smelters, seaside resorts, industrial towns, established vineyards, and superb beaches (including W.A.'s best surfing spot). The inland route takes the traveler to some good bushwalking trails, dams, waterfalls, and a historic structure or two.

TO BUNBURY

Rockingham

Facing the Indian Ocean, Warnbo Sound, and Shoalwater Bay, Rockingham (pop. 25,000), 47 km south of Perth, once a major seaport (1872-1908—before Fremantle grabbed the honors), is now a popular holiday resort.

Rockingham Museum, corner Flinders Lane and Kent St., is a social history museum with memorabilia related to the district's early settlers. Hours are Tues.-Thurs. and Saturday 1-4:30 p.m., Sunday 10 a.m.-4:30 p.m. Admission is $2. For information, phone (08) 9592-3455.

Safe **swimming beaches** are at the Foreshore Reserve, Rockingham Rd., and Point Peron, at the southern end of Cockburn Sound. (Point Peron is favored by photographers, who click with the superb sunsets.) Daily ferry service will transport you to **Penguin Island,** a colony of fairy penguins, and to **Seal Island,** a colony of guess what.

A good Sunday **market** is held on Flinders Lane, 9 a.m.-4 p.m.

Good-value **accommodations** are offered at **CWA Rockingham,** 110 Parkin St., tel. (08) 9527-9560. Two units house six to eight people. Budget-Inexpensive. **Rockingham Ocean Clipper,** Patterson Rd., tel. (08) 9527-8000, is a modern hotel with room service, pool, and TVs. Moderate. Campsites and on-site vans are available at **Cee and Cee Caravan Park,** 2 Governor Rd., tel. (08) 9527-1297, and **Rockingham Palm Beach Holiday Village,** 37 Fisher St., tel. (08) 9527-1515. Budget-Moderate.

Yachties should note that the annual **Cockburn Sound Regatta,** W.A.'s largest, takes place here between Christmas and New Year's.

For local info (including ferry schedules), see the **Tourist Centre,** 43 Kent St., tel. (08) 9592-3464. Hours are Mon.-Fri. 9 a.m.-4:30 p.m., Sat.-Sun. 10 a.m.-4 p.m.

Transperth buses will get you there from Perth or Fremantle. For information, phone (13) 2213.

Mandurah

Another 29 km south will bring you to Mandurah (pop. 11,000), one more beat-the-heat spot, situated at the entrance of Peel Inlet and the mouth of Harvey Estuary (where dolphins are occasionally sighted).

Hall's Cottage, on Leighton Rd., built in the early 1830s, is the local history museum. Hours are Sunday 1-4 p.m. Admission is $1.

Other historic structures are: **Christ Church** (1871), Scholl St. and Pinjarra Rd.; **Cooper's Cottage** (1845), Mandurah Terrace, near the bridge; **Eacott Cottage** (1842), Gibla St.; **Allandale** (1913), Estuary Rd., Dawesville (south of town); and **Hardy's Cottage** (built from local materials), Estuary Rd., Dawesville.

Kerryelle's Unique Collectors Museum, Gordon Rd., tel. (08) 9581-7615, exhibits collections of gemstones, seashells, coins, banknotes, stamps, old bottles, dolls, and model cars. Hours are Tues.-Fri. 10 a.m.-4 p.m., Sat.-Sun. 10 a.m.-5 p.m. **House of Dunnies,** Henry Rd., Melrose Beach (15 km south), features a series of handcrafted, folk dunnies (that means outhouses—a real Australian art form).

Estuary Drive, a detour from the Old Coast Road, is the scenic route to Peel Inlet and Harvey Estuary, weaving through bushland and picnic spots. The **Foreshore Reserve,** in central Mandurah, is home to Slim Jim, Australia's tallest cotton palm. About 60 years old, Jim stands 39-plus meters high.

Marapana Wildlife World, Paganoni Rd., tel. (08) 9537-1404, is W.A.'s first drive-through deer park and kangaroo sanctuary. Other wild things include donkeys, emus, and cockatoos. Visitors can feed the animals (food provided). Hours are daily 10 a.m.-5 p.m. Admission is $8.

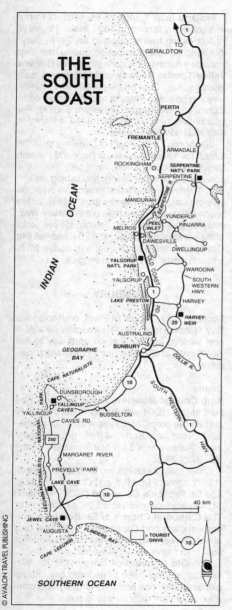

THE SOUTH COAST

TO GERALDTON

PERTH

FREMANTLE

ARMADALE

ROCKINGHAM

SERPENTINE NAT'L PARK
SERPENTINE

MANDURAH

SERPENTINE

YUNDERUP
PINJARRA

PEEL INLET

MELROS

DAWESVILLE

DWELLINGUP

YALGORUP NAT'L PARK

WAROONA

SOUTH WESTERN HWY.

YALGORUP

LAKE PRESTON

HARVEY

HARVEY WEIR

20

AUSTRALIND

BUNBURY

OLD COAST RD.

COLLIE R.

GEOGRAPHE BAY

CAPE NATURALISTE

DUNSBOROUGH

YALLINGUP CAVES

YALLINGUP

BUSSELTON

CAVES RD.

250

MARGARET RIVER

PREVELLY PARK

LAKE CAVE

JEWEL CAVE

AUGUSTA

FLINDERS BAY

CAPE LEEUWIN

SOUTHERN OCEAN

INDIAN OCEAN

SOUTH WESTERN HWY.

LEEUWIN-NATURALISTE NATIONAL PARK

0   40 km

= TOURIST DRIVE

10

© AVALON TRAVEL PUBLISHING

See a large variety of Australian birds in natural bushland and water settings at **Western Rosella Bird Park,** Old Pinjarra Rd., tel. (08) 9535-2104. Hours are daily 9:30 a.m.-5 p.m., closed Good Friday and Christmas Day. Admission is $6.

Brighton Hotel, Mandurah Terrace, tel. (08) 9535-1242, has basic pub rooms and counter meals. Inexpensive. Also centrally located, the **Foreshore,** Gibson St., tel. (08) 9535-5577, has motel rooms, plus air-conditioning, TVs, and a saltwater pool. Moderate. The **Albatross House,** 26 Hall St., tel. (08) 9581-5597, offers friendly B&B accommodations. Moderate.

Some of the many camping and on-site van facilities are: **Peninsula Caravan Park,** Ormsby Terrace, at the entrance to Peel Inlet, tel. (08) 9535-2792; **Belvedere Caravan Park,** 153 Mandurah Terrace, tel. (08) 9535-1213; and **Timbertop Caravan Park,** Peel St., tel. (08) 9535-1292. Budget-Moderate.

For tourist info, contact **Mandurah Tourist Bureau,** 75 Mandurah Terrace, tel. (08) 9550-3999. Hours are Mon.-Sat. 9 a.m.-5 p.m., Sunday 9 a.m.-4 p.m.

Transperth, tel. (13) 2213, and **Westrail,** tel. (08) 9326-2244, or (13) 1053, provide bus service from Perth and Fremantle to Mandurah.

Yalgorup National Park

About halfway between Mandurah and Bunbury, on a narrow coastal strip that includes Lake Clifton and Lake Preston, Yalgorup contains 11,545 hectares of heath, woodland, smaller lakes, interesting geological formations, and diverse bird- and wildlife (some birds migrate, visa-free, each year from the Soviet Union). Preston Beach, accessed through the park, offers good swimming and fishing. For information, phone (08) 9739-1067.

Warning: Tiger snakes are known to inhabit the paperbark swamps and sedge lands; additionally, the lakes are salty—be sure to carry freshwater on long bushwalks during summer.

Australind

The name is a contraction of Australia-India, derived from an 1840s plan to colonize the area and breed horses for the Indian army. The ambitious venture never got off the ground, but the name sure stuck.

Located on the eastern bank of Leschenault Inlet, Australind (pop. 2,900), along with neighboring Bunbury, is famed for blue manna crabs—thousands of which are caught in the inlet each season.

The **Gemstone and Rock Museum,** 267 Old Coast Rd., tel. (08) 9797-1241, contains displays of Bunbury agates and other Australian gemstones, natural crystals, as well as Aboriginal, American Native, and English stone artifacts, *and* a cactus garden. Hours are Tues.-Thurs. and Sat.-Sun. 10 a.m.-5 p.m. Admission is $2.

St. Nicholas' Church (1860), Paris Rd., is supposedly the smallest church (four by seven meters) in Western Australia—though the expanding congregation necessitated building a large adjacent edifice (circa 1987). **Henton Cottage** (1840), also on Paris Rd., once the Prince of Wales Hotel, is now an arts and crafts center.

The **scenic drive,** skirting the estuary, leads to crabbing and picnicking sites, while the **Collie River** offers recreational swimming, boating, and fishing.

Leschenault, 14 Old Coast Rd., tel. (08) 9797-1352, on the estuary, is a homey B&B with two guest rooms, TV lounge, and pool. Moderate. Campsites and on-site vans are available at **Leschenault Inlet Caravan Park,** Scenic Dr., tel. (08) 9797-1095. Budget-Moderate.

Most Bunbury-bound coaches from Perth call in at Australind.

The Inland Route

The South Western Highway runs from Perth, some 20 km inland, until it merges with the Old Coast Road at Bunbury. Various roads crisscross between the two highways, allowing travelers to venture inland through pine and jarrah forests or coastward en route.

Serpentine National Park (635 hectares), 52 km south of Perth on the western edge of Darling Scarp, consists of lots of hills with steep gullies, granite outcrops and slopes, and the Serpentine River flowing through the middle. The park's most popular facility is its natural rock pool, ideal for swimming. Steep trails make bushwalking difficult, and rockclimbing is not recommended. Admission is $6 per vehicle, $2 per bus passenger. For information, phone (08) 9525-2128.

Pinjarra (pop. 1,340), 86 km south of Perth, was settled by farmers in 1830, making it one of W.A.'s oldest towns. Located on the estuary, this agricultural and timber-producing township features a number of historic structures. **Hotham Valley Tourist Railway** operates steam train journeys, Aug.-Oct., on the preserved 1913 railway line between Pinjarra and the timber community of **Dwellingup.** Fares are $30-38. For information, phone (08) 9221-4444 in Perth, or (08) 9531-1908 in Pinjarra.

Waroona, 25 km south of Dwellingup, is the turnoff for Yalgorup National Park and Preston Beach. **Waroona Dam,** on Scarp Rd., is a powerboating, water-skiing, and fishing area.

In 1916, the state's first controlled irrigation scheme was built at **Harvey** (pop. 2,480), 28 km beyond Waroona. If you drive out to **Harvey Weir,** three km east off Weir Rd., you can still see some of the workers' campsites. The 20-meter-tall **Big Orange** houses a small zoo, a miniature train, arts and crafts, and fruit and veggies.

BUNBURY

Located 180 km south of Perth, on Koombana Bay, Bunbury (pop. 29,000) wears many hats—port, resort, industrial town, gateway to the Southwest, and blue-manna-crab-lovers' paradise.

Sights

King Cottage Museum, 77 Forrest Ave., was built in the 1880s with bricks made from clay dug on the property. Examine pioneer memorabilia Tues. and Sun. 2-4 p.m., or by appointment. Admission is $3. For information, phone (08) 9721-3929.

Other early structures are **St. Mark's Church** (1842), corner Flynn Rd. and Charterhouse St., and **St. Patrick's Cathedral** (1921), Parkfield St., the spire of which is a 1960s contribution. The **Cathedral Church of St. Boniface,** corner Parkfield and Cross Streets, though only about 25 years old, is impressive for its interior built from native blackbutt wood.

The **Old Convent of Mercy** (1860s), Wittenoom St., has been turned into city and regional art galleries and a community arts complex. Hours are daily 10 a.m.-5 p.m.

The **Boyanup Transport Museum,** South Western Hwy., Coombana Bay (20 minutes from Bunbury), houses the *Leschenault Lady* and *Koombana Queen,* two of Australia's oldest steam trains. Hours are daily 10 a.m.-4 p.m. For information, phone (08) 9731-5250.

Catch some great views from: **Boulter Heights,** Withers Crescent; the **Lighthouse,** Apex Dr. off Malcom St.; **Marleston Hill Lookout Tower,** Apex Dr.; and along **Ocean Drive,** which follows the coastline for eight km.

Big Swamp Bird Park, Prince Phillip Dr., tel. (08) 9721-8380, has a walk-in aviary with 2,000 birds, a wildlife and waterfowl wetland, and a penguin pool and cave. Hours are Wed.-Fri. 1-5 p.m., Sat.-Sun. and holidays 10 a.m.-5 p.m.

On Koombana Beach, the **Dolphin Discovery Centre,** tel. (08) 9791-8088, is a mini-Monkey Mia, where visitors can interact with playful bottlenose dolphins. Established in 1989, the dolphins "went public" shortly thereafter, and regularly come for feedings in the Inner Harbour—a flag signals their (and the tourists') arrival.

Accommodations and Food

Prince of Wales, Stephen St., tel. (08) 9721-2016, has spartan pub rooms. Inexpensive. **Clifton Beach Motel,** 2 Molloy St., tel. (08) 9721-4300, and **Admiral Motor Inn,** 56 Spencer St., tel. (08) 9721-7322, offer modern facilities. Moderate. The **Lord Forrest,** Symmons St., tel. (08) 9721-9966, is Bunbury's big luxury hotel. Expensive.

The YHA operates **The Residency Retreat Hostel,** corner Stirling and Moore Streets, tel. (08) 9791-2621. This lovely restored 1895 building offers $13 dorm beds. Budget. The **Wander Inn,** 16 Clifton St., tel. (1800) 064-704, offers hostel accommodations for $14-16 per night. Budget-Inexpensive. Kitchens and common areas are available at both hostels, but be sure to book ahead for high season (Dec.-February).

Grab campsites and on-site vans at: **Bunbury Village Caravan Park,** corner Bussell Hwy. and Washington Ave., tel. (08) 9795-7100; **Koombana Bay Holiday Resort,** Koombana Dr., tel. (08) 9791-3900; or **Punchbowl Caravan Park,** Ocean Dr., tel. (08) 9721-4761. Budget-Moderate.

For **food,** check out the numerous cafés around the town center, as well as the **Interna-**tional Food Hall, on Symmons St., and the **Centrepoint** shopping center.

Drooly's, on Victoria St., is a good local haunt ($6-10 entrees). Also on Victoria St., for Chinese food ($10-14), choose from the **Golden Flower** and the **Friendship.**

Try the counter meals ($5-10)—and the many beers on tap—at the **Rose Hotel** on Wellington Street. Meatheads can pig out at **Lump of Rump,** 119 Beach Road (lumps run about $14-18).

Foodies can do their nouvelle number at **Louisa's,** 15 Clifton St., tel. (08) 9721-9959, where some of the region's best country cuisine can be savored for $20-40.

Information

Tourist info can be obtained at the **Bunbury Tourist Bureau,** Carmody Place, in the old railway station, tel. (08) 9721-7922. Hours are Mon.-Fri. 8:30 a.m.-5 p.m., Saturday 9 a.m.-4 p.m., Sunday 9:30 a.m.-4:30 p.m., public holidays 10 a.m.-3 p.m.

Transportation

South West Coachlines, tel. (08) 9725-4366, operates a daily Perth-Bunbury service, continuing to Busselton. **Westrail,** tel. (08) 9725-5555 or (13) 1053, also provides daily service. Cost is $17.

Westrail's train Australind makes the trip twice a day for about the same fare as the bus. **Westrail Coaches** meets the train at Bunbury and go on to Busselton and Margaret River. Augusta is its last stop.

Bunbury City Transit, tel. (08) 9791-3111, covers the area from Australind to the north and south down to Gelorup.

FARTHER SOUTH

Busselton and Vicinity

Sheltered by Geographe Bay, Busselton (pop. 16,000) is a peaceful seaside resort not unlike Bunbury, 49 km to the north—a lazy place to fish, crab, and have beachy fun. It's also close to **Yallingup,** which some say is Australia's very best surfing beach.

The **jetty,** two km long, used to be the longest wooden jetty in the Southern Hemisphere until

1978, when Cyclone Alby shortened its act. At the corner of Queen and Albert Streets, see the Ballarat, a timber-hauling locomotive and W.A.'s first engine. Other historic sights are: **Wonnerup House and Old School** (1859), Layman Rd., Wonnerup; **Newtown House** (1851), Bussell Hwy., Vasse; and **St. Mary's Church of England** (1843), Queen St., the oldest stone church in the state.

The **Old Court House,** 4 Queen St., now completely restored, houses an art gallery, information center, book and craft shops, coffee shop, and artists' studios. Hours are Tues.-Sat. 10 a.m.-4 p.m. The **Old Butter Factory** (it's not "Ye Olde," but it has the same flavor), Peel Terrace, features 16 rooms of early pioneer furnishings, clothing, and artifacts, plus machinery and working models. Hours are Wed.-Mon. 2-5 p.m. Admission is $4. **Bunyip Craft Centre,** Bunyip Rd., Wonnerup, exhibits the wares of more than 150 craftspeople. Hours are Wed.-Mon. 10 a.m.-4 p.m. For information, phone (08) 9752-1159.

The **Oceanarium,** Geographe Bay Rd. near the jetty, displays local fish, including a white pointer shark and stingrays. Hours are daily 9 a.m.-9 p.m. Dec.-March, 9 a.m.-3 p.m. April-November. Admission is $4.

Slightly north of Busselton, **State Tuart Forest,** Bussell Hwy. between Capel and the Sabina River, is the world's only natural tuart forest. Some trees are estimated to be 300-400 years old.

Dunsborough, 24 km west of Busselton, is a pretty holiday town. For an impressive view of the Indian Ocean, continue another 13 km to **Cape Naturaliste Lighthouse** at the tip of Geographe Bay.

Yallingup Beach, eight km southwest of Dunsborough, is surf heaven according to national and international sources. Each November, the **Margaret River Surfing Classic** draws champions from around the world. Pick up a copy of the *Down Under Surf Guide* at the Dunsborough tourist office. It's full of information on wave and swell sizes and wind direction—and it's free.

Follow Caves Rd. to **Yallingup Cave,** off Caves Rd. north of Yallingup. Discovered in 1899, this limestone cave teems with stalactites, stalagmites, pillars, columns, flowstone, cave crystals, helictites, and straws. Hours are daily

9:30 a.m.-3:30 p.m. For information, phone (08) 9755-2152.

Accommodations: In Busselton, the **Geographe,** 28 West St., tel. (08) 9752-1451, and **Villa Carlotta,** 110 Adelaide St., tel. (08) 9754-2026, are comfy, homey B&B guesthouses. Inexpensive.

Motel Busselton, 90 Bussell Hwy., tel. (08) 9752-1908, offers good value motel rooms but is often heavily booked. Inexpensive.

The 1850s **Prospect Villa,** 1 Pries Ave., tel. (08) 9752-2273, is a lovely B&B, a short walk from Geographe Bay beaches yet still close to town. Expensive.

Broadwater Resort, corner Bussell Hwy. and Holgate Rd., tel. (08) 9754-1633, offers one- or two-bedroom apartments in the upper-price brackets, though sharing with others and cooking your own meals could cut costs considerably. Expensive.

This area has many caravan parks offering campsites and on-site vans. Some suggestions are: **Mandalay Caravan Park,** Bussell Hwy., tel. (08) 9752-1328; **Acacia Caravan Park,** Bussell Hwy., tel. (08) 9755-4034; **Kookaburra Caravan Park,** Marine Terrace, tel. (08) 9752-1516; and **Busselton Caravan Park,** 163 Bussell Hwy., tel. (08) 9752-1175. Budget-Moderate.

Hostel accommodations in Busselton are available at **Busselton Backpackers,** Jane St., one block from the tourist office, tel. (08) 9754-2763. Beds are $14, and bicycles are available to guests. Budget. Campsites and on-site vans are offered at **Yallingup Beach Caravan Park,** Valley Rd., tel. (08) 9755-2164, and **Caves Caravan Park,** corner Caves and Yallingup Beach Roads, tel. (08) 9755-2196. Budget-Moderate.

Information: For information about the Busselton area, contact the **Busselton Tourist Bureau,** Southern Dr. (in the civic center), Busselton, tel. (08) 9752-1288, or the **Dunsborough Tourist Centre,** Seymour Blvd., Dunsborough, tel. (08) 9755-3299. Both are open Mon.-Fri. 9 a.m.-5 p.m., Sat.-Sun. 10 a.m.-4 p.m.

Margaret River

Midway between Yallingup and Margaret River, along Caves Rd., is a cluster of wineries, with several more sprinkled around the Margaret River valley. Indeed, Margaret River (pop. 800), tiny though it may be, has come into its own as a wine-growing district that's giving the Swan Valley a run for the grapestakes. **Leeuwin Estate, Cape Mentelle,** and **Cullen** wineries are just a few of the delectable labels, now numbering about 50 in this region.

A tourist-oriented township, 47 km south of Busselton, situated on its eponym, Margaret River is enticingly close to pounding surf beaches and calm swimming bays.

The **Old Settlement Museum,** on the banks of the Margaret River, depicts 1920s settlement life with period farm buildings and machinery, along with crafts studios selling gift items. Hours are daily 10 a.m.-5 p.m., daily 10 a.m.-2 p.m. in winter, closed Christmas Day. Admission is $5. For information, phone (08) 9757-9335.

View displays of seashells at **Bellview Shell Museum,** Bussell Highway. Hours are daily 8 a.m.-6 p.m. Interesting buildings include **St. Thomas More Catholic Church,** Mitchell St., and the **Greek Chapel,** Wallcliffe Road.

Set in bushland, **Eagle's Heritage,** Boodjidup Rd., tel. (08) 9757-2960, boasts the largest collection of Australia's birds of prey. Hours are daily 10 a.m.-5 p.m. Admission is $4.

The **Marron Farm,** Wickham Rd., tel. (08) 9757-6329, 11 km south of town, produces thousands of the chestnut-like marron, which can be seen in their various stages of development. Swimming and picnic facilities are provided. Hours are daily 10 a.m.-4 p.m. Guided tours start several times each day.

Popular **Prevally Park,** south of the rivermouth, 10 km west of town, is known to have powerful surf. Follow Caves Rd. south through the lovely **Boranup Karri Forest.**

Mammoth Cave, 21 km south of Margaret River off Caves Rd., is noted for its fossil remains (including skeletons of Tasmanian tigers) and huge stalactites. **Lake Cave,** a few km farther south, reached via a natural winding staircase down into a vast crater, contains an underground lake. The big bonanza, however, is **Jewel Cave,** eight km before Augusta, on Caves Road. Western Australia's largest tourist cave features one of the world's longest straws (5.9 meters long and more than 3,000 years old), as well as gigantic pillars, grotesque formations, and a mysterious underground river. All caves are open daily except Christmas, with guided tours available several times a day.

Accommodations and Food: As with most wine regions, B&Bs are staked almost as often as the grapes. Some of the many choices include: **Margaret River Guest House,** 22 Valley Rd., tel. (08) 9757-2349; **Margaret House,** 5 Devon Dr., tel. (08) 9757-2692; and **1885 Inn,** Farrelly St., tel. (08) 9757-3177. Moderate-Expensive.

Hovering somewhere in the higher rungs are: **Bridgewater Bed and Breakfast,** Caves Rd., Margaret River, tel. (08) 9757-3129; **Rosewood Cottage,** Wallcliffe Rd., Margaret River, tel. (08) 9757-2845; and **Wild Brook Farm,** Caves Rd., Margaret River, tel. (08) 9757-3664. Expensive-Premium.

Properties where all the B&B stops are pulled out (sumptuous breakfasts, antiques and lace, country-weekend ambience, and bucolic everything) include: **Basildene Manor,** Wallcliffe Rd., Margaret River, tel. (08) 9757-3140; **Cape Lodge,** Caves Rd., Yallingup, tel. (08) 9755-6311; and **Gilgara Homestead,** Caves Rd., Yallingup, tel. (08) 9757-2705. Luxury.

The YHA **Margaret River Lodge,** Wallcliffe Rd., a few km out of town, tel. (08) 09757-2532, offers dorm and bunkhouse accommodations for $14 per night, plus bike rentals ($10), but shower and toilet facilities are outside the building. Budget. **Inne Town Backpackers,** Bussell Hwy., tel. (1800) 244-115, sits at the north edge of town and offers dorm beds for $14 for YHA members. Budget.

For campsites and on-site vans, contact **Margaret River Caravan Park,** 36 Station Rd., tel. (08) 9757-2180, or **Riverview Caravan Park,** 8 Willmott Ave., tel. (08) 9757-2270. Budget-Moderate.

For cheap pub food, try the **Settler's Tavern,** Bussell Highway. The **1885 Inn,** on Farrelly St., has continental cuisine, superb regional wines, and expensive prices ($20-40 for entrees, sans wine). For everything in between, you'll find a host of diners and cafés along Bussell Highway. Another top dining choice is **Flutes Café,** on Caves Rd., Willyabrup, tel. (08) 9755-6250, where you can dine on local venison, crayfish, and other contemporary Australian cuisine, in a sublime setting, for about $50-60 pp.

Or pick your own strawberries (Oct.-April), raspberries, boysenberries (Dec.-Jan.), and kiwi fruit (May-Aug.) at **Berry Farm Cottage,** Bessell

Rd., tel. (08) 97575-5054. Jams and wine are available for purchase. Hours are daily 10 a.m.-4:30 p.m.

Information: Winery maps and other tourist information are available at **Margaret River Tourist Bureau,** corner Tunbridge Rd. and Bussell Hwy., Margaret River, tel. (08) 9757-2911. Hours are daily 9 a.m.-5 p.m.

Augusta

Situated near Australia's southwestern tip, Augusta (pop. 470) sits 320 km from Perth and is W.A.'s third-oldest settlement. Blue waters and white beaches, surfing and swimming sites keep holidaymakers happy.

The **Augusta Historical Museum,** Blackwood Ave., displays early shipping relics and historical exhibits. Hours are daily 10 a.m.-noon and 2-4 p.m. summer, 10 a.m.-noon winter. Admission is $2.

Hillview Lookout, Golf Links Rd. off Caves Rd., affords panoramic views and a directional plate to help you pick out nearby landmarks. **Cape Leeuwin Lighthouse,** at the end of Cape Leeuwin Rd., marks the junction of the Indian and Southern Oceans, and functions as an important meteorological station. Open to visitors daily 9:30 a.m.-3:30 p.m. Admission is $4.

Nearby, see the waterwheel, built in 1895 to provide water for lighthouse builders, now encrusted in salt deposits.

Accommodations: Inexpensive holiday flats with kitchen facilities are offered at **Riverside Cottages,** Molloy St., tel. (08) 9758-1545. **Augusta Hotel Motel,** Blackwood Ave., tel. (08) 9758-1944, has moderately priced hotel rooms

but costlier (and more modern) motel units. Moderate-Expensive.

The **YHA,** corner Bussell Hwy. and Blackwood Ave., tel. (08) 9758-1280, also affectionately known as "Baywatch Manor Resort," is clean and cozy. Beds run $15 per night, and bike rental is $5 per day. Inexpensive.

Doonbanks Caravan Park, Blackwood Ave., tel. (08) 9758-1517, features a riverfront location with campsites and on-site vans. Budget-Moderate.

The **Augusta Hotel,** Blackwood Ave., offers an à la carte food-service area ($9-16), as well as the usual counter-meal setup. **Squirrels,** next door, has a good selection of sandwiches and gourmet health food ($6-10). **Cosy Corner Café,** also on Blackwood Ave., features low-brow (but tasty) meals in the $12-16 range.

Information: Augusta Information Centre, 70 Blackwood Ave., Augusta, tel. (08) 9758-1695, assists with local inquiries. Hours are Mon.-Fri. 8:30 a.m.-5 p.m., Sat.-Sun. 8:30 a.m.-1 p.m. (open weekends only in winter months).

Events

Surfers and their groupies from all over the world converge the third weekend in November for the **Margaret River Surf Classic,** held about nine km east of town.

Transportation

Daily buses operate between Perth and the Busselton/Margaret River/Augusta region. For information and bookings, contact **South West Coachlines,** tel. (08) 9324-2333, or **Westrail,** tel. (13) 1053.

THE SOUTHWEST

A few different routes will take you through Western Australia's southwest to the coastal region, known as the "Great Southern," with glorious beaches, rugged ranges, capes and parks, holiday resorts, and historic settlements. The South Western Highway travels inland from Bunbury, meeting the coast (and the South Coast Highway) at Walpole. The Albany Highway runs *way* inland in a southeasterly direction from Perth, connecting with the coastal highway at Albany. Other itineraries include the Great Southern Highway from Perth, Vasse Highway (from Busselton), the Brockman Highway (north of Augusta), and the Muirs Highway (between Manjimup and Mount Barker).

THE SOUTH WESTERN HIGHWAY

Leaving Bunbury, you'll journey into **Donnybrook,** the center of Western Australia's oldest apple-growing region, where Granny Smith is queen of the crop (try to make this trip in late October when it's apple blossom time). Many artsy-craftsy shops and studios permeate this area. Farther along the landscape gives way to rolling hills, pine plantations, jarrah and karri forests, and—eventually—the big, blue sea.

One particularly scenic detour is the stretch from Balingup, 29 km beyond Donnybrook, to **Nannup,** an old timber town on the Vasse Highway. The narrow, winding, 45-km drive crosses, then follows, the Blackwood River.

Westrail buses serve South Western Highway towns and most Vasse Highway communities several times each week. **South West Coachlines** also travels into some areas.

Bridgetown
Settled in 1857, Bridgetown (pop. 1,520) is a peaceful little community 95 km south of Bunbury in the heart of jarrah land. Visit **Bridgedale,** 1 Hampton St., the town's oldest house, built in the 1860s and restored by the National Trust. Hours are Wed.-Sat. and Monday 2-5 p.m., Sunday 11 a.m.-1 p.m. and 2-5 p.m.

The **Brierly Jigsaw Gallery,** Hampton St., is supposedly the country's only public jigsaw gallery. The collection includes puzzles from all over the world, and visitors are invited to go to pieces over unfinished works. Hours are Thurs.-Mon. 10 a.m.-4 p.m. Admission is $4. For information, phone (08) 9761-1740.

Good bushwalking and picnic spots are at **Bridgetown Jarrah Park** on Brockman Highway and **Blackwood River Park** at the southern edge of town.

Carnaby Butterflies and Beetles, Bridge St., is 31 km northeast in Boyup Brook. The collection contains many rare specimens and is reputed to be the largest outside of the British Natural History Museum. Hours are daily 10 a.m.-4 p.m.

The **Bridgetown Hotel,** 38 Hampton St., tel. (08) 9761-1030, offers pub rooms with breakfast included. Inexpensive. **Riverwood House,** South Western Hwy., tel. (08) 9761-1862, is a nicely done, no-smoking-allowed B&B. Moderate. Campsites and on-site vans are available at **Bridgetown Caravan Park,** South Western Hwy., tel. (08) 9761-1053. Budget-Moderate.

Pick up tourist info at the **Bridgetown Tourist Bureau,** Hampton St., tel. (08) 9761-1740. Hours are daily 9 a.m.-5 p.m.

Manjimup
You can't miss the fact that Manjimup (pop. 4,150), 37 km from Bridgetown, is the gateway to the Tall Timber Country—timber arches signal your arrival at both edges of town. Karri trees, more than a century old, are abundant here.

Bone up on the local timber industry at **Timber Park,** corner Rose and Edwards Streets. The complex houses Timber Park Gallery, Bunnings' Age of Steam Museum (W.A.'s only timber museum), displays of vintage machinery and implements, and various other attractions. For a close-up look at the industry, put on a pair of sturdy shoes and visit the **Bunnings Diamond Mill,** Eastbourne Road. Tours are available Monday, Wednesday, and Friday at 1:30 and 3 p.m.

Seven km down Seven Day Road, **Fonty's Pool,** once used to irrigate veggies, has been converted into a much-used swimming pool.

King Jarrah, three km along Perup Rd., is a 1,200-year-old tree with nearby walking trails. **Diamond Tree Tower,** 10 km south of town, sports a fire lookout atop a 51-meter karri tree and is usually crawling with tourists.

A bit of log and decking is all that remains of **One Tree Bridge** on Graphite Rd., 22 km from town. A couple of km from the bridge stand **The Four Aces,** 300- to 400-year-old giant karri trees.

Manjimup Caravan Park, Mottram St., tel. (08) 9771-2093, has campsites and on-site vans, as well as a bunkhouse with dorm-type accommodations. Budget-Moderate. **Fonty's Pool Caravan Park,** Seven Day Rd., tel. (08) 9771-2105, is another option. Budget-Moderate.

The **tourist bureau,** corner Rose and Edwards Streets, provides local information. Hours are daily 9 a.m.-5 p.m., closed Christmas Day and Good Friday. For information, phone (08) 9777-1083.

Pemberton

Set amid luscious karri forests, Pemberton (pop. 870) is reached via the Vasse Highway turnoff, 15 km south of Manjimup, or along the Vasse Highway from Nannup (76 km).

The **Pioneer Museum,** Brockman St., houses records, photos, and machinery from the early forestry settlement. Hours are daily 9 a.m.-5 p.m. Admission is $2.

Restored **Brockman Saw Pit,** on the Pemberton-Northcliffe road, depicts lumber-cutting methods of bygone days. The **Pemberton Sawmill,** conversely, is highly automated and one of the largest in the Southern Hemisphere. The tourist bureau can arrange tours.

Follow the signs to **Gloucester Tree** off Brockman St., the world's highest fire lookout tree. The view from up top is great, but don't attempt the dizzying 60-meter climb unless you're in good shape and vertigo-free!

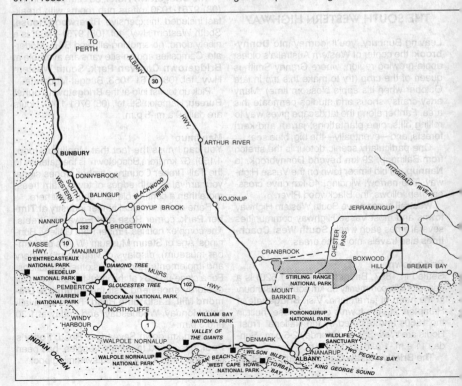

The **Rainbow and Tramway Trails** were the original 91-mm gauge railways that transported karri logs to the sawmill back in the 1920s. Sights along the Rainbow Trail include **Big Brook Arboretum** and **Big Brook Dam** (popular for fishing, canoeing, and sailboarding). Take a four-hour forest ride across rivers, streams, and old wooden bridges on the 1907 replica **Pemberton Tramway.** Fares are $15 to Warren River, $21 to Northcliffe. For bookings and information, phone (08) 9776-1322.

Other pretty spots around Pemberton are **Beedelup Falls**, off Vasse Hwy., and the **Walk Through Karri,** in Beedelup National Park (this 400-year-old tree has a hole you can stand inside). **Warren National Park** also contains huge karri trees.

Trout lovers and fishers might want to visit **King Trout Farm**, Northcliffe Rd., tel. (08) 9776-1352, or **Karri Valley Trout Farm**, Old Vasse Hwy., tel. (08) 9776-2048. Both offer fishing gear rentals and cooking facilities.

Shops that sell local timber crafts are: **Fine Woodcraft,** Dickinson St.; **Outpost Art and Crafts,** Brockman St.; **Warren River Arts and Crafts,** 63 Jamieson St.; and **Pemberton Arts and Crafts,** Broadway Avenue.

Accommodations in town are available at **Gloucester Motel,** Ellis St., tel. (1800) 65-1266, and **Forest Lodge Resort,** Vasse Hwy., tel. (08) 9776-1113. Moderate. **Pump Hill Farm,** Pump Hill Rd., tel. (08) 9776-1379, offers mudbrick cottages, with fireplaces and cooking facilities. Expensive.

The **YHA Hostel,** Pimelea Rd., tel. (08) 9776-1953, sits in the middle of the state forest, about 10 km northwest of town. Dorm beds run $14 per night. Budget.

On-site vans and tent sites can be found at **Karri Valley Resort,** Vasse Hwy., tel. (08) 9776-

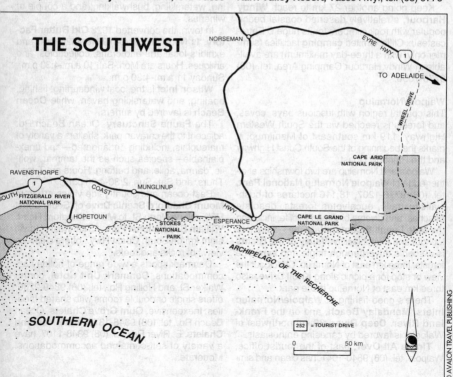

THE SOUTHWEST

NORSEMAN

EYRE HWY. 1

TO ADELAIDE

4 WHEEL DRIVE

RAVENSTHORPE

1

SOUTH FITZGERALD RIVER NATIONAL PARK

COAST

MUNGLINUP

HWY

CAPE ARID NATIONAL PARK

HOPETOUN

STOKES NATIONAL PARK

ESPERANCE

CAPE LE GRAND NATIONAL PARK

ARCHIPELAGO OF THE RECHERCHE

SOUTHERN OCEAN

252 = TOURIST DRIVE

0   50 km

© AVALON TRAVEL PUBLISHING

2020, or **Pemberton Caravan Park,** Pump Hill Rd., tel. (08) 9776-1300. Budget-Moderate.

Campsites with limited facilities are offered at **Pemberton Forest Camp** and **Warren National Park.** For information, phone (08) 9776-1200. Budget.

Tourist information is available at **Pemberton Tourist Centre,** Brockman St., tel. (08) 9776-1133. Hours are daily 9 a.m.-5 p.m.

Beyond Pemberton

Northcliffe, 28 km southeast of Pemberton, features more virgin karri forests. **Northcliffe Forest Park,** adjacent to town, is an ideal place to bushwalk, especially when the wildflowers are in bloom (Sept.-Nov.). The park is also home to the twin and hollow-butt karri trees. The **Pioneer Museum,** Wheatley Coast Rd., displays early settlement artifacts. Hours are daily May-Aug. 10 a.m.-2 p.m. Admission is $2.

Keep going another 27 km to reach **Windy Harbour,** a relatively deserted coastal beach popular with rock climbers for its huge D'Entrecasteaux Cliffs. Limited **camping** facilities (summer only, with a three-day maximum) are available at Windy Harbour Camping Area, tel. (08) 9776-7056.

Walpole/Nornalup

This coastal region with luscious bays, coves, and forests is reached via the South Western Highway, 119 km southeast of Manjimup. It marks the beginning of the South Coast Highway and the Rainbow Coast.

Walpole and Nornalup are two townships at either edge of **Walpole Nornalup National Park,** tel. (08) 9776-1207, 18,116 hectares of bushwalking trails, eucalyptus forests, desolate beaches, and diverse bird- and wildlife, including the **Dale Evens Bicentennial Tree**—a fire tree lookout and tourist facility. **Valley of the Giants** is a scenic drive through tingle and karri tree forests, three km east of Nornalup. Check out the view or stop for a picnic along **Knoll Drive,** also three km east of Nornalup in the park.

There's good fishing at **Walpole/Nornalup inlets, Mandalay Beach,** and on the **Frankland River. Deep River,** 36 km northwest of Walpole, is favored by canoeing enthusiasts.

Tingle All Over, east of the tourist office, Walpole, tel. (08) 9840-1041, has clean and simple rooms with sinks, though you'll have to walk to the showers. Inexpensive. Book ahead for dorm beds at the **Dingo Flat YHA Hostel,** Dingo Flat Rd. off Valley of the Giants Rd., tel. (08) 9840-8073. Beds are $8 per night (the property is on a cattle and sheep station). Budget. Campsites, on-site vans, cottages, and cabins are available at **Rest Point Tourist Centre,** Walpole Inlet, tel. (08) 9840-1032. Budget-Moderate.

For tourist information, contact **Walpole Tourist Bureau,** Pioneer Cottage, Pioneer Park, tel. (08) 9840-1111.

Denmark

No, this is not a Danish settlement. Denmark (pop. 2,000), 66 km east of Nornalup, was named for Dr. Alexandra Denmark, an 1800s naval physician. It's a favorite of surfers and hippies. Located on the Denmark River, recreational opportunities include surfing, swimming, fishing, waterskiing, bushwalking, and a couple of wineries.

In town, the converted 1928 **Old Butter Factory,** 11 North St., tel. (08) 9848-2525, sells and exhibits local arts and crafts, collectibles, and antiques. Hours are Mon.-Sat. 10 a.m.-4:30 p.m., Sunday 11 a.m.-4:30 p.m.

Wilson Inlet is the local windsurfing, fishing, boating, and waterskiing haven, while **Ocean Beach** is favored by surfers.

The **Fauna Sanctuary,** Ocean Beach Rd. adjacent to the caravan park, shelters a variety of marsupials, including endangered—and unexplainable—species such as the tammar, woillie, darma, agile, and bettong. Hours are Tues.-Thurs. and Sat.-Sun. 2:30-4:30 p.m.

Best ocean and countryside views are from **Mount Shadford Scenic Drive** off South Coast Hwy., along North St. to Mount Shadford Road. **William Bay National Park,** 15 km west of town, eight km off South Coast Hwy., offers close-up views of rocks and reefs.

Denmark sports a wide range of holiday accommodations. **Denmark Unit Hotel,** corner Walker St. and Holling Rd., tel. (08) 9849-2206, offers single or double rooms with shared facilities. Inexpensive. **Gum Grove Chalets,** Ocean Beach Rd., tel. (08) 9848-1378, and **Riverbend Chalets,** E. River Rd., tel. (08) 9848-1107, have a variety of self-contained accommodations. Moderate.

To be swathed in pure luxury (at luxurious prices), book at the secluded 60-acre **Karri Mia Lodge,** Mount Shadford Rd., tel. (08) 9848-2255. Go for one of the tower suites with spas and ocean views. Luxury. For a low-key farm stay, three rooms and two cottages are available at **Rannoch West Holiday Farm,** South Coast Hwy., tel. (08) 9840-8032, a working ranch near Valley of the Giants forest. Moderate.

The **YHA Hostel** is at **Wilson Inlet Holiday Park,** Ocean Beach Rd., tel. (08) 9848-1267. Beds cost $10, and facilities include a tennis court and boat hire. Book ahead. Budget.

Campsites and on-site vans are available at **Rivermouth Caravan Park,** Inlet Dr., tel. (08) 9848-1262, and **Rudgyard Beach Holiday Park,** Rudgyard Rd., tel. (08) 9848-1169. Budget-Moderate.

Satisfy burrito cravings at **Bandalero's Mexican Restaurant,** on Holling Road ($9-16 for the whole enchilada). **Blue Wren Café,** on South Coast Hwy., and **Mary Rose,** on North St., are other possibilities, along with **Figtree Bistro,** on Strickland Street. All three serve sandwiches, salads, and bistro fare, ranging $6-16.

If you visit in December, January, or on Easter Saturday, drop by the annual **Arts and Crafts Market Days,** along the Denmark River, where all kinds of goodies are for sale.

For tourist information, contact **Denmark Tourist Bureau,** Strickland St., tel. (08) 9848-2055. Hours are daily 9 a.m.-5 p.m.

ALONG THE ALBANY HIGHWAY

From Perth, the Albany Highway passes through a hodgepodge of timber, sheep-farming, and mixed agricultural districts and small service towns. En route, **Williams, Arthur River,** and **Kojonup** are smattered with assorted historic buildings, crafts galleries, picnic areas, and simple accommodations. **Cranbrook** is an access point for Stirling Range National Park. Turn off at **Kendenup** to see the site of W.A.'s very first gold find.

Mount Barker

Though the local industries are mainly sheep and cattle grazing, Mount Barker (pop. 1,520), some 359 km southeast of Perth, is also known for its wine production. Eyeball panoramic views of the area from atop the 168-meter-high TV tower on **Mount Barker Hill.**

The **Old Police Station,** Albany Hwy., built by convicts in 1867, has been preserved as a museum with period furnishings and pioneer artifacts.

Mount Barker Tourist Bureau, 57 Lowood Rd., tel. (08) 9851-1163, provides local information and maps to the wineries. Hours are Mon.-Fri. 9 a.m.-5 p.m., Saturday 9 a.m.-2 p.m., Sunday 10 a.m.-2 p.m., closed Christmas Day.

The Stirlings and the Porongurups

Sounds like the guest list for an amusing country weekend, doesn't it? Nope—these are two mountain ranges (and national parks) that rise dramatically from the surrounding flat, agricultural plains. Both parks are close enough to Albany for a day outing.

Stirling Range National Park (115,671 hectares)—about 66 km long and 18 km wide—is filled with mountains, valleys, cliffs, delicate wildflowers, eucalyptus forests, rare plants, profuse bird- and wildlife, and moody mountain views. **Bluff Knoll** (1,073 meters) is W.A.'s third-highest peak, and the park's most popular climb, followed by **Toolbrunup** (1,052 meters) and **Ellen Peak** (1,012 meters and a *hard* trek). You must obtain permission from the ranger on duty before embarking on any climb. If you don't feel like walking, a scenic drive will take you through the center of the park. For more information, phone (08) 9827-9230.

Closer to Albany, **Porongurup National Park** (2,401 hectares) features karri forests, excellent birdwatching, panoramic views, easy walking tracks, and some of the world's oldest rock. The best bushwalks are to **Castle Rock** (570 meters), **Hayward's Peak** (610 meters), **Devil's Slide** (671 meters), **Nancy Peak** (662 meters), and **Morgan's View** (662 meters). For information, phone (08) 9853-1095.

Campsites with limited facilities are available at Stirling Range National Park, tel. (08) 9827-9230. Budget. Cabins, campsites, and on-site vans are also available at **Stirling Range Chalet and Caravan Park,** Chester Pass Rd., South Borden, tel. (08) 9827-9229. Budget-Inexpensive.

At Porongurup, **Karribank Country Retreat,** Main St., tel. (08) 9853-1022, offers modern rooms plus swimming pool, tennis court, and golf course. Moderate. Adjacent to Karribank, **Porongurup Caravan Park,** Main St., tel. (08) 9853-1057, rents campsites and on-site vans. Budget-Inexpensive.

ALBANY

Albany (pop. 30,000) is Western Australia's oldest settlement and, because of its superb Princess Royal Harbour, it remained the state's principal port for years. Since its creation in 1826 as a military outpost to ward off French colonists, Albany (called Frederickstown until 1832) has served as both a whaling port and coaling station. Situated 409 km southeast of Perth, this town is presently known as the Great Southern's commercial center as well as a tourist resort.

Historical Sights

Albany has preserved a number of its colonial buildings; most are on or around York St., Stirling Terrace, and the harbor foreshores.

The **Residency Museum,** Residency Rd., sits on the exact site where Major Edmund Lockyer and his merry band of convicts landed in 1826. Built in 1850, the museum was formerly the local magistrate's home and a naval training facility. Exhibits concern regional history, geography, and environment. Hours are daily 10 a.m.-5 p.m., For information, phone (08) 9841-4844.

Explore a full-scale replica of Lockyer's brig *Amity,* Port Rd., near the museum. You can go below deck and imagine how some 45 men and accompanying livestock survived in the cramped quarters. Hours are daily 9 a.m.-5 p.m., closed Christmas Day. Admission is $2. For information, phone (08) 9841-6885.

The one-time convict-hiring depot and **Old Gaol** (1851) in Stirling Terrace now serves as a museum with WW I and II relics, pioneer tools and equipment, and Aboriginal artifacts. Hours are daily 10 a.m.-4:15 p.m., closed Christmas Day and Good Friday. Admission is $4, and also includes visits to the **Patrick Taylor Cottage.** For information, phone (08) 9841-1401.

The restored **post office** (1870), Stirling Terrace, once housed the customs and bond store, court, holding cells, magistrate's and jury rooms. These days it comprises an Inter-Colonial Communications Museum and a restaurant. Hours are daily 10 a.m.-5 p.m.

Constructed of wattle and daub, **Patrick Taylor Cottage** (1832), Duke St., is thought to be Albany's oldest building. The cottage contains thousands of items, including early costumes, old clocks, and kitchenware. Hours are daily 2-4:15 p.m. Admission is $4, which also entitles entry to the **Old Gaol.** For information, phone (08) 9841-1401.

Strawberry Hill Farmhouse, Middleton Beach Rd., built in 1836, is W.A.'s oldest farm. Originally the private home for the government resident, the two-story stone house has been restored by the National Trust. You can take tea in the adjoining miner's cottage. Hours are daily 10 a.m.-5 p.m., closed during June. Admission is $3. For information, phone (08) 9841-3735.

Other historic structures include: **St. John's Church of England** (1848), York St., the first church consecrated in Western Australia; **Albany Town Hall** (1888), refurbished in 1983 and converted into the Albany Town Theatre; **Vancouver Arts Centre** (1880s), used for regular arts and crafts exhibitions; and **Princess Royal Fortress** (1893).

Other Sights

Dog Rock, a huge granite outcrop near the corner of Middleton Rd. and Young St., resembles the head of a big dog.

Emu Point, where Oyster Harbour enters the sea, is a favorite place for boating, swimming, and windsurfing. Other good swimming sites are **Middleton Beach, Ellen Cove,** and **Jimmy Newell's Harbour,** south of town.

Mount Clarence offers the best views plus a recast of the original Desert Mounted Corps memorial erected at Suez in 1932. You can see bullet marks in the granite blocks, transported from Suez. **Mount Melville** and **Marine Drive Lookout** offer other wide-eye panoramas.

On the coast, 21 km south of Albany, **Torndirrup National Park** affords a number of spectacular sights including the blowholes, Natural Bridge, and The Gap. To reach the park, follow Frenchman Bay Road.

At the end of Frenchman Bay Rd., **Whaleworld,** the former whaling station responsible for taking up to 850 whales each season (until operations ceased in 1978), now serves as a museum. Have a whale of a time learning the history of Albany's oldest industry (30-min. tours are offered on the hour, 10 a.m.-4 p.m.). Hours are daily 9 a.m.-5 p.m. Admission is $7. For information, phone (08) 9844-4021.

Two Peoples Bay, 24 km east of Albany along Two Peoples Bay Rd., features more pretty beaches and a nature reserve that protects a small colony of noisy scrub birds. Believed to be extinct, the birds were rediscovered in 1961. Other nearby attractions are **Two Peoples Marron Farm,** Two Peoples Bay Rd., and **Valley Ponds Trout Farm,** Gull Rock Road.

Accommodations and Food

Colonial Guesthouse, 136 Brunswick Rd., tel. (08) 9841-3704, and **Middleton Beach Guesthouse,** 18 Adelaide Crescent, tel. (08) 9841-1295, are B&B offerings. Inexpensive.

Modern motels are: **Travel Inn,** 191 Albany Hwy., tel. (1800) 24-6144; **Amity Motor Inn,** 234 Albany Hwy., tel. (08) 9841-2200; and the **Albany International Motel,** 270 Albany Hwy., tel. (08) 9841-7399. Moderate. Heaps of others are scattered around town and along Albany Highway. One of the better and costliest accommodations is **Balneaire Seaside Resort,** 27 Adelaide Crescent, Middleton Beach, tel. (08) 9842-2899. The 17-apartment complex offers fully equipped villas with kitchenettes, VCRs, laundry service, and other amenities. Expensive. Even more luxurious, **The Esplanade Hotel,** Middleton Beach, tel. (08) 9842-1711, beckons with its views to everywhere and the usual mega-plethora of amenities. Premium.

The **Albany Bayview Backpackers YHA Hostel,** 49 Duke St., tel. (08) 9842-3300, offers communal facilities and dorm beds for $14 per night but fills up quickly. Budget.

You'll find many caravan parks to choose from. Some offering both campsites and on-site vans are: **Mount Melville Caravan Park,** 22 Wellington St., tel. (08) 9841-4616; **Middleton Beach Caravan Park,** Flinders Parade, Middleton Beach, tel. (08) 9841-3593; **Panorama Caravan Park,** Frenchman Bay Rd., tel. (08) 9844-4031; and **Emu Beach Caravan Park,** Medcalfe Parade, Emu Point, tel. (09) 9844-1147. Budget-Moderate.

Looking for food? Stirling Terrace is filled with fill-you-up eateries. For burgers, pancakes, and other light meals ($6-10), try **Dylan's on the Terrace,** 82 Stirling Terrace, tel. (08) 9841-8720. **Kooka's,** at 204 Stirling Terrace, tel. (08) 9841-5889, offers excellent fresh and nouvelle-ish cuisine ($18-26 entrees) in a colonial cottage with a kookaburra theme. Meals are in the expensive range and reservations are advised. For moderately priced pasta and steaks ($10-16), along with an exquisite harbor view, head over to the 1870s **Earl of Spencer,** corner Earl and Spencer Streets.

For Asian fare, try **Lemon Grass Thai,** 370 Middleton Rd., or **Three Plenties Palace** Chinese restaurant, York Street. Entrees range $8-14.

The **Health Nut,** corner of York and Peel Streets, is the perfect spot to load up on healthy snacks for camping and hiking treks.

Information

For a free copy of *Albany Experience,* a local mini-guide, or for other info, contact the **Albany Tourist Bureau,** Proudlove Parade, tel. (08) 9841-1088. Hours are Mon.-Fri. 8:30 a.m.-5:30 p.m. Sat.-Sun.; public holidays 9 a.m.-5 p.m.

Pick up street maps and other road info at the **Royal Automobile Club,** 110 Albany Hwy., tel. (08) 9842-1210.

Transportation

Ansett Australia, tel. (13) 1300, and **Skywest,** tel. (08) 9334-2288, operate daily flights from Perth Airport to Albany (about $180).

Westrail, tel. (13) 1053, provides daily coach service from Perth ($42) and travels to Denmark four times a week ($53).

If you're driving, the Albany Highway from Perth (409 km) should get you here in under five hours. The South Western and South Coast Highways from Bunbury (402 km, not counting detours) will take about the same time.

Louie's Bus Service, the local transport company, travels weekdays and Saturday mornings to points along the Albany Highway, as well as to Middleton Beach, Spencer Park, and Emu Point.

Rental cars are available from **Avis,** tel. (08) 9842-2833; **Budget,** tel. (08) 9841-2299; and **Albany Car Rentals,** tel. (08) 9841-7077. Rates are about $65 per day with unlimited km.

Contact the **Albany YHA Hostel** for bicycle hire outfits (about $10 per day) and cheap tours into the Stirling Ranges or up and down the coast ($20-45). The **tourist bureau** can also arrange local tours.

THE WESTERN BIGHT

From Albany to Esperance, the South Coast Highway teases its way along the western end of the Great Australian Bight—a 480-km odyssey through capes and parks, bays and beaches.

Ravensthorpe

A former gold and copper mining town, Ravensthorpe (pop. 330) is 114 km northeast of Jerramungup.

Cocanarup Homestead, classified as a historical site by the National Trust, is made up of several century-old stone buildings. The early 1900s **Dance Cottage Museum** is home to the local historical society's memorabilia collection. The old smelter sits three km from town, while ruins of a baked-out bakery and a played-out gold mine can be explored at **Kundip,** some 20 km farther. If you want to check out the **Ravensthorpe Range** at the northern end of Foater Road, beware of the old mine shafts in that area!

Ravensthorpe Motel, junction Hopetoun and Esperance Roads, tel. (08) 9838-1053, and **Palace Motor Hotel,** tel. (08) 9838-1005, both offer comfortable accommodations. Inexpensive-Moderate. Campsites are available at **Ravensthorpe Caravan Park,** Morgan St., tel. (08) 9838-1050. Budget.

Local info can be obtained at the **Ravensthorpe Tourist Information Centre,** Morgans St., tel. (08) 9838-1277. Hours are Mon.-Fri. 8:30 a.m.-5 p.m.

Below and Beyond Ravensthorpe

Hopetoun, situated on the coast 50 km south of Ravensthorpe, offers more secluded bays, beaches, inlets, and fishing holes. Whales can often be seen near these shores in August and September.

Fitzgerald River National Park, accessed either from Hopetoun, Jerramungup, or Bremer Bay, features 240,000 hectares of sand plain, river valleys, narrow gorges, rugged ranges, coastal cliffs, sandy beaches, visible wildlife, and approximately 1,350 species of wildflowers

and native plants. Check in with a ranger before you go bushwalking, and be sure to carry plenty of water. Swimmers should be aware of dangerous coastal rips. Some park areas are restricted at certain times of the year. For information, phone (08) 9835-5043.

Stokes National Park (10,667 hectares), reached via gravel roads off the South Coast Highway east of Young River, is a coastal region for bushwalking, ocean fishing, inlet swimming, and birdwatching (seals have been sighted, too). Facilities are limited and you must carry your own water. For information, phone (08) 9876-8541.

ESPERANCE

Beautifully situated across from the Archipelago of the Recherche, 730 km southeast of Perth, versatile Esperance (pop. 11,500) wears three hats—seaport, seaside resort, and agricultural center.

Named for the French frigate L'Esperance in 1772, the town was settled in 1863 when the Dempster brothers arrived with their families after an overland trek. Some 30 years later, with the advent of gold exploration, Esperance boomed as a port, then faltered again when the gold rush rushed out. Then, shortly after World War II and after a lot of research, it was discovered that trace elements were missing from the surrounding soil, which prohibited agriculture. The situation was remedied and voila—a rich agro-center and grain-loading port.

Sights

Esperance Municipal Museum, James St., features early machinery, tools, furnishings, and—best of all—a big Skylab display (Esperance was the lucky spot where Skylab decided to fall to earth in 1979). The museum park also houses **Craft Village,** where you can buy locally produced arts and crafts. Hours are daily 1:30-4:30 p.m. Admission is $3. For information, phone (08) 9071-1579.

The original **Dempster Homestead,** Dempster and Emily Streets, is privately owned and can be admired only from the road.

The **Australian Parrot Farm,** Fisheries Rd., Yarrumun, exhibits a large number of parrots, pheasants, guinea fowl, and peafowl, plus a collection of more than 2,000 vintage bottles. Hours are daily 9 a.m.-5 p.m. For information, phone (08) 9076-1284.

Salt-tolerant algae and saline are what makes **Pink Lake** pink—and sometimes purple. Some years, as much as 500,000 tons of salt are dredged from the lake, which is three km out of town along Pink Lake Road.

Twilight Beach Scenic Drive leads from town up to Observatory Point and Lookout, then to Pink Lake. **Rotary Lookout,** on Wireless Hill, affords yet another town-and-bay vista.

Twilight Cove, near the town center, is a good, safe swimming and fishing beach.

Islands and Parks

The **Archipelago of the Recherche,** also known as the Bay of Isles, is comprised of approximately 100 islands with sandy beaches, turquoise waters, plentiful waterbirds, and seal and penguin colonies. The MV *Cape Le Grand II* makes scenic two-hour cruises of the archipelago, or the MV *Sea Lion* will take you over to Woody Island—a wildlife sanctuary—for a five-hour picnic trip (January, February, and major holidays). For information, phone (08) 9071-1772.

Cape Le Grand National Park (31,390 hectares), 48 km southeast of Esperance, has some dynamite coastal scenery. Sand plains, freshwater pools, swamps, and massive granite outcrops (Mt. Le Grand, 353 meters, is the highest) make up the remaining terrain—home to birds, reptiles, gray kangaroos, possums, and bandicoots. A marked 15-km walking trail will lead you along the coast from Cape Le Grand to Rossiter Bay. Come September through November, when the wildflowers are in bloom. For information, phone (08) 9071-3733.

Cape Arid National Park (279,415 hectares), 125 km east of Esperance, can be reached by conventional vehicle, but tracks within the park are suitable only for four-wheel-drive (weather permitting). Cape Arid also features splendid coastal scenery, granite outcrops, and excellent lookouts as well as diverse fauna. You must obtain permission from a park ranger before rock climbing; swimmers should be wary of rips. Cape *Arid* also translates as *bring your own water.* For information, phone (08) 9075-0055.

Accommodations and Food

Pink Lake Lodge, 85 Pink Lake Rd., tel. (08) 9071-2075, offers affordable, well-maintained rooms. Inexpensive.

Self-contained holiday flats are available at: **Captain Huon,** 5 the Esplanade, tel. (08) 9071-2383; **Esperance All Seasons,** 73 the Esplanade, tel. (08) 9071-2257; and **Esperance Beachfront Resort,** 19 the Esplanade, tel. (08) 9071-2513. Moderate.

The YHA-affiliated **Blue Waters Lodge,** Goldfields Rd., tel. (08) 9071-1040, is two km east of the town center. Eight dorm and two twin rooms accommodate 110 happy hostelers. Dorm beds cost $14 per night. Budget. **Wirraway House Esperance Backpackers,** 14 Emily St., tel. (08) 9071-4724, offers kitchen and lounge facilities, $14 dorm beds, and inexpensive double rooms. Budget-Inexpensive. Book both hostels way in advance for crowded summer months.

Rent a campsite or on-site van at **Bather's Paradise Caravan Park,** corner Westmacott and Chaplin Streets, tel. (08) 9071-1014; **Bushland Holiday Village,** Collier Rd., tel. (08) 9071-1346; **Esperance Bay Caravan Park,** corner the Esplanade and Harbour Rd., tel. (08) 9071-2237; or **Pink Lake Caravan Park,** Pink Lake Rd., tel. (08) 9071-2424. Campsites with limited facilities are offered at both Cape Le Grand and Cape Arid National Parks. Budget-Moderate.

Numerous coffee shops, cafés, and fish-and-chip shops provide belly stuffers. **Spice of Life,** Andrew St., leans toward the vegetarian appetite. **Esperance Café,** Andrew St., and **Village Café,** Dempster St., are both a cut above the ubiquitous takeaway fare. Meals at both range $9-16.

Information

For tourist and tour information, contact the **Esperance Tourist Bureau,** Dempster St., in Museum Village, tel. (08) 9071-2330. Hours are daily 9 a.m.-5 p.m.

Transportation

Ansett Australia, tel. (13) 1300, and **Skywest,** tel. (08) 9334-2288 in Perth or (08) 9071-2002 in Esperance, fly daily from Perth to Esperance, and **Goldfields Air Services,** tel. (08) 9093-2116, makes a once-a-week trip from Kalgoorlie via Norseman.

Twice each week the Prospector Perth-Kalgoorlie train connects with a Westrail coach to Esperance. If you'd rather take the bus all the way, Westrail coaches also depart Perth for Esperance twice a week. For information, phone (13) 1053.

The YHA hostel rents **bicycles** for $10 per day.

If you're heading up to the goldfields region, take the Coolgardie-Esperance Highway north out of town, straight up to Coolgardie (375 km north of Esperance and 39 km southwest of Kalgoorlie), or turn onto the Eyre Highway at Norseman (207 km) for the eastward trek across the Nullarbor Plain.

THE WHEATLANDS

Don't be put off by the boring name—this agricultural heartland, stretching from Perth to Coolgardie and north of Albany to the Great Eastern Highway, has some wild rock formations, Aboriginal rock carvings, and worth-a-stop historical sights.

YORK TO HYDEN

Beginning at the Avon Valley, weave and wind your way through side ways and byways to various wheatlands attractions, ending at the simply *awesome* Wave Rock.

The Yoting-Kellerberrin Road, beyond the small wheaty township of Quairading (166 km east of Perth), accesses both **Kokerbin Rock,** with caves, a lookout, and a scenic drive, and **Mount Stirling,** a huge granite outcrop often climbed for the view.

Bruce Rock, 77 km east of Quairading, is another noteworthy outcrop. **Bruce Rock Museum,** 24 Johnson St., contains pioneering items. Hours are daily 10 a.m.-4 p.m. Admission is $3.

Situated 68 km southwest of Bruce Rock, **Corrigin** (pop. 840) dates back to the 1880s. The **Pioneer Museum,** corner of Kunjin Rd. and Kirkwood St., displays early machinery and pioneering memorabilia. Hours are daily 10 a.m.-4 p.m. Admission is $3.

Locally produced handicrafts can be purchased at the **Craft Cottage,** Walton Street. Hours are Mon.-Fri. 10 a.m.-5 p.m., Saturday 9:30-11:30 a.m.

Gorge Rock, 23 km southeast of Corrigin, is a swimming area created from a dammed gorge. **Jilakin Rock,** 50 km southeast, through Kulin, is a gray granite monolith overlooking a 1,214-hectare lake surrounded by bushland.

Wave Rock, three km outside Hyden and 108 km southeast of Corrigin, is the destination of most wheatlands travelers. This enormous 50-meter-high granite rock formation—shaped by wind and rain—is estimated to be 2.7 billion years old. It resembles a huge curling wave made even more distinctive by vertical bands of color on its sloping face. A marked track will lead you around the base of Wave Rock over to **Hippo's Yawn,** another unique outcrop. **Bates Cave,** 21 km northwest of Hyden, features Aboriginal hand paintings.

Dieps B&B, 17 Clayton St., tel. (08) 9880-5179, is a friendly establishment. Inexpensive. **Hyden Hotel,** 2 Lynch St., tel. (08) 9880-5052, is another option in this area. Moderate.

Campsites are also available at **Wave Rock Caravan Park,** Wave Rock, tel. (08) 9880-5022. Budget.

THE GREAT SOUTHERN HIGHWAY

Situated on the Avon River, 66 km south of York, **Beverley** is known for its **Aeronautical Museum,** Vincent St., with displays of aviation equipment, model airplanes, and the *Silver Centenary,* W.A.'s first privately made airplane. Hours are daily 10 a.m.-4 p.m. For information, phone (08) 9646-1555.

Historical buildings include **St. Paul's Church** (1862), Avon Dr., **St. John's in the Wilderness** (1895), Dale-Beverley Rd., and Beverley's oldest surviving building (now a museum), **Dead Finish** (1872), 138 Vincent Street.

Narrogin (pop. 5,000), 137 km south of Beverley, is the commercial hub of this district. The **Court House Museum,** Norseman Rd., gives insight into early industry and society. Hours are Tuesday, Friday, and Sunday 2-4:30 p.m.

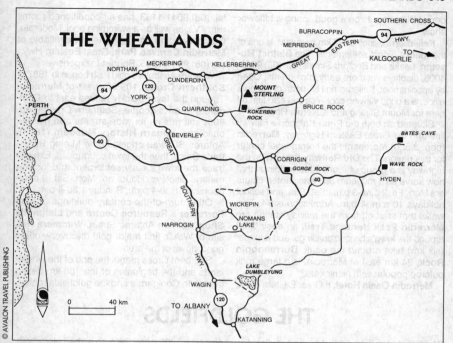

THE WHEATLANDS

Albert Facey's Homestead, on the road between Wickepin and Nomans Lake, was built by the colorful character of the same name. Facey's autobiography, *A Fortunate Life,* later became a TV miniseries. The homestead is open Mon.-Fri. 9 a.m.-5 p.m. Admission is $4.

Attractions around **Wagin,** 50 km down the highway, include the **Giant Ram Tourist Park** (the ram is 15 meters long and seven meters high and called the "largest (fake) ram in the Southern Hemisphere"), **Wagin Historical Village,** and nearby **Mount Latham,** for rock climbing and bushwalking. **Puntapin Rock** is another large, intriguing rock formation. **Lake Dumbleyung,** 39 km east of Wagin, is the spot where Donald Campbell broke the world water speed record in 1964. Around a portion of the lake is a nature reserve with varied birdlife, a scenic drive, and a lookout point.

Settled in the 1840s, **Katanning** (pop. 4,415) mixes a bit of history with modern services. The **Old Mill** (1889), Main St., houses early machin-

ery, equipment, and a crafts shop. Hours are Mon.-Fri. 10 a.m.-4 p.m., Saturday 10 a.m.-noon. Admission is $2.

The Great Southern Highway joins the Albany Highway 85 km south of Katanning.

THE GREAT EASTERN HIGHWAY

The 500-km stretch from Northam to Kalgoorlie is also known as the Goldfields Heritage Trail and follows the original 1860s route established by surveyor Charles Hunt.

Meckering, a little rural town 133 km east of Perth, was severely damaged in a 1968 earthquake. Though the town was immediately rebuilt, you can see mementos of the destruction at the tourist center gazebo.

The Municipal Museum at **Cunderdin,** 24 km east, displays assorted vintage farm machinery, tractors, photos, and other relics. Hours are daily 10 a.m.-4 p.m. Admission is $2. Cunderin Hill itself puts on a good spring wildflower show.

Kellerberrin, another 47 km eastward, is one of the route's oldest settlements. The **District Museum,** Leake and Bedford Streets, tel. (08) 9045-4006, displays yet more early implements. Open by appointment. Kellerberrin Hill, north of the post office, is a good viewing spot. You can also turn off here for Mount Stirling and Kokerbin Rock.

Situated on both the Perth-Kalgoorlie railway line and the Great Eastern Highway, **Merredin** (pop. 3,520) represents the commercial center for this region. The **Old Railway Station** on the highway is a group of four 1920s buildings that now serve as a museum and arts center. Hours are Mon.-Fri. 9 a.m.-3 p.m., Sat.-Sun. and school holidays 10 a.m.-4 p.m. Admission is $4. Two walks that start off from the railway station are **Merredin Peak Heritage Trail,** an easy jaunt around the town's historic buildings, and a longer (six km) hike around the peak. **Burracoppin Rock,** 24 km east of Merredin, is a large rock outcrop popular with picnickers.

Merredin Oasis Hotel, 8 Great Eastern Hwy.,

tel. (08) 9041-1133, has air-conditioned rooms with TVs, as well as a swimming pool. Moderate. Campsites and on-site vans are available at **Merredin Caravan Park,** Great Eastern Hwy., tel. (08) 9041-1535. Budget-Inexpensive.

Western Australia's gold rush began in 1887 at **Southern Cross,** 109 km east of Merredin. Though the fever quickly moved east to Coolgardie and Kalgoorlie, Southern Cross (pop. 800) still retains its wide streets and historic buildings. **Yilgarn History Museum** (1892), Antares St., was originally the Mining Registrar's Office, then the town courthouse. Exhibits trace the town's early settlement and include mineral displays. Hours are Mon.-Sat. 9 a.m.-noon and 1:30-4 p.m., Sunday 1:30-4 p.m.

Other turn-of-the-century buildings are the **Forrester's Resource Centre** and **Lisignolis Shop,** both on Antares Street. **Wimmera Hill,** site of W.A.'s first major gold discovery, offers good views of the area.

Southern Cross marks the end of the wheatlands and the beginning of the 188-km desert stretch to Coolgardie and the goldfields region.

THE GOLDFIELDS

Western Australia's goldfields are hot, flat, and extremely arid, punctuated with deserted outposts, preserved ghost towns, and its semi-thriving hub, Kalgoorlie. The streets are wide, shoot-'em-out affairs (made that way so camel trains could turn around easily), and many of the buildings exude the wealth and opulence associated with gold frenzy. Try to ignore the cranes, conveyers, and tailings dumps, and envision the Golden Mile's hundred mines all flourishing simultaneously.

History

Until that 1887 gold strike in Southern Cross, Western Australia received merely poor-relative status from the eastern colonies. But what brings relatives flocking faster than gold? Though the Southern Cross find quickly ran dry, in 1892 prospector Arthur Bayley (acting on a hot tip given by a man he'd saved from death) staked a claim at Bayley's Reward, a huge gold reef about three km east of Coolgardie. By 1900, the town's population soared to 15,000, dropping consid-

erably by 1905 when the rush rushed elsewhere. Bayley's Reward, however, continued to produce gold until 1963.

In 1893, Irish prospectors Paddy Hannan, Tom Flannigan, and Dan Shea found gold near the site of the present Mount Charlotte Mine. Though surface gold soon ran out, a bigger and deeper find was discovered along the Golden Mile (reputedly the world's richest square mile of gold-bearing earth), prompting companies and diggers to go underground. At one time, the Golden Mile boasted more than 100 working mines.

One enormous problem was the lack of water, or the pollution of what water there was: miners were dropping like flies from thirst and disease. Engineer C.Y. O'Connor came up with the perfect invention—a 563-km wood and pitch water pipe from Mundaring Weir, near Perth, to Kalgoorlie. Mocked and taunted by ignorant disbelievers, O'Connor nonetheless persevered with his pipeline. Unfortunately, three days after the water pumps were started and there was still nary a trickle, the despondent O'Connor shot himself to death—not realizing the water would take two weeks to travel such a distance. Dead or not, he'd solved the problem. By 1903 water began filling Kalgoorlie's new reservoir.

KALGOORLIE

"Queen of the Golden Mile," Kalgoorlie (pop. 20,000) sits 596 km east of Perth at the end of the Goldfields Heritage Trail. Kalgoorlie goldfields continued to produce during the lean 1920s, ebbing and falling during depression

and war. Just as the mines were faltering economically, the 1960s nickel boom brought renewed prosperity—and tourism—to town. Today, life centers around the "Super Pit," a working gold mine operated by Kalgoorlie Consolidated Gold Mines—supposedly the largest hole in the Southern Hemisphere. This is a working town, and virtually every aspect of it, from employment to entertainment to daily necessities—plays a role in the continuing quest for gold. Tourists are tolerated, but it's probably ill-advised to kick back here for long without joining the *very* serious workforce.

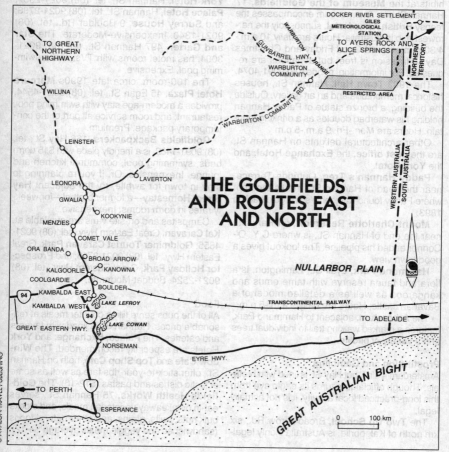

THE GOLDFIELDS AND ROUTES EAST AND NORTH

Sights

Kalgoorlie's biggest tourist attraction is **Hannan's North Tourist Mine,** off Goldfields Hwy., on Eastern Bypass Rd. (on the Golden Mile). See mining memorabilia and the inner (or under) workings. Visitors can take a 30-minute surface tour, 90-minute underground tour, or both. Tours depart several times daily and cost about $14 each, though you can explore the surface displays on your own, for free. Hours are daily 9 a.m.-5 p.m. For information, phone (08) 908-914074.

Learn the history and development of W.A.'s goldfields through displays and hands-on exhibits at the **Museum of the Goldfields,** 17 Hannan Street. The museum encompasses the teensy **British Arms Hotel,** supposedly the narrowest pub in Australia. Hours are daily 10 a.m.-4:30 p.m., closed Good Friday and Christmas Day. Admission is free, but donations are requested. For information, phone (08) 9091-4074.

The 1903 **Town Hall,** Hannan St., houses historical memorabilia and an art gallery. Outside the building, a bronze statue of Paddy Hannan holding his waterbag doubles as a drinking fountain. Hours are Mon.-Fri. 9 a.m.-5 p.m.

Other architectural delights on Hannan St. are the **post office,** the **Exchange Hotel,** and the **York Hotel.**

Paddy Hannan's Tree, Outridge Terrace, near the head of Hannan St., marks the spot where Paddy found Kalgoorlie's first gold back in 1893.

Mount Charlotte Reservoir, off Park St., near the end of Hannan St., is where C.Y. O'Connor ended his pipeline. The lookout gives a good town view.

Hammond Park, Lyall St., Lamington, is a flora and fauna reserve with tame emus and kangaroos as well as a detailed model of a Bavarian castle. Hours are daily 9 a.m.-5 p.m.

The **Arboretum,** adjacent to Hammond Park, features a marked walking trail to individual trees and a variety of birdlife.

Prostitution and Gambling

Amsterdam it ain't, but Hay St. is lined with brothels. Though officialdom turns its eagle eye from this long-practiced local activity, it is not actually legal.

The **Two Up School,** Broad Arrow Rd., six km north of Kalgoorlie, is Australia's only legalized bush two-up school. This famous Aussie gambling game has been played in Kalgoorlie since the beginning of the gold rush. Hours are Mon.-Sat. 1:30 p.m.-dark, Sunday 11 a.m.-dark. Closed on race days and the mine's payday. Don't bring alcohol, and don't come if you're under 18 years old. For information, phone (08) 9021-1413.

Accommodations

Would you want to stay anywhere but one of the classic old pubs? Find rooms at: the **Exchange Hotel,** Hannan St., tel. (08) 9021-2833; **York Hotel,** Hannan St., tel. (08) 9021-2337; **Palace Hotel,** Hannan St., tel. (08) 9021-2788; and **Surrey House,** 9 Boulder Rd., tel. (08) 9021-1340. Inexpensive-Moderate. The **Star and Garter,** 497 Hannan St., tel. (08) 9021-3004, has motel rooms with TVs, and a swimming pool. Expensive.

The 100-room, circa late 1990s **Mercure Hotel Plaza,** 45 Egan St., tel. (08) 9021-4544, provides a modern-age stay with swimming pool, restaurant, and room service all part of the contemporary package. Premium.

Goldfields Backpackers, 166 Hay St., tel. (08) 9091-1482, is a friendly place with $15 dorm beds, swimming pool, communal kitchen and lounge. Inexpensive. Or, if you're planning to stay in town for awhile, try the adjacent **Hay Street Homestay**—a former brothel—for weekly rates in dorm rooms. Inexpensive.

Campsites and on-site vans are available at: **Kal Caravan,** Great Eastern Hwy., tel. (08) 9021-4855; **Goldminer Tourist Caravan Park,** Great Eastern Hwy., tel. (08) 9021-3713; and **Prospector Holiday Park,** Great Eastern Hwy., tel. (08) 9021-2524. Budget-Moderate.

Food

All of the pubs serve filling counter meals at reasonable prices. Hannan St. is lined with taverns and eateries. The **Palace, Exchange,** and **York** Hotels are especially recommended. **The Window Cafe** and **Top Shop Café,** both on Hannan St., offer stick-to-your-ribs fare as well as some eclectic dishes and pastas ($12-16). The **Goldfields Health Works,** 75 Hannan St., serves eat-in or takeaway vegetarian meals, and stocks bulk nuts, fruits, grains, and other natural foods (sandwiches and veggie meals average $8-12).

If you've just hit gold, reserve a table at the very expensive **Amalfi,** 409 Hannan St., tel. (08) 9021-3088. This long-established restaurant is famous for its scaloppini as well as contemporary Australian dishes ($28-40). **Basil's on Hannan,** 168 Hannan St., tel. (08) 9021-7832, serves moderately priced pasta dishes, seafood, and a popular Sunday brunch ($14-28).

Kalgoorlie brews its own beer, aptly named **Hannan's.**

Shopping

Got that gold fever? You can buy prospecting supplies and metal detectors at **International Lapidary,** 67 Hannan St., tel. (08) 9021-3017, or rent equipment through the tourist office.

Information

For local information and tour bookings, contact **Kalgoorlie-Boulder Tourist Centre,** 250 Hannan St., Kalgoorlie, tel. (08) 9021-1966. Hours are Mon.-Fri. 8:30 a.m.-5 p.m., Sat.-Sun. 9 a.m.-5 p.m.

A branch of the **Royal Automobile Club** is at the corner of Hannan and Porter Streets. For information, phone (08) 9021-1511.

For **emergencies,** dial 000 or the **Kalgoorlie Regional Hospital,** tel. (08) 9080-5888.

Transportation

Both **Ansett W.A.,** tel. (13) 1300, and **Airlink** (book through Qantas) fly to Kalgoorlie daily from Perth. **Goldfields Air Services,** tel. (08) 9093-2116, does the Esperance-Norseman-Kalgoorlie route every Tuesday.

Greyhound Pioneer, tel. (13) 2030, stops in Kalgoorlie en route to the capital cities; **Westrail,** tel. (08) 9326-2222, or (13) 1053, operates four times weekly between Kalgoorlie and Esperance; and **Goldfields Express,** tel. (08) 9021-2954 or (1800) 620-440, does a twice-a-week run between Kalgoorlie and Perth, venturing into northern towns.

The Indian-Pacific and Trans-Australian trains both stop at Kalgoorlie on their way to and from Perth several times each week. The Prospector leaves East Perth Rail Terminal every day for the eight-hour trip ($60, including a meal). For information and bookings, phone Westrail, tel. (08) 9326-2222, or (13) 1053 (book this one ahead).

The local **bus** operates regular runs between Kalgoorlie and Boulder for $2 each way. The tourist center has timetables.

Taxis are available 24 hours a day; a ride between the town and the airport is about $15. For bookings, phone (08) 9021-2177.

All of the major car rental firms are at Kalgoorlie Airport.

Bicycles can be hired for $14 per day from **Johnston Cycles,** 76 Boulder St., tel. (08) 9021-1157.

Goldrush Tours, Palace Chambers, Maritana St., tel. (08) 9021-2954, offers a variety of guided tours and excursions, including town tours, gold detector tours, ghost towns, and in-season wildflowers.

VICINITY OF KALGOORLIE

Looking for gold? It's still out there. Grab a metal detector and join other weekend prospectors, but be sure you're well prepared—carry water, spare parts, and good maps. Check in with the tourist center and Royal Automobile Club before venturing out into this rugged, remote region. Both Boulder and Coolgardie are popular pit stops. Good luck.

Boulder

Boulder (pop. 5,600) is actually a satellite town of Kalgoorlie, built during the boom to service the Golden Mile. Boulder Block pubs used to see nonstop action, but alas, the town is much quieter these days.

The **Boulder Town Hall,** on Burt St., features an ornate clocktower and an exhibition of works by local artists. Next door, the **Goldfields War Museum** houses military artifacts and vehicles but—as of press time—was closed for renovations. For information, phone (090) 93-1083.

The 1897 Boulder City Railway Station is home to the **Eastern Goldfields Historical Society** and its historical and pioneering exhibits. Hours are daily 9-11:30 a.m.

The **Cornwall Hotel,** on Hopkins St., is another gorgeous old grand dame.

Coolgardie

You won't find the frenzied boom town of 1892. Settled into ghost-town retirement, Coolgardie (pop. 900), 40 km southwest of Kalgoorlie, is still a popular stopping place for gold-era aficionados. You'll easily get a sense of what this town was like in its glory just by the size of the streets and structures.

Details of Coolgardie's history can be gleaned from the 150 markers placed about town; they recount the original use of each building. An index to the markers is posted near the **Goldfields Exhibition** on Bayley Street. The exhibition relives Coolgardie's not-so-humble beginnings and includes goldfields memorabilia and a 35-minute video. Hours are daily 10 a.m.-5 p.m., closed Christmas Day. Admission is $4. For information, phone (08) 9026-6090.

The **Old Railway Station,** Woodward St., serves as a transport museum and features a display of Modesto Varischetti's rescue. The name doesn't ring a bell? In 1907, Modesto became trapped by floodwaters while 300 meters underground and was rescued by divers some 10 days later. Hours are Sat.-Thurs. 8:30 a.m.-4:30 p.m., closed Christmas Day. Donations re-

quested. For information, phone (08) 9026-6388. **Ben Prior's Open Air Museum,** Bailey St., is an amazing assortment of gold-boom junque sitting by the edge of the road. Open daily. Admission is free.

Warden Finnerty's House, Hunt St., belonged to the gold rush rule maker. Hours are Tuesday 1-4 p.m. and Sunday 10 a.m.-noon. Admission is $2.

Before jails were built, prisoners were chained to the **Gaol Tree,** on Hunt St., over the old railway bridge. The attached leg irons are replicas. **Bayley's Reward,** Kalgoorlie Rd., is the site of Coolgardie's first gold find. **Coolgardie Cemetery,** Great Eastern Hwy., west of town, has some interesting old graves and headstones, including those of a few Afghan camel drivers.

Learn the history of camels in the goldfields and take a ride yourself at the **Camel Farm,** Great Eastern Highway. Hours are daily 9 a.m.-5 p.m. Admission is $2 (rides are $4, and multiday treks are available). For information, phone (08) 9026-6159.

THE CANNING STOCK ROUTE

This old stock route, spanning 1,750 km from Wiluna to Halls Creek in Western Australia, is the harshest, lengthiest, most difficult (and probably most expensive) 4WD journey in Australia.

In the early 1900s, pastoralists in the Kimberley region had become desperate for an overland route by which to move their livestock south to the monied meat-eaters in the goldfields. An outbreak of cattle tick had banned all ship transport along the coast—the southern graziers were taking no chances that it would spread to their land. But the Kimberley cattlemen made an interesting discovery: conveniently, the nasty little ticks simply died during the trip across the sizzling desert.

So the Kimberley boys pressured the government to put up some money for a stock route, and in 1906, Alfred Canning—surveyor extraordinaire—was hired to make a preliminary exploration. His report was favorable—he could sink 54 wells, approximately 20 km apart. Canning and his construction party went to work, completing the route between March 1908 and April 1910. The first stock trod the path in 1911.

In 1929, a team led by William Albert Snell refur-

bished the wells up to No. 35, and Canning himself (retired by then) finished the job. In 1942, fear of a Japanese invasion of northern Australia spurred another refurbishment—just in case citizens and livestock had to flee the area.

In their prime, the wells each possessed a hand-operated windlass, two buckets, a whip-pole for water-hauling, and a galvanized steel trough for cattle-watering. Unfortunately, since 1958—when road trains made the route obsolete and it was abandoned—the wells have been desecrated by termites, rust, and fires; some retain only a bit of wood, ironwork, and the odd bucket.

Warning: This is an extremely arduous journey, requiring major preparations, a top-notch 4WD vehicle, permits from pastoralists, two-way radios, a *lot* of fuel, and other provisions. There is *no* help along the way. Increasingly, travelers are *dying* on this journey. It should only be undertaken late April until early October, with June through August being the best months. The Royal Automobile Club publishes an excellent map and can provide you with information, but even their literature carries red-ink warnings.

Queen Victoria Rock Nature Reserve, Queen Victoria Rock Rd., is a huge rock surrounded by woodlands, with a walking trail across the rock and up to the summit. You might be able to sight the "freckled duck," one of the world's rarest waterfowl, at **Rowles Lagoon,** Bonnie Vale Road. Rock climbing is popular at **Cave Hill Nature Reserve,** Sunday Soak Track. **Burra Rock Nature Reserve,** Burra Rock Rd., offers rock exploration, swimming, and wide views.

The **Denver City Hotel,** Bayley St., tel. (08) 9026-6031, one of the beautiful original hotels, offers simple pub rooms. Inexpensive.

All of the interstate coaches stop in Coolgardie on the way to and from Kalgoorlie. **Bonnie Vale Station,** 12 km away, is a stop for Kalgoorlie-bound trains.

Kambalda

Kambalda, 55 km south of Kalgoorlie, was originally a gold-mining town called Red Hill (1897-

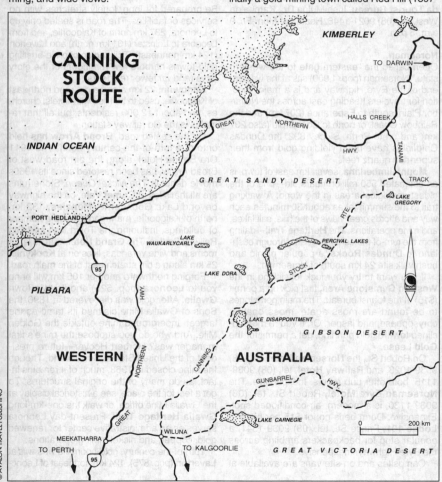

© AVALON TRAVEL PUBLISHING

1906). Regaining new importance—and a new name—when nickel was discovered in 1966, Kambalda continues to exist as a major mining center of the region. Situated on the shores of saltwater Lake Lefroy, Kambalda is a popular spot for weekend land yachting.

Red Hill Lookout offers vantage points of the town, lake, and surrounding countryside. **John Hill View Point** will give you a vantage point of the mine and slime dump.

Pick up permits to visit the mines at **Kambalda Tourist Bureau,** Irish Mulga Dr., Kambalda West, tel. (08) 9021-1446. Hours are Mon.-Fri. 9 a.m.-5 p.m.

Norseman

Often called the "eastern gate to the western state," Norseman (pop. 1,900) sits at the western end of the Eyre Highway and is a major junction for travelers heading east across the Nullarbor Plain, south to Esperance (207 km) and the Rainbow Coast, or north to Coolgardie (also 207 km) and on to Perth. Since 1892, the Dundas Goldfields have been yielding gold from their super-rich quartz reef.

Mount Jimberlana, seven km east of town, is an estimated 550 million years old—one of the oldest geological areas in the world. A walking trail to the summit takes about 30 minutes each way and affords great views of the hills, salt lakes, and mine operations. The **Heritage Trail**—dating from the turn-of-the-century—leads through bushland to **Dundas Rocks,** a popular picnic and bushwalk site 24 km south of Norseman.

If you want to try your luck fossicking in the **Western Gemstone Area,** first pick up a permit ($15) at the tourist bureau. The main gemstones to be found are moss agate, moss opalite, chrysophase, and jasper. Or, if you're more inclined toward gold panning, get a permit for the **Gold Lease.**

On Robert St., the **Norseman Hotel,** tel. (08) 9039-1023, and **Railway Hotel,** tel. (08) 9039-1115, both offer pub rooms. Inexpensive. The **Norseman Eyre Motel,** Robert St., tel. (08) 9039-1130, is a modern, air-conditioned spot. Expensive. Dorm beds go for $15 per night at **Lodge 101,** Prince St., tel. (08) 9039-1541, a popular stop for backpackers ambling across the Eyre Highway. Inexpensive.

Campsites and on-site vans are available at

Gateway Caravan Park, tel. (08) 9039-1500, on Prinsep Street. Budget-Moderate.

Goldfields Air Services, tel. (08) 9093-2116, can put down in Norseman on its Kalgoorlie-to-Esperance service. All of the interstate coaches stop in Norseman on the way to and from Kalgoorlie.

NORTH OF KALGOORLIE

Be prepared for long, lonely stretches with no services or facilities. The road is sealed only up to Leonora, 237 km north of Kalgoorlie, and from Leonora to Leinster (131 km north) and Laverton (124 km northeast). This region of once-bustling gold towns harbors few reminders of the glory days (and *far* fewer residents).

Kanowna, 22 km along a dirt road northeast of Kalgoorlie, used to be filled with hotels, churches, and about 12,000 residents, but all that remains is the old railway station.

On the sealed road, **Broad Arrow** has held onto one turn-of-the-century hotel. The 1911 Ora Banda Hotel, along the dirt road west of Broad Arrow, has been restored since its 1960s movie debut in *The Nickel Queen.* Stone ruins are all that's left of **Comet Vale,** on the highway beyond Lake Goongarrie. **Menzies,** 132 km north of Kalgoorlie, managed to keep a number of buildings, including the Town Hall and Old Railway Station. The **Grand Hotel,** with its large rooms and wide verandas, lives on at **Kookynie,** 25 km along a dirt stretch east of the main road.

Forging northward another 105 km will bring you to **Leonora** (pop. 525) and its twin town **Gwalia.** After gold was discovered in 1896, the Sons of Gwalia Mine claimed its fame as the largest underground mine outside the Golden Mile. And who do you suppose the mine's first manager was? Herbert Hoover—future president of the United States. Small world. Though the mine closed in 1963, much of it remains intact, as do many of the original structures. To get a feel for the place, see a historical display at the Gwalia Mine office, or walk the one-km-long **Gwalia Heritage Trail.** Present-day Leonora serves as an administrative center for renewed gold, copper, and nickel mining operations.

Turn-of-the-century, gold-boom life was *wild* at **Laverton** (pop. 875), 124 km northeast of Leonora, until the gold (and the town) died out in the early 1900s. The 1970s Poseidon nickel boom—and the huge Windarra Mine—have considerably revived Laverton, often used by visitors as a base from which to explore surrounding ghost towns and gold mines.

North of Leonora, the sealed road ends 131 km away at Leinster, another nickel-producing town. Following the unsurfaced road 166 km northwest will take you to **Wiluna** (a has-been 1930s arsenic-mining community), and then to **Meekatharra** (183 km west), on the Great Northern Highway between Port Hedland and Perth.

The sealed portion of the **Warburton Community Road** to Ayers Rock (1,033 km northeast) ends at Laverton. If you intend to travel this route, make sure you have a well-equipped 4WD or conventional vehicle with good ground clearance (the road is not suitable for caravans

or trailers). You will also need permits to enter Aboriginal lands en route and enough fuel for a 600-km stretch. Check on current road conditions at the Laverton Shire Council and notify police of your intended departure and arrival times. Due to intense heat, travel is *not* recommended November through March. Fuel, food, supplies, and camping facilities are available at **Warburton Roadhouse,** 692 km from Leonora.

The road joins 45 km of the Gunbarrel Highway near Giles Meteorological Station (230 km northeast of Warburton), crosses the Northern Territory border at Docker River Settlement, bringing you to Uluru (Ayers Rock) and Yulara another 233 km east. When you reach the border, you'll see the memorial plaque to Harold Lasseter (of Lasseter's Folly fame), who claimed to have found a magnificent gold reef out there and died trying to find it again.

red kangaroo

THE NORTH COAST

The northern part of Western Australia has undergone so much expansion that, in 1976, the Brand Highway was opened to smooth the way for travelers who had previously relied on the Midlands Road up to Dongara (80 km longer and with many more stops). Above Geraldton the Brand becomes the North West Coastal Highway, linking with the Great Northern Highway from Port Hedland to Broome and through the Kimberley. Collectively, all of these roadways are still Highway 1, the sealed route that circles Australia.

It's a 1,780-km journey from Perth to Port Hedland, passing through the state's Midwest, Gascoyne, and Pilbara regions. The coastal road only really becomes coastal as it nears the Midlands Road junction; until then it runs about 40 km inland. Both the inland and coastal highways are *hot* during summer months.

PERTH TO GERALDTON

The Brand Highway cuts into the Great Northern Highway 55 km northeast of Perth. It's 150 km to the turnoff for Cervantes (pop. 240), a fishing town established in 1962, and the closest town to **Nanbung National Park.** A spectacular site within the park is The Pinnacles, calcified spires of widely varying shades, sizes, and shapes, scattered eerily amid 400 hectares of yellow and ochre sand. Some of the long-eroded formations are thought to be 30,000 years old. Several lookouts over the desert and coast can be accessed via a 500-meter walking trail. The best time for Pinnacle viewing is sundown. Day tours depart Cervantes Service Station daily at 1 p.m. For park and Pinnacle information, contact the **Department of Conservation and Land Management,** tel. (08) 9652-7043.

Warning: Bushwalkers should be wary of **kangaroo ticks**—use the appropriate repellent.

To reach **Jurien,** a tiny rock lobster port on a sheltered bay, follow the side track 50 km north of Cervantes. **Drovers Cave National Park,** six km east of Jurien, has some good bush-

walks, but all of the numerous caves have been locked up.

Greenhead, 56 km north of Jurien via the gravel Jurien Rd. or the sealed Brand Highway, features safe swimming, skin diving, and all kinds of fishing. **Leeman,** a short distance away, is also a relaxed fishing village.

Dongara (pop. 1,155) and neighboring **Port Denison** are holiday resorts and crayfish ports that touch the coast 359 km north of Perth. **Royal Steam Roller Flour Mill,** Walldeck St., is part of a restored village that includes the 1870 Old Dongara Police Station and Tourist Information Centre. Hours are Mon.-Fri. 9 a.m.-5 p.m., Sat.-Sun. 10 a.m.-2 p.m. The 1870 **Russ Cottage,** Port Leander Dr., is furnished with period items. Hours are Sunday and public holidays 2-4 p.m. Admission is $2.

The National Trust has classified a number of stone buildings at **Greenough,** an 1850s wheat-farming hamlet 41 km north of Dongara. The **Pioneer Museum,** Wonga Park, will fill you in on local folklore. Hours are Sat.-Thurs. 10 a.m.-4 p.m.

Midlands Road

The old Midlands Rd. begins 30 km farther up the Great Northern Highway, past the Brand Highway turnoff. This is well worth the drive in spring when the wildflowers put on a stupendous show.

At **Coorow,** you can detour 12 km west along Greenhead Rd. to Perth Basin, one of the world's deepest sedimentary basins. **Yarra Yarra Lakes,** between Carnamah and Three Springs, is a salty lake system with some wild color variations (red, green, and blue), plus prolific birdlife. Climb to the top of **Mingenew Hill** for excellent east and west views of the Irwin Valley.

Wildflower Way

One more alternate route to Geraldton is Wildflower Way, which runs parallel to the Midlands Rd. beginning at Wubin, off the Great Northern Highway, and continuing 222 km to Mullewa, where you hook up to Highway 123 west. **Mullewa** (pop. 918), a sheep and wheat farming town-

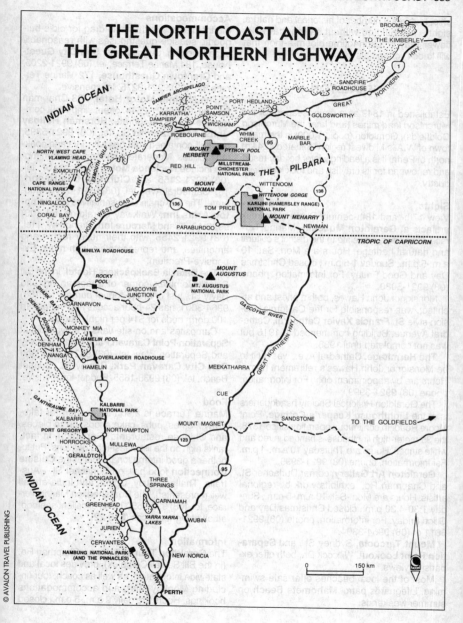

THE NORTH COAST AND THE GREAT NORTHERN HIGHWAY

ship, features a number of historical and natural sights. It should go without saying that Wildflower Way is a springtime bloom-a-thon that will knock your petals off.

GERALDTON

Established in 1849 as a major seaport for the Murchison lead mines (and later the Murchison Goldfields), Geraldton (pop. 21,000) is the major town of W.A.'s Midwest region. Situated 424 km north of Perth, it is a leading winter holiday resort and renowned for its crayfish and rock lobster industry.

Sights

View 17th- and 18th-century Dutch shipwreck artifacts at **Geraldton Museum,** Marine Terrace. Other displays relate to the district's cultural and natural heritage. Hours are Mon.-Sat. 10 a.m.-5 p.m., Sunday 1-5 p.m., closed Christmas Day and Good Friday. For information, phone (08) 9921-5080.

Monsignor John Hawes, both a priest and architect, was responsible for the California-mission-style **St. Francis Xavier Cathedral,** Cathedral Avenue. Building commenced in 1916 but was not completed until 1938.

The **Hermitage,** Cathedral Ave., was built to be Monsignor John Hawes's retirement home. Hours are by appointment only. For information, phone (08) 9921-3999.

The Geraldton Historical Society headquarters is at the **Lighthouse Keeper's Cottage,** Point Moore Road. In continuous operation since 1878, the 35-meter-high lighthouse is banded in red and white stripes. Hours are Thursday 10 a.m.-4 p.m. For information, phone (08) 9921-3999.

Geraldton Art Gallery, corner Durlacher St. and Chapman Rd., exhibits work by regional artists. Hours are Mon.-Sat. 10 a.m.-5 p.m., Sunday 1:30-4:30 p.m., closed Christmas Day and Good Friday. For information, phone (08) 9921-6811 or (08) 9964-3304.

Mount Tarcoola, Sydney St., and **Separation Point Lookout,** Willcock Dr., both offer expansive views.

Most of the local beaches offer safe swimming. Lifeguards patrol **Mahomets Beach** on summer weekends.

Accommodations

Marine Terrace is the main drag for oldie-but-goodie seaside guesthouses with reasonably priced lodging. Suggestions: **Sun City Guesthouse,** 184 Marine Terrace, tel. (08) 9921-2205, and **Grantown Guesthouse,** 172 Marine Terrace, tel. (08) 9921-3275. Inexpensive.

The **Mariner Motor Hotel,** 298 Chapman Rd., tel. (08) 9921-2544, offers simple but comfortable rooms. Moderate. **Horsman Holiday Units,** 144 Fitzgerald St., tel. (08) 9921-5395, has self-contained cottages with TVs and cooking facilities. Moderate. Other mainstream motels include **Hacienda Motel,** Durlacher St., tel. (08) 9921-2155, and **Club Sun City Resort,** 137 Cathedral Ave., tel. (08) 9921-6111. Moderate. The two chain representatives are **Hampton Arms Inn,** Walkway Geraldton, tel. (08) 9926-1057, and **Mercure Inn,** Brand Hwy., tel. (08) 9921-2455, with their ritzier rooms and amenities, and representative high rates. Expensive-Premium.

The **Batavia Backpackers Hostel,** in the Bill Sewall Complex, corner of Chapman Rd. and Bayly St., just near the tourist bureau, tel. (08) 9964-3001, has 24-hour access and more than 100 dorm beds for $14 per night. Budget.

Campsites and on-site vans are available at **Separation Point Caravan Park,** corner Portway and Separation Way, tel. (08) 9921-2763, and **Sun City Caravan Park,** Bosley St., Sunset Beach, tel. (08) 9938-1655. Budget-Inexpensive.

Food

Marine Terrace is also the location for take-aways, cafés, pubs, cake shops, pizza places, and Chinese restaurants. Geraldton, in fact, ranks high on the list of fast-food heavens. Put together a good international meal at the **Cuisine Connection** food hall, on Durlacher St.—Australia, Thailand, Italy, China, and India are all well represented. The **Boatshed,** on Marine Terrace, tel. (08) 9921-5500, has excellent seafood, albeit at higher prices ($16-22).

Information

The **Geraldton Tourist Bureau,** Chapman Rd. (in the Bill Sewall Complex), provides local and statewide information, as well as coach, tour (including Monkey Mia), and accommodations bookings. Hours are daily 9 a.m.-5 p.m., closed

Christmas Day and Good Friday. For information, phone (08) 9921-3999.

Transportation
Both **Ansett Australia,** tel. (13) 1300, and **Skywest** (book through Ansett) fly between Perth and Geraldton. Check with the tourist bureau for current regional airlines that connect to other W.A. locations.

Westrail, tel. (13) 1053, and **Greyhound Pioneer,** tel. (13) 2030, both provide regular coach service to and from Perth. Northbound buses travel Highway 1 en route to Broome and Darwin. The coach terminal is in the same building as the tourist bureau.

A **local bus** provides service to neighboring communities. For information, phone (08) 9921-1034.

Avis, Budget, and Hertz have Geraldton agencies. Hire bicycles for $10 per day from **Batavia Backpackers Hostel,** corner Chapman Rd. and Bayly St., tel. (08) 9964-3001.

FARTHER NORTH

Beyond Geraldton
Leaving Geraldton, the Brand Highway metamorphoses into the North West Coastal Highway. **Northampton** (pop. 750), 50 km north, was a favorite Aboriginal site until lead and copper mines were established in the 1840s. Today the community prospers from the surrounding farmlands. Constructed of local sandstone, **Chiverton House Folk Museum** (1868-75), North West Coastal Hwy., houses a collection of early machinery and memorabilia. Hours are Thurs.-Sun. 10 a.m.-noon and 2-4 p.m. For information, phone (08) 9934-1215.

Horrocks Beach, 22 km west of Northampton, features a reef surrounding its five-km swimming beach, as well as good fishing (kingfish, whiting, herring, skippy, tailor, and rock lobster). The **Bowes River** turnoff, four km south of Horrocks, is the location for a number of ancient Aboriginal cave paintings. Bowes River is another jumpin' fishing spot.

Port Gregory, 43 km northwest of Northampton, is the Midwest coast's oldest port, and nearby **Lynton** is a former convict-labor hiring depot. Though the town is defunct, many of the old ruins can still be seen.

From Lynton, follow Yerina Springs Rd. north, then turn east on Ogilvie West Rd. to **Hutt River Province,** where self-appointed "Prince Leonard" is ruler. Having seceded from the Australian Commonwealth in 1970, Prince Leonard's kingdom rakes in revenue from special stamps, money, souvenir items, tearooms, a swimming pool, and other tourist snares.

Kalbarri
Situated where the Murchison River meets the Indian Ocean, Kalbarri (pop. 820) is a holiday resort famous for its gorgeous gorges and terrific fishing. This is also the area where the Dutch ship *Zuytdorp* was wrecked *and* the long-ago home of a 400-million-year-old, two-meter-long scorpion known as the eurypterid.

Kalbarri National Park (186,096 hectares) features awesome sandstone cliffs and banded-in-red gorge walls (formed 400-500 million years ago). The fossil tracks of prevertebrate marine creatures have been located in the sandstone. The park also harbors a wide variety of wildlife and flora; try to come during the spring wildflower season. **Ross Graham** and **Hawk's Head** lookouts provide dynamic gorge views. A 35-km scenic drive leads to **The Loop** and **Z Bend,** two other spectacular viewing perches. Ongoing road upgrades provide easier access to prime inland gorge attractions, including The Loop and Z Bend. Park facilities include short and long walking trails as well as picnic sites. Carry your own drinking water. Admission is $5 by machine (only coins are accepted). For information, phone (08) 9937-1140.

Jake's Corner, a few km south of Kalbarri, has some of W.A.'s best surfing breaks. **Red Bluff,** just south, is where you can see tracks left by the ancient eurypterid (possibly the first creature to have walked on land) and explore frozen, tearlike threads of rock and other intriguing formations (also thought to be 400 million years old).

Rainbow Jungle, Red Bluff Rd., is lush with palms, ferns, tropical plants, rare and tropical birds, and fish. Open Tues.-Sun. 10 a.m.-5 p.m. Admission is $6. For information, phone (08) 9937-1248. **Fantasyland,** Grey St., combines collections of dolls, marinelife, fossils, and gemstones. Every morning at 8:45 a.m., the proprietor feeds pelicans on the foreshore opposite. Hours are Sun.-Fri. 9 a.m.-noon and 1:30-5 p.m.,

Saturday 9 a.m.-noon. Admission is $5. For information, phone (08) 9937-1062.

Sailboats, canoes, surf cats, and pedal boats can be hired at **Kalbarri Boat Hire,** tel. (08) 9937-1245, on the foreshore across from Murchison Caravan Park. **Kalbarri Sports and Dive,** Grey St., tel. (08) 9937-1126, hires diving equipment and offers instruction.

Av-er-est, Mortimer St., tel. (08) 9937-1101, offers good-deal weekly rates on self-contained holiday units with TVs and cooking facilities. Inexpensive. Holiday units include **Kalbarri Reef Villas,** Coles St., tel. (08) 9937-1165, and **Sunsea Villas,** Grey St., tel. (08) 9937-1187. Moderate.

Kalbarri Backpackers, 2 Mortimer St., tel. (08) 9937-1430, caters to travelers with 24-hour check-in and $14 dorm beds. Budget. Rent campsites and on-site vans at **Kalbarri Tudor Caravan Park,** Porter St., tel. (1800) 68-1077, and **Murchison Caravan Park,** Grey St., tel. (08) 9937-1005. Budget-Moderate.

Westrail, tel. (13) 1053, operates bus service three times a week, in each direction. A shuttle connects with **Greyhound Pioneer,** tel. (13) 2030, on its thrice-weekly runs along the North West Coastal Highway.

Rent bicycles at **Murchison Cycle Hire,** Porter St., tel. (08) 9937-1105, for about $10 per day. For local tours (including a cruise up the Murchison River on the *River Queen*), contact **Kalbarri Travel Service,** Grey St., tel. (08) 9937-1104. Full-day hikes in the park, including pickup from accommodations, are offered three times a week by **Kabarri Safari Tours,** tel. (08) 9937-1011. For other tours and information, check in with the tourist bureau, south of Woods St., tel. (08) 9937-1104.

AROUND SHARK BAY

The Overlander Roadhouse (179 km north of Kalbarri) marks the turnoff from the North West Coastal Highway to Shark Bay, site of the first European landing on Australian soil (Dutchman Dirk Hartog in 1616).

Stromatolites, among the world's oldest living fossils, can be seen in **Hamelin Bay's** clear, shallow waters. **Shell Beach,** near Nanga via Denham Rd., is created from billions of minute shells packed about 20 meters deep. Actual

---

DOLPHIN ETIQUETTE

Please—Monkey Mia is *not* a dolphin Disneyland. These babies are not trained for your pleasure. When you're wading with the dolphins, observe the following rules:

- Wade about knee-deep.
- Don't approach the dolphins; let them approach you.
- Never touch, or put anything into, a dolphin's blowhole.
- Don't touch a dolphin's head, dorsal fin, or tail (pat gently along the side of the body).
- Do not scare the dolphins with loud noises.
- Don't try to swim with the dolphins—and don't reach over them for any reason.
- Check with rangers before feeding—the dolphins are fussy about their food.
- If a dolphin gives you a fish, don't give it back. Accept it and say "thank you."

one of the untrained dolphins at Monkey Mia

MARK MORRIS

---

shell "blocks" (compacted by nature) have been constructed by locals along the Shark Bay foreshore. **Freshwater Camp,** Nanga's pioneer homestead, features the usual relics.

One-time pearling port **Denham,** 48 km northwest of Nanga, sits on the west side of Peron Peninsula (just above the 26th parallel) and is Australia's westernmost town. Sightseeing **cruises** and fishing trips depart from Denham Jetty. For cruise bookings and information on other local tours, contact **Shark Bay Tourist Information Centre,** 83 Knight St., tel. (08) 9948-1253.

Well-posted signs lead to **Monkey Mia,** one of the country's—and the world's—most unusual natural attractions, 25 km northeast of Denham. Since 1964, when a woman from one of the area's fishing camps began the practice, dolphins have regularly come up to these shores to be hand-fed by rangers and throngs of visitors. These sweet mammals will only accept whole fish, not any that have been gutted or gilled. Obey rangers' instructions on feeding and petting. Feeding times usually take place at intervals between 8 a.m.-1 p.m. An information center provides educational exhibits and videos on dolphin behavior. Fresh fish are sold for your feeding pleasure. Hours are daily 7:30 a.m.-4:30 p.m. Admission is $5. For information, phone (08) 9948-1366.

Bay Lodge, 109 Knight Terrace, Denham, tel. (08) 9948-1278, is a YHA associate. Backpackers' accommodations run $12 per night, while self-contained holiday units are in the higher price brackets. Budget-Moderate. Other self-contained units are **Denham Villas,** 4 Durlacher St., tel. (08) 9948-1264, and **Hartog Holiday Villas,** Denham-Hamelin Rd., tel. (08) 9948-1323. Moderate. **Heritage Resort Hotel,** Knight Terrace, tel. (08) 9948-1133, with deluxe facilities, is the deep-pockets choice. Expensive.

Campsites and on-site vans are available at: **Denham Seaside Caravan Park,** Knight Terrace, tel. (08) 9948-1242; **Shark Bay Caravan Park,** Spaven Way, off Durlacher St., tel. (08) 9948-1387; and **Monkey Mia Dolphin Resort,** tel. (08) 9948-1320. Budget-Moderate.

Local restaurants offer the usual counter meal and takeaway fare. The **Old Pearler Restaurant,** Knight Terrace, Denham, tel. (08) 9948-1373, is built out of shell blocks. Food is on the upmarket side and reservations are recommended ($15-22 entrees). The **Shark Bay Hotel** is your counter-meal stop ($6-12).

Skywest tel. (08) 9334-2288, flies several times each week between Perth and Shark Bay.

Greyhound Pioneer, tel. (13) 2030, will drop you at the Overlander three times a week; from there, a Denham Tourist Centre shuttle will transport you to Denham and Shark Bay ($25). For information, phone (08) 9948-1253.

A local bus departs Denham for daily forays to Monkey Mia. Check with the tourist office for fares and schedules.

For tourist information and a list of tour operators that will take you dolphin-spotting on the way to Monkey Mia, check in with **Shark Bay Tourist Bureau,** 71 Knight Terrace, tel. (08) 9948-1253. **Denham and Monkey Mia Booking Office,** also on Knight Terrace, tel. (08) 9948-1056, is another tour- and holiday organizer.

CARNARVON

Positioned at the mouth of the Gascoyne River, Carnarvon (pop. 6,900) is known as the tropical gateway to the north. This seaside commercial center is famed for its tropical fruit plantations (particularly bananas) and its mile-long jetty, beloved by fishers. This was also the spot about which Captain Dirk Hartog and various other explorers said such lousy things, but post-jetty, big-banana Carnarvon has redeemed itself. After all, the place can't be all bad if the fish come up to the foreshore to be hand-fed.

Carnarvon Museum, Robinson St., features historic displays and a shell collection. Hours are Mon.-Fri. 9 a.m.-5 p.m., Sat.-Sun. 9 a.m.-noon and 2-5 p.m. For information, phone (08) 9941-1146. Other local relics—including a whale bone arch—can be seen at **Pioneer Park,** Olivia Terrace.

Ponder trial plantings of tropical fruits and winter veggies at **Gascoyne Research Station,** South River Rd., North Carnarvon. Hours are Mon.-Fri. 8 a.m.-5 p.m. For information, phone (08) 9941-8103.

Check with the tourist office for directions to the former **NASA Tracking Station** (closed in 1975).

Pelican Point is a good swimming and fishing site five km from town. Other top fishing spots include **Dwyer's Leap** and **Prawn Jetty Beach.**

Practicalities

Oldish, cheap pub-hotels are: **Gascoyne Hotel,** Olivia Terrace, tel. (08) 9941-1412; **Port Hotel,** Robinson St., tel. (08) 9941-1704; and the **Carnarvon Hotel,** Olivia Terrace, tel. (08) 9941-1181. Inexpensive.

Both **Carnarvon Close,** 96 Robinson St., tel. (08) 9941-1317, and **Carnarvon Beach Holiday Resort,** Pelican Point Rd., tel. (08) 9941-2226, offer self-contained holiday units. Moderate.

The **Backpackers Paradise**, Robinson St., tel. (08) 9941-2966, has beds for $14 per night—and only two beds per room—still, it is pretty sparse and attracts an odd mix of guests. Budget. Centrally located **Carnarvon Backpacker's**, 50 Olivia Terrace, tel. (08) 9941-1095, has communal facilities and charges $13 per night, with bargains on weekly rates. Budget.

Among the numerous caravan parks offering campsites and on-site vans are: **Plantation Caravan Park**, Robinson St., tel. (08) 9941-8100; **Carnarvon Caravan Park**, Robinson St., tel. (08) 9941-8101; and **Star Trek Caravan Park**, North West Coastal Hwy., tel. (08) 9941-8153. Budget-Moderate.

The Gascoyne, Port, and Carnarvon Hotels all have similar counter meals at reasonable prices ($5-10). Robinson St. is the food strip: fish and chips, pizza, and the ubiquitous coffee lounge.

Tel-O-Mac, 280 Robinson St., tel. (08) 9041-1873, sells fishing, camping, and diving gear.

For local information, including tours, bicycle rentals, and fishing charters, contact **Carnarvon District Tourist Bureau**, 6 Robinson St., tel. (08) 9941-1176. Hours are daily 9 a.m.-5 p.m.

Daily Perth-Carnarvon flights are operated by **Ansett Australia**, tel. (13) 1300. Carnarvon is a regular stop on the north-south **Greyhound Pioneer** route, tel. (13) 2030, and is also served by **Westliner**, tel. (08) 9250-3318.

VICINITY OF CARNARVON

Oyster-picking and crayfishing are specialties at the **Blowholes**, 70 km north of Carnarvon, via Pt. Quobba Road. Salt headed for Japan is loaded at **Cave Cuvier**, a deep natural port some 30 km north of the Blowholes.

Rocky Pool is a deep, freshwater swimming pool, on Gascoyne Junction Rd., 55 km inland. **Gascoyne Junction**, another 122 km east, is a gateway to the rugged Kennedy Range, full of wildlife, Aboriginal caves, rock paintings, and semiprecious gemstones. Gascoyne Junction Hotel, constructed of corrugated iron, is a famous old bush pub.

Mount Augustus, a 289-km gravel drive from Gascoyne Junction, is the world's largest monocline, measuring 717 meters above the surrounding plain (1,105 meters above sea level),

and it remains one of Australia's best-kept secrets. Mount Augustus National Park, only just proclaimed in 1989, is also noted for Aboriginal rock paintings and unusual flora and fauna. Coach tours and scenic flights operate out of Carnarvon. **Mount Augustus Outback Tourist Resort**, tel. (08) 9943-0527, at the foot of the rock, offers campsites and moderately priced units.

CONTINUING NORTH

The Ningaloo Reef

You'll be able to view everything from humpback whales to egg-laying turtles around this mini-Great Barrier Reef, one of the world's major reef systems. Running 260 km along the North West Cape from Exmouth to Amherst Point, Ningaloo Reef—far more accessible than Queensland's Great Barrier—is fast becoming a snorkeling, scuba diving, fishing, and boat-trip mecca. Get there before the developers do!

Also, environmentalists are concerned about this region, now that the North West Cape region is heavy into offshore drilling. State legislation in 1994 decreed drilling in the fragile marine park to be off-limits, but only time will tell whether the law holds.

The turnoff from North West Coastal Highway is just past the Minilya Roadhouse, 142 km north of Carnarvon.

Coral Bay, 78 km from the roadhouse (you'll cross the Tropic of Capricorn about midway), is the main entry point to **Ningaloo Marine Park**, just meters offshore. The reef covers more than 5,000 square km of the Indian Ocean, is made up of almost 200 types of coral, and shelters incredibly diverse marinelife—from teensy tropical fish to scary-looking whale sharks—in its crystal waters. Five shipwrecks around Ningaloo Station provide additional fun for divers. Sign up for a tour aboard the *Sub-Sea Explorer Coral Viewer*, tel. (08) 9942-5955, a semisubmersible viewing craft, or contact **Ningaloo Bay Resort**, tel. (08) 9942-5932, for a glass-bottom boat cruise. **Ningaloo Reef Dive Centre**, tel. (08) 9942-5824, runs a full program of diving courses and rents necessary equipment. For game and deep-sea fishing charters, contact **Coral Bay Adventures**, Robinson St., tel. (08) 9942-5955, or the Tourist Information Centre.

The 50-bed **Ningaloo Bay Resort and Coral Bay Backpackers,** just beyond the Reef Café, tel. (08) 9942-5932, has $15 beds, including linens, in twin rooms. Inexpensive.

Bay View Holiday Village Caravan Park, tel. (08) 9942-5932, offers campsites, cabins, chalets, and on-site vans. Budget-Moderate. Self-contained holiday units are higher priced at **Ningaloo Reef Resort,** tel. (08) 9942-5932, but facilities include tennis courts and hired boats. Expensive.

You'll need a 4WD to access most of **Cape Range National Park** and its 50,831 hectares of coastal scenery, limestone rocks, and gorges. Marked bushwalking trails lead to some of the gorges and lookout points. **Lightfoot Heritage Trail** is a seven-km walk through rugged limestone formations. First-come, first-served campsites are available at selected locations. Come April through October for best weather. For information, phone (08) 9949-1676.

Coral Bay **Tourist Information Bureau** located in Coral Bay Arcade, tel. (08) 99422-5988, can assist with accommodations, tours, and fishing charters.

Exmouth

Exmouth (pop. 2,750), at the tip of the peninsula and 155 km north of Coral Bay, is also popular for fishing, diving, and other beach activities. The town was founded, however, as late as the 1960s to service and house personnel at the joint U.S./Australian naval base at the top of the North West Cape. Used as an Allied base known as "Potshot" during WW II, the facility has ostensibly been used to maintain international contact with U.S. Navy vessels (including submarines) via 13 very low frequency radio transmitters. If the oil tycoons have their way, proceeding with offshore drilling around Ningaloo Marine Park, Exmouth may soon become their "company town."

Take steep **Lighthouse Drive** for panoramic views of the reef, cape, and communication towers.

Potshot Hotel Resort, Murat Rd., tel. (08) 9949-1200, offers a wide range of accommodations—hotel and motel rooms, family apartments, and campsites in price ranges to suit all. Budget-Expensive. For other campsites and on-site vans, contact: **Exmouth Cape Tourist Village,** corner Truscott Crescent and Murat Rd.,

tel. (08) 9949-1101; **Lighthouse Caravan Park,** Vlaminghead Peninsula, tel. (08) 9949-1478; or **Ningaloo Reef Accommodation and Caravan Park,** Yardie Creek Rd., tel. (08) 9949-1389. Budget-Moderate.

For reef dives and equipment hire, contact **Exmouth Diving Centre,** tel. (08) 9949-1201, an outfit that claims the world's premiere whale shark team.

Collect tourist information and book reef or fishing tours at **Exmouth Tourist Bureau,** Payne St., tel. (08) 9949-1176. Hours are daily 9 a.m.-5 p.m.

Ansett Australia, tel. (13) 1300, flies every day except Saturday between Perth and Exmouth.

Several-times-weekly Perth-Exmouth bus service is provided by **Greyhound Pioneer** , tel. (13) 2030, and **Westliner,** tel. (08) 9250-3318.

Avis, tel. (08) 9949-2492, and **Budget,** tel. (08) 9949-1534, both on Murat Rd., rent cars for about $65 per day. Hire **motorcycles** or be lead by pros at **Norwest Cape Classic Tours,** Fyfe St., tel. (08) 9949-1220.

THE PILBARA COAST

The coastal portion of the Pilbara region is a cluster of early pioneering towns getting fat off their own natural resources and the rich inland mines. The Burup Peninsula area harbors some 10,000 ancient Aboriginal petroglyphs, most depicting the wildlife of the time.

Karratha (pop. 8,400), on Nickol Bay about 530 km northeast of Minilya Roadhouse, was established mainly because of the Hamersley Iron Project. Additional growth can be attributed to the Woodside Petroleum Project, which has developed a gigantic natural gas reserve on the North West Shelf. The **Woodside LNG Visitors' Centre,** tel. (08) 9158-8100, will acquaint you with the project—at least one side of it. Hours are Mon.-Fri. 9 a.m.-4:30 p.m. during winter months.

The 3.5-km **Jaburara Heritage Trail,** beginning at the water tanks, will lead you to Aboriginal carvings, grinding stones, shellfish middens, and taboo spiritual sites.

Up the road, **Dampier** (pop. 2,500) was built in the 1960s to serve as port facility for Hammersley Iron. The **Dampier Archipelago,** which the town faces, has a more exciting history of shipwrecks, whaling, and pearling. Boating and fishing these waters (with reefs containing more than 200 species of living coral) are primary pastimes.

Roebourne (pop. 1,700), 32 km southeast of Karratha, is known as "Gateway to the Pilbara." Established in 1864 along with the gold and copper mines, Roebourne is the oldest town in the northwest, as evidenced by its many remaining early stone buildings.

Aiming toward Cape Lambert, **Cossack,** the northwest's first port, once known as Tien Tsin Harbour, also has preserved its beautiful stone buildings. Nearby, **Wickham** is another iron ore company town. **Point Samson,** though modernized, is still a lovely little fishing village.

Accommodations in this area are on the expensive side. Deluxe accommodations can be found at **Karratha International Hotel,** Karratha, tel. (08) 9185-3111, or **Mercure Inn Dampier,** the Esplanade, tel. (08) 9183-1222, where you can retreat to a modern air-conditioned room in the midst of this rugged region. Premium-Luxury.

Victoria Hotel, Roe St., Roebourne, tel. (08) 9182-1001, has simple pub rooms. Inexpensive. The least expensive motel is **Point Samson Lodge,** Samson Rd., Point Samson, tel. (08) 9187-1052. Moderate. Campsites and on-site vans, probably your best bet, are available at: **Karratha Caravan Park,** Mooligum Rd., Karratha, tel. (08) 9185-1012; **Harding River Caravan Park,** De Grey St., Roebourne, tel. (08) 9182-1063; and **Solveig Caravan Park,** Samson Rd., Point Samson, tel. (08) 9187-1414. Budget-Moderate.

Forget the shopping center food and go to Point Samson for fresh fish 'n' chips and other seafood. **Moby's Kitchen,** tel. (08) 9187-1435, specializes in fresh local seafood in a garden setting overlooking the ocean, plus offers takeaways ($12-18, eating in).

For Roebourne area tourist information, contact: **Karratha and Districts Information Centre,** Karratha Rd., tel. (08) 9144-4600, or **Roebourne Tourist Bureau,** Queen St., Roebourne, tel. (09) 9182-1060. For **emergencies,** dial 000.

Ansett Australia, tel. (13) 1300, flies daily to Karratha from Perth. For bus info, contact **Greyhound Pioneer,** tel. (13) 2030, or **Westliner,** tel. (08) 9250-3318.

Vicinity of Roebourne

Traveling 60 km inland on the Wittenoom Rd. will bring you to **Python Pool,** a former oasis for Afghan camel drivers *and* for the area's many pythons.

Millstream-Chichester National Park (199,710 hectares), 60 km farther, forms an odd contrast to its semiarid surroundings, with natural springs, permanent river pools, lily ponds, and groves of date palms (thought to have been brought by the camel drivers). Carry your own food and water, and be prepared for heavy rain and rough roads. Camping is allowed in designated facilities. For information, phone (08) 9184-5144.

Back on the North West Coastal Highway, 78 km east of Roebourne, the 1887 **Whim Creek Hotel** was a rowdy Outback pub, built to serve the Whim Well Copper Mine. Historic photos are on display, and today's brew is on tap.

Port Hedland

Established originally as a service center for the surrounding cattle stations, Port Hedland (pop. 11,600), 1,762 km from Perth, is now the major deepwater port for the megabuck Pilbara iron ore industry—visited by some of the world's biggest ships. By tonnage, it is Australia's biggest port. The entire town and **South Hedland,** its satellite, live and breathe for those rich inland mines. And, as if those miners aren't salty enough, the real stuff is produced a few km away, where huge salt dunes encrust the landscape.

Pretty Pool, behind Cooke Point Caravan Park, is a favorite spot for fishing and shell collecting. Wear sturdy shoes if you want to walk on the reef at low tide—these waters are full of venomous stonefish.

For the most part, Port Hedland accommodations are comparatively high in price. **Pier Hotel,** the Esplanade, tel. (08) 9173-1488, is the best deal, and next best is **The Esplanade,** corner of Anderson St., tel. (08) 9173-1798. Moderate-Expensive.

Port Hedland Backpackers Hostel, 20 Richardson St., tel. (08) 9173-3282, offers dorm beds for $14 per night, sheets included. Budget.

Campsites and on-site vans are available at: **South Hedland Caravan Park,** Hamilton Rd., South Hedland, tel. (08) 9172-1197; **Dixon's Port Hedland Caravan Park,** opposite the airport, tel. (08) 9172-2525; and **Cooke Point Caravan Park,** Athol St., tel. (08) 9173-1271. Budget-Moderate.

Food is the usual coffee lounge, pub, and supermarket put-togethers. The **Hedland Hotel,** corner Lukis and McGregor, does the best counter meals ($8-14). The **Coral Trout** has excellent fish in both its restaurant ($14-20) and takeaway section.

For local information and tour bookings, contact **Port Hedland Tourist Bureau,** 13 Wedge St., tel. (08) 9173-1711. Hours are Mon.-Fri. 8:30 a.m.-5 p.m., Sat. 8:30 a.m.-3:30 p.m., Sun. noon-4 p.m.

Port Hedland Airport is an international gateway. **Garuda** provides service between Port Hedland and Bali.

Ansett Austrlia, tel. (13) 1300, operates daily flights to Port Hedland from Perth. Frequent flights serve Broome, Derby, and Darwin. **Greyhound Pioneer,** tel. (13) 2030, and **Westliner,** tel. (08) 9250-3318, make regular runs between Perth and Port Hedland; to Broome; and to Darwin.

Avis, Budget, and **Hertz** have agencies at Port Hedland Airport, and a taxi into town runs about $20. **Hedland Bus Lines,** Schillaman St., tel. (08) 9172-1394, operates Mon.-Sat. between Port Hedland and South Hedland. The Backpackers Hostel rents **bicycles.**

THE GREAT NORTHERN HIGHWAY

Though the coastal route to Port Hedland is more interesting, the inland Great Northern Highway is actually more direct. From Perth, the highway travels northeast through the Midwest and Pilbara regions, veers coastward at Newman, meeting up with the North West Coastal Highway 42 km south of Port Hedland.

Perth to the Pilbara

Up the highway, 132 km northeast of Perth, **New Norcia** is a strange contrast to other country towns. Founded in 1846 by Benedictine monks who came to inflict their gospel on the Aborigines, the Spanish monastic community consists of the monastery, church, old mill, jail, hotel, and the original boarding schools (now used as a Catholic college). The Benedictine monks still

live and work there, much as they used to. The **Museum and Art Gallery** relates the town's history and also houses a **Tourist Information Centre.** Hours are daily 10 a.m.-4:30 p.m., closed Christmas Day and Good Friday. For information, phone (08) 9654-8056.

Mount Magnet, Cue, and **Meekatharra**—560, 640, and 760 km respectively from Perth—are old Murchison River goldfields. Gold is still being mined at Mount Magnet. Nearby **ghost towns** include Austin (20 km south of Cue), Cuddingwarra (10 km west), Pinnacles (24 km east), Reedys (60 km northeast), and Tuckanarra (40 km north).

Prospecting for gold is still popular at **Sandstone,** 158 km east of Mount Magnet, which is also surrounded by a myriad of abandoned mining settlements. From Meekatharra, it's 183 km of unsealed road to Wiluna, where the road turns south to Kalgoorlie, 534 km away (with the 166-km Wiluna-Leinster portion unsealed).

The Pilbara

This region encompasses 510,335 square km of isolated territory, rugged ranges, deep gorges, gigantic mining operations, company towns, and enormous wealth. Come see men and their ultra-big monsters rip the earth apart and extract its riches, then cart it off to Port Hedland for worldwide shipment.

More than 100,000 tons of iron ore are produced daily at **Newman,** 422 km north of Meekatharra, then shipped via private railway to Port Hedland and the big blue yonder. **Mount Newman Mining Company** operates free tours of its Mount Whaleback Mine (reputedly the world's largest open-cut mine). Tours depart Mon.-Fri., except public holidays, at 8:30 a.m. and 1:30 p.m. For information and bookings, phone (08) 9175-3200.

Please, stay *out* of **Wittenoom!** Yes, it *is* the heart of the Pilbara, and it sits at the mouth of the breathtaking Wittenoom Gorge. However, in this instance, the word "breathtaking" is given a whole new meaning: asbestos. Wittenoom mined blue asbestos 1937-66, when the mine closed and the population dropped from 1,500 down to 60. The fact is, the road is *still* paved with blue asbestos. The Australian government would like to forget Wittenoom ever existed—in fact has been systematically buying up the town's buildings and then demolishing them. The place is virtually a ghost town these days, though local Aborigines with land claims and some government officials would like to see the place make a comeback.

Karijini National Park (formerly Hamersley Range National Park) is reached via a newly sealed road off the Great Northern Highway, 180 km west of Newman. The 617,606-hectare park encompasses a variety of spectacular gorges, stony watercourses, and permanent pools, as well as Mount Meharry (1,245 meters), Western Australia's highest mountain. Campsites with limited facilities are available.

The park service warns visitors to keep out of Yampire Gorge, where extensive main tailings can cause serious health risks. Furthermore, alternative routes should be used—if you are traveling through the gorge, keep your car windows closed! For information, contact the **Department of Conservation and Land Management,** tel. (08) 9143-1488.

Tom Price, W.A.'s highest town, at 747 meters, and **Paraburdoo,** on the edge of the Hamersley Range, are two other company towns south of Wittenoom that rail their ore production over to Dampier. Continuing along the Wittenoom Rd. (Highway 136) will take you to the North West Coastal Highway.

Another off-the-beaten path from Newman is along unsealed Highway 138. **Marble Bar** (pop. 357), 306 km north, is reputedly Australia's hottest place. It was hot gold-wise, too, with more than two million ounces produced since an 1891 discovery. The town was named for the Marble Bar, Australia's only jasper bar, easiest seen where it crosses the Coongan River, 10 km west of town. You're not allowed to chip at it, but you can get a sample at the jasper deposit on the road to Comet Mine. The **Comet Mine,** 10 km south of town, is still operating and features a souvenir shop with beautiful rocks, including the regional Pilbara jade. This whole area offers superb fossicking.

Goldsworthy, almost at the coast, was the Pilbara's first iron ore town, and it thrived until mining shifted eastward to **Shay Gap.** Both towns took the brunt of Cyclone Enid when it hit in 1980.

As the Great Northern Highway merges with the North West Coastal Highway, south of Port Hedland, it remains the Great Northern Highway throughout the Kimberley region and almost to the Northern Territory border. It's 610 km from Port Hedland up to Broome. **Eighty Mile Beach** and several roadhouses provide diversions along the way.

THE KIMBERLEY

This is it—the last outpost, the frontier for which Daniel Boone would give the coonskin off his cap for the chance to explore. Even with phones, faxes, and the sealed highway, this 350,000-square-km region is remote and rugged, and *was* sparsely traveled until it hit the cover of *National Geographic* and prime-timed its way onto the "must-be-seen" travel circuit.

Though an 1885 gold find at Hall's Gap provided the first lure to this isolated area, it was soon supplanted by cattle ranching, and—thanks to the successful Ord River Irrigation Scheme—tropical fruit production for both domestic and worldwide markets.

The Kimberley is a magical haven of desert ranges, Outback stations, tropical forests, raging rivers, national parks, and more, more, more. The weather is a big drawback, however. It's best to travel here April-Sept., during the Dry.

At other times of the year, not only do temperatures swelter above 40° C, but the very wet Wet swells rivers, floods roads, leaves settlements stranded, blackens tempers, and renders attractions inaccessible. Also common are bone-biting cold nights, May-July. You'll need a well-equipped 4WD for off-highway exploration.

BROOME

As the "Gateway to the Kimberley," Broome (pop. 8,500) is one of the hottest (in both temperature and popularity) destinations in the country. Situated 2,353 km northeast of Perth, this dusty, cosmopolitan town is filled with boab trees, red dust, and oodles of character (and characters).

Pearls before swine—or at least cattle—certainly held true here. Beginning in the 1880s, the gung-ho pearling industry provided work for about 400 luggers (boats) and 3,000 workers, contributing 80% of the world's mother-of-pearl until the advent of plastics. Now only a few luggers remain, in conjunction with established cultured pearl farming. But there's beef, and *plenty* of it; Broome's modern meatpacking industry can process some 40,000 head of cattle each season.

Though the Japanese targeted Broome during WW II, evidence of damage by both sides can be seen in the wrecked carcasses of Allied flying boats in Roebuck Bay and the Japanese plane engines mounted near the Continental Hotel.

The Asian pearlers contributed to Broome's rich cultural mix, mini-Chinatown, and atmospheric appeal for a new breed of travelers—backpackers, frontrunners, high-lifers, and the eco-kitsch—and the Aboriginal community has jumped onto the tourist bandwagon as well.

Chinatown

Bounded by Carnarvon St. and Dampier Terrace, Short St. and Napier Terrace, "Chinatown" basically refers to Broome's older section—once alive with saloons, billiard parlors, boardinghouses, and pearling sheds—now lined with restaurants, souvenir shops, and ubiquitous pearl purveyors.

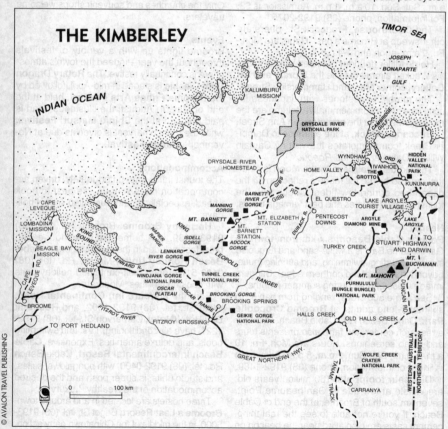

THE KIMBERLEY

Dating from 1916, **Sun Pictures,** near the corner of Short and Carnarvon Streets, is one of Australia's few remaining open-air cinemas. Regular screenings of not-terribly-old releases show nightly. Admission is $9. For program information, phone (08) 9192-1077.

The glass-encased model of a **Chinese temple** sits on Dampier Terrace, near Short Street.

Other Sights
The **Broome Historical Society Museum,** Saville St. (in the old customs house), presents pearling-era items, historical displays, and a shell collection. Hours are Mon.-Fri. 10 a.m.-4 p.m., Sat.-Sun. 10 a.m.-1 p.m. Admission is $3. For information, phone (08) 9192-2075.

The **Courthouse,** Frederick St., offers another sweep at Broome's past. Hours are Mon.-Fri. 9 a.m.-noon and 1-4 p.m.

Horrie Miller (founder of Ansett WA) displays his Wackett aircraft outside the **Library and Art Gallery,** corner Mary and Hammersley Streets.

The marble headstones with Japanese inscriptions and a commemorative column are the most interesting at the **cemetery** on Ann Street.

Buccaneer Rock, at the entrance to Dampier Creek, commemorates the visit by Captain William Dampier and the *Roebuck.*

The **Golden Staircase to the Moon** is an effect created by the full moon's reflection off the ocean bed during low tides. Check with the tourist bureau for dates and best vantage points.

Nearby
Popular **Cable Beach,** six km from town on Gantheaume Bay, is a white-sand and turquoise stretch for surfing, swimming, and sunning (nude, beyond the rock at the northern edge). Stingers invade these shores during summer months.

See some 500 crocs, ranging from babies to six-meter-long adults, at **Broome Crocodile Park,** Cable Beach Rd., Cable Beach. Primarily a research center, the farm also presents tours and video screenings. Hours are Mon.-Fri. 10 a.m.-5 p.m., Sat.-Sun. 2 p.m.-5 p.m. Admission is $10. For information, phone (08) 9192-1489.

Dinosaur footprints, 130 million years old, are visible at low tide at Gantheaume Point, seven km south of Broome, at the end of Cable Beach. If you're not able to see the real thing, cement casts are displayed near the beacon on the cliff. **Anastasia's Pool,** a humanmade rock pool north of Gantheaume Point, fills up at high tide for those who want to take a dip.

Birdwatchers can view more than 200 species of their feathered friends at the **Broome Bird Observatory,** 18 km east of town on Roebuck Bay. Hours are Tues.-Sun. 8 a.m.-noon and 2-5 p.m. For information, phone (08) 9193-5600.

Cape Leveque Road, from Broome to Cape Leveque Lighthouse, spans a distance of around 200 km. Sights along the way include the Beagle Bay and Lombadina Aboriginal communities and their beautiful churches, plus another at One Arm Point, beyond Cape Leveque Lighthouse. Only the churches and souvenir shops welcome travelers.

Events
Broome lights up with a variety of festivals throughout the year—indeed the town's atmosphere is continually festive. The **Rotary Dragon Boat Classic** is staged in mid-April, followed by the **Broome Fringe Arts Festival,** held at the end of May. In August, the illustrious pearl is paid homage at the **Shinju Matsuri Festival,** while the mango harvest is given its due at November's **Mango Festival.**

Accommodations
The tourist influx has, unfortunately, driven accommodation rates way up. It's best to book ahead, especially during Australian school holidays.

Harmony Broome, Broome Rd., tel. (08) 9193-7439, is a home-like guesthouse with breakfast included in the tariff. Moderate. **Cable Beach Holiday Units,** Murray Rd., tel. (08) 9193-5173, offers self-contained holiday units with cooking facilities. Moderate.

Both the **Mercure Inn Continental Hotel,** Weld St., tel. (08) 9192-1002, and **Roebuck Bay Hotel/Motel,** Carnarvon St., tel. (08) 9192-1221, have air-conditioning, TVs, and swimming pools, and deluxe amenities. Expensive. **Cable Beach Intercontinental Resort,** Cable Beach Rd., tel. (08) 9192-0400, with bungalows, suites, and studio units, is super posh and the desired accommodation of the wealthy. Luxury.

Three hostels are located in and around town. **Broome's Last Resort,** Bagot St., tel. (08) 9193-5000, in the middle of the Chinatown party action, offers $13 dorm beds, laundry facilities, and free shuttle transportation to the bus station. Budget. Close to the beach, **Cable Beach Backpackers,** Lullfitz Dr., tel. (08) 9193-5511, has a pool, kitchen and laundry facilities, and a free shuttle around town and to transportation stations. Budget. The hands-down favorite, however, is **Kimberley Klub,** Frederick St., tel. (08) 9192-3233, a friendly place with pool, recreation room, volleyball court, kitchen facilities, open-air lounge, veranda, and $14 dorm beds. Budget.

Campsites are located at **Broome Vacation Village,** Port Dr., tel. (08) 9192-1057; **Cable Beach Caravan Park,** Millington Rd., tel. (08) 9192-2066; **Roebuck Bay Caravan Park,** Walcott St., tel. (08) 9192-1366; and **Broome Caravan Park,** Great Northern Hwy., tel. (08) 9192-1776. Budget-Moderate.

Food

The sometimes-too-lively **Roebuck Bay Hotel** in Chinatown serves a good range of counter meals for lunch and dinner, and more high-brow fare ($13-16 entrees) in its restaurant section.

For Chinese in Chinatown, try **Wing's** on Napier Terrace and **Murray's Asian Affair** on Dampier Terrace (entrees $10-14). **Chin's Chinese Restaurant,** Hamersley St., offers Asian specialties at moderate prices ($12-16), plus takeaways.

Blooms Cafe, Carnarvon St., serves large breakfasts ($9-12), changing blackboard menus ($10-16), and outdoor people-watching seating. **Charters,** in the Mangrove Hotel, enjoys a wonderful reputation for its seafood specialties ($14-18).

Conti Bar and Bistro in the Mercure Inn Continental Hotel offers daily changing menus, with emphasis on seafood, in the moderate-and-up price range ($14-26).

For your splurge in fine dining ($50 pp, average), Broome's best is the **Club Restaurant** at Cable Beach Club, where only fresh ingredients are used. For reservations (required), phone (08) 9192-2505. **Lord Mac's** is a more casual spot to watch the hot sun slip away over a cold beer.

Shopping

Scads of shops will be happy to sell you **pearl jewelry** at expensive prices. Some high-quality outlets are: Paspaley Pearling, Short St.; Lin-

ney's, Dampier Terrace; and the Pearl Emporium, Dampier Terrace.

Browse for local Aboriginal arts and crafts at **Matso's Gallery and Coffee House,** Hammersley Street.

Information and Services

For tourist information and local tour bookings, contact **Broome Tourist Bureau,** corner Great Northern Hwy. and Bagot St., tel. (08) 9192-2222. Hours are daily April-Nov. 8 a.m.-5 p.m., and in other months, Mon.-Fri. 9 a.m.-5 p.m., Sat.-Sun. 9 a.m.-1 p.m.

Dial 000 for police, medical, or fire **emergencies. Broome District Hospital,** Robinson St., tel. (08) 9192-1401, has a casualty department, and you'll find the local **police** at the corner of Hamersley and Frederick Streets, tel. (08) 9192-1212.

Transportation

Ansett Australia, tel. (13) 1300, offers scheduled service from Perth and Darwin. Services on Qantas' **Airlink** are comparable. Book Qantas flights through **Harvey World Travel,** Paspaley Shopping Centre, Chinatown, tel. (08) 9193-5599.

Greyhound Pioneer, tel. (13) 2030, operates regular bus service to Broome from Perth and Darwin. The local office is at **Broome Travel,** Hamersley St., tel. (08) 9192-1561.

The **Town Bus** runs two shuttles that circle Broome and also run out to Cable Beach and Gantheaume Point. For schedules and information, phone (08) 9193-6000.

Major car rental firms are represented at the airport, with prices beginning at about $65 per day. Contact: **Avis,** 14 Coghlan St., tel. (08) 9193-5980; **ATC Rentacar,** tel. (08) 9193-7788; or **Hertz,** 29 Frederick St., tel. (08) 9192-1428.

Broome is an easy town for cycling. **Broome Cycle Centre,** corner Frederick and Hamersley Streets, tel. (08) 9192-1871, rents bicycles for $10 per day, with a break for weekly rentals.

Tours

Many local and extended tours depart Broome. For example, you can take a glorious twilight cruise aboard a yacht, a pseudo-lugger, or on *The Cornelius*—an authentic pearl lugger. Cost is around $65, including beer or wine. Book this and other tours through the tourist office.

Kimberley Hovercraft will take you for a one-hour glide over Roebuck Bay for $50. For information, phone (08) 9193-5025.

Inquire at the tourist office for the latest on bushwalks, 4WD safaris, and Harley rides.

DERBY

Broome may be the "Gateway to the Kimberley," but Derby (pop. 5,000)—at the heart of many scenic attractions—has been dubbed "Gateway to the Gorges." Situated on the King Sound shore 220 km northeast of Broome, this port town was lively during the 1880s gold boom, until it, too, went the cattle route. More recently oil, diamonds, and, of course, tourism have played an important role in the town's development as both an administrative center and a base for travel to some of W.A.'s most stunning gorges.

Sights

The **Derby Cultural Centre,** Loch St., exhibits Aboriginal artifacts, local arts and crafts, Jowlaenga sandstone, and a palm tree botanic garden. Hours are Mon.-Wed. and Friday 10 a.m.-4 p.m., Thursday 1-7 p.m., Saturday 8 a.m.-noon. For information, phone (08) 9191-1712.

At the corner of Loch and Elder Streets, the 1920s **Wharfinger's House,** built for the harbormaster, typifies tropical architecture.

The original **Old Derby Gaol,** dating from the 1880s, is situated next to the modern-day Derby Police Station.

The present **jetty,** constructed in 1963-64 to replace the original 1885 wooden structure, is used mainly for fishing or observing the tidal movements (tides up to 11 meters give this the highest tidal range of any wharf in the Southern Hemisphere).

Estimated to be 1,000 years old, the hollow **Boab Prison Tree,** seven km south of town, was used as an overnight "holding cell" for prisoners on their way to Derby.

Pigeon Heritage Trail details the adventures of an Aboriginal outlaw and folk hero named Pigeon who was shot and killed in 1887, following a three-year standoff with police and white settlers.

The self-guiding tour is presented in two stages—one from Derby, the other from Windjana Gorge. The tourist bureau provides brochures.

Events

The annual two-week **Boab Festival** in late June and early July presents a rodeo, mardi gras, street parties, arts and crafts exhibits, and mud football.

Accommodations and Food

West Kimberley Lodge, corner Sutherland and Stanwell, tel. (08) 9191-1031, and **Spinifex Hotel,** Clarendon St., tel. (08) 9191-1233, offer guesthouse lodging. Inexpensive. Another possibility is **Derby Boab Inn,** Loch St., tel. (08) 9191-1044. Moderate. **King Sound Tourist Hotel,** Delewarr St., tel. (08) 9193-1044, has quality rooms at higher prices. Expensive.

Derby Backpackers Lodge, next to the bus station, tel. (08) 9191-1233, has $10 beds, free linens, and kitchen and laundry facilities. Budget.

Derby Caravan Park, Rowan St., tel. (08) 9191-1022, has campsites and on-site vans. Budget-Inexpensive.

The **Spinifex Hotel,** Clarendon St., and the **Derby Boab Inn** both serve moderately priced counter meals ($9-14). **Lwoy's,** on Loch St., offers a Chinese fix ($10-14), and **Wharf's Restaurant,** on the jetty, specializes in seafood ($14-19).

Information

Walking maps, tourist literature, and tour bookings are available at **Derby Tourist Bureau,** Clarendon St., tel. (08) 9191-1426. Hours are Mon.-Fri. 8:30 a.m.-4:30 p.m., Saturday 9 a.m.-1 p.m.

For emergencies, dial 000; the **police,** tel. (08) 9191-1444; **hospital,** tel. (08) 9193-3333; or **Royal Automobile Club** agency, tel. (08) 9191-1256.

Transportation

Daily flights from Perth or Darwin are operated by **Ansett Australia,** tel. (13) 1300. The local Ansett office is at 14 Loch St., tel. (08) 9193-1488.

Greyhound Pioneer, tel. (13) 2030, and **Westliner,** tel. (09) 250-3318, run buses to Derby from Broome, Port Hedland, Perth, and Darwin.

Cars can be rented through Avis, tel. (08) 9191-1357, or Budget, tel. (08) 9191-2044, and begin at $70 per day.

The tourist bureau can arrange scenic flights to Koolan and Cockatoo Islands, as well as to some of the other Buccaneer Archipelago islands, but they start at $125 pp, with a four-person minimum. **Buccaneer Sea Safaris,** tel. (08) 9191-1991, will cruise you along the Kimberley coast.

GIBB ROAD

This 705-km back road is used primarily to transport beef from the Kimberley's huge cattle stations to ports at Derby and Wyndham. It's also the most direct route over to Wyndham, with convenient, if not always easy, access to the majestic gorge country and—for the well-prepared adventurer—to places where no one else has ever set foot! Although it's possible for conventional vehicles in excellent condition to negotiate this harsh road (a combination of bitumen, gravel, and natural earth, marked with some very large pits and pocks), a 4WD is advisable. Make this trip only April-Nov., and carry plenty of extra supplies. Petrol is available approximately midway at Mount Barnett Station.

The road to Windjana and Tunnel Creek Gorges shoots off Gibb Rd. 120 km east of Derby. **Windjana Gorge** features awesome multicolored cliffs that rise 90 meters above the Lennard River (which rages during the Wet, trickling down to a few pools during the Dry). **Windjana Gorge National Park** (2,134 hectares), part of the Napier Ranges, is home to a variety of native fauna—including crocodiles. Campsites with limited facilities are available May-October. For information, phone (08) 9191-5121.

Pigeon's first victim, Constable Richardson, was killed at **Lillmooloora Police Station,** a couple of km beyond Windjana Gorge.

Aptly named **Tunnel Creek,** about 35 km south, has cut a 750-meter-long tunnel through the Oscar Range. A central shaft exposes natural light. During the Dry, the tunnel can be explored, but bring a torch or lantern, be ready for a short wade through cold water, and watch out for flying foxes. Aboriginal cave paintings can be seen near the tunnel's north end. From Tunnel Creek,

it's 68 km to the Great Northern Highway and another 37 km to the roadhouse services at Fitzroy Crossing.

Back on Gibb Road, you'll mosey along the foothills of the King Leopold Ranges, a rugged area of tall granite outcrops, then you'll pass through Ingliss Gap to the top of the range before dipping down to the Broome Valley. Along the way are sidetracks to **Lennard River Gorge, Isdell Gorge,** and **Adcock Gorge.**

Replenish petrol (no LPG) and other supplies at **Mount Barnett Station,** 308 km east of Derby, on the banks of the Barnett River. Campsites with limited facilities are available. For information, phone (08) 9191-4649 or (08) 9191-7007. **Manning Gorge,** on Mount Barnett Station, offers swimming, fishing, and a two-km walking trail to a waterfall.

Forging onward, the turnoff to **Barnett River Gorge** is another 22 km. Moderately priced accommodations and cheap campsites are available at **Mount Elizabeth Station,** tel. (08) 9191-4644, 30 km off Gibb Road. The station also operates 4WD tours and scenic flights.

You must know where you are going, what you are doing, and—probably not a bad idea—who you are doing it with before adventuring onto **Kalumburu Road.** This extremely isolated, rough, and rocky road is often closed. **Drysdale River Homestead,** 66 km from the Gibb-Kalumburu Road junction, is the last information center and service point. From there on out, you're on your own—*really* on your own. Many of the attractions, such as Mitchell Plateau and Drysdale River National Park, can only be reached by foot. And, if you do make it to **Kalumburu,** at the end of the 276-km haul, you'll discover that Kalumburu Mission is an Aboriginal reserve, requiring an entry permit that must be obtained in advance.

The next pit stop along Gibb Rd. is **Jack's Waterhole** (also sometimes called Joe's Waterhole), on the Durack River, a popular swimming, fishing, and camping stop. **Durack River Homestead,** tel. (08) 9161-4324, has moderately priced accommodations with all meals included. Four-wheel-drive tours of the region depart from here daily.

Home Valley Homestead, tel. (08) 9161-4322, is 56 km beyond Jack's (or Joe's). Accommodations, camping, and local tours also are available here. **El Questro Homestead,** tel. (08) 9161-4318, on the Pentecost River, has a fully self-contained stone cottage that accommodates six people, and a riverside camping area—it has been pushing for the yuppie/trendy/wealthy clientele (sumptious rooms in the old homestead run more than $500 pp, double occupany—though that includes meals). Budget-Luxury.This is the last facility on Gibb Road. It's 33 km to the junction of the Great Northern and Victoria Highways, where you go north to Wyndham or continue east to Kununurra.

THE GREAT NORTHERN HIGHWAY

Fitzroy Crossing and Vicinity

From Derby, it's 214 km to the gravel road north to Windjana Gorge and Tunnel Creek National Parks, and another 42 km to **Fitzroy Crossing** (pop. 500) on the Fitzroy River. Basically a cattle town, this little township is enjoying the fruits of Kimberley's popularity, providing services to travelers, either about to cross the river or stranded because of the Wet's floods, and giving access to **Geikie Gorge National Park** (3,136 hectares), 21 km northeast. The 14-km-long gorge cuts through a fossilized "barrier reef" dating from the Devonian period some 350 million years ago, and fossil deposits can be seen in the limestone cliffs. The park is filled with interesting vegetation and abundant wildlife, including sawfish and stingers (usually found only near the sea), freshwater crocodiles, kangaroos, and wallabies. The park is open April-Nov. (depending on the river's level). Boat tours of the gorge depart daily at 9:30 a.m. and 2 p.m. For information, call (08) 9191-5121.

The historic 1890s **Crossing Inn** (oldest pub in the Kimberley), near Brooking Creek, tel. (08) 9191-5080, offers B&B rooms, campsites ($5 pp), and plenty of local color. Budget-Moderate.

During the Dry, campsites with limited facilities are available within the park; in Fitzroy Crossing, try the **Fitzroy River Lodge Caravan Park,** tel. (08) 9191-5141, or **Tarunda Caravan Park,** tel. (08) 9191-5330.

Brooking Gorge is also close to Fitzroy Crossing, but inquire first at Brooking Springs Station both for directions and permission to cross the privately owned land. Budget-Inexpensive.

Fitzroy Crossing Tourist Office located at the entrance to town, tel. (08) 9191-5355, is closed Nov.-March.

Halls Creek and Vicinity

The turnoff to Tanami Track is 272 km beyond Fitzroy Crossing and 16 km before Halls Creek—then it's another 114 km of unsealed road south to **Wolf Creek Crater National Park** (1,460 hectares). Discovered in 1947 (but probably dating back a couple million years), the crater measures 835 meters wide and 50 meters deep, and is the second-largest meteorite crater in the world. The road is usually accessible May-Nov., but check at Halls Creek for current conditions, or call (08) 9168-0200. **Carranya Station,** tel. (08) 9168-8927, seven km south of the crater, provides limited supplies and camping facilities.

Western Australia's first gold rush took place in 1885 at **Halls Creek** (pop. 1,000), although the gold dried up just a few years later. Now the center of the vast East Kimberley beef lands, you can still see crumbling reminders of the old gold days at the town's original site, 15 km away along Duncan Road. **Mount Bradley Mine** off Duncan Rd. is one of the region's original mines (some shafts are still open—and deep—so take care when walking around). You can still see the rusting machinery left behind at the **Ruby Queen Mine,** abandoned in the 1970s.

Good local swimming and picnic spots are at **Caroline Pool, Sawpit Gorge,** and **Palm Springs. China Wall,** on the way to old Halls Creek, is a natural white-quartz formation that resembles a mini-Great Wall of China.

Moderately priced, basic cabin accommodations with air-conditioning are available at **Shell Roadhouse,** 31 McDonald St., tel. (08) 9168-6060. Lodging in the expensive range is offered at the **Kimberley Hotel,** Roberta Ave., tel. (08) 9168-6101—though there's a cheap backpacker section. **Halls Creek Caravan Park,** Roberta Ave., tel. (08) 9168-6169, has campsites and on-site vans. Inexpensive.

Fresh bread is baked Mon.-Sat. at **Halls Creek Bakery,** Great Northern Highway. The **Kimberley Hotel** has the usual counter meals ($5-10) and a higher-quality bistro (the bar here has a readily apparent black/white border).

Halls Creek Information Centre, Great Northern Hwy., tel. (08) 9168-6262, is open May-Sept.; info is also available at the shire office, Thomas St., tel. (08) 9168-6007. In emergencies, dial 000; the **police,** tel. (08) 9168-6000; or **hospital,** tel. (08) 9168-6002.

One of Australia's greatest natural wonders is the 208,000-hectare **Purnululu National Park** (formerly Bungle Bungle National Park), with its amazing tiger-striped rock formations banded with black lichen and orange silica, plus thousands of low, domed, beehive-appearing peaks. Though Purnululu was only "discovered" in 1983, the place was no secret to the Kidja Aboriginals—and now no secret to tourists who may well turn this area into the next Uluru (Ayers Rock). Vegetation is composed of everything from the Bungle Bungle fan palm to spiniflex and eucalpyts. Access to the park (a *very* rough 55 km from the Great Northern Hwy., 108 km from Halls Creek) is difficult, limited only to 4WDs with good clearance, and only April-October. Check on road and weather conditions beforehand. Daytime temperatures can be extreme, and visitors must carry water.

Hikes can be taken to **Echidna Chasm** in the north, **Cathedral Gorge** in the south, and **Piccaninny Gorge,** an intense 18-km roundtrip. Entrance fee is adult $11, child $1. Because of the fragile ecology and travel difficulty, many visitors choose to take a scenic flight (departing from either Halls Creek or Kununurra) over the park—inquire at both tourist offices. **Camping** is permitted at Belburn Creek. For information, contact the **Department of Conservation and Land Management,** P.O. Box 242, Kununurra, WA 6743, tel. (08) 9168-0200.

The Great Northern Highway calls into **Turkey Creek Roadhouse,** tel. (08) 9168-7882, 53 km north of the Purnululu turnoff. The roadhouse offers petrol, overnight accommodations, and 4WD Bungle Bungle tours.

Sorry, sparkly-eyed readers, they won't let you into the **Argyle Diamond Mine** up the road from Turkey Creek unless you book an air or coach tour from Kununurra through **Belray Diamond Tours,** tel. (08) 9168-1014 (about the same cost as a small diamond). Discovered in 1979, this is purportedly the world's largest diamond deposit. Its annual production of 30 million carats includes white, champagne, cognac, and rare and valuable pink diamonds.

From Turkey Creek, it's 151 km to the Great Northern and Victoria Highways junction, from where you proceed north to Wyndham or east to Kununurra.

WYNDHAM

Western Australia's northernmost port welcomes you with a 20-meter-long concrete "Big Croc" sculpture at the town's entrance—a replica of the salties that inhabit its waters. Situated on Cambridge Gulf, at the end of the Great Northern Highway, Wyndham (pop. 1,500) is nicknamed the "Top Town in the West." During the Halls Creek gold rush days, the town prospered, then declined, made a comeback in 1919 when the Meatworks was established, then fizzled again after a 1985 fire closed the plant down. Today it survives mostly on tourism and as a service center for surrounding pastoral and Aboriginal communities.

Sights

What do you think about a spot called **Blood Drain Crocodile Lookout?** Located on the gulf side of the Meatworks complex, the adjacent creek once was used as a blood drain. Well, guess who came for dinner? And about 20 of them at a time! Since the Meatworks closed and the blood stopped flowing, fewer crocs dropped by until feeding began in 1987. Inquire at the Tourist Information Centre for feeding times and tide charts (they eat an hour before the full tide).

Five Rivers Lookout, at the top of the Bastion Range, offers magnificent views of the Forrest, Pentecost, Durack, King, and Ord Rivers, as well as the port, Meatworks, surrounding gulf, and mudflats. Sunrise and sunset are the best viewing times.

Three Mile Valley, a miniature East Kimberley Range, is reached via Five Rivers Road. Rough gorges, splintered rocks, clear pools, and colorful vegetation closely duplicate the larger range. Walking trails lead to a variety of good sites.

Aboriginal rock paintings depicting spiritual figures and animals are located on the road to Moochalabra Dam. Built to provide the town's water supply, the dam also makes a good picnic spot and fishing hole.

The **Grotto,** a rockbound waterhole off the Wyndham-Kununurra Road, is a favorite swimming spot. **Prison Tree,** King River Rd., is a huge boab tree lockup dating back to the 1890s.

Pay your respects to the historic dead at the **Gully, Bend,** or **Afghan** cemeteries.

Accommodations

It's sparse pickings up here. A reasonably priced choice is **Gulf Breeze Guest House,** tel. (08) 9161-1130, with single and double rooms, and $10 dorm beds. Budget-Inexpensive. Nicer rooms and more amenities are offered at **Wyndham Town Hotel,** 19 O'Donnell St., tel. (08) 9161-1202, and **Wyndham Community Club,** Great Northern Hwy., tel. (08) 9161-1130. Moderate-Expensive. **Three Mile Caravan Park,** Baker St., tel. (08) 9161-1064, offers campsites and on-site vans. Budget-Moderate.

Information

Wyndham Tourist Information Centre, O'-Donnell St. (in the Old Port Post Office), provides tourist literature, including a brochure detailing the heritage trail. For information, phone (08) 9161-1054. Hours are daily 8 a.m.-5 p.m.

For emergencies, dial 000; the **police,** tel. (08) 9161-1055; **hospital,** tel. (08) 9161-1104; or local **Royal Automobile Club,** at Branko BP Motors, Great Northern Hwy., tel. (08) 9161-1305.

Transportation

Ansett Australia, tel. (13) 1300, has daily flights to Perth-Kununurra, as well as a Darwin service.

From Kununurra, **I.J. and S.A. Thorley,** tel. (08) 9161-1201, provide daily coach transport to Wyndham. Fare is $28 one-way.

Rental cars begin at about $70 per day and are available at Branko BP Motors, Great Northern Hwy., tel. (08) 9161-1305.

KUNUNURRA

Where were *you* in the sixties? Kununurra (pop. 2,100) was just being born as center of the Ord River Scheme, the Kimberley region's successful irrigation project. Then, in 1979, it was a double whammy when the world's largest diamond deposit was discovered south of town at Smoke Creek. Surrounded by water, natural attractions, birds, and wildlife, Kununurra is a travelers' stopover en route west to Broome (1,057 km) or east to Darwin (825 km).

Sights

The **Zebra Rock Gallery,** Packsaddle Plains Rd., features displays of this unusual striped rock found

---

LOOKALIKES

The vicinity of Kununurra is inundated with lookalike rock formations:

Shark Fin Tree, on Parker Rd., looks like

City of Ruins, Weaber Plains Rd., which looks like

Zebra rocks, in the East Kimberleys, near Kununurra, which look like

Sleeping Buddha, along the Ord River on Victoria Highway, which looks like

Elephant Rock, an end-on view of the Sleeping Buddha, which looks like

Sleeping Mummy, which looks like **Sleeping Buddha,** which looks like **Elephant Rock,** which looks like . . . you?

---

only near Kununurra. Hours are daily 8 a.m.-6 p.m. For information, phone (08) 9168-1114.

Collections of Aboriginal artifacts are displayed and sold at **Waringarri Aboriginal Arts,** Speargrass Road. This Aboriginal-run outlet offers boomerangs, didgeridoos, paintings, spears, fighting sticks, and many more crafts. Postcards, books, and music are also for sale. Hours are Mon.-Fri. 9 a.m.-5 p.m. For information, phone (08) 9168-2212.

Kelly's Knob, near the town center, is a 191-meter-high viewpoint over the town, Ord River, and surrounding farmlands.

Adjacent to town, artificial **Lake Kununurra** has a wealth of wildlife and vegetation both on the lake and in the wetlands. Boat cruises are available.

The town fishing hole is **Ivanhoe Crossing,** a permanent waterfall on the Ord River near the Ivanhoe Station Homestead.

About three km out of town, **Hidden Valley National Park** (1,817 hectares), also known as Mirima National Park, is referred to as a "mini-Bungle Bungle." Features of this 300 million-year-old region include scenic gorges, rugged sandstone hills, Aboriginal rock art, abundant birdlife, and short walking trails. For information, call (08) 9168-0200.

Created by the Ord River dam, **Lake Argyle,** 72 km south of Kununurra along Parker Rd., contains nine times the water of Sydney Harbour.

Rugged islands—which used to be mountain peaks—support a large number of birds and wildlife. Watch for Aboriginal rock paintings during the drive in. Boat cruises on Lake Argyle depart daily. **Diversion Dam,** which holds back the waters of Lake Kununurra, is located just outside of town. This area is a hot spot for travelers seeking casual employment picking fruit at local farms.

Moved from its original Lake Argyle site, the reconstructed **Argyle Homestead Museum,** Parker Rd., provides the history of early settlers' lives. Hours are daily 9 a.m.-4 p.m.

Accommodations

Seasons up here mean as much to travelers as to Aborigines when it comes to accommodations rates—there can be a wide variation. If you come during low (inferno-hot) season, you might well get an inexpensive deal at a "better" place.

Good, modern air-conditioned accommodations are available at **Country Club Hotel,** Coolibah Dr., tel. (08) 9168-1024; **Kimberley Court Motel,** corner River Fig Ave. and Erythrina St., tel. (08) 9168-1411; and **Hotel Kununurra,** Messmate Way, tel. (08) 9168-1344. Moderate-Expensive. **Mercure Inn Kununurra,** corner Duncan Ave. and Messmate Way, tel. (08) 9168-1455, and **Lake Argyle Inn and Tourist Village,** Parker Rd., tel. (08) 9168-7360, offer costly but comfortable rooms and corresponding amenities, and Lake Argyle Inn also has cheap campsites. Premium-Luxury.

Choose from two **hostels: Desert Inn Oasis** (most popular, and closest to town), Trustania St., tel. (08) 9168-2702; or **Kununurra Backpackers,** 111 Nutwood Circle, tel. (08) 9169-1998 or (1800) 641-998. Dorm beds range $14-16.

Campsites are available at: **Hidden Valley Caravan Park,** Weaber Plains Rd., tel. (08) 9168-1790; **Kimberleyland Holiday Park,** Duncan Hwy., tel. (08) 9168-1280; **Town Caravan Park** (on-site vans, too), Bloodwood Dr., tel. (08) 9168-1763; and **Kona Lakeside Caravan Park,** tel. (08) 9168-1031, a bit out of town, but worthwhile for its lakeside location and prolific bird population. Budget-Moderate.

Food

Gulliver's Tavern, corner of Konkerberry Dr. and Cotton Tree Ave., is a local watering hole

that also serves counter meals ($5-8) as well as some more upmarket dinners ($9-6) in the dining room.

The **Kununurra Hotel** is another counter-meal establishment. **Chopsticks,** a decent Chinese restaurant ($10-16), is housed inside the **Country Club Hotel** on Coolibah Drive.

Snackers might try **Hot Gossip Café** (burgers around $6) or **Chit Chats Chinese** ($8-14 entrees), both nestled inside the Kununurra Shopping Centre. **Valentines Pizzeria,** on Cottontree Ave., tosses up pies and pastas ($7-12).

Information and Services

For information on local attractions and tours, contact **Kununurra Visitors' Centre,** Coolibah Dr., tel. (08) 9168-1177. Hours are daily 8 a.m.-5 p.m.

For emergencies, dial 000; the **police,** tel. (08) 9169-1122; **hospital,** tel. (08) 9168-1522; or **Royal Automobile Club,** tel. (08) 9168-2236.

Transportation

Ansett Australia, tel. (13) 1300, has a daily Perth-Kununurra flight, as well as service from Broome and Darwin. Ansett's local office is in the Kununurra Shopping Centre, tel. (08) 9168-1622.

Greyhound Pioneer, tel. (13) 2030, stops through on the Darwin-Perth route.

For **bicycle rentals** ($10 per day), inquire at any of the hostels or the visitor center.

Rental cars start at $70 per day and are available from **Avis,** Bandicoot Dr., tel. (08) 9168-1258; **Budget,** Mango St., tel. (08) 9168-2033; and **Hertz,** Poinciana St., tel. (08) 9168-1257.

A full range of **tours** depart from Kununurra to surrounding sights. Book with the visitor center or the YHA Hostel (you'll get a discount if you're staying there). Just a few choices include the increasingly popular Purnululu scenic flights, horseback treks through the Kimberley Ranges, Ord River cruises, Lake Argyle cruises, and an extensive range of 4WD safaris and coach excursions.

From Kununurra, it's 513 km along the Victoria Highway to Katherine, junction of the Victoria and Stuart Highways. Proceeding 321 km north on the Stuart Highway (also called the Track) will bring you into Darwin—a kangaroo hop from Indonesia.

GLOSSARY

You only *think* they speak English down here. They don't—they speak Australian. It's *like* English, but there are some important differences and many linguistic idiosyncracies ("filet" is pronounced "fill-ette," for instance). As you're trying to decipher an Australian's conversation, one factor that may render many words very foreign-sounding is the habit of shortening the noun and then adding "y" or "ie" to the end ("brekkie" for breakfast, "telly" for television). Similarly, you'll hear many speakers adding an "o" to the end of a person's name ("Johno," for example). But those guidelines alone won't resolve all your difficulties. Following is a list of unique terms you may find useful.

A

abo—derogatory term for Aborigine (best avoided!)
amber fluid—beer
Anzac—Australia and New Zealand Army Corps
arvo—afternoon
avago—have a go, take a try (also "avagoyermug")
award wage—minimum pay rate

B

back o'Bourke—in the middle of nowhere (also "back of beyond")
Backpackers—hostel
banana bender—a Queenslander
barbie—grill or barbecue
bail out—go home early
barra—barramundi
barrack—to cheer on or root for a team
bathers—bathing suit (really heard only in Victoria)
battler—one who struggles
beaut or beauty—great, wonderful
bikies—motorcyclists
billabong—pond or waterhole in an otherwise dry riverbed
billy—a tin can with a wire handle; **billy tea** is bush tea boiled in such a container over a campfire

biscuit—cookie
bitumen—a sealed or surfaced road
black stump—the back o'Bourke begins at the black stump
bloke—a man
blowies—blow flies
bludger—lazy person
blue—fight
bluey—anyone with red hair
bonnet—the hood of a car
bonzer—terrific
boomer—huge
boot—the trunk of a car
booze bus—the Breathalyzer police van
bottle shop—liquor store
brekkie—breakfast
brolly—umbrella
Buckley's—no chance
bull bar—extra-large front bumper designed for protection against animals on the road
bungarra—a large goanna, especially Gould's goanna (an Aboriginal food source)
bunyip—mythical swamp dweller
bush—anyplace outside a city
bushbash—travel through dense bush
bush tucker—Outback grub
bushrangers—Wild West-type outlaws (though some were good guys)
bushwhackers—hicks
BYO—bring your own (booze); a restaurant that permits patrons to bring their own liquor

C

campervan—small motorhome
caravan—holiday trailer
cark it—to die
carn—rallying cry at football games
cheeky—sarcastic, insolent, rude
chips—French fries
chook—chicken
chunder—vomit
clobber—clothes
cobber—old-timer's term for "mate"
cocky—a farmer
coldie—a beer
come good—turn out okay

compo—compensation (e.g., "worker's compo")

cooee—originally an Aboriginal shouting-distance greeting

cordial—concentrated fruit drink

corroboree—an Aboriginal meeting, usually with song, dance, and ceremonies

counter meal—pub food

cozzies—bathing suit (from "costume," as in swimming costume)

crook—sick

crow eater—a South Australian

cuppa—tea or coffee

cut lunch—sandwiches

D

daggy—unfashionable (from dag, the dirty lump of wool on a sheep's bottom)

daks—trousers

damper—bush bread cooked on an open fire

Darwin stubby—Darwin's two-liter beer bottle

dead set—"Really?"

dero—derelict

didgeridoo—Aboriginal men's wind instrument

digger—a miner; a soldier or veteran; an old-timer

dill—idiot

dilly bag—Aboriginal woven-grass carrying bag

dinkum—honest, true

dinky-di—genuine

donk—automobile engine

don't come the raw prawn—"Don't fool me!"

doona—feather-filled blanket

drongo—stupid person

duco—automobile paint

duffing—cattle-stealing

dunny—an outhouse

E

earbash—nonstop chatter

ensuite—private bathroom attached to a room

Esky—cooler (from the popular Eskimo brand name)

F

fair go—an equal opportunity

fall pregnant—get pregnant

feral—bush-living hippy

financial—to be in good monetary condition

flagon—two-liter wine bottle

flake—shark meat (the fish that usually goes with your chips)

flat out—busy

floater—meat pie floating in pea soup

flog—to sell, steal, or beat

footy—football

footpath—sidewalk

fossicking—gem- or rockhounding

G

galah—a fool or idiot (also a noisy parrot)

garbo—trash collector

g'day—hello

gibber—stony desert

good on ya—good for you, well done

good oil—good information or ideas

grazier—big-time sheep or cattle farmer

The Green—The Wet, in the Kimberley

H

hire—rent

homestead—station owner or manager's residence

hoon—a jerk or noisy rabble-rouser

Hughie—sometimes God, sometimes just the god of surf and rain

hump—to carry

humpy—temporary bark hut used by Aborigines

I

icy pole—popsicle

J

jackeroo—male ranch hand

jillaroo—female ranch hand

joey—pouch-riding baby kangaroo or wallaby

journo—journalist

jumbuck—sheep

jumper—sweater

K

Kiwi—a New Zealander

knackered—extremely tired

knocker—someone who criticizes others

Koori—Aborigine from southeastern Australia

L

lay by—lay away (to hold something in a store or shop)

licensed—(of a restaurant) permitted to serve alcohol

lollies—candy

M

mad as a cut snake—*really* crazy or crazy mad

magic—good

manchester—household linen items

mate—friend or casual aquaintance

matilda—swag

middy—medium-size beer glass

milk bar—corner shop or convenience store

milko—milkman

missus—wife or girlfriend

moke—a jeep (also "mini-moke")

mozzies—mosquitoes

mud map—rough hand-drawn map

mulga—the bush

Murri—Aborigine (usually Queensland)

muster—round up sheep or cattle

N

nappy—diaper

never never—way out in the Outback

new Australians—newer immigrants (usually non-British descendants)

newsagent—convenience store selling newspapers and magazines

no hoper—loser

no worries—no problem

nought—zero

nulla-nulla—Aborigines' wooden club

O

ocker—a brash, rude Aussie

offsider—an assistant

on the piss—out drinking

ordinary—not good

OS—overseas

Outback—Australia's (and one of the world's) most remote regions

Oz—Australia

P

papaya—tropical melon

pastoralist—a really big-time grazier

pavlova—traditional dessert of cream and meringue

pensioner—retiree, someone on an old-age pension

perve—stare at lustily

petrol—gasoline

piss—beer, booze

pissed—drunk

piss weak—no guts

plonk—rot-gut wine

pokies—poker or slot machines

pom—an English person

postie—a mail person

powerpoint—electrical outlet

prawn—shrimp

Q

Queenslander—a house, built up off the ground to maximize natural cooling

R

rapt—*really* pleased or enraptured

ratbag—mild trouble-stirrer

ratshit—lousy

rego—car registration

return—roundtrip

ridjy didge—the genuine article

right—okay ("She'll be right, mate.")

ripper—good, great, terrific

road train—a semi truck tractor with several trailers

rockmelon—canteloupe

rollies—roll-your-own cigarettes

rooted—tired

ropable—intensely angry or fiery-tempered

rubbish—garbage (also, to tease)

S

sandgroper—a Western Australian

sandshoes—sneakers

sanger—sandwich

sauce—usually ketchup

schooner—large beer glass

scrub—bush

seppo—an American

serviette—napkin

shanty—typically, an unlicensed pub in goldmining enclaves

shark biscuit—body-board surfer

sheila—woman

she'll be right—no problem

shoot through—leave quickly

shout—a round of drinks ("It's your shout" means it's your turn to buy the round)

sickie—a day off work (often not having anything to do with sickness)

side—team

singlet—sleeveless T-shirt

slab—four six-packs of tinnies/stubbies

smash repair shop—auto body shop

smoko—tea break

snag—sausage

sparky—electrician

spunk, spunky—good-looking

station—a large ranch or farm

stickybeak—nosy or curious person

stinger—box jellyfish

stuffed—exhausted, beat

sunbake—sunbathe

super—superannuation, pension

surfies—surfers

swag—bedroll containing one's possessions (often carried over the shoulder)

sweets—dessert

T

ta—thank you

TAB—shop where bets are placed

tacker—toddler

takeaway—takeout, food to go

tall poppies—successful people

taxi rank—taxi stand

tea—dinner, supper, evening meal

terra nullius—the outrageously racist claim of the Australian government that no one had lived on the continent before 1788

thingo—a thingamabob

thongs—flip flops

tinny—can of beer

tomato sauce—ketchup

torch—flashlight

truckie—truck driver

true blue—honest, real, dinkum

tucker—food, grub

two-up—Aussie gambling game

U

uni—university

unsealed—unpaved

upmarket—upscale

ute—pickup truck

W

waddy—Aborigines' wooden club

wag—to cut school

walkabout—set out on a long walk with no particular destination in mind

wanker—jerk

weatherboard—wooden dwelling

whinge—whine

willy-willy—small dust storm

wobbly—shaky behavior

wowser—a tightass, prude

Y

yabber—jabber, chat

yabby—small freshwater crayfish

yahoo—loud, ill-mannered person

yobbo—an unmannered, brash person

BOOKLIST

The majority of books listed can be purchased at either chain or independent bookshops in Australia, and many are available in the United States. Australian embassies and consulates often house libraries with a wide range of reference and reading matter. The most comprehensive collections are found at the Australian High Commission (London), the Australian Embassy (Washington, D.C.), and the Australian Consulate (New York). **Biblio Quest International,** P.O. Box 687, Bowral, NSW 2576, tel. (1800) 06-7877, e-mail: bookfind@biblioquest.com.au, is a worldwide database of old and rare books, and of those recently out of print. It specializes in Australian titles. For purchasing books over the Internet, surf the web to www.amazon.com.

ABORIGINAL CULTURE, HISTORY, AND STUDIES

Berndt, Ronald, and Catherine Berndt. *The Speaking Land: Myth and Story in Aboriginal Australia.* Penguin, 1989. Nearly 200 myths from a variety of Aboriginal societies and cultures are compiled in this first-of-a-kind anthology.

Broome, Richard. *Aboriginal Australians.* Allen and Unwin, 1982. A black response to the white invasion spanning 1788-1980.

Dixon, R.M.W., and Martin Duwell, eds. *The Honey-Ant Men's Love Song & Other Aboriginal Song Poems.* University of Queensland Press.

Edwards, W.H. *An Introduction to Aboriginal Societies.* Social Science Press, 1988. Though mainly a college text, this volume is an excellent introduction to Aboriginal economic, social, religious, and political organizations and values.

ABORIGINAL WRITINGS

Davis, Jack, Stephen Muecke, Mudrooroo Narogin, and Adam Shoemaker, eds. *Paperbark: A Collection of Black Australian Writing.* University of Queensland Press, 1989. More than 40 black authors have contributed oral literature, poetry, drama, novellas, and other literary forms.

Gilbert, Kevin, ed. *Inside Black Australia: An Anthology of Aboriginal Poetry.* Penguin, 1988. Diverse voices from riverbanks, universities, jail cells, urban ghettoes, campfires, and reserves.

Headon, David, ed. *North of the Ten Commandments.* This anthology of Northern Territory writings is filled with insights and discoveries from a wide range of contributors.

Morgan, Sally. *My Place.* Fremantle Arts Centre Press, 1987. A powerful and poignant autobiography that traces three generations of Aborigines.

Narogin, Mudrooroo. *Master of the Ghost Dreaming.* HarperCollins, 1993. In this book by the first Aboriginal novelist, Jangamuttuk, the custodian of the Ghost Dreaming, uses his shamanist powers to will his tribal people to their land.

Narogin, Mudrooroo. *Wild Cat Falling.* HarperCollins, 1993 (orig. 1964). The first novel ever published by an Aboriginal writer, this is the study of an Aboriginal youth who is convicted of petty theft, jailed, and then plunked back out into society.

Narogin, Mudrooroo. *Wildcat Screaming.* HarperCollins, 1993. This satirical sequel to *Wild Cat Falling,* written 27 years later by Australia's most prolific Aboriginal author, sees our fellow back in jail.

Neidjie, Bill, Stephen Davis, and Allan Fox. *Australia's Kakadu Man.* Bill Neidjie, one of the last of the Kakadu tribe, passes along some of his people's ancient wisdom through text and color photos.

Nunukul, Oodgeroo. *My People.* Jacaranda-Wiley, 1981. Oodgeroo was formerly known as Kath Walker. This provocative book of poems is now in its third edition.

Nunukul, Oodgeroo. *Stradbroke Dreamtime.* HarperCollins, 1993. The Aboriginal author has penned a two-part book: the first half is a childhood memoir, the second contains Aboriginal folklore tales.

ART AND PHOTOGRAPHY

Bachman, Bill. *Local Colour.* Odyssey, 1994. A hardback coffee-table edition with 354 exquisite and unique photographs. Bachman, king of Outback photography, supplies his own insightful and humorous text, supplemented by that of award-winning Western Australian author Tim Winton.

Bachman, Bill. *Off the Road Again.* Lothian, 1989. A terrific compendium of both quirky and mystical Outback photos.

Coleman, Peter. *Bruce Beresford: Instincts of the Heart.* Angus and Robertson, 1993. An in-depth study of the Aussie director with film credits such as *Driving Miss Daisy, Tender Mercies,* and *Breaker Morant.*

Granville, James. *Australia the Beautiful.* Weldons, 1983. This glossy volume of photography and text will take you on a pictorial journey of the continent and its inhabitants.

Isaacs, Jennifer, ed. *Aboriginality: Contemporary Aboriginal Paintings and Prints.* University of Queensland Press, 1992. This lavish, revised edition showcases 25 contemporary artists committed to expressing their cultural heritage in a variety of vibrant works.

Isaacs, Jennifer. *Australian Aboriginal Paintings.* Weldons, 1989. A selection of traditional can-

vas and bark paintings from tribes of Arnhem Land and the western desert regions, including translated information from the artists.

Spencer, Sir Walter Baldwin. *The Aboriginal Photographs of Baldwin Spencer.* Viking, 1987. A coffee-table edition of the widely acclaimed Aboriginal photos, taken by Sir Walter 1894-1927, on expedition in northern and central Australia.

AUSTRALIAN CLASSICS

Baynton, Barbara. *Bush Studies.* Angus and Robertson. A female view of bush life told through a collection of stories.

Clarke, Marcus. *For the Term of His Natural Life.* HarperCollins/Angus and Robertson. An Australian literary classic depicting the gruesome life inside a penal colony.

Clark, Manning. *A Short History of Australia.* Penguin, 1987. The acclaimed historian's abridged and accessible version of his five-volume *A History of Australia.*

Franklin, Miles. *My Brilliant Career.* HarperCollins/Angus and Robertson. The novel-turned-film of a smarty-pants young woman coming of age in turn-of-the-century Outback Australia.

Herbert, Xavier. *Capricornia.* HarperCollins/Angus and Robertson, 1977. Originally published in 1938, this elaborate saga portrays the mistreatment of half-castes in Australia's north.

Stowe, Randolph. *The Merry-Go-Round in the Sea.* Penguin. A classic story, against a World War II backdrop, of a young bloke coming of age in Outback Western Australia.

BUSH BALLADS AND YARNS

Edwards, Ron. *The Wealthy Dog.* Rams Skull Press. Classic Australian yarn-spinning—a genre of its own, akin to the "tall tale."

Lawson, Henry. *The Best of Henry Lawson.* Angus and Robertson. Bush ballads and poems from one of the country's most famous balladeers and poets.

Paterson, A.B. "Banjo." *Collected Verse.* Harper-Collins. A selection of bush ballads and poems from the country's *most* famous balladeer and poet.

Semmler, Clement, ed. *Banjo Paterson.* University of Queensland Press. A collection of classic works—many depicting Outback characters—by Andrew Barton "Banjo" Paterson of *Man from Snowy River* fame.

FICTION, LITERATURE, AND SOME HYPE

Bryson, John. *Evil Angels.* Bantam. Saga of the 1980s Lindy Chamberlain trial and media event, in which she swore her baby was carried off by a dingo from an Uluru (Ayers Rock) campground. Ultimately tried, convicted, then released, Lindy's story is *still* being bandied about. (She was played by Meryl Streep in the movie version.)

Facey, A.B. *A Fortunate Life.* Penguin, 1988. An Australian best-seller, written by Bert Facey (published when he was 87 years old), describing the life of this extraordinary man.

Flood, Tom. *Oceana Fine.* Allen and Unwin, 1989. An award-winning fantasy/thriller/whodunit novel set in Marvel Loch, Western Australia—a place of myth and mystery.

Keneally, Thomas. *The Chant of Jimmy Blacksmith.* Penguin. A very disturbing and brutal account of the inner psyche and outer workings of an Aboriginal criminal.

McCullough, Colleen. *The Thorn Birds.* Avon Books. Be-still-my-heart saga (and miniseries), set in Western Australia, of lusty forbidden love between priest and parishioner.

Morgan, Marlo. *Mutant Message Down Under.* HarperCollins, 1994. The unlikely tale of a middle-aged Missouri woman "chosen" by a small Aboriginal tribe to become privy to their culture, dreams, and way of life—all in the span of four months. Oh *pleeease!* Originally, this self-published book was sold as fact, but the HarperCollins edition sensibly carries a disclaimer and catalogs the work as fiction.

Pritchard, Katharine Susannah. *Coonardoo.* HarperCollins/Angus and Robertson, 1975. This story of interracial love between a white station owner and his Aboriginal housekeeper was hot stuff in 1929 when it was first published.

Shute, Nevil. *A Town Like Alice.* Published in 1950, *Alice* was the first widely read Outback-themed novel. *In the West* (1953) and *Beyond the Black Stump* (1956) were other Outback-based Shute follow-ups.

White, Patrick. *The Aunt's Story.* Penguin, 1948. White, Patrick. *The Tree of Man.* Penguin, 1955. White, Patrick. *Voss.* Penguin, 1957. Australia's Nobel prize winner portrays Outback life, hardships, and characters in his heavy epic works.

Winton, Tim. *Cloudstreet.* Graywolf. The superb Mr. Winton spins an engaging tale of two families sharing a household in postwar Perth.

Wongar, B. *The Last Pack of Dingoes.* Angus and Robertson, 1993. Aboriginal and non-Aboriginal cultural differences exposed through clever short stories that combine an intriguing blend of political critique with mythological beliefs.

Wongar, B. *The Track to Bralgu.* HarperCollins, 1993. An enlightening though hardly upbeat short-story collection depicting the Aborigines' trials and tribulations.

GENERAL INTEREST

Antipodes. American Association of Australian Literary Studies (190 6th Ave., Brooklyn, NY 11217). A twice-yearly Australian literary journal featuring Aussie poetry, fiction, essays, book reviews, and literary scene updates.

BP Touring Atlas of Australia. Viking O'Neil, 1999. This large-format, fully indexed road atlas contains easy-to-read maps, including key maps and capital city maps.

Dunstan, Keith. *The Amber Nectar*. Viking O'Neil, 1987. A book celebrating the brewing and imbibing of Australian beer.

Goodwin, Ken, and Alan Lawson, eds. *The MacMillan Anthology of Australian Literature*. MacMillan, 1990. Thematically organized sketches, narratives, speeches, poems, and historical and biographical material.

Hirst, Robin. *Pocket Guide to the Southern Skies*. Dynamo Press, 1985. Get your bearings on the Southern Cross, Magellan's Clouds, and other phenomena of the southern skies.

Johansen, Lenie. *The Dinkum Dictionary: A Ripper Guide to Aussie English*. Viking O'Neil, 1988. More than 16,000 entries of slang, usage, and Aussie vernacular.

Mayo, Oliver. *The Wines of Australia*. Faber and Faber. Tipple over Aussie-made vintages and their vintners.

Warren, Mark. *Atlas of Australian Surfing*. HarperCollins, 1997. Good guide to riding Australia's famous waves.

HISTORY

Aitchison, Ray. *The Americans in Australia*. AE-Press, 1986. Americans have exerted considerable influence in Australia.

Cannon, Michael. *Who Killed the Koories?* Heinemann Australia. A no-bedtime-lullaby of the violent clash between inland-bound settlers and Aborigines in 1840s New South Wales.

Grant, Joan, ed. *The Australopedia*. McPhee Gribble/Penguin Books, 1988. Informative descriptions for young readers about the workings of Australia after 200 years of civilization.

Gunn, Aeneas. *We of the Never Never*. Random Century Australia, 1987. This turn-of-the-century account of Outback pioneer life and Aboriginal encounters is an Australian classic.

Hawke, Stephen. *Noonkabah*. Fremantle Arts Press. A former Premier's son relates the early 1980s headlock between Aborigines and the Labor Party over oil exploration near Fitzroy Crossing.

Hughes, Robert. *The Fatal Shore*. Collins, 1986. The best-seller that traces the country's convict origins, beginning with the 1788 arrival of the First Fleet.

Isaacs, Jennifer. *Pioneer Women of the Bush and Outback*. Weldons, 1990. Learn how ordinary bush and country women coped with daily life and hardships beginning from the last century onward.

Pilger, John. *A Secret Country*. Knopf. Read all about Aboriginal maltreatment, racism, British nuclear experiments, and other political and social dirt—spewed forth by a genuine-born Aussie bloke.

Rajkowski, Pamela. *In the Tracks of the Camelmen*. Angus and Robertson, 1987. The lowdown on some of Outback Australia's most intriguing pioneers.

Rosser, Bill. *Up Rode the Troopers: The Black Police in Queensland and Dreamtime Nightmares*. University of Queensland Press. Nineteenth-century Queensland's dispersion methods for ridding the land of Aborigines, along with reasons why the indigenous people had little chance of resistance.

Sherington, Geoffrey. *Australia's Immigrants, 1788-1988*. Allen and Unwin, 1990. This recently revised volume explores the role migration has played in Australian society.

Webby, Elizabeth. *Colonial Voices*. University of Queensland Press, 1989. An anthology with glimpses of 19th-century historical events as well as daily life.

Whitlock, Gillian, and David Carter, eds. *Images of Australia*. University of Queensland Press. This introductory guide to Australian studies includes historical development, Aboriginal culture, muliculturism, bush legends and suburban lifestyles.

NATURAL HISTORY

Bush Dwellers of Australia. Australian Government Publishing Service. A second edition with color shots of critters you're apt to encounter out bush.

Cogger, Harold G. *Reptiles and Amphibians of Australia*. More than 800 species are featured in photos and line drawings.

Dangerous Australians: The Complete Guide to Australia's Most Deadly Creatures. Bay Books, 1986. Read up on venomous and dangerous wildlife, creepies, and crawlies.

Ellis, G., and S. Cohen. *Outdoor Traveler's Guide: Australia*. HarperCollins/Angus and Robertson, 1988. This descriptive guide—containing many color photos and maps—embraces Australia's geography, vegetation, wildlife, parks, and natural areas.

Flood, Josephine. *The Riches of Ancient Australia*. University of Queensland Press Australia. Follow the continent's prehistoric heritage in this book complete with maps, photos, and drawings.

Longhurst, Peter. *Bush Strokes*. Bay Books, 1987. A full-color portfolio of 20 native Outback animals, combined with informative text.

MacKness, Brian. *Prehistoric Australia*. Golden Press, 1987. Catch up on four billion years of the continent's evolution.

Phillips, Bill. *Koalas: The Little Australians We'd All Hate to Lose*. Australian Government Publishing Service. Learn more about the koala and its fragile existence.

Slater, Peter. *The Birdwatcher's Notebook*. Weldons, 1989. A field notebook with useful sighting charts, birdwatching techniques, bird characteristics, and much more birding info.

Triggs, Barbara. *The Wombat: Common Wombats in Australia*. The New South Wales University Press. Wombats, wombats, and more wombats: One-third of this book is photographs.

Webb, G., and C. Manolis. *Australian Freshwater Crocodiles*. Webb., G., and C. Manolis. *Australian Saltwater Crocodiles*. G. Webb Pty. Ltd. Both 33-page texts feature color photos of fascinating and terrifying crocs.

TRAVEL INSPIRATIONS

Chatwin, Bruce. *The Songlines*. Viking, 1987. In this superb account, the author chronicles his life with central Australian Aborigines and helps demystify some of the cultural complexities.

Davidson, Robyn. *Tracks*. Allen and Unwin, 1982. An interesting tale of a determined woman who walks alone with her camels from Alice Springs to the Western Australia coast.

Hawthorne, Susan, and Klein, Renate, eds. *Australia for Women: Travel and Culture*. Spinifex Press, 1994. Rural and urban Aboriginal and Australian women share their culture and experiences in this unique compendium specifically for women travelers.

Stewart, D., ed. *Burnum Burnum's Aboriginal Australia, a Traveler's Guide*. Angus and Robertson, 1988. A large hardback volume that sets you exploring the country from an Aboriginal viewpoint.

INDEX

CAVES

CHURCHES/TEMPLES

CRUISES/BOAT EXCURSIONS

GARDENS/FLOWER SHOWS

New South Wales
Almond Blossom Festival: 58
Alpine Wildflower Festival: 174
Australian National Botanic
    Gardens: 160
Blue Mountains Rhododendron
    Garden: 191
Bougainvillea Festival: 58
Festival of Gardens: 183
Floriade: 58
Japanese Garden: 203
Mount Tomah Botanic Gardens:
    194
North Coast Botanic Garden:
    247
Royal Botanic Gardens: 103
Tulip Time Festival: 152
Wagga Wagga Botanic
    Gardens: 178
Western Australia Wildflower
    Festivals: 58

Northern Territory
Alice Springs Desert Park: 327-
    328
Bougainvillea Festival: 286
Darwin Botanic Gardens: 281
Mecca Date Gardens: 319
Olive Pink Flora Reserve: 317-
    318

Queensland
Anderson Park Botanic
    Gardens: 428
Brisbane Botanic Gardens: 353
Cairns Botanical Conservatory:
    444
City Botanic Gardens: 358
Flecker Botanic Gardens: 444
Ju Raku En: 369
Lamington National Park: 350
Mt. Coot-tha Park: 358
Rockhampton Botanic Garden:
    403

South Australia
Arid Lands Botanic Gardens:
    560
Bicentennial Conservatory: 489,
    491
Gamble Cottage Garden: 491
Himeji Gardens: 491
Melaleuca Nursery: 536
Mt. Lofty Botanic Gardens: 506
Museum of Economic Botany:
    489, 491
Nagawooka Flora Reserve: 522
Rose Display Garden: 520
Soldiers Memorial Gardens:
    525
Veale Gardens: 491
Wittunga Botanic Garden: 491

Tasmania
Allendale Gardens: 647
Bridestowe Estate Lavender
    Farm: 667
Royal Tasmanian Botanical
    Gardens: 609

Victoria
Ballarat Botanic Gardens: 710
Begonia Festival: 710
Carlton Gardens: 686
Fitzroy Gardens: 686
Geelong Botanic Gardens: 720
National Herbarium: 686
Rhododendron Gardens: 687
Rosalind Park: 717
Royal Botanic Gardens: 686
Seawinds Botanical Garden:
    775
Sunraysia Oasis Botanical
    Gardens: 748-749
Wombat Hill Botanic Garden:
    713

Western Australia
Alan Green Conservatory: 799
Big Brook Arboretum: 835
Kings Park: 803
Queens Garden: 803
Rainbow Jungle: 855
White Gum Flower Farm: 823

GREAT BARRIER REEF

HIKING

HISTORY/CULTURE MUSEUMS

LIGHTHOUSES

MARITIME MUSEUMS/MONUMENTS

MUSIC VENUES

NATIONAL PARKS

(continued on next page)

N

RAINFORESTS

RESERVES/CONSERVATION AREAS/NATURE PARKS

STATE PARKS/RECREATION AREAS

ZOOS/WILDLIFE PARKS

ABOUT THE AUTHORS

Marael Johnson has been exploring and writing about Australia since 1983. She has freelanced as an area editor, researcher, and writer for many Fodor's Travel Guides (specifically in the Australia, New Zealand, and South Pacific regions) and has reviewed Australia's hotels and resorts for *Star Service Worldwide Hotel Guide*. She is the author of *Outback Australia Handbook* (Moon Travel Handbooks)—winner of a Society of American Travel Writers' Lowell Thomas Award, *San Diego Agenda* (Fielding Worldwide, Inc.), *Why Stop? A Guide to California Roadside Historical Markers* and *Why Stop? A Guide to Louisiana Roadside Historical Markers* (Gulf Publishing Co.). She is co-author of Fielding's Hawaii and Bahamas guides and contributing author to Microsoft's *Automap* and Fielding's *World's Most Dangerous Places*. She is an active member of the National Writer's Union and the Society of American Travel Writers.

Australian Andrew Hempstead has spent many years exploring, writing about, and photographing Australia. In addition to co-authoring this book, he is the author of *Alberta/NWT Handbook* and *Canadian Rockies Handbook* and co-author of *British Columbia Handbook* (Moon Travel Handbooks). He has been writing since 1989, when, after leaving a promising career in the field of advertising, he took off for Alaska, linking up with veteran travel writer Deke Castleman to help research and update the fourth edition of *Alaska-Yukon Handbook* (Moon Travel Handbooks). Andrew has also traveled to New Zealand on assignment to write and photograph for Moon Publications and The Guide Book Company, and traveled purely for pleasure through most of the United States, Europe, the South Pacific, and India.

When not working on his books, he is happiest hiking, fishing, golfing, camping, and enjoying the simple pleasures in life, such as skimming stones down on the river.

MOON TRAVEL HANDBOOKS

LOSE YOURSELF IN THE EXPERIENCE, NOT THE CROWD

For more than 25 years, Moon Travel Handbooks have been the guidebooks of choice for adventurous travelers. Our award-winning Handbook series provides focused, comprehensive coverage of distinct destinations all over the world. Each Handbook is like an entire bookcase of cultural insight and introductory information in one portable volume. Our goal at Moon is to give travelers all the background and practical information they'll need for an extraordinary travel experience.

The following pages include a complete list of Handbooks, covering North America and Hawaii, Mexico, Latin America and the Caribbean, and Asia and the Pacific. To purchase Moon Travel Handbooks, check your local bookstore or check our Web site at **www.moon.com** for current prices and editions.

"An in-depth dunk into the land, the people and their history, arts, and politics."
—*Student Travels*

"I consider these books to be superior to Lonely Planet. When Moon produces a book it is more humorous, incisive, and off-beat."
—*Toronto Sun*

"Outdoor enthusiasts gravitate to the well-written Moon Travel Handbooks. In addition to politically correct historic and cultural features, the series focuses on flora, fauna and outdoor recreation. Maps and meticulous directions also are a trademark of Moon guides."
—*Houston Chronicle*

"Moon [Travel Handbooks] . . . bring a healthy respect to the places they investigate. Best of all, they provide a host of odd nuggets that give a place texture and prod the wary traveler from the beaten path. The finest are written with such care and insight they deserve listing as literature."
—*American Geographical Society*

"Moon Travel Handbooks offer in-depth historical essays and useful maps, enhanced by a sense of humor and a neat, compact format."
—*Swing*

"Perfect for the more adventurous, these are long on history, sightseeing and nitty-gritty information and very price-specific."
—*Columbus Dispatch*

"Moon guides manage to be comprehensive and countercultural at the same time . . . Handbooks are packed with maps, photographs, drawings, and sidebars that constitute a college-level introduction to each country's history, culture, people, and crafts."
—*National Geographic Traveler*

"Few travel guides do a better job helping travelers create their own itineraries than the Moon Travel Handbook series. The authors have a knack for homing in on the essentials."
—*Colorado Springs Gazette Telegraph*

MEXICO

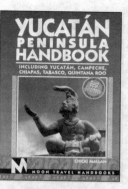

"These books will delight the armchair traveler, aid the undecided person in selecting a destination, and guide the seasoned road warrior looking for lesser-known hideaways."
—*Mexican Meanderings* Newsletter

"From tourist traps to off-the-beaten track hideaways, these guides offer consistent, accurate details without pretension."
—*Foreign Service Journal*

Archaeological Mexico	**$19.95**
Andrew Coe	420 pages, 27 maps
Baja Handbook	**$16.95**
Joe Cummings	540 pages, 46 maps
Cabo Handbook	**$14.95**
Joe Cummings	270 pages, 17 maps
Cancún Handbook	**$14.95**
Chicki Mallan	240 pages, 25 maps
Colonial Mexico	**$18.95**
Chicki Mallan	400 pages, 38 maps
Mexico Handbook	**$21.95**
Joe Cummings and Chicki Mallan	1,200 pages, 201 maps
Northern Mexico Handbook	**$17.95**
Joe Cummings	610 pages, 69 maps
Pacific Mexico Handbook	**$17.95**
Bruce Whipperman	580 pages, 68 maps
Puerto Vallarta Handbook	**$14.95**
Bruce Whipperman	330 pages, 36 maps
Yucatán Handbook	**$16.95**
Chicki Mallan	400 pages, 52 maps

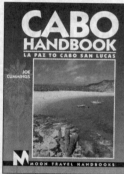

"Beyond question, the most comprehensive Mexican resources available for those who prefer deep travel to shallow tourism. But don't worry, the fiesta-fun stuff's all here too."
—*New York Daily News*

LATIN AMERICA AND THE CARIBBEAN

"Solidly packed with practical information and full of significant cultural asides that will enlighten you on the whys and wherefores of things you might easily see but not easily grasp."

—*Boston Globe*

Belize Handbook	**$15.95**
Chicki Mallan and Patti Lange	390 pages, 45 maps
Caribbean Vacations	**$18.95**
Karl Luntta	910 pages, 64 maps
Costa Rica Handbook	**$19.95**
Christopher P. Baker	780 pages, 73 maps
Cuba Handbook	**$19.95**
Christopher P. Baker	740 pages, 70 maps
Dominican Republic Handbook	**$15.95**
Gaylord Dold	420 pages, 24 maps
Ecuador Handbook	**$16.95**
Julian Smith	450 pages, 43 maps
Honduras Handbook	**$15.95**
Chris Humphrey	330 pages, 40 maps
Jamaica Handbook	**$15.95**
Karl Luntta	330 pages, 17 maps
Virgin Islands Handbook	**$13.95**
Karl Luntta	220 pages, 19 maps

NORTH AMERICA AND HAWAII

"These domestic guides convey the same sense of exoticism that their foreign counterparts do, making home-country travel seem like far-flung adventure."

—*Sierra Magazine*

Alaska-Yukon Handbook	**$17.95**
Deke Castleman and Don Pitcher	530 pages, 92 maps
Alberta and the Northwest Territories Handbook	**$18.95**
Andrew Hempstead	520 pages, 79 maps
Arizona Handbook	**$18.95**
Bill Weir	600 pages, 36 maps
Atlantic Canada Handbook	**$18.95**
Mark Morris	490 pages, 60 maps
Big Island of Hawaii Handbook	**$15.95**
J.D. Bisignani	390 pages, 25 maps
Boston Handbook	**$13.95**
Jeff Perk	200 pages, 20 maps
British Columbia Handbook	**$16.95**
Jane King and Andrew Hempstead	430 pages, 69 maps

Canadian Rockies Handbook	**$14.95**
Andrew Hempstead	220 pages, 22 maps
Colorado Handbook	**$17.95**
Stephen Metzger	480 pages, 46 maps
Georgia Handbook	**$17.95**
Kap Stann	380 pages, 44 maps
Grand Canyon Handbook	**$14.95**
Bill Weir	220 pages, 10 maps
Hawaii Handbook	**$19.95**
J.D. Bisignani	1,030 pages, 88 maps
Honolulu-Waikiki Handbook	**$14.95**
J.D. Bisignani	360 pages, 20 maps
Idaho Handbook	**$18.95**
Don Root	610 pages, 42 maps
Kauai Handbook	**$15.95**
J.D. Bisignani	320 pages, 23 maps
Los Angeles Handbook	**$16.95**
Kim Weir	370 pages, 15 maps
Maine Handbook	**$18.95**
Kathleen M. Brandes	660 pages, 27 maps
Massachusetts Handbook	**$18.95**
Jeff Perk	600 pages, 23 maps
Maui Handbook	**$15.95**
J.D. Bisignani	450 pages, 37 maps
Michigan Handbook	**$15.95**
Tina Lassen	360 pages, 32 maps
Montana Handbook	**$17.95**
Judy Jewell and W.C. McRae	490 pages, 52 maps
Nevada Handbook	**$18.95**
Deke Castleman	530 pages, 40 maps
New Hampshire Handbook	**$18.95**
Steve Lantos	500 pages, 18 maps
New Mexico Handbook	**$15.95**
Stephen Metzger	360 pages, 47 maps
New York Handbook	**$19.95**
Christiane Bird	780 pages, 95 maps
New York City Handbook	**$13.95**
Christiane Bird	300 pages, 20 maps
North Carolina Handbook	**$14.95**
Rob Hirtz and Jenny Daughtry Hirtz	320 pages, 27 maps
Northern California Handbook	**$19.95**
Kim Weir	800 pages, 50 maps
Ohio Handbook	**$15.95**
David K. Wright	340 pages, 18 maps
Oregon Handbook	**$17.95**
Stuart Warren and Ted Long Ishikawa	590 pages, 34 maps

Pennsylvania Handbook	**$18.95**
Joanne Miller	448 pages, 40 maps
Road Trip USA	**$24.00**
Jamie Jensen	940 pages, 175 maps
Road Trip USA Getaways: Chicago	**$9.95**
	60 pages, 1 map
Road Trip USA Getaways: Seattle	**$9.95**
	60 pages, 1 map
Santa Fe-Taos Handbook	**$13.95**
Stephen Metzger	160 pages, 13 maps
South Carolina Handbook	**$16.95**
Mike Sigalas	400 pages, 20 maps
Southern California Handbook	**$19.95**
Kim Weir	720 pages, 26 maps
Tennessee Handbook	**$17.95**
Jeff Bradley	530 pages, 42 maps
Texas Handbook	**$18.95**
Joe Cummings	690 pages, 70 maps
Utah Handbook	**$17.95**
Bill Weir and W.C. McRae	490 pages, 40 maps
Virginia Handbook	**$15.95**
Julian Smith	410 pages, 37 maps
Washington Handbook	**$19.95**
Don Pitcher	840 pages, 111 maps
Wisconsin Handbook	**$18.95**
Thomas Huhti	590 pages, 69 maps
Wyoming Handbook	**$17.95**
Don Pitcher	610 pages, 80 maps

ASIA AND THE PACIFIC

"Scores of maps, detailed practical info down to business hours of small-town libraries. You can't beat the Asian titles for sheer heft. (The) series is sort of an American Lonely Planet, with better writing but fewer titles. (The) individual voice of researchers comes through."

—*Travel & Leisure*

Australia Handbook	**$21.95**
Marael Johnson, Andrew Hempstead,	
and Nadina Purdon	940 pages, 141 maps
Bali Handbook	**$19.95**
Bill Dalton	750 pages, 54 maps
Fiji Islands Handbook	**$14.95**
David Stanley	350 pages, 42 maps
Hong Kong Handbook	**$16.95**
Kerry Moran	378 pages, 49 maps

Indonesia Handbook	**$25.00**
Bill Dalton	1,380 pages, 249 maps
Micronesia Handbook	**$16.95**
Neil M. Levy	340 pages, 70 maps
Nepal Handbook	**$18.95**
Kerry Moran	490 pages, 51 maps
New Zealand Handbook	**$19.95**
Jane King	620 pages, 81 maps
Outback Australia Handbook	**$18.95**
Marael Johnson	450 pages, 57 maps
Philippines Handbook	**$17.95**
Peter Harper and Laurie Fullerton	670 pages, 116 maps
Singapore Handbook	**$15.95**
Carl Parkes	350 pages, 29 maps
South Korea Handbook	**$19.95**
Robert Nilsen	820 pages, 141 maps
South Pacific Handbook	**$24.00**
David Stanley	920 pages, 147 maps
Southeast Asia Handbook	**$21.95**
Carl Parkes	1,080 pages, 204 maps
Tahiti Handbook	**$15.95**
David Stanley	450 pages, 51 maps
Thailand Handbook	**$19.95**
Carl Parkes	860 pages, 142 maps
Vietnam, Cambodia & Laos Handbook	**$18.95**
Michael Buckley	760 pages, 116 maps

OTHER GREAT TITLES FROM MOON

"For hardy wanderers, few guides come more highly recommended than the Handbooks. They include good maps, steer clear of fluff and flackery, and offer plenty of money-saving tips. They also give you the kind of information that visitors to strange lands—on any budget— need to survive."

—*US News & World Report*

Moon Handbook	**$10.00**
Carl Koppeschaar	150 pages, 8 maps
The Practical Nomad: How to Travel Around the World	**$17.95**
Edward Hasbrouck	580 pages
Staying Healthy in Asia, Africa, and Latin America	**$11.95**
Dirk Schroeder	230 pages, 4 maps

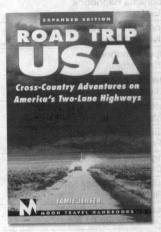

U.S.~METRIC CONVERSION

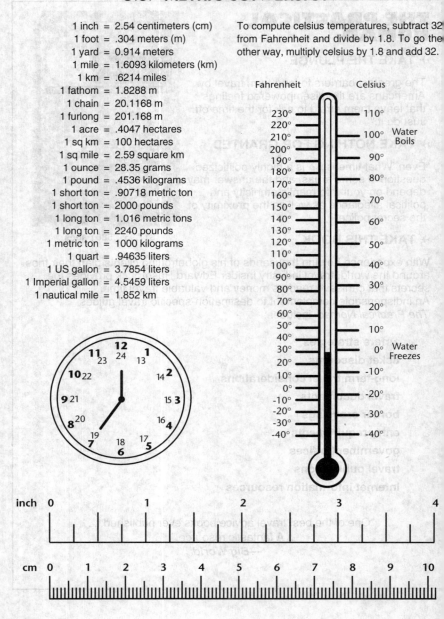

1 inch = 2.54 centimeters (cm)
1 foot = .304 meters (m)
1 yard = 0.914 meters
1 mile = 1.6093 kilometers (km)
1 km = .6214 miles
1 fathom = 1.8288 m
1 chain = 20.1168 m
1 furlong = 201.168 m
1 acre = .4047 hectares
1 sq km = 100 hectares
1 sq mile = 2.59 square km
1 ounce = 28.35 grams
1 pound = .4536 kilograms
1 short ton = .90718 metric ton
1 short ton = 2000 pounds
1 long ton = 1.016 metric tons
1 long ton = 2240 pounds
1 metric ton = 1000 kilograms
1 quart = .94635 liters
1 US gallon = 3.7854 liters
1 Imperial gallon = 4.5459 liters
1 nautical mile = 1.852 km

To compute celsius temperatures, subtract 32 from Fahrenheit and divide by 1.8. To go the other way, multiply celsius by 1.8 and add 32.

Fahrenheit   Celsius

230° — 110°
220° —
210° — 100° Water Boils
200° —
190° — 90°
180° —
170° — 80°
160° —
150° — 70°
140° —
130° — 60°
120° —
110° — 50°
100° —
90° — 40°
80° — 30°
70° —
60° — 20°
50° —
40° — 10°
30° — 0° Water Freezes
20° —
10° — -10°
0° —
-10° — -20°
-20° — -30°
-30° —
-40° — -40°

inch 0   1   2   3   4

cm 0 1 2 3 4 5 6 7 8 9 10

Next time, make your *own* hotel arrangements.

Yahoo! Travel